The
Jazz Book
From Ragtime to the 21st Century

Seventh Edition
Revised and Expanded

Joachim-Ernst Berendt
and
Günther Huesmann

Translated by H. and B. Bredigkeit,
Dan Morgenstern, Tim Nevill, and Jeb Bishop

Lawrence Hill Books

Library of Congress Cataloging-in-Publication Data
Berendt, Joachim-Ernst, 1922-2000.
  [Grosse Jazzbuch. English]
  The jazz book : from ragtime to the 21st century / Joachim E. Berendt
and Günther Huesmann ; translated by H. and B. Bredigkeit ... [et al.].
  — 7th ed., rev. and expanded.
    p. cm.
  Includes bibliographical references and index.
  Discography: p. 669
  ISBN 978-1-55652-823-1 (pbk.) — ISBN 978-1-55652-820-0
(hardcover) 1. Jazz—History and criticism. I. Huesmann, Günther,
1957- II. Title.
  ML3506.B4513 2009
  781.6509—dc22

                                                2008053770

Cover and interior design: Jonathan Hahn
Cover photo: Miles Davis at Shrine Auditorium, September 15, 1950,
with Budd Johnson on saxophone and Bobby Tucker on piano
© Bob Willoughby/Redferns

New material in the 2009 edition was translated from the German
by Jeb Bishop

Seventh edition
Published by Lawrence Hill Books
An imprint of Chicago Review Press, Inc.
814 North Franklin Street
Chicago, Illinois 60610
ISBN 978-1-55652-820-0 (cloth)
ISBN 978-1-55652-823-1 (paper)
Printed in the United States of America

One does not come to know something unless one loves it.
—*Goethe*

You've got to love to be able to play.
—*Louis Armstrong*

The most important contribution you can make to the tradition is to create your own music, create a new music.
—*Anthony Davis*

In music there is something more than melody, something more than harmony. There is the music!
—*Giuseppe Verdi*

Contents

Preface ix

The Styles of Jazz 1

Around 1890: Ragtime 4
Turn of the Century: New Orleans 6
The Teens: Dixieland 9
The Twenties: Chicago 10
The Thirties: Swing 12
The Forties: Bebop 14
The Fifties: Cool Jazz, Hard Bop 17
The Sixties: Free Jazz 20
The Seventies 32
The Eighties 42
The Nineties 55
    Outlook: Jazz in the Age of Migration 72

The Musicians of Jazz 77

Louis Armstrong 78
Bessie Smith 87
Bix Beiderbecke 89

Duke Ellington 94

Coleman Hawkins and Lester Young 101

Charlie Parker and Dizzy Gillespie 109

Miles Davis 120

John Coltrane and Ornette Coleman 136

John McLaughlin 153

David Murray and Wynton Marsalis 162

John Zorn 180

The Elements of Jazz 193

Sound and Phrasing 193

Improvisation 196

The Arrangement 202

The Blues 206

Spiritual and Gospel Song 216

Harmony 221

Melody 226

Rhythm, Swing, Groove 232

The Instruments of Jazz 245

The Trumpet 245

The Trombone 267

The Clarinet 279

The Saxophones 293

    The Soprano Saxophone 294

    The Alto Saxophone 302

    The Tenor Saxophone 315

    The Baritone Saxophone 339

    Saxophone Groups 345

The Flute 349

The Vibraphone 358

The Piano 363

Organ, Keyboards, Synthesizer, Electronics 397

    Hammond Organ 398

    Keyboards and Synthesizer 404

    Samplers and Electronics 410

The Guitar 416

The Bass 441

The Drums 467

The Percussion Instruments (Cuban, Salsa, Brazilian,

African, Indian, Balinese) 501

The Violin 519

Miscellaneous Instruments 530

    Accordion 532

    Tuba 534

    Harmonica 536

    French Horn, Oboe, English Horn, Bassoon, Shells 537

    Mandolin, Banjo, Cello, Daxophone 539

    Non-Western Instruments 542

        The Oud 543

        Asian Stringed Instruments 544

        Kora 546

    Mixing Board 547

The Vocalists of Jazz 549

The Male Singers 549

The Female Singers 563

The Big Bands of Jazz 587

Fletcher Henderson and the Beginning 588

The Goodman Era 589

The Black Kings of Swing 591

Woody Herman and Stan Kenton 594

Bebop Big Bands 596

Basie as Basis 598

Gil Evans and George Russell 600

Free Big Bands 602

Rock Big Bands 609

Big Bands Forever: The Seventies 611

Back to the Basics and Postmodernism: The Eighties 614

Repertory Orchestras, Europe, and the Diversity

of Styles: The Nineties 618

The Small Bands of Jazz 627

The Small Swing Bands 628
Bop and Cool 630
First High Points of Integration 632
From Hard Bop to Free 634
Ornette and After 637
The Seventies 639
  Neobop 639
  AACM 640
  Jazz-Rock and Fusion 642
The Eighties 646
  New Straight-Ahead Jazz 647
  The Avant-Garde Discovers the Tradition 648
  World Jazz 650
  Free Funk 651
Since 1990: Stylistic Diversity and the Art of Interaction ... 652

Toward a Definition of Jazz 661

Discography 669
Index 735

Preface

When Joachim-Ernst Berendt's voice, with its characteristic combination of urgent murmuring and sensuous whispering, was heard in the jazz programs of Germany's Southwest Radio, listeners who otherwise never listened to jazz somehow felt as if he were speaking directly to them. Jazz critics tend to be didactic. Berendt's tone was something different: the tone of the seducer and the prophet. This emphatic intonation made him famous. Whether you agreed or disagreed with what he was saying, he touched you. He moved his listeners and his readers with an appeal to both heart and soul; in one of his favorite phrases, he "spoke to the senses."

Berendt achieved his greatest success as a kind of mediator, building bridges between musicians and listeners. He wasn't afraid of sounding passionate. His speech was rhythmically brusque, sometimes emotionally provocative and polarizing. He transferred the intensity so often spoken of in jazz into his words, and in this way managed to close, at least to some extent, the gap between words and the world of music.

His impassioned plea for a "more conscious listening" went beyond the purely musical. For Berendt, the conscious, intensive experience of music was part of working for a more just social order, a better world.

Like no other writer on music, he made palpable the idea that spirituality is an essential aspect of music and of the experience of music. Spiritual and sensuous experience of music beyond material analyses: to bring people close to this was his great gift, exercised in books such as the present volume, *Nada Brahma, Das Dritte Ohr* [*The Third Ear*], and his audio books. Joachim-Ernst Berendt brought the quality of jazz into

ix

speech: a spontaneity and an enchantment that for at least a moment went beyond rational thought.

The present book was the first book about jazz that I ever read. It was given to me by some friends when I was sixteen years old. I opened it up and was immediately entranced. It made me so curious about the sounds of jazz that I have remained attached to this music ever since. Even today, after twenty years of professional work as a music journalist and radio writer, jazz is for me the most exciting and most alive of all musical traditions.

My enthusiasm for jazz, and my first encounters with it, quickly brought me into contact with the original author of this book. When Joachim-Ernst Berendt asked me if I would like to take over responsibility for the continuation of *The Jazz Book*, my immediate answer was yes. I consider it a high honor to continue the work of writing this book, which in its many editions has served and helped four generations of jazz fans, as well as newcomers to jazz.

It has been my good fortune to work on three revisions of this standard reference work: in 1981 as an assistant, in 1989 as a revising editor, and in 2005 as author. In each of these roles, I've considered it to be a particular challenge to do justice to the growing diversity of the jazz scene to at least some extent.

Since the last revision of this book in 1989, the jazz scene has undergone explosive growth. In order to keep the book to a manageable size, some shortening and simplification has been unavoidable. Musicians who from a contemporary point of view no longer appear to be essential have been removed. Other musicians are mentioned only in passing. Nonetheless, as far as I can judge, all of the jazz musicians who have contributed to developing styles are represented.

The Jazz Book may be read selectively. In particular, the order in which the chapters are read is up to the reader. It is completely appropriate to begin with one of the chapters about a particular instrument, and from there to continue to "The Elements of Jazz," and to learn about the great musical personalities of jazz.

With regard to those personalities, in the earlier stylistic periods of jazz, the selection of which musicians to write about was almost automatic. Since the seventies, however, there are no longer individual musicians who can by themselves represent the development of a decade. For example, for the nineties it would also have been possible to choose Dave Douglas, Bill Frisell, or Uri Caine, but no musician combined the stylistic and genre-bridging tendencies of the jazz of the nineties in such a fascinating way as John Zorn did in his many musical projects.

Jazz styles do not succeed one another at intervals of ten years. At least since the seventies, the division into decades has served more as a means of chronological orientation than of stylistic classification. Experts should keep in mind that this book is also intended as an introduction; it is hoped that it can open the door for anyone interested in the world of jazz, regardless of whether they have any prior knowledge of it.

"Jazz is dead": this slogan has popped up again and again since the end of the twenties. Today as well, there are voices repeating this chorus. In reality, today jazz is more vital and diverse than ever.

For historical reasons alone, it would be advisable to think carefully before accusing contemporary players of a lack of stature or weak musicianship. Many of the musicians who are today celebrated as heroes of modern jazz—John Coltrane, Eric Dolphy, Thelonious Monk—were misunderstood in their own time and were strongly criticized for the music they played. In some cases, their now-undisputed status as great figures did not come to them until years after their death, leading clarinetist Don Byron to remark sarcastically, "There's nothing easier to love than a dead black man in general."

In the nineties, attempts were frequently made to pit the European jazz scene and the American jazz scene against one another, elevating one and denigrating the other, depending on the particular point of view. I see no reason to join these battles. However, in this book I have acknowledged the growing importance of European jazz.

I am also not interested in choosing sides in the "innovation versus tradition" debate that has raged since the nineties. In jazz there is a complex tension between tradition and innovation, both of which are inherent in the music. The obsessiveness with which the "Young Lions" embraced the jazz tradition in the nineties, celebrating and examining it from a contemporary perspective, has often been criticized as curatorial, more concerned with re-creation than with creation. Sometimes this criticism was justified, but the emphasis with which African American musicians placed the jazz tradition in the center of their music also has a great deal to do with the fact that African American music was primarily handed down as an oral tradition. Constant re-examination and questioning of a heritage that is transmitted orally is an unavoidable necessity.

Trumpeter Clark Terry provided what is perhaps the best description of the learning process of a jazz musician. Terry sees three stages in the development of the improvising musician: "imitation, assimilation, innovation." Only a few musicians will succeed in achieving the final stage of this process. But this does not mean that all the other players who assimilate and refine existing playing styles are performing less valuable work. Bassist John Golsby comments: "Let us not forget that it is the development of new techniques and musical ideas that brings about progress and growth in the jazz tradition."

In jazz criticism, there is a strong tendency to value innovators over those who develop and refine styles. As understandable as this tendency is, it conceals an essential impetus in the development of jazz, because often it is precisely those thousands of players, who absorb these new techniques and refine, develop, and differentiate them in personal ways, who make it possible for innovations to survive and to become an integral part of the jazz tradition. Without a relation to jazz tradition, innovation is not possible. As trumpeter Eddie Henderson says, "You can't be in the present if you haven't been in the past."

However, excessive respect for the jazz tradition also has something crippling and rigidifying about it. Anyone who regards the masterpieces of jazz as if they are unalterable edifices gives up the right to develop his or her own vision. Jazz is the sound of change, of transformation, expansion, and development. In this music, nothing stays the same. Bassist Ben Allison says, "Bebop was a music of its time. But today, hot dogs don't cost five cents anymore." And pianist Uri Caine adds, "The real tradition of jazz is permanent innovation."

We hope that this book will communicate a feeling for the jazz tradition in its entirety—the flowing, streaming quality of its development. Building on the innovations of other musicians, the give-and-take between improvisors: this is the jazz tradition. But jazz also includes plurality. For this reason, from a certain point of view, today many jazz traditions are "the tradition," whether you're talking about American jazz, European jazz, "world jazz," electric jazz, etc. This book aims to present all of them, without the prejudices, exaggerations, and ideological rigidity too often found in jazz criticism.

I'd like to quote the words of Joachim-Ernst Berendt here: "Creative artists in all spheres are of the opinion that the critic's main task doesn't involve criticizing but rather describing—that is, promoting understanding. I have always felt this to be my main goal. To be sure, this book is filled with criticism, but the idea of critically assessing every single musician would amount to overestimating the role of the critic, resulting in the know-it-all pedantry of which musicians (and other artists) have accused critics ever since (jazz) criticism came into being."

One of the many fascinating experiences that jazz has to offer is that of seeing how musicians again and again manage, within this tradition, to develop and add an unmistakably individual voice—one that the listener recognizes immediately, like the voice of a good friend on the telephone. The search of every jazz musician for an unmistakable style is also a search for the "inner voice." Guitarist John Scofield shares this insight: "I like what Charlie Haden said: Everyone has his own sound. It's there. You just have to believe in yourself enough to let it out."

In the nineties, jazz underwent globalization at a dizzying pace. The higher degree of synthesis in contemporary jazz is based not only on a greater integration of old and new, but also on increasing openness to other musical traditions. It's true that interest in African, Latin American, and Asian music is found throughout the entire history of jazz, but in the nineties this reached new heights. Contributing to this was not only the melting pot of New York, but also European jazz, with its cultures of migration. Here, the musicians of "imaginary folklore" showed a well-developed personality—despite postmodernism's slaughterhouse of styles, they were able to preserve regional cultural diversity in their jazz.

Jazz *is* world music, and has been ever since its beginning—a musical art form that grew on American soil out of the interaction of the very different African and European musical traditions. The stories that jazz tells us are messengers and ambassadors between the world's cultures. One often gets the feeling that jazz musicians are decades ahead of the world's societies in their cultural dialogues.

As the importance of migration increases in jazz, critics have spoken of "ghettoization." But in jazz there can be no "clash of civilizations" (in Samuel Huntington's formulation), simply because this music was based from the beginning on mixing. Despite the repressive, racist circumstances in which it arose, jazz came not from limitation but rather from crossovers and mutual influence between widely differing African, European, and American musical cultures—in short, from a dialogue. Jazz is a kind of bastard. And it will always remain so, in the future more than ever.

As globally as jazz has developed and will doubtless continue to develop, its core legacy will always be one that was formulated first of all by African Americans. The message of jazz is not only "Be yourself." Jazz is also telling us "Free yourself." Jazz is a music of community, of being together, of sharing, of skill, of negotiation: ultimately, of the ability to communicate.

The dialogical character of jazz conceals an emancipatory element. Improvised music is found all over the world, but jazz teaches the lesson of nonconformity. The communicative impulse that African Americans developed in jazz brought a new quality into the history of music: the idea, transmuted into sound and rhythm, of individuality, equality, dignity, and freedom. As trumpeter Wynton Marsalis puts it, "The power in jazz comes from the musical freedom of speech."

The jazz of the nineties showed that the attempt to make classic elements such as blues, Swing, groove, or standards part of the music is an important aid but not an absolute necessity. The essence of jazz is deeper than that. It is rooted in a musical ethics of improvisational self-determination, individuality, responsibility for oneself, and freedom.

Jazz is not only the "only procedural art form that has developed a tradition" (Diedrich Diederichsen). It is also, as Max Roach put it, a "democratic art form." I would count myself happy if something of this essence of the music were expressed in the pages of this book.

In writing this book, I often had the feeling that it would be necessary to invent a new language to do justice to the uniqueness of this music. As musical development pushes ever forward, subtle differentiations increase, and unorthodox stylistic combinations come to predominate, words often fail before the diversity and depth of the music. Or, as Kodwo Eshun put it, "language drags its fat ass behind the sound."

In the end, nothing is more important than hearing jazz. For this reason, this edition includes a completely revised discography prepared by Thomas Loewner, enabling the reader to gain rapid access to the most important recordings of the musicians mentioned in the text.

A book such as this one is necessarily based on works that came before it. We are indebted above all to: Leonard Feather's *Encyclopedia of Jazz*, André Hodeir's *Jazz—Its Evolution and Essence*, and Peter Niklas Wilson's *Hear and Now*. Particularly inspiring to me were those books written in intensive cooperation with musicians, such as Paul F. Berliner's *Thinking in Jazz*, Nat Shapiro and Nat Hentoff's *Hear Me Talkin' to Ya*, and the *Rough Guide to Jazz*, written by three practicing jazz musicians—Ian Carr, Brian Priestley, and Digby Fairweather.

The fine stylistic branching of jazz, its permanent musical growth, and the mutual give-and-take between its musicians make it an exciting musical adventure. I consider it to be a great privilege to participate in this adventure as a mediator between musicians and listeners.

I also felt the need to retain Berendt's tone as much as possible, and I am pleased that there are sections in the book, such as in the chapters "Coleman Hawkins and Lester Young" or "Charlie Parker and Dizzy Gillespie," in which nothing, or only the absolute minimum, was changed.

This revised edition is also a thank you to Joachim-Ernst Berendt, who influenced my professional development more than anyone else. Above all, however, it is a thank you to all of the musicians who have made jazz, for me, the most diverse and alive of all forms of music. I'd also like to thank my wife, Christiane Gerischer, and Martin Rubeau, who again and again gave me the courage to finish this job, even in the moments when it seemed too much for me.

GÜNTHER HUESMANN, Langerwisch, summer 2005

The Styles of Jazz

Jazz has always been the concern of a minority—always. Even in the age of Swing, the thirties, the jazz of creative black musicians was—except for very few recordings—recognized by only a few. Still, taking an active interest in jazz means working for a majority, because the popular music of our times feeds on jazz: all the music we hear in TV series and elevators, in hotel lobbies and in ads, in movies and on MP3 players; all the music to which we dance, from Charleston to rock, funk and hip-hop; all those sounds that daily engulf us—all that music comes from jazz (because their beats came to Western music through jazz).

Taking an active interest in jazz means improving the quality of the "sounds around us"—the level of musical quality, which implies, if there is any justification in talking about musical quality, the spiritual, intellectual, human quality—the level of our consciousness. In these times, when musical sounds accompany the takeoff of a plane as well as a detergent sales pitch, the "sounds around us" directly influence our way of life, the quality of our lives. That is why we can say that taking an active interest in jazz means carrying some of the power, warmth, and intensity of jazz into our lives.

Because of this, there is a direct and concretely demonstrable connection between the different kinds, forms, and styles of jazz on the one hand and the periods and spaces of time of their creation on the other hand.

The most impressive thing about jazz, aside from its musical value, in our opinion is its stylistic development. The evolution of jazz shows the continuity, logic, unity, and inner necessity that characterize all true art. This development constitutes a whole, and those who single out one phase and view it as either uniquely valid or as an aberration destroy this wholeness of conception. They distort that unity of large-scale evolution without which one can speak of fashions, but not of styles. It is our conviction that the styles of jazz are genuine and reflect their own particular times in the same sense that classicism, baroque, romanticism, and impressionism reflect their respective periods in European concert music.

Let's suggest one way of getting an impression of the wealth and scope of the different jazz styles. After reading about the early styles, ragtime and New Orleans, skip a few chapters and jump into the one on free jazz, listening to some of the characteristic records as well (which can easily be found with the help of the discography at the end of the book). What other art form has developed such contrasting, yet clearly interrelated, styles within a span of only fifty years?

It is important to be aware of the flowing, streamlike character of jazz history. It certainly is no coincidence that the word *stream* has been used again and again by jazz critics and musicians in connection with different jazz styles—interestingly enough, as "mainstream" first for Swing jazz, later for the main tendency of today's jazz, or as in "third stream." There is one mighty stream that flows from New Orleans right up to our contemporary music. Even breaks or revolutions in this history, such as the emergence of bebop or, later, free jazz, appear in retrospect as organic or even inevitable developments. The stream may flow over cataracts or form eddies or rapids from time to time, but it continues to flow on as ever the same stream. No one style "replaces" another; one isn't "better" than another. Each incorporates what went before—*everything* that went before.

Many great jazz musicians have felt the connection between their playing styles and the times in which they live. The untroubled joy of Dixieland corresponds to the days just prior to World War I. The restlessness of the Roaring Twenties comes to life in the Chicago style. Swing embodies the massive standardization of life before World War II; perhaps, to quote Marshall Stearns, Swing "was the answer to the American—and very human—love of bigness." Bebop captures the nervous restlessness of the forties. Cool jazz seems to reflect the resignation of men who live well yet know that H-bombs are being stockpiled. Hard bop is full of protest, soon turned into conformity by the fashion for funk and soul music. This protest gains uncompromising, often angry urgency in free jazz, which characterized the period of the civil rights movement and the student revolt. In the seventies there was a renewed phase of consolidation. Some aspects of jazz-rock went along with the age's faith in technology. The jazz of the eighties, on the other hand, expresses much of the skepticism of people who live amid affluence but also know where ongoing unquestioned progress has brought them. In its pluralism and its aggressive multistylistic tendencies, the jazz of the nineties is a reaction to the data explosion of the information age. What has been said in such a generalized and simplified way here is even more applicable to the many different styles of individual musicians and bands.

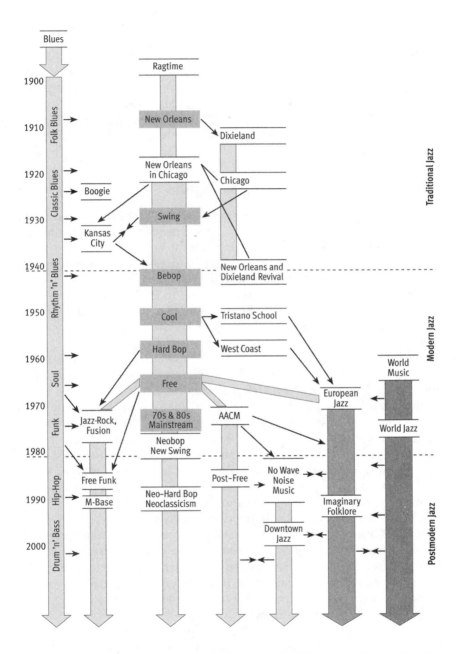

The development of jazz, with the blues as backbone, and showing the post–free-jazz stylistic delta.

Many jazz musicians have viewed attempts at reconstructing past jazz styles with skepticism. They know that historicism runs counter to the nature of jazz. Jazz stands and falls on being alive, and whatever lives, changes. When Count Basie's music became a worldwide success in the fifties, Lester Young, who had been one of the leading soloists of the old Basie band, was asked to participate in a recording with his old teammates for the purpose of reconstructing the Basie style of the thirties. "I can't do it," Lester said. "I don't play that way any more. I play different; I live different. This is later. That was then. We change, move on." Obviously, this is also true about contemporary reconstructions of historical jazz styles.

Around 1890: Ragtime

Jazz originated in New Orleans: a truism, with all that is true and false about such statements. It is true that New Orleans was the most important city in the genesis of jazz. It is false that it was the only one. Jazz— the music of a continent, a century, a civilization—was too much in the air to be reducible to the patented product of a single city. Similar ways of playing evolved in Memphis and St. Louis, in Dallas and Kansas City, in other cities of the South and Midwest. And this, too, is the hallmark of a style: different people in different places making the same (or similar) artistic discoveries independently of each other.

It has become customary to speak of New Orleans style as the first style in jazz. But before New Orleans style developed, there was ragtime. Its capital was not New Orleans but Sedalia, Missouri, where Scott Joplin had settled. Joplin, born in Texas in 1868, was the leading ragtime composer and pianist—and thus we have made the decisive point about ragtime: It was largely composed, primarily pianistic music. Since it was composed, it lacks one essential characteristic of jazz: improvisation. Yet ragtime swings, at least in a rudimentary sense, and so it is considered part of jazz. And the practice of not only interpreting rags but also using them as themes for jazz improvisations began quite early.

What today seems the epitome of ragtime—the piano rags of Scott Joplin and others—is in fact a late peak in a long development involving an abundance of ragtime forms: vocal ragtime songs, Texan banjo rags (which musicologists assume served as the basis for piano ragtime), ragtimes for brass bands and rags for strings, and ragtime waltzes written by composers who were often more popular than Joplin, even though today they are only known to specialists.

Posterity only remembers the "classic" piano ragtime. Justly so, since it crystallized not only the most artistically valuable aspects of ragtime but also the elements that were to influence jazz most (whereas ragtime songs became important for the tradition of the popular song).

"Classic" ragtime seems to be composed in the style of nineteenth-century piano music. Sometimes it appears to adhere to the trio form of the classical minuet; at others it consists of several successive formal units, as in the waltzes of Johann Strauss. It is, however, important to realize—and this characterizes the complexity of the development of African American music—that the forms of ragtime also have African origins. Additive forms are even more important in African than in European music. In ragtime, European music and African music met as equals for the first time in America.

Pianistically too, ragtime reflects much of nineteenth-century music. Everything of importance at that time can be found there, from Chopin and above all Liszt to marches and polkas, all recast in the rhythmic conception and dynamic way of playing of African Americans. And that was also how it was perceived: ragtime is, as the name suggests, "ragged time." Unlike in European music, rhythm dictates the melody.

Ragtime was particularly popular in the camps of workers building the great railroads across the American continent. Ragtime was heard everywhere—in Sedalia and Kansas City, in St. Louis and Texas, Joplin's home state. The composers of rags hammered their pieces into player-piano rolls, which were distributed by the thousands.

That was way before the time of the phonograph, and at first little was known about all this. Only in the fifties were substantial numbers of the old piano rolls rediscovered, sometimes quite accidentally in places like antique stores and junk shops, and transferred to records.

Aside from Joplin, there were many other ragtime pianists: Tom Turpin, a St. Louis bar owner (particularly melodically inventive); Joseph Lamb, a textile merchant (celebrated for the complex motivic interweavings in his rags); Louis Chauvin; May Aufderheide; and, above all, Eubie Blake. At the age of ninety, Blake made a spectacular comeback at the great 1973 Newport–New York Jazz Festival and even had his own Broadway show in the late seventies. Blake made thousands of young people who no longer knew what ragtime was "rag conscious" once again. He died in 1983, just a few days after his hundredth birthday.

There were several whites among the great rag pianists around the turn of the century, and it is significant that even experts were not able to detect differences in playing style between blacks and whites. Ragtime, as Orrin Keepnews once put it, is "on the cool side."

Scott Joplin was a master of melodic invention. He was amazingly productive, and among his more than thirty rags are such melodies as "Maple Leaf Rag" and "The Entertainer" (which became immensely popular in 1973, almost sixty years after Joplin's death, through the motion picture The Sting). In Joplin, as in ragtime per se, the old European tradition merged with the black rhythmic feeling. Ragtime, more than any other form of jazz, may be described as "white music, played black."

How much Joplin was at home in the European tradition is apparent not only in the construction of his rags, but also in the fact that he composed a symphony and two operas.

Among the first musicians to liberate themselves from the strictures of the composer-imposed interpretation of rags and take a freer and more jazzlike approach to melodic material was Jelly Roll Morton, one of the important musicians with whom the New Orleans tradition begins. "I invented jazz in 1902," he once claimed, and on his business card he described himself as "creator of ragtime." Both statements are hyperbole, but Morton is important as the first known jazz pianist who truly improvised on themes, mostly his own, that were rags or derived from ragtime music.

In Morton we recognize for the first time the decisive fact that the personality of the performing musician is more important in jazz than the material contributed by the composer.

Jelly Roll carried the ragtime tradition to the Chicago of the Roaring Twenties, and even to California. Other pianists—James P. Johnson, Willie "The Lion" Smith, and young Fats Waller—kept ragtime, or at least the ragtime tradition, alive in New York during the twenties. At that time, apart from the "boogie-woogie" musicians, there was scarcely a jazz pianist whose origins could not be traced, in one way or another, to ragtime.

Turn of the Century: New Orleans

At the turn of the century, New Orleans was a witches' cauldron of peoples and races. The city had been under Spanish and French rule prior to the Louisiana Purchase. French and Spaniards, followed by English and Italians, and lastly joined by Germans and Slavs, faced the descendants of the countless Africans brought here as slaves. And among the black population as well there were differences in nationality and culture no less significant than those, say, between the whites from England and the whites from Spain.

All these voluntary and involuntary immigrants loved first of all their own music: what they wanted to keep alive as sounds of home. In New Orleans, people sang British folk songs, danced Spanish dances, played French dance and ballet music, and marched to the strains of brass bands based on Prussian or French models. Hymns and chorales of Puritans and Catholics, Baptists and Methodists could be heard in the churches; mingled with all these sounds were the "shouts" of the black street vendors, and the black dances and rhythms. As late as the 1850s, blacks congregated periodically in Congo Square to perform voodoo rites, thus preserving a cult with origins in ancient African traditions. Recent converts to Christianity, they celebrated the new god in song and dance much as they had honored the deities of their native land. Old New Orleans must have been an incredibly musical city. We know of some thirty orchestras from the first decade of the twentieth century. To appreciate what that means, you have to know that the Crescent City had little more than two hundred thousand inhabitants then. And in a city of that size, there were thirty orchestras, playing a vital, new kind of music.

All this created an atmosphere that made the New Orleans of those days a symbol of strange, exotic romanticism for travelers from all parts of the earth. It is certainly a myth that this city in the Mississippi River delta was the sole birthplace of jazz, but New Orleans was indeed the point where many important aspects of the music first crystallized. New Orleans was a watershed—for the music of the countryside, such as the work songs of the black plantation laborers; for the spirituals that were sung during the religious services for which they gathered under open skies; and for the old "primitive" blues-folk songs. All these things merged in the earliest forms of jazz.

W. C. Handy, the blues composer, related that the music played in Memphis around 1905 was not very different from that of New Orleans. "But we didn't discover until 1917 that New Orleans had such music, too," Handy said. "Every circus band played this way." The entire Mississippi delta was full of the new sounds—all rising independent of each other. "The river and the city were equally important to jazz."

New Orleans, in spite of this, held a special place. Well into the thirties, more than half of the important jazz musicians came from there. Four reasons may have been decisive:

- First, the old French-Spanish urban culture of the Crescent City, favoring cultural interchanges, unlike other American cities where Puritanism and Victorian values predominated.

- Second, the tensions and challenges arising from the fact that, as we shall see, two decidedly different black populations confronted each other here.

- Third, the intense musical life of the city in terms of European "serious" and popular music, to which the blacks were constantly exposed.

- And finally, the fact that all these varied elements came together in Storyville, the city's red-light district, relatively free of prejudice or class consciousness.

The two African American populations of New Orleans were the Creoles and the "American Negroes." However, obviously, the Creoles, in the geographical sense, were just as "American" as other blacks— perhaps even more so. The Creoles of Louisiana emerged from the old French colonial culture. They were not, like other blacks, descendants of slaves who had gained freedom at the end of the Civil War. Their ancestors had been free much longer. Many of them had been freed by rich French planters or merchants for reasons of distinguished service. The term *Free Negro* was an important one in old New Orleans.

The Creole African Americans had made French culture their own. Many were wealthy businessmen. Their main language was not English but Creole, a French patois with admixtures of Spanish and African words. Their names were French: Alphonse Picou, Sidney Bechet, Barney Bigard, Albert Nicholas, Buddy Petit, Freddie Keppard, Papa and Louis deLisle Nelson, Kid Ory, etc. It was an honor to be a Creole. Jelly Roll Morton took great pains to make clear that he was a Creole and that his real name was Ferdinand Joseph LaMenthe.

Compared to the Creoles, the American blacks were "more African." Their masters were of Anglo-Saxon origin, and thus they were not exposed to the more liberal social attitudes of the French-Spanish orbit. The American blacks constituted the poor black proletariat of New Orleans. The Creoles looked down on them with a particular class- and color-consciousness that "at that time was even more prejudiced to other blacks than the attitude of white people to the colored generally was," as guitarist Johnny St. Cyr put it.

Consequently, there were two very different groups of New Orleans musicians, and the difference found expression in the music. The Creole group was more cultured and educated (skilled in reading notes), the American more vital and spontaneous (handing down its music orally). But, as is so often true in such cases, it was clear early on that the really outstanding players combined elements of both these traditions. The most convincing example was pianist, composer, and orchestra leader Jelly Roll Morton.

The main instrument of the Creole group was the clarinet, which has a great tradition in France. The old French woodwind tradition remained alive well into the thirties in the playing of the leading Swing clarinetists. In fact, Eric Dolphy, in the late fifties, was the first to drop it totally.

In New Orleans itself, the Creole/French influence can hardly be overestimated. Many of the things that gave the city the fascinating atmosphere, without which its jazz life would have been inconceivable, stem from France. Thus, there is the famous Mardi Gras, which has become the expression of the city's lust for life. Even the funerals, during which a band escorts the deceased to the cemetery with sad music and then leads the procession back home with joyful sounds, derive from a French custom; it prevails to this day in rural districts of southern France.

In the mingling of the many ethnic and musical strains in New Orleans, which occurred almost automatically in the laissez-faire climate of Storyville, New Orleans style was born. It is characterized by three melody lines, generally played by cornet (or trumpet), trombone, and clarinet. The lead is taken by the brilliant sound of the cornet, effectively contrasted by the heavy, weighty trombone. The clarinet entwines the two brasses in an intricate pattern of melodic lines. This front line is supported by the rhythm section: string bass or tuba, drums, banjo or guitar, and occasionally piano.

The early New Orleans rhythm is still very close to European march rhythm. The peculiar "floating" effect of jazz rhythm, stemming from the fact that 1 and 3 remain the strong beats but 2 and 4 are accented, is as yet absent. The stress is still on 1 and 3, just as in a march.

The early New Orleans jazz bands resembled the marching and circus bands of the day in other respects too, such as instrumentation and social function.

New Orleans style is the first example of "hot" playing. *Hot* connotes the emotional warmth and intensity of the music and has come to stand for the peculiar sound, phrasing, "attack," and vibrato that characterize this style. From that point on, all these musical elements become individualized. The instrument is not so much played as made to "talk"—to express the individual feelings of the musician.

The Teens: Dixieland

In New Orleans, playing jazz was not exclusively a privilege of the black man. There seem to have been white bands almost from the start. "Papa" Jack Laine led bands in New Orleans from 1891 on. He is known as the father of white jazz. Bands traveled through the city on carts, known as band wagons, or marched along the streets. When two bands met, a contest, or "battle," ensued. It sometimes happened that black and white bands became engaged in such contests, and when the white band was led by Papa Laine, it often "blew out" its opponent.

From the earliest time, there was a white style of playing jazz: less expressive, but sometimes better versed technically. The melodies were smoother, the harmony "purer," the sonorities not so unorthodox. There were fewer bent notes, less expressive vibrato, fewer portamenti and glissandi. Whenever these effects were used, there was an element of self-consciousness involved, of knowing that one *could* also play "legitimately"; often the music approached the eccentric, even the downright comic. In contrast, the music of the black bands, whether joyful or blue, always contained the aspect of *having* to be that way.

All the successful early white bands stem from Papa Laine. And there is no doubt that the first successful groups in jazz were white (due to easier access to the means of production and to records): first and foremost the Original Dixieland Jazz Band, and then the New Orleans Rhythm Kings. The ODJB, as it has come to be known, with its punchy, collective style (there were almost no solos), made many early jazz standards famous. Among them were "Tiger Rag" and "Original Dixieland One-Step" (recorded in 1917) and "At the Jazz Band Ball" (recorded in 1919). The

New Orleans Rhythm Kings, with their two outstanding soloists, Leon Rappolo, clarinet, and Georg Brunis, trombone, devoted more room to solo improvisation. They first recorded in 1922 and became famous in the early twenties.

In 1917, the ODJB played at Reisenweber's Restaurant on Columbus Circle in New York and made a tremendous hit. From that time on, the word *jazz*—at first usually spelled "jass"—became known to the general public. Bandleader Tom Brown claims to have used the word publicly for the first time in Chicago in 1915. But it appears as early as 1913 in a San Francisco newspaper. Prior to that, *jass*, and the earlier *jasm* and *gism*, were in use as slang expressions for speed and energy in athletic pursuits, and in sexual contexts as well.

It has become customary to label all New Orleans European-American jazz "Dixieland," thus separating it from essential New Orleans style, but the borderlines remain fluid. Especially in later years, with black musicians playing in white bands or vice versa, it no longer made any sense to argue about which style was being played.

The origin of the word *Dixieland* has been the subject of much speculation and legend. One story has it that the term stems from the ten-dollar bills used in Louisiana, on which the French word *dix* (ten) appeared alongside the English *ten*. Yankees were said to have called the region Dixieland, after the money, and then named the music after the region. According to another theory, the term comes from the name of Jeremiah Dixon, one of the land surveyors for whom the Mason-Dixon Line was named.

With ragtime, New Orleans, and Dixieland, the history of jazz begins. What was earlier belongs to what the late jazz historian Marshall Stearns called "jazz prehistory."

Jazz was born in the encounter between black and white. That is why it originated where this meeting took place in the most intensive fashion: the southern part of the United States. Until this day, jazz is conceivable only in terms of this interaction. It loses its fundamental rationale when one or the other element is overemphasized, or even given a status of exclusiveness, as has been done.

The contact between cultures that has been so important in the evolution and development of jazz symbolizes that spirit of "togetherness" per se that characterizes jazz in musical, national, international, social, sociological, political, expressive, aesthetic, ethical, and ethnological terms.

The Twenties: Chicago

There are three essential things about jazz in the twenties: the great period of New Orleans music in Chicago, classic blues, and Chicago style.

The development of New Orleans jazz in Chicago is generally connected with the entry of the United States into World War I. This connection appears somewhat dubious but may, along with other factors, have played a certain role. New Orleans became a war port. The secretary of the navy viewed the goings on in Storyville as a danger to the morale of his troops. Storyville was closed by official decree.

This decree deprived not only the ladies of Storyville but also many musicians of their daily bread—particularly the pianists mainly employed in Storyville, at that time known as "professors." Even before that, hundreds of other musicians for whom Storyville wasn't as important had already experienced economic hardship. Many left town, most of them to Chicago. The Windy City on Lake Michigan had previously been a source of fascination for many New Orleans musicians. Now came the great exodus of New Orleans musicians to Chicago, and it is clear that this was only a part of the general migration of blacks from south to north. The first jazz style, though called New Orleans, actually had its really great period in the Chicago of the twenties. It was in Chicago that the most famous New Orleans jazz recordings were made, as the phonograph became increasingly popular after World War I.

King Oliver was the leader of the most important New Orleans band in Chicago. It was here that Louis Armstrong formed his Hot Five and Hot Seven, Jelly Roll Morton his Red Hot Peppers, Johnny Dodds his New Orleans Wanderers, etc. What is known as New Orleans style today is not the archaic and barely recorded jazz that existed in New Orleans in the first two decades of the twentieth century, but the music made by New Orleans musicians in Chicago during the third decade.

The blues also had its great period in the Chicago of the twenties. Certainly blues songs existed before there was jazz, at least from the late nineteenth century. In those days, they were heard in the rural districts of the South, mostly without a steady jazz beat and often lacking the standard twelve-bar pattern that characterizes the blues today. Itinerant blues singers traveled from town to town, from plantation to plantation, with a banjo (or guitar) and a bundle containing all their worldly possessions, singing those songs with the drawn-out "blue" notes known today as "country" blues.

When the first marching bands began to play in New Orleans, there was a difference between their budding "jazz" and the blues. But soon the rural blues began to flow into the mainstream of jazz, and from then on jazz and blues became so interwoven that, as Ernest Borneman has written, all of jazz is "nothing but the application of the blues to European music, or vice versa." Even the most modern and "freest" jazz musician of today is indebted to the blues; in fact, blues consciousness is higher in today's jazz than in many previous styles.

The twenties are considered the period of "classic" blues. Bessie Smith was its greatest singer. In later chapters, Bessie Smith herself and the harmony, melody, and form of the blues will be discussed. It is with good reason that the blues are treated in a special section as an element of jazz. It was not only a certain style of jazz in the early times, but it has left its mark on all forms of jazz and on the whole history of the music. The intention here is to give a summary of the development of jazz in its entirety for easier orientation in the following chapters.

Around the great jazz instrumentalists from New Orleans and the famous blues singers there developed in Chicago a jazz life hardly less active than that of New Orleans in the Golden Age. Centered on the South Side, Chicago's African American district, it lacked the happy exuberance of the old New Orleans days but reflected the hectic pace of the metropolis and, increasingly, the problems of racial discrimination.

Stimulated by the jazz life of the South Side, young white high school and college students, amateur and professional musicians, began to develop what has been called Chicago style. They had become so inspired by the greats of New Orleans jazz that they wanted to emulate their style. As imitation, their music was unsuccessful; instead they came up with something new: Chicago style. In it, the profusion of melodic lines, so typical of New Orleans style, is more or less absent. The voicings, if there is more than one line, are in most cases parallel. The individual has become the ruler. From this point on, the solo becomes increasingly important in jazz. Many Chicago-style recordings consist of hardly more than a sequence of solos or, in jazz terminology, choruses.

Only then did the saxophone, which to many laypeople represents jazz incarnate, begin to gain importance. Chicago may be considered the second "cool" style of jazz (the first being piano ragtime). Bix Beiderbecke is the foremost representative of this style, which will be discussed at greater length in the section about him.

The Thirties: Swing

The older styles of jazz are grouped together under the heading "two-beat jazz." Toward the end of the twenties, the two-beat styles seemed all but exhausted. In Harlem, and even more in Kansas City, a new way of playing developed around 1928–29. With the second great exodus in jazz history—the journey from Chicago to New York—Swing begins. Swing may be characterized as four-beat jazz, because it puts stress on all four beats of the bar. This is true in general, but as is so often the case in jazz, there are confusing exceptions. Louis Armstrong (and some Chicago-style players) were already conversant with four-beat style in the twenties. On the other hand, Jimmie Lunceford's big band at the height of the Swing era employed a beat that was simultaneously 2/4 and 4/4.

The word *swing* is a key term in jazz, and it is used in two different senses. This may lead to a certain amount of confusion. First, swing connotes a rhythmic element from which jazz derives the tension classical music gets from its formal structure. This swing is present in all styles, phases, and periods of jazz. It is so essential that it has been said that if music does not swing, it is not jazz.

The other use of the term refers to the dominant jazz style of the thirties—the style through which jazz won its greatest commercial success before the emergence of fusion music. In the Swing era, Benny Goodman became the King of Swing.

There is a difference between saying that a jazz piece swings and that it *is* Swing. Any jazz tune that is Swing also swings—if it is any good. But, conversely, not all jazz that swings is necessarily Swing. In order to avoid confusion, it was suggested in an earlier edition of this book that the *style* Swing should be capitalized, while lowercase swing should connote the rhythmic element. Many jazz scholars all over the world have adopted this practice. In the Rhythm, Swing, Groove chapter, the nature of swing (lowercase) will be described further.

One feature of the Swing era was the development of big bands. In Kansas City (e.g., in the bands of Bennie Moten and later Count Basie), the "riff" style developed. This was an application of the old, important call-and-response pattern (originating in Africa) to the sections of a large jazz band. These sections are trumpets, trombones, and saxes. The riffs (emphatic two- or four-bar phrases that are repeated) put the "heat" into big-band jazz; in Kansas City orchestras and jam sessions, these riffs were often invented on the spot in order to stoke the fire under the soloist. Another contribution to big-band jazz was made by the white Chicago style: a more "European" approach to the music. In Benny Goodman's band, the different styles flowed together: some New Orleans tradition, through Fletcher Henderson, who arranged for the band; the riff technique of Kansas City; and that white precision and training through which this brand of jazz somehow lost so much of its expressivity. On the other hand, the easy melodic quality and clean intonation of Goodman's band made it possible to sell jazz to a mass audience.

It only seems to be a contradiction that the individual soloist gained in importance alongside the development of big bands. Jazz has always been simultaneously collective and individualistic. That jazz, more than any other music, can be both at the same time clarifies much about its nature. This is jazz's particular characteristic (we'll talk about it later), mirroring the social situation of the modern era.

Thus, the thirties also became the era of great soloists: the tenor saxists Coleman Hawkins and Chu Berry; the clarinetist Benny Goodman; the drummers Gene Krupa, Cozy Cole, and Sid Catlett; the pianists Fats Waller and Teddy Wilson; the alto saxists Benny Carter and Johnny Hodges; the trumpeters Roy Eldridge, Bunny Berigan, and Rex Stewart; and many more.

Often these two tendencies—the orchestral and the soloistic—merged. Benny Goodman's clarinet seemed all the more glamorous against the backdrop of his big band. Louis Armstrong's trumpet stood out in bold relief when accompanied by a big band. And the voluminous tone of Coleman Hawkins's or Chu Berry's tenor sax seemed to gain from the contrast to the "hard" sound of Fletcher Henderson's big band.

The Forties: Bebop

By the end of the thirties, Swing had become a gigantic business enterprise. It has been called the greatest music business of all time (which was true then, but the record sales of the thirties and forties were modest compared to the dimensions of today's music business). The word *Swing* became a marketing device for all sorts of goods, from cigarettes to articles of female clothing, while the music, conforming to general commercial demands, often became a matter of endlessly repeated clichés.

As is so often the case in jazz when a style or way of playing becomes too commercialized, the evolution turned in the opposite direction. A group of musicians who had something new to say found each other in a healthy, although not in all cases deliberate, reaction against the general Swing fashion.

This new music developed—at first in spurts—originally in Kansas City and then, most of all, in the musicians' hangouts in Harlem (particularly in a place called Minton's Playhouse) and once again at the beginning of a decade. Contrary to what has been claimed, this new music did *not* develop when a group of musicians banded together to create something new, at whatever cost, because the old was no longer a draw. The old style drew very well—it was still the "greatest music business of all time." Nor is it true that the new jazz style was shaped as a conscious effort by an interrelated group of musicians. The new style was formed in the minds and instruments of different musicians in different places, independent of each other. But Minton's became a focal point, as New Orleans had been forty years earlier. And just as Jelly Roll Morton's claim to have invented jazz was absurd, so would be the claim of any musician in the forties to have "invented" modern jazz.

The new style was eventually named bebop, a word that seemed to mirror the vocalization of the then best-loved interval of the music: the flatted fifth. The term *bebop* came into being spontaneously when someone attempted to "sing" these melodic leaps. This is the explanation that trumpeter Dizzy Gillespie, one of the main exponents of the new style, gave for the origin of the term *bebop*. There are as many theories about the origin of this word as there are about most jazz expressions.

The flatted fifth became the most important interval of bebop, or, as it was soon called, bop. Until then, this device would have been felt to be erroneous, or at least "wrong" sounding, although it might have been used in passing chords or for the special harmonic effects that Duke Ellington and pianist Willie "The Lion" Smith liked to use as early as in the twenties. But now it characterized an entire style, as the narrow harmonic base of earlier jazz forms was constantly broadened. Within ten or twelve years (as we shall see) the flatted fifth was to become a "blue note," as common as the undetermined thirds and sevenths familiar in traditional blues.

The most important musicians who gathered at Minton's were Thelonious Monk, piano; Kenny Clarke, drums; Charlie Christian, guitar; trumpeter Dizzy Gillespie; and alto saxist Charlie Parker. The latter was to become the real genius of modern jazz as Louis Armstrong was the genius of traditional jazz.

One of these musicians—Christian—not only belongs among the founders of modern jazz but also among those who fashioned from Swing the foundations for its development. There is a whole group of such pioneers, at once the "last" generation of Swing and the pathbreakers for bop. And almost every instrument had its own bebop pioneer: among trumpeters, it is Roy Eldridge; among pianists, Clyde Hart; among tenors, Lester Young; among bassists, Jimmy Blanton; among drummers, Jo Jones and Dave Tough; among guitarists, Charlie Christian.

To the listener of that time, the sounds characteristic of bebop seemed to be racing, nervous phrases that occasionally appeared as melodic fragments. Every unnecessary note was left out. Everything was highly concentrated. As a bop musician once said, "Everything that is obvious is excluded." It is a kind of musical shorthand, and you have to listen to it in the same way you would read a stenographic transcript, establishing ordered relationships from a few hasty signs.

The improvisations are framed by the theme presented (often in unison) at the beginning and the end of each piece, generally played by two horns, in most cases a trumpet and saxophone (archetypically, Dizzy Gillespie and Charlie Parker). This unison alone—even before the musicians began to improvise—introduced a new sound and a new attitude. Music psychology knows that unisons, wherever they appear—from Beethoven's "Ode to Joy" and even earlier in the main motif of the Ninth Symphony's first movement to North African Bedouin music and to the choirs of the Arabic world—signal, "Listen, this is *our* statement. It is *we* who are talking. And you to whom we speak, you are different from us and are probably our opponents."

Confronted by this then avant-garde bop sound, many friends of jazz didn't know what to make of this new turn in the evolution of the music. With great determination, they oriented themselves backward, toward the basic forms of jazz. "Simple" music was demanded. There was a New Orleans renaissance—or, as it was called, revival—that spread all over the world.

This development began as a sound reconsideration of the roots of jazz—the tradition that to this day nourishes jazz in all its forms and phases. But soon the revival led to a simplified and cliché-ridden "traditional" jazz from which African American musicians turned away. (With the exception of the surviving New Orleans jazz musicians, for whom traditional jazz was the logical form of expression, no important black musicians participated in the Dixieland revival—strange as this may sound to some.) Amateurs often worked against the commercialization of Dixieland, but they regularly fell victim to it themselves as they attained professional status.

After World War II, the "jazz boîtes" in Saint-Germain-des-Prés in Paris became the headquarters of the traditional movement, fortified with existentialist philosophy. But soon the young existentialists discovered that their philosophy was better suited to a music that did not reflect the happy, carefree attitudes of the early years of the century, but rather the unrest of their own times. They gravitated toward more contemporary jazz forms, and the center of the movement shifted to England. In that country, Dixieland concerts were organized with the same commercial effort and success as presentations of rock 'n' roll singers.

In this section, bebop and the New Orleans revival have been contrasted in the same way that they appeared to be in contrast to each other to jazz fans at that time: as extremes of antagonistic opposition. Today—and actually since the genesis of free jazz in the sixties—these poles have approached each other, for today's young listener can no longer appreciate this contrast. To him, Charlie Parker is just as much a part of the jazz tradition as Louis Armstrong.

In describing bebop, we have used terms like *racing, nervous, melodic fragments, cipher, hasty.* But in the face of what is racing, nervous, fragmented, and hasty in today's scene, most of the jazz of the forties seems of almost classic completeness to the young listener today. One can only hope that listeners and critics of today's jazz learn from this development and use greater caution in the application of extreme words and concepts. The critics who foresaw the "end of jazz" or even the "end of music" in reaction to the "nervousness" of bop seem a bit ridiculous today, but there were a lot of them once. They are here today, too, in reaction to what seems nervous and loud.

It is appropriate here to pause and consider what has become of the great musicians who created bebop. In the eighties and nineties, only one of them, Max Roach, was still creatively active in the vein of the scene of the forties: with his contemporary percussion group, for instance; or in his duo concerts with avant-garde musicians like Cecil Taylor, Anthony Braxton, and Archie Shepp; or playing together with string quartets or with the Beijing Trio, inspired by Chinese music. Another of the bop fathers, Dizzy Gillespie, was still creative in the bebop style until his death in 1993. The others have either become artistically rigid or have died—most of them after psychological or physical illness, after heroin or alcohol addiction. And even though they died young (Charlie Parker, for example, was thirty-four), they were past the peak of their creativity at the time of their deaths, at an age when other artists often only begin to gain real stature.

Compare the bebop musicians with the creative personalities of European art—figures like Stravinsky or Schoenberg, Picasso, Kandinsky, or Chagall. They lived to a ripe old age and remained creative, and the whole world respects and admires them. For the creative musicians of bebop, however, early death was often the rule, and nobody is writing papers and essays about it. That seems to be the toll jazz artists in America have to pay to society, which accepts it without batting an eyelash.

But that is also the backdrop that makes this music so powerful and impressive and that makes the work of these soon rigidified or perished artists seem that much more admirable. And it is no accident that at the end of the seventies we witnessed a bebop revival that hardly anyone would have forecast some years ago. Bebop has become the embodiment of classical modernity in jazz. Indeed, in the jazz of the nineties and later, it became such a dominant factor that Scott DeVeaux could write: "In order to understand jazz, you have to understand bebop." An entire generation of young people plays this music, and today, in the first decade of the twenty-first century, more than ever before. They won't suffer breakdowns or die from heroin like their forerunners. This revival is occurring over fifty years after Charlie Parker's death, sixty years since Bud Powell's first breakdown, and fifty-five years after bop trumpeter Fats Navarro died, right after his twenty-sixth birthday.

The Fifties: Cool Jazz, Hard Bop

Toward the end of the forties, the "unrest and excitement of bop" were more and more replaced by a tendency toward calm and smoothness. This trend first became apparent in the playing of trumpeter Miles Davis. As an eighteen-year-old, he had played in Charlie Parker's Quintet of 1945 in the turbulent style of Dizzy Gillespie; not much later, however, he began to blow in a relaxed and "cool" manner. The trend also showed up in the piano improvisations of John Lewis, an anthropology student from New Mexico who traveled with Dizzy Gillespie's big band to Paris in 1948 and only then decided to remain in music; and in the arrangements Tadd Dameron wrote in the second half of the forties for the same Gillespie big band and for various small combinations. Miles Davis's trumpet solos of 1947 with Charlie Parker, such as "Chasin' the Bird," or John Lewis's piano solo in Dizzy Gillespie's version of "'Round Midnight," recorded at a 1948 concert in Paris—these are the first cool solos in jazz history, excepting Lester Young's tenor sax solos with Count Basie from the late thirties, in which he paved the way for the cool conception even before the bebop era had begun.

With these three musicians—Miles Davis, John Lewis, and Tadd Dameron—the style known as cool jazz begins.

The cool conception dominates all the jazz of the first half of the fifties, but it is notable that it found its most valid and representative expression at a moment almost coincidental with its origin: in the famed recordings of the Miles Davis Orchestra, which was formed for a brief engagement at New York's Royal Roost in 1948 and was recorded by the Capitol label in 1949 and 1950. In the chapter dealing with Davis, this group—of decisive importance to the ensemble sound and musical conception of the decade—will be discussed in detail.

Lennie Tristano (1919–78), a blind pianist from Chicago who came to New York in 1946 and founded his New School of Music there in 1951, gave a theoretical foundation to cool jazz through his music and thinking. The musicians of the Tristano school (notably altoist Lee Konitz, tenorman Warne Marsh, and guitarist Billy Bauer) were to a large extent responsible for the layman's idea of cool jazz as cold, intellectual, and emotionless music. However, there can be no doubt that Tristano and his musicians improvised with remarkable freedom, and that linear improvisation stood at the center of their interests. Thus Tristano let himself be advertised as Lennie Tristano and His Intuitive Music; he wanted to emphasize the intuitive character of his conception and ward off the lay opinion that his was an intellectually calculated music. Still, Tristano's music held for many listeners a coolness often bordering on a chill. The evolution of modern jazz soon found less abstract, more sensuous and vital forms. The problem was, as Stearns has said, "to play cool without being cold."

The influence of the Tristano school has remained traceable throughout all of modern jazz, however far removed from the Tristano-ite mode of coolness. This is true harmonically, but most of all in a distinct preference for long, linear melodic lines.

After Tristano, the center moved initially to the West Coast. Here evolved, directly connected to the Miles Davis Capitol Orchestra, a "West Coast jazz," often played by musicians who made their living in the Hollywood studio orchestras. Trumpeter Shorty Rogers, drummer Shelly Manne, and clarinetist-saxophonist Jimmy Giuffre became the style-setting musicians of the West Coast. Their music contained elements of the academic European musical tradition; direct and vital jazz content was often pushed into the background. The experts frequently pointed out that New York remained the true capital of jazz. This was where real and vital jazz was made: modern, yet rooted in jazz tradition. West Coast jazz was confronted with "East Coast jazz."

Since then, it has become apparent that both "coasts" were not so much stylistic entities as advertising slogans promoted by record companies. The real tension in the evolution of the jazz of the fifties was not between two coasts but between a classicist direction and a group of young musicians, mostly of African American origin, who played a modern version of bebop, so-called hard bop.

The new fifties jazz classicism—as French critic André Hodeir has called it—found its "classics" in the music Lester Young and Count Basie had played in the thirties, first in Kansas City and later in New York. Many musicians from either coast, white and black, were oriented toward this music: Al Cohn, Joe Newman, Ernie Wilkins, Manny Albam, Johnny Mandel, Chico Hamilton, Buddy Collette, Gerry Mulligan, Bob Brookmeyer, Shorty Rogers, Quincy Jones, Jimmy Giuffre. In the fifties, a massive number of "Count Basie tributes" were recorded. Basie's name stands for clarity, melodiousness, swing, and certainly that "noble simplicity" of which Winckelmann, a German scholar of the eighteenth century, spoke in his famous definition of classicism. (It is amazing how often it is possible to employ, almost literally, the words of the German classicists of the Goethe period when speaking of jazz classicism. One needs only to substitute for the names and concepts from Greek art and mythology Count Basie and Lester Young, swing, beat, and blues.)

Confronting this classicism stood a generation of young musicians whose foremost representatives lived in New York, though few of them were born there. Most were from Detroit or Philadelphia. Their music was the purest bop, enriched by a greater knowledge of harmonic fundamentals and a greater degree of instrumental-technical perfection. This hard bop was the most dynamic jazz played in the second half of the fifties—by groups under the leadership of, among others, drummers Max Roach and Art Blakey and pianist Horace Silver; by musicians like trumpeters Clifford Brown, Lee Morgan, and Donald Byrd, and tenor men Sonny Rollins, Hank Mobley, and others, including initially John Coltrane.

In hard bop, something new was created without sacrificing vitality. All too often, the new in jazz can only be attained at the expense of vitality. Drummer Shelly Manne, for example, had to pay for the amazing musical refinement of his playing with some reduction in directness and vitality. His colleague Elvin Jones, on the other hand, managed to discover rhythms that simultaneously possess a complexity of structure *and* a vitality the likes of which, in such a relationship, were previously unheard of in jazz. Horace Silver rediscovered new ways of combining the thirty-two-bar song structure, which is the foundation for most jazz improvising, with other forms—combining them into "groups" of forms (as had been done in similar fashion by the ragtime pianists, Jelly Roll Morton, and other musicians of the early jazz period under the influence of both European and African additive styles). Tenor saxophonist Sonny Rollins created through his improvisations grandiose structures, which at that time were considered "polymetric," while striding across the given harmonic materials with a freedom and ease that not even the Tristano school could match.

Marshall Stearns said:

> Indeed, modern jazz as played in New York by Art Blakey and his Messengers, Jay and Kai, Max Roach and Clifford Brown, Art Farmer and Gigi Gryce, Gillespie, Davis, and others . . . has never lost its fire. The harmonies of cool jazz—and bop—were taken over, the posture of

resignation disappeared, the light sound remained, but the music always has a biting sharpness. In a word: It has changed, but fundamentally it remained "hot" and "swinging." . . . The word *cool* has lost its meaning—unless it is taken in a general sense of "sensitive" and "flexible."

The last sentence applies to both directions of the jazz of the fifties: Basie-Young classicism and new bop.

It is also true of both movements that they had found a new relationship to the blues. Pianist-composer Horace Silver—and with him a few others—broke through with a manner of playing known as funky: slow or medium blues, played hard on the beat, with all the feeling and expression characteristic of the old blues. And not only the blues, but also the gospel songs of black churches began to play a new, powerful role in jazz: in a playing style called soul, connected again with Horace Silver, but also with singer and pianist Ray Charles and vibraharpist Milt Jackson. Jazz musicians of all persuasions on both coasts threw themselves into funk and soul with notable enthusiasm. They did so in a manner that, since musical reasons are not readily apparent, leads one to conclude that extramusical influences were present.

The tendency toward funk and soul expresses the wish to belong and the desire for something offering a semblance of security in a world of cool realism. Soul with its roots in the music of the gospel churches, experienced a large-scale success in popular music during the late sixties; funk, which comes from blues, did the same in the seventies. The important thing is to remember that both were born from jazz or, more generally, from black tradition and feeling.

This tendency toward a feeling of security and belonging became even clearer a decade later, in free jazz. Albert Ayler, for example, transplanted circus, country, and marching music—clearly motifs from the safe and sane "good old days"—into his free, atonal, ecstatic improvisations. Other free-jazz musicians overemphasized their hate for the white world and found a substitute realm of group acceptance and security in communion with those who shared this hate—a psychological reaction familiar to anyone conversant with psychoanalysis.

During the cool-jazz period, the contrapuntal and linear music of Johann Sebastian Bach fulfilled this need to belong in the Modern Jazz Quartet of pianist John Lewis. A whole tide of jazz fugues rose in the first half of the fifties; it subsided as power and vitality returned to the scene with hard bop.

The Sixties: Free Jazz

These are the innovations of the jazz of the sixties—free jazz:

1. A breakthrough into the open space of "free tonality."

2. A new rhythmic conception, characterized by the disintegration of meter, beat, and symmetry.

3. The flow of "world music" into jazz, which was suddenly open to all the great musical cultures—from India to Africa, from Japan to Arabia.

4. An emphasis on intensity unknown to earlier styles of jazz. Jazz had always been superior in intensity to other musical forms of the Western world, but never before had the accent been on intensity in such an ecstatic, orgiastic—sometimes even religious—sense as in free jazz. Many free-jazz musicians actually made a "cult" of intensity.

5. An extension of musical sound into the realm of noise—having to do not so much with ugliness, unrest, aggression, or violence as with a sheer enjoyment of sound for its own sake.

Around the early sixties, jazz music broke through into the realm of free tonality, or even atonality, as concert music had done forty or fifty years earlier. Jazz specialists had expected this development for some fifteen years; it was anticipated in Lennie Tristano's "Intuition" and "Digression" of 1949; some important musicians of the fifties, particularly George Russell and Charles Mingus, paved the way for it. A "new music," a "new jazz," was born like many innovations in the arts, initially relying on shock value. The power and hardness of the new jazz, along with a revolutionary, partially extramusical pathos, affected the jazz scene of the sixties vehemently. This vehemence was even stronger because so many things had been bottled up in the fifties, when the breakthrough was imminent but was avoided with almost pathological anxiety. All these bottled-up things came down like an avalanche on a contented jazz public, which had accommodated itself to Oscar Peterson and the Modern Jazz Quartet.

For the younger generation of free-jazz musicians, the music preceding them had been depleted in terms of playing and procedural possibilities, harmonic structure, and metric symmetry. It had become rigid in its clichés and predictable formulas, similar to the situation twenty years earlier when bebop was created. Everything seemed to run according to the same, unchangeable pattern in the same, unchanging way. All possibilities of traditional forms and conventional tonality seemed exhausted. That is why the young musicians searched for new ways of playing; in the process, jazz again became what it had been in the twenties when the white public discovered it: a great, crazy, exciting, precarious adventure. At last, there was collective improvisation again, with lines rubbing against and crossing each other wildly and freely. That, too, is reminiscent of New Orleans—with modifications to be discussed later.

Don Heckman, the critic and musician, once said, "I think there's been a natural tendency toward this freeing of the improvisatory mind from harmonic restrictions throughout the history of jazz."

In jazz, free tonality, however, is understood in a basically different way from that of European concert music. The free jazz of the New York avant-garde around 1965 featured—much more so than, say, the "serial" European avant-garde music—so-called tonal centers (see the section dealing with harmony). This means that the music loosely partakes in the general gravitation from the dominant to the tonic but has a wide range of "freedom" in all other aspects.

This development was so spontaneous and nonacademic that the European term *atonality* cannot be used in an exclusively academic sense. Small wonder that many free-jazz musicians expressed their explicit contempt for conservatory music and its vocabulary (Archie Shepp: "Where my own dreams sufficed, I disregarded the Western musical tradition altogether"). In free jazz, atonality—or better, "free tonality"—has a wide range of meaning: it includes all steps, from the intimated "tonal centers" to complete harmonic freedom.

In spite of the brevity of its history, jazz has a much longer atonal tradition than European art music. The shouts and field hollers, the archaic blues of the southern plantations—indeed, nearly all musical forerunners of jazz—were "free tonal," often simply because the singers didn't know anything about European tonality. In the old days of New Orleans, too, there were musicians unconcerned with harmonic laws. Certain Louis Armstrong records from the twenties ("Two Deuces" with Earl Hines, for example) are among his most beautiful, though they contain notes that are "wrong" in terms of European academic tonality.

In other words, there is a tradition of atonality—or of harmonic freedom—in the whole history of jazz, while atonality in European music was first introduced by an avant-garde—the "classical" avant-garde beginning with Arnold Schoenberg, Anton Webern, and Alban Berg. Thus, jazz atonality became the meeting ground for tradition and avant-garde—a truly advantageous point of departure rarely encountered in an art in flux!

There is no doubt that musicians like Ornette Coleman, Archie Shepp, Pharoah Sanders, and Albert Ayler were closer to the "concrete," folk-music-like harmonic freedom of the field cry and of the archaic folk blues than to "abstract," intellectual European atonality. Ornette Coleman, for instance, didn't realize that there was also free tonality in European music until he met John Lewis and Gunther Schuller in 1959–60. At that time he had already developed his own musical concept. Free jazz is a part of jazz tradition, not a break with it.

For a number of years we were at a point where the freedom of free jazz was often understood as freedom from any musical system formed in Europe, with the emphasis on "formed in Europe." The formal and harmonic emancipation from the music of the "white continent" was a part of a greater racial, social, cultural, and political emancipation. "Black music," as it was interpreted by many of these musicians and by LeRoi Jones (Amiri Baraka), one of their most eloquent spokesmen, became "blacker" than ever before in this process of breaking its strongest link with the European tradition, the harmonic laws. (See the quotes by Jones and one of his associates in the section on Ornette Coleman and John Coltrane.)

There is a parallel between jazz and modern European concert music, but only insofar as both displayed a growing disgust with the mechanistic, machinelike character of the traditional system of functional harmonics. This system had become a roadblock in the development of the musics by increasingly substituting for individual decisions its own functional mechanics, and its abolition was a legitimate development familiar from many other arts, cultures, and traditions. When a structuring principle has been worn out and the creative artists become convinced that within its limits everything possible has been said, the principle must be abandoned.

All new jazz styles have created new rhythmic concepts. Free jazz is no exception. Two basic facts determine the different rhythmic concepts in the history of jazz from New Orleans to hard bop: A fixed meter, generally 2/4 or 4/4 (until the emergence of the waltz and other uneven meters in the fifties), is carried out constantly. Second, the jazz beat produces accents that do not necessarily correspond to those a classically trained musician would place within that same meter. Free jazz demolished the two pillars of conventional jazz rhythm—meter and beat. The beat was replaced by the pulse, and the meter, which was passed over by some free-jazz drummers as if it did not exist, was replaced by "free playing," not bound by a regular rhythm or meter, in which wide arches of rhythmic tension are built up with an incredible intensity. (More about this in the sections on rhythm and the drums.) Sunny Murray, one of the leading free-jazz drummers, called traditional drum rhythm "cliché beats" that are "like slavery or poverty. Freedom drumming is an aspiration toward a better condition."

Just as important to jazz as harmonic and rhythmic innovation was gaining access to world music. Jazz developed within a dialectic—the meeting of black and white. In the first sixty years of jazz history, the counterpart of jazz was European music. Interaction with the European musical tradition was by no means a marginal activity. Nearly all styles of jazz came into being in and through this dialectical interaction.

In the process, the realm of what was meant by "European music" grew continually larger. To the ragtime pianists of the turn of the century, it meant the piano compositions of the nineteenth century. To the New Orleans musicians it meant French opera, Spanish circus music, and European marches. Bix Beiderbecke and his Chicago colleagues of the twenties discovered Debussy. The Swing arrangers learned orchestration skills from the late romantic symphonic period. Finally, when the development had gone beyond cool jazz, jazz musicians had incorporated almost all elements of European music they could possibly use, from baroque to Stockhausen.

Thus, the role of European music as the stimulating counterpart of jazz—at least as its only counterpart—had run out. Aside from this musical reason, there were extramusical ones—racial, social, and political—as we have already mentioned. This is why jazz musicians discovered new partners with growing fervor: the great non-European musical cultures.

The Arabic and Indian cultures and musics at first held a special fascination. There had been Islamic tendencies among African Americans since the midforties, since the time, in other words, when modern jazz originated. Dozens of jazz musicians converted to Islam and occasionally took Arabic names. For a couple of years, drummer Art Blakey was known to his Muslim friends as Abdullah Ibn Buhaina; in the forties, saxophonist Ed Gregory had already become Sahib Shihab.

In this turning away from "the white religion," the emancipation from the white man was given particularly effective expression. James Baldwin, the African American poet and writer, said, "Whoever wishes to become a truly moral human being must first divorce himself from all the prohibitions, crimes, and hypocrisies of the Christian church. If the concept of God has any validity or any use, it can only be to make us larger, freer, and more loving." Millions of black Americans believed—"after two hundred years of vain attempts"—that the Christian God could not do that. For that reason, said Baldwin, "it is time we got rid of Him."

It was only a small step from religious conversion to Islam to a growing interest in Islamic music. Musicians like Yusef Lateef, Ornette Coleman, John Coltrane, Randy Weston, Herbie Mann, Art Blakey, Roland Kirk, Sahib Shihab, and Don Cherry in the United States, and, among others, George Gruntz and Jean-Luc Ponty in Europe—many of them not Muslims by faith—expressed their fascination with Arabic music in compositions and improvisations.

Even stronger than Arabic music was the interest in Indian music with its great classical tradition. What fascinated jazz musicians most about Indian music was, above all, its rhythmic wealth. The great classical music of India is based on talas and ragas.

Talas are rhythmic series and cycles of immense variety, from 3 to 108 beats. You have to be aware that Indian musicians and sophisticated listeners are able to appreciate even the longest tala—108 beats—as a series and as a predetermined musical structure and to recall it as such.

Talas usually have a great wealth of rhythmical structuring possibilities. A tala consisting of ten beats, for example, can be conceived as a series of 2-3-2-3 or 3-3-4 or 3-4-3 beats. Within the series, there is ample room for free improvisation; the improvising musicians can wander far away from each other. But the tension characteristic of Indian music is to a large extent founded on the fact that the individual lines of improvisation finally must meet again on the first beat, "one"—the so-called *sam*. After the widely diverging melodic movements, this meeting very often is felt like an almost orgiastic relief.

It is this rhythmic wealth of Indian music that particularly attracted modern jazz musicians. They wanted to liberate themselves from the 4/4 uniformity of the metrically conventional, constant jazz beat, while at the same time searching for rhythmic and metric structures that created a jazzlike intensity.

In contrast to the rhythmically well-defined tala, the *raga* is a melodic row in which many elements categorized in numerous ways in European music come together: theme, key, mood, phrase, and the form determined by the melodic flow. A particular raga may require, for example, that a certain note can be used only after all other notes of the raga have been played. There are ragas that can be played only in the morning, at night, at full moon, or only with religious thoughts in mind. And, above all, ragas are "modes," which makes them correspond ideally to the tendency toward modality in modern jazz (cf. the section on harmony).

A large number of jazz musicians studied with the great masters of Indian classical music. The word *classical,* by the way, should be read with emphasis, because this is not folklore music. It is as "classical" as the corresponding music in European culture. The openness with which dozens of jazz musicians of the fifties and sixties have approached the world's great traditional musical cultures went far beyond comparable developments in modern European concert music. Overwhelming intensity and complexity were generated when Don Ellis derived big-band compositions, such as "3-3-2-2-2-1-2-2-2" and "New Nine," from Indian talas; when Miles Davis and Gil Evans transformed Joaquin Rodrigo's "Concierto de Aranjuez" into Flamenco jazz; when Yusef Lateef converted Japanese, Chinese, and Egyptian elements into blues on his record *A flat, G flat and C*; and when Sahib Shihab, Jean-Luc Ponty, and George Gruntz played with Arab Bedouins on the album *Noon in Tunisia*. Compared to that, Debussy's, Messiaen's, and Roussell's use of Indian and Balinese sounds and the influence of Chinese rhythms on the modern German composer Boris Blacher seem timid and marginal.

The new jazz musicians opened themselves up to the world's musical cultures with a fervor whose messianic, all-embracing gesture of love was manifest in many of their album titles: in Albert Ayler's *Spiritual Unity* and *Holy Ghost*; Don Cherry's *Complete Communion*; Carla Bley's *Communication*; Alexander von Schlippenbach's *Globe Unity*; Yusef Lateef's *Try Love*; Ornette Coleman's *Peace*; John Coltrane's "Love," *A Love Supreme*, "Elation," and *Ascension*; or in tunes such as "Sun Song," "Sun Myth," and "Nebulae" from *Heliocentric Worlds* by Sun Ra and his Solar Arkestra. The message of these titles could be felt when seen in a single context: "spiritual unity to complete communion and communication with the globe as a unity—and, through that, love and peace for everybody and salvation in pan-religious ecstasy . . . cosmic ascension and elation to mythological suns and nebulae and heliocentric worlds."

It is important to note that the jazz musicians merely emphasized artistically and musically what the more aware members of the black community were realizing extramusically. In March 1967, for instance, teachers and students of a predominantly African American New York high school boycotted all concerts of classical European music, not because they were not interested in European concert music (quite the contrary—musical activity at this school was above average) but because they felt it was wrong to be offered only concerts of European music, not jazz or Indian, Arabian, African, etc., music: "This selection is arbitrary, based on European history, not ours."

The opening of musical sounds into the realm of noise had to do with both world music and even more so with increased intensity. Their explosive intensity—"high-energy playing"—literally burst open the conventional sound barriers of the instruments of many free-jazz musicians. Saxophones sounded like the intensified "white noise" of electronic music, trombones like the noises of conveyor belts, trumpets like steel vessels bursting from atmospheric pressure, pianos like crackling wires, vibraphones like winds haunting metal branches; collectively improvising groups roared like mythical, howling primeval creatures.

Kodwo Eshun has remarked that in the free jazz of the sixties, the musicians became "power plants tapping into a universal sound." Free jazz has a particular relationship to musical energy; its extreme compression of sounds and rhythms, and its emphasis on physicality and the body, are what set free jazz apart from the sonic experimentation of Western "new music." The high intensity of free jazz, and its groove, energetic despite its abstractness, are rooted in the jazz tradition.

The border between musical sound and noise, which seems so clear and natural to the average listener, is not physically definable; it is founded on traditional, tacit conventions. Fundamentally, music can use anything audible. In fact, this is its goal: the artistic utilization of what is audible. This goal cannot be reached when only some sounds are deemed suitable for music while all others are branded inappropriate.

Pianos can be played not only on the keys but also inside, on the strings; violins can be beaten; trumpets can be used (without mouthpiece) as blowpipes. People ridiculing these ways of playing instruments simply prove that to them, music is nothing but fulfilling conventional rules. An instrument exists to produce sounds. There are no laws governing the procedure of this production. On the contrary, it is the job of the musician to continually find new sounds. In doing so, he or she can use conventional instruments in new ways, or invent new instruments, or further develop conventional instruments. This job has become a major challenge for many musicians. For an edition of the avant-garde magazine *Microphone*, many modern British percussionists wrote detailed, page-long statements, but jazz drummer Tony Oxley simply wrote one sentence: "The most important activity for me is the enlargement of my vocabulary." This opinion is characteristic of many contemporary musicians.

We are living in an age that has created new sounds of unimaginable variety: jet planes and atomic explosions, the noises of oscillation and the ghostly crackling in the assembly buildings of precision industry. Big-city dwellers are subject to a barrage of decibels that people of former times not only would have been unable to withstand physically, but that would have cast them into paroxysms of psychological confusion. Scientists have amplified the sounds of plant growth by millions of decibels so that they become a deafening roar. We now know that fish, deemed to be the quietest of all creatures by the romantics of the last century, exist in an environment of continual sounds. Every human being alive today is affected by this expansion of the realm of the audible. Are musicians, whose subject is sound, supposed to be the only ones unaffected?

The listener must give up the idea that free jazz is an unstructured music in which improvisation takes place aimlessly, each player blithely playing whatever he or she likes with no sense of coherence. All good music, including free jazz, is structured; it uses a vocabulary, a system of rules. However, free jazz takes advantage of the recognition that, in contrast to earlier jazz styles, this system of rules is no longer externally predetermined and accepted as a fixed quantity, but rather is grounded in, and develops from, the playing itself. Freely improvised music is based on the desire to renegotiate the rules of playing on every occasion.

The free improviser must therefore above all possess the quality that is perhaps the last thing that the uninitiated listener associates with free jazz: discipline. In a musical situation in which the rules of playing can be reconceived every time, the player cannot indulge in navel-gazing, but must be capable of introspection, of listening to him- or herself while simultaneously paying attention to the others. This requires a quality that John Coltrane, in his mature free-jazz period, called "selflessness."

"Improvised sound leads inward, not outward," says music journalist Peter Niklas Wilson. For this reason, he and others have spoken of an "ethics of improvisation." The composer Cornelius Cardew, who was strongly attracted to the ideas of free jazz and himself practiced free improvisation, listed seven "virtues" of improvisation: simplicity, integrity, selflessness, forbearance, preparedness, and—surprising only at first glance—identification with nature. (The seventh, perhaps more genuinely surprising, is "the acceptance of death," which Cardew relates to music's essential ephemerality.)

The notion of unlimited musical freedom of speech, upheld as an ideal by many musicians in the early phase of free jazz, is an illusion. As liberating as free jazz was from obsolete norms, roles, and clichés, it inevitably developed norms, roles, and clichés of its own. Sun Ra sometimes called free-jazz musicians the "freedom boys" and related this idea to that of jail. Many free-jazz musicians might think they were playing in the moment, following nothing but spontaneous inspiration. "No," said Sun Ra: "we're in jail, but we're in the freest jail in the world."

Even in the "freest" free jazz, where improvisation takes place with no prior explicit agreements, there are still implicit rules at work. Whether in the power playing and high-energy sounds of Albert Ayler, Cecil Taylor, and Peter Brötzmann, or in the finely woven sonic textures of bands such as AMM or the Music Improvisation Company, the unarticulated rules and laws are what create musical coherence and structure.

The term *free*, taken in isolation, can be misleading. When Ornette Coleman gave a concert in Cincinnati, Ohio, in 1961, the organizers advertised the concert as "Ornette Coleman—Free Jazz Concert." The crowd that showed up for the performance took this at face value and protested the fact that they were required to pay an entrance fee.

Within a few years, free jazz became a richly varied means of expression, mastering the gamut of human emotions. We should free ourselves from the misconception that this music only voiced anger, hate, and protest. This highly one-sided impression was created mainly by a small group of New York critics and musicians who were far from representative of all of free jazz. Besides the protest, there was the hymnlike religious fervor of John Coltrane, the joyous air of the folk musician in Albert Ayler, the intellectual yet humorous coolness of Paul Bley or Ran Blake, the cosmic amplitude of Sun Ra, the sensitivity of the early Carla Bley.

During the sixties, increasingly, young musicians and jazz fans all over the world were finding their way to the new sounds. While critics and unappreciative fans were still crying "chaos," the new jazz was finding its audience—not only in the United States but also in Europe, where an autonomous type of free music, European free jazz, evolved. Free jazz finally gave European jazz an unmistakable identity. With free jazz the emancipation of European jazz got under way—not coincidentally somewhat later than American developments in the midsixties. Only with liberation from functional harmony and ongoing rhythm did European musicians really liberate themselves from imitation of American jazz. Of course, there had already been Django Reinhardt—the great exception—who exerted a stylistic influence on American jazz. But up to that point European musicians had been spellbound by American models.

It's interesting that initially, with the emergence of free jazz, nothing changed in this imitative relationship. Just as they had previously copied and imitated Swing and bebop, cool jazz and hard bop, European musicians now copied and imitated the free jazz of Ornette Coleman, Cecil Taylor, and Albert Ayler. But in doing so they also absorbed free jazz's explosive inner message, which says that no musical rule is self-evident.

It may sound paradoxical, but European musicians found themselves because they copied American free jazz. By taking over this model of negotiating rules during the act of playing, they were thrown back on themselves. A vacuum developed that European adherents of free jazz had to fill, and they filled it in a highly individual, diverse, and colorful way. There can be no doubt that free jazz was the crucial stimulus for the emancipation of European jazz.

Various languages of free jazz, often intermingling during international encounters, immediately developed in Europe, establishing diverse national and regional characteristics. Interest in the sound's inner life predominated on the English scene among such musicians as guitarist Derek Bailey, saxophonist Evan Parker, and drummer Tony Oxley. Nowhere else in Europe were subdued, fragile, transparent, fragmented sonic experiments and sound collages taken so far as in England. This trip into sound's nuclear center automatically resulted in British free-jazz musicians—particularly subtly, the group AMM—becoming involved in electronic music. The Netherlands were dominated by a free jazz characterized by biting wit and mocking humor and propelled by an inclination toward burlesque and parody. Musicians like Misha Mengelberg, Han Bennink, and Willem Breuker developed theatrical elements out of their playing. A predilection for weight and power was apparent in West German free jazz, whether in Peter Brötzmann's frenetic overblown performances or in Manfred Schoof's and Gunter Hampel's emphasis on clarity. At the end of the sixties, free jazz also got under way in the German Democratic Republic (the former East Germany), with such an emphasis on accuracy and order (despite multiple incursions of irony) that people talked about a "Prussian" variant of free jazz.

Peter Niklas Wilson has pointed out that a schism occurred early in the history of European free jazz. British improvisers found the massive sonic salvos of Peter Brötzmann to be "Teutonic," and Brötzmann's LP title *Machine Gun* reinforced such martial associations. On the other hand, British improvised music, inspired by the pointillistic music of composer Anton Webern and emphasizing individual sonic events over linear development, was dismissed by Brötzmann as symptomatic of an "English disease." Both approaches to playing—high-energy power playing on the one hand and quiet, fragile sound exploration on the other hand—produced wonderful results, and mark the extreme poles of the spectrum of European freely improvised music.

One claim kept appearing in the countless critiques that this new style of music spawned: the new freedom would ultimately end in chaos. However, after understandable initial elation over the new freedom, the musicians began to emphasize that freedom was not the only point. Sunny Murray, the free-jazz drummer already mentioned, said, "Complete freedom you could get from anyone who walks down the street. Give them $20, and they'll probably do something pretty free." Similar statements have been made with increasing frequency since the end of the sixties. One reason for this is certainly that musicians became more aware that free jazz was developing its own clichés. And soon these free-jazz clichés—lacking a tradition—appeared even emptier than the clichés of conventional jazz that had just been so eagerly destroyed. In this way the majority of free-jazz musicians developed a new, dynamic interest in the jazz tradition. But there are other reasons why chaos is an inappropriate concept. Let's take a look at the history of European music.

Three times in that history, a "new music" appeared. First, there was *Ars Nova*, appearing around 1350; its most important composer was Guillaume de Machaut. Two and a half centuries later, around 1600, *Le Nuove Musiche* came into existence with the monodical music of the *Stilo Rappresentativo*, centering on composers like Orazio Vecchi and Monteverdi. Both times, secular and religious musical authorities agreed that the new music meant the beginning of chaos in music. From this point on, that fear never vanished: Johann A. Hiller spoke "with disgust" of Bach's "crudities." Copies of the first edition of Mozart's quartets were returned to him because the engraving was "quite imperfect." "Many chords and dissonances were thought to be engraving faults" (Franz Roh).

The reactions of critics contemporaneous with Beethoven are applicable to today: "All neutral music specialists were in full accord that something as shrill, incoherent, and revolting to the ear was utterly without parallel in the history of music." (This about the overture to *Fidelio*!) Brahms, Bruckner, and Wagner at one time or another were all in the "guild of chaotics." Then came the third "new music"—with all the well-documented scandals, misinterpretations, and misunderstandings. One need only recall the turbulence at the premiere of Stravinsky's *Sacre du Printemps* in Paris in 1913; the various Schoenberg scandals; or the premiere of Debussy's *Pelléas et Mélisande* in 1902 (it was labeled "brain music" and an example of "nihilistic tendencies"). Today, all this music is considered "classical." Hollywood composers are using harmonies and sounds borrowed from it.

It was similar in jazz. At first, the "new music" from New Orleans sounded chaotic to the "legitimate" ear: a wild, free departure to a confusing new land. However, by the turn of the fifties, New Orleans jazz had become party music for the young bourgeois.

When bebop appeared in 1943, the nearly universal opinion was that chaos had finally taken over, that jazz was nearing the end. Today, Dizzy Gillespie's trumpet and vocals sound as gay and familiar to us as "When the Saints Go Marching In."

The conclusion to be drawn from all this is that the word *chaos* is merely a refrain that rhymes with *history of music*, as simply as *fun* and *sun*. *Free jazz* also rhymes with it very well.

Free jazz wants to force us to cease understanding music as a means to self-affirmation. Human beings, who build fuel cells and send satellites to Mars, have better means of self-affirmation. And the person whose racial problems and power politics are still in the style of the nineteenth century does not deserve self-affirmation anyway.

By self-affirmation in music we mean the way all of us have learned to listen to music: always anticipating a few bars ahead, and when it comes out exactly (or at least nearly) as expected we feel confirmed and note with pride how right we have been. Music has had no other function than to cause such self-esteem. Everything has worked out perfectly. The few places where things deviated have simply increased the fascination.

Free jazz must be listened to without this need for self-affirmation. The music does not follow the listener anymore; the listener must follow the music—unconditionally—wherever it may lead. The members of a German avant-garde group, the Manfred Schoof Quintet, have spoken of the absolute "emptiness," the tabula rasa indispensable to that kind of musical experience. It was observed in the United States that children could be enraptured by free jazz. They simply listen to what is happening—and a lot is! Wherever the sounds go, children follow. There is no place in their minds or sensory systems that, in the middle of each musical phrase, demands this is the way it must continue; that is where it has to go; if it does anything else, it is "wrong." They demand nothing, and so get everything. The adults, however, for whom a piece of music—or a poem or picture—has almost no other function but to fulfill their demands, should not fool themselves. Except for guaranteed self-affirmation, they get nothing.

Free jazz is not a completed jazz style with fixed rules. It emphasizes the character of improvisation as an open process. Because free-jazz and freely improvising musicians take this challenge seriously, they have succeeded over the last forty years in constantly refining and differentiating their improvising.

During the eighties and nineties, European free-jazz players such as Derek Bailey, Evan Parker, and Misha Mengelberg came to have greater influence on the American free improvisation scene—not just on John Zorn, but also on younger musicians of the Chicago scene such as Ken Vandermark, Hamid Drake, and others, whose playing relates explicitly to the European lineage of free players.

And in the nineties, the interest in free jazz grew even greater due to players such as David S. Ware, Charles Gayle, and Matthew Shipp. Paradoxically, this "free-jazz renaissance" took place not so much among hard-core jazz followers as among experimental rock groups such as Sonic Youth, who found in the unbridled sonic language of free jazz an inexhaustible source of inspiration for postpunk and postmetal music.

Free jazz lives. Nothing illustrates the ongoing fascination of free improvisation better than the conversion of pianist Keith Jarrett, who, on his 2001 CD *Inside Out,* moved away from romantic/impressionistic playing in favor of free improvisation. Jarrett says, "People who don't 'understand' free playing (like Wynton Marsalis, Ken Burns, etc.) are not free to see it as an amazingly important part of the true jazz history. Where's the form? Don't ask. Don't think. Don't anticipate. Just participate. It's all there somewhere inside. And then suddenly it forms itself."

The Seventies

Up to this point, we have been able to match each decade with a particular style—certainly at the cost of some fine distinctions, but with greater clarity as a result. With the beginning of the seventies, we have to drop this principle. This decade showed at least seven distinct tendencies:

1. Fusion or jazz-rock: the combination of jazz improvisation with rock rhythms and electronics.

2. A trend toward European romanticist chamber music, an "aestheticization" of jazz, so to speak. Suddenly, large numbers of unaccompanied solos and duos appeared on the scene, often without any rhythm section—no drums, no bass. Much that had been considered essential to jazz was dispensed with: explosive power, hardness, tremendous expressiveness, intensity, ecstasy, and no fear of "ugliness." As an American critic put it, jazz was being "beautified"—or as we just put it, "aestheticized."

3. The music of the new free-jazz generation. When fusion music took over the scene in the early seventies and immediately became a commercial success, many critics wrote that free jazz was dead. But that was a rash judgment. Free music had gone underground (and "underground" back then also meant to Europe). The years 1973–74 marked the comeback of free playing, centered on the Chicago-based AACM, an association of musicians founded by pianist-composer Muhal Richard Abrams. In the course of the seventies, free-jazz musicians, spearheaded by the AACM players, became increasingly prominent, stressing transparent structures and a restless quietness. And it only seems contradictory that the free jazz of the AACM was more consciously oriented toward composed structures and genre-bridging sounds on the one hand, while on the other it related strongly and deliberately to the African roots of black music. The AACM musicians no longer called their music "jazz" but, proudly, "Great Black Music." (More about the AACM appears in the section on jazz groups.)

4. An astonishing comeback for Swing. Suddenly there was an

entire generation of young musicians who appeared to be playing
rock or fusion but in fact were making music reminiscent of
the great masters of the Swing age—tenor saxophonists like
Ben Webster and Coleman Hawkins, and trumpeters like Harry
Edison and Buck Clayton. The most successful of these young
musicians were tenor sax player Scott Hamilton, trumpeter
Warren Vaché, and guitarist Cal Collins. Reissues of classic
Swing recordings attracted astonishing interest.

5. An even more amazing and widespread comeback for bebop,
   sparked off by Dexter Gordon, the great tenor saxophonist. For
   many years he had led a withdrawn existence in Europe (mainly
   Copenhagen), but then, in late 1976, he went to New York to
   appear at the Village Vanguard club. What was supposed to
   be a short engagement led to a triumphant comeback for both
   Gordon (who remained in the States until his death in 1990) and
   bebop itself.

   This was the third bebop wave in jazz history, following the
   original bebop in the forties and hard bop in the second half
   of the fifties. Just as hard bop incorporated the experience of
   cool jazz (particularly the extended melodic phrases), the new
   bebop at the end of the seventies similarly took into account all
   that had happened in the interim. The work of two musicians
   who were no longer alive, Charles Mingus and John Coltrane,
   seemed to be omnipresent in this new bebop. But there were also
   musicians whose way of playing bebop responded to experiences
   of free jazz, thereby creating a kind of "free bop." They included
   drummer Barry Altschul and saxophonists Arthur Blythe, Oliver
   Lake, Dewey Redman, and Julius Hemphill.

6. European jazz found itself. This development opened up with
   the free jazz of the sixties. New, however, was the fact that
   European music now went beyond the more confined sphere
   of free jazz and also included tonal ways of playing. Just as the
   African American musicians of the AACM remembered their
   African roots, European players often started reflecting their
   own origins.

   Some European musicians sought their identity by relating
   to the tradition of European concert music—in the tonal sphere
   particularly to romantic and impressionist music, and in the
   realm of free jazz to modern concert music from Webern by
   way of Berg to Stockhausen, Boulez, Nono, Rihm, and above all
   Eissler and Weill.

   Others found roots and stimuli in European folklore, the
   ethnic music of their cultures, and others again in world folklore
   and the great non-European musical cultures.

These spheres of influence often existed in a multifaceted state of tension, particularly in the continued confrontation with, and examination of, American jazz influences.

7. The gradual development of a new kind of musician who moved between jazz and world music, transcending and integrating these approaches.

Among all these trends, there were countless overlaps and interconnections. All of these playing styles developed through the interaction of free jazz with conventional tonality and musical structure, traditional jazz elements, modern European concert music, and elements of exotic musical cultures (India, above all), with European romanticism, blues, and rock. "There's no longer just a free style of playing; it's all together," said clarinetist Perry Robinson. Of course, the fundamentally new aspect was that the categorical nature of all these elements was dissolving. The elements no longer existed as distinct entities, as in earlier amalgams; they lost their singular nature and became pure music.

The question of what goals the freedom of the sixties had set for itself found its answer in the music of the seventies. The musicians understood why freedom had been necessary: not so that everyone could do as they pleased, but rather to enable jazz musicians to freely make use of all the elements whose authoritarian and automatic characteristics they had overcome.

Harmonically, for example, jazz musicians did not abandon all harmony by learning to play with "free tonality." They merely liberated themselves from the automatic, machinelike functioning of conventional school harmony that, once a certain harmonic structure had been established, determined all harmonic progressions. The free-jazz musicians broke through this authoritarian circularity of the harmonic process. By doing so, they were that much better equipped to play aesthetically "beautiful" harmonies.

Another example may be found in rhythm. In the seventies, it became clear that the regular meter of conventional jazz was not dissolved in order to destroy it, as it appeared to some fanatics in the initial phase of free jazz. Rather, it was dissolved because the automatic, mechanistic nature of the constant beat was in question. Indeed, an even, constant meter had become so taken for granted during the first sixty years of jazz history that personal artistic decisions in this realm were more or less impossible. But after the first half of the sixties, nothing in rhythm was taken for granted any longer. Now, all kinds of rhythms and meters, constant or not, could be, with that much more freedom and independence.

Free jazz was a process of liberation. Only now could the jazz musician be really free—free also to play all the things that were strictly taboo for many creative musicians of the free-jazz period: thirds and triads, functional harmonic progressions, waltzes, songs and four-beat meters, discernible forms and structures, and romantic sounds.

The jazz of the seventies melodicized and structuralized the freedom of the jazz of the sixties. To the nonspecialist, the seventies were primarily the decade of fusion music or, as it is often called in Europe, jazz-rock. But, as already mentioned, there were a lot of elements besides jazz and rock that were fusioned into this music.

The first signs of fusion could be seen in the late sixties in groups like the Gary Burton Quartet, flutist Jeremy Steig's Jeremy and the Satyrs, pianist Mike Nock's Fourth Way, the Charles Lloyd Quartet, the Free Spirits of guitarist Larry Coryell, Tony Williams's first Lifetime group, the group Dreams with saxophonist Michael Brecker and trumpeter Randy Brecker, and various so-called compact big bands modeled after Blood, Sweat & Tears.

Interestingly enough, the fusion development was initially much stronger in Great Britain (beginning in 1963), but it also came to an end much faster there (around 1969) than in the United States. With a bit of exaggeration one could say that in Great Britain the sixties were already the decade of fusion music, in groups like the Graham Bond Organisation of organist Graham Bond; Colosseum and Cream; Soft Machine; and in musicians like guitarist John McLaughlin, bassist Jack Bruce, drummers Ginger Baker and Jon Hiseman, and saxophonist Dick Heckstall-Smith.

And yet, it was no doubt Miles Davis who made the breakthrough for fusion jazz with his album *Bitches Brew*, released in 1970. Miles was the first to reach a balanced and musically satisfactory integration of jazz and rock. He was the catalyst of jazz-rock—not only with his own records, but also because many of the decade's important players emerged from his groups.

The point in time when all this occurred is noteworthy. As we mentioned, *Bitches Brew* was released in 1970, the time of the *Götterdämmerung* of the rock age: Jimi Hendrix, Janis Joplin, Brian Jones, Jim Morrison, and Duane Allman died; the Beatles broke up. The worst disaster of the rock age occurred in Altamont, California, at a Rolling Stones concert: four persons died, hundreds were wounded; all the wonderful good will of Woodstock was destroyed; and Woodstock—the miracle of the "Woodstock Nation," of a new, young society full of love, tolerance, and solidarity—showed its true business face. In New York and San Francisco, the Fillmore East and Fillmore West, centers of rock music, closed their doors for the last time. Suddenly the rock age had lost its drive; the age had lost its rock. No new groups or individual artists were appearing on the scene to tower above it. Toward the end of this period, Don McLean sang the sad, resigned refrain about the "day the music died" in his hit song "American Pie," the closing hymn of the rock age. It was interpreted that way by the whole world. The song stayed on the charts for weeks.

All that has been enumerated here happened between 1969 and 1972. The new jazz developed in exact parallel to these events, integrating rock and jazz. The year 1969 marked the release of Miles Davis's *In a Silent Way*, the album that paved the way for *Bitches Brew*. In 1971, Weather Report and the Mahavishnu Orchestra were formed. From 1972 on, the new jazz was here, full-fledged, with all the groups to be introduced in the "Jazz-Rock and Fusion" section of the chapter on bands. The rock age (or at least the best elements of it) flowed into the new jazz. The new jazz sensitized the rock music of the sixties, as the latter had similarly sensitized the rock 'n' roll of the fifties.

This point becomes clearer when one notes that there was a rock influence on jazz in four essential aspects: the electronicization of instruments, rhythm, a new attitude toward the solo, and—connected with that—a stronger emphasis on composition and arrangement as well as on collective improvisation. In each of these aspects, jazz-rock made more sophisticated a characteristic of rock that rock musicians were unable to develop further.

In the area of electronics, several instruments and accessories were added to the store of jazz instrumentation, usually divided into two groups. The first group comprised electroacoustic instruments that mechanically generate sound and then electronically amplify and treat it: electric pianos, clavinets, guitars, saxophones, trumpets, and even drums. They were often used in connection with wah-wah and fuzz pedals, echolettes, phase shifters, ring modulators, and feedback units; varitones, multividers, harmonizers, etc., for octave duplication and automatic harmonization of melodic lines; and double-neck guitars, combining the possibilities of both six-string and twelve-string guitar or of guitar and bass. The second group included instruments where sounds are generated completely electronically: organs and other keyboards, and above all a great variety of synthesizers, monophonic (i.e., capable of playing only one note at a time) at the start of the seventies, then becoming polyphonic, and with greater dynamic control, in the eighties.

Recording technology achieved similar importance. The modern recording studio had become so important that it has assumed the stature of an "instrument" of equal value to those played by the musicians. A good recording engineer had to have the same background knowledge and the same sensitivity as a musician—plus all the required technological expertise—because he or she "played" the controls and devices. The musicians, on the other hand, had acquired a level of technological know-how scarcely lower than that of many an engineer. Manipulating sound had become an art; with the aid of such devices as phasers, flangers, or chorus machines, sound was made to change, scintillate, "migrate."

At a superficial first glance, the tempting impression is that the jazz musicians simply took over all this equipment from rock and pop music; but on closer inspection, one discovers that the electric guitar, for example, was first featured by Charlie Christian in 1939 in Benny Goodman's sextet. And the electric organ first became popular in black rhythm and blues music, played by such musicians as Wild Bill Davis; it found its way into mass consciousness through the great success of jazz organist Jimmy Smith after 1956. The music world first became aware of the sparkling sound of the electric piano through Ray Charles's hit "What'd I Say" in 1959. White rock music did not incorporate the instrument until Miles Davis recorded *Filles de Kilimanjaro* with Herbie Hancock and Chick Corea on electric piano in 1968. The first experimentation with electronically amplified horns, varitones, and multividers was done by jazz musicians Sonny Stitt (1966) and Lee Konitz (1968). The synthesizer comes from concert music, where it had been developed and tested in the studio since 1957 by R. A. Moog in cooperation with Walter Carlos. But the first public synthesizer concert was given by a jazz musician: pianist Paul Bley, who performed on a Moog synthesizer in 1969 in New York's Philharmonic Hall. Ring modulators, phase shifters, and feedback techniques were also first developed in the electronic studios of concert music.

The impression that all these sounds are sounds of rock is essentially the result of the gigantic publicity machine of the rock media and the record industry. Thus these sounds reached general mass consciousness. It must be seen, however, that the production of "purely" electronic sounds first came from avant-garde concert music. The pioneer work in electrically amplifying and electronically manipulating conventional instruments was done predominantly by African American musicians, as was acknowledged by Charles Keil and Marshall McLuhan.

In this connection, it might be interesting to remember that it was an African American singer in the thirties, Billie Holiday, who was the first to realize the potential of the microphone for a completely new use of the human singing voice. It has been said that the Billie Holiday style, which at the time was felt to be new and revolutionary, consisted mainly in "microphonizing" the voice, in a way of singing unthinkable without the microphone. This "microphonic" style has become so commonplace for all kinds of popular music that hardly anyone can imagine how revolutionary it was when Billie Holiday created it.

Not only the instruments but also the auditory needs of modern man have been "electronicized"—of modern man from all social strata and classes, from the slums and ghettos to the music festivals of the intellectual world. Electronics, according to American composer Steve Reich, have become "ethnic"; electronics "transport" the music that "the people" want to hear, as animal hide and wood once transported the music in Africa. The music of an era is always transported by that element that is the general determinant of life. Today that function is carried by electronics.

The question of loudness also belongs in this context. This point caused the outsider as many problems as did the constant beat of the basic meter fifty years ago. So many things were said about loud volume. We heard them all: that it was physiologically wrong, incommensurate with the potential of the human ear; that it therefore endangered the auditory faculties or eventually destroyed them. There was always an otologist who could confirm this "from daily experience," and the press loved to print things like that. However, increased volume also could create new sensibilities. In the sixties, nobody would have been able to discover as many subtleties as could be heard a decade later in the gale-force range of sound waves generated by the Mahavishnu Orchestra or Weather Report, for example. The new volume was a new challenge.

At a time when the sounds of our daily lives reached decibels of unimagined dimensions, music could not remain fixed to the volume of yesterday or the day before. That would have meant relinquishing the artistic breakthrough into the auditory ranges in which we lived, in the sense sketched in the section on the jazz of the sixties regarding the question of "noise."

So much for electronics. Now let's consider rhythm. The inadequacies of the jazz-rock combinations of the sixties were due mainly to the fact that the conventional rock rhythms of the popular groups were much too undifferentiated to be of interest to such a highly sensitized music as modern jazz. Already in the early sixties, drummers like Elvin Jones, Tony Williams, and Sunny Murray were beating out rhythms without equal in Western music in their highly stratified complexity and intensity. In the face of this, the work of even the best rock drummers seemed regressive. Interestingly, only jazz drummers had generally been successful in dealing with the extroverted, aggressive attitude of rock rhythms in such a way that structures corresponding to the high standards of jazz were produced. In the early seventies, the leading drummers in this field were Billy Cobham (of the first Mahavishnu Orchestra) and Alphonse Mouzon (of the first Weather Report). Both formed their own groups later.

The third aspect of the rock influence on jazz is the new approach to the solo. In all its periods, jazz always had its true culmination in the solo improvisations of outstanding individual artists. However, in the sixties—first in the United States, then even more in Europe—an increasing number of free-jazz collectives came into being who began to doubt the validity of the conventional solo principle. Many of these jazz musicians, consciously or subconsciously, felt that the practice of individual improvisation, in which only the top individual performance counts, reflected all too faithfully the performance principle of the capitalist system. Parallel to the growing social and political criticism of this principle (in fact, even a few years before its rise), a questioning of the value of the principle of individual improvisation had begun. The tendency to improvise collectively became stronger and stronger. The way for this was paved by bassist Charles Mingus, in whose groups there was a lot of free collective improvising as early as the late fifties. At the time it could not be foreseen that just a few years later such "collectives" would be the hallmark of an entire musical development—in Europe even more so than in the United States. Bands of the caliber of the Mahavishnu Orchestra showed such a high degree of complex interplay when improvising that one could barely tell which of the five musicians was leading at any given moment, not to speak of soloing in the traditional sense. Pianist Joe Zawinul said about his early band, Weather Report, "In this group, either nobody plays solo, or we all solo at the same time."

From the start, record companies and producers played a bigger role in jazz-rock and fusion music than in any of the preceding jazz styles. They had a larger say about what was going to be recorded than the musicians themselves. And they made these decisions more with business than music in mind. Within a span of about five years, the musical impetus of fusion jazz got bogged down by this—in much the same way that, half a decade before, it got bogged down in Great Britain within five years' time.

In jazz-rock, an emphasis on virtuosity and a "higher-faster-louder" mentality took hold, criticized by guitarist John Scofield as the "fusion curse": "What I hate about fusion is the gymnastics." As early as 1975, critic Robert Palmer wrote:

> Electric jazz/rock fusion music is a mutation that's beginning to show signs of adaptive strain. . . . Fusion bands have found that it's a good idea to . . . stick with fairly simple chord voicings. Otherwise, the sound becomes muddy and overloaded. This means that the subtleties of jazz phrasing, the multilayered textures of jazz drumming, and the music's rich harmonic language are being abandoned.

The seventies produced an overwhelming inundation of jazz-rock records. Which have endured? At the highest quality level, certainly the records from the early, experimental phase of jazz-rock: the two initial Miles Davis jazz-rock albums (and most of the rest of them), all the records of the first Mahavishnu Orchestra (none by the other Mahavishnu formations!), a couple by Chick Corea's Return to Forever, by the Herbie Hancock Sextet, and by Weather Report, and four or five other albums. Not much, really, if you consider that during the peak of bebop—or during the Swing age before that—important, timeless recordings came out month after month; today, over fifty years later, these are reissued because they have brilliantly stood the test of time.

Many of the best jazz-rock musicians felt a deficit in their music. Especially during the second half of the seventies, they increasingly returned to acoustic music in studio work or in concerts. ("Acoustic music" is the name for all nonelectronic sounds of conventional instruments—not a particularly fitting term, since of course all music is "acoustic.") When two of the most successful jazz-rock artists, Herbie Hancock and

Chick Corea, went on their great 1978 duo tours, they dispensed with all the electronics they normally used and played only on the good old concert grand piano. And beginning in 1976, the group V.S.O.P. brought musicians together on acoustic instruments who had been particularly successful in electronic jazz-rock, among them Herbie Hancock, Tony Williams, Freddie Hubbard, and Wayne Shorter. It was striking how all these musicians really blossomed when they were finally able to play "just music" again on "normal" instruments without all the complicated electronics.

One of the main reasons why rock elements could be integrated so smoothly into jazz is that, conversely, rock has drawn nearly all its elements from jazz—especially from blues, spirituals, gospel songs, and the popular music of the black ghetto, rhythm and blues. Here the regular, steady rock beat, the gospel and soul phrases, the blues form and sound, the dominating sound of the electric guitar, etc., had all been in existence long before the appearance of rock. Drummer Shelly Manne once said, "If jazz borrows from rock, it only borrows from itself." A key figure in this development is blues guitarist B. B. King, who originated almost every element in the music of today's young rock and Top 40 guitarists. Among these, one of the most successful is Eric Clapton, who was honest enough to admit: "Some people talk about me like a revolutionary. That's nonsense—all I did was copy B. B. King." This is what vibraharpist Gary Burton meant when he said, "There is no rock influence on us. We only have the same roots."

We have talked about the way in which improvisation became increasingly collective. You could hear this trend in the most diverse modern jazz styles, from free jazz to contemporary mainstream and on to fusion jazz. But as is almost always the case in jazz, it also had its countertrend, toward the solo unaccompanied by a conventional rhythm section, a trend initiated by alto saxophonist Anthony Braxton and vibraharpist Gary Burton. There were many such unaccompanied solo or duo performances in the late sixties and afterward, from pianists McCoy Tyner, Chick Corea, Keith Jarrett, Cecil Taylor, Oscar Peterson; saxophonists Archie Shepp, Steve Lacy, and Roland Kirk; vibraharpist Karl Berger; trumpeter Leo Smith; trombonist George Lewis; guitarists John McLaughlin, Larry Coryell, Attila Zoller, John Abercrombie, and Ralph Towner; violinists Zbigniew Seifert and Billy Bang; and many others. In Europe there were solo recordings from Gunter Hampel, Martial Solal, Derek Bailey, Terje Rypdal, Albert Mangelsdorff, Alexander von Schlippenbach, and John Surman; and in Japan from Masahiko Satoh and others.

Certainly, there had been earlier unaccompanied jazz solos. Coleman Hawkins recorded the first a cappella horn solo in 1947, "Picasso." Above all, unaccompanied playing was favored by the great pianists, from the ragtime masters around the turn of the century to James P. Johnson and Fats Waller and on to Art Tatum and beyond. As in almost all areas of jazz, Louis Armstrong was a forerunner in the field of the unaccompanied solo, too: in his duet with Earl Hines in 1928, "Weather Bird," and in dozens of solo cadenzas and solo breaks.

However, these musicians merely paved the way for what was, in the first half of the seventies and beyond, a clear tendency reflecting the social alienation and the isolation of the jazz musician—and, in general, of modern man—the opposite of the collective spirit described earlier.

The trend toward the unaccompanied solo performance in the seventies was a romantic tendency—away from the loudness of electronic amplification and toward an intimate, extremely personalized, and sensitized form of expression, a symptom of a growing trend toward a new, objective, clear romanticism. It was only fitting that in the history of this solo and duo movement (and also in the parallel movement toward an "aestheticization" of jazz) Europe played a special role. The Munich record company ECM developed a concept and sound that became exemplary for this tendency toward the accent on aesthetics.

The gradual emergence of a new type of musician (which had already begun in free jazz, but was now becoming more of a worldwide tendency) was of greater importance in the seventies than most of the trends already described. On the one hand, this new type of musician remained in touch with the jazz scene; on the other hand, he or she used jazz only as a starting point, or even as merely one component among many others. These artists integrated elements from a large number of musical cultures into their music—above all from India and Brazil, but also from Arabia, Bali, Japan, China, the various African cultures, and many others, and occasionally also from European concert music. They felt what McCoy Tyner put into these words: "I see connections between all these different kinds of music. The music of the whole world is interrelated. . . . What I see in music is something total." And free-jazz trombonist Roswell Rudd, who was professor of music ethnology at the University of Maine, said:

> We're slowly starting to understand that there really is such a thing and that you can play it: world music. . . . Today, we can listen to the musics of the whole world, from the Amazon jungles to the Malaysian highlands and to the recently discovered native people of the Philippines. All that music is now at our disposal. . . . What's really important now is a new kind of hearing and seeing, right through these cultures.

The prototype of this new breed of musician was Don Cherry (who died in 1995), the former partner of Ornette Coleman. In the early sixties, we could still call him a free-jazz trumpeter. But what was he to be called in the seventies? In that span of time, Cherry became more deeply involved in the musics of the world than just about any other musician. And he also learned to play instruments from different cultures: from

Tibet, China, India, or Bali. His own answer to the question was, "I'm a world musician." And he called his music "primal music."

The development toward this new type of musician was initiated by John Coltrane, even though he himself was not yet of that type. Clarinetist Tony Scott, who spent years in Asia and was one of the first to incorporate elements of many Asian music cultures, and flutist Paul Horn, who recorded a number of moving solos at the Taj Mahal in India, fit this description as early as the sixties. During the seventies, more and more of these improvisers moving between jazz and world music emerged, and this trend continued (see the following section). Among the second generation of jazz-meets-world-music players were such artists as American sitar and tabla player Collin Walcott, Brazilian guitarist and composer Egberto Gismonti, the members of guitarist Ralph Towner's group Oregon, and Stephan Micus. In the seventies, there in fact existed a music center whose program included world music: the Creative Music Studio of German vibraharpist Karl Berger in Woodstock, New York. Said Berger, "When we started here in the early seventies, we may have called ourselves a 'jazz school.' But what actually interests us today, what we do and play and teach here, that's world music."

The Eighties

No single style can illustrate eighties jazz. On the one hand, the jazz of the eighties unceasingly fragmented and transcended stylistic limits. Just because it did that, and because it exploded categories and ignored de-limitations in an incessant process of blending and intermingling, eighties jazz was syncretistic and eclectic. Never before—not even in the seventies when this development was already emerging—had there been such an astonishingly colorful juxtaposition, so joyously undertaken, of so many different trends and styles. The exciting and fascinating thing about eighties jazz was its enormous diversity.

On the other hand, transcending stylistic boundaries became such a formative component in the jazz of the eighties that this freedom from any circumscribed style became the decade's "style." Aware of its abundance and diversity, and conscious that this style entails an open-minded attitude toward playing rather than an actual style, jazz became postmodern. It's a trend that continues in jazz today.

Up until the sixties the development of jazz followed a clear-cut, binding line of progress. The currently topical and most recently developed style was viewed as being not only the most up-to-date but also the most musically apposite compared to what preceded it. The jazz world of the eighties abandoned this perspective. Postmodern jazz says that no style explains the world on its own, none is better than another, and that every style is musically acceptable—not only contemporary and modern jazz, but also traditional forms of playing, from hard bop back to bebop, Swing, New Orleans jazz, and even earlier elements. And the musicians quickly applied what we have said about style in general to all forms of music. All musical means, not just those belonging to jazz, are usable and may be mixed and amalgamated with one another.

Belief in the equal value of all musical genres and styles is thus the foundation of postmodern jazz. Three aspects have therefore determined jazz since 1980:

1. All of a sudden, everything dating back to before the onset of the New Jazz—the great heritage and legacy of jazz—became available to the improvising musician. The eighties' improvised music involved an intensive dialogue with jazz tradition.

2. Postmodern jazz creates unity amid the multiplicity of differing and disparate stylistic elements. It plays with contradictions and rapid paradoxes by integrating contrasting elements into a whole. "The harmony of the disharmonious" is a principle often found in postmodern jazz.

   In the jazz of David Murray, John Zorn, Louis Sclavis, or even the playing of a conservative like Wynton Marsalis, it often happens that two or more stylistic layers are combined without "mixing" them. Borrowing a term from architect Charles Jencks, we can then speak of "double coding" or "multi-coding."

3. The art of quotation became a decisive force in the jazz of the eighties. As drummer David Moss has said, this is a "music of hyphens" in which musical fragments are quoted, paraphrased, compared, and combined.

In the early forms of jazz, a musician spent a lifetime mastering a single style. At least since the eighties, young musicians master several styles and ways of playing simultaneously, often with such sovereign virtuosity that it's scarcely possible to assign them to a single category. Collin Walcott, the tabla virtuoso and sitar player who died in 1984, time and again said that he felt like a musical nomad—neither an Indian musician, jazz stylist, salsa player, nor African percussionist, but rather someone who roams around between these spheres. "More and more musicians have this background, knowing a little bit about many things and usually not the least about something specific," he said. "It's like walking a tightrope. When I feel bad, I think I'm a dilettante, but when things are going well, I feel I know a lot." Alto saxophonist and composer John Zorn adds:

Because of the explosion of recordings, people of our generation have been exposed to more music than any other in the history of the world because of the recording boom. As a kid I listened to my father's jazz 78s, blues, pop, and rock on the radio—I was really into surf music— and at eighteen or nineteen, I started studying jazz saxophone. All of these musics made me who I am. . . . In a sense my music is rootless since I draw from all these traditions; I don't hold to any one camp.

Postmodern jazz musicians are primarily multistylists because they believe that stylistic purism is a fraud.

The freedom of eighties jazz was freedom of choice—the possibility, as pianist Anthony Davis put it, "of feeling no restraints in taking something over from any conceivable source of influence."

This went along with a pointed criticism of the avant-garde. Postmodern jazz musicians questioned the received maxims and unspoken taboos of free jazz. Real freedom, felt by an increasing number of musicians at the start of the eighties, is only possible for someone who can both apply and decide between everything offered: between free meter and playing with beat, open form and the thirty-two-bar standard form, free tonality and major-minor triads, free jazz and world music, bebop, minimal music, rock, New Orleans jazz, trash rock, tango, hip-hop. . . . The message of eighties jazz was "Anything goes."

People have attacked multistylistic jazz and its colorful amalgams for being flashy and arbitrary products of fashion. But in an age when we in our modern communication society experience a deluge of information, and the distances between countries and cultures become ever smaller, musicians are constantly exposed to the greatest possible diversity of sounds, melodies, and stimuli. They're absolutely bombarded with musical information. "The influences are inescapable," said drummer David Moss. "They are just there. We can't get away from them. We hear them all the time."

The development of postmodern jazz thus also has its cultural, social, and political catalysts. The exuberant eclecticism and colorful games played with disparate stylistic elements, wittily mixing and recombining them, constitute a simultaneously despairing and creative attempt at establishing meaning and relationship in a world of fragmentation and dissolution. At a time when digital and computerized communication technologies have brought us a gigantic overabundance of information, a musician's world appears as a huge heap of resounding shards out of which he or she has to construct a personal, individual view of reality. Truth as a unified whole is hardly achievable in postmodern jazz, or in the other arts. Only a patchwork, a cacophony of partial truths, exists.

It goes without saying that yearning for the whole is still present, even if ironically, in this process of assembling stylistic fragments—a yearning for security, which the invocation of jazz tradition has time and again rekindled. The jazz of the eighties was predominantly conservative. It isn't just a coincidence that this traditionalist, historicist phase of development was paralleled by a resurgence of political conservatism in the Western world (Reaganomics, Thatcherism, etc.).

"There are hundreds of styles today," according to electric bassist and producer Bill Laswell. Nevertheless, a number of eighties ways of playing jazz were more dominant and important than other equally interesting developments. They're listed sequentially here for clarity's sake, but it's important to see that they didn't exist in isolation. Delimitations are fluid and all conceivable permutations exist. The important eighties jazz tendencies are the following:

- Post–free-jazz view of the jazz tradition: developing from the sound of what was formerly the jazz avant-garde, in the eighties more and more musicians began to incorporate the great heritage of the jazz tradition into contemporary improvisation. Here, elements of free jazz are combined and mixed with traditional styles.

- The musicians of the new mainstream and neobop reacted in a consciously conservative countermovement to the above direction. They played with a *view of the jazz tradition from the vantage point of classic modern jazz*, picking up where the seventies bebop revival left off. Ostentatiously excluding any trace of free jazz, they continued and developed the results of classic modern jazz in a contemporary form. American critic Gary Giddins called this neobop movement "neoclassicism," but the term is a bit misleading. The relationship of the new mainstream players to the jazz tradition was more one of conservation and restoration, whereas the relation of the musicians coming out of the avant-garde to the jazz heritage was more strongly motivated by a desire for contemporary dialogue with that heritage. It would therefore make more sense to regard the attitude toward tradition of the musicians coming from free jazz as *neoclassic*, while the bop-inspired players of the eighties are better seen as *classicists*. The classicism of neobop also brought with it a renewed emphasis on craftsmanship in jazz.

- With jazz-rock as a model, *free funk* came into being—a combination of free horn improvisations with the rhythms and sounds of funk, new wave, and even punk.

- The dialogue of jazz with the world's musical cultures continued: more and more improvising musicians cultivated a *world jazz*, integrating elements of Asian, African, Indian, Middle Eastern, and many other musical cultures into their playing.

- The friction between free jazz on the one hand and rock and punk on the other gave rise to *noise music* (also called *no wave* or *art rock*)—a lurid mixture of free-jazz improvisation and the wild, unruly sounds and rhythms of punk, heavy metal, trash rock, minimal music, ethnic music, and numerous other influences.

Regarding the dialogue of the avant-garde with the jazz tradition: by the start of the eighties the achievements of free jazz, principally through the AACM from Chicago and the Black Artists Group from St. Louis, had become so defined in terms of melody and structure that one could no longer speak of free jazz as strictly defined. The current of free jazz flowed into the mainstream of eighties jazz. When the avant-garde trio Air released its *Air Lore* album in 1979, which links free jazz with Scott Joplin's ragtime melodies and Jelly Roll Morton's New Orleans sounds, it was a sensation. At that time, when the avant-garde world was preoccupied with permanent innovation, it still took courage to turn again to the old masters of jazz. But it wasn't long before free-jazz players' return to the imposing achievements of jazz heritage became something that was taken for granted.

It was alto saxophonist Arthur Blythe who provided a slogan for the contemporary look back at the history of jazz, with the title of an album he recorded in 1980: *In the Tradition.* All the important musicians within this direction, coming from free jazz and entering into a dialogue with jazz's legacy, really did play in the tradition: pianist and composer Muhal Richard Abrams; saxophonist, flutist, and composer Henry Threadgill and his sextet; tenor saxophonist David Murray and his octet and big band; trumpeters Lester Bowie and Olu Dara; bassist Dave Holland; flutist James Newton; and many others.

The style that a seventies neobop musician reconstructed could still be defined with a degree of precision: updated bebop adapted to contemporary tastes. But what style does someone like former free-jazzer David Murray reconstruct in his work since the eighties? You hear everything in his music: from the collective improvisations of New Orleans jazz to the Duke Ellington Orchestra's jungle sounds, from the turbulent motivic vortexes of bebop by way of the tempo displacements of a Charles Mingus to the emphatically overblown sounds of free jazz and the shuffle meters of rhythm and blues. That is astonishingly different from earlier retrospective currents in jazz, such as the forties New Orleans revival or the neobop of the seventies. The post–free-jazz traditionalist doesn't reconstruct a single style, but rather views jazz tradition as a whole.

To be sure, eighties neoclassicist jazz had a conservative tendency, but some critics failed to see it wasn't only nostalgic. Its adherents modernized and updated jazz tradition, making it of contemporary interest. They integrated (in the best sense of the word) the music—not just returning newer jazz to its roots but also moving in the other direction, filling traditional forms with present-day awareness—and highly infectiously and vitally, too. That's what was involved when trumpeter Lester Bowie said, "We are trying to take what has gone before, mill it around in our minds, add some of *us* to it, and then: this is *our* vision of what has happened."

As so often in jazz, the new relationship to what went before became most apparent in rhythm. More and more musicians who were formerly associated with the pulse structures of free jazz found their way back in the course of the eighties to playing with a regular beat. What was frowned upon by many representatives of free jazz and thought a cliché even in the structured free jazz of the seventies—the time-playing, the playing with an ongoing fundamental rhythm—was suddenly viewed with respect again. More and more musicians discovered, going beyond the tacit self-restrictions of free jazz, that playing with a specific meter involves certain irreplaceable qualities. Interestingly, they didn't simply take over the classic time-playing but rather permeated that with the unconfined, flowing rhythms of free jazz, refracting the conventional rhythms of bebop, Swing, New Orleans jazz, etc., and enriching them with updated elements. What such free-jazz musicians as Albert Ayler or Ornette Coleman felt cautiously is celebrated and lived by musicians since the eighties with enormous vitality and openness. They affirm that free tonality begins not with free jazz but with country blues and archaic New Orleans jazz, and that the liberation of meter wasn't an invention of sixties jazz but is basically present in everything that goes back (by way of bebop, Swing, and the march rhythms of New Orleans parades) to African American music's enormously flexible way of treating meters.

Free jazz developed new clichés even though it deliberately broke with old ones. Neoclassic jazz of the eighties—this is the difference—broke with clichés by consciously retaining and playing with them while maintaining (alongside all the quotation, humor, and parody) a profound respect for the great legacy of jazz tradition. "Nothing is contemporary," said guitarist John Mclaughlin, "unless you feel the tradition behind it."

The first neoclassicist (although unknowingly) was Duke Ellington. More than anyone else in the abundantly rich history of jazz, Ellington linked innovation with tradition, creating something modern by referring back to the great old forms of African American music. It's not just accidental that eighties jazz was so shaped by numerous tributes to Ellington. James Newton, the World Saxophone Quartet, Chico Freeman, and many others dedicated entire albums to Duke. Many musicians intuitively sensed the parallels linking Duke Ellington and the jazz of the eighties. Both moved in realms beyond categories, dissolving such restrictions in their playing.

The classicist neobop movement developed, in many cases, as a blunt, critical opposition to the free retrospection of the jazz tradition. To be sure, it too updated jazz tradition (in this sense, its "classicism" is indeed often "neo"), but, deliberately distancing itself from free jazz, it pursued the course prepared by seventies neobop, further developing and disseminating the legacy of bebop. At the start of the eighties, more and more young musicians built on the great tradition of Charlie Parker, Dizzy Gillespie, Thelonious Monk, Fats Navarro, Clifford Brown, Bud Powell, and others, but since then so many nonbop elements—modality (see the section on harmony), tempo displacements, formal freedoms, and, occasionally, all the older, premodern jazz styles—have been flowing into this revival that neobop can no longer be narrowly defined. The stream of neobop thus enters into the jazz classicism of the eighties. The basic elements of neobop are: playing over "changes" (the predetermined chord sequences of a fixed form, or "chorus"), tonality, and a regular beat. This music is, as its practitioners call it, "straight-ahead," because it emphasizes continuity of line and the regularity of its fundamental rhythm.

All the important new straight-ahead musicians (including trumpeter Wynton Marsalis in his early work, saxophonists Donald Harrison and Bobby Watson, trumpeter Terence Blanchard, pianist Mulgrew Miller, drummer Jeff "Tain" Watts, and bassist Charnett Moffett) were united by the certainty that bebop is *the* foundation of modern jazz. Nevertheless, these musicians updated and modernized not only bebop, but also everything that led up to the beginnings of free jazz: John Coltrane's modality, Wayne Shorter's abstract hard bop, the harmonic and rhythmic daredevilry of the legendary second Miles Davis Quintet, the melodic complexity of the early Eric Dolphy, etc. All that was no longer merely a refreshing contribution to the bebop style, as in neobop, but stood alongside it as something of equal value.

Some critics charged the new straight-ahead musicians with copying the masters of bebop—and very badly at that, "with mistakes in syntax and grammar." But there's no doubt that it was just these supposed mistakes—so-called errors of harmonic, melodic, and rhythmic character—that constituted the charm of neobop. Classicism's splendid young drummers—Watts, Marvin "Smitty" Smith, Ralph Peterson, and others—built on the rich bebop tradition: from Max Roach and Art Blakey by way of Roy Haynes to the rhythmic advances of Tony Williams and Elvin Jones. Nevertheless, their playing sounded contemporary and different; it was more powerful, aggressive, and hard. They played the rhythms of modern jazz with an awareness of the fact that fusion and jazz-rock existed at the same time. They carried something of the energy and weight of rock-oriented styles into the new bop. Of course, that did involve "mistakes in syntax and grammar," but obviously every innovation in jazz, every attempt at autonomy and individuality—whether of a stylistic or a personal nature—begins with such deviations from existing rules and structures, with "mistakes."

Also astonishing about the new mainstream jazz was that it showed what great possibilities of differentiation could exist within similarity. Eighties classicism demonstrated as clearly as any other jazz style that "sounding like" and "reminiscent of" still contained niches for "sounding like myself." Both in the course of a concert and often within a piece or even a phrase, tenor saxophonist Branford Marsalis was reminiscent of Joe Henderson, and then again of Buddy Tate and Don Byas, of John Coltrane and Sonny Rollins. Yet no one charged Marsalis with imitation. He always sounded like himself. It may seem paradoxical, but the more he paraphrased and alluded, the more individual he became.

Some eighties jazz (not just straight-ahead jazz) succumbed to the danger entailed in such a process: the quotation used as a cue remained a fragment and an empty phrase. No quotation, no matter how brilliant, permits a jazz musician to avoid his or her greatest challenge: to creatively charge improvised lines with a distinctly personal sound. Musicians have time and again pointed out that any quotation must really be felt and lived if it is to be more than a theatrical effect.

A main feature of the jazz of the eighties was the relationship of tension between neoclassicism and classicism, as defined above. Both directions cultivated a dialogue with the history of jazz; both reevaluated that tradition from the perspective of the eighties. But the new hard bop began from the idea that jazz has a tradition of conservation, while the neotraditionalists coming from free jazz emphasized the fact that jazz has a tradition of renewal and innovation, extending, as drummer Beaver Harris put it, "from ragtime to no time."

Development of free funk in the eighties was largely unaffected by the dialectic between classicism and neoclassicism. Free funk caught up with what seventies jazz-rock either neglected or simply forgot. It utilized the means accessible to free jazz for liberating and opening up the rhythms and melodies of jazz-rock. And, conversely, free funk with its danceable funk and rock rhythms transmitted symmetry, motor energy, and tangible physicality to free jazz. At the start of the eighties, the interpenetration of jazz and rock again became, for a brief time, an exceptionally exciting, infectious adventure.

It is striking that this process of liberation began at a time when signs of stagnation were unmistakable in fusion and jazz-rock, in 1977 with Ornette Coleman's *Dancing in Your Head* album. Ornette's Prime Time band's seething "free" funk rhythms and electrifying untempered collective improvisation didn't only indicate a way out of the dead end reached by a jazz-rock that had run out of ideas. *Dancing in Your Head*, and later *Body Meta*, were also years ahead of the whole of free funk.

To be sure, there had been previous experiments aimed at melding free jazz and funk. In his 1968 album *New Grass*, Albert Ayler mixed elements of rhythm and blues and soul with free jazz. At the beginning of the seventies, Rashied Ali, once the drummer in John Coltrane's last band, headed a group that played free funk. In 1974, the Human Arts Ensemble, grouped around drummer Charles Bobo Shaw in St. Louis, recorded free-jazz improvisation linking rock, rhythm and blues, and funk.

Yet there is no doubt that Ornette Coleman achieved the first artistically satisfying integration of free jazz and funk rhythms on *Dancing in Your Head*.

Ornette Coleman guided and influenced free funk in the same sovereign fashion as Miles Davis shaped and advanced jazz-rock. From Coleman came everyone of significance in the eighties border area between free jazz on the one side and the rhythms of funk, rock, and pop on the other: drummer Ronald Shannon Jackson and his various Decoding Societies, guitarist James "Blood" Ulmer, and electric bassist Jamaaladeen Tacuma (who all played in Ornette's Prime Time band). But also musicians and groups without any close personal contact with Coleman were lastingly influenced by his music: the Slickaphonics around trombonist Ray Anderson, the Five Elements with alto saxophonist Steve Coleman, saxophonist Greg Osby, the band Defunkt led by trombonist Joseph Bowie, the Noodband in Europe, saxophonist Kazutoki Umezu in Japan, and others.

Even though the rhythmic patterns produced by seventies jazz-rock drummers went considerably beyond rock rhythms, they were a step backward compared with the complex and multilayered rhythms of modern jazz. Their symmetry and two-beat regularity seemed rigid and schematic. Free funk at long last opened up jazz-rock rhythms. All of a sudden funk rhythms *breathed*. They were extended and compressed. The meter was suddenly reinterpreted and played with in a multitude of ways.

All the same, it gradually became apparent during the eighties that the rhythmic patterns in funk could only be liberated to a certain extent, or else they lost the very feature that characterized this music: its motor-power and dance-oriented rhythmic impetus. Funk's riff techniques and its ostinato interlocking figures are diametrically opposed to the open form and liberated conception of free jazz.

Free and funk thus clash. Since that is the case, free funk always fluctuated between two tendencies: either transposing the pulsating funk rhythms into metrically free playing, thereby losing funk qualities, or stressing funk's rigid beat, thereby restricting free jazz's melodic and harmonic independence.

It is part of the diversity and complexity of eighties jazz that many musicians don't regard this inner contradiction within free funk as disturbing. On the contrary, it inspires them to creativity. Drummer Ronald Shannon Jackson masterfully incorporated this conflict within the rhythmic concept underlying his group Decoding Society. There the freely flowing slow rubato horn themes constituted an intensively provocative contrast to Jackson's strongly pulsating, funk-inspired rhythmic figures.

On the other hand, it was clear that conflicts of such intensity could not be maintained over the long term, so it wasn't surprising that free funk—in amazingly similar fashion to jazz-rock—began to show clear-cut signs of fatigue after a brief and vehement flourishing at the start of the eighties.

Free funk's dilemma very much involved the fact that its rhythms rarely contained the interactive, group-forming qualities present in all great jazz rhythms. The relative compactness of such ostinato patterns created problems for what is indispensable in living, vital jazz as created by all the great drummers from New Orleans to free jazz: musical conversation and open dialogue.

That's why free funk—again astonishingly like jazz-rock—gave rise to only a few records satisfying the highest artistic demands: above all Ornette Coleman's *Dancing in Your Head*, some early recordings by Jackson's Decoding Society (*Street Priest* and *Nasty*), and some work by James "Blood" Ulmer (*Odyssey*). Coleman, with his Prime Time band, still remains the leading figure in free funk, even more than twenty-five years after *Dancing in Your Head*, because he mediates, unifies, and integrates in an environment that obstructs mediation, unification, and integration.

Parallel to free funk flowed a stream (with many branches leading in other stylistic directions) that first bore fruit in the seventies: the further development of the encounter between jazz and the world's musical cultures. When, at the end of the sixties, Don Cherry spoke of bringing jazz into a dialogue with African, Asian, Middle Eastern, and Latin American music—in short, of making a "world music"—he was almost the only one doing so. Twenty years later, this kind of musical exchange between cultures was practically taken for granted. World music went from being a visionary movement to being a profitable branch of the popular music industry. In 1987 the recording industry began to use the term *world music* as a label for marketing all the popular music trends of the non-Western world. For reasons of simplicity, and also in order to better distinguish it from this "world music," we will use the term *world jazz* for music that brings together jazz and non-Western musics.

World jazz got under way in the sixties as an additive process. Jazz musicians added what interested them—Indian, Balinese, Japanese, African, and Brazilian elements—to what they already played. Only in the seventies did this world music achieve initial high-quality artistic results, blending and integrating the various influences.

Since 1980 this process of interpenetration has proceeded further, even more intensively, within groups such as Codona and Oregon and with musicians like percussionist Okay Temiz, bassist David Friesen, the Europe-based oud player Rabih Abou-Khalil, saxophonist Charlie Mariano, Swedish percussionist Bengt Berger, trumpeter Jon Hassell, percussionist Naná Vasconcelos, and many others.

Because world jazz goes beyond categories, and was doing so already in the seventies, it was *the* catalyst for syncretic, eclectic, and style-dissolving forms in the eighties. More than any other stream in jazz, perhaps even more than free jazz, the encounter between jazz and world music called into question divisions between styles, forms, and categories that were taken to be binding. The jazz musician who sought dialogue with musicians from other cultures thus became the prototype of the multistylistic musician, because he or she sought unity in diversity. Trombonist Roswell Rudd said, "We discovered Pygmy music and realized that it's our own music." And Karl Berger, for years the director of the Creative Music Studio in Woodstock, New York, concurred: "When you listen to all the different musics, you suddenly become aware that they all have something in common. They all share the same roots."

Many musicians believed that their musical travels to other cultures were in reality trips within themselves. During his world music courses at Woodstock, Berger time and again stressed, "Listen into yourself. Find everything in yourself."

Consider drummer Ed Thigpen, a man of the older conservative jazz generation, completely different from youthful world-jazz musicians. When T. A. S. Mani, the South Indian percussionist, explained in 1984 a difficult 11/8 rhythm frequently found in Indian music but nowhere in jazz, Ed responded (once he'd "understood" the rhythm and played with a group of Indian musicians for a couple of minutes), "It's funny but somehow I knew all that. As if it had always been in me. Who knows?"

That sense of recognition was already felt by the man who sparked off this fusion of jazz and world music: John Coltrane, who died in 1967. When he first became acquainted with Indian and Arabic music, he thought he was really hearing a music hidden within himself—"a trip into your inner self." So this was the psychological motivation for the world-jazz movement—the discovery of musical archetypes.

Percussionist and sitar player Collin Walcott loved saying that "world music" was a model of how people on our overpopulated planet could live together more humanely and thoughtfully.

On the other hand, the eighties showed clearly that someone who viewed African, Tibetan, Balinese, Brazilian, etc., material as inter-changeable didn't achieve any genuine integration. Some early attempts at world jazz produced terribly superficial results. Many musicians have constantly stressed that you must be aware of the significance and mean-ing of what you want to amalgamate if the individual elements are to be melded into a whole.

The music of other cultures can't be learned in crash courses. If mu-sicians in a non-Western culture require half a lifetime (wiser musicians would say an entire lifetime) to penetrate and incorporate the symbolical, mythical, religious, and functional aspects of their music, then it would be presumptuous to assume that a jazz musician could internalize the riches of such music within a short period or even after years of hard study. The problem was even more acute because the world-jazz musician was usually involved in several different musical cultures rather than a single one.

World jazz thus tended toward superficiality—inherently rather than because of lack of interest. Stature and integrity were required if that danger was to be avoided. Astonishingly, many musicians were successful there. The "colonialist plundering of the self-service shops of global musical cultures," which was also a part of this movement, paled into insignificance alongside the high artistic achievements of this encounter of jazz and world music.

Noise music, or no wave, developed alongside world jazz, much influenced by it. People have gotten used to viewing no wave as incorporating all the multitudinous tendencies, ways of playing, and fashions resulting from the friction between free jazz on the one hand and, on the other, punk, experimental rock, minimal music, ethnic elements, and various other influences. The proliferation of labels was as rampant as the musical outcome was diverse: art rock, punk jazz, out music, fake jazz, etc. Despite all their differences, these styles were unified by the fact that their bizarre, eccentric playing around with mosaiclike stylistic elements evaded any clear-cut categorization—hence no wave, a music directed against all waves and fashions even though some of it showed unmistakable signs of modishness.

Among the outstanding musicians in this area were alto saxophonist and composer John Zorn; guitarists Arto Lindsay, Fred Frith, and Elliott Sharp; saxophonist John Lurie; drummer David Moss; scratcher Christian Marclay; keyboardist Wayne Horvitz; harpist Zeena Parkins; bassist Bill Laswell; and others.

No wave or noise music employed the means developed by punk, trash rock, minimal music, and numerous other influences in pursuing what free jazz started—the emancipation of noise. It broke even more shockingly, aggressively, and wildly with what previously seemed musically valid and binding, transposing all the everyday sounds that surround us into improvised music.

In the process, no wave musicians went beyond the restrictions free jazz imposed on itself with the same élan and radicality once directed by free jazz against functional harmony, beat, and tonality. Noise music called into question what was self-evident for free jazz in at least four areas:

1. Noise musicians separated themselves from free jazz's ideas about development. Instead of extended arches of ecstatic tension, often long prepared in collective improvisation, short, isolated sound events were stressed. Noise music and no wave musicians disintegrated and atomized the prolonged formal processes of free jazz, turning them into rapidly changing sound events.

   Free jazz integrated sounds; no wave isolated them. The musical fracture was noise music's most important method, and its favorite medium was the collage—the linking of apparently unrelated musical processes and sounds. It goes without saying that musical relationships and order developed on a superordinate level but were disrupted and teased ambivalently.

2. Free jazz's ideas about tempo were intensified and accelerated. No Wave concentrated the pulse of free jazz to establish highly charged tempos where time was foreshortened. Pieces and forms became ever more compressed and shorter at these frantically breakneck speeds. Percussionist and singer David Moss: "If a piece lasts for a minute, that's sometimes too long for us."

3. Free jazz rejected much that went before but persisted unwaveringly with the idea of craftsmanship and virtuosity. Noise music broke with even that ideal. Out of protest it incorporated the dilettantish, kitschy, and banal, all the acoustic junk that surrounds us day in and day out, ironically fragmenting, distancing, and parodying.

4. Noise musicians played without free jazz's utopias. The ominous, fragmented sound of noise music and no wave completely abandoned any belief that music could directly bring about political and social change. The vision of a better, more humane world was replaced by the noise musicians' sober, cynical "that's how it is" attitude, criticizing the inhospitability of cities and the madness of an ecologically butchered and militarily overarmed world by reflecting and dismantling reality in all of its brutality and aggressiveness.

Of course, some of those features, attributed here to noise music and no wave, could also be found in isolated examples of free jazz. The difference between the two ways of playing consisted, however, in the fact that noise music overstated and exceeded, more cheekily and ambivalently, what was merely suggested in some aspects of free jazz.

There was much talk of noise music and no wave as destructive. But it wasn't the no-wave musicians who were aggressive, brutal, and violent; it was the conditions of existence influencing their penetration of the acoustic environment. Ever since art has existed, the charge has always been the same. Artists are made responsible for something to which they, as sensitive, alert human beings, are usually the first to draw attention. "Just ride a bike down Broadway about one in the afternoon, and you'll experience everything that's in our music," said saxophonist and composer John Zorn.

In conclusion, we would like to stress once again that neobop, neoclassicism, free funk, world jazz, and noise music were not ways of playing isolated from one another. Indeed, they often appeared in colorfully confusing admixtures. The situation was complicated even further by the fact that many musicians openly jumped around between these ways of playing and trends. It became increasingly impossible to assign a musician's way of playing to a single category. That was astonishingly different from previous decades when a single style usually predominated, with at most two others making themselves felt.

The Nineties

At the beginning of the nineties, the stylistic delta of jazz had become immeasurably broad. With its style- and genre-bridging tendencies, jazz had ensured that hybrid ways of playing, stylistic mixtures of every conceivable type, had become commonplace. At the same time, the boundaries between jazz and other kinds of music had become extremely permeable. American critic Tom Piazza says: "The sense of why jazz was important—of what jazz was in the first place—had become diluted; the music needed a revivifying, organizing metaphor." This felt need was vehemently addressed by a group of musicians who, supported by some critics, united under the rallying cry: "We need a canon."

"We need a canon": the man who first raised this cry, and gave it its rhetorically sharpest and most radical formulation, as well as its strongest musical emphasis, was Wynton Marsalis. The trumpeter, composer, and bandleader wanted to give back to jazz that which (as he saw it, at any rate) it seemed to have lost after thirty years of free jazz, twenty years of jazz-rock, and ten years of the hyphenated styles of postmodern jazz: commitment, classicism, and fixed rules.

Whether one approved of the Marsalis canon or not, it became binding for a whole generation of young musicians at that time, the "young lions." Like Wynton Marsalis, they performed in custom-tailored suits, and like their idol, they were dedicated to a conservative style of playing that, taking bebop as its starting point, cultivated a new valuation of the jazz tradition.

The "young lions" set out to give jazz a feeling of wholeness and continuity. They wanted to tell stories instead of deconstructing, to serve rather than to provoke. Their conservative tendencies were reflected in their improvisations, which did not seek to modify and invent, but rather to affirm and rediscover. According to Branford Marsalis, "before you can liberate yourself from the burden of jazz history, you have to carry it for a while."

The new conservatives in straight-ahead jazz set up their standards, and, as doubtful as many of the positions they staked out may have been (as will be seen), they succeeded in creating thoroughly personal playing styles. The mastery with which they handled the great heritage of jazz was astonishing; they "played" the jazz tradition like an instrument.

In January 1991, New York's Lincoln Center established a permanent jazz division, with Wynton Marsalis as its artistic director. The launching of this venture was supported by an endowment of $3.4 million, intended to ensure that Jazz at Lincoln Center would operate at the same cultural level as the Metropolitan Opera, the Juilliard School of Music, the New York City Ballet, or the New York Philharmonic.

In terms of cultural politics, the message being sent was important. For the first time, African Americans were given the leading role in an important part of America's cultural establishment. With a budget of $2.3 million, the programmers sought to define a canon of the classic masterpieces of jazz.

According to Albert Murray, a cultural critic and mentor to Marsalis, the Lincoln Center program aimed at radiating the qualities of "affirmation, majesty, and sophistication." The question as to how jazz could survive the "onslaught of pop music" and the "death of the great jazz masters" was answered by Jazz at Lincoln Center by an emphasis on the "eternal values" of jazz: values that Marsalis believed he had found in the elements *blues*, *swing*, *groove*, and in the classic jazz standards.

The program was correspondingly conservative. It gave priority to the straight-ahead jazz of the young lions, and presented retrospective celebrations of the heroes of the Swing era, bebop, hard bop, and New Orleans jazz. But all the developments in jazz that came after these—avant-garde/free jazz, hip-hop jazz, jazz-rock, European jazz, world jazz—were ignored. As Stanley Crouch put it, "As far as I'm concerned, call it new music, call it 'imaginary folklore,' but please don't call it jazz."

Jazz at Lincoln Center (JLC) became the focal point of the conflict between old and new ways of thinking in jazz, and JLC's programming ignited debates that became quite bitter. The "tradition versus innovation" argument became so polemical and polarized that newspaper headlines appeared referring to the "New York jazz wars."

"These Armani jazzers with their standards, they aren't risking anything," charged clarinetist Don Byron. Trumpeter Lester Bowie saw them as "museum curators," and believed that "rebellion is the real tradition of jazz." Tenor saxophonist Gary Thomas added: "To whoever wants to use tradition as a club to beat down those who stand outside it: fuck the tradition!"

In fact, Wynton Marsalis and the young lions paid a high price for recognition by the American cultural establishment: the exclusion of large parts of contemporary jazz. Marsalis castigated free-jazz musicians as "a lost patrol," and his mentor and champion Stanley Crouch referred to black musicians returning to African roots of jazz as "painted warriors with spears." According to Crouch, the last twenty-five years of the twentieth century could best be viewed as a "Dadaist period" in jazz history. In the end, the results of the jazz avant-garde, jazz-rock, and world music had nothing to contribute to the canon of classical masterpieces.

"The bebop cats and the classical musicians have one thing in common," counters guitarist Vernon Reid. "Both of them say: we're the ones playing the *real* thing, so give *us* the money."

There are two ways of viewing the jazz tradition. Percussionist Hamid Drake makes a distinction between "small tradition" and "great tradition." The "small tradition" represents imitation, the continuation or expansion of a particular style. The "great tradition," in contrast, is carried on by players who look for points of friction with the tradition that is handed down to them. The "great traditionalist" proceeds from a paradox: he remains true to the old masters by continuing their refusal to compromise. "The essence of the music is change itself," says composer Muhal Richard Abrams.

As justified as some of the criticism of the retro trends of the nineties is, some of the charges leveled against neoconservative jazz have turned out to be exaggerated. Most of the young lions were not engaged in simply re-creating jazz history. Rather, they wanted to grasp its innermost essence in the hope of finding themselves by measuring themselves against the standard of history. Many improvisers, such as tenor saxophonist Joshua Redman, trumpeters Nicholas Payton and Roy Hargrove, pianists Benny Green and Cyrus Chestnut, succeeded in this quest. It sounds paradoxical, but neoconservative musicians also contributed to the evolution of jazz. They demonstrated the inexhaustible richness of subtlety and possibilities of differentiation that can be found in the combination and reevaluation of traditional forms of playing.

The fear that the increasing institutional support of jazz in the United States would cause entire creative streams of jazz development to dry up has not come to pass. Rather, the opposite is the case: the increased attention benefited jazz as a whole. And by the end of the nineties, Lincoln Center proved willing to relax its strict canonical rules and to modernize its program.

"The 'jazz wars' have nothing to do with creativity," said trumpeter Dave Douglas in early 2000. Tenor saxophonist David Murray added: "Can I just say what I'd like to see at the end of all this arguing? Respect between musicians working in different parts of the jazz community. There is no reason why people should not respect each other just because they're working in different musical genres."

The bebop boom of the nineties brought with it an intense reevaluation of craftsmanship. Connected with this, jazz pedagogy experienced strong growth, and both contributed to and profited from the success of the young lions.

In 1975 Ellis Marsalis, Wynton and Branford's father, was playing with tenor saxophonist Sonny Stitt. Branford, who at the time was fifteen years old and full of veneration for the greats of the jazz tradition, played something for the master saxophonist. "Oh, that's all right. You're working on the shit." Branford said, "Well, you know what that shit is, Mr. Stitt." He went, "No, son. I can curse. You can't."

On the one hand: "Jazz is one of the least learnable art forms" (Keith Jarrett). Can you teach a young player to sound like an older, mature musician? "No," says saxophonist David "Fathead" Newman, "you have to *live* and *hear*."

On the other hand: jazz pedagogy works. Today, young, ambitious jazz musicians spend less time learning in clubs and jam sessions and more time in schools, with their jazz programs and workshops. "New York has changed," says saxophonist Marcus Strickland. "I think that school has replaced the street as the network." The history and development of jazz pedagogy, its opportunities and its dangers, move between these extremes.

The world of jazz education offers musicians a stable, even lucrative, occupation. This new generation of players/teachers disproves the proverb "those who can, do; those who can't, teach." Jazz musicians today, young and old, increasingly regard universities, not "the street," as the main place where talented aspirants go to learn.

In 1972 only fifteen universities and colleges in the United States offered degree programs in jazz studies. By September 1998, the number was more than one hundred. The magazine *Jazz Times* reported in 1992 that in America alone over one hundred thousand students were involved in jazz pedagogy. At that time, the International Association of Jazz Educators (IAJE) had more than seven thousand members in thirty-two countries around the world.

In order to give themselves legitimacy in the eyes of their classical music colleagues, many jazz teachers sought formulas and codes that would raise jazz to the level of a classical art form. They found this above all in the music of bebop, which is to some extent notable according to Western standards, and which has the advantage that it can be described according to the rules of functional harmony.

The meteoric rise of jazz pedagogy has led to the propagation of a way of playing that can best be described as "conceptualized bebop." Despite its stylistic openness, the codified, formal elements are so predominant in this music that drummer Kenny Washington remarked, "Musicians today are not into feeling. Younger cats don't even like to play the blues. They feel as though it has already been done. The blues is beneath them."

Whether consciously or unconsciously, jazz pedagogy has oriented itself toward the ideals of classical music. The teachers emphasize notation and harmony, the learning of particular melodic models (patterns) and note choices, and precision of articulation. But jazz teachers who proceed in this manner forget that the uniqueness of the music of Lester

Bowie, Joe "Tricky Sam" Nanton, Peter Brötzmann, or Jan Garbarek stems precisely from the fact that these instrumentalists modulate timbres in their own unique fashion. It's true that anyone who wants to improvise on standards needs to learn about harmony. But, according to David Ake, "It is less clear, however, why harmonic theory should predominate to the virtual exclusion of all else in jazz improvisation courses or why written material should hold such a privileged position in college-level jazz pedagogy."

For example, it would not be difficult to teach the shrieks and sounds of the free-jazz saxophonists. But to play in the manner of late Coltrane, Evan Parker, or Albert Ayler would undermine the classical "authority" of the teacher, and the necessity of the teacher's "precise" and "objective" instructions. The uniqueness of these sounds cannot be notated. For this reason, this music has no place in institutional jazz pedagogy, so that pianist and composer Anthony Davis justifiably complains: "It's so sad that pedagogy cannot incorporate the entire American experience." Fortunately, the fixation of jazz pedagogy on classical elements is being called more and more into question, even by teachers. There are many alternatives to the rituals of codified, rigid teaching. Steve Coleman, for example, teaches his extremely rhythmically complex compositions by having his students (in Banff, Canada) play them back by ear. Teachers are becoming more and more conscious of the importance of rhythmic and timbral elements, or intuitive hearing. A good jazz musician never stops learning. "Education is a forever process," said trombonist Slide Hampton—at the age of seventy. Thus, it would also be wrong to assume, as is sometimes done, that contemporary jazz would be better off if there were no such thing as jazz pedagogy. The opposite is the case. All the great jazz musicians who have given and continue to give jazz its creative impulse in the nineties and the early twenty-first-century—Jason Moran, Brad Mehldau, Branford Marsalis—emphasize that without the impetus that their careers received from jazz colleges and universities, mentors and teachers, they wouldn't be what they are today: creative improvisers with their own unmistakable musical identities.

Says pianist Jason Moran:

> Jazz education works. I had Jaki Byard every Monday. It couldn't get any better than that. But it's up to the student. Before they decide to get to learn jazz in school, they have to have an idea what they want to do, who they want to be. I saw a student in Brazil, and he was wondering about schools in New York. I pointed to his head, and I said, "That's where your school is."

At first glance, the jazz of the nineties seems to be all about restoration and conservatism. In reality, jazz did not lose any of its curiosity. In the nineties, the jazz scene was more diverse, colorful, and original than it had ever been before. Independent of the neoconservative jazz of the young lions, and sometimes in direct contrast to it, there developed at least six tendencies that were decisive for jazz in the nineties (and among which, of course, all possible overlaps could also take place):

1. The New York downtown scene became a catalyst for the multistylistic tendencies of jazz.

2. The development of "imaginary folklore." This largely coincided with the growth of European jazz consciousness.

3. The incorporation of sampling and remixing into jazz. This extended from free improvisers to players who used elements of hip-hop, drum 'n' bass, and techno in their improvisations.

4. The blossoming of "M-Base" music. This style of improvising through highly complex metrical and rhythmic labyrinths was the specialty of the musical collective that formed under this name.

5. The jazz scene underwent a very rapid rate of globalization. World jazz made a quantum leap in popularity. Immigrants expressed their different ways of life and cultural experiences in the language of jazz. More and more non-Western musicians put their stamp on the music.

6. An unusually large wave of song and vocal jazz. This was triggered by the success of the singer Diana Krall, whose mass popularity, previously considered unlikely, was quickly surpassed by the seven Grammy awards won by vocalist Norah Jones. Since the end of the nineties, jazz singers have scored great successes with their treatments of standards from the Great American Songbook and with their own songwriting (more about this in the chapter on "The Singers of Jazz").

From the shrill, colorful legacy of noise music and new wave, integrating and further developing these sounds, at the end of the eighties a dynamic experimental music scene arose on Manhattan's Lower East Side—the New York "downtown scene."

"What's coming out of this scene is undoubtedly hybrid music," said alto saxophonist and composer John Zorn. "It's the result of people who grew up in the sixties and seventies and for most of their conscious life have heard and experienced music from all over the world."

One of the most important statements of the downtown scene was: unity no longer exists. Instead, there's plurality. The impertinent, exuberant playing with quotation in this music marked an aesthetic of musical disintegration that, paradoxically, sought cohesion. A characteristic of the downtown scene was its unbridled polystylism.

The pluralism of the downtown scene had nothing to do with arbitrariness, but with the multiplicity of diversity and differing commitments. "A lot of people have a hard time classifying me stylistically," said guitarist Jim O'Rourke, a musician close to the downtown scene. "They say I'm just doing a bunch of different things that have nothing to do with each other. I don't see it that way. For me, it's all connected. The common denominator is difficult, almost unsolvable situations from which I have to liberate myself aesthetically and in which I can learn something new."

The downtown scene was the child of the city of New York. Its music tended toward loudness, density, and extreme sounds. Its uninhibited bricolage and multistylistic pastiches (Thomas Miessgang has called this a "cut-and-paste aesthetic") became the sonic lingua franca of the downtown scene. In its jumble of styles and quotations and its combinations of contradictory musical languages and idioms, the downtown scene reminds us that jazz is a music of curiosity, rebellion, unrest, and protest. The downtown sounds came from a world in which the tempo of musical perception had accelerated enormously. For this reason, the music often sounds restless, truncated. "We hear music the same way we see films," said pianist Uri Caine, "with fast edits, jump cuts, and abrupt scene changes."

"In our time, we're inundated with music from all periods and genres," said trumpeter Dave Douglas. "How to make a synthesis of it—that's the big question." All the important New York downtown musicians, including alto saxophonist John Zorn, pianist Uri Caine, clarinetist Don Byron, guitarist Marc Ribot, keyboardist Jamie Saft, percussionists Joey Baron and Bobby Previtte, violinist Mark Feldman, and, of course, Douglas, found their own personal answers to this question.

Many of the stylists of the New York downtown avant-garde intuitively felt and experienced the particular closeness of jazz to the great non-Western musical cultures. They experienced the richness of the world's music as an important inspiration. For this reason, it is hardly surprising that a large number of musicians of non-European origin—immigrants and musicians whose lives span multiple cultures—made creative contributions to this scene, such as Brazilian percussionist Cyro Baptista, percussionist Susie Ibarra (of Filipina descent), Japanese musician Ikue Mori, Cuban-American percussionist Roberto Rodriguez, and others.

The diverse origins of these musicians alone indicate how multilayered the involvement of the downtown scene was with the sounds of the world's great musical cultures. In addition, during the nineties the world-music-inspired improvisations of the downtown musicians showed two tendencies that were characteristic of this scene:

1. Close to the time of the revival of klezmer music, but
   experimentally broadening and radicalizing it, Jewish downtown

musicians incorporated new and old elements of their musical culture. They created a new multistylistic klezmer jazz. This led to the development of what has been called a "Radical Jewish Culture" (after the series of recordings of the same name on John Zorn's Tzadik label).

2. There was a notable turn by many New York jazz musicians toward the melodies and rhythms of Balkan folk music (further discussed in the section on "imaginary folklore").

With regard to "klezmer jazz" and radical Jewish culture, many musicians saw in Jewish music a welcome alternative to the dogmatism of the young lions movement, and "an effective antidote to the African American cultural genealogy of the young lions/straight-ahead scene" (Peter Niklas Wilson).

Just as the black musicians of the AACM found in "Great Black Music" the roots of an avant-garde approach to jazz that bridged genres and styles, the musicians of the downtown scene have found in Jewish music the roots for a new kind of hybrid jazz. "We didn't have an ethnic identity," said keyboardist Anthony Coleman, "and then we found this thing that was cool and that had as much funkiness as the blues, or the other kinds of black music that we were trying to steal."

Other New York downtown musicians, such as trumpeter Frank London or drummer Joey Baron, emphasized the closeness of Jewish music to the blues. The affinity went beyond a preference for lowered scale degrees, or "blue notes" (see page 208). This is because, like in the blues, in Jewish music emotional extremes such as ecstatic joy and pain, sadness and happiness, can coincide in a moment. Clarinetist Ben Goldberg summed it up paradoxically: "Klezmer gave me a way of playing the blues without playing the blues."

It is notable that the new klezmer jazz gave many musicians that sense of identity that seems easily lost in the overflowing stylistic diversity of multistylistic jazz. Jewish music offered the downtown improvisers a way of keeping warm in the cold wind of postmodernism. But what is "Jewish music"? What makes it sound "Jewish"? The downtown musicians were constantly answering this question anew, and every musician had a different answer. Anthony Coleman said it's not enough to play a few Middle-Eastern-sounding scales: "I can put on a cowboy hat and really feel like an American." But this was a limited approach. The more interesting approach was to play a Jewish music that had never existed before: "a music beyond orthodox clichés."

Afrobeat, Latin music, samba, free jazz, klezmer: for Frank London, the trumpeter of the Klezmatics, all this was part of his Jewish heritage. He had lived and played all these musics, and therefore celebrated them in his own jazz (with, for example, his Shekhina Big Band) as a seamless whole. Clarinetist David Krakauer's band Klezmer Madness used post-Hendrix sounds and noise elements to break away from the clichés and rigidified forms of orthodox Jewish music, while still preserving the great heritage of klezmer music.

The music of the new Jewish downtown scene grew out of a paradox. On the one hand, it overcame the arbitrariness of postmodernism by turning to its Jewish roots. But at the same time it incorporated all the stylistic diversity gained by postmoderism into its invention of a new music. For Frank London, Jewish music stood for both at once: an age-old tradition and constant reinvention. "The point is not to mix free jazz and klezmer," said clarinetist Ben Goldberg. "I can hear all the modern elements in klezmer: fantastic melodies, a special relationship to harmony, style, vocabulary, madness."

It is a mark of John Zorn's position as the engine and integrating figure of the downtown scene that he also was a trailblazer in the encounter between jazz and new and old Jewish music. He supplied the initial spark for this movement when in 1992 he organized a program of "new Jewish culture" for the Art Project festival in Munich. In a manifesto, Zorn called for a "Radical Jewish Culture": for New York's pastiche music to contribute to the renewal of Jewish culture. It took only a few years for this vision to become sonic reality.

With his quartet Masada, John Zorn created *the* model for an approach to improvising that interpreted Jewish music from an individual, modern perspective. On his record label Tzadik, he established the series "Radical Jewish Culture," under which heading there have appeared over seventy CDs to date, on which more than two dozen artists and groups have articulated their own visions of contemporary Jewish music. Every one of these artists has a different, individual answer to Zorn's question: "What, for you, is new Jewish music today?" The power of the new Jewish downtown jazz was also attested to by the fact that it was increasingly spreading internationally. Bands from Berlin (Ahava Raba, Paul Brody's Sadawi), London, Kraków, and Paris became part of the inner circle of John Zorn's "radical Jewish culture."

All these musicians were fascinated by the idea that it was possible to create a Jewish music without preconceptions, dogmas, and clichés. When the Jewish trumpeter Paul Brody was asked what to him was the "radical" part of "Radical Jewish Culture," he replied: "That on Jewish holidays I'm just as happy to cook Arab food for my children as Jewish food. That falafel has a place on my table next to matzo bread."

"Much of what is most original and most vital in jazz today comes from Europe," said American jazz critic Dan Ouellete in 2003, writing in the American jazz magazine *Down Beat*. Another critic put it more provocatively: "Jazz has moved to Europe."

The fact is that in the nineties, European jazz developed to a level equal in musical value to anything in American jazz and became particularly rich in creative approaches. A large contribution to this was the development of what was called "imaginary folklore," originated in Europe as early as the seventies. The two driving forces behind this movement were a) the French musicians' initiative Association à la Recherche d'un Folklore Imaginaire (ARFI), around the Lyon-based clarinetist Louis Sclavis, and b) the Norwegian saxophonist Jan Garbarek, whose reflections on Scandinavian folklore and Balkan moods proved early on that a contemporary European jazz could be created from reflection on one's own roots.

The musical explorations of the imaginary folklorists were based on what has been called an art of allusion. Motives were constantly heard that sound as if they originated in folk music, but that were in fact new, invented by the jazz musicians themselves. According to musicologist Ekkehard Jost, "the folklore to which the musicians related here was not a really existing one, but one that they found within themselves, that formed a part of their own multicultural identity." Alluding to and hinting at the past in this way, these musicians were inventing new folkloristic elements in the spirit of the twentieth and twenty-first centuries.

For example, French bassist Renaud Garcia-Fons made music in which elements of Syrian, Spanish, Turkish, Arabic, and French music flowed together into a pan-Mediterranean world jazz. Elements of flamenco rhythms, Arabic *maqam* improvisations, hymns from the Middle Ages, and Sephardic melodies constantly surfaced, but these combined to form a truly new improvised music.

Italian clarinetist Gianluigi Trovesi worked in a similar way. His improvisations are informed by the saltarello dances of the Florentine Renaissance and the music of the *ars nova*, as well as by the folk melodies of his native Bergamo, serial music, Italian banda groups, and the film scores of Nino Rota. All this was added to his deep knowledge of the jazz tradition of Charlie Parker, Eric Dolphy, Ornette Coleman, and the "new thing" sounds of the jazz avant-garde.

"Jazz is a great, broad river," said Trovesi, "and when it gets close to the sea, it opens up into a delta. The delta is the place where the European musicians were deposited. They use the water from the jazz stream and from the sea; they use both jazz and the traditional historical musics of their own countries."

Like Trovesi, the "imaginary folklore" musicians reflected their own backgrounds in the telling of their personal jazz stories. Spanish pianist Chano Domingo combined the jazz tradition with the melodies and rhythms of flamenco; kaval flutist Theodosii Spassov brought Bulgarian hora melodies into contemporary jazz; Armenian-Turkish percussionist Arto Tuncboyacian used the sounds of the Caucasus and Anatolia in Western European improvisations.

Italian writer Umberto Eco: "Here we are in the presence of a new transversality where distinctions of genre are vanishing . . . that the meeting of apparently incompatible traditions conjures up the ghosts of non-existent musical families."

The European jazz scene profited from two things: first of all from the immeasurable richness of cultural regional differences and folkloric traditions, and second of all from the fact that European countries became a preferred destination for emigrants, promoting transcultural experiences (as was also the case in the United States toward the end of the nineteenth century).

Thus, the polyglot character of European jazz is one of its most interesting features. Typical regional characteristics quickly developed. The electronic experiments of the Norwegian scene, including players such as Bugge Wesseltoft and Nils Petter Molvaer, and groups like Supersilent and Jaga Jazzist, were particularly impressive in their refreshing combination of styles and genres and integration of European pop trends. Jazz in Great Britain profited to a particular degree from the cultural heritage of its Caribbean immigrants and their British followers, so that London developed its own European variant of a black jazz, with musicians including Courtney Pine, Soweto Kinch, and Denys Baptiste. The French jazz scene, including groups such as the Sclavis/Texier/Romano Trio, and Renaud Garcia-Fons, showed a particular sense for bright harmonies and refined tone colors, and a connection to the delicate melodies of "imaginary folklore." In the Netherlands, a vital scene blossomed between jazz, free improvisation, and new music, with improvisers including Wolter Wierbos, Ab Baars, and Tobias Delius. In Vienna, a new electronics scene established itself around players such as Christian Fennesz and Martin Brandlmayer, using laptop computers to create an art situated between jazz, pop, and composed music.

The first fully formed European jazz musician was guitarist Django Reinhardt, in the thirties. In his famous solos with the Hot Club of France, this gypsy musician forced European jazz to reinvent itself, confronting it with the idea of becoming a more self-aware music that reflected its own environment and its own roots. For the first time, Balkan melodies and grooves found their way into jazz, at first as an exceptional case. In the nineties, however, jazz musicians' interest in the melodies and rhythms of Southeast Europe and the East had become so strong that a New York critic spoke of the "Balkanization" of contemporary jazz. New York's downtown musicians made Balkan music the center of their musical investigations. Jazz musicians from Western Europe were more and more interested in "odd meters" (asymmetrical time signatures) and the folklore melodies of Bulgaria, Romania, etc. And more and more Balkan and Eastern European musicians were becoming creative figures in the rapidly globalizing jazz scene.

It seems as though the odd meters and richly ornamented melodies of Southeastern Europe and the Mediterranean were particularly close to the spirit of jazz—closer, in any case, than the Western European musical aesthetic based on classical forms of expression.

Balkan music is "blue." As Serbian pianist Bojan Zulfikarpasic explains, this is true already due to the fact that "it comes from an ambiguous mixture of exuberance and melancholy." Musicians have also discerned a spiritual relation to the blues in its tendency to microtonally "flatten" certain notes.

Balkan wedding bands, with their powerful, swinging drum patterns and vital drive, were often reminiscent of the Second Line rhythms of New Orleans jazz. The remarkable ease with which Balkan musicians improvise over odd rhythms has already had an influence on musicians of classic modern jazz, such as Lennie Tristano, Dave Brubeck, and Don Ellis. "I think American musicians are always looking for humanity and seriousness," said trumpeter Dave Douglas. "And you can find these ingredients on an elementary level in almost every Balkan music production."

In the midnineties, many musicians and bands of the New York downtown scene began to incorporate the melodies and odd rhythms of Balkan music into their own jazz, such as Pachora, Dave Douglas's Tiny Bell Trio, and Brad Shepik's Commuters. When these musicians and bands improvised over the irregular meters of Balkan and Eastern music, they weren't trying to reconstruct traditional folklore. Rather, they were playing Eastern music from the vantage point of a new jazz sensibility. Many of the pieces played by the quartet Pachora sounded as if they could have been played in Balkan wedding bands for centuries. But the melodies were new creations. "Ninety-nine percent of the music comes from us, even if sometimes it doesn't sound like it," said guitarist Brad Shepik.

Shepik, a New Yorker, had never been to Bulgaria, nor had he visited Egypt, Morocco, or Tunisia. Does this make the stories told in his "world jazz" less true—stories in which Maghreb, Eastern, and especially Balkan musical elements collide with the experimental spirit of the New York downtown avant-garde?

Brad Shepik and the other downtown musicians were not practicing a kind of musical cannibalism. The irregular rhythms of Balkan folklore became an integral part of their musical experience and of their lives, via the Internet, CDs, and New York's Balkan community. "When people hear us, they ask us where we come from," said Shepik. "We tell them: from today's Brooklyn."

Norwegian saxophonist Jan Garbarek spoke of this as well. The more he became involved with Indian music, the more conscious he became of how important the Balkan region is for the path that Eastern music took into Central and North Europe. The Balkan region is a kind of interface between the East and the West, and this may help explain the region's cultural richness. Its melodies and rhythms have always fascinated, stimulated, and inspired jazz musicians. "For me, Balkan music is like a flying carpet," said Macedonian guitarist Vlatko Stefanoski. "I can use it to go anywhere."

In the nineties, a new class of instruments arose that permitted jazz musicians to create and modify sounds in completely new ways. These instruments—samplers and computers, particularly laptops—existed in the eighties, but it was not until the nineties that they became practical, portable, reliable, and affordable enough to become an important part of many jazz groups. "Today's generation of electronic gadgetry allows for far more sophisticated experimentation than the old wickka-wickka sound of turntable scratching or a basic sample loop for musicians to improvise over," writes British jazz critic Stuart Nicholson. "Now the improviser's art can be played out against a new sonic backdrop colored by fragments of electronic sounds, rhythms, and samples swimming through the music."

Improvising with samplers has contributed a great deal to the rejuvenation of electronic jazz. "Sampling offers an undiscovered universe of sounds and textures," said arranger and saxophonist Bob Belden. According to Greg Tate, "Sampling gives you a technique of being able to collaborate with all the periods of black music on one chip."

The sampler is a sort of universal instrument that virtually contains all the other instruments, because it can imitate, "create," and quote them. The sampler gives the musician the power of recombination—and here it is absurd to accuse the musician (as some critics have done) of theft. A sample is a musical snapshot from another time. Samples become art only after the musician has appropriated, transformed, and shaped these sonic building blocks. As Afro-British music journalist Kodwo Eshun said: "The sampler insists that you have to know which sounds you love."

Electronic jazz gave stimulating impulses to the jazz of the nineties. At least four trends crystallized out of this creative use by jazz musicians of samplers and electronics. Of course, there were also many overlappings and mixtures between these directions:

1. Jazz meets hip-hop. Drummer Albert "Tootie" Heath: "I like having a beat in the music. That's why I listen to hip-hop, because they have a serious beat."

   With its loops and sampling, hip-hop lifted grooves instead of venerating ancestors. Many hip-hoppers turned to jazz remarkably often for their samples, using snippets from great jazz recordings by Art Blakey, Sonny Rollins, Charlie Parker, and Miles Davis. It was only fair for jazz musicians to respond with their own version of jazz and hip-hop beats.

   In the search for new sounds, since the end of the eighties

the encounter with the sounds of hip-hop, rap, and soul provided an ideal source of inspiration for improvising. This was due not least to the fact that rap and hip-hop reminded them of their own roots. Max Roach, one of the founders of modern jazz drumming: "In hip-hop beats, I hear the fast rhythms of bebop."

The early hip-hop jazzers, such as Gary Thomas, knew intuitively that rap and hip-hop are the current version of what improvising jazz musicians were trying to do with poetry and jazz as early as the sixties, such as Charles Mingus with Langston Hughes and others. If jazz musicians were borrowing from the newest forms of black music, they were really borrowing from themselves.

The way sampling is used in hip-hop has often been criticized as uncreative. But the borrowing of loops and the layering of texts over older songs did not necessarily lead to gutting and plundering. The sampler made it possible to make music without being able to play a conventional instrument. Hip-hop musicians could create an original piece of music by assembling fragments of existing pieces. As in jazz, this involved improvising—the ability to think quickly and to be creative in the moment.

Above all, African American musicians saw the potential for resistance and protest in rap's improvising and the bass-heavy sounds of hip-hop. "A lot of people today think the kids who are rapping just want to complain," said tenor saxophonist Gary Thomas, "but the opposite is true. These kids are angry, and they have every right to be. Racism, for example. The air we breathe is saturated with it. The end of racial segregation did not remove racism."

In the nineties, rap and hip-hop underwent a transformation from an urban folk art to a global phenomenon, and therefore also to a big business. Only a tiny portion of what was put on the market as "music from the streets" had any real street cred. "The problem with hip-hop," according to Q-Tip, "is that the second the businessmen see they can make money with it, the whole thing becomes corrupt."

2. Drum 'n' bass meets jazz: "When I hear Roni Size, I hear Tony Williams," said arranger Bob Belden. Along with Belden, countless other jazz musicians discovered in the nineties that the hyperactive rhythm of drum 'n' bass represents a variability similar to the differentiated rhythms that jazz musicians have prized in modern jazz for decades.

Drum 'n' bass was created in London's multicultural club culture. Its fractal, intricate rhythms, or breakbeats, are rooted in reggae music, which in turn is rooted in rhythm 'n' blues and American jazz. The rhythms of drum 'n' bass and jungle have a peculiar effect: the music that is actually "straight-ahead" gets tangled up in conflicts with itself. Drum 'n' bass rhythms have a kind of "irregular regularity," and this is what makes them related to jazz rhythm. They act like "grooves tattooed on the body," and "make you into a stepper moving with heightened reflexes. Listening sharpens your senses until they stick out like thorns," said Kodwo Eshun.

Jazz musicians have found this internal rhythmic tension, heightened by speed and a kind of hecticness, to be a powerful stimulus to improvisation. In particular, a striking number of European musicians and bands used elements of drum 'n' bass and jungle and the electronic grooves of club music as bases for exciting improvisations. These include, in Norway, Bugge Wesseltoft, Nils Petter Molvaer, and the group Jaga Jazzist; in Great Britain, Matthew Herbert; in France, the Swiss trumpeter Erik Truffaz. Americans who found inspiration in this area of intersection include trumpeter Graham Haynes, saxophonist Bob Belden, trumpeter Tim Hagans, and others. In their examination of drum 'n' bass, all these bands and musicians gave the breakbeats a melodic-harmonic and interactive dimension that drum 'n' bass itself, with its fixation on rhythm, had practically forgotten.

For this reason also, jazz musicians have enthusiastically worked with drum 'n' bass DJs. Because these DJs make music in the moment, they don't use fixed methods or become stale. "I like the speed of drum 'n' bass," said guitarist Derek Bailey, "you can't hang around with that shit."

3. Nu jazz (or "lounge jazz"), also known in the early nineties as "acid jazz." Nu jazz is the name given to jazz music that is inspired by pop, soul, and hip-hop and is concerned above all with the dance-oriented elements of these musics. In this area, with many concessions to tastes of the moment, the following musicians were successful in the nineties: St. Germaine, Soel, the French band No Jazz; in Germany, Roberto Di Gioa, Joo Kraus, The Nighthawks, and others.

At the beginning of the nineties, many musicians attempted to bring the group elements of jazz and pop into harmony with one another, using electronics and improvisation. *Acid jazz* (the term was coined by London DJ Gilles Peterson) began as a fresh, stylistically open music in which hip-hop rhythms and soul melodies were combined with jazz improvisation without preconceptions. Successful bands in this area included US 3,

Jazzmatazz, and U.F.O. Later, however, after record companies discovered the commercial potential of this hybrid music, the approach narrowed to become a stale concoction of soul garnished with some jazz elements. A significant part of the success of nu jazz and acid jazz was due to the fact that DJs, in their turntable playing, rediscovered classic hard-bop recordings. It became fashionable to sonically reprocess, or remix, the great melodies and solos that jazz musicians played in the fifties and sixties on Blue Note and Prestige recordings.

Not all the musicians who took on this challenge were up to it. Particularly in the area of dancefloor jazz, groove stealing was more common than creativity. Many dance floor remixes of classical jazz recordings sound superficial in comparison with the originals. "It's as if they were rewriting the Bible!" complained drummer Rashied Ali. "This kind of remixing is the same thing as blasphemy." Bill Laswell, on the other hand, proved that there can be creative remixes in his sensitive, distinctive rethinking of the early jazz-rock recordings of Miles Davis on the CD *Panthalassa*.

4. Free electronics. There has always continued to be an interest in live electronics in free jazz and in freely improvised music. But the emergence of digital signal processing and computer-based technologies that are portable, affordable, and reliable took the possibilities of live electronics to a completely new level. Laptop improvisation and playing with DJs and computers opened up unsuspected new possibilities for free improvisers.

In the mideighties, probably no free-improvising musician would have believed that a DJ could provide inspiration for his playing. Ten or fifteen years later, the proof was there: players coming out of free jazz, such as Evan Parker, Derek Bailey, Matthew Shipp, William Parker, Tim Berne, and many others, collaborated as a matter of course with new electronic musicians.

The main accusation that critics leveled against the new use of electronics in jazz was always the same. They bemoaned the technological disembodiment of the musician. Kodwo Eshun said: "Machines do *not* alienate us from our emotions; quite the contrary. Sound machines *amplify* what is felt, and spread it over a broader emotional spectrum than what has ever been done before." And, in terms prophesied by Marshall McLuhan, Eshun spoke of how digital electronics was making us into electronic tribes. In fact, the broad possibilities offered by digital electronics, from sampling to turntablism to remixing and DJ culture, greatly expanded jazz's improvisational vistas.

On the other hand, technology alone, no matter how advanced, is not a substitute for musical growth. Innovation in jazz is not determined by technological progress; it is a purely musical matter. "All music has to be organic, has to come from the earth and the soul to be meaningful. Electro-acoustic music is no different," says trumpeter Dave Douglas.

"What is M-Base?" asked Cassandra Wilson, early in her career. "More and more I'm finding out that it's a way of life. It's a way of deciding to live the truth. . . . It's a spiritual movement."

At the end of the eighties, a musicians' collective was founded in Brooklyn under the name "Macro-Basic Array of Structured Extemporisations," or M-Base. M-Base was a melting pot of a wide variety of musical backgrounds and experiences. Nonetheless, the music of M-Base had a salient characterizing feature: constant rhythmic change. Complex, constantly changing meters were *the* trademark of M-Base music. In addition, the music tended toward funkiness and toward the street rhythms of black music. M-Base stood for the sounds of an improvising generation of musicians who grew up with funk, rock, and rhythm 'n' blues. Motown plus irregular meters: that was M-Base, with the addition of the entire spectrum of new possibilities opened up by the multistylistic jazz of the nineties.

The central figure of the M-Base movement was alto saxophonist Steve Coleman. He got the idea for his ambitious approach to improvising over changing meters while practicing one day in a park in his native Chicago. While he was playing, he watched some bees flying nearby. The rotation of their wings and the organized swarming of their bodies inspired Coleman to imagine a particular rhythmic concept: improvising "within interwoven cyclical structures."

In the title track of the recording *Drop Kick* by Steve Coleman's Five Elements, the saxophone, the piano, and the rhythm section of bass and drums each play in different meters (polymetry). In the middle part of the piece, the "bridge," Coleman improvises over a twenty-beat meter subdivided into cycles of 4 1/2, 5, 5 1/2, and 5, which are in turn superimposed over an underlying thirty-beat structure and displaced against it.

Coleman and his musicians were often asked how they were able to spontaneously improvise over these extremely complex rhythms and meters. But every time they were asked about the technical aspects or the counting of meters, formulas, and cycles, they answered: "intuitively."

For Coleman, M-Base was an approach to life, not a musical style. He called his group improvisations "collective meditations." According to him, music was a symbolic language "for expressing the nature of the universe—a force that sends out consciousness-expanding vibrations." He organized melodies and rhythms according to principles of kabbalah and astrology. He combined rhythms in the ratio of the golden mean and of the constellations. He grouped chords according to geometric formulas and mystical numerological symbols.

"M-Base is a way of thinking about creative music," said Steve Coleman. "It's the ability to see intuition and logic as a 'science' that gives African, and African American, music its particular quality and its particular character. Western cognition fundamentally separates the intuitive from the logical."

Intuition plus logic: Indian-American pianist Vijay Iyer, who began working with the M-Base collective at the end of the nineties, called this consciousness "Afrological" (a term borrowed from trombonist George Lewis). In Afrological consciousness, interaction and personal storytelling are primary. The focus is on exchange, transformation, and a flow of ideas that "conditions the communication between cultures," said Iyer. "Whatever M-Base is, I feel that it addresses these global, transcultural issues, and it does so from a growing complex of Afrological viewpoints."

Outlook: Jazz in the Age of Migration

Jazz is the sound of migration, and has been from its beginning. Without the great migrations of the nineteenth century, the cultural melting pot of New Orleans would never have come into being, and the encounters between races, nationalities, and cultures that gave rise to jazz would not have been possible. Fundamentally, the legacy of jazz—musical freedom of speech—is a reaction (the "triumph of the soul") to the painful experience of a migration imposed by violence: the uprooting and enslavement of millions of Africans, brought across the Atlantic unwillingly, in a black diaspora.

Jazz is, in the truest sense, world music: a hybrid. For this reason, jazz has contributed perhaps more than any other Western music to the continuing interaction and mutual influence of cultural forms. More and more players from Africa, Asia, and Latin America are putting their own creative imprint on the rapidly globalizing jazz scene. In this way, the development of new musical languages between cultures has brought new qualitative changes in jazz.

When, in the seventies, Don Cherry and Collin Walcott spoke of crossing boundaries between cultures, and were the first to realize this dream in music, they were considered utopian thinkers and were laughed at by critics. Today, their vision of a "world music," or an improvised music that operates between cultures, has become an accepted reality due to migration and globalization. No one today would dream of calling it crazy when, for example, French-Vietnamese guitarist Nguyên Lê mixes his European jazz experience with melodies and rhythms from Southeast Asia, or when the Turkish ney flutist Kudsi Erguner incorporates Middle-Eastern Sufi music into contemporary jazz.

Today, Asian music can be heard almost everywhere on Earth. People of Asian origin are found throughout Europe, North America, and Africa. And the general statements made here about Asian music are equally true of African music, Arabic music, Indian music, and many others. The Tunisian oud player Dhafer Youssef says, "Now I know that I don't have to be in Africa in order to have African ideas. And some of the best African musicians live in Europe. If you want to find a good Iranian dumbek player, just look around France."

In the world's great cities, today an enormous variety of musical languages, competing or overlapping with each other, constantly encounter one another. They combine to form complex patchwork styles. Ethnomusicologists speak of "modern diasporas." In these diasporas, finding one's identity means not just recognizing the other, the foreign, or "the difference" (Stuart Hall), but living this experience. This attitude promotes mixture, openness, evolution. The modern diasporas are characterized by this hybridness.

The jazz of the nineties is cross-cultural. In the United States alone, the large number of mixtures has resulted in the development of two notable trends:

1. The new quality of the encounter between jazz and Latin American music. The music of musicians like tenor saxophonist David Sànchez and alto saxophonist Miguel Zenón from Puerto Rico, or trumpeter Diego Urcola and pianist/arranger Guillermo Klein from Argentina, is no longer Latin jazz in the conventional sense (Latin music garnished with some jazz-inspired solos), but "jazz-Latin." These musicians play with a sovereign mastery (not previously present in the same way in Latin music) of the great heritage of jazz, refining and renewing it by weaving Latin American influences into it.

   More and more Latin American jazz musicians are enriching the contemporary jazz scene. And this development will continue. The fact that the largest minority group living in the United States today is no longer African Americans but rather Latino-Americans will certainly have an effect on the future development of jazz. "In my opinion, the future of jazz will be the exploration of the rhythmic diversity of Latin America," says percussionist Bobby Sanabria. "In my opinion, the future of the music will be about exploring the rhythm structures of Latin America. We have twenty-two countries in Latin America. Colombia alone has like over 160 rhythms or stylistic musics. . . . I mean, there's so much unexplored territory."

2. The music of Asian-Americans. After Hispanics and African Americans, people of Asian descent are the third largest

minority in the United States. The binary conception of "black" and "white" has long been a distraction from the fact that a constantly growing number of Americans of Asian origin are making important contributions to contemporary improvised music. Musicians like pianist Jon Jang, saxophonist Fred Ho, koto player Miya Masaoka, and Filipina-American percussionist Susie Ibarra have a deep knowledge of Western improvisational styles, while simultaneously having a special connection with their Asian cultures. This connection has less to do with traditional values than with new outlooks and conceptions.

It is revealing that these musicians, rather than turning first to their own ethnic backgrounds, see themselves primarily as members of the jazz community, operating in this community with a great stylistic openness while still retaining a strong consciousness of roots and regional particularities in their playing. This flexibility means that their jazz does not require a regional "branding." For example, Puerto Rican tenor saxophonist David Sànchez, when he plays a solo in the Sonny Rollins tradition, sounds just as individual and convincing as he does when playing over bomba rhythms. Nguyên Lê, the Vietnamese-French guitarist from Paris, plays just as brilliantly and masterfully when he plays "pure" new jazz as when he combines jazz and Vietnamese music.

Today, jazz styles coincide with ethnicities and nations less than ever before. In a globalized, networked world, jazz in the American and European mold is increasingly losing its claim to be the sole representative of this music. These musics are now partners in a wider field; the hierarchy between Western jazz and the music of "other cultures" has collapsed into mutual curiosity. In the nineties, jazz became a music of universal communication, connection, and inspiration. Senegalese fashion designer Oumou Sy speaks of *metissage*, the mixture of everything with everything.

Many African American jazz critics have mixed feelings about these developments. But the fear that "world jazz" is a movement intended to neutralize the "African American aesthetic" in jazz is, in the end, unfounded. There is no right of ownership of jazz. "Play your own song": this challenge from African American tenor saxophonist Lester Young is being met today by more and more musicians outside American and European forms of expression. And, in incorporating local, regional characteristics—Chinese, Japanese, Vietnamese—and all the transcultural experiences that they have lived into jazz, they are expanding, evolving, and revolutionizing the music.

The future of jazz lies in its intercultural potential. All the developments brought by today's globalization, described by cultural anthropologists using terms like *hybridization*, *creolization*, *bastardization*, have been present in jazz since long before talk of the "cultural technology of the future." As trombonist George Lewis puts it, improvisation in jazz is "transcultural of necessity and by its nature."

More than any other Western music, jazz is becoming something like a transmission belt in the invention of a new music between cultures. Composer and guitarist Steve Martland says: "The music of the future will be a hybrid, a colorful mixture, a standard borne above all by asylum-seekers, refugees, and migrants. They don't have any money and they don't have any means of production, but they have the visions that will shape the sounds of the future."

The Musicians of Jazz

"I play what I live," said Sidney Bechet, one of the great men of old New Orleans. And Charlie Parker stated, "Music is your own experience, your thoughts, your wisdom. If you don't live it, it won't come out of your horn."

We shall see how the unmistakable sounds of the great jazz soloists, right down to technical elements, depend on their personalities. The jazz musician's life is constantly transformed into music—without regard for "beauty," "form," and the many other concepts that mediate between music and life in the European tradition. That is why it is important to speak of the lives of the jazz musicians and why the jazz enthusiast's desire to know the details of their lives is legitimate. And it is also legitimate that such details make up a great part of the literature of jazz. They help us understand the music itself and thus are quite a different story from the details fan magazines report about the lives of Hollywood stars.

"A person has to have lived to play great jazz, or else he'll be a copy," said Milt Hinton, the bassist. Only a few musicians who exemplify this dictum could be selected for this book. But they are musicians in whom the history of a style is involved, with each one representing a specific style or period. Louis Armstrong stands for the great New Orleans period; Bessie Smith for the blues and jazz singing; Bix Beiderbecke for Chicago style; Duke Ellington for orchestral Swing; Coleman Hawkins and Lester Young for combo Swing; Dizzy Gillespie for big-band bebop, Charlie Parker for small-group bebop (and modern jazz itself); Miles Davis for the whole development from cool jazz to jazz-rock; Ornette Coleman and John Coltrane for the jazz revolution of the sixties; John McLaughlin for the fusion music of the seventies; David Murray and

Wynton Marsalis for the jazz classicism of the eighties; and John Zorn for the explosion of stylistic diversity in the nineties.

Louis Armstrong

Until the rise of Dizzy Gillespie in the forties, there was no jazz trumpeter who did not stem from Louis Armstrong—or "Satchmo," as he was called—and even after that, every player has been at least indirectly indebted to him.

The immense size of this debt became clear when impresario George Wein made the 1970 Newport Jazz Festival into one big birthday celebration for seventy-year-old Armstrong. (Satchmo claimed to have been born on July 4, 1900, but Gary Giddins has established that his baptismal certificate states August 4, 1901.) World-famous jazz trumpeters competed for the most appropriate homage to Louis. Bobby Hackett called himself "Louis Armstrong's number one admirer." Joe Newman took exception: he himself should be called Louis's "A-number one fan." Jimmy Owens said that if he could not claim to be Armstrong's number one fan or even A-one fan, he was at least his "youngest fan." Dizzy Gillespie said, "Louis Armstrong's station in the history of jazz . . . all I can say is *unimpeachable*. If it weren't for him, there wouldn't be any of us. So I would like to take this moment to thank Louis Armstrong for my livelihood."

Musicians other than trumpeters have also expressed their great debt to Armstrong. Frank Sinatra has pointed out that Armstrong made an art of singing popular music. Wynton Marsalis said, "You can find bass players and entire trombone and saxophone sections who try to sound like him, and arrangers who write Armstrong licks."

When Louis Armstrong died on July 6, 1971, Duke Ellington said, "If anyone was Mr. Jazz, it was Louis Armstrong. He was the epitome of jazz and always will be. Every trumpet player who decided he wanted to lean toward the American idiom was influenced by him. . . . He is what I call an American standard, an American original. . . . I love him. God bless him."

Louis Armstrong spent his youth in the turmoil of the great port on the Mississippi—in New Orleans's old Creole quarter. His parents—his father was a factory worker, his mother a domestic—were separated when Louis was still an infant. Nobody paid much attention to him. Once or twice the authorities considered putting him in a reformatory, but nothing was done until, one New Year's Eve, Louis fired a pistol loaded with blanks in the streets. Then they put him in the reformatory. He became a member of the school choir that performed at funerals and festivities. Louis received his first musical instruction on a battered old cornet from the leader of the reform school band.

One of the first bands in which Louis played was that of New Orleans's leading trombonist, Kid Ory. Little Louis happened to be passing by with his cornet as Ory's band was playing in the street. Somebody asked for whom he was carrying the instrument. "Nobody. It's mine," said Louis. Nobody would believe him. So Louis started to blow . . . and was hired on the spot.

During World War I, when the red-light district of Storyville was closed down by the secretary of the navy and the great exodus of musicians had long been underway, Louis was among those who remained. He did not go to Chicago until 1922, when King Oliver sent for him to join his band, then playing at the Lincoln Gardens. King Oliver was the second "King of Jazz" following the legendary New Orleans trumpeter Buddy Bolden (who never made any recordings). Louis Armstrong was to become the third king.

Oliver's band—with the King himself and Louis on cornet, Honoré Dutrey on trombone, Johnny Dodds on clarinet, his brother Baby Dodds on drums, Bill Johnson on banjo, and Lil Hardin on piano—was then the most important jazz band. When Armstrong left it in 1924, it began to decline. To be sure, Oliver made several good recordings in later years (such as the 1926–27 series with his Savannah Syncopators), but by then other bands had become more important (Jelly Roll Morton's Red Hot Peppers, Fletcher Henderson, young Duke Ellington). The end of Oliver's career presents the tragic spectacle of an impoverished man, without teeth, unable to play and earn money to live, hiding from his friends because he is ashamed and yet was once king of jazz. Here is an example of the tragedy of artistic existence, and there are many such tragedies in the annals of jazz. Louis Armstrong escaped this fate in an almost supernatural way. The ups and downs that characterize the lives of so many jazz musicians hardly ever affected him. For him there was only one direction: up.

It is a mark of Louis Armstrong's superiority that throughout his long career he had only two ensembles worthy of him—actually only one, because the first of these was a group organized for recording purposes only: Louis Armstrong's Hot Five (and later, Hot Seven) from 1925 to 1929. The other was the Louis Armstrong All Stars of the late forties, with trombonist Jack Teagarden, clarinetist Barney Bigard, and drummer Sid Catlett. With these All Stars—and they really were—Armstrong won tremendous acclaim all over the world. With them he gave one of the most famous concerts of his career in Boston in 1947; it was later released on record.

The musicians who surrounded Satchmo in his Hot Five and Hot Seven are among the great personalities in traditional jazz. Johnny Dodds, the clarinetist, was there, as was trombonist Kid Ory, who many years earlier had given Louis a job in New Orleans. Later, pianist Earl Hines was added. He created a style of piano playing based on Armstrong's trumpet that became (and still is) a model for many pianists throughout the world.

Louis Armstrong's Hot Five and Hot Seven were the right soundtrack for the new world of atomic particles, moving pictures, instant communication, Freudian psychology, the automobile, "stream of consciousness" literature, Cubist and Dadaist art, and the Manhattan skyline. African American writer Robert B. O'Meally has gone so far as to suggest that the Hot Five and Hot Seven recordings contain a hidden strategy for survival in modern times. Armstrong's power of asserting himself as an individual soloist in a group, the ability to swing through all the ups and downs of life, made him "the bluesy wounded healer," someone who helps us not just to survive, "but, as Faulkner once put it, to prevail."

There are few artists whose work and personality are as closely joined as Armstrong's. It is almost as if they had become interchangeable, and thus even the musically flawed Armstrong was made effective through his personality. In the liner notes to a record taken from Edward R. Murrow's film, *Satchmo the Great*, Armstrong said:

> When I pick up that horn . . . the world's behind me, and I don't concentrate on nothing but that horn. . . . I mean, I don't feel no different about the horn now than I did when I was playing in New Orleans. No, that's my living and my life. I love them notes. That's why I try to make them right. . . . That's why I married four times. The chicks didn't live with that horn. . . . I mean, if I have an argument with my wife, that couldn't stop me from enjoying the show that I'm playing. I realize I could blow a horn after they pull away. . . . I've expressed myself in the horn. I fell in love with it and it fell in love with me. . . . What we play is life and a natural thing. . . . If it's for laughs, for showmanship, it would be the same as if we were in a backyard practicing or something. Everything that happens there is real. . . . Yeah, I'm happy. Doing the right thing, playing for the highest people to the lowest. . . . They come in Germany with them lorgnettes, and looking at you and everything, and by the time they get on the music, they done dropped the lorgnettes, and they're swinging, man! . . . When we played in Milano, after I finished my concert . . . I had to rush over to the La Scala and stand by those big cats like Verdi and Wagner . . . and take pictures, 'cause they figure our music's the same. We play them both from the heart.

In such passages more is revealed about Armstrong's nature and music than from all the words a critic can say about them. The musical findings are, anyhow, as simple and immediate as the music itself: Louis Armstrong made jazz "right." He brought together emotional expression and musical technique. After Armstrong, it is no longer possible to make excuses for wrong notes with claims of vitality or authenticity. Since Armstrong, jazz has to be just as right as other music.

A brilliant article written on the occasion of Armstrong's death by critic Ralph Gleason has this to say:

> He took the tools of European musical organization—chords, notation, bars, and the rest—and added to them the rhythms of the church and of New Orleans and (by definition) Africa, brought into the music the blue notes, the tricks of bending and twisting notes, and played it all with his unexcelled technique. He went as far with it as he could by using the blues and popular songs of the time as skeletons for his structural improvisations.

Many of the young people who love to use the term *revolution* have forgotten that Armstrong was the greatest of all jazz revolutionaries. They may be thinking about Charlie Parker or Cecil Taylor and Albert Ayler when they talk of musical revolutions. But the difference between the music before Armstrong and what he made of it is greater than the difference between the music before Parker or Taylor or Ayler and what they made of it. So, the jazz revolution started by Armstrong is certainly the greater one.

A young fusion drummer, Bob Melton, was right when after Armstrong's death he wrote in a letter to the editor of *Down Beat* magazine:

> We've lost some great ones in the last five years. . . . Today we lost the most daring innovator of all. . . . I'm young, a "long-hair," a "jazz-rock" drummer. . . . I've just played over and over about twenty times a 1947 Town Hall concert track of "Ain't Misbehavin'" with Pops. . . . I've played it over that many times because in the last three years I've been filling my head with "free" tenor men and rock guitarists, and I've forgotten how audacious—is that the word?—I've forgotten how *outrageous* it *really was*. . . . I mourn especially that so many of my genera-tion . . . never heard Pops' message, and might not have listened if they had. You know that line of bull about not trusting anybody over thirty? Pops is one of the few people in this century I trusted!

Some in the media have tried to portray Louis Armstrong as a kind of emotional "child of nature," constantly grinning and joking, playing the "Hello Dolly" clown. But, as Wynton Marsalis has said, Armstrong was "jazz's first intellectual," because he was the first to *consciously* swing.

Louis Armstrong made the rhythmic quality of swing an essential element in jazz. In early New Orleans jazz, many musicians still phrased in ways long established in march music and the ragtime tradition: rhythmically angular, stiff, and by today's standards prudish. Of course, musicians were beginning to produce rhythmically rounded, springy, swinging phrasing, but in those days swing was a secondary business, almost as expendable and interchangeable as dynamics and tremolos. It could be used, but it didn't have to be. Since Louis Armstrong, jazz without swing has been unthinkable. With Satchmo, flexible triplet jazz phrasing gets under way, and it immediately starts with a high point—and not only with regard to its relaxed feeling. Much of what Louis Armstrong sang and played—his nuances of phrasing and his highly exciting rhythmic stretchings and curtailings—was so boldly in advance of its time that it pointed the way toward aspects of modern jazz phrasing. Satchmo made swing the lifeblood of jazz. The rhythmic quality of swing in Armstrong's playing is, as critic André Hodeir wrote, "the manifestation of a personal force of attraction," an expression of emotional intelligence—the ability to spontaneously find the right way to meet life at every moment.

The abandonment of two-beat jazz and transition to playing over four beats began with Louis Armstrong, too. He also introduced solo playing into jazz long before it became customary in the Chicago style. His explosive inventiveness literally blew apart the brief and constrained variations of New Orleans jazz, giving rise to expansive and enormously compelling solos. He didn't improvise *over* a musical theme so much as *away* from the theme *to* his own, personal melodic lines. This was the legacy of his sound: let yourself go, play all the thoughts, inspirations, and feelings that you can find in yourself. Don't play just any melody: play yourself, and make the world a richer place.

Between the Armstrong of the Hot Five and Hot Seven and the Armstrong of the All Stars of the forties and fifties stands the Armstrong of the big bands. This period began when Armstrong became a member of Fletcher Henderson's orchestra for a year, starting in 1924 immediately following his departure from King Oliver. Armstrong brought so much stimulation to the rather commercial and mediocre Henderson aggregation of the time that one could say the year 1924 marks the real beginning of big-band jazz. There is a lot of significance and logic in the fact that Armstrong, the most important personality of the New Orleans jazz tradition, was cofounder of the jazz phase that years later replaced the great era of New Orleans: the Swing era of the thirties, with its big bands. Even with the recordings of his Hot Five and Hot Seven, however, Armstrong soon placed himself beyond the New Orleans form, with its three-voiced interweaving of trumpet, trombone, and clarinet. Armstrong is the man who, precisely with the most significant records of the Hot Five and Hot Seven, dissolved this fabric—an achievement characteristic of many stylistic developments in jazz. Again and again, the important personalities within a style have paved the way for the next style when at the zenith of their own. Only the fans demanded a standstill in one particular style. The musicians have always wanted to go on.

Armstrong's playing in Fletcher Henderson's band at the Roseland Ballroom in New York was a sensation among musicians. Armstrong himself found much inspiration in the (for that time) compact section sounds of the big band. Later he became convinced that his trumpet could unfold better against the backdrop of a big band than with a small ensemble—a feeling not shared by many jazz fans.

This feeling may be related to the fact that from the start Armstrong wanted to reach a larger audience—a wish that perhaps was the prime mover of his musical career. Louis Armstrong was at once both the first icon of twentieth-century popular music and the first musician to make jazz into art. "There is a definite implication that Louis had a primary interest in pleasing his audiences," George Avakian stated. Many jazz fans ignored Armstrong's success in the hit charts with "Hello Dolly" with a determination that could imply that they were somewhat discomforted by this success. For Armstrong, however—and maybe even more so for his wife, Lucille—the real climax of his career came in 1964, when he took the top spot on the record charts away from the reigning Beatles and held it for weeks with "Hello Dolly."

Louis Armstrong transposed more pop music into jazz than any other musician. Conversely, he translated jazz so convincingly and artistically into pop music that even when he sang the schmaltzy hits of the day, something of jazz's power, warmth, and vitality still shone through.

If twentieth-century popular music viewed as a whole constitutes a single, unceasingly flowing river, which arises in the blues and jazz and then branches into an ever-broader delta of rock and pop, funk and disco, rap and hip-hop, then Louis Armstrong symbolizes the oneness holding this river together. No one else made more vividly apparent all the streaming currents linking jazz and popular music.

To Armstrong, singing was at least as important as trumpet playing—not just during his final years when, sometimes hardly able to blow his horn because of failing health, he remained a brilliant singer. During all phases of his career, he knew he could reach a larger audience as a singer than as an instrumentalist. His singing—husky, hoarse, squeezed, rough—shocked listeners in the twenties. Here was someone who dared, in a world still shaped by Victorianism and bourgeois hypocrisy, to transform what he thought and felt into music, directly and honestly. The carefree naturalness and sincerity with which Louis Armstrong made music was an important sign of the times for the contemporary public. His voice, his trumpet, said "Show your feelings." That became a message for the century. The entire world understood it. By now there are hundreds of singers who express their own feelings, not just jazz singers. Any rock singer does so, and almost every pop singer. The fact that no one today is shocked any longer about a singer expressing what he or she feels indicates, more than anything else, Louis Armstrong's status. Armstrong was once alone there; now there are thousands. In the history of music, it is rare for a musician to be equally innovative as a singer and as an instrumentalist. As jazz critic Stanley Crouch put it, "It was as if Beethoven were to stand up and sing."

Rex Stewart, himself a trumpeter (in fact, one of the best), had to admit:

> Louis has bestowed so many gifts upon the world that it is almost impossible to assess in which area his definitive impact has been most felt. My vote would be for his tremendous talent of communication. As profoundly creative as his trumpet ability is, I would place this in a secondary position. He was revered mostly by other professionals, whereas his gravel-voiced singing has carried his message far and wide, to regions and places where not only was the music little known, the language foreign, but where there also was the further barrier of a political system having labeled jazz as decadent. But when Satchmo sang, the entire picture changed. People saw the truth.

In a television program produced on the occasion of the 1970 Newport Jazz Festival, Louis said:

> Well, people love me and my music and, you know, I love them and I have no problems at all with people. The minute I walk on the bandstand they know they're going to get something good and no jive and they know what they're there for and that's why they come. . . . I'm the audience myself. I'm my own audience, and I don't like to hear myself play bad or something, so I know it ain't no good for you. . . . Some of the critics say I'm a clown, but a clown, that's something great. It's happiness to make people happy. Most of those critics don't know one note from the other. . . . When I play, I just think of all my happy days . . . and the notes come by themselves. You've got to love to be able to play.

During all of Armstrong's life, again and again, there was talk of the impending "end of jazz music" or "death of jazz" in papers and magazines, from the twenties right on up into the nineties. The communicative genius in Armstrong never believed such talk. He told Dan Morgenstern:

> I'd get me a record company and record nothing but what people said was finished—and we'd make a million dollars. You get those boys blowing out there—waitin' for that one gig, that one recording session, and we'd get together and set up, you know—we wouldn't go wrong. Everybody's looking for that top banana, but they're asleep on the good music that started all this.

Wynton Marsalis likens Louis Armstrong to Merlin the magician. "Armstrong brought back a real joy to music," says Wynton. "Anything you want, he has it—warmth and intelligence, worldly and provincial, spiritual and tawdry, down home but sophisticated. The most complex player there's ever been, yet he can still sound like a country boy."

Louis Armstrong's success is, in a very important sense, the success of his personality. Anybody who knew him or worked with him can tell of an experience that illuminates his warmth and sincerity. In 1962 Joachim Berendt produced a television show in New York with the Armstrong All Stars. Only a short time before, Satchmo had been on camera sending regards to his German fans, asking them to have his *sauerkraut* and *wurst* ready for his upcoming tour. Then he and the crew were done; in a few minutes the studio had become dark and empty. Berendt was next door, discussing the editing of the film. Satchmo, surrounded by a throng of fans, had left. About forty-five minutes later, the elevator door opened and out came Louis Armstrong, to tell Berendt that he had already been sitting in a taxi when he realized he had not said good-bye. Somewhat in doubt, Berendt suspected he had forgotten something. No, said Satchmo, he had just come back up to say good-bye. Which he did—and then he left. Jack Bradley, the jazz photographer, commented, "Yes, that's the way he is."

In the sixties, it became fashionable to call Armstrong an "Uncle Tom" who had not shown any involvement in the African American liberation struggle. However, when, in 1957, militant whites prevented black schoolchildren from attending classes, and were supported by Arkansas governor Orval Faubus—and President Eisenhower declined to condemn this behavior—Satchmo said to a reporter of the Grand Forks (North Dakota) *Herald*, "The way they are treating my people in the South—the government can go to hell! The president has no guts!" And then he canceled a tour of the Soviet Union organized by the State Department, refusing to go abroad for a government led by such a president. "The people over there ask me what's wrong with my country. What am I supposed to say? I have had a beautiful life in music, but I feel the situation the same as any other Negro." His words resounded around the globe. And when, in 1965, police brutally beat blacks in the protest march in Selma, Alabama, organized by Martin Luther King Jr., Armstrong told a reporter, "They would beat Jesus on the cross if he was black and marched."

Louis Armstrong had human solidarity and human compassion, but he was not a political man. In his music, he remained an unshakable optimist. He never let anything or anyone in the world take away his sense of the joy of life, not even his anger over racial prejudice, segregation, and discrimination. "He loves people so much, he would even find good in a criminal. He is not capable of hate," a British critic once wrote.

In Louis Armstrong's music, the cry of the mistreated soul, as heard in blues singers and in sublimated, imploded form in Billie Holiday, is transformed into a jubilant affirmation of life, despite all life's tribulations. Why were we put on this earth? Armstrong's answer was simple and clear: not to make money; not to atone for our sins; not to suffer. We are here to enjoy life, despite the obstacles it puts in our way. Armstrong's trumpet rejoices, exults in being human. It wants to celebrate life now, in this moment, not to wait until the revolution has claimed all its victims. But the spontaneity and joy of life of his melodic lines can obscure the high degree of technical mastery with which he controlled his improvisations. Armstrong was a consummate technician. His "tags"—responses in the low register to his high-note phrases—are legendary. His trumpet playing was unparalleled in its physical brilliance. His intonation was perfect, his articulation clean and consistent.

"Of how many American artists can it be said that they formed our [i.e., the twentieth] century?" asked American musicologist Martin Williams, who then answered, "I am not sure about our writers, painters, our concert composers. But I am certain Louis Armstrong has formed it."

In a television program on the occasion of Louis Armstrong's death, Joachim Berendt said:

> There is no sound today on radio, television, or record which could not somehow be traced back to Armstrong. He must be compared with the other great innovators in the arts of this century—Stravinsky, Picasso, Schoenberg, James Joyce. . . . He was the only native American among them. Without Armstrong, there would be no jazz—without jazz, there would be no modern popular music and no rock. All the sounds that surround us daily would be different without Satchmo; they would not exist without him. If it had not been for Armstrong, jazz would have remained the local folk music of New Orleans—as obscure as dozens of other bodies of folk music.

"Folk music?" Louis once asked. "Why, daddy, I don't know no other kind of music *but* folk music. I ain't never heard a horse sing a song."

Soviet poet Yevgeny Yevtushenko wrote this poem in the days when the news of Louis Armstrong's death was going around the world:

> Do as you did in the past
> And play.
> Cheer up the state of the angels,
> And so the sinners won't get too unhappy in Hell
> Make their lives a bit more hopeful
> Give to Armstrong a trumpet
> Angel Gabriel.

Bessie Smith

Papa, Papa, you're in a good man's way
Papa, Papa, you're in a good man's way
I can find one better than you any time of day.

You ain't no good, so you'd better haul your freight
You ain't no good, so you'd better haul your freight
Mama wants a live wire, Papa, you can take the gate.

I'm a red hot woman, just full of flamin' youth
I'm a red hot woman, just full of flamin' youth
You can't cool me, daddy, you're no good, that's the truth.

"There was no pretense. It was the real thing: a woman cutting her heart open with a knife until it was exposed for all to see," Carl Van Vechten wrote.

Bessie Smith is the greatest of the many singers from the classical period of the blues, the twenties. She made 160 records, was featured in a movie short, and was so successful at the peak of her career during the early and mid-twenties that her record sales saved the old Columbia Record Company from bankruptcy. Nearly thirty million Bessie Smith records were sold. Bessie was the "Empress of the Blues."

Her personality had an awesome effect. She often elicited responses from her listeners similar to religious experiences. They would shout "amen" when she finished a blues number, as they did after spirituals or gospel songs in churches. At this time, nowhere else could one see as clearly the relationship between spirituals and the blues.

Mahalia Jackson, the great singer of the modern spirituals, the gospel songs, said, "Anybody that sings the blues is in a deep pit yelling for help." The blues tells of many things that have been lost: lost love and lost happiness, lost freedom and lost human dignity. Often the blues tells its story through a veil of irony. The coexistence of sorrow and humor is characteristic of the blues. It is as if what one is singing about becomes more bearable because it is not taken quite seriously; even the most desperate situation may reveal something amusing. At times, the comic element arises because one's misfortune is so limitless that it cannot be presented in adequate words. And always there is hope in the blues. As in "Trouble in Mind": "I won't be blue always 'cause the sun will shine in my back door some day."

Bessie Smith sang like someone who hopes that the sun one day will shine in her back door. And the sun did shine. Bessie earned a great deal of money, but she lost it all. She spent it on drink and on whatever else she wanted; she gave it away to relatives and people who seemed needy, or lost it to the men she was in love with.

Bessie Smith was born on April 15, 1894, in Chattanooga, Tennessee. Nobody took care of her, but she started to sing early. One day, blues singer Ma Rainey—the "Mother of the Blues"—came to town. She heard Bessie and took her in tow as a member of her troupe.

Bessie sang in the circus and tent shows in the cities and towns of the South. Frank Walker heard her and signed her to a contract. In 1923 she made her first record: "Downhearted Blues." It was a sensation. It sold eight hundred thousand copies—almost all bought by African Americans. However, only one of her records was a real success among the white audience of those years, and that one for the wrong reason: her "Empty Bed Blues," recorded in 1928 with trombonist Charlie Green, which was banned in Boston as obscene. "But," said George Hoefer, "it's hard to believe that the Boston censor understood the words, not to speak of the music. The word *bed* alone did it."

Aside from Bessie, there were many divas of the classic blues: Ma Rainey; Mamie Smith, who in 1920 had made the first African American recording of a blues vocal; Trixie Smith and Clara Smith, like Mamie, not related to Bessie; Ida Cox, who made "Hard Times Blues" and was rediscovered and recorded in 1961 when she was past seventy; and Bertha "Chippie" Hill, who recorded "Trouble in Mind" with Louis Armstrong in 1926 and again with Lovie Austin's Blues Serenaders in 1946. But Bessie towers above them all.

It is hard to describe the magic of her voice. Maybe it is that its hardness and roughness seem to be edged with deep sorrow, even in the most frisky and humorous songs. Bessie sang as a representative of a people that had lived through centuries of slavery and, after emancipation, often had to live through human situations that seemed worse than the darkest days of slavery. The fact that her sorrow found expression, without a trace of sentimentality, precisely in the rough hardness of her voice may be her secret.

On her recordings Bessie Smith often had first-rate accompanists—musicians like Louis Armstrong or James P. Johnson, Jack Teagarden, Chu Berry, Benny Goodman, Tommy Ladnier, Eddie Lang, Frankie Newton, Clarence Williams, and more of the best jazz musicians of the day. Fletcher Henderson—director of the then-leading jazz orchestra—was responsible for her supporting combos for several years and placed his best men at her service.

No female singer in jazz is not influenced to some degree, directly or indirectly, by Bessie Smith. Louis Armstrong said of her, "She used to thrill me at all times, the way she would phrase a note with a certain something in her voice no other blues singer could get. She had music in her soul and felt everything she did. Her sincerity with her music was an inspiration."

Her decline began in the later twenties. By 1930, Bessie Smith, who five years earlier had been the most successful artist of color (and one of the most successful in America), was in such dire straits that she had to accept bookings no longer in the great theaters of the North but back where she had started from: rural traveling shows in the Deep South.

On September 26, 1937, Bessie Smith died after a highway collision near Clarksdale, Mississippi. In an earlier edition of this book, a story of Bessie Smith's death was retold that reflected a belief still widespread in jazz circles: the singer died because the white hospital to which she was taken after the accident refused to treat a black patient; she bled to death "on the steps" of this hospital.

While it must be granted that this story reflects the situation of the American Deep South at that time, it has been proven that the jazz world was misinformed in the case of Bessie Smith. She was taken to a black hospital in Clarksdale, no further from the scene of the accident than was the white hospital. She did not awaken from her coma, and died the same day.

But the story of Bessie Smith's life and work does not end here. In 1971, Columbia Records rereleased the complete life work of Bessie Smith on five double albums. The Empress of the Blues thus received an honor unprecedented at that time in popular music: thirty-four years after her death, she gained worldwide fame for the second time. Marketing analyses have shown that mainly young people bought the results of this "most important and biggest single reissue project in history." This shows that the words of Bessie Smith's great fan and rediscoverer, John Hammond, were understood: "What Bessie sang in the twenties and thirties *is* the blues of today."

As a result of this renaissance of the music and name of Bessie Smith, her grave (a hardly identifiable hill in range 12, lot 20, section 10, of the Mount Lawn Cemetery in Sharon Hill, Pennsylvania) finally received a headstone. Black Philadelphia citizens and Janis Joplin, the white singer from Texas who had learned so much from Bessie, contributed toward the $500 bill for the tombstone. The inscription reads, "The Greatest Blues Singer in the World Will Never Stop Singing—Bessie Smith—1894–1937."

Bix Beiderbecke

Bix Beiderbecke is among those musicians so well hidden by the myth that has evolved about them that it is difficult to discover the reality of the man. He was an inhibited person who never seemed satisfied with his achievements and always set unattainable goals for himself. "I think one of the reasons he drank so much was that he was a perfectionist and wanted to do more with music than any man possibly could. The frustration that resulted was a big factor," said trumpeter Jimmy McPartland, who came particularly close to him musically.

Paul Whiteman related:

> Bix Beiderbecke, bless his soul, was crazy about the modern composers—Schoenberg, Stravinsky, and Ravel. . . . One evening I took him to the opera. It happened to be *Siegfried*. When he heard the bird calls in

the third act, with those intervals that are modern today, when he began to realize that the leitmotifs of the opera were dressed, undressed, disguised, broken down, and built up again in every conceivable fashion, he decided that old man Wagner wasn't so corny after all and that Swing musicians didn't know such a helluva lot.

Why Bix played in the dance orchestras of Whiteman and Jean Goldkette has often been misunderstood. The fans usually say he had to because he could not make a living from jazz. But Bix was one of the most successful musicians during the second half of the twenties. He was in a position to play where he wanted and always earn enough money. George Avakian said, "No one put a pistol in his back to make him join these bands." Actually Bix joined Whiteman—the epitome of commercial music of the day—because he was fascinated by the fancy arrangements written for the band. Here he could at least hang on to a reflection of the colorful orchestral palettes of Ravel, Delius, Stravinsky, and Debussy.

And thus it was—later in the thirties and forties—that record collectors all over the world bought the old records of Paul Whiteman to listen over and over again to eight or sixteen bars of solo blown by Bix. These recordings have repeatedly been reissued up to this day. (Indeed, no other musical form from the first half of the century has remained so alive on records as jazz.) When Beiderbecke's work in Whiteman's orchestra is viewed from a contemporary perspective, the difference between it and the jazz records made by Bix with his friends is really not too great. Few of the musicians with Bix on his own recording dates could shine his shoes. Not much lasts on them aside from Bix's cornet: the ensemble passages he leads and the solos he improvises.

Bix Beiderbecke is, more than any other musician, the essence of Chicago style. The following musicians—although some only stem from it and gained real importance in other styles—also played in the Chicago style: saxophonist Frankie Trumbauer; trumpeters Muggsy Spanier and Jimmy McPartland; drummers Gene Krupa, George Wettling, and Dave Tough; the Dorsey Brothers (Jimmy on alto and clarinet, Tommy on trombone); tenor man Bud Freeman; violinist Joe Venuti, one of the few jazz violinists of those times; guitarists Eddie Lang and Eddie Condon; trombonists Glenn Miller and Jack Teagarden; clarinetists Pee Wee Russell, Frank Teschemacher, Benny Goodman, and Mezz Mezzrow; pianist Joe Sullivan; and a dozen or so others.

Their history is tragic in more ways than one. Rarely was so much enthusiasm for jazz concentrated in any single place as among them. Even so, most of their records from the period are unsatisfactory. The chief reason may be that there was no single band that, on a higher level, represented Chicago style per se. There is no ensemble like Louis Armstrong's Hot Seven or Jelly Roll Morton's Red Hot Peppers, which immediately come to mind when New Orleans style is mentioned; or like the bands of Count Basie or Benny Goodman and the Teddy Wilson combos in Swing; or the Charlie Parker Quintet in bop. From an ensemble point of view, Chicago style failed to produce a single satisfying recording. Almost always, only solo passages are remarkable: the unmistakable clarinet sound of Frank Teschemacher, the tenor improvisations of Bud Freeman, the "cool" alto lines of Frankie Trumbauer, and most of all Bix Beiderbecke's cornet.

It has been argued that Chicago style is not really a "style." Its best recordings, indeed, come so close to Dixieland or New Orleans that what is most typical of Chicago style seems to be only the unfinished quality of its few fine records. And yet, there are a few musical signposts—mainly the rather novel emphasis on solo contributions—that differentiate Chicago from New Orleans and Dixieland. Most of all, the *human* unity and rapport among the Chicagoans was so strong and was reflected in their music with such immediacy that one hesitates—even now—to tear them apart on theoretical and academic grounds.

Bix Beiderbecke was born in Davenport, Iowa, in 1903, the son of a family of German immigrants. His ancestors had been clergymen and organists in Pomerania and Mecklenburg for generations. One of his father's given names was Bismarck, and this name—shortened to Bix—was inherited by the son. As a boy, Bix sang in the chorus of the Lutheran church in Davenport. His grandfather led a German male glee club.

Bix was a musical prodigy. At the age of seven, he was able to play back by ear any melody played for him on the piano, in any key. He rebelled against learning to read music just as he rebelled against having his protruding ears stuck back on his head with plaster. He was able to play everything he heard. He took his first piano lessons with Professor Charles Grade. Bix's brother remembers:

> Bix would persuade Professor Grade to play next week's lesson "to hear how it sounded." When the professor returned the next week, Bix would play it exactly as he had heard it. If the professor had made any mistakes the previous week, those mistakes were included in Bix's performance. Finally the professor caught on to Bix's deception and informed Mother that he could no longer teach the piano, and he meant it as a compliment!

It is said that he first became acquainted with jazz through the riverboats that docked on the Mississippi; some of them had bands from New Orleans, and the music carried across the water. And he learned to play the cornet the same way he had learned piano: by imitating the sounds of jazz that he heard coming over the river, and by listening to the recordings of his favorite band, the Original Dixieland Jazz Band. He learned to play the solos of trumpeter Nick LaRocca note for note by slowing down the gramophone.

Soon Bix became so absorbed in music that people began to think him a bit strange. He was expelled from school because he was interested only in music. The image of young Beiderbecke wandering the streets like a dreamer, his beat-up cornet wrapped in newspaper, became proverbial to all who knew him.

With Beiderbecke, German romanticism—and the whole spectrum of feelings that belongs to it—entered jazz. Perhaps it was this romantic heritage, fraught with yearning and melancholia, that created in Bix a state of mind similar to that which had come to black people through their American experience. What to the great New Orleans musician was the musical heritage of Africa, if preserved only subconsciously, was to Beiderbecke the "Blue Flower" of German romanticism. He was a Novalis (a lyric poet of German romanticism [1772–1801]) of jazz, transported into the jazz age of the roaring twenties with all the life-hungry characters of F. Scott Fitzgerald.

He didn't understand it when his fans would ask to hear his famous breaks and solos, or why he played this or that, and how he arrived at it. And when somebody took up a trumpet and played one of his legendary solos note for note, Bix was not impressed in the least. "I don't feel the same way twice," he said. "That's one of the things I like about jazz. I don't know what's going to happen next. Do you?"

Bix Beiderbecke was the first European-American jazz cornetist who was able to make a broad, lasting impression on musicians playing African American jazz. Rex Stewart learned Bix's solo on "Singing the Blues" by heart. With regard to harmony, Bix's influence went well beyond his own instrument. Not just trumpeters and cornet players, but also saxophonists and clarinetists analyzed, studied, and copied his solos. "He could find notes that no one else could find," said Bing Crosby. Jimmy McPartland remembers: "Bix! What can you say about him? For me, he was the greatest! What a sound! What a feeling for melody!

Beiderbecke was, aside from the old ragtime pianists, the first great "cool" soloist of jazz history. From his cool conception a line leads straight to Miles Davis. His ideas and his style were based not so much on rapid, technical playing as on originality, feeling, and sound—what musicians call "soulful playing." Once, when tenor saxophonist Sid Stewart accused Bix of being "stingy with notes," and told him he should "play a little flashy stuff," Bix replied, "Sid, the trouble with you is you play so many notes but they mean so little."

At eighteen, he began to play in public. In 1923 he was with the first real Chicago-style band, the Wolverines. In 1924 he met saxophonist Frank Trumbauer, with whom he made many of his finest records. There followed jobs with a variety of groups—with Jean Goldkette, Hoagy Carmichael, and other bands—until, by the late twenties, Bix was among the select musicians who gave the music of Paul Whiteman its jazz spice.

Bix Beiderbecke was the most brilliant musician of Chicago jazz. His harmonic sense was far ahead of that of his contemporaries. As early as the twenties, he was playing whole-tone scales and experimenting with augmented chords and elevenths, with quartal melodies (based on the interval of a fourth) and altered chords—ideas that did not become part of the general currency of modern jazz until much later. To traditional jazz musicians, his playing was so foreign that he was sometimes accused of playing out of tune. "Now and then we would incorporate these refined little things in our pieces," said Bix's colleague, the clarinetist Pee Wee Russell, "that were so daring, or rather so far ahead of their time, that more than once the manager would come to us in a fit, and ask us 'For God's sake, what are you doing?'"

Around 1927 a lung complaint became noticeable. Bix paid no attention. He played and played, and when he wasn't playing, he drank or went to symphony concerts. He experimented in the harmonic world of Debussy, primarily at the piano. He wrote five piano pieces that captured Impressionism in astonishingly refined, jazz-conscious fashion. The titles are revealing: "In the Dark" and "In a Mist," perhaps his best-known composition. About the origins of this piece, pianist Fred Bergin says:

> One morning Bix and I came out of our room under the pavilion after spending the whole night drinking gin and listening to Stravinsky's *Firebird*, with nothing but a red light over the record player. We walked along a little street that led down to the lake. The sun was coming up, and the fog that had crept over the lake during the night began to thin out. A sandpiper was running along the shore, and Bix was fascinated by the way it moved. He asked me if I saw what he saw: the rhythms of the bird's movement reminded him of morning gymnastics. I agreed with him, but I think my gin-soaked eyes weren't really seeing anything. Bix told me he wanted to capture this scene in a piece for solo piano that he was working on just then.

As a trumpeter he was mainly a jazz musician; at the piano he was rather more indebted to the European tradition.

On March 12, 1928, Maurice Ravel visited a recording session of the Paul Whiteman Orchestra in New York's Liederkrantz Hall. Whiteman played for Ravel the pieces "Metropolis" and "Suite of Serenades." Ravel showed polite interest, but not much enthusiasm about Whiteman's music. The thing that really fascinated him, however, was Bix Beiderbecke's playing.

"Sometimes we would transcribe Bix's solos note for note and then hand them out so the ensemble could play them," said Frankie Trumbauer. "Bix took one look at the notes and said 'Man, that's impossible.'"

Bix's health was deteriorating visibly. Finally, Whiteman sent him to Davenport for a rest. (He kept him on salary.) But it was too late. Bix could not stay home long. A woman—one of the few in his life—persuaded him to move to Queens and got him an apartment.

Bix spent the last weeks of his life in the apartment of bassist George Kraslow. Here something occurred that is characteristic of the love Bix inspired in everyone. He was in the habit of getting up around three or four in the morning to play his cornet. It is hard to imagine a jazz musician doing such a thing without bringing down upon himself the wrath of all the neighbors. Nothing of the sort happened. The neighbors told Kraslow, "Please don't mention we said anything. We would hate for him to stop."

In August 1931, Beiderbecke died of pneumonia in Kraslow's apartment. In Germany, on the "Lüneburger Heide" south of Hamburg, there are still Beiderbeckes. We asked them about Bix once. They had never heard of him.

Duke Ellington

Duke Ellington's Orchestra was a complex configuration of many spiritual and musical elements. To be sure, Duke Ellington's music was created here, but it was just as much the music of each individual member. Many Ellington pieces were genuine collective achievements, but Ellington headed the collective. Attempts have been made to describe how Ellington recordings came into being, but the process is so subtle that verbalization appears crude. Duke, or his alter ego, the late arranger and jazz composer, Billy Strayhorn, or one of the members of the band would come to the studio with a theme. Ellington would play it on the piano. The rhythm section would fall in. One or another of the horn men would pick it up. Baritone saxophonist Harry Carney might improvise a solo on it. The brass would make up a suitable background for him. And Ellington would sit at the piano and listen, gently accenting the harmonies—and suddenly he'd know: This is how the piece should sound and no other way. Later, when it was transcribed, the note paper only happened to retain what was, in the real meaning of the word, improvised into being.

It would be difficult to say who got more from the other in this mutual give-and-take—Ellington from his musicians, or the musicians from Ellington. The Duke Ellington Orchestra spoke with a unified voice, and yet was a unique instrument for individual expression. "You have to write with particular people in mind," said Duke. "You're writing for their abilities and their natural strengths, and you give them musical settings where they can give their best. . . . My band is my instrument."

The dynamic willpower with which Ellington communicated his ideas to his musicians, while at the same time giving them the impression that he was only helping them to unfold and develop their hidden powers, was one of his many great gifts. Owing to this relationship, which can barely be put into words, everything he wrote seemed to be created for him and his orchestra—to such a degree that hardly anyone can copy it. Once, it is said, Paul Whiteman and Ferde Grofé, his arranger, went night after night to the club where Ellington was playing, because they wanted to assimilate some of Ellington's typical sounds. Finally they gave up: "You can't steal from him." Duke Ellington was the great sonic sensualist of jazz, a wizard of sound whose sophisticated, scintillating timbres have a real power to move the listener. The unmistakably individual sound of each member of his orchestra was no accident—it was the defining feature, the organizing force of his music.

Duke Ellington wrote countless popular melodies—melodies in the genre of Jerome Kern, Richard Rodgers, Cole Porter, or Irving Berlin. But even the most popular among them—"Sophisticated Lady," "Mood Indigo," "Creole Love Call," "Solitude,"—radiate an elegance and refinement without equal in the Great American Songbook.

When Ellington was eighteen, he wanted to become a painter. By becoming a musician he only seemed to have abandoned painting. His compositions, with their many colors of timbre and harmony, are musical paintings. Sometimes this is revealed by the titles: "The Flaming Sword," "Beautiful Indians," "Portrait of Bert Williams," "Sepia Panorama," "Country Girl," "Dusk in the Desert," "Mood Indigo," and so forth. Even as a conductor, Ellington remained the painter: in the grand manner in which he confronted the orchestra and, with a few sure movements of the hand, placed spots of color on a canvas made of sounds.

It may be due to this that he perceived his music as "the transformation of memories into sounds." The memories are pictures. Ellington said, "The memory of things gone is important to a jazz musician. I remember I once wrote a sixty-four-bar piece about a memory of when I was a little boy in bed and heard a man whistling on the street outside, his footsteps echoing away."

Again and again Ellington expressed his pride in his African American heritage. Many of his larger works took their themes from black history: "Black, Brown, and Beige," the tone painting of the American Negro who was "black" when he came to the New World, became "brown" in the days of slavery, and today is "beige"—not only in his color, but in his being as well; "Liberian Suite," a work in six movements commissioned by the small republic on the west coast of Africa for its centennial; "Harlem," the work in which the atmosphere of New York's black city has been captured; "Deep South Suite," which reminds us of the locale of the origins of jazz; or "New World A-Comin'," about a better world without racial discrimination.

"I want to create the music of the American Negro," Ellington once said, placing the accent on "American." He was conscious of the fact that the African American had more in common with the world of the white man than with that of black Africa. To a man who once wrote him that he should take his jungle music and go back to Africa as soon as possible, he replied with extreme courtesy that this unfortunately was impossible, inasmuch as the blood of the American Negro in the course of generations had become so mixed with that of the letter writer that he would hardly be accepted there. But if it were all right with the writer, he would go to Europe. "There we are accepted."

Many critics have said that Ellington often comes too close to European music. They point to his concern with larger forms. But in this very tendency is revealed a feature of the molding of these forms that is certainly not European. Ellington always wrote his tone poems, suites, medleys, and potpourris with an awareness of the fact that his musicians were first of all improvisers.

In 1923 he joined a five-piece combo, which already included three of his later-to-be famous instrumentalists: Otto Hardwicke, alto sax; Sonny Greer, drums; Arthur Whetsol, trumpet. The combo took the name The Washingtonians, from the capital city where Ellington was born in 1899 and where he spent a sheltered, carefree youth.

The Washingtonians went to New York where, as Duke told it, they sometimes had to split a hot dog five ways to keep from starving. After six months they gave up.

Three years later, Ellington tried again. This time it worked. Soon he was playing in Harlem's most expensive nightspot, the Cotton Club, located in Harlem but nevertheless catering to white tourists—to give them the feeling that they had "really been to Harlem." Ellington's first famous records were made: "East St. Louis Toodle-oo," "Jubilee Stomp," "Birmingham Breakdown," and "Black and Tan Fantasy," with its quotation, much-discussed at the time, from Chopin's *Marche funèbre*.

The germ cell of his Cotton Club orchestra was preserved by Ellington well into the fifties. No other band leader has known so well how to keep an orchestra together. While other successful bands had personnel changes every few months, Ellington in twenty years only had six or seven significant alterations. Among the important soloists with Ellington at the Cotton Club were trumpeter Bubber Miley, trombonist Joe "Tricky Sam" Nanton, and baritone saxophonist Harry Carney. Ellington created his "jungle style" with Miley and Nanton. The expressive growl sounds of trumpet and trombone reminded listeners of voices moaning in a jungle night. The "jungle" association that this music created was so strong that listeners often called out, "Why don't you get out of the jungle and go back to Harlem where you belong?" The anecdote comes from Langston Hughes, the poet of Harlem, who added, "The inhabitants of Harlem didn't know anything about the jungle, and didn't care about it. They didn't identify themselves with Africa. Hot jazz was more important to them."

The jungle style is one of the four styles identified with Duke Ellington. The other three are (in a somewhat simplistic but synoptically clear grouping) "mood style," "concerto style," and "standard style," which came rather directly from Fletcher Henderson, the most important band leader of the twenties, and initially did not contribute much that was new. What it did have to offer, though, was clothed in typically Ellingtonian colors and sounds. In addition, of course, there is every imaginable mixture of these styles.

The mood style is melancholy and partakes of blues feeling, even in pieces that are not really blues. Ellington's most ambitious compositions in terms of tonal color are linked to this mood style. "Solitude," which says more in three minutes about the feeling its title describes than many a bulky book, is the most famous example.

As far as the concerto style is concerned, there are really two: real, small concertos for different soloists in the Ellington orchestra (such as the famous "Concerto for Cootie" for trumpeter Cootie Williams) and the aforementioned attempts to write jazz in larger forms.

The history of Duke Ellington is the history of the orchestra in jazz. No significant big band—and this includes commercial dance bands—has not been directly or indirectly influenced by Duke. The number of innovations and techniques introduced by Ellington and subsequently picked up by other orchestras or players is unrivaled.

In 1927 he was the first to use the human voice as an instrument. The voice was Adelaide Hall's; the tune, "Creole Love Call." Later, he was to create similar effects with Kay Davis's coloratura soprano. Today, the expression "voice as instrument" has become a household phrase.

With his 1937 recording "Caravan," a tune written with his Puerto Rican trombonist Juan Tizol, he paved the way for what has been called "Cuban jazz" since the forties—what is today called "Latin jazz": the combination of Latin American rhythms with the melodies and harmonies of North American jazz.

Duke Ellington was first to use so-called reverberation, or "reverb," in recording. Today, the use of reverb is taken for granted. In 1938 Johnny Hodges's solo on "Empty Ballroom Blues" was the first solo ever to be recorded with reverb.

In the thirties, Ellington was the first to experiment with the use of stereo microphone placement. He anticipated the use of two basses, which was to become fashionable in the sixties, by thirty years.

Toward the end of the twenties there is evidence of the flatted fifth, the interval so characteristic of bop, in more than one Ellington piece.

With his baritone saxophonist, Harry Carney, Ellington created a place for the baritone in jazz.

For years, the history of the jazz bass was so closely tied to the Ellington orchestra that it might be as appropriate to discuss it here as in the later section about the bass. There is a straight-line development from the first recording with amplified bass—"Hot and Bothered" with bassist Wellman Braud in 1928—to the playing of Oscar Pettiford and especially of Jimmy Blanton, who as a member of the Ellington band around 1940 made the bass the instrument it is in jazz today.

With Duke Ellington we discover for the first time in jazz how sound becomes independent. The discovery that sound itself, that tonal color, can be a uniquely determining element (just as important as rhythm, melody, and harmony) was first made by Duke Ellington, long before it became a standard feature of sixties jazz. Everything involved in ensemble sound and jazz instrumentation derives almost exclusively from Ellington.

Most important of all, Ellington was decades ahead of his time in solving the paradox of integrating composed music into predominantly improvised music. Duke didn't compose for instruments. He wrote for individuals. Ever since Duke Ellington, jazz composition, if it strives for quality, must entail dialogue between the composer and the performers. Out of composing (an individual's inner monologue) he made an act comprising an exchange of musical ideas between creator and interpreter. Without such empathy and understanding of the character of the particular musicians involved, jazz composition is no longer conceivable. On the level where jazz compositions are written today, Ellington was almost alone between 1925 and 1945. Only then came all the others: John Lewis, Ralph Burns, Jimmy Giuffre, Bill Russo, George Russell, Gerry Mulligan, Charles Mingus, Carla Bley, Gil Evans, Oliver Nelson, Toshiko Akiyoshi, Muhal Richard Abrams, Henry Threadgill, David Murray, Edward Wilkerson, Maria Schneider, Klaus König, Wynton Marsalis, Mathias Rüegg, Dave Douglas.

"Jazz is freedom of expression," said the Duke. For this reason, he was never bound by the rules and regulations of style. In many of Ellington's compositions, the combinations and colorations of sound go beyond even the sonic visions of European composers such as Stravinsky and Schoenberg. As one musician said, "Some of his voicings and orchestrations were so unique that you couldn't even tell from listening to the records which instruments were playing. You had to see the band live to find that out." But Duke Ellington didn't break the rules out of a desire to be subversive. He broke with convention only because convention was an obstacle to the development of his personal expression. And thus he was led to revel in sounds that were outrageous by Swing-era standards: stark dissonances and chromaticism, polytonal transitions, deviations from form, extreme registers, and unusual voicings. The astounding thing was: Ellington broke the rules, but everyone loved it.

Incomparable, too, is the way in which Ellington dealt with the problem of the piano in jazz (about which we will hear later). The piano became an extension of his conducting hands. He played only what was most necessary, indicated harmonies, bridged gaps, and left everything else to his musicians. His piano breaks were like a drummer's. Duke often executed them without using the piano stool, but they are filled with admirable tension, and when he played one of his rare solos, one feels to this day his roots in the old, genuine ragtime.

Ellington's two most famous orchestras were that of the late twenties, with Bubber Miley and "Tricky Sam" Nanton, and that of the early forties, with bassist Jimmy Blanton and tenor man Ben Webster. Modern big-band jazz begins with the latter; "Ko Ko" is its best-known piece. After that, there was occasional talk about the decline of Ellington. Some people advised him to disband his orchestra, or to keep it together for only a few months of the year and spend the rest of his time composing. But Duke needed his musicians: "I want to have them around me," Leonard Feather quoted him, "to play my music. I'm not worried about creating music for posterity; I just want it to sound good right now!"

Besides, Duke Ellington himself put an end to the "decline" of which hasty critics had spoken. This occurred at the Newport Festival in 1956. Ellington was billed as just another of the many attractions. Nobody expected anything out of the ordinary, but his appearance proved to be the climax of the whole festival. Duke played his old (1937) "Diminuendo and Crescendo in Blue," one of his first extended compositions; Paul Gonsalves blew twenty-seven choruses of stimulating tenor sax on it, and the band generated a vitality and drive the likes of which had not been heard from Ellington in a long time.

It was one of the great jazz nights of the fifties. And what had been forgotten for a few years again became apparent: Duke Ellington was still the "grand old man" of big-band jazz. A string of new masterpieces came into being, first and foremost the Shakespeare suite *Such Sweet Thunder*, dedicated to the Shakespeare Festival at Stratford, Ontario. With its spirited glosses, persiflages, and caricatures of great Shakespearean characters, it is one of the most beautiful of the larger Ellington works.

Ellington constantly rewrote the parts of his compositions. At any given time, the orchestra's repertoire might include six or seven different arrangements of a given piece. And, when a new musician joined the band, trumpeter Benny Bailey remembers that "no one told you which one was the current version."

Conversely, Ellington's musicians never played an arrangement twice the same way. They loved to refine each piece with improvised additions and deviations. In this way, new arrangements came into being night after night, concert after concert.

In 1967 Billy Strayhorn died; in 1970, altoist Johnny Hodges. Since the death in 1932 of trumpeter Bubber Miley, who together with Ellington had formed the jungle style with his "growl playing" between 1925 and 1929 (and who was replaced by another outstanding soloist, Cootie Williams), Ellington had not taken any personal loss so hard as the deaths of these two great musicians. The rich, sensuous solos of Johnny Hodges had reflected almost uninterruptedly since 1928 (for forty-two years!) the romantic, sensuous, impressionistic side of Ellington's character. Composer and arranger Billy Strayhorn had contributed many important pieces to the band's repertoire, such as "Lush Life," "Chelsea Bridge," and "Take the A Train," the theme song of the Ellington orchestra. As an orchestrator, he tuned in to Duke so perfectly that even specialists often were hard put to differentiate between what was written by Ellington and what by Billy "Sweet Pea" Strayhorn.

But Strayhorn's death unearthed once again a host of new creative powers in Ellington. During the sixties, he had increasingly left the main composing and arranging work to Strayhorn. Now he began—alone again—to take the initiative himself. A large number of important new great works were created: the *Sacred Concert* and, following that, *Second Sacred Concert*; Duke Ellington's *70th Birthday Concert* (chosen in 1969 as "Jazz Record of the Year" all over the world); the "Far East Suite" (in which Ellington reflects on a tour of Asia, sponsored by the State Department, in a highly personal manner); and, above all, the *New Orleans Suite*, which became the 1970 "Jazz Record of the Year." In the latter recording, Ellington salutes the New Orleans heritage of the jazz tradition and transforms it into Ellingtonian music.

Jazz specialists have said that the years after Strayhorn's death comprise one of the richest and most fruitful periods in Ellington's fifty-year life's work—in terms of composition as well as the number of concerts and tours by the Ellington orchestra.

In 1970 the Ellington band went on one of the longest tours ever made by a jazz orchestra: the Soviet Union, Europe, Latin America—all without a break, for three months. And again and again, one had the impression that seventy-year-old Ellington was the youngest, most active, most dynamic man in this orchestra of his juniors. Often, when the other band members seemed to drift into sweet slumber behind their music stands, Ellington would fascinate his audience with his humor, spirit, and charm. And when his musicians would be exhausted toward the end of a concert, he would gather a small group of four or five soloists and create with them rare apexes of youthful vitality.

In 1969 we turned the Berlin Jazz Days into a grand birthday celebration for the seventy-year-old Ellington, and dozens of famous musicians—not only the older generation, but also personalities like Miles Davis and Cecil Taylor—paid tribute to Duke. And a critic wrote that Ellington had been "the youngest musician at the whole festival."

Five years later, on May 25, 1974, Duke Ellington—the "Great Orchestrator of Jazz"—died of pneumonia in a New York hospital. Just a couple of weeks before, *Down Beat,* on the occasion of his seventy-fifth birthday, had dedicated to him a whole issue full of congratulations. From Leonard Bernstein to Miles Davis, the music world paid homage to him. Drummer Louis Bellson, possibly, found the most moving words: "You, the *maestro,* have given me a beautiful education musically and have guided me to be a good human being. Your valued knowledge and friendship will be with me forever. You are the model citizen of the world. Your music is Peace, Love, and Happiness."

Duke Ellington's music will remain with us—not only in the Duke Ellington Orchestra, which was taken over by his son Mercer after his death and which continued to play the compositions of the Grand Old Man into the eighties, but also, from the nineties to today, in the Lincoln Center Jazz Orchestra and in the other large orchestra projects of trumpeter Wynton Marsalis, who is keeping Ellington's brilliant sound world alive.

Also in the nineties, countless repertory bands competed to see who could best celebrate and pay tribute to Ellington's music. Despite the technical brilliance of many of these groups, critics and musicians often were dissatisfied with the approach of many of them, seeing them as seeking to internalize the Ellington tradition without creating anything new.

Pianist Uri Caine says, "If you really want to play Duke Ellington, you have to hear how relaxed and open Duke Ellington was. Then you can't sound like a high school big-band playing Duke Ellington charts. Which only makes Ellington all the more mysterious—he always found a way to make the old sound new again."

Today's avant-gardists and traditionalists alike pay homage to Ellington; both the apologists for traditional values in jazz and the defenders of today's New Thing cite him as a major source of their musical ideas.

First and foremost, though, Duke Ellington's music continues to live in the hundreds of musicians who learned from him and who, in turn, have passed on their experiences and developments to their students and successors: a stream of "Ellingtonia" that will continue to flow as long as there is jazz.

Coleman Hawkins and Lester Young

Until the late sixties, when the guitar and electronic instruments came into the foreground, the sound of modern jazz was—to use a favorite term of arranger Bill Russo—"tenorized." The man who tenorized it was Lester Young.

More important jazz musicians play tenor saxophone than any other instrument. The sound of the Miles Davis' Nonet has been described as the orchestration of Lester Young's tenor sound. The other important jazz sound of the fifties—the "Four Brothers" sound of the Woody Herman band—is tenorized, too. The tenor men who played it, almost all other important tenorists, and even trumpeters, trombonists, pianists, alto and baritone saxists of the cool jazz of the fifties—all were influenced by Lester Young.

Lester Young became a trailblazer of modern jazz because he liberated the saxophone from the sonic ballast with which it had been saddled since New Orleans jazz. Lester Young's triumph was to free the melodic line from these unwieldy shackles. He was the first to give the saxophone the lightness and mobility that made possible all the modern ways of playing it.

With Lester "Prez" (from President) Young, cool jazz, the jazz of the fifties, began long before there was bebop, the jazz of the forties. It began with the solos played by Lester in the old Count Basie band: "Song of the Islands" and "Clap Hands, Here Comes Charlie," recorded in 1939; "Lady Be Good," recorded by a Count Basie combo in 1936; or even earlier, when Lester became a member of Fletcher Henderson's band in 1934. Lester reminisced:

> The whole band was buzzing on me because I had taken Hawk's place. I didn't have the same kind of sound he had. I was rooming at the Hendersons' house, and Leora Henderson would wake me early in the morning and play Hawkins' records for me so I could play like he did. I wanted to play my own way, but I just listened. I didn't want to hurt her feelings.

Coleman Hawkins and Lester Young—these two names designate two great eras of jazz. Since "Bean" and Prez both played tenor, and since each of them holds approximately the same position in the phase of jazz he represents, no two other personalities could show more clearly how wide the scale of being and meaning in jazz really is. At one end stands Coleman Hawkins—the extroverted rhapsodist with the dark, voluminous tone and the fast, strong vibrato. Hard and gripping on fast pieces, erotically expressive on slow numbers, always vitally communicative, never shying away from quantity in utterances or notes, he is a Rubens of jazz. And opposite him stands Lester Young—the introverted lyricist with the supple, soft tone and the light vibrato, friendly and obliging on fast pieces, full of tender abandon on slow numbers, reserved in utterance, never stating a nuance more than is absolutely necessary. He is a Cézanne of jazz, as Marshall Stearns has called him, which not only indicates his artistic but also his historical position: As Cézanne paved the way for modern painting, so Young paved the way for modern jazz.

It would be an oversimplification, however, to assign one man to the jazz tradition and the other to modern jazz. Both stem from the tradition; both were "modern."

Lester Young was a master of "horizontal" playing, or an approach oriented more toward the linear development of melodies, while Coleman Hawkins was a virtuoso of "vertical" playing, missing no opportunity to fill out the chord structure underlying his choruses with his rhapsodic, arpeggio-rich playing. George Russell compared these two contrasting styles to the image of a steamboat stopping at different stations along a river, each smaller town standing for a chord and each larger city standing for "tonic destinations." "Hawkins solos are like the trips of a local steamer with stops at each town along the way, whereas Young solos are like the trips of an express steamer that stops primarily at the larger towns" (Paul F. Berliner).

Coleman Hawkins emerged from the Jazz Hounds, the group accompanying blues singer Mamie Smith. Lester Young was born near New Orleans and in his youth received the same impressions that affected the old New Orleans musicians: street parades, Mardi Gras, and New Orleans funerals. When the modern jazz of the forties sprang up, Coleman Hawkins was the first noted "traditional" jazz musician to play with the young bebop revolutionaries. And in the second half of the fifties, the period just preceding the death of Young (who after years of almost constant indulgence in alcohol and marijuana was only a shadow of his former self), the man who preceded him—Coleman Hawkins—retained his old, indestructible vitality and power.

Hawkins is the "father of the tenor saxophone." To be sure, there were some tenor players before him, but the instrument was not an acknowledged jazz horn. At that time it fell into the category of strange noise makers, like the euphonium, the sousaphone, or the bass sax.

Coleman Hawkins was twenty-one when he came to New York with Mamie Smith in 1923. He was playing blues and jazz in the style of that time, similar possibly to King Oliver and Louis Armstrong, and he was one of the few black musicians who played with the young Chicago-style jazzmen. That same year, he joined the first important big band—Fletcher Henderson's—and remained until 1934. He was the first real tenor saxophone soloist, in the sense of the great virtuosos of the Swing period. He was one of the first to make records with the young European musicians who were just then beginning to hear the jazz message: in 1934 with Jack Hylton in England, in 1935 with the Ramblers in Holland and with Django Reinhardt in Paris. And as modern jazz began—as we have mentioned—he was again one of the first to participate. Hawkins could always be found where original jazz was being created.

Tenor saxophonist Joe Lovano says, "He could play any song, any chord progression and it wasn't the thing you were listening to. You were hearing the man and the feeling and the sound. . . . He played with such a driving force, but also with that lyrical beauty."

His first famous solo on record was the 1926 rendition of "Stampede" with Fletcher Henderson. In the Henderson orchestra, he cultivated a dynamic breadth and a fullness of sound that enabled him to blow entire solos over seven or eight other horns. "He had one of the deepest, most beautiful, resonant sounds on his saxophone. It was almost like a bass," says bassist Charlie Haden.

In 1929 came "If I Could Be with You" with the Mound City Blue Blowers, who included some of the Chicago-style practitioners. Then in 1934, again with Henderson, "Talk of the Town"—probably the first great solo ballad interpretation in jazz history, the foundation for everything now meant by ballad playing in modern jazz. (Miles Davis said, "When I heard Hawk, I learned to play ballads.") Then came the European recordings, such as "I Wanna Go Back to Harlem" with the Dutch Ramblers and "Stardust" with Django Reinhardt. When Hawkins returned to the United States in 1939, he almost immediately scored the greatest success of his career: "Body and Soul," a jazz record that became a worldwide hit and the model for all jazz ballad playing thereafter. Hawkins could not understand it: "I've been playing like that all my life. . . . It wasn't anything special." In 1943 he blew a breathtaking solo on "The Man I Love" with Oscar Pettiford's bass and Shelly Manne's drums, and then in 1947 came "Picasso"—a long improvisation for unaccompanied tenor saxophone, based on the harmonies of the piece identified with Hawkins, "Body and Soul." It is reminiscent in structure and delineation of Johann Sebastian Bach's Chaconne from the D-minor Partita for solo violin, and full of the same baroque vitality and linearity.

On all these records, and in almost everything he ever played, Hawkins was the master of the chorus, of improvising on a given chord scheme. A Hawkins solo, it has been said, is the classic example of how to develop a solo statement from a phrase. And almost every phrase Hawkins has blown could itself be used again as the theme for a jazz improvisation. There is only one musician who can be compared to him in this respect, the one who in almost every other respect is his opposite: Lester Young.

While everything about Hawkins the human being is simple and comprehensible, everything about Lester is strange and incomprehensible. A booking agent, Nat Hentoff related, gave up working with Lester because he couldn't talk to him. "I'd talk to him," the agent said, "and all he'd say was 'Bells!' or 'Ding dong!' I finally decided I'd go to Bellevue if I wanted to talk to crazy people."

According to legend, he left the Count Basie band, from which he emerged and with which he was connected as Hawkins had been with Fletcher Henderson's band, because Basie had set a recording date for a Friday the thirteenth—and Lester refused to play on that day.

His jargon was almost a language in itself, which made it hard for people to understand him in conversation. No one has coined as many jazz expressions as he—right down to the word *cool*—so that not only the style, but also the word as an expression for something someone likes, stems from him. He called his colleagues "lady" and addressed club owners as "Prez"; he called the army "Mr. Hangman," and he asked pianist Bobby Scott about his "left people" when he wanted to tease Scott about the habit (shared by many modern pianists) of running hornlike lines with his right hand while the left hardly came into play. Norman Granz said that Lester for a time pretended to be speaking a foreign language: "It was gibberish, but he did it with a straight face and with conviction."

When, in the Basie Orchestra, someone missed a note, or a new musician joined the band and his playing was a little off, Young would take a little bell out of his pocket and ring it. If something particularly bothered him, he would play the first measure of "Running Wild." This was his reaction to musicians who didn't have their own stories to tell. "I try not to be a repeater pencil," he said, "I don't want to be a parrot."

Lester, or "Prez," had the sensibility of a Baudelaire or James Joyce. "He lives in his own world," an agent said about him. What was outside of this world was, according to Lester's convictions, not in the world at all. But this world of his was a wonderful world, a world that was mild and friendly and lovely. "Anything that hurts a human being hurts him," said drummer Jo Jones.

Dancer Rudolf Nureyev once said that the great dancer is not the one who makes a difficult step look easy, but rather the one who makes an easy step look interesting. He could have been talking about Lester Young's playing. Lester could make even the simplest phrases sound exciting. He did not hide behind a façade of ornaments and mannerisms. His playing reflected his vulnerability and sent the message: your sound is the window onto your soul. When you're soloing, you're letting out your thoughts and feelings. Every solo has to tell a story, and the story has to be true, has to reflect the ideas and feelings of the moment. And if it's not your own story, then forget it.

Jo Jones said: "Everyone playing an instrument in jazz expresses what's on his mind. Lester would play a lot of musical phrases that were actually words. He would literally talk on his horn. That's his conversation. I can tell what he's talking about in 85 percent of what he'll play in a night. I could write his thoughts down on paper from what I hear from his horn. Benny Goodman even made a tune out of a phrase Lester would play on his horn—'I want some money.'"

Because Lester talked on his horn, he loved to listen to singers: "Most of the time I spend in listening to records is listening to singers and getting the lyrics to different songs."

When improvising on a melody, Lester Young attempted to convey the lyrics of this melody to the listener directly and without the aid of words. Thus, he recorded some of his most beautiful solos as accompanist to singer Billie Holiday, the greatest female singer since Bessie

Smith—perhaps simply the greatest, in any case the personification of Swing singing, as Bessie Smith was the personification of the classic blues. The way in which Prez backed "Lady Day"—the name he gave her—set the standard for accompaniments to singing in jazz, with such pieces as "Time on My Hands," "Without Your Love," or "Me, Myself, and I." The two musicians sounded as if each was able to read the other's thoughts, to feel what the other was feeling. Saxophone and voice become one, are woven so tightly together that they fuse into a perfect balance of spirit and devotion.

What Lester tells us when he improvises freely on his tenor sax might sound something like this: "I was born near New Orleans, August 27, 1909. I stayed in New Orleans until I was ten. During the carnival season we all traveled with the minstrel show, through Kansas, Nebraska, South Dakota, all through there.

"I played drums from the time I was ten to about thirteen. Quit them because I got tired of packing them up. I'd take a look at the girls after the show, and before I'd get the drums packed, they'd be gone.

"For a good five or six years after that I played the alto, and then the baritone when I joined Art Bronson's band. Ran away from my father when I was about eighteen. . . . I joined Art Bronson and his Bostonians. Played with him for three or four years . . . anyway, I was playing the baritone, and it was weighing me down. I'm real lazy, you know. So when the tenor man left, I took over his instrument.

"Used to hear the Basie band all the time on the radio and figured they needed a tenor player. They were at the Reno Club in Kansas City. It was crazy, the whole band was gone, but just this tenor player. I figured it was about time, so I sent Basie a telegram.

"But Basie was like school. I used to fall asleep in school, because I had my lesson, and there was nothing else to do. The teacher would be teaching those who hadn't studied at home, but I had, so I'd go to sleep. . . . You had to sit there and play it over and over again. Just sit in that chair.

"I joined Fletcher Henderson in Detroit in 1934. Basie was in Little Rock then, and Henderson offered me more money. Basie said I could go . . . was with Henderson only about six months. The band wasn't working very much . . . then back to Basie until 1944 and the army."

The army broke Lester Young, according to Nat Hentoff. He was harassed, and his individuality and sensitivity were deadened, in the way armies all over the world deaden individuality and sensitivity. Through the army, hate came into his life—hate particularly for whites, or so Hentoff supposed. For a musician whose message was lyricism, tenderness, and amiability, there was not much left.

The other thing that oppressed him, subconsciously and sometimes consciously, was the fact that almost every tenor player was playing à la

Prez, until during the last years of his life Sonny Rollins and the musicians of his school came up. The worst thing was that there was a man who often played a "better" Lester Young than Lester himself: Paul Quinichette, whom Lester called "Lady Q." Lester's manager tells of the time when both were playing at Birdland—the famous, now defunct jazz club in New York—and Lester came off the stand saying, "I don't know whether to play like me or like Lady Q, because he's playing so much like me."

It was a peculiar brand of irony: on the one hand, nothing underlined Lester's enormous artistic success more than that an entire generation of tenor men should play like him; on the other hand, as an uncompromising individualist he found it intolerable that they all should play like him, and he like them. "They're picking the bones while the body's still warm," said Young.

Most of the records Lester made in the fifties—such as the ones for Norman Granz's Verve label—were only a pale reflection of the great "President of the Tenor Saxophone." But often there were sparks, and one could still feel something of the genius of this great musician—for instance, on the record *Jazz Giants of 1956* with Teddy Wilson, Roy Eldridge, Vic Dickenson, and other great Swing musicians.

For years Lester traveled with Norman Granz's concert unit, Jazz at the Philharmonic, all over the world. Night after night, he witnessed how Flip Phillips brought audiences to their feet with the exhibitionism of his tenor solos. He disliked this ecstatic way of playing tenor, but it reached the point where he himself often utilized it—and from this, too, he must have suffered. For years Lester Young lived almost uninterruptedly in a state of intoxication, until, in March 1959, he died after a tragic engagement at the Blue Note, a Paris jazz club. Ben Benjamin, the club owner, reported, "Lester was very sick when he worked for me. He was almost apathetic. He wanted to go home because, as he said, he couldn't talk to the French doctors. He had ulcers, and I think he drank a little too much."

Lester came back to New York in time to die. On the early morning of his arrival, he died in the Hotel Alvin, on the "musician's crossroad" at Fifty-Second Street and Broadway where he had lived during the last years of his life.

The only thing Lester retained throughout the crisis periods of his life, and down to his last days, was his sound—as Coleman Hawkins retained his. "The only thing nobody can steal from you is your sound. Sound alone is important," Hawkins once said.

French saxophone expert Jean Ledru has created a complicated theory of the relationship between volume, air column, length of melodic phrases, number of notes, loudness, articulation, mouthpiece, reed, and everything else that can affect a tenor saxophonist's playing. In this way, he has shown that there is a necessary connection between a saxophonist's sonority and everything he or she plays. This provides an academic basis for the conviction of many jazz scholars that in jazz nothing is as important as tone formation, and that this is the actual element by which jazz differs from European music.

In Lester Young's playing, the tone is not a fixed quantity. It constantly follows a strangely flowing movement: upward, downward, with subtle vibratos, the tiny up-and-down sliding movements of portamenti and glissandi, and constant modification of tone color. Lester's sound is the art of evasion, a crystallization of unapproachability. Using alternative, or "false," fingerings, he was able to produce wah-wah effects similar to those created by trumpet players using mutes, and to shade one and the same note with an enormous variety of feelings. He pushed the registers of the saxophone to their limits. "I'm trying to further develop my saxophone sound," he said. "I want it to sound like an alto, a tenor, and a bass, and I'm always trying to take it further."

Lester's sonority stems from Frankie Trumbauer and Bud Freeman, the Chicago-style musicians. "Trumbauer was my idol. . . . I imagine I can still play all those solos off the records. He played the C-melody saxophone. I tried to get the sound of a C melody on a tenor. That's why I don't sound like other people. . . . I did like Bud Freeman very much. Nobody played like him." The line that leads from Chicago style via Lester Young to cool jazz is direct.

The name of Lester Young even stands at the beginning of bebop. Kenny Clarke told about it:

"They began to talk about Bird [Charlie Parker] because he was playing like Prez on alto. People became concerned about what he was doing. We thought that was something phenomenal because Lester Young was the pace setter, the style setter at that time. . . . We went to listen to Bird at Monroe's [a Harlem club] for no other reason except that he sounded like Prez . . . until we found out that he had something of his own to offer . . . something new."

And Parker himself said: "I was crazy about Lester. He played so clean and beautifully, but I wasn't influenced by Lester. Our ideas ran on differently."

Indeed, these were two different directions. It would be possible to show that modern jazz as a whole, even up to free jazz, has developed in the counterplay of the ideas of Lester Young and Charlie Parker. Lester came first; then, when Parker arrived, *his* influence became dominant. But then, in the fifties, Prez's hour struck again, with a host of musicians playing "cool" à la Lester Young, until finally, with the coming of hard bop, Bird's influence again assumed overwhelming importance. And with this Bird influence, with the sonority of Sonny Rollins's tenor sax, we return (and so the circle of this chapter closes) to Coleman Hawkins. His hard, dramatic style now was in the right place, after Lester Young's desire to make the world "nice and cozy" had proven vain, although it had been shared by all jazz musicians for so many years. Hawkins, whose career preceded Young's by almost ten years, also survived Lester by ten years. His health was as robust as his playing (with the exception of the last years of his life), and only weeks before his death—in June 1969—he appeared in concerts and on television. The tenor saxophonists of free jazz who meanwhile had so radically changed jazz—Archie Shepp, Pharoah Sanders, Albert Ayler, and others—all agreed on who had given the first impulses to those expanding inflections of tenor sound that were their main focus: Coleman Hawkins. Archie Shepp said it clearly: "I play Hawk today."

For Coleman Hawkins, this whole rich era he had lived through—from Mamie Smith in 1922 to the post-Coltrane period in 1969—was not as varied as it seems to us today. It was *one* style and *one* era. The style was jazz; from the beginning until today and beyond, it was the era of jazz. Progress was a foreign word to Hawkins. He once said to critic Stanley Dance, "What Charlie Parker and Dizzy were doing was 'far out' to a lot of people, but it was just music to me." And he made recordings with the young bebop people only because "they needed help." When Dance talked to him about Mamie Smith and Fletcher Henderson and the good old days, Hawkins said, "I don't think I ever was a child."

Charlie Parker and Dizzy Gillespie

"Just a week before his death," Leonard Feather said, "Parker ran into Gillespie at Basin Street. He was desperate, pitiful, pleading. 'Let's get together again,' he urged Dizzy. 'I want to play with you again before it is too late.'"

"Dizzy can't get over Bird saying that to him," recalled Loraine, Dizzy's wife. "His eyes get full of water even now when he thinks about it."

Charlie Parker and Dizzy Gillespie are the Castor and Pollux of bebop.

Charlie Parker came from Kansas City. He was born on August 29, 1920. When he died in 1955, the doctors who performed the autopsy said that he might as well have been fifty-five.

Dizzy Gillespie came from South Carolina. He was born on October 21, 1917. In all phases of his life he appeared to be five to eight years younger than he was.

Both grew up in the world of racial discrimination and from early youth experienced the humiliations that are a part of it.

Nobody cared much about young Charlie. Throughout his youth, he lacked love and the warmth of the nest.

None of the few family members close to Parker were musical. At thirteen, he was playing baritone horn. A year later, alto sax was added.

It has always been a mystery why Parker became a musician. The alto saxophonist Gigi Gryce—one of his best friends—said: "Parker was a natural genius. If he had become a plumber, I believe he would have been a great one."

At fifteen, Parker was forced to earn his own keep. "We had to play," he said, "from nine in the evening to five in the morning without a break. We usually got $1 or $1.25 a night."

In 1937, at seventeen, Parker became a member of Jay McShann's band, a typical Kansas City riff and blues orchestra. Parker said he was "crazy about Lester Young," but it is questionable whether he had a real model. It is probable that his colleagues at first considered his style terrible because he played "different" from anybody else.

Parker's real schooling and tradition was the blues. He heard it constantly in Kansas City and played it night after night with Jay McShann.

Dizzy had a sheltered youth and grew up in a well-ordered family environment.

Gillespie's father was an amateur musician. He taught his kids to play several instruments. At fourteen, Dizzy's chief horn was the trombone. A year later, trumpet was added.

It seemed decided from the start that Dizzy would become a musician. He studied theory and harmony.

At fifteen, Dizzy completed the studies paid for by his father.

In the same year—1937—Dizzy took over Roy Eldridge's chair in Teddy Hill's band. Roy was Dizzy's great model. The Hill band had grown out of the Luis Russell orchestra, and Russell himself had taken over the King Oliver band in 1929. Thus, the jazz genealogy from Dizzy back to King Oliver and Louis Armstrong is surprisingly short.

Gillespie, too, had roots in the jazz tradition, but it was rather the happy tradition of New Orleans and Dixieland music.

The titles of the first records made by both men are symbolic:

Parker recorded "Confessin' the Blues" on April 30, 1941, in Dallas, Texas, with Jay McShann's band (however, there are earlier recordings, e.g., a 1940 radio session with the Jay McShann Band. The oldest surviving documentation of Parker is an unaccompanied saxophone solo based on "Honeysuckle Rose" and "Body and Soul," recorded by another musician in 1940).

Gillespie recorded, in mid-1937, just after becoming a member of Teddy Hill's band, Jelly Roll Morton's "King Porter Stomp."

Parker at first did not get far from Kansas City. He lived a dreary, joyless life and became acquainted with narcotics almost simultaneously with music. It is believed that Parker had become a victim of "the habit" by the time he was fifteen. He was called "Yardbird." Every musician has a different story about where this nickname came from, but all agree that it refers to a chicken destined for the cooking pot.

Gillespie went to Europe with Teddy Hill's band in the summer of 1937. Teddy Hill wrote, "Some of the guys threatened not to go if the frantic one went, too. But it developed that youthful Dizzy, with all his eccentricities and practical jokes, was the most stable man of the group. He was able to save so much money that he encouraged the others to borrow from him so that he'd have an income in case things got rough back in the States."

The inhibitions and complexes of his life began the moment he became a musician. Parker played with Jay McShann until 1941. Once he landed in jail for twenty-two days when he refused to pay his cab fare and wounded the driver with a knife. Then he fled to Chicago. He arrived there dirty and tattered as if he had "just got off a freight car." But he was playing "like you never heard."

Gillespie was successful from the moment he began to play. In Paris it was first noticed that his playing was different. A French drummer wrote at the time, "There is in the band of Teddy Hill a very young trumpeter who promises much. It is a pity that he has no opportunity to make recordings here. He is—along with trombonist Dickie Wells—by far the most gifted musician in the band. His name is Dizzy Gillespie."

For three months he was a dishwasher in a Harlem restaurant. Sometimes he didn't even have a horn to play on. "I was always in a panic" is one of his best-known quotes. He slept in garages. "Worst of all was that nobody understood my music."

When Parker once played in a jam session in Kansas City with members of the Basie band and nobody liked what he was blowing, drummer Jo Jones, as an expression of his feelings, took his cymbal off and threw it almost the entire distance of the room. Bird just packed up his horn and went out.

Parker said, "I'd been getting bored with the stereotyped changes that were being used all the time at the time, and I kept thinking there's bound to be something else. I could hear it sometimes, but I couldn't play it.

"Well, that night I was working over 'Cherokee,' and, as I did, I found that by using the higher intervals of a chord as a melody line and backing them with appropriately related changes, I could play the thing I'd been hearing. I came alive."

Parker said that in order to

Upon his return from Europe, Gillespie became a successful musician, playing in different bands. In 1939 he became a member of Cab Calloway's orchestra.

Cab Calloway didn't like the way Gillespie played, nor did he care for Gillespie's penchant for practical jokes and, occasionally, for quarreling also. During an engagement in Hartford, someone (not Dizzy) threw a spitball out on the stage, hitting the bandleader. After the curtain, Cab blamed Diz, "and an argument ensued," bassist Milt Hinton related. "Cab made a pass at Dizzy, and Dizzy came at him with a knife. I grabbed Diz's hand . . . but Cab was nicked in the scuffle. Cab hadn't realized he'd been cut until he was back in the dressing room."

Gillespie said, "When I was growing up, all I wanted to play was Swing. Eldridge was my boy. All I ever did was try to play like him, but I never quite made it. I'd get all messed up because I couldn't get it. So I tried something else. That has developed into what became known as bop."

One of the first records Gillespie made with Cab Calloway's band had the odd title, "Chop, Chop, Charlie Chan," on March 8, 1940. A dozen years later, Parker appeared on the last record made by Dizzy and Bird together under the pseudonym "Charlie Chan." (Chan was his wife's first name.)

increase the power and focus of his sound, he played with the hardest reed he could find, at first putting a tenor saxophone reed on the mouthpiece of his alto saxophone. This produced a sound that was fundamentally different from the soft, warm, older sounds characteristic of the Swing era. Parker's sound is hard-edged, rich in overtones, and without the sweetness that was so characteristic of older, vibrato-laden styles of alto playing, such as that of Benny Carter and Johnny Hodges.

Gillespie was "like a painter who takes a can of paint and just throws the whole thing at a canvas and tries to make something out of it, playing with great daring in between the spaces of time and sound," said Lonnie Hillyer.

Barry Harris said, "Dizzy can take a phrase that you never thought could be played in a certain space, and he'll just cram it in there and make it work beautifully."

When he was not playing with Jay McShann, Parker pulled through with menial jobs. He participated in every jam session he could find.

Starting in 1939 Gillespie had begun to arrange. Successful bands like Woody Herman's, Jimmy Dorsey's, and Ina Ray Hutton's bought his arrangements.

In 1941 Parker came to New York with the McShann band. They played at the Savoy Ballroom in Harlem.

Gillespie came by to sit in.

Bird and Dizzy had met in Kansas City in 1939, but it was most likely on this night that they really played together for the first time.

Soon the McShann band left New York. Parker went along to Detroit. Then he no longer could stand the routine arrangements and left the band, without saying anything. He never cared much for big bands.

Gillespie evolved more and more into a big-band musician. After the row with Calloway he worked in the big bands of Benny Carter, Charlie Barnet, Lucky Millinder, Earl Hines (1943), Duke Ellington, and Billy Eckstine (1944).

After he left the McShann band, Parker went almost daily to Minton's in Harlem. A band consisting of pianist Thelonious Monk, guitarist Charlie Christian, trumpeter Joe Guy, bassist Nick Fenton, and drummer Kenny Clarke was playing there. "Nobody," Monk was to say later, "was sitting there trying to make up something new on purpose. The job at Minton's was a job we were playing, that's all." Yet Minton's became the point of crystallization for bop. There Parker and Gillespie met again.

Monk relates that Parker's ability and authority were immediately accepted when he began to show up at Minton's. All could feel his creative productive genius.

Gillespie said, "Charlie Parker was the catalyst, he was the one that founded the style."

Billy Eckstine related, "Now Diz is like a fox, you know. He's one of the smartest guys around. Musically, he knows what he is doing backwards and forwards. So what he hears—that you think maybe is going through—goes in and stays. Later, he'll go home and figure it all out just what it is."

Parker and Gillespie became inseparable. In 1943 they played together in Earl Hines's band; in 1944 they were both with Billy Eckstine. In the same year they co-led a quintet on Fifty-Second Street, which became the "Street of Bop." They also made their first joint recording in 1944. Gillespie said that sometimes when he and Bird played together, it sounded as if a single horn were playing.

Tony Scott said, "And Bird came in one night and sat in with Don Byas. He blew 'Cherokee' and everybody just flipped. . . . When Bird and Diz hit the Street regularly a couple of years later, everybody was astounded and nobody could get near their way of playing music. Finally, Bird and Dizzy made records, and then guys could imitate and go from there. Everybody was experimenting around 1942, but nobody had set a style yet. Bird provided the push."

In Leonard Feather's words, "Dizzy's followers were aping his goatee, beret, and glasses, even his gait." Gillespie created then what was to go around the world as "bebop fashion." Fan magazines advertised "bebop ties."

Parker had found, in the quintet format of bebop, the instrumentation most congenial to him: sax, trumpet, and rhythm trio. The Charlie Parker Quintet became as significant to modern jazz as Louis Armstrong's Hot Five had been to traditional.

Deep inside, Gillespie was a big band man. In 1945 he founded his first own big band. From 1946 to 1950 he had large bands almost steadily. In 1948 he took one to Europe. His Paris concert had long-lasting effects on European jazz.

It becomes clearer: Gillespie in those days was the most frequently mentioned bebop musician. If he did not bring to this music the creative impulses that radiated from Parker, he gave it the glamor and power without which it could not have conquered the world.

Billy Eckstine said, "Bird was responsible for the actual playing of [bebop], more than anyone else. But for putting it down, Dizzy was responsible."

With his Charlie Parker Quintet, Bird made the most important combo recordings of bebop: "Koko," based on the changes to "Cherokee"; "Now's the Time," a blues; "Chasin' the Bird," with the fugato entry of trumpeter Miles Davis, commencing the fashion of fugues and fugatos in modern jazz; "Embraceable You," the first classic modern jazz recording based on themeless improvisation (even though, as André Hodeir shows, that was hinted at in "Koko"); and countless others. Accompanied by Erroll Garner he recorded "Cool Blues," relating coolness and the blues in the title itself.

"Things to Come" became the most important record of the Gillespie big band, an apocalyptic vision of the things that were to come: a broiling, twitching mass of lava out of which for a few seconds arise ghostly figurations, to disappear again at once. But above it all the clear and triumphant sound of Gillespie's trumpet. "Music of chaos," as some people said then, but also music about man's victory over chaos!

Parker's alto sax became the most expressive voice of modern jazz—each note arising from the blues tradition, sometimes imperfect, but always from the depths of a tortured soul.

Gillespie's trumpet became the clearest, most clarion-like, and yet most flexible trumpet voice in the history of jazz. Almost every phrase he played was perfect.

Parker's rhythmic sense was explosive. One musician said, "The rhythms of his solos are so strong that you could put almost any notes to those rhythms and they would still sound great."

Bird became the basic improviser, the chorus man par excellence, interested more than anything in the flow of the lines he played. "He was like Midas,"

Gillespie became more and more interested in the percussive aspects of the new jazz. "I'm a rhythm man," he said. "Rhythm is the foundation of the building. If you don't take care of the foundation, the building collapses." In the words of Billy Eckstine, "If you ever listen to Diz humming something, he hums the drum and bass part and everything said Chico O'Farrill, "everything he touched musically turned to gold." Parker made the nineteen-year-old trumpeter Miles Davis a member of his quintet—the man who was to become the dominant improviser of the next phase in modern jazz. Parker encouraged Davis, who had begun à la Gillespie and Parker, to find a style of his own.

Years later, when Parker was under contract to Norman Granz, he recorded with Machito's orchestra. But the results were hardly representative of Bird. Parker's formula remained the quintet: the smallest instrumentation in which it was possible to create "form" through the unison statement of theme at beginning and end, while retaining complete improvisatory freedom for the remainder.

Speed was at the core of Parker's personality. His wild, excessive life was as fast as his music. He led many different lives, each intensely and to the hilt: intellectual, drug addict, philosopher, playboy, responsible father of a family, ladykiller.

The only place where he wasn't torn and driven and was able to be at peace with himself was in his music. Critics named this frenetic new style "bebop."

In Parker's words: "I'd be happy if what I played would simply be called 'music.'"

because it all fits in with what he's doing. Like 'Oop-Bop-Sh'Bam.' That's a drum thing. And 'Salt Peanuts' was another. It was a drum lick."

Gillespie was interested in Afro-Cuban rhythms. He played with musicians from the Cuban orchestra of Machito. In 1947 he added the Cuban percussionist Chano Pozo to his band and thus brought a wealth of ancient West African rhythms and drum patterns into modern jazz.

To the question of how the future of jazz would develop Gillespie answered, "Probably it will go back to where it all started from: a man beating a drum."

Gillespie, educated in music theory, did a great deal to expand the harmonic vocabulary of jazz. As Doc Cheatham said, "Dizzy really straightened out jazz, by inventing new bridges for pieces like 'I Got Rhythm.'"

On another occasion, Parker said, "Life used to be so cruel to musicians, just the way it is today. They say that when Beethoven was on his deathbed he shook his fist at the world because they just didn't understand. Nobody in his own time ever really dug anything he wrote. But that's music."

According to Leonard Feather, Gillespie never took himself, or the music he created, as seriously as did the countless music lovers and musicians who have spent so much time investigating, discussing, and imitating everything.

In 1946 Parker had the first major breakdown of his life. It came during the recording of "Lover Man" at the Dial studios. When Parker came home after the session, he started a fire in his hotel room and ran, naked and screaming, into the hall.

In the eighties, a critic remarked: "The other musicians who took part in the incubating process that evolved into bop today are dead, or struggling intermittently with the drug habit. Gillespie apparently has never suffered any major frustration or neurosis."

According to Orrin Keepnews, "There can be little doubt that he was a tortured man, and there are several who emphasize his loneliness." Often he would stay up all night, riding aimlessly around on the subway. As a musician, on stage, he never developed the ability to "sell" himself and his music. He just stood there and played.

The more it became apparent that Gillespie could not keep his big band together permanently, the more consciously he became the comedian of his music. As the "clown of bebop" he attempted to sell that which otherwise had proven itself unsaleable. He was not only the best trumpeter of bop but also one of its foremost vocalists. Always, he retained controlled superiority.

In the years 1948 to 1950, both Dizzy and Bird made recordings with large string ensembles—Bird in New York, Dizzy in California. This was to become the only major financial success of Parker's career. The fanatics among the fans beat their breasts: Bird and Dizzy had gone commercial. It was revealing how differently the two reacted:

Parker, for whom recording with strings was the fulfillment of a lifelong wish, and for whom the strings represented that aura of the symphony he had always admired, suffered from the prejudiced judgment of the fans.

Gillespie, for whom the string recordings actually had meant not much more than another record date, made fun of the ignorance of those who talked about commercialism.

Parker was never satisfied with himself. He never knew how to answer the question of what recordings he thought to be his best. In answer to the question about his favorite musicians, a jazz man only came in third place: Duke Ellington. Before him came Brahms and Schoenberg; after him, Hindemith and Stravinsky. But more than any musician he loved Omar Khayyám, the Persian poet.

Leonard Feather: "Charlie drank more and more in a desperate attempt to stay away from narcotics while still avoiding the terrors of sober reality."

At a time when there was hardly a musician playing anywhere in the world who was not in some degree or fashion under Bird's influence—when this influence had even penetrated into the world of dance and pop music—Parker was only playing occasionally. According to Orrin Keepnews, "He had given up the fight toward the end. In 1954 he sent [his former wife] Doris a poem. . . . In part it sets forth a credo that might easily have been his own: 'Hear the Words! Not the doctrine. Hear the speech! Not the meaning. . . . Death is an imminent thing. . . . My fire is unquenchable.'"

On March 12, 1955, he died. He had been watching television, laughing at a joke on *The Tommy Dorsey Show*.

The Parker myth began almost immediately. Among those who paid him tribute was disc jockey Al "Jazzbo" Collins: "I don't

In 1954, at a birthday party for his wife, somebody fell over Gillespie's trumpet and bent the horn so that the bell pointed upward. "After his anger had subsided," Feather reported, "Dizzy tried to play the horn and found that the sound seemed to reach his ears better. . . . The next day he went to a trumpet manufacturer to ask whether he could put the idea into mass production." Gillespie wanted to take out a patent. But it was discovered that a similar instrument had been patented 150 years earlier.

Gillespie became the first "world statesman" of the international jazz tours organized by the U.S. State Department. With the help of funds from Washington, he managed to put together a big band again. He went on worldwide tours—first to Asia and southeastern Europe, later to Latin America. In Athens he gave the most triumphant concert of his career at the height of the Cyprian crisis of 1956. The Greeks were furious at the Americans. The headlines in the newspapers asked why the Americans were sending a bunch of jazz musicians instead of guns to chase the British out of Cyprus. Gillespie's concert began in a very tense atmosphere. But when the four white and nine black musicians swung into Gillespie's "Tour de Force," written shortly before the tour, the audience broke into wild applause. All Athens was filled with enthusiasm over the Gillespie band, and the political believe that in the whole history of jazz there was a musician more recognized and less understood than he."

"Bird Lives!" This is still true—and especially today. Since the fifties, all the important altoists in jazz have been shaped directly by Parker: Ornette Coleman, Phil Woods, Lee Konitz, Charlie Mariano, Sonny Stitt, Gary Bartz, Jackie McLean, Cannonball Adderley, Anthony Braxton, Oliver Lake, Richie Cole, Arthur Blythe, Paquito D'Rivera, Christopher Hollyday, Greg Osby, Antonio Hart, Stefano di Battista. Around the mideighties, a young musician emerged who has gained status as a kind of "present-day Bird": Steve Coleman.

climate changed so markedly that a newspaper stated, "Dizzy Gillespie is a better diplomat than all the diplomats the U.S.A. ever had in this part of the world."

More than anyone else, Gillespie carried the bop idiom through all subsequent styles and ways of playing: cool and hard bop, free, and rock-influenced—and yet, he remained unmistakably Dizzy Gillespie.

He toured worldwide with his United Nations Orchestra in the eighties and nineties. In this big band, musicians from all over the world combined styles from North and South America and the Caribbean with the legacy of bop. When Gillespie was engaged for an "exclusive concert" at an upscale club in Turkey, he noticed a group of street kids standing outside, peering over the wall. Before he started to play, he asked the club owner to let the young people in, saying "Man, we're here to play for all the people."

He wrote in his autobiography that his greatest wish was to be remembered as a friend of humanity. Gillespie died on January 6, 1993.

Trumpeter Wallace Roney: "No one, not even Miles, was able to take what Dizzy played further. The way Dizzy articulated still hasn't been equaled today."

Saxophonist Joe Lovano says, "For me, Dizzy Gillespie was the most modern player, period. He made so many young trumpeters sound old. Modern doesn't mean

young. Modern means having a
concept and a way of developing your playing that's free. Free,
because you've mastered a deep
concept of melody, harmony, and
rhythm that lets you be creative.
No limits! Jazz is about expression and imagination."

The new bebop had become a major style at the end of the seventies, and,
in the classicism of the eighties and nineties, became so definitive that
"bop" essentially became synonymous with "jazz." Young musicians are
now playing Parker's compositions more frequently than in the fifty years
since his death.

And since the end of the eighties, the bebop renaissance has received
new life in the form of countless reissues of recordings. As different as all
today's young musicians sound, in their playing they all agree with Steve
Reich, who said of Parker that "it's like asking what you think about
Johann Sebastian Bach—he's simply the standard by which everyone else
is measured."

Miles Davis

"Don't we have to admit," asked André Hodeir as early as 1956, "that
the only complete aesthetic achievements since the great period of Parker
and Gillespie belong to Miles Davis?" And the British critic Michael
James stated, "It is no exaggeration to say that never before in jazz had
the phenomenon of loneliness been examined in so intransigent a manner
[as by Miles Davis]."

Our first quotation establishes the historical situation of Davis's music, the second its aesthetic situation. Both were contained, at least up
to the beginning of the seventies, in the sound with which he blew. His
tone—one of great purity, full of softness, almost without vibrato or attack—represented an image of the world; in each sound of Miles this
image was contained.

Davis's sound created an impression of lyrical indifference to the
world and a stimulating mixture of aggression and melancholy. It could
also sound triumphant, but this was a triumph of interiority over the
victorious nature of the trumpet.

Arranger Gil Evans said, "Miles couldn't play like Louis [Armstrong]
because the sound would interfere with his thoughts. Miles had to start
with almost no sound and then develop one as he went along, a sound
suitable for the ideas he wanted to express. He couldn't afford to trust
those thoughts to an old means of expression."

Gil Evans is the man who translated the Miles Davis sound into orchestral terms. Evans arranged for the Claude Thornhill band during the

forties, when Lee Konitz was in the band. He said, "At first, the sound of the band was almost a reduction to an inactivity of music, a stillness . . . everything was moving at a minimum speed . . . and was lowered to create a sound. The sound hung like a cloud."

When improviser Davis and arranger Evans met, it was one of the great moments in the history of jazz. The result was the Miles Davis Nonet, formed for a two-week engagement in September 1948 at the Royal Roost and actually in existence only for those two weeks. "The instrumentation," Evans recalled, "was caused by the fact that this was the smallest number of instruments that could get the sound and still express all the harmonies the Thornhill band used. Miles wanted to play his idiom with that kind of sound." This band consisted of Miles on trumpet, a trombone (J. J. Johnson or Kai Winding), two saxophones (Lee Konitz, alto; Gerry Mulligan, baritone), and, as sound factors, two instruments rarely used in jazz: French horn and tuba. In addition, there was a rhythm section of Al Haig or John Lewis on piano, Joe Shulman or Nelson Boyd on bass, and Max Roach or Kenny Clarke on drums.

Mulligan and Lewis also arranged for this group, but its sound was created by Evans in collaboration with Davis. Evans also arranged its two most significant pieces, "Boplicity" and "Moon Dreams." With these pieces, the texture of sound that became a model for the entire evolution of cool jazz was created. It was, of course, more than just the Thornhill sound with fewer instruments. It was a conscious step back from the melodic and rhythmic complexity of bebop: a darker, more cultivated sound, very gently filled with secrets. Rhythmically, it presented a soft, smooth surface in a way that was almost provocative at the time. The most "modern" piece recorded by this group was "Israel" by John Carisi, a trumpeter and student of the modern symphonic composer, German-born Stefan Wolpe, with whom many first-rate jazz musicians have studied. "Israel" is a minor blues, and characteristically this piece, whose harsh, brittle sounds opened new tonal horizons, remains indebted to the core of the jazz tradition: the blues.

This 1948 Miles Davis Nonet, recorded by Capitol in 1949 and 1950, was bigger than a small group and smaller than a big band. In 1957 Davis went a step further. He recorded with a large orchestra, and naturally he asked Evans—of whom little had been heard in the interim—to do the arrangements. "Gil," says Gerry Mulligan, "is the one arranger I've ever played with who can really notate a thing the way the soloist would blow it." And Miles himself said: "I haven't heard anyone that knocks me out as consistently as he does since Charlie Parker."

For the album *Miles Ahead*, Evans put together a unique big band. There was no saxophone section, but in its place—alongside the conventional trumpets and trombones—there was a strange, unreal-sounding combination of French horns, tuba, alto saxophone, clarinet, bass clarinet, and flute. In some of the pieces—like the title piece, a theme by

Davis—Evans realizes a "continuation" of the Nonet sound; here it becomes apparent which big-band sound the Nonet aimed at: not the sound of Claude Thornhill in the late forties, but rather the sound of this Gil Evans–Miles Davis big band of 1957. It has consciously been stripped of every trace of heated attack. It is calm, lyrical, static—each climax planned way in advance. Broad lines are always preferred, in terms of melody as well as dynamics. But it moves above the old, swinging, pulsating rhythm, laid down by Paul Chambers, bass, and Art Taylor, drums.

The working relationship between Davis and Evans, symbiotic in the best sense of the word, continued until Evans's death in 1988. As an arranger, Evans gave Davis context, structures, and new sounds. For his part, Davis gave Evans the inspiration to break out of his almost mystical withdrawnness, and provided an outstanding soloistic force for his textures. Trumpeter Ian Carr says, "It was a total cooperation. The soloist didn't just understand the score, he took part in its shape and its atmosphere; the composer didn't just understand the soloist, he knew how to intuitively create contexts that expand the soloist's stylistic elements."

Further climaxes in the Evans-Davis collaboration were reached with the album of Gershwin's music from *Porgy and Bess* (1958) and, above all, with the great *Sketches of Spain* (1959), incorporating Spanish, flamenco-conscious compositions. Here, too, Davis made a decisive contribution to a jazz tendency that since has steadily gained in importance: the dialogue between jazz and world music.

There can be no doubt: Davis was an improviser. But he improvised out of a great feeling for arrangement and composition. Probably eighteen-year-old Davis, when he asked Dizzy Gillespie and Charlie Parker how to play right, took Gillespie's advice literally: "Learn to play the piano, man, and then you can figure out crazy solos of your own." Marshall Stearns, who tells of this, concluded, "It was the turning point in the playing of Miles Davis." This fits in with Evans's story of the Royal Roost engagement: "There was a sign outside: 'Arrangements by Gerry Mulligan, Gil Evans, and John Lewis.' Davis had it put in front; no one before had ever done that, given credit in that way to arrangers."

Until the midfifties, Davis had made his most beautiful recordings in quartets, accompanied only by a rhythm section, often with John Lewis or Horace Silver on the piano. Up to that time, he had never had lasting success with audiences. Then, at the 1955 Newport Festival, the turning point came.

All of a sudden, the name of Miles Davis—until then known only to informed fans and critics—could be heard everywhere. From then until his death in 1991, success never left him. For the first time in jazz history, the best-paid and most successful musician of an era was not white, but black—Miles Davis. It is self-evident why Miles became the model for a whole generation of black musicians, not only musically, but in terms of personality as well. Proud black parents—even in Africa—began to name their sons "Miles" or even "Miles Davis."

The quintets Miles Davis led after that are of crucial importance. Two have been particularly influential. The first—with John Coltrane (tenor), Paul Chambers (bass), Red Garland (piano), and Philly Joe Jones (drums)—set standards for those that followed, indeed for all quintets in modern jazz from 1956 to today. After this quintet, which attained peaks of interaction within hard bop between 1955 and 1957, even greater achievement seemed scarcely possible. But Miles Davis was an exception, so just a few years later he got together another quintet that was artistically the equal of the first and perhaps even greater in the interaction of its members. This quintet stayed together from 1964 to 1968—longer than any other of Davis's groups—with young musicians at that time inspired by free jazz: Herbie Hancock (piano), Wayne Shorter (tenor saxophone), Ron Carter (bass), and Tony Williams (drums). People have rightly become used to calling this the "second" Miles Davis Quintet even though it came very much later in the chronology of Davis quintets. Both musically and in terms of the influence exerted and standards set, this group followed from where the first quintet had stopped. The second Miles Davis Quintet was an important model for "acoustic" quintets in the seventies mainstream, and it was by far the chief source of inspiration for the groups involved in the hard-bop revival of the nineties.

A specialty of the "second" Miles Davis Quintet was what were called "pulse pieces." In these pieces, such as "Gingerbread Boy" from the 1966 record *Miles Smiles*, the beat is pulsing and free of accents, independent of bar lines or four-bar formal phrases.

Davis was a bandleader who had the will and the courage to learn from his younger, adventurous, virtuosic sidemen. He was able to digest new developments in the music and then to build on them by communicating to his sidemen his vision of a music yet to be played, like a beacon. "Miles was the only bandleader who paid his musicians not to practice at home," says Wayne Shorter. "Miles wanted it always fresh."

Another greatly influential Davis band was the *Kind of Blue* group (1959) with pianist Bill Evans. Here the new freedom just recently discovered by musicians like Mingus, Coltrane, Evans, and Davis himself for the first time became a group-integrating force, leading to a lyricism and sensitivity unknown in this kind of music until then. The history of over thirty years of jazz combos has been shaped by Miles Davis's groups, indicating the extent to which Davis has influenced the development of modern jazz beyond the realm of the trumpet.

An important factor in Davis's great popularity also is his way of playing the muted trumpet—almost as if he were "breathing" into the microphone through the mute. The solo he recorded in this manner on

Thelonious Monk's "'Round Midnight" was particularly successful; the muted solo on "All of You" has been praised, especially by musicians, as one of the most beautiful jazz solos of the fifties. Even more than his open-horn playing, Miles's muted work makes it apparent that there is no definitive attack. No longer does the sound begin in one definite, clearly stated moment, as it does in traditional jazz and particularly with most other trumpeters. His sound begins in a moment that cannot be grasped; it seems to come out of nowhere, and it ends equally undefined. Without the listener quite knowing when, it fades into nothingness. And yet, as arranger Gil Evans has indicated, this sound, apparently so fragile and timid, contains an incisive intensity, a strength and presence in expression never attained by anyone else on the Harmon mute (a stemless mute made from aluminum). Since Davis first used such a Harmon mute for "Oleo" in 1954, its employment has become so customary in jazz, rock, pop music, and even modern concert music that it must be stressed: Davis first made this sound popular.

Davis's muted trumpet playing close to the microphone showed early traces of two important aspects of his later work: first, his then-developing feeling (in the midfifties!) that electronics are "the continuation of music by other means"; and second, the unconditional striving for success he shares with Louis Armstrong, his true antipode. Davis's ambitions often caused him to listen with special care to and absorb the music of successful players—in the midfifties (as Gunther Schuller has shown) to someone like pianist Ahmad Jamal, in the late sixties to Jimi Hendrix, James Brown, and Sly Stone, and in the eighties to Prince, Michael Jackson, and Cyndi Lauper.

But let's return to the fifties: Davis was the most significant creative musician of a movement in jazz best defined as having applied the findings of bop to Lester Young. The basic difference between Young's music and that of Davis and his followers is that Davis played with the knowledge that between himself and Lester there was bop. André Hodeir's remark, "Miles Davis is the only trumpeter who could give to Parker's music that intimate quality in which lies a considerable part of its charm," may be interpreted in this sense. The "intimate quality" is Lester Young.

This intimate quality was also found in the simplicity of Davis's playing. No other musician in jazz developed simplicity with such refinement and sophistication. The basic contradiction between complexity and simplicity ceased to exist in his playing. Davis made an art out of the conscious control of sound and silence. "Miles was *the* authentic minimalist, (where, although there were so few notes, there was so much *in* those few notes)," as Keith Jarrett, Gary Peacock, and Jack DeJohnette have pointed out. "No matter how much 'noise' there was around him, Miles always came from silence, the notes existing in a purity all of their own." Producer and arranger Quincy Jones said, "Miles always played the most unexpected note, and the one that is the perfect note."

In his desire to play simply, Davis (since the second half of the fifties) tended to free his improvisations from the underlying structure of chord changes. He based his solo work on "scales." About his big-band version of Gershwin's *Porgy and Bess*, Davis said, "When Gil wrote the arrangement of 'I Love You, Porgy,' he only wrote a scale for me to play. No chords. This gives you a lot more freedom and space to hear things." One of Davis's most influential compositions, "So What," is based in its first sixteen measures on a single scale; relieved in the bridge by another scale, it returns to the first scale for the final eight bars.

Davis, and with him John Coltrane, who then was in Davis's Quintet, made this method of improvisation based on scales standard practice for the whole jazz world, thus creating the last step required for the total freedom of free jazz. This is also referred to as "modal" improvisation. (See the section dealing with harmony.)

In his trumpet playing, Davis always seemed to be trying to discover what could be left out. Jazz critic Peter Niklas Wilson correctly observed that Davis's sense of *space* was not a private space but a collective one, a communal space. The often cryptic instructions that Davis gave his musicians "were intended to thin out the music . . . , to create room to listen, to hear each other."

"Don't play what's there," Davis often said to his musicians, "play what's *not* there."

The simple phrases, often consisting of only a few notes, that Davis made up on these modal scales have not only an aesthetic but also a practical basis. From the point of view of instrumental technique, Davis's abilities as a trumpeter were limited, especially when he is compared to his chief competitor among modern classic jazz trumpeters, Dizzy Gillespie, a masterful musician who seems able to execute anything conceivable on his horn. If Davis wanted to maintain himself alongside Gillespie, to top him in popularity, he had to make a virtue of his instrumental limitations. Hence the cult of simplicity.

This "sophistication of simplicity" may be related to the fact that Davis—no matter how many avenues for new possibilities in jazz he may have opened—very often chose tradition when faced with a choice between it and avant-garde. He once complained that pianist Thelonious Monk was playing "wrong chords," though no doubt Monk's chords were not "wrong," but merely more abstract and modern than was suitable to Davis's conception at the time. Davis complained bitterly to the recording director who had hired Monk for a record date. The results, however—whether Davis liked it or not—were some of the most important and artistically successful recorded works of the fifties (Miles Davis, *Bag's Groove*, on the Prestige label).

A further example of Davis's traditionalism is the sharp words with which for years he assessed one of the most important members of the jazz avant-garde, the late Eric Dolphy—some of them insults that Davis had to retract in later years.

When an ultramodern fanatic once called Art Blakey "old-fashioned," Davis said, "If Art Blakey is old-fashioned, then I'm white." About the avant-garde of the sixties, he said, "What's so avant-garde? Lennie Tristano and Lee Konitz were creating ideas fifteen years ago that were stranger than any of these new things. But when they did it, it made sense."

Once, when tenor saxophonist Stan Getz was making some snide remarks about Coleman Hawkins being basically "old-fashioned," Davis rebuked him by pointing out that, if it weren't for Hawk, Getz probably would not be able to play as he did.

Often Davis made harsh judgments—not only about outsiders (which would be understandable), but also about his colleagues. In a "Blindfold Test" with critic Leonard Feather, Davis voiced such gross insults in connection with many well-known jazz musicians that *Down Beat* magazine hesitated to spell out all his four-letter words. Reputable musicians like Clark Terry, Ellington, Dolphy, Jaki Byard, Cecil Taylor, and others were insulted by Davis at that time.

On the other hand, it must be seen that no other musician—with the exception of Charles Mingus, George Russell, and Dolphy—led the "tonal" jazz of the fifties closer and closer to the "free tonal" jazz of the sixties with such increasing consistency as Davis. Justifiably, Dan Morgenstern calls Davis one of the "spiritual fathers" of the new jazz. In the midsixties, the members of the previously mentioned second quintet played "free" or almost free on their own records (mostly on the Blue Note label): Tony Williams (drums), Herbie Hancock (piano), Ron Carter (bass), and Wayne Shorter (tenor)—musicians discussed in the instrument sections. Only Davis himself avoided the final step across the border at that time. But the relevant fact remains that the free tonal musicians also admired him greatly and looked up to him as an example.

Davis's goal in this area of tension between traditionalism and avant-garde was not license, but rather controlled freedom. "Look, you don't need to think to play weird. That ain't no freedom. You need controlled freedom."

With this "controlled freedom," Davis was diametrically opposed to many extreme avant-garde musicians of the sixties. But in the context of the new jazz of the seventies, and to an even greater extent, postmodern jazz since 1980, "controlled freedom" was the actual watchword—no longer just for Davis's music, but for a whole generation of young musicians continuing where Davis's electric jazz (discussed below) only seemingly leaves off.

In 1972 Japanese critic Shoichi Yui went so far as to speak of Davis as the "absolute apex of the development of jazz up to this point." He held that Davis was superior even to Louis Armstrong and Charlie Parker, each of whom led the way in jazz for only a few years, while Davis was the dominating personality from the end of the forties until his death in 1991—"longer than anybody else." Davis always seemed to be a step ahead of the general trend of development in jazz. "It's like a curse—I have to keep changing," he once said.

It is hard to say which is more admirable: the power with which a musician like Parker made a host of creative, new recordings within the span of just a few years in a concentrated, explosive eruption, or the longevity with which Davis, for almost half a century, continued to set new signposts relevant to the majority of jazz musicians.

In order to be able to gain a perspective on this half-century, one should remember that Davis basically went through five different stylistic phases, including all the overlaps and interconnections that, of course, existed between these phases:

1. Bebop: from playing with Charlie Parker from 1945 to 1948.

2. Cool jazz: from the launching of the Miles Davis Nonet in 1948 to the big-band recordings with Gil Evans in 1957–58.

3. Hard bop: from the success of the first Davis quintet with John Coltrane in 1955, via the many subsequent Davis quintets and the sextet with Cannonball Adderley and Bill Evans, to 1963 (during this period, an increasingly clear tendency toward modal improvisation).

4. Controlled freedom: The second Miles Davis quintet (1964–68) abstracted modal playing so that it almost became free jazz without Miles ever completely crossing the dividing line.

5. Electric jazz: from *In a Silent Way* (1969) and *Bitches Brew* (1970) by way of the pared-down funk of *We Want Miles* (1982) to the pop of *You're Under Arrest* (1985) and *Tutu* (1989), through the later hip-hop jazz of *Doo-Bop* (1991).

The term *electric jazz* aptly characterizes the music Davis made since *Bitches Brew,* incorporating electronic sounds. Records like *Jack Johnson* and *Live Evil* also belong to this movement, with such musicians as saxophonist Wayne Shorter and British guitarist John McLaughlin, and, above all, with the collective sound of different pianists playing electric instruments. Among the latter were such players as Chick Corea, Larry Young, Herbie Hancock, Keith Jarrett, the Brazilian Hermeto Pascoal, and the transplanted Viennese Joe Zawinul, who played a special role in this phase of Davis's work. Davis began to electrify his music after he heard Zawinul playing the electric piano in Cannonball Adderley's 1966 hit "Mercy, Mercy, Mercy."

Even more important, however, were the impulses given by rock and funk musicians like Jimi Hendrix, James Brown, and Sly Stone. Davis's electric music of the seventies set a standard for musical excellence that rock musicians would do well to learn from. At the same time, he made jazz accessible to a young audience coming from rock. Filled with self-assurance, Davis declared that he could form a better rock group than even Jimi Hendrix.

Davis's change-over from "acoustic" to electric jazz didn't occur all of a sudden; it was the outcome of a prolonged process of feeling his way and experimenting, leading to innumerable studio sessions between 1967 and 1970.

Davis's circumspect and highly cautious approach to this transition suffices to refute the critical charge that with his 1970 *Bitches Brew* he had decided to "sell out." Davis was not an unconditional innovator. The fact that he put off and held back from stylistic changes until they finally became unavoidable accords with his basically conservative nature. "Do you know why I don't play ballads any more?" he asked pianist Keith Jarrett at the start of the seventies. "It's because I love to play them so much."

With its electric sounds and its bubbling keyboard textures, its hypnotic ostinatos and grooves, *Bitches Brew* was a radical departure from any conventional jazz aesthetic. The creation of moods and grooves, atmospheres and textures, was more important than the perfect solo. And here again, Miles's sense of space became a central principle of organization. Guitarist Carlos Santana says that he learned from *Bitches Brew* "that you have to let the music breathe, and that space is the way to make a rock guitar solo sound like something different than a machine gun." With *Bitches Brew*, even more than in the earlier *In a Silent Way*, the recording studio itself plays a key role as an instrument alongside the others. And the player of this instrument, who became Davis's key collaborator, was Teo Macero. The creative contribution that Macero (a Juilliard-trained composer) made to the electric Miles recordings has never been properly acknowledged, but his influence on Miles's music of the seventies is perhaps comparable to the influence that Gil Evans had in the forties and fifties with his refined tone colors: both created a context that let Davis develop his potential to its fullest.

The working approach that Davis and Macero developed in the studio was to always have the tape running, whether during rehearsal or an official "take." After the band had jammed something in the studio, Davis and Macero would reassemble the material, using tape editing, loops, echo and reverb, delay, and phase shifting to create a new sonic fantasy after the fact—a way of creating a composition from recorded improvisations.

Recalling the *Bitches Brew* recording sessions in his autobiography, Miles said, "It was just like one of those old-time jam sessions we used to have up at Minton's back in the old bebop days." The subtle difference was that tape editing was used to create a structure later from what was originally a spontaneous session.

Some critics made the accusation that Davis played only a small part in the tape-editing process, leaving most of it to Macero, who was considered a "Paganini of tape cutting." But Miles never left any room for doubt as to who the captain of the ship was—he always had the last word. One of Miles's greatest strengths lay in the freedom that he allowed his musicians. Davis's and Macero's collaborative adventure in tape editing began in 1969, with the piece "Circle in the Round," released in 1979 on the record of the same name, and reached a first high point with *Bitches Brew*. From then on, the combination of Miles's reduction to the essential and Macero's compositional abilities as an editor set the direction for electric jazz.

From 1968 to 1975, Davis's music developed and changed so rapidly that his label, Columbia, could barely keep up with it in the records they released. The album *On the Corner* made excessive use of loops, delays, and wah-wah effects. It was distressing not just to jazz critics, but also to musicians and general listeners. Miles's biographer Bill Cole called it "an insult to the intellect of the people." Saxophonist Stan Getz complained, "It sounded like they were gathering at the elephant graveyard. . . . That music is worthless. It means nothing, there is no form, no content, and it barely swings."

On the Corner was a further revaluation of all jazz values. Many of the elements that had been so important in Miles's music up to that time (despite all his innovations), such as improvisation and melody, receded into the background. Grooves and textures took on even more importance. Many DJs of the later remix scene have said that *On the Corner*, and Davis's other electric recordings, anticipated what today's turntablists are doing with loops, samples, and grooves. Creative "ambient" musicians, such as Brian Eno, and "trance" musicians have acknowledged the strong influence that Miles's electric music of the seventies had on them.

One of Davis's fans once approached him during his electric phase and said to him, "Miles, you're my man, but I don't get this new thing you're playing." Miles immediately replied: "Am I supposed to wait for you?"

What is interesting is the fact that Miles Davis's music (after *In a Silent Way*, which was indeed a study in silence) became more and more percussive, particularly after he hired the percussion player Mtume, a man inspired by African music. Davis paid tribute to the opening of jazz to world music by using Indian instruments like the sitar and tabla drums.

Miles now played trumpet with a wah-wah pedal and through an amplifier. In most cases, the pure, clear, "lonely," always somewhat sad sound of the earlier Miles is hardly recognizable. He explored the wah-

wah pedal to the limits of its technical and musical possibilities. No one who plays an electrically amplified trumpet today can do so without referring to Davis's results.

Davis, the electric trumpeter, has sometimes been accused of breaching jazz tradition. In fact his use of the wah-wah pedal brings the jazz trumpet full circle. This electronic equipment was originally devised to allow rock guitar players to achieve effects corresponding to the wah-wah sounds—the rough growl and muted effects—of brass. Miles's use of the wah-wah pedal was nothing but a return to the jungle sounds of Ellington trumpeters Bubber Miley and Cootie Williams, of course modified and transformed into the electronic age's awareness of sound.

From an orchestral point of view, the electric Miles was also more strongly connected to the jazz tradition than many critics, brought up on conventional jazz sounds, were willing to admit. At the end of the sixties, Davis and Evans had talked about putting together a big band, but financial obstacles prevented them from realizing this idea. With the arrival of electronic instruments, Miles as a bandleader had for the first time his own orchestral possibilities, and he exploited them to their full extent on his records, in his use of the Fender Rhodes piano, electric organ, electric guitar, and the possibilities of the recording studio.

Davis is nowhere closer to his idol Duke Ellington than in the futuristic experiments of his early jazz-rock period. Like Ellington and his orchestra, the electric Miles became a master of the manipulation of tone colors. But his records were not a conservative look back at the heritage of jazz, but rather offered new sound worlds, sonic utopias for contemporary society.

The electrifying success of the "electronic Miles" led to a point when the world of rock and popular music wanted to seize upon Miles Davis. In the summer of 1970, when he was supposed to play with rock musicians like Eric Clapton and Jack Bruce at the Randall's Island Festival in New York, Miles had music people all over the world holding their breath for several weeks, but then he said no; he wouldn't play except with his own group. "I don't want to be a white man. Rock is a white man's word."

Miles Davis had the same kind of leadership position in the jazz scene of the early seventies as Louis Armstrong or Charlie Parker had during earlier jazz periods. But he did not play his role with Satchmo's natural ease. Davis, exactly like Armstrong, wanted to "make it" with a large audience. But he reflected the pride, self-assurance, and determination to protest of the black generation of his time. He played "black music," but he also had to acknowledge the fact that his audience—the buyers of his records and the listeners at his concerts—was mainly white. In a revealing interview with Michael Watts of the London publication *Melody Maker*, Miles said, "I don't care who buys the records as long as they get to the black people so I will be remembered when I die. I'm not playing for any white people, man. I wanna hear a black guy say, 'Yeah, I dig Miles Davis.'"

The cover of Miles's album *On the Corner*, for instance, consciously aimed—according to the trumpeter's express wishes—at the black market: a comic-strip-style display of a group of dancing, "hip" street blacks, with slogans like "Vote Miles" and "Free Me" on their shirts and hats.

Again and again, he said to dozens of critics and reporters, "I just do what I feel like doing." He sometimes played with his back to the audience. Miles said, "What should I do? Smile at 'em?" And then comes the sentence that reappears so often: "I just do what I feel like doing."

Davis's charisma often took astounding forms. Miles was involved in violent public encounters twice. Once, gangsters shot at him when he was sitting with a woman in his parked car in Brooklyn. He set a reward of ten thousand dollars for the capture of the two assailants. Nobody collected the reward, but a few weeks later, the two gangsters were mysteriously shot.

Several years earlier, Miles was standing in front of the Birdland club on Broadway when a white policeman asked him to move on, then hit him over the head with a club. "The cop was killed, too. In a subway," Miles claimed.

His attitude toward the white world was totally unconciliatory, and thus stood in contrast to the models up to that time for the way that African American musicians had dealt with the white establishment. The blunt, brusque manner in which, even in the fifties, Davis spoke out about racism and discrimination made him something of an iconic figure in the struggle to improve living conditions for African Americans. Trumpeter Eddie Henderson tells the story of a 1961 club appearance at San Francisco's Blackhawk: "One night, a woman of southern persuasion kept heckling Miles to play 'Bye Bye, Blackbird.' She kept insisting and Miles kept looking at her funny. So Miles walks off the stage and tells Guido [the club owner], 'Get this bitch out of here,' and Guido got her out of there and then Miles played 'Bye Bye, Blackbird.'"

Miles Davis was a devoted sports car fan. In 1972 he broke both ankles in an accident. After that, and especially after hip surgery some time later, he rarely appeared in public. This retreat into seclusion certainly involved musical and psychological as well as medical reasons. He wanted to be "the greatest," not just because he'd become used to that but because this aspiration was the mainspring of his musical and personal development. In the midseventies, Miles's music had become so ornate and disoriented that he could no longer be sure of his preeminence.

After 1972 Davis's music became ever denser, more African and percussive: the spacious keyboard sounds of *In a Silent Way* and *Bitches Brew* gave way to dark, claustrophobically dense forests of percussion, with hypnotic funk rhythms and bass riffs. Miles now often had all the instruments (except the percussionists) play with wah-wah pedals. The result was a cooking, seething cosmos of exploding rhythms and sounds in which the Miles Davis Group sounded like a West African drum ensemble transposed into the age of rock and electronics. Amid such extreme density, hardly any space remained for the unique Miles Davis radiance, and, his health declining, he played his trumpet less and less. Everything in Miles's music from 1972 pointed toward a withdrawal, and yet the shock impact was considerable when in 1975 he quit the scene for six years. It wasn't just coincidental that this period of silence was also the time when fusion and jazz-rock stagnated most strikingly.

"Let's all just *forget* about Miles Davis, huh?" wrote an irritated *Down Beat* reader in 1980 when there were innumerable rumors about the possibility of the trumpeter's comeback. "I'm so sick and tired of readers bitching and moaning about his lack of new recordings and his apparent disdain for his audience. . . . Miles is not a god." Yet Miles was treated like a god when, after six years of expectation and speculation, he finally made his comeback at the 1981 New York Jazz Festival. He played great music, driving his group of predominantly young musicians to a climax of glowing, incandescent beauty. He blew more and better trumpet, without distancing electronic equipment, than in the years before his withdrawal. At last it was there again: the warm, dark Davis glow—simultaneously triumphant and resigned.

Stylistically there was nothing new. Miles Davis still played jazz-rock and fusion, stimulated, it's true, by eighties funk rhythms and pop sounds, but time and again interwoven with flashbacks: from the early fusion Miles back by way of the *Porgy and Bess* phase at the end of the fifties to the blues Miles of cool jazz and hard bop. It was obvious that Davis had lived in such isolation that he was unaware of how much had in the meantime changed through such manifestations as noise music, free funk, and world music.

The jazz world expected superhuman feats from Miles. He had already changed the course of jazz three times—it wasn't fair to demand that he do so a fourth time. Davis had done enough.

After his comeback, Miles's jazz-rock became more and more transparent. This tendency toward increasing clarity was reflected in the movement away from sonic ritual, back to a rediscovery of the song. The hypnotic tangles of percussion and sonic fog banks of the seventies disappeared. Psychedelic ambiguity gave way to the clarity of groove and song structures. Davis gave up the wah-wah pedal and echo effects, concentrating again on playing with the Harmon mute.

The high points in this phase of economically played jazz-rock occurred between 1980 and 1985. During that period he produced, in pure and undistorted fashion, what was constantly promised but hidden by his predilection for sonic experimenation: vital, gripping, crisp funk, with interludes of swing feeling, remembrances of the blues, and a deliberately interactive approach among the musicians. Of importance here were his various groups with drummer Al Foster (who had already played with Miles in the seventies), electric bassist Marcus Miller, and guitarists Mike Stern and John Scofield. They in particular concentrated funk on the essentials, exerting an enormously passionate, gripping, and concentrated impact. The album *We Want Miles* (1982) was a climax in this interactive, economically played funk, and was awarded a Grammy. They set standards for group cohesion—a virtue by no means taken for granted in jazz-rock up to that time. Davis's view became a leading principle in eighties jazz-rock: "It must be a team."

Also important are the albums *Decoy* (1983) and *You're Under Arrest* (1984–85), on which Miles developed a highly chromatic version of funk. The material for the pieces was often derived (e.g., in the piece "What It Is") from solos by guitarist John Scofield, whose angular, blues-inflected chromatic and melodic lines were transcribed by Gil Evans and other musicians and arranged to form new melodies.

After 1984 Miles's music was increasingly influenced by pop. Recordings like *Tutu* and *Amandla* finally made him a superstar of jazz. He might have found inspiration in eighties pop music—Michael Jackson, Ashford & Simpson, and above all Prince—after his comeback, but it was in 1984 that Miles started to take over pop hits (including Michael Jackson's "Human Nature" and Cyndi Lauper's "Time After Time"), playing them almost literally, which didn't exactly please jazz fans. The more he turned toward the song forms of contemporary popular music, the more obviously he put his concept of lean, collectively improvised jazz-rock on the back burner.

As early as the fifties, Miles had taken up popular songs and integrated them into his jazz repertoire. "My Funny Valentine" and "Autumn Leaves" were nothing but pop songs at the time, but critics have rightly shown that Davis cultivated them through the brilliant flights of his improvisations, thereby elevating them to new levels of quality. But in the eighties, it seemed as if he were merely copying pop hits note for note. Davis was said to have lost his ability to make something artistically worthwhile out of the simple songs of pop music.

Yet there's no doubt that simply through the expressive power of his sound, Miles did make something new out of these songs. Pianist Keith Jarrett correctly says that Davis's achievement consists of the fact that "sound itself can say as much, if not more, than a lot of phrases." Anyone who from the sound of a single note can create the expressiveness for which others require torrents of notes doesn't need to resort to digressive improvisation.

On *Tutu* (1986), arranged and produced by electric bassist Marcus Miller, Miles increasingly returned to melody. The sonic picture is more and more dominated by polyphonic synthesizers and drum machines, more use is made of samples, and the studio production includes more and more overdubs, with limited space for improvising.

For these reasons, critics, comparing Davis's early electric music to his music of the eighties and nineties, tried to find a "break" between the adventurous, avant-garde jazz-rock he played in the seventies and the more melodic, "poppier" Miles of the eighties and nineties. But the "pop" Miles was just as close—maybe even closer—to the sources of his music than in his earlier electric phase. When, between 1968 and 1983, he played highly abstract music, he relied on two of his main strengths: his inimitable trumpet sound and his capacity for melodic invention. Guitarist John Scofield: "After so many years of playing really 'out' music, it was great to hear him play songs again. People were so happy to hear him play a melody again."

Trombonist J. J. Johnson: "Miles is doing his natural thing. He's putting it in today's setting, on his own terms. If you put Miles and his new group in the studio and record them on separate mikes, and then you cut the band track and you just played the trumpet track, you know what you'd have? The same old Miles. What's new is the frame of reference."

In the eighties and nineties, Miles Davis was closer to Louis Armstrong than ever before. He started his career soundwise as an antipode to Satchmo, but he ended it as Armstrong's fellow. Both broke through the division between jazz and pop, showing the way ahead. Just as Satchmo once filled the songs and hits of popular music with jazz feeling, so too did Miles Davis breathe life into pop music.

As a soloist, after his comeback Miles experienced peaks and valleys in close proximity. There were moments when his playing attained moving splendor and dazzling greatness, as in "Back Seat Betty" (1982), a textbook example of how a solo should be developed in jazz-rock, or—even more impressively—in a blues ("It Gets Better," 1983) where he blows an enthralling long solo that sparked off a renaissance for slowly played blues in eighties jazz. But you couldn't help hearing when Miles's playing was off form, and the fragility of his intonation was sometimes so obvious that only Davis's phenomenal sound spared him from what would have happened to other trumpeters in similar circumstances.

More important than the soloist in the eighties was Miles Davis the orchestrator and catalyst of groups. He possessed the rare gift of achieving extraordinary cohesion among a band, charging it with human and musical intensity without having to give special instructions. For Keith Jarrett and Jack DeJohnette, Miles the bandleader was "a medium, a transformer, a touchstone, a magnetic field." Other musicians who played in his bands are astonishingly unanimous that Miles's presence was so strong that it alone was sufficient to release powers and abilities no one, least of all themselves, ever thought they had.

The most striking aspect of his comeback, however, was that Miles Davis demonstrated fresh characteristics as a human being. To the astonishment of his listeners, he now gave the audience a friendly wave. He made fun of himself on stage. He demonstratively hugged his musicians after a good solo. He was now so obliging toward jazz fans and journalists that hardly anyone would think that this used to be the reclusive, contemptuous Miles. "Yes," he confessed to journalist Cheryl McCall, "I'm an entertainer."

"If I ever look back, I'll die," Davis once said. In 1991 he looked back, twice in quick succession: in retrospective concerts at jazz festivals in Montreux and in Paris at La Villette. In Montreux he played the legendary music that he had recorded at the end of the fifties with his musical soul mate, Gil Evans. Supported by a hand-picked orchestra conducted by Quincy Jones, he played pieces from the albums *Birth of the Cool*, *Miles Ahead*, *Porgy and Bess*, and *Sketches of Spain*. In Paris, at the La Villette festival, he appeared with a selection of world-class players who had come through his working bands and who paid tribute to their mentor with music from his long career, from cool to pop. They included John McLaughlin, Herbie Hancock, Joe Zawinul, Wayne Shorter, Chick Corea, Dave Holland, Al Foster, and John Scofield.

Twelve weeks later, Miles was dead. He died on September 28, 1991. Paul Tingen wrote: "Rather than dramatize the situation, and assume that he died because he looked back, it appears that he looked back because he was aware that he was dying."

Miles died before finishing production work on the album *Doo-Bop*, a mixture of jazz and hip-hop. Nonetheless, in the jazz world it was taken as an act of compensating justice for the album to be released posthumously. Many hip-hop productions had imitated Davis and his trademarks, such as his playing with the Harmon mute, often via cutting and sampling. Now it was only fitting for the original to reply with his own mixture of hip-hop beats and trumpet solos. And Miles made his reply in the brilliant manner that was his, uninfluenced by the stiff backbeats added later by producer Easy Mo Bee.

"You want me to tell you where I was born—that old story?" Miles once responded when he was relatively young, in the fifties. "It was in good old Alton, Illinois, in 1926. I had to call my mother a week before my last birthday and ask her how old I would be. . . .

"There was a very good instructor in town. He was having some dental work done by my father. . . . 'Play without any vibrato,' he used to tell us. 'You're going to get old anyway and start shaking.' . . . That's how I tried to play—fast and light, and no vibrato.

"By the time I was sixteen . . . Sonny Stitt came to town with a band and heard [me] play. He told me: 'You look like a man named Charlie Parker and you play like him, too. Come with us.'

"The fellows in his band had their hair slicked down, they wore tuxedos, and they offered me sixty whole dollars a week to play with them.

I went home and asked my mother if I could go with them. She said no, I had to finish my last year of high school. I didn't talk to her for two weeks. And I didn't go with the band, either.

"I knew about Charlie Parker in St. Louis—I even played with him there, while I was still in high school. We always used to try to play like Diz and Charlie Parker.

"When we heard that they were coming to town, my friend and I were the first people in the hall, me with a trumpet under my arm. Diz walked up to me and said, 'Kid, you have a union card?' I said, 'Sure.' So I sat in with the band that night. I couldn't read a thing from listening to Diz and Bird.

"Then the third trumpet man got sick. I knew the book because I loved the music so much I knew the third part by heart. So I played with the band for a couple of weeks. I just *had* to go to New York then. . . .

"A friend of mine was studying at Juilliard, so I decided to go there, too. I spent my first week in New York and my first month's allowance looking for Charlie Parker.

"I roomed with Charlie Parker for a year. I used to follow him around, down to Fifty-Second Street where he used to play. Then he used to get me to play. 'Don't be afraid,' he used to tell me. 'Go ahead and play.'. . .

"If you can hear a note, you can play it. The note I hit that sounds high, that's the only one I can play right then—the only note I can think of to play that would fit. You don't learn to play the blues. You just play. . . .

"Do I like composing better than playing? I can't answer that. There's a certain feeling you get from playing that you can't get from composing. And when you play, it's like a composition anyway."

John Coltrane and Ornette Coleman

The jazz of the sixties was dominated by two towering personalities: John Coltrane, who died quite unexpectedly in July 1967, and Ornette Coleman. One must appreciate the difference between these two in order to realize the extent of their influence and appreciate the scope of the expressive possibilities of the new jazz. Neither man is a revolutionary, and if the effect of their work nevertheless was such, this was not their wish. Both came from the South: Coleman was born in Texas in 1930, Coltrane in North Carolina in 1926. Both are solidly rooted in the blues tradition: Coleman more in the country tradition of the folk blues, Coltrane more in the urban rhythm and blues tradition.

Coltrane had a relatively solid musical education within the limits possible for a member of the black lower middle class (his father was a tailor). Coleman's parents were too poor to be able to afford music lessons for him; Ornette acquired his musical tools on his own. No one told him that a saxophone is notated differently than it is tuned. So, at the age of fourteen to fifteen—a crucial phase in his development—he played everything written "wrong" in the academic sense. Critic Martin Williams takes this to be a decisive reason for the harmonic uniqueness Coleman displayed from the start.

Whenever young Ornette played, he made a kind of music whose harmonies, sound, and instrumental technique could be placed only with difficulty within the conventional framework of jazz, blues, and rhythm 'n' blues—that is, within the musics to which he related most in terms of style, inclination, expression, and origins. He remembered, "Most musicians didn't take to me; they said I didn't know the changes and was out of tune." He said about one of his first leaders, singer-guitarist Pee Wee Crayton, to whose rhythm and blues band he belonged, "He didn't understand what I was trying to do, and it got so he was paying me not to play." Nightclub owner and bassist Howard Rumsey recalled, "Everybody—the musicians, I mean—would panic when you'd mention Ornette. People would laugh when his name was brought up." This is placed in correct perspective if we remember that Lester Young in the Fletcher Henderson band and young Charlie Parker in Kansas City triggered similar reactions.

In contrast, Coltrane—or, as he was called, "Trane"—was accepted from the start. His first professional job was in 1947 with the Joe Webb rhythm 'n' blues band from Indianapolis, with singer Big Maybelle. After that, he played mainly in better-known groups, mostly for lengthy periods—Eddie "Cleanhead" Vinson (1947–48), Dizzy Gillespie (1949–51), Earl Bostic (1952–53), Johnny Hodges (1953–54), until, in 1955, Miles Davis hired him for his quintet and he gained immediate fame with his solo on "'Round Midnight." It must be clearly understood: he was accepted and successful within the jazz that was accepted and successful at the time.

Ornette Coleman's emergence, however, came as a shock. He had to take work as an elevator operator in Los Angeles because the musicians would not accept him. Since his elevator was seldom in demand, he would stop it on the top floor and study his harmony books. Then, in 1958–59, producer Lester Koenig recorded the first two Coleman albums for his Contemporary label: *Something Else: The Music of Ornette Coleman* and *Tomorrow Is the Question*. A few months later, Coleman attended the Lenox School of Jazz. Many famous musicians were teaching there: Milt Jackson, Max Roach, Bill Russo, Gunther Schuller, John Lewis. Yet, after a few days of the summer courses, the unknown student Ornette Coleman had attracted more attention than all the famous teachers.

Right away, John Lewis decided that "Ornette Coleman is doing the only really new thing in jazz since the innovations of Dizzy Gillespie and Charlie Parker in the forties and since Thelonious Monk." The leader of the Modern Jazz Quartet described the way Coleman played on his plastic alto with his friend Don Cherry, who used a miniature trumpet, as follows: "They're almost like twins. . . . I can't imagine how they manage to start together. Never before have I heard that kind of ensemble playing."

Although Coleman was not at all trying to bring about a musical revolution—he always only wanted to make his own music, and otherwise be left alone—there was suddenly the feeling in the jazz world of 1959 that this was a turning point, that a new style was beginning with Ornette Coleman: "He is the new Bird!"

The harmonic freedom characteristic of all the music played and composed by Coleman has been particularly well described by George Russell:

> Ornette seems to depend mostly on the overall tonality of the song as a point of departure for melody. By this I don't mean the key the music might be in. . . . I mean that the melody and the chords of his compositions have an overall sound, which Ornette seems to use as a point of departure. This approach liberates the improviser to sing his own song, really, without having to meet the deadline of any particular chord.

Ornette himself feels that the rules of a music must be found within the musician himself rather than being based on harmonic principles imposed from outside. "When you get up on the morning, you have to put your clothes on before you can go out and get on with your day. But your clothes don't tell you where to go; they go where you go. A melody is like your clothes."

He called this his "harmolodic system": each harmony is, as this name suggests, established only by the melodic line. The system has influenced many other jazz musicians, such as guitarist James "Blood" Ulmer, and also the teaching at the Creative Music Studio of German-born vibraharpist Karl Berger, in Woodstock, New York.

The harmonic freedom that Coleman had achieved from the start in a manner self-evident to him, John Coltrane had to struggle for in a slow, laborious development spanning an entire decade: from the first cautious attempts at "modality" with Miles Davis in 1956 to *Ascension* in 1965.

It is a fascinating, exciting "adventure in jazz" to follow, via recordings, the logical consistency of this process of development. In the beginning stands the encounter with Miles Davis and modality. That means no more improvisation on constantly changing chords, but rather on a "scale" that, unchangingly, underlies the whole melodic activity. It was a first step into freedom. In spite of the tense, aware attention with which the jazz world was observing this development in all its phases, it was never made clear precisely whether Davis or Coltrane had taken the first step. This is fitting, because the step was not taken consciously. It "happened"—as something does that is "in the air."

The second phase, beginning in 1957, was the collaboration with Thelonious Monk (though Trane returned to Miles after that; only in 1960 did he permanently separate from him). Coltrane himself was best qualified to discuss Monk: "Sometimes he would be playing a different set of altered changes from those that I'd be playing, and neither one of us would be playing the changes to the tune. We would reach a certain spot and if we got there together we'd be lucky. And then Monk would come back in to save everybody. A lot of people used to ask us how we remembered all that stuff, but we weren't remembering so much. Just the basic changes and everybody tried anything they wanted to."

It was around this time that Coltrane developed what Ira Gitler named "sheets of sound," the playing of many notes so rapidly so as to create an impression of a unified sonic expanse. This was best described by LeRoi Jones (now Amiri Baraka): "That is, the notes that Trane was playing in the solo became more than just one note following another. The notes came so fast, and with so many overtones and undertones, that they had the effect of a piano player striking chords rapidly but somehow articulating separately each note in the chord, and its vibrating subtones."

Many of the recordings that Coltrane made in the second half of the fifties for Blue Note or Prestige are exemplary for this way of playing—on Prestige, for example, with the Red Garland Trio; on Blue Note, for instance, *Blue Train*. The critic John S. Wilson wrote that "he often plays his tenor sax as if he were determined to blow it apart." In *Jazz Review*, Zita Carno coined that often-quoted sentence: "The only thing you can, and should, expect from John Coltrane is the unexpected." It is one of the few statements about Coltrane that are equally true about all his stages.

The critics at that time overlooked a fact musicians probably felt instinctively—that the sheets of sound had an immediate rhythmic effect that was at least as important as the harmonic effect: If the notes were no longer definable as eighths, sixteenths, or thirty-seconds, becoming more like quintuplets, septuplets, and nonuplets, then the symmetry of the relationship to the underlying meter was gone, too. The sheets of sounds, therefore, were a step toward substituting for the simple regularity of the conventional beat the flowing, vibrating quality of the pulse—a conception that Elvin Jones, starting in 1960, arrived at in the Coltrane Quartet, and young Tony Williams, beginning in 1963, in the Miles Davis Quintet.

When Coltrane signed exclusively with Atlantic Records in 1960, the sheets of sounds soon moved into the background—although, until his death, Trane on many occasions proved that he had not lost the technical ability necessary to play them. Instead of "shreds of sounds" and sheets of sounds, there was a strong concentration on melody: long, widely curved lines that condensed and dissolved according to an immanent, nonapparent principle of tension and relaxation. One had the feeling that Coltrane first had to supply the harmonic and rhythmic prerequisites so that he could deal more exclusively with the musical dimension that interested him most—melody. It was Coltrane the melody man who for the first time had a real hit with a large audience—with "My Favorite Things," in its original version a somewhat simple-minded waltz from a Richard Rodgers musical. Coltrane played the piece on the soprano sax with the nasal sound of a shinai (an Indian double-reed instrument) or a zoukra (a kind of Arab oboe). From the constant, always just slightly altered repetition of the notes of the theme, he built an accelerating monotony previously unknown in jazz, but akin to aspects of Indian and Arabic musics.

Around this time, he claimed that Eastern and Asiatic music interested him, and he proved it a year later (1961) with *Olé Coltrane* (which is also inspired by Spanish-Moorish music) on the Atlantic label. After he had moved to the Impulse label, on the momentum of his success with *My Favorite Things*, he made further records of the same orientation: in *Africa Brass* (1961) he reflected his impressions of Arab music, and in *India* (1961), with the late Eric Dolphy on bass clarinet, of classical Indian music. Just how much he admired Indian music is shown by the fact that a few years later he named his second son Ravi—after Ravi Shankar, the great Indian sitar player.

It is certainly not presumptuous to believe that Coltrane—considering that conventional tonality, stemming from European music, had meanwhile been stretched almost to the breaking point—found in the modes of Indian and Arab musics a freedom and openness that Western functional harmony, no matter how expanded, could not offer. Under the influence of Indian music, Coltrane increasingly broke with the system of chord-dominated music. Instead, beginning with "My Favorite Things," he made playing around a drone, or several drones, the central element of his music.

From 1960 on, Coltrane led a quartet including—with occasional substitutions or additions—Elvin Jones (drums) and McCoy Tyner (piano). The bass spot changed several times—a sign of Coltrane's continually developing conception of the basic harmonic (and rhythmic) tasks of the bassist. From Steve Davis, he went first to Art Davis, then to Reggie Workman, and finally to Jimmy Garrison—the only musician whom Coltrane retained in his quartet until the end, even after the great change of 1965. Incidentally, Coltrane was fond of using two bassists.

This John Coltrane Quartet—with, above all, Jimmy Garrison—was a perfect group. It followed the intentions of its leader with marvelous empathy, up to the crucial change in 1965. At that point, Coltrane needed a totally "free" drummer—Rashied Ali—and an equally "free" pianist—he chose his wife, Alice Coltrane.

Before that, in 1964, a record was created that for many is the apex of Coltrane's work: *A Love Supreme*—a singular, great prayer of hymnic intensity. Coltrane wrote the lyrics himself: "Let us sing all songs to God to whom all praise is due. . . . I will do all I can to be worthy of Thee o Lord. . . . I thank You God. . . . Words, sounds, speech, men, memory, thoughts, fear and emotions—time—all related. . . . They all go back to God." At the end of this prayer appear the three words that most aptly characterize the music the quartet plays to these lyrics: "elation, elegance, exaltation."

An outsider may not have expected such religious testimony from the then most-discussed modern jazz musician. But Coltrane, not unlike Duke Ellington, frequently dealt with religious matters during his varied career. In 1957 Coltrane had an experience of religious awakening that enabled him to overcome his heroin addiction. He said that he experienced, through the grace of God, "a spiritual awakening." And in 1962 he said, "I believe in all religions," to which LeRoi Jones commented that music for Trane was "a way into God." Many of his recordings have titles inspired by religion. One of them is called *OM*. According to Nat Hentoff, "To Coltrane, however, music—his reason for being in music—was to become part of the source of consciousness from the beginning of time. . . . To John, *OM* was 'the first vibration—that sound, that spirit which set everything else into being,' and he wanted to connect, to enter into, that universal, transcendent peace."

Coltrane saw religion as a hymn of praise to the cosmos that is God, and to God who is the cosmos. The psalmlike monotony that builds whole movements of the four-part *Love Supreme* on a single chord (a drone), and in this manner seems to lead from nowhere to everywhere, is for him an expression of infinity as sound. In many records made after that, Coltrane again took up religious topics, for instance, in *Meditations*. "Father, Son, and Holy Ghost" and "Love"—religious love—are two of the movements on this album.

In the meantime, the culmination of a process that had been going on for years—at first unnoticed by the jazz public—and the real jazz surprise of the winter of 1964–65 had taken place: John Coltrane, personally and musically, had joined the New York avant-garde. In March 1965 he played at the New York Village Gate in a musically, as well as socially and politically, revealing free-jazz concert of "new black music," produced as a benefit performance for LeRoi Jones's short-lived Black Arts Repertory Theatre/School.

On several records, Coltrane employed the star quality of his name to help young, little-known, uncompromising free-jazz musicians reach a wider audience. And recordings made by tenor saxophonist Archie Shepp at the Newport Jazz Festival of that year were coupled with a Coltrane performance on the Impulse label. This meant the decisive breakthrough for Shepp.

A few days before the Newport Festival, on June 28, 1965, *Ascension* was produced. This was Coltrane's first record to be tonally "free." Coltrane gathered almost all the important musicians of the New York avant-garde: three tenormen—Trane himself, Pharoah Sanders, and Archie Shepp; two trumpeters, Freddie Hubbard and Dewey Johnson; two altoists, John Tchicai and Marion Brown; two bassists, Art Davis and Jimmy Garrison; and McCoy Tyner on piano and Elvin Jones on drums. Marion Brown, attempting to describe the mad intensity of *Ascension*, which at the time seemed to strain the limits of the appreciable and physically tolerable, said, "You could use this record to heat up the apartment on those cold winter days." It is hymnlike, ecstatic music of the intensity of a forty-minute orgasm.

With *Ascension* Coltrane reached a harmonic freedom Coleman had achieved many years before. However, how much more overpowering, gripping, aggressive is the freedom of *Ascension*! It is what the title implies: an ascension into heaven, from humanity to God, taking in both— the divine and the human, the whole cosmos.

Compared to that, Ornette's freedom seems lyrical, quiet, melodious. It is illuminating that the structure of *Ascension*, consciously or unconsciously, follows a structural scheme Coleman had used five years earlier on his record *Free Jazz* (Atlantic). (This was where that term, later applied to so much of the jazz of the sixties, appeared for the first time: on a 1961 album by Ornette Coleman!) It was a collective improvisation by a double quartet, in which the Coleman Quartet (Don Cherry, trumpet; Scott La Faro, bass; Billy Higgins, drums) faced another quartet (Eric Dolphy, bass clarinet; Freddie Hubbard, trumpet; Charlie Haden, bass; Ed Blackwell, drums). From the dense complexity of collective parts rubbing against each other, a solo emerged that led to another set of collective playing, from which was born—in precisely that sense: free solos born in painful labor—the next solo.

During the years when Coltrane underwent his dynamic development, breathlessly attended by the jazz world, things became relatively quiet for Ornette Coleman. For two years, he lived in nearly total seclusion in New York.

It has been said that he played so little then because he was unable to find work. But the opposite is true: he was showered with tempting offers but did not want to play in public. He was developing his music; he composed and learned to play two new instruments: trumpet and violin. He also worked on compositions for string quartet (which he gave Béla Bartók–like sounds) and for other chamber music ensembles—among them the score for Conrad Rooks's film *Chappaqua*. The director found himself wondering if he should use music "in itself so beautiful," and feared that it would take away from the force of the film. Rooks commissioned a new score from Ravi Shankar and Ornette's *Chappaqua*—scored for Coleman's trio, Pharoah Sanders (tenor), and a chamber ensemble of eleven musicians—was released only as a record (on Columbia).

In early 1965, Coleman reentered public life at the Village Vanguard. Only now was the album Coleman had recorded before his voluntary retirement (in 1962 at a concert at New York's Town Hall) released (on ESP). Further Coleman records were made in Europe. It was the year when *A Love Supreme*, though not recorded then, was released as well as *Ascension*—perhaps the richest jazz year since Charlie Parker and Dizzy Gillespie made their great recordings during the forties.

It was also in 1965 that Coleman went on a European tour. It was a surprise to the jazz world that he, who had turned down all offers for years, now signed a contract—accepting Joachim Berendt's invitation to appear at the Berlin Jazz Days. He arrived with a trio consisting of himself, bassist David Izenzon, and drummer Charles Moffet. At the Berlin Sportpalast he scored such a terrific success that the man who had been expected to make the hit of the evening, Gerry Mulligan, had a fit of anger. In the Stockholm restaurant Gyllene Cirkeln, Ornette recorded two albums that soon appeared on Blue Note and are comparable in lyrical beauty to Coltrane's *A Love Supreme*. Swedish critic Ludwig Rasmusson wrote in the liner notes:

> The content of his music is mostly pure beauty, a glittering, captivating, dizzying, sensual beauty. A couple of years ago nobody thought so, and everyone considered his music grotesque, filled with anguish and chaos. Now it is almost incomprehensible that one could have held such an opinion, as incomprehensible as the fact that one could object to Willem de Kooning's portraits of women or Samuel Beckett's absurdist plays. Thus Ornette Coleman has been able to change our entire concept of what is beautiful merely through the power of his personal vision. It is most beautiful when Coleman's bass player, David Izenzon, plays bowed bass with him. Then, it is almost hauntingly beautiful.

A comparison of Coleman's *At the Golden Circle* with Coltrane's *A Love Supreme* shows most clearly the basic difference between the two musicians: Coleman's quiet, naturally balanced, static character versus Coltrane's dynamic nature. Both play—in the simple, naive sense of the word—beautiful music. The music of both is immensely intense. But in Coltrane's music, the dynamic nature of the intensity ranges above the static quality of beauty. In Ornette Coleman's music, the reverse is true.

That is also why it is not surprising that almost all of Coltrane's recordings are conceived from the improvisatory point of view (including his compositions!), while in Coleman's work, composition is perhaps as important as improvisation. Coleman is a passionate, dedicated composer. There is an illuminating story—critic John Tynan tells it—that Coleman, in Los Angeles in 1958, was at a point where he simply no longer knew how to make ends meet. Filled with despair, he went to record producer Lester Koenig and asked him to buy some of his compositions. Ornette did not ask for a recording date; he only wanted to sell his compositions. He believed that to be a more promising avenue; his first thought was that the compositions would be a way out. And Ornette's first recording on the Contemporary label was made only because Koenig asked him to play the compositions on the alto saxophone.

Later, when there were heated discussions in the jazz world about the pros and cons of Ornette Coleman's music for years, it became apparent that even the critics who rejected Ornette as an improviser recognized the beauty and competence of his compositions. Today, fifty years later, it is clear that Ornette Coleman is one of the most gifted and influential composers of themes in the history of jazz. Because of their elemental melodic power, more of Ornette's compositions—"Ramblin'," "Blues Connotation," "Lonely Woman," "Broadway Blues," etc.—have become part of the standard jazz repertoire than those of any other musician of the sixties. Coleman the composer was accepted faster than Coleman the improviser. One of the main reasons why Coleman managed to withdraw from the jazz scene for two years was that his creative genius can be satisfied for long periods by composing alone. More often than most other free-jazz musicians, he speaks of "tunes" or "songs": "If I play an F in a tune called 'Peace' I don't think it should sound the same as an F that is supposed to express sadness."

Ornette's message was as simple as it was radical: pitch should be determined by the mood of the improvising musician, his momentary thoughts and feelings, not by the academic rules of music. Ornette Coleman's greatest influence on the jazz avant-garde lies in the freely flowing melodies that he spontaneously composes as an improviser.

Coleman's music is distinguished by a strict refusal to subject his music to the dictates of a standardized harmonic sequence. Ornette believes that the essence of improvisation is not compatible with predetermined schemata and patterns, be they harmonic, rhythmic, or formal. The improvised line should not be determined by a predetermined form; rather, improvisation should itself *create* form.

The fact that Coleman taught himself to play trumpet and violin is also connected with the priority of sound over determinate pitch. One should judge the way Ornette plays his self-taught instruments in this light. Certainly he is a perfect instrumentalist only on the alto sax. But the crux of the matter is missed if one speaks of the amateurish nature of his violin and trumpet playing. The criteria for amateurishness refer back to the "professionalism" of academic music. Ornette, however, plays the violin left-handed and tunes it as if it were played right-handed; he does not bow it, but rather beats or fiddles it with unorthodox arm movements. He is not interested in the note he might generate, but rather in the sound he can gain from sounding as many strings as possible at once. What is left of the conventional violin when Coleman plays it is only its external shape. He plays it like an independent, newly discovered instrument. And he produces exactly those effects required for his compositions. There—and nowhere else—is where the criterion lies, and that criterion is met brilliantly by Ornette's violin playing. "I can't talk about technique because it is ever-changing. That's why for me the only method for playing any instrument is the range in which it is built. Learned technique is a law method. Natural technique is nature's method. And this is what makes music so beautiful to me. It has both, thank God."

In the eighties and nineties, Coleman's violin and trumpet playing were less emphasized. He used them only episodically, particularly toward the end of live appearances. But his daring adaptation of two instruments completely foreign to him did have an influence on the following generation of improvising musicians. For example, the multi-instrumental work of musicians from the circle of the Chicago AACM, such as Anthony Braxton, the Art Ensemble of Chicago, Leroy Jenkins, or Leo Smith would hardly be conceivable without Ornette Coleman's multi-instrumental explorations.

Coleman is the master of an immense compactness. His improvisations are made up of motives that are melodically independent of the theme, and that he develops with a remarkable logical consistency. Working independently of choruses, or chord sequences that underlie the improvisation, he develops connections from a stream of consciousness, comparable to that found in James Joyce, in which one motive arises from the next, is reformulated, and thus leads to a new motive. Musicologist Ekkehard Jost has called this approach to improvisation "motivic chain association." Ornette's outstanding sense of musical unified construction became even clearer when he (finally!) found a horn partner with whom he really enjoyed playing: tenorman Dewey Redman. Through him, Coleman found his way back to quartet music. And two musicians who had already been connected with Ornette in his early days, bassist Charlie Haden (with whom he also made great duo recordings) and drummer Ed Blackwell, joined the new quartet. The latter comes from New Orleans, where Ornette so often played in his youth, and does with the rhythm 'n' blues patterns of the South basically the same thing Ornette did with the Texas blues: he abstracts them.

"Coleman has proven that he has the most comprehensive concept of musical order outside predetermined form that we have heard in the jazz avant-garde," writes Stanley Crouch. Almost everything Ornette plays or composes seems to be cut from the same cloth. For that reason, Coleman's recorded pieces usually are significantly shorter than Coltrane's. Listening to Coltrane meant witnessing a laborious birth. Hearing Ornette means viewing the newborn creature.

Archie Shepp commented on this phenomenon:

> One of the many things [Trane] accomplished was the breakthrough into the concept that a jazz musician need not—could not—be limited to a solo lasting a few minutes. Coltrane demonstrated that a man could play much longer, and that in fact it was an imperative of his conception to improvise at great length. I don't mean that he proved that a thirty- or forty-minute solo necessarily is better than a three-minute one. He did prove, however, that it was possible to create thirty or forty minutes of music, and in the process, he also showed the rest of us we had to have the stamina—in terms of imagination and physical preparedness—to sustain these long flights.

This indeed touches on one of the more superficial among critical opinions: that the great old musicians—King Oliver, Lester Young, Teddy Wilson—were able to express all they wanted in one or two choruses of sixteen or thirty-two bars, and that it simply indicates lack of conciseness that such contemporary musicians as Coltrane (and many others since him) play such lengthy solos. In fact, the older musicians recorded short solos because records at that time usually only afforded some three minutes of music. But when they were able to play the way they really wanted, in jam sessions or clubs, they preferred, even back then, to play relatively long solos. Great music—from European symphonies to the ragas and talas of India—requires time. Only the commercial Top 40 hit is satisfied with two or three minutes.

But back to Ornette Coleman. The playing of rubato ballads, of slow pieces in a free tempo (which has become so popular in contemporary jazz from Keith Jarrett by way of Pat Metheny to Shannon Jackson and others), derives from one single point: Ornette Coleman and his celebrated 1959 "Lonely Woman."

His aspiration to make his music all by himself and the periods of withdrawal from the public eye certainly say something about his problems in dealing with the world around him. John Coltrane was a builder of groups. Ornette Coleman is alone. He is filled with a deep mistrust of society. To him, agents and managers automatically are people who want to cheat him. Almost all his managers were originally his friends, but as soon as Ornette would ask them to manage him, the friendship would quickly end. His mistrust, often unfounded, would create such unpleasant situations that soon there would be a reason for his suspiciousness.

In a 1965 interview with Dan Morgenstern he said:

> As a black man, I have a tendency to want to know how certain principles and rights are arrived at. When this concern dominates my business relationships, I'm cast into schizophrenic or paranoid thinking. . . . I do not wish to be exploited for not having the knowledge or know-how

required for survival in today's America. It's gotten so that in your relationships to every system that has some sort of power, you have to pay to become part of that power, just in order to do what you want to do. This doesn't build a better world, but it does build more security for the power. Power makes purpose secondary.

We believe Coleman's origin in Texas and the world of country blues cannot be overemphasized. For good reason he made his first records—as a sideman, of course—in the early fifties with blues singer Clarence Samuels (who had been with the Jay McShann Band, the orchestra in which Charlie Parker got his start). Elsewhere (in the free-jazz section), we have shown that Ornette's free harmonic conception is a direct result of the harmonic freedom Southern country and blues musicians have always had.

Ornette's breaking away from the standard twelve-bar blues form is not due to a desire to distance himself from the roots of the blues, but is rather a deliberate addressing of the origin of the blues. Tenorist Archie Shepp—one of the great musicians of the new jazz—said:

It was Coleman who, in my opinion, revitalized and refurbished the blues idiom without destroying its simplistic milieu. Far from taking it beyond its original intentions, Coleman restored [the blues] to their free, classical [African] unharmonized beginnings. I have always felt that this early work of Ornette's was much closer to the "old thing"—hoedowns, foot-tappin'—than the new. Certainly Blind Lemon Jefferson and Huddie Leadbetter must have played thirteen, seventeen, twenty-five bar blues. Regardless; no pundit would have been foolish enough to label them avant-garde.

And critic A. B. Spellman said, "Ornette's music is nothing but the blues." Ornette is a total blues musician. And if conventional jazz includes only two—or rather, since the advent of bebop's flatted fifth, three—blue notes, it can be said that Coleman has turned the whole scale into blue notes. Almost all his notes are bent up or down, off-pitch, tied, flatted, or augmented—in short, vocalized in the blues sense. Remember his statement that an F in a tune called "Peace" should not sound the same as an F in a context that is supposed to express sadness? Precisely that is a blues musician's concept. And if, after years of conventional jazz, this concept is found astonishing—because all Fs, whether concerned with peace, sadness, or whatever, simply must have the identical pitch—this merely illustrates the influence of the European tradition—an influence that Ornette eliminated, at least in this realm.

The ease with which Ornette deals with free tonality has been contrasted with Coltrane's immensely tense, complex relationship to it. This became clear when, right after *Ascension*, the album *Coltrane—Live at the Village Vanguard Again* was released. At this point, Coltrane could no longer play just with the musicians who'd been with him for so many years. He founded, as we have mentioned, a new group, a quintet, with Pharoah Sanders as a second tenor sax voice, Trane's wife Alice Coltrane on piano, drummer Rashied Ali, and, as the only holdover from the old quartet, bassist Jimmy Garrison. When Coltrane plays on this record well-known themes from his earlier recordings—"Naima" or "My Favorite Things"—one feels that he loved these themes and would have preferred to continue playing them as they appeared to him as themes, if only he would have been able to express within them everything he so much wanted to express! If John Coltrane had seen a possibility of reaching, by conventional means, the degree of ecstatic heat he was aiming for, he would have continued to play "tonally" to the end.

Coltrane hesitated for a long time. He needed ten years to take the step he finally took in 1965, and that a whole generation of musicians in this era took in one day. Anybody who hears the sermonlike, sublimely swinging lines of "Naima" understands: this musician mourned for tonality. He knew how much he had lost with it. And he would have loved to return to it, had he not, during these ten years, again and again run into the limitations of conventional tonality before having been able to express all that seemed necessary to him.

The "sound playing," rich in noises, that New Orleans jazz musicians briefly employed at the high points of their "hot" solos—growls, tooting, squeezing—are extended by Coltrane to form glowing, freely tonal solos, storms of intensity lasting half an hour or more. Tenor saxophonist Charles Lloyd says, "In my view, Bird discovered the atom, but Trane split it."

Jazz is a music of intensity, and John Coltrane made the most intense statements ever made on the tenor saxophone. "When Trane played in the so-called free style it was the best and it still is because you could hear that he had all the other stuff together," says Dave Liebman. "He had all the ground work laid." Ernie Watts adds: "It's like a compendium of all of the possibilities that are available, sonorically, in the saxophone. It's an incredible study of saxophone sounds and nuances and all the capabilities with the instrument that we normally don't even delve into."

It was only for the sake of increased intensity that Coltrane hired a second tenorist. In terms of physical power and the ability to bring forth the wildest and most unbelievable sounds on his instrument, the man he chose was certainly, after Albert Ayler, the most amazing tenor player in the field: Pharoah Sanders. In interaction with him, Coltrane became even more intense.

Coltrane totally exhausted himself in this process and had to cancel a European tour in the fall of 1966. That is why he began to need frequent recuperation breaks. Repeatedly, during such breaks friends would anticipate that this particular one would last a year or so. But just weeks later, Trane would be on the scene again, carrying on with the tearing, ecstatic power of his jazz and love hymns.

The liver ailment doctors determined as the cause of his death may merely have added the final blow to the complete exhaustion resulting from a life led ceaselessly at the edge of humanly possible intensity.

Again and again, he seemed to be totally drained of all energy after his concert appearances. He was like a relay runner: at a certain point, he would hand the torch to Pharoah Sanders, who then had to press forward—even *more* powerfully, intensely, and ecstatically, yet without the hymnlike power of love that radiated from Coltrane.

Tragically, there was one musician among the persons close to Coltrane who had—and still has—this power of love, but she was not able to express it musically, at least not on the high level associated with Trane. In 1967, when Trane died, she had not yet emerged clearly in the jazz world, but then, she became the purest and clearest successor and heir to the spiritual message of John Coltrane. This was his wife—pianist, harpist, organist, and composer Alice Coltrane—or, as she was known when vibraharpist Terry Gibbs introduced her in the early sixties, Alice McLeod; or, as she later called herself in accordance with her religious conviction, Turiya Aparna.

For her record *Universal Consciousness*, Alice enlisted the cooperation of Ornette Coleman. Thus a circle closed. Ornette shaped, or at least essentially determined, a violin sound for Alice without equal among the numerous string experiments in modern jazz, purposely avoiding the standard aesthetics of beauty and homogeneity. The four violinists were from the most diverse schools: two from concert music, Julius Brand and Joan Kalisch; one a free-jazz man, Leroy Jenkins; and the fourth a soul musician, John Blair. These four, in pieces like "Oh Allah" and "Hare Krishna," play a dense texture of sounds that combine the complexity of avant-garde concert music with traditional jazz intensity, the spiritual power of John Coltrane with the tradition of bebop and blues.

Ornette Coleman loves violins. He admires (as did Charlie Parker twenty years earlier) the great tradition of European concert music. Again and again, he has presented compositions for symphony orchestra, chamber ensembles, and string quartets—most impressively in *Skies of America*, recorded in 1972 by the London Symphony Orchestra conducted by David Measham. However, Ornette Coleman remains a jazz musician, even when composing for symphony orchestra. The symphony orchestra to him is an enlarged "horn" on which he improvises.

Ironically, Coleman's admiration for strings and the wealth of harmonics produced by the sound of a symphony orchestra was also the decisive factor that led to electrical amplification of his music from the midseventies. For Ornette "a guitar can sound like ten violins," so he logically equipped his groups with a choir of amplified guitars. In a process of increasing compression, he ultimately ended up with two electric basses and two electric guitars. The instrumentation alone made Ornette's music more and more rock-oriented. And it received an additional push toward funk when drummer Ronald Shannon Jackson joined the band in 1975. Never before was Ornette's rhythm 'n' blues background so profoundly apparent as in his Prime Time bands of the eighties and nineties. His albums *Dancing in Your Head* (1977) and *Body Meta* launched free funk with a big bang (see the section on "The Eighties").

Ornette opened up funk on all levels—melodic, rhythmic, harmonic—to free improvisation, making it interactive. By breaking with the static elements in this music, he liberated it for interaction and group thinking.

A striking aspect of Ornette's Prime Time bands was his return to the principle of doubling instruments, as first successfully applied in the 1960 *Free Jazz* album. This time, however, there were not two equal, opposing quartets, but two trios fulfilling different roles. While the first band (Calvin Weston, drums; Al MacDowell, electric bass; and Charles Ellerbee, guitar) provided a foundation of impetuously "free" funk rhythms, the other trio (Jamaaladeen Tacuma, electric bass; Bern Nix, electric guitar; and Denardo Coleman, drums) commented freely on those rhythms.

Those two levels collided with enormous power and energy in the Prime Time band's collective improvisations. Above this dazzlingly pulsating bedrock of free melodies and bubbling funk rhythms floated—outshining everything else—Ornette's alto playing, in which (as if in some huge, dazzling glass) all the band's complex lines combined as a single, songlike, glowing white beam.

Ornette's encounter with Berber musicians, the Master Musicians of Joujouka, in Morocco in 1973 (documented in a piece on the *Dancing in Your Head* album) impressed him to such an extent that from then on he had his Prime Time band play in nontempered tuning, inspired by non-Western musical cultures. The Joujouka musicians, adherents of a branch of Sufi mysticism, do not understand music as "art for art's sake," but rather as a magical healing ritual—an attitude congruent with that of Ornette, who has always sought a music that could help improve human existence. Ornette speaks of music in the so-called Third World as the only avant-garde left to our century: "Nontempered instruments can arouse an emotion that doesn't exist in Western music. I mean, European music is very beautiful, but the musicians that play it don't always get a chance of expressing it that way because they have spent most of their energy perfecting the unison of playing together by saying 'You're a little flat' or . . . 'a little sharp.'" It's obvious who makes his appearance behind this love for untempered non-Western music: Ornette Coleman, the blues musician.

Many critics complained about the thunderous volume marking Ornette's Prime Time band. But there's no doubt that Ornette's free funk could not be experienced without this immense loudness. For Ornette knows that high volume changes sound. It elevates aspects of the sound spectrum into the realm of the perceivable, making accessible previously inaudible regions of harmonics. It is precisely because Ornette's band played up to the limits of physically bearable storms of sound that his music discovers new tonal and expressive possibilities with whirring, shimmering overtone melodies encasing his free funk in an iridescent net. Since the Prime Time band played in nontempered tuning and the instruments seemed to be microintervallically "detuned" among themselves, these harmonics collide with the force of elementary particles, generating new series of partials through this process of friction like a melody playing itself in an unending sequence. Rock guitarist Lou Reed has never made a secret of the fact that Ornette Coleman influenced him to play the electric guitar, not as a "normal" instrument, but rather as a feedback instrument, with free pitch manipulation. The young Reed had heard Coleman's music while standing in front of the New York jazz club Five Spot in 1959 (he couldn't afford the entrance fee). Later he said, "Ornette's free jazz made me think, what a great thing to do on an electric guitar!"

Ornette's free funk seemed shrill and deafening to the contemporary public. In fact, as also became obvious in his Prime Time music, Ornette Coleman is an absolute melodist. Even at the start of the sixties when he transformed jazz with enormous revolutionary energy, Ornette was much too much of a melodist to have sacrificed the beauty of a melodic line to the energetic power of "free" noise playing. The same is true of free funk. His improvisations signify nothing less than "beautiful" music—clear, singing, wonderfully balanced alto saxophone lines. It's among the great (and unfortunate) ironies of jazz history that one of African American music's greatest melodists, of all people, shocked the jazz world with his trailblazing changes. Ornette has twice decisively influenced the development of jazz. Both times he did so (also) as a grandiose melodist.

Ornette's theory of harmolodic music says that all musical elements—melody, harmony, rhythm, tempo, meter, and phrasing—should be equal, which seemingly contradicts what has just been said. The secret of his harmolodic music ultimately entails melodization of all the musical parameters. "Harmony, movement, rhythm—they can all become a melody," said Ornette.

Peter Niklas Wilson writes, "Coleman's path after 1960 showed that he wasn't at all interested in destroying form, tonality, harmony, or meter; rather, he wanted to flexibilize and individualize them. Form should not be predetermined, but should rather grow out of the playing process, but with the same strictness as a predetermined pattern."

While Ornette Coleman was blazing new trails in his harmolodic music, his alto sax playing attained "classical" status. When he recorded the *In All Languages* double album in 1987, that was programmatic in character. Ornette devoted an entire record to the music of the celebrated, reunited "classic" quartet (with Don Cherry, trumpet; Charlie Haden, bass; and Billy Higgins, drums), while on the other disk he played contemporary free funk with his Prime Time band. Ornette subtitled the album "30 Years of Harmolodic Music," often presenting interpretations of the same pieces by both bands—for instance, "Peace Warrior," "Space Church (Continuous Services)," and "Feet Music"—thus providing fascinating documentation of his music's unbroken development and continuity.

Song X, the album that many believe to mark the high point in Coleman's eighties music making, came out in 1986. Characteristically, this record was created in conjunction with another great jazz melodist, guitarist Pat Metheny, who mainly employed a guitar synthesizer here. The two of them—joined by bassist Charlie Haden and two drummers, Jack DeJohnette and Denardo Coleman—made ravishing music. Ornette inspired Pat Metheny to play the wildest and most intense lines he had ever played up to then. In pieces like "Endangered Species" and "Song X," Coleman himself discovered long, singing improvisations of raging beauty—more expansive and intense than with the Prime Time band, where he usually holds back somewhat so as not to disrupt group coherence. Ornette proudly compares the intensity and spirit of this album with John Coltrane's *Ascension*.

Coltrane's music has become even more vital in the years since his death, triggering developments everywhere, from rock to jazz, in the most diverse of transitional stages.

The hymnlike element prevalent on the entire contemporary jazz and rock scene comes from Coltrane, above all from *A Love Supreme*. When the Miles Davis influence subsided during the midseventies, it turned out that Coltrane was now the most intensively influential musician on the jazz scene. In fact, a "John Coltrane classicism" developed that is comparable to the Count Basie and Lester Young classicisms of earlier years.

The history of contemporary jazz since 1960 has been impressively and extensively shaped by the contrasting styles of these two musicians. In the sixties both exerted an equally intense influence, but the seventies were dominated by Coltrane. In the eighties it was exactly the other way around. Now Ornette Coleman was the outstanding figure, heading the scene. In the jazz classicism of the nineties, John Coltrane again became the leading figure.

No jazz of the last fifty years was so deeply rooted in the cry of the blues as that of Ornette Coleman. At the same time, John Coltrane was, both for the neobop straight-ahead musicians and "young lions" and for the free players in Europe and the United States, a symbol of an inexhaustible drive to musical exploration. Coltrane's sound is the sound of the joy of discovery, the "sound of surprise," as critic Whitney Balliett once famously described the essence of jazz.

To his friends, Coltrane was a marked man, at least after *A Love Supreme*. He already knew back then that his sounds were shaping the jazz of his times, and he suffered from this responsibility. He saw himself too strongly as a ceaseless seeker to be able to enjoy the fact that the whole jazz world now praised each of his statements as "the last word."

In answer to the question whether there would ever be an end to the development that had already led him through a half dozen different ways of playing since the midfifties and the Miles Davis Quintet, Coltrane told Nat Hentoff, "You just keep going all the way, as deep as you can. You keep trying to get right down to the crux."

If Ornette Coleman is the phoenix whose music from the start was revealed to us—if not in its mature form, then at least in its basic conception—as if it had sprung from the head of Zeus, then Coltrane was a Sisyphus, who again and again—from the very bottom up to the mountaintop—had to roll the hard, cumbersome rock of knowledge. And perhaps, whenever Coltrane got to the top, Coleman would already be standing there in his resplendent circus suit, playing his beautiful melodies. But the music John Coltrane would blow then, from the top of the mountain, standing next to Ornette, was imbued with the power of the pilgrim who had reached yet another station on the long, thorny road to knowledge (or might we better say, because it was Coltrane's conviction, to God), and who knew there were many more stations to come—though in the months of exhaustion preceding his death, he no longer knew how to go on.

John McLaughlin

No single musician could represent the jazz of the seventies. Jazz had become too wide. McCoy Tyner, Keith Jarrett, Chick Corea, Joe Zawinul and Wayne Shorter, Herbie Hancock, Dexter Gordon, and others were all of equal stature. And above all, Miles Davis (especially during the first half of the decade) and John Coltrane (in the late seventies) were still dominating figures. Beyond them, the jazz scene was split—into acoustic jazz on the one hand, and electric jazz on the other, but actually into many more subgroupings.

And yet, there was *one* musician of that decade (and also of the early eighties) who belonged to all these groupings. He played blues and bebop, free and fusion and world jazz, and, above all, he felt bound to electric as well as to acoustic music: John McLaughlin.

The following interview took place in 1980 in John McLaughlin's Paris home. McLaughlin is among those contemporary musicians who are so articulate that the interviewer merely has to give the cues, so the questions are only included if they are necessary to an understanding of the context. Further information about McLaughlin can be found in the sections on the seventies, the guitar, and the bands of jazz.

JOHN McLAUGHLIN: I was born in 1942 in a little village in Yorkshire. My father was an engineer; my mother used to be an amateur violinist. There was always a very good atmosphere toward music in the house, which I am eternally grateful for. Classical music. The Three B's: Beethoven, Bach, Brahms. When I was about nine, my mother sent me to have piano lessons. Later we moved up to Northumberland—close to the Scottish border. Every summer the Scottish bagpipe bands used to come. Sometimes they had six or seven bagpipes, with three or four drummers—they had great drummers. Swinging in their own way. They had a big effect on me.

When I was about ten, there was the beginning of the blues revolution in England. The blues started underground among the students. One of my brothers had a guitar. He taught me three chords, and from that day on, everything was decided. I completely fell in love with the guitar. I started listening to musicians like Muddy Waters, Big Bill Broonzy, Leadbelly. [While John said this, I saw that he still had records by these musicians in his library; they were just above the record player, so he apparently still plays them. —J. E. Berendt] So I had all this music just thrown at me. It was fantastic. Incredible.

When I was fifteen, I was able to take my guitar and a little amplifier and go to a pub on a Sunday night where they had a jazz club, and I would say, "Please let me play a tune with you." And they said, "OK, come in." And they would play some very fast tunes and they would burn me out completely, but it was a very good experience. I went home and I realized I still had much to learn.

Around that time I started to listen a lot to Django Reinhardt and Tal Farlow. They were my heroes on guitar. They still are. Maybe that's why I like violinists so much—because I loved Django and Stephane Grappelli.

When I was sixteen, I went on the road with a traditional jazz band called Professors of Ragtime. This got me to London, which, of course, was the center of jazz in England. In those days there were two clubs: the Marquee and the Flamingo. They were great. Everybody met everybody there, and the attitude was that everybody could play with everybody. So this is what I did. I remember jam sessions with everybody and anybody.

I remember the Rolling Stones coming in for an audition. I didn't care much for them. They were out of tune, and I didn't think they were swinging, but at least they were playing Muddy Waters's blues tunes.

I started to play with the Graham Bond Organisation and with Alexis Korner. Alexis had everybody in his band at some point. But Miles Davis's recordings with the Gil Evans big band really did it for me. Miles crystallized a new school of music, and I immediately felt, "That is my school." But I kept on playing rhythm 'n' blues and it was great, because they were playing real jazz solos. It was blues, but at the same time, it was much more than blues.

I played with Eric Clapton and Dick Heckstall-Smith and Ginger Baker and everybody, but I now must talk about Graham Bond. He meant a lot to me. I had grown up in an ordinary school where the teacher taught religion in a very dry way. He did not understand what religion—and Christianity—really means. He was not a living Christian. I never went to church, but Graham Bond—God rest his soul—really was a seeker. He was interested in the invisible things in life. He introduced me to a book about ancient Egyptian culture, and I got very interested in this because, for the first time in my life, I realized that a human being is much more than meets the eye. Later, I discovered a book by Ramana Maharshi, and the first thing I saw was a photo of Ramana Maharshi, and this was the first picture of someone I could consider to be enlightened—an enlightened human being, and it meant very much to me. I began to realize that India as a culture and as a nation has treasures waiting to be discovered.

At this time I was friends with a guitar player by the name of Jim Sullivan, a well-known pop musician. So we were hanging out together, and we both became members of the London Theosophical Society. One day he played a record of Ravi Shankar. I couldn't understand it, but there was something which grabbed me. In the notes on the jacket I read the same things I was reading in that book by Ramana Maharshi, so I realized there is a connection between the music and the wisdom. And I knew I had to listen more in order to understand this connection.

At this time I was just scuffling along. Living from hand to mouth. Impossible to make any money. So I had to do sessions: pop sessions with people like Tom Jones, Engelbert Humperdinck, and Petula Clark. Musically it was terrible, and after some time this session thing was driving me completely crazy. I had to do it in order to survive, and yet more things were happening musically that I wanted to do. Finally, one day I woke up and I said to myself, I cannot do this any more. And I got into my car and I just drove, and I didn't stop until I got to Northern England and I stayed with my mother. It was a question of sanity for me.

I didn't want to go back to London. So I decided to go to the Continent and just play the kind of music I wanted to play. The first offer I got was from Gunter Hampel in Germany, so I went there playing free music for about half a year or so.

I am very glad I had the experience with Gunter. I know, idealistically, it's right to play free music, but there is always a big "but." Because for the most part it is indulgent; this is my real opinion about free music. In order to really play it, first of all, harmonically and melodically you have to know everything, and then you have to be a real big person, a developed human being.

When I was playing with Gunter, I lived in Antwerp, so I could go back to England every now and then. We had a little band with bass player Dave Holland and drummer Tony Oxley, and it was fantastic. I did a record called *Extrapolation* with Tony Oxley and John Surman on baritone and soprano saxophone. And of course we all were proud when Dave was leaving for New York to play with Miles. Imagine, an Englishman to play with Miles—it was unheard of at that time. A real coup!

A few months later, in November of 1968, I got a call from Dave. He was in Baltimore, and guess who he was with? I said, "Miles." "No," he said, "Tony—Tony Williams—and he wants to talk to you." Tony said he would like to form a band, and he would like to have me. Jack DeJohnette had played him a tape he had done with me a few months before while he was in London with Bill Evans. So I said, "When you are ready, just call me."

In early 1969 he called again. So I left the first week of February for New York. Two days later I was in the studio with Miles. That was incredible. You must understand, New York was the ultimate for any European jazz player. And to be able to go there and to play in New York—it was just unbelievable for me!

Tony Williams and Dave Holland were playing with Miles. So immediately I met everybody. Miles and Wayne Shorter and Chick Corea and Jack DeJohnette and Gil Evans! Imagine! Like a dream coming true!

I'll never forget one night in that week. Miles was talking with Louis Armstrong and Dizzy. I wish I had had a camera. The three of them together! Just to see those guys together was so beautiful for me.

On my second day in New York, Tony had to go to Miles's house to pick up some money. So I went along. Miles had a record date the day after. Miles knew that Tony would leave him in order to have a group with Larry Young on organ and me. But Miles didn't want him to leave. He loves Tony. Miles said to me, "Why don't you bring your guitar tomorrow?" Tony wasn't terribly happy about that, because suddenly there was a little competition between Miles and Tony. For me, of course, it was the ultimate. It was the last thing I could expect. But now comes the next day [the recording session for *In a Silent Way*]. Chick Corea was there. And Joe Zawinul and Herbie Hancock. That I was fortunate enough to be invited, to be there at the right moment, was really nothing I could have created. It was just like a blessing.

We had a tune [the record's title track] by Joe Zawinul—with lots of chords. Miles said, "Well, John, why don't you play it on the guitar?" I said, "Do you want all these chords? That's going to take me quite a while to work it out." And now I had my first experience with Miles's way of directing. He wanted me to play the tune with just one chord! And then suddenly everybody was waiting for me to start the tune, and

I didn't know what to do. I had no idea. Miles said, "Well, you know the chord." So I gave him the chord. That's all. Two chords, in fact. I started to play, and I realized the light is on; and I played the first solo, Wayne Shorter played the tune, Miles and Wayne played it together. I was confused, but I was playing on instinct. And then we played it back, and I was shocked how beautiful it was. And I realized: Joe Zawinul had brought the tune in, and Miles, in one minute, had brought the real essence, the beauty out of it. I was astonished to see how he could hear all that and just bring it out. That was one of the great things in Miles, how he brought the extraordinary out of his surroundings.

Afterwards, Miles asked me to join his group. Again, it was unbelievable for me. Imagine—I had to turn down Miles! Because it was more important for me to go with Tony Williams. I had compositions. And I realized, with Tony I would have more of a chance to play them than with Miles.

Eventually, Lifetime, our band with Tony Williams and Larry Young, was working. There was very little money involved, but musically, it was fantastic, and we couldn't believe that Columbia was turning us down. We played an audition for a guy called Al Kooper who was with Blood, Sweat & Tears. And he said no. I lost all my respect for him immediately because we were burning.

JOACHIM BERENDT: So this was your first experience with the music business in America? What do you think about the jazz business?

McLAUGHLIN: I don't think they understand jazz in America. They are so far from reality. Even after eleven years in the U.S.A., I know they don't understand their own music. They don't know how to market it. In Europe and in Japan it's so much better, because people really love the music. It has always been recognized as an art form over here. In Europe, whoever does business with you deals with you on the psychology that you are an artist. But in America they don't look at it that way. Of course, there are a lot of people who love and enjoy jazz in America. But as far as the business is concerned, it's terrible. There are no festivals as you have them in Europe. So when I first encountered these problems, I was quite surprised, because I thought they would have it much more together. In fact, it was one of the shocks of my life when we made that first record with Tony Williams and when they mixed it and the sound was just terrible, and I realized they had no respect for the music and the musicians. Really, I was shocked.

BERENDT: And of course, later it turned out that everybody was blaming Tony and the musicians for the bad sound. It did a lot of harm to Lifetime. . . . However, John, I always felt you have been relatively lucky in your career—businesswise. When I look at what happened to Tony Williams, to Ornette, to Cecil Taylor, to so many others who had bad managers and agents during most parts of their careers, I really think you have been lucky.

McLAUGHLIN: And yet I have been betrayed, people have taken money from me, and often enough I have been in very difficult positions. I'll never forget my first experience with Douglas Records. I met the man and I thought he's a real nice guy. But the first record I made for him—*Devotion*, with Buddy Miles on drums and Larry Young on organ—was a terrible experience. After I recorded it, I went on tour with Tony Williams, and when I came back, he had finished the album, mixed it, cut this out and that, and there were parts in it which I didn't recognize any more as part of our music. I was in total shock.

BERENDT: How much did they pay you?

McLAUGHLIN: I got paid about two thousand dollars.

BERENDT: That's all? For a famous record that was sold all over the world and is still selling?

McLAUGHLIN: No, not for one record. I got two thousand for the two records I did for them—for *Devotion* and *My Goal's Beyond*. . . .

BERENDt: . . . the one with the solo side. This is the record that really established solo guitar playing in jazz—the forerunner of hundreds of solo guitar records that followed—and, in my opinion, it still is the most beautiful of all of them. . . . Well, from Douglas you went to Columbia, which at that time was considered the best of all the companies—jazzwise.

McLAUGHLIN: Well, here I am ten years later [in 1981], and I have to leave Columbia. They have to pay me for leaving. Because they think that only electric music is worth marketing. Which I think is disgraceful to the American people. And it's patronizing. They are looking at it from a hamburger point of view.

BERENDT: Please, tell me about Sri Chinmoy, the guru you had at that time.

McLAUGHLIN: Well, just before I went to America, I started to do yoga exercises every day in the morning. I arrived in America, and being in Manhattan, I thought I had to get myself more together. So I did more exercises. I was doing one hour and a half in the morning and one hour and a half in the evening. Just yoga. So after a year of doing this, I felt great physically, but I thought I was missing the interior thing. So I went to meditate with different teachers, most of them Indians. And then suddenly one day, Larry Coryell's manager introduced me to Sri Chinmoy. Immediately I felt good about him. He said some important things to me. About music and spirituality. My question was, "What is the relationship between music and the spiritual consciousness?" And he answered, "It's not so much what you do, but what's important is the consciousness with which you do it. For instance, a street sweeper can sweep his street perfectly and at the same time have great satisfaction from doing it. He can even get enlightened. The important thing, always, is the state of your consciousness because it determines (1) how you do it, and (2) the quality of what you do, and (3) the quality of what you are. So if you are a musician and you work toward enlightenment, your music will automatically be part of it." Of course, this was a great answer, so I subsequently went to see him several times, and after a few weeks, I became a disciple.

BERENDT: But a couple of years later, the jazz media made a big thing out of you leaving Chinmoy.

McLAUGHLIN: I never left him.

BERENDT: I expected that answer.

McLAUGHLIN: I will never leave him, because I love him. He is a great man, he is an enlightened man. And that's the greatest thing any human being can be, because it takes an incredible amount of work. . . . The only thing that I disagree with are the formalized things. . . . This to do and this not to do. I cannot do this because I have to go on as a musician. I have to go on tour.

Anyway, let's go back to 1971. Miles suggested I should have my own band. I had met Billy Cobham on one of Miles's dates, and I looked around for a violin player. I had spoken to Jean-Luc Ponty while I was in Paris. He said no. He wouldn't want to come to America. (Two years later he did!) A few weeks later, I found Jerry Goodman. And Miroslav Vitous, the bass player, called me and said, "Joe Zawinul and Wayne Shorter are founding a group together, called Weather Report. We want you to come with us." And I said, "Well, that's really nice, but I got something to do myself." And Miroslav said, "If you need a piano player, call Jan Hammer. He is also from Czechoslovakia, and he is playing with Sarah Vaughan." So this was the Mahavishnu Orchestra: Jan Hammer, Billy Cobham, Jerry Goodman, and, of course, I had Rick Laird on bass, because I knew him from way back in England, and we used to play a lot together. Right from the beginning, we had a beautiful rapport. One evening I was telling Sri Chinmoy that I got a band together and I wanted to give it a name, and he said, "Well, call it the Mahavishnu Orchestra." I said, "Mahavishnu Orchestra? This is going to take everybody out!" "Just try it anyway," he said. So we tried it, and it was great for a year. We really identified with it—with the sound and the energy. And the music was amazing. Of course, I had expected it would work, but I didn't expect a big success like that. We just worked and played and things were great.

Part of the fun was that I kept living my own life the way I wanted to. People were very interested in it. They asked me lots of questions about

Sri Chinmoy and all the spiritual things—meditation and India and religion. But of course none of the other musicians went into that. Gradually, they resented it. I felt we would have worked it out, but the real problem was with Jan Hammer and Jerry Goodman. They were really heavily against it. Finally, it became a big psychosis. So we went to Japan, and it didn't get better. It got worse. So when we came to Osaka, I said, "Look, why doesn't anyone say one word to me? If you have something on your mind, just say you hate me, just tell me. It's OK. Tell me, and things will get better." But neither of them would say a word, and Rick Laird told them, "Why don't you tell him? You are always talking to me when he is not around." So I felt they were determined to go out, and I realized this is the end of the band. It also had to do with success. You know, success is hard to take.

BERENDT: To me, the Mahavishnu Orchestra—the first one—was the greatest of all the jazz-rock bands. Both its records were just terrific—*Birds of Fire* and *Inner Mounting Flame*. Some time later, you had a second Mahavishnu Orchestra, but I always felt you no longer reached that type of height and intensity and inspiration and density.

McLAUGHLIN: We reached it more rarely. It did happen, I think, about two nights in a year. For me, this record *Visions of the Emerald Beyond* (with the second Mahavishnu Orchestra and a string quartet) was one of the greatest I ever made. And then I did *Apocalypse* with Michael Tilson Thomas conducting the London Symphony Orchestra.

BERENDT: But meanwhile Shakti had happened. I still remember the sensation—after all that electric high energy: you playing with those Indian guys—all acoustic music, you being the only Westerner in the group.

McLAUGHLIN: In fact, we had played together before the first Mahavishnu Orchestra had finished. I had some friends and they had a music shop and I told them, I am looking for somebody who can teach me about Indian music. So I took some vocal lessons—Indian singing—and the mrindanga player there (south Indian percussion) was L. Shankar's uncle. So I met L. Shankar, the violin player. I'll never forget when Jean-Luc Ponty arrived from California to join the second Mahavishnu Orchestra. Shankar and I had been hanging out that day, so they met—the two violinists, Shankar from India and Jean-Luc from France. And then L. Shankar started to play, and I saw that look of amazement on Jean-Luc's face—I've never seen anything like this in my life.

I was so lucky to have some lessons from Ravi Shankar and other masters of Indian music. I love India, its music and its spirituality, its religions. The spirituality *is* the music. You can't separate the two, like you can in the West.

I had met Zakir Hussain, the tabla player, at Ali Akbar Khan's school for Indian music near San Francisco. Khan-sahib, the great master sarod player, was just sitting there in his chair listening to both of us playing, and after we finished, I said that I never played with anybody like that.

I did three records with Shakti. But Columbia just didn't go along with it.

BERENDT: So you went back to electric music because Columbia told you to?

McLAUGHLIN: You can't say this. You know, jazz music and Western har˘ monies are part of me. I cannot suppress it. Not that I have suppressed it in Shakti, but I was preoccupied with Indian music, which has its own kind of discipline. Shakti really stayed together for quite some time. So I wanted to go back to Western music. It's a part of me I cannot deny. So I really had a desire to play chords and to play with a drummer and a bass player, and that's why I made this record *Johnny McLaughlin—Electric Guitarist*. In a way it was like going back to my beginnings, and, of course, it also was a reunion with almost all the Mahavishnu players. It was like forgetting all those old problems and just playing music.

BERENDT: For many people there is almost a schism between electric and acoustic music.

McLAUGHLIN: Both are part of me. There is a style of music and a style of playing I can only do on an electric guitar, and there is another style I like to do on acoustic guitar.

BERENDT: When I presented the Mahavishnu Orchestra at the Olympic Games Jazz Festival in Munich in 1972, I considered you, more or less, a European musician, but you talked to me about New York. "It only could have happened there," you said. And: "New York makes you strong. It really is *the* jazz city." But now, ten years later, you live in Paris. And you have a French wife. And your wife is a classical musician. And you have an apartment at the Pont Neuf in Paris. Are you coming back to your European roots?

McLAUGHLIN: In a sense, yes. I think New York has changed. America has changed. America may, at some point, enjoy a renaissance of music, but I don't know when this will happen. Right now, the situation for music is better in Europe than it is in America.

BERENDT: How do you feel about fusion?

McLAUGHLIN: I think a lot of fusion music is not true fusion. If a musician is being pushed to play a certain kind of music or if he feels he has to do something with a different beat in order to become popular, then this is basically against the spirit of music and against the spirit of jazz—that's all. The fusion has to happen inside you, otherwise it's not going to happen at all. It becomes only pseudofusion. There is so much pseudomusic around.

You can't say, "Let's put it with a disco beat. Or let's do it with a rock beat." It won't have any weight. It won't carry any conviction. That's why I don't listen too much to that kind of music anymore. I'm not deeply touched by it. And I have to be deeply touched, otherwise it's not worth it. I want something to really grab my insides. That's the music I take along when I go on tour.

BERENDT: What do you take along?

MCLAUGHLIN: I take Coltrane, Miles; I take some gypsy music. I have a cassette of a great Indian *nagaswaram* player. And a beautiful Indian tabla player. And I take some Chopin on the road. And some Schumann.

David Murray and Wynton Marsalis

The most important development in jazz in the eighties was that young musicians learned to improvise in all the historical styles. In notable contrast to earlier generations of musicians, they had at their command an encyclopedic repertoire of playing styles that made it possible for them to carry on an intensive dialogue with the jazz legacy in its entirety. It is the reevaluation of jazz tradition, not its negation, that brought jazz furthest in the eighties and nineties. For the first time in the history of jazz, dialogue with the past became more important than a visionary look into the future—a dialogue in which examination of jazz's rich legacy held more promise than utopias. There wasn't, however, any single binding principle regulating encounters with jazz tradition: there were innumerably many. Nowhere else in eighties jazz did the immense range of neoclassicism become so clearly evident as in the differences between the music of David Murray and Wynton Marsalis. Both used a retrospective view of jazz's history as a vantage point from which to create something new. Both reinvigorated a feeling for standards in jazz, thereby establishing new standards. Both took advantage of a pool of information that had never before existed with regard to jazz improvisation. And yet, as we will see, the difference between them could hardly have been greater. After twenty years of free jazz's destruction of norms and clichés, and after ten years of fusion music's superficial formulas and mannerisms, Wynton Marsalis and David Murray used classical elements to give jazz new impetus.

Hans-Jürgen Schaal on David Murray:

Wild, passionate, powerful, massive—David Murray blows gospel, free, blues, swing, funk. The phrases spilling from his horn glow with the magic of the history of black saxophone playing. Murray loves the soft tremolo, gruff multiphonics, the leap from the growl to the falsetto.

And no one can match his playing in the extreme high register. His eyes
roll behind almost-shut lids, a saxophonist on the path to jazz ecstasy.

The first thing you notice about the sound of David Murray's tenor
saxophone is indeed its enormous robustness, weight, and intensity—a
sound that tastes of rich loam and earth: rustic, effusive, brimming with
wild passion and the full weight of the blues. Jazz critic Stanley Crouch
extols David Murray's ability "to summon fifty years of saxophone techniques in two or three phrases, to pivot from harmonic sophistication to
rhythm and blues squeals, from cleanly articulated tones to percussive
blurs and blat sounds, or from swelling melody to swirls of color."

Everything that David Murray plays issues from tremendous inner
intensity. His tenor saxophone seems to move in a trance—wending and
climbing, bobbing and weaving a serpentine path through wildly fulmi-
nating climactic lines, supported by Herculean feats of circular breathing.
This is the same abandonment and ecstasy, the same spirit possession, that
can be experienced day in and day out in the gospel services of black communities. "The church I come from is the Pentecostal Church of America
where African rituals have been preserved and people become possessed
by spirits," said Murray. "Then they speak in tongues they themselves
don't understand. . . . It's the same when we've reached a certain plateau
in our music. Sometimes I have the feeling that I could step out of my
body and observe myself as I'm playing. I see myself playing. I don't think
about it. Someone else does that."

David Murray's improvisations are the very incarnation of musical freedom, confirming Ornette Coleman's declaration that "the best
statements Negroes have made of what their soul is have been on tenor
saxophone."

The self-evident rawness, vitality, and naturalness so characteristic of
David Murray's music making contrasts strongly with Wynton Marsalis's
inclination toward clarity, logic, and unification. Wynton's trumpet
sound radiates total purity. Ulrich Olshausen: "No other trumpeter in
the world today has the technical resources that Marsalis has. A talent
like his probably doesn't come along more than once or twice in a century." Marsalis's lucid mastery of instrumental technique on the trumpet
is the greatest jazz has seen since Dizzy Gillespie. Many critics are even
of the opinion that, as far as technical ability goes, Wynton is superior to
Dizzy. His tone is crystal clear, his gestures are round and luminous, his
lines precise and polished. His unbelievable fluency is seen above all in
his mastery of playing in the high register without any trace of shrillness.
Nonetheless, there is no doubt that Wynton's trumpet playing comes out
of a concentrated expressiveness—a fire, but an intellectual, cool one,
reminiscent of the cool flame of a Miles Davis, but without Miles's sadness and world-weariness. Rather, Wynton's playing is overlaid with a

significant intellectual component, an almost scientific relationship to the blues.

Wynton Marsalis was the main catalyst of the jazz renaissance of the eighties and nineties. In the reevaluation of traditional approaches to playing, no musician had more imitators than he did—and no one polarized the jazz scene to the extent that he did. "My guiding principle is: never discard anything," says Marsalis. "The whole emphasis on constant innovation that we learned in the sixties is false, because we were cut off from the roots. The job is not to imitate what our forefathers did, but to transfer the power of their playing into our time." According to Wynton, the job of a musician is to again take up lines of tradition that have vanished, to study the masterpieces of jazz and to learn from them, and to measure oneself against them according to one's own individuality and personality. Marsalis's emphasis on the jazz tradition gained him the reputation of being a bebop revivalist. But, starting around 1989, he went much further back than that, orienting his trumpet playing toward the old masters of the jazz trumpet, and his compositional work in the direction of Duke Ellington and New Orleans jazz. At the beginning of the nineties, Wynton Marsalis had become a leading figure for a generation of young musicians, standing for a renaissance and transformation of traditional ways of playing jazz.

In contrast to the loose dress codes of the jazz avant-gardists, Wynton and his acolytes, the "young lions," dressed in elegant, custom-tailored suits, sophisticated ties, and finely crafted shoes, all intended to underline the seriousness of their musical efforts. This deliberately well-groomed appearance was adopted not only for reasons of fashion: "One hundred and fifty years ago, I would've been a slave; fifty years ago, I would've had to sit in the back of the bus, like my father did. Today, I don't have to do that any more," said Wynton. And, when a white critic referred, somewhat derogatorily, to Marsalis and the "young lions" as "young men in suits," Wynton responded, "So how should I come out on stage? Naked?"

Albert Murray, the African American writer and sociologist, and a mentor to Wynton Marsalis, added, "The most radical thing that a dark-skinned American can do is to look good, to be well-dressed, to have good manners, and to show a good upbringing; that's the most dangerous son of a bitch in this country!"

The success that Wynton Marsalis enjoyed in the nineties was unprecedented. *Life* magazine, in its July 1995 issue, named him one of the "50 Most Influential Boomers," and *Time* magazine included him in their 1996 cover story on "America's 25 Most Influential People."

Wynton Marsalis has mastered the art of moving compellingly and conclusively from one note to the next with such uncanny perfection that the listener is first amazed and then convinced, "This is it! This is exactly how it must sound!" Some critics contend that this highly organized mixture of mental clarity and precision is no more than a slick abstraction. In fact, there can be no doubt that this spontaneously fused crystalline containment is far superior to the efforts of those who resort to preestablished formulas, let alone composition. In Wynton's interviews, logic is one of his favorite concepts to invoke.

Wynton Marsalis comes—like Louis Armstrong and Jelly Roll Morton—from New Orleans, where he was born on October 18, 1961. He grew up in modest black middle-class surroundings. His father, Ellis, was a recognized jazz pedagogue and pianist who had played with Cannonball Adderley and Ornette Coleman, but who had relatively few playing opportunities in New Orleans, because in that city's jazz scene, fixated on older historical styles, a postbop pianist like Ellis was considered a modernist.

"Racism is the main problem of our society," Wynton remembers. "As a child, I found out what it means to be called a 'nigger.' There's no delete key for that."

At the age of six, Wynton received his first trumpet. "Miles, Clark Terry, Al Hirt, and my father were all sitting around a table in Al's club in New Orleans. . . . My father, just joking because there were so many famous trumpeters sitting there, said, 'I better buy Wynton a trumpet.' And Al said, 'Ellis, let me give your boy one of mine.' But Miles said, 'Don't give it to him. Trumpet's too difficult an instrument for him to learn.'" Fifteen years later, in the 1982 *Down Beat* readers poll, it wasn't Miles, after having made his anxiously awaited and spectacular comeback to the jazz scene in the previous year, who was voted musician of the year, but rather Wynton Marsalis—and for nothing less than "Jazz Album of the Year," as well as in the trumpet category. Having entered the scene only two years before, Wynton walked away with first place, while Miles had to settle for second. Since then Wynton's success in such polls has remained unbroken.

Wynton gained his musical skills at the Ben Franklin High School and the New Orleans Center of Creative Arts (NOCCA). Because his father taught a jazz course at NOCCA, it was decided that Wynton would follow the classical course, learning jazz at home. In contrast to many other musicians of his generation, from the age of twelve, Wynton studied jazz and classical music at the same time: Bird along with Bach, Coltrane along with Corelli, Monk along with Mozart. His contemporaries didn't understand his musical preferences: "When you said you played classical music, they laughed in your face. 'Classical music, man, give me a dollar.'"

He played in guitarist Danny Barker's marching band, in funk groups, and blew first trumpet in the New Orleans Civic Orchestra (in which he was at the time the only nonwhite musician). "Every year," said Wynton, "there was a competition for soloists, and the three winners then performed in youth concerts with the New Orleans Philharmonic.

No one thought I had a chance. 'Who wants to hear a trumpeter play a concerto?'" At fourteen Wynton won the competition. As winner of the first prize, he performed Haydn's trumpet concerto with the New Orleans Philharmonic, followed two years later by Bach's Brandenburg Concerto no. 2 in F Major. His successes in the world of classical music led to appearances with the New York Philharmonic and the Cleveland Orchestra under conductors including Leonard Bernstein, Zubin Mehta, and Seiji Ozawa.

Compared with Marsalis, David Murray's musical development was completely unacademic. He taught himself to play the saxophone. He was born in Berkeley, California, on February 19, 1955. His mother was a respected gospel pianist, his father a preacher in the Missionary Church of God and Christ. At the age of eight, David started play-ing alto sax in the Murray family's band, which accompanied gospel services ("the first night I got my saxophone, I played in church"). By twelve he was blowing in a rhythm and blues group. Shortly afterward he tried his luck as a street musician, wearing a headband and strum-ming a guitar à la Jimi Hendrix on Berkeley's Telegraph Avenue. "I wanted to be Jimi Hendrix. I'm a black hippie." At fifteen he headed an organ trio in the San Francisco area. The lineup of organ, saxo-phone, and drums was very popular in the black neighborhoods of the time, and the electrified, wildly cooking sounds of this particular con-stellation demanded an absolute maximum of physical and emotional involvement from a saxophonist. It was during this period that David Murray, inspired by an unaccompanied solo concert by Sonny Rollins, switched to tenor sax. "I knew then that I couldn't play the alto saxo-phone any more. It doesn't have enough substance." Murray added, "When I was growing up, everyone was trying to play all the Coltrane solos. So I told myself, 'Maybe I shouldn't study his solos because in five years all these people will sound the same.' I was right. They all sound the same."

He studied with John Carter and Bobby Bradford at Pomona College in Los Angeles. Paradoxically, when he first went to New York in 1975, it wasn't as a musician, but rather to write a thesis for his diploma: "The Saxophone after Ornette Coleman." He interviewed musicians including Ornette, Cecil Taylor, and McCoy Tyner. When he met with saxophonist Dewey Redman and played for him, Redman told him: "Put down the pencil and pick up the horn." By the end of his stay in New York, Murray was spending more time on gigs than on field research. He became a participant in the Greenwich Village/Lower East Side loft scene, which continued and developed the free-jazz tradition.

"David Murray," wrote American jazz critic Martin Williams, "ex-plored his horn to the extent of finding and using several notes on the top of the tenor sax that nobody knew were there before." Indeed, David

Murray has uniquely, for traditional styles of playing, developed the ec-static overblown playing opened up by free-jazz saxophonists. Murray comes in part from Albert Ayler, the free-jazz tenorist who died in myste-rious circumstances in 1971 after having become *the* master of overblown free playing, while on the other hand Murray also comes from the sen-sual vibrato playing of Swing-era tenor players such as Paul Gonsalves, Ben Webster, and Lester Young.

Greg Tate remembers Murray's first appearances on the New York loft scene:

> There was the big brawny vibrato of the Webster/Shepp school, the slip-pery melodic invention of Rollins and Gonsalves, and Ayler's ghastly braying, neighing and whinnying. There was also something I had only heard before in Jimi Hendrix's ectoplasmic "Band of Gypsies" version of "Machine Gun": a ghostly harmonic shimmer leaking out of his lin-gering overtones—his version of the blues came with accompanying poltergeists.

In an exciting process, Murray has brought two improvisational directions—modern and old—into balance with each other. He has, step by step, melodized and "tonalized" Ayler's overblown playing of free jazz—characterized by spectral arcs of sound and sharpened microtonal lines—without taking away any of his music's wildness, fire, and ecstasy. Conversely, he revitalized the classic tenor sonority of the Hawkins-Webster-Rollins lineage by opening it up to the incandescent lines of energy playing.

It is fascinating to follow how Murray gradually applied orthodox overblown free-jazz playing to increasingly concrete melodic figures. His debut album, *Flowers for Albert*, recorded in 1976, is still strongly under the influence of Albert Ayler's eruptive cascades of sound. But within a year, in *Live at the Manhattan Ocean Club*, Murray was already point-ing the way toward what he would increasingly refine and develop in the eighties and nineties, together with drummer Jack DeJohnette, with gui-tarist James "Blood" Ulmer, with the World Saxophone Quartet (which he cofounded in 1976), and above all with his own groups. His over-blown playing finds its way back to the song form and to recognizable melodic figures. "I love the song form," he says. "The way I play is to-tally related to the song form. . . . The song form will always live. If you listen to music today on the radio, the problem is the absence of it—in Rap, for instance." Murray's approach already showed this tendency to-ward song form, tonality, and beat when as a twenty-year-old he came to New York in 1975 and established himself in the front ranks of the jazz avant-garde. "A lot of people from California have more of a melodic sense of hearing things than people over on the East Coast—musicians like Charles Mingus, Eric Dolphy, and Ornette Coleman. Ornette's not from California, but everybody from Texas is from California, really," Murray said.

Four years after David Murray moved to New York, Wynton Marsalis followed suit, enrolling in the Juilliard School of Music in 1979 in order to prepare for a concert career in classical music. In 1980 he went on a European tour with bop drummer Art Blakey's ten-piece band. Shortly afterward he became a member of Blakey's legendary Jazz Messengers and stayed with Blakey until 1982. "If it hadn't been for Art Blakey," explained Wynton later, "I wouldn't be playing jazz. I never had the intention of doing that professionally. It was Art Blakey who gave me the chance to play every night."

Wynton's playing is a grandiose synthesis of the best that the history of the jazz trumpet can offer—from Louis Armstrong's rhythmic exuberance by way of Dizzy Gillespie's exultant high notes, Clifford Brown's warmth, Miles Davis's cool poetry, and Freddie Hubbard's powerful attack, up to Don Cherry's swirling melodic sounds (see the section on the trumpet). And yet everything that Wynton plays derives from his highly imaginative personality's capacity for integration. Wynton Marsalis quotes less than he paraphrases—using his own gestures and vocabulary to circumscribe, cultivate, and apply to the present what his predecessors have expressed, equally individually, as the truths of jazz.

Wynton Marsalis is the first musician to have mastered both jazz and European concert music in such sovereign fashion, and furthermore to find acceptance and acclaim in both worlds. Maurice Andre, who has himself done so much to uphold and interpret the literature of classical trumpet playing, has called Wynton Marsalis "potentially the greatest trumpet player of all time." And Ron Carter, celebrated jazz bassist, believes Marsalis to be "the most interesting young musician since the sixties." Marsalis is the only musician ever to win a Grammy in both the jazz and classical categories in the same year (1983).

Wynton Marsalis went the way that, as he stresses, "I had to go." The more difficult way of proving himself as a black musician in a world of concert music shaped by European standards, and then, after enjoying great success, withdrawing from the attractions of the classical music business. He could have pursued the career of a highly paid concert trumpeter, living in luxury in conditions that were much less physically demanding. But Wynton, for thoroughly political reasons, chose the African American heritage of jazz. "I think—I *know*—it's harder to be a good jazz musician at an early age than a classical one. In jazz, to be good means to be an individual, which you don't necessarily have to be in classical music performance." He continued: "The techniques of sax players Charlie 'Bird' Parker and John Coltrane, drummer Art Blakey, pianists Art Tatum and Thelonious Monk . . . require more understanding of composition than Bach or Bartók. It is harder to play good jazz well than classical. Jazz is the classical music of our century."

What Wynton Marsalis and his pupils, the "young lions," sought were the essentials of jazz. Wynton's outlook is explicitly conservative. In his view, the indispensable fundamentals of jazz are: blues, standards, a continuous swinging beat, tonality and functional harmony, refined craftsmanship on one's instrument, and a mastery of the jazz tradition, from New Orleans jazz up to the early (and still tonal) music of Ornette Coleman. Everything beyond that—avant-garde and free jazz, hip-hop jazz, jazz-rock, European jazz, Asian improvisation—is, for Marsalis, a false path.

Wynton's choice of words is often polemic. He has denigrated rap as "hormone-driven pop music." He says that he's happy not to be a hip-hop musician, "because you don't have to keep reaching for your pipe in public." Marsalis denounced Miles Davis's pop-based music of the eighties: "He's like a general who has betrayed his country."

Anyone who expresses himself in these terms shouldn't be surprised to be on the receiving end of equally vehement counterattacks. One critic gave him the title of the "jazz resurrection machine." Another critic said of Marsalis's highly virtuosic trumpet playing, "The whole technique serves only to put the past in a pristine museum display case." In 1997 pianist Keith Jarrett said, in a furious article in the *New York Times*, "Wynton imitates other people's styles too well. You can't learn to imitate everyone else without a real deficit. I've never heard anything Wynton played sound like it meant anything at all. . . . His music sounds like a talented high-school trumpet player to me. . . . He's jazzy the same way someone who drives a BMW is sporty."

Marsalis responds to such attacks with his characteristic mixture of polemics and calm: "You can't enter a battle and expect not to get hurt." His irrepressible drive to challenge others and to get into arguments has brought him into conflict not only with critics and musicians remote from his own circle, but also with, for example, his idol Miles Davis.

When Wynton and Miles met for the first time, Miles greeted him with the words "So, here's the police . . . " And when, at the 1986 Vancouver Jazz Festival, Wynton tried to join, unannounced, a performance by Miles's electric band, Miles stopped the band as soon as Wynton started to play and said, "Come back tomorrow."

It's evident that the young Marsalis mastered instrumental technique to such perfection that his creative ability was overshadowed. That is especially apparent in his first recordings with Art Blakey and in his debut album *Wynton Marsalis* (1981). Despite the polished brilliance of these recordings, they were nonetheless plagued by etudelike, virtuoso scale playing.

It's certainly not just by chance that Wynton's playing underwent a fundamental change after his mideighties decision to concentrate exclusively on jazz. (Since then he has performed European concert music only sporadically.) His playing increasingly lost its traces of slickness and became rhythmically more and more round, refined, and spontaneous.

In the course of that development Wynton Marsalis acquired a rare mastery of rhythmic nuance. His skill in placing a note just where it's "due" is truly breathtaking. The music of his quintet with Branford Marsalis (saxophone) and Kenny Kirkland (piano) and of his quartet with Marcus Roberts (piano), Bob Hurst (bass), and Jeff "Tain" Watts (drums) gained him a reputation as a bebop nostalgist. But his ability to manipulate tempo and meter goes well beyond that of his models: John Coltrane, Charles Mingus, and above all the second Miles Davis quintet. The music is indeed straight-ahead, and unquestionably has the characteristics that Wynton has designated essential to jazz, such as tonality, beat, walking bass, and chord changes. But it also has a metrical variance and flexibility that had not been seen in jazz up to that point. Critic Martin Williams correctly noted in 1987 that "there are signs that Wynton's work is more than just a brilliant synthesis of the past." His growth as a trumpeter has above all been rhythmic. His original contribution involves *metrical variance*—the absolute virtuosity and freedom with which Wynton and his musicians improvise with, and over, constantly changing meters. The meter is no longer rigidly predetermined; it can mutate and change into as many different forms as can the melodic and rhythmic elements. However, Wynton imposes one limiting condition: no matter how freely the musicians manipulate the meter, they must always resolve it correctly within the preexisting form of the piece. In the artfulness with which they improvise with different meters, creating polymetric or bimetric ambivalence, Marsalis's groups of the eighties are without parallel in jazz. His music of this period is a modern continuation of the bebop conception, an interpretation of jazz history.

Listen, on the other hand, to David Murray, and you seem to be encountering the primal forces of sound. "The sound, that's first," he once said, and indeed his sound is so powerful that, like Coleman Hawkins and Ben Webster, or Albert Ayler, Murray does not need to use a microphone in his club concerts. Murray's playing, like his composition, is saturated with the earthy, raw, squeezed sounds of jazz—with the passionate vocalized wailing of archaic New Orleans jazz, with the powerfully eruptive tones of swing tenor horns, with the exciting jungle cries of the Ellington orchestra, with the throaty timbre of the blues, and with the ecstatic outbursts of free jazz that by now can almost be called traditional. David Murray thus mainly chooses and updates those elements from the legacy of jazz where the emphasis is on expressive sound production.

David Murray admires big bands. That is already apparent in the fact that the saxophonists who, after Albert Ayler, greatly influenced him often recorded with big bands: Paul Gonsalves and Ben Webster with the

Duke Ellington Orchestra, Coleman Hawkins with Flechter Henderson, and Lester Young with the Count Basie Orchestra. So it's not surprising that Murray's music, whether in smaller groups or solo concerts, is almost overwhelmingly orchestral with a "love for bigness" in sound: compact, massive, and resolute, and, despite its melodic sensibility, always a little raw and gruff. About his love of orchestral texture, he says, "If I can't play music that's on the edge, I'd rather die."

Throughout the eighties Murray's love of big bands increasingly led him toward composition. He has recorded many of his great works—"Flowers for Albert," "Last of the Hipmen," and "Dewey's Circle"—with all possible lineups (and this ability to keep himself fresh by leading several groups at once—quartet, octet, big band, etc.—is one of his specialties). Each of these versions has been successful on its own terms. But the interpretations become increasingly mature, unified, and dynamic as the number of players increases. "Arrangements are like children," according to Murray. "They have to grow."

Exceptional praise has been directed toward the compositions and arrangements for his famous octet, which made its debut appearance at New York's Public Theatre in 1978. It must certainly be ranked one of the outstanding groups of the eighties and nineties. Like his idol, bassist Charles Mingus, Murray had always dreamed of heading a big band. Like Mingus, he was forced by financial circumstances to make do with a medium-sized ensemble; like Mingus, Murray also made a virtue out of necessity. Whenever Murray's dream has come true and he has managed to put together a big band, critics and musicians have concurred that as a composer, Murray convinces more with his octet.

"I'm trying to be like a vessel in which the antique and the modern, tradition and the avant-garde, can mix." David Murray's mastery of disrupting stylistic norms is perhaps even more apparent in his compositions than in his tenor playing. His music is more than just a dazzling reevaluation of jazz tradition; it addresses the entire spectrum of black music: bebop, free jazz, rhythm 'n' blues, African, soul, Swing, and right back to the cradle of New Orleans—in a synthesis that is reflective, freely interpreted, and not just a restoration of the past, but a transformation into something new. His music never merely speaks through the tongues of others. They speak through him in his own voice.

Anyone who links so many influences—uniting and reassessing the work of Duke Ellington, Charles Mingus, King Oliver, Jelly Roll Morton, and Albert Ayler—runs the risk of superficiality, a lack of commitment. David Murray found his own way out of that danger. The many fragments encountered in his music aren't lifeless, interchangeable material. Just as in a gospel service, the calls and responses from individual members of the congregation occur independently, coming together in a process of unceasing intensification to form a multivoiced choir where every voice is a recognizable part of the whole and yet retains its own individual character. Similarly, the many influences in Murray's music overlap and cohere as voices with which he, like a preacher, conducts an ongoing ecstatic dialogue.

Especially from the point of view of harmony, everything David Murray plays and composes has a direct connection to the music of the African American church. In gospel church services, the members of the congregation engage with the music independently of one another, resulting in a kind of accidental polytonality, different tonal centers at the same time. Something like this happens in David Murray's compositions. The natural, relaxed way in which he achieves polytonality, and his masterful free treatment of contrapuntal ideas, comes from the gospel community. Free jazz plays a role here only as a reinforcing element.

Wayne Saroyan remarks:

> The intriguing element of Murray's writing is the melodic structure of his songs. As hard and free as Murray can sometimes blow, his writing always returns to a sense of the familiar. His melodies linger in the mind, nested against the soulful improvising that, like that of Lester Young, Ben Webster, or Coleman Hawkins, becomes a well thought-out story, framed by a musical narrative thread. It's one of Murray's enduring musical strengths: as a storyteller, he's making the music both accessible and relevant to his audience, whether he's moving into uncharted territory or returning to his R&B roots.

"I'm not very interested in what people will think about my music after I'm dead," said David Murray once. "I want to hear it now." Similar to Sonny Stitt, he has been accused of not being able to say no to any recording opportunity. Among living jazz musicians, Murray is by far the most recorded. Under his own name, and with the World Saxophone Quartet, he has released more than 220 albums—not counting the more than one hundred records on which he appears as a sideman or a guest. "Murray's discography gives new meaning to the phrase 'an embarrassment of riches,'" writes American critic Gary Giddins. "Several of his recordings . . . are among the benchmark achievements in the postmodern era, and others attest to a consistency that is rare in any era."

Ming, the 1980 album where Murray first presents his celebrated Octet—with Anthony Davis (piano), Henry Threadgill (alto sax), George Lewis (trombone), Olu Dara (trumpet), Butch Morris (cornet), Wilbur Morris (bass), and Steve McCall (drums)—is a key work of eighties jazz. Here Murray for the first time presented in music his conviction—never before expressed with such multistylistic breadth—that "the entire legacy of jazz is avant-garde" (Stanley Crouch). Murray's music doesn't pontificate on jazz history, but makes surprisingly and sensuously clear how revolutionary the collective improvisations of New Orleans jazz are, how forward-looking the jungle sounds of the Duke Ellington Orchestra, how excitingly revolutionary Charlie Parker's bebop and the Charles Mingus Band's liberation of tempo. Murray uncovers what lies at the heart of traditional elements, pointing toward the development of contemporary jazz. This is even more impressively achieved on the 1982 album *Home*, where his octet once again mixes and fuses all the great aspects of black music even more boldly and freely: gospel sounds, free jazz, Afro-Caribbean music, Delta blues, soul, etc. "With every sound, he brings the tradition to life for us," writes Hans-Jürgen Schaal.

Like David Murray, trumpeter Wynton Marsalis has played his way through almost the whole of jazz history, taking up and reinterpreting whatever is of relevance for his individual and critical revaluation. All the same, in this stock taking of jazz tradition he has been shaped and influenced by one musician more than any other: Miles Davis. More than any other band, Wynton's quartet of the second half of the eighties advanced and refined Davis's concept of "controlled freedom." As discussed above, his bands have attained rare mastery, particularly in playing with changing rhythms, shifting tempos, and superimposing different meters. Every new album Marsalis released in the eighties brought further intensification and refinement of rhythmic nuances. And each time you thought he had finally reached the limits of prowess, he surprised with fresh metric possibilities and new rhythmic finesse. The peaks here are *Marsalis Standard Time Vol. I* (1987), an album where he throws fresh metrical light on "standards," the great songs from American popular music; *J Mood* (1986), on which he celebrates the blues (Wynton: "The blues is the soil of American music"), and *Live at Blues Alley* (1988), which is particularly impressive in its stirring, intense interplay.

By the end of the eighties, Wynton's concept of rhythmic density had attained such complexity that further refinement seemed scarcely possible. It is characteristic of his dynamic development and of his constantly self-critical attitude toward his own music that at this point he felt that a change of style was unavoidable. He turned away from contemporary bebop (a kind of "high energy bop" with crazily rapid tempos, aggressive rhythms, and complex metric superimpositions), which had shaped his playing up to that time, toward "softer," more relaxed rhythms, and more traditional aspects of jazz.

This transformation, documented in the 1989 album *The Majesty of the Blues*, was not, as some critics thoughtlessly contended, a nostalgic retrograde step. It is the logical outcome of Wynton Marsalis's musical development. After he had extensively investigated and refined the entire rhythmic foundation of postbop, the aspect of sound—timbre—became increasingly important in his music making.

That becomes apparent in his greater use of all sorts of mutes (plunger, derby, cup mute, etc.) and a more expressive, blues-related articulation—the *dirty* sounds that Wynton now explores with the accuracy and discipline he had previously devoted to bop-oriented phrasing. Since 1988, Wynton's roots in New Orleans jazz, until then concealed and only indirectly apparent in his playing, have thus increasingly moved into the foreground. Now he deliberately reflects the tradition of archaic jazz with its expressiveness: in dirges, call-and-response structures, vital melodies, exuberant Mardi Gras rhythms, and humorous sounds—all this even though the bop element continues to be active in his music.

During the nineties, Wynton incorporated into his playing, in a virtuosic and personal way, all the "old" trumpet techniques that had been neglected since the advent of bebop, adding them to his vocabulary and transforming them. The musicians of modern jazz had broken with these techniques in the midforties because at that time they seemed to have hardened into clichés. But now Marsalis found in them an inexhaustible source of material that could be used to make his playing individualized and personal—for example, Louis Armstrong's "rips" (sliding up to a note from underneath rather than hitting it directly), the elaborate mute and "growl" techniques of King Oliver, Rex Stewart, and Cootie Williams, or in Ray Nance's ability to give one note infinitely many different shades of color. Trumpeter Steven Bernstein says, "You know what's so great about Wynton? He's done so much good for trumpet players. . . . It's funny. When I talk to other trumpeters, they complain: man, we quit playing that stuff in 1940. And I answer them: yeah, and that's exactly why that stuff is so hip today, because nobody's played it for sixty years."

Marsalis said:

Everything you ever need to know is in New Orleans jazz. Duke Ellington knew that better than anybody! You have a polyphonic conception of improvisation, high stylization of the blues, a virtuosic concept of the solo, the tradition of ensemble playing with interludes and parts . . . riffs, breaks, timbral effects, a unique concept for playing the bass, tuba, saxophone, and drums—with a new instrument that never before existed: the drum set. Everything you could want is there. I guess when I was growing up, I had no idea that's what it was. I just thought it was some old people in some club playing for some tourists.

There's no doubt that Wynton's musical world—even where it appears to be pure, vibrant jazz—is shaped by the aesthetic standards of Western art. When American journalists Rafi Zabor and Vic Garbarini interviewed Marsalis and keyboardist Herbie Hancock for *Musician* magazine in 1985, Wynton told them, "Anybody can say 'I have emotion.' I mean, a thousand trumpeters had soul and emotion when they picked up trumpets, but they weren't all Louis Armstrong. Why?" Herbie Hancock answered first: "Because he was a better human being." And then Wynton Marsalis: "Because Louis Armstrong's technique was better. . . . Who's to say that his soul was greater than anyone else's? How can you measure soul? . . . Soul is part of technique. Emotion is part of technique. Music is a craft, man."

Zabor and Garbarini commented:

> What bothered him about the notion of soul as conventionally applied is the racist subtext. Black musicians are expected to be 'soulful' and inarticulate, to perpetuate the myth of the gifted primitive whose sources of inspiration are racial and mysterious, and therefore *not his own*, which is to say he is not a conscious artist in the deific Western sense of the term, and even if a genius, one of automatically the second rank.

So the motor for Wynton Marsalis's musical development is this: he aspires to be an artist in the Western sense of the word, recognized as someone who is *consciously* creative. That explains his emphasizing of intellect over emotion, the vehemence with which Marsalis applies the standards of European musical aesthetics to jazz, and his exaggerated purism. "If you don't believe in intellect," he says, "you cannot develop as a musician." Wynton Marsalis rejects the devaluation of "black life" by speaking emphatically of jazz as a "noble art form." In almost every interview, he speaks of the musical excellence, responsibility, nobility, and constant striving for freedom in black music—thus also arguing "that social equality of black Americans with white Americans should now be followed by cultural equality" (Broeking).

Against the prejudice that the musical abilities of black people are "innate," Wynton Marsalis cites the creative intellectual achievements of black jazz musicians. For Wynton, the black man is not a "noble savage," but rather a hero in a thousand forms whose historical creativity is reflected in a series of masterpieces: "Jazz is the classical music of the twentieth century."

When asked to name his favorite composers, Marsalis names—immediately after Duke Ellington—Beethoven, "because of the consciousness of his music, even more than his style."

Wynton Marsalis's perfectionism and work ethic are perhaps the greatest obstacle to his work as a bandleader. One critic has called the Marsalis band "the paradise of a control freak," and in fact his groups sometimes suffer from his tendency to closely monitor and control everything. At the same time, there is no doubt that his quartet of the eighties, with Marcus Roberts, and his septet of the nineties, with trombonist Wycliffe Gordon, pianist Eric Reed, and drummer Herlin Riley, set new standards for the multi-stylistic reworking of the jazz heritage (particularly his septet, with the eight-CD box set *Live at the Village Vanguard*).

While for Wynton Marsalis "soul" is an invention of the white man aimed at degrading black music, for Murray every phrase he plays is bursting with proud black soul-consciousness and soul-feeling. "My experience comes more from rhythm 'n' blues than from anywhere else," Murray has said. Where Marsalis's traditionalism is tinged by the standards of European musical aesthetics, David Murray's music draws its substance from acknowledgment of the African roots of black music, often to such a vital and exuberant extent that one seems to be listening to African music through a veil of jazz, soul, and blues. South African bassist Johnny Dyani (d. 1986), who liked playing with Murray and did so on many occasions, once said, "Sounds like the kind of music we play at home." Dyani conjectured that Murray had certainly "lived in Africa in a previous incarnation."

David Murray's interest begins with the roots of jazz and ends at the outer edges of the African diaspora. No other jazz musician did as much as he did in the nineties to bring contemporary jazz together with other musicians of the black diaspora. David Murray is a kind of jazz ambassador, searching for musical encounters, exchanges, and collaborative projects. Since 1995 he has lived in Paris, using the multicultural metropolis as a platform for collaboration with African and Afro-Carribean musicians from many different countries. When a journalist asked him whether he felt that he was part of the black community in the United States, he answered, "My community is the world."

In 1994 he played at the Banlieues Bleues festival in Paris with Senegalese sabar master Doudou N'Diaye Rose (the composer of Senegal's national anthem, said to know more than a thousand rhythms). They traveled together to Dakar for workshops and concerts. The recording that came out of this encounter, *Fo Deuk Revue*, tries to answer the many questions about cultural identity, tradition, roots, and history that black people from Dakar to New York have asked themselves. In the Wolof language, *fo deuk* means "Where do you come from?" The recording *Fo Deuk Revue* is a grooving mixture of turntablism, Senegalese hip-hop, delicate West African percussion, the Islamic Tukulor songs of the Wolof people, and contemporary Afro-American jazz. In David Murray's music, the dialogue between jazz and world music is not a one-way street. It's a communication based on mutual respect and give-and-take on both sides. Murray says, "I'm ready for the next John Coltranes to come from somewhere else. They might not be coming from North Carolina or New Orleans. Maybe they'll come from Dakar or Nigeria or Guadeloupe or Martinique. Maybe they'll come from Scandinavia—I don't know." In his search for the roots in the soul of black music, David Murray travels the world ceaselessly. He has led countless workshop orchestras as offshoots of his big band. He has played with musicians from the Ivory Coast, Senegal, and Ghana, has improvised with the band Dieuf Dieul from Dakar, bringing fouta music (an urban, modernized form of traditional Islamic Tukulor music) together with contemporary jazz.

On the recording *Creole* (1997), his jazz quartet meets the hypnotic Afro-Caribbean grooves and trance rituals of music from Guadeloupe (with singer Guy Konket and percussionist Klod Kiavue). With the Gwo-Ka musicians of Guadeloupe and singer Fontella Bass, in 1999 he produced a moving gospel project, the recording *Speaking in Tongues*, in which his octet together with Caribbean musicians plays music derived from the black tradition of spirituals.

And in 2002 he formed in Cuba, with musicians from Havana, a Latin big band, for which he wrote compositions in which the figures of Cuban *bata* percussion are transferred to the melodic textures and section playing of a jazz big band.

For himself, he refuses the label of "world musician." "Some guys go around the world and get some music and it's a postcard thing. They don't get into the real fabric of the music. They just take stuff. . . . I could never be that way. That disgusts me. It's like you're a thief. My idea was to get *into* Cuban music."

The key that Murray uses to "get *into*" is the blues. His music emphasizes the African "hinge" in the blues. "The two essential elements of jazz from the U.S. are gospel and blues. When you take those two elements out, I don't know what you get. But the Europeans have to take those two elements out, because they have a difficult time with them. . . . I'm not saying they're not using the *forms*. I'm talking about the *feelings*."

In the nineties, David Murray undertook a "great crossing" in his music, a kind of reversal of the "middle passage," by following the lines of tradition of black music back to their roots, from America to the Caribbean, and from there through West Africa to Central and South Africa. Through his encounters with African and Caribbean musicians, he globally expanded the field of improvised "Great Black Music" to include the polyphony of South African Zulu choirs, the vocal and percussion techniques of Senegal's Wolof, the supple rhythms of Martinique, and the hypnotic beats of Guadeloupe's Gwo-Ka music. Poet Blaise Ndjehoya, also known as Coffin Mokassa, wrote of Murray's world jazz projects, "Odysseus no longer lives in the West. His ship has strayed . . . into the heart of darkness."

While David Murray has internationally expanded the consciousness of the global force of black music in improvisational projects spanning the globe, Wynton Marsalis has helped raise the cultural status of jazz in North America to a new level. In 1987 Marsalis was named the artistic director of Jazz at Lincoln Center. The prestigious New York–based project has a multimillion-dollar endowment. With Wynton Marsalis, and his advisers Albert Murray and Stanley Crouch, African Americans for the first time were in charge of a leading cultural institution in the United States. Jazz at Lincoln Center (JALC) became a powerful vehicle for Wynton's related projects of preserving jazz and expanding the scope of jazz pedagogy. Since its foundation, Jazz at Lincoln Center has performed invaluable services in spreading awareness of jazz, with its concert series, appearances by the Lincoln Center Jazz Orchestra and other groups, television documentaries and programs, workshops, and a library of jazz scores. The success of these programs stands symbolically for the decisive role that Wynton Marsalis and the "young lions" have played in emphasizing the authority of tradition-conscious musicians in defining jazz.

Although he had always been a target for jazz critics, he now began to receive even harsher disapproval from them. These criticisms were three-fold. First of all, critics accused him of nepotism and cliquish behavior in the handing out of compositional commissions and performance oppor-tunities. Second, the JALC program was criticized for being too inflexibly traditional, because it excluded representatives of the jazz avant-garde and the political left, let alone players from the outer edges of improvised music. Wynton responded to this charge: "A log can lie on the bottom of the river forever, but it still won't turn into a crocodile."

Third, the most severe criticism, from mostly white critics, was that Marsalis was practicing a kind of "reverse racism" in his management of JALC. He was accused of ignoring the historical contributions of white jazz musicians in his concert programming, and of largely excluding white musicians in his selection of the members of the Lincoln Center Jazz Orchestra. Wynton responded that the real reason why he was so strongly attacked for his programming policy at Lincoln Center was that a black jazz musician had been appointed director of such a prestigious program. In an interview with Christian Broeking, he said, "Today's crit-ics act like slave owners. We aren't going to solve racial problems on the stage of Jazz at Lincoln Center. The social construction of black people is already wrong enough. What percent of Negro blood does it take exactly to be a black person? How does a black trumpeter play who studied with a German immigrant—half white, half black?"

Trumpeter Terence Blanchard added, "The journalists counting up white and black at JALC ought to take a look at the New York Philharmonic and ask themselves why there are so few black people in that orchestra. . . . Accusing Wynton of racism is cheap."

The vehemence with which Marsalis maintains that the black jazz tradition is the ne plus ultra of improvised music has a reasoned basis. According to Wolfgang Knauer, Marsalis's effort—as well as that of his mentor Albert Murray—to control the definition of what is and isn't jazz "is also a struggle against the appropriation of this musical tradition by non-Americans, and above all against the evolution of the stylistic lan-guage of jazz so as to incorporate influences that are in fact quite remote from its origins."

Wynton Marsalis could have earned millions of dollars if he had chosen a solo career and worldwide tours with his septet and quartet. Instead, he decided to devote the majority of his time to being artistic director of Jazz at Lincoln Center and bandleader of the Lincoln Center Jazz Orchestra.

Since the beginning of the nineties, in addition to his work for JALC, Wynton has devoted himself increasingly to composition. He has written an impressive number of works that reflect the legacy of jazz—Coltrane, Monk, Mingus, spirituals, and blues—in modern, Ellingtonian colors. His tendency toward ambitious large-scale forms is also a sign of his admiration of Ellington ("Duke is one of the foundations of the music"), and his extended pieces have irritated critics much as Ellington's did in their day. In 1992 he released *In This House, on This Morning*, a multipart suite for his septet based on forms from African American church music (spirituals, gospel). In 1993 there followed the suite *Citi Movement and Jazz: Six Syncopated Movements*, written for the New York City Ballet, in which he captured the tempo and pulsing life of America's great cities. He has written string quartets, such as *At the Octoroon Ball* (1995), and ballet music, such as *Sweet Release* (1996) for the Alvin Ailey American Dance Theater. However, the crowning achievement of his work as a jazz composer is the three-hour jazz oratorio *Blood on the Fields*, for which he was awarded the Pulitzer Prize in 1997—the first jazz musician ever to receive this honor.

Blood on the Fields is both a historical examination of the African American experience and a commentary on present-day America. The story begins on a slave ship but quickly becomes a parable about African American identity and U.S. history. *Blood on the Fields* celebrates the contribution that African Americans made to the liberal and democratic values of American society, a society that Wynton sees as essentially hybrid, "incontestably mulatto."

For Wynton Marsalis, the symbol of African American humanity is the blues, whose subject matter is triumph and rebellious joy—not defeat and depression:

> Jazz is an art form and it expresses a Negroid point of view on life in the twentieth [and twenty-first] century. It is the most modern and profound expression of the way Black people look at the world. . . . Negroes didn't accept what was handed down to them, they put those things together in the symbolic form of art and proved that you could use those same principles of respect for the individual and collective expression in artistic *performance*. That was a major event in the history of the world and in the history of art.

Blood on the Fields modulates through asymmetrical forms, in many keys. Its basis is the blues and all of its incarnations, but Marsalis also incorporates spirituals and chorales, contrapuntal textures, Latin rhythms, Mardi Gras melodies from New Orleans, European marches, bebop harmonies, modal improvisation, and swing. It is a powerful stylistic pastiche of the history of jazz, in which Marsalis, with his characteristic tendency toward pomposity, but also with a real sense for integration, brings together influences from Ellington to Mingus, from Igor Stravinsky to Leonard Bernstein.

In *Blood on the Fields*, Wynton Marsalis's band functions like a chorus in ancient Greek theater—affirming, negating, or commenting on the action with improvised interjections. When, as the piece progresses, the protagonists gain more and more freedom, the musicians correspondingly gain more and more space for improvisation. Marsalis's tendency toward monumental forms was also seen in December 1999 when he premiered his work *All Rise* at New York's Avery Fisher Hall, with over 200 musicians, including the New York Philharmonic, the Lincoln Center Jazz Orchestra, and the Morgan State University Choir.

Marsalis's work as teacher and jazz pedagogue is perhaps equally as important as his work as a trumpeter, bandleader, composer, and orchestra director. Wynton is a passionate mentor who has presented his musical message to thousands of young musicians in master classes and seminars, workshops, radio and TV programs, and lectures. His commitment has created a new level of consciousness for the greatness of the jazz tradition, and has helped to develop a network of younger players familiar with almost the entire history of jazz. Tom Piazza: "He has awakened more interest in jazz than anyone else in the last twenty years."

John Zorn

John Zorn has significantly changed and expanded our conception of what diversity in jazz means. His music can be heard as a call to a new way of experiencing, or even living, plurality.

In the seventies, a jazz musician could still probably call him- or herself versatile if he or she had mastered three or four styles. At that time, it was a significant achievement for a player to have the vocabularies of free jazz, bebop, and jazz-rock at his or her fingertips. John Zorn radically expanded this kind of versatility.

"What I completely reject," says the saxophonist and composer, "is the idea that music is a hierarchy: the so-called more complex forms, such as classical music, are higher than jazz, which in turn is more complex and therefore higher than the blues, which is higher than pop music, or whatever. All of them are on the same level! And all of them should be respected in the same way."

This radical democrat of musical postmodernity is serious about this. In John Zorn's music, Bugs Bunny stands alongside Pierre Boulez and bebop; hillbilly music next to Ornette Coleman; death metal next to Stravinsky; drunken cocktail piano next to Japanese court music;

Beethoven next to Brötzmann and the Beatles. "All the genres are the fucking *same*," says Zorn.

In other words: no one musical style alone can explain the world. And if this is true of styles, it's even more true for genres, media, traditions, and cultures. Zorn's music not only notes this, but, in its most provocative, radical moments, screams it out in its very form: any leveling out of diversity is suppression, is violence.

John Zorn is not so easy to grasp; he doesn't fit into any one pigeonhole. He has written pieces for string quartet and for symphony orchestra; he's played freely improvised music; has jammed with death metal bands; has organized moving tributes to hard bop; has played with blues legends like Albert Collins and Big John Patton; has brought klezmer music into the twenty-first century; and has composed film scores of great musical value. But the works that have made him the postmodern musician par excellence are his collage pieces, such as *The Big Gundown, Spillane*, or *Godard*, which brought Zorn out of the shadows as a creative outsider and made him world famous.

"My music is ideal for impatient people, because it is packed full of information that changes very quickly." In John Zorn's collages, no one musical image lasts very long; they constantly collide with other stylistic images tumbling through musical space equally chaotically and quickly, flashing particles that collide with and pulverize one another. "That's the most important thing for me," he says, "abrupt stylistic changes, executed very cleanly. From one world to the next, never staying on one thing for a long period of time. Always defining a particular thing, and then moving very quickly to something different."

It's a unique, wild celebration of speed. In the rush of acceleration, the headlong change of styles, messages, and images, Zorn has found his language: throwing quick ideas together sharply and humorously, a kind of furious "channel surfing." Zorn has explored the possibilities of collage playing so deeply that groups working with similar elements, no matter how hard they may try to distinguish themselves, always somehow wind up sounding like John Zorn. His technique is one of intensification, of the most extreme abbreviation—an entire novel expressed in an epigram, using the tactic of ambushing the listener. In the shimmering dizziness of haste, the essence of the moment, anything seems possible except one thing: the imposing ego of a single style. "If a piece sounds the same at the end as at the beginning, I've already heard it."

Zorn's entire musical development can be related directly to his love of cartoon music (in particular that of Carl W. Stalling). In this music there is no development toward a goal, no slow buildup, but rather an incessant, hectic, anarchic bombardment of atomized, abbreviated sounds. Zorn has radicalized this discontinuous, nonlinear relation to time found in cartoon music, and transposed it to the field of improvised music. "My music is not a slow evolving of the music from thing to thing. . . . It's more like boom-boom-boom, those really fast changes from one world to the next, never staying on any one for a long time, always defining a certain thing, then moving on to something else very quickly."

John Zorn's method is cinematic. He is a master of setting, using compressed, abbreviated gestures to create atmospheres, spaces, and moods that appeal so suggestively to the listener's visual imagination that images appear immediately in the head.

Zorn's music is not only allegorical, imagistic, visual; his music *is* film. Images masterfully edited together in a way that would have earned the admiration of the great masters of film montage: Pudovkin, Eisenstein, Balasz. Every change of style in Zorn's music is like coitus interruptus: a sequence always stops just as it reaches the height of excitement.

Every successful collage contains a contradiction—the contradiction between disintegration, the dissolution of a whole, on the one hand, and integration, the creation of unity, on the other hand. The relation between integration and disintegration can take on many forms here. Zorn's music, particularly his early music, is radical because it shifts this balance so far in the direction of disintegration. Stylistic collision as guiding aesthetic principle: for John Zorn, cracks, fractures, and separations become a permanent crash test of rapidly changing sound worlds. Rupture has never sounded so logical.

It is a paradox: Zorn's music sounds excessively "tailored." But in preparing his pieces, he avoids any later editing in the studio. "People often assume that the fast changes in my music are a result of tape editing. Nothing could be further from the truth," says John Zorn. "There are no tape edits in my music, ever." Instead, Zorn uses the flow of the moment, even when he is using the studio itself as an instrument.

> What I do is done live in the studio. We'll rehearse the first six-second segment, put it on tape, roll the tape back to the top, rehearse the next section, then roll the tape again and get ready for section two while we listen to section one. As soon as section one is over I give the cue, they come in with the next section and we punch it in. We have A and B tracks—this way there's always a slight overhang, slight decay—as A is still fading out B is already in there. There's a kind of organic glue, as if the sections were growing one out of the other instead of chopped up and pasted together. At the end of one day of work usually I have about three minutes of music.

In the age of computer technology, it would be very simple to produce these breaks with a mouse click or the press of a key. But John Zorn insists, with a radicality verging on narrow-mindedness, on the presence of the physical. The breaks and cracks in the music are, as it were, going through the bodies of the musicians playing it. Whereas many postmodern artists want to make the body disappear, or make it into part of a machine, John Zorn puts it in the center, makes it into "the subject of the suffering of dismemberment," as Thomas Miessgang has said. Zorn's collages are indeed often deliberately constructed "like Frankenstein's monster." But, although the breaks and seams always remain audible when styles, genres, moods, and atmospheres collide with one another in Zorn's pieces, on a higher level they communicate the art of elegant melding.

John Zorn's music is not an embrace of multiculti-supermarket culture, nor of an arbitrary "anything goes" aesthetic. Jazz music is authentic only if the actual life story of the person making the music is sublimated in it. Zorn can be accused of many things, but not of falsifying his own development in his music.

Everything about him is there in his music: the boy brought up on television and radio; the enthusiastic teenager obsessed with the cartoon music of Carl Stalling; the aficionado of concert music who experienced his first concert of John Cage's music at age fifteen like a physical impact; the obsessive record collector listening in zigzag fashion across all genres and styles; the cinephile who felt shivers up and down his spine the first time he heard Ennio Morricone's film music; the avant-gardist who experienced Ornette Coleman's music as a revolutionary act of liberation and pogo dancing as an expression of protest.

"What you're definitely *not* hearing in John Zorn's music," says American critic Gene Santoro, "is a bored lack of attentiveness, a self-indulgent and superficial meandering. Just the opposite, in fact: it's a provocative representation of and challenge to the hurtling, increasingly atomized bombardment of information that marks life in our hustling, decontextualizing times."

Zorn's collages are often thematically expressed, and, despite their internal splintering and fragmentation, achieve unity on a higher-level narrative plane. The recording *Spillane* paints an acoustic panorama of the detective films of the fifties: depravity and danger, gambling joints and strip clubs, smoky dive bars and suburban movie theaters, loneliness, murder, and betrayal—the entire ambience of film noir captured as a musical action film. The piece "Shuffle Boil," dedicated to the great jazz pianist and composer Thelonious Monk, is built around Monk's trademark elements of oblique humor, blues, silence, space, and innovation. In the piece "Godard," Zorn translates the cinematic language of director Jean-Luc Godard and the jump-cut techniques of the French New Wave into the field of improvised music.

Zorn's musical range, as annoyingly broad as it may seem at first, also has its trademark characteristics, recurring features, and *topoi*. One of them is his love of the musically dubious, impenetrable, and ephemeral, which features prominently in his whirling cosmos of styles and quotations: schmaltzy cocktail piano, sappy B-movie themes, fake jazz, pathetic copies of country and western music, overwrought free-jazz assaults, consciously informal blues, saccharine film music choirs, Okinawan reggae, etc.—but without smoothing any of this out, passing judgment on it, or presenting it as parody; rather, always keeping it just on the edge of tipping over, half-smiling and half-seriously, a singular epiphany of the mundane and trivial, a celebration of life as it presents itself, equal parts humor and severity.

"That's the secret of a Duke Ellington concept, where you give something to someone and they transform it through their personal filter," says John Zorn. "And when you find someone whose filter interacts with yours in a very creative, helpful way, then you've got a member of the group. Then you've got a pool."

Zorn is not only the best-known musician of the New York downtown avant-garde, but also its most brilliant integrative figure. His groups and projects have consistently catalyzed the New York downtown scene.

Just as, in Duke Ellington's orchestra, each musician has a personal sound, an unmistakable timbre in the music, in Zorn's groups each musician contributes a different style, a different genre. Where Ellington's orchestra was a chorus of irreplaceable sound colors, the music of Zorn's ensembles is an unchained polyphony of genres and styles. "Each musician has his own musical world in his head," says Zorn, "so that, whether he likes it or not, as soon as he gets involved with something, is interested and excited, he's gonna add his world to it. That makes my piece, my world, deeper."

Zorn's influence on the musicians of the East Village in the nineties and early 2000s was so inescapable that he was referred to as the "puppet master of the downtown scene." "Is Zorn a tyrant?" asked one critic, only to answer the question himself: "As far as his music goes: yes. He is the autocratic regisseur of his cinematic musical dramas, and the others dance to his tune like the players at the Charenton Hospice under the direction of De Sade."

In fact, the opposite is true. Practically everyone who has worked with Zorn has been influenced by his ideas, and yet has only profited in his or her own musical personality from the experience. Just as the saxophonist has undoubtedly profited from the personalities of his collaborators—and there's no doubt that he has done so immensely—these musicians have also learned from Zorn's ideas.

It's often overlooked, but it must be acknowledged: under Zorn's influence, the previously ethereal, floating playing of guitarist Bill Frisell became harder-edged, more rock-influenced, more experimental. Drummer Bobby Previte, who previously composed only fairly simple free-bop pieces, came through Zorn's influence to the bizarre interweavings of styles and genres that gained him a wide reputation. And keyboardist

Wayne Horvitz, coming from New Music and free jazz, was inspired by Zorn to weave wonderful, melancholy melodic creations. The list could continue indefinitely of names that are well-known today as leaders in innovative, creative music: guitarist Marc Ribot, accordionist Guy Klucevsek, drummer Joey Baron, guitarist Arto Lindsay, laptop specialist Ikue Mori, turntable artist Christian Marclay.

It's an ideal combination of give-and-take. Without the contributions of these musicians, without their creative presence, John Zorn would still be what he was in the midseventies: a freakish, noise-oriented saxophonist who played free jazz and composed New Music. But, conversely, it was Zorn who, with his gift for integration and his musical ideas, first brought together all the scattered stylistic energies of downtown New York under the umbrella of a common vision. His compositions are more than the sum of the ideas of all the musicians involved.

Zorn's principle of fragmentation, the postmodern confrontation of different elements, functions both within a single piece (*Spillane*, *Godard*) and also between various tracks of a CD (for example, on the recording *Radio* with his band Naked City, or on the Masada sampler *Voices in the Wilderness*). In fact, this has been characteristic of his entire development as saxophonist and composer, which has followed a course like that of a "chameleon racing through a paintbox" (*Down Beat* magazine). For this reason, all the attempts to find order in Zorn's cosmos of gleefully provocative stylistic contradictions are somewhat futile. Nonetheless, Zorn's musical development can be divided into at least eight categories, which in no way are to be seen as following one another strictly chronologically, but rather overlap and intersect with one another in various ways:

1. John Zorn, free improviser. This category includes the two solo albums *Classic Guide to Strategy Vol. 1* and *Vol. 2*, as well as the recording *Yankees* with trombonist George Lewis and guitarist Derek Bailey. In this role, John Zorn perfected playing with duck calls and other game calls (ordinarily used by hunters to attract game), and on the saxophone mouthpiece alone, developing an unruly, protest-laden, furious sonic vocabulary. Zorn has about sixty of these game calls, which he originally tried out in New York hunting stores. "Now they don't even let me in the stores anymore (*laughs*). . . . I mail order them."

2. John Zorn as creator of "game pieces," as they are known. Influenced by the aleatoric works of New Music composers like Pierre Boulez, Christian Wolff, and Karlheinz Stockhausen, Zorn wrote compositions in which musicians, using a predefined symbolic language, play according to rules taken from various sports or games. Using hand signals, bodily movements, and

written signs, the improvising musicians can intervene in the composition as it develops, in order to trigger abrupt changes or to bring their fellow musicians in or out of the music. Pieces like *Cobra*, *Lacrosse*, *Hockey*, and *Track and Field* were designed with improvisers in mind. "My first decision, which I think was the most important, was never to talk about language or sound at all. I left that completely up to the performers. . . . I can talk about *who* and in what *combinations*, but I can't say what goes on. I can say, 'A change will happens *here*,' but I can't say what kind of change it will be." *Cobra* is the high point of Zorn's game pieces, with the most complex structure.

3. "File card" pieces. Zorn's compositional approach resembles the work of a film director more than that of a conventional composer writing notes on paper. His compositions often consist of short instructions and associations which, written on file cards, are deliberately vaguely formulated, relying heavily on the imagination of the improvising musicians.

These file card pieces contain instructions such as: "Try to avoid the paths with the energy units until you're ready to attack a monster," or "Noise of a car accident, while someone plays the flute."

In his file card pieces, John Zorn is generally guided by visual impressions. When someone asked him what a file card piece would look like if he were to write a piece about China, he said "Legend of the Mountain . . . Chinese drums and flutes . . . thunder . . . rain and thunder . . . balladeer *pipa* in the castle . . . cat transformation . . . birds in the trees."

The recordings *Godard* and *Spillane* are probably the pieces that show the strongest imprint of Zorn's file card method. They have a breathtaking, explosive stylistic diversity, and yet they radiate a remarkable sense of unity. On the CD *Spillane* alone— inspired by pulp detective novels of the fifties and the associated film noir atmosphere—sixty stylistic segments are crammed into twenty-five minutes. Nonetheless, Zorn succeeds in welding all of these divergent elements together by relating them to an overarching organizational concept. "In the file card pieces, I needed something to tie all the different genres of music together, so I used dramatic subjects, like Mickey Spillane or Jean-Luc Godard. Each moment of music related to the dramatic subject in some way."

4. The group Naked City. By the beginning of the nineties, Zorn was becoming increasingly tired of the file card concept. "Sometimes we'd do fifty takes of one moment of music that lasted only six seconds." As a result, Zorn started the band

Naked City in order to reproduce live onstage the hectic stylistic pivots that up to that time had been laboriously (and expensively) realized in the studio. Naked City is, as Simon Hopkins put it, "a whole city crammed into two- or three-minute bursts." The music, performed by guitarist Bill Frisell, keyboardist Wayne Horvitz, electric bassist Fred Frith, and singer Yamatsuka Eye, is a lightning-fast cultural massacre, a compression of the history of music in the twentieth century into the blink of an eye. Zorn says:

> Naked City started with rhythm and blues/*Spillane* kind of things, then went into this hardcore [punk rock] period. That came about, I think, because I was living in Japan and experiencing a lot of alienation and rejection. I had a lot of anger in me, and that came out in this hardcore music. . . . My interest in hardcore also spurred the urge to write shorter and shorter pieces. How can you create a ten-second piece that has integrity? That's not so easy.

5. John Zorn as a link between hardcore punk rock and free jazz. This aspect is particularly prominent in the band Painkiller, with electric bassist Bill Laswell and drummer Mick Harris (of the band Napalm Death). This is where the furious side of John Zorn as saxophonist is most clearly expressed, appearing onstage in a T-shirt bearing the slogan "Die, Yuppie Scum!" and unleashing a firestorm of noise on the audience. "The connection between free jazz and hardcore seemed so natural to me. . . . When Ornette Coleman's music came out for the first time, it was a shock. That impact, that shock, is what I wanted—like a fist in the face."

Zorn's involvement with hardcore, punk, noise, and death metal is the expression of his desire to play the role of agent provocateur. This shocking, obscene side of Zorn is expressed in titles like "Purgatory of Fiery Vulvas" or "Mantra of Resurrected Shit," and cover sleeves featuring gruesome images of medical pathology, sadomasochistic pornography, horrible photographs of murder victims, corpses torn into pieces in massacres. The group CAAAV (Committee Against Asian-American Violence) attacked Zorn for the cover images of his recordings *Torture Garden* and *Leng Tch'e*, charging that these images were degrading to people of Asian descent. Zorn responded by releasing these CDs in a "black box" package in which the controversial art is concealed. Zorn says, "You should ask heavy metal groups if they feel guilty because some guy flips out listening to their music and kills three people. They have been asked and their response is, hey, it's not our fault. And they're right, it's not their fault."

Zorn's violations of taboos are in fact part of a time-honored tradition. The art movements Dadaism and Fluxus, and the musical genres of punk and death metal, show the same impulse: to use shock and disgust to awaken feelings that can shake the viewer or listener out of complacency or apathy, leading to what can be a renewed examination of morality.

Nonetheless, critics accused Zorn of sadomasochistic posing, with a ritualized element. One journalist wrote, "If you live in a state of basic alienation, you have to shock yourself in order to experience anything."

6. John Zorn as jazz interpreter, and his tributes to the great figures of the jazz tradition. It may seem paradoxical that John Zorn of all people, the symbol of the avant-garde, has recorded some of the most moving and most original tributes to the jazz tradition. Zorn's jazz homages are concerned more with paying musical tribute to jazz's knotty original figures and creative outsiders than to the giants of the mainstream. The CD *News for Lulu*, for example, honors almost-neglected hard-bop stylists such as Hank Mobley, Kenny Dorham, and Freddy Redd, while the recording *Voodoo* is dedicated entirely to the unjustly obscure pianist Sonny Clark. Zorn's recordings in this vein will be listened to with great enjoyment even after jazz-historical nostalgia has faded and bop revivalists no longer enjoy the benefits of fashion.

Certainly, John Zorn isn't playing traditional bebop on these recordings. This is a new take on bop, not so much commentary as a kind of criticism—in the sense of the completion of the past from the standpoint of the present. Zorn: "So it wasn't solo, solo, trade fours, head at the end, etc. I said, we're all blowing all the time—no soloists, everybody plays whatever they want whenever they want, and we do short versions. It seemed to make sense. Taking the music somewhere rather than just *regurgitating* it."

This is an understanding of tradition that is diametrically opposed to the bebop renewal coming from the camp of Wynton Marsalis. That is "an attitude where the jazz past is like a museum," Zorn says about Marsalis. "You know, these guys are doing it so much like it was originally done, there is literally no point in them doing it. It's *pathetic*. . . . I think it's racist in a certain way. Anything that excludes other interpretations or other forms of expression is, I think, racist."

7. John Zorn as new music composer. Although his name often appears in books about new music from the United States, Zorn has generally been ignored by the classical music establishment.

Zorn himself is at least partly responsible for this. Works such as *Rituals* (1998) or *Chimeras* (2001) show good postserial craftsmanship and ambitious encoding techniques, but not much more. The rapid stylistic pivots, so exciting in bands such as Naked City, have a strangely flat effect in classical pieces such as *Cat o' Nine Tails* (1998) for string quartet. Zorn's compositions are at their liveliest when their creator has a very direct relationship to the interpreter, whose strong ability to personalize sound is given wings by Zorn's works. For this reason, when Zorn's compositions are played by classical ensembles, they sometimes sound arbitrary, because in the world of classical music this improvisational flexibility and the drive toward strongly individualized sounds is not really present. "Telling Anthony Coleman that he should play the soundtrack to the first scene of Edgar G. Ulmer's novel *Detour*, or telling Bobby Previte to play drums like a sixteen-year-old on an acid trip—this is highly private communication that anyone else would misunderstand, and that works only because we have a unique personal relationship." Zorn is not being vague when he speaks of a "private code" at work in his communication with his musicians. He calls his players his family. "You can't go to Gidon Kremer and say, 'Give me a car crash.'"

8. Zorn's explorations of Jewish music, and his approach to what he calls "Radical Jewish Culture." This continuing development in his music is so important for Zorn that we will examine it in more detail below.

In 1992 John Zorn was at the first major peak of his fame. All of his musical projects seemed to set new standards for contemporary avant-garde music. But then, this iconoclast of the postmodern—"Downtown's Master of the Unsuspected"—suddenly brought out an acoustic quartet playing "klezmer music and jazz," as it has been called.

In this band, Masada, Zorn seemed for once to seek stylistic unity. With this group, he showed that he could play, compose, and lead a band in the manner of a traditional jazz musician. Naked City and Painkiller were assaults on the senses. Masada, in contrast, is concerned with contemplation of Jewish identity and the heritage of Jewish music. For the first time in his career, Zorn put his Jewish roots at the center of his musical interests. "I don't know why it happened," he says, "but suddenly it was like a strange kind of inspiration. All of a sudden I realized that most of the musicians I was close to were Jewish. It was like: wait a minute, how is it that all these musicians are Jewish? I started to get interested in that. And I still don't know if I have an answer to it."

This all began in 1992, when Zorn premiered his piece *Kristallnacht* at the Munich Art Project Festival, simultaneously publishing a manifesto in which he called for a "radical new Jewish culture." The CD *Kristallnacht* is a search for Zorn's Jewish roots, but it is just as much a confrontation, demand, a cry of resistance and rebellion. The CD begins with musical reminiscences on ghetto life in the *shtetl* (overlaid with sounds from historical Nazi speeches). This is violently obliterated by a hellish twelve-minute section: in "Never Again," jagged, high-pitched electronic sounds (in the liner notes, Zorn warns the listener that hearing damage could result from listening at high volume) bombard sad, proud folk melodies. *Kristallnacht* is an attempt to document recent Jewish history from as many points of view as possible. Its seven movements tell the story of the Jewish experience, of survival and Holocaust, the formation of a Jewish state, the Jewish diaspora and the desire, or refusal, to assimilate, and the basic problems of fanatical religious fundamentalism. The piece ends in the present in New York. Zorn says, "We are *garin*—the new settlement."

On the CD *Alef*, and on many other records, John Zorn cites Gershom Scholem, the Kabbalah historian and teacher of Jewish mysticism:

> There is a life of tradition that does not merely consist of conservative preservation, the constant continuation of the spiritual and cultural possessions of a community. There is such a thing as a treasure hunt within tradition which creates a living relationship to tradition and to which much of what is best in current Jewish consciousness is indebted even where it was—and is—expressed outside the framework of orthodoxy.

Over the course of four years, Zorn composed more than 205 pieces in rapid succession that combined Middle Eastern scales with the possibilities of the new jazz. "Masada came about because I'd always wanted to write a book of melodies. Again, it was a challenge—I had never done this before. Ornette Coleman's compositions—wow—what a book of tunes—incredible! I wanted to contribute something like that."

This Masada songbook became not only the foundation for the "Radical Jewish Culture" movement that Zorn called for; it also served as a point of departure for the wild, exciting improvisations of his Masada quartet, which became one of the best-integrated bands in nineties jazz.

The music, played by trumpeter Dave Douglas, bassist Greg Cohen, drummer Joey Baron, and Zorn on alto saxophone, oscillates between resistance and exuberance, refusal and joy. Beyond the virtuosity and technical mastery with which Masada handles the material, there is a deep understanding for a particular energy beneath the music: the cry of the blues, found equally in Ornette Coleman's music and in Jewish music. Critics thought that they had quickly found the formula: Masada = Ornette Coleman + klezmer. In fact, Masada is much more than this. Masada includes Sephardic music, Balkan rhythms, melodies from Romania and Bulgaria, boleros, free bop, boogaloos and dirges, Hasidic wedding and funeral music, and the entire context of jazz, rock, world music, trash, and noise (though applied here in a more refined fashion) that is central to Zorn's commitment to musical diversity. But here, unlike the eighties, Zorn does not engage in labyrinthine stylistic destruction, but rather functions as a great improvising alto saxophonist, telling musical stories as entities.

He gave the Masada pieces titles in Hebrew and Aramaic, naming them after legendary Biblical locations, mythical characters, and parables from the Old Testament and the Kabbalah: *Paran* (the desert Paran, where the Israelites camped, led by Moses; site of God's appearance to Moses), or *Neshamah* ("Soul"), *Kodashim* ("Holy Things"), *Halom* ("Dream"), *Mochin* (Aramaic: "to protest"), *Lachish* (city conquered by the Israelites after a two-day siege; Joshua "killed everything living there with a sharp sword"), *Avelut* ("grieving"), *Ziphim* ("bristles"), *Lebaoth* ("things to come"), *Rahab* (1: prostitute from Jericho, saved by Joshua's scout, and spared when the city was taken; 2: a monster from Babylonian mythology, symbolizing primordial chaos), *Jair* ("may God enlighten"), *Tzofeh* ("to track down"), and *Zebdi* ("My Gift").

The covers of his CDs featured Jewish symbols and Hebrew inscriptions, stars of David, and liturgical objects from Jewish antiquity.

The project quickly drew criticism. Zorn's "radical Jewish music" was said to show a tendency toward political Zionism. His call for a Jewish cultural renaissance was suspected of being ideologically motivated. And in fact, at the beginning of the twenty-first century, with the escalation of bloody violence in the Middle East, the slogan "Radical Jewish Culture" sounded out of place, almost intolerably cynical. After September 11, 2001, a New York avant-garde guitarist distanced himself from Zorn's "radical Jewish culture" onstage during a performance, saying that he did not want to play in the name of a religion that called itself radical—and was applauded for this.

However, it is hardly plausible to call a CD series "Zionist" in which, for example, in 1997 the recording *The Revenge of the Stuttering Child* appeared: on this recording, Palestinian poet Ronny Sonneck reads his poems in English and Arabic over sensitive arrangements written by Elliott Sharp (a Jewish musician) for guitar, electric mandocello, mandolin, bass clarinet, saxophone, computer, harp, accordion, cello, piano, and dumbek (an Arabic drum).

The accusation of religious and ethnic segregation, which critics have repeatedly launched against Zorn's "Radical Jewish Culture" concept, also misses the mark. Zorn's Masada projects include both Jewish musicians and musicians of other origins and other faiths, such as trumpeter Dave Douglas in the Masada quartet, or clarinetist Matt Darriau in the Paradox trio.

In Zorn's "Radical Jewish Culture," there is no promised land. And there are no restrictive definitions. For John Zorn, being Jewish is an open question, not a list of enumerable musical qualities. "I realized that a Jew is someone who naïvely believes that if he gives selflessly to his host culture he'll be accepted. But we are the world's outsiders. . . . This is what was attractive to me about the tribe—the culture of the outsider."

Zorn's Masada music is not radical politically, ethnically, or ideologically. It is radical because it distinguishes itself adamantly both from the mainstream of the orthodox Jewish community and from the American cultural mainstream. For John Zorn, the shtetl long ago became part of the global village, in a multistylistic, provocatively individual manner. That, and not the mistaken political and ideological implications, is what is really radical about Zorn's radical Jewish music.

Zorn's work with Masada and his pride in Jewish culture provide a view in miniature of the complex and paradoxical interaction between a profound rootedness in popular culture on the one hand, and on the other hand an imaginative departure from the mainstream. Like Zorn's series of recordings under the title "Radical Jewish Music" on his label Tzadik, Masada understands Jewish music to include not only klezmer, but also all the other styles and genres that Jews of all historical periods have lived, composed, and performed. "All these kinds of music, from Mahler's symphonies to Burt Bacharach's pop songs and Lou Reed's dissonant rock, are reflected in the Masada songbook. . . . This is music that refuses categorization, but remains true to its elements."

Zorn's restless spirit of innovation within the context of traditional Jewish consciousness has resulted in a creative output that is truly protean. In 1998 alone, eleven new recordings appeared under John Zorn's name. Seven of these were on his own label Tzadik, which in Hebrew means something like "charismatic leader who accomplishes righteous actions." In the first four years of the Tzadik label, Zorn released, as producer, more than 142 albums by various artists. Many of these came from musicians who, without Zorn, would have had no other opportunity to release their work.

Zorn has proved that his Masada music can be played in any conceivable instrumentation. He has organized an electric version of the band, Electric Masada, in which he combines Miles Davis's electric music of the seventies with Middle Eastern scales. For the Bar Kokhba string trio, he has transposed Masada music into a chamber-music context. And, for Masada's tenth anniversary in 2003, he organized interpretations of his Masada songs by the widest conceivable variety of musicians: from punk bands to Ukrainian bandura ensembles, from trash-rock groups and classical chamber ensembles to solo guitarists and jazz sextets, from Sephardic folk bands to noise ensembles. Through it all, he is there at every turn, in all his eclecticism and stylistic diversity, in the full growth and maturity of his new Jewish Masada world. "I'm not afraid of styles," he says. "I like them all."

The Elements of Jazz

Sound and Phrasing

What particularly distinguishes jazz from classical European music is sound. Crudely put, the difference is this: in a symphony orchestra, the members of, say, the string section, will wish to play their passages as homogeneously as possible. This means that each member of the section must have the same ideal of sound and know how to achieve it. This ideal corresponds to transmitted cultural standards or aesthetics: an instrument must have a "beautiful" sound.

For the jazz musician, on the other hand, it is of no particular importance to conform to a commonly accepted conception of sound. A jazz musician has his own sound. His highest goal is to develop, as David Murray has put it, a "signature sound"—a sound that makes him or her unmistakably recognizable. The criteria for this sound are based not so much on standardization as on emotionality and expressivity. To be sure, the latter are also found in European music. But in jazz, expression ranks above euphony, while in European music euphony is more important than expression.

Thus, one may find in jazz a tendency contradictory to standarized aesthetics—but this tendency does not imply that jazz of necessity must be "unaesthetic." It does imply, however, that an artistic music is conceivable that conforms to the highest standards of jazz and yet is contrary to received aesthetic conventions.

The self of the musician is clearly reflected, in the most immediate and direct fashion, in the nonstandardized sound of the great jazz improvisers. In jazz, there is no bel canto, no "schmaltzy" violins, but hard,

193

direct sounds—the human voice, plaintive and complaining, crying and screaming, sighing and moaning. The instruments are expressive and eruptive, not filtered through any regulations or rules of sound. That is why the music made by a jazz player is "true" in a much more concrete sense than that made by the average player of European music. The majority of the one hundred or two hundred musicians in a large symphony orchestra probably do not feel the "titanic struggles" that occur in Beethoven's music, nor do they fully sense the secrets of form that are the basis of symphonic music. But a jazz musician, even in a big band, senses and feels, knows and understands what he plays. The lack of understanding among the "civil service" musicians in the symphony orchestras, of which so many conductors have complained (especially where modern music is concerned), is unthinkable in jazz.

Because a jazz musician's playing is "true" in a direct, naive, and "primitive" way, it may possess beauty even when it contradicts aesthetic standards. One could say that the beauty of jazz is ethical rather than aesthetic. To be able to respond to jazz means first and foremost to be able to feel this kind of beauty.

The first word the layperson thinks of when jazz is mentioned— "hot"—is not just a matter of rhythmic intensity. It is first of all a matter of sound. One speaks of "hot intonation."

The personal, inimitable sound of a great jazz musician is the reason for something that always astonishes the outsider: that the jazz connoisseur is able to recognize, after relatively few notes of music, who is playing. This certainty does not exist in classical music, where it is only with difficulty that one can guess who is conducting or playing certain parts in a symphonic orchestra.

Sound in jazz is—to give a few examples at random—the slow, expressive vibrato of Sidney Bechet's soprano sax; the voluminous, erotic tenor sax sound of Coleman Hawkins; the earthy cornet of King Oliver; the jungle sound of Bubber Miley; the elegant clarity of Benny Goodman's clarinet; the sorrow and lostness of Miles Davis or the victoriousness of Louis Armstrong; the lyrical sonority of Lester Young; the gripping, concentrated power of Roy Eldridge; the clear glow of Dizzy Gillespie; or the joyful melancholy of Jan Garbarek.

In the older forms of jazz the shaping of sound is more marked than in the more recent ones. In the newer forms, an element that often was absent in earlier times is added: jazz phrasing. Trombonist Kid Ory, for example, played phrases that existed in circus and marching music at the turn of the century and are not necessarily jazz phrases. Nevertheless, what he plays is clearly jazz—because of his sound. Stan Getz, on the other hand—especially the Getz of the fifties—has a sound that, when isolated from its surrounding elements, is not so far removed from "classical" saxophone sound. But he phrases with a concentrated jazz feeling no symphony player could emulate. There are modern jazz recordings (e.g., some by Jimmy Giuffre, violinist Zbigniew Seifert, or cellist Erik Friedlander) that are very close to the chamber music of modern "classical" composers. Yet the phrasing is so definitely jazz that the music is felt to be jazz even when a regular beat is not present.

Thus one notes a shift in emphasis from sound to phrasing in the history of jazz (and back, to a certain degree, from phrasing to sound with some free-jazz and postmodern players)—in a sense that will be clarified later in our final chapter.

Sound and phrasing can represent everything of importance in jazz to the extent that a jazz musician, were he to play a piece of European concert music, could transform it into "jazz"—even when playing his part note for note.

The sound of jazz and the jazz phrasing connected with it are the "blackest" elements in jazz. They lead back to the shouts of Southern plantation slaves and from there, back to the coasts and the kingdoms of Africa. Along with swing, they are the sole predominantly black elements in jazz.

One might compare the sound that African Americans, in the formative years of jazz, coaxed from their European instruments to the situation in which the Africans deported as slaves to the New World were forced to speak European languages. It has been pointed out that the "singing" way of speaking peculiar to the southern United States can be traced back to black influence, and it is ironic that even those Southerners who have no other word than *nigger* for a black person also speak in this manner. Originally, the word was nothing but the black way of saying "Negro." In the same sense, jazz sound and jazz phrasing came from nothing but the black way of playing European melodies on European instruments. And this way—like black Southern speech—has penetrated the white world so completely that it has conquered audiences in this white world; it is often employed by white musicians as legitimately as by blacks.

From the vantage point of sound it becomes clear that the question of a musician's skin color remains superficial unless due regard is had for the underlying complexities. From the inner conviction that most of the creative jazz musicians were black, Roy Eldridge once claimed that he could always distinguish a white musician from a black one. Critic Leonard Feather gave him a blindfold test: Eldridge had to listen to a number of unfamiliar records and judge from them. It turned out that he frequently erred about race. In spite of this, Feather did not, as he believed, disprove Eldridge's point to show that black and white jazz musicians sound alike. He only pointed up the many sides of the problem.

On the one hand, Fletcher Henderson, black, wrote the arrangements without which Benny Goodman, white, might not have become the "King of Swing." On the other hand, Benny Goodman played these arrangements "better" with his white orchestra than Henderson did with his black orchestra—according to any standard, even that of black musicians.

Furthermore, in reverse: Neal Hefti, white, wrote some of the most brilliant arrangements for Count Basie's black band. But Basie's band played them "better" than Hefti's own band, which consisted mainly of white musicians.

Finally: As early as the fifties (i.e., before the time of today's avant-garde), Charles Mingus, black, was an exponent of an experimental, deliberately abstract tendency one would almost certainly ascribe to a white rather than to a black musician—if all the generalizations we carry to the race problem made any sense. On the other hand, even before the hard-bop movement, white musicians such as Gerry Mulligan and Al Cohn again and again pointed to the importance of beat, swing, and blues; of originality, vitality, and simplicity. In other words, they did what the simplistic average judgment would sooner have expected of black musicians.

Always, there is this duality when the question of race arises in jazz—and not only in jazz. It is impossible, especially for a European writer, to do more than acknowledge both points of view.

Improvisation

*"If a species can't improvise, it dies out." *—Derek Bailey

A hundred and fifty years ago our ancestors went to hear Beethoven and Hummel and Thalberg and Clementi improvise richly and splendidly; and before that to the great organists—to Bach, Buxtehude, Böhm, Pachelbel; not forgetting Samuel Wesley, though he came later. Today we have to go for the same sort of musical performance to Lionel Hampton, Erroll Garner, Milt Jackson, Duke Ellington, and Louis Armstrong. I will leave you to digest the implications to be drawn from that curious circumstance.

Burnett James made these remarks in an article about improvisation in jazz.

Indeed, during the whole history of jazz, from New Orleans to today, jazz improvisation has been accomplished according to the same techniques as employed in old European music: with the aid of harmonic structures (which, however, in free jazz became so open that they are barely structured any longer).

On the other hand, from the beginning of the nineteenth century, improvisation atrophied in European music to such a degree that today even leading soloists sometimes are unable to make up the cadenzas left open to improvisation in the great classical concertos. Concert performances today are judged according to "authenticity"; that is, whether a piece of music is played or sung as the composer "meant it to be." But if, for example, we were to perform a Vivaldi concerto or a Handel sonata as the composers wrote them, we would simply be "interpreting" a bare, skeletal framework of notes. The entire improvisatory force and freedom of Vivaldi's and Handel's music—and, in general, of all of baroque and prebaroque soloistically conceived music—have been lost to the ideal of "authenticity." Arnold Dolmetsch has said that the omission of ornamentation—the improvised embellishment of the notated music—is as "barbaric" as would be the removal of the flamboyant Gothic architectural ornamentation from a cathedral with the excuse that one preferred a simpler style. The jazz musician (if he is playing tonally) improvises on a given harmonic structure. That is exactly what Johann Sebastian Bach and his sons did when playing a chaconne or an air: they improvised on the harmonies on which the melody was based, or embellished the given melody. The whole technique of ornamentation—the embellishment of melody—that flowered during the baroque period still survives in jazz—for instance, when Coleman Hawkins played his famous "Body and Soul." And the ground bass, organ point, and cantus firmus of the old music came into being to give structure to improvisation and to make it easier, in the same sense that jazz musicians today use blues chords and the blues form, and the chord changes of standards, to give shape to their improvisations. Winthrop Sargeant speaks about harmony in this sense as a "controlling structural principle in jazz."

Of course, it is not as if the early jazz musicians had consciously taken over the improvisational techniques of the old music. They knew nothing of Bach and all these matters, and the parallels that exist here are meaningful precisely because they developed unconsciously: the result not of the same but of a related basic musical feeling. On the contrary, the parallels between jazz and old music become suspect when they are practiced deliberately and when, because similarities in improvisational methods do exist, the two forms are thrown into one pot. Nor does the relationship in conception that stands behind all this stem from the old European music. It is a conception basic to *all* musical cultures in which it is "more important to make music yourself than to listen to the music of others," in which the primeval nature of the relationship to music does not allow for any questions of interpretation or conception to arise, in which the music is judged not according to what it means but to what it is. There are such musical cultures and styles in Africa as well as in Europe, in America as well as in Asia. One might even say that almost all musical cultures anywhere in the world have this common basic conception, with the exception of the music that flowered in nineteenth-century Europe, and that still rules the musical sensibilities of the white world.

The essence of improvisation includes a liking for spontaneity and a positive attitude that lets the musicians believe in the possibility of successful playing even given all the surprises and difficulties that can arise in a musically open situation. This attitude includes the conception that apparent "mistakes" actually open windows onto a new, previously hidden world, accessible by finding a logical way to integrate the "mistake" into a convincing whole. "Jazz is a particular way of approaching life," says Paul F. Berliner.

Jazz, then, has improvisation. But the problem of improvisation is not exhausted with this conclusion. It begins with it. The statement "There is improvisation in jazz" is a truism so widespread that many fans and laypeople proceed to conclude from it that if there is no improvisation in a piece, it is not jazz. Yet Humphrey Lyttelton, the most brilliant representative of traditional jazz in Europe, once said, "In the full sense of 'composing extemporarily,' that is, without preparation, improvisation has proved to be not essential to, and practically nonexistent in, good jazz."

Most jazz improvisation is based on a theme. Usually, it is a standard song in thirty-two-bar form—excluding the free jazz of the sixties and the more complex song forms that came into use in the subsequent decades—the AABA form of our popular tunes in which the eight-bar main theme (A) is first presented, then repeated, then followed by a new eight-bar idea, the so-called bridge, (B). In conclusion, the first eight bars are sounded once more. Or it may be the twelve-bar blues form, about which more will be said in the section about blues. The jazz musician places new melodic lines over the given harmonies of the song or the blues. This is done by embellishing or making slight alterations in the songs or blues (André Hodeir calls this manner of improvising "paraphrasing"), or by creating entirely new melodic lines over the given harmonies (a manner of improvising that Hodeir calls the "chorus-phrase").

The decorative, embellishing "paraphrase" was the main improvisatory device of the older jazz forms. Clarinetist Buster Bailey related, "At that time [1918] I wouldn't have known what they meant by improvisation. But embellishment was a phrase I understood. And that was what they were doing in New Orleans." The "chorus-phrase," on the other hand, which creates entirely new melodic lines, is the main improvisatory manner of modern jazz. Its possibilities are vast. Example 1 shows, in the top row, the beginning of the song, "How High the Moon," the favored theme of the bop era, with its related harmonies, and in rows a, b, and c three different improvisations on it by three leading jazz musicians. One can see at a glance that three completely different melodic lines have come into being. There is no connection between these three lines as far as melody is concerned, but the connection is given through the harmonic structure of "How High the Moon": the same harmonies constitute the basis for three very different improvisations.

This example was transcribed from an RCA record that does not even give a clue to the original theme in its title, "Indiana Winter." The three choruses (that is what improvisations on the harmonies of a theme

Example 1

in the number of bars corresponding to that theme are called) cited in the example were played by trombonist J. J. Johnson, trumpeter Charlie Shavers, and tenorman Coleman Hawkins.

The habits of jazz ensure that the most important jazz themes repeatedly become the foundations for the improvisations of jazz musicians. These themes are called "standards," because they are standard references that enable jazz musicians to be as creative in their improvisation as possible. Standards are played day after day and night after night in hundreds of clubs and concert halls. After one hundred or two hundred choruses, a musician may arrive at certain phrases that then will crop up more and more frequently in the playing of the tune. After a while something like an "ideal chorus" on the respective theme will have developed.

Many choruses have become so famous that the listener would be disappointed if the musician who made them up were suddenly to play something different. King Oliver's "Dippermouth Blues," Alphonse Picou's "High Society," Charlie Parker's "Parker's Mood," Ben Webster's "Cotton Tail," Stan Getz's "Early Autumn," Bix Beiderbecke's "Singing the Blues," Louis Armstrong's "West End Blues," Lester Young's "Song of the Islands," Chu Berry's or Coleman Hawkins's "Body and Soul," Miles Davis's "All of You," Coltrane's "My Favorite Things," Chick Corea's "Spain," Pat Metheny's "Are You Going With Me," Wynton Marsalis's "J Mood"—these (written down as they came to mind) are high points one would be loath to see transplanted to other peaks, especially as one cannot be sure they would be peaks. On the contrary, such a result would be unlikely. It would be foolish to claim that choruses that are among the greatest in jazz cease to be jazz when repeated. Thus, what is created by improvising and, having proved to be of value, is repeated, also belongs to improvisation.

This concept of the once-improvised is important. It makes clear that what was once created by improvising is linked to the musician who created it. It cannot be separated from him or her, notated, and given to a second or third musician to play. If this happens, it loses its character, and nothing remains but the naked formula of notes.

At this point, the distinction between improvisation and composition becomes more differentiated. European music, insofar as it is notated, is capable of limitless reproduction by anyone who possesses the instrumental, technical, and conceptual capacities to grasp it. Jazz can be reproduced solely by the musician who produced it. The imitator may be technically better and intellectually superior but still cannot reproduce the music. A jazz improvisation is the personal expression of the improviser and of his or her musical, spiritual, and emotional situation.

In other words, the concept "improvisation" is actually inaccurate. A jazz musician who has created a chorus is at one and the same time improviser, composer, and interpreter. In jazz—even in arranged jazz, as will be shown later—these three aspects *must* be in evidence lest the music become questionable. In European music they *can* be separated without affecting the quality of the music. On the contrary: the quality may improve. Beethoven was considered a poor interpreter of his own music; others were able to play it better. Miles Davis in his formative years was, as far as technique is concerned, not an outstanding musician. Yet it is unthinkable that a technically better-equipped trumpeter should have copied his phrases and, playing them note for note, have played a "better Miles Davis" than Miles himself. To express it as a paradox: Miles might have been only a fair trumpet player, but he was the greatest interpreter of his own music one could wish for. Indeed, the spiritual power of his improvisations had impact and influence even on trumpeters who were technically superior.

An improvised jazz chorus stands in danger of losing its authenticity and of becoming dishonest and untrue when it is copied by someone who did not create it. Given the multiplicity of human experience, it is inconceivable that the "other" could play from the identical situation from which the "one" improvised a chorus. The relationship between the music heard and the person who created it is more important to jazz improvising than complete lack of preparation. When copying and imitation occur without proper preparation, jazz is in greater danger than when, after hour-long, systematic preparation, phrases are created that belong to the player as expressions of artistic personality. This is the meaning of the passage from Humphrey Lyttelton quoted earlier. A musician as different from Lyttelton as Shorty Rogers means the identical thing when he said, "In my opinion all good jazz musicians are composers. I have utilized them as composers by having parts in which I merely wrote instructions and left the rest to the men to compose spontaneously, mutual instinct being the connecting link between us." (In other words, between arranger and improviser.) Misha Mengelberg, the Dutch pianist, speaks of improvisation as a process of "instant composing," thus expressing the identity of improviser, composer, and interpreter in a different way.

This identity of improviser, composer, and interpreter is what is meant when we speak of improvisation in jazz—not a wild, head-on extemporization. The identity of improviser, composer, and interpreter has to be fulfilled also by the arranger who—aside from relating what is to be improvised to what has been once-improvised—finds the real justification for his position in the fact that he can sometimes respond more satisfactorily to the demand for the identity of improviser, composer, and interpreter than the spontaneously improvising soloist can. Jack Montrose, one of the leading arrangers on the West Coast, said:

> The jazz writer forms a unique contrast to his colleagues in other fields of musical composition in that his ability to *write* jazz music is a direct extension of his having acquired the ability to play it first. He must have shared the experience of creating jazz music, the *jazz experience*. It is my contention that jazz music bearing the stamp of true authenticity has never been written except by composers who have first attained this prerequisite.

Elsewhere, Montrose contended that as long as the music is the work of a jazz musician, jazz will be the result.

We shall discuss this more extensively in the next section, but for now we propose six points that may serve as a summary of the problem of improvisation in jazz.

1. The once-improvised is equal to improvisation.

2. The once-improvised can be reproduced by the one who produced it, but by no one else.

3. Both improvisation and the once-improvised are personal expressions of the situation of the musician who produced them.

4. The concurrence of improviser, composer, and interpreter belongs to jazz improvisation.

5. Insofar as the arranger corresponds to point 4, his or her function differs from that of the improvising-composing interpreter merely in terms of craftsmanship and technique: the arranger writes, even when writing for others, on the basis of experience as an improvising-composing interpreter.

6. Improvisation—in the sense of points 1 through 5—is indispensable to jazz; improvisation in the sense of complete unpreparedness and unlimited spontaneity *may* occur but is *not* a necessity.

The Arrangement

Many jazz lovers and almost all laymen believe there is a contradiction between improvisation and arrangement. Because, in their view, improvisation is decisive, the presence of an arrangement must automatically indicate a state of decadence since "the more arrangement, the less improvisation."

Jazz musicians—not just today, but from the start of jazz, or at least from the great days of New Orleans jazz in Chicago—are of another opinion. They see the arrangement not as an inhibition of the freedom to improvise but as an aid. It is a matter of experience that the possibilities for free and unlimited improvised solo playing are particularly enlarged when the soloist knows what the other musicians are doing. With an arrangement, the soloist knows. Many of the greatest improvisers—first and foremost Louis Armstrong—have demanded arrangements. Only to a superficial observer does it appear contradictory that Fletcher Henderson on the one hand was the first jazz arranger with a precise conception, while on the other hand his orchestra offered greater freedom of improvisation than almost any other big band of its day.

In the relationship between arrangement and improvisation there is an inherent tension, which can be fertilized to an unimagined extent. Jelly Roll Morton told his musicians, "You'd please me if you'd just play those little black dots—just those little black dots that I put down there. If you play them, you'll please me. You don't have to make a lot of noise and ad-lib. All I want you to play is what's written. That's all I ask." And despite this, clarinetist Omer Simeon—long a member of Morton's bands—and guitarist Johnny St. Cyr said, "Reason his records are so full of tricks and changes is the liberty he gave his men. . . . He was always open for suggestions." This is the tension that has to be dealt with in art, and one cannot do much theorizing about it. In the early days of the Ellington orchestra, all the band members felt they were playing what they wanted; yet each note was "Ellingtonian."

Arrangements came into being as early as the formative years of jazz. Even the early jazz musicians—King Oliver, Jelly Roll Morton, Clarence Williams, Louis Armstrong—arrived through improvisation at set, repeatable turns of ensemble playing, and once their effectiveness had been tested, these turns remained. This shows how rapidly improvisation is transformed into arrangement. What was once-improvised yesterday has perhaps already become a permanent arrangement by tomorrow.

George Ball related how the New Orleans Rhythm Kings—the most successful Dixieland band between 1921 and 1925—did this kind of thing

by predetermining definite parts for each man to play; by introduction of patterns, simple though they were, and a more even rhythmic background. Arrangements were, of course, impossible as we know them today, if only from the fact that the most important members of the melody section, Mares, Rappolo, and Brunis, could not read music. [Elmer] Schoebel nevertheless spent numberless rehearsals drilling these men in their parts, which we might call arranged, although not a note of music was set down for them, and which the performers had perforce to learn by sheer memory.

Perhaps the misunderstanding arises from the fact that the term *arrangement* has not been precisely defined. There is a tendency to speak of arrangements only when something has been notated beforehand. But it is easy to see that it is actually only a question of procedure whether a certain passage actually has been written down in advance or has merely been discussed. Arrangement begins the moment something is agreed upon in advance. It is immaterial whether this is done in writing or orally.

Since the thirties, the expression "head arrangement" has gained currency among big bands. In the bands of Fletcher Henderson and Count Basie or in the first Woody Herman "Herd" of the forties, it was common practice to establish only the first twenty-four or thirty-two bars of a piece; the remainder was left to the improvisatory capacities of the musicians. This term also makes clear how inevitable and organic is the development from improvisation through the once-improvised to the arrangement.

Since there is no contradiction between arrangement and improvisation, the latter has not faded into the background by reason of the progressive development of the former in jazz history. Improvisation and arrangement have both developed equally. Charlie Parker, Miles Davis, and John Coltrane—and later, even more so, Albert Ayler, Evan Parker, and other free-jazz musicians—command a freedom of improvisation that King Oliver, Louis Armstrong, or Bix Beiderbecke never possessed at the zenith of traditional jazz. This can be determined quite rigorously: often several masters of one title are recorded until recording director and musicians are satisfied. On several available versions of a given piece by Armstrong or Beiderbecke, for example, the solos vary, but they are, by and large, quite comparable; structure and line were changed only rarely. Takes by Charlie Parker, however, differ so markedly that one might say that a new piece was created each time. Of the four takes of Parker's "Cool Blues," recorded in immediate succession on the same day (only the final one was approved by Parker for use as a master take), three were put on the market under different titles: "Cool Blues," "Blowtop Blues," and "Hot Blues"—and to a certain degree they are all different "pieces."

Thus it is not contradictory for musicians who are members of groups dependent on arrangements to speak of improvisation as the "key word."

John Lewis, the maestro of the Modern Jazz Quartet, where arrangements and composition are of decisive importance, has said, "Collective improvisation is what makes jazz singular." And clarinetist Tony Scott, who has undertaken many interesting experiments as arranger and jazz composer, said during a roundtable discussion at Newport in 1956 that jazz was more likely to progress through improvisation than through writing.

Clearly, the arrangement can only fulfill its task when the arranger lives up to the demands expressed by Jack Montrose at the end of the last section: he must be a jazz musician and a jazz improviser. In the entire history of jazz there is no exception to this basic rule. It is significant that it is not possible to speak of the arrangement in jazz without mentioning improvisation.

Insofar as the arranger has to be an improvising jazz musician, it is only a small step from arranger to jazz composer. The actual contradiction is not between improvisation and arrangement, but between improvisation and arrangement on the one hand and composition on the other. Because improvisation is of such importance in jazz, the music has arrangements but very few compositions that are completely "composed through." European music, at least since romanticism, is a composed and compositionally grounded music, so it has practically no improvisation aside from "aleatorics" in modern concert music (but that is a different matter, which, with its theory-laden clumsiness, casts further light on the strained attitude of the concert musicians toward improvisation!).

Thus the "jazz composer" is a paradox. *Jazz* means improvisation, and *composer*—at least in Europe—means the exclusion of improvisation. But the paradox can be fruitful: the jazz composer can structure music in the sense of the great European tradition and nonetheless leave room for jazz improvisation. Most of all, the composer can write what he or she structures in the sense of the European tradition in a jazz manner. There can be no doubt that jazz is subordinate to European music as far as formal structure is concerned and that it might gain if mastery of form and structure becomes possible in jazz, provided nothing is lost of the elements in which the singularity of jazz is contained: vitality, polyrhythms, immediacy of expression—in short, all that is jazzlike. From this point of view, Stravinsky's dictum that composition is "selective improvisation" acquires a much greater degree of importance for the jazz composer than it can have for the composer in the European tradition.

Here it is helpful to remind oneself that the terms *composition* and *improvisation* are to some extent relative. The two musical procedures are not antagonistic. Every form of composition contains improvisational elements, consciously or unconsciously. Conversely, every improvisation, even the wildest, "freest," collective improvisations of free jazz, includes preformulated patterns, licks, and elements used by the players—that is, composed structures. The difference between composition and improvisation is a matter of degree, determined by the way in which composed and improvised elements relate to one another in these two approaches to making music.

Since the fifties, musicians such as Jimmy Giuffre, John Lewis, Horace Silver, Bill Russo, Ralph Burns, Oliver Nelson, Charles Mingus, Carla Bley, Chick Corea, Muhal Richard Abrams, Henry Threadgill, Vince Mendoza, Maria Schneider, and Klaus König have given new meaning to the term *jazz composer*, with credit to both elements of the term. But only Duke Ellington, who has been jazz "composer" since the midtwenties, stands on the level of the truly great jazz improvisers—the level of Charlie Parker, Louis Armstrong, Lester Young, Coleman Hawkins, John Coltrane, Miles Davis. . . .

The jazz composer and arranger thinks of him- or herself primarily as an organizer, someone who provides the players with ideas (rhythmic patterns, riffs, scales, harmonies, formal structures, sonic textures, etc.). A basic part of jazz composition is the selection of particular musicians who will interpret the parts in the context of the music being played. Starting with Duke Ellington, all great jazz composers have had an unerring sense for this selection of players.

Beyond all these considerations, of course, stands the kind of composer who could be found in jazz from the very start: the musician who simply writes twelve-bar blues or thirty-two-bar song themes, supplying himself and his players with materials for improvisation. This line leads straight from early musicians—Jelly Roll Morton, for example—through, say, Fats Waller in the twenties and thirties and Thelonious Monk from the forties on to the well-known improvisers of modern jazz who write (or wrote) much of their own material: Sonny Rollins, Miles Davis, John Coltrane, Herbie Hancock, Wayne Shorter, Muhal Richard Abrams, Kenny Wheeler, Gianluigi Trovesi—in fact, practically everyone who plays improvised jazz. This sort of composing is directly related to the improvisatory process, without detouring through the arrangement. Of course, there are many gradual stages—from simple sets of changes and themes merely setting up a blowing line to the complex jazz composition, formally structured and scored for many voices. All of these steps build on each other so organically that the erection of boundaries appears more or less arbitrary.

The relationship between arrangement and improvisation reflects the frequently posed question about the relationship between the collective and the individual in jazz. Jazz has been called "the music of the collective" as well as "the music of boundless individualism." But the symphony orchestra, in which a hundred musicians subordinate themselves, almost in self-sacrifice, to a single will, is collective to a much greater degree. And a disdain for rules, regulations, and laws would seem to be a prerequisite for "boundless individualism." Jazz shows no signs of such disdain.

What happens in free jazz only *seems* to follow different laws. Certainly, it has none (or only very few) of such tonal written-down scores as those written by Oliver Nelson or Gerry Mulligan or Gary McFarland for the big bands. But in the sonically innovative big bands of free jazz, such as the orchestras of Anthony Braxton or Barry Guy, Alexander von Schlippenbach's Globe Unity Orchestra, or Misha Mengelberg's ICP Orchestra, notated passages are not a rare occurrence. In these groups, the limited options offered by traditional notation have been expanded or even completely replaced by graphic notation. Moreover, the concept of arranging in free jazz actually returns to the position it had at the beginning of jazz history—to the orally predetermined arrangements of the King Oliver Band or of the New Orleans Rhythm Kings. And that same fruitful and inspiring tension between the freedom of the improvisatory principle and the order of the arrangement that existed in the other jazz styles is retained for example in the "conductions" of Butch Morris or John Zorn's game pieces (both examples of directed improvisation). Of course, there is, aside from that, also the kind of improvisation that entails no predetermination, in which there is no trace of arrangement whatsoever. The impression grows stronger, however, that such total lack of restraint was only a passing stage within the process of liberation during the sixties. After that, the musicians gained a much more relaxed attitude toward composition by using compositional processes to structure the lessons learned through the experience of free improvisation.

At any rate, since the arrangement had been growing in scope and importance for so many years, it was logical that improvisation—and finally, following the freeing of improvisation, composition as well—should do the same. With his usual cogency, Dave Brubeck summed it up: "Jazz is about the only form of art existing today in which there is freedom of the individual without the loss of group contact." This coexistence of collectivism and freedom expresses what we characterized as "the sociological situation of jazz" at the start of this book.

The Blues

Two jazz critics, a recording director, and a musician were discussing "if the blues is essential to the jazz idiom." Pianist Billy Taylor, the participating musician, said, "I don't know of one giant—early, late, midthirties, or cool—who didn't have a tremendous respect and feeling for the blues, whether he played the blues or not. The spirit of it was in his playing or he wasn't really a giant as far as jazz was concerned." Nesuhi Ertegun, vice president of Atlantic Records, added, "Let me ask you one question. Do you think a man like Lester Young would play a tune like 'Body and Soul' in the same way if he had never played the blues?" Billy Taylor's answer was "No." And Leonard Feather summarized: "I think what it all boils down to is that the blues is the essence of jazz, and merely having a feeling for blues means having a feeling for jazz. In other words, the chords or the notes of the chords which are essential for blues are the notes that are essential for jazz—the flat third, flat seventh, etc." To which Billy Taylor countered:

> Well, I hesitate to oversimplify in that particular case because I tend to go back to the spirit. It's not the fact that a man on certain occasions would flat a certain note, bend a note or do something that is strictly a blues-type device. It's just that whatever this nebulous feeling is—the vitality they seem to get in the blues—whatever it is makes the difference between Coleman Hawkins's "Body and Soul" and a society tenor player's "Body and Soul."

It becomes clear from this discussion that the blues can be defined in several ways: emotionally, racially, sociologically, melodically, harmonically, and formally. Nearest at hand and most useful at this point is the emotional definition. Leadbelly, a singer from the olden days when the blues was wholly a folk art, set down the emotional definition in incomparable fashion:

> Now this is the blues. No white man ever had the blues, 'cause nothin' to worry about. Now, you lay down at night and you roll from one side of the bed to the other all night long—you can't sleep . . . what's the matter? The blues has got you. You get up and sit on the side of your bed in the mornin'—may have your sister or brother, your mother and father around but you don't want no talk out of 'em . . . what's the matter? The blues has got you. Well you go and put your feet under the table and look down on your plate—got everything you want to eat—but you shake your head and get up and say, "Lord! I can't eat and I can't sleep! What's the matter with me?" Why, the blues has got you, wanna talk to you.

Bessie Smith sings, "Nobody knows you when you're down and out." And John Lee Hooker: "I've got the blues so bad, it's hard to keep from cryin'." In "Trouble in Mind Blues" it goes, "If you see me laughin', I'm laughin' just to keep from cryin'."

This emotional definition also holds true for the blues when it is happy and full of humor, as it often is. The blues artists in whose work there are as many happy as sad blues—such as Big Bill Broonzy or later B. B. King or Otis Rush—have included themselves in this emotional definition of the blues.

Next to the emotional stands the melodic, harmonic, and formal definition. T-Bone Walker, the blues singer, has said, "You know, there's only one blues, though. That's the regular twelve-bar pattern and then you interpret over that. Just write new words or improvise different and you've got a new blues."

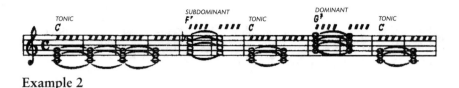

Example 2

As a general rule, the blues strophe consists of twelve bars, based on the most fundamental of all chords: tonic, dominant, and subdominant.

This twelve-bar chord structure is, exceptions aside, consistent—from the earliest blues (insofar as they already conform to the manifest blues pattern) down to the most complex blues improvisations of the modern musicians, who expand the harmonics in the most subtle way but of course without disturbing their basic function. The twelve-bar form is the standard form of blues. There are various other forms of blues that deviate from it.

The blues melodies and blues improvisations that rest on this twelve-bar chord structure derive their peculiar fascination from the "blue" notes. At one time, people assumed they were the product of a difficulty—of the problem that arose for the enslaved blacks deported from Africa to the New World when they had to adapt their pentatonic system (consisting of five notes) to our heptatonic scale (seven notes). In order to make the third and seventh steps of our scale accessible to their own musical sensibility, they had to flatten them. Although that can result in what traditional European functional harmonics would call "diminution," it is in principle a different process. In this process, the "minor third" and the "dominant seventh" (to use conventional musical terms that are in fact out of place here) became blue notes. That happened without recourse to the minor or major keys, which in European music govern the diminution of certain steps.

In the meantime this "theory of incapacity" seems increasingly shaky. It's not just that heptatonic systems are to be found in Africa and don't create any difficulties there. The frequency, tension-building pregnancy, and purposefulness with which blue notes appear in early blues and jazz also indicate that these "unstable" notes were intentional right from the start, and were deliberately used to make the music sound better.

Later, when the bebop musicians introduced the flatted fifth, this note, too, became a "blue" note—at first in the minor blues, then in all kinds of blues music—equal to the blue notes of the third and seventh steps.

In the blues a conventionally tonic or dominant chord frequently appears under a blue note, so that the major third may be played in the bass, and the minor third in the treble. This creates frictional sounds, which certainly can be interpreted as arising from a friction between two different harmonic systems: the chord structure, which corresponds to the European tradition, and the melodic line, with its blue notes originating in African music.

Example 3 shows a very typical melodic line. Every other note is a blue note. The traditional blue notes at the third and seventh steps are marked by a single arrow; the double arrows indicate blue notes originating in the flatted fifth. The C chord is the basis for the whole cadence, unharmed by the constant friction. Each blue note thus stands before a "normal" note, into which the blue note resolves, so that the cadence actually is nothing but a sequence of tension and relaxation, repeated six times. The tendency in jazz to create tension only to dissolve it immediately and then to create new tension that is again dissolved here becomes particularly clear. These tensions do not have the broad span they possess in European music.

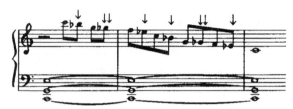

Example 3

Since the blues notes are generally resolved by a note that lies one half tone lower, there is a strong tendency in the blues toward descending melodic lines, as Example 3 also shows. It is a melodic line that occurs, in this or similar form, in thousands of jazz improvisations, within and outside of blues. It also shows how all jazz is saturated with blues elements—whether an actual blues tune is involved or not.

The twelve blues bars consist of three four-bar phrases, developed in such a way that a statement is made in the first four, repeated (over different harmonies) in the following four, and a "conclusion" drawn from it in the final four.

Sara Martin sings:

Blues, Blues, Blues why did you bring trouble to me?
Yes, Blues, Blues, Blues why did you bring trouble to me?
O Death, please sting me and take me out of my misery.

This threefold form, with its double question and contrasted answer, creates a finite and compact mode of expression comparable to the important "minor forms" of art, from a literary standpoint as well. The causal interconnection of form and content fulfills the highest criteria of form. It is astonishing that the highest ideal of Western art—the unity of form and content—is approximated in the "proletarian" and "Negroid" world of the blues, and so tightly and clearly that the relationship between them becomes "causal."

The finite blues form was of course not given from the start, neither musically nor textually. When looking at old folk blues, one must conclude that the threefold four-bar AAB structure was present in the beginning merely as an "idea," which was approximated and deviated from. This idea of the blues form became increasingly crystallized over the years, and today it is so pure that nonconformity to it is generally felt to be an error. But in the great, "classical" period of the blues it was no error not to conform.

Harmonically as well, there were many "errors" in the old, "primitive" blues. The singers floated with sovereign ease above certain basic chords, doing much as they pleased. Big Bill Broonzy often pointed out that to be emotionally right was much more important than to be formally and harmonically correct.

The blues singer generally fills the three four-bar phrases only up to the beginning of the third, seventh, and eleventh bar. The remainder of each phrase is at the disposal of an improvisation called a "break," a short, cadenza-like burst that sets off the preceding from the following phrase. These one and a half bars of the classic blues break are the germ cell of jazz improvisation as a whole, with its fascinating interplay of forces between the unbounded freedom of the soloist and the obligation toward the collective of players.

The blues lyrics correspond in level to their form. According to Jean Cocteau, the poetry of the blues was the only substantial contribution to genuine folk poetry in the twentieth century. Alfons M. Dauer goes so far as to maintain that the blues is primarily a kind of poetry. Everything of importance in the life of the blues singer is contained in the lyrics of the blues: love and (often disguised) racial discrimination; prison and the law; floods and railroad trains and the fortune told by the gypsy; the evening sun and the hospital—just to mention a few of the favorite subjects of blues singers. Life itself flows into the lyrics of the blues with a surprising straightforwardness and directness to which nothing in Western poetry—and this goes for folk poetry as well—is comparable.

The majority of blues deal with love. Love is viewed, simply and clearly, as that toward which love aims, yet it is able to remain love—even when it reflects the kind of war between the sexes sociologists have found to be very frequent in the black ghettos and neighborhoods, resulting from centuries of disrupted black family structures, during and also after slavery. At a time when everyday love poetry has barely risen above the level of "Roses are red / Violets are blue," the blues reflects that lofty, unsentimental stature and strength of the emotions and the passions that we know from great literature. Not a single blues is on the housemaid level of "Too Young," and yet the blues belongs to the world of those who have supplied an entire continent with domestics, butlers, and nursemaids!

There are funny blues and fast blues. But mainly blues is the music of a first rural, then urban proletariat whose life is filled with suffering. The social origins of the blues are at least as important as the racial ones. We know of very few genuine, authentic blues in which it is not obvious at once that the singer is of the proletariat. It would not make sense for members of the "aristocracy" to sing the blues: they don't have the blues.

It is not without reason that references to "having" or "not having" the blues are made time and again in blues lyrics. You have to have the blues to be able to sing them. "The blues are a part of me," said singer Alberta Hunter.

From its mood and atmosphere the blues achieves continuity—something it seems to be lacking to a notable degree at first glance. It almost seems as if lack of coherence—in other words, diametrical opposition to all that stood for art in the Western sense until the end of the nineteenth century—is a mark of the blues (which, of course, also has to do with the oral tradition of the blues). Lines and verses put together from the most varied blues and songs are linked up, unconcerned with what we call narrative logic and context. Sometimes the singer himself seems to be the actor, and then a third person is acting. A moment ago the subject was a "he," and now it is a "she" . . . we were in the past, now we are in the future . . . suddenly, we switch from singular to plural.

Even those blues songs clearly created by a single person seem to show that their author was not particularly worried about continuity of content. In the "Old New Orleans Blues," although unquestionably committed to old New Orleans by title and theme, the next-to-last verse takes us to Memphis, while in the final verse the topic is the lantern swinging in the wind outside the window behind which the singer is sleeping. The "Two Nineteen Blues" first deals with the railroad and then suddenly with a streetwalker, and so forth. Dozens of blues furnish examples of this "blues discontinuity," while it seems quite difficult to find a blues in which each word follows logically from the foregoing. It would be wrong to conclude that this stems from an inability to create continuity. No, continuity is not the point. The lines and verses have an impressionistic quality. They relate to each other as do the spots of color in a painting: if you stand close, you cannot tell why there is red next to blue, or green next to orange, but as soon as you take a few steps back, it all blends into a whole. The "whole" of the blues is the mood, the blues atmosphere. It creates its own continuity. Into the blues mood flows whatever comes up—events, memories, thoughts, fancies—and out comes, always, the blues.

Everything that exists in the world of the singer goes through the blues; all is contemporaneous. Nothing can be outside. Blues singer Big Bill Broonzy tells about how when he was a boy, he and his uncle caught a big turtle:

We drug him home and my uncle told me to make him stick his neck out of his shell. I took a stick and put it in front of him. The turtle caught hold of the stick and couldn't turn it loose. So my uncle said, "Hold his head right there, and I'll cut it off." My uncle took the axe and cut the turtle's head off and we went in the house and stayed there a while. When we came back, no turtle. So we looked for him and turtle was nearly back to the lake where we caught him. We picked him up, brought him back to the house, and my uncle said, "There's a turtle who is dead and don't know it." And that's the way a lot of people is today: they got the blues and don't know it.

At the beginning of the blues stand the work songs and field hollers: the simple, archaic songs sung by African Americans at work in the fields or on the levees. They were sung because it was easier to work to the rhythm of a song than without it. The rhythm had an effect on the singers, making even those perk up who otherwise would have worked sluggishly or not at all: "Lawd, cap'n, I's not a-singin'—I's just a-hollerin' to help me with my work." That's why the white man wanted to see the black sing. "A singing Negro is a good Negro," is the way French critic François Postif described the attitude of a plantation owner or prison warden.

Folk song and folk ballad, frequently in the "white" sense, joined with work song and field holler. There were the old rounds with the regular, happy repetition of a refrain of a few lines, sung by the chorus of listeners.

Blind Lemon Jefferson, Big Bill Broonzy, Leadbelly, Robert Johnson, Elmore James, Blind Boy Fuller, Rev. Gary Davis, Bukka White, Blind Willie McTell, Big Joe Williams, Sonny Terry, Brother John Sellers, John Lee Hooker, and Lightnin' Hopkins are famous representatives of blues folklore. Most accompanied themselves on guitar, and they often are wonderful guitarists (e.g., Lonnie Johnson and Lightnin' Hopkins). Other blues singers (e.g., Sonny Terry or the late Little Walter and Sonny Boy Williamson) knew how to coax amazing sounds from a harmonica. Others recorded with well-known jazz musicians backing their folk-rooted blues vocals.

In most cases, the accompanying instrument meant more to the blues singer than mere background: it was a partner in conversation. It would inspire and excite; it could make comments in affirmation or protest; it anticipated or completed an idea.

Under no circumstances should the reader assume that we are speaking of things related to a distant past. Almost all well-known commentators on blues have consciously or unconsciously nurtured this feeling, as if they were the last of their profession with just time enough left to document a vanishing folklore art form. A feature of the white man's relationship to folklore of all kinds is that he links it to nostalgia, sentimentality, memories of the "good old days." As far as the blues is concerned, this response is wrong.

There are more blues movements and blues styles today than ever before, and they all live side by side. Not one of the old blues forms—folk blues, country blues, prison blues, archaic blues, Cajun blues—has become extinct. In fact, new ones were added: city blues, urban blues, jazz blues, rhythm 'n' blues, soul blues, funky blues, hip-hop blues. In addition there are different regional styles. The most easily recognizable are Mississippi blues (rough, archaic), Texas blues (mobile, flexible, jazz-related), and East Coast blues, from Florida or Tennessee, for example (often permeated with white country and hillbilly folklore). The folk blues of Texas and of the Midwest (the so-called territories) shaped the California big-city blues; the folk blues of Mississippi, with Memphis as the core, shaped the Chicago big-city blues. But in this case, too, the mixtures are no less interesting than the pure forms, which are illusory in the blues world, anyway—blues is by nature a mixture. The success of the Memphis blues in the sixties—of Albert King, to name one, but also of soul singers like Otis Redding—lies precisely in its combination and urbanization of elements from Mississippi and Texas.

Almost all important blues singers are at home in several forms and styles—not only in the sense that they developed from one form to the other, as from country blues to city blues and on to contemporary urban blues (e.g., Muddy Waters, Howlin' Wolf, B. B. King, Otis Rush), but also in the sense that they may practice several forms simultaneously, for example, John Lee Hooker, Johnny Shines, or Louisiana Red, who kept switching between folk, country, and city blues; or Jimmy Witherspoon, T-Bone Walker, Ray Charles, who all frequently played with jazz musicians; or Gatemouth Brown, who mixed practically everything: blues, jazz, country, Cajun, etc.

Since the midfifties, the blues has penetrated popular music to a degree unimaginable up to then. First, black rhythm 'n' blues—the rocking music of the black South and of the Northern ghettos—led into rock 'n' roll. Bill Haley and Elvis Presley were the first white rock 'n' roll stars, but immediately following came black artists—Chuck Berry, Fats Domino, Ray Charles—who enjoyed an immense success on the white pop scene that would have been considered impossible even shortly before. By 1963 the best of rhythm 'n' blues had become so closely linked to the mainstream of American popular music that *Billboard* magazine temporarily suspended separate listings of "Rhythm and Blues" and "Pop." Separate listing was resumed later, but the magazine kept changing its policy; it had become uncertain. Outstanding black talent is also now part of the white scene. Younger readers will hardly be able to appreciate how unusual that once would have been. The term *rhythm and blues* was only introduced in the late forties. Up to then, the term was *race records*. This label makes it clear that for fifty years black music had been played in a ghetto that was noticed by the white world only indirectly at best: by letting its own musicians degenerate, play down, drain, what in its authentic black form remained unknown to most of the white audience.

It was through musicians like Bill Haley, Elvis Presley, Chuck Berry, Fats Domino, Little Richard, and others, that the blues literally demolished the popular music of Tin Pan Alley and its babbling about schmaltzy, kitschy, dishonest feelings. If much of today's popular music is more realistic, clear, honest, and at the same time more poetic, musical, and often emotionally richer than popular music before the midfifties (leaving disco music aside), then this must be ascribed to the penetration of white popular music by the blues. Blues—and black music in general—has always *been* what white popular music has only recently become: realistic and full of social involvement, a commentary on the everyday life and problems of those who sang it.

What happened during the fifties was only the preparation for the "decade of rock," the phrase frequently applied to the sixties. For the United States, it was Bob Dylan; then, initially in Great Britain and later simply for the whole world, it was the Beatles—and also the Rolling Stones (who took their name from a Muddy Waters blues)—who created a new musical consciousness, so that artists who just shortly before had been the personification of high musical standards (think of Frank Sinatra!) within a few years became "old fogeys" when confronted with this new consciousness. The musical standards of the world of popular music demolished in the process were the symbols of the moral, social, and political standards of the bourgeois world that had created the old pop music. These standards were the real target of the new movement.

Bob Dylan, the Beatles, the Rolling Stones—they all are unthinkable without the blues. The Beatles came from rhythm and blues, particularly Chuck Berry. Dylan comes from Woody Guthrie and the American folklore at whose center stands folk blues. For half a year he lived with blues singer Big Joe Williams. It has been said that Dylan was "the first true poet of popular music." But in so saying, hundreds of black folk-blues singers who, since the turn of the century—and perhaps even earlier—have been the "true poets of popular music," are forgotten.

"If there was another name for rock 'n' roll, it would be Chuck Berry," said John Lennon. (Berry is one of the big stars of blues and rhythm 'n' blues.)

It has been said that the Beatles and Bob Dylan changed the musical and social consciousness of a whole generation. In this context, it is important to realize that this change of consciousness is based on the blues and would have been impossible without it. British guitarist Eric Clapton made this very clear when he said, "Rock is like a battery. Every so often you have to go back to the blues and recharge."

To be sure, from the standpoint of jazz and authentic blues, much of the blues derivations played in the rock era of the sixties and the rock 'n' roll of the fifties were inferior to the pure, uncommercialized product. But this holds true only for a minority of jazz and blues connoisseurs. For the majority, the reverse is valid: through the blues, popular music attained a qualitative level previously unthinkable. This development continued. The stream of black music flowing into white rock and pop music became wider and wider, in fact, so wide that there was no, or almost no, difference anymore between black and white popular music. "Funkiness" became the fashionable be-all and end-all of commercial rock music during the seventies; funk, though, came from the black ghetto and the blues—like rap and hip-hop ten years later.

At first, pure blues consciousness among white audiences and musicians was stronger in Britain than in the United States. Most of the successful British pop and rock musicians of the sixties for years had studied, imitated, and copied black blues singers and blues instrumentalists, and on that basis, they found their own styles.

Since the late fifties, there had been a true "blues movement" in Great Britain, led by a guitarist and vocalist who was born in Vienna, educated in France, and settled in England—Alexis Korner—and later also by John Mayall. One could indulge in all kinds of speculation as to why this contemporary "blues consciousness" originated in Britain rather than the United States, though the British Isles are much farther away from the creative blues centers of the American South or Chicago's South Side than are New York or Los Angeles. The question can be asked, Were there too many prejudices against black blues in the United States, and did the American music world jump on the blues wagon only when it was realized how much money British groups like the Rolling Stones—or later Led Zeppelin or John Mayall—were making from the blues?

Another point cannot be made without bitterness: it was white musicians who were making fortunes in the British and American scenes with black blues, while the black creators of this music (apart from a few exceptions) were still the obscure voices of an excluded underclass.

At the beginning of this section, we quoted Leadbelly: "No white man ever had the blues." For decades, the blues were thought to be the "last retreat" of black music that no white man would ever be able to penetrate. In all areas of a music originally created by blacks, whites again and again had been more successful, had made more money than the black creators: Benny Goodman and Artie Shaw in Swing, Stan Getz and Dave Brubeck in cool jazz, and all the others. Only in blues did the whites not succeed in producing really convincing sounds.

Since the sixties, parts of this "last bastion" have also been conquered. There are some white musicians who, at least as instrumentalists, can play authentic black blues. As we said, Britishers Alexis Korner and John Mayall paved the way for this, but both are still far away from the authenticity reached by the musicians following them: guitarists Eric Clapton or Rory Gallagher, then also Americans, guitarist Mike Bloomfield and Johnny Winter; or harmonica players Paul Butterfield, Charlie Musselwhite, and Paul Osher, all of whom learned in Chicago's black South Side (especially from Muddy Waters); guitarists Duane Allman, Stevie Ray Vaughan, Duke Robillard, Derek Trucks, and pianist-guitarist Dr. John; the musicians of the blues-rock group Canned Heat; and others.

Still, there is a difference. White blues—especially where it is artistically serious—is more precious, more "accurate," cleaner, less expressive, and also more vulgar, less subtle, and less flexible than black blues.

Charles Keil tells of a survey about the nature of blues and soul made by a black Chicago radio station among its audience. In the answers, again and again the word "mellow" recurred. They're "mellow," the blues and soul. And "mellow" is exactly what white blues is not; and when they become mellow, they generally cease to be blues.

Not without reason, white blues player John Mayall, a man who should know and whom it concerns directly, has said, "When we talk about blues, we mean black blues. That's the real blues for us."

However, the sociological and social side of this matter should not be overlooked. The blues is black music for one thing, because the living conditions of blacks in parts of the South and in the Northern ghettos were, and largely still are, so different from those of whites, not only in degree, but more important, in essence. The late American critic Ralph Gleason speculated that to the extent that this changes, white blues musicians will gain "equality" with black blues musicians. At the beginning of the twenty-first century, it seems obvious that it will be a long time before that day arrives.

Spiritual and Gospel Song

The singer who comes closest to Bessie Smith in vocal power and expressiveness is not a blues singer but a gospel singer: Mahalia Jackson, who died in 1972. The gospel song is the modern form of the spiritual, the religious song of the African American—more vital, more swinging, more jazzlike than the old spiritual, which frequently shows a closeness to European church music, and above all a proximity to the white spirituals of the nineteenth century (which are often overlooked by the "race-romancers").

The blues is the secular form of spiritual and gospel song. Or the other way around: gospel song and spiritual are the religious forms of the blues. Thus it is not only in a relative, but in a literal sense that blues singer Alberta Hunter said, "To me, the blues are—well, almost religious. . . . The blues are like spirituals, almost sacred. When we sing the blues, we're singin' from our hearts, we're singin' out our feelings." And blues singer T-Bone Walker said:

> Of course, the blues comes a lot from the church, too. The first time I ever heard a boogie-woogie piano was the first time I went to church. That was the Holy Ghost Church in Dallas, Texas. That boogie-woogie was a kind of blues, I guess. Then the preacher used to preach in a bluesy tone sometimes. A lot of people think I'll become a minister if I stop working as a singer, because of the way I sing the blues. They say I sound like a preacher.

For the Africans who were taken to North America as slaves, religious songs were an important means of survival in the black diaspora. In spirituals and gospel songs, they expressed to God their belief in a better future. It was a call to freedom, and later, after the abolition of slavery, the hope for a better life without racial discrimination and social disadvantage.

As religious as many spirituals sound, in some situations they contained secret messages that slaves could use to communicate about their intentions and their plans to escape. A song about the "River Jordan" referred not only to the metaphorical, biblical river, but also to the real-life Ohio River, which at that time was the border to the Northern states that slaves sought to cross in order to escape slavery. Many spirituals, such as "Steal Away to Jesus" or "Sweet Canaan," are a call to independence. They could be used to indicate when the coach would come that would take the escapee to freedom ("Swing Low, Sweet Chariot"). Fleeing slaves could be warned against traveling by land and advised instead to wade through water in order to throw the bloodhounds off the scent ("Wade in the Water").

In spirituals, Jesus, Mary, and all the Christian saints become, in a sense, members of the slave community. They become comrades in suffering: Sister Mary, Brother Jesus, Brother Paul. By singing joyfully about them, the people taken from Africa also celebrate the spirits of their forefathers, their ancestors. In the spirituals, Moses is not only a biblical figure, but also an ancestor watching over the fate of the slaves and pointing the way to freedom. This invocation of the spirits remains part of African American music today. The more emphatic and personal it becomes, the more successful it is. And this truth in expression, the *testifying* that is so important in gospel music, is also the point of the individualized sounds of jazz, though of course there it is transformed and modernized. David Murray says, "It's enough to make one long note your own. If you can do that, then thousands of others will also naturally be yours."

The visitor to a church in Harlem or on Chicago's South Side will not find a great contrast to the ecstatic atmosphere that might be found at a jazz concert by, say, Lionel Hampton. There are the identical rhythms, the same beat, the same swing in the music, and frequently, jazz-associated instruments—saxophones, electric guitars, drums, and more recently keyboards. The visitor will hear boogie-woogie bass lines and blues structures and see enraptured people beating time with their hands and feet and sometimes even dancing.

Natalie Curtis Burlin describes a church service in the South:

> Minutes passed, long minutes of strange intensity. The mutterings, the ejaculations, grew louder, more dramatic, till suddenly I felt the creative thrill dart through the people like an electric vibration; that same half-audible hum arose—emotion was gathering atmospherically as clouds gather—and then, up from the depth of some "sinner's" remorse and imploring came a pitiful little plea, a real Negro "moan" sobbed in musical cadence. From somewhere in that bowed gathering another voice improvised a response; the plea sounded again, louder this time and more impassioned; then other voices joined in the answer, shaping it into a musical phrase; and so on, before our ears, as one might say, from this molten metal of music a new song was smithied out, composed then and there by no one in particular and by everyone in general.

Modern gospel songs are mostly composed pieces, marketed as sheet music. But these pieces are used freely in church services—certainly not quite as freely as jazz musicians treat a theme, but still as a basis for individual activity and interpretation. Leading black writers like Langston Hughes, who died in 1967, are sometimes authors of gospel lyrics. And the sheet music is often printed in larger editions than commercial tunes.

The most important gospel singer was—and will remain—Mahalia Jackson, born in New Orleans. In 1945 she became famous almost overnight with her recording of "Move On Up a Little Higher," a best seller in the category of the big hits: more than eight million records sold!

Through Mahalia Jackson, the white world for the first time became familiar with the art of gospel singing on a broader scale. Actually, the whites heard only Mahalia Jackson. Gospel music still is the real underground art form of black America: a flourishing art full of power and vitality. Yet, the average white American has no idea of the wonderfully enraptured life that unfolds in the black churches each Sunday.

Under the impression of the breadth of today's jazz scene, jazz fans will have a hard time accepting the fact that there are far more gospel groups than jazz bands. To give an idea of this wealth of the gospel scene, we mention here only the most important gospel artists and groups—only those, that is, who are equal to the best jazz players and bands.

Among the female singers: Inez Andrews, Marion Williams, Delois Barrett Campbell, Bessie Griffin, Shirley Caesar, Dorothy Love, Edna Gallmon Cooke, Marie Knight, Willie Mae Ford Smith, Queen Esther Marrow, and Clara Ward.

Of the male singers: Robert Anderson, Alex Bradford, James Cleveland, Reverend Cleophus Robinson, R. H. Harris, Jessy Dixon, Isaac Douglas, Claude Jeter, and Brother Joe May.

The outstanding female gospel groups include the Davis Sisters, the Stars of Faith, the Angelic Gospel Singers, the Barrett Sisters, the Robert Patterson Singers, the Caravans, Liz Dargan and the Gospelettes, the Roberta Martin Singers, and Sweet Honey in the Rock.

The male gospel groups we should cite are the Five Blind Boys of Mississippi, the Brooklyn All Stars, the Gospel Clefs, the Gospelaires, the Fairfield Four, the Gospel Keynotes, the Highway QCs, the Mighty Clouds of Joy, the Pilgrim Travelers, the Pilgrim Jubilee Singers, the Soul Stirrers, the Swan Silvertones, the Swanee Quintet, the Blind Boys of Alabama, the Supreme Angels, and the Violinaires.

And finally, some of the best gospel choirs: the Gospel Singers Ensemble, Rosie Wallace and the First Church of Love, the Staple Singers, the Faith and Deliverance Choir, the Thompson Community Singers, Mattie Moss Clark and the Southwest Michigan State Choir, J. C. White and the Institutional Church of God in Christ Choir, Harrison Johnson and His Los Angeles Community Choir, Walter Hawkins and the Love Center Choir, the Edwin Hawkins Singers, the Garden State Choir, the Harlem Gospel Singers, Linda Tillery and the Cultural Heritage Choir, the Brockington Ensemble, the B.C. + M. Mass Choir, and the Montreal Jubilation Gospel Choir.

Of special importance is the aged Bishop Kelsey in Washington, D.C. On some of his records, such as *Little Boy*, one hears how in the course of his sermon Rev. Kelsey gradually becomes the lead singer and how the sermon turns into the gospel singing of the entire congregation. Almost nowhere else does the flowing transition between speech and music—characteristic of black music—become so clear as in this vital passage between sermon and gospel song.

Many preachers and male gospel singers are masters of falsetto singing, which moves the male tenor or baritone voices far beyond their usual range into that of the female soprano—and even higher than that. This manner of singing was practiced in Africa for centuries as a sign of highly potent, bursting manhood. It moved from spiritual and gospel song to the blues and, far beyond that, into modern jazz (as in Leon Thomas) and into the contemporary rock and soul music of Prince and Michael Jackson. It certainly can also be perceived in the high "falsetto" playing of the post-Coltrane tenor saxophonists.

In gospel communities, a prayer is considered good only if it is moving. To move someone who's suffering, to induce a state of spiritual excitement, is, for African American gospel musicians, the fastest route to Jesus. Questions of musical style are not important here. There are gospel songs that use rhythms from country and western, bluegrass, mambo, waltzes, boogie-woogie, and hip-hop. In the age of music videos, there are gospel rap songs.

But most of all, gospel songs have a strong, full jazz beat. In gospel songs, as in blues, there is everything that can be found in daily life: elections, skyscrapers, railroads, telephones. It may appear naive to white people—with our characteristic notion of intellectual superiority—when someone expresses in song the wish to talk with the Lord on the telephone, or travel to heaven in a Pullman car. Yet, in the great period of European religious art, it was no different: the Flemish painters transferred the story of the crucifixion to the landscape of the Lowlands; and in the Christmas songs of Silesia, the people sing about the birth of Christ as if it had taken place in the ice and snow of their own mountains.

Spiritual and gospel songs are not, as is often thought, something belonging to history—something that existed at the beginning of jazz somewhere in the Southern countryside. Quite the opposite: in the course of jazz development, they have grown more effective, more dynamic and alive. From the fifties on, gospel and soul have broken into other areas of black music on a wide front; initially into jazz. Milt Jackson, the leading vibraharpist of modern jazz, once answered the question of where his particular style and soulful playing came from: "What is soul in jazz? It's what comes from inside. . . . In my case, I think it's what I heard and felt in the music of my church. That was the most important influence of my career. Everybody wants to know where I got my 'funky' style. Well, it came from the church."

Bassist and composer Charles Mingus emphasized that his jazz would be inconceivable without his experience of the spirituals and gospel music that he regularly heard in Pentacostal churches. His recording "Wednesday Night Prayer Meeting," with Pepper Adams (baritone saxophone), Booker Ervin (tenor saxophone), and Jimmy Knepper (trombone), is a moving portrait of the experience of a gospel service: the calls of the faithful to the Creator, the trances that overcome them, the driving out of evil spirits by the preacher, the speaking in tongues, the collective religious ecstasy experienced by the congregation.

Musicians such as Milt Jackson, Horace Silver, and Ray Charles generated a "soul wave" in the second half of the fifties that got its crucial impulse from gospel music and has been breaking into popular music since the sixties. Some of the most successful rock and soul singers of the sixties and seventies would be unthinkable without their gospel background: Otis Redding, James Brown, Aretha Franklin, Little Richard, Wilson Pickett, Isaac Hayes, and Marvin Gaye, for example.

Soul is secularized gospel music. And many of the best soul singers, even at the high points of their careers, still love to sing in gospel churches for a black audience—Aretha Franklin, for instance.

Some jazz specialists claim that gospel music was more important in the development of the contemporary sounds of rock, pop, and jazz than was the blues. As Charles Keil pointed out, "there are still at least forty store-front churches for every joint where blues or jazz is played in Chicago, the blues capital of the world." Young African Americans are thus forty times more likely to hear gospel music than they are the blues.

Jazz and gospel singing are related in yet another respect: many of the best female jazz singers got their start in church—Sarah Vaughan, for instance, who carried Charlie Parker's conception into jazz singing; or the late Dinah Washington, the successful "Queen" of rhythm and blues, who not only sang but also played piano in church; or Aretha Franklin.

The late Sister Rosetta Tharpe sang in the thirties with the Swing bands of Cab Calloway and Lucky Millinder and had a successful night-club act, but before she became known in the jazz world, she had sung in church. Afterward she again returned to gospel singing. One of the best-known composers of gospel songs—Thomas A. Dorsey—got his start in Chicago in the twenties and early thirties as a blues lyricist, singer, and pianist.

Danny Barker, the guitarist, said about Bessie Smith, "If you had any church background, like people who came from the South as I did, you would recognize a similarity between what she was doing and what those preachers and evangelists from there did, and how they moved people."

Harmony

In terms of harmony and melody, jazz does not offer much of a revolutionary nature, at least not until the beginning of free jazz in the sixties. Paradoxically, there is in this very fact a difference between jazz and concert music. In the realm of European notated musical culture, what is new and revolutionary is always first and foremost in terms of melody and harmony. Jazz, on the other hand, though among the most revolutionary developments in the arts of the twentieth century, is mostly traditional in respect to harmony and melody. Its newness is based on rhythm and sound.

Almost the only novel and singular thing in jazz in the harmonic domain are the blue notes. Aside from these, the harmonic language of conventional jazz—that is, of the jazz prior to and apart from free playing—is identical with that of popular dance and entertainment music. The harmonies of ragtime, Dixieland, and New Orleans jazz are—beyond blue notes—identical with the harmonies of polkas, marches, and waltzes. They are based on the tonic, the dominant, and the subdominant, and on their subsidiary functions. Bix Beiderbecke brought certain Debussy-like chords and whole-tone effects into jazz. The great Swing musicians added the sixth to the major triad, and "enriched" sevenths with ninths or even elevenths. Since bebop, passing chords ("substitutes") are placed between the basic harmonies of a piece, or the basic harmonies are extended through "alternations." Jazz musicians are (or at least were during the bebop and cool-jazz periods) proud of the developments in this realm of their music, and among them there was much talk of harmonic problems; but these problems, viewed from the position of European music, are more or less "old hat." Only very few chords with augmented or diminished fifths and ninths, characteristic mainly of modern jazz, do not exist in this form in conventional music, especially when such intervals occur in combinations. For example, harmonies occur that may have a flatted fifth in the bass and an augmented fifth in the treble, and above this one may occasionally find a diminished or augmented ninth. Example 4 shows two such chord combinations, with their respective resolutions.

Example 4

Example 5 shows the first four bars of the song "I Can't Give You Anything But Love," popular since the twenties. (A) indicates the simple, almost primitive harmonies on which the jazz improvisations of that day were based, while (B) shows how the harmonies were altered in later years—during the transition from Swing to bop. No doubt the simple harmonies of (A) might just as well stem from a European folk dance. The more modern harmonies of (B) could also be employed in modern popular music.

Example 5

The development of jazz harmonies from ragtime and New Orleans jazz to bebop and cool jazz are not peculiar to jazz. They run parallel to and are "synchronized" with harmonic developments in popular music from the polka to the slickly orchestrated sounds of Hollywood movie music. André Hodeir surmises that jazz was influenced by pop music in this respect—a thought that lies near to hand since jazz musicians, who listen open-mindedly to everything they deem valid or worthy of imitation in any kind of music, heard that here was something that could be learned and applied to what seemed to them not very highly advanced in their own music. The harmonic language of jazz, according to Hodeir, is "largely borrowed." Because this is so, it is quite in accord with the main line of jazz tradition. It is peculiar to the genesis of jazz that it "borrowed" and united the best of two divergent musical cultures: European and African. Even among the first African Americans who composed rags, played New Orleans jazz, and sang blues and spirituals, there were some who recognized or, at least, felt somehow that there was nothing in their own musical past that came even close to the ripe and rich harmonic expression in European music. On the other hand, there was nothing in European music that could come even close to the expressive power of "black" sonorities and to the vitality of Africa's rhythmic tradition. Thus both musical cultures contributed their "specialty."

The way in which these European harmonies are deployed in jazz—the "changes"—does however follow its own rules. As a rough simplification, it can be said that in contrast to European music, in which harmony creates structural stability by demarcating large formal segments, jazz harmony is fundamentally based on a rapid sequence of tension and release.

In bebop and cool jazz, harmonies can be varied just as melodies were the basis for variations in traditional jazz. Thus Example 5 shows eight harmonies in the modern (B) version as compared to four in the old (A). The latter only has chords that are closely related to C major. The modern version, however, creates a singable bass line that stands in contrapuntal relationship to the melodic line. The entire harmonic picture is loosened up and enriched. The chord sequence itself shows a steady succession of tension and relaxation, in terms of the tensions so important to jazz. Most of the added chords in the modern version (B) are terminal chords, having a tendency to resolve in the subsequent chord. The older version (A) shows only one resolution, in the fourth bar; the modern version shows three such processes. This, too, indicates how jazz history demonstrates an ever stronger and more intense concentration of jazz-like, tension-creating and tension-dissolving elements.

In the modern version a whole new chord structure comes into being. But this chord structure is not so new that it fails to indicate in each chord its relationship to the original harmonies. The new chords, so to speak, stand in place of the handed-down chords, which is why they are called substitutes. The tonal relationship of the whole remains as ordered and neat as one could desire.

Many laypeople and friends of traditional jazz not conversant with the harmonic vocabulary of bop at first reacted to its sounds as "atonal." Atonality, as the word itself makes clear, means that the music has no relationship to a tonal center and has no tonal center of gravity. But this is not the case in the prevalent forms of modern jazz before free music—and even there, only in rare instances. If many listeners cannot hear the harmonic centers of gravity, it is not because these centers are lacking, but because the listener's ear is unaccustomed to these harmonies. Indeed, harmony in music is a matter of custom. Any harmonic system, even in its most far-reaching variants, can be assimilated by the ear after a period of listening—even when the initial impression has been that of absurdity.

Altogether, the development of harmony in jazz and modern concert music shows many parallels—with jazz tending to lag considerably behind. The flatted fifth—the bebopper's favorite interval in the forties—in many respects corresponds to the tritone, which plays an important role in modern concert music: in Hindemith, Bartók, Stravinsky, Honegger, Milhaud, etc. Hindemith devoted much space to the tritone in *The Craft of Musical Composition*, one of the main theoretical works on modern concert music. In this work he states, "With increases in distance the familial relationship is loosened until at the utmost note—the augmented fourth or the diminished fifth—the tritone, it barely remains noticeable." Elsewhere Hindemith says that the tritone is indifferent to the harmonic base. Thus Hindemith feels that the flatted fifth does not destroy tonality but stands in a neutral, "indifferent," relationship to it. This is felt by jazz musicians as well. This "indifference" is the real reason for the popularity of the tritone in modern jazz. The tritone that, according to Hindemith, "neither belongs in the region of the harmonious, nor can be regarded as discordant," has renewed an old jazz tradition: the preference for the shimmering and the ambiguous, which can also be found in the blue notes of the blues. It was no accident that the flatted fifth—as its novelty started to fade—began to take on the function of a blue note. Example 3 (in the section on the blues) shows the degree to which blue notes and flatted fifths have become equivalent.

The flatted fifths and blue notes of jazz and the tritone of modern symphonic music thus do not point toward a dissolution of tonality, but toward its loosening and broadening. The presence of the flatted fifth and blue notes in jazz can be explained from the same point of view from which Hindemith explains the tritone in the new symphonic music: "Harmonic and melodic power are arrayed in opposition." Where the harmonic power is weakest—in the flatted fifth—the melodic power is strongest. And power of melodic line is what counts.

The bop musicians who were the first to use flatted fifths frequently— Charlie Parker, Dizzy Gillespie, Charlie Christian, Thelonious Monk— certainly did not have the faintest notion of the tritone or of Hindemith's *Craft of Musical Composition*. In their own way they arrived at solutions that Hindemith (whose name stands here for an entire direction in modern concert music) had derived from European musical tradition. This phenomenon, by the way, appears not only in the harmonies but also in the sound character of the music. The sounds of the Miles Davis Nonte—in pieces like "Moves," "Budo," or "Israel"—are remarkably similar to those in Stravinsky compositions such as "Dumbarton Oaks Concerto," "Symphony in C," or other works from his classicist period.

The first few traces of the dissolution of conventional tonality began to show a couple of years after the initial phase of bebop in some jazz forms of the fifties—as in the work of Lennie Tristano, Charles Mingus, or George Russell. Russell, who wrote the famous "Cubana Be-Cubana Bop" for Dizzy Gillespie's big band in the late forties, created a system of tonality that he called the "Lydian Chromatic Concept of Tonal Organization." In many respects it resembles the scales of the old Hellenistic music. Lennie Tristano, with musicians of his school, created a freely improvised piece in 1949 (i.e., long before free jazz) called "Intuition," in which Wolfgang Fortner—a well-known contemporary German symphonic composer—found tendencies toward the twelve-tone system.

Musicians like Tristano, Russell, Jimmy Giuffre, and Mingus paved the way for that sudden and explosive harmonic freedom that made jazz burst at the seams around the turn of the fifties. Free jazz, whose first outstanding representatives were Cecil Taylor and Ornette Coleman, finally rejected the laws of conventional functional harmonics. Sounds and lines rub against each other freely and hard, lending an ecstatic character to the music to a degree that goes far beyond what might have been felt as "ecstatic" in earlier jazz forms.

On the other hand, even in many of the freest jazz recordings, the music remains related to what musicians call "tonal centers." The word *tonal*, however, is not used in the sense of functional harmonics but is simply supposed to indicate certain crucial points—centers of gravity—from which the musicians take off, and to which they find their way back.

In the sections about Miles Davis and John Coltrane, we used the term *modal*. In the manner of improvisation developed in jazz by Davis and Coltrane, the harmony is no longer determined by the constantly changing chords of a harmonic structure; every chord that corresponds to the "mode," to the scale, is allowed. This is a way of playing that has been in existence for centuries in many of the great non-Western musical cultures—the Arab and the Indian cultures, for example, but also in some European folk music traditions. On the one hand, it allows harmonic freedom; on the other, it prevents arbitrariness. Modal playing also means a further Africanization of the music, away from the "dictatorship" of European harmonies toward the free harmonization that exists in many African musical cultures (not only in the Arab and Muslim ones). The jazz of the seventies and eighties combined the freedom of free jazz with the harmonic possibilities of previous jazz styles. The new aspects it achieved in terms of harmonies were rooted mainly in the virtuosity and sovereignty with which harmonies from the most varied sources were dealt with. In pianist Keith Jarrett's playing, for example, one may find side by side, held together by modality, blues chords, Debussy-like whole-tone harmonies, traces of medieval ecclesiastical keys, baroque and romantic elements, non-European elements such as Arab *maqam* improvisations, and the whole range of harmonic possibilities of conventional jazz and free jazz. Often, all these elements occur in such immediate transitions that even specialists can no longer localize the sources, but they appear in an order that seems necessary and logical, although no known theoretical system could explain the necessities and logic of such an order. That is exactly where freedom is founded: no longer on freedom of tonality but rather in the mastery with which all the elements of tonality and atonality, European, non-Western and jazzlike, classical and modern, are utilized. Thus, freedom also includes the freedom to be free and the opposite: to forego being free, if that is what the musician wants.

This is also how the missionary and sectarian character of the freedom of the free jazz of the sixties—a conception of freedom that condemned all nonfree playing as not only musically but also politically, socially, and morally regressive—was overcome.

Melody

If one proceeds from the assumption made by modern musical theory that there is no basic difference between melody and harmony—melody is "horizontal harmony," harmony is "vertical melody"—almost everything that can be said about jazz melody has already been said in the preceding section. In the early forms of jazz there was hardly anything that could be called a "jazz" melody—with the exception of melodies containing blue notes (Example 3 in the blues section). The melodies were fundamentally similar to those of circus and march music, to the piano and drawing room music of the late nineteenth century. To the degree in which jazz phrasing gained significance, melodies began to evolve in terms of this phrasing—so thoroughly that this manner of phrasing finally changed and shaped the melodic flow itself, and something that might be called jazz melody came into being.

Jazz melody is primarily marked by its flowing character. Insofar as the melodic development is expressed in improvisation, there are fewer repeats, such as are often used structurally in European music. Repeats are largely excluded, to begin with, because the improvising soloist mainly assembles musical elements intuitively and spontaneously, and so is unable to repeat large parts of what he has just played without first having recourse to close study of a possible recording. Repeats are part of the relationship of music to time. When a melody is repeated, it is lifted out of the flow of time. It is as if one were to bring back a span of time that has already passed in order to relive it once more. The rarity of repetition in the flow of chorus improvisations makes it clear that jazz is more closely related to the realm in which music occurs—time—than is European music. The phenomenon of swing and other peculiarities of jazz also point to this. To give it pointed expression: if music—as almost all philosophies of music hold—is *the* art expressed in time, then jazz corresponds more fundamentally to the basic nature of the musical than does notated European music.

Jazz derives one of its unique traits from the fact that it is instrumentally conceived. André Hodeir, who has expressed the most succinct ideas about the problems of melody and harmony in jazz yet published, said, "Composers in the European tradition conceive a phrase by itself and then make it fit the requirements of a given instrument. The jazz improviser creates only in terms of the instrument he plays. In extreme instances of assimilation, the instrument becomes in some way a part of him."

Since the instrument and, through it, the musician are "projected into" the melody, things like attack, vibrato, accentuation, rhythmic placement, etc., are so closely connected with a jazz melody that it may become meaningless without them. A European melody always exists "in the abstract" as well, but the jazz melody exists only in its concrete relationship to the instrument on which it is played and to the musician who plays it. It becomes nonsense (in the literal sense of the term) when it is removed from its creator and his instrument. This is the reason why most attempts to notate jazz improvisations have remained unsatisfactory. The fine points of phrasing, attack, accentuation, expression, and conception cannot be expressed in notation, and since everything depends on these subtleties, notation is largely unsatisfactory. When jazz melodies separated from these subtleties appear on note paper, they often seem primitive and banal.

In the course of jazz development, the improvisers have developed a facility for projecting subtleties into jazz that cannot be expressed in words. In order to accentuate the flowing character of jazz melody, the oppressively dotted quarter and eighth notes so typical of the jazz of the twenties have been dispensed with. Ever since the forties, this kind of punctuation has been regarded as "corny"; it can still be found in popular music, especially when nostalgia for the "good old days" is in order. (But all of a sudden there were several free-jazz musicians, most notably Albert Ayler, and then later alto saxophonist Henry Threadgill in nineties jazz, who had fun with such "old-fashioned" march, polka, and circus elements!) Miles Davis, Lee Konitz, and Lennie Tristano have fashioned a manner of improvisation in which eighth note stands next to eighth note, almost without punctuation. Here are lines that look in transcription as "European" and "symphonic" as one could imagine. But when such lines are played by Davis or Konitz or almost any significant jazz musician today, they become the very essence of concentrated "jazzness." The jazz character no longer lies in the crude, external punctuation and syncopation of notes; it lies in subtlety of conception. That is what Fats Waller and so many other jazz musicians mean when they say, "Jazz isn't *what* you do, it's *how* you do it."

Because all these refinements (almost ephemeral but extremely important differentiations in attack, phrasing, vibrato, accentuation, etc.) were further developed, it has become increasingly possible to incorporate the beat—the rhythm section—into the melody line. More and more one can hear unaccompanied jazz solos of similarly concentrated jazz essence as a solo improvisation with a rhythm section. We noted in the section on the jazz of the seventies that Coleman Hawkins was the first to record a whole piece without rhythm accompaniment: "Picasso," in 1947. This record was the real forerunner of those long, free-swinging unaccompanied improvisations and cadenzas played by Sonny Rollins—or, for instance, in Germany by Albert Mangelsdorff—that became something of a trend during the seventies, often filled with hidden romanticism.

One could say that from the midfifties on, it became the jazz improviser's prime concern to play long, flowing lines without crudely external jazz effects, and nonetheless to convey real jazz intensity. This is also the source of the "flowing," "pulsating" rhythmic conception developed by such musicians as drummer Elvin Jones in John Coltrane's group or Tony Williams with Miles Davis.

It is only a step from here to the melodies of many free-jazz musicians, who in the realm of melody more than anywhere else retained all elements of post–Lester Young and –Charlie Parker jazz phrasing, in addition to an ecstatic intensity that has its roots way back in Africa. With other free-jazz musicians, the pendulum swung in the opposite direction again: away from the emphasis on phrasing to the accent on noise-enriched sound production—in the sense of Bubber Miley's "jungle sounds," for example, of which we spoke in the section on sound.

The ability to simply let certain notes "go by the board" becomes particularly important in the organic course of a jazz melody line. Anyone who has notated jazz improvisation knows of this phenomenon, which André Hodeir has pertinently called a "ghost note." The note is here, one hears it quite clearly, and it has to be included in the notation. Yet one does not hear it because it was played but because it was *not* played; it was merely felt and hinted at. The theme to be improvised on has become less and less important in the course of jazz development. The embellishment and ornamentation of the theme, so important to the old jazz, recede further into the background. They still exist in the interpretation of "ballads"—slow pieces with melodies or chord structures that appeal to jazz musicians. Otherwise, improvisation became so free that the melody of a theme is hardly of significance. Often it cannot be recognized even at the start. Since the fifties, the jazz musician who plays fast pieces im-

Example 6

provises not so much on a theme as on the harmonies of this theme. And thus, as Hodeir has said, the jazz variation is a "variation on no theme at all."

Example 6 clarifies the process of untying the jazz improvisation from the theme. The example is transcribed from a record by the Max Roach Quintet, "Prince Albert," and the actual theme is Jerome Kern's "All the Things You Are." The first bars of this melody are in row (a). Above the harmonies of this theme (b), trumpeter Kenny Dorham and tenor saxophonist James Moody have placed a riff figure (c)—a new theme closer to their jazz conception. This theme of "All the Things You Are" is never even heard on the record. The musicians improvise on the new theme that was gleaned from the harmonies (in jazz terminology, chord changes) of "All the Things You Are," and on which in turn alternated harmonies can be based. One of these improvisations and its related harmonies can be found in rows (d) and (e) (with a flatted fifth in the fourth bar).

Clearly, this chain can be extended. A new riff can be based on the (e) changes, and this riff can become the basis for a different improvisation that in turn possesses alternations. The relationship to the theme is retained in all cases, and the jazz man—if he is knowledgeable—at once feels that somewhere "All the Things You Are" was the starting point.

Many melodies and standards that have become well-known in jazz are based on the harmonies of other themes and standards. Examples include Sonny Rollins's "Oleo" and Charlie Parker's "Anthropology," both based on "I Got Rhythm," Parker's "Donna Lee," based on "Indiana," and his "Warming Up a Riff," based on "Cherokee." Examples could be multiplied indefinitely. There is therefore a tradition in jazz in which the melodic and harmonic initial material of themes is carried further and developed in a modified, renewed, personal form. Frank Tirro has called this the "silent theme tradition" in jazz.

This is radical usage of a tenet basic to all forms of music in which improvisation is alive (such as baroque music) and in which the melody (or its harmonies!) is used as material. It is not a cause unto itself, as it is in music of the romantic period. When the melody is a cause unto itself, it becomes sacrosanct. Since our musical consciousness is romanticized, we are accustomed to regarding melodies as sacrosanct, and thus many people have no feeling for the "materiality" of melody.

Johann Sebastian Bach still had this feeling. It was not the melody that played a role, as in romantic music, but what one made of it. *Executio* took precedence over *inventio*: execution came before invention, whereas the musical conception of romanticism created a mystique of invention and placed it above all else. Because Bach regarded music as working material, he was able to take melodies from other masters of his time (such as Vivaldi) and use them for his own purposes without acknowledging his source. According to contemporary conception this is plagiarism. But to Bach it seemed all right, and exactly in this sense it seems all right to jazz musicians. Melody is the material, and so one can do with it as one wishes, with the proviso that what is made of this material should make musical sense.

The art of inventing new melodic lines from given harmonies has become increasingly differentiated in the course of jazz development. Often on older jazz recordings the improvisation actually only consists of taking the harmonies apart. Notes that in the basic chords were superimposed on one another are strung out in the melodies. The melodic movement has the flavor of cadenced triads and seventh chords. The melodies of modern jazz are more closely meshed. It no longer depends on interpreting the chord but on placing against it a contrasting, independent melodic line. This creates tension between the vertical and the horizontal, and the old jazz tendency to find possibilities for tension is thus nourished.

The jazz melody—aside from free playing—mainly obtains its structure from the twelve-bar form of the blues or the thirty-two-bar AABA form of the popular song, and in the newer stages of jazz, also from several irregular forms. There is a tendency among jazz musicians to cross over formal sections. Here, too, the indebtedness of music to time becomes clear. This crossing over the formal sections would be misread if one were to conclude that it results in a dissolution of form. The periodic form—predetermined by the chord structure—remains intact. In free jazz it was dissolved, but this amounted only to its replacement by more open, flexible, nonperiodic formal structures. Not following the formal bar structure is perceived as something special and out of the ordinary. One might almost say the formal structure is accentuated by the fact that it is not accentuated. Here, too, a new possibility for creating tension has been discovered: tension between the given, retained form and the free line that swings above it.

Related to the tendency to play across structural sections and displace them unexpectedly is the preference for long melodic lines in modern jazz—lines much longer than in the older forms.

Kenny Clarke and Mary Lou Williams claim that the pioneers of bop consciously crossed bar lines so that musicians who were trying to "steal" their ideas would not be able to get themselves organized. Thelonious Monk said, "We're going to create something that they can't steal because they can't play it." Drummer Dave Tough told of the first time he walked into the place on Fifty-Second Street where Dizzy Gillespie was playing: "As we walked in, these cats snatched up their horns and blew crazy stuff. One would stop all of a sudden and another would start for no reason at all. We never could tell when a solo was supposed to begin or end. Then they all quit at once and walked off the stand. It scared us." But, as Marshall Stearns points out, about a year later the selfsame Dave Tough was playing with Woody Herman's band some of the things that had scared him.

Independent of the structuring of four- or eight-bar sections, blues choruses, or thirty-two-bar song strophes is the natural structuring of tension and relaxation. The free-jazz musicians often went so far as to set this "organic form" in the place of predetermined, mostly four-bar-based structures. A collectively improvising free-jazz group creates its own form by "breathing," in the sense that the interaction of the musicians determines the form, not vice versa. This achievement of free jazz has also proven of lasting importance for the jazz of the subsequent decades: even younger musicians who have returned to conventional, functional tonality, as within "neo-classicism," love to create their own "breathing" forms independent of twelve-bar, sixteen-bar, or thirty-two-bar structures. More and more, one can also hear combinations of predetermined and breathing structures.

It is illuminating that the way for this was paved by the Kansas City jazz of the thirties, the so-called riff style: the riff creates tension, and the subsequent improvised melodic line creates relaxation. The strong, rhythmic, heavily accentuated ostinato phrases called "riffs," often only two or four bars in length and capable of being repeated until the thirty-two-bar song entity has been filled, are excellently suited to the creation of tension.

Guitarist Charlie Christian—one of the musicians who played a part in the creation of modern jazz—built up his solos in such a way that new riff elements were constantly opposed to new melodic lines. His solos are sequences of riffs and free-swinging melodic lines, the riffs creating tension, the melodic lines relaxation. Christian's manner of improvising was adopted by many musicians and has had great influence—consciously and unconsciously.

This relaxation—the moment of relief—goes further and deeper than is familiar from European music. Naturally, the aspect of tension and relaxation belongs to every organic musical art. In jazz, however, it is projected into the old call-and-response principle of African music. In the improvisations of Charlie Christian, the riffs are the "calls," the subsequent free-swinging lines the "responses." In other words, the lead singer no longer holds a conversation with the answering chorus of listeners—as in African music or in the spiritual—but the improvising soloist holds a conversation with himself. The loneliness—the "alienation"—of the creative jazz musician could never be made clearer than through this fact. Everything that goes into the give-and-take between call and response within the communion of a spiritual-singing congregation or a West African cult is now concentrated in the improvisation of a single soloist.

Of course, this thought must not be pursued too far. The principle of call and response is not projected merely in the single individual. The "call" of the riff is frequently played by the other musicians during the improvisation (which means during the "response" of the soloist), and it is possible in this way to create an intensity that carries everything with it. This intensity is rooted in concentration. Call and response no longer follow each other but are sounded simultaneously. The different melodic ideas of the different personalities communicate with each other; this is part of the lifeblood of jazz.

In the preceding discussion we have repeatedly used the word *relaxation*. To be "relaxed" has become an expression in the language of musicians as well as of jazz critics—and, as Norman Mailer has shown, an ideal in the lifestyle of jazz musicians and, in general, of people who want to be "in." From that vantage point, it has had a deep influence on the entire American lifestyle. Statements on European concert music rarely if ever use *relaxation* as a critical term.

Rhythm, Swing, Groove

Every ensemble playing tonal jazz, be it large or small, consists of a melody section and a rhythm section. To the former belong instruments such as trumpet, trombone, clarinet, and the members of the saxophone family; to the latter, drums, bass, guitar, and piano—only insofar as they do not step out in solo roles of their own, of course.

There is tension between the melody and rhythm sections. On the other hand, the rhythm section carries the melodic group. It is like a riverbed in which the stream of the melodic lines flows. Tension exists not only between the two sections but within each group as well; in fact, this can go so far as to mix up the actual functions of the two sections. It is not uncommon in modern jazz that "melody instruments" take over rhythm functions while "rhythm instruments" play the melody part. In free jazz those functions are so intertwined that the separation between melody and rhythm sections often seems to have been abandoned.

Thus a many-layered rhythm is created that thoroughly corresponds to the many layers of melody found in, say, the music of Johann Sebastian Bach. To claim, as some people still do, that the rhythm of jazz is nothing but primitive pounding merely reveals that such a person disregards the fact that rhythmic possibilities are as inexhaustible as melodic and harmonic ones. The lack of such feeling is of course in line with Western musical development. Hans H. Stuckenschmidt, one of Europe's leading music critics, and thus not a man of jazz but of concert music, once spoke of "the rhythmic atrophy in the musical arts of the white race." It is oddly ironic that the oft-heard complaint of primitiveness, directed against jazz and other similar phenomena, here turns back on the world from whence it came: against the European-Western world, in which there is this strange gap between admirable development of melodic, harmonic, and formal elements and, as Stuckenschmidt said, the atrophy of things rhythmic.

Not that there isn't any rhythm in European music. There are great rhythmic creations—for example in Mozart and Brahms, even more so in avant-garde concert music—but even these pale when compared to the grandiose rhythms of Indian or Balinese music, with traditions of rhythmic mastery as long and honorable as those of Western music in respect to form. One does not have to think only of jazz when it comes to recognizing the inferiority of rhythmic elements in notated European music.

It is simply an inferiority of rhythmic sense. What every street urchin in the Near East can do—beat out with arms and legs on boxes and pots rhythmic structures in which three or four different rhythms are complexly entwined—is seldom possible for the percussionist of a symphony orchestra within the European tradition. In symphony orchestras, three or four different percussionists are frequently needed to achieve such complexity.

In jazz, the multiplicity of rhythms is anchored in the "beat": a regularly accented basic rhythm, the beating heart of jazz—or, as drummer Jo Jones has put it, "even breathing." This fundamental rhythm is the organizing principle. Through it, the musical happenings are ordered. It is maintained by the drummer or, in classic modern jazz, often only by the steady 4/4 ("walking") of the bassist. This regulatory function corresponds to a European need. Certainly swing is connected with an African feeling for rhythm. But in spite of this—as Marshall Stearns has pointed out—there is no swing in traditional African music. Swing arose when African rhythmic feeling was applied to the regular meter of European music, in a long and complex process of fusion.

In the styles of jazz can be found certain basic rhythms, represented in simplified fashion by Example 7. This example represents the drum part. The notes in the lower row are played on the bass drum, those on the bottom on the snare drum (in the jazz-rock example: center row), and the crossed notes on the cymbal. The carrier of the basic beat in New Orleans, Dixieland, Chicago, and Swing style is the bass drum; in bebop and cool jazz it is the cymbal. The rhythmic accents are indicated by >.

Example 7

In New Orleans style and ragtime (a), the rhythmic emphasis is on the so-called strong beats: on 1 and 3, just as in march music. From here on, jazz rises to an ever-increasing rhythmic complexity and intensity. Dixieland and Chicago style (b), as well as New Orleans jazz as played in Chicago during the twenties, shifts the accents to 2 and 4, so that while 1 and 3 remain the "strong" beats, the accent now is on 2 and 4. Thus the peculiar "floating" rhythmic atmosphere from which swing takes its name was created.

Both New Orleans and Dixieland rhythms are two-beat rhythms insofar as the bass drum, carrier of the basic beat, is assigned two beats per measure. Of course there were exceptions. Louis Armstrong—always the Swing man!—requested drummer Baby Dodds to play an even four beats. Subsequently, Swing style was founded on four beats to the measure (c) but tends to emphasize 2 and 4. Up to this point, jazz rhythm had an almost staccato beat, with its concomitant punctuation: the cymbal beat in the Swing example. Bebop brings a further concentration, replacing staccato largely with legato (which is often phrased like a triplet). The rhythm becomes—as French drummer Gerard Pochonet has said—a *son continu*, a continuous sound. The cymbal sounds steadily—thus the *son continu*. In this *son continu* the rhythm gains the presence of an uninterrupted sound that, like a river, carries and immerses all that is happening in the music. On his other instruments—primarily on the snare drum—the drummer executes all kinds of rhythmic accents that emphasize the basic rhythm:

it is not so much "beat out" as it is "encircled." The deliberate insertion of accents on the bass drum, with which bebop drummers commented on the soloists' melodies, is known as "dropping bombs." Compared to the rhythmic dynamism of bop, the rhythm of cool jazz often seems like a step backward, combining rhythmic features of Swing and bop.

At the bottom of Example 7 (e), there is a rhythm sample of fusion music (one of many possible ones!). Here the two-beat rhythm returns, in disguise. The snare drum (center row) hints at it. The bass drum accents the basic rhythm by encircling it.

For free jazz, there is no basic formula that can be notated. The beat is replaced by what many jazz musicians call "pulse": a pulsating, percussive activity, generally rapid and free, in which single beats, standing by themselves, can no longer be perceived. Here several tempos, all different from each other, can coexist next to and on top of each other! The free-jazz drummers use many rhythmic formulas that have been developed through jazz history, plus a host of new rhythms taken from African, Arabian, Indian, and other non-Western musics, occasionally also from European concert music. Many musicians for whom the freedom of free jazz not only represents a liberation from conventional harmonies, but also has racial, social, and political implications, emphasize African elements—from pride in their own African roots.

It is often proposed that within free jazz, swing—that basic constituent element without which jazz is unthinkable—has ceased to exist. But what has ceased to exist is merely a certain metric symmetry. Our musical instincts used to perceive swing as rooted just in the friction between the symmetry of conventional, fundamental rhythm and the asymmetry of the various counter- and cross-rhythms that move above this fundamental rhythm and "contradict" it. Actually, what happened was that, in an even more concentrated and radical manner than when bebop rhythm was created, swing has been moved more "inward." Some contemporary musicians have learned to produce swing through phrasing (and thus to include it in the flow of the melody line) to such an extent that they find the kind of swing that depends on the mere symmetry of a steady, basic beat, or on just a steady bass beat, much too obvious, limiting, and static. (But since the seventies, there is also the sheer lustful joy of accenting—and overaccenting!—conventional Swing and Swing rhythms again.)

When bebop came into being, the majority of critics and fans also responded: "This music doesn't swing any more!" But just a few years later, when they had grown accustomed to the new rhythms, these same critics and fans said, "It swings more than ever." And even Dixieland bands used bebop drummers in their rhythm sections.

Jazz of the seventies and eighties was in a similar position vis-à-vis the jazz of the sixties as, twenty years earlier, cool jazz was vis-à-vis bebop: the use of elements of earlier jazz forms was—in light of the newly gained freedom—once again held in high esteem. In addition, there are the rock elements, of which we spoke in the section about the seventies. The absence of a stylistically generally binding rhythmic principle has been even more apparent since 1980. In postmodern jazz—beyond any schematism—all the rhythmic models of jazz, and even rhythms from outside jazz, can be amalgamated and combined. The fact that even symmetrical meters and a regular beat provide opportunities for rhythmic individuality was a discovery often and gladly made in recent jazz.

In these computerized times, we have come to call jazz-rock or fusion rhythms "binary," differentiating them in this way from the "ternary" ones of conventional jazz forms. Jazz-rock is based on steady eighths—a fact that explains the close relationship of rock, jazz-rock, and fusion rhythms to Latin music. Drummers like Billy Cobham and Pierre Courbois pointed this out at an early stage of the development. Conventional jazz rhythms, in contrast, are based on a triplet structure, that is, on a ternary rhythm feeling.

American jazz critic Martin Williams said:

> "Jazz" eighth notes, the "jazz" triplet: they are not the superficialities or the ornaments of a musical style. In jazz they have always been among the fundamentals. One of the unwritten (and undiscussed) laws of jazz has been that each of the great players has found his own way of pronouncing the triplet, expressed or implied—and Roy Eldridge's triplet doesn't sound like Louis Armstrong's; Miles Davis's didn't sound like Dizzy Gillespie's; Lester Young's triplet was unlike Coleman Hawkins's; and Stan Getz's is unlike Lester Young's.

This enormous abundance of individually varied rhythmic forms is among the most fascinating artistic outcomes of jazz. In keeping with the splendor of jazz's many rhythmic forms, there doesn't exist, up to the present day, any form of notation, graphic representation, and computer analysis capable of satisfactorily registering the subtlety of these rhythmic processes, which differ not just stylistically but also in terms of specific distinctions between groups and individuals.

And yet what happens rhythmically in many contemporary jazz groups is still shaped according to bebop models where the triplet feeling is most productive. They can be found everywhere in today's jazz—even in those contemporary jazz forms that are all but totally out of contact with bop in terms of sound, melody, and harmony.

The tension-filled complexity of these bop structures was clarified many years ago by Miles Davis, when he said:

> Like, we'd be playing the blues, and Bird [Charlie Parker] would start on the eleventh bar, and as the rhythm section stayed where they were and Bird played where he was, it sounded as if the rhythm section was on 1 and 3 instead of 2 and 4. Every time that would happen, Max [Roach,

the drummer] used to scream at Duke [Jordan, the pianist] not to follow Bird but to stay where he was. Then, eventually, it came around as Bird had planned and we were together again.

Davis called this, according to Marshall Stearns, "turning the beat around," and Miles added that it so bewildered him at first that he "used to quit every night."

Stearns has shown, on the basis of African recordings, that no style of jazz before free jazz was rhythmically closer to Africa than bebop. The simple, marchlike meters of New Orleans and of Dixieland were replaced by rhythmic structures in which polyrhythmic African practices seem suddenly to have come to life again.

All this took place without any direct contact between the urbanized modern jazz musician and West African rhythms. It is as if the musicians have subconsciously relived once more an evolution that their ancestors had gone through centuries ago—or conversely: as if they have shaken off habits rooted ultimately not in their own, but in European tradition, becoming increasingly "free," rediscovering, consciously *and* unconsciously, their true rhythmic heritage. This is also supported by the fact that in free jazz—as with drummers Sunny Murray, Milford Graves, and Rashied Ali—there was a further "Africanization" of jazz rhythms.

As early as the fifties, Art Blakey traveled to West Africa to become acquainted with old African rhythms. Even earlier, in the late forties, Dizzy Gillespie had hired the conga drummer Chano Pozo, who was still a member of an African sect in his native Cuba, where West African traditions remained alive to a much greater degree than in North America.

Meanwhile, what used to be the exception has almost become the rule on a host of jazz recordings: frequently, percussionists who are exponents of Africanizing rhythms—Latin Americans and Africans—are included as equal partners in the rhythm sections of jazz groups. No longer do we have to face a flaw that used to be so prevalent in earlier combinations of jazz and African rhythms—a rhythmic gap.

But all these remarks are insufficient. It may be possible to write down and notate the most complex rhythms by Max Roach or Art Blakey—or today, Tony Williams, Billy Cobham, Jack DeJohnette, and Jeff "Tain" Watts—only to discover that what has been written down and copied is merely a miserable skeleton of what the music really sounded like. You see, it swung, and swing cannot be notated. It cannot even be grasped in words. "It's a real simple thing," said Jo Jones, "but there are some things you can't describe, some things that never have been described. . . . The best way you can say what swinging is, is you either play with a feeling or you don't. It's just like the difference between receiving a genuine handshake or a fishy one."

Jo Jones thinks that the difference between jazz and European music lies in swing. In European music—"that approach to music is scientific"—the musician plays the notes that are placed before him or her. If one is sufficiently musical and has studied music, one can play the required parts. But in order to play jazz it is not sufficient to be musical and to have studied music long enough: you also have to swing. Almost all important representatives of modern jazz have studied music, and it is part and parcel of a good musician that he should know and understand his craft. But the decisive part cannot be taught: swing. One can hardly say what it is.

In the course of jazz development, swing became ever more far-reaching and concentrated. According to André Hodeir:

> The phenomenon of swing should not be regarded as the immediate and inevitable result of a confrontation between the African rhythmic genius and the 2/2 beat. What we know about primitive jazz excludes the hypothesis that swing sprang into being like a spark at the collision of two stones. Pre-Armstrong recordings reveal, on the contrary, that swing was merely latent at first and took shape progressively over a long period.

The aspect of serenity and relaxation belongs to swing. Jo Jones said, "Another thing about rhythm is that when an artist is performing on his instrument, he breathes in his normal fashion, and he has a listening audience that breathes along with him."

Steadiness of natural conditions of breathing creates the uniqueness of swing. There are never two possibilities. "The only way I can describe swing," said ragtime pianist Wally Rose, "is it's the kind of rhythmic movement where you can place a note where and when it is due. The only thing that keeps you together is when the whole band meets on this beat, meets on the split second you all think the beat is due. The slightest deviation from that causes tension and frustration."

Swing gives jazz its peculiar form of precision, which cannot be compared with any kind of precision in European music. Conductors and composers of symphonic music have been among the first to admit this. The difference between the precision found in Count Basie's band and the precision of the best European orchestras—jazz as well as symphonic—is due to the fact that Basie's precision stems from swing, whereas the other kind of precision is the result of rhythmic standardization. Basie's musicians feel that the note is due, and since they all feel this at the identical moment, and form the basis of swing, everything is precise in a direct, unfettered way. The kind of precision gleaned from academic tradition, on the other hand, is less direct and less unfettered.

To swing belong, furthermore, the multiple layers of rhythm and the tension between them—the displacements of rhythmic accents and all that we have said about them. This displacement is called "syncopation" in European music. But the use of this term in jazz reveals an essential misunderstanding of the nature of jazz. In European music syncopation signifies a clearly defined shift of emphasis within the bar. The accent falls precisely at the midpoint between two beats. In jazz the displacements of accent are freer, more flexible, and more subtle. The accent can now be anywhere between two beats—precisely where the musician feels it is "due." This accent moves away from the beat but simultaneously stresses it, so it is termed "off-beat."

It must be clear by now: swing is not the task of a drummer who has to "swing" the soloists. A jazz musician who does not swing—all alone and without any rhythm section—is no jazz musician. Thus the considered opinion of many modern musicians that it is almost as possible to swing without a drummer as with one: "The drive that creates the pulsation has to be within yourself. I don't understand why it should be necessary to have someone else drive you," said Jimmy Giuffre. Nat Hentoff remarked, "The ability to swing must first be contained within each musician. If he is dependent on a rhythm section . . . he is in the position of the rejected suitor who can't understand that one must be capable of giving love if one wishes to receive it."

It becomes increasingly clear that such paraphrases, by the musicians themselves or by sympathetic critics, are more satisfactory elucidations of the phenomenon of swing than "exact" explanations made by musicologists who have no feeling for swing. It is particularly unedifying to see swing explained as off-beat accentuation, which is so often the case. Off-beats—in other words, the accentuation away from the beat—do not of necessity produce swing. Most non-Western music, and even European folk music and modern pop music (even where it doesn't swing), is full of off-beats.

Equally unsatisfactory is the attempt (frequently found in writings on jazz) to equate jazz's triplet feeling with the phenomenon of swing. Certainly there are connections, but the mere fact that many jazz musicians (say, John Coltrane in his later periods, Eric Dolphy, or David Murray) have largely or completely abandoned triplet phrasing and yet swing with the greatest of ardor, intensity, directness, and vitality speaks against an identity between jazz triplets and swing.

Some of the most concise thoughts concerning swing have been expressed by the Swiss musicologist Jan Slawe. In his *Versuch einer Definition der Jazzmusik,* in the context of rhythm and meter, he states:

> The main concept of jazz theory is "formation of conflict"; originally, these formations of conflict were rhythmic in nature, existing in the antagonism between simultaneously executed, different segments of music-filled time. . . . The fundamental nature of swing is expressed in the rhythmic basis of the music as a whole. . . . In particular, swing postulates a regularity of time in order to simultaneously be able to negate it. The particular nature of swing is the creation of rhythmic conflicts

between the fundamental rhythm and the rhythm of the melody; this is the musical-technical cornerstone of jazz.

But these definitions, too, remain unsatisfactory. Meanwhile, so much has been written about swing that one might tend to accept once and for all the dictum that swing cannot be verbally expressed. Maybe this is because swing involves a feeling for time for which there is no precedent in European music. Ethnology has shown us that the African's sense of time—and, in general, that of many cultures—is more holistic and elementary than the clock-based time sense of the Westerner. Swing developed when the two concepts of time met. In all the polyrhythms of traditional African music, often much more complex than those of jazz, there is still no swing—as is the case in European music. One might assume that its nature is rooted in the overlapping of two different conceptions of time.

Musicology knows well that music may occur in two different conceptions of time. Stravinsky called these "psychological" and "ontological" time. Rudolf Kassner spoke of "lived" and "measured" time. These two kinds of time cannot be equalized in those aspects of our being that count most: one second of pain becomes an eternity, and one hour can be but a fleeting moment in a state of happiness. This is of significance to music. Music is art in time, as sculpture is art in space, and painting the art of the plane. But if music is art in time, we may ask which time: psychological or ontological, relative or absolute, lived or measured?

This question can be answered only in respect to one particular musical style. It has been said that the relationship between lived and measured time is of considerable formative consequence to music. Thus romantic, and particularly late romantic, music is almost exclusively an art of lived, psychological time. Private and subjective experience of time is primary here. On the other hand, the music of a Bach is almost exclusively in measured, objective, ontological time, related in each note to the movement of the cosmos, to which it is of no concern whether a minute seems to us like an eternity, or eternity like a minute.

The question is, Which is the time of swing? And here it becomes clear why Westerners must "leap over the shadow of their time sense" if they want to find out about swing. For there can be no doubt that swing is related to both levels of time at once—to measured, objective time and to lived, psychological time. By the same token, it is also related to both an African and a European sense of time. Swing is rooted in the awareness of a simultaneously desperate and joyous inability to find a common denominator for lived and measured time. More precisely: a common denominator for lived and measured time has been found, but the listener is aware of a duality—in other words, he or she is aware of swing.

Paul F. Berliner writes:

> Among all the challenges a group faces, one that is extremely subtle yet
> fundamental to its travels is a feature of group interaction that requires
> the negotiation of a shared sense of the beat, known, in its most success-
> ful realization, as striking a groove. Incorporating the connotations of
> stability, intensity, and swing, the groove provides the basis for "every-
> thing to come together in complete accord."

Groove is a phenomenon of perception that relates both to musical
structure and to musical process. The term *groove* is used in many different ways in jazz. Its use changes depending on whether one is talking
about the communication within a group or about particular parts of the
musical structure.

In relation to the plane of musical appearance, that is, structure,
groove is present when overlapping rhythmic patterns mesh with one
another until an effect of self-propulsion arises, creating an impression of
inexorability that is at the same time completely unforced—a sensation
"that pushes you from behind until you're as funky as a locomotive"
(Kodwo Eshun).

That quotation gets at a feature that is indispensable for the sense of
groove: closely connected with groove is the feeling of a motoric attraction that irresistibly draws in players and listeners alike. Groove appeals
to musicians' and listeners' bodies; it is a strong energy that compels
movement. The more intensely a piece of music creates a drive to movement, the stronger its groove. In both African American music and in
centuries of African music, a good groove is always the promise of a
good dance.

In African American music, groove is therefore proof of the highest
degree of rhythmic ability. In response to all the ink spilled by theoreticians on the subject of groove, guitarist Bo Diddley said: "Save yourself
all that trouble. I *have* the groove."

Groove is a more general, more comprehensive concept than swing.
Anyone who swings necessarily grooves, but not everyone who grooves
also has swing. Almost all pop music grooves. Many of the works of
Johann Sebastian Bach groove as well, as does the music of the Balkans,
Balinese *ketchak* dance, or South Indian mridanga music, even though
the explicit concept of groove certainly did not exist during the baroque
period, or in many traditional non-Western cultures today.

The word *groove* has various connotations in English, including
its reference to the grooves of a record. In African American slang, "to
groove" means to feel good. Anything that can be enjoyed is "groovy."
Someone who "grooves" has mastered the art of a positive approach
to life, a certain way of thinking and acting. Among the disadvantaged
African Americans of slave society, victims of discrimination, someone

who "grooved" had a competitive advantage, because it feels good to know how to make the best of your circumstances. In jazz, the term *groove* regularly comes up as a way of describing a particular relationship within the rhythm section. If, for example, the bassist's phrasing and the drummer's rhythm work together so well that a heightened sense of the beat (or, in free jazz, the pulse) results, and is communicated and shared among the musicians, you have a groove. Because of the eminently important significance of the groove, in jazz the rhythm section has a special responsibility. They are not, as nonmusicians sometimes think, a part of the group subordinated to the soloists; rather, they are the center and the heart of the group. Because the rhythm section forms the "groove anchor" of a band, musicians place great emphasis on the importance of the interaction, the togetherness, of rhythm sections. Over the course of jazz history, again and again bassists and drummers have emerged between whom a more successful rhythmic communication took place than between others. For example, in the John Coltrane Quartet, Jimmy Garrison and Elvin Jones had this transcendent surefootedness, as did Tony Williams and Ron Carter with Miles Davis, Jaco Pastorius and Peter Erskine with Weather Report, Palle Danielsson and Jon Christensen with Jan Garbarek. "For things to happen beautifully in the ensemble, the drummer and the bass player must be married," says drummer Charlie Persip. "When I listen to the drummer and the bass player together, I like to hear the wedding bells."

Groove has to result from a mutual understanding. It is an element of interaction, a particular rhythmic attunedness to the other musicians. When a piece of music grooves, musicians have a powerful rhythmic relationship to each other. Someone who is grooving is in a communicative mode. For this reason, a good groove is a living expression of successful musical-rhythmic community; it creates security—musical, rhythmic, human, and cultural. "When we are in the same time feeling, the same rhythm as the others (or in the groove, as you say in music), we create a relationship that goes beyond the purely verbal, into the bodily dimension," writes vibraphonist Christopher Dell.

As strange as it may sound, this coming into agreement between musicians, this synchronicity, does not mean that all the players are doing the same thing. The power of the groove consists in a paradoxical interplay between rhythmic uniformity and micro-rhythmic deviation. The overall feeling is one of togetherness, a constant coordinated musical-rhythmic movement, and a communal experience. At the same time, however, the individual parts are also moving out of phase, in constant friction with one another, in the manner of a deviation from an imagined unison. Charles Keil calls these intentional, gradual deviations from a basic pulse, which both confirm the whole and create friction, "participatory discrepancies."

Groove comes into being when rhythmic relationships happen that are simultaneously synchronous with one another and displaced, or out of phase. This oscillation between rhythmic synchronization and deliberate minute deviations from the basic pulse are the basis of the groove's power.

But groove is not an exclusive property of rhythm sections. *All* the musicians of a jazz group have to groove in order for that shared sense of the beat (in free jazz, the pulse) to happen in which the contradiction between rhythmic synchronicity and microrhythmic deviation creates an agreeable sense of relish and tension.

Even musicians playing alone can groove. But here, too, for example in the monologue of an unaccompanied solo concert, there is still an element of interaction. An unaccompanied solo player grooves only if he or she places rhythmic accents so as to create a feeling of carrying on an internal dialogue with him- or herself—a sense of successful communication between the breath, the limbs, the brain, etc. A groove develops only if the listener is carried along by the rhythm, and can actively groove along with it.

Groove happens whenever a strong rhythmic self-propulsive effect takes over. The power of the rhythm then prevails to such an extent that it seems as though the players themselves are not controlling the music. "Every jazz musician wants to be locked in that groove where you can't escape the tempo," says Franklin Gordon. "You're locked in so comfortably that there's no way you can break outside of it, and everyone's locked in there together. . . . These are the magical moments, the best moments in jazz."

This self-propulsive effect depends prominently on repetition. Rhythmic repetition, whether it be the ostinato funk patterns of jazz-rock, the riffs of Kansas City jazz, or simply the cyclical patterns that drummers and bassists play as accompaniments, have a stimulating, intensifying effect on the feeling of the groove.

Groove means rhythmic security. Just as the stylus of a record player is carried through the regular rotations of the groove of the LP, and is guided securely from the beginning to the end of a record, the strong rhythm of repetitive structures, or patterns, carries musicians securely from the beginning to the end of a piece of jazz. Electric bassist and arranger Marcus Miller says, "Groove is when a rhythm in the music is repeated endlessly. It literally feels like you're in a groove. You feel like you're out of pocket, not moving. But the music keeps going, on and on. And even though it's changing only imperceptibly, it gets bigger and bigger, like a snowball rolling down a hill—that's groove."

Part of the complexity of the phenomenon of groove is that repetition is nonetheless not a necessary condition for the feeling of groove. Freely improvised music, with its "breathed" figures and lack of repetition, can also groove.

In a more narrow, exclusive sense, groove refers to those rare moments of successful improvisation in which the musicians have the feeling of being so tightly connected to one another that feelings of happiness occur, which musicians have compared to the experience of trance and ecstasy, religious experience, or the intensity of orgasm. "Groove is when you are lifted up, when you're in the zone," says David Sanborn. "Groove is when you're in the right place at the right time." Characteristic of this intense groove experience is that the musician simultaneously feels completely melded with the other musicians and completely "in himself." "When you're grooving, it's like you're in the Garden of Eden," says Herbie Hancock.

Thus, groove refers to the development by the musicians of a shared sense for the beat in which the tension between rhythmic synchronicity and microrhythmic deviation is perceived to create a pleasurable, enjoyable tension. These are rhythmic accents that are more subtle than the rubato or syncope of Western music.

In fact, the chronological "channel" for these microrhythmic deviations, that is, the temporal space within which gradual deviations from the basic pulse are felt to be exciting, is indeed very narrow. Musicians have an intuitive feeling for the boundaries of these "slots," and accents that fall outside this time frame are felt to be jarring and false. Although subtle fluctuations within the groove are possible, musicians strive to avoid larger changes in the tempo, or in the pulse in free jazz. This "time channel" varies from musician to musician and from style to style, but it certainly exists, and its exploitation in order to create microrhythmic deviation seems to be essential to living, grooving music.

From all this, it can be concluded that groove, with all its freedom for deviation, is closely connected to a heightened sense of rhythmic precision—but this is a precision that is living and that leaves room for the personality of the musicians of the group, instead of imposing itself on them.

Freddie Green, the guitarist of the Count Basie Orchestra, played almost nothing but quarter notes for fifty years, but he microrhythmically phrased these quarter notes in such a refined, individual way that he was able to make the Basie big band groove like no other. Bassist Red Mitchell, an admirer of Green's playing, once presented his idol with a poem expressing the idea that what's important is not so much rigid, metronomic time, but rather sound and soul, communication and love, support and bounce.

"Yeah, I couldn't have said it better than that," answered Freddie Green.

Whereupon Red Mitchell, hoping to learn more about the secret of groove, asked Green, "Can you verbalize how you do what you do?"

"Well, you gotta get the first beat right."

Mitchell wasn't sure what that meant. "You mean one of each bar?"

"No, the very first beat of the whole tune. If you get that right, you got a good crack at the second. If you don't, forget it."

The Instruments of Jazz

The Trumpet

*Hold the trumpet up proudly, and you can become
a priest, a shaman, or a griot.*
—Wynton Marsalis

The trumpet has been called the "royal instrument of jazz" because its sound is so piercing and brilliant that in almost all ensemble passages in which a trumpet takes part, the lead is almost automatically assigned to it. This happens in the New Orleans collective as well as in the ensembles of the big bands, which are almost always dominated by the trumpet section.

With the trumpet belong the cornet, on the one hand—particularly in the older forms of jazz—and, the fluegelhorn, on the other—in the newer styles. In the early days of jazz, *trumpet* almost always meant cornet. Later on, there were few cornetists, probably because the trumpet offers greater range and technical possibilities. Nevertheless, cornetist Rex Stewart ranks as one of the greatest technical virtuosos of the "trumpet" up to the beginnings of bop. Other technically able "trumpeters"—mainly in the realm of Dixieland—stayed with the cornet, among them Wild Bill Davison and Muggsy Spanier. In modern jazz Nat Adderley and occasionally Clark Terry, among others, used the cornet; in free jazz Bobby Bradford and Butch Morris. In some modern forms of jazz, however, the fluegelhorn became popular due to its round, flowing sound. There are fluegelhorn players in jazz who manage to lend their instrument a saxophone-like suppleness, and who yet are able to preserve the brilliance of the brass sound. Among the best fluegelhorn players are Art Farmer, Thad Jones, Jimmy Owens, Roy Hargrove, the Dutch player Ack van Rooyen, Canadian-born Kenny Wheeler, who lives in England, the German player Claus Stötter, and, again, Clark Terry.

The first generation of jazz cornetists is that of Buddy Bolden—the legendary progenitor of New Orleans jazz, who regrettably played before the era of recorded jazz music—and his contemporaries, active around the turn of the twentieth century and immediately thereafter. They played jazz or similar music—we might call it ragtime and march music with hot intonation. To this generation belong Freddie Keppard, Emmanuel Perez, Bunk Johnson, Papa Celestin, and above all King Oliver. Keppard had a suspicious attitude toward recording, and played with a handkerchief covering his right hand so that other players would not be able to "steal" his fingerings. King Oliver's recordings, on the other hand, provide rich material for study. They have that rough, earthbound, hard sound, still lacking the triumphant tone that Louis Armstrong gave to the jazz trumpet.

The earliest period of jazz was an epoch of great sound discoveries. In the quest to individualize their sounds, African American trumpet players competed to see how many different "vocal" sounds they could get out of their instrument. In New Orleans jazz, and later in Swing, it was not unusual for a trumpeter to have as many as ten mutes.

In finding ways to charge the sound with individual expression, the imagination of these trumpet players knew no limits. At first, they experimented with placing beer glasses, ashtrays, paper bags, wooden balls, boxes, etc., into the bell of the trumpet. Later, commercially produced jazz mutes came on the scene, which were in some cases so successful that they eventually found their way into symphony orchestras.

King Oliver said, "I am the guy who took a pop bottle and a rubber plunger and made the first mute ever used in a horn, but I didn't know how to get the patent for it and some educated cat came along and made a fortune off of my ideas." This story is probably an invention, but we mention it here nonetheless because it provides a revealing picture of the circumstances under which African American jazz came into being. King Oliver was the musician who made the most creative and wide-ranging use of mutes in New Orleans jazz.

Tommy Ladnier links this sound to a strong and expressive blues feeling, accentuated primarily in the lower registers of the instrument. Initially, Ladnier stems wholly from Oliver. In the twenties, he traveled as far as Moscow, billed as "Tommy, the talking cornet." Ladnier, born in 1900, belongs to Louis Armstrong's generation, but one feels inclined to place him earlier in terms of musical conception. We have spoken of Armstrong in a special section. He did not switch from cornet to trumpet until 1928. Armstrong is the measure for all jazz trumpeting up to this day.

Among the musicians who played most à la Armstrong were Hot Lips Page, Teddy Buckner, and Jonah Jones. Page, who died in 1954, was active in the Kansas City circle of musicians from the late twenties to the midthirties. An exceptional blues player, he sometimes played so much like Armstrong that he could be mistaken for him. As a singer, too, he was astonishingly close to Armstrong. Page was the undisputed master of "growl" playing, that earthy, "squeezed"-sounding, vocal tone-bending that is capable of producing a wide variety of colorations (another master of this kind of playing was, later, Cootie Williams). In jazz, the growl is a rough, "dirty" sound that can be produced on brass instruments in two different ways: by "fluttering" the tongue rapidly while playing, or by making guttural sounds in the throat.

Now, back to the first generation of white trumpet (and cornet) players, beginning with Nick La Rocca, founder of the Original Dixieland Jazz Band. His cornet in a way retained the sound of the circus trumpeters of the turn of the century, in paradoxical contrast to his preposterous claims that he and his white orchestra had been the first jazz band.

In the realm of the old Dixieland, but considerably more musical and differentiated, was the trumpeting of Sharkey Bonano. He and Muggsy Spanier are among the white trumpeters who frequently are counted by traditional jazz fans among black New Orleans rather than white Dixieland. Spanier made the first Chicago-style recordings in 1924 with his Bucktown Five. In 1939 he had a short-lived band—Muggsy Spanier's Ragtime Band—that made a deep and lasting impression with its musicianly and original Dixieland music. In 1940 he made records with Sidney Bechet, accompanied by guitar and bass only, that are a kind of "chamber music" of traditional jazz.

Along the line originating from La Rocca, but more polished and musical, are Red Nichols and Phil Napoleon, two musicians representative of "New York style." This term is common usage for the music of the white jazz musicians in New York during the twenties and early thirties, who did not have the privilege of steady, stimulating contact with the New Orleans greats, as did their colleagues in Chicago. On the other hand, they were often ahead of them in terms of academic training, technique, and craftsmanship. Comparison between Nichols and Bix Beiderbecke illuminates this point: Nichols's blowing was perhaps even more clean and flawless than Bix's, but he could not approach Bix where sensitivity and imagination were concerned. Both Napoleon's Original Memphis Five and Nichols's Five Pennies found great favor with their kind of "purified" jazz, especially with commercial audiences.

Bix Beiderbecke brought elegance and cool introversion to the sound of the jazz cornet. He had more followers than any other white cornetist of his time. Bunny Berigan, Jimmy McPartland, and Bobby Hackett are among these. The Bixian conception can be pursued well into cool jazz. Many solos by Miles Davis, and even more by Chet Baker, sound as if Beiderbecke's Chicago style had been "transformed" into modern jazz— although, of course, there is no direct link between Bix and Miles.

Stylistically, the most significant of Beiderbecke's followers was Bobby Hackett. Hackett was a genuine master of the art of playing standards, the great songs of popular music in America. His "traditional" jazz playing was spiced with many harmonic and rhythmic experiences from much more "modern" periods of jazz.

Rex Stewart, although not a Beiderbecke successor, copied some of Bix's solos during the years when Beiderbecke was the talk of all jazz musicians, mainly—with the Henderson band of 1931—Bix's celebrated "Singing the Blues," one of the most famous trumpet solos in jazz history.

With Stewart we arrive at a group of trumpeters who might be described as "Ellington trumpets." These are first and foremost the "jungle-style" trumpeters.

The first in this group was Bubber Miley, who died in 1932 and who gave the Ellington band of the twenties the characteristic coloration that until this day is associated with Ellington. Bubber was first influenced by King Oliver: if one recalls Oliver's most famous solo—"Dippermouth Blues"—it illuminates how direct the link is to Miley's famed solo on Ellington's first version of "Black and Tan Fantasy," which Bubber cocomposed.

Miley made the "wah-wah" sound, closely connected with the "jungle" style, world-famous. Unusually, he played his trumpet with a small cornet mute inserted in the bell, while simultaneously using his left hand to manipulate a rubber plunger in front of the bell in order to create a wide variety of "wah-wah" sounds, variously modulated and squeezed, from the already-muted tones.

Ellington remained interested in the retention of the "Miley color." Stewart, Cootie Williams, Ray Nance, Clark Terry, and others had to see to this during various epochs in Ellington's career. Cootie Williams played growl trumpet with particular expressiveness and strength. He was known as the "master of a thousand sonorities." No one else matched him in the number of sounds he was able to bring forth from the trumpet using the plunger—speechlike, heartfelt "talking" sounds. He is the soloist on one of Ellington's most significant recordings, *Concerto for Cootie* (1940). Stewart, who died in 1967, has often been admired for the lightness and assurance with which he could play at even the most rapid tempos—and very expressively, at that.

An element of Stewart's style was the half-valve technique: the valves of the trumpet are pressed down only halfway. Clark Terry transplanted this style of playing into modern jazz. Terry has created a unique, completely personal style, with a joyful, fat sound animated by his characteristic pitch bending, and is perhaps the only modern trumpeter prior to free jazz who did not become enmeshed in the back-and-forth between Dizzy Gillespie and Miles Davis. And, above all, Terry is master of intelligent musical humor.

All trumpeters mentioned up to now actually belong to the immediate Armstrong school. In contrast to this school stands what might be called, for simplification, the Gillespie school. It, too, is a product of what had come before. The Gillespie tradition actually begins long before Dizzy, with Henry "Red" Allen. Allen, who died in 1967, took King Oliver's place in the Oliver band when it was taken over by Luis Russell in 1929. In his playing, the shift in emphasis from sonority to phrasing was indicated for the first time—if only in spurts. When compared to his contemporaries, Allen plays more legato than staccato, in a more flowing manner, connecting rather than separating his phrases.

The tendency toward this kind of playing becomes more marked with a group of trumpeters who came after Allen: Roy Eldridge, Buck Clayton, and Harry Edison. Eldridge, who died in 1989, became the most important exponent of his instrument between Armstrong and Gillespie. Fluidity now became an ideal for jazz trumpeters. The saxophone is the most "fluid" of jazz instruments, and here was revealed for the first time the impact of the saxophone on the sonority of modern jazz. Eldridge once said, "I play nice saxophone on the trumpet." He later abandoned this saxophone emphasis in his playing, but it remained an active influence. He had a rough, scratchy sound, and became well-known for his emotional way of building solos: playing riffs in the high register, leading to rhythmic climaxes.

Buck Clayton and Harry Edison, finally, played the most gentle and tender trumpets of all the Swing musicians. Edison earned his nickname "Sweets" because he loved to eat anything sweet. But his nickname applies also to the supple tenderness of his playing. Harmonically speaking, he is the most "modern" trumpet before Gillespie, while Clayton, who died in 1991, still tends more toward traditional harmonies. Both were among the star soloists of the classic Count Basie band of the late thirties. In the fifties, Edison, who died in 1999, became a busy Hollywood studio musician who participated in recording sessions with stars like Frank Sinatra and later in New York in jazz and rock productions. No other trumpeter so completely expresses the sensitivity of classic modern jazz in the idiom of Swing style.

Clayton is frequently mentioned when Ruby Braff's antecedents are under discussion. Braff (d. 2003) is a unique stylistic phenomenon: a trumpeter of the jazz generation of the fifties who took his cues not from Dizzy or Miles, but from the trumpeters of the earlier jazz tradition—a perfectionist of the Swing cornet, full of grace and charm in Swing and Dixieland. In the seventies he co-led a quartet with guitarist George Barnes, whose Swing was characterized by a floating weightlessness. This

Swing tradition is still alive, as in Warren Vaché, who became prominent at the end of the seventies, or today through Randy Sandke, both of whom remain very much indebted to Swing in everything they play.

Jazz trumpeters began early to make use of the stimulating effects of the highest registers of the instrument, playing far above conventional trumpet range. As with everything else in the history of the jazz trumpet, this, too, begins with Louis Armstrong, who found notes on the trumpet that simply did not exist according to the standards of European trumpet literature at that time. But Charlie Shavers, an unusually brilliant all-around Swing trumpeter, was the musician who most influenced the high-note specialists: "Cat" Anderson and Al Killian with Duke Ellington, and eventually Maynard Ferguson, who became known as a member of Stan Kenton's orchestra. Kenton scored with the record sales of Ferguson's skyscraper-climbing escapades, but the critics were almost unanimously antagonized by the tastelessness of this way of playing. Later, Ferguson showed that he was a musician with real jazz feeling and tremendous swing, mainly with his wildly swinging big bands, which he led in the late fifties in the United States, later in Great Britain (more about that in the section on the big bands).

With astonishing ease and assurance, Ferguson, who died in 2006, played things other trumpeters would consider impossible. Most of all he does not just scream and screech when playing at skyscraper heights; even up there he hits each note accurately and phrases musically. Not until the end of the seventies did he meet with a real competitor in this field: Cuban-born Arturo Sandoval, who further developed Ferguson's high-flight trumpeting with fiery élan and captivating relaxation, linking (when playing in the Irakere big band until 1981 and then in his own groups) this form of high-note playing with Dizzy Gillespie's bop brilliance.

A particular kind of high note playing developed within the big bands. In order to be better able to lead a trumpet section, lead trumpeters are generally outstanding high-register players. For example, Australian big-band trumpeter James Morrison, in the nineties, played in a muscular style that ascended to stratospheric, whistling heights. But Morrison, despite his brilliance, also tends to fall into the trap of circus-like high-note demonstrations played for effect, sometimes playing two trumpets at once.

"There's a terrible misconception of lead playing," says trumpeter Marcus Printup. "Many people think lead playing is a lot of high notes. That is one aspect of playing lead. But it's more about phrasing." Outstanding lead trumpet players in jazz include Ernie Royal, Snooky Young, Cat Anderson, Jon Faddis, Bobby Shew, and, in contemporary jazz, Alex Sipiagin and Jeremy Pelt.

Dizzy Gillespie based his style of playing on the instrumental achievements of Eldridge and on the stylistic contributions of the other bop pioneers: antipodal to Armstrong and yet only comparable to him in power and brilliance. Gillespie, too, has been discussed in a separate section.

Just as all trumpeters of traditional jazz come from Armstrong, so do all modern trumpeters stem from Gillespie. The four most important in the forties were Howard McGhee, Fats Navarro, Kenny Dorham, and young Miles Davis. The early death of Fats Navarro was as lamented by the musicians of his generation as Bix Beiderbecke's passing had been mourned by the musicians of the Chicago period. Fats's lithe, assured playing was a forerunner of the style practiced by the generation of hard bop since the late sixties, combining the melodic arcs of Miles Davis with the fire of Dizzy Gillespie. In his autobiography, *Beneath the Underdog*, Charles Mingus makes Fats Navarro into an emblematic figure of modern jazz.

Miles Davis began as a Dizzy imitator, just as Dizzy had begun by imitating Eldridge. But he soon found his own, completely new style. Miles is the founder and chief representative of the second phase of modern jazz trumpeting: lyrical arcs of melody in which the sophistication of simplicity is admirably cultivated, even less vibrato than Dizzy—and all this with a tone less glowing than loaded with coolly smoldering protest. After Davis, the development of jazz trumpeting first took place in the interplay between Dizzy and Miles, frequently spiced with a shot of Fats Navarro (into whose place Clifford Brown later stepped). Kenny Dorham proved himself to be a musician in this mold who by no means received the recognition due his talent. His warm, soulful playing radiates great harmonic knowledge.

Chet Baker, Johnny Coles, and Art Farmer are all stylistically close to Miles Davis, but only Chet was directly influenced by Miles. Baker played his way to sensational success with his solo on "My Funny Valentine," recorded in 1952 with the Gerry Mulligan Quartet. For a short time he dominated all jazz polls. His phrasing was so supple that he occasionally was chided as "feminine." Today that would be a compliment. No other trumpeter, apart from Miles, captured the phenomenon of loneliness and sadness so movingly as Chet Baker, who died in 1988 (who also made a name for himself as a vocalist). Every note he played was like parting from a good friend. It often seemed as if he were "singing" rather than blowing his trumpet, with such a floating, melancholy lightness that when he put aside his horn to sing, the voice seemed a logical continuation of his trumpet playing.

Art Farmer, who lived in Europe for many years and died in 1999, played with particular sophistication; his expressive powers on flugelhorn seemed to be unlimited, and on muted trumpet he combined liquid mobility with soulful expressiveness. Art, and along with him Johnny Coles, were the only modern trumpeters who could equal the lyrical intensity of Davis without imitating him—in their own unmistakable ways. And it is indeed illuminating that just these two trumpeters, who were above any attempt at copying Miles, came closer to him in expressiveness than all the many musicians directly influenced by him. Art Farmer also emerged in 1952 from the same Lionel Hampton band that brought to light classic modern jazz's most highly praised trumpeter next to Miles Davis: Clifford Brown, who died in 1956 in a tragic automobile accident. "Brownie," as he was called, further developed the playing style of Fats Navarro. In many respects, he—and, of course, Navarro—are the "fathers of the hard-bop trumpet." The black musicians untouched by cool jazz had continued to play bop in the first half of the fifties, but hardly anyone took notice. It was Brownie's success that initiated the breakthrough of hard bop. Clifford Brown played with a mobility and tone quality that made the trumpet sound almost like a woodwind instrument. He was able to create excitement without playing a lot of high notes, because his rhythms and the logic of his lines created tension. Clifford Brown made hard bop logical. Before John Coltrane, no one made the complicated linear style of bop sound more focused and inevitable than Brown. At the same time, his lines communicated soul, warmth, and an unbounded optimism. After his untimely death, a Clifford Brown myth developed, comparable to the Beiderbecke legend. Clifford Brown's influence was also apparent in seventies neobop and—more strongly still—in the neo–hard bop of the eighties and nineties. There's scarcely a trumpeter in these two styles who didn't relate to Brown's mellow sound, harmonic flexibility, and austere phrasing.

The musical experience of cool jazz in the first half of the fifties and the vitality of the bop of the forties merged in hard bop. Donald Byrd, Thad Jones, Lee Morgan, Bill Hardman, Nat Adderley, Benny Bailey, Ira Sullivan, Yugoslavian Dusko Gojkovic, Ted Curson, Blue Mitchell, Booker Little, Freddie Hubbard, and Woody Shaw are all trumpeters in this mold.

Donald Byrd combined a certain academic solidity with so much professional flexibility that he became one of the most frequently recorded trumpet players of hard bop. In the seventies, he was successful playing a tasty brand of funk jazz, even though some critics objected to it. In 1993 he released the album *Jazzmatazz*, on which, working with the rapper Guru, he brought together elements of jazz and hip-hop. The results were mixed: the hip-hop rhythms and jazz melodies certainly groove, but they don't meld smoothly; the impression is often that they are tacked onto each other.

Thad Jones (d. 1986), an exceptional arranger, was co-leader of the Thad Jones–Mel Lewis Big Band until 1979. He stemmed from the Basie Orchestra, and he blew some of his first remarkable solos in the then experimental-sounding Jazz Workshops of Charles Mingus. Lee Morgan, who died in 1972, worked with Dizzy Gillespie's big band in the midfifties, and, as an eighteen-year-old, was featured extensively by Dizzy. He became (as a member of Art Blakey's Jazz Messengers) a frequently re-corded hard-bop musician. His sound was always an unfeigned reflection of his momentary mood. Morgan's fiery, compelling sound expresses hu-mor and a gift for constructing a solo as a long melody. This was a musi-cal architecture with heart and a grooving slyness that was closer to soul music than to the mathematical scales of the conservatories. One of Lee Morgan's trademarks was his personal approach to "half-valve" play-ing. In neobop, and among the "young lion" trumpeters of the nineties, Morgan's sound had a level of influence comparable to that of Clifford Brown or Freddie Hubbard (discussed below).

Among other creative hard-bop trumpeters who lived in Europe was Benny Bailey (d. 2005), who won many friends with his great, full sound—a true trumpet stylist and, in addition, one of the best lead trum-peters one could wish for in a big band.

The development of the trumpet, as far as it took place within "tonal" jazz, brought little that was stylistically new up to the late nineties—aside from an astounding perfecting of bop fire, which occurred in two thrusts forward: first in neobop at the end of the seventies and then in nine-ties neoclassicism. The most important trumpeters by far in the transi-tion from hard bop to neobop were Booker Little, Freddie Hubbard, and Woody Shaw.

Booker Little, who died far too young in 1961, first became known through his playing in the Max Roach ensemble. He opened up hard bop from the inside, as it were, to the innovations and freedoms to come in the jazz of the sixties. He was the first jazz trumpeter to improvise using wide intervallic jumps, not the more usual smaller tonal steps; it was no accident that he made some of his finest recordings with saxophonist Eric Dolphy, who played in a similar intervallic style. Little's motto was: "The greater the dissonance, the greater the sound." He was a master of an infinite variety of valve nuances, which he used to ornament notes by "scooping," or microtonal pitch deviations, giving his lines pathos and dignity.

Little was also a talented composer. His complex pieces have little in common with the conventions of hard bop. They are full of breaks and contrasts and have a bittersweet quality, alternating in their mood between light and shadow, combining consonance and dissonance within a narrow space. This complex, contradictory quality has made Booker Little an important point of reference for the postmodern jazz trumpeters of the early twenty-first century.

Freddie Hubbard, who died in 2008, was the most brilliant trumpeter of a generation of musicians who stood with one foot in hard bop and the other in fusion music. He played as inspiredly in Max Roach's ensemble as, for example, in Oliver Nelson's big band on *Blues and the Abstract Truth*, as well as on numerous records under his own name that vividly reflect the development of jazz from hard bop through free playing of the sixties to the electric sound of the seventies. Hubbard's trumpet playing resembled that of the early John Coltrane in some ways, with outstanding linear fluidity and a big, velvety, swaggering sound. The melodic self-assuredness of his lines was legendary: he hit the beat squarely in the middle, even when, as is sometimes the case, he relied a little too much on high-note effects. And since the eighties, in wonderful duo recordings with Woody Shaw and in albums with his own groups, Hubbard found a way back to his bop roots.

Woody Shaw (who died in 1989) is the link between Freddie Hubbard and Wynton Marsalis. He went his own way without making compromises, as the most inspired trumpeter of neobop. Shaw produced great work both with Eric Dolphy and in the band that Dexter Gordon headed during his triumphant 1976 comeback. He far outstripped anyone else in successfully integrating the outcome of modal jazz into bop, conclusively making improvisation with pentatonic scales (so beloved of modal players) bop-conscious and bop-accessible. One of his trademarks was a pronounced tendency toward quartal melodies (melodies built using the interval of a fourth). At the start of the eighties, he headed a much-lauded quintet with a front line consisting solely of brass—trumpet and trombone (Steve Turre).

In neobop, therefore, bop and modal jazz flow together with John Coltrane as the absolutely outstanding influence. Jack Walrath, Jimmy Owens, Eddie Henderson, Jon Faddis, Swiss-born Franco Ambrosetti, Lew Soloff, Hannibal Marvin Peterson, Terumasa Hino, and Randy Brecker represent the younger generation of such trumpeters. Over the years a number of them have taken up neobop alongside other styles, developing it further.

Randy Brecker, for example, became known as a fusion stylist (and will later be considered as such), but he also blows an unusually dynamic and vital neobop trumpet. In his powerful way of creating a climax, he transposes elements from jazz-rock to neobop, particularly impressively when playing during the eighties with Brazilian pianist Eliane Elias. Lew Soloff is a phenomenon: an excellent big-band specialist who made a name for himself in both the Thad Jones–Mel Lewis big band and in the orchestra created by Gil Evans, with whom he was closely linked for almost twenty years. He particularly likes the metallic, bronze register of the trumpet, and he is a specialist in making surprising changes of register. Jack Walrath from Montana, who played and served as an arranger in Charles Mingus's last band, blows his neobop trumpet with unexpected stylistic breaks, and often with tongue humorously in cheek.

Tom Harrell, who has worked with Horace Silver and Phil Woods, is the great lyricist of the renaissance of swinging mainstream trumpet. In this area, which often tends toward displays of technical brilliance, he is a master of subtle note placement, with a rare feeling of economy and balance. He never seems to play a superfluous note. Jon Faddis is one of neobop's most reliable lead trumpeters, endowing big bands with unusual brilliance. In addition he's a dazzling Dizzy Gillespie–inspired high-note virtuoso, who found his own style in the eighties.

Hannibal Marvin Peterson, who was first presented by Gil Evans, has mastered the entire range of jazz from Bessie Smith to Coltrane with so much energy and power that in the midseventies *The New York Times* dubbed him the "Muhammed Ali of the trumpet."

But bebop trumpeters of older generations also gained new, unexpected attention in the eighties. Particularly notable here are Red Rodney (who died in 1994) and Ira Sullivan, both of whom have a particularly vital feeling for the music of Charlie Parker. Besides trumpet, Sullivan also plays soprano, alto, and tenor saxophone; Rodney was a veteran of the Charlie Parker quintet and the great big bands of Jimmy Dorsey, Les Brown, and Woody Herman.

The fascination exerted in the eighties by the entire phenomenon of the new bebop, particularly on younger musicians, was clearly seen in the influence of Wynton Marsalis, who arrived on the jazz scene at a time when fusion and jazz-rock dominated the American market, and who became world-famous, and the leading figure of an entire generation of musicians, by playing acoustic straight-ahead jazz. Wynton Marsalis plays jazz in its noblest form, and he does so to perfection. He brings the image of classical music—order, discipline, and an air of luxury and exclusiveness—to his sympathetic jazz playing. Despite the retrospective character of his music, he has contributed a great deal to the development of trumpet playing. Wynton does not simply imitate a particular style—New Orleans Jazz, bebop, hard bop, or Swing—but rather includes in his music everything that these traditional styles mean to him: the way bebop sounds in *his* language, the way Miles Davis's influence is expressed in *his* sensibility, the way Louis Armstrong's classic approach is continued in *his* sound.

In this multistylistic conception, Wynton's approach goes beyond previous postbop approaches. Since the end of the eighties, no musician has done more for straight-ahead jazz than Marsalis. He is a serious technician whose lines and rhythms expand and contract in an original manner; he improvises in a highly compositional, logical fashion, with a slight Miles Davis influence and a certain undeniable New Orleans element in his sound (see also the chapter on "Wynton Marsalis and David Murray").

Wynton Marsalis stands at the head of a line of trumpeters who, coming from New Orleans, revitalized straight-ahead playing in the nineties, thus continuing the influential trumpet tradition of the Crescent City. Other musicians in this lineage include Terence Blanchard, Marlon Jordan, Nicholas Payton, Leroy Jones, and Irvin Mayfield.

When, in 1982, Marsalis left Art Blakey's Jazz Messengers, his place was taken by a nineteen-year-old trumpeter who, like Marsalis, came both from New Orleans and from the New Orleans Center for Creative

Arts (NOCCA): Terence Blanchard. Blanchard's style has a strong relationship to the melodies and rhythms of the Crescent City, with a particular love of Mardi Gras music, but also with a developed consciousness of the African roots of black music. With his very warm, delicate tone, he made original contributions to neo–hard bop in the quintet that he led in the mideighties with alto saxophonist Donald Harrison. Later, he was successful as a composer of film scores for Spike Lee's *Mo' Better Blues* and *Malcolm X*, and in Hollywood. "The trumpet is the mirror of the mind," he says. "It's time for musicians in my generation to throw away the shackles of the past, to investigate other areas."

The trumpet symbolizes power. One of the best demonstrations of this in the tradition-conscious acoustic jazz of the nineties and later is provided by Nicholas Payton. He became known in the bands of Elvin Jones and Clark Terry. Payton phrases with stamina and elastic power, combining a broad sound with a fluid eighth-note legato in the style of Freddie Hubbard. He has added elements of older jazz to postbop styles in a lively manner, for example in 1996, when he worked with the then ninety-one-year-old trumpeter Doc Cheatham (a veteran of the Louis Armstrong school), and on the recording *Gumbo Nouveau*, which brought traditional New Orleans sounds into an exciting post-bop context. Later, he developed an inspired fusion of jazz with hip-hop elements.

Irvin Mayfield is not only an outstanding neo–hard bop player, but has also convincingly brought Wynton Marsalis's legacy into the context of the melodies and rhythms of Afro-Caribbean music, particularly with the band Los Hombres Calientes.

Benefiting from the success of Wynton Marsalis, at the beginning of the nineties the "young lions" movement erupted, bringing jazz a wave of talented young trumpet players. Many of these musicians were not much more than puppets of the recording companies, who were hoping to make a fast buck from the hard-bop vogue, and these players disappeared as quickly as they emerged. In fact, many of the "young lions" trumpeters played better, from the point of view of instrumental technique, than their historical models—but without their authenticity and freshness. "I don't know what they're afraid of," said Lester Bowie. "It seems like they're afraid to live their own lives." One young trumpeter said, "Our generation feels the pressure of all this information." The fact that hundreds of stylists nonetheless emerged who found a personal voice within neo–hard bop was a sign of the diversity and strength of the acoustic jazz scene of the nineties.

What is striking about these trumpeters—to a greater degree than neobop trumpeters—is the eclectic way in which they relate to almost the entire history of tonal jazz trumpet playing, coupled, however, with three dominant influences: a blending of the swinging Miles Davis line with Clifford Brown's springy and warm hard-bop concept and a strong influence from Wynton Marsalis.

The most important players in this area are: Roy Hargrove, Wallace Roney, Ryan Kisor, Alex Sipiagin, Marcus Printup, Ingrid Jensen, Terrell Stafford, Jeremy Pelt, Greg Gisbert, Joe Magnarelli, Eddie Allen, Don Sickler, and David Weiss; in Germany, Till Brönner; in Great Britain, Gerard Presencer and Guy Barker; and in Italy, Flavio Boltro.

Of all the instruments of jazz, the trumpet is perhaps the most stubborn. "It sits there in a case surrounded by luxury, just waiting to mess somebody up when they pick it up," Dizzy Gillespie once said. But when Roy Hargrove plays it, it sounds as though playing the trumpet is the easiest thing in the world.

Hargrove doesn't really fit into the conservative pigeonhole of neo-traditionalism. He became world-famous after being "discovered," at the age of eighteen, by Wynton Marsalis at a workshop at a music school in Dallas, Texas; since then, his development has been constant. He combines, in his own, original manner, the round, warm hard-bop conception of Clifford Brown, with Freddie Hubbard's thrilling linear facility. His mastery in constantly setting himself new rhythmic challenges in playing over changes is unequaled. He has played with D'Angelo and with Erykah Badu, and had great success in 2003 with his band RH Factor—a jazz/neosoul project incorporating influences from hip-hop and drum 'n' bass.

Wallace Roney, from Philadelphia, blows a powerful Miles-inspired trumpet with an unmistakable dark, metallic timbre. In the early nineties, he was so much in demand among neo–hard boppers that he was simultaneously a member of both Art Blakey's and Tony Williams's groups, which demonstrates his range. He handles the conservative wing of classicism with its leaning toward hard bop as adroitly as he does the style's contemporary trend. He is a brilliant changes player, where he loves to create tension by using "out" chords in his lines.

It is striking that so many of the leading musicians of the neoconservative jazz of the nineties were trumpet players: Wynton Marsalis, Roy Hargrove, Nicholas Payton, Terence Blanchard, Wallace Roney. This phenomenon is due to the fact that the trumpet is an instrument that greatly favors conservative approaches to playing. Playing with sound, in the sense of freely improvised music, is more difficult to execute on the trumpet than on, for example, the saxophone.

Canadian Ingrid Jensen, known for her work with the Maria Schneider Orchestra, plays with remarkable grace, power, and sensitivity. Her agile playing links elements of Art Farmer and Woody Shaw. The playing of Jeremy Pelt, known for his work with the Mingus Big Band, tends toward drama and energetic interplay with the drummer.

In Europe as well, there are players who have personally adapted the Marsalis approach. Gerard Presencer provoked something of a scandal when, at the age of twenty, he was named director of the Jazz Department of the Royal Academy of Music in London. The elegance with which he has developed the legacy of Clifford Brown in various stylistic areas—neo–hard bop, jazz meets drum 'n' bass, big bands—is remarkable. Till Brönner improvises with cool elegance and maturity, and a virtuosity that is sometimes somewhat self-satisfied. He honors the great tradition of black jazz trumpet playing—Kenny Dorham, Freddie Hubbard, Clark Terry—by following an arc from hard bop to the soul and hip-hop beats of the nineties, programmed by DJs.

Now, let's move on to free playing; to do so we first have to go back in time. Don Cherry (d. 1995), the ground-breaking free brass player, played a cornetlike "pocket trumpet"—more or less a child's trumpet. When he became known in the late fifties as a member of the Ornette Coleman Quartet, he seemed to most critics merely a good friend of Ornette's who also happened to play the trumpet. However, in the interplay of this group, it became clear that Cherry was pursuing a way of improvising on the trumpet that was fundamentally new in jazz at that time. He became well-known for the sheer spontaneity of his playing, and his very melodic way of inventing lyrical lines that flow freely through time and space without being bound metrically. He later became a "poet of free jazz" of great, intimate, glowing expressiveness, commended even by so strict a critic as Miles Davis. During the midsixties, Cherry moved to Europe (he later returned to the States), where he made notable achievements—in a twofold sense. On the one hand, he created particularly unusual realizations of new large-orchestral jazz that excel over all other attempts in this direction with their melodiousness and charm. On the other hand, he became an exponent of "world jazz"—of the incorporation into jazz of elements of the great exotic musical cultures. Cherry assimilated Balinese, Indian, Tibetan, Arabic, Chinese, and African elements, often not only on his trumpet but also on various flutes and the *douss'n gouni* (a bowed harp from Mali).

The immensity of Cherry's importance is illustrated by the fact that all other free-jazz trumpeters stood in his shadow for years—the early Lester Bowie, Bobby Bradford, Wadada Leo Smith, Bill Dixon, and Butch Morris, among black musicians; Don Ellis and Mike Mantler among white ones; and Toshinori Kondo among the Japanese.

Ellis, who died in 1978 and who became known in the late fifties as a member of George Russell's sextet, scored a sensational success at the 1966 Monterey Festival, where he introduced his new big band. He played a custom-made "quarter-tone trumpet" that allows for the finest tonal nuances (before him, the Czech trumpeter Jaromir Hnilicka had already employed such an instrument, stimulated by the quarter-tone music of Czechoslovakian composer Alois Hába).

When, in 1964, Bill Dixon presented his legendary concert series "October Revolution in Jazz" at New York's Cellar Café, featuring musicians mostly unknown at the time such as Sun Ra, John Tchicai, Roswell

Rudd, Milford Graves, Paul Bley, David Izenzon, and his own sextet, he made a fundamental contribution to the formation of the free-jazz movement. In his trumpet playing, Dixon communicates an emotional investment in every note and phrase that he plays. His flugelhorn playing has an intimate quality, but he is also a master of "cluster" playing on the trumpet, using spitting, growling, whirling short phrases that are compressed to create an impression of several notes at once.

Wadada Leo Smith discovered the magic of silence and space for free jazz, making that the basis for his own notation (deviating from the standardized European system), which he calls "Ankras-mation." Smith's multilayered compositions seeking new sounds have also made an essential contribution to the structuring of free jazz since the seventies.

But in the eighties and nineties as well, there were trumpeters who refined and further developed post–free-jazz, avant-garde playing. Rajesh Mehta, an American trumpeter of Indian descent, combines the microtonal richness of Indian music with the rhythmic spirit of adventure and urge to freedom of the post–free-jazz avant-garde. In addition to a conventional trumpet, he plays an instrument of his own invention, the "hybrid trumpet," in which two trumpets are connected to one another by a complex system of tubes and valves, enabling him to produce an enormous variety of multiphonic sounds.

Like Mehta, Greg Kelley, Rob Mazurek, and Axel Dörner are abstract improvisers who have significantly expanded the boundaries of the trumpet and of music in their playing, which moves between free jazz, hard bop, noise, experimental electronics, and minimalism.

Axel Dörner, who lives in Berlin, says, "The trumpet is a difficult instrument to play. You have to produce the tone yourself using your lips—actually, using your whole body. What produces the tone is the lips, not a reed, as with the woodwinds, or the strings, as with the violin and piano."

Dörner is a master of circular breathing, and in his free improvisations and compositions he has achieved a kind of evolution of sound. Using extended playing techniques, he has greatly expanded the sound possibilities of the trumpet. He produces an enormous range of noises, multiphonics, and pedal tones (very low notes not considered part of the normal range of the trumpet), which he then shapes and develops into controlled structures inspired by Luigi Nono and Bernd Alois Zimmermann. But he is also fluent in "conventional" freely tonal playing, as he has proved in an original tribute to legendary jazz pianist Thelonious Monk, in collaboration with pianist Alexander von Schlippenbach.

The rediscovery of tradition is to be found in all styles of playing, from the new bebop to free trumpeters. Lester Bowie, who emerged from the AACM circle in Chicago, was in some respects the initiator of postmodern trumpet playing. He began as a free-jazz musician of the second generation, bringing to the free-jazz trumpet a sense of drama, structure, and sly humor. Later, he turned to more tonal ways of playing. In his "growl" playing, he was a kind of Cootie Williams of the avant-garde. Bowie's ability to manipulate and modify the sound of the trumpet appeared to be inexhaustible. "He gets certain timbres on trumpet that nobody has got since Miles," says Wynton Marsalis, who in some respects is situated 180 degrees opposite Bowie. Bowie once said, "The history of our music does not just go back to 1890 or to New Orleans. It goes back thousands of years! We try to express this with our music."

From Roots to the Source was thus the name Bowie gave to his early eighties band, forming a bridge between Africa, gospel songs, and contemporary jazz. In the eighties and nineties, his Brass Fantasy (eight brass instruments and a drummer) delighted listeners with adaptations of rhythm 'n' blues hits and pop songs—from Fats Domino to Whitney Houston—a modern extension of the New Orleans brass band tradition full of exuberance, wit, and sardonic joyousness. Bowie died in 1999.

Following Lester Bowie's achievements, the postmodern jazz trumpeters—Olu Dara, Baikida Carroll, Herb Robertson, Rasul Siddik, Stanton Davis, Ron Horton, Roy Campbell, Dave Ballou, and Paul Smoker—developed their own playing. Strikingly many adherents of this performance style—contrasting with modern playing's inclination toward suppleness and clarity—upgraded the earthy, speechlike sounds of archaic jazz, transforming them in contemporary presentations. Olu Dara, who previously played with Henry Threadgill and David Murray, has been particularly and impressively successful there. He blows the most melodic, earthiest cornet in multistylistic jazz. Mississippi and Texas reminiscences flow time and again into his inspired blues-saturated solos. His later move to world music, incorporating Mexican and Afro-Caribbean sounds as documented for example on the recording *In the World—From Natchez to New York*, was thus a natural, organic development.

Closely linked with that return to the trumpet sounds of archaic jazz is an astonishing (and until then scarcely expected) renaissance in playing with mutes. Herb Robertson, who became known during the eighties in groups with alto sax player Tim Berne, is a master of muted playing. Many trumpeters only use a single mute during a solo. Robertson deploys an entire arsenal, brilliantly changing them in the course of his solo. He inspires postmodern jazz with the whole range of jungle and plunger sounds, from Bubber Miley to Rex Stewart.

In contrast, Paul Smoker, Ron Horton, and Dave Ballou play with exceptionally flexible phrasing. They are stylistically nimble, linear-free bop players, distinguished by a joyful approach to improvisation and the ability to "let it go."

After Don Cherry and Olu Dara, the most persuasive trumpeter in world jazz is Jon Hassell, who comes from Memphis and has worked with such minimalist musicians as La Monte Young and Terry Riley. Hassell "dematerializes" the trumpet as no other player does. Not a gram of brass, not a gram of metal vibrates in his playing. Instead there is a stream of floating sounds and whispered notes whose breathy impact is closer to a voice than the blaring sounds of a trumpet. Stimulated by Miles Davis and ethnic music, he studied with Pandit Pran Nath, the Indian singer, transposing this song style onto his electronically distanced trumpet and utilizing the same microtonal, richly ornamented lines. Together with keyboardist Brian Eno he developed a concept of "Fourth World Music," uniting high-tech computerized sounds of the "First World" with the vital magical melodies and rhythms of the "Third World"—particularly impressively in an encounter with the Farafina group of African drummers from Burkina Faso in 1988.

"The trumpet and the drum are relatives," Dizzy Gillespie once said. Because the attack with which the jazz trumpet is usually played has a strong percussive energy, Latin-American and Caribbean stylists have naturally found their way to jazz trumpet playing. The most important and influential player in this regard, Arturo Sandoval, has already been mentioned above. Others include the Brazilian Claudio Roditi, the Argentinian Diego Urcola, the Cuban Jesús Alemañy, the New Yorker (of Puerto Rican descent) Ray Vega, and Americans Brian Lynch and Michael Philip Mossman.

In his lithe improvisations, Claudio Roditi combines the roots of bossa nova music with influences from Freddie Hubbard and Lee Morgan. Diego Urcola has opened hard-bop lines up to Argentinian tango and milonga figures in an especially virtuosic manner. Ray Vega and Jesús Alemañy, in their jazz improvisations, refer to Dizzy Gillespie and Clifford Brown as well as to the proud tradition of the *trompetistas* of *son* and salsa music: from Alfredo "Chocolate" Armenteros via Victor Paz to Roberto Rodriguez and Rene Lopez.

But non-Latino musicians also play over clave and *montuno* rhythms so convincingly that today they are accepted as great improvisers in Latin jazz just as much as in the new hard bop. Brian Lynch, for example, played with Eddie Palmieri and Horace Silver; Michael Philip Mossman played in Ray Baretta's band and was also music director of the Mario Bauzá band.

Let's turn to European trumpeters. Starting off from free jazz, in the sixties they quickly developed a style of their own, often with a striking liking for *melos*, as is indicated by the fact that during the seventies many moved on from free jazz into other directions. The most important among the older generation are Kenny Wheeler and Harry Beckett in England, Enrico Rava and Paolo Fresu in Italy, Tomasz Stanko in Poland, Hans Kennel in Switzerland, Bumi Vian and Thomas Gansch in Austria, Eric Vloeimans in the Netherlands, and, in Germany, Manfred Schoof, Herbert Joos, and Uli Beckerhoff; among the younger generation, the most important are Johannes Faber, Markus Stockhausen, Reiner Winterschladen, Claus Stötter, Thomas Heberer, and Ingolf Burkhardt.

The best-known, covering the widest musical range, is Kenny Wheeler: from free jazz to the aestheticized playing many jazz fans associate with the ECM record label. Of all the trumpeters living in Europe, Wheeler has had the strongest influence on the American jazz scene. He is one of those trumpeters who when soloing always finds a song and a great melody. He has been called the "glass blower of jazz." His solos radiate a refined melancholy whose floating mood emphasizes bitterness rather than sentimentality. Bert Noglik writes, "Kenny Wheeler's charm has to do with this 'in-between'-ness, this movement between a playing that grew out of bebop and a stylistic unboundedness that he found in free-improvisational circles."

With his recordings *Gnu High* (1976) and *Deer Wan* (1978), Wheeler earned a reputation as an incomparable jazz composer. His works open up a beautiful world of modern harmony and floating melancholy. Wheeler's compositional strengths include lush, unconventional melodies, stubborn chords, and unusual forms. "I think I've been doing the same thing ever since I was thirty. I try to find kitschy romantic melodies mixed with a little bit of chaos," he says jokingly.

Following Kenny Wheeler, Dutch trumpeter Eric Vloeimans plays jazz trumpet with chamber-musical brilliance. He is a stylist in twenty-first–century jazz comfortable in many different areas—free, rock, concert music, swinging—and his playing has deep roots in the jazz tradition.

Returning to the first generation of European jazz: almost as versatile as Wheeler is Manfred Schoof, from the traditional big band to the free jazz of the Globe Unity Orchestra, from bebop to a gentle, beautiful aesthetic. Schoof's trademarks are "skidding sounds," as musicologist Ekkehard Jost called his rapid, overlapping streams of sound, flowing together in virtuoso fashion.

Tomasz Stanko was another of the first trumpeters to find a European, jazz language of his own at the end of the sixties. His dramatic playing is full of scratchy, vocal sounds. Slavic *melos* and Coltrane-influenced modal pathos combine in his playing to form a jubilant melancholy. Stanko creates suspended sonic atmospheres in which his aggressive playing darts back and forth like a lightning bolt. At the beginning of the twenty-first century, he and his quartet, featuring Polish musicians two generations younger than him, found international success.

In Germany, in the nineties Thomas Heberer further developed Stanko's sound in his own manner. He is particularly convincing in his tributes to the music of Jelly Roll Morton and Louis Armstrong, moving humorously between the present and the past.

Another pioneer of European jazz is Enrico Rava. He is a master of melisma, in the Italian tradition, and plays in a "singing horn" style that has been part of jazz since its beginnings. Rava is influenced by Miles Davis, but has transposed Miles's sound to a jazz environment inspired by Italian opera, filled with *melos* and internal drama. Nat Hentoff writes that "in his music, nothing sounds prefabricated; everything comes from inside."

Another Italian trumpeter, two generations younger, is Paolo Fresu. He is from Sardinia, but has lived in Paris since 1996, and has become one of the most in-demand trumpeters on the continent. With his sensitive, tender lines, Fresu is a lyrical visionary of European jazz. Beginning from the sounds of the *bandas*, the Italian outdoor wind bands he grew up with, he has transformed the sound of Miles Davis into a Mediterranean jazz poetry sparkling with ideas. On the CD *Sonos e Memoria* (2001), he reworked influences from Sardinian folk music, with its typical sounds of the *launeddas* (multiple-pipe flutes) and the *canto de tenores* (archaic polyphonic Sardinian singing), using plain melodies, and moving between North African and European Mediterranean sounds. He has also used electronics to bring new life to the sound of the trumpet and to make it a continuation of the human voice.

Markus Stockhausen, son of composer Karlheinz Stockhausen, plays intuitive lines full of lucid power and spiritual interiority. His improvisations, incorporating elements of jazz, New Music, and world music, are examples of great composure and meditative concentration.

Some of these musicians also have a strong Miles Davis influence, including Miles's fusion music of the seventies and eighties. This is true for example of Uli Beckerhoff, Reiner Winterschladen, and Ian Carr. Carr has made a name for himself above all with the intelligent, harmonically stimulating music of his group Nucleus. Uli Beckerhoff combines great sensitivity with power, and is as experienced in acoustic playing as in fusion playing; his later music also includes elements of Miles's pop-influenced music of the eighties. Reiner Winterschladen, who became known in the eighties with the trio Blue Box, is a melodist at heart, whose unique sound, charged with energetic pressure and a sense of directedness, is as in demand in big bands as in small groups.

Among the trumpeters who have incorporated rock elements, Randy Brecker, Chuck Mangione, and Danish player Palle Mikkelborg require special mention. In the seventies, Mangione, with his catchy music, was particularly successful on the American college and university circuit. Palle Mikkelborg, who is also active as an arranger, Europeanized the Miles Davis concept in exemplary fashion, lyrically moderating the angry, rebellious fusion Miles and imbuing his music with a Nordic glow without reducing the pressure. Mikkelborg is one of the very few trumpeters after Miles who has found his own style on the wah-wah pedal. His use of other forms of electronic distancing is also particularly sensitive. The regard Mikkelborg enjoys is revealed too by the fact that his idol Miles Davis, who was generally hostile to making guest appearances, was willing to collaborate with Mikkelborg as soloist in one of Mikkelborg's orchestral compositions. The suite *Aura*, dedicated to Miles, was premiered in 1995 in Copenhagen and was later released as a recording. In his autobiography, Miles called it a masterpiece.

Randy Brecker—also an outstanding fluegelhorn player—became known through his work in Art Blakey's Jazz Messengers and in the Horace Silver Quintet. He became famous for his extroverted, staccato funk playing with the Brecker Brothers, a dynamic fusion band that he co-led with his brother Michael in the seventies (and in a re-formed version in the nineties). He probably is the trumpeter best versed in a technically complex kind of electric jazz. He is one of the busiest New York studio musicians, so he really knows about jazz rock: "Playing trumpet is often difficult in rock because you have to compete with all that electricity," he said. "Certain elements of jazz have come to rock, but rock people still can't improvise on the level of a jazz artist. As a jazz musician, you feel like yourself. As a rock musician, you feel like a star."

In the nineties, the jazz-meets-hip-hop movement provided new inspiration for rock-influenced trumpet playing. And here again, it was Miles Davis who, in 1991, provided the decisive impetus in this direction (as he had done twenty years earlier for jazz-rock), with his posthumously released album *Doo Bop*. While the stiff backing beats, added later by an outside producer (Miles died shortly before the CD was finished), make it difficult to discern exactly what Miles intended, *Doo Bop* had the effect of a beacon. Hundreds of trumpeters got the message immediately. Miles Davis's world-weary, sad sound, layered over digital, electronic beats: this combination became an aesthetic standard for jazz trumpeters who sought personal ways to incorporate elements from hip-hop, drum 'n' bass, ambient music, dancefloor, and neosoul into their jazz improvisations.

The most important musicians of this movement are, in America, Russell Gunn, Tim Hagans, Jeff Beal, Graham Haynes, and, in a certain sense, Roy Hargrove, as well as, in Europe, the French trumpeter Erik Truffaz, Norway's Nils Petter Molvaer, and, in Germany, Till Brönner and Joo Krauss.

Tim Hagans, whose phrasing is harmonically very deliberate, has, with Bob Belden and later with the Norwegian Norbotten big band, combined the break beats of drum 'n' bass with the structures of big-band jazz in a particularly effective manner.

Russell Gunn, also a very active neo–hard-bop musician, has created with his band Ethnomusicology a panorama of danceable black rhythms, celebrating funk beats, hip-hop, DJ samples, rhythm 'n' blues, house music, New Orleans swing, and bop rhythms as equally valid parts of black music.

Two Europeans have taken Miles Davis's sound further in a particularly sensitive and subtle manner, working in the area between jazz, drum 'n' bass, and electronica: the Swiss trumpeter Erik Truffaz, who lives in Paris, and the Norwegian Nils Petter Molvaer. In his rock-inspired bands, Truffaz is a master of a spare, atmospheric style—not so much an individual soloist as a group player. Truffaz is a natural trumpeter, even with his occasional use of reverb and echo effects. He and his group convert the inspiration that he gets from machine-generated beats, such as those in drum 'n' bass, trip-hop, and jungle, into a mostly acoustic music.

"What we like about this approach is the flexibility that it allows us to grow as a band. The connection between machines and human beings is definitely one of the twenty-first century's most important challenges," Truffaz says. "When there is a real fusion, then the machine becomes human."

This flowing together of humanity and technology is found in the trumpet playing of Nils Petter Molvaer. He creates a synthesis of acoustic playing and ambient sounds by combining the hard, fractal electrobeats of techno and drum 'n' bass with the floating, spacious approach to improvisation of Scandinavian jazz. Molvaer does for Miles Davis's world-weary sound what saxophonist Jan Garbarek did for John Coltrane's modal sound: he invests it with Nordic longing and mournful nostalgia. His horn sounds not so much like a trumpet as like a continuation of the human singing voice. "I'm excited to use my trumpet like other instruments, to internalize their feeling in such a way that I can carry it over to my trumpet. But these could also be influences from other musical cultures, other tonalities."

In acoustic playing as well, in the nineties approaches to the trumpet developed that are exciting and difficult to categorize. In particular, players from the United States, especially the New York downtown scene, have advanced postmodern trumpet playing by mixing various idioms. The best improvisers of this group include Steven Bernstein, Cuong Vu, Frank London, James Zollar, Taylor Haskins, Denver native Ron Miles, and, above all, Dave Douglas.

With their spontaneous, turbulent lines, Frank London and Paul Brody (who lives in Berlin) have developed contemporary jazz trumpet playing in the context of Radical Jewish Culture—Brody in smaller groups, and London in various bands that combine the grooves of Balkan brass-band playing with electric Miles and modern big-band sounds. London: "I'm not interested in klezmer *per se*, I'm interested in good music."

Ron Miles, who came to prominence in the Bill Frisell band, plays with a delicate sound and a beautiful, old, dark tone. Like Wynton Marsalis, he plays a Monette trumpet, a massive instrument with an integrated mouthpiece. The Monette trumpet is significantly heavier than a normal trumpet, and sounds somewhat different from the conventional instrument. "These trumpets don't sound like normal trumpets," says Steven Bernstein. "It's like the difference between a hollow-body guitar and a solid-body guitar."

Bernstein is the most humorous, crafty player of the postmodern jazz trumpeters, a charismatic bandleader (with the group Sex Mob) and an outstanding plunger player whose willingness to take musical risks has landed him in many pathbreaking musical situations. In the new jazz of his band Diaspora Soul, he has demonstrated that there are remarkable similarities and parallels between Jewish dance music on the one hand and Afro-Cuban music, rhythm 'n' blues, and New Orleans marching band music on the other. He has also made brilliant recordings with saxophonist Sam Rivers. The CD *Diaspora Blues* contains passionate free-jazz interpretations of traditional Jewish prayer songs and synagogue songs. "Jewish cantor singing is soul music. It's full of soul," says Bernstein, who sometimes plays slide trumpet, an instrument that is played using a slide like that of a trombone.

But the most impressive and influential trumpet player of New York's downtown scene is Dave Douglas. He is the true trumpet doyen of multistylistic jazz. In contrast to John Zorn, in whose Masada Quartet he plays, Dave Douglas is a master of the art of elegant melding, and is unequaled in his ability to combine sharply contrasting styles in a consonant manner. He plays with amazing facility and authority, and with a bell-like tone reminiscent of the cornet, often with an ironic vibrato. Douglas makes use of an enormous variety of sounds and registers of the trumpet, and humorously refers to earlier styles while also incorporating new sounds and elements in an unpretentious manner. Douglas has said that his main influences are Igor Stravinsky, John Coltrane, and Stevie Wonder. Although he has a strong background in classic modern jazz, having worked with the hard-bop band of Horace Silver, he constantly interrogates the boundaries of the genre, and with each new project evaluates the music from a different perspective. In addition to his influence as instrumentalist and bandleader, Douglas is also an important jazz composer, whose works play with the line between composition and improvisation in a subtle manner. He always finds an unmistakable group access to his compositions, and is moreover a politically and socially conscious and engaged musician.

Inspired by the worldwide success of Wynton Marsalis, the jazz classicism of the eighties and nineties brought significant advances in trumpet playing. But there was also a real boom in jazz trumpet playing in the colorful multistylism of the downtown scene and on the European scene. Never before in jazz have there been so many players with so many different approaches to the trumpet as there are today. This stands in marked contrast to earlier decades. After the saxophone-centric sounds of modern jazz in the forties and fifties, and the guitar- and keyboard-heavy sounds of the seventies, the trumpet has again become what it was at the beginning of jazz, from New Orleans to Swing: a lead instrument. As Dave Douglas says: "This is a great period for the trumpet."

The Trombone

The trombone began as a rhythm and harmony instrument. In the early jazz bands it was hardly more than a "blown bass." It supplied an additional harmonic background for the melody instruments—trumpet and clarinet—above which they could move, and it stressed the rhythmic accents. In big bands, the trumpets and trombones form the brass section, which stands opposite the reed section, the saxophone group. Both, brass and reeds together, form the horn section, whose counterpart and partner is the rhythm section.

In view of the substitute-bass role the trombone had to play in the marching bands of early New Orleans, it can be said that the style of the first jazz trombonist worth mentioning was already a sign of progress. This style is called "tailgate." The name stems from the fact that the trombonist took up more space than other musicians on the band wagons—the carts on which the bands rode through the streets of New Orleans on festive occasions—and had to sit as far back as possible, on the tailgate. There he had room to work his slide. The tailgate position made possible effective, glissando-like fills placed between the melodic phrases of the other horns. Kid Ory, who died in 1973, was the most important representative of this style.

A trombonist of very personal conception within the New Orleans tradition is Charlie Green. Bessie Smith liked his accompaniments—as in "Empty Bed Blues"—which gives an indication of his style: blues trombone full of extroverted, earthy sounds. He was a kind of Tommy Ladnier of his instrument.

The first jazz musician to play musically conceived, expressive, and melodically rich solos on the trombone was Jimmy Harrison, who died in 1931. Critics have called him the most important trombonist in the realm of the older styles. He was one of the leading soloists in Fletcher Henderson's band. And he was the first to at least come close to, if not yet attain, the biting sound of the trumpet on the trombone.

Miff Mole (d. 1961) is in many respects a white "counterpart" of Jimmy Harrison. Perhaps he lacked the former's mighty inspiration, but he was a flawless technician, and by his playing rather than Harrison's, the white musicians of the day were made aware of the fact that the trombone was about to achieve "equal rights." Miff's trombone was an important voice in the Original Memphis Five led by Phil Napoleon, and along with the latter and Red Nichols, he made up the "triumvirate" of memorable "New York–style" brass musicians.

The Chicago-style trombonists were also influenced by Mole—for instance, Tommy Dorsey and Jack Teagarden. Dorsey evolved in the thirties into the "Sentimental Gentleman," leader of a successful big band and eventually hardly a jazz musician anymore. Yet he always remained a player of great technical ability and soulful feeling. Teagarden was one of the few traditional jazz players who were especially respected by the cool jazz musicians of the fifties for his controlled, expressive sound and his supple lines. Bill Russo—a former Stan Kenton arranger and an excellent trombonist himself—praised him as "a jazzman with the facility, range and flexibility of any trombonist of any idiom or any time; his influence was essentially responsible for a mature approach to trombone jazz." Teagarden—or Big T, as he was called—was Louis Armstrong's favorite trombonist. Together, they played and sang on some of the most spirited and enjoyable duo recordings in jazz. Both as singer and instrumentalist, Teagarden was a blues man with a very modern, reflective attitude toward the blues.

There is a Duke Ellington group among the trombones as well, although they are not as closely related, stylistically, as the Ellington trumpets. These are Joseph "Tricky Sam" Nanton, Juan Tizol (from Puerto Rico), and Lawrence Brown. Tricky Sam was *the* great man of growl trombone. Even today, experts puzzle over exactly how he produced his earthy, dramatic tonal effects. His way of using a plunger mute in combination with a trumpet straight mute (a conical mute inserted into the bell) was uniquely his. Juan Tizol (coauthor with Ellington of the famous "Caravan," considered to be the most important early Latin jazz tune, though there were already Latin elements in Jelly Roll Morton's "New Orleans Blues" and in W. C. Handy's "St. Louis Blues" around the time of World War I) did not play the slide trombone, as do most jazz trombonists, but the valve trombone. He played it softly and sweetly, and occasionally became a trifle saccharine. His sound has been compared to that of a cello. Lawrence Brown, a cultivated melodist with a somewhat nasal, "leathery" sound and a spare vibrato, was a musician of strong personal warmth with a preference for tuneful (sometimes almost sentimental) melodies.

Benny Morton, J. C. Higginbotham, Vic Dickenson, Dickie Wells, and Trummy Young are the great trombonists of Swing style. Their playing shares a vibrant vehemence. Morton, Wells, and Dickenson were all heard with Count Basie's band. Morton had previously worked with Fletcher Henderson. His playing had an intense, blueslike quality—something on the order of a Swing fusion of Jimmy Harrison and Charlie Green. Dickie Wells has been described as a musician of "romantic imagination" by André Hodeir. He was a romanticist not in the sense of overblown pathos but in terms of a forceful, imaginative sensitivity. Much of this romanticism is contained in the incomparable vibrato of his trombone sound.

J. C. Higginbotham was the most vehement, powerful trombone of the Swing period—his tone sometimes reminiscent of the earthy, tight sound known in the twenties as "gutbucket" trombone. Sometimes he played with an abrupt explosiveness, as if the trombone had been struck rather than blown. Vic Dickenson had a lusty, pleasing sense of humor that sometimes seeped into even his slow solos. Dan Morgenstern once wrote about Dickenson, "When he picks up his trombone, he tells you a story that's personal through and through. His horn seems to be an extension of his body. The complete ease with which he masters it makes the instrument, which actually is a bit cumbersome, appear like the embodiment of elegance."

Trummy Young is to the trombone what Roy Eldridge is to the trumpet—a fulcrum linking Swing and bop ways of playing. From 1937 to 1943 he was one of the principal soloists in the Jimmie Lunceford band. His "Margie" was a particular success from that period. Louis Armstrong brought Trummy Young into his All Stars in 1952 as the replacement for Jack Teagarden. With this group Trummy popularized—and sometimes banalized—his style.

Directly linked to Trummy Young, in terms of tone related to the vehement verve of Swing trombonists like Benny Morton or J. C. Higginbotham, is the trombonist who created modern trombone style and remains its personification: J. J. Johnson. Before discussing him, we must mention a white trombonist, Bill Harris, master of a brilliant virtuoso technique. Harris was a member of Woody Herman's band from 1944 to 1946, again from 1948 to 1950, and later played with Herman again from time to time. His solo on "Bijou," recorded with Herman in the midforties, was the most admired trombone solo of the time. His personality was marked by the contrast between the piercing, springy style of his fast work and the polished, studied vibrato of his slow solos. The contrast is so pronounced one might think two musicians were involved, if one did not know that Harris, with his slightly professorial looks, was responsible for both. Next to J. J. Johnson, Harris, who died in 1973, was for years the strongest influence on trombonists.

J. J. Johnson became to trombonists what Dizzy Gillespie is to trumpet players; what he played was not just bop trombone but also "trumpet-trombone." He played his instrument with that brilliant glow long associated with the trumpet; no other trombone player before him accomplished this feat. But he also played muted: earthy, tight, reminiscent of Charlie Green's blues trombone but with all the mobility of modern jazz. Johnson went through the same development as Gillespie: from the nervousness of bop to great sobriety and quiet sovereignty. J. J., also an outstanding arranger, went to Hollywood in the late sixties to start a new career as film and television composer and arranger. When bebop returned in the eighties, he started again to play solo trombone—even *more* mature and mellow than during the period of his great success. This maturity shows in his statements, too: "A change in art shouldn't take place for novelty's sake, as in fashion. New styles in music or painting or poetry should result from a new style of thinking in the world. The next style in music will come from the heads and hearts of real artists and not from opportunists."

J. J. Johnson is the father of modern jazz trombone. He has the same significance for the instrument as Charlie Parker for the saxophone, and his influence on all the trombonists who followed him cannot be overstated. With his powerful sound and the great clarity and consistency of his ideas, J. J. was also a touchstone for the bop-inspired jazz of the nineties. "J. J. set a standard that remains unequaled today," says Steve Turre. He died in 2001.

Kai Winding (d. 1983) was the white counterpart of J. J. Johnson. Independent of J. J., he found a style often so reminiscent of J. J. that time and again they were mistaken for each other. It must be counted among the marvels of jazz that two musicians as different as Winding and Johnson should have arrived at similar styles. Kai, born in Denmark, was a member of Benny Goodman's band and later came to the fore through his playing with Stan Kenton; thus he was first and foremost a big-band musician. J. J. Johnson, from Indiana, black, combo-man of the bebop groups, came to the fore through his playing on Fifty-Second Street.

Ten years later, among the musicians of hard bop, Curtis Fuller, Jimmy Knepper, Julian Priester, Garnett Brown, and Slide Hampton (also notable as an arranger) are especially worthy of mention. Fuller is particularly typical of the Detroit generation of hard bop, and he is also a specialist in rapid, warm lines, notable for their full-toned fluidity and lightness. Fuller "saxophonized" the bop trombone approach of J. J. Johnson by incorporating elements of John Coltrane's early playing. In the seventies, he was one of the first to experiment with electric amplification of the trombone, with mixed results. Jimmy Knepper, associated for many years with Charles Mingus, blew a "piercing," vital trombone style in which Swing and bop elements are equally alive. Knepper and Garnett Brown were all-round trombonists who mastered everything from conventional big-band work to avant-garde experimentation. Julian Priester became known primarily through his subtle, intelligent work with the pianoless Max Roach Quintet of the sixties. He blew a tasteful jazz-rock trombone—from 1970 to 1973 in the Herbie Hancock Sextet, later in his own groups—and then returned in the eighties to acoustic music making, particularly impressively in sophisticated yet raw recordings with bassist Dave Holland. Slide Hampton, with his octet of 1959, "modernized" the classic Miles Davis Capitol Band of 1949, giving it a touch of soul. For years Slide lived in Europe, playing in the most diverse groups, from quartet to big band. He was connected with the great tenorman, Dexter Gordon (who died in 1990), in a very fruitful cooperation that initially took place in Europe in the sixties. Ten years later, in the United States, Slide Hampton was also the man behind the most impressive mass trombone effort in jazz so far: his *World of Trombones*, recorded in 1979, at first employed no fewer than nine excellent trombonists, among them

Janice Robinson and Curtis Fuller. In 2002, for the CD *Spirit of the Horn*, he expanded the World of Trombones to include twelve trombonists, including top-shelf soloists like Benny Powell and Steve Davis.

Among other post-Johnson trombonists, Frank Rosolino's typically Italian feeling for effects, his temperament, and his sense of humor often stood out in Stan Kenton's 1953–54 band. In his countless appearances and recordings, he remained a bebop man until his tragic death in 1978. Carl Fontana played without Frank's striving for effects, but with great flexibility and feeling for harmonic subtleties. He, too, was a big-band musician and emerged from the bands of Kenton and Woody Herman. Further trombonists of this line are Frank Rehak and Eddie Bert—the latter a particularly temperamental improviser, also influenced by Bill Harris.

Rehak, Bert, Al Grey, Bill Watrous, and, most of all, Urbie Green are flexible trombonists, able to cope with any style or demand. Green, who became known through his work in the Benny Goodman band of the fifties (during which stint he often stood in for Benny) has said, "My playing has been compared to almost every trombonist who ever lived. The reason probably is that I had to play in so many different styles— Dixieland, lead à la Tommy Dorsey, and later, modern jazz." To this flexibility, Al Grey added the aspect of humor, which has always had an especially live tradition among the trombonists—from tailgate style through Vic Dickenson and Trummy Young up to Albert Mangelsdorff and Ray Anderson, whom we will discuss later. Grey was a big-band veteran: from Benny Carter and Jimmie Lunceford to Lionel Hampton and Dizzy Gillespie up to Count Basie.

Among the most significant trombonists of the sixties are Jimmy Cleveland, the previously mentioned Curtis Fuller, and Bob Brookmeyer. Cleveland was a "super J. J.," whose brilliant tromboning often seemed almost explosive, especially since this explosiveness was combined with the fluency of a saxophone in the most natural way.

Valve trombonist Bob Brookmeyer, on the other hand, is a musician of modern Lester Young classicism, who "cooled off" the tradition of his hometown, Kansas City, in quite a remarkable way. With Jimmy Giuffre, he recorded an album entitled *Traditionalism Revisited* that demonstrates the classicist position: the jazz tradition viewed from the standpoint of modern jazz long before that became fashionable in postmodern jazz. Here, famous old jazz themes—such as Louis Armstrong's "Santa Claus Blues" and "Some Sweet Day," King Oliver's "Sweet Like This," Tommy Ladnier's "Ja-Da," and Bix Beiderbecke's "Louisiana"—are transported into the world of modern jazz. Since the seventies Brookmeyer has made a name for himself as an excellent arranger: first in the Thad Jones–Mel Lewis orchestra, and in the nineties with European groups like the WDR Big Band or the New Art Orchestra.

Mike Fahn, an alumnus of the Maynard Ferguson band, is a technically skillful postbop soloist with a bronzed, fiery sound, and is continuing Brookmeyer's valve trombone lines into the twenty-first century.

Among the trombonists who carried on, refined, and played the J. J. Johnson tradition in a contemporary way in the seventies are Janice Robinson, Bruce Fowler, Tom Malone (who plays thirteen instruments besides the trombone), and Jiggs Whigham, who formerly headed the Jazz Department of the Cologne Music Academy. Wayne Henderson, Glenn Ferris, Fred Wesley, and Brazilian Raul de Souza took this playing style into jazz-rock, funk, and fusion, in many records that are highly electronicized. With his disco-oriented music, de Souza achieved a success comparable, among trombonists, to Tommy Dorsey's in the thirties.

In the eighties and nineties, Glenn Ferris made a particularly successful return to acoustic playing. His phrasing has an almost cellolike mobility, and this fluidity has led to his being called the "Stan Getz of the trombone." "He sings more than blows," says one critic. "The trombone is a difficult instrument," says Ferris. "In order to play fast lines, you have to make acrobatically fast movements with the slide. Nobody wants to watch you fighting the slide."

Fred Wesley plays the most humorous, muscular funk trombone imaginable. With the JB Horns in James Brown's band, with Maceo Parker, and with his own group, he has proved that you can swing convincingly even in rock and soul contexts.

The jazz classicism of the eighties and nineties did not bring much in the way of new stylistic discoveries on the trombone, but the refinement of J. J. Johnson's legacy was expanded and deepened. The best players in this direction include, in the United States, Steve Davis, John Fedchock, Delfeayo Marsalis, and Andre Hayward, and in Germany, Henning Berg and Ludwig Nuss. These are all individual players with a highly rhythmic command of the instrument and a well-thought-out directedness in their bop-influenced improvising. "That's one thing that bebop did," says Slide Hampton. "It gave you the experience you need to improvise in an organized way."

The more clear and "beautiful" one's tone on the trombone is, the more precise and dynamically propulsive the rhythms can be. Steve Davis has brought this maxim of bop playing into the twenty-first century in a particularly impressive manner. He has played with Chick Corea and with Jackie McLean, and his resilient legato improvisations show a love of vital interaction with drummers and pianists. Above all, though, Davis is a master of playing over chord progressions, or changes. Both in his masterful interpretations of standards and in his effortless, focused playing over the complex changes of his own compositions, he achieves his stated goal: "I really want to sing a song in my solo." Davis, and many of the trombonists named above, although they play with great virtuosity in small groups, have a notably strong connection to the world of the big bands. The powerful, earthy sound of the trombone has a natural tendency toward the orchestral. This is particularly true of the bass trombone, whose technical possibilities have been developed by jazz players far beyond its original function as a "substitute bass," while also retaining its supporting, anchoring role. Two of the best bass trombonists in contemporary jazz are Dave Bargeron and Douglas Purviance. Bargeron, who also plays tuba, is one of the most sought-after New York studio musicians, and set new standards in jazz-rock with his solos in the band Blood, Sweat & Tears. Douglas Purviance is also an in-demand, highly versatile musician in New York's mainstream big-band scene, such as the Vanguard Jazz Orchestra.

In free jazz, Grachan Moncur III, Roswell Rudd, Garnett Brown, and the early Joseph Bowie, among others, gained prominence—all musicians who widen and inflect the sound spectrum of their instrument, including noise elements in their music. Roswell Rudd deserves special attention in this field as he has a certain Dixieland and blues approach to his tonally free excursions. His "smears"—the deliberate, raucous bending of the trombone tone—are legendary. His playing is very extroverted, and shows an influence from the angular lines of pianist Thelonious Monk. Through the vocal qualities Rudd incorporates in his playing, he discovered the great musical cultures of the world: "Suffice it to say that vocal techniques I had associated at one time only with the jazz singers of my own country were revealed to be common to the oldest known musical traditions the world over. What I had always considered the epitome of musical expression in America, the blues, could be felt everywhere in the so-called folk world."

Rudd was connected with soprano saxophonist Steve Lacy (who died in 2004) in a particularly fruitful partnership. Characteristically, both got into free playing directly from Dixieland, skipping the stages in between.

Joseph Bowie incorporated the free-jazz trombone in the realm of free funk, particularly vitally in the eighties and nineties with his band Defunkt.

Actually, the trombone scene—more so than any other instrument, with the exception of the clarinet—atrophied during the sixties. Some of jazz's best trombone players, among them J. J. Johnson, Kai Winding, and Bill Harris, were practically absent from the scene. In the jazz polls, no instrument had fewer entries than the trombone. In this situation, European trombone players, somehow, took over: Paul Rutherford in Great Britain, Eje Thelin in Sweden, and, most important, Albert Mangelsdorff in West Germany. They developed new styles of playing, creating a lively, flourishing trombone scene again.

Mangelsdorff (d. 2005) emancipated the long lines of alto player Lee Konitz—under whose influence he began in the fifties—in a gradual and seemingly necessary process, becoming ever freer harmonically, until they were "freed"—in the exact sense of the word. Mangelsdorff's constant seeking and finding expanded the limits of what was possible in modern jazz trombone playing. In his pioneering exploration of multiphonics, and his famous tremolo, he played intervals, sounds, and harmonies that were long considered impossible on the instrument. From the beginning of the seventies, Mangelsdorff developed a technique that permitted him—as the first trombonist in jazz—to play "chords" on his instrument. By blowing one tone and simultaneously singing another, usually higher, tone, Mangelsdorff gave the vocal tone the sound quality of the trombone. Taking these two tones as his starting point, Mangelsdorff created—simultaneously!—three- and four-note chords by playing with the combination tones generated through the friction between the blown and sung tones. This deliberate use of "multiphonics"—multivoiced sounds on an instrument that usually only produces single notes—wasn't specifically discovered by free-jazz players in the sixties. Performers of traditional jazz, such as tenor saxophonist Illinois Jacquet in the forties, knew about them. But nowhere has the art of multiphonic playing been so cultivated and advanced as in free jazz. More among saxophonists than trombonists, multiphonics, with such tenor players as Dewey Redman, Evan Parker, or Archie Shepp, often became more important than the de facto blown notes.

Mangelsdorff made many of his best records with important American drummers like Elvin Jones, Alphonse Mouzon, and Ronald Shannon Jackson. In his long solo appearances—without rhythm section—he managed to keep audiences attentive to his music through the wealth of his ideas and sounds. Without recourse to folklore or to elements from classical or new music, his playing, solely through its swinging energy and rhythmic emotionality, played an important part in awakening a specifically European jazz consciousness. From the sixties, his name constantly appeared in the leading spots of the American jazz polls, even though he did not live in the United States. (Generally, Europeans achieve this kind of recognition in America only if they decide to live there.) Even if Mangelsdorff is left out of account, the European trombone scene—with its striking love for experimenting with multiphonics—is richer than the American. Eje Thelin from Sweden and Conrad Bauer from [East] Germany have developed, independently of Mangelsdorff, a similarly sovereign soloistic and chord-based approach to the trombone.

Worthy of mention among the second generation of European free-jazz trombonists are Günter Christmann from [West] Germany, Willem von Manen from the Netherlands, the Italian Giancarlo Schiaffini, Johannes Bauer from [the former East] Germany, and, above all, Johannes's previously mentioned brother Conrad. Conrad Bauer probably plays the most flowing free-jazz trombone. At the beginning of the seventies, with the quartet Synopsis, he was an important voice in the jazz of what was then East Germany. Going against all the conservatory rules, he has developed a new way of playing that is smooth without being cold, and operates, through circular breathing, with long-held, unbroken sounds that are inwardly varied and developed. Like Mangelsdorff he is a master of polyphonic playing; but whereas Mangelsdorff fosters and refines the tonal aspect of multiphonics, Bauer uses them as "free" tone colors, which can exert an almost noiselike impact. Conrad Bauer plays a tenor trombone with an additional valve section such as that found on bass trombones, allowing him to produce unusually overtone-rich, low sounds, as well as trills. In the search for new sounds, in the nineties he also played with samplers and with a MIDI (Musical Instrument Digital Interface) pedal, enabling him to carry on a creative "dialogue" with himself by recording and playing back passages and then playing along with them.

The younger European trombonists include Dutch Wolter Wierbos, English Annie Whitehead, French Yves Robert and Denis Leloup, Austrian Christian Radovan, who made his name with the Vienna Art Orchestra, Italian Gianluca Petrella, Swede Nils Landgren, and Germans Jörg Huke and Nils Wogram. Wierbos's playing is particularly striking. He energetically and grippingly opens up the tradition of free-trombone playing to the stylistic amalgams of contemporary jazz, effectively incorporating rock and bebop sounds as well as the growl techniques of swing trombonists. Annie Whitehead, who has played with Chris McGregor's Brotherhood of Breath, is a gripping soloist with a gift for the art of simple, unpretentious lines. Nils Landgren, "the man with the red trombone," is a highly energetic player. In his Funk Unit, he plays irrepressible, driving melodies and rhythms. As a sign of his stylistic breadth, he has also played modern jazz versions of Swedish folk songs in duo with pianist Esbjörn Svensson, and with trumpeter Tomasz Stanko he has created new treatments of Scandinavian church chorales as once sung by his forebears—pastors who lived on the island of Gotland.

Over the last two decades, Yves Robert has been one of the most important figures in new French jazz. With Louis Sclavis, whose band he played in, Robert crosses stylistic boundaries with ease. He combines a childlike sense of play with a strong sense of musical logic and adventure on his instrument. He uses extended playing techniques, including unusually high notes, multiphonics, and circular breathing, to create a warm, lyrical music that foregrounds the sensuous character of the sound. This preference of his may also account for the fact that Robert, who adapts his way of making music to each new project, tends to favor chamber-musical instrumentation in his highly dialogic way of playing.

Nils Wogram has an inexhaustible supply of ideas, and the nuances of his sound run from butter-softness to vocal growling. His stylistic flexibility is so great as to liberate the trombone from traditional expectations of its role. In his explosive solos, he incorporates influences of Gyorgy Ligeti, Ornette Coleman, drum 'n' bass, freebop, new music, world music, and minimalism as equally valuable elements. He is a master of swinging improvising over striking rhythmic changes and odd meters, convincingly combining abstraction and romanticism. His compositions are also remarkable, enabling him to "travel improvisational paths" in a music that seems to have no stylistic limits.

Since the seventies, the trombone scene has been revitalized in America in the realm of contemporary mainstream (mainly through Bill Watrous) and in free jazz, especially through George Lewis, who was first introduced by Anthony Braxton. Bill Watrous has a gymnastic virtuosity on the trombone, combining flexibility with an enormous range in his lively straight-ahead playing. He blows with a light attack and with brilliant technical mastery. But his playing also illustrates the limits of virtuosity. One of his colleagues says:

> There is a way of playing slide trombone . . . so that the trombone almost begins to play you. The instrument dictates to you what you will say. There are certain vanilla fudge areas in every instrument that make it so much fun to do certain things so well that you can't stop yourself from doing them. Therefore, instead of making a line, improvising truly, you become a purveyor of instrumental excellence, and that's a far cry from improvising.

Lewis, who belongs to the AACM, has studied philosophy, especially the German philosophers Heidegger and Husserl. The level of abstract thinking required for that can also be felt in his music. Lewis is also interested in computer music and other electronic sounds: "With the synthesizer, you have a whole new source of available sounds, rhythms, timbres, and colors. It's just a matter of organizing them rhythmically. I want to be able to do everything with it on the same level as on my trombone."

Another American trombonist who has taken free trombone playing into the nineties is Jeb Bishop. Then there's Nicholas Collins, who is not really a trombonist at all. After completing composition studies with Alvin Curran, Collins became a part of the New York noise music scene. He constructs his solos from contradictory stylistic snippets and found sounds. At one point, he used a trombone to control a sampler in such a way that the digital sound storage device was controlled by the slide of the trombone. In live concerts, Collins has also made some use of computers. His remarks about his digital "trombone playing" could also hold for any electronic musical instrument: "Computers, circuits, and processors are all just skeleton keys to get us into rooms that the landlord hasn't given us the right key for yet—the thief who makes too much noise rattling around will quickly be arrested."

Of all the brass instruments, the trombone is probably the least easily domesticated. Wildness and unpredictability have been part of its character since the beginning of jazz. It has an immediate, soulful quality that hits the listener in the gut. As Roswell Rudd put it: "You blow in this one end—and a sound comes out the other end that disrupts the universe." Modern approaches to jazz trombone playing coming from J. J. Johnson, with their cultivated bop rhythmic sense, are at bottom a valiant attempt to control this unpredictability. But in the nineties, trombonists increasingly found their way back to the older sounds of the jazz tradition, finding new colors by consciously using the "crazy" elements of their instrument, placing them alongside the achievements of modern jazz. Josh Roseman: "The stereotypical role of the trombone is just so radically in need of updating. . . . The instrument needed a PR face-lift."

The brass renaissance of the eighties and nineties included a striking number of trombonists who achieved further developments in jazz trombone playing, including Ray Anderson, Frank Lacy, Gary Valente, Steve Turre, Curtis Fowlkes, Art Baron, Dan Barrett, Avi Lebovich, Craig Harris, Wycliffe Gordon, Robin Eubanks, and Josh Roseman. The most vital of these players is Ray Anderson, who was also first presented by Anthony Braxton but lacks his abstractness. Anderson is a stylist full of drama and wild passion, who transposes the gruff, emotionally loaded sounds of the tailgate and gut-bucket trombone into the language of contemporary jazz. His style is one of rolling, swaying sounds and lines, an enormous range, and great stylistic flexibility. He's a strong player of gripping melodic lines and reminds us that one element has been more important in the history of the jazz trombone than in that of any other instrument (and it has certainly been part of the nature of the trombone from the start): humor. Frank Lacy, also a singer, became known for his work in the Mingus Big Band. His solos, full of character and intelligence, exploit the instrument's inherent unwieldiness in a distinctive way, also emphasizing its vocal nature. "For me, I think the trombone is the closest instrument to the human voice."

Gary Valente plays the most muscular, loudest trombone in postmodern jazz. His colossal sound recalls the renegade sounds of the prebop trombonists. His delightfully unruly lines have a razor-sharp intensity, full of gravity and power, and are heard to best advantage in the groups and big bands of Carla Bley.

If anyone has ever demonstrated the rewards to be gained from playing a trombone as if it were a percussive instrument, then that's Steve Turre from Omaha, Nebraska. His brilliantly articulated rhythmic lines carry on from where J. J. Johnson stopped, but his playing also reveals the influence of saxophonists and trumpeters: Charlie Parker, John Coltrane, Miles Davis, and Woody Shaw (in whose quintet Turre played until 1985). Turre, also an arranger, is one of the few trombonists to have completely mastered pentatonic playing, which is very difficult in terms of slide technique. He brought Afro-Cuban and Brazilian elements into postbop trombone in an especially convincing manner. Turre says, "Whatever's in you, it's going to come out of the horn—you can't fool it."

Turre has often played in Afro-Cuban and Puerto Rican salsa bands. Latin music has a strong brass orientation. Many jazz trombonists besides Turre, including Steve Davis and Nils Wogram, have played in Latin bands in addition to their jazz groups. Conversely, in the world jazz of the eighties and nineties, more and more trombonists found their way from Latin music to contemporary jazz playing. Besides Turre, the best Latin jazz trombonists are Barry Rogers, Juan Pablo Torres, William Cepeda, Joe Gallardo, Luis Bonilla, and Conrad Herwig.

Barry Rogers, who died in 1991, was justifiably considered the founder of solo trombone in Latin jazz, due to his powerful, heartrending solos over clave rhythms, for example in Eddie Palmieri's "La Perfecta" band. He took Afro-Cuban-inspired jazz trombone playing to a new level, with a colossal sound and explosive improvisations. In the seventies, he was also an in-demand studio musician in New York, for example with the Brecker Brothers and George Benson.

William Cepeda, son of the famous Cepeda family that has done so much for the tradition of Puerto Rican folk music, played in Dizzy Gillespie's United Nations Orchestra and with Lester Bowie. He calls his music "Afro-Rican Jazz," celebrating the heritage of Puerto Rican music and its African roots from a contemporary jazz perspective. "For years, there has been a fusion of Cuban rhythms with jazz. I love that music, but I wanted to create something that goes all the way back to my roots."

However, the most fluent Latin jazz trombonist is Conrad Herwig, also well-known as a neobop player. "I've always felt as a trombonist that I was a frustrated saxophone player," he says, which prevented neither Eddie Palmieri nor Dizzy Gillespie from employing him as a featured soloist in their various Latin-jazz projects. His solos are influenced by John Coltrane, Wayne Shorter, and Joe Henderson as much as by J. J. Johnson, Slide Hampton, and Frank Rosolino. For his CD *The Latin Side of John Coltrane*, a recording that makes a direct connection between the spirituality of Coltrane's music and the spirituality of Afro-Caribbean music, he received a Grammy award in 1998 for Best Latin Performance.

Craig Harris, who came out of the bands of Sun Ra and David Murray, plays strong, full trombone in the context of world jazz, for example with musicians from Turkish gypsy music. Together with Ray Anderson, Gary Valente, and tuba player Bob Stewart, in the early 2000s he founded a "Heavy Metal Quartet"—a massive collection of brass sound.

Wycliffe Gordon, a native of Georgia who came up through the bands of Wynton Marsalis, leans more toward traditional playing. Critic Dan Morgenstern has called him a "modern Tricky Sam Nanton." Gordon, who also plays trumpet, tuba, piano, bass, drums, and clarinet, plays a heavy trombone with a rare intuitive naturalness and courage. His playing is a development in the tradition of the "talking trombone," with all its growls and speechlike sounds, full of humor and soul. His solos have a direct connection to the sounds of the black Baptist churches of the South.

Robin Eubanks, from Philadelphia, has found a completely individual improvisational language in a realm between bop trombone and free trombone playing. His phrasing, inspired by saxophonist Wayne Shorter, is characterized by great control and harmonic abstraction. Of all the trombonists in contemporary jazz, he perhaps possesses the widest stylistic spectrum. His dark, powerful sound has exerted formative influence in a variety of directions: in alto saxophonist Steve Coleman's M-Base music, in the hard bop of Art Blakey's Jazz Messengers, in the ambitious new jazz of the Dave Holland Quintet, and in McCoy Tyner's modality. Eubanks said, "If you look at very different kinds of music from varying viewpoints, you discover what they have in common, which you would otherwise miss from a *single* viewpoint."

Another multistylist on the trombone is the musician whose name most often comes up today in discussions of advanced jazz trombone playing: Josh Roseman. Like Roswell Rudd, Frank Lacy, and Gary Valente, he's part of the tradition of "raw sound" playing on the trombone, with a rich, clattering tone, wild, potent lines, and his legendary "dog notes." He has an insatiable appetite for absorbing a wide variety of different styles. His band, the Josh Roseman Unit, kaleidoscopically combines an enormous range of influences: dreamlike jazzscapes, Jamaican ska grooves, Hermeto Pascual, Björk, M-Base, AACM. In his sounds and his phrasing, he has found his own solutions by combining opposites in his playing: vital grooves and powerful dynamism on the one hand, a sense of lightness and an "outside space" feeling on the other. "My favorite musicians have always made music that creates an inner connection to the laws of nature," he says. "It is an amoral instrument, potent and insoluble—and it has taken me on a wild ride. Extreme things happen when you unleash that kind of vibration. In the hands of a master it can cause people to question their place in nature."

The Clarinet

In all stages of jazz development, the clarinet has been a symbol of interrelation. The function of the clarinet in the old New Orleans counterpoint, filling in the space between the contrasting trumpet and trombone and entwining them like ivy, is characteristic. Not coincidentally did the clarinet have its greatest period during the Swing era, when jazz and popular music were largely identical.

Alphonse Picou (1878–1961) was the first clarinetist from New Orleans whose style became known. His famous chorus on "High

Society" is one of the most copied solos in jazz history. Down to this day, almost every clarinetist who plays "High Society" is quoting Picou—just as every trombonist who plays "Tin Roof Blues" is quoting from George Brunis's solo with the New Orleans Rhythm Kings, or playing it entire.

The second important clarinetist from old New Orleans is George Lewis—though his influence was felt much later, in the New Orleans revival of the forties and fifties. Lewis (1900–68) participated in New Orleans jazz life from the time he was sixteen. In the thirties, he worked on the docks until the New Orleans revival movement in the forties carried him to worldwide fame. In the music recorded by George Lewis then and in the fifties (initially with trumpeter Bunk Johnson, later with his own bands staffed with the best New Orleans–style musicians) the listening public, which was inundated with amateurish or commercialized New Orleans and Dixieland records, was reminded of the really authentic New Orleans jazz. Lewis's tenderly fragile clarinet playing, as in his classic "Burgundy Street Blues," on his many long, worldwide concert tours found admirers in many countries, including Japan.

It highlights the multiple layers of jazz development that the great triumvirate of the jazz clarinet—Johnny Dodds, Jimmie Noone, and Sidney Bechet—preceded Picou and Lewis in recording, while in a certain sense building musically and stylistically on their way of playing. Picou, Lewis, and, of course, Bechet, actually were merely the final representatives of a style cultivated in old New Orleans by many other Creole clarinetists. As late as 1964, on the island of Martinique, Joachim Berendt heard an eighty-year-old man play at a fair who sounded virtually like Sidney Bechet, and yet he had never heard the name of that great clarinetist. On the other hand, Bechet, when he came to Paris and was introduced to music from Martinique, played many pieces of Martiniquan folk music as if they were—as they actually could be—old Creole dances from New Orleans.

But back to the triumvirate: Dodds-Noone-Bechet. Noone is best known for the gentleness and subtlety of his tone. Compared to him, the improvisations of Johnny Dodds seem almost wild and brutal. Dodds, a master of the lower register of his instrument, was Louis Armstrong's preferred clarinetist during the time of the Hot Five and Hot Seven recordings. Bechet, finally, of whom we shall speak again in the soprano section, is the embodiment of the jazz *espressivo*. The fast, expressive vibrato of his clarinet produced a sound recognizable even to the jazz layperson. In France, where Bechet lived during his final years (he died in 1959), he was as popular as any pop star. And even when much in his playing seemed to have become mannered, it was one of the especially moving human experiences in jazz to see this white-haired, dignified man from old New Orleans play amid the young Dixieland existentialists in Saint-Germain-des-Prés.

In Paris, too, Albert Nicholas, the last great New Orleans clarinetist, made his home (he later moved to Switzerland, where he died in 1973), playing in a mild, technically masterful style that in the fifties became somewhat Bechet-like, yet always retained that wealth of ideas and mobility that Bechet often seemed to have lost in the final years of his life. Nicholas, also a Creole, emerged from the orchestras of King Oliver and Luis Russell, while the Bechet of the twenties is primarily represented by records made with the Clarence Williams Blue Five. In the thirties Bechet recorded with his own New Orleans Feetwarmers. Among his most important clarinet recordings are those he made with pianist Art Hodes in the forties.

Nicholas—along with Omer Simeon and Barney Bigard—belongs to what might be called the third generation of the jazz clarinet. Omer Simeon was Jelly Roll Morton's favorite clarinetist, while Barney Bigard became known mainly through the flowing, supple solos he recorded as a member of Duke Ellington's band from 1928 to 1942, and with Louis Armstrong's All Stars from 1946 to 1955, as one of the few jazz musicians who spent considerable time with both of these giants. Bigard (d. 1980) was a sorcerer of melody, with a pronounced "woody" sound and an inventive way of using arpeggios, his celebrated "waterfalls." He played with strong feeling and with a dynamic sense almost equal to that of Benny Goodman.

Bigard, though indebted to the New Orleans tradition, already belonged among the Swing clarinetists in his great period. Before going on to these, we must recapitulate the history of the white jazz clarinet. It begins with Leon Roppolo of the New Orleans Rhythm Kings, that famous white group of the early twenties. Roppolo is one of the Beiderbecke types so frequent in jazz who seem to burn themselves out in their music and their lives. The most important of his successors in the realm of Chicago style are Frank Teschemacher, Jimmy Dorsey, and Pee Wee Russell. All three played with Bix Beiderbecke. Teschemacher, who died in 1932, loved to connect and smear his notes, perhaps subconsciously feeling that this would make him sound more like a black musician. He was a great influence on the young Benny Goodman. Pee Wee Russell preferred the lower registers of the clarinet. He played with a vibrato and way of phrasing that puts him in a similar relationship to Lester Young and Jimmy Giuffre as Bix Beiderbecke seems to be to Chet Baker. His phrasing was unpredictable, sweet, and intelligent. Willis Connover dubbed him the "poet of the clarinet."

Finally, Mezz Mezzrow, a musician who gained renown through his friendship with the French jazz critic Hugues Panassie, must be mentioned among the Chicago clarinetists. From the standpoint of technique, he was mediocre, and as an improviser he often had to limit himself to stringing triads together. Still, he played with a feeling for the blues surprising in a white musician of his generation. "The race," Mezzrow wrote, "made me feel inferior, started me thinking that maybe I wasn't worth beans as a musician or any kind of artist, in spite of all my big ideas." Mezzrow's most important contribution is not so much his clarinet playing as his autobiography *Really the Blues*, in which the flavor of Chicago in the twenties, and even more, of Harlem in the thirties and forties, is so well captured that even Henry Miller expressed his enthusiasm.

It may be part of the instrument's nature that traditional jazz elements stayed alive for clarinetists way into the seventies and eighties, much more so than for most players of other instruments. This is true, for instance, for Bob Wilber, initially inspired by Bechet, and for Kenny Davern. Both combined the warmth of traditional playing with a feeling for looseness and a contemporary kind of elegance. Wilber once said, "I felt then [in the fifties] and even more so now that there's a *oneness* about jazz. Style shouldn't be a barrier between musicians."

But back to the thirties. The clarinetist of whom the layperson thinks first when jazz clarinet is mentioned is Benny Goodman. He, too, stemmed from the circle of Chicago style. He is the "King of Swing," whose scintillating and polished clarinet playing is the reason why the clarinet and the Swing era are largely synonymous. "B. G.," as he is known, was one of the great stylists of jazz, a musician of superlative charm, spirit, and gaiety. His clarinet playing is associated in equal degrees with his big-band recordings and those he made with various small combos: from the Benny Goodman Trio, with Teddy Wilson at the piano and Gene Krupa on drums, through the quartet in which Lionel Hampton first found public recognition, to the Benny Goodman Sextet in which guitarist Charlie Christian helped pave the way for modern jazz. In terms of expression, Goodman accomplished on the clarinet almost everything other instruments could not achieve until the advent of modern jazz. But he did this—and here is the heart of the matter—without the harmonic finesse and rhythmic complexity of modern jazz. This may be one reason for the disadvantageous position occupied by the clarinet in modern jazz. On the other hand, B. G. was a master of subtleties. His dynamics ranged smoothly, like those of no other clarinetist, from softest pianissimo to jubilant fortissimo. Particularly astonishing is the skill with which Goodman managed to play even the softest notes and still, even when playing with a big band, capture the attention of the listeners in the very last row of a large concert hall.

Other well-known clarinetists of the Swing era were Jimmy Dorsey, Artie Shaw (who from a technical point of view was sometimes more advanced than Goodman), and Woody Herman, both of whom had big bands to celebrate their clarinets in Goodmanesque fashion. Jimmy Hamilton, Buster Bailey, and, indirectly, Edmond Hall were also influenced by Goodman, as were all clarinetists who played alongside and after him—except Lester Young and the modern clarinetists who stem from him. Hamilton played solos with Duke Ellington that are softer and more restrained than even Goodman. If the theories of the jazz racists were correct, one would have to conclude—comparing Hamilton and Goodman on purely aural evidence—that the former was white and Goodman black, though the opposite is true. During the fifties, Hamilton, who died in 1994, evolved into an important clarinet voice in modern jazz, and it is regrettable that his name was so rarely mentioned in the same breath with Buddy DeFranco, Tony Scott, and Jimmy Giuffre. In the eighties he played in the Clarinet Summit, that imposing clarinet quartet whose members (apart from himself: Alvin Batiste, John Carter, and David Murray) with ease embraced four generations of clarinet playing—from Swing by way of bebop and free jazz to neoclassicism.

Edmond Hall, who died in 1967, was the most important black Swing clarinetist and, alongside Benny Goodman, the towering Swing stylist on this instrument. He had a sharp, biting tone that often stands in contrast to Goodman's suppleness. During the forties and fifties, Hall played with Eddie Condon's New York Dixieland bunch.

It is indicative of the organic tightness of jazz evolution that the approaches to the playing of different instruments have evolved on a parallel course. Nearly every instrument has its Roy Eldridge or Charlie Parker. The "Eldridge" of the clarinet is Edmond Hall; the "Parker" of this instrument became Buddy DeFranco, the first clarinetist who could outdistance Benny Goodman in terms of technique. He is an improviser of vital force, which led impresario Norman Granz to team him with Lionel Hampton and other great Swing musicians on numerous recordings. The brilliance of his playing is of such clarity it has sometimes been regarded as "cold." It is one of the paradoxes of jazz that the playing of so "hot" and basic an improviser as DeFranco should have impressed so many listeners as cold. It symbolizes the difficult, almost hopeless situation of the clarinet in classic modern jazz that the brilliant DeFranco finally resigned himself to taking over the direction of the Glenn Miller Orchestra "for reasons of economic survival . . . playing tiresome music and adding nothing to his own development," as Leonard Feather put it. In the eighties and nineties he played jazz again with great success—in recordings with pianist Oscar Peterson as well as with vibraphonist Terry Gibbs, with whom he headed a quintet. Here at last he found the artistic challenge his playing demanded.

It does not contradict Buddy DeFranco's position as the "Charlie Parker of the clarinet" to point out that a European musician was the first, strictly speaking, to play bebop on the clarinet. This was the Swede Stan Hasselgard. Benny Goodman made him a member of his sextet in the spring of 1948, the only clarinetist he ever tolerated alongside himself. A few months later, in November of the same year, Hasselgard was fatally injured in an automobile accident. Hasselgard was the second European jazz musician to create a recognizable personal style of his own, admired even by American jazz musicians. The French Sinti guitarist Django Reinhardt, who had a considerable influence on almost all jazz guitarists between the late thirties and the late forties, was the first.

After DeFranco's speed and "coldness," the spareness and "warmth" of Jimmy Giuffre seemed even stronger. His sound was perhaps the most "clarinetish" of all the clarinetists. Initially, Giuffre played almost exclusively in the low register of his instrument—the so-called chalumeau register. He on occasion pointed out that he did this because he was technically unable to do anything else. In fact, making the transition from low to high register fluently is the greatest problem involved in playing this instrument.

Giuffre's technical handicap became a stylistic identification. The dark warmth of his playing at last seemed to embody what had been missed for so long: a modern clarinet conception somehow corresponding to the "Four Brothers" sound of the tenor saxophonists. But Giuffre played his clarinet much as Lester Young had played his twenty years before—on the few recordings Prez had then made on this instrument: in 1938 with the Kansas City Six, and around the same time with Count Basie's band. Many experts do not doubt that Lester, had he played it more often, would have become as important on the clarinet as he was on the tenor. Lester himself said he played clarinet so rarely mainly because he could not find an instrument that suited him.

The paradox of the situation is that cool jazz actually has only two clarinetists whose playing corresponds to the cool conception in a narrower definition—Lester Young and Jimmy Giuffre—whereas among the tenor saxophonists the Lester Young sound was multiplied to such a degree that the tenor man seemed to be living in a world of mirrors. Indirectly, however, a few tenor men have extended the cool Lester Young conception when occasionally playing clarinet: Zoot Sims, Buddy Collette, and others. But this was usually perceived only as a surprising side effect, not as a genuine style—as, for example, Sims's way of playing tenor.

But back to Giuffre. During the second half of the fifties, he moved away from his preference for the low register of his instrument, probably because the success of his dark-toned playing forced him to play clarinet so much that he overcame his technical handicap. From the sixties on, Giuffre stood out as a sensitive musician, presenting a restrained, chamber-music–like cool free jazz.

Two other important musicians who took up the struggle with the difficult position of the clarinet in jazz are the German Rolf Kühn and the American Tony Scott. From 1956 to 1969, Kühn lived in the United States, and John Hammond called him "a new Benny Goodman" then. Leonard Feather found that "Kühn had the misfortune to enter the jazz scene at a time when his chosen instrument had suffered an apparently irreversible decline in popularity. Had it not been for these circumstances, he might well be a major name in jazz today." In the sixties and seventies

Kühn incorporated a lot of modern impulses, at first from Eric Dolphy and later from free jazz and fusion music. His great stylistic breadth enabled him to make a comeback in the nineties that brought him together with Ornette Coleman, Michael Brecker, and Peter Erskine.

Tony Scott was a true "jam session" musician, with an immense drive to play and, above all, with the "loudest sound of all clarinetists" (Perry Robinson). He was a genuine clarinetist who felt the music through his horn, undisturbed by the unfavorable stylistic situation of the instrument. "I don't like funerals," said Scott when it seemed in the late fifties that the jazz clarinet was finally laid to rest. "That's why I went to Asia."

In Asia, Scott inspired and trained dozens of musicians. What all those "Americans in Europe" accomplished together, Scott achieved almost alone in the much more extended Asian territory. From Taiwan to Indonesia, from Okinawa to Thailand, he passed the message of genuine jazz on to a whole generation of young jazz musicians.

Of course, the dilemma of the clarinet—that it simply didn't seem to fit into the "saxophonized" sound of classic modern jazz—was not solved by Scott's flight to Asia. A solution was initiated by the great avant-gardist Eric Dolphy, who died in Berlin in 1964—however, not so much on clarinet as on bass clarinet.

Never before had the bass clarinet been a true jazz instrument. Dolphy turned it into one—with searing, wild emotional expression and also with a physically immense power that gave his listeners the feeling that he was not playing the traditional bass clarinet, which had always appeared somewhat old-fashioned, but rather a totally new instrument that had never been heard before.

Dolphy's work on the bass clarinet was all the more revolutionary because the instrument had previously been used in jazz only sporadically. It was considered a curiosity, and it is a sign of the lack of success with which New Orleans jazz musicians attempted the instrument that the first use of bass clarinet on record—"Someday Sweetheart," recorded by Jelly Roll Morton's Red Hot Peppers in 1926—is one of the lesser-known Morton recordings. At that time, Omer Simeon's bass clarinet playing was still fairly awkward and rhythmically stiff, functioning more like a substitute for the bass than as an instrument in its own right.

In contrast, Harry Carney's bass clarinet playing, which included the use of circular breathing, represented a step forward. Unlike his heavy baritone saxophone playing, Carney approached the bass clarinet as a tender ballad instrument, whose warm, dark sound lent subtle atmospheric effects to the slower pieces of the Duke Ellington Orchestra.

The bass clarinet has an organic, natural sound. "It gives people the feeling that someone's blowing on a part of a tree," David Murray once said. The dark, warm, mysterious, slightly "snorkelly" sound of the bass clarinet is ideal for coloristic effects, as Harry Carney was the first to realize. In a similar, but modern, way, Bennie Maupin used the bass clarinet in the psychedelic atmospheres and floating sounds of the early jazz-rock of Miles Davis's *Bitches Brew*, as an instrumental voice used to add an element of mysterious "fog" to the sound. Marcus Miller is a player who has carried the suggestively atmospheric Maupin sound into twenty-first-century pop jazz.

But this is getting ahead of our story. To return to Eric Dolphy in the sixties: compared to the infrequent use of the instrument in traditional jazz, his bass clarinet playing was pathbreaking. With his wide interval jumps and wild, tearing sounds, he made the bass clarinet an instrument capable of expressing the entire spectrum of human thoughts and feelings. In the wake of Dolphy, hundreds of musicians took up this instrument, especially in Europe, where many musicians, mostly saxophonists, took it on as an additional instrument. For example, Willem Breuker from Holland, Englishman John Surman, the Germans Gunter Hampel and Gebhard Ullmann, and, especially, Italy's Gianluigi Trovesi developed their own approach to the bass clarinet. While Dolphy's playing has eccentric edges and angles, Surman's bass clarinet lines are more round and flowing, describing soft diatonic arcs.

For most musicians, however, the bass clarinet remained a secondary instrument. Only Michel Pilz, Rudi Mahall, Michel Portal, Gianluigi Trovesi, and Louis Sclavis have been able to give such complete expression to themselves on the bass clarinet that they concentrated on this instrument right from the start. Strikingly, many of these players come from the rich Francophone traditions of clarinet playing: Pilz from Luxembourg and Portal and Sclavis from France.

In contrast to the standard clarinet, the bass clarinet enables tone colorations like those prized by jazz saxophone players: vocal, raw, overblown sounds. As an expert in overblown playing whose furious lines contrast miraculously with the gentleness and warmth of his tone, Michel Pilz plays nothing but bass clarinet, and he has brought Dolphy's legacy into the ecstatic free collective improvisations of the Globe Unity Orchestra. And Rudi Mahall "saxophonizes" the bass clarinet like no one else, using raw, abstract, rough lines inspired more by the snarling baritone saxophone sound of Pepper Adams, or the playing of earthy tenor saxophonists, than by clarinetists. His humorous, subversive playing and his deep knowledge of the jazz tradition are particularly effective in his duos with pianist Aki Takase, and in the band Die Enttäuschung [The Disappointment].

As stated, through the end of the sixties it seemed as though Eric Dolphy had said everything there is to say on the bass clarinet. But then, with the emancipations that developed in European jazz, players emerged whose bass clarinet and standard clarinet playing, were expanded and rejuvenated through their reflection on their own background in folk music, classical music, etc. Multi-instrumentalist Michel Portal was, already in the sixties, the first clarinetist to find a genuinely European jazz voice on the instrument. A Frenchman, he comes from the concert hall and new music, having worked with Pierre Boulez, Luciano Berio, and Karlheinz Stockhausen. As a bass clarinetist he links the dancelike impulse and the joyous liveliness of southern French folk music with free jazz's explorative awareness of sound. He also often works with attractive electronic transformations.

Gianluigi Trovesi is the doyen of Italian jazz. His playing combines American and European influences. His solos are strongly rooted in traditional Italian folk music. He has found a personal way of translating saltarello music (an Italian dance form in 3/4 or 6/8 time dating from the thirteenth century and originally played on the baroque flute) to the bass clarinet, by combining these melodies and rhythms with elements from blues, twelve-tone music, chanson, and avant-garde jazz. His compositions for his octet refract the history of jazz through a prism, incorporating European elements from at least six different centuries—Gregorian chant, bel canto arias, traditional dances and folk songs, to "little stories" full of emotion, irony, and suffering. Umberto Eco has written of Trovesi that "there is nothing more seductive than artfullness, when it has the humility to disguise itself as artlessness." Trovesi never considered himself to have made a break with the American jazz tradition. "In my own music, I simply wanted to reincorporate all the musical elements that I had lost along the way."

Louis Sclavis from Lyon, cofounder of the ARFI (Association pour la Recherche d'un Folklore Imaginaire), which he later left, became known for his impressive performances with the Workshop de Lyon and the La Marmite Infernale orchestra. Few players have had as lasting an influence on European jazz in the last twenty years as Sclavis. "His legendary reputation is due to the extraordinary flexibility with which he finds human warmth in even the most abstract concepts," writes Wolf Kampmann.

Sclavis is a melodic wizard, who plays brilliantly soft, radiant lines that balance free imagination and strict discipline in an archaic perfection. Sclavis began as one of the integrating figures of the "imaginary folklore" movement, a music that is sometimes entertaining and bucolic, sometimes dark and disturbing, and that creates a strangely folkloric impression despite the fact that it contains little actual folk music. This is an invented folklore, a brilliantly conceived free space of the creative imagination. Later, Sclavis incorporated influences from European art music into his improvisations. His interest in European composers such as Luciano Berio, Pierre Boulez, and Brian Ferneyhough was overlooked by many people whose attention was focused on his influence as one of the outstanding figures of the "imaginary folklore" movement. Sclavis considers his main instrument to be the bass clarinet. In 1998, with Jacques Di Donato and Armand Angster he formed the Trio de Clarinettes, which combined free improvisation with imaginary folk melodies. In the nineties, with Henri Texier and Aldo Romano he made two extended tours of West and South Africa. The resulting music, documented on the recording *Carnet de Routes*, is one of the most successful fusions of African and European sensibilities.

It is striking that there has been no musician on the bass clarinet who has founded a "school" in the way that, for example, Charlie Parker or John Coltrane did for saxophonists. While Eric Dolphy and, in Europe, Louis Sclavis have had a considerable influence on bass clarinet playing, it is remarkable that even their innovative playing has never become a standard to be emulated for bass clarinetists. Both of these musicians are inspirational not so much stylistically as due to the resoluteness with which they brought the bass clarinet into the foreground and gave it their own personal sound.

The fact that the bass clarinet has no "founding fathers" of this sort is an advantage. "Because you don't have a model that you measure yourself against in your head, you feel freer," says Louis Sclavis. "Compared with many other instruments, on the bass clarinet, it's considerably easier to be yourself."

Among the Americans who should be mentioned in this context are Douglas Ewart, Hamiet Bluiett, David Murray, John Purcell, Marty Ehrlich, and Bob Mintzer. In contrast to his earthy, vital tenor saxophone playing, Murray plays bass clarinet with a tender sound, but also often plays the instrument percussively, using the "slap-tongue" technique. Bluiett plays the alto clarinet, whose appearance often leads to it being mistaken for the bass instrument. He attracted attention in the eighties with the Clarinet Family, to date the most colorful and opulent concentration of clarinet sounds in jazz: eight clarinetists and a rhythm section, reflecting and updating the instrument's entire history from New Orleans to free jazz.

John Purcell, who became known in Jack DeJohnette's and Muhal Richard Abrams's groups, is—like Anthony Braxton (still to be discussed)—one of the few real multi-instrumentalists. He phrases with equally remarkable expressiveness and steadiness on the bass clarinet, and also oboe, English horn, and the soprano and tenor saxophones so that no distinction can be made between primary and secondary instrument. Marty Ehrlich is almost his equal: a musician who can cope with all styles in postmodern jazz and whose love of rich colors and contrasts is to be heard in his bass clarinet, as well as in his alto sax and flute phrasing. And Bob Mintzer, with his flexible, inventive, swinging lines, has proved that the bass clarinet also has a place in today's hard bop.

Beyond the avant-garde, the mainstream also flowed into the music of the seventies, eighties, and nineties, through such clarinetists as Bill Easley, Bill Smith, Ken Peplowski, Paquito D'Rivera, Richard Stolzman, Swedish-born Putte Wickman, England's Tony Coe, and, particularly brilliant,

Eddie Daniels. In 1988 Putte Wickman made ambitious duo recordings with bassist Red Mitchell. He cultivated the charm of the swing clarinetists while spicing it with a bolder modern harmonic openness. Ken Peplowski combines the friendly, attractive tone of Benny Goodman with the rhythmic flexibility of Buddy DeFranco. Tony Coe, whose clarinet playing is decidedly unorthodox, has an unusual position in this grouping. His playing combines traditional and avant-garde techniques, and swings, even at fast tempos, into the highest registers of the instrument.

Most successful of all in the eighties and nineties was Eddie Daniels, who started out as a tenor sax player and won a reputation as an experienced studio musician. The clarinet became his chief instrument in 1985. A year later the readers of *Down Beat* chose him as the best clarinetist (and in many following polls, too)—a category that, unlike any other, had been absolutely dominated for decades by the grand old masters of the instrument. Daniels—a "Wynton Marsalis of the Clarinet," according to Leonard Feather—further developed Buddy DeFranco's concept of the bop clarinet in unique fashion, with enormously supple, flowing lines bubbling over with a wealth of ideas and a special feeling for the music of Charlie Parker. "The clarinet has the widest range of all woodwinds. It has one of the warmest sounds. . . . It's been the most neglected instrument since the bebop era primarily because it is one of the hardest," said Daniels.

The fact that the clarinet experienced a timid comeback in the eighties was also partly thanks to Daniels. But more important still have been performers coming from "free" playing, which they often developed in a variety of directions. Anthony Braxton, J. D. Parran, Perry Robinson, Michael Moore, German Theo Jörgensmann, Hungarian Lajos Dudas, Canadian Francois Houle, and, most important of all, John Carter made people almost forget the instrument's shortcomings—its lack of tonal sharpness and physical presence—by using the clarinet's rich register for a shimmering palette of highly diverse sounds.

Multi-instrumentalist and composer Braxton is a masterly player of the entire spectrum of clarinets from the soprano to the contrabass, creating linearly ordered sounds that to many listeners seem abstract, despite their having attained worldwide success in the seventies.

Perry Robinson has played with the Jazz Composers Orchestra and Roswell Rudd, with Charlie Haden and Sunny Murray, with Gunter Hampel, and with Dave and Darius Brubeck; all those names testify to his universality. Already in the seventies he took free jazz, cool jazz, bop, swing, and rock to that postmodern style that was to become a matter of course in the eighties. "We want to be able to play any kind of music and yet we want to be ourselves," he said. "The clarinet, it's incredible, because you have these different sounds. The only frustrating thing about it that has to be overcome somehow is that it's too small; it won't carry the weight when you're trying to get through. I made a study of it, and I learned a lot of things about sound, about overblowing."

Theo Jörgensmann transposed the open expressiveness of free playing into bop and modal jazz—as a specialist in making surprising changes of register, utilizing with particular sensitivity his instrument's dark, warm register, reminiscent of Jimmy Giuffre. In the eighties, Jörgensmann headed the CL-4 clarinet quartet, discovering unusual sounds in the borderline area between jazz and new music.

John Carter (d. 1991) was at one time a Texas companion of Ornette Coleman, but only became famous in the eighties. A sparkling, subtle melodist within tonally free jazz, his playing was deeply rooted in the great tradition of the jazz clarinet. He enriched modern clarinet playing with exciting whirling sounds (based on circular breathing) and unusual altered chords that extend into the region of polyphonic playing. Carter was also a master of the extreme high register. Where other clarinetists took an easier way, noisily overblowing their instrument, Carter did something much more difficult. He played elastic, absolutely sure notes—tonally free and in tempered tuning, up to three octaves above the instrument's normal range. In the eighties, Carter also became an important composer, a master of extended form who achieved a rare balance between notated and improvised parts. His *Roots and Folklore: Episodes in the Development of American Folk Music* marked a peak of unification. This composition, consisting of five suites documented on five records, stands alongside Duke Ellington's *Black, Brown & Beige* and Wynton Marsalis's *Blood on the Fields* as probably the most successful and creative tone poem depicting over two hundred years of black culture in America: from deportation and slavery by way of emancipation and rural black folklore to the urbanization of modern blacks.

What John Carter began has been emphatically carried forward since the early nineties by Don Byron. With his resolute, aggressive playing, he has brought the clarinet back as an equal partner in contemporary jazz. Don Byron is widely known for his lack of musical boundaries. In 1993 he made the recording *The Music of Mickey Katz*, in which he presented classic Jewish music in a new light, years before klezmer jazz became fashionable. He has realized exciting new Latin-jazz projects, has played Brahms and Schumann, and has improvised in hip-hop, funk, and free contexts. Like Charles Mingus, Byron is a critical, and sometimes cynical, commentator on political and social issues in the United States, including racial ones.

After Benny Goodman, jazz clarinet was generally played with almost no vibrato. Byron has given it back this expressiveness, as well as great dynamic range. He is a gripping improviser with a hearty tone, biting rhythmic intensity, and an impeccable melodic sense of direction. It's no accident that Byron often plays with dynamic, interactive drummers, such as Ralph Peterson or Pheeroan AkLaff. His clarinet lines interact with the rhythmic energy of drummers in a particularly exciting way. For this reason, his band Music for Six Musicians is the perfect vehicle for his jazz clarinet, due to its unorthodox combination of Afro-Caribbean and Latin-American rhythms and new jazz.

Don Byron says: "The clarinet puts you in a situation that's kind of unique. There's no way to play the clarinet without playing classical music." For decades, this was the dilemma of the jazz clarinet. In American modern jazz, coming from bebop, the classical legacy of the clarinet was felt to be an obstacle, a difficulty for expressive playing. But in the multistylistic jazz of the eighties and nineties, the clarinet's roots in classical music are no longer a problem for jazz clarinet players. Rather, in particular for European musicians, this legacy is a treasure trove and a source of inspiration that they can use freely.

Michael Riessler has created a new jazz from the roots of European art music and folk music that combines composition and improvisation in a playful way. Riessler is a master of "polyphonic" playing, producing the impression of several notes at once through circular breathing and special fingering and embouchure techniques. His music has room for many identities. Jazz, tarantellas, French barrel organ music, early music, avant-garde—all these are superposed in his music, as though sheets of film were placed on top of one another, ultimately melding together to form a whole.

In the multistylistic jazz of the nineties and the beginning of the twenty-first century, jazz clarinet made an unexpected comeback. While the iconic jazz instrument, the saxophone, is little-used in classical music and in folk music, the clarinet has, in addition to its jazz heritage, a rich classical and folkloristic tradition that expands its possibilities, rather than standing in the way of them. Thus, it is not surprising that it was above all European players who, besides Byron, gave contemporary jazz clarinet playing in the nineties a boost that before then would hardly have been considered possible. Besides the above-discussed Sclavis, Trovesi, and Riessler, these players include Gabriele Mirabassi, Ab Baars, Klaus Dickbauer, Jürgen Kupke, and Claudio Puntin.

Gabriele Mirabassi, who came to prominence through his playing with Rabih Abou-Khalil, plays like a modern-day, "imaginary folklore" version of Barney Bigard, ornamenting his chamber-music-like solos with lithe lines that move between classical music and regional folklore. Mirabassi is unusually playful and assured as a dialogist. His light jazz is full of melodic gems, with Mediterranean flair and a strong tendency toward Brazilian rhythms—in Europe, Mirabassi is justly considered an outstanding expert on Brazilian *choro* music, the precursor of all Brazil's popular music forms.

Swiss clarinetist Claudio Puntin is, like Chris Speed (see below), an extremely legato player, phrasing in a soft, smooth, connected manner, yet with rhythmic force. His group Mondo, a trio with Chinese *ghuzeng* player Wang Yong and Argentinian percussionist Marcio Doctor, creates meditative world jazz with chamber-music qualities. In 2004 Puntin and Mirabassi founded the World Clarinet Quartet.

Louis Sclavis, Gianluigi Trovesi, and Gabriele Mirabassi are the clarinet triumvirate of Europe's "imaginary folklore." Other notable players connected to this movement include the Americans David Krakauer, Ben Goldberg, and Matt Darriau, who are the most prominent of an outstanding group of klezmer jazz clarinet players. Evan Ziporyn and, representing New York's Balkan jazz movement, Chris Speed should also be mentioned here.

David Krakauer, with his energetic, ardent playing, influenced by John Coltrane, Sidney Bechet, and Charlie Parker, is the outstanding protagonist of new klezmer jazz. At the same time, he represents the conservative but unorthodox wing of New York's "Radical Jewish Culture." "I want my music to be klezmer, not some sort of a fusion mishmash," he says. The name of his band Klezmer Madness indicates his program. In this group, he humorously and turbulently turns traditional Jewish melodies on their head—such as "Kale Mazel Tov" or "Kusatzke," but also Balkan dances such as the Bulgar—by combining them with elements of Hendrix, blues, funk, and electronica. Ben Goldberg, in his New Klezmer Trio, treats new and old Jewish melodies with a free-floating tonality inspired by free improvisation. "In klezmer music, the clarinet is often reminiscent of the human voice," says Krakauer, explaining why so many clarinetists have been attracted to the klezmer tradition. "People talk a lot about the laughing or crying of the klezmer clarinet. But for me it also sounds like prayer and celebration. It has a relationship to the liturgical music of the cantors, even though it's purely secular dance music."

Evan Ziporyn, who also subjects the clarinet to radical electronic transformations, explores a particularly rhythmically complex territory between new jazz and Indonesian music. Chris Speed, known from the band Pachora, is a master of a kind of "flutelike" playing, using laconic, smoothly flowing legato lines to bring the odd meters of new Balkan jazz and the ornamented lines of Eastern European music into new jazz.

In "imaginary folklore," there are more leading stylists on the clarinet than on any other wind instrument. This is because the clarinet, beyond its classical tradition, has roots in many folkloric traditions: Greek and Turkish gypsy music, klezmer, Balkan folk music, Brazilian *choro* music. Improvisation is an important part of all these traditions.

It is therefore also not surprising that these relationships also run in the other direction. Players who come more from world music than from jazz are increasingly seeking dialogue with new jazz: Paulo Moura in Brazil, Giora Feidman in Israel, Mustafa Kandirali in Turkey, Ivo Papasov in Bulgaria.

At the beginning of the twenty-first century, the clarinet is back. This is a remarkable contrast to the situation in the previous few decades, when the clarinet was perceived to be a little dusty and antiquated, and was thought to have little chance of finding a place in modern jazz. Today, more and more interesting players are emerging, intense stylists like Greg Tardy, Klaus Dickbauer, and Ab Baars. All these personal approaches to playing the clarinet demonstrate its amazing versatility.

The Saxophones

The ideal jazz instrument is one that can be as expressive as the trumpet and as mobile as the clarinet. The instruments of the saxophone family combine these two qualities, which are in extreme opposition where most other instruments are concerned. That is why the saxophone is important to jazz. But it became important only at the start of the thirties. One can hardly speak of a New Orleans saxophone tradition. The few saxophonists active in New Orleans were looked upon with the expressions reserved today for sousaphone or theremin players, regarded as odd characters rather than musicians. Generally, the saxophone belonged to sweet bands and popular dance music rather than jazz. During the days of Chicago style, things changed. It is noteworthy that the New Orleans Rhythm Kings were without a saxophone when they came to Chicago from New Orleans in 1921; yet when they obtained the engagement at Friar's Inn that was their springboard to fame, they were urged to include a saxophone. The saxophonist stumbled and staggered about amid the collective ensemble of the Kings, and never really found his place. As soon as the band quit the job at Friar's Inn, he was let go.

Since no jazz tradition existed for the saxophone, the clarinet tradition had to do for jazz-minded saxophonists. The importance that the saxophone—primarily the tenor—has achieved in modern jazz immediately becomes clear when one realizes that at the outset of its jazz career, the saxophone was played more or less like a peculiar sort of clarinet, whereas since the fifties jazz clarinetists often have had a tenor-sax approach to their instrument.

The saxophones range downward from soprano (and sopranino) through alto, tenor, and baritone to bass (and contrabass). The most important in jazz are the first four.

Adrian Rollini played Dixieland and Chicago-style music on the bass sax with its hollow, somewhat burping sound, with great agility and basically with the same intention that motivated Boyd Raeburn to use the instrument as the lowest voice in the sax section of his modern big band: to give depth and bottom to the sound spectrum.

In many contemporary jazz saxophone ensembles and other bands, such as those of Carlos Actis Dato or Steffen Schorn, the bass saxophone acts as a kind of gruff, heavy groove engine. A handicap of this bass voice of the saxophone family is the difficulty in centering pitches on it, and thus a tendency toward indistinct intonation: a handicap that, of course, improvising musicians have turned to their advantage in their search for new musical challenges, in the manner typical of jazz. Musicians inspired by free jazz, such as Joseph Jarman and Roscoe Mitchell of the Art Ensemble of Chicago, or Vinny Golia, have been particularly attracted to the noisy elements of the bass saxophone in their sonic explorations. This has sometimes resulted in exotic "squawking" sounds such as those produced on other saxophones (not just the bass) at the very beginning of the instrument's history in early New Orleans jazz.

Scott Robinson and Anthony Braxton, coming from diametrically opposed standpoints, have brought bop velocity to the bass and contrabass saxophones. Braxton has done so with the subversive lines of a musician finding new sounds in the sonic stew of freebop, while Robinson has used it to enrich his neo–hard bop with energetic, massive lines.

The bass sax has nevertheless remained an outsider instrument.

The Soprano Saxophone

The soprano saxophone continues where the clarinet leaves off—because of its loudness, for one. It has the most disproportionate history of all instruments in jazz, even more disproportionate than the violin. In the beginning, there was only Sidney Bechet. Today, there are hundreds of sopranoists. A tenor man is no longer acceptable in countless big bands and studio orchestras if he does not double on the soprano. In fact, things have been somewhat reversed since the seventies: often the soprano became the main instrument and the tenor the second one.

For decades we were told that soprano sax was used so rarely because of the difficulty in playing it "clean." It's a recalcitrant instrument, sometimes referred to disparagingly as the "fish horn." Its high notes necessarily sound "out of tune." Today, however, we know that this is the very advantage of the instrument: The "dirtiness" of sound, which has been of great importance in all phases of jazz history, is an integral part of the soprano. One could almost say that the soprano tends to flatten each note, to turn it into a "blue note," to turn the whole scale "blue." This is a tendency imminent from the start in folk blues and the archaic jazz forms. The three classical blue notes of jazz are compromises with the European harmonic system. Actually, the music of the African and the African American tends toward slanting each individual tone, toward not accepting a note as it is, toward transforming each note as a personal statement. The soprano does all this in an exemplary manner: it "Africanizes." The thesis that this is its actual strength can even be verified in a test: there are sopranoists who have managed to produce "clean" sounds in spite of all the technical difficulties of the instrument—Lucky Thompson (d. 2005), for example, who in the sixties transferred the perfect beauty of his tenor sound to the soprano. But he remained relatively unsuccessful, in spite of the high degree of sophistication of his playing. He is admired, but failed to truly excite and move.

Sidney Bechet is the Louis Armstrong of the soprano saxophone—he had Armstrong's majestic expressiveness. During the span of his rich life, which led from the New Orleans of pre–World War I days to the Paris of the fifties, he changed—gradually at first, but then more and more decidedly—from clarinet to soprano sax. It has been said he did so because with advancing age, the soprano became easier for him, since it requires less air for full-volume play. His main reason, however, was that the soprano makes possible a wider range of expression, and the maximum of *espressivo* was Bechet's main goal. His "bleating," expressive vibrato was called a "talking vibrato" because of its closeness to joyful, jubilant speech. Bechet repeatedly emphasized: "I am a storyteller," and it is fitting that his tours in the twenties began under the billing "Sidney Bechet, The Talking Saxophonist." For good reason he has been called the forefather of the great ballad tradition of jazz. For the outsider, this tradition begins with Coleman Hawkins's "Body and Soul" in 1939. But actually, it began much earlier—with Sidney Bechet (and, of course, like all things in jazz, with Louis Armstrong!).

Bechet had only a few soprano students: Johnny Hodges, Don Redman, Charlie Barnet, Woody Herman, Bob Wilber, Kenny Davern—and in a certain sense, even in the Coltrane era, Budd Johnson and Jerome Richardson. They all applied their Bechet experiences to the stylistic periods to which they belonged. Hodges, the most famous soloist of the Duke Ellington Orchestra, was devoted to expressiveness in a way similar to Bechet. But the soprano solos he played with Ellington in the twenties and thirties seem pale compared to the power of his alto sound. Hodges gave up the soprano altogether after 1940. Perhaps he also felt that playing the soprano would always keep him somewhat in the shadow of the great Bechet, to whom he was indebted in many ways. Toward the end of his life, when the soprano sound became fashionable, Ellington wanted Hodges to give it another try, but there was not time. Hodges died in 1970.

The close proximity between Hodges and Bechet in this aspect is made clear by Woody Herman: if he derives from Hodges as an alto player, he stems from Bechet as a soprano man.

John Coltrane was also among Bechet's students on this instrument. I (Joachim-Ernst Berendt) know this from personal experience: from the turn of the fifties into the sixties, Coltrane repeatedly had me send him soprano records by Bechet, especially from his French period, so he could study them. With his solo on "My Favorite Things" in 1961, Coltrane created a sweeping breakthrough for the soprano sax (see also the section on Coltrane).

The development of the soprano saxophone again displays the continuity of growth so very characteristic of jazz: from New Orleans—from Sidney Bechet in this case—to the modern and complex creations of Coltrane and Wayne Shorter and to their "students" and contemporaries.

Coltrane retained the expressiveness and "dirtiness" of Bechet. But for Bechet's majestic clarity, which is reminiscent of Louis Armstrong, he substituted an Asiatic meditativeness. Coltrane's soprano sound calls to mind the *shenai* of northern Indian music, the *nagaswaram* of the music of southern India, and the *zoukra* of Arabian music. His soprano sound virtually demands modality. It becomes particularly clear at this point what modality actually is: the equivalent in jazz to the *maqams* of Arabic music and the Indian *ragas*.

Without Coltrane's soprano work it is hard to conceive of the whole Asiatic movement in jazz—not only in the area of the soprano, but transcending to all other instruments. This is particularly true of those instruments that, since the sixties, have increasingly been incorporated into jazz or were imbued with a new approach: violin, flute, bagpipes, oboe, English horn, up to the Arabic instruments themselves, such as oud, *ney*, *kanun*, etc. In fact, we must say that these instruments were incorporated into jazz or experienced changes in approach precisely because Coltrane's way of playing the soprano became the great example.

Still, Coltrane was not the first to play a modern type of jazz on the soprano sax. The first was Steve Lacy. We have already mentioned his peculiar development in the section on the trombone, in connection with Roswell Rudd. He moved from Dixieland directly to free jazz, bypassing the usual waystations of bebop and cool jazz. Quite to the contrary, he did not discover bop until after he had been playing free jazz. In 1952 he played Dixieland with musicians like Max Kaminsky, Jimmy McPartland, and Rex Stewart; in 1956 he played with Cecil Taylor; and in 1960 with Thelonious Monk. He was one of the few horn players—and probably the only white among them—who fully understood and assimilated Monk.

The stations of Lacy's development—Kaminsky, Cecil Taylor, Monk—indicate his originality. He was a stimulating thinker on his instrument, uncompromising in his tone, his articulation, the logic of his ideas. Lacy was the first well-known soprano saxophonist in jazz who made the soprano his main instrument right from the start without deriving his way of playing from the clarinet, tenor, or alto sax. He could express himself so completely on this instrument that he didn't need any other. Lacy, who lived in Paris from the sixties and returned to America only shortly before his death in 2004, stands outside the three main currents in soprano playing: Sidney Bechet, John Coltrane, and Wayne Shorter. He was the first to produce sounds by blowing "in reverse": not by blowing into the instrument, but by sucking air "backward" through the horn. Many others have since adopted this way of playing. Lacy was also a master of overblowing the horn to produce clearly intoned overtones. Bruce Ackley, known for his work with the ROVA Saxophone Quartet, was one of the few musicians who could advance Lacy's brittle, angular playing in the eighties. Canadian Jane Bunnett has brought the wild energy and explosive rhythms of Afro-Cuban music to Lacy's laconic sound. Since her first visit to Cuba in 1981, she has incorporated the sound of her soprano so convincingly into contexts of *son*, rhumba, guiro, and *guaguanco*, in her work with Cuban pianist Hilario Durán, percussionist Tata Güines (d. 2008), or the Afro-Cuban Rhumba All-Stars, that Cuban musicians call her "Havana Jane." "You don't have to be Austrian to play Mozart," says exiled Cuban alto saxophonist Paquito D'Rivera. "She knows more about contemporary Cuban music than I do."

Leonard Feather surmises that Coltrane first became interested in the soprano saxophone through Steve Lacy. This is suggested by the fact that before Lacy joined the Thelonious Monk Quartet, Coltrane had played with Monk. The club in which Monk then could be heard regularly was the Five Spot in New York, the meeting place of the in-group of jazz. No doubt Coltrane must have heard Lacy there.

"My Favorite Things," as we have said, became a hit. Soon, big bands and studio orchestras jumped on the soprano bandwagon. The range of the saxophone section was extended. Some arrangers became specialists in incorporating soprano sounds into this range: Oliver Nelson, Quincy Jones, Gil Evans, Gary McFarland, Thad Jones, and, later, Toshiko Akiyoshi and Maria Schneider.

The soprano not only took up the legacy of the clarinet; in a certain sense it was also heir to the tenor saxophone. Since free jazz, many tenor men love to "overblow" their instruments in a way reminiscent of the falsetto sound of blues and gospel vocalists, driving into the range of the alto and soprano sax. In this way the tenor becomes "two or even three instruments in one": tenor, alto, and even soprano. This tendency to play "high" has always been part of jazz. A hot way of playing is frequently achieved by playing high, in a way that prompted the German ethnomusicologist Alphons Dauer to suspect that the term *hot* actually was derived from the French *haut*—high. It is obvious that the overblown tenor saxophone is a very ecstatic, intensive instrumental sound on the one hand, but that it is musically rather limited on the other. No doubt, the soprano continues where the overblown tenor leaves off. In this way a tenorist who overblows the instrument and also plays the soprano commands the entire range, from the lowest tenor tones to the flutelike heights of the overblown soprano saxophone. Thus it is no surprise that a host of soprano players were initially specialists of falsetto tenor, among them Pharoah Sanders, Archie Shepp, Roscoe Mitchell, Joseph Jarman, Sam Rivers, James Carter, and Englishmen Evan Parker and John Surman (whose main instrument at first was the baritone and who first used the soprano only as a "falsetto baritone," until he made an increasingly decisive switch from baritone to soprano). Further discussion of the musicians whose main instruments are tenor, alto, or baritone will be found in the chapters dealing with those instruments.

Other important soprano saxophonists after Coltrane include altoist Charlie Mariano and tenor players Dave Liebman, Roland Kirk (who included the soprano-like *manzello* among his various instruments), Zoot Sims, Gary Bartz, René McLean, and, most important of them all, Wayne Shorter (who influenced many of those previously named).

Charlie Mariano is a great master of melody. He has been the most successful at bringing the "Asiatic sound" of the soprano saxophone into jazz communication with Carnatic South Indian music, for example with the Karnataka College of Percussion. His rich, full, golden soprano sound radiates wisdom and a unique melancholy, more optimistic than sentimental.

Many tenor saxophonists who play soprano saxophone as a second instrument use it in ballads, as a welcome contrast to the more powerful tenor, which they play in faster pieces. This tradition, which began so impressively with John Coltrane, became over the decades a kind of reflex that actually limited the freedom of the soprano, as it increasingly took on the role of the preferred voice for slow pieces.

Dave Liebman broke with this cliché more radically and virtuosically than anyone else. He began his career by in fact conforming to this preconception, in the Elvin Jones group. But in the Miles Davis group in the seventies, where his main instrument was tenor saxophone, he began to use the soprano more intensively, until in 1980 he gave up tenor entirely in favor of soprano (though since 1996 he has sporadically returned to the tenor).

As a tenor saxophonist, Liebman comes from John Coltrane, but on the soprano he has developed his own approach, independent of Coltrane, Bechet, Lacy, and Shorter. The intentionally "dirty" sound of his intuitive, finely chiseled lines gives the soprano a greater expressive range. In freely tonal, unaccompanied duos, or in the chamber-music setting of his quartet Quest, Liebman plays the soprano in a more unruly, rhythmic, spacious, hard manner than is normally done on the instrument. In brief, Liebman gives the soprano saxophone an earthiness that is more usually found in trumpet playing or tenor saxophone playing.

Wayne Shorter, who came out of one of Art Blakey's Jazz Messenger groups, became known as *the* saxophonist of the Miles Davis Quintet from 1964 to 1970. *In a Silent Way* of 1969 was the first record on which he played soprano. Apparently, he and the producers thought this to be such a minor point that not even the personnel identifications on the record indicate his soprano contribution. But the jazz world immediately noticed and listened. *Bitches Brew*, produced a year later, is unthinkable without Shorter's soprano sound. His soprano playing made such a strong impression on Miles Davis that Miles from that time onward no longer engaged any sax players who couldn't also play soprano, which often resulted in horn players who had started with tenor and alto having to learn the soprano as well. Shorter aestheticized Coltrane's legacy. Miles plus Trane = Shorter; that is, Shorter combines Coltrane's meditativeness with Miles's lyricism. His soprano sound has, in a way, the expressiveness described in the beginning of the chapter on Miles Davis: loneliness, forlornness, "the sound floats like a cloud." As a soprano player (more perhaps than as a tenorist!) Shorter ranks among the truly great improvisers in jazz. The tone alone implies the music and the complete musical personality of the improviser.

Shorter loves Brazilian music. One of his masterpieces is the transformation of "Dindi"—one of the earliest bossa compositions, dedicated by Antonio Carlos Jobim to the late Sylvia Telles, the first singer of bossa nova, into an exciting, hymnal, free-jazz excursion, which yet retains in every note some of the Brazilian tenderness. Shorter was part of Weather Report, one of the most successful of all fusion groups from its beginnings in 1970 until its dissolution in 1985. The lyricism and melodic luminosity of Shorter's sound stood out from the electronic sounds of this group as a reminder that human musical thinking was at work.

Due to its high register, the soprano saxophone is better able to penetrate the dense sound masses of electric jazz than other saxophones. But it was Shorter's style—refined, simple, melodic, with occasional outbreaks of rapid passages—that was the main reason for the soprano's rise to the spot of most favored horn in jazz-rock and fusion music. Some of the musicians who have blown the soprano in records with fusion, rock, and funk music are Ernie Watts, Tom Scott, Ronnie Laws, Grover Washington, Kenny G. (alias Gorelick), Bendik (alias Bendik Hofseth), George Howard, Bill Evans (no relation to the pianist with the same name), and, in Europe, chiefly Barbara Thompson from England.

As a soprano saxophonist Wayne Shorter has been just as influential as John Coltrane and Sidney Bechet. Of the many soprano sax players who followed the Shorter line in the eighties, the most important are Branford Marsalis (a year older than his brother Wynton), Greg Osby, and, above all, Jane Ira Bloom. No saxophonist has so sovereignly transposed, and further developed, the loneliness and forlornness of Shorter's soprano sax sound into eighties and nineties jazz classicism as Branford Marsalis. Branford's warm and tender soprano also made a decisive contribution to the poetic impact of Sting's pop music.

If Sting headed the best-integrated pop band of the eighties, he ultimately owes much to Marsalis, who, like the other jazz players in Sting's band (pianist Kenny Kirkland, bassist Daryl Jones, and drummer Omar Hakim), staked the openness and warmth of musical dialogue against increasing mechanization and computerization in the pop sector.

Greg Osby, who also plays alto sax, encapsulated and abstracted Shorter's concept particularly effectively in recordings of M-Base music. Jane Ira Bloom is, after Steve Lacy, one of the only players who right from the start has been able to express herself exclusively on the soprano saxophone. She has a full, fat sound. Her chromatic, lyrical soprano playing tends toward an intuitive approach that emphasizes the freedom of the line over close adherence to harmony. The characteristic features of Bloom's playing are unusual melodies and "doublings" of sound, which she achieves through a combination of unusual fingerings and embouchure techniques. She also has a notable ability to create new forms, and has discovered unique sounds in the combination of acoustic playing with live electronics. She was the first musician to receive a compositional commission from NASA as part of their Artist Program, and in 1993 the International Astronomical Union named a newly discovered asteroid, number 6083, after her.

With Wayne Shorter, the great *melos* tradition of the soprano saxophone begins—a tradition that is all the more impressive because new players are constantly adding new facets to the delicate, intimate character of the instrument. These include Andy Sheppard, Anatoly Vapirov, and Stefano di Battista in Europe, Michael Blake and Jimmy Greene in the United States, and Christine Jensen in Canada.

Some of these players, and even more so those belonging to free jazz, make it especially clear that the soprano comes closer to an African sound and intonation than the other saxophones. Important free players to gain attention as sopranoists can be found mainly in and around the AACM: Anthony Braxton, Joseph Jarman, and Roscoe Mitchell, as well as, from the Black Artists Group, Oliver Lake and Julius Hemphill. Occasionally, Jarman produces that typical growl sound that Sidney Bechet so movingly employed in the lower registers to create his blues and ballad renditions. Hemphill dedicated one of his works to the West African Dogon people, who live in total seclusion in Burkina Faso, making references not only to their music but also to their mythology.

The soprano saxophone is an instrument that does not have as great a weight of tradition behind it as some others. Everyone who learns it has the opportunity to approach it anew. Nowhere is this clearer than in the striking music of Evan Parker. Parker, an Englishman, plays the soprano saxophone as if it had just been invented. No other soprano saxophonist equals the imaginative facility with which he shapes overtones. He is a master of circular breathing, which he uses to play endless, scintillating streams of notes and sounds that extend for many minutes without pause, traveling through entire spectra of timbres "like an acoustic rainbow" (Thomas Miessgang).

Parker is one of the originators of European free jazz. He was a member of drummer John Stevens's Spontaneous Music Ensemble, and founded the Music Improvisation Company with guitarist Derek Bailey.

His soprano playing stands at the forefront of an entire improvisational direction of free jazz. He is the main representative of what can be called "laminar" playing, in which sonic blocks and bands are layered over one another, in contrast to "atomized" playing, which is focused more strongly on isolated, individual sounds.

Evan Parker has become one of the most influential saxophonists of the avant-garde since John Coltrane. On the basis of his soprano improvisations, a lineage of players has emerged who have further developed this repetitive, sonically discursive approach to free playing: John Butcher in England, Hans Koch in Switzerland, Wolfgang Fuchs and Dirk Marwedel in Germany, and, in some respects, Ned Rothenberg and Michael Riessler, whose work is closer to the multistylism of postmodern jazz.

Before Evan Parker, Joe Maneri developed his own way of phrasing microtonal lines on the soprano saxophone. Maneri, who studied twelve-tone composition with Joseph Schmid (a pupil of Alban Berg), makes use in his improvisations of a microtonal system that divides the octave into seventy-two steps. Maneri plays with an energetic drive that is absolutely foreign to the world of academic music. He has said, "If rhythm doesn't have creative energy for me, five thousand microtones aren't going to help." The Lithuanian Petras Vysniauskas is a poet of Eastern European avant-garde jazz. In contrast to his teacher, Vladimir Chekasin, known for his wild phrasing, Vysniauskas is attracted to breathing, open structures. "In Lithuanian folk songs, I hear echoes of the music of John Coltrane," he says.

Coltrane's legacy also continues in the field of contemporary mainstream jazz, where influences from Shorter and Liebman often accompany that of Coltrane. Noteworthy players here are John Purcell, Chris Potter, Sam Newsome, Steve Wilson, Roger Hanschel, Ted Nash, and, last but not least, John Coltrane's son Ravi Coltrane.

John Purcell brought intimate moments to the playing of the World Saxophone Quartet, and is also an original composer. Roger Hanschel, a member of the Cologne Saxophone Mafia, has individualized the spiky, fine sound of the sopranino saxophone more than anyone else in Europe.

But the "pure" Bechet legacy also continues, touched more by Swing than by Coltrane and Shorter. It is represented in an exemplary manner by Bob Wilber and Kenny Davern (who later returned to clarinet), on individual records as well as in their joint *Soprano Summits*.

"Pure" soprano playing, in the vein of the contemporary aestheticism, is especially cultivated by Norwegian Jan Garbarek and American Paul Winter, but also by some of the musicians named earlier, such as John Surman.

In his duos with Jack DeJohnette and in chamber-musical settings, Surman is a master of circular breathing and of the expansion of the soprano's sound using electronics. His hypnotic melodies, which move ambiguously between minor and major tonalities, sound as if they could be centuries old. In 1979 he used studio overdubbing techniques to record the solo album *Upon Reflection*, in which he transformed the melodies of British madrigals, Irish jigs, and Scottish reels and laments into a cathedral of soprano sounds.

The clear, elegiac sound of Jan Garbarek has attracted particular attention. His music, with its jubilant melancholy and plaintive joy, is some of the most personal and distinctive jazz to come from Europe. Garbarek, with his ascetic, intense melodies, has demonstrated that jazz saxophone playing is not about the number of notes, but rather about making each note a powerful expression of the player's feelings, both in his own groups, which use sources from Scandinavian folklore, and in collaborations with Eberhard Weber, North Indian musicians, and the Hilliard Ensemble (in adaptations of liturgical songs of the early Renaissance).

Surman and Garbarek are the main representatives of a generation of players who build on the diverse musical heritage of Europe, including in their new jazz influences from folklore, classical music, and also American, African, and Asian music. Such players also include Louis Sclavis, Gianluigi Trovesi, Karl Seglam, Julian Argüelles, Liudas Mockunas, and others.

The Alto Saxophone

The history of the alto saxophone actually begins in the Swing period. To the clarinet triumvirate Jimmie Noone–Johnny Dodds–Sidney Bechet of the twenties corresponds a duo of altos that set the pace for everything played on this instrument during the thirties: Johnny Hodges and Benny Carter.

The Duke Ellington musician Johnny Hodges, who died in 1970, was a melodist of the rank of Armstrong or Hawkins. His warm, expressive vibrato and his way of melting notes in erotic glissandos made the Hodges sound one of the best-known instrumental signatures in jazz. Hodges was the first great "sound player" of the alto saxophone. He had the ability to make every note "blossom" with many inflections, projecting more emotion and subtleness in one note than other musicians do in entire lines. Dark, tropical warmth seems to lie in this sound, an erotic vibrancy which may occasionally approach sentimentality on slow pieces. At faster tempos, Hodges remained the great, gripping improviser he had been since joining Duke Ellington's band in 1928.

Among the many Hodges disciples, Woody Herman for many years was one of the best known. Herman blew Hodges-inspired solos that stood in pronounced and sometimes amusing contrast to the more modern conceptions of the young musicians in his band.

Benny Carter (1907–2003) was Hodges's opposite. Where the latter loved melancholy and earthiness, Benny Carter had a buoyant clarity and airiness. Hodges was like a seducer on his instrument; his saxophone seemed to beguile with every note, draping the notes in a sonic erotomania. Carter, on the other hand, was a man of elegance, whose sleek, almost vibratoless lines suggested that he was convinced that the alto saxophone should sound like a great, dignified singer. During the forties Carter settled in Hollywood, where he started a second career as arranger and composer for film and television studios. Carter was one of the most versatile musicians in jazz, of equal importance as alto saxist, arranger, and orchestra leader, and also a notable trumpeter, trombonist, and clarinetist. We shall have more to say about Carter in the chapter on big bands.

The maturity of the Hodges-Carter constellation seems all the more astonishing when one considers how few notable alto players preceded them. There was Don Redman, who as an arranger had a great impact on the development of the big-band sound of the twenties and early thirties and who played occasional alto solos with his bands; and then there was Frank Trumbauer among the Chicago-style musicians, who recorded with Bix Beiderbecke. Trumbauer did not play the E-flat alto, but its relative, the C-melody saxophone. His clear, cool lines had a certain influence on the early style of Lester Young.

After Hodges and Carter, the whole development of the alto saxophone is concentrated on one towering personality: Charlie Parker. In the section dedicated to him and Dizzy Gillespie, we have attempted to clarify his singular position. Parker possessed both Hodges's emotionality and Carter's clarity. His importance was so great initially that there was hardly another bop altoist worth mentioning. The sole exception was Sonny Stitt, who vacillated between alto and tenor, and who, strangely enough, developed independently of Parker a Bird-like alto style of great clarity and bluesy expressiveness.

There was one realm that stayed relatively free from bebop way into the fifties: "jump," a style of playing (and dancing!) popular in Harlem and other big-city ghettos. Three of its outstanding players were alto saxophonists: Earl Bostic, Louis Jordan, and Johnny Hodges. The latter was—mainly in those few years of his career when he was not a member of the Ellington band—a player of dynamic jump rhythms, as in records with organist Wild Bill Davis. In the late forties, long before the great rock 'n' roll era, Bostic scored hits of rock 'n' roll proportions with his *Flamingo* and other records. And Louis Jordan found a way of playing that combined Benny Carter's mobility with blues-drenched humor and a sense of fun. His commercially successful orchestra developed a riff-based style that was a forerunner of rhythm 'n' blues.

While all the other instruments during the great days of bop produced important musicians in addition to the leading representative on the respective horn, the alto saxophone (apart from Sonny Stitt) had to wait for the start of the cool era for a considerable figure to emerge.

This was Lee Konitz, who came out of the Lennie Tristano school. The abstract, glittering alto lines Konitz played around the turn of the forties on his own and Lennie Tristano's recordings later became more singable, calmer, and more concrete. Lee said that "in jazz, playing with feeling is more important than playing with emotion." In the meantime, Konitz has absorbed and incorporated into his music many of the jazz elements since then—and some of Coltrane and of avant-garde jazz—and yet he has always remained true to himself. Konitz has such a mastery of the harmonic implications on which his solos are based that his lines communicate a sense of "free" improvisation even when they are based on songs and standards. This has probably also been the basis of his constant development. In the seventies he gained special attention with a unique nonet. After that he increasingly became a sensitive specialist in high-quality unaccompanied duos as principally documented in recordings with such pianists as Harold Danko, Hal Galper, and Michel Petrucciani, and also with trombonist Albert Mangelsdorff and drummer Matt Wilson.

After Charlie Parker and Lee Konitz, the development of the alto saxophone takes place in the interplay between them. Art Pepper found his way toward a mature, Parker-influenced style of deep emotionality. Pepper, who spent more time in jails and reformatories than outside them, is an especially distressing example of the disastrous effect that heroin has had on the lives of some jazz musicians. He told about it in his autobiography, *Straight Life*, which appeared in 1979 and initiated his comeback. The book is a moving document of the depressing conditions under which so many jazz musicians have to live. He died in 1982.

Paul Desmond was a particularly successful figure of the Konitz line as altoist in the Dave Brubeck Quartet—and surely the most significant jazz talent in this well-known group: a lyricist of the alto sax and a master of lucid, brightly swinging lines. He was also the composer of "Take Five," which was the first jazz piece written in a 5/4 meter, and with which Dave Brubeck's group made it into the pop charts.

The most significant altoists of West Coast jazz were Bud Shank, Herb Geller, and Paul Horn. Shank was one of the first jazz musicians to play with one of the great masters of classical Indian music. As early as 1961 he was recording with sitar master Ravi Shankar. Herb Geller, who moved to Germany, has much of the clarity of Benny Carter, but of course it is a Carter style that is touched by what came afterward, especially by Bird.

The power of Parker's personality gains full clarity when it is realized that the Bird influence—after the ideas originating with Konitz had been digested—did not recede during the late fifties but rather increased steadily: Lou Donaldson with his strong hard-bop emotions; Sonny Criss; Charles McPherson, who stems from the Detroit hard-bop circle; Gigi Gryce and Oliver Nelson, who were also outstanding arrangers; and, finally, Frank Strozier and James Spaulding, who both mark the transition to free jazz—all of them have, in the final analysis, their roots in Charlie Parker. This is true also of the three most important musicians of this group: Jackie McLean, Cannonball Adderley, and Phil Woods. Jackie McLean played with more inflections of swinging edginess and sharpness than all the other bop-inspired alto saxophonists. His soulful playing, whose frequent sourness of pitch had a certain sarcastic humor, combined Parker's blues feeling with a freer, more uninhibited mode of expression.

Cannonball Adderley came to New York on the recommendation of blues alto saxophonist Eddie "Cleanhead" Vinson. In the Miles Davis Sextet, and in his own groups at the end of the fifties, he played solos that have become classics. His joyful, decorative lines were simultaneously earthy and cultivated. His nimble playing contributed a great deal to the injection of a strong blues feeling into hard bop. His solos maintained an almost classical balance between the refined quality of modern jazz and the strong expression of the jazz tradition. And, as we will see, it is perhaps this classicism that made Adderley one of the heroes of the neo–hard-bop "young lions" in the eighties and nineties. Cannonball was also successful playing funk with his quintet shortly before his death in 1975, and produced exquisite improvisations in soul and rock contexts as well.

No other altoist transformed the Charlie Parker heritage so consistently into contemporary jazz as Phil Woods. His full, springy, triplet-based bop rhythmic sense is without equal. Swiss critic Peter Rüedi called him (in 1972) "the most complete alto player in today's jazz." It is significant to note that this completeness was shaped by the awareness of all the way stations Woods had passed through in twenty-five years: Lennie Tristano's institution, Jimmy Raney's cool jazz, George Wallington's bop, Dizzy Gillespie's and Quincy Jones's big bands. . . . Since the end of the seventies Woods has found in Richie Cole an altoist who carries on in the realm of neobop from where the older man stops, thus underlining the continuity of the Parker heritage up to the present. Cole combines effervescent joy in playing with burning intensity.

While Bird's way of playing still dominated the scene, Ornette Coleman appeared at the Lenox Jazz School, which was under John Lewis's direction, in the summer of 1959. In the section devoted to him, the musical revolution this towering musician instigated is discussed in detail. The fact that he—like all genuine innovators—did exactly what was "in the air" is illustrated by other musicians taking similar roads at about the same time, or just after him, without being directly influenced by him. Among the alto saxophonists in this group, we should particularly mention Eric Dolphy, who died in 1964, but whose influence still affects today's scene. Dolphy (who based his playing somewhat more on functional harmonics than Coleman) came out of Chico Hamilton's and Charles Mingus's groups and made great recordings with trumpeter

Booker Little and with his own groups. With his emotionally charged intonation, the wild, free flight of his ideas, and his wide intervallic leaps, he created effects on a par with those of Ornette Coleman. The degree to which free playing was "overdue" is also demonstrated by the fact that in Great Britain Jamaican-born Joe Harriott developed—around 1960 and independently of Coleman and Dolphy—a high-quality free bop that never gained the recognition it merits.

The breakthrough created by Ornette Coleman and Eric Dolphy had an especially liberating effect on the alto players. Among the first to be affected were John Tchicai, Jimmy Lyons, and Marion Brown (who combines the virtuosity and the clarity of a man like Benny Carter with the possibilities of free jazz), followed by Byard Lancaster, Carlos Ward, and, from the AACM, Anthony Braxton, Joseph Jarman, Roscoe Mitchell, Henry Threadgill, and John Purcell, as well as Julius Hemphill and Oliver Lake, both from the Black Artist Group in St. Louis.

Brown's development is typical: from a "wild" free player when he entered the scene in the midsixties to a musician who now commands the entire stylistic range of his instrument. Altoist Tim Berne has said of Oliver Lake, member of the World Saxophone Quartet (discussed below), "He can play the outest shit and it sounds like he's playing funk. He's just so *soulful.*" Lake's music is shaped by inimitable feeling for the unity of black music—whether in the context of his avant-garde quartet or in his Jump Up band inspired by reggae melodies and African highlife rhythms. "It's all the same thing: dealing with the blues," said Lake.

Jarman and Mitchell are founding fathers of the Art Ensemble of Chicago (which is mentioned in the combo section). The contrast in their playing was particularly highlighted when, in the Art Ensemble of Chicago, they played simultaneously with and against each other: Jarman's phrasing tends more toward an "African" sound, while Mitchell has developed a minimalistic, intellectually dry approach to the alto saxophone. But the contrast is also seen in their respective musical projects: Jarman has combined his far-ranging improvisations with modern black poetry; Mitchell has also developed into an outstanding solo performer on unaccompanied alto saxophone, with a fragile, economical style of playing.

Having similarly wide stylistic range in their playing are the following non-Americans: Japanese-born Akira Sakata, Englishmen Trevor Watts and Mike Osborne, (former East) German Ernst-Ludwig Petrowsky, and South African Dudu Pukwana, with his exciting combination of Bantu music and Bird.

Anthony Braxton, also mentioned in the chapter on jazz in the seventies, has expanded the vocabulary of the alto saxophone to include spectacular sounds and textures. He has created a body of work that is so extensive that even Braxton experts have difficulty gaining a complete overview of it. Braxton is equal parts improviser and composer. In the band Circle with Chick Corea, Dave Holland, and Barry Altschul, and with his quartet, he has enormously expanded the sonic repertoire of the jazz avant-garde. His melodic lines are abrupt and jagged, even more so than those of Eric Dolphy, leading critics to accuse him of playing too "cerebrally" and of not swinging. Braxton's genial reply was that in the fifties Lee Konitz and Paul Desmond had been accused of the same thing, only to later become "an accepted part of the jazz canon."

Beginning in 1968 with the recording *For Alto*, and in countless solo concerts, Anthony Braxton brought unaccompanied alto saxophone playing to a new level. This music includes linear sound and noise studies of astonishing formal variety, with unorthodox phrasing and articulation: extreme dynamic register contrasts, vocalized passages of sound and noise, percussive slap-tongue staccatos, and frayed, darting zigzag runs. But it is perhaps even more as a composer than as an improviser that Braxton has created a new musical universe. His oeuvre is extensive and abstruse, with graphically titled pieces and abstract terminology, sometimes creating such a cryptic impression that Braxton has been accused of pseudointellectualism. In fact, Braxton's compositions are highly refined, individual attempts to "steer" improvisation, to make it more directed. His philosophy of music is stated in his extensive writings, primarily his three-volume *Tri-Axium Writings*.

Since the midnineties, Braxton has increasingly worked with a principle of musical reduction, in what he calls "Ghost Trance" music. This approach is inspired by ritual elements of Native (North) American Indian, Persian and African trance music, and Gregorian chant. Braxton says, "I maintain that music is not identical with sound. Music is what's behind the sound, the spiritual information that is transported by the sound. I insist on this point."

The degree to which Ornette Coleman shapes the contemporary alto saxophone scene also becomes apparent in the fact that his influence in the jazz of the eighties and nineties did not decline but rather increased. It's striking how many alto saxophonists—far more than other horn players—have also made a name for themselves as composers, here also clearly following on from Coleman. Besides Braxton, these include Henry Threadgill, Julius Hemphill, John Zorn, and Tim Berne. Threadgill and Hemphill reevaluated the jazz tradition from an avant-garde standpoint, while Zorn and Berne further developed Coleman's legacy in the stylistically ramified realm of postmodern jazz.

Henry Threadgill, who became known for the transparent music of the Air trio, excited attention in the eighties with his Sextet, which is in fact a septet with two drummers used by Threadgill as one voice. In the 1988 *Down Beat* poll, critics mentioned him in no fewer than eleven categories, including alto saxophonist, flutist, baritone saxophonist, big-band leader, composer, and arranger. His compressed, dramatic alto playing stresses the instrument's vocal qualities with concentrated originality. His Sextet compositions are full of morbid, somber, ironic tanginess, celebrating the diversity of the jazz tradition with raw energy, in tight, well-thought-out voicings. The use of low instruments, such as tuba and French horn, allows Threadgill to cloak his melodies in a trancelike, euphoric, mysterious layer of sound. Threadgill is an expert in the imperceptible blending of composition and improvisation. This allows him to seamlessly unite the legacy of free jazz with New Orleans dirges and funeral marches, with Ellington and Mingus. "The total vocabulary is valid, you don't throw away anything," said Threadgill. Nevertheless, "Tradition is a background of ingredients; in itself it's nothing. If you can't make something out of it, the world can do without it." The idea of double instrumentation is one Threadgill also continued into the nineties, in, for example, his band Very Very Circus, which used two guitars, two tubas, etc. His oblique, well-conceived juxtapositions of different musical styles are not nostalgic meditations on jazz history, but rather raw attacks on clichés—a powerful, sophisticated, forward-thinking celebration of the past.

John Zorn began as a radical saxophonist in noise music, producing unusual, abruptly changing sounds from an arsenal of over sixty saxophone and clarinet mouthpieces as well as various bird calls (geese, ducks, etc., used as hunting decoys). He later developed into a gripping alto player who spins astringent, thrilling stories on his saxophone in, for example, the new Jewish jazz of his quartet Masada (more on Zorn in the chapter devoted to him above).

In the seventies Julius Hemphill (d. 1995) was a kind of multimedia specialist, working with actors and dancers, with film, video, and theater. He brought the Texas saxophonists' throaty timbre into avant-garde alto playing. Hemphill was a master of blues allusion; even in his freest improvising and his abstract compositions, he retained contact with the roots of black music. His solos sound completely unforced. His contributions as "one of the most important composers in creative music" (John Zorn) have often been overlooked. He wrote works of epic length for seven woodwind instruments (*Water Music for Woodwinds*), for the Arditti String Quartet (*One Atmosphere*), and for his sextet (*Long Tongue: A Saxophone Opera*). During his time in the World Saxophone Quartet, from its founding in 1976 until 1988, he was the composer of most of the group's pieces, including the most successful ones.

Tim Berne carries on from where his mentor Hemphill stops—as a rich melodist who, with his cutting, splintered sound, has at last liberated free jazz from the necessity of endless sequences of solos, developing precise strategies of communication. Berne considers himself primarily a group organizer and composer, and is a master of larger compositional forms. With his band Bloodcount, a jazz version of a chamber ensemble, in the nineties he developed paradigmatic examples of process-oriented improvising and composing. Long arcs of tension are slowly, dramatically, and carefully developed to extreme high points.

In 1996 he severed his ties with large record labels and started his own label, Screwgun. He has had a particularly fruitful collaboration with French guitarist Marc Ducret, who is Berne's equal in musical rebelliousness and melodic freedom.

Like Berne, the alto saxophonists of the M-Base collective are rooted in the multi-stylistic jazz consciousness of the eighties and nineties. David Binney, Rudresh Mahanthappa, and, above all, Steve Coleman and Greg Osby have at their disposal an inexhaustible stylistic palette, ranging from funk, rock, and rhythm 'n' blues to world music to the abstract conceptions of the AACM. At the same time, they have developed a genuine mastery of improvisation over intricate meters and through tortuous rhythmic labyrinths.

Steve Coleman has gone particularly far in abstracting from the legacy of Charlie Parker; his recordings with the Dave Holland Quintet are especially thrilling, but even more exciting and important is his work with his own band, Five Elements. In this group, he has incorporated elements of funk and hip-hop to create highly complex rhythmic textures that translate the motoric drive of street funk into asymmetrical melodies and rhythms. Later, he increasingly brought world music influences into his angular improvisations.

Coleman believes that the knowledge of the world's great ancient cultures, the wisdom of the ancient Egyptians and Sumerians, came to America from West Africa via the Africans who were brought as slaves to Haiti, Cuba, Puerto Rico, Brazil, and North America centuries ago. His musical projects can be understood as an attempt to make contact with this wisdom, and with ancient musical traditions and esoteric information.

No alto saxophonist has engaged as intensively with the roots of African music in the black diaspora as Coleman has. With his Five Elements, he has toured in Cuba, Haiti, Senegal, Brazil, Puerto Rico, and India, and has engaged in intensive exchange with the musics of these cultures.

He constantly emphasizes that his music does not have bar lines, not even the "odd meters" so often cited by critics. For Coleman, M-Base is, rather, a "non-Western concept" that goes back to African roots and to the experiences of the people of the black diaspora. "One of the main ideas in M-Base is growth through creativity. . . . This music is unique primarily in the areas of spiritual, rhythmic, and melodic development."

Coleman has not hesitated to take radical steps in distributing his music. Since 1996 he has made a large part of his previously commercially released music available for free downloading on the Internet (www. m-base.org). "Basically, greed runs the world today and it is because of this that the concept of ownership exists. . . . The quest for money, and material acquisition in general, is a barrier to spiritual development. . . . I believe that ideas should be an area that is common to all people."

Greg Osby, who first came to the fore with Jack DeJohnette and also belongs to the M-Base circle, worked independently of Coleman in developing a similarly angular, asymmetrical way of playing—to such an extent that he is sometimes mistaken for Coleman, even though his sound is darker and warmer, and his playing permeated by love of Wayne Shorter and Japanese music. Osby is the real stylistic chameleon of M-Base music; with each project, he seems to reinvent his music. He has developed a saxophone sound that radiates a rare melodic self-assurance and solid rhythmic confidence. He makes notes work that would sound questionable played by other players.

Coming from Coleman and Osby, Indian-American saxophonist Rudresh Mahanthappa has developed his own way of playing in which he has brought the rich ornamentation of Indian *dhrupad* singing and the complex rhythms of classical Indian music to the alto saxophone. David Binney, known for the driving rhythms of his electric band Lost Tribes, has in his acoustic groups revealed a pronounced sense of drama and a tendency toward atmospheres that are reminiscent of film music.

In the realm of fusion and jazz-rock, David Sanborn, Ernie Watts, Kenny G., and Chris Hunter have attracted particular attention along-side Elton Dean and Ian Ballamy in England, Sadao Watanabe in Japan, and Candy Dulfer in the Netherlands. Sanborn is especially influential. Even in the context of beautiful, smooth melodies, his lines preserve the characteristic cry of rhythm 'n' blues. Sanborn has inimitably "saxophonized" the vocal style of Stevie Wonder (with whom he played at the start of the seventies), assimilating Stevie's characteristically impassioned mordents and appoggiaturas and transposing them to passionate playing in the alto's highest register.

Older funk and soul saxophonists, such as Maceo Parker, who first became known for his work with James Brown, also attracted great interest in the nineties. Maceo Parker is a groove master par excellence. His riffs and licks are bursting with life and rhythmic vitality, and the "Maceo sound" has a rhythmic, soulful "bounce." The Dutch saxophonist Candy Dulfer combines Maceo Parker's vitality with David Sanborn's high-note playing, and has brought her funky alto saxophone to the rock and pop groups of Prince and Dave Stewart, in addition to her work with her own groups.

Beyond all that, there still flows—even for alto saxophonists—the mainstream, no longer nourished just by the Swing style but also by bebop and Coltrane. This is represented by John Handy, Paquito D'Rivera, Arthur Blythe, Eric Kloss, Charlie Mariano (who mainly lives in Germany), and contemporary straight-ahead swingers like Bobby Watson, Donald Harrison, Kenny Garrett, and Gary Bartz. D'Rivera, who comes from the Cuban band Irakere and has lived in the United States since 1980, plays the hottest postbop alto sax, combining Cuban music and Bird with his volcanic temperament and joy in communication. Donald Harrison and Kenny Garrett are particularly representative of the many alto players who have expanded Bird's legacy in conjuction with strong Coltrane influences. In the quintet Harrison headed in the mideighties with trumpeter Terence Blanchard, he extended the harmonic basis of bop's message particularly strongly, incorporating polymodal, bitonal, African, and Indian elements. After the group disbanded, Harrison went back to his native city of New Orleans, where he developed his concept of "nouveau swing": a music in which the rhythms of Mardi Gras, reggae, and calypso meet the melodic and harmonic sophistication of modern jazz.

The alto saxophone's sound is less powerful and muscular than that of the tenor saxophone—but Kenny Garrett's flamethrowing playing almost makes you forget this. He plays with a glowing, fiery expression. His tone is biting, with a caustic intensity that seems to bore into the listener. He's found a way to transfer the power of midperiod John Coltrane to the alto saxophone with very little loss of force.

Kenny Garrett is from Detroit, the city that produced so many of the musicians of hard bop. His presence in Miles Davis's band at the end of the eighties was a guarantee of musical fire. Whenever Miles, in his late days, faltered, Garrett sprang into the breach, dramatically raising the energy with his blazing solos. Later, in his own groups, Garrett played a quicksilver, high-energy postbop. His playing is characterized by a harmonically ambitious, exciting chromaticism. One American critic has remarked that in a world going more and more off the rails, Garrett's playing fits better than the friendly, obliging lines of a Phil Woods.

In contrast, Bobby Watson, who, like Harrison, first played with Art Blakey's Jazz Messengers and later led the New Horizon Quintet, plays neo–hard bop with a smile—full of high spirits and melodic optimism. He's enlivened contemporary straight-ahead jazz with light, sunny lines full of heart. The enormously powerful Arthur Blythe outstandingly exemplifies the fact that in eighties jazz it was traditionalists rather than avant-gardists who dominated the scene. In 1990 he became a full-time member of the World Saxophone Quartet. Blythe developed Parker's legacy particularly originally, but he was also influenced by Johnny Hodges, Maceo Parker, and Ornette Coleman—an excitingly expressive musician whose aggressive phrasing (cuttingly sharp and with a penetrating vibrato) impressively brings a modern style of playing into jazz's great alto sax tradition.

A special position is held by Gary Bartz, who became known playing with Miles Davis's electric band in the seventies, and later developed into a mature master of acoustic playing. Bartz has enriched the spirituality and modality of John Coltrane with an archaic blues sound and funk rhythms, and is skilled at multilayered vocalization of the alto saxophone's sound. In the seventies, he founded the band NTU Troop. The name of the group comes from the Bantu language. NTU means unity in all things: unity in time and space, life and death, the visible and the invisible.

"I play the alto saxophone because of Charlie Parker," Bartz once said. Like him, the "young lions" (younger than Bartz by two generations) in the eighties and nineties increasingly turned to Bird and to the legacy of bop, also adding many of the subsequent developments in jazz to their eclectic playing. In the neo–hard bop of the nineties, the following altoists were important: Abraham Burton, Antonio Hart, Vincent Herring, Steve Wilson, Myron Walden, Jesse Davis, Erin Fletcher, Switzerland's George Robert (strongly influenced by Phil Woods), Italy's Rosario Giuliani and Stefano di Battista, and, in Great Britain, Soweto Kinch, who was also successful in hip-hop jazz.

Abraham Burton, Vincent Herring, and Antonio Hart have developed Parker's legacy from the perspective of Cannonball Adderley's approach to playing. The powerful playing of Burton, who came through the band of Art Taylor, combines Cannonball's rhythmic drive with the hard-core bebop language of tenor saxophonists like Benny Golson and Sonny Rollins. He loves to play over a burning rhythm section. Stefano di Battista, who comes equally from Art Pepper and John Coltrane, is what jazz musicians call a "burner": a player whose lines radiate passionate heat. Di Battista, who has lived in Paris since 1992, has roughed up the smooth, fine sound of the alto saxophone as if with sandpaper. He unleashes such sharp and expressive sounds that he blows the cliché of the lack of rhythmic intensity of European jazz almost literally to pieces. In the year 2000, the great drummer Elvin Jones came to Brussels in order to record a couple of rhythm tracks for the recording *Stefano di Battista*. Jones was so impressed that he insisted that di Battista join his Elvin Jones Jazz Machine for a worldwide tour.

Antonio Hart is distinguished by a particularly "juicy," sensuous phrasing, full of a lust for life. His playing comes out of Cannonball Adderley, but with a consciousness of globalization, expanding and energizing his neo–hard bop with influences from the music of Senegal, Morocco, the Near East, and Latin America.

Steve Wilson subscribes to the idea that jazz makes sense only if it draws on the fullness of life, and not merely from the dusty vaults of jazz's past. Even when he's playing pure straight-ahead jazz, the listener can hear elements of funk, rhythm 'n' blues, and soul. He plays with a vocal, almost cellolike tone.

Myron Walden, who came through the band of Benny Golson, has cultivated Charlie Parker's legacy in an almost compositional style of improvising. His playing is influenced particularly by tenor saxophonists and trumpeters. His intelligent lines combine Bird's singing tone with the preaching sound of John Coltrane and the moody melodies of Wayne

Shorter, but also with elements of Miles Davis, Freddie Hubbard, and Booker Little.

The continuing impact of Parker's legacy becomes ironically clear in the fact that Frank Morgan, a musician from the second generation of bebop, was astonishingly successful in the mideighties: he was a passionate stylist who kept the Bird flame burning with throaty expressiveness. He died in 2007.

Particularly conservative, in the positive sense of the word that denotes proper respect for the great legacy of jazz, is the playing of Wes Anderson. In various groups and orchestras led by Wynton Marsalis, Anderson, with his blues-inflected, sensitive approach, has assumed a role similar to that played by Johnny Hodges in the Duke Ellington Orchestra.

In European postmodern jazz of the eighties, the alto saxophonists—Wolfgang Puschnig from Austria, Dutch-born Paul van Kemenade, the American Michael Moore, who has lived in Amsterdam since 1982, the Italians Carlos Actis Dato and Roberto Ottaviano, and the Germans Frank Gratkowski, Roger Hanschel, and Jan van Klewitz—are remarkable. They have found distinctively European approaches by examining the heritage of American jazz—often at a respectful distance—while integrating other influences. Before discussing these alto saxophonists, the Pole Zbigniew Namyslowski must be acknowledged, who already in the seventies had developed his own European jazz language. His sound has a melancholy Slavic glow that he applies to standards and the jazz tradition and to his treatments of Polish folk themes with equal mastery.

Wolfgang Puschnig, a founding member of the Vienna Art Orchestra, is a true original, whose phrasing is characterized by joy in playing and intelligent wit. He has maintained an unmistakable profile despite the many styles he has touched on: from world jazz with the Korean Samul Nori percussion group to an avant-garde duo with electronicist Roland Mitterer, from the Pat Brothers' advanced jazz-rock to Air Mail's contemporary jazz. In 1988 he made wonderful duo recordings with Carla Bley, Jamaaladeen Tacuma, Bob Stewart, etc.

Michael Moore is a kind of postmodern Lee Konitz. He avoids squalls of notes, playing in a pause-laden, epigrammatic style. He's a master of poetic spareness, providing a stark contrast to the turbulent, eclectic music of the band Available Jelly and the humorous, chaotic Clusone Trio—two of the bands that he plays in.

Paul van Kemenade, winner of the Dutch Podium Prize, is a cultivated groover and moaner. He combines the ideal of free playing with the soul-inspired ideas of a David Sanborn. Carlos Actis Dato's alto saxophone playing, with its turbulent, chaotic, anarchic lines, moves in a consciously ambiguous manner between slapstick and protest.

Frank Gratkowski, who lives in Cologne, says, "Jazz is not about a particular style, jazz is about a particular attitude." He has developed a wide range of alternative blowing and embouchure techniques on the alto saxophone. With his biting, bitter tone, he has found a very open way of combining improvisation and composition, in duo with pianist Georg Gräwe or in his own quartet with drummer Gerry Hemingway. For Gratkowski, compositions are not rigid instructions, but rather flexible structures that reveal themselves and evolve in the interaction between the musicians.

Perhaps Charlie Mariano from Boston possesses the widest range of styles of all alto sax players living in Europe. That may surprise American readers since Mariano has said, "My American career came to an end when I went with Toshiko to Japan in 1962." Mariano got started in 1941, still under the influence of Johnny Hodges. He played with Charlie Parker, initially forming his style after Bird. In the midfifties he was in the Stan Kenton orchestra, and in the early sixties with Charles Mingus. Then he went to Japan with Toshiko Akiyoshi, his wife at that time. There, and in Malaysia and India, he learned and worked on Indian music. Under the influence of Coltrane and Indian wind instruments, he took up the soprano saxophone and studied the *nagaswaram*, a kind of south Indian oboe. In the early seventies, he finally returned to Europe, opening himself up to the more ambitious and musicianly forms of jazz-rock. His development hasn't stood still over the course of forty years. His rich, golden sound combines an affirmation of life with tolerance and respect. Charlie Mariano was playing world music when very few people had any idea of the concept. In his encounters with non-Western musicians, he doesn't simply use the "exotic" as a backdrop for his own thing. In his collaborations with the Karnataka College of Percussion, he has made his alto saxophone an instrument of empathy and true encounter.

Other important alto saxophonists of world jazz include Talib Kibwe, who became known through his African-influenced playing with Randy Weston, Cuba's Yosvani Terry, and, especially important, Puerto Rico's Miguel Zenón. Zenón, who grew up in a poor area of San Juan and was first heard on the recordings of David Sànchez, is one of the musicians who are redefining Latin jazz. His dry tone, not at all "African American" sounding, and his sublime melodic sensibility contradict all preconceived notions about Afro-Caribbean music. He's the first alto saxophonist to have applied the ideas of Ornette Coleman to Afro-Caribbean music, using Ornette's singing, flowing pitch, in which every note can be a blue note. But Zenón's roots in this greatly expanded melodic space do not lie in rhythm 'n' blues and folk blues, but rather in the *bomba* and *plena* rhythms of Puerto Rican music. "My music is a melting pot in which I take advantage of the infinite possibilities of combining different musical elements—jazz, Latin music, American and European classical music, Puerto Rican rhythms and melodies. My music is a self-contained unity."

The Tenor Saxophone

The best statements Negroes have made of what their soul is have been on the tenor saxophone.
—Ornette Coleman

The evolution of the tenor saxophone is the reverse of that of the clarinet. While the latter begins with a wealth of brilliant names and then seems at first to ebb into a decrescendo—albeit a wavy one—the history of the tenor sax is one imposing crescendo. At the beginning stands a single man. Today there are so many tenor saxists that it sometimes becomes difficult even for the expert to survey the subtleties that distinguish them. We have said before that the sound of modern jazz was "tenorized," which it actually was after Lester Young, until in the course of the late sixties it was "guitaricized" and later "electronicized." "The tenor saxophone is such an expressive instrument," said Michael Brecker, "that everyone sounds different on it."

The single figure at the beginning is Coleman Hawkins. Until the end of the thirties, all jazz tenor playing took its cues from him: from his dramatic melodic structures, his voluminous sonority, and his rhapsodic improvisations. A Hawkins pupil then was quite simply anyone who played tenor. The most important are Chu Berry, Arnett Cobb, Herschel Evans, Ben Webster, Al Sears, Illinois Jacquet, Buddy Tate, Don Byas, Lucky Thompson, Frank Wess, Eddie "Lockjaw" Davis, Georgie Auld, Flip Phillips, Charlie Ventura, and Benny Golson. Chu Berry came closest to the master. During the second half of the thirties, while Hawkins was in Europe, he was a much sought-after musician, the man who first came to mind when a tenor was needed. One of his most famous solos was on "Ghost of a Chance." Arnett Cobb was a member of the Lionel Hampton band in the early forties. His playing can best be characterized by the way he was advertised after quitting Hampton: "The Wildest Tenorman in the World." Herschel Evans was Lester Young's opposite in the Count Basie band. Though Lester was the greater musician, Evans played the most renowned tenor solo in the old Basie band: "Blue and Sentimental."

"Why don't you play alto, man?" Evans used to tease Lester. "You got an alto sound." And Lester would tap his forehead: "There are things going on up there, man. Some of you guys are all belly." Basie found the contrast between the styles of Young and Evans so effective that he saw to a similar contrast in most of his bands from then on. In his fifties band, for instance, these roles were taken by the "two Franks": Frank Foster representing the "modern" trend, Frank Wess the Hawkins school. Later, Lockjaw Davis took Wess's place. Davis is a typical "Harlem" tenor, with hard, striking presence. Later in his career, Foster gained fame as an arranger, and in 1986, two years after Count died, he took charge of the Basie Orchestra.

Before Herschel Evans, there was a tenor man in Count Basie's first Kansas City band whose place he took: Buddy Tate. When Evans died in 1939, Tate returned to Basie. Later he dropped into comparative obscurity, until the mainstream wave of the fifties and sixties brought him renewed attention. For many years, he led his own band in Harlem, enriching the style of the classic Harlem big bands (as played in the old Savoy Ballroom) with modern rhythm 'n' blues tendencies. Tate and Arnett Cobb are typical "Texas Tenors," whose earthy, expressive playing is rooted in the emotional roughness of Texas blues, but simultaneously has the finesse of great, swinging art. (Other important Texas tenors include Herschel Evans, Illinois Jacquet, James Clay, and David "Fathead" Newman.) Cobb, called "the wild man" due to his extroverted style, and Tate, whose big, vocal tone and melodic directness made an impression on modern tenorists, are among the few musicians of their generation who even in the late eighties were still active.

Don Byas became known primarily for his "sensuous" vibrato and ballad interpretations. By Swing-era standards, he had an extremely flexible harmonic consciousness, which he got from his idol, pianist Art Tatum. "At that time, there weren't any tenor players who were listening to pianists, so I was ahead of everyone," Byas said. He played with Basie, was one of the first Swing musicians to work with the then-young bebop people, and made his home in Holland from the late forties on. He died in 1972.

Ben Webster, who died in Europe in 1973, was two things: a musician with a throaty, harsh vibrato on fast pieces, and a master of erotic, intensely felt slow ballads. Of all the musicians of the Hawkins school, he has had the strongest influence—on many musicians of modern and postmodern jazz as well. The writer Geoff Dyer described Webster's ballad playing most insightfully:

> He had a huge sound and hearing him coax it into such softness was like seeing a farm laborer holding a newborn animal gently in his hands, or like a man who's been working construction handing flowers to the woman he loves. On "Cottontail" he's got a sound like a prizefighter's fist, but he plays a ballad like it's a creature so fragile, so cold and close to death that only the heat of your breath can bring it back to life.

In the early forties, Webster was a member of the Ellington orchestra, with which he recorded one of his most famous solos—"Cotton Tail." Al Sears took Webster's chair with Ellington in 1943. His stylistic bent is indicated by a rhythm and blues piece, "Castle Rock," that he wrote for Johnny Hodges and became a hit. Later Paul Gonsalves became Ellington's featured tenor in the Webster tradition. Gonsalves's marathon tenor displays were legendary: fast, torrid runs in flowing motion, almost free from repeated notes and honks, yet more exciting—and musically more logical—than many solos played by tenor men whose honking ecstasy was outside the realm of music. Ellington took care to always have a musician who could take the spot of the great and, in the final analysis, unreachable Ben Webster.

A stylistic phenomenon is Benny Golson: a tenorist and arranger who emerged from the Dizzy Gillespie band of the midfifties and played with all the young modern musicians at the time. Nonetheless, he is cast in the mold of the rich, mature ballad style of Byas-Webster-Hawkins. In the fifties, he became, along with Horace Silver, one of the most important composers of hard bop. He created some of the most indelible melodies of this style between soul and jazz, standards with round, full melodic arcs and vivid harmonies, which jazz musicians have used ever since as vehicles for improvisation: "Stablemates," "I'll Remember Clifford," "Whisper Not," "Along Came Betty," and, particularly popular, "Blues March."

Illinois Jacquet, finally, is perhaps the "hottest," most exciting musician of the Hawkins school. Long before the modern free-jazz tenorists, he was able to extend the range of his instrument into the extreme heights of the flageolet. Jacquet came from Lionel Hampton's band, where he played his famous solo on "Flyin' Home." He is also renowned for his triumphs with the early tours of Norman Granz's Jazz at the Philharmonic. Jacquet said, "Granz owes the worldwide success of JATP to me!"

Georgie Auld, Flip Phillips, and Charlie Ventura are the leading white tenor men of the Hawkins school—the first two via Ben Webster. For years, Flip Phillips was used as an effective crowd-pleaser with the Jazz at the Philharmonic troupe. But in Woody Herman's band in the midforties, and later also on records and in concerts, Phillips played excellently structured ballads with a polished and "reduced" Hawkins sound. Charlie Ventura became known through the medium-sized groups he led on and off from 1947 into the fifties. During the bop era he performed under the banner of "Bop for the People" and contributed much to the popularization of bop.

Bud Freeman, the tenor voice of Chicago style, who touched Lester Young in his earliest period, preceded Coleman Hawkins. Bud became the most compelling Dixieland tenor, a state of affairs that did not prevent him from studying with Lennie Tristano in the fifties.

With these musicians we have for the present exhausted the Hawkins chapter of tenor history. Lester Young became the great man of the tenor in the forties, and particularly in the fifties, but then, tension between Hawk and Prez has remained alive—to the degree that a renewed predominance of the Hawkins tradition could be detected among the tenorists of the Sonny Rollins school after the late fifties.

What fascinates tenor players about Hawkins is, first of all, his big, strong, voluminous tone. What fascinates them about Lester Young is his lyrical, sweeping lines. Simplified, the tension that underlies the history of the tenor sax is the tension between Hawkins's sonority and Lester's linearity. This tension is already present in some of the tenor players who have been mentioned as representatives of the Hawkins line—Byas, Gonsalves, Phillips, and Ventura. To these must be added a group of tenor men who, stylistically speaking, are firmly in the Lester camp but show a noticeable tendency toward the Hawkins sonority. Gene Ammons, who died in 1974, is the most important. The son of boogie-woogie pianist Albert Ammons, he was in the Billy Eckstine and Woody Herman bands of the forties and moved into the limelight through the "battles" (those popular contests between two practitioners of the same horn) he fought with Sonny Stitt (on tenor!). He has the biggest, mightiest tone outside the Hawkins school: "Big as a house, a fifteen-story apartment dwelling, and very vocal, too," said Ira Gitler, who compared his playing with the blues singing of Dinah Washington.

Otherwise, the tenorists of the Lester Young school may be grouped—in much simplified terms—in two sections: the musicians who have linked Lester's ideas to the ideas of bop, and the school of modern Lester Young classicism, in which the bop influence receded in proportion to the youth of the musicians. The most important tenorists of the "Lester Young plus bop" direction are Wardell Gray, James Moody, Budd Johnson, and Frank Foster, as well as the forerunners of Sonny Rollins whom we shall mention later.

James Moody, altoist and flutist as well as tenor man, was one of the more remarkable musical personalities of the bop era, often filled with a rollicking humor that was replaced by maturity and mellowness during the seventies. Dizzy Gillespie hired him for his quintet in 1960 and again in 1980. Moody kept his freshness and openness into the beginning of the twenty-first century, always finding new and interesting paths for playing over changes. In 2003, at the age of seventy-eight, he recorded the CD *Homage*, on which he played together with well-wishers including Chick Corea, Herbie Hancock, Joe Zawinul, Kenny Barron, Horace Silver, and Marc Copland. "A man is the way he thinks. My wife says I'm seventy-eight going on eighteen, and that's how I feel." Budd Johnson (1910–84) emerged from the most influential big bands of the bop era—Earl Hines, Boyd Raeburn, Billy Eckstine, Woody Herman, Dizzy Gillespie—and was probably the only musician to play in all these great bands. Under this influence, he repeatedly reoriented his approach to playing to contemporary trends. He belonged to the handful of musicians of his generation who dealt with the musical movements of the seventies and eighties.

Wardell Gray, who died in 1955 under mysterious circumstances (his body was found in the desert near Las Vegas), was a musician of supreme importance. He had Lester's linearity, the phrasing of bop, and his own distinctive hardness of attack and sparkling mobility, all joined in convincing stylistic unity. It is fitting that such genuine Swing musicians as Benny Goodman and Count Basie were attracted by Gray but became aware of stylistic conflict when he began to play in their combos or bands. "The Chase," that characteristically titled tenor battle recorded in 1947 by Gray and Dexter Gordon (who is of similar importance and will be discussed later), still ranks among the most exciting musical contests in the history of jazz.

It should be noted that, initially, there were only a few tenor players who could be considered bebop musicians (in a strict sense). Wardell Gray, James Moody, Sonny Rollins (in his early career), Dexter Gordon, and Allen Eager were the only ones at the time. Lester Young's stature was still too great to allow a different development. Even a man like Sonny Stitt, who was, on alto, pure bop, clearly showed the Lester Young influence when he changed to tenor saxophone. In fact, up to the middle of the fifties, Lester's—not Charlie Parker's—importance for the tenor scene continued to grow!

Wardell Gray occupies a central position between the two tenor movements of the fifties: the "Brothers" and the Charlie Parker school led by Sonny Rollins. In the former, Lester Young celebrated his real triumphs. The abundance of names belonging to this Lester Young classicism will be categorized according to the manner in which the Basie-Young tendency has made itself increasingly felt. At the beginning of our list the bop influence is noticeable—Allen Eager, Stan Getz, Herbie Steward, Zoot Sims, Al Cohn, Bob Cooper, Buddy Collette, Dave Pell, Don Menza, Jack Montrose, Richie Kamuca, Jimmy Giuffre, and Bill Perkins. A remarkably large segment of these musicians either worked with Woody Herman or were more or less connected with the California jazz scene. That is where the "Four Brothers sound" developed in 1947. "We had a band," Stan Getz said, "in the Spanish section of Los Angeles. A trumpeter named Tony de Carlo was the leader, and we had just his trumpet, four tenors, and rhythm. We had a few arrangements by Gene Roland and Jimmy Giuffre." Roland and Giuffre, in other words, created the Four Brothers sound. The four tenors in this band were Getz, Herbie Steward, Zoot Sims, and Jimmy Giuffre.

At the time, Woody Herman was about to form a new band. He happened to hear the four tenors and was so taken with the sound that he hired three of them: Sims, Steward, and Getz. In place of the fourth tenor, he put Serge Chaloff's baritone, to add warmth to the tenor combination. The new sound was made famous by a piece written for Herman in 1947 by Jimmy Giuffre. It was called "Four Brothers"—thus the name of the sound. Along with the Miles Davis Capitol sound it became the most influential ensemble sound in jazz up to Miles Davis's *Bitches Brew*, and even after that it remained effective. Its warmth and suppleness symbolized the sound ideal of cool jazz.

In the years to follow, a succession of tenorists passed through the Four Brothers sax sections of various Herman bands. The first was Al Cohn, who took Steward's place as early as 1948. Then came Gene Ammons, Giuffre, and many others, down to Bill Perkins and Richie

Kamuca. Getz, who from the start of the Brothers counted as the primus inter pares, made some combo recordings (for Prestige) in 1949 with Sims, Cohn, Allen Eager, and Brew Moore in which the Four Brothers sound was celebrated by five tenorists.

The following passage by Ira Gitler—a critic with particular affinity for the modern tenor scene—will give an impression of the fine distinctions among these tenor players:

> An excellent example of inner differences in a similar area can be found in examining the work of Zoot Sims and Al Cohn and comparing it to the playing of Bill Perkins and Richie Kamuca. In the broad sense, all would be considered modernists in the Basie-Young tradition, but Sims and Cohn, who were originally inspired by Lester Young, grew up musically in the forties when Charlie Parker was at his peak and his influence at its most powerful. Although they do not play like Parker, they have been affected somewhat stylistically and very much harmonically.
>
> Kamuca [d. 1977] and Perkins [d. 2003] (active from the fifties), who for inspiration go back to the Prez of the Basie period and also to the Brothers (Sims, Cohn, Getz), are only touched by Bird through osmosis from the Brothers, and since it is twice removed, the traces are intangible.

The Parker traces are strongest in Allen Eager, as shown by the splendid, stimulating solos he played with the Buddy Rich big band around 1945. Getz is the towering figure in this school, an improviser in the sense of truly great jazz improvising and altogether one of the outstanding white jazz musicians. He is a virtuoso who can play anything possible on the tenor sax. It is this technical element that distinguishes him from most of his Brothers colleagues and their sophistication of simplicity (which in a sympathetic way, hides the fact that these players, too, are masters of technique). Stan became known mainly through his ballad interpretations. Nonetheless, during the fifties, he had a Parker-inspired affinity for very fast tempos. Some of the most exciting recordings of his career were made in 1953 at the Storyville Club in Boston with guitarist Jimmy Raney and at a 1954 concert at the Shrine Auditorium in Los Angeles with trombonist Bob Brookmeyer.

Stan Getz developed his characteristic airy, breathy sound further than anyone else, with soft tones in the low register and high notes as light as feathers. His harmonic sense was extraordinary, but he did not play over changes in as chord-oriented a fashion as Sonny Stitt or James Moody. He was more of an "ear player." He always played the essence of the melody.

In 1961 when bossa nova, with its poetic, charming songs from Brazil, entered the United States, Getz was introduced to this music by guitarist Charlie Byrd, just returned from Brazil. Initially with Byrd, later without him, he scored a number of great hits with Brazilian music.

It has been said so many times that Getz was inspired by the bossa nova and that he "owes everything" to it, that it is necessary to point out that earlier there had been a reverse influence: from cool jazz (where Getz has his roots) to the Brazilian samba. Only from the interaction between cool jazz and samba did the bossa nova emerge. Thus, a circle was closed when Getz "borrowed back" (as he himself expressed it) Brazilian elements. This may be one of the main reasons for the fascination of his "Brazilianized," melodic cool-jazz transformations, although some creative Brazilian musicians considered these recordings falsifications or bastardizations from a rhythmic point of view. It is interesting to remember that the characteristic switch from the choralelike cantilena to intensely rhythmic passages, so typical of Brazilian music, also existed in a different form in Getz's cool improvisations from the early fifties on, long before the emergence of bossa nova.

After the midsixties, when the bossa nova wave died down, Getz combined his classicist Lester Young legacy with some harder, more expressive ingredients, originating mainly in Sonny Rollins. The expressive range of this great jazz musician became continuously even more universal and towering up until his death in 1991.

Zoot Sims is considered the most swinging of the Brothers. He was an untrammeled, vital improviser with a certain knack for emphasizing the upper ranges of his instrument, lending to his tenor an occasional alto sound. Characteristically, he played alto, too; later, under the influence of Coltrane, he also played soprano with very personal inflections. His ideas had an intensive flow. Al Cohn is the most expressive representative of this post-Young school, emphasizing melodies and legato phrasing. He mirrored the *conscious* turn toward Basie-Young classicism—not only in his playing but also as arranger and leader on many recordings. The little twists and turns he gave to his smooth Lester Young tone made his playing especially expressive. For several years Cohn and Sims co-led a two-tenor quintet that—within the confines of their similarity—gained attractiveness from their subtle dissimilarity.

Most of the remaining musicians on our list of Lester Young classicists are representatives of West Coast jazz. Jimmy Giuffre's tenor playing had something of the quality of his clarinet—a great affinity for cool, "distilled" blue notes. His is a Young classicism based on a keen knowledge of modern "classical" chamber music and a deep love of folk melodies. Buddy Collette is one of the few black musicians in West Coast jazz, but his black roots are shown more by his alto playing, veering toward Parker, than by his relatively polished tenor sound. And Don Menza, who also is an excellent big-band arranger (for Buddy Rich, for instance), is among those who carried the Four Brothers sound close to Sonny Rollins in the seventies and eighties.

There is one European who belongs in the illustrious company of these Americans: the Austrian tenorist Hans Koller. It has so often been noted that the European jazz of the fifties was imitative, slavishly copying American originals, that it is important to see that the emancipation of European jazz did not begin with free jazz. Already in the fifties there existed independent European jazz dialects. Koller's tenor playing was an example. Koller, who died in 2003, toured with Dizzy Gillespie, Lee Konitz, and Stan Getz. His soloing, a blend of equal parts robustness and abstractness, was important in pointing the way for German postwar jazz. In 1970 Koller, who in the sixties had turned to abstract painting, returned to Vienna. He is the father figure of Austrian jazz, one of the few European musicians coming from cool jazz who was also recognized by his younger colleagues as an inspiration and model.

Several musicians will not fit into either of the categories into which we have attempted to divide the Lester Young tenors. Among them are Paul Quinichette, Brew Moore, and Warne Marsh. Brew Moore belongs in Lester's immediate vicinity, without the detour via fifties tenor classicism. He said: "Anyone who doesn't play like Lester is wrong." Warne Marsh was a product of the Tristano school. Marsh was said to play "tenorized" Lee Konitz, but he did have his own fluid style, full of unpredictable long lines that oscillated freely over the underlying form without regard for four-bar divisions. This style became so up-to-date again in the seventies and early eighties that Marsh was able to attract much attention with his duet records with musicians many years his junior, such as Pete Christlieb and Lew Tabackin.

So far, it might seem as if the contest between the ideas of Hawkins and Young in the evolution of the tenor sax had ended with complete victory for Young. This picture became blurred in the course of Sonny Rollins's overwhelming influence during the second half of the fifties. Rollins the improviser became so important one tended to mention him right after Miles Davis. Nonetheless, neither Sonny himself nor his way of playing were "new" in the strictest meaning of the word. From 1946 he played with many important bop musicians: Art Blakey, Tadd Dameron, Bud Powell, Miles Davis, Fats Navarro, Thelonious Monk, and others. His style involves combining Charlie Parker lines with the voluminous sound of Coleman Hawkins—which Sonny developed into his very own, angular, edged, immensely individual sound—plus that slight Lester Young influence that hardly any tenor player since Prez can completely escape.

This combination, which appeared so novel in the second half of the fifties, was comme il faut during the bop years. Not only Sonny Rollins played that way then. Sonny Stitt, and, most of all, Dexter Gordon are musicians of this lineage, related in many respects to the previously mentioned Lester-plus-bop line (James Moody, for instance). Sonny Stitt, who was also active as an alto saxophonist, played in Dizzy Gillespie's band in 1945. His tenor improvisations are constructed, motif by motif and line by line, with such convincing logic that his solos are "like a textbook of bebop" (David Murray)—with the crucial difference that his solos came not from conservatory étude books but from the free flight of his spontaneous imagination. Gordon was *the* bop tenor man, with all the quicksilver nervousness belonging to bop. At the same time, there is a sovereign relaxedness in his sound. His laconic manner of playing slightly behind the beat—"laid back"—is legendary. In 1944, in a recording of Billy Eckstine's big band ("Blowing the Blues Away"), Gordon and Gene Ammons founded the musical practice of "battles" and "chases" of which we have spoken already in this chapter. (There's more about Gordon later in this section.)

That Sonny Rollins nevertheless achieved primary importance so suddenly was due less to his innovations than to the temperament and vitality he brings to his improvisations—in short, to his stature. Rollins is the outstanding representative of *motivic improvisation*—his solos are masterful treatments and developments of motifs taken from the theme of the piece. Thus, he can afford to treat the harmonic structures on which he improvises with an astonishing lack of constraint and great freedom, and often indicate melody lines only with widely spaced staccato notes, satirizing and ironicizing them in this manner. It is a freedom similar to that of Thelonious Monk's piano improvisations. Both Monk and Rollins were/are New Yorkers, and there's that typically quick and dry New York sense of humor in their music. "Sonny Rollins fears nothing," said the French tenorist Barney Wilen at a time when he was one of the many young musicians of the Rollins school.

This school remained alive in the eighties and nineties. Rollins, who visited India and studied yoga and Asian religions, made most of his records in the fusion vein in the seventies. This displeased the jazz purists, but they overlooked the fact that Rollins retained more bop elements in the realm of jazz-rock than any other musician. He still displayed his most important asset: his sound, and his (occasionally somewhat sarcastic) humor. His family has roots in the Caribbean. Again and again, he has composed and included in his music calypsos and Latin themes and rhythms in general. In the eighties and nineties he amazed audiences with unaccompanied solo appearances in which he blew breathtakingly long improvisations.

Before turning to John Coltrane and the musicians of his school, we have first to mention a number of tenor players who are more or less independent of both the Rollins and the Coltrane schools—even though some of them may, in the course of their careers, have received impulses particularly from John Coltrane. They are Wayne Shorter, Hank Mobley, Johnny Griffin, Yusef Lateef, Charlie Rouse, Stanley Turrentine, Booker Ervin, Teddy Edwards, Roland Kirk, and Clifford Jordan.

In that group Wayne Shorter is the player who developed most imposingly: from the hard bop of Blakey's Jazz Messengers, where he made a name for himself at the end of the fifties by way of the second Miles Davis Quintet's controlled freedom, to the multielectronic sounds of the legendary Weather Report jazz-rock combo, to the more abstract, freer playing of his acoustic quartet at the beginning of the twenty-first century. His brittle, restrained, and yet full sound mediates distance to perfection. Shorter's trademark is an abstract shimmering quartal melody directed against conventional harmonic models but nevertheless preserving the foundations of tonal playing. "Wayne was always someone who experimented *with* the form," observed Miles Davis. That's probably why Shorter's work from the sixties—especially in the celebrated second Miles Davis Quintet—made a strong impression on the tenorists of postmodern mainstream jazz. As a composer he has written more modal compositions of lasting value than any other musician, pieces whose mood-rich melodiousness and economy have fascinated and challenged musicians up to the present day: "Nefertiti," "Footprints," "Yes or No," "Masqualero," etc. Shorter plays as he composes: economically and circumspectly. There isn't a note too many. According to Miles, "Wayne tells splendid stories."

Hank Mobley was a member of Miles's quintet before Shorter, in 1961–62. He had his own sophisticated style, with a velvety tone that hangs like a veil over his long, seemingly self-perpetuating lines. Stanley Turrentine applied a "rocking soul" approach to the "jumping" lines of Ben Webster and Coleman Hawkins. His open, blues-conscious playing had no sadness or anger in it. It communicated a danceable feeling, in which body, mind, and spirit—the inner and the outer—coincide in one swinging moment: in soul. Another signature of the "Big T" was his sweeping vibrato: "It's like laughter, like he's laughing" (Geoff Keezer).

The late Booker Ervin, who first became known through his association with Mingus, was one of the most solid improvisers of the early and midsixties, with a marvelous wealth of blues-inspired and vehement swing. Johnny Griffin was one of the fastest tenor players of his generation. The flawless speed of his cascading, arpeggiated improvisations over bop harmonies gained him the reputation of an outstanding straight-ahead player with razor-sharp timing.

Charlie Rouse was closely associated with the music of Thelonious Monk as only a few saxophonists have been. His playing always had a slightly dry, hoarse quality. He translated Monk's angular melodic language to the tenor better than anyone else, and spent eleven years in the band of the mysterious pianist.

Yusef Lateef stems from the Detroit circle of modern bop musicians. As early as the fifties, he became the first jazz musician to try to incorporate elements from Arabic and oriental musics into jazz, making inspiring, exciting recordings on which he (aside from tenor) blows such instruments as diverse flutes of often non-Western origin, oboe, and bassoon (used only rarely in jazz).

And then, there is Rahsaan Roland Kirk: a blind musician who came to Chicago from Columbus, Ohio, in 1960, with three saxophones hanging around his neck, sometimes playing them all simultaneously—and, on top of that, a flute and about a dozen other instruments—blowing on a siren between choruses.

Kirk, whose death in 1977 was mourned by the entire jazz world, was one of the most vital, most communicative of the modern jazz musicians. He was like the old folk musicians who packed up their bundle and wandered through the world. And, no doubt, he was a symbol of many things that have occurred in jazz during these years: sophistication rising from roots, naïveté from a genuine childlike attitude, sensitivity from vitality. Said Kirk, "People talk about freedom, but the blues is still one of the freest things you can play."

For Kirk, jazz was "black classical music." In his compositions and improvisations he deliberately elevated this tradition into a program, not in the sense of historicizing backward looks, but quite to the contrary by incorporating it into the sounds of the seventies. A few times he played with pop and rock groups: "I just want to play. I'd like to think I could work opposite Sinatra, B. B. King, the Beatles, or a polka band, and that people would dig it." Roland Kirk based his work on so many of the great black musicians—Duke Ellington, Charles Mingus, Sidney Bechet, Fats Waller, Don Byas, John Coltrane, Clifford Brown, Lester Young, Bud Powell, Billie Holiday, et cetera—that it may be stressed: Kirk played on the black tradition as if it were an instrument long before that became a matter of course in postmodern jazz. He said, "God loves black sound."

Eddie Harris (1934–98) was an original—a unique artist who experimented as early as the sixties with electric processing of the sound of the tenor saxophone, and who also played electric piano, organ, and a hybrid instrument: a trumpet played with a reed mouthpiece like that of a saxophone or clarinet. Harris's saxophone improvisations were the epitome of swinging "funkiness" long before the term *funk* became the standard expression for hipness in seventies fusion and jazz-rock. Harris's solos combined intense bop concentration with the rhythmic drive of boogaloo, soul, and rhythm 'n' blues. His composition "Freedom Jazz Dance," which became famous after the Miles Davis Quintet recorded it in 1966, is one of the rare jazz standards to have emerged from the sixties.

A distinction of many of these musicians—certainly of Sonny Rollins and Roland Kirk—is their relationship to rhythm. They play beyond the rhythm with the same free sweep that characterizes their approach to harmony; but since on the one hand they move far away from the basic beat while on the other never losing contact with it, they develop an intense, exciting rhythmic tension in which the real stimulation of their playing resides. In this respect, too, Rollins continues Charlie Parker's heritage. "Charlie Parker's Successors Play Tenor" said the headline in a

French jazz magazine as the Rollins influence reached its peak in the late fifties.

At this peak the Rollins influence changed over into the perhaps even more engulfing John Coltrane influence. Coltrane (see the section devoted to him and Ornette Coleman) became the teacher and master of most of the tenorists up to the present day—and not only of the tenorists.

The Coltrane "students" can be classified into two groups (similar to the groupings of the players of other instruments): those within the boundaries of tonality and those outside (with all the intermediate shades that must be called expressly to mind in such a generalized classification). Among the former the Coltrane model is stronger and more immediately perceptible, whereas the latter see Coltrane's impulses as "liberation" only in general terms, bringing their own individuality into play that much more clearly.

Members of the first group are musicians as diverse as Joe Henderson, George Coleman, Charles Lloyd, Joe Farrell, Jim Pepper, Sam Rivers, Billy Harper, and others. Henderson (1937–2001) led the great bop tradition exemplarily into the jazz of the post-Coltrane era. He had the darkest, "blackest" sound on the entire bop-oriented tenor scene. And a part of his mysterious effect was that he phrased softly and with great patience. From 1964 to 1966, Henderson played in the Horace Silver band, and in the seventies he played in Herbie Hancock's electric sextet. He was a master of thematic improvisation and had incredible "time"—that is, he knew how to put the right note at exactly the right spot. Guitarist John Scofield said:

> Joe Henderson is the essence of jazz. He embodies all the elements that came together in his generation: the mastery of hard bop and the avant-garde. He can play harmonically abstractly without getting away from the roots. He can play a blues shout the way Joe Turner would sing it, and then play the fastest, craziest, most angular atonal music you've ever heard. Who, on any instrument, plays better, more interestingly, and with more bite than Joe Henderson? He's my model in jazz.

In the nineties, Henderson, who until then had been a typical "musicians' musician," enjoyed great public success, finally receiving the recognition for his mastery and maturity as an artist that he had deserved already in the sixties and seventies.

Charles Lloyd led a group in the late sixties that was one of the forerunners of the jazz-rock bands. At the high point of his fame, Lloyd retired from music, disappointed with the music business. He returned to the scene in 1983, first with French pianist Michel Petrucciani and later with his own groups. Lloyd has made Coltrane's legacy lyrical and romantic as no other tenor saxophonist has done, often in collaboration with European musicians, such as the Swedish musicians Bobo Stenson and Anders Jormin. Charles Lloyd doesn't blow the saxophone so much as he "sings" it, in a song of sweet melancholy, with the Buddha-smile of Eastern wisdom. A critic wrote, "In Lloyd's sound, the spiritual energy of Coltrane seems to have been preserved as in a tabernacle."

Jim Pepper, who died in 1992, combined Coltrane with his American Indian roots. He was not a great technician, but had soul, and his solos created moods that came from the heart. In the jazz of the sixties, his composition "Witchi-Tai-To" was a much-played standard.

Like George Coleman, Sam Rivers played with Miles Davis during the sixties and with Cecil Taylor later on. Something like a father figure to the New York avant-garde loft scene in the seventies, he bridges over to the next group of tenor players.

Archie Shepp, Pharoah Sanders, Albert Ayler, John Gilmore, Fred Anderson, Dewey Redman, Frank Wright, Joe McPhee, Charles Tyler, as well as—among the younger generation—David Murray, Chico Freeman, Charles Gayle, and David S. Ware stem from the camp of the "free tonal" (to some ears even "atonal") avant-garde jazz. Shepp, an especially devoted, "angry" free-jazz man in the beginning, has meanwhile come to infuse the traditions of Coleman Hawkins, Ben Webster, and Duke Ellington with the experiences of free playing. Shepp's tenor sound has that cry that does not shrink from showing the wounds of the soul and the scars that the vicissitudes of the musician's life have left on his playing. No other saxophonist has so deep a knowledge of the African American tenor tradition. Evan Parker has gone so far as to say that Archie Shepp is the first postmodern tenor saxophonist. Even when playing radical free jazz with Cecil Taylor in 1960, Shepp's playing was related to older styles, to Coleman Hawkins and Ben Webster, to field hollers and rhythm 'n' blues. But his solos do not merely rummage virtuosically through a file cabinet of quotations—what is moving about his playing is its simple, expressive, vocal quality.

Like so many other musicians of his time, Albert Ayler's commitments went beyond the musical. "We play peace" was his oft-reiterated motto. In the freedom of his tenor breaks, Ayler (who developed his style more or less independently of Coltrane) referred back to tradition in an especially peculiar, folk-music-like manner, incorporating march and circus music of the turn of the century, folk dances, waltzes and polkas, or the dirges—the music of the old New Orleans funeral processions. His smeared streaks of sound in the tenor's stratospheric, overblown register, and his "rapid-fire staccato multiphonic salvos" (Peter Niklas Wilson) were especially influential in free jazz. Ayler's high-energy music is not about anger or wrath—it is peaceful and spiritual, and everything in it revolves around love. Ayler, who died in 1970 at the age of thirty-four (his body was found in New York's East River after he had been missing for twenty days), was "in many ways closer to [the old sound] of Bubber

Miley and Tricky Sam Nanton than to Parker, Miles, or Rollins," said Richard Williams. "He brought back to jazz the wild, primitive feeling which deserted it in the late thirties. . . . His technique knew no boundaries, his range from the lowest honks to the most shrill high harmonies being unparalleled."

Joe McPhee plays a calmer version of Ayler, seemingly lost in contemplation. Pharoah Sanders is the tenor man bursting with musicianly and physical power whom John Coltrane engaged in 1966 as the second horn player of his group, in order to grow through his challenge. Like others among the newer tenorists, he extends the range of the tenor sax, by means of overblowing, into the highest registers. The records he made for the Impulse label at the beginning of the seventies are legendary. They radiate a joyful, almost peacemaking atmosphere; characteristically, one of his best-known pieces has the refrain: "The Creator has a master plan / Peace and happiness for every man." Sanders transferred the glowing fire of black free jazz into tonal playing with melodic directness and with the same spiritual energy that infused his playing since the sixties. Sanders continued to develop this style—featuring expressive solos and ecstatic saxophone outbursts over a hypnotic, African, oscillating harmony—into the nineties, on CDs produced by bassist Bill Laswell, showing influences of Indian and African music, ambient music, and drum 'n' bass.

Around the turn of the decade from the sixties to the seventies, Dewey Redman finally became the congenial musicial partner whom Ornette Coleman—and later also Don Cherry—had been seeking for so long. He was one of the first players to have sung into the instrument while blowing it, intensively vocalizing and emotionalizing the tenor sound. Old and New Dreams is the name of the group Redman co-led with Cherry in the seventies and eighties, and that is exactly what they presented: new dreams of an old and basically timeless black tradition.

Then came postmodern jazz, with David Murray (see the section devoted to his work) providing a decisive impulse. Murray revitalized the classic Hawkins-Webster-Rollins tenor sonority by bringing the incandescent sounds of energy playing into this tradition. Other important tenorists who have reflected and modified the legacy of free jazz within the framework of a traditional way of playing include Chico Freeman, George Adams, Bennie Wallace, John Purcell, Ned Rothenberg, and Edward Wilkerson. All of them—except for Wallace—have had strong links with Coltrane's music, but their playing was/is so individual that they have eclectically reflected and integrated a large number of other tenor styles against that background. Freeman is a particularly intensive "inside-outside" player, "inside" implying that Freeman knows his tradition and "outside" that he ventures into free sounds. Freeman's special characteristic is that he often employs both approaches simultaneously rather than alternating between them. Chico learned such inside playing from his father, Von Freeman, who is also a tenorist, and the outside aspects come from his links with the AACM, the avant-garde group from his home city, Chicago.

George Adams, who became known through Charles Mingus and Gil Evans, allowed his vital, throaty improvisations to explode with such wildness in the horn's upper register that they time and again evoked the falsetto singing of gospel and blues, with the same intensity and ecstasy of expression. In fast pieces he built on Coltrane and Albert Ayler's overblown glissando style; in slow pieces he followed Ben Webster's velvety ballad sound. He said, "Sometimes even I think I'm not blowing a horn—I feel like I'm singing."

Tennessee-born Bennie Wallace was one of the few tenorists in the eighties and nineties who developed an individual style independently of the overpowering Coltrane influence. Wallace comes from Rollins, whose vehement and sardonic sound he has transformed with rhapsodic élan into an original musical language. Wallace blows what seem to be strange lines full of bizarre intervallic leaps, moving in a flash from the highest flageolet register right down to the depths and back again, incorporating influences from Don Byas, Eddie "Lockjaw" Davis, and the hoarse sounds of rhythm and blues tenorists into his humor-filled "zigzag" playing.

The free tenor style found particularly fertile soil in Europe. Some of these tenorists play in a style totally their own. Willem Breuker from Holland, already mentioned as a bass clarinetist, exerted a liberating influence—with his burlesque humor and clownlike music theater—in the midseventies, when European free jazz was marked by unspoken dogmas and exaggerated seriousness. He satirizes and defamiliarizes nineteenth-century popular music—polkas, operettas, waltzes, marches, tangos—and his parodies sometimes also become joyfully ironical attacks on the world of the avant-garde. He has been called the "Kurt Weill of jazz."

Germany's Peter Brötzmann blows his tenor clusters with an intensity usually only found among black musicians, yet in a way that is entirely his own. Brötzmann's playing reminded Don Cherry of a machine gun, and in fact one of Brötzmann's most influential recordings, which Steve Lake called "the first jazz album that can be called European," is titled *Machine Gun* (recorded 1968).

Brötzmann's frenetic, overblown playing, extremely loud and full of artillery-like attacks, has often been associated by critics with the first phase of European free jazz, the so-called *kaputtspielphase* (roughly translated, playing to pieces)—the radical first phase of free music, in which the aim was to destroy, and thereby overcome, obsolete models of playing. In the course of this process of liberation, however, Brötzmann constructed a saxophonic vocabulary that made him one of the most convincing storytellers of European free jazz. He is one of the wildest, most communicative improvisers of free jazz—a high-energy power player, but equally a master of fractured, stumbling ballads, a facet of his playing that is often overlooked.

Evan Parker from England has perhaps gone further than any other European tenorists in exploring overblown sounds. He has genuinely created a new style: abstract and minimalist, fluently melodizing the falsetto without any recognizable influence from John Coltrane and Ornette Coleman. Through virtuosic manipulation of noise-rich multiphonics and overtones, he succeeds in playing two or three phrases simultaneously. For Parker, free jazz is not a historical phase, but a living process, and this attitude is made clear by the fact that he has constantly continued to develop his playing by, for example, collaborating with live electronics players and computer/laptop players such as Lawrence Casserley and Walter Prati.

Evan Parker and Peter Brötzmann have had an influence not just in Europe but also on the younger American free scene. A clear example of this can be heard in the playing of the Chicago tenor saxophonist Ken Vandermark, who in 1999 was awarded a $265,000 grant from the MacArthur Foundation (popularly known as the genius grant). This prize had previously been awarded to musicians including Max Roach, Ornette Coleman, Cecil Taylor, and Anthony Braxton. Vandermark has adapted the free-jazz languages developed in Europe to experimental, post-AACM American jazz. His background includes rock and funk as well as jazz, and his solos are structured by rapid sequences of tension and release. In contrast to the exploratory playing of the first free-jazz generation, he has an affinity for rapid changes and surprising turns in his sonic textures.

Among the European tenorists in the realm of post–free jazz who sovereignly structured and molded the freedom gained, Anatoly Vapirov and Vladimir Chekasin from the former Soviet Union, France's André Jaume and Sylvain Kassap, Swiss-born Hans Koch and Daniel Schnyder, the Dutch musicians Tobias Delius and Peter van Bergen, and Germany's Alfred Harth, Mathias Schubert, and Gebhard Ullmann are remarkable.

Vapirov, who now lives in Bulgaria, transposes the gentle, soft saxophone sound of European concert music into free jazz, showing particular interest in the music of the Second Viennese School. Kassap is an exciting mixer of styles absolutely in accordance with the principles of postmodern jazz. Folklore, minimal music, free jazz, rock, and advanced European concert music make contact here in a kind of simultaneity of the disparate. Tobias Delius's playing is distinguished by great finesse and conspicuous brio. His freely tonal soloing darts through the great black tenor tradition, from the melodic density of Archie Shepp to the erotic whisperings of Ben Webster to the muscular proto-bop of Don Byas. At the beginning of the eighties, Alfred Harth imbued the somber visions and splintered sound collages of no wave with an unusual poetry and tonal warmth—without depriving the music of any of its charged protest and exciting provocations. Schubert is equally at home in straight-ahead and free settings, combining an intuitive force with a wild energy of attraction, as though his tenor was carried back and forth on waves of widely shifting feelings and emotions. Berliner Gebhard Ullmann cultivates a lively, freely tonal playing style with unusual forms, rooted deeply in the jazz tradition. In the nineties, he made the closest working contact of all German tenorists with players from the New York scene such as Ellery Eskelin, Tony Malaby, George Schuller, et cetera.

The number of good European tenorists, who have in their own way carried forward the Coltrane legacy, has by now become so great that we can only mention the most important here: Alan Skidmore, Andy Sheppard, and Julian Argüelles from England; Poland's Tomasz Szukalski, Leszek Zadlo, and Adam Pieronczyk; Swedish-born Lennart Aberg and Bernt Rosengren; Juhani Aaltonen from Finland; Frenchman François Jeanneau; and Germany's Heinz Sauer, Gerd Dudek, Johannes Barthelmes, and Christof Lauer. Skidmore, who became known with the European Jazz Quintet and the SOS trio, reflects the modality of middle-period Coltrane in his passionate linear playing. He was one of the first European jazz musicians to make contact with the South African jazz scene after the end of apartheid (and of the UN cultural boycott). With the Cape Town percussion group Amampondo, and later with Ubizo, he created a vital musical bridge between European jazz and Xhosa music. Sheppard, two generations younger, is an arch-melodist, playing the tenor softly and tenderly, almost like a caress, with a feeling for round, soft melodies. His playing is much admired by Carla Bley and Steve Swallow. Szukalski adds Polish folk music's dancelike element to Coltrane's language. Zadlo and Pieronczyk are emotionally enormously powerful stylists whose playing is deeply founded in the great black tenor tradition. In the realm of world music, Aberg has distinguished himself—in recordings with the Rena Rama and Oriental Wind groups—with succinct and sensitive arches of melody. Dudek fosters Coltrane's power within a sensitive, withdrawn style.

The "Europeanization" of Coltrane's legacy has been carried particularly far by Christof Lauer. Coming up through Albert Mangelsdorff's quintet, he has developed, in duo with pianist Jens Thomas and above all in his own groups, a risk-taking approach to playing that shows an understanding of the value of the roots of jazz. His stirring, intense playing is communicative and full of ideas. Lauer's predecessor in the Mangelsdorff quintet was Heinz Sauer, who has a throaty, compressed style in which the rough elements of the black tradition of tenor playing—Shepp/Sanders—are fused with a European melodic sensibility in a very personal manner.

Let's move on to the musicians influenced by rock and fusion. They include Wayne Shorter, Argentinian Gato Barbieri, Tom Scott, Wilton Felder, Ernie Watts, and Mike Brecker, and in the younger generation Bill Evans (not related to the pianist of the same name), Bob Berg, Gary Thomas, and Johannes Enders. The best known is Wayne Shorter, whose roots are in both Sonny Rollins and Coltrane. Shorter's outstanding tenure in the jazz-rock group Weather Report is discussed in the chapter on the soprano saxophone. After that group disbanded, he led his own fusion bands, in which he proved to be a composer of intricate compositions featuring complex contrapuntal figures, in stark contrast to the spare pieces of his modal period. The release of his 2002 recording *Footprints Live!* met with phenomenal success. This was not only Shorter's first live recording under his own name, but also a triumphant return to acoustic playing—his last previous recording with his own acoustic group had been the 1967 album *Schizophrenia*. Courtney Pine has said: "I'd send Wayne Shorter's music into space on the *Voyager* probe, as the representative of Earth's saxophone playing. For me, he has the greatest sound on the saxophone."

Nevertheless, Mike Brecker exerted even greater influence on tenor playing in jazz-rock than Shorter has, with his lightning lines shooting up to the flageolet register. Parallel to that he linked acoustic and electric playing to become a fiery, harmonically flexible postbop stylist, infusing the Coltrane legacy with the motor élan and impact of rock-oriented styles. Brecker thus called his music "electric bebop." In fact he was one of the few tenorists in the tonal sphere whose development of the Coltrane tradition was so original that they formed an unmistakably individual style of their own. That's why Brecker's sound—crystal clear, metallically cutting, and yet full of radiant power dynamically rising and falling—has become a determining color in postmodern jazz's tenor playing. George Duke has said: "Of all the sax players I've worked with, even back in the days of fusion, with Billy Cobham and those guys, Michael was always the melodic genius. He would string things together and play notes that nobody else would think about."

In the fusion music of the American West Coast, Ernie Watts was a top-shelf studio musician in the seventies. In the eighties, he played sophisticated straight-ahead jazz full of feeling in Charlie Haden's group Quartet West. His ornamented, highly decorative style has a patina of dreamlike enchantment and romanticism, yet is strongly rooted in the Coltrane legacy. Gary Thomas, one of the most creative saxophonists of the nineties, has expanded M-Base language with his dark, powerful tenor sound and his angular, adventurous playing. His attempts to combine rap with ambitious jazz playing were less successful. With his hard-bop tenor sound, coming from Coltrane, Shorter, and Henderson, Johann Enders has brought great warmth and a "third dimension" to electronic projects using samplers, computers, and DJs, for example in the band Tied, Tickled & Toe, and his own group Enders Room.

In the nineties, Michael Brecker was the most influential white tenorist. The extent of Brecker's impact on the tenor scene of that time is also shown by the fact that his influence is even increasing the more tenorists turn away from jazz-rock and take up neobop. Among the many tenorists inspired by Brecker, ensuring by way of the "Brecker bridge" that the Coltrane legacy stays alive, the most important are Bob Mintzer, Bob Malach, Larry Schneider, Bob Berg, Tony Dagradi, Rick Margitza, British-born Tommy Smith (who played with vibraphonist Gary Burton), Norwegian Bendik Hofseth (who made his name with the Steps Ahead group), Frenchman Sylvain Beuf, Tony Lakatos from Hungary, German Peter Weniger, and, especially influential, Chris Potter. Bob Mintzer and Bob Malach are studio musicians (and also important as big-band leaders and arrangers) who can cope with all technical and stylistic demands, in their own way processing Brecker's vocabulary in both jazz-rock and the progressive mainstream. One critic wrote, "Many jazz musicians play like they're driving in Manhattan with a street map. There are many paths that you can choose along the grid to get from A to B, but . . . once you've been on Fifth Avenue a few times, you recognize it if it comes up again. Chris Potter plays like he's walking in the woods with a compass. Every step is someplace new and fresh and unpredictable." Potter, who came up through trumpeter Red Rodney's band, has played solos of lasting value in the Dave Holland Quintet. His vocal style is the expression of an unrestrained, stormy imagination that lets him reflect an enormous variety of influences in his improvising: Lester Young, Miles Davis, Stravinsky, Mozart, Bach, the Beatles, Stevie Wonder, Joni Mitchell, the Meters, Indian rhythms, etc. His playing always has an air of risk and danger about it. He says, "The moments of greatest beauty and originality always seem to happen when there's no plan."

The other white tenorist who, alongside Brecker and Joe Lovano (discussed below), exerted particular influence in the seventies and eighties is Jan Garbarek from Norway. Don Cherry was the first to inspire Garbarek to integrate Scandinavian folk influences into his music. "Don changed my relationship to folk music, radically and in a way that determined my path." Garbarek dramatically cooled, elegized, and aestheticized the ardent "cry" of free-jazz tenorists—above all the late Coltrane, but also Albert Ayler and Archie Shepp. His playing, rich in pauses, expresses both sorrow and joy. Garbarek's tenor saxophone cries but doesn't lament. His lines open up areas of absolutely magical expansiveness—dream images interweaving elements of Scandinavian folk, free jazz, and Asian music rituals to create enraptured beauty. Garbarek is basically the only tonally playing European tenor saxophonist who has also influenced the American scene, which is all the more remarkable since his work has moved astonishingly far from the African American roots of jazz, stressing instead the sources of European music, especially of Scandinavian folk music.

At the height of Brecker's influence, a new element entered the equation: Brecker's metallic, hard, brilliant-edged sound found a direct counterpart in the playing of Joe Lovano. Lovano has brought warmth and an almost operatic, singing bel canto sound to post-Coltrane playing.

Most saxophonists coming from Coltrane play with a penetrating, metallic sound. Lovano, in contrast, has a warm, woody sound full of dynamic contrast between loud and soft, as though he caresses each note individually. Harmonically, he is very flexible and has a humorous way of playing at odds with the chords. In 1976 Lovano played in the big band of Woody Herman, and in 1980 he was in the Mel Lewis Orchestra. Like Brecker, he is an emphatically rhythmic improviser—he played drums for years before taking up the tenor. Great jazz drummers have sensed this intuitively, and have recruited him for their bands: Mel Lewis, Paul Motian, Elvin Jones, Peter Erskine.

Many of the tenor players of the nineties and later have incorporated elements of Lovano's playing: Seamus Blake, Mark Turner, Ravi Coltrane, even Chris Potter, as well as Joshua Redman (discussed below), and many other straight-ahead players, have all been touched by Lovano's warm, "human" sound.

Proceeding to neobop, we must first retrospectively discuss a senior figure in jazz whose name has already been mentioned several times in this section: Dexter Gordon, who died in 1990. Dexter, a musician whose wealth of ideas seemed inexhaustible, belongs to the generation of great bebop musicians. John Coltrane talked of Dexter as having been one of the few players who influenced him. Gordon in turn later took over elements of Coltrane's style. Like so many American jazz musicians, Dexter Gordon, disappointed by the U.S. scene, went to Europe at the start of the sixties and lived first in Paris and then in Copenhagen. For years he was one of the central figures on the European jazz scene. In 1976—as previously mentioned in another context—he returned to New York for a short engagement and thereby became *the* catalyst for bebop's comeback. Ten years later he played the main part in Bertrand Tavernier's film *'Round Midnight*, which uses elements from the lives of Bud Powell and Lester Young in a fictitious story set in fifties jazz clubs. Gordon's performance, as both actor and musician, made a considerable contribution toward *'Round Midnight*, being the first feature film to present a sensitive and undistorted picture of jazz musicians' lives and problems at that time. In the eighties, too, Dexter exerted a lasting influence on the tenor scene. His majestic sound and way of phrasing slightly behind the beat transmit mounting excitement to the highest degree.

But good old Swing also came back in the seventies, and after everything that has been written above, it's not surprising that the standard-bearer of the young Swing generation should be a tenor man: Scott Hamilton, already discussed in the chapter on jazz in the seventies. In the nineties, his fellow tenorist Howard Alden brought a personal version of Paul Gonsalves's full sound into his exciting neoswing.

Bop-oriented music has been played by so many musicians since the midseventies that here too we can only mention the most important:

Ricky Ford, Carter Jefferson, Bob Berg, Billy Pierce, Ralph Moore, Ralph Bowen, and Todd Williams belong to the first generation of neobop. Characteristically, most of them underwent a development that got under way in the second half of the seventies with the bebop revival, and then extended in the course of the eighties to the rich stream of neoclassicism into which there flowed, alongside bop as the chief component, many other influences (for the most part more modern): modal jazz, Coltrane, Shorter, and sometimes even elements from early free jazz and even the prebop era.

Ricky Ford, who became known through playing with Charles Mingus, is, among neobop tenor players, basically the only one who has been able to completely escape the overwhelming influence of Coltrane, pursuing instead the Rollins line with a love for Dexter Gordon.

Inspired by the success of Wynton Marsalis, since the mideighties a large number of tenor players have appeared on the scene who have carried on an intensive dialogue with the jazz tradition and the great heritage of the tenor saxophone, all from the vantage point of postbop. The most technically gifted, and most intelligent, player of this school is Branford Marsalis. From 1982 to 1985 he was a key member of Wynton Marsalis's quintet, and later made important recordings with his own groups, especially his risk-taking trio with Jeff "Tain" Watts. Branford's band Buckshot LeFonque, a meeting of jazz musicians, rappers, scratchers, and DJs, made creative contributions to hip-hop jazz.

Branford Marsalis achieves originality by reflecting past tenor styles in a personal manner. Earlier jazz tenor players were specialists—they cultivated individual styles. In contrast, Branford Marsalis, and the tenorists who came after him, have revitalized straight-ahead jazz with an explosive, eclectic stylistic diversity. Branford has a stupendous knowledge of the tenor tradition, and in his solos he distills the best of the tenor styles of the past—Sonny Rollins, John Coltrane, Buddy Tate, Joe Henderson, but also elements of Miles Davis and Louis Armstrong, forming focused, personal lines full of variety. "Young people should know early jazz. The more you learn, the more resources you have," says Branford.

Besides Branford Marsalis, the most important tenor player of the new acoustic jazz has been Joshua Redman (the son of saxophonist Dewey Redman). Originally, the younger Redman didn't want to become a jazz musician at all: he embarked on legal studies. More or less accidentally, the self-taught saxophonist went to New York, where, in 1991, he won the Thelonious Monk saxophone competition. Before long, his straight-ahead jazz records were selling like rock records. No one in jazz since Wynton Marsalis has excited more media interest and commercial success than Redman—all while playing uncompromising, acoustic, bop-influenced straight-ahead jazz.

Redman is strongly influenced by alto saxophonists, including Charlie Parker, Cannonball Adderley, and Ornette Coleman. He plays with enthusiasm and a striking zest for life, and is a master of emotional, soulful lines. "One thing I've learned about myself is that I'm eclectic, as a person and as a musician. I know that I'll never feel satisfied as a specialist in one type of music, or a representative of one style. There can't be a contradiction between being eclectic and being focused."

On the one hand, Branford Marsalis complained about the young tenor players of the nineties: "They all want to play like speed demons." In fact, the increasing availability of jazz educational programs and clinics has given these tenor players a technical ability that is the equal of, and in many cases even superior to, that of the great masters of jazz. The problem of this generation is not technique. Their problem is what to do with all that technique. In the nineties, many of the "young lions" seemed to lose sight of who they were amid all their virtuosic possibilities. Or, as David Murray put it, "They don't know what to play in order for their real soul to come out."

On the other hand, in no other area have so many players demonstrated the incredibly great potential for individuality in the sound of the tenor saxophone as in the new, swinging postbop. The "young lions" tenor players have sharpened the consciousness of, and raised the bar for, standards in jazz.

This internal contradiction, this "on the one hand / on the other hand," accompanied the development of the tenor saxophone in the nineties, and it is part of the "young lions" phenomenon that they were never quite able to completely resolve this contradiction.

Nonetheless, there are outstanding tenor improvisers who are making their mark in postmodern mainstream jazz. Bop-oriented straight-ahead jazz led to the emergence of many creative tenorists, who in many cases also later explored other stylistic directions. In addition to Branford Marsalis and Joshua Redman, these include, among black musicians, Don Braden, Mark Turner, Javon Jackson, Brice Winston, Ravi Coltrane (the son of John Coltrane), Gregory Tardy, Jimmy Greene, Victor Goins, Craig Handy, Tim Warfield, Marcus Strickland, and the English players Courtney Pine and Denys Baptiste, and, among white musicians, Ted Nash, Seamus Blake, Eric Alexander, John Ellis, Tim Ries, and Walt Weiskopf. This generation of tenor players grew up with pop and rock, funk and soul, and usually did not undergo jazz training until later. This wide spectrum of influences is reflected in their improvisations, even when they play "pure" straight-ahead jazz.

Don Braden replaced Branford Marsalis when Branford left Wynton Marsalis's quintet. Mark Turner is a tenor saxophonist who has a soft tone and a sharp mind. He incorporates the abstract playing of Warne Marsh into the Coltrane-Rollins lineage—a highly harmony-conscious player who doesn't simply follow the movement of the changes, but superimposes countermelodies on them that create great tension.

Marcus Strickland, who became known playing with Roy Haynes, combines energy with excitement, phrasing with an unbridled, adventurous force. Walt Weiskopf plays something like a melancholy Coltrane. Seamus Blake, who came up through Victor Lewis's group, comes more from Wayne Shorter, modernizing and developing Shorter's economical, legato approach, using pauses and fermatas as points of rest on the journey forward. Victor Lewis said that what separates Blake from all the "whiz kids" is that his "whiz"—his technical ability—ends with "dom." And, in fact, "wisdom" is not a foreign concept to these tenorists.

Courtney Pine, the black tenorist from England and the son of a Jamaican immigrant, is a phenomenon: a player who so effusively and energetically emotionalizes the Coltrane legacy that his lines explode climactically—from passion rather than calculation—into sounds reminiscent of such free-jazz tenorists as Albert Ayler and Archie Shepp. He unites humor with a profound feeling for the melodies and rhythms of Caribbean music. In 1987 his debut album reached the Top 40. In the nineties, he was responsible for some of the most successful attempts to fuse jazz with hip-hop, rap, and soul.

"Courtney Pine and his colleagues seem to have created a black British jazz scene out of nothing," marveled drummer Art Blakey at the end of the eighties. The kernel of this scene, formed by British musicians of Caribbean origin, was the Jazz Warriors big band founded by Courtney Pine. The most important black British jazz musicians of the eighties and nineties came from this band (just as the Loose Tubes, the white counterpart of the Jazz Warriors, produced the most important white British jazz musicians). Other notable representatives of the black British tenor scene include Denys Baptiste, who has transposed Sonny Rollins's freedom-loving rhythms and sardonic melodies into a highly fluid style of playing, and Steve Williamson, who has proved particularly adept at the odd meters and asymmetrical rhythms of M-Base music.

Before turning to the saxophonists of New York's downtown scene, a tenor saxophonist must be mentioned who in the nineties showed the greatest knowledge of the jazz tradition: James Carter, from Detroit. His technically adept playing has impressive force and dizzying scope. Carter has a comprehensive understanding and complete incorporation of the tenor saxophone's entire legacy, which he expresses with his own voice. The rigid battle lines between traditionalists and avant-gardists that were drawn in New York jazz in the nineties appear simply not to exist for Carter. He's the only tenorist who is equally recognized by the enemy camps around Wynton Marsalis and Lester Bowie, and who has worked with both of them. With his massive, glorious tenor sound, he is a particularly vocal, physical player, a subversive spirit and a stylistic juggler, who can move in one solo, or even one phrase, between Roland Kirk, Arnett Cobb, Albert Ayler, Eddie "Lockjaw" Davis, and Don Byas, while always keeping, in an unusual balance of aggressiveness and subtlety, his own unmistakable sound: harsh, romantic, expressive, sophisticated.

The originality of Carter's outspoken tenor playing lies in its candid, encyclopedic handling of the jazz tradition. It's as if Carter is having a conversation with the history of jazz, as if that history were an equal partner who can be revered but also, at times, challenged. Thus, in James Carter's tenor playing a love for the great jazz tradition exists alongside attacks and aggressive outbursts, dense flurries, and a unique, hysterical sense of humor.

"The young lions?" asked tenorist Roy Nathanson. "They should put 'em in the zoo, wait until they get old enough, then farm 'em out." In the nineties, Nathanson was one of the most colorful tenor players of New York's downtown scene. In his group Jazz Passengers, he thoroughly investigated turbulent playing with stylistic clichés. Other important tenor players of New York's downtown scene include Michael Blake, Peter Apfelbaum, Chris Speed, Ellery Eskelin, and Tony Malaby. With the Lounge Lizards, Michael Blake played spiky "punk jazz," but in contrast to this, his melodic playing radiates a calming sense of economy. Eskelin is one of the most underrated tenor players in New York. He's a master of virtuosic free playing over fixed forms. Peter Apfelbaum plays something like a "tenorized" version of Don Cherry. With his Hieroglyphics Ensemble, he has combined elements of jazz, Afrobeat, highlife, juju music, soul, reggae, and township jazz in a particularly melodic manner.

Apfelbaum's playing points toward a group of tenor players who are important in world jazz. These include the Hungarian Mihaly Dresch, the Israeli Gilad Atzmon, the Lebanese Toufic Farroukh, the South African McCoy Mrubata, the German Norbert Stein, and the Puerto Rican David Sànchez.

Dresch combines elements of the black tenor saxophone tradition, above all Archie Shepp, with Hungarian folk music. "Archie Shepp often plays melodies superimposed on rhythm; this is what makes his performance so spacious. Our folk musicians also often play with tempo in parlando fashion, less strict and somewhat rubato-like: this suited me well." Toufic Farroukh, who lives in Paris, represents a style in which Eastern Taquisi melodies, jazz, and electronic club beats form a new, suggestive fusion.

Influenced by the Lyon musicians' initiative ARFI, Norbert Stein has developed his own raw variant of "imaginary folklore." He developed his "patamusic," as he calls it, using the concept of "pataphysics" developed by the Frenchman Alfred Jarry in 1898—a "science of irreal logic," detached from standard causal thinking. In his various formations, from the Patahorns to the Pataorchestras, and in collaboration with Moroccan, Brazilian, and Indonesian musicians, Stein's postmodern playing with these widely differing stylistic elements demonstrates what his Patamusic is about: "Everything is changeable, mutable, reversible, and exchangeable: things, times, and spaces. But nothing is arbitrary—this simplicity is itself a multiplicity that's woven with itself and penetrates itself."

David Sànchez plays tenor as if the clave rhythm lives in his horn. One hesitates to call his music "Latin jazz," because in it the great black tenor tradition—Rollins, Coltrane, Shorter—meets the bomba and danza rhythms of Puerto Rico in such a convincing, style-bridging fashion. Sànchez, who grew up in San Juan, came to New York at the beginning of the nineties, where he found success with his reinvented Latin straight-ahead jazz. His saxophone playing has the rhythmic inevitability of a percussion instrument. He says, "When rhythms reach a certain intensity, it's like you're talking to someone."

The timelessness of the great black tradition nowhere becomes so convincingly apparent as on the tenor saxophone, also represented by older musicians who preceded the "young lions," like Dave Liebman, Sal Nistico, Pete Christlieb, Odean Pope, John Stubblefield, Jerry Bergonzi, Billy Drewes, Lew Tabackin, and many others who have already been mentioned (including the tenorists in the first Coltrane group and classicism). Tabackin, by the way, offers an interesting contemporary reflection of Sonny Rollins, whereas in the music made by most of the others John Coltrane remains vital in an endless variety of ways. Together with most neobop tenor players and adherents of the Brecker style, this group of musicians represents a Coltrane classicism, which got under way in the seventies and has intensified since the eighties. For over four decades, tenorists have lived off the legacy of John Coltrane's music, which nevertheless time and again offers astonishing and hitherto unsuspected openings for individuality.

No instrument suits jazz's tendency toward individualization of sound as well as the tenor saxophone. Its variety of timbres makes it the quintessential jazz instrument. Its possibilities of dialogue and reflection seem to be unlimited, so much so that Wynton Marsalis has said, "The saxophone is a thinking man's instrument."

The Baritone Saxophone

Baritone saxophonist Hamiet Bluiett: "Duke [Ellington] had two bands—he had his band and he had Harry Carney. . . . Harry's sound was as large as a big band." For decades, Harry Carney represented the baritone saxophone more monopolistically than any other jazz musician ever represented any other instrument. In 1926 Duke Ellington received permission from the Carney family to keep sixteen-year-old Harry in the band, and from that point until Duke died in 1974, Carney remained with Ellington. Five months later, Carney, who was almost synonymous with the history and the sound of the Ellington orchestra, died too. Carney was to the baritone what Coleman Hawkins was to the tenor—of equal power, volume, and expressivity. He played his instrument with all the dark force and roughness it embodies. "No baritone player should be scared of the noise his horn can make. Carney isn't scared," said Pepper Adams, a baritonist of the generation that in the late fifties took up the Carney tradition again. Until the midforties, Carney ruled royally over the baritone scene. Aside from him there was only Ernie Caceres, who managed to play Dixieland on the cumbersome horn, and Jack Washington, who provided a similarly professional and powerful foundation for Basie's sax section as did Carney for the Ellington band—without, of course, Carney's brilliance and stature. The role of the baritone seemed to have been fixed: its massive, hearty sound was usually used to "anchor" a big band.

Then came bop. And paradoxical as it might seem to play the nervous, mobile phrases of bop on the big horn, suddenly there was a whole row of baritonists. Serge Chaloff, who came from a Russian-Jewish family, was first. He applied to the baritone all the new things played by Charlie Parker—as Buddy DeFranco did on the clarinet and J. J. Johnson on the trombone. Chaloff is among the musicians who played big-band bop with Woody Herman's important 1947 band. Ten years later—when the original Brothers section was reconstructed for a recording date—he had to be taken to the studio in a wheelchair. A few months later, he was dead of cancer.

Leo Parker played a mixture of rhythm and blues and bebop. His big, heavy sound and fluent technique brought a gutsy blues feeling to the complex harmonies of bebop. In 1946, he played in the small group and big band of Dizzy Gillespie, and in 1947 he recorded with J. J. Johnson, establishing him as the most virtuosic representative of a modern direction of baritone playing rooted firmly in black dance music. (Until the advent of the electric bass, in rhythm and blues the baritone saxophone was usually used to reinforce the bass lines.)

The restless expressiveness of Serge Chaloff's and Leo Parker's baritone playing was smoothed out into cool sobriety by Gerry Mulligan. Mulligan (who died in 1996) began quite à la Chaloff in the combos of Kai Winding and Chubby Jackson toward the end of the forties. He worked in the big bands of Claude Thornhill and Elliot Lawrence and was one of the important participants in the Miles Davis Capitol sessions, also as an arranger. From 1951 on, he became the increasingly influential baritone voice of Basie-Young classicism. Given a choice between a chord or a melodic line, Mulligan always chose the melody. His playing was characterized by soft volume, careful control of tone colors, and a mild but energetic approach to swing. Mulligan is of great importance as baritone saxophonist, arranger, band leader, but most of all as a catalytic personality of cool jazz. Few musicians of modern jazz were so firmly rooted in the "mainstream" of the Swing era. His "meetings" on record (Verve) with such Swing musicians as Harry Edison, Ben Webster, and Johnny Hodges are impressive proofs of this. The famous pianoless quartet that first made the name Mulligan popularly known in the early fifties and will be discussed in our combo section was organized on the West Coast. Though he himself didn't want to be called a West Coast man, he had lasting influence there. From the end of the sixties, Mulligan repeatedly took the place of altoist Paul Desmond in the Dave Brubeck Quartet for different lengths of time.

The true baritone sound of West Coast jazz came from Bob Gordon, who—fatally injured in an automobile accident in 1955—was an improviser of sweeping vitality. He, too, was a musician of Basie-Young classicism. The records he made with tenorist-arranger Jack Montrose are among the most memorable combo recordings in West Coast jazz.

Independently of Mulligan and Gordon, Sweden's Lars Gullin found his own delicate approach to playing. After Django Reinhardt and Stan Hasselgard, Gullin was the third European jazz musician to have a lasting influence on American players. In 1959 he toured with Chet Baker in Italy, and played with Lee Konitz and Stan Getz. Lars Gullin transcends the heaviness of the baritone saxophone with a legato of unsurpassed fluidity, and was also one of the first European jazz musicians to reflect his own cultural roots in his music. His elegant, relaxed solos contain audible elements of Scandinavian folk music and nineteenth-century Swedish concert music.

Influenced more by Charlie Parker and the other great bebop musicians than by his own baritone colleagues on the East Coast, and later in Europe, Sahib Shihab developed into a baritonist who has received much too little recognition. Shihab plays his instrument with power and conviction, often also with ironic humor, totally free of any mannerisms, and beyond the three modern "baritone styles" signified by the names Chaloff, Mulligan, and Pepper Adams.

Another excellent, highly regarded bebop baritone saxophonist is Cecil Payne, a melodist par excellence. In the fifties and sixties, Charlie Fowlkes earned himself a solid reputation as a lively musician among the players with whom he made music firmly grounded in the healthy Basie tradition.

However, the man who got the whole new wave of interest in the baritone saxophone rolling was Pepper Adams (d. 1986). Before Adams, it seemed as if the possibilities of the baritone had been exhausted with Mulligan and the musicians of his generation and that the only thing yet to come could be an increase in perfection. This opinion was blown down by Pepper Adams's "sawing" sound. Pepper emerged in 1957 from the Stan Kenton band. There he was nicknamed "The Knife." Drummer Mel Lewis said, "We called him 'The Knife' because when he'd get up to blow, his playing had almost a slashing effect on the rest of us. He'd slash, chop, and before he was through, cut everybody down to size." Adams is one of the musicians who ebulliently negates the belief that one can distinguish between "black" and "white" in jazz. Prior to the appearance of his first photographs in the jazz magazines, almost the entire European critical fraternity thought him to be black. They were supported in this opinion by the fact that he comes from Detroit, the Motor City, which is the birthplace, physically and musically, of many black musicians of this style. Said Pepper, "Hawkins made a tremendous impression on me." "Pepper's sound was incredible," says Gary Smulyan. "So was his time, sense of humor, and harmonic ingenuity."

Other baritone players following in Adams's style include Nick Brignola, Ronnie Cuber, Charles Davis, Bruce Johnstone, Bob Militelo, Glenn Wilson, Jack Nimitz, and, of the younger generation, Denis DiBlasio, Scott Robinson, and Gary Smulyan. Most of them have worked in big bands, above all in Woody Herman's orchestra, which has been something like a breeding ground for good baritone players in modern jazz, from Chaloff in the forties to Brignola and Smulyan in the seventies. The latter has been neobop's outstanding voice on the baritone saxophone since the end of the seventies.

Because of its physical characteristics alone, the baritone saxophone is a heavy, burdensome instrument. But also from the point of view of playing technique, the "big horn," as players respectfully call it, presents obstacles. It puts up a fight, has to be mastered. This obstinacy requires a particular approach to playing. Nick Brignola said, "Every time I pick up the big horn, I'm challenging it as it challenges me. I have to conquer it and prove that I can play it with force and conviction."

Brignola, who died in 2002, had been the baritone's foremost neobop voice since the late 1970s. His fiery, long-spun lines reflected a mastery of substitutions (the use of alternate chords derived from the original harmony). "If you freeze a Brignola solo and review the pattern of notes, they are all essentially strings of melodies," wrote one critic. "Add to this another Brignola asset—his strong rhythmic trademark—and we arrive at a communicative brand of swing."

Looking back at the sixties: among the musicians inclined toward free playing, only two baritonists became internationally known in that decade: Pat Patrick, as a member of the Sun Ra Arkestra and, in Europe, Briton John Surman, whom Japanese critics of those days called "the most important baritone saxophone player of the new jazz." His improvisations always give an impression that something new is being created. With his vivid glissandos and swirling sounds, Surman has expanded the tonal range of the baritone—previously thought to be limited—into the overblown regions of tenorlike playing and far beyond. Up there he sounds sharp and raw, while in lower registers he emanates a gentle, warm, full sound. Since the midseventies his music has become increasingly aestheticized, more "beautiful," under the influence of a variety of elements: English and Scandinavian folk music, the polyphony of British sacred music, and the ostinato patterns of minimalism.

Swedish saxophonist Mats Gustafsson is an example of how the most powerful aspects of European free-jazz playing can be distilled into an unmistakable, individual baritone style. In his hymnlike improvisations, Gustafsson, who has played with Peter Brötzmann and Ken Vandermark, deconstructs Scandinavian children's songs and lullabies by producing differentiated split tones and overblown sounds from the heavy sound of the baritone. He creates these highly individual sounds by not just blowing into the baritone, but also screaming and roaring through it with his voice, in a highly emotional—and musical—way.

Amazingly few baritone players emerged from the free jazz of the sixties and later. Surman explains that the baritone—much more than other saxophones—naturally inclines toward certain standard phrases and effects, and in absolutely free playing it is strikingly liable to clichés. Only in the course of the seventies and eighties did the baritone scene start moving again with musicians like Henry Threadgill, Mwata Bowden, Vinny Golia, Fred Ho, Seppo Paakkunainen from Finland, German-born Bernd Konrad, and, above all, Hamiet Bluiett. Threadgill has been associated with both the free jazz of the Air trio and the neoclassicism of his own sextet. He plays his baritone with impressive ease as if it were a flute, and he is indeed also a convincing stylist on the flute. As a Chinese-American, Fred Ho (earlier known as Fred Houn) has developed a special feeling for linking African American and Asian musical styles. His baritone playing is characterized by powerful pentatonic lines. According to Ho, "Many Chinese songs have a quality very similar to the blues." His baritone playing has a bluesy hardness derived from Mingus and Julius Hemphill—expressive, earthy, and weighty. As a composer, Ho writes long suites that are explicitly political, often criticizing social conditions in the United States. He says, "Asian Americans are marginalized in jazz, because we're often still perceived as foreign, and anything we might have to contribute would be something 'exotic.'"

Hamiet Bluiett, who emerged from the Black Artist Group, dominates the baritone scene since the mideighties with a sovereignty matching Harry Carney's dominance of Swing and Gerry Mulligan's of cool jazz. He commands what is probably the most powerful baritone sound since Carney. He blows his horn with a vibrating intensity and power usually associated with big-band baritonists, but Bluiett has marvelously adapted his voluminous timbre to combo playing, first in free jazz and later in neoclassicism, and above all in the World Saxophone Quartet (still to be introduced). "Nobody puts more air into an instrument than Bluiett," says Don Byron. "You can't play a whole bunch of technical shit if you do that. His sound is like . . . BAM!" Independently of Surman, Bluiett has gained exceptional virtuosity in overblowing the baritone sax, driving it up three octaves above his instrument's normal range, full of the characteristic smears and growls of the blues. Later, he increasingly emphasized the low register of his instrument. He says, "Serge Chaloff played the baritone saxophone more like an alto. Mulligan played it more like a tenor—the way Lester Young would've played if he had played baritone. I play *baritone* baritone." Bluiett phrases with an alert awareness of the African roots of black music. He isn't simply a "free player." He, like so many tradition-conscious avant-gardists, plays "everything": free and blues, bop and Swing, Dixie and rhythm 'n' blues, commanding all those styles as if they were *one* music, which in fact is what Bluiett feels.

James Carter, discussed above as a tenor saxophonist, picks up on the baritone where Hamiet Bluiett leaves off. He plays like a kind of "super-Bluiett," with a similarly colossal sound, but taking the big horn even further with stupendous technical flexibility, extending it far into the realm of shrill overblown attacks. Carter is also a member of the group Baritone Nation, founded by Bluiett, the most imposing group yet assembled of baritone sounds—three big horns and Ronnie Burrage on drums.

Bluiett and Carter are a logical extension of the lineage of Harry Carney not only in terms of sound but also with respect to total flexibility. They have transcended the characteristic of their horn, making it almost a part of their bodies: using honks and slaps, vocalized overtones, and wide vibratos, and making percussive use of the keys.

But Harry Carney's sound has also been preserved and developed in conservative, swinging straight-ahead jazz. The man who has done the most in this regard in the last thirty years is Joe Temperley. An Englishman, he began, in 1974, completely under the spell of his idol, when he took over the chair that Carney had recently vacated (due to his death) in the Ellington Orchestra, led at that time by Mercer Ellington. From then to the turn of the millennium, Temperley played on countless recordings, with Benny Carter, Humphrey Lyttelton, and the Lincoln Center Jazz Orchestra among others, ensuring the survival and development of the warm, powerful Carney sound.

Claire Daly says, "When you're the baritone player in a big band, you're usually the guy behind the pole." The emancipation of the instrument to become a solo voice in fact took place, since the fifties, increasingly in the context of small groups—a tendency that became stronger at the beginning of the twenty-first century. Claire Daly is also such a small-group player. Although she was a member of the women's big band Diva for more than ten years, she is a specialist in small-group playing, conversant in a wide variety of styles—rock, free, groove, straight-ahead. Her self-confident sound is modeled on Sonny Rollins and Rahsaan Roland Kirk, but also on Leo Parker and Ronnie Cuber. She plays perhaps the most lyrical baritone saxophone in contemporary jazz. Because of her ability to artfully shape her baritone sound, Billy Taylor has compared her to tenor saxophonist Ben Webster.

In Europe, Cologne's Steffen Schorn developed an exciting playing style at the end of the nineties. No other baritone saxophonist understands as well as he does how to explore his horn's dynamic and sonic gradations with such a richness of variety. He studied under Sergio Celibidache and Hermeto Pascual, and has been a member of the Cologne Saxophone Mafia since 1994. In his powerful improvisations, he uses Brazilian and Indian elements to enrich an abstractly grooving approach.

The baritone saxophone is the sumo wrestler of the woodwinds. Its awkwardness is as much a part of its personality as its heavy weight. Claire Daly says, "Carrying it around is probably the most burdensome challenge. . . . Anybody who is a baritone player is like an acoustic bass player. Anybody who is out there playing this instrument is doing it because they are extremely driven to play it."

The number of jazz musicians who have mastered the big horn is therefore somewhat limited. Nonetheless, it has increased steadily in the last twenty years. Today, players like Claire Daly, Gary Smulyan, Steffen Schorn, and James Carter are making the baritone's voice heard in smaller configurations. So it doesn't require powers of clairvoyance to predict, as Hamiet Bluiett does, that "you're going to see more and more baritones. The baritone will be the lead instrument and not a complementary entity."

Saxophone Groups

Nowhere is the idea of open musical dialogue, characteristic of jazz, so clear-cut as in a saxophone quartet. And nowhere is that concept so completely, harmoniously, and vitally realized as in the World Saxophone Quartet (WSQ). In fact, its members really do sound like four people talking together in an ongoing exchange of overlapping statements and counterstatements. Certainly such dialogue is a key concept on the playing of "pure" saxophone groups. Since that concept can be implemented more clearly and with greater tonal homogeneity within the chamber-music-like context of a saxophone ensemble than in other "pure" groupings, there was a boom in saxophone groups during the eighties. When saxophonists David Murray, Julius Hemphill, Hamiet Bluiett, and Oliver Lake set up the World Saxophone Quartet in 1976, they were on their own. Even without a rhythm section, they swung more intensively and vitally than some good jazz groups with bass and drums. Today dozens of saxophone ensembles in jazz do just that. Under the influence of the World Saxophone Quartet, since the eighties so many of these saxophone ensembles emerged—sometimes even going so far as to include other reeds and even flutes—that such groups require a section unto themselves rather than being dealt with under combos.

The World Saxophone Quartet is jazz's most important and influential saxophone ensemble. But it wasn't the first. Long before the saxophone quartet was introduced into jazz, such groups existed in European (especially French) concert music. Their influence on the development of jazz ensembles was, however, astonishingly minimal. The jazz saxophone quartet arose out of the inner laws and logic of black improvised music.

In the beginning—as so often in jazz—was Duke Ellington. As early as the late twenties, Duke time and again featured his saxophone section in a way that went far beyond what was usual in the jazz of the day. Already with "Hot and Bothered," recorded in 1930, the Ellington orchestra's saxophone section acquired such presence and autonomy that it seemed less a functional part of the band than a single newly invented solo instrument. Then in 1947 came the Four Brothers sound in the Woody Herman Orchestra, accompanied by further concentration on the purely "saxophonic" in jazz. The Four Brothers' use of four saxophones shaped even the least detail in the orchestral sound, even the structuring of themes and arrangements. If anyone seeks the nucleus of the four-voiced saxophone quartet style, it is to be found here in the homogenous, transparent sound of the Four Brothers Band (and in the various combo recordings the Brothers saxophonists made without the big band).

So far as we know, the first all-saxophone group in jazz (without a rhythm section!) came, however, from Europe—from England, where in 1973 tenorist Alan Skidmore, baritone and soprano saxophonist John Surman, and altoist Mike Osborne formed the SOS group. The trio's free improvisations (documented on their one record, made in 1975) were still very much under the spell of the novelty of such an instrumental combination. The extent to which the idea of saxophone groups was in the air at that time is revealed by the fact that a year after SOS's formation, Anthony Braxton recorded his *New York, Fall 1974* album, already featuring Julius Hemphill on the alto, Oliver Lake on the tenor, and Hamiet Bluiett on the baritone. This is the earliest jazz recording of a saxophone quartet, and indeed it already expresses that spirit of permanent dialogue that would become so important for later saxophone ensembles (such as the Rova Saxophone Quartet, which cited this very recording as a reason for setting up). The *Saxophone Special* album—with Steve Lacy (soprano) and fellow saxophonists Trevor Watts, Evan Parker, and Steve Potts—dates from the same year.

Yet such precursors did nothing to change the fact that pure saxophone groups remained a curiosity in jazz. It was the World Saxophone Quartet that finally succeeded in making this "unusual" and "exotic" grouping an institution and even an autonomous instrumental genre. With its vital jump playing full of wildly exciting riffs—transposing the collective improvising of free jazz into swing and rhythm 'n' blues, into bebop and New Orleans jazz, Ellington and Mingus—the World Saxophone Quartet makes exemplarily clear what counts in such an ensemble. Here every player possesses an unmistakable, completely individual sound, and yet in collective improvisation they meld as *one* voice that goes far beyond what the sum of four parts can achieve.

Since there is no rhythm section in a saxophone quartet (the saxophonists themselves must fulfill that function), such an ensemble generally makes greater demands of the players' phrasing than a band with bass and drums. The World Saxophone Quartet pointed the way there. In its first concert—at Southern University in New Orleans in December 1976—the quartet was still backed by a rhythm group. But then financial difficulties forced the group to appear without bass and drums. From that moment the four musicians have so vitally and intensively transferred the beat to the saxophone lines, swinging so much to the point, that no one would think of asking what's happened to the rhythm section.

The tight-knit closeness with which the WSQ plays is seen also in the fact that replacing any one of its individual voices is extremely difficult. After Julius Hemphill left the group in 1986, his place was taken by a succession of saxophonists—James Spaulding, John Stubblefield, Arthur Blythe, Eric Person—until John Purcell finally introduced a certain calmness, using the sound of his saxello (alongside more standard reeds) to bring the WSQ's music to new heights.

In the meantime, the WSQ recorded with singer Fontella Bass (in 1992), with African percussionists (1995), and with drummer Max Roach (still unreleased). Although, after three decades, the WSQ's playing has become somewhat complacent and unchallenging, when it comes to groove and rhythmic drive they still stand head and shoulders above other saxophone quartets.

The Rova Saxophone Quartet, founded in San Francisco in 1977, became the most important saxophone quartet alongside the WSQ, coolly situated diametrically opposite that group. This ensemble (Larry Ochs, Bruce Ackley, Jon Raskin, and Andrew Voigt, who was replaced in 1988 by Steve Adams) demonstrates complexity and subtle inventiveness in the quest for new saxophone sounds. They perhaps even surpass the World Saxophone Quartet in that respect, but come nowhere near the older group's vitality and power. Compared with the WSQ's earthy, vehement playing, their music seems cool and abstract. Nonetheless, it is unusually rich and gripping. In its complex interweaving lines, which come from free jazz (above all Anthony Braxton), the Rova Saxophone Quartet links the spontaneous and the notated so artistically that even experts have difficulty in distinguishing between where composition ends and improvisation begins. How completely the musicians can give expression to themselves in this quartet also becomes apparent from the fact that as of the beginning of the twenty-first century, the individual members of the group generally have not felt much urge to make recordings outside the Rova context.

As different as the various instruments of the saxophone family sound, they still have great homogeneity of sound among them, similar to groups of string instruments. Because their timbres blend so thoroughly, saxophones playing as an ensemble have become something of a fixture in jazz. Of all such groups the Twenty-Ninth Street Saxophone Quartet (with Bobby Watson, Jim Hartog, Ed Jackson, and Rich Rothenberg) produces the most catchy melodic phrasing. In its gripping contrapuntal lines, the jaunty zest of bebop rhythms attractively encounters the hard-driving melodies and rhythms of street music—funk, rap, soul, and hip-hop. Whatever a saxophone quartet needs, the Twenty-Ninth Street Saxophone Quartet has it: balance and homogeneity. Tenorist Rich Rothenberg said, "In a big band the whole sax section is supportive, but here each of us is a section in and of ourselves."

The wave of saxophone quartets that emerged at the beginning of the eighties profited greatly from the art of unaccompanied solo playing that became a genre of its own in the jazz of the seventies. "When the idea of a saxophone quartet came up, it seemed completely natural," Oliver Lake said of the WSQ. "We were all able to carry an entire evening of unaccompanied solo playing, so it seemed easy to carry a whole evening of a saxophone quartet without a rhythm section."

Among the other important saxophone quartets that have in their own way refined the WSQ approach are the Your Neighborhood Saxophone Quartet and the Windmill Saxophone Quartet in the United States; Itchy Fingers and the Hornweb Saxophone Quartet from England; the Atipico Trio with Carlos Actis Dato in Italy; in Austria, the New Art Saxophone Quartet (also successful in classical chamber music) and the group Saxofour (including members Wolfgang Puschnig and Klaus Dickbauer); Position Alpha in Sweden; and, in Germany, the Kölner Saxophon Mafia and Gebhard Ullmann's group, Ta Lam. The Your Neighborhood Saxophone Quartet cultivates, in chamber music style, the great saxophone tradition established by Swing orchestras from Basie to Ellington. The Windmill Saxophone Quartet, based in Washington, D.C., has specialized in working with guest musicians on other instruments, such as pianists Ran Blake and Frank Kimbrough, bassist Ben Allison, and percussionist Mark Merella. The humorous improvisations of Itchy Fingers (Mike Mower, Martin Speaks, John Graham, and Howard Turner) offer a crazily fascinating kaleidoscope of styles, with Latin, pop, bebop, funk, and jazz-rock interweaving and superimposing to create ever-changing patterns. Itchy Fingers, who emerged from the twelve-piece group Orchester Hiatus, was originally not conceived as a saxophone quartet. Rather, the group was intended to substitute for the Hiatus ensemble, which was having money problems—so Mike Mower wrote arrangements for the saxophone ensemble as if it were a big band. Position Alpha bursts onto the saxophone ensemble scene with anarchic wit plus punk wildness and gloom, but its phrasing also demonstrates a special liking for the sea shanties of Swedish folk music.

However, the most creative and longest-lived saxophone ensemble in European jazz is the Cologne Saxophone Mafia, founded in 1982. This group represents a decidedly European approach to playing, combining humor with a love of large formal structures and complex harmonies in their powerful, groove-based chamber music. The Cologne Saxophone Mafia has found exciting ways to bring rhythmic diversity to the sound of a saxophone ensemble. Paradoxically, when the Cologne Saxophone Mafia reduced its size from six pieces to five pieces (1986), and then later became a quartet (2003), their sound became bigger, not smaller. This has to do on the one hand with the concentration of improvisational skill in the group—Roger Hanschel, Wollie Kaiser, Joachim Ulrich, and Steffen Schorn are some of the best improvisers in German jazz—and on the other hand with the fact that, over the course of two decades, the group has significantly expanded its sonic possibilities. Their instrumentation extends all the way from the rarely used B-flat tubax (a massive, custom-built saxophone pitched an octave below the bass saxophone) and the contra-alto clarinet to high instruments also rarely seen, such as the F mezzo-soprano saxophone and the sopranino.

It is important to realize that the development of pure saxophone groups particularly demands new ways of playing the low instruments. The baritone saxophone serves, often as harmony instrument, to carry the ensemble, and yet it must satisfy the requirement of being a fully functional and equal member of the group. Hamiet Bluiett's lines have helped shape the way the baritone is played in such saxophone groups: pulsating, forward-driving riffs, which nonetheless are time and again broken up like solos within ensemble playing. Following the model of Bluiett's improvisations—with the instrument the center of gravity on the one hand and a fully equal solo voice on the other—the baritone has been further developed in saxophone groups by many musicians: Jon Raskin, Jim Hartog, Tom Hall, Steffen Schorn, and Steve Adams.

All the saxophone ensembles mentioned here "celebrate" a wealth of new, unusual sounds that no one would have been able to foresee twenty or thirty years ago—a development that will continue.

The Flute

As recently as the fifties, the flute ranked among "miscellaneous instruments." But in proportion to the decline of the clarinet came the flute's ascendancy. At least since the late fifties, this instrument has taken the position of playful, airy, triumphant heights on jazz recordings that had been the domain of the clarinet during the Swing era, to which, since the midsixties, was added another "clarinet successor": the soprano sax under John Coltrane's influence.

Still, the flute has only a relatively short tradition in jazz. The earliest flute solo we know of is by Alberto Socarras (d. 1987) in "Shootin' the Pistol," a 1927 recording of the Clarence Williams Orchestra. Socarras's main instrument was the clarinet, and his flute phrasing had the angularity and stiffness of a musician who came from European concert music. Wayman Carver was the first jazz flutist who really has to be taken seriously. In "Sweet Sue," a 1933 recording of Spike Hughes and His All-American Orchestra, Carver plays with a suppleness that seems astonishingly modern. Chick Webb, too, occasionally used a flute in his orchestra of the early Swing era. But back then, the instrument still was a curiosity. Strange how suddenly this state of affairs changed when, in the early fifties, the appearance of a half-dozen jazz flutists—literally overnight—established the instrument in jazz. It wasn't until microphones began to be widely used that the technical conditions were created under which the "soft" flute, always at a disadvantage when competing with the penetrating sound of the saxophones and trumpets in the large dance halls of the twenties and thirties, could successfully be used as a solo instrument.

The first musician to record modern flute solos was tenor player Jerome Richardson, whose solo on "Kingfish," with Lionel Hampton in 1949, has a direct, vital bop feeling. Immediately after him, Frank Wess and Bud Shank stepped into the limelight. Wess (mentioned in the tenor saxophone chapter) was in Count Basie's orchestra. And in this band, whose name stands for Swing par excellence, he played the flute—still thought to be alien to Swing by many jazz fans—with the natural ease of his saxophone.

Wess symbolizes the breakthrough that led to the acceptance of the flute. The flute has difficulty in making itself heard, so it only had a real chance of getting across in the post–Lester Young era when people became generally aware of supple, springy, modern jazz phrasing taking precedence over expressive sonority. Lester Young is the "main culprit" in this shift of accent from sonority to phrasing, and thus jazz flutists are initially shaped in his mold. Wess illustrates this point almost ironically. As a tenorist, he clearly is of the Hawkins tradition; as a flutist, he is just as clearly of the Young line. Wess recorded some of his most interesting flute solos on a date in 1955 with Milt Jackson (vibraphone), Hank Jones (piano), Eddie Jones (bass), and Kenny Clarke (drums): *Opus de Jazz.*

Bud Shank was the most important West Coast flutist. He emerged from Stan Kenton's band, where, in 1950, he had already recorded an interesting flute solo showing Latin influences, "In Veradero." Later, his duets with Bob Cooper, into which Max Roach drummed swing, stirred much discussion. A strong Arabic and oriental tendency is detectable in Yusef Lateef, on flute as on his numerous other instruments. Aside from the usual concert flute, he has used a whole store of non-Western flutes: Chinese bamboo flute, a flute of Slovak folk origin, cork flute, the Arab ney flute, Taiwan flute, and a ma ma flute he constructed himself.

Other good jazz flutists are Sahib Shihab, James Moody, Herbie Mann, Sam Most, Buddy Collette, Paul Horn, Rahsaan Roland Kirk, Joe Farrell, James Spaulding, Eric Dixon, and Sam Rivers. It should be noted here that many of these musicians are saxophonists first and foremost and play the flute as a second instrument. This is true, for instance, of tenor and alto player James Moody (whom we have mentioned in the tenor section) who came out of the first bop circle of the forties. Although the flute is only one instrument among others for him, he has been considered one of the best jazz flutists for thirty years—a bebop man par excellence also on this instrument.

Sam Most started in 1948 as a clarinetist with Tommy Dorsey, but then changed to the flute because he felt that on it he could better express the modern ideas in his head. He was the first white flute player to successfully play bebop solos on his instrument, such as on "Undercurrent Blues" in 1953.

In the fifties, Sam Most and Herbie Mann contributed equally to the growing popularity of jazz flute. In 1955 they recorded and appeared in concert together, in cool but gripping flute "battles." At these concerts, Most's fans would chant the slogan "Most is the man!"—countered by Herbie Mann's fans with: "Mann is the most!"

In fact, Herbie Mann (1930–2003) subsequently became the most successful of all jazz flute players. In his brilliant solos, he created a secure place for the flute as a jazz instrument. The emancipation that Mann brought to the flute was clearly seen in the division of labor with which he played his instruments: he played the flute as his main instrument, and only occasionally picked up the tenor saxophone. He also incorporated many elements from other musical cultures in his jazz recordings: Brazilian, African, Arabic, Jewish, Turkish, and Caribbean. Although these "fusions" were often somewhat superficial—a "jazzing up" of folk music, rather than a real mutual encounter—Mann did help expand the stylistic spectrum of jazz.

In the seventies and eighties he also made rock, and finally even fusion, records. His record *Memphis Underground* (1968) appeared in sampled form in many of the dance-jazz remixes of the nineties.

Herbie Mann won the Reader's Poll of *Down Beat* magazine—*the* authoritative popularity poll of the jazz world—from 1957 to 1970— thirteen years! To everyone's surprise, Hubert Laws took over this spot as best-liked jazz flutist with a real classical sound. He has successfully attempted to create a number of jazz adaptations of classical music (compositions of Bach, Mozart, Debussy, Stravinsky, and others), but he has also made many jazz-rock and fusion records. In this context, Laws also took piccolo playing to a virtuosic level.

Paul Horn, who became known in the second half of the fifties for his work with the Chico Hamilton Quintet, in the early seventies made unaccompanied flute recordings in the Taj Mahal, on which the flute sounds echo back from the hundred-foot dome of the marvelous edifice "like a choir of angels" multiplied a hundredfold, as in an acoustic hall of mirrors: meditational mantras transformed into flute music. The success of this Horn record, *Inside*, was so great that it was later followed by a second one, this one recorded in the burial chambers of Egyptian pyramids (among them the famous Cheops pyramid). Horn later became a universal flutist within world music. He traveled through China and the Soviet Union and convincingly absorbed various non-Western flute techniques—Indian, Tibetan, Chinese, and Japanese—in his playing of the European concert flute. The "duets" he recorded with the songs of whales also attracted great interest.

New flutists keep coming. The reservoirs seem inexhaustible. More and more saxophonists choose the flute as a supplementary horn only to discover one day that it has become their main instrument—as happened to James Moody.

A special place is occupied by the outstanding avant-garde player Eric Dolphy, who died in 1964. His influence as an alto and bass clarinet player was felt immediately, from the early sixties on, while on flute the importance of his message was not realized by other musicians until the midseventies. Dolphy became interested in the experimental flute playing of Severino Gazzelloni, the pioneering Italian classical flutist. This resulted in a fruitful mutual influence between jazz and new music: when Dolphy was in Europe, he took lessons from the Italian musician, and dedicated the piece "Gazzelloni" to him (on the album *Out to Lunch*). In return, Gazzelloni was strongly impressed by the rhythmic innovations in Dolphy's flute improvisations. The genius of Dolphy's ideas already contained all of what "jazz flute" means on today's scene. His flute "message"—quite in contrast to what he expressed on his other instruments—was one of lightness and airiness. For people who knew Dolphy the man, there is reason to feel that his flute playing expressed more of his humanity, his soft-spoken gentleness and amiability, than the bursting expressivity of his alto style and the pain-filled eruptions of his bass clarinet improvisations. Dolphy often said that his flute playing was inspired by sounds and impressions from nature: the noise of the wind, the humming of the bees, the songs of the birds.

Strangely enough, the first to understand and elaborate on Dolphy's flute style were European musicians. They distinguish themselves through an awareness of classical traditions—musicians like the Bulgarian Simeon Shterev, Czechoslovakian Jiří Stivín, German Emil Mangelsdorff, Briton Bob Downes, and Dutchman Chris Hinze. Downes, who has also stepped out as a composer of contemporary ballets, belongs to the realm of classics as much as to jazz. Hinze plays mainly jazz-rock. Mangelsdorff has an especially full, rich sound. Stivín, also an excellent composer and altoist, is a virtuoso with Bohemian musicians' roots. Shterev commands the whole rich musical heritage of Balkan folk music.

Many of the flutists named above cultivate the "overblowing" technique where, through simultaneous blowing and singing or humming, two voices become audible (often through the resultant combination tones, even three or four voices)—creating jazz intensity of an astonishing degree. Anybody who knows the flute from classical music (from baroque music, for instance) may not immediately think of the flute as an instrument that lends itself to jazzlike intensity in the same terms as, say, the tenor saxophone. Only by way of the technique of overblowing has it gained this intensity, and only in that way could it have achieved its success on today's scene.

The first jazz musicians to overblow the flute, as early as the midfifties, were Sam Most and Sahib Shihab (whom we discussed in the section on baritone saxophone). Ever since the sixties, this technique has been employed by a growing number of flutists, most intensely by Rahsaan Roland Kirk, who when overblowing the flute didn't just sing into the instrument, like his predecessors, but also spoke, shouted, and screamed. He sometimes seemed to explode in a dozen different directions with the many different sounds he created simultaneously while blowing the flute (and, at the same time, blown through the nose, his so-called nose flute).

A master of overblowing is Jeremy Steig. He was the first flutist to structurally incorporate air and functional and finger noises into his music, while Kirk still used them mainly to increase ecstatic vitality. In 1976 Steig recorded some highly interesting chamber-music-like duos with bassist Eddie Gomez. Steig also integrated electric flute playing into an acoustic group context in an intelligent manner.

Flutists in the actual jazz-rock field are, among others, Dave Valentin, Tom Scott, Gerry Niewood, and the two jazzwomen Bobbi Humphrey and Briton Barbara Thompson. Dave Valentin, who studied with Hubert Laws, plays sunny, bright lines that derive their optimism and relaxation from the supple rhythms of Latin American, particularly Brazilian, music.

Two other flutists who have "Latinized" the ultra-virtuosic approach of Hubert Laws are the Cuban musician Orlando "Maraca" Valle and the Puerto Rican Nestor Torres. Maraca, who played in the group Irakere for six years, combines a brilliant classical technique with explosive Afro-Cuban melodies. With his group Y Otra Vision, a melting pot of the young Cuban jazz scene, he revitalized the tradition of *descarga* playing, a jam-session-like musical competition in which musicians spontaneously test each other, in the nineties.

Torres plays stratospheric solos in the flute's highest register. He arrived at his sensitive rhythmic approach and his high-note playing while working in salsa bands with the King of Mambo, percussionist Tito Puente. Puente gave him a tip: "In this type of music, to be heard, you have to stay up high and play in the third octave."

The flute has always been an instrument with a special affinity for world music—as early as the fifties through Yusef Lateef and Bud Shank, later particularly impressively through Paul Horn, and in the seventies, for instance, through Brazilian Hermeto Pascoal, who overblows the flute with truly passionate intensity. Bob Moses once called Pascoal "God on Earth." With his melodies full of warmth and humor, Pascoal (who, in addition to the flute, also plays accordion, saxophone, and keyboards, and makes use of household objects) displays an almost childlike joy in provoking musical chaos and guiding it onto orderly paths.

Among the important musicians, all greatly influenced by Eric Dolphy, who play more or less "free" flute (in that universal sense of "free" that evolved in the innovative dialogue with the jazz tradition) are Douglas Ewart, Henry Threadgill, Oliver Lake, Prince Lasha, George Adams, Gary Thomas, Dwight Andrews, Marty Ehrlich, and, most important of all, James Newton. No other jazz flutist has so individually and unmistakably reworked and developed Dolphy's legacy as Newton has. Newton possesses the most powerful flute sound—penetrating, strong, and full, but never loud despite the power involved, emanating an elegance reminiscent at times of the expressiveness of *shakuhachi* flute. One of the few jazz musicians whose main instrument is the flute, Newton has mastered the art of overblowing almost unsurpassably, playing up to four notes at once multiphonically, and demonstrating an astounding ability to sing and growl contrapuntal lines into the instrument while playing it. "A lot of the things I play where I use my voice are related to the way the brass instruments would growl in the Ellington orchestra," said Newton.

Newton recorded what he believes to be his most beautiful album (*Echo Canyon*) in Echo Canyon, New Mexico, a huge natural amphitheater formed by erosion, playing with the echoes thrown back from many directions as if answering partners standing everywhere on the edges of the canyon, and incorporating the sounds of nature—birds, coyotes, stones falling into the depths—into his performance.

In 2002 James Newton made headlines when he sued the pop band The Beastie Boys, who had sampled parts of his composition "Choir" in their hit "Pass the Mic." The suit was dismissed in federal court.

Newton's powerful, vocal style was absorbed and further developed in a personal manner above all by two flute players in the nineties: the Canadian Jane Bunnett and the American Nicole Mitchell. Bunnett, also an important soprano saxophonist, recorded exciting duos with her mentor, pianist Don Pullen, in 1989, on the CD *New York Duets*. In her flute playing, she uses an extremely expressive vibrato to give her warm, passionate sound an enormous variety of emotions, demonstrating a masterful control of dynamics. Mitchell, a member of the AACM and a classically trained musician, goes back to the African roots of Great Black Music in a particularly vital manner. She is one of the founders of Semana, the AACM's first all-woman band.

"If you play the flute, you run into a lot of widespread prejudice about this instrument and the sounds that come from it," a flutist once said. In fact, the flute is often almost automatically prejudged as having an ornamental, superficial character. This cliché, however unjustified, has sometimes been perpetuated by jazz flute players. Some flutists have a tendency to seek out settings in which it is easy to play the flute—they choose contexts in which they can play "flutently" (as Nicole Mitchell has put it)—quickly, lightly, and clearly. In opposition to this, New York flutist Jamie Baum has repeatedly sought out difficult group situations whose challenges help her playing to grow, such as dialogues with Dave Douglas, Randy Brecker, and others. Baum has also distinguished herself as a composer and bandleader, and plays dark, contrapuntal lines that retain a wonderfully swinging feeling despite their tendency toward abstraction.

Many of the flutists named here use what are called extended techniques, in addition to conventional playing. One player who has dramatically expanded the spectrum of these extended techniques, and thus the expressive possibilities of the flute, is the American Robert Dick. He has discovered a seemingly infinite variety of new sounds on the entire flute family, from the piccolo to the contrabass flute. In addition to circular breathing and multiphonics, which have over time become standard techniques, he makes use of unusual glissandi and tonal colorings, such as "whisper tones" in extremely low registers, as well as a very broad palette of percussive and vocal effects.

Dick lived in Switzerland for ten years before returning to New York, where he improvised with John Zorn and Ned Rothenberg. The intensity of his playing has earned him the nickname of the "Jimi Hendrix of the flute"—a comparison that may seem inapt in some respects, but is nonetheless insightful. In fact, Dick was inspired to expand his flute playing after hearing Hendrix and other rock guitarists in the sixties. He has discovered a range of sound possibilities for the flute comparable to that of these guitarists—not only through the innovative use of new techniques, but also through the invention of unusual instruments. In addition to the conventional arsenal of flutes, he plays an instrument with additional keys, and a flute that has a "glissando head joint"—a telescopic lever that functions something like a "whammy bar" on an electric guitar. Robert Dick's motto is: "If I can hear it inside me, I can play it."

Other jazz flute players whose playing has been influenced directly or indirectly by Robert Dick's extended techniques include the American John Savage, the Swiss flutist Matthias Ziegler, and Germany's Michael Heupel. Savage, who studied with Andrew Hill, uses extended techniques in the service of musical content, not instrumental tricks. Ziegler, who became known playing with bassist Mark Dresser, has an almost orchestral palette of flute colors and sounds. He has discovered unusual sonic structures, from sounds reminiscent of spherical choral harmonies to sounds resembling the sine waves of electronic music. Ziegler also plays a "Matusi flute" of his own invention, which has an additional membrane that vibrates sympathetically.

In the eighties and nineties, contemporary mainstream was played on the flute by, among others, Steve Slagle, Robin Kenyatta, Jerry Dodgion, Steve Kujala, Kent Jordan, Holly Hofmann, Ali Ryerson, and Anne Drummond. Jordan, who hails from New Orleans and is the son of saxophonist Kidd Jordan, blows the piccolo with stupendous virtuosity within the realm of neo–hard bop, emancipating this instrument, hitherto mostly serving a coloristic function, with an impressive sense of swing. Anne Drummond, who became known playing with Kenny Barron, cultivates a sensitive, legato approach oriented toward friendly, attractive Brazilan bossa melodies. Once in a while, Lew Tabackin, co-leader of the Akiyoshi-Tabackin Big Band, produces sounds reminiscent of Japanese *shakuhachi* flutes in his amazing virtuoso flute excursions played in a quartet or his big band. Tabackin remarked, "No wonder. With my wife being Japanese, you absorb these sounds automatically."

It is important to understand that *the* flute does not exist: no instrument is more varied. Every musical culture on earth has developed its own particular types of flutes. To the extent that jazz musicians incorporate the musical cultures of the world, they discover flutes. Joachim Berendt once did a record date with Don Cherry to which Cherry brought thirty-five different flutes—among them a ceramic Chinese shuan flute, a Latin American Maya bird flute, a Bengali flute, a bamboo flute, a metal flute (in B-flat), a plastic flute in C, American Indian flutes, Japanese flutes, etc.

There's a kind of natural flow in the way that jazz and the world's great musical cultures come together in this instrument, the flute.

In an earlier edition of the present book, we posited that a time would come when the horizon of the jazz flute would expand even further. That time has now arrived: since the nineties, flutists from Africa, Latin America, and Asia have introduced new flute sounds and techniques to world jazz.

Orlando "Maraca" Valle, discussed above, combines in his playing two lineages that had previously developed independently of each other. He comes both from the tradition of the great flute masters of Cuban *son*—players like Antonio Arcaño and Richard Egües—and from the Latin-inspired virtuosos of the jazz flute like Hubert Laws and Dave Valentin. In bringing together these two lines of influence, he has ignited an improvisational fire the likes of which have not been heard previously on his instrument.

Kudsi Erguner, the great master of Sufi music on the *ney* flute, moved to Paris in 1975, where, in collaboration with jazz musicians, he has brought new ideas and influences to the tradition of flute playing associated with dervish ceremonial music.

One of the greatest *shakuhachi* players in Japan (perhaps the greatest of them all), Hozan Yamamoto, has also played this immensely expressive bamboo flute—probably the most expressive instrument of the worldwide flute family—in a jazz context with his own kind of mastery. He has done so with, for instance, singer Helen Merrill and percussion player Masahiko Togashi.

Theodosii Spassov is a player who has both an exciting jazz sensibility and deep roots in the Balkan folk music of Bulgaria. He has played with Trilok Gurtu, Anatoly Vapirov, and Rabih Abou-Khalil, and plays the *kaval* flute with a revolutionary flexibility and stylistic openness. The kaval is a transverse flute made of wood that has six holes on its front. On the lower part of the flute, there are four additional small holes, called the "dyavolski dupki," or "devil's holes." These control the sound and the intensity of the tone. According to a Bulgarian legend, the devil stole the kaval flute from a sleeping shepherd. Intending to destroy it, the devil bored four small holes into the flute. But instead of destroying it, this made the instrument sound even more beautiful. The shepherd then played it, and in doing so vanquished the devil.

In traditional Bulgarian music, the kaval flute is played diatonically (i.e., within the notes of a particular scale). Spassov, however, plays it chromatically, using notes from outside the scale. He also uses special embouchure and fingering techniques to modify the sound of the instrument. By means of these innovations, Spassov has made the kaval flute into a flexible, powerful instrument—a fully capable solo instrument in the jazz sense.

Bansuri flutists Ronu Majumdar and Steve Gorn have introduced the artful sliding and ornamentation techniques of their Indian transverse flute, made of bamboo, into jazz—Gorn in collaboration with Glen Velez, and Majumdar in subtle dialogues with Jon Hassell and Dhafer Youssef.

But perhaps the most impressive flutist among the new European jazz immigrants plays the "conventional" European concert flute: Malik Mezzadri, or "Magic Malik." Born in the Ivory Coast and raised in Guadeloupe, he studied classical flute in Marseilles, and at the age of nineteen moved to Paris, where he became an active member of the scene of young jazz musicians. "In the jazz club you can meet Cuban musicians, Indian musicians, Serbo-Croat musicians—it's great." Magic Malik has played M-Base music in Steve Coleman's band, and in 1999 he started his own Magic Malik Orchestra, in which he combines radically different styles. He is often asked why a musician from Ivory Coast plays a form of jazz in which music from the Peruvian Andes, electronic club beats, Algerian rai music, classical music, African music, drum 'n' bass, fusion, and reggae all collide. Magic Malik answers: "In my music everything revolves around the heart, the brain, and the body. You can find these three components in every kind of music in the world. No matter how different the different kinds of music may sound structurally, everywhere the heart, brain, and body are involved. So you can build functional relationships to *all* kinds of music."

The Vibraphone

Percussion instruments (instruments that are struck or hit) tend to be used primarily as rhythm instruments. If such instruments additionally offer all kinds of melodic possibilities, it can be assumed that they would make ideal jazz instruments. In this sense, the vibraphone (or "vibes") is an ideal jazz instrument. The fact that so vitally rhythmic a musician as Lionel Hampton introduced it to jazz—or at least helped to do so—points in this direction. If it nevertheless has been slow to assert itself, it may be due to its inability to allow for the production of a hornlike jazz sound. The sound of the vibraphone can only be influenced indirectly, by way of its electrically adjustable vibrato, or by foregoing any electrical adjustment, or through the force—or sensitivity—with which it is struck.

Lionel Hampton (1908–2002) and Milt Jackson (1923–99) are the outstanding vibraphonists of the jazz tradition. Hampton was a volcano of energy who, like hardly anyone else, could carry thousands of people to a trancelike state of ecstasy by the sheer power (and, of course, showmanship) of his playing and performing. He loved to have a big band with trumpet, trombone, and sax sections behind him. His big bands often pounded away without consideration for intonation, blend, or precision, but Lionel Hampton, the vibraphonist, derived from the rhythmic riff orgies of his big bands even more inspiration and fire and power than he possessed on his own. Hampton's vital attack, percussive phrasing, and melodic inventiveness remain the standard for all jazz vibraphonists today.

Hampton and, a couple of years before him, Red Norvo introduced the vibraphone to jazz at the beginning of the Swing era. Their music demonstrates with exemplary clarity the contrasting possibilities open to the jazz vibraphone. To simplify somewhat, the vibraphone can be played in two ways: like a percussion instrument or like a piano. Hampton phrased percussively, Norvo pianistically. That is already apparent in their instrumental backgrounds. Hampton came from the drum set to the vibraphone, Norvo from the xylophone. Norvo (who died in 1999) is the father of the four-mallet technique of playing the vibes. He developed in a remarkably open way from Chicago style through Swing, bebop, and cool to mainstream jazz—with a special sensitivity for small chamber-music-like jazz groups.

Milt Jackson was fifteen years younger than Hampton. As Hampton's vibraphone career had started with Louis Armstrong and Benny Goodman, so Milt Jackson's began in 1945 with Dizzy Gillespie, in his groundbreaking bebop big band. "Bags," as Jackson was known, arrived on the scene at a time when the vibraphone was played percussively, using hard mallets. But Jackson used softer mallets to play flexible melodic lines, sounding "like a horn player and not like a novelty instrument," as vibraphonist Gary Burton put it. From 1951 onward Jackson was a member of the

Modern Jazz Quartet, which originated as the Milt Jackson Quartet and to begin with was hardly more than the combination of Milt Jackson's vibes and the rhythm section of Dizzy Gillespie's big band. The Milt Jackson Quartet became the Modern Jazz Quartet under the influence of John Lewis, and it has sometimes been said that the shape and form given by Lewis to this ensemble restricted Jackson's flow of ideas and improvisatory freedom. Jackson, however, has played the most beautiful solos of his career as a member of the Modern Jazz Quartet. As so often happens in jazz, the tension between the rigidity of the arrangements and the freedom of improvisation did not hinder the artist but rather inspired him.

Milt Jackson's improvisations deserve the adjective "flowing," more than any other kind of jazz. A provocative element of Jackson's playing is the seemingly unconscious way in which he makes the most complicated harmonies seem natural and organic. That is also one of the reasons why he is one of the great ballad players in jazz. He has articulated the most complete understanding of the bebop conception on the vibraphone. Already in the midfifties, Jackson was one of the first soul musicians. However far vibraphonists may have developed away from Milt's style, whoever plays vibraphone in contemporary jazz speaks of "Bags" with respect and admiration.

Of course, Jackson is not the only vibraphonist of his generation; others are Terry Gibbs, Teddy Charles, Cal Tjader, Vic Feldman, and the somewhat younger Eddie Costa, Tommy Vig, Lem Winchester, Larry Bunker, Charlie Shoemaker, and Mike Mainieri. Gibbs became known through his brilliant solo work with the Woody Herman band of the late forties. Even in later years, he remained interested in big bands and in the contrast between his vibraphone and the big-band sound. The big band is also where he developed his outstanding technique of playing in octaves. "In the big-band context, the vibraphone is not strong enough if you only play single notes, so you have to play octaves," says vibraphonist Bobby Hutcherson.

Cal Tjader was the first to use the vibes as a solo voice in Latin music. His blend of jazz phrasing with mambo, conga, bolero, cha-cha-cha, and other Latin rhythms is a valid and sophisticated development of Cuban jazz, as initiated by Dizzy Gillespie, Chano Pozo, and Machito in the great days of bop. Teddy Charles belongs among those musicians who, in the fifties, were already expanding tonality and preparing the way for free playing.

Lem Winchester, who died in 1961, was the first to display a feeling for the glittering, oscillating sound quality of his instrument, at first only in initial intimations. In the ensuing years, this manner of playing became more and more pronounced through musicians like Gary Burton, Walt Dickerson, Tom van der Geld, and Bobby Hutcherson. These are the players who after years of an unchallenged Milt Jackson reign have revolutionized the style of their instrument as dramatically as has happened only to the bass during this timespan. These musicians accomplished what Ornette Coleman had wanted to see replace the "old rules of play-ing": "a continuous exploring of all possibilities of the instrument." They found that the flittering, oscillating quality of sound that we mentioned in connection with Lem Winchester fits their instrument better than sim-ply "a continuation of standard bop by means of the vibraphone."

In Gary Burton's playing, sonic lyricism and percussiveness form a poetic unity—he plays with a fascinating combination of tender, floating lyricism and great virtuosity. No other vibraphonist has so comprehen-sively revealed his instrument's pianistic possibilities. He has developed further than anyone else the ability to play with three or four mallets simultaneously, creating refined chordal effects similar to those of pianist Bill Evans, who influenced him. Another influence was the country and hillbilly music of his home state, Indiana. Burton joins all these elements into a new, independent whole so securely that he has become successful far beyond jazz. It was Burton, too, who in the early seventies initiated the trend of that time toward playing without a rhythm section and who led this trend to its first big triumphs.

Walt Dickerson, who died in 2008, transferred the ideas of John Coltrane to the vibraphone. He loved exploring new sounds, and he, too, was an impressive improviser without accompaniment. But the central figure among contemporary vibraphonists (since the late sixties) is Bobby Hutcherson. He began his career with Archie Shepp's free jazz and also played jazz-rock, before developing in the eighties into an outstanding postbop performer on the vibes. Hutcherson took Milt Jackson's legacy furthest, masterfully incorporating Coltrane and the new vibraphone sound. He achieves a near-legato effect with his nimble mallet technique. He's an enormously complete player, unifying in his lines the possibilities open to the instrument, both percussive and pianistic. And he's also a magician of touch, excitingly diverse in the art of giving emotional shape to a piece and "molding" the sound. "It's not the note itself that counts," Hutcherson has said, "it's the story you tell in the note." Tom van der Geld is the most sensitive, most tender player among the new vibraphon-ists. Once in a while his improvisations sound as if the bars of his instru-ment were set vibrating not by being struck with mallets, but by a mild, warm wind. David Friedman has a brilliant, gripping sound, occasionally like a "modern Lionel Hampton," with a pronounced fondness for sur-prising technical effects. Off and on, he includes a second vibraphonist (and marimba player), David Samuels, in his group, "multiplying" the vibraphone sound in this way. Austrian-born Werner Pirchner produces previously unheard sounds from his specially constructed "tenor vibes."

Strikingly few vibraphone players became interested in the sounds of jazz-rock and fusion music. Among them are Roy Ayers, Dave Pike, Mike

Mainieri, Ruth Underwood, and Jay Hoggard. Mainieri uses electronics to alter the vibraphone's sound in a particularly subtle manner, including the incorporation of MIDI technology, in groups like Steps Ahead and N.Y.C.

Radically new ways of playing have been discovered by two German musicians who have made their home in the United States: Gunter Hampel and Karl Berger. Hampel (who has also distinguished himself as flutist, clarinetist, bass clarinetist, and pianist) is the more sensitive of the two; Berger (who heads the Creative Music Studio in Woodstock, New York) is the more dynamic, with bop roots that he has been developing in the direction of a wide and deep interest in world music. With his different groups, Hampel has created mesmerizing webs of sound, combining the vibraphone with flutes and saxophones played in the high registers.

A synthesis of all these tendencies has been created by four American players, who on the one hand play free and on the other command the entire tradition of their instrument: Bobby Naughton, Gust William Tsilis, Khan Jamal, and, above all, Jay Hoggard. Jamal made free-funk recordings with Ronald Shannon Jackson's Decoding Society. Hoggard is an enthrallingly emotional improviser of the tradition-conscious avant-garde, who possesses a fine sense for discovery of tonal parallels between, on the one hand, the vibraphone and, on the other, related instruments in non-Western music. In his playing he resorts to African *balaphon* techniques or the metallophones of Balinese Gamelan music. Since the mideighties he has inclined toward jazz-rock, but his appearances there are less expressive.

Simplifying somewhat, there have been three main trends in vibraphone playing since the eighties: percussiveness in the Lionel Hampton tradition, as exemplified by Jay Hoggard and David Friedman; the iridescent sensitivity initiated by such players as Gary Burton, Lem Winchester, Walt Dickerson, and Gunter Hampel, and carried on by Tom van der Geld and Khan Jamal; and, above all, as a balancing element mediating between those two ways of playing, the legacy of Milt Jackson, which lives on in the suppleness of Bobby Hutcherson and Steve Nelson.

Turning first to the more percussive approach, in postmodern jazz this sound is represented most impressively by Bryan Carrott, Monte Croft, Matthias Lupri, and Orphy Robinson. All these players utilize phrasing that is not as emphatically linear as that of the players in the Jackson/ Hutcherson lineage; rather, their improvisations are more angular, more abstract harmonically. For example, Bryan Carrott, who became known for his work in Ralph Peterson's Fo'tet, feels a closer relation to African *balaphon* playing than to the European tradition of mallet percussion.

The vibraphone is a particularly rigid instrument. Its hard metal bars seem especially resistant to the attempt to individualize its sound, and the unspecific sound of its electric vibrato contributes to the difficulty.

Perhaps because of this, the number of jazz vibraphonists who have created an original style has remained relatively small. Nonetheless, all the great vibes players in jazz have found personal ways of overcoming these handicaps. Bryan Carrott, for example, specializing in "flattening" pitches through a kind of "exaggerated" use of the vibrato and the pedal. In this way, he creates sonic effects that are the equal of the expressive note-bendings of a horn player or blues musician.

Monte Croft is a virtuoso of abstract, broken arpeggios, playing in a quirky style strongly influenced by Monk. In the playing of Britain's Orphy Robinson, the son of Caribbean immigrants, the vibraphone becomes a mirror of the black diaspora, reflecting and combining all the African lines of influence in black music: reggae, griot music, soul, funk, classics, and the avant-garde. Robinson says, "When I hear Monk, I hear reggae grooves."

The shimmering vibrato effect that gives the instrument its name also makes it ideal for achieving atmospheric, coloristic effects. Many jazz musicians use the transparent sound of the vibes to "soften" the sound and mood of their improvisations. Without detracting from the groove, the vibes can create a soulful and at the same time dreamlike, flowing feeling. Under the influence of Gary Burton and Lem Winchester, European players in particular have developed the instrument's iridescent character at the beginning of the twenty-first century; they include the Finn Severi Pyysalo and Germany's Franz Bauer, Rupert Stamm, and Christopher Dell.

Severi Pyysalo was discovered in 1982 at the Pori Jazz Festival, when he was invited to perform with Paquito D'Rivera and Sarah Vaughan. He is a wizard of the vibes, a virtuoso who uses the dreamlike quality of the instrument to paint sound pictures, for example in duos with saxophonist Peter Weniger and in works composed by Pyysalo for orchestra and jazz vibraphone.

Christopher Dell has intellectualized and abstracted Gary Burton's approach brilliantly; with his group D.R.A., he has brought the art of playing through metrical labyrinths and complicated rhythmic textures to a high level of mastery. Dell has also emerged as a significant theoretician of improvisation. His book *Prinzip Improvisation* [*The Improvisation Principle*] is a complex philosophical treatise in which Dell draws on the thought of Hannah Arendt, Kant, Socrates, and St. Paul in order to depict improvisation as an "embrace of spontaneity" and a "democratic, intuitive form of practical knowledge." Dell sees improvisation as having the potential for socially therapeutic effects.

Two musicians who have developed personal vibraphone styles in the New York downtown jazz scene are Bill Ware and Matt Moran. Ware uses a great deal of reverb, lending a grooving weight to the stylistic patchworks of the Jazz Passengers. Matt Moran, in contrast, is an intentionally "antivirtuosic" player (though he has no trouble playing fast lines) whose solos cross the boundary lines between composition, improvisation, and folk traditions. He is active in New York's Balkan-jazz scene as well as in innovative projects led by drummer John Hollenbeck and by tenor saxophonist Ellery Eskelin.

However, since the nineties the strongest branch of jazz vibraphone playing has been formed by the players continuing the lineage of Milt Jackson and Bobby Hutcherson. By far the three most important of these are Joe Locke, Steve Nelson, and Stefon Harris.

Stefon Harris picks up where Bobby Hutcherson leaves off. He has an amazing ability to make the vibes sing, kneading and modulating the sound of the instrument according to the emotional context. Harris became known at the end of the nineties through his playing with Wynton Marsalis and Greg Osby. Before taking up the vibraphone, he played classical percussion. He is the great multistylist of the jazz vibraphone, expanding the swinging postbop approach coming out of Hutcherson by incorporating influences from hip-hop, rhythm 'n' blues, and dancefloor, as well as African, Caribbean, and Latin music elements.

Unlike saxophonists or trumpeters, vibraphonists have no way of expanding the pitch range of their instrument through special techniques. The instrument's range is fixed by the number of bars. Mike Mainieri: "With a range of three octaves, you can run out of space pretty fast." Steve Nelson, who came to prominence in the Dave Holland Quintet, plays the vibes as if its range were unlimited. His solos, though complex, are fluent and melodic. In his tasteful, creative improvisations, he creates the illusion of constantly climbing lines, with surprising turns in every bar. Trombonist Steve Davis: "Steve is able to cast a 'musical spell' through the vibes."

Joe Locke is perhaps the fastest, most nimble player of this group. He has brought a particularly high degree of virtuosity to linear postbop vibes playing, and his extremely fluid playing creates sounds not unlike the "sheets of sound" previously associated only with saxophonists. Although Locke is a typical postbop player, he has also repeatedly sought out abstract, free contexts, including duos with Cecil Taylor. He breaks the rules from a standpoint of great consciousness of the jazz tradition: "Limits can give us great freedom. How can you break rules if you don't know anything about them? To improvise freely is the highest aim of improvisation, but there's no freedom without knowledge. But if you play free in a situation coming from the Great American Songbook, you're doubly free."

The Piano

Since the history of jazz begins with ragtime and ragtime was a pianistic music, jazz begins with the piano. Yet the first bands on the streets of New Orleans had no pianos—perhaps because pianos could not be carried around, but perhaps also because the piano could not produce the jazz sound that seemed essential to the early hot players.

The history of jazz piano is acted out between these two poles. The piano offers more possibilities than most other instruments used in jazz. It is not limited to playing one note at a time, as are the horns. It can not only produce rhythm but can also harmonize this rhythm. It can not only state the harmonies, as can the bass, but also connect them with other musical possibilities. But a horn line is more intense than a piano line.

In summary, we find that, on the one hand, the more the pianistic possibilities of the piano are exploited, the more the piano seems overshadowed by the hornlike, intense phrasing of jazz blowers. On the other hand, the more the pianist adopts the phrasing of the horns, the more he or she relinquishes the true potential of the instrument—up to a point that can represent "pianistic suicide" for anyone familiar with pianistic virtuosity in European music.

Art Tatum and Bud Powell (who was too great to be capable of such "pianistic suicide," though it did exist within the piano school he represents) signify the extremes of this last dichotomy. These extremes have been sharpened since the 1880s, when Scott Joplin began to play ragtime in the Midwest. Joplin was a "pianistic" pianist. In many respects he played his instrument clearly within the conventions of the nineteenth-century romantic piano tradition. (See the section on ragtime.)

Since New Orleans bands had no use for pianistic piano players, and since a hornlike piano style had not yet been "discovered," there was hardly one pianist in the jazz bands of old New Orleans. But there were pianists in the saloons and the bars, in the "houses" and cabarets—pianists in abundance. Every house had its "professor," and the professor was a pianist. He played ragtime piano. And even when he played blues and stomps and honky-tonk piano, ragtime was always in the background.

The great professor of New Orleans piano was Jelly Roll Morton, who died in 1941. Morton played ragtime piano with awareness of the marching bands on the New Orleans streets. Filled with pride at his certainly considerable accomplishments, he became almost paranoid: "I have been robbed of three million dollars all told. Everyone today [1939] is playing my stuff and I don't even get credit. Kansas City style, Chicago style, New Orleans style—hell, they're all Jelly Roll style."

The professors, the honky-tonk and "barrelhouse" pianists, existed in New Orleans not only before and during the period of the actual New Orleans style, but also after. However, only a few of them gained fame beyond the limits of the Delta City—for instance, Champion Jack Dupree, Huey "Piano" Smith, and Professor Longhair. Fats Domino (mentioned in the blues section and later again in the vocalists chapter), who stood at the center of the rock 'n' roll movement of the fifties, emerged directly from this tradition. Indeed, in the chapter dealing with jazz vocalists, we shall discuss the fact that New Orleans created styles twice in the history of African American music—not only during the era of New Orleans jazz, but also fifty years later in rhythm 'n' blues and in rock. The New Orleans piano professor bridges these two fields. Jelly Roll Morton made New Orleans jazz with his band; Fats Domino or Professor Longhair made rhythm 'n' blues and rock 'n' roll. Although separated by half a century, Morton and the rhythm 'n' blues pianists of the Crescent City all belong to the same professor and honky-tonk tradition.

Ragtime as played in the Midwest by Scott Joplin was clearly different from ragtime in New Orleans as played by Jelly Roll Morton, but both were music in which one could feel the elements of rag—the elements of "ragged time." Soon, there was ragtime in New York, and again it was different from the piano sounds in the Midwest and in New Orleans. From New York ragtime developed the great era of the Harlem jazz piano. But even if Scott Joplin played in Sedalia, Missouri, from the 1880s, and Jelly Roll Morton named 1902 as the year he "invented" jazz, and the first ragtime pianists played in New York and Harlem around 1910, this still does not prove that the line of evolution led directly from Sedalia over New Orleans to Harlem. Styles, as we have mentioned, develop when the time is ripe, independently of causal schemes of evolution.

James P. Johnson, who died in 1955, was the first important Harlem pianist. He was a schooled musician; from the beginning there were many academically trained musicians among the pianists, in contradistinction to the players of other instruments. James P. Johnson had studied with a pupil of Rimsky-Korsakoff, and late in his career, during the thirties, he composed a series of symphonic and quasi-symphonic works.

With Johnson is revealed for the first time an aspect of jazz piano at least as important as all the brilliant solo achievements: the art of accompaniment, the art of adapting oneself to a soloist, stimulating and giving him or her a foundation on which to build. Johnson did this in unsurpassed fashion for Bessie Smith—on "Preachin' the Blues" or "Backwater Blues," for instance.

Harlem of the twenties was a breeding ground for jazz piano. Duke Ellington related, "Everybody was trying to sound like the 'Carolina Shout' Jimmy [James P. Johnson] had made on a piano roll. I got it down by slowing up the roll. . . . We went out every evening regardless of whether we had money or not. I got a big thrill when I found Willie "The Lion" Smith [one night]. . . . We made the rounds every night looking for the piano players."

Willie "The Lion" Smith is another great pianist of the Harlem tradition of the twenties—a master of charming melodies, which he set off with the mighty rhythm of his left hand.

The Harlem pianists—Johnson, Smith, Ellington, Luckey Roberts, and young Fats Waller—played for "rent parties" and in "cutting contests," all part of the whirling jazz life of Harlem. At the rent parties, jazz was a means of getting up the rent for one's apartment in a friendly atmosphere, and the cutting contests were play-offs among the leading pianists, ending only when one man had definitively "cut" all the others. The most characteristic of their various styles was called stride piano. "Stride" means a constant, swinging alternation of a bass note (played on one and three) and a chord (played on two and four). The switch between the low bass note and the higher chord involves a further step, a stride.

The most important pianist to come out of this Harlem tradition was Fats Waller, who died at thirty-nine in 1943. Louis Armstrong said, "Right now, every time someone mentions Fats Waller's name, why, you can see the grins on all the faces." Fats was two men: one of the greatest pianists in jazz history and one of the funniest and most entertaining comedians of popular music—both of which he managed to combine with inimitable relaxation.

"Livin' the Life I Love" was the theme of his life and his music. He did not always bring it off; for all his comic sense, he still suffered when the public seemed to appreciate his showmanship more than his music. Gene Sedric, Fats's tenor man, said:

> Fats was sometimes very unhappy about his music. You see, he was appreciated for his showmanship ability and for that amount of piano that he played on records, but very few of Waller's record fans knew how much more he could play than what he usually did on records. He didn't try to prove anything by his singing. It was a matter of fun with him. . . . Yet he wanted to do great things on organ and piano—which he could do.

Elsewhere, Sedric said, "As for the record sessions, it seems like they would always give him a whole lot of junk tunes to play because it seemed as if only he could get something out of them."

As composer, Waller wrote some of the most beautiful jazz themes, equally agreeable to all styles. "Honeysuckle Rose" (whose chord progression became a favorite of the beboppers) and "Ain't Misbehavin'" are the most important. Before modern jazz musicians began to experiment with odd meters in the fifties, in 1942 Waller wrote the first great jazz waltz: "Jitterbug Waltz." "Waller," said Coleman Hawkins, "could write tunes as fast as he could play the piano."

His solos are a combination of opposites. They unite weight with delicacy, wild harmony with melodic clarity. As a pianist, Fats had the strongest left hand in traditional jazz—a left hand that could replace not only a rhythm section but a whole band. He was altogether an "orchestral" pianist; that is, his piano sounded rich and full like an orchestra. Quite relevantly, the most orchestral of all jazz pianists, Art Tatum, invoked Waller: "Fats, man—that's where I come from. . . . Quite a place to come from, too!"

The other great pianist to come from Fats Waller is Count Basie. Basie told of his first meeting with Fats: "I had dropped into the old Lincoln Theater in Harlem and heard a young fellow beating it out on the organ. From that time on, I was a daily customer, hanging on to his every note, sitting behind him all the time, fascinated by the ease with which his hands pounded the keys and his feet manipulated the pedals."

Even later, one could sometimes still hear in the piano solos Basie played with his band that he came from Fats Waller. He played a kind of "economized" Fats: an ingeniously abstracted structure of Waller music in which only the cornerstones remain—but they stand for everything else. Basie became one of the most economical pianists in jazz history, and the way he manages to create tension between often widely spaced single notes is incomparable. Many pianists have been influenced by this: Johnny Guarnieri in the Swing era and during the fifties, John Lewis, the maestro of the Modern Jazz Quartet, in whom one senses behind Basie's unconscious economy of means a sage knowledge of all that economy and abstraction imply in music and art. When musicians like Basie or John Lewis leave open spaces in their improvisations, it is more than just empty space; it is a medium of tension and relaxation every bit as important as any note they play.

However, another stream of jazz piano development flowed into Count Basie: the stream of great boogie-woogie pianists. Basie not only plays "economized" Fats Waller, but economized boogie as well.

In the early days, the ragtime and Harlem pianists always looked down a bit condescendingly on the "poor boogie-woogie piano players." Chicago became the center of boogie-woogie. Whereas Harlem rent parties and cutting contests jumped to the sound of stride piano, their counterparts on Chicago's South Side rocked to the beat of blues and boogie piano. Boogie-woogie, too, has its roots in the Midwest and Southwest, down to Texas. From Texas comes one of the few remarkable pianists who in the seventies and eighties still played genuine, uncommercialized boogie and blues piano: Sam Price. Memphis, St. Louis, and Kansas City were important boogie-woogie towns. Memphis Slim, who came from Memphis (d. 1988 in Paris), is among the more recent masters of boogie. He made a name for himself primarily as a blues shouter. There were many blues singers in the black sections of northern and southern cities who accompanied themselves with convincing boogie-woogie piano, or even were outstanding boogie soloists—for example, Roosevelt Sykes, Little Brother Montgomery, and above all, Otis Spann.

The boogie-ostinato—the sharply accented, continuously repeated bass figures—may have developed in the South from the banjo or guitar figures with which the blues singers accompanied themselves. Anyhow, blues and boogie have belonged together since their origin. The first boogies were played as blues accompaniments, and to this day almost all boogies are in the twelve-bar blues pattern. Often, the difference between blues and boogie is anything but distinct; as might be pointed out here, the notion that all boogie-woogie is fast and bouncy is an erroneous generalization. It is just as false as the idea that all blues are slow.

If the search for the origins of boogie-woogie takes us beyond the early banjo and guitar blues accompaniments, we arrive at a time when the differentiation between Latin American (rumba, samba, tango, etc.) and North American (ultimately jazz-influenced) music was not yet so distinct. Jimmy Yancey, the "father of boogie-woogie," and other boogie pianists have based some of their pieces on the bass figures of Latin American dances—Yancey's "Lean Bacon Boogie," for example, is based on a tango figure. In the last analysis, boogie is a sort of "arch-rhythm" of African American music, which is why one encounters it again and again in modern times—as "in disguise" in rhythm 'n' blues of the fifties, in soul music of the sixties, or in Muhal Richard Abrams's piano improvisations of the eighties and nineties, of course often in an alienated, abstract manner. That authentic boogie-woogie can still be alive and effective became apparent when a number of British rock and blues musicians formed Rocket 88 in 1978 on the occasion of the fiftieth anniversary of boogie-woogie (in 1928 Pinetop Smith had recorded his "Pinetop's Boogie-Woogie," which gave the whole style its name). Rocket 88 included, among others, Rolling Stones drummer Charlie Watts, British boogie team George Green and Bob Hall (on two pianos), as well as Alexis Korner, the father of British blues. Equally vital are the recordings made in the eighties by German-born Axel Zwingenberger together with blues singer Big Joe Turner and vibraphonist Lionel Hampton. All these musicians played boogie-woogie with the same cooking intensity that heated up the old boogie joints of twenties Chicago.

At that time, Jimmy Yancey, Pinetop Smith, Cow-Cow Davenport, and Cripple Clarence Lofton were the first important boogie-woogie pianists. Yancey was originally a tap dancer, which might have inspired his eight-to-the-bar playing.

Most brilliant of the boogie-woogie pianists was Meade Lux Lewis, who died in an automobile accident in 1964. His "Honky Tonk Train Blues," first recorded in 1929, achieved legendary status. In the midthirties, when the Negro audience for whom boogie-woogie had been played in the twenties on Chicago's South Side and elsewhere had long since gone beyond this style, the white world began to warm up to it. At that time, jazz critic John Hammond searched for Lewis and found him as a car washer in a suburban Chicago garage. At New York's Cafe Society, Hammond brought him together with two other pioneers of boogie-woogie piano: Albert Ammons and Pete Johnson. The records made by these three masters of boogie at three pianos are among the most exciting examples of boogie-woogie.

The third branch of pianistic development—hornlike piano playing—was the latest to evolve. Earl Hines has been called the first musician of this direction; in any case he is its most important pathbreaker. His playing has been called "trumpet style piano"—the mighty octave movements of his right hand sounded like a translation of Louis Armstrong's trumpet lines to the piano. But Hines (d. 1983) was a musician in his own right, filled with energy and humor and revealing musical and human development even in his old age. He is one of those fascinating personalities of jazz who have become legends in their own time.

No piano can sound "like a horn," but Hines is the founder of a school whose pianists realized lines—little by little at first, but more and more generally later—that may not have attained a hornlike expression but surely the contours of hornlike phrases. This school leads via Mary Lou Williams, Teddy Wilson, Nat "King" Cole, and, of special importance, Bud Powell, up to countless pianists of contemporary jazz.

Of special interest is Mary Lou Williams, since she lived through this entire school and developed parallel to it. Mary Lou (1910–81) is surely the most important female figure in the whole history of instrumental jazz. She began to play around 1927, in the blues and boogie-woogie style of the day. In Kansas City she became arranger and pianist for the Andy Kirk band. She wrote a number of arrangements—for Kirk, Benny Goodman ("Roll 'Em"), and Duke Ellington ("Trumpets No End," which is an arrangement of Irving Berlin's "Blue Skies")—that cannot be left out of any history of jazz. As a pianist she evolved through Swing and bop into a mature representative of modern jazz piano, which caused some to say that this "First Lady of Jazz" had no style of her own. She herself said with justified assurance:

> I consider that a compliment, although I think that everyone with ears can identify me without any difficulty. But it's true that I'm always experimenting, always changing, always finding new things. Why, back in Kansas City I found chords they're just beginning to use now. What happens to so many good pianists is that they become so stylized that they can't break out of the prison of their styles and absorb ideas and new techniques.

She demonstrated this openness toward new developments as recently as 1977, when she played a noted duo concert with the best-known player of free-jazz piano, Cecil Taylor.

In the Swing style of the thirties the Earl Hines direction is embodied first of all in Teddy Wilson. He connects it with the format of the great black Swing horn players and with the elegance and affability that

Benny Goodman brought to the jazz of that day. Wilson made Swing piano exquisite by removing the rumbling, heavy elements from Harlem stride piano. As a member of the Goodman combos and as leader of his own ensembles, Wilson participated in some of the best and most representative combo recordings of the Swing era. During the thirties, he influenced almost every pianist—including Mel Powell, Billy Kyle, Jess Stacy, and Joe Bushkin. Bushkin, of course, was also influenced by the "grand old man" of all jazz pianists: Art Tatum. Marian McPartland has transferred the elegance of Wilson—with whom she recorded a duo album—to mainstream jazz, incorporating many of the musical insights since then. She is one of those players who in the course of her life keeps growing in stature.

Everything created in the history of jazz piano up to the time of his renown—the midthirties—comes together in Art Tatum, with the addition of a pianistic virtuosity that has been compared to that of the great concert pianists, such as Rubinstein or Cherkassky, and that before him was unheard of in jazz. The cadenzas and runs, the arpeggios and embellishments of the virtuoso piano music of the late nineteenth century are as alive in his playing as a strong feeling for the blues, which he demonstrated in, say, his recordings with blues singer Joe Turner.

Tatum's improvising was so virtuosic that he gave the impression of playing with twelve fingers rather than ten. His lightning-fast arpeggios, dense chords, and daring pirouettes back and forth across the keyboard are without parallel in jazz. His harmonic conception seemed to transcend all formulas and concepts. His appearances in New York clubs attracted a cult following not only among jazz musicians, but also among classical concert pianists such as Leopold Godowsky, Vladimir Horowitz, and Walter Gieseking, all of whom made the pilgrimage to Fifty-Second Street's Onyx Club, where Tatum played regularly.

Nurtured on the piano techniques of the nineteenth century, Tatum showed a certain preference for the salon pieces of that time—such as Dvořák's "Humoresque," Massenet's "Elégie," and others of this genre, which didn't always satisfy the highest of artistic demands. But it is characteristic of the high esteem in which Tatum is held by almost all jazz musicians that a storm of protest arose when French jazz critic André Hodeir brought up this question of taste. Even musicians who otherwise could not be moved to write took pen in hand to send in glowing defenses of Tatum.

Tatum, who died in 1956, was a soloist—period. His piano was his best band. Aside from a few combo recordings with all-star personnel or the previously mentioned sessions with blues singer Joe Turner, he was accustomed to playing solo or with his own trio. Tatum continues to be influential—as on French pianist Martial Solal or Adam Makowicz from Poland, and indirectly also on dozens of piano players who today play virtuoso solo piano. In this sense it might be said that Art Tatum's universal piano approach has experienced its real triumphs since the seventies, over twenty-five years after this great musician's death. Russian-American Simon Nabotov is a pianist who continued Tatum's legacy in the multistylistic jazz of the nineties in incomparable fashion.

After Tatum, the counterplay between the pianistic and the hornlike conceptions of jazz piano becomes particularly marked. Bud Powell, who died in 1966 under tragic circumstances, was the primary exponent of the hornlike approach and, in general, the most influential pianist of modern jazz. At eighteen, he had already played with Charlie Christian and Charlie Parker at Minton's. He has been called the "Bird of jazz piano," and he was similarly tormented and threatened as a human being. After his creative period, from the midforties to the early fifties, he spent more than half his time in asylums. During this relatively long time, he often was only a shadow of the greatness he displayed in those few years when he actually created the modern piano style.

The problem of Powell is an intensification of the problem of the jazz musician in general: the problem of the artist who is creative within a socially and racially discriminatory world whose aggressiveness and lack of sensibility cannot possibly be borne by those artists who are neither willing nor able to play the game.

Powell created those sharply etched lines that seem to stand free in space like glowing metal that has hardened. Yet Bud is also a romanticist, whose "Glass Enclosure" (an original composition) or whose ballad interpretations—for instance, "Polkadots and Moonbeams"—have the gentle charm of Robert Schumann's "Scenes from Childhood." This tension between the hardness of his hornlike lines and his romantic sensibility is always present, and perhaps it was this tension between two ultimately incompatible extremes that also contributed to the tragedy of this wonderful musician. As a pianist, Bud Powell freed the left hand from its role as timekeeper. For Powell, the left hand is no longer a "virtual rhythm section," as it is in boogie-woogie or stride playing. Rather, it takes on the role of providing harmonic cues and support for the long, energetic, hornlike single-note lines played by the right hand. In this way, Bud Powell created the turning point toward modern jazz piano—in bop, the piano became a soloistic voice equal to that of the horns.

From Tatum comes the technique; from Powell, the style. Tatum set a pianistic standard that for a long time seemed unattainable. Bud Powell founded a school. Thus, there are more pianists in modern jazz who are "Powell students" than there are "Tatum students." Descended from Tatum are first of all Billy Taylor, Martial Solal, Hank Jones, Jimmy Rowles, Phineas Newborn, and Oscar Peterson (who, of course, are also influenced to a certain degree by Bud Powell and other pianists). Jones combines bebop and Tatum, leading this combination to ever greater maturity and integrity up to the present day—since the seventies also in impressive solo appearances. Solal is the great father figure of modern French jazz. His fairly abstract playing possesses French brilliance and Gallic humor and esprit. Sometimes the wealth of his ideas and intimations explodes like fireworks.

When in the course of the seventies Polish pianist Adam Makowicz came to the fore, it became apparent how strong the Tatum tradition still is. Makowicz plays a very concertlike, Chopinesque kind of Tatum style. Guided by John Hammond, the greatest talent scout of jazz, he moved to New York in 1978, where he stated, "What I am learning here is mainly rhythm." Simon Nabotov brought the Tatum legacy into the nineties with a pronounced sense of adventure and a humorous willingness to take chances. Like Tatum, Nabotov is fond of large, rhapsodically moving groups of notes, but he also deconstructs elements of traditional jazz piano by transforming them into "freer" ways of playing with gravity and sensitivity.

The most successful pianist of the Tatum school, however, is Oscar Peterson; time and again he has pointed out how strongly indebted he feels to Tatum. Peterson is a swinger of immense energy and gripping attack. In the seventies, when he started to give solo concerts (without the small groups with whom he had appeared until then), one could hear that the Harlem pianists—Fats Waller and James P. Johnson with their mighty bass lines, who in turn were Tatum's ancestors—had also left their mark on him.

If one wanted to find a way to distinguish Peterson from his idol and mentor Tatum, one way to do it would be to note that Peterson is, in addition to his abilities as a soloist, a brilliant accompanist. And Peterson's legendary trios, for example with Ray Brown and Ed Thigpen, are not just platforms for pianistic virtuosity, but are also masterfully integrated ensembles in which Peterson achieves new high points of interplay and group balance. Third, Peterson plays with an earthy, grounded swing. Tatum is the great harmonist of the jazz piano; Peterson is the most swinging of its powerful melodists.

In the meantime, Peterson has formed a school of his own. One of the pianists in this school is Monty Alexander, who combines an attack à la Peterson with the charm, and the ska and reggae grooves, of his native Jamaica.

From Bud Powell come Al Haig, George Wallington, Lou Levy, Lennie Tristano, Hampton Hawes, Claude Williamson, Joe Albany, Dave McKenna, Japanese émigré Toshiko Akiyoshi, Wynton Kelly, Russ Freeman, Harold Mabern, Cedar Walton, Mose Allison, Red Garland, Horace Silver, Barry Harris, Duke Jordan, Kenny Drew, Walter Bishop, Elmo Hope, Tommy Flanagan, Bobby Timmons, Junior Mance, Ray Bryant, Horace Parlan, Roger Kellaway, Roland Hanna, Les McCann, Austrian Fritz Pauer, and a legion of other pianists, including representatives not just of neobop (where many of those mentioned here are also to be found) but of neoclassicism, too.

Al Haig, Duke Jordan, and George Wallington played in combos on Fifty-Second Street during the formative years of modern jazz. Lennie Tristano (1919–78) is the head of the previously mentioned Tristano school, which had such great importance at the time of the crystallization of cool jazz. He played long, sweeping, sensitive melodic lines (often almost in the sense of Bach's linearity) over complex harmonic structures. As Lynn Anderson put it, "He was the first piano player to spontaneously improvise extended chord stretches. . . . He was the first to improvise counterpoint. . . . Another of his innovations was his conception of bypassed resolution, so that harmony does not always move in the way you think it should." Tristano anticipated the harmonic freedom of free jazz by as much as ten years.

Tristano's influence reaches across many styles. Among those pianists who have paid allegiance to him are Don Friedman, Clare Fischer, and, above all, Bill Evans; among the younger ones are Alan Broadbent, Connie Crothers, Ken Werner, Eric Watson, and John Wolf Brennan, all of whom show how alive the Tristano influence still is.

Russ Freeman and Claude Williamson are the main pianists of West Coast jazz. Hampton Hawes, who also lived on the West Coast (he died in 1977), does not fit in the West Coast bag. He had a strong blues and Charlie Parker feeling, which was very much rooted in his black heritage. Mose Allison (see also the section on vocalists) represents an intriguingly direct connection between old blues and folk songs and modern Bud Powell piano. Red Garland is a hard-bop pianist who sparkles with ideas. He became known through his work with the Miles Davis Quintet in the midfifties. He created amazing voicings, concise single lines that he played with the right hand and that stood in astonishing contrast to the explosive block chords in his left hand. After he left Davis, his place was taken first by Bill Evans (of whom more later) and then Wynton Kelly. Kelly's playing was not as harmonically refined as Garland's, but his bubbling, joyful lines had a swaggering swing and a timing that became a model for many neo–hard-bop pianists in the nineties. Miles Davis said, "Without Wynton, it's like coffee without cream." Kelly, and even more so Junior Mance, Les McCann, and Bobby Timmons, belong to the funk- and gospel-inspired hard-bop pianists. Timmons's compositions "Moanin'," "This Here," and "Dat Dere," written in the late fifties when he was in Art Blakey's Messengers and Cannonball Adderley's quintet, became highly successful. In the early seventies, Les McCann combined his soul piano conception, which he had presented with great success in the fifties, with contemporary electric sounds.

Ray Bryant is a master of expressive, highly rhythmicized blues lines, into which he time and again incorporates powerful boogie elements. Tommy Flanagan, a musician of the Detroit hard-bop generation, has found a delicacy in the "hardness" of hard bop that few others have. He has raised the art of accompanying vocalists to new heights; in 1962–65, he brought the best out of Ella Fitzgerald, for example. Until his death in 2001, he led one of the most consistent trios in mainstream jazz.

Barry Harris was always designated a "genius" by the musicians to come out of Detroit. He was the strongest and most individual personality behind the Detroit jazz scene and remained an important jazz pedagogue into the early twenty-first century. Horace Silver has extended the Powell heritage particularly convincingly—to a funk and soul-inspired playing style with firm, full melodies and rhythms full of riffs and grooves, coupled with an audacious sense of form and affable vitality, which has become a success formula for himself and his quintet.

"The idea of spontaneity is part of jazz, and Thelonious Monk played piano as if he'd never seen one before," wrote English writer Geoff Dyer. Monk sounded like no one else. He was a deliberately percussive player.

One of the important musicians from the in-group of the bop creators, his influence was realized only from the second half of the fifties on. He had hardly finished contributing to the invention of bop when he turned away from it to create something completely new. Monk "Africanized" the piano—the quintessentially European instrument—by playing it percussively, with a hard-edged attack. Monk played "al fresco–like," widely spaced, often barely indicated lines. In terms of the dissolution of the phrase as a unit and harmony as a functional system, he went further than almost anyone before free jazz. Much of what leads to Ornette Coleman, John Coltrane, Eric Dolphy, and all the other avant-gardists of jazz was heard for the first time in his music—anchored in a strong blues feeling and saturated with a mocking, burlesquing sense of humor. His playing, as innovative as it appeared, was nonetheless deeply rooted in jazz tradition, as became particularly clear when he included elements of stride piano in his playing, as if to deconstruct it. Monk's own themes, with their rhythmic displacements and irregular structures, are among the most original themes in modern jazz.

Monk was an innovator with a guaranteed sense of swing. For this reason, today he is revered equally by bop conservatives and by avant-gardists. The neoconservative jazz musicians around Wynton Marsalis maintain that Monk's music has no "out content"—that nothing in it bursts the boundaries of musical rules or logic. On the other hand, the avant-gardists in the jazz community emphasize the obstinate, recalcitrant aspects of Monk's music, its rebelliousness and nonconformity. In fact, both positions are accurate characterizations of Monk and his music, whose message is: be different than the others. Be yourself. Monk translated this attitude into music with more logic and more swing than anyone else.

Monk improvised like a composer thinking out loud at the piano. His angular, bizarre solos are certainly spontaneously invented, but they don't constitute chains of association detached from the theme. They are in fact so closely linked with his compositions, pursuing them so "logically," that they themselves seem "composed." Monk has seldom been successfully imitated on the piano—probably because his piano style entails continuation of composition (by other means) rather than jazz virtuosity as such.

The first musicians to take up Monk's musical language, further developing it in personal fashion, were Randy Weston, Herbie Nichols, and Mal Waldron. Weston, who besides Monk names Ellington as a model, lived in North Africa for years, where he also entered into an intense dialogue with the trancelike melodies and rhythms of Arab Gnawa music. Weston says, "I found out that many things I thought were modern have existed in Africa for thousands of years." Weston's piano playing is milder and more rhapsodic than that of Monk. His power, and the spare expressiveness with which he uses the piano's bass register, make his playing unmistakable. "I have a couple of nice drums there on the bottom," he says.

Nichols played in traditional and blues bands before he had an opportunity to present his bizarre and novel compositions. He died of leukemia, in poverty and virtually forgotten, in 1963. The trio recordings he made for the Blue Note label in 1955 were an early pointer toward the jazz avant-garde to come, with their delicate, unwieldy melodies and their abstract structures in which the drums functioned as an equal voice. Later free-jazz pianists such as Misha Mengelberg and Cecil Taylor would acknowledge the importance of the liberating influence that Nichols, after Monk, had on them. He was one of the true originals of jazz piano. Mal Waldron had great success in Japan during the seventies. His way of playing was referred to as "telegraph style": his phrases sounded like "long-long-short-long," like a mysterious Morse code. Waldron was the last accompanist for the great Billie Holiday. From then until his death in 2002, he developed an increasingly individual style in which "space" is very important. The courage to express oneself simply and starkly was especially strong in Waldron. He also discovered the "power of repetition" for modern jazz piano. He distilled the torrential melodic lines of bop into short, pregnant figures, which he insistently repeated to create harmonic, melodic, and rhythmic tension and novelty. In their obstinate insistence, these figures sounded like a Morse code from the future, messages written in a secret code of surprise.

An especially successful pianist was Bill Evans, who died in 1980. Evans was one of the few white musicians accepted within the narrower circles of hard bop; yet his style was completely different from that of other hard-bop pianists, much more sensitive and fragile. In today's terms, he was the first "modal" pianist. He was sometimes called an "American Chopin," with the eminent skill—without comparison in jazz—to make the piano sound in a way that places him (in terms of sound) in the vicinity of a pianist like Rubinstein. With his sensitive lines, he gave modern jazz piano a completely new lyrical dimension. Evans was the first to play jazz piano totally "pianistically," not percussively, as his predecessors had done. He made the piano sound like a singer. It is no wonder that such a unique and interesting combination of heterogeneous elements has been successful in commercial terms as well (in the Bill Evans Trio). Evans's work with other musicians—with Miles Davis or bass player Scott LaFaro, for instance—shows him to be, as German pianist Michael Naura said, "a musician who seems to register his environment in an almost spiritualistic manner. Only someone capable of total devotion can play a piano like that."

Bill Evans revolutionized the jazz piano trio, a genre that dates back to the twenties. After Evans, the jazz piano trio is a texture woven from three more or less equal voices. Bill Evans invented new forms of integration for the piano trio by erasing the previously automatic assignment of solo and accompaniment roles. To simplify somewhat, before the Evans Trio was formed in 1959, jazz piano trios played "two-dimensionally." On the one hand, the piano dominated and led; on the other hand, the rhythm section of bass and drums had the task of establishing the appropriate foundation. The Bill Evans Trio, however, was the first jazz piano group to play "three-dimensionally." Now each instrument in the trio could assume a leading role, which meant that bassist Scott LaFaro was by no means restricted to playing walking lines (with four quarter notes to the bar). He also phrased lines that were melodically and rhythmically independent of his supporting function. Paul Motian similarly developed a freer way of playing that extended time-keeping (marking the beat) and opened up additional melodic possibilities for the drums. By creating a new division of labor between the piano, bass, and drums, Bill Evans introduced to the piano trio an element that has since become the standard of successful music-making in this configuration: the freshness of equal dialogue.

It is illuminating that Evans has been a point of departure for a whole line of pianists. Don Friedman on the East Coast, with his sensitive and clear piano improvisations, Krzysztof Komeda from Poland, and Clare Fischer on the West Coast, who also has made a name for himself as an arranger, were the first, later followed by such younger players as Fred Hersch, Italian-born Enrico Pieranunzi, and Michel Petrucciani, a particularly impressive French performer.

Krzysztof Komeda (1931–69) is the legendary father figure of modern Polish jazz, also important as a composer. His pieces, tinged with Slavic melancholy, are some of the most beautiful and lasting contributions to European jazz. The best-known of them is "Sleep Safe and Warm," which he wrote for Roman Polanski's film *Rosemary's Baby*.

Enrico Pieranunzi's sparkling playing made him the doyen of the Italian mainstream scene. Few European pianists can match his rhythmic sensitivity and harmonic refinement.

Fred Hersch is an Evans-oriented pianist of great linear clarity. He excels in treating secondary voices so delicately and with such attention to detail that they become melodically interesting in their own right.

When Michel Petrucciani moved from Paris to America in 1981, only a few European jazz specialists knew about him. Then, at the age of eighteen, he played with saxophonist Charles Lloyd, and later with Lee Konitz and Jim Hall. From then until his unexpected death in 1999, his concert appearances were among the most moving occasions at all the big jazz festivals. When the dwarflike pianist, who had to be carried to the piano stool, started playing, he developed Evans's vocabulary so vitally and with such joy in risk taking that you'd think he was presenting a "percussionized" Evans, expanding his precursor's sensitivity with fiery élan and rhapsodic power. It is fitting that Petrucciani—whose improvisations also reflect Art Tatum, Maurice Ravel, and Claude Debussy—should have started out as a drummer.

But seventies and eighties aestheticism would also have been inconceivable without the Evans touch. Chick Corea, Keith Jarrett, Paul Bley, Steve Kuhn—"Evans is the father of them all," according to Michel Petrucciani. In the eighties and nineties there existed (as will be shown) a Bill Evans classicism.

Jaki Byard (who died in 1999) holds a special position. He emerged from the Mingus group, and on the one hand played very modern, nearly free improvisations with abrasive sounds; but on the other hand, he was rooted in the stride piano of the twenties. As early as the fifties, he was a musician with that total grasp of the black tradition, which Mingus and Roland Kirk set up as an ideal.

There are a few musicians who do not fit into the system we have tried to use in classifying the pianists. They should be discussed now, before going on. As a member of Lionel Hampton's band, Milt Buckner (who died in 1977) created a "block chord style"—with intertwined, parallel note movements—that has a strong, stimulating effect. With this approach, called the "locked hands" style due to the parallel movement of the two hands, he sometimes sounded as if he were transferring a whole trumpet section in all its sweeping brilliance to the piano.

British-born George Shearing incorporated Buckner's style into the sound of his quintet. Combined with the bop lines of Bud Powell, he developed this style into a success formula, but he also has a Chopinesque sensitivity.

Characteristically, the most sensational success has been enjoyed by the two pianists who are least definable in terms of schools: Dave Brubeck and Erroll Garner. Brubeck has incorporated a wealth of European musical elements, from Bach to Darius Milhaud (with whom he studied), in his playing—elements that in his music seem to be enveloped within a certain romanticism. The question whether Brubeck "swings" has been debated for years. Critics and musicians have attacked him for "pounding" the piano. But Brubeck is a marvelously imaginative and individual improviser. He and his alto saxophonist Paul Desmond mutually inspired one another almost in the intuitive way of sleepwalkers. Brubeck often finds his way to moving climaxes. The way in which he builds to these climaxes over wide stretches and seemingly "shores up" to them is unique and original.

Since Fats Waller, there has been no pianist whose name was so synonymous with exuberant joy as that of Erroll Garner. Garner is also comparable to Fats—and to Tatum—in his orchestral approach to the piano. He sovereignly commands the entire keyboard. *Concert by the Sea* is the title of one of his most successful records; the title is appropriate not only because this concert was recorded on the Pacific Coast, but also because Garner's piano cascades bring to mind the roar of the sea. The rhythmic independence that Garner achieved between the left and right hands was phenomenal. He was able to give each hand its own timing, and to bring these two rhythmic planes into an energetic relationship of tension. In addition to this, Garner was a master of fascinating relaxation. When he played, the listener sometimes felt that the beat had been delayed too long, but when it came, you knew it fell just where it belonged. Also masterful were Garner's introductions, which—often with cadenzas, often also with humorous intimations—seemed to delay the start of the theme and the beat further and further. Garner's worldwide audiences applauded enthusiastically when pianist and audience finally arrived "back home" again, in the well-known melody and the even better-known "Garner beat," with its even, "trotting" quarter-note chords in the left hand.

The familiar observation that the jazz pianist plays the instrument like a big band was particularly applicable to Garner, who never learned to read a note of music. He said, "I always play what I feel. I always feel like me, but I'm a different me every day. I get ideas from everything. A big color, the sound of water and wind, or a flash of something cool. Playing is like life. Either you feel it or you don't."

Garner was so singular and original that only two pianists are really related to him: Ellis Larkins and Ahmad Jamal. Larkins played some of the most beautiful piano accompaniments in jazz history, on a record of Ella Fitzgerald singing Gershwin. The younger Jamal occupied a curious position at the end of the fifties, evaluated in sharply contrasting fashion by musicians and critics. While most of the latter hardly considered him more than a gifted cocktail pianist, many musicians—primarily Miles Davis—have called him a towering "genius." Jamal's timing and combination of embellishment and economy are masterly. Gunther Schuller believes that Miles's high regard for Jamal is mainly due to the fact that the Davis of the fifties adopted certain ways of embellishing and, to a certain degree, his sophisticated simplicity from Jamal, and that Miles's great success began with this adoption. Since the eighties, Jamal has increasingly "Africanized" his concept of spareness and his feeling for the charged tension of pauses, using groove- and dance-conscious melodies and rhythms that point toward Africa in the context of his swinging mainstream piano.

Almost single-handedly, Cecil Taylor developed a language on the piano that was essential to the development of free jazz. Born in Long Island in 1929, Taylor was, at the end of the fifties, the first to draw the correct conclusion from his deep knowledge of African American music, Ellington's art of arrangement, and European composers such as Bartók: that the future of jazz lay in its liberation from norms of song form, rhythm, and tonality that had become restrictive.

In his clusters, racing across the entire keyboard of the piano, a cosmos of sonic and rhythmic invention oscillates and swings. The physical aspect of a Taylor performance, the stamina with which he brings his jarring, percussive clusters of sound from climax to climax over two hours or more, is so overwhelming that the delicate, detailed structure of the music is often concealed by its sheer physicality. It is one of the ironies of jazz history that the pianist who developed these blocks of sound with the greatest logical consistency was at first accused of chaos and anarchy.

Taylor's "free" motivic sequences are in fact deployed according to an easily understood pattern. The "call and response" structures of African music play an important role, as does the use of thesis and antithesis with subsequent development. Even the principle of thematic/motivic improvisation, identified in Sonny Rollins's playing by Gunther Schuller, can easily be heard in Cecil Taylor's playing—with the difference that it does not take place within the framework of a fixed form, and that it consists not so much of tonal elements as of sound blocks and groups of clusters that Taylor sets into relation with each other, constantly redeveloping them with a propulsive energy. Taylor himself has pointed out that he feels more at home in his own black tradition—above all, in Duke Ellington—than in European music. If you listen to him carefully, you can detect in his playing dozens of elements from the history of black piano music: blues cadenzas and bop phrases and boogie basses, but all of them as if they were encoded in clusters, only intimated, estranged, abstract, and—as soon as they are sounded—transformed into the next element in the gushing stream of idea after idea. His intensity consists not just of racing across the keyboard; it is fed by, as he put it, "the magical lifting of one's spirits to a state of trance. . . . It has to do with religious forces"—in the sense of the African tradition.

In his music, Taylor has emphasized his African and Indian roots and the trance aspect of the dance; one of his most famous statements is: "I try to imitate on the piano the leaps in space a dancer makes."

German pianist Alexander von Schlippenbach, strongly influenced by Taylor, has pointed out that any other pianist would be capable of generating such burning and bursting intensity for only a few minutes, and that it is incredible that Taylor is able to keep up such playing for an entire evening in long concerts or club appearances. In the eighties and nineties, Taylor's music became increasingly clear and spare, more impressionistic, and more tonal and calm in some passages—giving it even more power and capability of differentiation.

Cecil Taylor is the outstanding pianist in free jazz, but there are—independently of him or coming from him—an abundance of other pianistic possibilities in this field. First the American musicians. Important free-jazz pianists (who often developed in other directions) are Paul Bley, Carla Bley, Ran Blake, Sun Ra (famous mainly as the leader of his free big band), Dave Burrell, Bobby Few, Borah Bergman, Marilyn Crispell, Matthew Shipp, Vijay Iyer; and then, already as a bridge to the tradition-conscious avant-garde, Muhal Richard Abrams, Don Pullen, Anthony Davis, Amina Claudine Myers, Geri Allen, and Myra Melford. We can discuss only a few of these pianists in detail.

Paul Bley was the first pianist to play ballads in the spirit of free jazz (making him a source of inspiration for Keith Jarrett, discussed below). Bley can be seen as having built on the innovations of Ornette Coleman, in much the same way that Bud Powell did with respect to the achievements of Charlie Parker. Just as Powell translated Bird's quick bop lines to the piano, Bley transposed Ornette's freely singing motives to the keyboard, making him one of the piano's innovators in the sixties.

Ran Blake and Carla Bley are especially sensitive players. Ran, who has been influenced by Thelonious Monk, is a master of estranging standard tunes by the great writers of American popular music. He tears, shreds, and abstracts these tunes, transplanting them to a new musical world diametrically opposed to their original world (which certainly involves a sociocritical process). Carla Bley (more about her in the big-bands chapter) became known mainly as a player of her own tender, delicate compositions, perhaps the most original jazz compositions this side of Thelonious Monk. "Escalator over the Hill," the "chronotransduction" Carla created with writer Paul Haines, is the first successful magnum opus of postmodern jazz, which matured as early as 1971 to that colorful polystylism and category-transcending eclecticism that was to become a matter of course only ten years later in the eighties. The linguistic creation "chronotransduction" illuminates the point: time and space are being transcended in a musical and poetic sense.

Borah Bergman endowed free-jazz piano with lightness and elasticity. He possesses, as one critic said, "increased power and strength in his left hand." Often his Ornette-influenced left-hand lines sound as if they were played with both hands. Bergman thus attains total equality between the two hands. The most interesting and original advancement of the Cecil Taylor line in the eighties and nineties came, however, from a woman: Marilyn Crispell. Crispell, who first worked with Anthony Braxton's group and studied at Karl Berger's Woodstock Creative Music Studio, unites Taylor's enormous energy with Coltrane's spirituality. Like Taylor she came from classical concert music to jazz, and like Taylor she also studied at the New England Conservatory in Boston. But Crispell plays more lyrically, pointillistically. She breaks up Taylor's blocklike clusters and momentum into free, highly intense contrapuntalism, spiritually rather than materially inspired by baroque music, and Bach in particular. Crispell causes energy-charged particles of ideas to collide within fractions of seconds, and yet she does so with the sovereign and refined assurance of a post–free-jazz musician who has found the way from "controlled chaos" to more formally unified structures.

Muhal Richard Abrams is the "chief" (although he would object to that term) of the frequently mentioned AACM: one of the first pianists who deliberately moved on from free jazz to polystylism, incorporating the entire black tradition from ragtime and boogie onward into free playing. Like Abrams, Myra Melford comes from Chicago, and like him she also seems to have the entire jazz tradition under her fingers. In her free playing, she melds blues and boogie, barrelhouse and bop, with explosive force and a very open rhythmic feeling, creating lines of extraordinary contrapuntal density. She is a master of exciting tempo accelerations and retardations. The most vital and wildest pianist of the free-inspired reevaluation of the jazz heritage was, however, Don Pullen, who made his name in a quartet with tenor saxophonist George Adams. Pullen uniquely melodized cluster playing and made it tonal. He phrased impulsively raw clusters with his right hand and yet embedded them in clear, harmonically functional tonal chords simultaneously played with the left hand. Independently of Taylor he developed an entirely individual cluster technique. Unlike Taylor he didn't *strike* such clusters, but rather used the knuckles and side of his hand in sweeping across the keys, producing glissandolike, quasi-melodic streams of sound perpetuating the rawness and directness of the blues. "I like it down and dirty," he once said. A few years before his death in 1995, Don Pullen, in his band African-Brazilian Connection, incorporated world music elements, creating a vital, joyfully swinging jazz influenced by melodies from West Africa, Brazil, and the Caribbean.

Anthony Davis is a cool, aware player, who was also influenced by romantic and classical music (particularly chamber music) that he heard in the parental home. He is the most distinctive musician in a generation that discovered, within the realm of "free" jazz, the importance of composition for their playing. "I would like everything I play to be linked with what went before and what will come afterwards," he told Francis Davis, the U.S. critic. "Even when I'm improvising freely, I'm still thinking compositionally. . . . It amounts to the same thing." In 1985, his opera X—The Life and Times of Malcolm X was premiered.

Michele Rosewoman sensitively brought the percussiveness of Afro-Cuban rhythms, dating back to the ancient rituals of Yoruba culture, into contemporary jazz piano playing. Geri Allen from Detroit has attained particular pianistic originality in pursuing the postmodern principle of mixing styles. Allen, who became known playing with James Newton and with Steve Coleman, mainly comes from Cecil Taylor and Thelonious Monk, but her intricate, angular lines also provide exemplary illustration of multilayered jazz piano playing. They give voice to the romanticism of Chick Corea (still to be introduced), the percussiveness of African *balaphon* music, Count Basie's art of playing with pauses, and Ellington's feeling for tonal color. Tradition and the avant-garde have seldom coexisted alongside each other as closely as they do in Allen's playing. She phrases with great freedom and is equally fluent at playing "inside" and "outside," both rhythmically and harmonically. Above all, Allen plays the most original bass figures and ostinatos in contemporary jazz piano—full of tricky changes of rhythm and effective displacements and dissonances, accompanied by an admirable rhythmic flow and a strong feeling for the African roots of black music. Her piano often sounds like an "mbira with eighty-eight keys," like a giant westernized African thumb piano.

Like Allen, Indian-American pianist Vijay Iyer is one of the few pianists who has successfully internalized the M-Base aesthetic in his playing. For years, he was an important part of the groups of Steve Coleman, and names the percussive school of jazz piano as his influence: players like Cecil Taylor, Thelonious Monk, and Bud Powell. In his own jazz, inspired by the avant-garde, he uses the complex rhythmic patterns of South Indian drum music, combining these with the metric textures of M-Base music in a unique way.

Matthew Shipp, who emerged from the David S. Ware quartet, has set new standards in building bridges between free improvised music and electronica. In 2001, he was the curator of the "Blue Series" for the label Thirsty Ears, where he created a platform for the encounter of free jazz with DJs and electronicists. He made free jazz hip again by collaborating with sampler and computer artists. In his "merely" acoustic solo piano concerts, he is a specialist in "pantonal music." In his solos, he often juxtaposes smoothly flowing passages and hard, fierce clusters, razor-sharp block chords and impressionistic voicings, pointillistic flurries and calm passages of sound, creating rapid sequences of tension and release.

Taylor's message has also fallen on fruitful soil in Europe and Asia. There the important free pianists include Yosuke Yamashita and Aki Takase from Japan; Englishman Keith Tippett; Dutch-born Misha Mengelberg; Belgian Fred van Hove; Germans Alexander von Schlippenbach, Ulrich Gumpert, Achim Kaufmann, and Georg Gräwe; Swiss-born Irène

Schweizer and Sylvie Courvoisier; Frenchman Benoit Delbecq; Russians Vyacheslav Ganelin (immigrated to Israel in 1987) and Sergey Kuryokhin; and Giorgio Gaslini from Italy. Here, too, only a few musicians can be mentioned.

U.S. critics have accused Yosuke Yamashita of imitating Cecil Taylor, but he derives his ritualistic power and intensity (reminiscent of Taylor) from the Japanese rather than the American tradition, drawing on a centuries-old culture of fervency. Aki Takase merges filigrain style with a high degree of esprit and humor. She makes masterful use of numerous older elements of jazz, presenting them in a freer contemporary context in a personal matter. Takase is also a master of duo playing; her performances with Maria João, with Alexander von Schlippenbach, and with Rudi Mahall are brilliant examples of integration and sharp, cryptic interplay.

Keith Tippett plays a free jazz much influenced by ethnic music, where ostinato patterns and meditative structures, magical in their impact, are of considerable importance. His Centipede orchestra, bringing together fifty-one musicians from rock and jazz who recorded the *Septober Energy* album in 1971, was one of the crucial (and yet too little appreciated) seventies jazz groups extending beyond established frontiers.

Misha Mengelberg, who attracted attention as head of the Instant Composers' Pool, is inspired by Thelonious Monk and Herbie Nichols. He plays free jazz full of idiosyncratic, eccentric humor. He is a master of reduction and ambiguous allusion. His duo with drummer Han Bennink, reflecting the spontaneous happenings of fluxus art, is among the longest-lasting and most vital of European free-jazz combos.

Alexander von Schlippenbach heads the Globe Unity Orchestra, the first and longest-lasting European free-jazz orchestra (established in 1966), which has held together until today. Musicologist Ekkehard Jost calls Schlippenbach's sounds "rasping structures": highly energetic and unusually dense sounds, concentrating on color and rhythm.

Irène Schweizer is at the communicative, tranquil center of many women's ensembles in jazz such as the Feminist Improvising Group, but in her performances with male musicians her solos also achieve a high degree of interactive richness. Her clear phrasing is characterized by a high degree of percussiveness. Sylvie Courvoisier, who has lived in New York since 1998, crosses the boundaries between jazz and new music. Her lucid, dark music is full of complex structures and intuitive invention.

Inspired by John Cage, Benoit Delbecq has brought a large number of microtonal possibilities and floating sounds to the jazz piano by preparing the strings of the piano in an imaginative manner. Vyacheslav Ganelin was the main musical and dramatic force behind the Ganelin Trio from 1971 until its dissolution in 1989, which developed a completely individual form of free interaction in the former Soviet Union. This group cultivated an often parodistic, stylistic openness consciously directed against all of free jazz's dogmas, pursuing an ironical dialectic rooted in Soviet tradition.

In Europe, German pianist Georg Gräwe has developed and abstracted the Tristano approach in a way that carries it to the edge of new music, combining Tristano's rhythmic energy with the intellectual rigor of Arnold Schoenberg. Hans-Jürgen Osterhausen writes, "Gräwe achieves this seamlessly, developing a unique style that is truly his own. His music is full of finesse, and he has no fear of fast tempi."

Jens Thomas, who came to prominence in 1994 with his band Triocolor, also plays with a pronounced European sensibility. His spirited, freely tonal playing combines elements of new music and the traditions of late romanticism and impressionism with the entire legacy of jazz piano. His solos present a logically convincing reconciliation of opposites: Frank Zappa and Keith Jarrett, Arnold Schoenberg and Bud Powell, Wolfgang Rihm and Paul Bley. Jens Thomas describes his music as a "celebration of the moment"—a spontaneity of subtle, lyrical colors that can nonetheless escalate into frenetic improvisational tirades worthy of Cecil Taylor at his most ferocious.

With his sensitive playing and his freely tonal, exploratory sense of sound, Achim Kaufmann is one of the most interesting pianists in European post–free jazz. In collaboration with musicians from the Amsterdam scene, as well as with musicians from new music and underground rock in the nineties, he has found new forms of piano playing. He has made particularly sublime contributions in the gray area of overlap between composition and improvisation.

In any case, jazz piano playing is becoming more and more individualized—not only on the free side of Cecil Taylor but also among nonfree players. Among the latter there are also a number of pianists who defy categorization. Andrew Hill, originally from Haiti, has infused African elements from his Caribbean homeland into modern piano compositions and improvisations. "Really listen to the avant-garde, and you can hear African rhythms. You hear the roots of jazz," he said. The fact that the African, black nature of jazz not only is not being suppressed as the music's development continues, but on the contrary gains increasingly concentrated and valid prominence as the black music of America progressively throws off the shackles of European musical laws, becomes impressively clear in musicians like Hill—and also in Muhal Richard Abrams, Don Pullen, Geri Allen, and others.

Andrew Hill was also important as a composer and as a leader of ambitious, freely tonal small-group recordings, such as *Point of Departure* (Blue Note, 1964), in which he combined emotional depth with complexity. His pieces always end differently than they begin. Their rhythmically cross-displaced structures and block chords ignore all fixedly predetermined forms, yet create something of lasting tonal value. At the beginning of the twenty-first century, Hill enjoyed great success at international jazz festivals. Over the decades, his playing became more and more spare, but with the same passion for musical challenge.

Even more direct in his relationship to Africa is Abdullah Ibrahim (previously known as Dollar Brand), a musician from Cape Town, South Africa. He is an improviser of great spiritual power, and the first pianist to create an independent African jazz language on this archetypally European instrument. The Jazz Epistles, the group with which he recorded in Johannesburg in 1960, played "township bebop"—a music in which modern jazz and South African styles met as equals. In 1962 Ibrahim, sponsored by Duke Ellington, went into exile: first to Switzerland, and then to the United States, where he played with Max Roach and Gato Barbieri. Ibrahim's concerts draw the listener into a world of soft, trancelike melodies and rolling rhythms. His solos are wandering journeys through the emotions of the African soul and the history of jazz, from Zulu melodies to the chorales of South African black church music, from Monk and Duke Ellington (whom Ibrahim calls the "village elders") to the exuberant rhythms of the Cape Town Minstrel Carneval, to the Arabic sounds of the Cape Malays and the hypnotic ostinato melodies of Marabi music from the townships. Ibrahim says, "I'm a pilot. I direct my passengers to the dark corners of their souls, to places where they usually don't dare to go."

In 1983 Herbie Hancock topped the international charts with "Rockit," with rhythm tracks devised by bassist Bill Laswell and keyboardist Michael Beinhorn. That was not only the greatest instrumental hit in eighties pop music but also considerably influenced the rise of techno / hip-hop culture. And yet Hancock, despite his successes in funk and pop, has always remained a jazz man.

Herbie Hancock has progressively turned to "commercial funk" music—hardly jazz anymore—yet the jazz world keeps considering him one of its own, not only because his Blue Note records *Empyrean Isles* and *Maiden Voyage* from the sixties are among the few convincing tone poems jazz has brought forth, aside from the work of Duke Ellington. They are "tone paintings of the sea" comparable to Debussy's "La Mer" in concert music. Hancock is one of the important musicians who became known through their work in the Miles Davis Quintet in the sixties. As a pianist, Hancock has an unshakable internal feeling for form that makes it possible for him to play abstract harmonic and rhythmic ideas against the form, so that his melodies and groove-conscious ideas, not the chord changes, shape the improvisation. His own sextet (1971–73) presented one of the most interesting and musically most demanding solutions to the entire problem posed by electronics in jazz. The fact that Hancock didn't lose his jazz feeling even after he changed over to commercial funk became apparent with the group V.S.O.P. that he led for a few concert tours during the second half of the seventies (with Freddie Hubbard,

Wayne Shorter, Tony Williams, and Ron Carter—all on acoustic instruments). And it became even more apparent when he appeared with Chick Corea on two grand pianos—a great, worldwide concert event that also appealed to those who normally would not have attended such a concert but were lured by the names Hancock and Corea, well known from their commercial and electric recordings. Since then, Hancock switches successfully between the "acoustic" and "electric" camps—a musician who has developed his own unmistakable style in both spheres. Herbie Hancock has learned to express himself in very different musical idioms like no other pianist. In 1986 he won an Oscar for his film score to Bertrand Tavernier's 'Round Midnight.

Chick Corea is another musician from the Miles Davis circle. Interestingly enough, before getting into fusion music he played free jazz. At the start of the seventies he headed Return to Forever, one of the groups in which jazz-rock attained a never-to-be-repeated peak scarcely before the style had got going. Corea is an affable musician with a fondness for childlike fairy-tale moods and clear rhythms. He knows Bartók, loves Latin American and Spanish music, and is an outstanding composer. Critics have compared his charming tunes with famous piano pieces of the nineteenth century (by Schumann and Mendelssohn) but have failed to notice the imminent, highly sensitized jazz tension with which Chick Corea fills his romanticism.

Since the seventies, this "filling" of romanticism with modern tension can also be found in the work of other important pianists —for example in Keith Jarrett, Richie Beirach, Stu Goldberg, Art Lande, Denny Zeitlin, Walter Norris, Bob Degen, Ken Werner, Norwegian Bobo Stenson, Dutchman Jasper van't Hof, Makoto Ozone from Japan, German Wolfgang Dauner, Briton John Taylor, and, years before this trend began, Steve Kuhn. The first player who filled romanticism with modern tension was Bill Evans. Beirach's music often has the lovely simplicity of folk songs, and his music also has a high degree of abstraction. He demonstrated his powers of interaction particularly impressively in recordings with David Liebman. In the nineties, he presented jazz interpretations of classical composers including Bartók, Frederico Mompou, and Claudia Monteverdi. John Taylor is less dependent on the gracious lyricism that critics associate with Bill Evans's playing; instead, his crystalline playing has a powerful, abrasive attack and rhythmic drive.

Romanticism without moderation, and an intuitive sense of gripping melodies and harmonies, is the main characteristic of the most successful pianist of this kind and the most successful jazz pianist of the seventies: Keith Jarrett. He is a "pianistic totalizer" whose fingers—and, above all, head and heart—command almost everything ever played on a piano. His solo concerts are musical voyages not only through several centuries of piano history, but also through many landscapes of an ever more complex human psyche.

After giving up one-man appearances for a year and a half in order to distinguish himself as an interpreter of classical piano music (from Mozart by way of Bartók to Bach), Jarrett returned to solo jazz in 1985. "I came to know the world of classical musicians and saw almost nothing but frustration among those people—the higher their ranking, the more cultivated the frustration."

Jarrett has the ability to make his piano "sing," to such an extent that his playing gains a hymnlike and almost sacral quality. It was Coltrane who introduced hymnlike elements into jazz, but Jarrett is unrivaled in cultivating and transposing this dimension into metaphysical realms. His secret lies less in the melodies and harmonies he plays than in the quality of his playing. This often spiritual quality is linked with the fact that not since Bill Evans has there been another pianist with such a differentiated touch, an ability to "give life" to the notes, ranging—as critic Peter Rüdi says—across the entire spectrum: "from harplike arpeggios barely floating above silence to screaming, stinging fandango lines drawn with finger-breaking expressiveness." That's why Jarrett followers such as George Winston and Liz Story probably seem dreary and banal—they only imitate the surface without approaching the quality, which also involves "touch." Even when playing completely free, his music comes from a grandiose sense of melody.

All of the pianists in this "romantic group" are part of the already mentioned Bill Evans classicism, which developed out of the rediscovery of tonality and beat in the seventies and eighties. That is documented not only in the playing of such younger pianists as Michel Petrucciani and Fred Hersch but also in many jazz groups themselves. Since the eighties, more and more piano trios built on the achievements of the Bill Evans Trio. Especially successful was the Keith Jarrett Trio, whose unusually fresh and melodically mature interpretations of standards, the great timeless melodies of the Great American Songbook, achieved a new level. A similarly homogeneous and contemporary continuation of Evans's concept came from Chick Corea and his Akoustic Band.

Keith Jarrett is the hymnic singer among jazz pianists. Coming from the Bill Evans/Keith Jarrett line, in the nineties many pianists found their own personal version of this style, full of imagination and sensitivity: Brad Mehldau (discussed below), Robert Glasper, Marc Copeland, Bill Mays, and Bill Carothers in America. However, the melodic Evans/Jarrett approach has been particularly strongly developed in Europe, above all in Scandinavia and in the Slavic countries. Pianists in this lineage include, in Poland, Leszek Mozdzer and Marek Wasilewski; in Norway, Jon Balke, Christian Wallumrod and Kjetil Björnstad; in Sweden, Bobo Stenson and Esbjörn Svensson; in Denmark, Christian Dahl; in Germany, Florian Ross; in Portugal, Mario Laginha; and in Italy, Stefano Bollani.

In the midseventies, Bobo Stenson was a member of the Jan Garbarek quartet. He combined American and European jazz languages by introducing Swedish folk melodies and the European heritage of classical music to the Evans/Jarrett inspired style of playing. His freely flowing rubato playing and his outstanding feeling for space and atmosphere are also very European. Together with Anders Jormin on bass and Jon Christensen on drums, he has formed one of the longest-lasting piano trios in Nordic jazz.

Poland's Leszek Mozdzers has also shown an outstanding ability to incorporate European classical music into contemporary piano jazz—Frederic Chopin, Béla Bartók, Johann Sebastian Bach, and liturgical melodies from the Middle Ages. The great strength of this sensitive pianist is his ability to play freely without losing the melodic focus.

Stefano Bollani, who came from the band of trumpeter Enrico Rava, is the European jazz pianist whose attack has perhaps the greatest delicacy and refinement. He understands the many gradations of touch that exist between caressing the keyboard and pounding it. His playing does not have the solemn pathos of Jarrett, but rather has a pronounced sense of irony and Mediterranean humor. His solos are brilliant fireworks that incorporate influences from French *chanson*, ethnic music, the avant-garde, rock, and classical music.

Behind all these styles and streams, in fact feeding them all, flows the mainstream (in the sense of that main development line of jazz history that leads from bebop via Coltrane to contemporary music). Here, McCoy Tyner is the towering figure, in the seventies the number one pianist in most jazz polls of the world. He is the essence of jazz in the most powerful, swinging sense of that word. "McCoy Tyner plays piano like a roaring lion," said critic Bill Cole.

Tyner became known in the early sixties as the pianist of the classic John Coltrane Quartet. In the meantime (we have talked about it), the whole scene—jazz, jazz-rock, fusion, pop—has become unthinkable without Coltrane. And yet, today McCoy Tyner represents the Coltrane tradition more validly than any other musician. In fact, Tyner *is* that tradition: quietly serving, filled with seriousness and religiosity.

The first Tyner album voted "Record of the Year" (more would follow) was *Sahara* in 1972. In connection with it, McCoy quoted the Arabian historian Ibn Khaldoun: "This desert is so long it can take a lifetime to go from one end to the other, and a childhood to cross at its narrowest point." This quote is characteristic, because for McCoy Tyner, all of music is "a journey of the soul into new, uncharted territory." He said, "I try to listen to music from many different countries: Africa, India, from the Arabic world, European classical music. . . . All kinds of music are interconnected."

It is an enigma to other pianists how McCoy Tyner manages to get so much power out of the piano. Cecil Taylor's piano is similarly powerful, but he plays free music, where it is easier to reach that kind of energy level. Other pianists may pound the piano keys as hard as they can, and they would sound only half as powerful as McCoy. "You've got to become one with your instrument," he explained. "Like, you start learning an instrument—and at first the piano is nothing but an instrument. But after a while it becomes an extension of yourself, and you and your instrument become one."

It must be this "union" with his instrument that has enabled McCoy Tyner to find his own characteristic sound on the piano—very much in line with the great jazz horn players. Naturally, this is much more difficult on the piano than on a horn. McCoy is one of the few piano players who have done this successfully, which, he says, is one of the reasons why he does not use electric instruments: "Electric music is bad for your soul."

Many pianists are influenced, directly or indirectly, by Tyner: Hal Galper, John Hicks, Hilton Ruiz, Jorge Dalto, Henry Butler, JoAnne Brackeen, and from Germany, Joachim Kühn, the European pianist who has incorporated McCoy Tyner's style most convincingly. With bassist Jean François Jenny-Clark and drummer Daniel Humair, Kühn formed an improvising trio that was perhaps the most adventurous and convincing European jazz piano group of the eighties and nineties. Their style was completely free of American influences, yet remained characterized by a virile, powerful swing.

JoAnne Brackeen has also found her own voice. *Mythical Magic* is the title of one of her records—which is exactly what one feels when listening to her music: a ritual of mythical-magical power. Brackeen played with Art Blakey and Stan Getz and later with Joe Henderson prior to appearing in solo performances and with her own groups. She studied with Lennie Tristano—one of the many students in whom this great jazz teacher brought out their own identity. (Said Lennie, "Teaching is an art—as much as playing.")

It must also be said that JoAnne Brackeen was the first person to create a new image of the woman in jazz: the woman as a jazz musician—simply a jazz musician, without asking whether this musician is a man or a woman—and yet still a woman who will not let herself be exploited by men and by a male-dominated society, or even by the male-chauvinist music business; the woman and jazz musician who does not feel the need to escape from the implications of her situation into glamor or into flirting with the supposedly inescapable female inferiority in the man's world of jazz, or (as was somewhat the case with Mary Lou Williams) into religious faith. All this has never existed so purely, so totally, and so convincingly as with JoAnne Brackeen. At the end of the seventies, she was the first representative of a new type of female jazz musician, who does not merely talk about emancipation but *is* emancipated.

Of course, the spirit of Coltrane and Tyner can be also felt, directly or filtered, among those piano players who are affiliated with contemporary neobop and eighties/nineties neoclassicism. Onaje Allen Gumbs, Kenny

Barron, George Cables, Mickey Tucker, Don Grolnick, Jim McNeeley, Eliane Elias, Kenny Werner, and Mark Soskin, and then—leading to the realm of neo–hard bop—Mulgrew Miller, James Williams, Kirk Lightsey, and Larry Willis—each with his personal approach and, of course, influenced not only by McCoy but by other musicians, too. Kenny Barron played with the originators of modern jazz, including Dizzy Gillespie in the sixties. He plays swinging mainstream jazz piano as if all the bop clichés to which almost every young pianist today seems to succumb had never existed. He made moving duo recordings with Stan Getz, and continued the legacy of Monk in the group Sphere, which he co-led. His harmonically very flexible playing communicates passion and commitment beyond any feeling of competition.

Don Grolnick, who died in 1996, evolved toward the end of his career from a fusion keyboardist to a swinging acoustic pianist. He was a fabulous composer of new mainstream jazz. His harmonically delicate, groove-conscious pieces contain many moments of humorous surprise, effortlessly integrated.

Mulgrew Miller, who played with Art Blakey and Tony Williams, is especially successful at bop-oriented post-Coltrane playing. Miller emotionalizes the classicist jazz piano with his vital attack and a balanced sense of musical climaxes: sparkling, agile, impressive lines and firm chords full of unexpected turns.

James Williams, one of the most active sidemen in New York, is equally rooted in blues and in standards.

A large number of European players also belong in this context of progressive contemporary bop—in fact, so many that we can mention only three pronounced individualists here: Britons Stan Tracey and, as a real virtuoso, Gordon Beck; and the Spaniard (or as he would have called himself: Catalonian) Tete Montoliu (who died in 1997). Montoliu once said, "Basically we Catalonians are all black." And that's the way he played—perhaps the "blackest" of the European pianists, and yet rooted in the tradition of his native Catalonia, whose folk songs he has given moving interpretations. Tracey has occasionally been called a "British Thelonious Monk," but he is more than those words can express. His humor is typically British, full of understatement and intimations and often of sarcasm, too.

The comprehensive reevaluation of the jazz tradition that took place in the eighties from the vantage point of bop gave an immense boost to straight-ahead jazz piano. Spurred by the success of the "young lions" around Wynton Marsalis, legions of players flooded the scene. They form the largest group of contemporary pianists, especially since they are immediately related to those named above as the heirs of Bud Powell. In the nineties so many interesting piano stylists enriched the swinging mainstream that the *New York Times* spoke of a "golden age of jazz piano."

All these musicians have developed and refined straight-ahead playing by revitalizing and reflecting on the legacy of modern jazz piano (and in some cases also older traditional jazz) in a variety of mixed forms, with a certain tendency to prefer Herbie Hancock, McCoy Tyner, Bill Evans, Chick Corea, and Keith Jarrett.

A first impression of the breadth and the complex possibilities of this direction can be gained by comparing Marcus Roberts with Orrin Evans. Both of these pianists come from Monk and from Ellington, both identify themselves strongly with the jazz tradition, both tend toward unconventional forms while swinging fantastically, and yet their playing could hardly be more different. Roberts, who played with Wynton Marsalis, cultivates and sublimates many older styles in his rich, resonant sound—ragtime, Swing, blues, stride piano, and gospel—often finding new ways to play them simultaneously. In contrast, Orrin Evans has expanded the modern branch of straight-ahead playing (Hancock and Tyner) with exciting rhythmic changes and metrical pivots, up to tonal improvisation without chord changes, so that his refusal to call his music "neobop" is quite understandable.

These two styles—Roberts's and Evans's—mark two extreme points of this direction. We will rank this abundance of musicians contributing to straight-ahead piano approximately according to the way in which they combine modernist tendencies with an orchestral, traditional way of playing. At the head of this group are musicians in whose playing the influence of Herbie Hancock and Chick Corea can be detected: Kenny Kirkland, Stephen Scott, Renee Rosnes, Ed Simon, Joey Calderazzo, Mulgrew Miller, Kevin Hays, Bill Charlap, David Kikoski, Helen Sung, Geoff Keezer, Luis Perdomo, David Hazeltine, George Colligan, David Berkman, Xavier Davis, Kenny Drew Jr., Bruce Barth, Joel Weiskopf, Aaron Parks, Julian Joseph in England, Antonio Farao in Italy (particularly percussive in his phrasing), Michiel Borstlap in the Netherlands, Thierry Maillard in France and Robert Di Gioia in Germany, and then—already inclined more toward the orchestral dimension of the jazz piano—Cyrus Chestnut, Eric Lewis, Eric Reed, Bill Charlap, and Benny Green.

Kenny Kirkland, who died unexpectedly in 1998, played a kind of "super-Herbie Hancock," producing unpredictable harmonies and rhythmic ideas very interactively and with boundless energy. He was a member of Wynton Marsalis's quintet in the eighties, and played a particularly creative form of Latin jazz in his own bands.

David Hazeltine, coming from Cedar Walton and Barry Harris, composes melodies that are immediately accessible to any improvising musician of the neo–hard-bop school.

Canadian Renee Rosnes, who has played with Joe Henderson and Wayne Shorter, is one of the most lavish stylists in postbop, a great asset to any group. Her brilliant, virtuosic lines help other musicians shine.

Edward Simon, from Venezuela, bridges Herbie Hancock and Keith Jarrett, bringing the rhythmic force of Afro-Caribbean music to acoustic straight-ahead jazz with great classical aplomb.

David Kikoski, a member of drummer Roy Haynes's band for more than nineteen years, has distilled the rhythmically accurate, crystalline approach of Chick Corea into an exciting, percussive postbop style. He is at his best playing with dynamically interactive drummers, and also has a brilliant sense for Latin rhythms.

Cyrus Chestnut has a joyful, expansive style that is deeply rooted on the one hand in gospel and blues and on the other hand in the swinging, driving grooves of Erroll Garner. With his gift for dramatic effect, he's able to lift entire groups to a new plateau.

Benny Green, who played with Art Blakey and Betty Carter, is considered the legitimate successor of Oscar Peterson, not least because he recorded a duo record with Peterson in 1993. He carries on the opulent, harmonically broad playing of Peterson, Errol Garner, and Art Tatum in a particularly moving, convincing manner. Eric Reed combines Ahmad Jamal with the spiritual roots of his own gospel experience. Bill Charlap's energetic, focused playing brings new life to Broadway tunes and to the classics of the Great American Book. With Peter Washington and Kenny Washington, he led one of the most exciting trios of the new mainstream jazz.

In a piano trio, there are basically two possibilities for approaching improvisation: if the musicians exchange their ideas and inspiration in the manner of a dialogue, "tossing the ball back and forth," this can be called an "interactive" trio. The main emphasis here is on the meshing with one another, the dialogic exchange. If, on the other hand, the three musicians concentrate on the simultaneous creation and execution of a powerful rhythmic movement, this can be called a power trio. In this kind of group, the energy of the groove is most important.

The Ahmad Jamal Trio of the fifties is the prototype of the power trio. Here, everything is directed toward the resilient, explosive force of the groove. The Bill Evans Trio, on the other hand, is the archetypal interactive trio, raising the interaction between three equal forces to a high level of art.

This distinction between interactive trios and power trios was also useful in the nineties, when the piano trio experienced something of a renaissance as part of the rediscovery of the jazz tradition. (Of course, all conceivable combinations of the two approaches are also possible.)

The trio The Bad Plus (featuring pianist Ethan Iverson), the Jacky Terrasson Trio, and Jean-Michel Pilc's trio are the most impressive of the power trios, while the Brad Mehldau Trio and Jason Moran's Bandwagon are the outstanding examples of the interactive trio.

The members of The Bad Plus—pianist Ethan Iverson, bassist Reid Anderson, and drummer Dave King—have become known for the deconstruction and radical transformation of pop songs and drum 'n' bass music (by Björk, Aphex Twin, and Radiohead, for example). They don't parody these songs, but celebrate them, by elevating them to a new level through the incorporation of powerful jazz solos marked by the rhapsodic piano of the nineteenth century and by free passages.

Jacky Terrasson, who grow up in Paris and has lived in New York since 1990, has a breathtaking ability to reharmonize old melodies and to transform them into new thematic material. His interpretations of standards are like little symphonies, full of internal drama, with inspired changes of tempo and powerful dynamic fluctuations. Despite the complexity of his lines, he has an outstanding sense for strong, deep melodies: "Maybe I'm just a frustrated singer."

Jean-Michel Pilc, a self-taught pianist from France who has lived in New York since 1996, is a musician who has no fear of letting himself go. He brings jazz standards into the twenty-first-century with volcanic temperament and structural clarity. Of the many piano trios active in today's jazz, his has perhaps the greatest dynamic range. They explore the extreme possibilities of contrasts between loud and soft, from whispering pianissimo to powerfully roaring chords, to the point of ecstacy. "My roots are in the jazz of the twenties and thirties," says Pilc, who began playing traditional jazz and then skipped over bop to contemporary playing. "Rhythmically, I've drawn a great deal from that music. I see people today in the jazz schools starting with John Coltrane, which for me is completely absurd. And I can hear that absurdity in their playing."

At this juncture we must address a common prejudice, according to which power trios necessarily play loudly and intensely, while interactive trios necessarily play softly and with a chamber-music feel. The Swedish trio E.S.T. is characterized by ingenious lyricism and the magic of simplicity, and it has to be considered a power trio. In their elegiac, romantic improvisations, finely meshed grooves create a dreamlike effect. Their captivating songs, borrowed from the world of pop, do away with predictable solo routines. Instead, Esbjörn Svensson enriches his sensitive improvisations with judiciously applied elements of electronica, including looped drum 'n' bass melodies and atmospheric sounds that intensify the groove.

Of course, it is not true that there is no interaction in power trios—communication naturally takes place there as well. But here, the interaction between the musicians primarily serves the creation of an overall rhythmic energy that is as high as possible. Conversely, interactive trios of course also groove, but here priority is given to the motives that are exchanged back and forth between the instrumental voices. Outstanding contributions in this vein have come in particular from the Brad Mehldau Trio. Mehldau has been constantly compared to Bill Evans, a comparison that Mehldau vehemently rejects. No other pianist of the nineties has translated the feeling of lonesomeness into music in such a moving fashion as Mehldau. With his trio, including bassist Larry Grenadier and drummer Jorge Rossy, he has made an important contribution to the revitalization of the piano trio. The principle of contrapuntal improvisation is an integral part of this trio's conception. Mehldau "polyphonizes" contemporary jazz piano. He has developed the ability to improvise two or three melodies at the same time, each completely valid lines in their own right, that combine to form a polyphonic, multidimensional music.

In the course of this development, Mehldau's playing has increasingly moved away from the Bud Powell tradition of jazz piano, in which the right hand is used like a horn while the left hand plays accompanying chords in the low register "like a claw" (Mehldau). His solos are animated by a duality of innocence and irony, full of emotion yet held back in an introverted manner, which makes the music even more stimulating and appealing. In playing without chord changes, his trio has achieved rare melodic high points.

In the playing of Jason Moran, who came from the band of Greg Osby, tradition and the avant-garde, composed and improvised elements, are fused seamlessly. In his dark, clearly contoured lines, he takes a creative look at the constant flow of African American rhythms, from ragtime to bebop and from the AACM to hip-hop. His trio Bandwagon, with Tarus Mateen on bass and Nasheet Waits on drums, proves that even in playing over complex meters it is possible to reach the destination without making the distinction between "leader" and "sidemen."

As in Bandwagon, in other piano trios of the nineties innovative steps were taken in the area of the rhythm section. The growth in rhythmic ability in such groups was so enormous that the rhythm section is capable of inverting the normal trio hierarchy at any time. Or, as Jason Moran says, "Today you don't necessarily have to play 'free' to be free."

The development toward world jazz has also brought an abundance of new melodies and rhythms to piano groups, expanding the scope of jazz. In Latin jazz in particular, Cuban pianists have led the way; these include musicians with a pronounced percussive style and classical training, such as Chucho Valdes, Gonzalo Rubalcaba, Ramon Valle, Carlos Maza, Omar Sosa, and Emiliano Salvador. But musicians from the Caribbean and from Central and South America also made surprising and innovative contributions to Latin jazz in the nineties, including Danilo Perez from Panama, Hector Martignon from Colombia, Michel Camilo from the Dominican Republic, Puerto Rican New Yorker Eddie Palmeri, and Hernan Lugano from Argentina.

It is characteristic of all these pianists that they bring together jazz and Latin American elements às equals, coming from a deep knowledge of both idioms. Unlike earlier decades, neither element predominates; both aspects—sophisticated jazz harmony and a swinging mainstream approach on the one hand, and folk / Latin American styles on the other—blend organically.

The most impressive of these pianists is Rubalcaba, who was discovered by Charlie Haden in 1999 and has lived in South Florida since 1996. He is a great jazz improviser who combines explosive technique with sensitive depth. His piano playing has brought new perspectives to Afro-Cuban Jazz. His contribution has been to analyze, revise, expand, and bring a new quality to the abstraction and complexity of Afro-Cuban music from the vantage point of a passionate jazz sensitivity. His glissando-filled solos celebrate old Afro-Cuban traditions, including *danzon* (which has much in common with jazz harmonically), bolero, cha-cha, rumba, *nueva yoruba,* and *guacuanco*. Rubalcaba works with all these styles in order to expand them and to develop them further.

Rubalcaba's piano playing is typified by the Rachmaninoff-like power with which he uses the bass notes of the keyboard. He's also a master of ballad playing, bringing out the lesser-known romantic, melodic, and lyrical side of Cuban music.

Chronologically before Rubalcaba comes Chucho Valdes, leader of the band Irakere (also discussed in the chapter on big bands), who since the seventies has drawn on Afro-Cuban sources in his solo and trio concerts, raising them to a concert level with an intoxicating bravura technique. His flamboyant, expansive playing combines Errol Garner and Art Tatum with the Yoruba roots of Afro-Cuban music. Valdes is an expert at combining Afro-Cuban *bata* and *timba* rhythms with new rhythmic formulas. His unconventional use of percussion increased the polyrhythmic adventurousness of Latin jazz. Gonzalo Rubalcaba says: "I don't know of any other pianist before him who had his energy and power." Danilo Perez's playing is also rooted on the one hand in the jazz piano tradition (Thelonious Monk, Herbie Hancock, Bill Evans) and on the other hand in the folk music of his native Panama. As a member of the acoustic quartet of Wayne Shorter, he has shown an exceptional feeling for organic development and concise, clear solos. His ability to simultaneously layer several different stylistic elements is phenomenal—for example, Duke Ellington in the left hand combined with Panamanian melodies in the right hand and Cuban rhythms in the middle. For all their abstraction, his solos have a dancelike quality. As a pianist, Perez was the first to bring many of the rhythms of Latin American music to jazz—in particular the Panamanian *atraverso, tamborito,* and *punto* rhythms, which, like Cuban music, have a close connection to New Orleans rhythms. Perez has also incorporated the dark percussive colors of the *caja* drum, which sounds very African. Perez says: "When I listen to Monk, I hear percussion. When I listen to Duke Ellington, I hear percussion."

Michel Camilo is perhaps the most joyful and most polyglot of the contemporary Latin pianists—a fiery, eclectic musician whose blues-tinged solos reflect not only the *pambiche* rhythms of his native Caribbean islands, but also Cuban bolero, Argentinian tango, and the *buleria* figures of Spanish flamenco. He sometimes showcases his incendiary technique—his racing octave runs are legendary.

In Europe as well, numerous pianists have made important contributions to world jazz. The most important of these are Aziza Mustafa Zadeh from Azerbaijan, Mikhail Alperin from Russia, Chano Dominguez from Spain, and the Serbian-Bosnian pianist Bojan Zulfikarpasic, who lives in Paris.

Aziza Mustafa Zadeh enjoyed great public success in the nineties. At the age of seventeen, she won the Thelonious Monk competition in Washington, D.C. Critics have carped about her divalike air and her bizarre self-dramatizations—in interviews, she has sometimes said that she is the "reincarnation of an Azerbaijani princess." Her sensitive, pathos-filled solo concerts present improvisations rich in nuance, in which she combines a Bill Evans–influenced approach with the eruptive Eastern lines of Azerbaijani *mugam* music. Brilliant pianistic fireworks full of heart and soul, opulent Eastern scales, Bach and Monk, Chopin and Bud Powell, the music of the Caucasian shamans and the lyricism of Keith Jarrett all meet in her performances. When she was once asked why, as an Easterner, she plays jazz, she answered that *"mugam is* jazz. In the music of Azerbaijan there is a great deal of improvisation. So when I add jazz to *mugam*, I'm playing a kind of double jazz."

Chano Dominguez, born in Cadiz, has played with Wynton Marsalis and with the Lincoln Center Jazz Orchestra. His jazz piano sounds like a flamenco guitar with eighty-eight strings. Dominguez creates an artful integration of flamenco and the standard tradition of American jazz from Thelonious Monk and Bud Powell to Art Tatum. In his playing, flamenco "dances" on the keyboard of the piano so convincingly that Andalusian music is joined seamlessly to the playing of jazz standards, as if flamenco dancing and handclapping had always been part of the jazz tradition. In fact, the rhythms of flamenco—the *bulerias*, fandangos, *alegrias*, tangos, and rumbas—have a similarity to jazz rhythms. Both are very warm, direct, and emotional. Chano Dominguez's jazz has the quality of duende—the word that flamenco musicians use when the music has a particularly intense feeling. "When you hear a saxophonist play with a lot of swing, lots of feeling—that is also duende," says Dominguez. "I play jazz in Spanish."

Bojan Zulfikarpasic enriches contemporary French jazz with the spirit in the soul of Balkan folk music. He was a member of the groups of Louis Sclavis and Henri Texier, and his own groups are mainstays of European jazz. Starting from Herbie Hancock, Chick Corea, and Keith Jarrett, Bojan Z (as he calls himself for the sake of simplicity) creates a bridge from contemporary European jazz to the odd rhythms and vital, ornamental melodies of Balkan music. He arrived at his unique playing style when he discovered that the rhythms and meters of Balkan music "develop exactly the same power and energy that a good swinging rhythm has." As a Serb of Bosnian origin, Bojan Z was so to speak caught in the middle during the Balkan war. He commented on the absurdity of that war by combining Serbian, Croatian, and Bosnian folk music elements in his own music. More than just a symbolic gesture, this was music against the barbed wire in the heart. "If people could only feel as deeply as this music, the world would be a better place," wrote saxophonist Dave Liebman about Bojan's piano playing.

Hans Lüdemann, also a wonderfully abstract, freely tonal player, has transferred the pentatonic melodies and patterns of West African mbira and *balaphon* music to his European piano improvisations, in collaboration with, among others, *balaphon* virtuoso Aly Keita and with kora player Tata Dindin.

Uri Caine is the outstanding pianist of New York's downtown scene. He plays like a postmodern Herbie Hancock. In his trio, he has developed the postbop approach of the sixties with highly chromatic, strongly rhythmic motives. He attracted attention in the nineties with his arrangements and group projects: joyful, courageous adaptations of classical composers, including Mahler, Bach, Beethoven, and Schumann. The question whether, in these projects, Caine intended to denigrate or make fun of this classical music was much discussed. But Caine's classical adaptations are not traditional treatments, but transformations. From the vantage point of a jazz musician, he found new aspects in the music of Mahler by creating puzzlelike cross-connections between this music and many contrasting styles and genres: DJ music, baroque music, klezmer, hip-hop, rock and alternative music, mambo and free jazz.

One of the strengths of Caine's music is that it demonstrates that multiplicity does not have to end in a pluralistic collapse, but can be organized in such a way that each element retains its individuality and its power while becoming part of a convincing whole. Caine's working process is different from that of John Zorn, with whom Caine has a close musical partnership. Instead of making styles collide with each other like particles in the manner of Zorn, provoking radical fractures, Caine is a master of the combination and fusion of different idioms. Caine says: "Putting things together that originally didn't belong together—that's how all music comes into being, until it becomes an accepted quantity, and is no longer perceived as strange."

Organ, Keyboards, Synthesizer, Electronics

The organ. Originally, it was the dream of exalted church music, resounding in hallowed cathedrals, the "royal instrument" of the European tradition (Ligeti: "the largest prosthesis in the world").

The realization of this dream was the starting point of the organ in jazz. It began with Fats Waller.

John S. Wilson wrote, "Like the inevitable clown who wants to play Hamlet [Fats] had a consuming desire to bring to the public his love of classical music and of the organ." And Waller himself, in reference to a Chicago music critic who had written that "the organ is the favorite instrument of Fats's heart, and the piano only of his stomach," said, "Well, I really love the organ. . . . I have one at home and a great many of my compositions originated there."

To be sure, the organ was also the instrument of escape for Fats Waller: it symbolized a world—a distant, unattainable world—in which the artist is accepted solely on the basis of his musical abilities, without racial or social prejudice and also without regard for his talents as showman and entertainer. If one hears the organ records made by Fats Waller—such as his famous version of the spiritual "Sometimes I Feel Like a Motherless Child"—one encounters an element of sentimentality that makes it clear that Waller had only a fuzzy notion of the world into which he wanted to escape.

The instrument that Fats Waller truly loved was the great church organ of the European tradition, the pipe organ. Once, in Paris, he had an opportunity to play the organ in the cathedral of Notre Dame. It was, as he put it, "one of the greatest moments in my life."

Fats Waller passed his love for the organ on to his best-known pupil—Count Basie, whose organ playing is (almost) as light and spare as his piano style. Basie, however, played the electric organ because it had become obvious in the meantime that the pipe organ can be used in jazz only with great difficulty. The pipes sound too slowly because the distance between the console and the pipes is too long and mechanically involved. That's why it is very hard to swing on a pipe organ. "On a normal pipe organ," Clare Fischer said, "the lag is about half a beat behind, which plays hell with your mind when you're trying to play rhythmic music. It makes it impossible to play jazz."

It was Fischer who in 1975 made probably the most swinging (and musically most interesting) pipe organ recordings, on a small "chamber organ," where the distances the air column has to travel are relatively short. Among the Europeans, Belgian Fred van Hove has developed his own style of playing (free) jazz on a pipe organ, with gigantic sound columns and imposing clusters. The rich free duets recorded by Hans Günther Wauer, cathedral cantor at Merseburg, Germany, and drummer Günter "Baby" Sommer have also been much praised.

Hammond Organ

Meanwhile, and in a general sense, the term *organ* in jazz refers to the electric organ, in any of the many different types (each with its own sound) available on the market.

From Count Basie and Fats Waller come the many organists who have been inspired to use the instrument for a kind of rhythm and blues.

The first of these were Wild Bill Davis, who introduced the legendary Hammond B-3 organ to jazz, and Milt Buckner, who always played with a bassist, because he was too short to reach the bass pedals. They both played in a style influenced by the big bands, full of blues-soaked riffs, bright, swelling chords, and frequent use of the volume pedal.

In America's black neighborhoods the organ has been a particularly popular instrument together with guitar or tenor saxophone (in both cases with drums but without bass, since the bass lines can be played with the organist's feet or on the instrument's bass register). Among the organists who continued to play such a variant of rhythm and blues twenty years after Wild Bill Davis and Milt Buckner, while incorporating much that happened, musically and stylistically, since then, were Jack McDuff, Johnny Hammond, Don Patterson, Lou Bennett, Richard "Groove" Holmes, John Patton, Lonnie Smith, Jimmy McGriff, Charles Earland, and many others. Shirley Scott brought some of the relaxation and amiability of Erroll Garner to this way of playing. Charles Earland was a master of the "drone" technique often favored in this style, in which melodies and chords are layered and developed, building tension, over sustained bass notes. The bluesy tension this creates is increased to almost unbearable high points before the resolution occurs. After Ray Charles (who also played organ) became successful, not only the blues, but also the soul and gospel element of the black churches became significant for practically dozens of organ players.

The traditional Hammond sound takes up so much sonic space that conventional jazz organ playing requires a certain percussive approach, simple and to the point. A host of rock organists took over the traditions of rhythm and blues and of gospel music—among others, Stevie Winwood (in his early phase), Al Kooper, and the black, particularly soul-oriented musicians Billy Preston and Booker T. Jones.

"The organ was the first synthesizer." Even if this statement by Bill Kirchner is not true from the point of view of musical technology—the synthesizer produces the tone completely electronically, while the (early) Hammond organ produces the sound electromechanically—it nonetheless gets at what jazz musicians were doing with the Hammond organ: constantly modifying the sound. The thirty different switches, keys, and sliding bars, and the variable adjustment of the Leslie rotating speaker, provided infinite sound possibilities. In this way, organists became experts at shaping unique sounds, each with his or her own identifiable sonic "signature." Historian Bob Porter says, "The perfect mastery of all the characteristics of the Hammond organ gives these artists the ability to identify themselves with clearly distinguishable sounds. The listener hears immediately: that's Groove Holmes, or Jack McDuff, or Jimmy McGriff, or Jimmy Smith."

These settings are often guarded by the organists as though they were alchemical secrets. Sound engineer Rudy Van Gelder, who recorded many

of the classic organ records for the Blue Note label in the fifties and sixties, says that many jazz organists were careful to put the drawbars of
the instrument back to the neutral position at the end of each recording
session.

Musicians like Richard "Groove" Holmes, Jimmy McGriff, Charles
Earland, Booker T., Billy Preston, and many others bring to mind that
the technique of playing the Hammond organ was already well developed in the gospel churches when it was only in its infancy in jazz. It
is important to note that the organ implies a totally different musical
background for black and white audiences. For both, the organ may
come from church. But "church" for African American listeners is associated with the cooking sounds of the gospel churches, while white
listeners might have Johann Sebastian Bach in mind. "I remember it very
clearly," says tenor saxophonist James Carter, "this fat organ sound
as the foundation—it was as if someone was pouring gasoline on the
fire."

We have gone somewhat ahead in time to clarify the position of the
blues and soul tradition in jazz organ playing. Before the road was free to
travel by all the organists coming after Wild Bill Davis and Milt Buckner,
Jimmy Smith had first to appear on the scene. He was the first to improvise walking lines using the bass pedals: continuous quarter-note lines
so supple and swinging that they could have been played by Ray Brown
or some other master jazz bassist. Smith did for the organ what Charlie
Christian had achieved for the guitar: he emancipated it. Only through
him did the organ gain equal footing with the other instruments in jazz.
Probably his most important record, made in 1956, is an improvisation
on Dizzy Gillespie's "The Champ." Nobody had accomplished this before: achieving effects on the organ reminiscent of a bebop big band—in
this case of the most exciting Dizzy Gillespie big band of the late forties—by employing a high, overpowering dynamic range built on wide,
steadily rising arcs of sound.

Smith can also be compared to Christian because he was the first
to consciously play the organ like an electronic instrument, similar to
Christian's transition from acoustic to electric guitar. Certainly, Wild Bill
Davis, Milt Buckner, and others played Hammond organ before Jimmy
Smith. But they played it more like a piano with an electric organ sound.
It was left to Smith to realize that the Hammond B-3 organ is an independent, new instrument that has only the keyboard in common with the
piano or the conventional organ. Indeed, the realization that electronics
do not simply amplify an instrument but rather make of it something
new took a long time to be generally accepted. Electronics, we emphasize
again, meant a revolution—for organs, guitars, violins, bass, and other
instruments.

During the sixties and seventies, Smith made many commercial pop-
jazz recordings of doubtful value. But that does not detract from his his-

toric achievement: he made the organ a vehicle for jazz improvisations of the highest artistic quality.

Smith came on the scene in 1956. Nine years later came the next step in the development of the organ, through Larry Young (who later took the Muslim name Khalid Yasin). Young, who died in 1978, played the organ in the spirit of middle-period John Coltrane. It is illuminating that he became well known at the moment when Smith, through continuous repetition of blues and soul clichés, more and more seemed to have become a roaring "Frankenstein of Hammond Castle." Understandably, organists and audiences initially became enraptured with the instrument's immense range of dynamics, its fortissimo possibilities. Young discovered the potential of the organ played pianissimo.

"There is an individuality in his music that leaves behind all the nervousness and manneredness of which the organ is capable," writes Cordelia Scherwitz. "His warm, mostly vibratoless tone, his linear, spare voice leading, and his improvisational focus on melodic development radiate a calm and grace that are something new on this difficult instrument. The 'Coltrane of the organ,' as he was sometimes called, not only gave the organ back its original spirituality, he also intellectualized it."

Young was the first to realize the modal conception on the organ, and belongs to the generation of musicians that carried the Coltrane legacy into advanced rock. He was a member of one of the most important early jazz-rock bands—the trio Lifetime, with Tony Williams and John McLaughlin—and he also played in sessions with Jimi Hendrix (of which bootleg recordings exist). It is regrettable that he never got to enjoy great commercial success. But Young's influence (in the form of his typical binary, eighth-note-based rhythmic feel) is omnipresent in the organists of modern jazz and rock. It is especially notable in the two British players Brian Auger (who, like Young, also made recordings with Tony Williams) and Mike Ratledge (of the group Soft Machine).

In Europe, Frenchman Eddie Louiss (whose family comes from Martinique) has developed the Coltrane influence into an individual, hymnlike, singing, triumphant style, with some Caribbean-Creole overtones. Musicians like Carla Bley, Amina C. Myers, Clare Fischer, Joey DeFrancesco, Cuban Chucho Valdez (from the Irakere group), English-born John Taylor, Wojciech Karolak from Poland, Germany's Barbara Dennerlein, and, especially originally, Arturo O'Farrill also created interesting organ sounds during the seventies and eighties. But in general, organ playing in jazz stagnated for a while after Larry Young. This was mainly because at the end of the sixties, the organ was pushed aside to some extent by the development of new electric and electronic keyboard instruments, including the electric piano and the synthesizer. For club gigs, the heavy Hammond B-3 organ, which weighs about four hundred pounds, was at a decided disadvantage compared to the lighter, newer instruments. After Larry Young's death, the Hammond B-3 entered years of decline. Experts spoke of jazz organ playing as a dying art form. But in the midnineties, "the beast," as jazz musicians affectionately and respectfully call the B-3, made a sudden comeback. Partly because interest in the great sounds of the jazz tradition increased enormously in the nineties, a renaissance of organ playing came about, bringing many new, young, exciting players who brought fresh perspectives to the instrument.

Another reason for the return of the Hammond organ is its unique, clear, "horn-like" sound. It is certainly no accident that the Hammond revival came about at the moment when digitized and computerized musical instruments became established in jazz, including samplers, hard disks, and laptops. In the age of digital sound machines, the classic sound of the Hammond seemed to be the epitome of warmth, earthiness, and human feeling.

But instead of merely looking backward with a retro sound, the new generation of organists also found new possibilities of expression on the instrument. Two branches of contemporary organ playing developed: the updated continuation, in the nineties and later, of the Larry Young tradition, in players like Barbara Dennerlein, Larry Goldings, John Medeski, Dan Wall, Jimane Nelson, and Sam Yahel, and the post–Jimmy Smith lineage, heard in the bluesy hard-bop playing of players like Joey DeFrancesco, Melvin Rhyne, Tony Moreno, Chris Foreman, and Dan Trudell.

The German organist Barbara Dennerlein has the greatest stylistic breadth and openness of all these musicians. She expands the classic American jazz organ tradition, from Jimmy McGriff to Jimmy Smith, with her own European jazz sensibility. Dennerlein expands the organ sound by combining her classic Hammond B-3 with samplers and synthesizers, using MIDI technology. As a composer, she has expanded the Charlie Parker–influenced Hammond organ tradition to a more open, more modern style, incorporating funk, free playing, blues and Latin, Swing and rock. Above all, however, she has raised playing with the foot pedals to a new level of virtuosity and rhythmic independence.

John Medeski, leader of the successful trio Medeski, Martin & Wood, is on a constant search for new sounds on his Hammond A-100. Among organists, he has most successfully translated the style of Jimi Hendrix to jazz Hammond playing. His organ sound is distinguished by dark, deliberately "dirty" low notes.

Larry Goldings, who became known playing with Maceo Parker and Michael Brecker, says, "If the organ doesn't sound warm, I hate it." Goldings, who plays a CX-3, is also an outstanding pianist, and specializes in playing bass lines not with the foot pedals, but rather with the left hand on the keyboard, which gives his solos their characteristic rhythmic airiness and extraordinary lightness. Goldings is the leader of one of the longest-lived organ trios in contemporary jazz—since 1988, with guitarist Peter Bernstein and drummer Bill Stewart, he has cultivated a very interactive playing style that departs from the one-dimensional approach of traditional organ trios, bringing new adventures to mainstream jazz.

Joey DeFrancesco, who played with Miles Davis and with John McLaughlin, is the "hottest" of all contemporary jazz organists. In his blazing solos, he is a master of building bebop steam with Coltrane's rhythmic intensity. He has an affinity for exciting, fast tempos and is a master of long, polished lines. He makes particularly effective and powerful use of the Hammond B-3's fast attack, in the bluesy hard-bop tradition. Melvin Rhyne is more pianistically oriented; he has a more refined musicality than the standard grooving, funky playing in the style of Don Patterson.

Wayne Horvitz is an organist who cannot be classified in any of the above categories. He became known through his work with John Zorn and Naked City, and is the most interesting organist of the New York downtown scene. In contrast to Zorn, he does not make use of virtuosic "jump cuts," but rather uses stylistic layering techniques, which he cultivates and controls with great logical force. Horvitz's organ playing features short, almost staccato notes, differing from the predilection toward long-held notes that is standard among B-3 players.

Today there are organs whose sounds are produced digitally using contemporary sampling technology. But all these instruments seek to emulate the fat, warm, clear sound of the legendary Hammond B-3, its fast, rhythmic attack, and its characteristic humming, clicking, percussive noises.

In world jazz, Cheick Tidiane Seck, a Malian living in Paris, has made impressive contributions on the Hammond organ in the area between jazz-rock and the griot music of the Mandinka. He has made particularly sensitive recordings with the great master of mainstream piano, Hank Jones. Lucky Peterson and Neal Evans (from the trio Soulive) play the heaviest, most powerful organ in funk and neosoul contexts. Don Pullen revitalized organ playing by bringing free elements into his blues playing. Craig Taborn has used the Hammond organ in post–free-jazz contexts in a particularly convincing manner. And Rob Burger has integrated organ playing into the stylistic patchworks of the New York downtown scene.

The jazz organist has to coordinate more elements than any other instrumentalist, with the exception of the drummer. The left foot plays the pedals; the right foot controls the volume; the left hand plays the bass together with the pedals, and the right hand is responsible for the melody. Simultaneously, Hammond B-3 players are constantly also modifying the instrument's sound by manipulating the stops (drawbars) or varying the settings of the Leslie cabinet (an amplifier with a built-in rotating speaker).

Joey DeFrancesco says, "There are 250 million sound combinations on a Hammond organ." But every musician improvising today on this re-born instrument, regardless of generation or stylistic direction, is subject to DeFrancesco's Law: "If you want to play organ, you have to put soul in it. If the organ groove isn't right, forget it!"

Keyboards and Synthesizer

Since the beginning of the seventies, a new group of musicians has developed who do play the organ but whom we hesitate to call organists in the sense of the term as used so far in this section. For them, the organ is one instrument among several others: acoustic and electric piano, synthesizer, clavinet, and such accessories as wah-wah pedal, fuzz, vibrator, Echoplex and Echolette, phase shifter, ring modulator, etc. These musicians are referred to as "keyboard artists." And indeed, the only thing all the instruments they play actually have in common is the keyboards.

Joe Zawinul, a prototype of these new keyboard players, sat at the center of half a dozen different instruments, like an astronaut in the cockpit of his spaceship, surrounded by a mass of electronics that could hardly be increased. Almost ironically, the good old sound of the acoustic piano was also there, produced by a Yamaha *electric* (!) grand piano.

Joe Zawinul's importance for synthesizer playing in jazz can hardly be overemphasized since he led the way in completely transcending the instrument's mechanical, technical, and electronic rigidities. Zawinul "humanized" the synthesizer. Of all synthesizer players, he produced the most organic sounds, full of warm, mellow, rich colors.

Before Zawinul, Paul Bley, Richard Teitelbaum, Sun Ra, and Wolfgang Dauner wrested unfamiliar tonal colors and sounds from the synthesizer within sixties free jazz—more exciting and stimulating than much that followed in jazz-rock and fusion. Paul Bley gave the first public synthesizer concert in 1969, in New York's Philharmonic Hall. Sun Ra played a prototype of the Minimoog synthesizer before it was available on the market. Ra always said that he had borrowed the instrument from Robert Moog and simply never gave it back. Ra hated the preset sounds programmed by the manufacturer. Sun Ra biographer John Szwed says:

> Instead, he fooled around with the instrument until it sounded totally different. In his very first electronic recordings, he was assisted by synthesizer pioneer Gershon Kingley, who came to the studio and adjusted the instrument. But the collaboration didn't work out at all. Sun Ra began to argue with Kingley immediately, saying; "All that sounds too conventional to me. I want different sounds, wilder sounds."

And yet it certainly wasn't just chance that almost none of the many sounds these musicians discovered were sufficiently satisfying to retain their interest for any length of time. The synthesizer thus gained a tendency toward tonal arbitrariness. Revealingly, all those musicians, except for Teitelbaum, time and again changed over to the piano. Among the early jazz synthesizer players, working electronically in the tonal sphere, were saxophonists Oliver Nelson and Dick Hyman. Viewed from today, their somewhat timid presentations suffered from a striking tonal poverty. Only Joe Zawinul, surmounting the two extremes of synthesizer playing—tonal arbitrariness and tonal poverty—gave the instrument an autonomous and fully matured sound aura. That's why Zawinul is as important for jazz synthesizer playing as Jimmy Smith is for the organ. Zawinul's multielectronic keyboard approach gave the band Weather Report a textural depth that was previously not possible in a group of that size (a quintet). He was able to express himself on the synthesizer so completely that, unlike most fusion keyboardists, he did not find it necessary also to use the acoustic piano. His preeminence is also confirmed by the fact that he cannot be assigned to either of the two basic ways of playing the synthesizer (soon to be discussed here) but is equally influential in both. Later, after the breakup of Weather Report in 1985, Zawinul at first succumbed, in his unaccompanied solo appearances, to a tendency to strive for effects. From the nineties, his group Syndicate featured synthesizer playing in a ferociously grooving world-jazz setting.

Since the first generation of synthesizers could only be played monophonically, performers phrased vehemently as soloists, creating long, digressive phrases in the same way as guitarists link long chains of single notes. Among the soloists who gained an international reputation for this style are the following keyboardists (who naturally mastered other ways of playing, and later developed in different directions): Chick Corea, Jan Hammer, George Duke, Barry Miles, Mike Mandel, Patrice Rushen, Bob James, Richard Tee, Dave Grusin, Joe Sample; and among the younger generation, Scott Kinsey, Wladislaw Sendecki from Poland, Brazilian Eliane Elias, Cuban-born Gonzalo Rubalcaba, Denmark's Kenneth Knudson, and Django Bates from England, who plays with droll wit and great intelligence.

Two keyboardists, Chick Corea and Jan Hammer, have been particularly successful in the sphere of solo synthesizer playing. Corea has cultivated the rich, warm tonal colors of the Minimoog in his fine-spun, imaginative interweavings of line. Among the great paradoxes of keyboard development is Corea's utilization in the eighties of sinfully expensive, highly refined digital equipment for "imitating" that "cheap," simple Minimoog analog sound that he unmistakably made his own at the start of the seventies. "Advances in keyboard technology," said a well-known keyboardist, "don't guarantee an improvement in actual sound quality. Many older analog synthesizers have characteristic sounds and personalities unmatched by today's digital dream machines." And in fact, in the first decade of the twenty-first century the analog Minimoog enjoyed a comeback similar to that of the Hammond organ and the Fender Rhodes electric piano. Adam Holtzman, who played with Miles Davis, prefers the analog Moog synthesizers to the newer digital instruments, precisely for their organic keyboard sounds. It is striking that this phenomenon is a constant factor in the history of keyboard instruments: the electric or electronic instruments that are initially perceived as new and technologically "cold" become, twenty or thirty years later, models of a "warm," "human" sound ideal—not only because players and listeners have become accustomed to their sound, but also because they now communicate a sense of safety and security, compared to a new generation of keyboard instruments that now in turn sound technologically cold because they are unfamiliar. It is therefore advisable not to immediately condemn new developments in keyboard and electronics technology as "inhuman"; a few decades from now, such judgments may well appear bizarre.

Jan Hammer, who became known through the Mahavishnu Orchestra, played "the best jazz-rock guitar" (Wolfgang Dauner) on the Minimoog in the first half of the seventies, with distortions à la Jimi Hendrix. In the keyboard realm Hammer is the real master of pitch bending (achieved through manipulating a wheel or stick alongside the keyboard), which permits smaller and more subtle tonal nuances than the half tones usually available on a keyboard. Hammer later commercialized and trivialized his music.

Herbie Hancock stands apart from this "soloistic group." He mainly made his name in jazz-rock as a soloist on the electric piano and clavinet while remaining strikingly restrained on the synthesizer. Nevertheless, Hancock merits prominence among the pioneers of synthesizer playing. Hancock is the master of synthesizer funk, unequaled in the conception and development of powerfully interlocking rhythms and grooves. He produced the most refined rhythmic superimpositions and intermeshings of electronic sound. The intensity of sound mixtures and the funkiness his sextet attained between 1971 and 1973 were unique in jazz-rock for their open group conception, and have been influential on new genres of electronic music like techno, drum 'n' bass, and new jazz. On the electric piano as well, he found a completely individual approach to rhythmic placement and orchestration.

Herbie Hancock is an inventor of playing textures on keyboards. Toward the end of the seventies, solo playing became hackneyed. Musicians regarded endless synthesizer lines as being superficial and egomaniacal. More and more keyboardists, helped by the emergence of polyphonic synthesizers, all of a sudden turned to inventing refined sound textures, patterns, and layerings. Solo playing wasn't, of course, completely renounced but clearly moved into the background. The important players of such textures, alongside Herbie Hancock and naturally Joe Zawinul, are Wayne Horvitz, Lyle Mays, Geri Allen, Adam Holzman, John Irving III, Kenny Kirkland, Mitchell Forman, Scott Kinsey, Jim Beard, Andy Milne, James Hurt, Harold Budd, German-born Rainer Brüninghaus, and, from Britain, John Surman, John Taylor, and Brian Eno. Wayne Horvitz, who emerged from the New York downtown scene and now lives in Seattle, is a master of the personalization and emotional charging of stylistically heterogeneous keyboard sounds. In contrast to most keyboardists, who prefer fat, dense sounds, Horvitz is a master of uniquely "thin," bizarre, droll sounds. He uses these sounds to create spare sonic atmospheres that are charged with internal drama and nourished by a cynical sense of humor. At the end of the eighties, Horvitz found ways to fracture and denature the cool, metallic, shining, dark sounds typical of the first digital synthesizer (and one of the most popular): the Yamaha DX-7. Compared with the horrendously expensive technology employed by other keyboard greats, he used cheap and simple equipment—and yet produced more exciting and more stimulating sounds than people who were then employing keyboard "altars" costing hundreds of thousands of dollars.

Lyle Mays, who is deeply rooted in jazz tradition, plays particularly vividly: pastel-like, delicately dense superimpositions of chords and sounds permeated with unsentimental romanticism and melancholy, like a sensitive electronic pendant to Bill Evans's piano music. Mays specializes in mixing piano and keyboard sounds so sensitively that he produces a kind of "acoustic synthesizer" feeling that is unmistakably his. He can also develop highly contrapuntal drama, and he played a great part in the sound of Pat Metheny's music. He has played with Metheny since 1976, and it's scarcely possible to distinguish which elements in the Metheny Band come from Mays and which from the guitarist. The fact that Mays's own projects have been less convincing demonstrates the quality and inwardness of this "musical symbiosis." John Surman is a specialist in "sequencing"—the development of complex patterns, repeated as often as wished, which he likes to overlay with long saxophone improvisations. Rainer Brüninghaus has impressively transposed the repetitive patterns of Balinese gamelan and minimal music into synthesizer playing.

The three most important keyboardists of the New York downtown scene, who in the nineties gave the music around John Zorn an unmistakable keyboard signature, are Wayne Horvitz, Anthony Coleman, and Jamie Saft. Coleman and Saft have, in the context of "radical Jewish music," investigated the roots and perspectives of Jewish music in a particularly fascinating manner, creating cross-connections to a large number of other styles and genres.

Saft plays keyboards in John Zorn's band Electric Masada. In the midnineties, he was one of the first musicians in New York to combine jazz with influences from techno and drum 'n' bass in live performance. His "extreme dubs" leave the "higher/faster/louder" mentality of jazz-rock far behind. Instead, the personality of his playing is expressed as the construction and deconstruction of surrealistic sound tableaux in which he uses new sounds to reflect on the roots of Jewish music.

Keyboardist Jim Beard made the most personal continuation and development of the Joe Zawinul approach in the nineties, using polytonal turns full of oblique humor, and smug melodies that humorously evoke circus and fair music. In the M-Base context, Andy Milne has impressively demonstrated an ability to organize rhythms in a musical world of labyrinths, in particular in his playing with alto saxophonist Steve Coleman. Milne's keyboard playing is characterized by intelligence, abstraction, and harmonic surprises.

The wave of keyboard artists that has been inundating the scene since the early seventies has produced surprisingly few individualists. Musicians with a sound unmistakably their own can be counted on two hands.

And yet, the electronic keyboard instruments are indispensable for today's jazz, as we have shown with what we said about electronics in the chapter about jazz styles. We live in an electronic world, which implies electronic sounds, which in turn imply electronic keyboards. It also is a phenomenon of volume; electronic instruments can be heard better because they are easier to amplify and to control. In a way, the sound of the electric piano is to that of its acoustic sister instrument what the vibraphone is to the marimba; it is clearer, more sparkling, more precise—that is, more percussive. That is certainly one of the main reasons why the electric piano made its breakthrough so swiftly.

Carla Bley has pointed out that the lack of individualism has to do not only with the instruments, but also with the record industry: "There is such a trend toward superclean sound in the industry that all these things will become depersonalized. They are trying to get rid of personalities, to make everyone sound like a million other people. Maybe that's so people can be replaced by other people and nobody will have the industry over a barrel."

This situation is even more paradoxical when you consider that the synthesizer offers millions of different sounds, making it the perfect tool for personal expression. "Keyboard players are confronted with almost too many options when it comes to formulating an identifiable sound," said Adam Holzman. The wealth of variety that the synthesizer offers is also its most crucial problem: it is too easily used for pure effects, cheap sound imitations, and incongruous playing around with the sound. "There are a number of keyboard synthesizer players who don't have a lot of technical means but have these programs," said John McLaughlin. "And today's factory programs are becoming so complex and interesting, software development is snowballing, but these people with slight means are able to get a good sound and get by. From the playing point of view, we have to distinguish the difference. It's one thing to play sounds, and it's another to play and *play*." In contrast to traditional instruments, electronic devices are still generally *operated* rather than *played*. This means that the production of the sound is much less direct, and usually less intuitive, than in the case of instruments that have been adapted to human physicality over a centuries-long process of development and refinement.

It is the dialectic of the great instruments in the history of music that they offer their players resistance. Personalities grow with the resistances they meet and deal with. And exactly because the electronic instruments make many things so easy—because they initially level out resistance—individuality is difficult to achieve on them.

It fits into this picture that keyboard artists mainly play fusion or dance music, in other words a kind of music primarily produced from a commercial point of view. This music is not only supposed to be successful as fast as possible; most of it is also supposed to be off the market again soon in order to make room for new "products." And it also fits this picture that, interestingly enough, those musicians who found a personal expression on keyboards had already developed this personality on the acoustic piano—musicians like Kenny Barron, Barry Miles, and Bill Evans. The latter succeeded in realizing the entire rich and brilliant sensitivity of his acoustic piano on the electric instrument as well.

Nowhere was the latent inferiority complex originally present in the keyboard scene so apparent as in the meaningless but understandable attempt to produce exact electronic emulation of the natural harmonics familiar to us from the venerable old instrumental tradition. An imitation syndrome shaped the synthesizer scene considerably. All creative synthesizer players in jazz are characterized by their surmounting of this syndrome.

If we say that a saxophonist has an individual sound, that's a mighty understatement. In reality great jazz saxophonists avail themselves, whether consciously or not, of a multitude of the most differentiated, nuanced sounds. The sound spectrum inclusive of the buildup and decay of tones is constantly changing. Every modification of embouchure, every change in the air column or lip tension, every nuance of phrasing (whether loud or soft, deeper or higher, legato or staccato) transforms the parameters of saxophone sound. There doesn't as yet exist any synthesizer capable of producing all those enormously complex sound processes.

The synthesizer doesn't justify its musical existence by copying natural harmonics. That is only meaningful for the record industry, which can thereby rationalize away studio musicians, but it has become apparent that the industry can't ever do so completely. Every new musical instrument demands a new way of playing and an aesthetic of its own. In the realm of the synthesizer, only the initial stages of such an aesthetic are apparent. "The instrument is a lot further ahead than most of the players," said British rock synthesizer player Rick Wakeman. "The technology is racing ahead of the musicians."

The synthesizer, developed by R. A. Moog in the late fifties, gained sudden popularity in 1968 through the worldwide success of Walter Carlos's record *Switched-On Bach*, which presented electronic versions of some of Johann Sebastian Bach's compositions. Here, the electronics simulated the original instrumental voices; there were hardly any signs yet of a truly autonomous use of the new sounds and new instrumental possibilities. The first artists, besides Carlos, to experiment with the synthesizer in an effort to create really new and original sounds were not jazz players but musicians of different types of music—for example, John Cage and Terry Riley.

In jazz the new possibilities of the synthesizer that make up its actual attraction were used most creatively by players like Paul Bley, Sun Ra, Richard Teitelbaum, George Lewis, Joe Gallivan, Pete Levin, and the German Wolfgang Dauner. These musicians have produced sounds never previously heard, and have refuted the argument leveled so often against the synthesizer, and against electronics in general, that they sound mechanical and "inhuman." This was done most convincingly by Sun Ra through the boiling intensity of his synthesizer improvisations, and also by a player like Terry Riley through his spirituality, and by Richard Teitelbaum through his very personal intellectual level.

There are constant additions on the synthesizer and accessory market. Specialists have pointed out that even after forty years, the development is only in its beginning stages. There is a new kind of jargon that goes along with electronics. Insiders use it as a sort of ritual language: pink noise, white noise, phasing, sawtooth wave, sequencer, shatter, square wave, sine wave, trigger, trigger pulse, low-pass, high-pass, band-pass, and so on.

In the meantime, the synthesizer scene has become so extensive that almost every instrument can now employ MIDI (musical instrument digital interface) for operating a synthesizer without using a keyboard. On the one hand, the time has long passed when keyboardists were alone in using synthesizers. Now guitarists (by way of the guitar synthesizer), saxophonists (through EWI or Pitchrider), trumpeters (through EVI), drummers (through Simmons), etc., also preside over an abundant world of synthesizer sounds. On the other hand, the electronic sounds of wind, string, and percussion instruments have become so similar to keyboard sounds that the electronic scene largely seems to be "keyboardized" even when that isn't the case. This development sometimes even takes on paradoxical aspects when instruments with natural harmonics imitate electronic sound generators that previously served to copy such instruments. Nonetheless, some musicians have been able to employ these new technologies creatively. (We consider the guitar synthesizer and the synth-drums in the sections on the control instruments.)

Samplers and Electronics

The electronic scene has become even more complex through the development of samplers—digital equipment for storing sounds, making it possible to record, store, and then call up and use sounds at whatever pitch required by way of control equipment, such as a keyboard. The real attraction of samplers is that musicians can now employ the sounds of instruments they cannot play in terms of the technical skills involved. "I can't play drums at all," said guitarist Henry Kaiser, "but thanks to microcomputer technology it becomes possible for me to play things and express myself musically in ways I couldn't before." Among the first keyboardists who have taken playing with samplers beyond the usual imitation of natural harmonics to the point of individual musical creativity are Bob Ostertag, Peter Scherer, Wayne Horvitz, Austrian-born Wolfgang Mitterer, and Heiner Goebbels from Germany.

In the eighties, samplers were still outrageously expensive devices, difficult to operate, with limited memory and long load times. Today, with the appropriate software any laptop computer can be used as a sampler, and the access to the stored sounds and to all the parameters of the music takes place in real time. The functioning of the sampler is respectful and predatory in equal measure. The sampler makes it possible to access an archive of sounds and to sonically denature, manipulate, and modify them in any conceivable manner. An improvising sampler artist works on the sound the way a sculptor works on a piece of material. He or she shapes, models, and modifies previously found blocks and fragments of sound by sonically processing them and reassembling them.

However, because the sampler removes sounds from their original environment, it has a fundamental tendency to decontextualize them and to make them anachronistic and anonymous—to depersonalize them. As music journalist Peter Niklas Wilson correctly observed, "A bass line played by Ray Brown on a recording made in the fifties, and then inserted into an improvisation in the nineties using a sampler, is no longer just a Ray Brown bass line, but rather an historical quotation of a Ray Brown bass line." Sampler playing is therefore less about the "what" and more about the "how." The context is more important than the sound itself. Virtuoso electronicists such as DJ Spooky, DJ Olive, DJ Logic, DJ Soul Slinger, France's Eric M., Japan's Otomo Yoshihide, or Germany's Frank Schulte have all liberated DJing from the cage of its function as an aid to partying, making it into an exciting, open, improvisational art. The possibilities offered by electronics gave an unexpected new impulse to free improvised music and to free jazz. It is true that there had already been an interest in live electronics in free jazz and free-improvised music. For example, at the end of the seventies Richard Teitelbaum and George Lewis were already experimenting with the use of computers (still extremely expensive and difficult to use at that time) whose interactive software reacted to inputs from free-jazz soloists. But the advent of computer-supported technologies that were easily portable, affordable, and reliable brought the possibilities of live electronics to a completely new qualitative level.

A fundamental distinction can be made between two different types of sampler playing: detailed processing of the sound, like working on a sculpture, on the one hand; and on the other hand, the assembly of small fragments to form collage structures. The first group includes players like Bob Ostertag, Ikue Mori, Frank Schulte, John Wall, John Coxon, Ashley Wales, Christian Fennesz, Christof Kurzmann, Walter Prati, Marco Vecchi, and Lawrence Casserley, all of whom process and shape sound. The second group of sampler players includes musicians like David Shea, Otomo Yoshihide, DJ Spooky, DJ Olive, John Oswald, and Eric M, who favor a strongly collage-oriented approach, assembling fragments. The use of short time segments—snippets, quotations, shards—to move the listener is part of the excitement of the art of sampling. By making the cut audible, the patchwork becomes a means of expression. As Mark Sinker has said, it's as if "you're seeking the universe in a grain of sound."

The American David Shea does something similar when, in his pancultural sampler improvisations, he uses filmic elements like jump-cut/cross-cut techniques to achieve an almost visual, "narrative" dimension. DJ Spooky, aka Paul D. Miller (and also known as That Subliminal Kid), has overturned all hierarchies with his encyclopedic use of global music history. He has improvised with Steve Reich, Ornette Coleman, and Matthew Shipp, and has found radical, convincing solutions by demonstrating musical cross-connections between contrasting idioms. Japan's Otomo Yoshihide has brought the splintered sounds of noise music into the area of electronics in a particularly effective manner, with a sense of speed and colliding sound blocks also fed by Asian ideals of intensity.

"The machine is something that takes you outside yourself, but I'm actually finding the machine is allowing me to connect more inwardly with myself." The speaker is pianist Matthew Shipp, who broke new ground with his recordings bridging free improvised music and electronics, on the label Thirsty Ear. For saxophonist Evan Parker, the advantage of electronic musicians resides precisely in their ability to break with and abstract away from reality: "They can dehumanize these overhumanized sounds."

Fundamentally, however, the function of the sampler does not differ from that of a conventional jazz instrument: it is used to individualize sounds. The sampler doesn't care who you are. Therefore, you have to make it clear to the sampler who you are. Or, as electronics and sampler virtuoso Bob Ostertag says, "The sound has to have something to do with my own life."

Ostertag is the player who has developed the sound-sculpting approach the furthest artistically. He is the reigning master of the use of loops (repeating passages of recorded sound). Ostertag modifies, layers, and develops his loops with such a richness of variation that they no longer resemble the loops used in commercial music in any way.

For laptop improvisers as well, who in their live performances work "only" with a hard disk and software, it is as if they were their own DJs. Software programs are now available that offer laptop players databases of hundreds of sounds that they can load and process in real time. And, of course, they also have real-time access to all the other musical parameters: loop positions, filter settings, pitch, formants, etc. The biggest problem in improvising with laptops is the lack of physicality of the playing. The physical, sensual moment that connects the body of the musician to the instrument in the case of conventional instruments is reduced in the case of the laptop to only a few keystrokes and mouse movements. Thus, the "playing" of computers and laptops is often itself virtual—and in this genre it sometimes happens that the musicians become tools of the technology that they are using so that the listener can't tell which sounds are being produced spontaneously and which are simply played by the execution of a program.

All the best laptop improvisers are distinguished in that they have found ways to overcome this handicap. These include, in Europe, Christian Fennesz, Christoph Kurzmann, and Wolfgang Mitterer, and, in the United States, Ikue Mori and DJ Spooky, among others.

"In 1985 did any improviser think that fifteen years later improvised music would be getting important inspiration from DJs?" asks music journalist Felix Klopotek. "And in 1995 had any techno adherent ever thought that the image of the DJ as virtuoso could be saved only by liberating the DJ from the cage of functionality, making him into, for example, an improviser?"

DJs operate in flux. They don't fix processes or let them solidify. This makes them ideal improvisers. The dialogue of jazz musicians with DJs in other idioms has its limits, however. Derek Bailey, who repeatedly sought out playing situations with drum 'n' bass musicians, and who created some of the most lasting artistic achievements in the field of free improvisation, sums it up as follows: "Playing with machines is suicide. Because they can play for days without stopping."

Just as the synthesizer will never replace the grand piano, electronic media (samplers, laptops, etc.) will never be able to replace playing on acoustic instruments. They are an alternative in the best sense of the word—not a replacement, but an enrichment. With respect to improvisation, electronic instruments do not differ at all from conventional instruments. The improvising DJ or electronic musician qualifies as an outstanding jazz musician in the same way conventional instrumentalists do: through the capacity for interaction and dialogue.

Particularly impressive in this respect is the improvisation of Ikue Mori. She began as the drummer of the no wave band DNA, which also included Arto Lindsay, and progressed from there to playing three drum machines; later she transposed the sounds that she had invented with these electronic instruments to laptop playing. Her surreal sounds, always a little glassy and metallic, are so personal to her that she is immediately recognizable. Her sensitivity in the creation of textures and timbres is consistently ear-opening and surprising. Trumpeter Dave Douglas says, "When you find yourself wondering where a sound is coming from, it's usually Ikue."

Austria's Wolfgang Mitterer, who came to electronics from organ playing, plays with particular intensity and complexity. He is a master of the assemblage of opposites to form unpredictable musical events, as well as of dynamics—from extremely soft sounds to montages of exploding sonic shrapnel.

Jazz electronicists have also made fresh contributions to the music in the area between club beats, lounge jazz, and improvised music. The Norwegian scene, particularly in Oslo, has proven especially creative, diverse, and original in this respect, including artists like keyboardist Bugge Wesseltoft, guitarist Eivind Aarset, trumpeter Nils Petter Molvaer, and the groups Supersilent and Jaga Jazzist.

These and other Norwegian musicians associated with the labels Jazzland and Rune Gramofone have succeeded in using computer-supported technologies in such a way that they are not just fashionable effects, but rather a genuine artistic means of expression and creation of music. "Electronics is an extra instrument," says Norwegian Helge Sten, who became known through his improvisations with the band Supersilent.

In England, Matthew Herbert (coming from drum 'n' bass) and the bands Spring Heel Jack (in collaboration with Evan Parker, Kenny Wheeler, Han Bennink) and the Bays have created exciting music using samplers.

An improviser and bandleader who has mastered all the instruments discussed in the keyboard chapter—synthesizer and Fender Rhodes, as well as sampling and organic drum programming—and who has used this approach to create perhaps the most complete architecture of electronic sounds is Norway's Bugge Wesseltoft. He has transposed the rhythmic pull of club music (which grabs the listener immediately) into jazz in a congenial manner, and makes particularly imaginative use of the possibilities of electronic real-time improvisation through live sampling of himself and his band.

"Electronics sound interesting whenever you push them past their boundaries," says Wesseltoft. In his "New Conception of Jazz," as he calls it, the keyboards and electronics do in fact sound organic, like natural extensions of the body. The way in which Wesseltoft brings together jazz improvisation and club beats is also fascinating—in round, wide arcs of tension constructed with great mastery.

Returning to keyboard playing: every synthesizer player needs knowledge of programming in order to achieve a personal sound. However, the confrontation with algorithms, envelopes, oscillators, etc., brings aspects of mathematics and engineering into the creative musical process, obstructing the principle of intuitive, spontaneous discovery of sound, so important in jazz. The synthesizer enforces a "technocratization" of musical thinking. That tendency is even more apparent in the second generation of digital synthesizers. Since the programming of synthesizers has become a laborious science of its own, many keyboardists have their sounds made to measure by program writers. Herbie Hancock, for instance, first called on Patrick Gleeson, creator of the music for Coppola's film *Apocalypse Now*. These programmers became so important that in fusion music they received credit on albums just like the musicians involved. It is certainly not just chance that creative keyboard-players—musicians like Joe Zawinul, Sun Ra, Lyle Mays, Wayne Horvitz, Wolfgang Mitterer, Bugge Wesseltoft, and others—exclude the programmer as middleman and search for new sounds themselves.

"I definitely went through a period of experimenting with machines," says George Duke. "All my tracks started sounding computerized. A lot of life got taken out of it. You have to be real careful with synthesizers. . . . I'm from the Miles Davis school. Let a few quirks in there, to make it a little more human . . . let a few mistakes in there, let it fly."

Finally, let's return once more to the organ. Outside the realm of jazz, although with clear repercussions for it, Terry Riley developed his own way of playing the organ. The music of Riley—one of the founders of the musical movement called minimalism—cannot be categorized—neither as jazz nor as rock nor as avant-garde concert music—but it has influenced musicians from all these fields (Don Cherry, for example, or the British group Soft Machine or composer Steve Reich, to mention three names from three fields). Riley is far from playing the organ with the kind of technical brilliance and loudness taken for granted among contemporary organists. He plays at a low volume, carefully, moderately, as a sort of aid to meditation. His music is supposed to be felt more than heard. It is music as much for the aura of a person as for his ears. Riley's music is modal, but it is not so much Coltrane's modality—even though "jazz ears" may perceive it as such—as it is the modality of Asia, above all of Indian ragas. And yet it is Western music, played on modern Western electronic instruments. Riley's music has been called "minimal music," since it hardly seems to change. The listener has the impression that the same tonal movements are constantly being repeated; but in the course of these repetitions, imperceptible changes take place, so that at the end of a Riley piece something new, something different is reached, while the listener is still under the impression of hearing the same tonal movements, phrases, and sounds with which the piece began a long time ago. Riley's phrases are "mantras" that develop and grow in meditation—hardly noticed by the meditating subject—and begin to be effective in a spiritual world, according to their own laws. Riley has dematerialized the organ—certainly a significant accomplishment with an instrument that just a short while before (as with Jimmy Smith and Jack McDuff or with rock players like Keith Emerson or Rick Wakeman) had seemed to be one of the most material, robust, and solid of all instruments. But he also brought the organ back to where it had been before it became electronic: to the spiritual realm—not, however, to a regressive spirituality, but rather to one that progresses into new spaces not only of sounds but of consciousness.

The Guitar

The history of the modern jazz guitar begins with Charlie Christian, who joined Benny Goodman in 1939, and began to play in the Minton circles shortly thereafter. He died in 1942. During his two years on the main jazz scene, he revolutionized guitar playing. To be sure, there were guitarists before him; along with the banjo, the guitar has a longer history than any other jazz instrument. But it almost seems as if there are two different guitars: as played before Charlie Christian and as played after.

Before Christian, the guitar was essentially an instrument of rhythm and harmonic accompaniment. The singers of folk blues, work songs, and blues ballads accompanied themselves on guitar or banjo. In the whole field of jazz prehistory—the field of the archaic, West African–influenced folk music of the southern slaves—the guitar (or banjo) was the most important and sometimes sole instrument. This was the beginning of the tradition that singers like Robert Johnson, Leadbelly, and Big Bill Broonzy carried into our time, playing rich and long melodic lines that jazz guitarists per se discovered considerably later.

The surveyable history of the jazz guitar begins with Johnny St. Cyr and Lonnie Johnson. Both are from New Orleans. St. Cyr was an ensemble player, with the bands of King Oliver, Louis Armstrong, and Jelly Roll Morton in the twenties; while Johnson, almost from the start, concentrated on solo work. The contrast between the rhythmic chord style and the solo-type, single-note style that dominates the evolution of the guitar is emphasized from the very beginning in St. Cyr and Johnson.

The supreme representative of the rhythmic chord style of playing is Freddie Green, the most faithful of all Count Basie band members, from 1937 until the Count's death in 1984. (Green himself died three years later.) Indeed, what is meant by the concept "Basie" is in no small degree to Freddie Green's credit: the tremendous unity of the Basie rhythm sections. Nowhere else in jazz did rhythm become "sound" to the degree it did with Basie, and this sound, basically, is the sound of Freddie Green's guitar. He hardly ever plays solos or is featured, yet he is one of the most dependable guitarists in jazz history. His playing is often felt more than heard, and yet it has a rhythmic power and presence that charges the sonic space between the drums and bass with a resilient, propulsive energy, a kind of rhythmic grease.

Experts today are still amazed at Freddie Green's development of his singular style. He placed his fingers on the strings in order to form a particular chord, but then would press down only some of the strings within this chord shape, while muting the other strings with his fingertips. This was the essence of his style: he played "chords that contained only one clearly sounded note" (Dr. Mark Allen). Green is the only guitarist who surmounted the breach created by Charlie Christian as if there had been no breach at all. Green, by the way, has a very prosperous successor in the seventies rock, jazz-rock, funk, and soul scene: Cornell Dupree, who plays the kind of dependable rhythm guitar that Green played for six decades in the Basie band. His playing, of course, is enriched by the many developments in the music since then.

Lonnie Johnson was the main influence on Eddie Lang, the most important Chicago-style guitarist, and he also made duet recordings with him. Lang came from an Italian background and reflects the tendency toward the *cantilena* and the *melos* of the Italian musical tradition noticeable in so many jazz musicians of Italian origin. The other important Chicago-style guitarist is Eddie Condon, more influenced by St. Cyr, purely a rhythm player and, until his death in 1973, the tireless guiding spirit of the Chicago-style scene in New York.

If you had heard everything played by these guitarists well into the second half of the thirties, and then had gone to Europe to hear Django Reinhardt, you would have understood the appeal that Django had. He couldn't read or write much more than his own name, but when he played, he created new, undreamt-of musical worlds on the guitar. His solos are bursting with surprises, like a fire into which someone is throwing wood as fast as he can. Django came from a Roma family that had trekked through half of Europe and was mainly at home in Germany and Belgium (where he was born). He still lived in his family's caravan during the height of his fame as a jazz musician in the thirties and forties. On November 2, 1928, his caravan went up in flames, and Django was severely injured. Doctors said he would never play guitar again, because two of the fingers on his fretting hand were crippled. But, through sheer willpower, he taught himself to play again, developing unorthodox fingerings in a "two-finger system," and inventing ideas that many uninjured guitarists would never have found. Django's playing vibrates with the string feeling of his people—whether they play violin, like the Hungarian gypsies, or flamenco guitar, like the Spanish gypsies of Monte Sacre. All of this, combined with his great respect for Eddie Lang, came alive in Django Reinhardt's famed Quintet du Hot Club de France, consisting solely of stringed instruments: three guitars, violin, and bass. The melancholy strain of the ancient gypsy tradition lent a magic to Reinhardt's music; down through his last years (he died in 1953), he found his greatness in slow pieces. He composed fragments of symphonies, masses, theater music to texts of Jean Cocteau, and dreamlike tone paintings such as "Nuages," admired by composers of all musical styles. Often the very titles of his compositions capture the enchanted atmosphere of Django's music: "Douce Ambiance," "Mélodie au Crépuscule," "Song d'Automne," "Daphne," "Féerie," "Parfum," "Finesse." In 1946, none other than Duke Ellington took Django Reinhardt on an American tour.

Django Reinhardt was the first musician to invent a truly European jazz language on his instrument. As he played his great solos in the thirties, Roma musicians forced European jazz to reinvent itself—forced it to become a more self-conscious music that reflected its own environment and roots. According to a Roma legend, "Django" means "I am awakening."

Django was also the first European whose influence could likewise be felt on the American scene, in countless guitarists. In fact, even a non-guitarist like pianist John Lewis named Django as a man who had influenced him through the climate of his music. Lewis named his composition "Django," one of the Modern Jazz Quartet's most successful pieces, in memory of Reinhardt. Since the eighties, many guitarists have continuously showed allegiance to Reinhardt—in the United States, for instance, Earl Klugh, mandolin player David Grisman (see "Miscellaneous Instruments"), Larry Coryell; in Europe, French guitarists Christian Escoudé, Boulou Ferré, Biréli Lagrène, Mark Fosset, Stochelo Rosenberg, and Romane (all six of these from Roma and Sinti families), as well as the splendid and absolutely original Belgian guitar virtuoso Philip Catherine. It was above all Catherine's sound that made Charles Mingus call him "Young Django."

The phenomenon of Django has often been cause for amazement. How was it possible for such a musician to emerge from the European world? In all probability, the only possible explanation—if one is not satisfied with the statement that Django simply was there—is sociological: European Sinti and Roma were in a social situation comparable to African Americans. Again and again, ethnic minority groups have been the sources of great jazz musicians: in the United States—besides blacks—Jews and Italians; and in the Europe of the thirties and forties, particularly Jews; and, in present-day jazz, immigrants from Asia, Africa, and Latin America. Here, too, it once again becomes clear that authentic jazz, undictated by the music business, is a cry for freedom, whatever the ethnic environment and whatever the style.

Django's position as an outsider is somewhat related to that of Laurindo Almeida (d. 1995), a Brazilian musician of the rank of the great concert guitarists, such as Segovia or Gomez. Almeida employed the Spanish guitar tradition within jazz initially, in the late forties, as a member of Stan Kenton's band. The solos he played on some of Kenton's recordings emanate more warmth than almost anything else in the cold and glittering music of that phase of Kenton's development. In the seventies and eighties, he was one of the L.A.4, with altoist Bud Shank, bassist Ray Brown, and drummer Jeff Hamilton. They were quite successful with their mixture of classical and Latin American music plus jazz.

Another guitarist who loves to mix different kinds of music is Charlie Byrd, who died in 1999. He really is in command of everything that can be expressed on the guitar, from Bach to Brazilian bossa nova.

The connection of the Iberian baroque guitar tradition with the modern age (and also with a West African rhythmic feeling coming from the Yoruba tradition) was made even more convincing by the great guitarists of Brazil. The five best-known are Baden Powell, Bola Sete, Egberto Gismonti, Vinicius Cantuária, and Romero Lubambo. Powell was the most original and rhythmically most dynamic of them. Sete, who lived in the United States from 1960 until his death in 1987, and who played with Dizzy Gillespie, named Reinhardt and Segovia as his important influences. Gismonti, a self-taught musician who studied with Amazon Indians and has been known to use fishing line on his ten-string guitar, has developed an innovative, futuristic music from the rich spirit of Brazilian folk traditions. In the seventies Gismonti appeared with Norwegian saxophonist Jan Garbarek and American bassist Charlie Haden. They played a kind of music that transcends style and geographical borders—world music in the best sense. As a composer and pianist, Gismonti has developed his own kind of chamber music that emphasizes his Afro-Brazilian roots and combines them with classical elements in a brilliantly virtuosic manner.

For Vinicius Cantuária, bossa, jazz, and rock are "three planets that move in one and the same orbit." A singer and guitarist, it was not until he went abroad, to New York, that he was able to develop his full potential as a Brazilian musician, he says. In collaboration with noise musicians such as Arto Lindsay and jazz musicians such as Bill Frisell, Cantuária created urbane jazz bossas with a cosmopolitan flair. Cantuária is from the Amazon region, and came into contact relatively late with Afro-Brazilian forms of *musica popular brasiliera*, so that his floating songs and tender, slightly angular melodies more strongly reflect his Indian roots. Romero Lubambo has worked with Dizzy Gillespie, Paquito D'Rivera, and singer Diane Reeves. He is a decidedly orchestral player who has brought elements of bossa nova guitar to the new jazz of the New York downtown scene.

But back to Django Reinhardt (whose music also featured, in a totally different cultural environment but in a similar process of acculturation, many Ibero-Spanish elements). The melodic lines he initially played on unamplified guitar seemed almost to cry out for the technical and expressive possibilities of the electrically amplified guitar. Charlie Christian gave the electric guitar such renown that almost all guitarists switched from acoustic to amplified instruments at the turn of the thirties. Yet Christian was not the first to play amplified jazz guitar. First came George Barnes and Eddie Durham, the arranger, trombonist, and guitarist in the bands of Jimmie Lunceford and occasionally Count Basie. The earliest electric guitar solo we know of on record was played by Durham in Lunceford's 1935 version of "Hittin' the Bottle." In Basie's 1937 recording of "Time Out," the contrast between Freddie Green's rhythm acoustic guitar and Durham's solo electric guitar is charming. More recent guitarists as well— for example, Tal Farlow in the fifties, John McLaughlin in the seventies, Pat Metheny in the eighties, or Bill Frisell in the nineties—have frequently made use of the possibilities for contrast between electric and acoustic guitar. As far as Durham and Barnes are concerned, however, they did not yet know how to exploit fully the potential of the electric guitar. They continued to play it as if it were the old acoustic instrument, only electrically amplified—as in the seventies many pianists initially approached the electric piano as if it were a grand, but with an electric sound. An outstanding musician was needed to recognize the new possibilities of the electric guitar. Charlie Christian (d. 1942) was that man.

Christian is comparable to both Lester Young and Charlie Parker. Like Young, he belongs to the Swing era and to the pathbreakers; like Parker, he belongs to the creators of modern jazz.

Christian is the outstanding soloist on some recordings made privately at Minton's around 1941: "Charlie's Choice" and "Stomping at the Savoy." These records were later issued publicly and must be regarded as the first of all bebop records.

Christian charted new territory in terms of technique, harmony, and melody. Technically, he played his instrument with a virtuosity that seemed incredible to his contemporaries. The electric guitar in his hands became a "horn" comparable to the tenor sax of Lester Young. His playing has been described as "reed style"; he played with the expressiveness of a saxophone.

Harmonically, Christian was the first to base his improvisations not on the harmonies of the theme but on the passing chords that he placed between the basic harmonies. Melodically, Christian smoothed out the tinny staccato that almost all guitarists prior to him had employed into interconnected lines that radiated some of the atmosphere of Lester Young's phrases. Not surprisingly, Christian had played tenor sax before becoming a guitarist.

Gary Giddins says, "Christian was an innovator not because he went electric, but because he had to go electric to play what he heard in his head." Blues guitarist B. B. King says, "I don't think that there is a guitar player who has come along after him in the field of jazz, blues, or rock that hasn't been influenced in some way by the genius of Charlie Christian."

Whoever comes after Charlie Christian has his roots in him. To begin with, there is the first generation of "post-Christian" guitarists: Tiny Grimes, Oscar Moore, Irving Ashby, Les Paul, Bill de Arango, Barney Kessel, and Chuck Wayne. The most important is Barney Kessel (1923–2004), who, as a member of the Oscar Peterson Trio and with his own groups, made many Swing-oriented recordings in the United States and in Europe. He had an unmistakable way of highlighting his flexible melodic lines with strong accompanying block chords. Strange how that which had seemed revolutionary in Christian appeared in Kessel, since the end of the fifties, conservative and not very daring. In the early fifties, Les Paul had an immense commercial success with recordings in which he overdubbed different sounds and tracks of electronically manipulated guitar voices. At the time, these techniques were put down in jazz circles as "extramusical trickery." Only from today's vantage point is it clear that—long before Jimi Hendrix and all the others about whom we will talk later—Les Paul was the pathbreaker of modern electronic manipulation of sound.

If Kessel could be designated the most rhythmically vital guitarist of the jazz of the fifties, Jimmy Raney was harmonically the most interesting and Johnny Smith is the one with the most subtle sound. But before Raney and Smith came Billy Bauer. He emerged from the Lennie Tristano school, and in the early fifties played the same abstract, long lines on the guitar that Warne Marsh played on tenor or Lee Konitz on alto. With Konitz, Bauer made duet recordings—just guitar and alto sax—among them, the slow, deeply felt "Rebecca"—one of the first duets in modern jazz that, even at that time, pointed toward the rich duo culture that evolved from the seventies. Jimmy Raney was also indebted to the Tristano school, but his melodies were more concrete and singable, with a flowing articulation. Where Bauer played "dissonant" chords and pointed leaps in which the thresholds are barely exploited, Raney featured richly nuanced harmonies, whose interrelatedness seems rounded, logical, often almost inevitable. Johnny Smith unfolded these harmonies to the last note. A whole universe of satiated, late-romantic sounds evolved—the world of Debussy's *L'Après-Midi d'un Faune* brought into jazz; a fatigued, decadent faun who relaxes in the warm sun of late summer . . . or in "Moonlight in Vermont." The mood of this ballad has never been more subtly captured than by Johnny Smith.

All this came together in the lyrical playing of Tal Farlow, who died in 1998. Farlow initially stems from Raney, but with his big hands he had possibilities quite different from those of Raney, who only played single-finger style. After Tristano, and before Sonny Rollins, hardly any jazz musician swung such long, ceaseless, seemingly self-renewing lines above the bar lines of choruses, sequences, and bridges as Farlow. But these are not the abstract lines of Tristano; they are the concrete lines of early jazz classicism. Farlow had an enormous, dark, deep sound, and was also known as Mr. Wide Interval.

Beyond the Bauer-Raney-Farlow constellation, yet inspired by it, stand the other guitarists of modern jazz: Jim Hall, Herb Ellis, Les Spann, Gabor Szabo, Grant Green, the early George Benson, Kenny Burrell, Larry Coryell, and finally the most significant, Wes Montgomery. Jim Hall—with his beautifully melodious, tuneful improvisations—gained renown, initially, through his work in the Chico Hamilton Quintet and in Jimmy Giuffre's trio; Herb Ellis became known through his long cooperation with Oscar Peterson. His drive is legendary. "If you didn't swing, he would make you swing," says Les Paul. Ellis often combines the stylistic elements of Christian with a shot of blues and country music (in which he has roots).

It is difficult to play in the bebop idiom without playing long strings of eighth notes. Grant Green found a way to do it with different lines, making bop guitar simpler and purer. Jim Hall's wonderfully melodious, songful improvisations and clear, lucid tone were first heard in the Chico Hamilton Quartet and in the Jimmy Giuffre Trio. Hall developed a relatively "free" conception of guitar playing already in the fifties. In his liner notes for the Jimmy Giuffre LP *Piece for Clarinet and String Orchestra / Mobiles* (1960), Hall was the first—before the free-jazz musicians—to speak of jazz as a principle of "instant composition"; over the decades, his lines have characteristically become more and more open and free. At a time when less and less was heard from the other great cool-jazz guitarists (Farlow, Raney, and Bauer), Hall became a master of delicate, sensitive guitar improvisations that have long left behind the confines of cool jazz and, since the seventies, can be considered the truly ageless jazz guitar style. In this sense, Hall, who in the nineties made wonderful duo recordings with his fellow guitarist Pat Metheny, has become *the* timeless jazz guitarist par excellence.

Detroit-born Kenny Burrell, with his tasty, earthy sound and brilliant articulation, could be designated *the* outstanding hard-bop guitarist, but he has grown in the most diverse directions, on electric as well as Spanish guitar. The integrity and steadiness of his improvisations is appreciated by many musicians. He has played with Dizzy Gillespie, Benny Goodman, Gil Evans, Astrud Gilberto, Stan Getz, and Jimmy Smith—which proves his versatility and openness. His economical approach to playing is also notable. "With Kenny, nothing is wasted," says Russell Malone.

The late San Francisco critic Ralph Gleason said that Wes Montgomery, who died in 1968, was "the best thing to happen to the guitar since Charlie Christian." Wes was one of three musical Montgomery brothers from Indianapolis (the others are pianist-vibraphonist Buddy and bassist

Monk), who first became known in San Francisco. He combined a fascinating, at the same time almost inconceivable octave technique with hard and clear self-restraint, in statements in which the blues and the Charlie Christian tradition figured prominently—even when he moved into pop-jazz, as he did frequently during the last years of his life.

Wes Montgomery's development exemplifies the way in which so many jazz musicians become subject to the marketing process of the industry. His producer, Creed Taylor, produced him strictly from a market point of view, with string orchestras and commercial tunes. He did not even allow him to play the kind of music really near and dear to him on every third or fourth album, which would have been the least you could have expected, as critic Gary Giddins once remarked. In 1962 Wes said in a *Newsweek* interview, "I know the melody and you know the melody—so why should I turn around to play the melody?" But only a few years later, he did nothing but play melody. Toward the end of his life, Wes said, "I'm always depressed by the result of my playing."

Wes Montgomery's legacy was carried on by many musicians, but especially so by two players who are diametrically opposed to each other: Pat Martino and George Benson, the latter in a commercial direction, the former in the opposite. From a rhythmic perspective, however, the two also have contrasting styles. While Benson continues the swinging, triplet-based aspect of Wes Montgomery's playing, Pat Martino has carried Montgomery's legacy further with a binary approach oriented more toward duple rhythms. Martino was one of the first jazz guitarists to combine postbop playing with modal ideas and rock-influenced phrasing. His playing has the verve of a lightning-fast thinker. His lines follow a rhythmic and melodic stream of consciousness that develops a breathtaking pull. In his solos, a constant flow of sixteenth notes, he has brought the art of placing modal melodies over angular chords to an astonishing level of perfection.

George Benson, at first solidly within the great black guitar tradition, in the course of the seventies became *the* guitar superstar, with recordings selling in the millions. Along with Herbie Hancock he was at that time the bestselling musician of modern jazz. As a hard-bop guitarist, Benson brought the expressive possibilities of string bending back to the guitar—the characteristic stretching and relaxing of notes, coming from the blues, that had been almost totally abandoned by modern jazz guitarists in their quest to make their lines rounded and clear. As a fusion musician and vocalist, he achieved an astonishing level of virtuosity by singing along in perfect unison with his fast, flexible guitar lines. He plays fantastic grooves with a vibrato all his own. However, the clichéd, sugary songs of his fusion records also met with criticism. Singer Betty Carter commented in a *Rolling Stone* interview, "It's like George Benson . . . the way he can play, why does he have to sound like Stevie Wonder to make money?" And Benson himself said, "I'm not there to educate an audience; I'm there to play for them." It is Benson's singing, of course, that made him so popular on records.

But we have advanced too far. In the meantime, a "guitar explosion," as the British *Melody Maker* called it, had taken place—a widening of the guitar scene by a factor of hundreds, if not thousands, within the span of a few years. Up to that point, the tenor sax had been the major instrument; now suddenly it was the guitar. Even psychologists have dealt with this phenomenon. Both instruments, they claim, are "gender symbols"— the tenor being a male symbol, the guitar, with its shape reminiscent of the human female figure, a female one.

Three musicians were the actual igniters of the sixties' guitar explosion, each in a different field of music: Wes Montgomery in jazz, B. B. King in blues, and Jimi Hendrix in rock.

B. B. King is the father of all guitar playing in rock and popular music of the sixties and seventies. He "rides" on the guitar sound: he lets it approach, jumps in the saddle and bears down on it, spurs it on and gives it free rein, bridles it again, dismounts, and jumps on the next horse: the next sound. It was King who fully realized the development that began with Charlie Christian: the guitar sound grew increasingly longer, was further and further abstracted from the instrument. Of course, this development began in fact before Christian: at the moment when first the banjo, then the guitar were used in African American music. It leads straight from the metallic chirpings of the banjo in archaic jazz (so brief in duration one often could barely hear them), through Eddie Lang and Lonnie Johnson, who (still without electric potential) waged a constant battle against the brevity of their sounds, and via the saxophone style of Charlie Christian and the great cool guitarists of the fifties, to the biting, concise lines of B. B. King—and from him, as we shall see, on to Jimi Hendrix. This development has a single goal: the continuous, determined elongation and the related individualization and malleability of the sound (which, however, as it became easier and easier to realize technically and electronically, finally began to lose its attraction). The aim of this development—the fact that one can do almost whatever one wants with the sound of the guitar, more so than with any other instrument—may have been the main reason for the immense progress and popularity of guitar playing in the sixties and seventies.

In the sixties and early seventies, B. B. King represented the apex of a development that points back to the history and prehistory of the blues. A particularly significant role in the transformation of the rural blues guitar into the "riding" guitar phrases of B. B. King was played by T-Bone Walker, who died in 1975. As we mentioned in the blues section, the South Side of Chicago has been a center of the blues tradition—with guitarists like Muddy Waters, Jimmy or "Fast Fingers" Dawkins, Buddy Guy, and Otis Rush. There was a white guitarist who stems from the

Chicago school of guitar playing, influenced greatly by Muddy Waters, and who stood solidly in this tradition: Mike Bloomfield. About Otis Rush it is said that he carries on where B. B. King left off, playing the King style even harder and more charged with electric and emotional tension. Among the guitarists bridging the gap to rock are Albert King, John Lee Hooker (with his inimitable minimal blues style), Albert Collins (the "Master of the Telecaster"), Jimmy Johnson, Luther Allison, Taj Mahal, Clarence "Gatemouth" Brown, Stevie Ray Vaughan, Robert Cray, Ronnie Earl, Lucky Peterson, Corey Harris, and Keb' Mo'. Said Collins, "I wanted to play jazz. I wanted to sound like Kenny Burrell. . . . I've been known as a blues player, but I wanna be more than a 'rock-blues' guitarist." Cray epitomizes the contemporary blues musician: a stylist who doesn't only play "down home" blues but is also a master of soul, funk, and rock, making clear their links with the source: the great legacy of black music.

Similarly intense sounds have been developed in gospel church services on the pedal steel guitar, by players like Derrick Campbell and Robert Randolph. In contrast to the shimmering sounds of country and Hawaiian guitar, these players use "cooking" sounds that give the instrument a particularly powerful expressive force. In contrast to the conventional guitar, the pedal steel guitar is not worn on the body, but stands on legs in the manner of a table. A metal slide bar is moved back and forth over the strings, which are raised away from the fingerboard. The pedal steel guitar is capable of bending and sliding notes to a much greater degree than the ordinary guitar. Because such pitch modulations are so easy to play on it, in African American gospel music, the instrument functions something like a "preacher," forming the point of communication between God and the congregation.

Modern pedal steel guitarists include Dave Easley, Daniel Lanois, Greg Leisz, and Robert Randolph. Randolph is particularly impressive, bringing the "grounding" energy of the pedal steel and its incandescent, ecstatic possibilities into contemporary jazz with great virtuosity.

The third great musician who, with Wes Montgomery and B. B. King, ignited the guitar explosion is Jimi Hendrix. Hendrix—born in 1942 as a "black Indian" in Seattle, Washington, died in 1970 in London as a world star—is surrounded by a halo of myths. Among instrumentalists, he was the real genius of the rock age of the sixties. Hendrix was the musical symbol of the counterculture of the sixties, comparable only to Bob Dylan. At the legendary Woodstock Festival, he shredded the American national anthem, but what he really meant was America itself. He ripped the anthem with machine guns, tore it to shreds with bomb explosions and the sound of children moaning.

Hendrix had strong links with jazz. Critic Bill Milkowski points out that at the end of his career the guitarist had grown weary of rock's simple forms and was devoting more attention to jazz. Hendrix jammed with Roland Kirk and later even with Tony Williams. He dreamed of a big band with vocal backing. Preparations were being made for working with Gil Evans when Hendrix unexpectedly died.

Hendrix has been dead for over twenty years, and there are more than half a hundred books about him. There are complicated analyses of his playing technique: his use of wah-wah pedals and whammy bars; how he used rings and bottle necks and occasionally even his teeth; how he played not only on his guitar but also "on" his amplifier, with switches and controls; how he retuned his instrument, fast as lightning, in the middle of a song, employing totally unusual tunings; the way he seemed to drum his guitar rather than pick it; the way he played with his own feedback, waiting for it and then answering it, returning it to the amplifier, as if asking questions that he then would try to reply to, which would lead to further questions. Often it seemed as if the feedback was his real partner, more so than the rhythm sections that never really satisfied him.

Jimi's actual accomplishment was to open the music to electronics. Electronics became his instrument, while the guitar served only as a control device. He was the first to explore the wide, unfathomable land of electronic sounds, the first to play "live electronics"—more than all of those who use this catch phrase today—and the first to transform electronics into music with the instinct of a genius, as if plucking the strings of an instrument made of waves, rays, and currents. Whatever can be called electronics in today's music—in jazz, jazz-rock, fusion, rock, pop, techno, drum 'n' bass—came from Jimi Hendrix. And that applies to guitarists as much as to electric piano and synthesizer or sampler players, and even to horn players who use electronics, as long as they employ them as more than a gimmick or a gag.

Jimi Hendrix spoke of his guitar as his lover. He got high just from playing it. But he also beat it, destroyed it, burned it—onstage. It was love and hate at the same time, a kind of sadism that was also masochism, as if someone were losing his mind, a lover who could neither give nor receive true love.

So these are the pillars of today's guitar playing: Wes Montgomery, B. B. King, and Jimi Hendrix. Many guitarists have built their structures on these pillars, but none as brilliantly as John McLaughlin. His range extends from folk blues and Django Reinhardt through the great guitarists of the fifties—in particular Tal Farlow—to the Indian sitar (see also the sections about jazz of the seventies, McLaughlin himself, and the small groups of jazz).

McLaughlin has played the most diverse kinds of music—free jazz in Europe (with Gunter Hampel, for example), fusion with Miles Davis, highly electronicized music with his Mahavishnu Orchestra, Indian music with his group Shakti, solo guitar and duets with French guitarist Christian Escoudé. But whatever he plays cannot be thought of separate from his spirituality. "God," he said, "is the Master musician. I am His instrument."

McLaughlin's 1983 trio recordings with Al Di Meola and Spanish flamenco guitarist Paco de Lucia are an exhilarating feast of acoustic guitar playing, taken on the highly electronicized fusion scene as a sign. Legions of "pure" acoustic guitar ensembles emulated the example set by this trio. Less successful was the reestablishment in the eighties of the Mahavishnu Orchestra, whose highly charged sounds then seemed anachronistic. But in his group Remember Shakti, formed in 1999 with tabla player Zakir Hussain, he returned to playing a version of world jazz that brought new dimensions to the fruitful mutual interaction of Indian music and jazz.

The guitar scene continues to explode. In order to get an even halfway correct picture, we can form the following groupings (remembering that they all blend into one another): rock, jazz-rock and fusion, folk jazz, free, free funk, no wave, cool, traditional neobop neoclassicism, postmodern jazz, and world jazz.

Most directly rooted in Hendrix (and in the blues) are the rock players whom we can only mention summarily in this context: Eric Clapton, Duane Allman, Carlos Santana (who is influenced by Latin music and by Coltrane's spirituality, and who has made recordings with John McLaughlin), Jeff Beck, Adrian Belew, Robert Quine, Derek Trucks, Prince, and Frank Zappa—to name only a very few. Zappa was perhaps the most individual of all rock guitarists, with a forceful obliqueness and bracing venom in his lines, which expanded the limits of expression on the guitar. The influence of Johnny "Guitar" Watson and of Greek bouzouki players can be heard in his fingerings and ornamentations, and his style was so unique and personal that it is difficult to imitate.

In diametrical opposition to these rock musicians stand those players who have transposed the tradition of the cool guitarists from the fifties to today's jazz. The most important of them, the one who was already active during those years, is Jim Hall, whom we discussed earlier. "The quiet American" is what *Melody Maker* called him when he appeared in London. Even when playing electrically, he sounds as if he has an "acoustic" sound. "Even though I never got to work with Lester Young, that's the sound I try to get from my guitar."

Other guitarists who deserve mention in this context are Hungarian-born Attila Zoller, Canadian Ed Bickert, and Americans Howard Roberts, Doug Raney (the son of Jimmy Raney, whose tradition Doug carries on), and Jack Wilkins. Zoller, a master of sensitive restraint, was initially indebted to the Lennie Tristano school. As the first among the guitarists, he transferred the long, singable melody lines he had learned back then into the freer realm of the new jazz, as in his collaborations with pianist Don Friedman. Bickert made recordings with Paul Desmond, the "poet of the alto saxophone," and Bickert's style is just as "poetic." Wilkins, perhaps the most talented of the younger guitarists of this direction, has become known through his work in trombonist Bob Brookmeyer's group.

Let's move on to the largest grouping, the jazz-rock and fusion guitarists. This grouping incorporates extreme positions: rock and blues on the one hand, cool and bebop on the other. This extensive group of jazz-rock guitarists falls into two almost diametrically opposed categories, with of course constantly fluctuating boundaries. On the one side the emphasis is on virtuoso playing, with its sweeping gestures and expansive improvisations. Steve Wakeman has compared this use of the electric guitar to that of a "techno-phallus." This group is predominantly shaped by older players who still phrase in the spirit of new departures and the striving for peak technical achievement; creative, virtuosic players who characterized early jazz-rock: Joe Beck (who was chronologically the first), Larry Coryell, Pete Cosey, Eric Gale, Earl Klugh, Al Di Meola, Lee Ritenour, Allan Holdsworth from England, Holland's Jan Akkermann, and Finland's Jukka Tolonen. Younger masters have also pursued virtuosity in the eighties and nineties: most importantly Stanley Jordan, Charlie Hunter (the most important of these), Kevin Eubanks, Robben Ford, Rodney Jones, Scott Henderson, Frank Gambale (recognizable by his unique vibrato), Dave Fiuczynski, Biréli Lagrène from France, and Germany's Michael Sagmeister.

Larry Coryell was already playing jazz-rock music in the midsixties, when nobody even knew the term, in the Gary Burton Quartet and in the group Free Spirits. His major influences were Jimi Hendrix and John McLaughlin: "Jimi is the greatest musician who ever lived, as far as I'm concerned." But then he added, "I hate him, because he took everything away from me that was mine." And about John McLaughlin: "McLaughlin heard me in England, and I still hear some of my own style coming back at me. Then, when he came to the United States, I started listening to him. It's a two-way street." Coryell hails from Texas, which is his third major influence: "If you listen to me carefully, it must come through that I'm from Texas." In the early seventies, Pete Cosey brought the Hendrix sound to the dark, psychedelic sound paintings of the electric Miles Davis band.

At the outset of his career, Al Di Meola recorded a wonderful duet album, transcending all musical cultures, with the great Spanish flamenco guitarist Paco de Lucia; but he never subsequently fulfilled the promise of this duet. His brilliance, albeit very superficial, nevertheless continued to fascinate. Lee Ritenour probably is the busiest guitarist on the Los Angeles fusion scene, but also has a solid feeling for swing and blues, coming from Wes Montgomery. Allan Holdsworth, who emerged out of Soft Machine, has impressively transposed Coltrane's "sheets of sound" into jazz-rock guitar playing, with extremely fast lines that combine an ultra-legato feeling with sophisticated harmonies. With his IOU trio at the start of the eighties he made an important contribution toward a new, more economical concept of jazz-rock. Many guitarists who play fast sound fast—and not much else. When Holdsworth plays fast, he does it from a balanced melodic sensibility. Dave Fiuczynski plays adventurous ideas at light speed—sleek, racing, contorted lines. Larry Coryell says: "I sat next to him every week for a year when I did the Mingus Guitars thing and I kept thinking I was sitting next to the soul of Eric Dolphy entering a guitar player."

Stanley Jordan and, a generation younger, Charlie Hunter have revolutionized the technical aspect of guitar playing. As a street musician in New York, Stanley Jordan's tapping technique attracted such attention that George Wein presented Jordan in the 1984 New York Jazz Festival. Jordan doesn't pluck his guitar. He gets the strings to sound by tapping with the fingertips of both hands on the fingerboard just as if it were a piano keyboard. Tellingly, Jordan says he developed this technique so as to attain the "orchestral" capacities of a pianist.

Jordan wasn't the first person to develop "tapping" (also known as "hammering"). He was preceded by Jimmy Webster (who in addition wrote a guide to this way of playing), Eddie Van Halen, David Torn, and Adrian Belew. Those guitarists, however, mainly used tapping as not much more than ornamentation and one playful method among many others, whereas Jordan makes this technique into the basis for his playing—with such rich polyphonic interweavings that you get the impression that two guitarists are playing here rather than one.

On the other hand, critics have noted the thinness of Jordan's sound and the problems created by trying to integrate his polyphonic concept, so fascinating in solo appearances, into a group.

Charlie Hunter, who comes from San Francisco, found his way to jazz from hip-hop. He derives his guitar style from the organ playing of Jimmy Smith and Larry Young, by adapting the heavy bass lines and broad chords of the Hammond B-3 to the guitar. Hunter is a "guitar wizard," a virtuoso who sounds like a one-man duo on an eight-string guitar of his own invention. This hybrid instrument, with three bass strings and five guitar strings, makes it possible for him to play deep, rich bass lines, chords, and melodic single lines simultaneously. In his trio, he is an interactive and groove-oriented player who combines funky vamps—the ostinato structures of funk—with ingredients from rhythm 'n' blues, hard bop, and hip-hop. Hunter says, "In the beginning, people would say, 'He can't do what a guitar player and a bass player can do. It's so limiting.' Yeah, it is, but I don't want to sound like a guitar player and a bass player; I want to sound like the eight-string guitar." Larry Coryell remarked: "He'll save a lot of money on sideman costs."

Tuck Andress and Philip DeGruy are two other guitarists who have expanded contemporary jazz guitar playing with unusual techniques and instruments. With the singer Patti, Tuck Andress formed the popular duo Tuck & Patti, using unusual percussive and tapping techniques to create rhythmically unbelievable effects in his full playing. Philip DeGruy uses a "guitarp"—a combination of a seven-string guitar and a ten-stringed harp—to play a virtuosic jazz full of stylistic pranks and humorous allusions.

So much for the representatives of deliberately virtuosic jazz-rock and crossover playing. The other group of guitarists puts the emphasis on deliberately economical use of the guitar with less lavish, more concise phrasing, concentrating on what is essential and on creating an atmosphere. The early representatives of this way of playing included Larry Carlton, Steve Khan, Terje Rypdal from Norway, and German-born Volker Kriegel, and Toto Blanke. But most of the stylists within this group come from the second and third jazz-rock generations, and their deliberately economical playing is a reaction to their precursors' often unrestrained virtuosity. Their number includes Pat Metheny, John Scofield, Hiram Bullock, Mike Stern, David Torn, Christy Doran, Eivind Aarset, and Wayne Krantz. Terje Rypdal, one of the progenitors of Nordic jazz, paints pictures on his guitar, reminiscent of the fjords and dark mountain lakes of his Norwegian homeland. Hiram Bullock, first presented by David Sanborn and Gil Evans, plays a funky jazz-rock guitar with oblique humor and biting irony, also full of witty harmonic deviations. Steve Khan was also among the first fusion guitarists, but in the eighties he played purified jazz-rock that had shed all unnecessary pomp. His quartet with bassist Anthony Jackson, drummer Steve Jordan, and percussionist Manolo Badrena exerted an astonishing (and much too little remarked) reformist influence on the jazz-rock of that time. Mike Stern, who became known through Miles Davis, is a master of bebop-inspired jazz-rock playing on the solid-body electric guitar. His knowledge of the standards of the Great American Songbook is exceptional in the jazz-rock field. Stern phrases clear, undistorted legato lines precisely on top of the beat, thereby gaining unusual drive and power. David Torn mixes Hendrix's wild, distorted sounds and Allan Holdsworth's complex harmonic sense, much influenced by ethnic music. Swiss guitarist Christy Doran has a strong connection to rock. He is imaginative in his use of delay effects, and his complicated pieces—with the band OM, among others—were influential in European jazz-rock. In Nordic jazz, Norway's Eivind Aarset is the master of playing with the guitar sampler. He has a unique sense for integrating dance beats and ambient sounds into his dramatic, melancholy sonic language.

By far the most important musicians in this group are, however, Pat Metheny and John Scofield. Metheny is a magician of melody. He plays songlike, mellifluous, warm, clear lines, constantly renewing themselves from within and extending over a great dynamic range. His improvisations are founded on harplike, floating electric guitar sounds rich in harmonics—with his celebrated "chorus sound," named after the device that duplicates the note being played, but modified by a sine wave sweeping at low pitch and depth. It's one of the most copied sounds of the eighties and nineties, but no one masters it so completely as Metheny. It is in his rare ability to make synthetic sounds seem "organic" that Metheny demonstrates such sensitivity. Critics have found fault with the cloying character of his music and the rococo ornateness of his quasi-symphonic arrangements. Even amid their tropical extravagance of weltschmerz, kitsch, and angelic sweetness, Metheny's improvisations uphold that love of clarity, homogeneity, and balance that have brought him a following of millions. Of all the guitarists in contemporary jazz, he is the most sophisticated harmonically. His wealth of melody seems inexhaustible.

Pat Metheny was also the first person to play the guitar synthesizer like an autonomous new instrument, beyond all sounds imitative of keyboards and unlike his otherwise more ethereal playing: angular, biting, penetratingly intense sounds. In "Endangered Species" (1986), a recording from Ornette Coleman's album *Song X*, Metheny gained an ecstatic element. However, his brief excursions into free jazz in the nineties—including some with Derek Bailey—seem to have had only a therapeutic function, and have not been followed up in his own groups.

Metheny's playing of the guitar synthesizer fulfills the jazz guitarist's dream of greater physical presence. The first step involved was the changeover from banjo to guitar. Then came Charlie Christian's use of the electric guitar, and next Hendrix's elongation of guitar sound. And now with Pat Metheny, the instrument (but only on the guitar synthesizer) attains a new, augmented dimension of tonal penetration that actually achieves (rather than merely strives for) a hornlike impact. Other musicians playing the guitar synthesizer include John McLaughlin, John Abercrombie, Bill Frisell, and Harry Pepl from Austria. The extent to which Metheny's improvisations uphold both jazz tradition (bebop, Jim Hall, and Wes Montgomery) and the country music of his home state Missouri became clear when he recorded—together with tenorists Dewey Redman and Mike Brecker, bassist Charlie Haden, and drummer Jack DeJohnette—the *80/81* double album, one of the most beautiful eighties jazz recordings.

John Scofield, who became known through playing with Billy Cobham and Miles Davis, has one of the most personal guitar sounds in contemporary jazz. He combines a strong feeling for bebop with blues and rock influences. He unites the legato feeling of Jim Hall and Wes Montgomery with B. B. King's biting blues and funkiness. Scofield, who also presented himself as a splendid neobop stylist, phrases jazz-rock with a rhythmic elasticity and glowing ardor that helped move this often cool realm, dazzling with technical skills, toward unanticipated warmth, with soulful, inventive improvisations. His trademark is his "sandpaper sound" (Vernon Reid)—a super-dry tone that he uses to play excitingly organic lines. Derek Trucks: "There's just a weird, beautiful uneasiness about his playing that's instantly recognizable." In the three years when Scofield played with Miles Davis, he brought many creative elements to the trumpeter's music, as soloist and composer. Scofield was as important for the "funky Miles" of the eighties as Wayne Shorter had been in the sixties.

Scofield has remained constantly inventive, developing interesting, individual sounds into the twenty-first century in his playing between go-go and acid jazz with the trio Medeski, Martin & Wood, or with his band Überjam, in which he plays guitar sampler and incorporates elements from drum 'n' bass. Scofield says:

> Guitar certainly has its place in jazz. . . . The guy who maybe had more to do with the invention of bebop was a guitar player. Guitar is also the number one instrument of rock 'n' roll and pop music and we've been influenced by that music too. . . . Every time I sit down and pick up a guitar, it's there . . . that open chord is there. And that leads you to another place than if you were a piano player or a tenor player. I could more easily live in the insulated world of II-V-I and jazz harmony—if I played another instrument. But guitar always, to me, it slams me out of that.

Scofield's wealth of unusual intervallic leaps and original runs have influenced countless guitarists (often alongside influences from Pat Metheny and Bill Frisell), including Leni Stern, Mitch Watkins, Kurt Rosenwinkel, Mimi Fox, England's Mike Walker, and John Schroder from Germany. Kurt Rosenwinkel, who emerged from the Electric Bebop Band of drummer Paul Motian, is one of the most unmistakable players of the early twenty-first century—a decidedly flowing, lyrical stylist who plays complicated lines with a clear but warm tone. His advanced harmonic logic is spiced with a "spectral," echo-expanded sound. Rosenwinkel is also a visionary composer, with an infinitely sensitive way of layering electronic sounds, borrowed from ambient music, dub, and drum 'n' bass, and manipulating them intelligently.

In some ways folk-jazz guitarists are related to jazz-rock players. That becomes particularly apparent in the music of Steve Tibbetts from Minneapolis. His magical sound paintings range from highly electronic, distorted, rocklike guitar sounds to the meditative acoustic tones of ethnic music (mainly Indian and Tibetan). Independently of Hendrix he developed his own way of playing with extreme feedback. Considering how deeply rooted the guitar is in the ethnic music of many cultures, the existence of these folk-jazz guitarists is not surprising. Apart from Steve Tibbetts they include such different musicians as Alex de Grassi, William Ackerman, Leo Kottke, Ry Cooder, John Fahey, Richard Leo Johnson, Joel Harrison, Doug Wamble, and Michael Hedges. Hedges plays a steel-string guitar and particularly relishes harplike, "open" string sounds full of a percussive quality. Joel Harrison plays American roots music on his fretless guitar, going back to the sources of traditional folk melodies in order to rearrange them from a contemporary jazz perspective. Doug Wamble is also a walking compendium of Americana, incorporating country blues, gospel, swing, and free jazz in an organic approach.

Parallel to the development of rock music, in which the guitar assumed a dominant role, the pioneers of free jazz radically changed the conception of how the instrument should sound. The first musician to play free-jazz guitar in the sixties was Sonny Sharrock, who played with Pharoah Sanders, Don Cherry, and the punk jazz group Last Exit. French guitarist Noël Akchoté has gone as far as to say that Sonny Sharrock is and will always be the "only free-jazz guitarist." "Why? Because no one except him dared to liberate himself so completely. Everything about him was about breaking the bounds, was explosive, extreme, without a scrap of convention." Sharrock played the instrument with guitar picks held in his mouth, shattering them under the enormous pressure; he played percussively behind the bridge, from the top to the bottom, from the front and from the rear, hit the strings with a slide, and never neglected an opportunity to reinvent this piece of wood with strings stretched across it. For him, supposed mistakes were not mistakes at all, but rather windows onto a new, previously hidden world.

Anyone who played free improvised guitar after Sonny Sharrock came from him. The first to do so were Michael Gregory Jackson, James Emery, Eugene Chadbourne, and England's Derek Bailey and Keith Rowe. Later came Germany's Hans Reichel, Uwe Kropinski, and Helmut "Joe" Sachse; Americans Jim O'Rourke and Nels Cline; Austrian Burkhard Stangl; and France's Jean-Marc Montera and Noël Akchoté. Probably the most radical of these free players is Bailey, a musician unusually fond of musical dialogue, who, with his differentiated, splintered sounds and pointillistic free lines, is a proponent of "non-idiomatic music"—music that attempts to do away with preconceptions and that strives for complete openness of musical communication. Bailey is one of the outstanding conceptualists of European free jazz, whose music has also had an enormous influence on American free improvisers. In the seventies, he was a member of the Spontaneous Music Ensemble, an important group of European free jazz. In the nineties, he constantly sought out encounters with musicians from other styles and genres: Chinese *pipa* players, drum 'n' bass musicians, DJs, guitarist Pat Metheny. Through all of it, he charged his variegated, imaginative "knitting needle" sounds with individuality, always further developing them.

Keith Rowe plays the most imaginative free jazz on the "tabletop guitar"—an approach in which the guitar is laid on a table, and its strings are prepared with the insertion and application of various metal objects and then played with iron bars, needles, small electric motors, violin bows, etc. Rowe is a master of intensive investigation of material. No guitarist has taken the concentrated examination of individual sounds as far as he has in his sonic microcosm. "It's almost like looking into a microscope. You really get pulled in, and the objects get bigger and bigger," he says.

The unusual quietness and persistence of Rowe's playing is also notable, in its use of extraordinarily quiet, still, "flat" sounds. This approach to playing with the surface of noise, which he developed in the group AMM with great patience and doggedness, has made him, quite unintentionally, one of the father figures of industrial and ambient music.

Eugene Chadbourne deconstructs styles and genres with explosive energy. His solos use virtuosically cut-out snippets of clichéd elements from country, free, rock, and folk, reassembling them into a universe of "crazy" sounds. His absurd, rebellious pastiches have an arbitrary, casual effect, but their greatest strength lies precisely in this indeterminacy.

Hans Reichel came to freely improvised music from blues and rock (Hendrix and Zappa). He is a guitarist, composer, designer, inventor, and instrument builder. He has seldom been satisfied with materials as he finds them. On his self-built instruments, which include movable pickups, guitars that can be played forward and backward, and instruments with twenty-three strings and four necks that are played behind the bridge and can be folded up, he plays a free jazz that is not shockingly avant-garde, but rather shockingly melodic, with shimmering overtones and strange, fragile floating sounds full of friendliness and humor. Reichel says, "I am not a tinkerer, but a musician."

American Jim O'Rourke, who has played with Sonic Youth, produces unique sounds on the acoustic guitar without using effects devices or amplifiers. More so than his model Derek Bailey, he also includes tonal elements and a greater sense of restfulness in his improvisations. France's Noël Akchoté is influenced by Ornette Coleman and John Cage, in his guitar music free of all rules and routines. He also incorporates elements of rock and *chanson* guitar into his playing, not as styles but as reference points in the creation of something individual. Noël Akchoté makes noises and sounds enigmatic, strangely mysterious. He specializes in dark, expanded floating sounds that consciously play with the diffuse sides of the electric guitar—overtones, notes on the verge of feeding back, the hums and clicks of the guitar amplifier, oscillating sound pulses, and vibratos that rotate in space like fields of radiation. Akchoté's music is animated by the details of sound gradation and sound transformation—"wrong is right and less is more."

James "Blood" Ulmer, who made his name in Ornette Coleman groups, has been more successful than anyone else in making the transition from free jazz to free funk. His concise, refractory, deliberately spluttering lines build a bridge from free jazz back to the original blues and to funk, concretizing the former and musicalizing the latter. Ulmer's motto: "Jazz is the teacher; funk is the preacher."

Among the other important free-funk guitarists are Kelvyn Bell with his striking emphasis on "smeared" phrasing; Jean-Paul Bourelly, who transposes an aggressive, venomous post-Hendrix sound with elements of hip-hop and rap into the unruly language of free funk; Bern Nix; Charles Ellerbee; and Vernon Reid. Bourelly has constantly sought out collaborations with musicians from West Africa and the Caribbean, such as Senegalese percussionist Doudou N'Diaye Rose and the Haitian band Ayibobo, with whom he developed an exciting "voodoo jazz." Vernon Reid became known through his playing with the hard rock band Living Colour. He is one of the founders of the Black Rock Coalition, and leaves plenty of room for free musical adventures in his Hendrix-influenced playing. His playing demonstrates that volume creates not only power but also new subtleties. "Above a certain volume, the electric guitar takes on totally different characteristics. The guitar is malleable; when it's hot, when it's really high, it becomes even more sensitive," says Vernon Reid.

Particularly original new sounds in the eighties and nineties came from the no wave guitarists, the players who most consistently pursued the demolition of stylistic categories in postmodern jazz. Although they are influenced by free jazz, they transcend that by making numerous other fragments collide in their playing: punk and ethnic music, avant-garde and rock, minimal music and folk. Among the interesting guitarists here are Arto Lindsay, Henry Kaiser, Fred Frith, Elliott Sharp, Rhys Chatam, Franco-Canadian René Lussier, Frenchman Marc Ducret, and German Caspar Brötzmann. Arto Lindsay grew up in Brazil, the son of an Amercian missionary. He makes the guitar sound like "a collapsing twenty-story glasshouse." He shaped such splintering, crashing, somber sounds when working with the Golden Palominos and alto saxophonist John Zorn. He later developed into a poet of the New York downtown scene, whose laconic, melancholy songs and bizarre, lithe melodies equally reflect his western and his Brazilian roots. In Henry Kaiser's playing the guitar is transformed (with assistance from computers, MIDI, rhythm machines, and other digital aids) into a "crazy" turbulent orchestra. There Kaiser batters and integrates extremely disparate musical styles—Korean music and Delta Blues, Vietnamese traditions and punk, Captain Beefheart and Ali Akbar Khan. Fred Frith is the most adventurous and flexible musician of this group. He played with the group Henry Cow in 1968, played punk jazz in the eighties with Massacre, and played flipped-out collage music in John Zorn's band Naked City in the nineties. Frith is a wizard of freely flowing, delicate sonic textures, an intrepid explorer of the outer edges of rhythm, harmony, and texture. René Lussier plays "imaginary folklore" full of droll humor. His lines often meticulously follow the course of French-Canadian linguistic patterns. Hence the vocal quality of his playing.

Self-taught guitarist Marc Ducret is one of the most personal voices to emerge from European jazz in the nineties. He brings new sounds and challenges to the guitar, combining *melos* with abstraction and uniting a round, flowing quality with deliberate angularity. Ducret came to post–free jazz from tonal playing. The clarity of his playing is fascinating; his feeling for pointed, brilliant sounds and transparent forms, and his intellectual sharpness and emotional presence, are remarkable. Since 1991 he has worked regularly with alto saxophonist Tim Berne, making him one of the few European musicians recognized by the New York downtown avant-garde as an equal partner, constantly participating in projects on that scene.

Diametrically opposed to the free and no wave players, to use another pair of contrasts, are the guitarists who remained connected with the Swing tradition. Among them are George Barnes (d. 1977), George van Eps (who gave up playing with a plectrum in favor of fingerpicking, becoming the founder of playing on the seven-string guitar), Bucky Pizzarelli, Cal Collins, Chris Flory, and the best known of them, Joe Pass, who died in 1994. In the early seventies Barnes co-led a quartet with Ruby Braff. Pizzarrelli plays block chords on a seven-string guitar with propulsive energy. Pass was an extraordinarily virtuosic, orchestral player who specialized in accompanying his melodies and chords with walking bass lines. He made recordings with many of the important jazz musicians of Norman Granz's Pablo label, among them Ella Fitzgerald and Oscar Peterson. He was a master of ballad playing as well as of swinging jam sessions. Like tenor man Scott Hamilton and trumpeter Warren Vache, Cal Collins, Jimmy Bruno, Howard Alden, and (the younger) John Pizzarelli are part of the new Swing movement that has been crystallizing since the end of the seventies.

Finally, the contemporary mainstream—which extends from bebop by way of Coltrane to the neoclassicism of the "young lions," where the all-dominant influence of Wes Montgomery lies—developed further within a large number of individual styles. John Scofield, Emily Remler, Bruce Forman, Joe Diorio, Joshua Breakstone, Peter Leitch, Henry Johnson, Rory Stuart, and others are among those who are a part of this mainstream. The best known is the already mentioned Scofield, whose trio—together with Steve Swallow (electric bass) and Adam Nussbaum (drums)—set standards for guitar groups in eighties jazz classicism, with its angular rock- and blues-imbued neobop improvisations integrated to an extent never previously experienced in such guitar trios.

The guitarists of the new mainstream jazz and of neoclassicism have demonstrated since the early nineties that there are infinite possibilities for further developing and refining classic jazz guitar styles in order to arrive at a personal approach to playing, with a strong emphasis on bop roots. Important stylists in this group include Mark Whitfield, Russell Malone, Peter Bernstein, Anthony Wilson (also known as an arranger and composer), Howard Alden, Jonathan Kreisberg, Joshua Breakstone, and Jesse van Ruler.

Mark Whitfield is the prototypical "young lions" guitarist. When he came on the scene at the beginning of the nineties, his bop-rooted, tradition-conscious playing displayed such breathtaking technical brilliance that he was accused of being cold and impersonal. Nonetheless, Whitfield, whose lines reflect elements of George Benson, Wes Montgomery, Grant Green, and Joe Pass, has made his playing unmistakable, with a pure, classical tone and nimble articulation. His experience includes collaborations with veterans like Ray Brown, Tommy Flanagan, and Brother Jack McDuff.

Russell Malone, who has worked with Diana Krall and Benny Green, improvises with white-hot fire and passion. The sheer musicality and bravura with which he has reinterpreted the classic guitar styles of jazz are stunning. He combines an appealing, bluesy guitar sound with a strong attack, a powerful vibrato, and an inexhaustible supply of harmonic ideas. His time feeling is as solid as a drummer's. George Benson: "He plays the biggest chords in the world."

Peter Bernstein is a lyrical, lightheartedly swinging guitarist. He has Grant Green's sense of droll simplicity and eloquent spareness, making him one of the most sought-after sidemen in the jazz of the nineties, for example with Joshua Redman, Dr. Lonnie Smith, and others. Howard Alden plays all the classic jazz styles from the Swing era to modern jazz with abandon. Another important guitarist in neoclassical mainstream jazz is the classically trained Adam Rogers, whose playing is strongly influenced by saxophonists. He has played electric guitar in bands including Lost Tribes and the Brecker Brothers. His energetic, intense playing brings the flow of Pat Martino and George Benson to neoclassicism, with fluent, round, soft lines full of pointed equilibrium.

Before turning to the guitarists of world jazz, three particularly individual musicians, who don't fit into any of the above groups, must be mentioned: John Abercrombie, Ralph Towner, and Bill Frisell. Abercrombie first became known playing in Billy Cobham's jazz-rock band. He has gone on to become one of the great, sensitive poets of contemporary guitar playing. In 1974 he made highly regarded recordings with Jan Hammer and Jack DeJohnette. Since 1986 he has led an exquisite trio with bassist Marc Johnson and drummer Peter Erskine. Abercrombie is a master of combining and weaving notes together in a style full of feeling and variety. In his highly legato playing, he moves between freedom and predetermined structure; his dark, gliding melodies are full of secrets and melancholy. He has made postfusion guitar playing relevant in the neobop era with ethereal lines and harmonically complex voicings that he adapts to any context, from a trio to a big band. On the guitar synthesizer he plays massive, penetrating power chords, which constitute a powerful contrast to the fragility of his actual guitar lines. He says: "I always think that the guitar is the most wide-reaching instrument, in a way, because it crosses all these boundaries. Tenor players get more into the legacy of what jazz tenor is about. For me, the guitar definitely has a strong legacy, but there seems to be more room for development and experimentation."

Ralph Towner, leader of the group Oregon, began as a pianist and still plays the instrument. His acoustic classic guitar playing is molded by this piano element. Towner studied in Vienna, and he admits to not being quite sure which side he is more indebted to: European music—in particular music from Vienna, that is, Viennese classicism, romanticism, and avantgarde (Schoenberg, Webern, etc.)—or jazz. "I wasn't on the jazz scene until I got a classically oriented technique on the guitar. . . . I do find acoustic instruments more sympathetic than electric instruments. . . . I treat the guitar quite often like a piano trio. If I'm playing alone, it's almost like a one-man band approach," he said.

In eighties and nineties postmodern jazz, Bill Frisell was the guitarist with the greatest stylistic range: from Eberhard Weber's sonically beautiful jazz to the free funk of the Power Tools trio, from the Bass Desires quartet's contemporary mainstream to the radical collage and noise music of John Zorn's Naked City.

Frisell brings hidden things to the surface, things that we normally see only in dreams. No other guitarist negates the harsh percussive moment that occurs when striking a string so completely as Bill Frisell. His lines seem to come out of nothingness and to vanish back there again—atmospheric floating sounds becoming louder and softer, notes sliding like wax dripping from a candle. "Bill is one of the great orchestrators, like Joe Zawinul; he's a painter," says John Scofield. At the same time, Frisell's playing also has a tricky, self-aware side, like a humorous "Monk of the guitar." Leni Stern observes, "He can take the corniest thing and make it sound like twentieth-century classical composition." Frisell played the clarinet before moving to guitar. Characteristically, it is the warm, wafting sounds of woodwind that made an unmistakable mark on his original style. Frisell "breathes life" into the jazz guitar. His music is a fascinating "Americana," created from many different, contrasting American sources, and drawing the essential ingredients from them—from country and rock, Nashville and Aaron Copland, Charles Ives and the blues, John Philip Sousa and Jimi Hendrix. John Scofield has called Bill Frisell's music "the most unique concept in guitar today."

At the beginning of the twenty-first century, Bill Frisell has not lost his sense of musical surprise. With his group The Intercontinentals, he incorporates influences from Africa, South America, Asia, and the Balkans. Frisell says, "Sometimes you hear music from the Middle East and you think: damn, that sounds like a blues guy from Louisiana."

A guitarist whose playing combines the best of Bill Frisell and John Abercrombie is Ben Monder. He can play chord melodies like a keyboardist, using difficult, large intervals, and he has a particular sensibility for beautiful, dark harmonies.

Perhaps the most important achievements of the guitarists of world jazz are to be found in their revitalization and expansion of modern jazz guitar playing with their respective cultural backgrounds. These include South Africans Louis Mhlanga and Jimmy Dludlu, with the melodies and rhythms of the Xosha and Zulu; Spain's Gerado Nunez and Tomatito, with elements of flamenco; Macedonia's Dusan Bogdanovic, Miroslav Tadic, and Vlatko Stefanovski, with the odd meters and ornamented melodies of Balkan folk music; Uzbekistan's Enver Izmailov, with the exuberant rhythms and melancholy moods of Crimean music; and many others.

Here as well, we must limit ourselves to only a few musicians. Three particularly brilliant individualists of world jazz are Nguyên Lê, Enver Izmailov, and Brad Shepik.

"I'm the personification of the fusion of two cultures," says Nguyên Lê, who grew up in Paris, the son of Vietnamese parents. From the perspective of a musician who grew up as it were "between" two cultures, Le has created a new jazz with a strong sense of urgency. His Asian musical heritage is unmistakably audible in his original European jazz-guitar playing. Critic Urlich Olshausen writes:

> What is so fascinating in Nguyên Lê's guitar playing is not so much the ruptures, but rather the brilliance with which he combines apparently disparate elements to form an unmistakable musical identity. He oscillates between luxuriant Asiatic ornamental melody and Hendrix-inspired power rock. He makes a transition from Asiatic trance music, detached from the world, to the wild, electric energy of jazz-rock. Every note Le plays is a small sonic cosmos in itself, leading its own life made up of many small tones, massaged by the art, grounded in Asia but felt as European, of many different vibrato, bending, and glissando techniques.

Nguyên Lê combines Jim Hall and Jimi Hendrix with the meditative, floating sounds of Asian music and folk music influences from the whole world. "You can learn a great deal from all the musical traditions of the world. There are so many fantastic sitar players or mandolin players. And that's what interests me today: what can I learn from them?"

Uzbek guitarist Enver Izmailov, whose parents were Crimean Tatars, picks up where Stanley Jordan leaves off with his virtuosic tapping style. With his two-handed "hammered" playing, Izmailov set new standards in the nineties for polyphonic guitar jazz. Using a tapping technique, in which the guitar strings are not plucked, but rather are struck against the fingerboard using the fingertips, Ismailov achieves orchestral effects compared by critics to a piano or a harpsichord. His jazz brings together the worlds of Uzbek music and the richness of Crimean culture, but also includes the music of the Tatars, with melodies and rhythms from the Mediterranean, India, and the Balkans.

The West African (from Mali) guitarist Ali Farka Toure has incorporated influences from Western blues, making his guitar improvisations fresh and modern. When he plays, the listener hears the roots of the music that led to the blues of a John Lee Hooker. Conversely, African American Taj Mahal, a master of acoustic blues, has expanded the perspectives of black music in his encounters with musicians from Africa, including Mali's Toumani Diabaté, and from Hawaii.

American Brad Shepik is the string virtuoso of New York's new Balkan jazz scene. He has introduced non-Western string instruments such as the saz, and also the Portuguese tamboura, to the jazz of the downtown avant-garde. In the Tiny Bell Trio, with Dave Douglas, or in the band Pachora, he combines the fluidity of Kenny Burrell and the soulfulness of Grant Green with lines of tradition that reach back beyond Mississippi Delta blues—with elements of Balkan music and music from North Africa and the Middle East. Many of his pieces sound as if they'd been played for centuries in Balkan wedding bands. But Shepik himself says: "I play neither traditional jazz nor traditional Balkan music." When he improvises over the delightfully irregular meters of Balkan folk music and of the East, he's not concerned with reconstructing traditional music. Nor does he wish to elevate the music of other cultures to something supposedly "higher" in a jazz sense. He plays Eastern music from the vantage point of a contemporary jazz sensibility.

Via Brad Shepik, we have arrived at a consideration of the important guitarists of the New York downtown scene: Gary Lucas, David Tronzo, Brandon Ross, Marc Ribot, Oren Bloedow, and Tim Sparks.

In the context of "Radical Jewish Culture," Tim Sparks, Oren Bloedow, and Gary Lucas have brought new perspectives to the jazz guitar. Lucas, a former member of Captain Beefheart's band, is stylistically uncategorizable. He combines Wagner with Jewish and Chinese music, blues, and Sun Ra. He sees himself as a "musical humanist," treating all cultures with the same respect. Brandon Ross has made interesting recordings with Cassandra Wilson and Henry Threadgill. His playing, coming out of James "Blood" Ulmer, is distinguished by a feeling for raw, atmospheric, convoluted textures, from free playing to grooves. David Tronzo is one of the few guitarists capable of playing slide guitar over changes. With his broken phrasing, he has expanded the possibilities of his instrument, like a "slide Monk."

However, the most complete guitarist on the downtown scene is Marc Ribot, who became known through his playing with John Zorn. He has all the sounds and techniques ever played on the electric guitar at his fingertips. And he combines these often diametrically opposed approaches in such a way that they make sense and are integrated in a compellingly logical manner. Ribot's genre-bridging consciousness of tone colors, and his encyclopedic knowledge of jazz, rock, world music, blues, and classical music are unique. Ribot is one of the few musicians capable of playing standards and traditional pieces using new, expanded techniques without sounding ironic. "Marc Ribot is one of the true revolutionaries of the guitar," says John Zorn. "It's not that he can do just about everything that's possible (and many things that are considered impossible)—he's completely *rethought* the guitar—its role, what it does, what it sounds like."

With his band Los Cubanos Postizos, in the nineties Ribot celebrated the music of Cuban *tres* player Arsenio Rodriguez—and created, with exiled Cuban musicians and players from New York, a "prophetic" Cuban jazz that provided a creative counterpart to the many *son* and *rumba* imitations that were in vogue at the time.

The guitar has come a long way—from the African banjo to the instrument of John McLaughlin and Marc Ribot, from folk blues to the guitar synthesizer. Like the flute, the guitar is an archetypal instrument. The Greek god Pan, the Indian god Shiva, and Aztec gods have blown on flutes; angels and Apsaras (the female heavenly beings of Hindu mythology) have played guitars. Psychologists have noted both the phallic symbolism of the flute and the guitar's resemblance to the female body. As the lover approaches the beloved's body, so does the guitarist court the body of the guitar, caressing it until it is no longer merely receptive, but responds in kind. The guitarist and the instrument symbolize a pair of lovers, and thus symbolize love itself.

The Bass

In 1911 Bill Johnson organized the Original Creole Jazz Band, the first real jazz band to go on tour from New Orleans. He played bowed bass. In the course of a job in Shreveport, Louisiana, he broke his bow. For half the night, he had to pluck the strings of his bass. Ostensibly, the effect was so novel and interesting that the jazz bass has been played pizzicato (i.e., plucked) ever since.

This tale, told by jazz veterans from New Orleans, is probably an invention, but it has the advantage of reflecting much of the spirit of those years. Thus, it is "true" on a higher level. On the everyday level, the string bass had much competition from the tuba in old New Orleans. The tuba tradition was so strong that even thirty years later, many of the great Swing bassists—such as John Kirby and Red Callender—still played tuba. Various New Orleans jazz bassists played tuba in open-air marching band concerts, while preferring the string bass in dance halls.

The bass provides the harmonic foundation for the jazz ensemble. It is the backbone of a jazz group. At the same time, the bass has a rhythmic task. Since bop, the four even beats to the measure played by the bass (called "walking bass") are often the only factor keeping the basic rhythm firm. Since the plucked string bass can fulfill this rhythmic function more precisely, fluidly, and with longer note durations than the blown tuba, bass replaced the tuba at an early date. Thirty-five years later, the electric bass established itself next to the "acoustic" contrabass. The evolution thus moved from tuba via stand-up bass to electric bass guitar. In the course of this development, the rhythmic impulse became stronger, more prominent, and more precise. At the same time, on the other hand, the sound became less personal and direct due to electrification. Many of the great bassists have pointed out that the acoustic bass is such a sensitive, highly developed instrument that it will never be replaced by modern electronics. In the meantime it has become apparent that the stand-up bass has an ideal median position between the two extremes of the tuba on the one hand and the electric bass guitar on the other, because it fulfills the needs of sound and rhythm optimally.

All bassists of traditional jazz refer back to Pops Foster. Foster worked with Freddie Keppard, King Oliver, Kid Ory, Louis Armstrong, Sidney Bechet, and all the other New Orleans greats. He can easily be identified by his "slapping" technique (today also called slap technique). This way of letting the strings snap back against the fingerboard of the bass—rejected by the bassists of the fifties as a sign of extreme technical inability, but used again by the free-jazz bassists to increase sound and intensity—gave Foster's playing much of its rhythmic impact. In slap bass playing, an old African aesthetic tradition also lives on: the idea that noises, used as colorations of the notes, are not a disturbing element, but rather are "the salt in the soup"; the idea that noise elements give soul to the melodies and rhythms. During the thirties, Foster was chosen several times as the "all-time bassist" of jazz. In 1942 (the year when Jimmy Blanton, the man who had "emancipated" the bass, died) he went to work for the New York subway system but resumed his playing career when the traditionalist revival began. He died in 1969.

In New Orleans jazz, it was still standard for the bassist to alternate between plucking, bowing, and slapping the instrument within a single piece. The function of the bassist was to support the band rhythmically. Solos were few, the harmonic conception was simple, and the lines, with their tendency toward staccato (i.e., short) durations, were reminiscent of tuba parts. Nonetheless, they swung with the greatest vitality. Pops Foster said, "Just play one go-to-hell note, as long as it swings."

The bassist who developed the change from bowed to pizzicato to the fullest extent was Wellman Braud, who was deeply rooted in the New Orleans tradition. From 1926 to 1935 he was a member of the Duke Ellington Orchestra, where his driving but steady two-beat rhythm ensured an irresistable groove. His big, spacious sound radiated rhythmic energy. The short break that he played in 1927 with Ellington's band in the piece "Washington Wobble" is perhaps the first recorded pizzicato bass solo. Steve Brown was the slap virtuoso of white Chicago jazz; his percussive solos were featured in the orchestras of Jean Goldkette and Paul Whiteman.

John Kirby (d. 1952), Milt Hinton (d. 2000), and Walter Page (d. 1957) are the great bassists of the Swing era. Kirby, who emerged from the Fletcher Henderson band in the early thirties, was leader of a small group in the late thirties that cannot be omitted from the history of the jazz combo. Walter Page was a member of the classic Basie rhythm section, which was shaped by the sound of Freddie Green, already mentioned in the guitar section. Walter Page is the key figure in the decisive evolution of jazz bass playing—the transition from the two-beat feeling of New Orleans jazz to the softer, more flexible quarter-note playing of the Swing era. In the Basie orchestra of the thirties and forties, he established the walking bass as a standard element of jazz. Jo Jones, this rhythm section's drummer, says that it was Page who really taught him to play in Kansas City: "an even 4/4."

Milt Hinton combined perfect time with humor and a percussive sound. He was one of the most in-demand session musicians of the Swing era; due to the inexorability and the balacing essence of his bass lines, he was also known as The Judge. Milt Hinton developed the slap technique to an unsurpassable level of mastery, including virtuosic triplet slaps. Lonnie Plaxico: "Most of the young electric guys who are slapping don't realize where that technique comes from. Milt was doing it decades ago."

Further Swing-era bassists who should be mentioned are Slam Stewart and Bob Haggart. Stewart is best known for the way he sings in octaves with his arco playing: the humming effect of a bee, which can be very amusing if not heard too often. Later, Major Holley also played in a similar manner, but Holley sings in unison with his bowing. In 1941, Bob Haggart scored a big hit with "Big Noise from Winnetka." In this piece, drummer Ray Baudoc plays rhythms on the G string of Haggart's bass with his sticks, while Haggart simultaneously fingers different notes.

Generally speaking, the history of the bass can be approached from the same point of view as that of the guitar. As modern guitar history begins with Charlie Christian, so the story of modern bass starts with

Jimmy Blanton. Both Christian and Blanton stepped onto the main jazz stage in 1939. Both died of tuberculosis in 1942. In two short years, both revolutionized the playing of their respective instruments, made "horns" of them. This function was established as clearly in the duo recordings made by Blanton in 1939–40 with Duke Ellington at the piano as it was by Charlie Christian with Benny Goodman during the same period. The Ellington band of the early forties is considered the best band of Ellington's career primarily because Jimmy Blanton was on bass. He gave the Ellington Band an especially high degree of rhythmic-harmonic compactness. Blanton was twenty-three when he died. He made the bass a solo instrument.

Blanton was the first bassist to improvise long, continuous melodic jazz lines distinguished by their clarity from the thick, "grumpy" sounds of traditional jazz. "His notes sang, rather than thumped," says bassist Reggie Workman. And Blanton was one of the first players to integrate ornaments into walking bass lines.

From Blanton stretches the impressive line of modern jazz bassists. Oscar Pettiford is the second. Soon after the death of Blanton he became Ellington's bassist. And as Duke had recorded duets with Blanton's bass, he now made quartet recordings with Pettiford on cello. Harry Babasin was the first jazz cellist, but Pettiford was the man who gave the cello its place in jazz. The road from the deeper sounds of the bass to the higher range of the cello seemed a natural consequence of the evolution of the bass from harmonic to melodic instrument. Since then, there have been other bassists, too, who have chosen the cello as secondary instrument, as did the late Doug Watkins, and later Ron Carter, Peter Warren, and Dave Holland, until finally, in today's jazz, the cello has become an autonomous solo instrument. Musicians like Abdul Wadud, Vincent Courtois, Hank Roberts, Tristan Honsinger, Kent Carter, and Frenchman Jean-Charles Capon play it. (For more details, see the section "Miscellaneous Instruments.")

A good jazz bassist should have team spirit, melodic mobility, and a refined feeling for harmony and rhythm—but above all he has to have a grooving propulsion, the magical ability to give a tempo that forward momentum (without speeding up the beat) that makes a band "feel good."

Pettiford, Ray Brown, and Charles Mingus are the great post-Blanton bassists. Pettiford, who died in Copenhagen in 1960, was the definitive bebop bassist, the first to apply the complex musical language of modern jazz to the bass. He played on Fifty-Second Street in the midforties with Dizzy Gillespie, really disseminating the new "Blanton message." In the fifties he was the busiest bass player on the New York scene. Several times during his career Pettiford organized big bands for recording purposes. His mobility on the bass was consistently amazing. He knew how to create tones on the bass that sounded as if he were "talking" on a horn. Pettiford expanded the modern foundation that Jimmy Blanton had created by inventing lines that functioned as perfect countermelodies to those of the soloists. As an accompanist he created uniform, accurate walking lines of sheer power, with a joyful feeling, and with inimitable melodic note selection. As a soloist, he played fully realized melodies, and not, like his idol Blanton, lines made up of elements of scales and triads. In the two years before his death, when he lived in Europe (first in Baden-Baden, then in Copenhagen), he had a strong and lasting influence on many European musicians.

Ray Brown (1926–2002) is considered the most dependable and swinging of bass players in classical modern jazz. He was featured in a bass concerto, "One Bass Hit," recorded by Dizzy Gillespie and his big band in the late forties. Brown was the preferred bassist for Norman Granz's record productions. Pianist Oscar Peterson, in whose trio Brown played for fifteen years, said: "He can lift a whole band and make them play better than they have ever played before. And he can do it tune after tune, night after night."

Brown's style is a further development of the Jimmy Blanton approach. "I took my bass from school home with me every day and practiced with Blanton records. The length of his notes was what spoke to me."

Ray Brown was one of the great rhythm section accompanists in modern jazz. With his gorgeous, woody sound and his unshakeably steady way of "pushing" the beat—placing notes precisely so that they land in the right spot to create rhythmic drive—he gave the jazz bass a rare dynamic radiance that has been imitated by thousands of players, but rarely achieved. "The Ray Brown sound is synonymous with modern jazz walking bass, and he ranks among the elite of the tradition," writes John Goldsby (to whose book *The Jazz Bass Book—Technique and Tradition* we are indebted as an important source).

Brown's solid solos are rich in arpeggios and triplets. Although he did not become a bandleader until relatively late in his career—1984— in his trio and in encounters with countless young musicians he helped put many of the "young lions" on a swinging track with his powerful beat.

Charles Mingus, who died in 1979, is of overriding significance, not only as a bass player, but also as a band leader. Mingus, who called jazz "black classical music," had an especially keen awareness of the black musical tradition, long before that became the norm, and he really lived this tradition. In the early forties, he briefly played traditional jazz with Kid Ory. Then he joined Lionel Hampton, whose best band—that of 1947—gained much from Mingus's arrangements and personality. Through his work with the Red Norvo Trio in 1950–1951, he won renown as a soloist. Subsequently, he increasingly turned his attention to breaking new paths for jazz, never fearing powerful and exciting harmonic clashes. Mingus never gave in to the pressure to play only a single style. His compositions are like stylistic rollercoasters in which the bass absorbs, in unsuspected rhythmic and metric changes, everything he could improvise on: blues, Blanton, flamenco, European concert music, gospel, Charlie Parker, and anything else that provided an opportunity for spontaneous dialogue between the tradition and the avant-garde (or a mixture of the two). There was probably more collective improvisation in the Mingus groups of the fifties and early sixties than in any other significant jazz combo of that time. As a bassist, Mingus led and held together the many different lines and tendencies that took shape within his groups with the certitude of a sleepwalker. He was a wonderfully recalcitrant bassist—even when "merely" accompanying, he was a genius of querulous challenge and furious musical interruption. His playing was temperamental, aggressive, and had incredible rhythmic propulsion. More than any other musician, he paved the way for the free, collective improvisations and the elastic, open formal structures of the new jazz. In Mingus's hands, the bass was a bubbling cauldron of constantly changing feelings, from anger, protest, and wrath to tenderness and poetic lyricism. When someone asked him for advice, he'd say: "Do as much as you can, man." The duets of Mingus on bass and the great avant-gardist Eric Dolphy on bass clarinet offer some of the strongest emotional experiences in all of jazz.

The triumvirate Pettiford-Brown-Mingus seems even more brilliant when seen in the light of a host of other outstanding jazz bassists of that generation, among them George Duvivier, Percy Heath, Tommy Potter, Curtis Counce, Leroy Vinnegar, Red Mitchell, Paul Chambers, Wilbur Ware. . . .

Duvivier was a "musicians' musician," highly regarded by musicians for his assurance and dependability but less known to the general public. Percy Heath became a much admired musician through his unerring time feel and sovereignly supportive playing in the Modern Jazz Quartet (of which he was a member for four decades). Leroy Vinnegar turned the California-based rhythm sections built around Shelly Manne upside down, insofar as Manne found many melodic potentials in the drums, while Leroy's bass delivered the rhythmic foundation that made the swing felt. He, and before him Curtis Counce, who died in 1963, and later Monty Budwig, Carson Smith, and Joe Mondragon, were among the most frequently recorded bassists on the West Coast. Red Mitchell's accompanying lines were full of swing and consistent inventiveness. He was a mainstay of the West Coast jazz scene in the fifties and early sixties. Mitchell tuned his bass in fifths, giving him a larger range. With his inimitable two-finger pizzicato technique (which he bequeathed to Scott LaFaro), he developed a lyrical, interactive style with a brilliant feeling for form, space, and tension. For Mitchell, jazz was a "search for identity." When asked how one goes about that, he replied: "Say something.

That's the most important thing. *How* you say it is important, but I don't think it's quite as important as *what* you say."

Paul Chambers, who died in 1969, had the expressiveness and vitality of the Detroit hard-bop generation. His time feeling was an important part of the forward-driving energy of two of the essential bands of modern jazz: the Miles Davis Quintet and the John Coltrane Quartet. He was a team player, full of subtlety and finesse. His solos, filled with eighth notes, sang and swung with an infectious, danceable beat. Independently of the sound ideals of classical music, Chambers developed a virtuosic approach to bowing the bass, spicing his blues-inflected solos with a rasping, grainy arco sound and with many slurs—sliding between notes with glissandi—that give his playing a vocal quality. Above all, though, Paul Chambers had what jazz musicians call "big ears": his contrapuntal lines react spontaneously to the melodies played by the soloists. He and drummer Philly Joe Jones formed one of the hottest rhythm sections in hard bop. Freddie Hubbard: "Paul thought like a horn player." Because his rounded, supple lines maintain an ideal balance between a supportive function and a melodically "emancipated" way of playing, they radiate classicality to a particular degree. It is fitting that the bassists within modern classicism have time and again referred to Chambers.

Wilbur Ware, who died in 1979, was a unique soloist and the chosen bassist of Thelonious Monk—probably the most empathetic Monk ever had. He had a powerful, percussive sound whose clarity was unsurpassed. While other bassists of modern jazz took up the harmonic and melodic aspects of Jimmy Blanton's legacy, Ware paid particular attention to the development of Blanton's rhythmic approach. He left space between the notes and played notes of different lengths in his walking lines, creating great variability in the rhythmic flow.

Ware shaped not just the notes but also the spaces between the notes, making his playing very convincing rhythmically. He said that a bassist has to know when to "get on off" the beat—when to release the string in order to achieve a particular percussive sound and rhythmic force. Each in their own way, all the great jazz bassists are masters of this release technique. They know that the swing feeling of the jazz bass comes from the space between the notes, and every jazz bass player has a personal way of playing that space.

With Chambers and Ware, we have arrived within the circle of hard-bop bassists: Jimmy Woode (who emerged from the Duke Ellington band, and became one of the most indispensable "Americans in Europe"), Wilbur Little, Jymie Merritt, Sam Jones, the late Doug Watkins, Reggie Workman, and others belong to this group. Some of them have been pathbreakers for the development that was carried out by Charlie Haden and Scott LaFaro: the second phase of the emancipation of the bass, after the first one associated with Jimmy Blanton and Oscar Pettiford.

Scott LaFaro, tragically killed in a 1961 auto crash at twenty-five, was a musician on the order of Eric Dolphy, creating new possibilities not from disdain for the harmonic tradition but from superior mastery of it. LaFaro was the "pioneer of facility on the bass" (George Duvivier). The "democratic" playing of the Bill Evans Trio was largely based on LaFaro's agile, complex, contrapuntal lines. It was as if he had decided not simply to walk, but to become an equal voice. Hearing LaFaro improvise with the Bill Evans Trio makes clear what the bass has become through its "second emancipation": a kind of superdimensional, low-register guitar whose sound has so many diverse possibilities as would have been thought impossible for the bass only a short time before, but that still fulfills the traditional functions of the bass. LaFaro fundamentally changed the way bassists interact in groups when they improvise. Said bassist Dave Holland, "The bass has become something like the fourth melody voice in the quartet. Wasn't Scott LaFaro the major reason for that?" When jazz critic Stanley Crouch dared, in the nineties, to write in the magazine *Jazz Times* that LaFaro's approach was "antiswing" and "too European," readers protested furiously. David Finck: "Any bassist who denies the contributions of LaFaro probably cannot play the instrument in tune above fourth position."

Jimmy Garrison (who died in 1976) was the bassist in the classic John Coltrane Quartet at the beginning of the sixties. He developed Scott LaFaro's "guitar sound" into a "flamenco guitar sound"—for example, in the long solo that he plays at the beginning of the 1966 recording of Trane's hit, "My Favorite Things." Perhaps even more amazing technically was the bass work of David Izenzon (who died in 1979) in the Ornette Coleman Trio during the midsixties. He presented his "guitar-like" bass sounds with the drive of a percussionist.

Although the bass is one of the quieter instruments, it has an immense influence in jazz groups. Beyond its supporting function, it plays a uniting role. The bass mediates between different instruments and roles, between elements of harmony and of rhythm, connecting the soloists to the rhythm section. Of the jazz instruments, the bass is the great mediator and uniter. It supports and it builds. And when it is played well, it inspires the band, introducing new ideas and group interactions. In the ensembles of jazz, it has thus played a significant part in bringing together different personalities from different styles and instruments. As Paul F. Berliner says, "Bassists are always concerned with things like continuity and development."

Since the turn of the fifties, Charlie Haden has frequently worked with Ornette Coleman, and he was—in the beginning perhaps even more so than Don Cherry—an essential partner. His Liberation Music Orchestra, for which Carla Bley writes arrangements, expands not only musical but also political consciousness: music conceived as the guiding torch of freedom, using themes and recordings from East Germany, Cuba, the Spanish Civil War, and the Latin American liberation movements.

Haden revolutionized the harmonic concept of bass playing in jazz. He was the first bassist who consistently avoided playing *changes* or following preestablished harmonic schemes, but instead created a solid harmonic foundation out of the passage of independent melodies. In technical terms Haden isn't a virtuoso. His virtuosity lies on a higher level—in an incredible ability to make the double bass "sound out." Haden cultivates his instrument's gravity as no one else in jazz: with an unfathomably dark resonance and an earthiness of timbre, endowing even apparently "simple" lines with an affecting quality. He is a master of simplicity, which is among the most difficult things to achieve.

These, then, are the "headwaters" from which the bass mainstream flows through the sixties, seventies, and eighties—with musicians like Richard Davis, Rufus Reid, Ron Carter, Gary Peacock, Steve Swallow, Barre Phillips, Eddie Gomez, Marc Johnson, Cecil McBee, Buster Williams, Cameron Brown, Mike Richmond, Avery Sharpe, Neil Swainson, Ed Schuller, David Friesen, Glen Moore, Rob Wasserman, Hungarian-born Aladár Pege, Henri Texier, Jean-François Jenny-Clark and Didier Levallet from France, Germans Günter Lenz and Dieter Ilg, Swedish Palle Danielsson, Denmark's Niels-Henning Ørsted Pedersen and Mads Vinding, and George Mraz and Miroslav Vitous from Czechoslovakia.

Because of this wealth of players, we can give special mention to only a few. Richard Davis is perhaps the most versatile of all bassists. He is one of those universalists who have mastered with equal perfection everything from symphonic music to all kinds of jazz, all the way from bop to free playing.

Ron Carter's sound is so personal that he is recognizable after just a few notes, like the handwriting of a good friend on a postcard. Carter was the bassist in the second Miles Davis Quintet. With drummer Tony Williams and pianist Herbie Hancock, in this band he created a new way of playing time, improvising harmonically open bass lines that gave the other musicians room to abstract away from the original chords. Todd Coolman: "No matter what Tony Williams was experimenting with—polyrhythms, playing across the bar lines, metric modulations—he could always count on Ron Carter to point the way to 'one.'" Ron Carter is one of the most-recorded bassists in jazz. He is a master of right- and left-handed rhythmic ornamentation, integrating hammer-ons (striking the strings against the fingerboard with the fingers of the fingering hand), pull-offs (plucking the strings with the fingering hand while lifting the fingers off the fingerboard), and dead notes (muted notes) into his swinging lines.

Coming from the acoustic bass, Carter has mastered a wide range of instruments: first the cello, and since 1976 a "piccolo bass"—an instrument of baroque music—in cellolike tuning. Carter plays the piccolo bass, which is to the contrabass approximately what the violin is to the viola, with the brilliance and lightness of a pizzicato concert violin and, at the same time, with the drive of a jazz player like Oscar Pettiford.

Ron Carter in a *Down Beat* interview:

> The term "liberation of the bass" has such negative overtones to it—it means that someone has been in bondage up to this point. . . . I've never felt inhibited in what I was trying to play. I didn't necessarily feel that I was a bass in a rhythm section that played behind or accompanied a soloist, that my function was just a function. . . . Since the music the electronic bass is predominantly used in is so different from the acoustic bass, it's like comparing apples and oranges. I don't see the electric bass as having any major input in regard to the development of the upright bass at any time.

Like all jazz bassists before him, Scott LaFaro played on gut strings, without amplification. In the sixties, bassists such as Ron Carter began increasingly to use steel strings with lower tension, and the use of electric pickups and amplifiers also became widespread—all of which altered the instrument's sound drastically. Notes became longer and more connected to each other; soloistic lines became more mobile. A bassist using a pickup has a large variety of sounds at his disposal; as John Goldsby has remarked, this is "both a blessing and a curse."

Gary Peacock, Steve Swallow, and Europe-based Barre Phillips are particularly sensitive and immensely agile bassists who have brought melodic freedom to the LaFaro approach. Peacock has played both free jazz with Albert Ayler and melodic standards in the Keith Jarrett Trio, of which he has been the bassist since 1983. He is one of the most intuitive, intense listeners among bassists, with an unconditional desire to give everything in the moment, and a readiness, rare even in jazz, to enter into unknown musical territory with deep confidence.

Eddie Gomez is the most resplendent player extending the virtuoso Scott LaFaro line. He is the bassist who had the longest tenure—eleven years—in the Bill Evans Trio. Charles Mingus appointed Gomez, a Puerto Rican, as stand-in when the bandleader's state of health prevented him from playing in recordings. Gomez phrases masterful melodic lines on the bass as if he were playing an oversized cello. His emancipated playing with its brilliant singing sound reaches up to the highest registers. At the same time, he "percussionizes" bass playing: his pizzicato lines seem to be "drummed." Gomez is a master of plucking the G string by way of an abrupt, sideways flicking of the finger, creating a tearing, splitting sound—similar to the slap technique but more supple because the string doesn't smack against the fingerboard.

Particularly worthy of notice among bassists from the younger generation influenced by Gomez are John Patitucci (who made a name for himself with Chick Corea), Marc Johnson, and Dieter Ilg from Germany. Patitucci, who has also played with Wayne Shorter, has a wonderful classical sensibility and an agility derived from fusion. He is a brilliant technician with a perfectionist streak. He has developed a personal sound on the bass, with particular, recognizable "signature" lines of his own. He integrates African and Brazilian elements into his playing.

Marc Johnson, who emerged from the Bill Evans Trio of the late seventies, is the outstanding legato player among contemporary bassists—a master of the art of connecting notes smoothly, creating the impression that the right hand isn't plucking so much as the left hand is simply fingering notes. Johnson also has a highly developed solo conception, a beautiful linear, melodic style heard in the context of his band Right Brain Patrol. He is a master of anticipation, of inducing and introducing harmonic changes, transcending the chords with an airy rhythmic feeling. In his group Bass Desires, he made a decisive contribution toward his instrument, gaining unexpected acclaim in eighties jazz-rock, with hip reggae and rock grooves woven into his jazz playing.

Among the other bassists who have brought the warmth and relaxation of upright bass playing into a jazz-rock-oriented context, giving the style an unanticipated boost, are Charnett Moffett, Lonnie Plaxico, Steve Rodby, and Norway's Ingebrigt Flaten.

Earlier, in the seventies, Stanley Clarke had already played acoustic bass very convincingly in the jazz-rock context of Chick Corea's electric band Return to Forever—a contribution that is often overlooked due to his reputation as an electric bassist.

Like Marc Johnson, Dieter Ilg is a melodist at heart and a fundamentally legato player, an expert at smoothly connecting notes with a warm, dark sound. In the eighties, he made a name for himself as a swinging accompanist in new mainstream jazz, playing with Albert Mangelsdorff and with the West German Radio (WDR) big band. From there, he developed into a player distinguished by his great flexibility in the polyglot field of multistylistic jazz. Ilg has incorporated elements of German, British, and French folk songs into his music. The historical appropriation of German folk songs by the Nazis, and their later nostalgic trivialization, has not prevented him from finding a way of using them that is sensitive and free of kitsch. Ilg says, "In the beginning there was the folk song. Its abuse came later."

Charnett Moffett, son of drummer Charles Moffett, played in Wynton Marsalis's band at the age of sixteen. Since then he is viewed as one of the most flexible bassists on the contemporary scene—from a traditional mainstream player à la Ray Brown by way of extension of the Paul Chambers tradition within neoclassicism to the fusion sounds of electric bassist Stanley Clarke.

Bassists are team players. Perhaps more than players of any other instrument, they feel responsible for the balance and stability of a jazz group. Cecil McBee, Ray Drummond, and Buster Williams are masters in this regard: they cultivate and update the Coltrane tradition on the bass in a way similar to McCoy Tyner on the piano. David Friesen and Glen Moore have come to the fore in the sphere of world music with a number of chamber-music-like recordings: Friesen, for instance, in a duo with flutist Paul Horn, with an absolutely original sound produced by a self-constructed "Oregon bass," and Moore in the group Oregon. Aladár Pege, bass teacher at the Hungarian National Conservatoire in Budapest, has been extolled as a "simply incredible bass miracle in terms of playing technique." His performance at the Jazz Yatra at Bombay in 1980 so moved Charles Mingus's widow that she gave him one of her husband's basses as a present. Since then Pege has several times taken the place of the great Mingus in the Mingus Destiny group. Miroslav Vitous was a founding member of the first Weather Report in 1971. He's a specialist in unconventional bowing, even up to the highest, elegiacally "singing" register. Henri Texier has been called the "knotty oak" of French jazz—since the sixties his playing has been an unshakable center of gravity for contemporary currents in French jazz. Texier always makes the drummer sound good. In the nineties, he became one of the outstanding figures of the French "imaginary folklore" movement. For example, in the trio Carnet de Routes with clarinetist Louis Sclavis and drummer Aldo Romano, or in his own Azur Quintet, he has created a melodically refined European jazz illuminated by elements from the world's great musical cultures—Arab, West African—but also by the folk music of his Celtic homeland. Avery Sharpe has been McCoy Tyner's favorite bassist since 1981, matching the pianist's percussive intensity. He ironically calls himself a "frustrated drummer."

The most-recorded bassist in Europe was the Dane Niels-Henning Ørsted Pedersen (who died in 2005). During the last four decades, whenever an American soloist on tour in Europe needed a bassist, Niels-Henning was almost always the musician to get the call. In this way, he came to play with Bud Powell, Quincy Jones, Roland Kirk, Sonny Rollins, Lee Konitz, John Lewis, Dexter Gordon, Ben Webster, Oscar Peterson, and dozens of other famous musicians. Pedersen was one of the technical giants of modern jazz bass playing. Most modern jazz bassists play using three fingers of the right hand. Pedersen used all four fingers, with various plucking and attack techniques. Because Europe has a great tradition of classical music, many European jazz bassists have taken advantage of their classical education—which helps to explain why European bassists have increasingly become part of the jazz scene since the seventies.

Sweden's Palle Danielsson is an extremely round melodic player who since the seventies has been part of one of Europe's best and longest-lived rhythm sections, with drummer Jon Christensen. Both these musicians have played in the bands of Jan Garbarek and in Keith Jarrett's European quartet, providing a solid rhythmic foundation for wonderfully open, spacious improvisations.

Palle Danielsson has pointed the way toward a distinctively Scandinavian approach to jazz bass playing, distinguished by a beautiful tone. Other bass players in this Nordic school include Norway's Arild Andersen and Eivind Opsvik, Denmark's Lars Danielsson and Chris Minh Doky, and Finland's Pekka Sarmanto. Although Arild Andersen adapted regional folk music in a free-jazz context as early as 1972 (on the album *Triptykon*, under Jan Garbarek's leadership), it wasn't until the early nineties that he began to engage intensively with Scandinavian folk music. In his band Masqualero, he cultivates a highly developed interactive approach to playing, with full, rich melodic arcs.

Denmark's Lars Danielsson is also an excellent cellist, and is the great "singer" of Scandinavian jazz bassists: an advocate of melody who retains his sense of sonic purity, precise intonation, and lyricism even when playing extremely energetic, vital rhythms. Anders Jormin has played in the band of saxophonist Charles Lloyd. His bass playing is distinguished by restfulness and meditative security. At times, his deep, round sound and his dry, percussive approach are reminiscent of a lower-tuned sarod (the Indian stringed instrument).

Like Andersen, Jormin, and Danielsson, many other European bassists have incorporated folk-music elements into sensitive, rhythmically vital playing. These include Poland's Vitold Rek, who uses the melancholy melodies and dance rhythms of Slavic folk music, Portugal's Carlos Bica, who uses the sadly beautiful melodies of fado (the "Portuguese blues"), Germany's Dieter Ilg, with his use of Scottish, Irish, and German folk songs from the seventeenth to the nineteenth centuries, Italy's Paolo Damiani with his use of Sicilian songs, and Spain's Javier Colina, who uses the melodies and rhythms of flamenco. One of the most brilliant and imaginative bassists of the "imaginary folklore" movement has been France's Renaud Garcia-Fons, also known as the "Paganini of the bass." He is able to make his warm, singing bass sound like an Arab oud or fiddle, a flamenco guitar, or an Indian sarangi. He has also taken arco playing (playing with the bow), often somewhat neglected in jazz, to a new high point of virtuosity. Using an enormous variety of bowing techniques, he plays things on the bass that were previously considered simply impossible. Garcia-Fons studied with François Rabbath, the great Syrian classical bass virtuoso. Through Rabbath, he discovered the great Arab and Eastern music tradition:

I had a dream about a bass—half Gypsy, half Mauritanian—that traveled from India to Andalucia, passing by the Mediterranean from north or south. Yet the bass is neither a traditional nor an oriental instrument. But its range of sonorities and the way it is played upon—both pizzicato and *con arco*—seem to make it comfortable in the neighborhood of certain instruments at home in the oriental world.

Garcia-Fons's recordings, such as *Oriental Bass* (1997) and *Navigatore* (2001), are lushly orchestrated, glittering recordings with a tendency toward perfectionism—a uniquely raucous celebration of Mediterranean music in which his bass reflects everything that has accumulated in the Levantine cultural universe over the centuries: flamenco, Sufi music, Ottoman art music, medieval lute music, fandango and fado, Sephardic melodies, Italian tarantellas. These records are soulful musical journeys through Mediterranean culture, an apotheosis of cultural transitions and of the dialogue between East and West.

It is striking that French jazz has more talented bassists than other European jazz scenes. The French tradition of stringed instruments, with its preference for warm, round, glowing tone colors, has had an extraordinarily advantageous effect on the formation of a strong lineage of modern French jazz bassists, beginning with Jean François Jenny-Clarke and Henri Texier, continuing with Michel Benita, Remi Vignolo, Patrice Caratini, Jean-Paul Celea, and Bruno Chevillon, up to today's players like Sebastian Boisseau, François Moutin, and Renaud Garcia-Fons. Perhaps, then, it is no accident that the most interesting and densest concentration of bass sounds so far achieved came from France: the Orchestre de Contrebasses, founded in 1981 by Christian Gentet. This group includes six bassists, who use their instruments to perform all the functions ordinarily performed by other instruments in their masterful, imaginative journeys back and forth across many different styles and genres of music.

Jean François Jenny-Clarke (who died in 1998) and Jean-Jacques Avenel are two European bassists who have received far too little recognition. Jenny-Clarke found surprising turns of phrase and played unpredictable solos in the freely tonal jazz of the Joachim Kühn Trio. Avenel has incorporated African melodic and rhythmic elements into his European jazz bass playing, and is also a master of overtone playing—and, incidentally, is one of the few Europeans to have mastered the kora, a West African harp.

François Moutin became known through his playing in the group of drummer Daniel Humair. His pizzicato playing in the high register of the bass is unique among European players.

Claude Tchamitchian, a Frenchman of Armenian descent, plays with amazing lightness despite all his rhythmic force. Germany's Sebastian Gramss is the leader of the band Underkarl, which became known in the late nineties with oblique, extremely compressed cover versions of jazz, pop, and rock classics.

Niels-Henning Ørsted Pedersen summarized the situation of the bass on today's scene in the following way:

> The bass has become more and more independent as an instrument. In the older jazz there was a very strong connection between instrument and solo, and it's my opinion that a solo should not be determined by the instrument. What I like today is that you've left the point behind where you have technical difficulties; there's no reason to be impressed by anything, just go for the music.

In a countermovement to the "emancipated" playing of the sixties and seventies, in the eighties and nineties many bassists returned to fundamentals. Instead of going for agile, solo-type lines as in the "cello school of bass playing" (Branford Marsalis), they concentrated on their instrument's powerful deep dimension. In their striving for melodic flexibility, many bassists may have made their instrument more quickly playable—by working with pick-ups (contact microphones) that brighten the sound or by lowering the height of the strings from the fingerboard—but they often achieved a thinner, less full tone.

That's where the eighties/nineties "fundamentalists" of bass playing set to work. They consciously reflect the deep, powerful sound quality of the bass, its gravity and supportive weight and its natural sound, while their interest in virtuosic solo flexibility somewhat recedes. Strikingly, most such players come from the sphere of neotraditional jazz (or at least closely related to it, alongside other ways of playing). They include Bob Hurst, Reginald Veal, Lonnie Plaxico, Charles Fambrough, Ira Coleman, and Santi DeBriano. All these bassists are strongly influenced by Paul Chambers. The classical qualities of the jazz bass—its accompanying and support function—and its deep, powerful natural sound are emphasized by these players without entirely giving up the soloistic possibilities achieved by earlier players. Some bass players in this direction, including John Clayton, Bob Hurst, and Reginald Veal, have returned to unamplified playing (not using electric pickups) in order to achieve a more natural bop sound with as much "wood" in the tone as possible.

Other players in this direction include Christian McBride, Ugonna Okegwo, Rodney Whitaker, Michael Hawkins, Eric Revis, Reuben Rogers, Essiet Essiet, Belden Bullock, James Genus, Peter Washington, Ben Wolfe, Doug Weiss, Dwayne Burno, Darek Oleszkiewicz, John Goldsby, and John Clayton. All these bassists are "masters of the basics." They are able to create a bass part that has its own melodic and rhythmic value, thus simultaneously playing a foundational role and an interactive one in the group.

Christian McBride is the most powerful, vital bass player of the new swinging mainstream jazz, and is also the most-recorded jazz bassist of the bop renaissance of the nineties. His phrasing is reminiscent of a modern Ray Brown, with clear, chiseled melodic contours and an irresistible, joyful swinging quality. McBride played for fifteen years with Wynton Marsalis, and later played with Art Blakey and with Joe Henderson. As a soloist, he quickly outgrew the "young lions" pigeonhole. He seems to be a postbop bassist in an almost classical mode, and yet his lines also clearly show the influence of seventies pop, soul, and funk, from James Brown to Sly Stone—a tendency that is heard all the more clearly when he plays electric bass (virtuosically, yet not quite as convincingly as his acoustic playing) in jazz-rock contexts.

Lonnie Plaxico is an enormously supple, powerful bassist who has performed with such different drummers as Art Blakey and Jack DeJohnette.

A jazz bass line should produce a mood and force that inspires the other musicians to give their best. This, rather than virtuosic soloing, is the standard by which a bass player's playing is judged. A good illustration of this is provided by a jazz veteran who began his career playing hard bop in the fifties, and who has played electric bass since the midseventies: Bob Cranshaw. Although he is not notable as a soloist, his playing is so reliable and masterful in its note selection and rhythmic power that he has been Sonny Rollins's first-choice bassist for more than forty years. A skilled bass accompanist like Cranshaw is "subordinate" only in a superficial sense. In reality, he is an equal partner in the creation of the music, as important and indispensable as the soloist whose playing he helps to sound good.

Beyond the mainstream, we find—as with the other instruments—players of free music on the one hand, and fusion and jazz-rock players (who mostly use the electric bass) on the other. (Here, too, one must realize that, particularly today, many musicians have become so versatile that they can belong to the most diverse stylistic camps. We will list them in the groupings where they are most often found.) Important free bassists are Buell Neidlinger, Peter Warren, Sirone, Henry Grimes, Alan Silva, Malachi Favors, Fred Hopkins, John Lindberg, Rick Rozie, William Parker, Britons Barry Guy, Paul Rogers, and Brian Smith, Japanese Yoshizawa Motoharu, Katsuo Kuninaka, and Yosuke Inoue, Austrian Adelhard Roidinger, Norwegian Arild Andersen, Dutchmen Arjen Gorter and Maarten Altena, Germans Peter Kowald and Buschi Niebergall, South African Johnny Dyani, and Joëlle Léandre from France. What the bassists of free jazz put into question with their extended techniques and new ways of playing the instrument was not at all, as laypersons often assume, the supporting role of the bass, but rather the hierarchy between the melody instruments and the rhythm section. The free improvising of these bassists shows that the bass *can* play an accompanying role (in the end, this is one of its greatest strengths), but that it no longer *has to* do this as was done in earlier jazz styles: when the musical context requires it, the bass can be a lead voice, or a voice on an equal footing with the others. As Barre Phillips put it: "You don't have to do that same damn old thing. You can do something else."

Musicians like Neidlinger, Sirone, and Silva belong to the first generation of free players. Neidlinger and Sirone worked with Cecil Taylor, Silva with Sun Ra's orchestra. Malachi Favors played bass in the Art Ensemble of Chicago, where his simple, deeply felt playing connected the music to the roots of "Great Black Music." Arild Andersen could be called an especially "romantic" player. Yoshizawa Motoharu's immensely intense bass is deeply rooted in the Japanese tradition, as was Johnny Dyani's (d. 1986) in the tradition of his native South Africa. Maarten Altena and Peter Kowald have particularly persisted in breaking with the principle of ongoing rhythm demanded of conventional bass playing.

Peter Kowald (1944–2002) was the most dynamic and interactive bassist in European free jazz. His free playing was filled with humanity and warmth. The great concentration and virtuosity with which he shaped new sounds was remarkable. He made even the most complicated alternative techniques sound simple and natural, such as playing on and behind the bridge of the bass, using unusual harmonics and double-stops (two notes at once), percussively hitting the strings, fingerboard, and body of the instrument, using his chin to press the strings down, etc. At the end of the sixties, Kowald was still a radical exponent of the *Kaputtspielphase* school of free playing, vehemently breaking with the norms and clichés of tonal playing. This meant, above all, questioning the bass's "slavish" role as an accompanist. Later, Kowald developed into a mature traveler of the world's musical cultures, transcending cultural and regional differences in his constructive improvised dialogues with musicians from Japan, China, and Mongolia. Kowald said: "North Americans, Japanese, Greeks, Russians, South Americans, Indians, Australians can all play together from their own experience immediately—that is, without any prior agreements by way of compositions or anything else. Improvised music is world music."

France's Joëlle Léandre is a virtuoso of a highly developed, dramatic free approach to arco playing. She is more interested in sound for its own sake than in fixed pitches or conventional melodic roles, and uses the bow to shape these sounds "like a sculpture." Her complex arco textures have given the bass a spectrum of new expressive possibilities as wide and imaginative as the pizzicato playing of Peter Kowald, Fred Hopkins, or William Parker. Like Léandre, England's Barry Guy is at home both in free improvisation and in new music. He has worked both with composer Iannis Xenakis and with the Spontaneous Music Ensemble. At the end of the nineties, he began to use a five-stringed bass, using the bow to produce long, virtuosic chains of harmonics and harmonic chords with a flowing character.

William Parker and Dominic Duval are exceptionally powerful bassists of the New York free-jazz scene. They are among the few bassists not overwhelmed by the elemental force of the cluster-based playing of pianist Cecil Taylor (with whom they have both worked). Duval, with his virtuosic arpeggios, tends more toward freely tonal playing. Parker is the definitive drone player of free jazz, a master of greatly varied ostinatos that give his free improvising a dark, trancelike character. In the early twenty-first century, Parker was particularly involved with collaborations with DJs and improvising electronicists.

Following directly from the free bassists are those musicians who, in accordance with the style-transcending tendencies of postmodernism, reflect on the jazz tradition from a free, undogmatic perspective. They are headed by Dave Holland, and then come Fred Hopkins, Mark Helias, Anthony Cox, John Lindberg, Lindsey Horner, Mark Dresser, Jaribu Shihad, and Swiss-born Martin Schütz. As bassist, composer, and bandleader, Dave Holland (from England) has continued the Mingus legacy into the present in a particularly impressive and influential manner. With his exciting reinterpretations and abstractions of traditional jazz elements, he is one of the freest-thinking bassists in jazz. Miles Davis recruited Holland for his electric band in the late sixties. Holland says, "I'm trying to use my instrument to influence, expand, and change the sound of the other instruments." In fact he is a master of exchange and mutual interplay, an approach that he raised to the level of an art highly charged with feeling in his groups of the late eighties and nineties. His compositions seem to be improvisational puzzles, full of complex rhythms and metrical superpositions, and yet Holland improvises over them with a looseness and intensity as if they were the easiest thing in the world. He has an unerring ability to make highly gifted young players enthusiastic about his music, so that his bands have become catalysts of the New York jazz scene. Holland: "If you don't move forward in your development as a musician, you're moving backwards."

Pianist Michael Naura writes:

> When it comes to rhythm, the corona of an ensemble is essentially shaped by the bassist. If the bassist is really good, there's something almost maternally protective about him. Bass monsters like Mingus, Ray Brown, or Dave Holland—mothers of bassism! When you're on stage with giants like that, they give you superhuman powers. I've experienced it myself. You play three times better, I swear.

Fred Hopkins (who died in 1999) was the bassist in Air and the Henry Threadgill Sextet. A master of "sliding" playing, of all post–free-jazz bass players he possesses the fullest sound, resonating powerfully—as a critic once said—"like a giant suspension bridge of dark wood." Mark Helias started with Anthony Braxton, and from that avant-garde stance has worked step by step backward through the legacy of jazz. His lines are so flexible and full of ideas that they unfold particularly well when not overlaid with other harmony instruments. Anthony Cox, who first played with the bands around James Newton and Muhal Richard Abrams, is one of the most inspired and flexible ostinato players among contemporary bassists—an unusually elegant, supple stylist with a strong sense of the African roots of black music. John Lindberg played with Anthony Braxton and is the foundation of the String Trio of New York. Mark Dresser, first presented by Anthony Braxton and Ray Anderson, is one of the busiest collaborators of the New York downtown scene. He has an especially dark, woody, natural sound and has made marvelous recordings with the string trio Arcado and with the Masada String Trio.

Other important bassists of the New York downtown scene are Greg Cohen, Drew Gress, Ben Allison, Michael Formanek, Ed Howard, and Trevor Dunn. Greg Cohen is a rock-solid player who seeks emotional depth and sympathetic deliberateness in his playing. He is one of the bassists, inspired by Charlie Haden, who seek to play nothing superfluous—not an outstanding soloist, but the ideal "anchor" with every note he plays, particularly in John Zorn's Masada. Drew Gress is one of the most sought-after bassists in contemporary jazz due to his rhythmic finesse and his detailed harmonic sense. His solid time, perfect intonation, and deep sound have made him the favored bassist of subtle, rhythmic pianists including Fred Hersch, Marc Copland, and Simon Nabatov. When a great jazz bassist like Gress "accompanies," this does not mean self-effacement or subordination, but rather an equal partnership, like accompanying a traveler along part of the way. A gifted bassist can, in fact, use well-directed interventions and supportive commentary to help decide and determine the course of the music. "When you start analyzing great jazz bass lines . . . they're like Bach," says Chuck Israels.

Ben Allison is a bassist and composer of controlled freedom. "The wild, expressionistic days of post–free jazz are over," says Allison, one of the founders of the musicians' initiative known as the Jazz Composers Collective. "Today, the task is to explore the middle area, the space between tradition and modernity." Consequently, Allison's bass lines follow fixed structures but allow room for controlled, effective rule-breaking. In his band Medicine Wheel, composition and improvisation are fused in such an organic, living manner that they are experienced not as opposites but as commonalities. Allison says, "You can only make jazz if you start from something existing. And you can only make jazz if you move toward something new."

It is striking that the contemporary bass scene includes a particularly large number of players who are difficult to categorize stylistically.

Perhaps more than other jazz instrumentalists, bassists are valued for their flexibility and stylistic mobility. Rufus Reid says, "A bassist has to have an open mind. I like to have the right feeling for the music, but still be free within the context—I can't play with Tommy Flanagan the way I play with Jack DeJohnette."

Important contemporary bassists who resist stylistic categorization, and who can't really be assigned to any of the directions named above, include Larry Grenadier, Scott Colley, Reid Anderson, and Chris Wood. Larry Grenadier, who came through the band of vibraphonist Gary Burton, has an unmistakable sound of his own. His playing is extremely convincing, with its exceptionally clear tone and strong sense of rhythmic placement. In the Brad Mehldau trio, he has expanded the melodic possibilities of jazz bass playing. Scott Colley became known workng with Jim Hall, and he shares Hall's sense of melodic subtlety and rhythmic finesse. Everything that Colley plays seems to have deep meaning. His ability to combine foundational playing with abstraction and flexibility has made him one of the most sought-after bassists in contemporary jazz. Reid Anderson and Chris Wood are powerful bassists and strong improvisers whose multi-stylistic playing brings something of the subversive energy of rock to jazz bass playing. Wood works in the trio Medeski, Martin & Wood, and Anderson works in the trio The Bad Plus.

We turn now to the bassists of world jazz, many of whom also work in other areas as well. Again, for reasons of space only a few of these musicians will be considered here. First, looking back, a musician must be acknowledged who in the fifties was one of the first musicians to integrate non-Western musical elements into the jazz vocabulary. Ahmed Abdul-Malik recorded with Thelonious Monk and with Art Blakey. On his own albums, such as *East Meets West* (1959), he applied the *maqam* and *taqsim* improvisations of Arabic music to modern jazz. Malik was born in New York to Sudanese parents. His interest, which at the time did not receive the attention it deserved, was to show that the original contribution of African music to the development of jazz was not limited to influences from West and Central Africa, but also included North African and Arabic elements.

However, in the forties and fifties the most widely propagated contributions to a way of playing jazz that took full advantage of non-Western elements came from the bassists of Latin jazz, reacting to the development of "Cubop." In Cuban music, the bass practically never plays on the "one" (the downbeat of a bar) in its accompaniment patterns. These heavily "offbeat" bass figures, with their strict bond to the Latin clave rhythm, are called *tumbao*. Due to its openness to improvisation, the *tumbao* combines well with jazz playing. The Cuban musician Cachao, known as the King of Mambo, was as pathbreaking in this respect for Latin jazz bass playing as Charlie Parker was for bebop. Cachao is considered one of the founders of *descarga* music, which introduced "jam session" elements, and thus the spirit of jazz, to Cuban music. Cachao had an explosive bowing technique, in the *danzon* style, and was also a pioneer in the percussive use of the body of the bass.

All Latin jazz bassists, traditional and contemporary, follow in the footsteps of Cachao, who died in 2008. The contemporary bass players here include Puerto Rico's Andy Gonzales, John Benitez, and Carlos Henriques, Austria's Hans Glawischnig, and the Cubans Jesus Lopez Cachaito and Lazaro Rivero Alarcòn. The contribution of these musicians has been to combine the Cachao approach with elements of classic jazz walking bass, expanding it in a personal manner. Andy Gonzales is particularly impressive here. For example, in the band Fort Apache, led by his brother Jerry Gonzalez, he has applied the *tumbao* style to deep, warm Latin grooves, bringing it to new heights by uniting Monk, Mingus, and the *montuno* style of Cuban bassists.

Brazil's Nilson Matta has incorporated samba elements into contemporary jazz bass playing. Matta has played with Joe Henderson and with Claudio Roditi, and his lines sometimes suggest, as Brazilian bassists understand, that the essence of samba comes from the *surdo* drum, the low-pitched drum played with felt mallets.

Omer Avital is an Israeli of Moroccan-Yemeni descent, living in New York. He has incorporated Arabic influences, as well as Jewish melodies and rhythms, into his jazz in a particularly convincing manner. Like many bassists of the nineties, Avital's playing shows a consciousness of Charles Mingus's lines, with the same physical energy that demonstrates that the bass is as much the engine of a band as the drummer is.

In Europe, Gary Crosby, an Englishman of Caribbean descent, created an exciting fusion of reggae, ska, and jazz ("skazz," as he calls it) in the nineties with his band Jazz Jamaica. The nephew of Jamaican guitarist Ernest Ranglin, Crosby is one of the central integrating figures of black British jazz, and is an important musical representative and intellectual of the London black community. As loose and joyously grooving as his British reggae jazz may sound, for the bassist the relationship to his Caribbean roots is a question of identity. Crosby says, "Many people don't understand at all that this is a very serious thing for us. We're not just playing reggae music, we're playing our culture."

It took years for electric bass players to solve the problems they had with their sound—the dull, somehow always empty tone of the instrument. Their dilemma was this: on the one hand, the electric bass had more flexibility, its sound (and volume!) fit better into electric groups; on the other hand it lacked expressivity and didn't sound "human," but technical. Monk Montgomery was the first bassist to make serious use of the electric bass in jazz. In the early fifties, he played swinging lines on a Fender bass guitar with great flexibility. But he was unable to solve the problem of the lack of individuality of the instrument's flabby sound.

The first player to initiate a change in the early seventies was a rock bassist: Larry Graham of Sly and the Family Stone. He did something that bass teachers of the academy would strictly forbid: he played, incredibly percussively, with his thumb. In the black rock and rhythm 'n' blues production of Motown Records, this thumb style became something like a trademark: the bass played with such intensity that its strings occasionally hit the wood of the instrument, just like the old New Orleans slap bass. Stanley Clarke combined this thumb style with Scott LaFaro's technique (and was immensely successful in the seventies with his fusion music). LaFaro's technique had already been used on the electric bass by Steve Swallow. His wiry, brittle, and yet warm, full sound and his melodious lines constitute one of the most unmistakable styles in the realm of the electric bass, unfolding with great sensitivity in his performances with, for example, Carla Bley. Swallow's sound has continued to gain in weight over the years. John Patitucci: "It's an electric but sounds acoustic. Swallow is one of the few electric bass players who sounds like a real, bona fide jazz musician."

The problem was finally solved, however, by Jaco Pastorius from Florida, who became famous overnight in 1976 when he played with Weather Report but who died tragically early in 1987. The significance of Pastorius's playing for the electric bass is comparable to Charlie Parker's importance for the (alto) saxophone. No electric bass sound has been more widely admired and copied than Jaco's. "He taught us that the bass can be anything—a piano, a conga drum, a saxophone," says Jeff Andrews. Another electric bassist adds: "Jaco opened the door, and we walked through it."

On his fretless instrument, Pastorius combined the thumb approach and LaFaro's flexibility with an octave technique associated up to that time with guitarist Wes Montgomery but considered out of reach for bassists. He added as well an iridescent flageolet technique and virtuosic chordal playing. Pastorius thereby became the real "bass sensation" of the seventies. Only through him did the electric bass gain complete emancipation. All of a sudden the electric bass possessed what Oscar Pettiford had made the chief criterion for all jazz bass playing: "Humanity, expressivity, emotionality, the ability to tell a story." Said Pastorius, "I play the bass as if I were playing a human voice. I play like I speak. I like singers."

Most electric bassists who play in a funk style use a percussive, edgy phrasing, at the expense of melody. Jaco Pastorius integrated groove-oriented, funky playing with melodic richness, becoming both a great rhythmic player and a still-unexcelled melodist on his instrument.

If there's a high point in the consistently high-quality development of the jazz-rock group Weather Report, then it was in the time from 1976 to

1981 when Pastorius played there. As arranger, composer, and producer, he constituted (to a greater extent than Wayne Shorter) the ideal creative counterpart to Joe Zawinul. Zawinul admits that he asked the unknown Pastorius, after hearing him for the first time on a tape, whether he could also play the electric bass. "He was playing so fast and so fluid, unlike any electric player at that time, that I thought it was an upright bass."

Jaco's playing, mastering the instrument into its highest register, made the use of the fretless electric bass popular. Like Miles Davis's Harmon mute sound, which became an iconic model for muted jazz trumpet playing, Jaco's warm, overtone-rich electric bass sound became a model for almost all electric bassists who came after him.

However, among the other important electric bassists we must first mention five musicians who predate the development just discussed: Jack Bruce, Chuck Rainey, Eberhard Weber, Michael Henderson, and Hugh Hopper. Jack Bruce was a member of the celebrated group Cream, which in the sixties was involved in then-new sorts of jam sessions and blues-inspired rock improvisations. Even though he was closely linked with the British rock scene, Bruce made several recordings with jazz musicians, including Charlie Mariano, Carla Bley, and Kip Hanrahan. In the seventies, Eberhard Weber developed—independently of Jaco Pastorius—a singing, "humane" way of playing the electric bass. His pervasively warm sound floats with the lightness of an imaginary chorus of angels. Weber is a very intuitive player with a beautiful sound, playing dreamlike, elegaic melodies on a five-stringed upright bass, and combining them with agile, lively rhythms. He has talked about his sense of allegiance to the European tradition, bringing elements from that tradition (above all from romanticism) and also from Steve Reich's minimal music into his own playing and that of his group Colours. Michael Henderson is probably the most underrated bassist ever to work with Miles Davis. In the psychedelic jazz-rock of Miles's electric band at the beginning of the seventies, he created dark, hypnotic riffs full of soul and funk feeling, combining rhythmic sophistication with a minimalist approach to improvising. Hugh Hopper was linked with Soft Machine. Alphonso Johnson, Jaco's predecessor in the group Weather Report, was a particularly elegant, versatile, much-employed performer on the West Coast fusion scene in the seventies and eighties.

All electric bassists after Pastorius refer to Jaco in the same way as all saxophonists after Charlie Parker relate to Bird. Correspondingly long is the list of musicians who individually cultivate Pastorius's legacy: Will Lee, Abe Laborial, Jeff Berlin, Mark Egan, John Lee, Percy Jones, Gary Willis, Tom Barney, Marcus Miller, Bill Laswell, Victor Bailey, Gerald Veasley, Daryl Jones, Jeff Andrews, Jimmy Haslip (of the Yellowjackets), Kim Clarke, Lincoln Goines, Denmark's Bo Stief, Swedish-born Jonas Hellborg, Lawrence Cottle from England, and Spaniard Carlos Benavent.

"That's the problem with fretless. Anytime you play one, everybody immediately goes, 'Jaco!'" says Will Lee. All the more astonishing, then, that this lineage has produced so many individual players. Jeff Berlin is the only electric bassist Bill Evans ever allowed to play with him, matching the pianist's sensitivity. He has a great mastery of diverse "hammer-on" techniques. During the seventies Bo Stief was the most sought-after electric bassist on the European scene. Victor Bailey followed Pastorius in Weather Report in 1981. Starting from Jaco's warm sound, he found his own virtuosic voice on a bass with frets. He transcends the technical aspect of the instrument as few other electric bassists do, combining integrity with a warm, woody sound. "I'm a song person," he says. Gerald Veasley says, "Sometimes you get so awed by what people are doing technically that you're not really about the content, but with Victor, it's all about content." Michael Manring uses hammer-on techniques to play two electric basses simultaneously, like a keyboard. John Patitucci, who became known through playing with Chick Corea, has particularly advanced phrasing on the relatively rare six-string electric bass, making use of the entire tonal register and harmonic range of an instrument that is so difficult to master. Even before Patitucci, Anthony Jackson drew attention to the possibilities open to the six-string electric bass with a profoundly deep dryness of sound and a masterful ability to construct brilliant countermelodies, which made him much in demand among many other musicians, including Steve Khan and Gerry Mulligan.

Jaco Pastorius brought virtuoso electric bass playing to a high point and, some musicians believe, its apogee for the moment. At the start of the eighties, at any rate, emphasis on solo virtuoso performance seemed played out. More and more, bassists concentrated on their instrument's earthy, robust, supportive qualities, paralleling in striking fashion developments in the sphere of the double bass. However, similar outcomes often arise independently of one another, as was the case here. The return to the earthiness of the electric bass resulted from the laws inherent in the instrument itself. Two musicians showed the way ahead, leading to completely different outcomes: Marcus Miller and Bill Laswell. Miller economized and pared down the Pastorius legacy, bringing it back to the foundations. Miller's springy rhythms optimize swinging intensity in the realm of the electric bass. His playing is extremely funky—his rhythms groove with a catlike suppleness, like a panther poised to leap. But even in his slapped lines, as percussive as they are, the melody always comes through. "No matter how much he's playing on the bass he stays close to the melody" (Richard Bona). In his concentration on the essentials he's a fellow spirit to Miles Davis, which a musician with Miles's nose immediately recognized. He engaged Miller not only as bassist in his band (the most supple electric bassist Miles has ever had in a band) but also as producer, composer, and arranger for three albums (*Tutu*, 1986; *Siesta*, 1987; and *Amandla*, 1989), a privilege only previously accorded

Gil Evans. Critics in fact noticed similarities in the way Miller and Evans arrange. According to Miller, "The bass is there to supply a foundation for the rest of the music. The guys who excite me most are the guys who can supply the foundation and still be interesting."

Bill Laswell, who is also a successful producer and supplied the rhythm tracks for Herbie Hancock's hit "Rockit," minimalizes the Pastorius approach by way of the vibrant vehemence and brusqueness of punk. But he also allows elements from rap, reggae, and free jazz to flow into his music. He plays somber, low lines full of "dirty" timbre and weight. His band Material was one of the most important eighties no wave groups. He later played free jazz with heavy metal influences in the Last Exit band. "I don't want to have the bass competing up on top with guitars and brass," Laswell said. "I want to feel the bass as a foundation."

Among the other electric bassists who refine and expand the Pastorius style, making it simpler and more elemental, are Daryl Jones, Lonnie Plaxico, Jeff Andrews, Lincoln Goines, Kim Clarke, and Germany's Alois Kott and Stefan Rademacher. Daryl Jones combines a fat, robust sound with a feeling for paring down, so that he acted as an unshakeable anchor in the Miles Davis and Sting bands. Kim Clarke became known through her playing with the group Defunkt and with George Gruntz.

In African jazz as well, the Pastorius sound has had a strong influence, largely because Weather Report's album *Black Market* (the first one on which Jaco appeared with the band) incorporated African influences, and was a huge hit in Africa. The three most important jazz electric bassists from Africa are Cameroon's Richard Bona and Etienne Mbappé, and South Africa's Bakithi Kumalo.

Bona and Mbappé became known playing with Joe Zawinul's band Syndicate, and Kumalo became known through his work with Hugh Masekela. Bona, who comes from a small village in Cameroon, has combined Jaco's approach with a sensitive consciousness of African music. "The record *Jaco Pastorius*, with his solo on 'Donna Lee,' changed my life," says Bona. Bona's first instrument was an electric bass that was ready for the scrap heap. He was so poor that he had to steal bicycle brake cables to use as strings on the instrument. The brake cables are much thicker than the standard bass strings that Bona plays today, which may be the origin of his virtuosic attack and the extreme fluidity with which he plays virtuosic, Jaco-inspired lines on the instrument.

With his warm, round lines and his angelic but masculine singing, Bona has created an optimistic, melodic African jazz that imaginatively undermines the preconception that African music has to be about percussion and trance. Bona's mild, friendly songs are deeply rooted in the African *griot* tradition, the tradition whose music forms the historical consciousness of West African communities, and that serves as a means of communication of messages, wisdom, and appeals between the ancestors and the living.

Outside the Pastorius school, although much stimulated by Jaco, are the free-funk bassists: Jamaaladeen Tacuma, Melvin Gibbs, Albert MacDowell, Kevin Bruce Harris, and Amin Ali. All these musicians, except for Harris, can be assigned, more or less closely, to the circle around Ornette Coleman's harmolodic music. Jamaaladeen Tacuma (formerly known as Rudy McDaniel) was for a long time linked with Coleman's Prime Time band, and he was involved in the *Dancing in Your Head* recording. Tacuma changed the role of the electric bass. Most electric bassists play static riffs, but Tacuma opens them up into free tonality, bringing about an unceasing process of melodic renewal by continuing and modulating the initial melody. Tacuma thus succeeded in simultaneously providing a foundation and being equally important as melodic soloist. Ornette Coleman called him the "master of the sequence." Melvin Gibbs, who emerged from Ronald Shannon Jackson's Decoding Society, produces metallic, angular, vehemently forward-thrusting lines.

The number of electric bassists working outside fusion and jazz-rock is comparatively small. Nonetheless, there are players who have succeeded in revealing new aspects of the instrument. Skuli Sverisson, Tony Scherr, and Stomu Takeishi are three extremely flexible, rhythmically solid electric bassists who have become important in the multistylistic New York downtown scene. Takeishi has taken Jaco Pastorius's fretless sound the furthest in New York's experimental avant-garde contexts. His lines are unusually sensitive and rhythmically open. Stuart Liebig and Tarus Mateen have played electric contrabass guitar in avant-garde jazz contexts, both with very elastic phrasing: Liebig with alto saxophonist Julius Hemphill, and Mateen in the trio Bandwagon, led by pianist Jason Moran.

In the field of M-Base music, Matthew Garrison and Anthony Tidd have shown great virtuosity in playing in complex meters and rhythms. Garrison, the son of John Coltrane's bassist Jimmy Garrison, plays arpeggios with an extremely smooth and mobile fluidity that is unequaled among electric (and acoustic) bassists.

Finally, we must acknowledge an electric bassist who does not fit into any of the categories discussed so far: Victor Wooten, who became known playing in the fusion/crossover groups of banjoist Béla Fleck. Wooten is a musical pyrotechnician with a brilliant technique, who plays bizarre, wild, dense solos using slap techniques in both hands. He has an immense stylistic vocabulary: from classical music to bebop, from country to rock and blues.

Jazz has made the bass, the "clumsy elephant" of the symphony orchestra, into a highly sensitive instrumental voice commanding the whole range of expressive possibilities—to a point where bassists like Dave Holland, Peter Kowald, or David Friesen can successfully play solo concerts that are filled with musical tension and beauty. Bassists have become technical wizards, under the influence both of developments in electric bass playing and the refinement of bass technique in classical music. When you consider that Pastorius can handle Charlie Parker's "Donna Lee"—a tune that has driven many a horn player to exasperation—as if it were the easiest thing in the world, then you start to realize what kind of development the jazz bass has gone through since the days of Jimmy Blanton.

At the conclusion of this bass section, let's once again quote the veteran bassist Ray Brown:

> Take a guy like myself, who's been playing the bass since he was fourteen. I've seen this instrument go from a slapped, two-beat instrument into complete freedom with people like Stanley Clarke. . . . I have been cast in situations where the guy says, "You're free." I said, "Wait a minute. I don't know if I want to be free," I've talked to kids who don't know anything but freedom. They don't know what it's like to play time and enjoy it. . . . And yet, I like what's happening to the bass. Some of the young people I have heard play the bass like a guitar, and it's fantastic. But I also still enjoy going someplace and seeing somebody playing time with a good sound—that will never be replaced! It's like a heartbeat.

The Drums

To a person raised in the tradition of European concert music, jazz drums initially appear to be noisemaking devices. Paradoxical as it may seem, this is because the drums were introduced for this very purpose in European music. The timpani parts in Tchaikovsky or Richard Strauss, in Beethoven or Wagner, are "noisemakers" insofar as they are intended to create additional intensity and fortissimo effects. The music "happens" independently of them; the musical continuity would not break down if they were left out. But the beat of the jazz drum is no mere effect. It creates the space within which the music "happens": the musical continuity would sometimes be disrupted if there were no chance of constantly "measuring" it against the beat of a swinging drummer. Jazz rhythm, as we have already shown, is an ordering principle.

It was no accident that there were no drum solos in the early forms of jazz; indeed, there were no drummers then with developed individuality. Concerning early jazz history, we know of Buddy Bolden and Freddie Keppard and the Tio family; we know of trumpeters, trombonists, even violinists; but we hardly know anything of drummers. Since the beat was the ordering principle (and only that!) the drummer had no task but to mark the beats as steadily as possible, a task that was performed the worse the less neutrally (i.e., the more individually) he drummed. Only later was it discovered that an additional element of the tension so important to jazz could be gained from the individuality of a drummer—without loss to the ordering function. Quite the contrary: unvaried, metronomic regulation developed into organically nuanced artistic order.

Unlike a metronome, whose "tick-tock" rigidly stays on its own path, the jazz drummer holds the tempo and also functions as a part of the highly nuanced interaction between the musicians—a factor that helps to create and to define the quality of the improvising. Drummers are like the navigators of jazz. They do not merely accompany; rather, they also point the way, define the course. If the drummer is off course, the whole ship sinks.

The modern drum kit, or drum set, was not invented by one person at a particular point in time. Rather, it evolved in a continuous process of development around the turn of the twentieth century, a process in which musicians and instrument builders were equally involved. Around 1890, musicians in New Orleans and elsewhere began to use the drums of military bands in such a way that one musician played the snare drum and the bass drum simultaneously. In 1909 instrument builder William F. Ludwig built the first bass drum pedal. Although percussion devices had been previously known that were operated by hand or by foot, Ludwig's pedal was a breakthrough, enabling easier and faster playing of the bass drum with the foot.

The drum kit existed in rudimentary form as early as the twenties. A New Orleans jazz drummer might for example play on a set made up of snare drum, Chinese tom-toms, wood blocks, cowbells, and small cymbals, as well as a bass drum to which another cymbal or a triangle might be attached. Similar sets were used in vaudeville revues, often with bizarre additions such as bird calls, whistles, sirens, and wind machines used for theatrical effects. The first drum sets were also called traps, after an English slang word for a funny apparatus.

Of course, African American musicians in New Orleans were the first to transform this circus/special effects equipment into a fully valid tool for polyrhythmic improvisation. "Jazz drumming has no precedent in music history," writes Stanley Crouch. "It is an original way of putting together and playing drums and cymbals, which introduced a new kind of virtuosity demanding independent coordination of all four limbs."

At the beginning stand Baby Dodds and Zutty Singleton, the great drummers of New Orleans. Zutty was the softer, Baby the harder. Zutty created an almost supple rhythm; Baby was vehement and impulsive—at least in the terms of that day. Dodds was the drummer in King Oliver's Creole Jazz Band, later with Louis Armstrong's Hot Seven. He can be heard on many records with his brother, clarinetist Johnny Dodds. Baby was the first to play breaks: brief drum eruptions, which often fill in the gaps between the conclusion of a phrase and the end of a formal unit or which set off solos from each other. The break is the egg from which drummers—primarily Gene Krupa—hatched the drum solo.

Sonny Greer was a powerful and sensitive (compared to other early jazz drummers) player whose coloristic abilities were displayed in a particularly opulent fashion in Duke Ellington's orchestra from 1919 to 1951. Don Byas said, "It's funny, for alone or with another band he was nothing exceptional. But he fitted with the Duke as has no one else!" Greer played a drum set that included timpani, vibraphone, tubular bells, Chinese temple blocks, and gongs, thus anticipating a tendency that became widespread among jazz drummers in the sixties: the augmentation of the drum set with other, coloristic percussion instruments.

Oddly enough, white drummers initially expressed more strongly the tendency toward accentuating the weak beats (2 and 4) so characteristic of jazz. The first two are the drummers of the two famous early white bands: Tony Spargo (Sbarbaro) of the Original Dixieland Jazz Band and Ben Pollack of the New Orleans Rhythm Kings. Pollack later founded one of the first larger jazz-oriented dance bands in California (1925) in which many musicians who began in Chicago style—among them Benny Goodman, Jack Teagarden, and Glenn Miller—first became known. In the late twenties, Ray Bauduc held the drum chair in the Pollack band. Bauduc is one of the best white drummers in the New Orleans–Dixieland tradition.

Within the Chicago-style circle "white" drumming developed in a different direction: toward virtuoso play with rhythm, in which the play occasionally became more important than the rhythm. The three most important Chicago drummers were Gene Krupa, George Wettling, and Dave Tough. George Wettling was the only one who remained true to the musical tradition of Chicago style until the end of his life (he died in 1968). Wettling was also a gifted abstract painter. He remarked that jazz drumming and abstract painting seemed different to him only from the point of view of craftsmanship: in both fields, he felt rhythm to be decisive. To someone who expressed amazement that Wettling should be both abstract painter and jazz drummer, he conveyed his own surprise that he should be the only one active in both spheres, since in his opinion they belonged together. George Wettling was one of those fascinating personalities who demonstrate the unity of modern art simply through their work.

Gene Krupa, who died in 1973, became the star drum virtuoso of the Swing era. "Sing Sing Sing," his feature with the Benny Goodman band, in which he played a long solo (in part with Benny's high-register clarinet soaring above him), drove the Swing fans to frenzy. Technically, Krupa was topped only by the drummers of modern jazz. He was the first who dared to use the bass drum on recordings in the twenties. It had been the practice to dispense with recording this part of the drummer's equipment, due to the danger that its reverberations would cause the cutting needle to jump on the still rather primitive recording equipment.

The most important drummer of the Chicago circle is Dave Tough, who died in 1948. He, too, was a man who knew something about the unity of modern art—if not as a painter, then as a would-be writer. Throughout his life, he flirted with contemporary literature as Bix Beiderbecke had flirted with symphonic music. Tough was one of the most subtle and inspired drummers of his time. To him, the drums were a rhythmic palette on which he held in readiness the right color for each soloist. He gained his greatest fame around 1944 as the drummer in Woody Herman's "First Herd." He helped pave the way for modern jazz drumming, as did Jo Jones with Count Basie's band, and it is interesting to note how an Anglo-American and an African American drummer arrived at similar results more or less independently of each other.

More about Jo Jones later, but let us point out that here is a fact vividly illuminating the element of inevitability in jazz evolution. Aside from Baby Dodds, the white Chicago drummers hardly drew much from black drummers; they all came mainly from Tony Spargo and Ben Pollack. Even though there were constant relations with black musicians, one could say that for twenty years "white" and "black" drumming in the main developed independently of each other. Nevertheless, the two evolutionary branches arrived at similar results. Dave Tough prepared the way for the new style in Tommy Dorsey's band, which he joined in 1936. At this time, Jo Jones was doing basically the same thing with Count Basie.

Jo Jones developed under the influence of the great black New Orleans and Swing drummers. Along the line leading from Baby Dodds to Jo Jones, there are four important drummers. The most important is Chick Webb, whose elemental power conjures up a giant rather than the crippled, dwarfish man he actually was. Chick Webb and, among white drummers, Gene Krupa, were first in the line of the "drummer leaders," big band leaders whose instrument was drums. This line was later continued brilliantly by Mel Lewis, Buddy Rich, and Louie Bellson. Webb was a drummer with a magnetizing aura. There are recordings of his band in which his drums are barely audible, and yet each note conveys the excitement that emanated from this amazing man.

Big Sid Catlett, Cozy Cole, and Lionel Hampton follow Webb. Big Sid (d. 1951) and Cozy were Swing drummers par excellence. Cozy made his first recordings in 1930 with Jelly Roll Morton. In 1939 he became the drummer with Cab Calloway's band, in which he was frequently featured in solos. In the late forties, he was the drummer in Louis Armstrong's best All-Star group, and in 1954 he founded a drum school with Gene Krupa in New York.

Cole and Catlett were for a long time considered the most versatile drummers in jazz, equally in demand for combo or big-band work, for New Orleans, Dixieland, and Swing recordings (and Catlett even in a few records important in the history of bop)—in other words, in all the different fields in which other drummers specialized. Catlett was with

Benny Carter and McKinney's Cotton Pickers in the early thirties, then worked with Fletcher Henderson. At the turn of the thirties, he was Louis Armstrong's preferred drummer. "Swing is my idea of how a melody should go," he said—not a scientific definition, but a statement that the musicians of the time, and jazz fans of all times, have understood better than all the fancy theories.

The difference between traditional and modern drumming becomes clear when one compares Cozy Cole and Jo Jones. Both are great, bubbling, storming, exciting musicians, but Cole is completely absorbed in the beat, staccato fashion, and relatively unconcerned with musical shading of what the horns are playing. Jones also creates an imperturbable, vital beat, but in more legato fashion, carrying and serving the musical happenings and accompanying the different parts of a solo with changing colors of toms, snare, hi-hat, and cymbals. Jo Jones was the first, before the drummers of modern jazz, to play accents on the bass drum, instead of using it to mark the quarter-note pulse of the 4/4 beat, as was standard in the Swing era. The Count Basie rhythm section in its classic period (with Jones's drums, Freddie Green's guitar, Walter Page's bass, and Basie's piano) was known as the All American Rhythm Section. Max Roach: "Of every three beats a drummer plays, two came from Jo Jones."

Jo Jones is the first firmly committed representative of the even four-bar unit. He said, "The easiest way you can recognize whether a man is swinging or not is when the man gives his every note its full beat. Like a full note four beats, and a half note two beats, and a quarter note one beat. And there are four beats to a measure that really are as even as our breathing. A man doesn't swing when there's anticipation." Kenny Clarke followed this dictum through: the even four beats became the *son continu*—the ceaseless sounding of the rhythm. The basic beat was displaced from the heavy, pounding bass drum to the steadily resounding ride cymbal, and the hi-hat was used to mark "two" and "four."

Clarke, the drummer of the Minton circle that included Charlie Christian, Thelonious Monk, Charlie Parker, and Dizzy Gillespie, is the creator of modern drum technique. It seems to us that he is often overlooked in this capacity by jazz friends in the United States, perhaps because he lived in Paris from 1956 until his death in 1985 and became the respected father figure of all the many Americans then living in Europe. "Klook," as he was called, had an irresistibly driving way of swinging on the ride cymbal. The interactive accents he used on the snare, the tom-toms, and the bass drum made him a master of classic modern jazz drumming, whose playing was entirely in the service of the group.

Max Roach (d. 2007), of course, developed this manner of playing to its most complete maturity. He was the prototype of the modern percussionist: no longer the more-or-less subordinate "drummer" who must beat out his even 4/4, but an accomplished musician who has studied, generally is able to play an additional instrument, and often knows how to arrange. It is almost the opposite of what used to be: once, drummers almost always were the least schooled musicians in the band; today they are often the most intelligent, as interesting in personality and education as in their playing. Roach once said, "To do with rhythm what Bach did with melody." This was not just meant as an impressive slogan; jazz rhythm has literally achieved the multilinear complexity of baroque play with melodic lines.

Roach was the first to drum complete melodic lines. There are private recordings, made at the historic bop sessions at the Royal Roost in New York in the late forties, on which Roach, in dialogue with Lee Konitz, consistently completes phrases Konitz has started. You can sing along with Roach's drumming just as well as with Konitz's alto playing. And vice versa: what Lee plays on alto is rhythmically as complex as what Max plays on the drums. The drums are no longer exclusively a rhythm instrument, and the alto sax is no longer just a melody instrument. Both have enlarged their range in a complex joining of what earlier could more readily be distinguished as "melody," "harmony," and "rhythm" than today. Thus, Roach could manage without a piano in his quintet of the late fifties. His sidemen vividly said, "He does the piano player's comping on the drums."

Roach effectively destroyed the belief that jazz can swing only in 4/4 time. He played entire drum solos in thorough, accurately accented waltz rhythm and swung more than many a musician who limits himself to 4/4. And he superimposed rhythms tightly and structurally, almost as in polyrhythmic conterpoint, such as 5/4 over 3/4. Roach did all this with a lucidity and restraint that gave meaning to his expression "I look for lyricism." No one proved more clearly than Roach that lyricism—poetic lyricism—can be conveyed through a drum solo. His *We Insist! Freedom Now Suite* is one of the most moving jazz works dedicated to the black civil rights movement in America.

Max Roach founded entire drum ensembles—in 1970 the M'Boom group: ten drummers of percussionists superimposing rhythm with a complexity and differentiation that make the phrasing of similar groups in modern concert music seem naive and clumsy.

Of all the players of the bebop generation, Max Roach developed furthest and opened himself stylistically most imposingly. He is the only drummer to have been involved in the trailblazing recordings of no fewer than three jazz styles: in the 1945 Charlie Parker Quintet shaping bebop, in the 1949–50 Miles Davis Nonet forming cool jazz, and in the midfifties the Max Roach–Clifford Brown Quintet opening the way for hard bop. His group at the end of the seventies was one of the germ cells for the neobop scene. And at the start of the eighties he also demonstrated his powers of rhythmic and melodic communication in "free" duo concerts and recordings with musicians like Archie Shepp, Anthony Braxton, and Dollar Brand; in the nineties he did the same in world jazz improvisations with the Beijing Trio. The dialogues he undertook with avant-garde pianist Cecil Taylor, recorded live at a New York concert in 1979, are among the most exciting duo experiences jazz has to offer. Said free-jazz drummer Jerome Cooper, "Before this concert, I thought that Max Roach was the king of bebop drummers. Now I know he's the king of the drummers."

Meanwhile, it has become obvious: the drums became a melody instrument . . . or more precisely, became a melody instrument *as well*. Certainly the drums did not suddenly give up their rhythmic function. Through the increasingly complex, more musical conception of rhythmic function, the melodic function arose by itself. Logically and inevitably, the drums went the way of all the instruments in and around the rhythm section. First came the trombone, which had only furnished the harmonic background in New Orleans; Kid Ory began, with his tailgate effects, and Jimmy Harrison completed, with his solo work with Fletcher Henderson, the emancipation of the trombone. Then came the piano, which insofar as it was used at all in New Orleans bands, was purely a rhythm-and-harmony instrument. Earl Hines emancipated it: not relinquishing the rhythmic-harmonic function but opening the way toward a hornlike one. Guitar and bass went a similar way. The evolution of the guitar from Eddie Lang to Charlie Christian is one of increasing emancipation. On the bass, Jimmy Blanton brought about this emancipation with one stroke. And finally Kenny Clarke and Max Roach made the drums an "emancipated instrument."

The interest expressed by Roach and the bop musicians in West African–influenced Cuban rhythms thus appears logical. Art Blakey was the first jazz drummer to go to Africa, in the early fifties, and study African rhythms and incorporate them into his playing (see also the section on percussion). He made duet recordings with the Cuban bongo drummer Sabu that are a constant interplay between jazz and West African rhythms; *Nothing But the Soul* (1953) is the characteristic title of one of these recordings. (It was the first time that the word *soul* was used in a jazz title; a couple of years later it designated a playing style in jazz, and later in rock and in pop music.) In the late fifties (i.e., before Roach) Blakey put together whole percussion orchestras: four jazz drummers (Jo Jones among them) and five Latin drummers, using all kinds of rhythm instruments and playing together under the slogan "Orgy in Rhythm." And, of course, once the drums were emancipated—that is, once they acquired melodic possibilities from the complexity of the rhythms—orchestras of percussionists had to become possible, just as there are orchestras made up of brass players or saxophonists.

Later, other drummers also formed percussion ensembles, including those formed in Europe in the seventies and eighties, such as the much-praised Family of Percussion, led by Swiss drummer Peter Giger. Characteristic of these efforts is the fact that the African influence, and the influence of the other great rhythm traditions of the world's music, have continually gained in importance for jazz drummers. Many theoreticians and ethnomusicologists believe that the African heritage was strongest in the original jazz forms and has been lessened ever since. In reality, however, jazz instrumentalists—and mainly drummers, in parallel with their growing political and sociological awareness and identification—have infused more African elements into jazz since the days of free jazz than the instrumental, urban jazz music from New Orleans via Chicago to Harlem ever had to show.

From the fifties until his death in 1990, Art Blakey did more for up-and-coming musicians than all the jazz conservatories, music colleges, and clinics of the day, with all their theories and seminars, put together. So many musicians emerged out of his diverse Jazz Messengers groups— a "university" of *lived* rather than pontificated jazz intensity—that only the most important can be mentioned here: Wayne Shorter, Lee Morgan, Freddie Hubbard, Woody Shaw, Keith Jarrett, Chick Corea, JoAnne Brackeen, Mulgrew Miller, Curtis Fuller, Slide Hampton, Bobby Watson, Terence Blanchard, Donald Harrison, Wynton and Branford Marsalis, Wallace Roney, Robin Eubanks, Steve Davis, and Christian McBride. "Don't play yesterday's shit; play your thoughts and feelings from today," Blakey urged his musicians. "Go find your own sound."

Blakey was the wildest and most vital of all the jazz drummers to emerge from bop. His driving playing illustrates a phenomenon observed by Steve Barrios: "Drummers are always leaders, whether it's the drummer's band or not." Blakey's rolls and explosions are famous. Compared to him, Max Roach seemed more subdued and intellectual.

Philadelphia-born "Philly" Joe Jones (d. 1985) merged the two approaches. He played with the explosive vehemence of Blakey, but he also had elements of Max Roach's musical cosmopolitanism. In the first Miles Davis Quintet, with John Coltrane and Red Garland, Jones's shrewd, intelligent playing ignited a rhythmic fire that made him the most interactive drummer of hard bop. His trademark was the "Philly lick": striking the rim of the snare drum on each fourth beat, thus establishing tension in preparation for the first beat of the following measure. Clarence Penn said: "Philly's playing was effortless. When he played drums, it was like listening to butter."

Even more transparent—in the refined sense this word has acquired in the terminology of cool jazz—is the playing of Joe Morello. He had the maturity, if not the vitality, of Max Roach, with a nearly somnambulistic feeling for the improvisations of his colleagues. Morello joined the Dave Brubeck Quartet in 1957. Through him, Brubeck gained a rhythmical awareness that he had lacked before. Ten years later, Alan Dawson replaced Morello for a while. Dawson also taught percussion at Berklee College in Boston, the most famous of jazz schools. He combined intellect and spirit with a swing and drive that harked back to the great drummers of the jazz tradition. The great rhythmic independence with which he musically coordinated all four limbs remains a point of reference for drummers today, such as Gene Jackson and Billy Kilson. Particularly integrated into melodic play is the drum work of Connie Kay with the Modern Jazz Quartet (see also the chapter dealing with jazz combos).

The drummers of hard bop—Art Taylor, Louis Hayes, Dannie Richmond, Pete LaRocca, Roy Haynes, Albert Heath, and (although he has gone far beyond hard bop) Elvin Jones, to mention only the most important—link back to Blakey and Roach. Dannie Richmond (d. 1988) was the only musician to remain affiliated with Charles Mingus for a considerable time. In the combo chapter, we will point out how important he was for the togetherness of Mingus's music (and in the seventies and eighties for the continuation of his legacy). Art Taylor's crystalline cymbal sound came more from Max Roach and from Kenny Clarke, while his playing on the toms came more from Philly Joe Jones. Louis Hayes, who became known playing with Cedar Walton, has one of the best cymbal sounds since Kenny Clarke. His boiling hard-bop style inspired Kenny Washington to remark, "That right hand will swing you into bad health."

Roy Haynes is a master of that "hipness" that eludes verbal description and that is so important not only for the music but also for the lifestyle of the jazz musician. His crisp, polyrhythmic sound has an inimitable driving quality. Haynes's reflexes are extremely quick. "You say something to him and he responds instantly. That way on the drums, too," said Anthony Roney.

Haynes is the most restless, subversive drummer in modern jazz. This observation applies equally to his style and to his career. In 1949 he took over the drum chair in the Charlie Parker Quintet; later he played in the bands of John Coltrane, Stan Getz, and Pat Metheny, and developed into one of the great drum masters of the jazz scene, continuously leading his own group from the seventies into the beginning of the twenty-first century.

Roy Haynes was the first, in the fifties, to liberate hi-hat playing from its static accompanying role. Instead of simply playing the hi-hat regularly on beats two and four (of a 4/4 bar), he uses it to play variable accents, creating such a driving rhythmic dance in its interplay with his ride cymbal that the hi-hat becomes a coloristic element rather than a timekeeping one.

But above all, Roy Haynes is less cymbal-oriented than most other drummers of modern jazz. Rather, his great interactive mobility is expressed in the form of many unexpected accents between the snare drum and the bass drum. When he was asked once where he got his ideas for these original snare/bass drum combinations, he answered: "Watch [boxer] Sugar Ray Robinson . . . and dancers."

Roy Haynes's playing forms a kind of hinge between the rhythms of bop and the drum approaches of the sixties, because "even before Elvin Jones, he introduced a new triplet feel." (Tony Williams). Elvin Jones—the third member of the family from Detroit, which gave us two other remarkable talents in pianist Hank and trumpeter-composer Thad—played a kind of "superbop" that musicians felt to be a new way of "turning the rhythm around"—after all that had already been done in this area by Charlie Parker and Kenny Clarke. In a period when one could hardly imagine that further concentration and compression of the rhythmic happenings in jazz were possible, Elvin Jones and his cohorts proved that the evolution continued. There has been further development, too, in the field of "encircling" the basic rhythm. The less the drummers play "on" the beat and the more they play "around" it, the more elemental is the perception of the basic rhythm—almost paradoxically. "It's less, and yet more," said John McLaughlin about Elvin Jones.

Elvin Jones was not only a master of this hyperbolically swinging triplet feel, but was also the outstanding example of dynamic control of the drums, from peaks of volume down to the softest playing. David Liebman says, "That's one of Elvin's greatest contributions: his dynamic breadth." It's almost impossible to imagine John Coltrane's music without Elvin Jones. Although Coltrane's quartet mostly played original compositions by Coltrane, Elvin can rightly be considered as "co-composer" of them in view of the way that his contemplative force and the glowing ecstasy of his rhythms vitalized and expanded them. In the duo "battles" that Jones played with Coltrane, his drums sometimes create the impression of a wave "that never completely breaks, like a wave that never stops breaking" (Geoff Dyer).

When Elvin Jones died in 2004, countless jazz musicians expressed their admiration. But perhaps the best-formulated tribute to him came from a rock musician, Carlos Santana:

> When I hear Elvin's music, I hear the pyramids, I hear African and pre-Columbian music, and I hear the future. Elvin is the beat of life itself, and his music transcends "clever" or "cute" or any superlatives. When he and Coltrane played and everyone else in the quartet dropped out, that's what Jimi Hendrix would play if he was still alive . . . because there is nothing more pure or vibrant than Coltrane and Elvin. . . . For me, Elvin was Número Uno, forever, for all ages, for all existence.

Before we can attempt to show where this development has led, we must refer to a number of drummers who stand outside the realm of these tendencies and represent a basically timeless modern Swing approach, in which new developments are less of a stylistic nature but tend more toward even greater professionalism and perfection. *The* main representative of these drummers is Buddy Rich (d. 1987), a ne plus ultra of virtuoso technique. His astonishing drum solos and no less astonishing personality were highlights of the big bands of Artie Shaw, Tommy Dorsey, and Harry James, as well as of his own brilliant big bands. Mel Lewis: "He could make a big band sparkle." At a drum workshop at the 1965 Newport Festival, Rich "stole the show" from all the other drummers—and among them were Art Blakey, Jo Jones, Elvin Jones, Roy Haynes, and Louie Bellson. However, Rich often gives one the impression that he is a great vaudeville artist—a circus artist who performs the most breathtaking *salti mortali* without a net—rather than a genuine jazz musician in the sense of Roach, Blakey, or Elvin Jones. It certainly is of psychological interest that Buddy Rich was born into a family of vaudevillians.

Louie Bellson, also an excellent arranger, put *two* bass drums in the place of one, and played them with an agility comparable to the footwork of an organist. During his years with Duke Ellington (1951 to 1953) the band gained a new, typical "Bellson" sound. Ellington's Sam Woodyard retained the two bass-drum setup, and fifteen years later double bass drums became standard equipment for many rock drummers.

The name Denzil Best stands for a way of playing known as "fill-out" technique. Kenny Clarke, Max Roach, and Art Blakey "fill in" the musical proceedings, placing their accents wherever they deem appropriate. This is the "fill-in" technique. But Best "filled out" the musical space evenly, placing no (or hardly any) accents but stirring his brushes continuously on the snare drum, and thus creating his own special *son continu* swing. This, too, was an end result of the legato evolution initiated by Jo Jones and Dave Tough. After the great success of the George Shearing Quintet around 1950, where Best was a member, his way of drumming has been copied in hundreds of cocktail-lounge groups.

From Dave Tough descend a number of excellent big-band drummers, such as Don Lamond, Dave's successor with Woody Herman, or Tiny Kahn, who died much too young and also was a gifted arranger whose themes are still being played. Other drummers of this lineage are Gus Johnson, J. C. Heard, the late Osie Johnson and Shadow Wilson, as well as Oliver Jackson, Grady Tate, Mel Lewis, Sonny Payne, and Rufus Jones.

Wilson, Gus Johnson, and Payne were Jo Jones's successors in the Basie band, a lineage continued into our present time by Butch Miles, Dennis Mackrel, and Kenny Washington. Heard participated in many of Norman Granz's Jazz at the Philharmonic tours and was in some respects a "modernized" Cozy Cole or Sid Catlett. Grady Tate was much in demand for modern Swing recordings. Mel Lewis (see also the big bands chapter) turned the great big-band drum tradition of men like Chick

Webb, Dave Tough, and Buddy Rich into a contemporary art. Lewis was a minimalist—an expert in the economical use of notes, movement, and energy. He never played more than what was necessary.

There are two ways to play drums in a big band: with an orchestral, extroverted approach, or more privately, oriented toward the sound of a smaller group. Just as Buddy Rich epitomized orchestral big-band drumming, Mel Lewis was a paradigmatic example of the approach inspired by small groups. Like Dave Tough or Sid Catlett, he brought the free spirit and sense of mutual trust inherent in small-group playing to the big-band context. This dialogue-friendly lightness was an indication of his roots: "I'm a bebop player."

On the West Coast, Shelly Manne took a step that was as logical as Art Blakey's, though it led in the opposite direction. Manne was the absolute melodist among jazz drummers. His way of playing was spare and subtle, spirited and animated, but frequently quite removed from what swing means in terms of the line leading from Webb to Blakey. On the other hand, Manne showed that he could swing—as in the famous quartet recording of "The Man I Love" (with Coleman Hawkins and Oscar Pettiford) from the midforties, or in the many recordings he made on the West Coast—from the fifties until his death in 1984, when he began to include fusion elements, too. He became well known through many dozens of records that made the term "West Coast jazz" a trademark.

The "in group" of New York jazz—that small elite from whence almost everything important in jazz originates—has gone even further. Its development leads from Elvin Jones (here we tie up with the paragraph in this section where we first mentioned this outstanding drummer) via Tony Williams to Sunny Murray, and from there to Billy Cobham and Jack DeJohnette.

Elvin took the *son continu* that began with Kenny Clarke to the extreme limits of what is possible within the framework of a symmetrical meter. He went to the extreme limits, but not beyond. When Coltrane wanted him to go further, Jones resigned from the Coltrane group in an act of great inner consequence. He was replaced by Rashied Ali, in whose playing the meter initially was totally dissolved (but who has since returned to recognizable meters). Jones, however, remained one of the great, independent jazz drummers until his death in 2004, in his own band, the Jazz Machine—a musician who refers to Coltrane on the drums as convincingly as does McCoy Tyner on the piano.

Meanwhile, in 1963, Miles Davis had hired Tony Williams (only seventeen at the time) for his quintet. Williams arrived—from a different point of origin—at a similar reduction of the jazz beat to a nervelike vibration and swing. In the section about jazz rhythm, we spoke of the fact that there is a certain physiological parallel to this reduction: from heartbeat to "pulse." Thus, a new physiological level, heretofore virtually blocked to musical approaches, was made accessible. The physiological level of great classical music was breathing; that of "classic" jazz reflects the heartbeat, that of the new jazz, the pulse.

When the attempt is made to describe the virile playing of this drummer, the concept of "aggressive elegance" quickly comes up. In the percussive firestorms that Williams unleashed, the remarkable subtlety and sensitivity of his playing are always surprising. This sensitivity is created by the silvery vibration and pulsation of his cymbals. One of Williams's trademarks is that he accents all the quarter notes with the hi-hat, four beats per bar, in contrast to many drummers, who use the hi-hat to accent only beats two and four.

Tony Williams was the motoric catalyst of the second Miles Davis Quintet. "The direction the band moved in depended on Tony," said Miles in his autobiography. In the Davis quintet, Williams created unique rhythmic high points through his ability to ignore conventional forms and to play across bar lines and formal units without losing his feeling for the overall form. This was because Williams played the meter less than other drummers, establishing instead a beat that flowed freely across the four-beat units of the bars, and used metric modulation (i.e., switching between tempos related by mathematical ratios) to create spaces for improvisation that were new at the time. For example, in the piece "Nefertiti," from Miles's 1967 album of the same name, the conventional hierarchy of the jazz group is turned "on its head." The only soloist here is the drummer, while the traditional solo instruments—trumpet and saxophone—provide the accompaniment by constantly repeating the theme. Williams's playing on "Nefertiti" is an outstanding example of the construction of a drum solo over a melodic-harmonic ostinato, and the use by a single drummer of a drum set to create orchestral melodies and harmonies.

When bop returned in the eighties and nineties, Tony Williams formed his own acoustic quintet, playing his own compositions, which engage with the legacy of classic modern jazz from a contemporary viewpoint. Sonically, he had long since evolved. Under the influence of his experience playing jazz-rock (discussed below), his playing became heavier, harder, and edgier, now oriented more toward the tom-toms than toward the cymbals, but in no way less challenging. In this way, as a bandleader Tony Williams (who died in 1997) served as mentor to a series of musicians who, through his band, succeeded in making the leap from "young lion" status to that of masterful stylists of the new mainstream jazz. These include trumpeter Wallace Roney, saxophonist Bill Pierce, bassists Charnette Moffett and Bob Hurst, and pianist Mulgrew Miller.

Before Tony Williams, however, three drummers who had worked with Ornette Coleman since 1959 had already shown that the "liberation" of the rhythm does not just mean a liberation from the function of the drummer. These three were Billy Higgins, Ed Blackwell, and Charles

Moffett (who died in 1997, and who has been described as a "Sid Catlett of free jazz"). Moffett was a percussionist strongly rooted in tradition, with a colossal swing, but was also flexible enough to execute spontaneous changes in tempo or, when the situation called for it, to abandon timekeeping completely and to move to free playing. Blackwell was from New Orleans, and said that he saw no contradiction between what the drummers of his hometown have always been doing and the new conception. In general terms, it is important to realize that Higgins and Blackwell—to a certain extent also Moffett—played mainly metrically with Ornette. It only sounded "revolutionary," while it was "traditional" at the same time.

Blackwell's unmistakable signature was a melodic drumming style influenced equally by African polyrhythms and by New Orleans beats. He combined a quick liveliness with a light touch and, for example in collaboration with Don Cherry and Dewey Redman, was able to play fast without sounding rushed, which is difficult for many drummers. "He played rhythms rather than time," said Don Cherry.

Billy Higgins, who died in 2001, played the drums with effervescent joy, warmth, and energy. His swing is very powerful, with stylistic feeling, taste, and a smiling, dancing elegance. Higgins not only had a strong right hand with which he created a captivating, shimmering pulse on a ride cymbal through which rivets had been placed (Higgins: "the cymbal—it's like the maitre d' of the drum set"), but also had a strong left hand, and was able to play the drum set as a whole. "The drum set is like a family. Each component of the drum set is different; to make them all sound as *one*—where each voice gets its own due—that's the whole secret. . . . If you muffle one drum, then it's not in the family anymore and you can't get the pure notes out."

The most extreme representative of the possibilities of free-jazz rhythm, however, was and still is Sunny Murray. In a radical fashion, the marking of the meter is here replaced by the creation of tension over long passages. When Murray was with Albert Ayler in the midsixties, especially when Ayler was playing folk-music themes, there were clearly perceptible metric pulses in the horn melodies, but Murray just didn't seem to consider them. He played above—and often enough even against—the meter with pulsating beats that seemed to be collecting energy, and suddenly he broke out into wild rolls utilizing the entire spectrum of his instrument. These were eruptive "knitting needle percussion structures" that seemed on the point of bursting with intensity. "Murray," wrote Valerie Wilmer, "seems obsessed with the idea of strength and intensity in music."

There can be no doubt that Murray's music swings with an immense density and power. It swings without beat and measure, meter and symmetry—all that which only recently was thought indispensable to swinging—simply by virtue of the power and flexibility of its tension arcs. One is tempted to wonder whether this fact might not call for revision of all previous swing theories, because this way of playing creates tension, too; in fact, it increases tension, in an ecstatic sense, far beyond anything previously known. And swing in earlier jazz can be subsumed under this, too: swing as element of tension building.

Murray said, "I work for natural sounds rather than trying to sound like drums. Sometimes I try to sound like car motors or the continuous cracking of glass."

Obviously, Murray is not the only drummer of this kind. Other drummers of the "first generation" of free jazz are Milford Graves, Beaver Harris, Barry Altschul (in the beginning of his career), as well as the previously mentioned Charles Moffett and Rashied Ali—and (worthy of special attention) Andrew Cyrille. Milford Graves is a master of the layering of irregular rhythms, which he is able to contract and expand in an elastic pulsation of time layers. Felix Klopotek says, "You have to imagine that like this: three people are walking down the street together; sometimes one of them sets the tempo, sometimes the other one, and the third one stays still and then runs quickly behind the one in front. . . . How many drummers are playing? One. Graves's music is different: polymetric." Rashied Ali has said that in free jazz, the drummer's job is to play time without marking time.

Cyrille made important rhythmic contributions to Cecil Taylor's music from 1964 to the midseventies, played with Illinois Jacquet as well as with West African drum groups from Ghana, and is conversant with the different kinds of European percussion music. At the risk of oversimplification, he could be called the intellectual among free-jazz drummers. He has an unmistakably clear cymbal sound.

Cyrille captured the attitude of many of these drummers to swing:

"Swing" is the natural psychic response of the human body to sound that makes a person want to move his or her body without too much conscious effort. . . . In a more abstract sense, "swing" is completely integrated and balanced sound, forming a greater, spiritual-like, almost tangible magic sensibility of being—the conscious knowledge that something metaphysical is happening.

This "first generation" of free drummers was the point of departure for a second and third generation, of whom we will speak later.

Rock rhythm is not very flexible. In some respects, it returned to Cozy Cole and Sid Catlett of the thirties; it reverted the accent away from the cymbals and back to where it had been—to the bass drum and the tom-toms. Thus, it cannot react as easily and effortlessly to the soloists' playing as a rhythm "played on top." But it is clearly defined. One can always tell where "beat one" is, which occasionally was no longer possible in the playing of jazz drummers in the sixties.

The task of the new type of drummer to gain significance since the beginning of the seventies was, in other words, to merge the emotionalism and communicative power of rock with the flexibility and complexity of jazz. The drummers who first accomplished this are Tony Williams, Alphonse Mouzon, and Billy Cobham. We have already mentioned Williams. He long played the "freest" rhythms in the realm of jazz-rock, and he was only later surpassed in this respect by Ronald Shannon Jackson. In the band Lifetime, with John McLaughlin and Larry Young, in 1969–70 he played with volcanic intensity across the boundaries between rock, jazz, and the avant-garde. Of all the pioneers of jazz-rock drumming, Tony Williams had the greatest stylistic breadth. On his record *The Joy of Flying* (1976), he plays both with fusion keyboardist Jan Hammer and with avant-garde pianist Cecil Taylor.

Billy Cobham accomplished his pathbreaking contribution in John McLaughlin's first Mahavishnu Orchestra, where his displays of power and virtuosic compactness made him famous. A master of one-handed press rolls, he led his own groups after that, but he hasn't reached the level of his Mahavishnu playing. Mouzon's development shows a similar problem. He was, on the one hand, a founding member of Weather Report and, on the other, one of McCoy's Tyner's sidemen in the early seventies, playing "acoustic" jazz in the Coltrane tradition—both of these styles on the highest level. During the late seventies Mouzon repeatedly said that he considered himself not a jazz but a rock musician; the rock world, however, obviously has problems accepting him as one of its own, because his playing is too complex and too demanding for a rock context.

The panorama of first- and second-generation contemporary jazz-rock and fusion drummers built on the foundation laid down by Williams, Cobham, and Mouzon, is so wide that, again, only a few can be named: Steve Gadd, Peter Erskine, Lenny White, Gerry Brown, Steve Jordan, John Guerin, and Al Foster. Among the Europeans of this group (even though they play with a kind of "European understatement" that differentiates them from their more aggressive American colleagues) are Dutchman Pierre Courbois, the French-Italian Aldo Romano, and Fredy Studer from Switzerland.

Steve Gadd, known through his work with Stuff and Steps Ahead, was the most successful and most demanded studio drummer of the seventies and eighties. Developing Tony Williams's style, he created the "dry" studio sound that served hundreds of drummers as a model. In the nineties Gadd's precise and clever style was refined and taken further, with complex virtuosity, by Dave Weckl. Lenny White from Jamaica (strikingly many jazz-rock drummers—including Billy Cobham—come from the Caribbean area) was involved in Miles's 1969 *Bitches Brew*, and he also played with Larry Coryell and Chick Corea. Peter Erskine, who was in Stan Kenton's big band, helped solve Weather Report's protracted rhythmic problems when he was with the group from 1976 to 1982, forming in conjunction with Jaco Pastorius one of jazz-rock's most creative rhythm sections.

If there was something akin to a constant musical axis in Miles's seventies and eighties bands, then it was the link that welded the trumpeter to Al Foster from 1972 to 1985. Miles's belief in an ongoing beat found its ideal counterpart in Foster's imperturbable timing. They were so attuned to one another that Foster often foresaw and initiated unexpected transitions between Davis's pieces, implementing such developments with sleepwalking ease. More than almost any other musician, Foster carried a swing feeling into jazz-rock rhythms, and he also integrated elements of the New Orleans tradition (such as its march rhythms, which have a uniquely supple quality compared with brisk Prussian marches) into that context.

Pierre Courbois was a significant influence on the entire European scene in the early seventies with his group Association P.C., but he has since grown away from this style of music. This is true also of several other players we have named: for instance, Peter Erskine (to whom we'll return later) and Lenny White, who first played fusion with Chick Corea's group Return to Forever, but then also bebop and even experimental bop with Heiner Stadler.

Jon Hiseman, Robert Wyatt, John Marshall, Bill Bruford, and Simone Phillips are part of the British scene. Hiseman drums in the successful United Jazz and Rock Ensemble. His playing grooves in such a precise, calculated manner that he has been both praised and criticized for it. As early as the late sixties, Robert Wyatt, in the British group Soft Machine, was creating a network of sensitive rhythms that were ahead of what most other drummers on the early jazz-rock scene were able to play then, even in America.

Bill Bruford is a master of jazz-rock drumming over complex meters. His angular playing was inspired by the odd-time-signature playing of Joe Morello (Dave Brubeck's drummer). Bruford is also a master of synthesizer drum playing. He drums, instead of on skins, on flat rubber pads where an impact creates an electrical impulse triggering a synthesizer. In his Earthworks group Bruford thereby achieves melodic and sonic effects that virtually match those of a keyboardist. Talk of playing drums "melodically" thus takes on a more tangible reality, opening up new chordal, harmonic, and sonic possibilities for drummers.

Aldo Romano has developed a very "French" style of jazz-rock playing, full of joie de vivre and a lightness pleasantly contrasting with the more powerful drumming of jazz-rockers. Fredy Studer from Switzerland is a specialist in sensitive and subtle jazz-rock rhythms with a great feel for differentiated cymbal sounds. Mark Nauseef has linked jazz-rock elements with world music from India, Asia, and Bali in original fashion.

The "daddy" of European jazz-rock drummers is Ginger Baker. After he became world famous in the sixties in the blues-rock group Cream, he spent several years in Nigeria studying African percussion music. Later, in the seventies and eighties, he tried a comeback with his tom-heavy sound, but did not succeed, because (like his colleague on bass, Jack Bruce) Baker has power and musical fire but has not been able to keep up with the technical playing standards meanwhile achieved.

Following the first and second generation of jazz-rock drummers, there is a series of players who have developed the ostentatiously virtuosic tradition of jazz-rock drumming in the eighties and nineties under the influence of many other styles. The most important of these players are Dennis Chambers, Terri Lyne Carrington, Paul Vertigo, Dan Gottlieb, Will Calhoun, Kenwood Dennard, Robby Ameen, Adam Deitch, Billy Martin, Dave King, Marcus Baylor, Will Kennedy, Nathaniel Townsley, Poogie Bell, and, in Europe, France's Phillipe Garcia, Switzerland's Jo Jo Mayer, and Germany's Wolfgang Haffner.

Dennis Chambers credits his reputation as a powerhouse drummer to a trajectory that has taken him from the P-Funk of George Clinton to the complex contemporary jazz of John Scofield. Chambers represents the summit of virtuosic funk technique, occupying the space between funk and jazz with irresistibly fat grooves. His energetic rhythms made him one of the most in-demand studio drummers of the nineties.

Will Calhoun, a former member of the band Living Colour, moves between funk, rap, and contemporary jazz in his Afrocentric, politically motivated jazz-rock. Will Kennedy and Marcus Baylor both became known through their technically highly developed, sophisticated playing in the fusion band The Yellowjackets.

Terri Lyne Carrington, under the influence of Jack DeJohnette (discussed below), has brought rhythms to jazz-rock drumming that are as complex as they are sensual. She sees herself as a "sculptor of rhythms." On first listening, she comes across as an expert at a kind of abstractly swinging power playing. On closer listening, she proves to be adept at the circumspect coloring of rhythms, a masterful shaper of drum sounds.

Most of these musicians have also used drum machines and drum computers. However, it is notable that they have used these electronic devices either in combination with conventional drum set playing or have eventually abandoned them in favor of the traditional drum kit. This is not because a drum machine is incapable of swinging, as is often thought—the machine certainly can swing if it is expertly programmed. Rather, the result lacks the physical directness and the spirit of spontaneous communication that makes the good jazz drummer so indispensable.

The advent of affordable, portable samplers that make improvisation possible in real time has also provided drummers, since the beginning of the nineties, with electronic tools that enable them to make spontaneous use of loops, rhythms, and all other parameters of sound. It is thus not surprising that since the midnineties a series of jazz-rock drummers have emerged who use these new electronic possibilities in parallel with their conventional drum set playing. The original contributions in this regard came from Europe, particularly from players associated with the new Norwegian electronic scene based in Oslo. These include Anders Engen (in the band of Bugge Wesseltoft), Rune Arnesen (with Nils Petter Molvaer), and Martin Horntveth (in the group Jaga Jazzist). These drummers use electronic loops to create "unplayable" rhythms, which they elegantly combine with their acoustic drumming.

The American drummer Adam Deitch has, for example in the John Scofield Band, made particularly successful use of loops and electronic sampling as a logical extension of acoustic jazz-rock drumming. France's Philippe Garcia, who became known through his playing with Erik Truffaz, has taken a different route: on his stripped-down acoustic drum set, he plays fast breakbeats and drum 'n' bass rhythms with such virtuosity that he becomes a kind of acoustic, "human," beat box.

Wolfgang Haffner is one of the most emancipated and diverse drummers in Europe. He is a sought-after freelancer and studio drummer, but also an exquisite swinger who played for example with Albert Mangelsdorff. At the beginning of the twenty-first century, he developed from an elegant rhythmicist to a sensitive composer. In his pieces, he creates atmospheric groove tableaux that are pleasantly distinct from the storms of breakbeats that one might normally expect from a drummer who had flirted with jungle and house music.

Similarly diverse is the panorama of free drummers whose second and third generations lead into the free-jazz inspired look at jazz tradition. These players include Phillip Wilson, Don Moye, Steve McCall, Barry Altschul, Pheeroan Ak Laff (Paul Maddox), Thurman Barker, Bobby Battle, Warren Smith, and, among younger musicians, Gerry Hemingway, Hamid Drake, Susie Ibarra, Tani Tabbal, Gerald Cleaver, Dylan Vanderschyff, George Schuller, Greg Bendian, and Alex Cline. Strikingly, all of these drummers, despite their ties with free jazz, have incorporated influences from outside the avant-garde, judiciously adding rhythmically free passages to their playing in a meter. That doesn't mean that the freedom previously gained has now been renounced, but rather that the dialogue with "more traditional" ways of playing has been expanded and refined. Wilson, Moye, and McCall are close to the AACM, even though Wilson changed to a different kind of music at the end of the sixties. He played in the Paul Butterfield Blues Band but later returned to free music when his AACM colleagues finally gained recognition in the United States in the second half of the seventies. During the eighties he performed with Lester Bowie's Brass Fantasy. Moye, linked with the Art Ensemble of Chicago, makes particularly impressive use of the African legacy of black music. His knowledge of the wide range of African rhythms seems inexhaustible. By incorporating a large number of percussion instruments—African, Arab, Indian—Moye has moved past the limitiations of the traditional drum set sounds, finding a new diversity of colors and textures. His impulsive style, with its air of ritual, has influenced many drummers who today integrate many different percussion colors and elements of hand drumming, as well as unorthodox stick techniques, such as Susie Ibarra, George Schuller, Kenny Wollesen, or Hamid Drake.

Steve McCall (d. 1989) lent a light and breezy quality to the rhythms of the trio Air. Barry Altschul had already played free bop with Circle when that term didn't yet exist. He's a master of rim shots (striking the rim of the snare drum), and the way he creates intensity and tension by his very restraint is inimitable.

Gerry Hemingway, who became known through his playing with Anthony Braxton, is the real "family man" of the post–free-jazz drummers. His pugnacious, tension-filled rhythms generate a peculiar attractive force. He plays drums with a particular resonance and a feeling for "mature" orchestration, so that it is not very surprising that he prefers to use old drum sets from the forties and fifties. Hemingway says, "It takes a while for an instrument to get its own sound, and these drums have been hit many times."

Susie Ibarra studied with Milford Graves and played in the quartet of David S. Ware. An American of Filipina descent, her playing has attracted the attention of the great figures of freely improvised music due to the delicacy and intelligence with which she enriches and expands the powerful pulse playing of free jazz. "People often misinterpret this music and think that 'free jazz' or 'free anything' is loud noise or coming from anger," she says. "But the music I play has emerged from forty years of studied development. . . . True 'freedom' can only come from discipline." Ibarra has unlocked the various sound possibilities of percussion by playing in a "tuneful" manner—"a different sound with every stroke."

Hamid Drake, based in Chicago, has created an exciting synthesis of free pulse playing and grooves. He is the most vital and gripping of the new post–free-jazz drummers, equally at home playing driving Afro and reggae grooves with Pharoah Sanders or playing completely free pulse structures with Peter Brötzmann.

Guillermo E. Brown has combined the possibilities of free drumming with tendencies from new electronic music in a particularly convincing manner, using breakbeats from drum 'n' bass as well as rhythms from hip-hop, jungle, and house music. He confidently plays as if the long-standing schism between free-jazz and jazz-rock musicians had never existed. For Brown, Weather Report's *Heavy Weather* and Cecil Taylor's *Dark to Themselves* have the same inspiring, innovative spirit: the quality of seeking, moving ahead into new sonic spaces and dimensions. "I grew up with the computers as another limb so I feel totally comfortable improvising in this way." Brown uses the drum machine in a way that

Max Roach always demanded from the conventional drum kit: he makes it "breathe."

Turning to the European scene, we must first mention the "daddies" of free drumming there: the Swiss Pierre Favre and Dutchman Han Bennink, the former perceptive and sensitive, the latter vital and gripping. More than any other drummer today, Favre is able to produce percussion "sketches" so vividly that one can almost "see" them as pictures: a Sunday morning in Switzerland or a young girl on her way to school. While Bennink's sound is especially convincing and developed on the skins, Favre is particularly impressive on cymbals, gongs, and other metal percussion instruments. Even before their American colleagues, both Favre and Bennink utilized the rich arsenal of percussion instruments employed today by so many drummers: instruments of Africa, Brazil, Bali, Tibet, India, and China.

Han Bennink unleashes the primal force of percussion like no other European jazz drummer. He celebrates the original impulse of drumming: its vital attack. At the end of the sixties, in the first phase of European free jazz, he played groundbreaking rhythms in the bands of Willem Breuker and Peter Brötzmann. Bennink's improvising is so wild that he effectively determines the direction of the music even in large groups. Later in his career, softer aspects were added, in an original mixture of neo-Dadaist and metrical elements. Of the free-improvising drummers of Europe, Bennink is the most swinging and the most grooving. He has great control of all the approaches to drumming: from free pulse playing to West African grooves to shuffle, boogie, and rock rhythms, all the way back to the beats of New Orleans and Swing drummers like Baby Dodds and Sid Catlett, including the humorous tradition of vaudeville and circus drumming. This diversity made it particularly easy for him to adapt to the multistylistic trends of jazz in the nineties, for example in exciting performances with the Clusone Trio.

In the sixties, the sheer quantity of Bennink's arsenal was astounding; it seemed that it could never be large enough—tabla, Chinese gongs, bass timpani, temple blocks, vibraphone, talking drum, sheets of metal, saws. Today, he generally plays on a drum set provided by the concert promoter. The idea of the giant drum kit is one that he has abandoned—not least because it was so often copied. He takes only his snare drum along to his gigs, because, as he says, he finds it "tasty." "For me it's important to go back to the origin of drumming, to bring the 'jazz aspect' back into it. I've gotten to the point where all I need is a couple of matchsticks."

In England, John Stevens (d. 1994), in the Spontaneous Music Ensemble, developed the idea of an egoless, complementary playing style using noises and textures. He was a master of "atomized" sound playing, in which the drummer is less interested in linear development than in the abrogation of the hierarchical relationship between the soloists and the accompanists.

Bennink and Stevens can certainly be considered founders of something like a European percussion lineage. From that lineage stem the Swiss Peter Giger, Reto Weber, and Marco Käppeli; Italian-born Andrea Centazzo; Sweden's Sven-Åke Johansson; the Finn Edward Vesala (who has also studied Balinese music); Britons Tony Oxley and Paul Lytton; as well as Germans Paul Lovens (who became known through his involvement with the Globe Unity Orchestra), Detlef Schönenberg (who played in one of the most interesting seventies European duos, with trombonist Günther Christmann), Willi Kellers, and Günter "Baby" Sommer.

Starting from aesthetically opposite premises, Paul Lovens and Paul Lytton have arrived at similar sonic results. Both play drums with high velocity, intensity, and polyrhythm, and yet they are fundamentally different with regard to group dynamics. Lovens, for example in Globe Unity Orchestra, is more of an interventionist, while Lytton, for example in his work with Evan Parker, understands particularly well how to make complementary, completing rhythmic contributions. Sweden's Sven-Åke Johansson is also a representative of classical European free-jazz drumming. For example in duo with Alexander von Schlippenbach, he has introduced neo-Dadaist aspects into free-improvised drumming, such as theatrical gestures and the use of accordion, voice, and bizarre objects such as shoe trees. The subtle irony and virtuosity of his playing is also visible in his group Moderne Nordeuropäische Dorfmusik [Modern Northern European Village Music], for example in a composition/improvisation for five tractors.

For more than thirty years, England's Tony Oxley has assembled his personal drum set—but without including a snare drum, normally considered indispensable. Instead, he plays on a set that he has modified with small objects, wires, screws, nuts and bolts, cheese slicers, and a giant cowbell, also using electronics to modify the sounds of many of these elements. Oxley's playing has an extremely developed sense of flow in its use of colors and textures, a "polyrhythmic primeval forest of shimmering textures of breathtaking density, and yet also crystalline transparency" (Peter Niklas Wilson). Oxley uses these sounds to complement the playing of Cecil Taylor in such a sensitive manner that he has been one of Taylor's preferred drummers since the late eighties.

Günter "Baby" Sommer is the outstanding drummer in European post–free jazz. He is a master of magical intensity and enormous drive with a captivating sense of breaks and rests accompanied by an almost "Prussian sense of order," that is time and again dialectically disrupted. Sommer is the most melodic drummer in the sphere of freely improvised music. He has extended his drum set by adding kettle drums, tubular bells, and other percussion instruments, producing such clear and finely meshed sounds that you sometimes forget it's a drummer playing here.

In the former Soviet Union, Vladimir Tarasov developed an individual free style independent of the European free-jazz tradition. He also plays in symphony orchestras and was a member of the Ganelin Trio until its dissolution in 1987. His playing is particularly percussive. Tarasov links the pulse techniques of free jazz with traditional swinging phrases, marches, circus music, and Lithuanian folk music, ironically disrupting all of those elements in a multitude of ways.

Finally, we must mention the Japanese free drummers Masahiko Togashi, Shota Koyama, and Takeo Moriyama. Togashi plays "spiritual" percussion music in which can be found elements from the Japanese musical and spiritual tradition, including Zen. There is hardly another free-improvising percussionist today in whose music "space"—the emptiness between the beats—has such significance and is filled with so much content. Moriyama and Koyama are very wild and intense players, with a kind of intensity that is fed not only from black music but also from traditional Japanese sources.

An important step beyond all these drummers—Americans, Europeans, and Japanese—was taken around the turn of the seventies by Ronald Shannon Jackson. One of the musicians at the 1980 Moers Festival in Germany said, "In a sense, Ronald is doing what Elvin Jones did in the early seventies. As Elvin emancipated the bop rhythms then, so Ronald Jackson is emancipating the rock and funk rhythms today." Jackson is the main free-funk drummer—not only because of his new, impressive polyrhythms but also because he has managed to transmit these polyrhythms to his compositions and to the music of his group, Decoding Society.

What is new about free funk is first of all, as is usually the case in jazz, the rhythm. This links the physical directness and power of jazz-rock with the independence and flexibility of free playing. Motor drive plus pulse: no one has driven that formula to such shattering intensity in climaxes of rhythmic energy as Ronald Shannon Jackson. He first became known through playing with Albert Ayler, Ornette Coleman, and Cecil Taylor. At the start of the eighties he made some trailblazing recordings with his Decoding Society, particularly influenced by Coleman's harmolodic music, but later never regained the high level of that time. In the Last Exit band he played a heavy-metal-oriented free jazz.

Other important free-funk drummers include Calvin Weston and Cornell Rochester, both of whom have played with guitarist James "Blood" Ulmer. Closely related to the free-funk drummers are those drummers who fuse elements of funk, soul, and hip-hop with the technical challenge of playing in abstract meters. Sean Rickman, Mark Johnson, Dafnis Prieto, Paul Samuels, Gene Lake, Gene Jackson, and Rodney Green are the most important drummers in M-Base music—all masters of delicate rhythmic changes and complex metrical layering.

With his mixture of funk and free forms, Sean Rickman is one of the most impressive drummers of the early twenty-first century. He plays the drum set as if it were a band. He has applied the results of his study of African, Indian, Arab, and Cuban musical cultures to achieve a rare level of mastery in the superposition and manipulation of abstract meters. His drum figures play an active part in shaping the songs of Steve Coleman's group Five Elements, instead of "merely" carrying and intensifying the groove. Rickman has practiced this "compositional drumming" with a boisterous spirit of interaction in the fusion band Dapp Theory and in his own group, combining sharp, hard, clear intensity with a friendly lightness.

Rickman's successor in Coleman's band was Dafnis Prieto, who has augmented the M-Base drumming approach with techniques from conga playing and the Afro-Cuban scene (Prieto is from Cuba). Gene Jackson, Gene Lake, and Rodney Green have all worked in the group of alto and soprano saxophonist Greg Osby.

Nasheet Waits is a master of controlled freedom whose drumming has been compared with a "force of nature." In Jason Moran's group Bandwagon, or in the trio led by Fred Hersch, he includes a healthy portion of rhythmic unpredictability in his virile, high-frequency poly-rhythms. The son of percussionist Freddie Waits, he has a crisp snare drum sound and a particularly well-developed ability to resolve freely flowing rhythms within fixed formal structures, with an admirable open-ness for all kinds of music, from James Brown to Indian tabla playing to hip-hop.

Like free-funk drummers, noise music and no wave percussion-ists similarly extend and update the treasure trove of experience gained in free jazz. David Moss is the most important representative of that direction. He drums something of the aggressiveness of punk and the harshness of avant-garde rock into the differentiated pulsations of free jazz. Moss is a master of the noise collage, one of the most imagina-tive of today's creators of short, abruptly changing sounds, incorporating toms, gongs, cymbals, balloons, toys, vocal effects, and all possible and seemingly impossible generators of sound. This man has so much sound within himself that he only need roll up a piece of paper and music comes into being.

The "hostile" camps of jazz-rock and free music are reconciled in the field of drumming, too, by the players of contemporary mainstream (also the reason why an especially large number of them have been in the limelight of both styles): Billy Hart, Stu Martin, Clifford Jarvis, Al Foster, Idris Muhammad, Adam Nussbaum, Woody Theus, Freddie Waits, Wilbur Campbell, Mickey Roker, Terry Clarke, Frank Butler, Jake Hanna, Jeff Hamilton, Bob Moses, Paul Motian, Joe LaBarbera, Elliot Zigmund, Ronnie Burrage, France's André Ceccarelli, Jon Christensen from Norway, Swiss-born Daniel Humair (who lives in France), Poland's Janusz Stefanski, Austrians Wolfgang Reisinger and

Alex Deutsch, and Germans Thomas Alkier and Wolfgang Haffner, among others.

Billy Hart is an immensely empathetic drummer, one of the most intensive as well as swinging on the scene today, who plays a kind of "sensitized Elvin Jones." Also having their base in Elvin Jones are Eddie Moore, Janusz Stefanski, Woody Theus, and Al Foster. In his swinging, triplet-based cymbal sound, and his bop-conscious, resilient rhythms, Foster cultivates a fat rhythmic momentum. His razor-sharp interventions and his ability to reduce or to compress volume and rhythmic complexity depending on the needs of the improvisational context made Foster (who formerly played with Miles Davis) one of the most sought-after drummers in New York in the eighties and nineties.

Stu Martin (d. 1980) came out of Quincy Jones's band of the early sixties. He commanded a particularly wide musical spectrum, including even Eastern European and Jewish music. Freddie Waits, Horace Arnold, and Wilbur Campbell are members of the Max Roach percussion group mentioned earlier. Mickey Roker was Dizzy Gillespie's favorite drummer in the seventies. Idris Muhammad (who made influential rhythm and blues recordings as a studio drummer under the name Leo Morris) picks up where Ed Blackwell leaves off. He incorporates the Second Line grooves and the crisp funk rhythms of New Orleans into a style that opens the bop tradition up to influences from Africa, the Caribbean, and India. Jake Hanna and Jeff Hamilton are true Swing men, referring back to the music of the great classic Swing tradition. Hamilton's delicate, strongly swinging work with the brushes (wire brushes used instead of sticks, for quieter playing) is legendary. In bands led by Ray Brown and Diana Krall, he became one of the scene's best trio drummers. Bob Moses, in a career that has taken him from the early Gary Burton quartet to his own bands, has distanced himself increasingly from the cymbal-based sound of classic modern jazz. Instead, the compositional element has become more important for him. The magic of his compositions lies beyond technical refinement, and has more to do with their atmospheric qualities—groove, imaginative sound-painting, Moses's sense for strong rhythms and simple melodies, and a particularly blues-conscious approach to "pastel power drumming": combining refinement and sensitive detail with vigorous power.

Daniel Humair is the "most swinging" of all European drummers—a musician who very much enjoys communicating, and whose inventive, springy playing, finding freedom even within formal structures, is also appreciated by American stylists. His expansion and contraction of rhythms in response to his perception of the overall rhythmic state of energy of the music is so concentrated, adventurous, and yet clear, that he achieves a transformation of the role of his instrument—the drums become timekeeper, energy source, and soloist simultaneously. Humair's motto: "Without consciously calculated improvisational risks, there's no musical freedom. And without the breakthrough into musical freedom, there's no real swing."

Coming from Humair, and further developing his approach, in France a series of creative drummers have found their own European colors and rhythms: Christophe Marguet, Erik Echampard, Joel Allouche, Maxime Zampieri, Stéphane Huchard, Patrice Heral, and Tony Rabeson (whose music also reflects his Malagasy roots).

Norway's Jon Christensen is not so much a "straight-ahead" musician as a "painter" in percussion: a Nordic impressionist of rhythm whose unpredictable patterns can lead groups in entirely new directions. His sensitive, spacious playing has helped shape the music of Jan Garbarek, as well as Keith Jarrett's European quintet. Christensen is a master of sensitive, finely meshed "binary" rhythms that, in contrast to the rolling, springy, triplet-based playing of most jazz drummers, is based on units of two notes to the beat.

The Italian drummer Aldo Romano, who lives in Paris, plays in a raw, carefree style. He moves energetically between metrically free and metrically bound playing. He has no fear of going outside the academic boundary lines of jazz. His compositions, for the Sclavis / Texier / Romano Trio or for his own band Palatino, have a recognizably French-Italian flavor, comprising bop influences as well as Mediterranean melodies and folkloric dances, and also including influences from classical music.

Humair, Christensen, and Romano form the triumvirate of European jazz drumming. Their work has been as innovative and influential in the field of time-bound playing as that of Han Bennink and John Stevens in the area of free drumming. The line of younger European jazz drummers coming from these three is discussed below.

Three of the drummers named above have played with Bill Evans, and all are characterized by the sensitivity of Evans's music: Paul Motian, Elliot Zigmund, and Joe LaBarbera. Motian plays rhythms of stimulating, extravagant beauty. He has an incredibly sophisticated way of playing "primitively," with a unique sense of reduction. His explosive but sensitive touch and his highly reactive rhythmic sense contributed to forming the ensemble sound of the Keith Jarrett Quartet. In his own Electric Bebop Band—which included Joe Lovano in the eighties and Kurt Rosenwinkel in the nineties—he plays with a complete sense of adventure and discovery, letting all the sounds around him flow into his rhythms. This is ultimately what improvisation is about: listening and reacting.

No other drummer, however, dominated eighties and nineties jazz so sovereignly and originally as Jack DeJohnette, who influenced many of the previously mentioned players. He is the most complex drummer on the contemporary scene, and has introduced new rhythms to jazz in countless recordings with other musicians and with his own group, Special Edition. DeJohnette has both: Tony Williams's filigrain and Elvin Jones's vitality.

He calls his music multidirectional and open to an imposing range of styles, and that characterizes his impressive range of playing: jazz-rock, reggae, free jazz, neobop, aestheticism, blues, etc.

Jack DeJohnette is a dialogic player. Even when he plays unaccompanied solos, he creates a constant dialogue between the parts of the drum set: he thinks orchestrally.

Jack DeJohnette's drum playing possesses an intoxicating abundance of colors and rhythmic movements. One of the most fascinating moments in jazz is provided by the experience of how DeJohnette dissolves the beat into complex "four-voiced" polyphonic patterns, allowing the rhythmic focus to move around the entire arsenal of his drum set as a motive, in the same way as the leading voice migrates between instruments in a polyphonic piece. It's revealing that DeJohnette started out as a pianist; he has also appeared on recordings as such.

DeJohnette is also an outstanding writer, but in contrast to most other drummers, his works do not immediately reveal themselves as "drummer's compositions." Indeed, a certain type of very obvious "drummer's writing" has been prevalent in almost all tunes composed by drummers so far—from Sid Catlett and Cozy Cole to Billy Cobham and Alphonse Mouzon.

Jack DeJohnette is the "father" of multistylistic drum playing. From DeJohnette comes (and he is the source of reference for) the new type of percussionist who by now plays, develops, and integrates so many styles—far beyond the degree of versatility and technical competence always demanded of drummers—that he can no longer be assigned to any single category.

The most important among such drummers today are Peter Erskine, Joey Baron, Bill Stewart, Brian Blade, Matt Wilson, Bobby Previte, Billy Kilson, and Ralph Peterson Jr. Erskine, who has made recordings with such groups as Steps Ahead and Bass Desires but also with guitarist John Abercrombie, plays with great clarity, combining power with elegance. His range of rhythmic coordination is especially captivating. Erskine says, "What makes one drummer's beat sound different from another is the space between the notes. It doesn't have to do with technique or sticking, it's just the shape between the notes." Bill Stewart's playing is a powerful celebration of lightness, sensitivity, and elegance. His playing is based on Tony Williams as much as on Ed Blackwell. Stewart has lightning-fast rhythmic reflexes and takes great joy in commenting on the music as it happens, framing the ideas of the soloists and making stimulating contributions to the exchange without cluttering up the musical space. When Stewart plays, he plays the whole song, with a great sense of flow, an excellent touch, and creative "out-of-time" accents. Brian Blade, known from the bands of Joshua Redman and Wayne Shorter, is the most exquisite of contemporary jazz drummers, matching fire with musicality and great intensity with total sensitivity. He raises the classical modern drum vocabulary to a new level by playing with intelligent roughness and a beautiful drum sound, further developing the percussion languages invented by Jo Jones, Max Roach, Tony Williams, and Jack DeJohnette. He combines power and subtlety to produce a unique flow in which, as he says, "spirit and groove" are fused inseparably. Blade is thoroughly schooled in the tradition of intensity of jazz drumming and yet has also incorporated something into his contemporary playing that he learned as a child in gospel church services, accompanying his father's preaching on the drums: the fact that in a group the jubilant sound of the community is stronger than the lamentation of the individual; that the "we" comes before the "I." His most important principle: "Serve the community first."

Brian Blade is the jazz drummer who today makes the most complete use of the total dynamic range of the drums—from explosions to dramatic, sensitive whispering. He says:

> I love harmonies. And usually harmonies give me rhythmic ideas, more than the other way around. That sounds strange. People always think that a drummer's interested above all in beats. And then comes the harmonic sound. But for me it works the other way. Every drummer should know that: even a drummer in the wildest underground rock band is partly responsible for the harmonic movement.

Billy Kilson plays in the bands of Dave Holland with an exciting, unrestrained energy, tuning his drums like a rhythm 'n' blues drummer, and playing rhythms of extraordinary flexibility and ecstatic density.

Marvin "Smitty" Smith has worked with David Murray, Wynton Marsalis, Sting, Sonny Rollins, Steve Coleman, Hank Jones, and Art Farmer, and was a member of Dave Holland's celebrated quintet. He has a particularly warm, deep, and dark sound, which partly results from his playing the bass drum with two foot pedals instead of one. Matt Wilson swings with great determination and a light, fine sense of irony. Like Joey Baron, he is one of the few contemporary drummers to have developed a personal approach to playing with brushes. Similar to Matt Wilson, Thomas Crane is a hard-swinging drummer adept at creating moments of surprise in the context of a "freer" style. Ralph Peterson Jr. has updated the vital Art Blakey tradition in his own Fo'Tet and with Michael Brecker. Peterson's playing is interactive, dynamic, and loud—maybe sometimes a little too loud. He is an aggressive, forward-driving drummer who sovereignly drums away the schism between the "hostile" trends of neobop and the post–avant-garde as if there had never been a breach.

The drummers of New York's downtown scene play across stylistic boundaries with the greatest abandon. They rhythmically embody the downtown propensity for juggling different styles in an extremely colorful, original manner, often showing a preference for hairpin stylistic turns, collage elements, and quick jumps between starkly contrasting genres. Joey Baron is the most important drummer of this group, but others in this area, like Jim Black, Bobby Previte, Kenny Wollesen, Michael Sarin, Tom Rainey, Ben Perowsky, Satoko Takeishi, John Hollenbeck, and Ben Wittman, are Baron's equal in richness of expression.

Joey Baron has been called the "Gene Krupa of the downtown scene." He's played swinging mainstream jazz with Carmen McRae and Dizzy Gillespie, as well as avant-garde jazz with Tim Byrne and John Zorn (Baron is probably Zorn's favorite drummer). Baron's playing can ignite an entire band. He is a humorous, loud, interactive player, a "kick-ass" player in the argot of musicians, due to his aggressive, refreshingly "juicy" style, loose and relaxed. You can hear his Southern roots in his earthy drumming, filled with a soulfulness that gives it emotional immediacy.

The drummer Jim Black, originally from Seattle, has a similar stylistic openness. He provided the rhythmic heartbeat in Dave Douglas's Tiny Bell Trio, as well as in Tim Berne's band Bloodcount. Black invents sharp rhythms that are capable of going anywhere stylistically—from grunge rock to avant-garde jazz, from swinging big-band drumming to Balkan grooves, from bop to rock, and so on. He has a particularly refined sense for mixing the sound of the classical drum set with other percussion instruments and with laptop electronics.

Bobby Previte's playing is characterized by taste, wit, and speed. He's an eclectic drummer who never wears the diversity of his influences on his sleeve, but rather bundles them into atmospherically dense, mood-rich compositions, in which he incorporates elements of minimalism, rock, and Afrobeat to form an organic development within circular patterns.

Tom Rainey is a classic "musicians' musician"—not so well known to the public, but highly rated among musicians. His attractive rhythms show a well-developed ability to confound expectations. He's capable of playing across metric patterns and free structures without losing his sense of form.

Ben Perowsky is a multistylist with perfect time. He has played in the jazz fusion band Lost Tribe, and with Don Byron. Kenny Wollesen has a remarkable feeling for the essential—he can hold an ensemble together with just a few strokes (an ability that, he emphasizes, he learned from the "old school"). Wollesen combines great melodic sensibility with a tendency toward very drastic patterns.

Compared with the flamboyant colorfulness of such postmodern drummers, the representatives of neoclassicism seem more concerned with stylistic rectitude, which has led some people to charge them with "purism." In fact, however, neoclassicist drummers—Jeff "Tain" Watts, Herlin Riley, Kenny Washington, Carl Allen, Tony Reedus, Victor Lewis, Leon Parker, Cindy Blackman, Lewis Nash, Adonis Rose, Ali Jackson, Damion

Reed, Joe Farnsworth, Eric McPherson, Jaz Sawyer, Yoron Israel, Sylvia Cuenca, Jason Marsalis, T. S. Monk, Keith Copeland, Winard Harper, and England's Mark Mondesir—play eclectic rhythms, just like other contemporary drummers, except that neoclassicists constantly refer back to bop-oriented rhythms. They reflect and modernize all the rhythms that have existed from Max Roach and Art Blakey by way of Philly Joe Jones to the refinements of Elvin Jones and Tony Williams. Nevertheless, their playing is fundamentally different from that of bebop drummers. They often drum more powerfully, explosively, and communicatively, out of the experience of a generation that has not only experienced bop but also free jazz, rock, and jazz-rock. The drums accordingly intervene, moving from an accompanying role to near equality with the soloists.

Jeff "Tain" Watts, who made his name with Wynton Marsalis's band, is such a drummer, "filling" bebop with controlled freedom and the entire spectrum of music between the new jazz and jazz-rock. He is one of the most experienced and most respected drummers in contemporary jazz. "Tain" plays like a more radicalized, more intense Elvin Jones, charging Jones's rhythmic concept with Afro-Cuban elements and rock influences. Watts is a powerhouse of rhythms—his aggressive drum style sometimes sounds like two drummers. His "clattering" playing was once compared to a drum set "falling down a flight of stairs." But at the same time, Watts's playing proceeds from an outstanding consciousness of form. With his flexible polyrhythms, he has found new ways of risk-taking playing with complex meters and structures.

In 1988 Herlin Riley took over from Watts as the drummer in Wynton Marsalis's group. More than any other musician, Riley played an important part in Marsalis's turn toward older forms of jazz. Riley was particularly important in enriching neoclassic jazz in the nineties with rhythms from the New Orleans tradition. Riley turned classical modern jazz drumming formally on its head by redefining its relationship to the Second Line rhythms of New Orleans. This is because in New Orleans jazz, the drumming comes "from the bottom up"—with a lot of activity on the bass drum and snare drum, whereas in bebop the drummer plays more "from the top down," emphasizing cymbal sounds. Riley is the most impressive contemporary drummer in a line of jazz drummers who, building on the accomplishments of Baby Dodds and Ed Blackwell, have preserved and refined the rhythmic legacy of New Orleans: Adonis Rose, Idris Muhammad, Jason Marsalis, and Ali Jackson (who, although he comes from Detroit, can play New Orleans grooves better than any other drummer not a native of the Crescent City).

Victor Lewis and Tony Reedus came from the central groups in eighties neobop around trumpeter Woody Shaw and saxophonist Dexter Gordon. Despite his virtuosity, Joe Farnsworth is a dynamically grooving accompanist. Leon Parker, from the Jacky Terrasson Trio, has developed a uniquely full and firm approach to the ride cymbal. He's a master of a suspenseful, less-is-more expressiveness, but in the midnineties decided to abandon drum set playing in favor of other percussion instruments, where he has developed a convincing way of playing post-Afrobeats. Cindy Blackman, who played with Wallace Roney, follows from Tony Williams's power drumming just as Kenny Washington does from the melodic clarity of Max Roach. Washington is a kind of walking encyclopedia of classic modern drumming. With his clean cymbal sound and his rumbling, wide-open beat, he is an expert stylist of postbop. Cindy Blackman, who has also played in the rock band of Lenny Kravitz, is, besides Terri Lyne Carrington, the most successful female jazz drummer in the new mainstream jazz. Many drummers create drama in their music by at first holding back and then, in a final chorus, playing soloistically and in an overpowering fashion against ostinato figures. In contrast, Cindy Blackman creates unpredictable curves of musical energy. Her volcanic playing is more responsive to the immediate musical surroundings provided by her fellow players than to rigid formulas and patterns.

Postbop, straight-ahead drummers are often accused of simply copying the past without ideas of their own—and, in fact, it's probable that in no other area has there been such a shocking lack of ideas and willingness to take risks as at the height of the neo–hard-bop "young lions" movement. On the other hand, the accusation of imitation leveled against straight-ahead players by critics has often been based in a lack of discernment on the part of the critics. The creative neoclassical players—and there were many of them—played fundamentally different rhythms than the drummers of classic modern jazz, even though these younger players came from bop and played in postbop idioms. The different relationship to rhythm was shown in their various influences. Thus, just as the drummers of seventies neobop, such as Victor Lewis and Tony Reedus, belong for example to a generation that had grown up with Motown and James Brown, the straight-ahead drummers of the nineties grew up with hiphop and rap—influences that can be heard in their playing. Even when playing in swinging postbop styles, the "purest" neo–hard bop, something of the energy and the vibration of the different cultural environment is audible. This simply means that the drummers of contemporary straight-ahead jazz reflect the social and cultural conditions of their time, just as the pioneers of bop and postbop did in their time.

This is nicely illustrated by two drummers who began within the relatively narrow circle of neo–hard bop and later developed in other stylistic directions: Clarence Penn and Eric Harland. Both these musicians have opened up the triplet-based swinging drumming style of postbop to other stylistic influences. Penn came to jazz from orchestral percussion, and has played with, among others, Betty Carter and Dave Douglas. He has a big sound and a wonderful sense of elegance, simplicity, and spareness, seeming to caress the drum set more than he hits it. Nonetheless, he produces a unique "pushing" energy. Eric Harland also plays with a fine sense of style and complexity. He has worked with Charles Lloyd and with Andrew Hill, and his swinging playing reflects free elements as much as it does influences from drum 'n' bass, soul, and hip-hop.

The extent to which the role of the drummer has evolved can also be seen in the great assuredness with which more and more contemporary drummers act as band leaders. Many of these drummer/leaders are distinguished in that they are not only excellent rhythmicists, but are also often remarkable composers. These include Victor Lewis, Matt Wilson, Cindy Blackman, Ralph Peterson Jr., Bobby Previte, Terri Lyne Carrington, Aldo Romano, Wolfgang Haffner, and Bill Bruford. Victor Lewis's words may be taken as representative: "Most people think that when drummers compose . . . they hum into a cassette or something and then let somebody transcribe it. I want people to know that I do my writing at the keyboard just like most other composers."

A drummer who does not fit into any of the categories named above is the Spanish (or Catalan, as he would insist) musician Jorge Rossy. His playing is very "un-percussion-like." He's a robust, space-conscious swinger who gives the soloist room to breathe. In the Brad Mehldau Trio, he wonderfully surrounds the pianist's lines with a great deal of space.

Drummers in Scandinavia have developed a similarly plastic, spacious approach, and a variant of Nordic drumming all their own. The most important of these, in whose footsteps all the others more or less follow, is Norway's Jon Christensen, already mentioned above.

Audun Kleive, also from Norway, continues where Christensen leaves off. Kleive, who has played with Terje Rypdal and Marilyn Mazur, is an expert in the reduction of the drum set to a few components. He has intensively combined Christensen's approach with jazz-rock grooves, creating enormous internal rhythmic tension.

Sweden's Magnus Öström has been part of the E.S.T. Trio, led by pianist Esbjörn Svensson, for more than ten years. Öström, as well as Norway's Rune Arnesen, has integrated elements of drum 'n' bass and techno into contemporary jazz drumming in a particularly sensitive manner.

Other important European jazz drummers of the eighties and nineties include Italy's Roberto Gatto (a swinger par excellence), Ettore Fioravanti (with a particularly "singing" style), and Tiziano Tononi (whose "Mediterranean AACM rhythm" is inimitable); Hungary's Elemar Balasz; England's Martin France, Steve Arguelles, and Steve Noble; France's Patrice Heral; Switzerland's Lucas Niggli; and the Germans Jochen Rückert and John Schröder.

Many of these drummers are notable in that, compared to the aggressive, vital playing of their American counterparts (who are more interested in constantly refining and perfecting their time playing), they play more spaciously and atmospherically, with more focus on textures and colors. For example, France's Patrice Heral, who has played with Markus Stockhausen and with Dhafer Youssef, is an expert in the refined, virtuosic treatment of the drum set with a large number of percussion instruments. In addition to conventional playing, he has also applied the entire expressive spectrum of hand percussion to the drum set by using all the parts of his hands in his strikingly virtuosic playing. Jo Jones in the Swing era, Connie Kaye in the Modern Jazz Quartet, Han Bennink in free jazz, and Joey Baron in New York downtown jazz had all already incorporated hand percussion into jazz drumming, but Patrice Heral is the first to create the feeling that this approach has become an art in itself.

Lucas Niggli is an enthusiastic collaborator and a sensitive high-frequency player whose transparent, precise playing reflects the influence of his mentor Pierre Favre. Having grown up in the "anything goes" atmosphere of the eighties, Niggli has played rock and jazz, new music and madrigals, big-band charts and avant-garde rock. But his playing is not about the fusing of different stylistic elements. Instead, he focuses stylistic diversity like a photographer who deliberately "zooms in" on individual elements and rhythms, leaving other elements and rhythms "out of focus" in the background. Niggli says, "Anyone can channel-surf—zooming in is an art."

Steve Argüelles, influenced equally by Tony Oxley and by Elvin Jones, is also a multistylistic European master. He's developed a personal approach to drumming that combines influences from world music and pop music with tonal approaches to playing and free jazz. Arguelles's strength is his strong rhythmic and melodic feeling. "Variation is what interests me," he says. "If it's strictly rhythmic and modal, or strictly colors, I get bored."

The drums are the key to a jazz group. John Scofield says, "A band is only as good as the drummer. I feel like you can't have a band unless you have a great drummer." For this reason, drummers, perhaps more than other jazz instrumentalists, find themselves in a delicate position of responsibility. "The drummer has to be a balancing act," says Jack DeJohnette. "The drummer also has to be able to motivate, keep it interesting and inspire the players. If the drummer's not setting some motion you can build from, then it can destroy the whole thing."

It's no wonder that the American drummer Keith Copeland decided to become a drummer after hearing recordings of Art Blakey. These records led him to conclude that "the drums basically control everything that's happening in the rest of the group."

The fact that, in the course of jazz history, the capacity of drummers to inspire and to motivate has continuously increased is not just the result of a permanent process of rhythmic refinement and stylistic development—which is in itself so fascinating that a jazz history could be written from the perspective of the drums—but rather is also connected with the special multicultural situation of the instrument. "The drum set is an invention of African Americans," says Guillermo E. Brown. "Additionally, it's an amalgamation that reflects our own American situation. The bass and snare, from Europe. The toms from Africa. Cymbals from Turkey and Asia. . . . "

It is therefore not too surprising that the drummers of world jazz, and later of other styles as well, found it particularly easy to incorporate into contemporary jazz drumming elements of their own cultural background and experience. Such musicians include, among others, France's Cyril Atef, Brazil's Duduka da Fonseca (with his flowing, light brushes playing in the samba genre) and Paolo Braga (outstanding in the fusion of bop and samba elements), Ivory Coast's Paco Sery (who, in Joe Zawinul's Syndicate, played a great mixture of funk and Afrobeat), Cameroon's Brice Wassy, and America's Scott Amandelo.

As impressive as the results were of the "Cubop" (Cuban music meets bebop) of the forties, and of the subsequent Latin-jazz styles, at the beginning of the encounter between jazz and Cuban music, jazz drummers and Afro-Cuban or Afro–Puerto Rican percussionists felt a strange misalignment of their rhythms with one another. The swinging, triplet-based jazz beat and the binary clave rhythms of Latin music seemed to be incompatible with each other past a certain point. At first, Latin-jazz drummers solved this problem by favoring one rhythmic approach over the other, usually by providing an underlying clave beat and then layering triplet-based swinging jazz improvisations over it. In contrast, the new drummers of contemporary Latin jazz close the gap through an equal mastery of both approaches—the ternary bop rhythm and the binary Afro-Cuban or Puerto Rican clave rhythm. Drummers in this category include Steve Berrios (an American of Puerto Rican descent), Horacio "El Negro" Hernandez, and Adam Cruz, as well as Cubans E. J. Rodriguez, Ignacia Berroa, and Ramses Rodriguez Baralt. Berroa has, for example with Gonzalo Rubalcaba, transferred Cuban percussion rhythms to the jazz drum set in a particularly exciting fashion.

It is important to understand that this encounter of classic modern jazz rhythms with folk elements is not a simple addition of jazz to world music or vice versa; rather, the mutual interpenetration of the various elements creates a qualitatively new approach to playing percussion.

One drummer who provides a brilliant illustration of this, and who has a comprehensive mastery of all these rhythmic tendencies—4/4 jazz swinging as well as the entire spectrum of Latin and jazz-rock approaches—is Antonio Sanchez, a Mexican musician who became known through his playing with Pat Metheny. He combines the Jack DeJohnette approach with complex Cuban and Brazilian rhythms, and has developed an outstanding sense of dynamics in his fast, finely woven interplay between the snare and the hi-hat.

It is strange how the development of the drum has taken place in pairs, from the beginning until today. We discussed how Jo Jones came up with results in the thirties in Count Basie's band that were quite similar to those reached independently by Dave Tough with Tommy Dorsey. Among the bop drummers, there is on the one hand "wild" Art Blakey and on the other intellectual Max Roach. During the sixties, Elvin Jones stood in opposition to Tony Williams. Or among the free drummers: "racing" Sunny Murray here and complex Andrew Cyrille there. Or in Europe: dynamic Han Bennink and sensitive Pierre Favre. Similarly poised in opposition among the drummers of the eighties are Billy Cobham (or, if you wish, Ronald Shannon Jackson) and Jack DeJohnette, or, today, the heavy, "hard" style of Jeff "Tain" Watts and the refined, transparent playing of Bill Stewart. In fact, this polarity can be found right from the beginning of drum development, even in New Orleans: "wild" Baby Dodds on the one hand and Tony Spargo, who incorporated European elements into the music of the Original Dixieland Jazz Band, on the other. ("European elements" back then, however, meant marching band and circus music.)

The Percussion Instruments (Cuban, Salsa, Brazilian, African, Indian, Balinese)

Percussion instruments used to be side instruments for drummers. However, in the course of the sixties, the store of percussion instruments became so immense that a new type of musician, the percussion player, evolved. The percussionist must be distinguished from the drummer, even though there are countless drummers who are *also* percussionists, and vice versa.

Initially, most of the percussion instruments came from Latin America: claves, *chocallo* (also referred to as shaker), guiro (also named gourd or, in Brazil, *reco reco*), *cabaza*, maracas, *quijada*, *cencerro* (or more simply, cowbells), *cuica*, bongos, conga, timbales, *pandeiro*, and so on. Then other instruments were added, from India, Tibet, China, Japan, Bali, and Africa (where most of the Latin American percussions have their roots anyway). Airto, the renowned Brazilian percussionist, spent years before his move to the United States traveling through Brazil—through the Amazon jungle, the dry Northeast, and the Matto Grosso prairie—where he collected and studied about 120 different instruments.

The father of all percussionists relevant to the modern jazz scene is Chano Pozo from Cuba (his complete name was Luciano Pozo y Gonzales). Unlike many other conga players of that time, he was not primarily "just" an accompanist, but was also an exciting soloist and composer who made fundamental contributions to the formation of New York jazz in the forties. He infused Cuban melodies and rhythms into Dizzy Gillespie's big band of 1947–48 and became the great catalyst for so-called Cubop. The leading figure of this music, however, is Dizzy Gillespie, the only jazz improviser of his generation who could improvise as comfortably on Latin rhythms as on jazz rhythms—often favoring the former, which he considered less "monotonous." (Chano and other Cuban percussionists often emphasized the upbeat of the fourth beat of the bar, or the "and of four," so that many listeners became unsure of where the "one" fell.) Although Chano Pozo could not read music, he composed many of the classics of Cubop, including substantial parts of the masterpiece "Manteca" with Dizzy Gillespie, by singing the parts out loud to Dizzy.

Some of the tunes the Gillespie band recorded with Chano Pozo— "Cubana Be-Cubana Bop," for instance, or "Woody 'n You," "Afro Cubano Suite," or "Algo Bueno"—are bacchanals of rhythmic differentiation. "You could never predict what the guy was going to do next," said arranger Mario Bauzá. "Chano had millions of ideas. He never played the same thing on conga like all conga players around. He always found something to fit in different."

Chano Pozo was an impulsive personality, always prepared to defend his honor. Friends said he always carried five or six knives with him. His exaggerated machismo and turbulent, conflicted life landed him repeatedly in dangerous situations. He spent his money on clothes and jewelry, took taxis for trips of three blocks, hid pesos in his shoes, and changed his expensive suits several times a day. Chano Pozo died in a stabbing in 1948 in East Harlem's Rio Café. There have been rumors that he was slain because he had made public—and thus desecrated—the secret rhythms of the Nigerian Abaquwa cult, to which he had belonged in Cuba. But this is a myth: in fact he was killed in a dispute with a drug dealer. The rhythmic power of this mysterious Cuban conga player is illuminated by the fact that Gillespie, though he often employed several Latin American percussionists at one time, never again was able to achieve the effects he had reached with Chano Pozo alone.

Similar to how all jazz alto saxophonists relate to and recall Charlie Parker, all conga players in Latin music are related to Chano Pozo. Pozo showed the way: he transformed the conga from an accompanying instrument into a full-fledged solo instrument. Almost all later developments in conga playing are based in his work.

The Cuban wave reached its first high point between the late forties and the midfifties. Not only did Dizzy Gillespie play Cuban rhythms again and again, but so did the favorite white big band, Stan Kenton's: in 1947, for example, with their successful version of "The Peanut Vendor," in "Chorale for Brass, Piano, and Bongo," or in the "Fugue for Rhythm Section" with bongo player Jack Costanzo. Later, Kenton used Carlos Vidal on conga, Machito on maracas, and others in pieces like "Machito," "Mambo in F," "Cuban Carnival," and "Cuban Episode."

In 1956, Kenton premiered a grand suite devoted to Latin (and above all Cuban) music: "Cuban Fire," written by Johnny Richards and featuring six Latin percussionists.

The Latin bands enjoying the greatest recognition in the jazz world of the fifties were, in New York, the orchestra of Machito (alias Frank Grillo) with the inspired and jazz-experienced arranger and trumpeter Mario Bauzá (who had also done arrangements for Chick Webb's and Cab Calloway's bands and gave Dizzy Gillespie key tips for the establishment of Latin jazz) and that of timbales player and arranger Tito Puente; and on the West Coast, the band of Perez Prado, with Kenton-like brass effects and a new kind of rhythm, the mambo—the first Latin dance to originate in the States (influenced by Mexican rhythms). "Rumba with jitterbug" is how *Down Beat* defined the mambo, which was quite a hit in the midfifties.

Also influenced by Stan Kenton, Tito Puente developed his own orchestral Latin jazz—brass-heavy and with sharp percussion accents, crowned with his exciting timbale solos. He was known as the King of Mambo and said, "I love excitement."

Machito frequently played and recorded with jazz musicians—first with Charlie Parker (starting in 1948) and later with Brew Moore, Zoot Sims, Stan Getz, Howard McGhee, Herbie Mann, and others. Machito's alliance with Parker was instigated by jazz impresario Norman Granz, mainly because Cubop was a widespread fashion back then. Parker was not nearly as accomplished on Cuban rhythms as Gillespie. Above all, it was Machito who nurtured the realization in the jazz world that it is wrong simply to add a Latin percussion player to a conventional jazz rhythm section—as was usually the case then (and often later). Instead, complete Cuban rhythm sections must be formed where the Latin percussionists are conversant with jazz and the jazz drummers with Latin American music. Such a group usually would employ several Latin percussion players, and the bassist would have to command the bass lines of Latin music (*tumbao* playing, described in the section on the bass) with as much ease as those lines he normally would play.

Among the significant Cuban percussionists of those years were conga players Carlos Vidal, Candido, Carlos "Patato" Valdes, and Sabu Martinez, and bongo player Willie Rodriguez. They made recordings with many jazzmen: Vidal with Stan Kenton, for instance; Candido with Gillespie (playing a relaxed style called walking conga); Sabu with Gillespie and Art Blakey.

Carlos "Patato" Valdes, who died in 2007, is the great melodist of conga playing, with very effective use of tuning of the Latin percussion (to the notes E, G, and C). Although he was always somewhat in Chano Pozo's shadow, he created a strongly swinging style with his low-tuned drums. In the fifties, his music was not so much Latin jazz as a kind of "jazz Latin."

On the West Coast, the vibraphonist and bongo player Cal Tjader (d. 1982) had worked since 1954 on an intelligent and spirited combination of jazz with Latin music, often revealing Mexican elements. His tasteful synthesis of cool jazz elements with Latin rhythms found a large audience beyond jazz fans. Tjader came from the George Shearing Quintet of 1949. Jazz critics have written a lot about the peculiar sound of this group, but the Shearing Quintet was also important in terms of rhythm, as a jumping-off point for a number of Latin percussionists who later became known through their own recordings: timbales player Willie Bobo, conga player Mongo Santamaria, and conga and bongo player Armando Peraza.

During the late fifties, Cuban music became considerably less alluring. A second wave came in the seventies in the shape of salsa, which since then has been sustained not only by Cuban musicians but also by players from Puerto Rico and other Latin American countries. Its centers are where most of these ethnic groups are concentrated in the United States: New York and Miami. *Salsa* means "sauce" and has been defined as "Cuban plus jazz," with elements of blues and rock. Fania Records has been quite successful in bringing together salsa and jazz musicians for studio dates and also for large concerts, as in New York's Yankee Stadium and in Madison Square Garden. Among the best-known "Fania All Stars" are Mongo Santamaria, Ray Barretto, Larry Harlow, Willie Colon, and the musical director of Fania Records, Johnny Pacheco. He patterned the All Stars primarily on the Cuban *conjuntos* (medium-sized ensembles composed of percussionists and horn players). Pianist and bandleader Eddie Palmieri (who was inspired first by Bud Powell, later by McCoy Tyner) created a salsa concerto style with pieces in larger forms, earning him the title of a "Duke Ellington of salsa." His wild piano introductions are legendary, with a rhapsodic tinge that becomes an exciting, forceful energy when Palmieri stokes his Latin jazz orchestra with glowing vamps (ostinato figures in the clave rhythm). In contrast to many other Latin bands that play more standardly, Palmieri's bands represent a modern, updated style that has attracted top jazz soloists like trumpeter Brian Lynch or alto saxophonist David Sanborn.

Ray Mantilla, a New Yorker with Peruvian–Puerto Rican roots, played with Art Blakey's Jazz Messengers and on Max Roach's classic *Freedom Now!* He was the first North American *conguero* to set foot on Cuban soil after the Cuban Revolution, in 1977 with Dizzy Gillespie's band. Mantilla's style is friendly and mild, emphasizing the drum's character as an accompanying instrument. According to him, the credo of the Latin percussionist is: "The main thing is to keep the music fresh."

From the sixties, when he appeared on the scene, into the eighties, conga player Mongo Santamaria (d. 2003) was the most influential Cuba-style percussionist for more than thirty years, with a host of recordings in the fields of Cuban as well as jazz and rock music (plus all imaginable mixtures). He wrote the jazz standard "Afro Blue," which has been recorded by such musicians as John Coltrane, Dizzy Gillespie, and Cal Tjader, among others. Santamaria also scored the first real salsa hit in the midsixties with his version of Herbie Hancock's composition "Watermelon Man." Since that time his music has been studied by Latin percussionists (and also by many jazz drummers) as diligently as Chano Pozo's work was studied in the forties and fifties. The great melodic re-laxedness of his playing, his inner peace and simultaneous strong rhyth-mic force have had a significant influence on the contemporary conga scene, for example on Poncho Sanchez (discussed below). Also of great significance is timbalero Willie Bobo, who made records with, among others, Miles Davis, Stan Getz, and Cannonball Adderley.

Two great "traditional" Afro-Cuban percussionists who often came into contact with jazz musicians, for example in Jesús Alemañy's band Cubanismo, are Changuito and Tata Güines. Güines plays with striking simplicity and clarity. Changuito has become legendary for his diversity and interactive flexibility as an accompanist and soloist.

Meanwhile, there is a whole generation of Latin musicians born not in Cuba or Puerto Rico or elsewhere in Latin America, but in New York, mostly in the Barrio district of East Harlem. Ray Barretto, Ray Mantilla, Johnny Pacheco, and Eddie Palmieri are among them. As can be eas-ily understood, these musicians have an additional interest in North American music, particularly jazz. But the dictum that you have to be a Latino to play outstanding Latin music still seems to hold—with a few exceptions. The first such exception was Cal Tjader, whose heritage is Swedish (certain non-Latin elements can be perceived in the "coolness" of his music).

Birger Sulsbrük from Denmark, African American Bill Summers, and drummer Don Alias were others. Sulsbrük has even managed, as a European, to assimilate Cuban rhythms so completely that he is recog-nized by Latino musicians. Alias is Anglo, but grew up with Cubans; he is not only an excellent jazz drummer but also a brilliant conga player, with a relaxed, calm feel.

Ray Barretto, who died in 2006, was known among musicians as "Mr. Hard Hands"—not just because of his large hands, but also due to his exceptionally hard-hitting playing. During the seventies salsa vogue, he led perhaps the most powerful of the *conjunto* bands, in which he mixed elements of Arsenio Rodriguez's Cuban *son* music with the urban fire of New York styles. In the nineties his group New World Spirit had an even more conscious orientation toward the roots of jazz. He replaced the traditional bongo or timbale players with a drummer, giving Latin jazz a greater harmonic and melodic flexibility. Barretto had probably the greatest knowledge of jazz of all conga players, and was a veteran of the jazz standard repertoire. "I didn't want to sound like other so-called Latin-jazz bands," he said. "They were just about playing bebop heads on a traditional Latin rhythm section. That is just one step removed from dance music. . . . I wanted to get closer to the source of jazz. . . . The Latin flavoring comes from me, but my role as a drummer is first to be an accompanist. . . . A lot of Latin jazz drummers kind of play the way they would play in a Latin band situation and the rhythm tends to dominate the melody and harmony."

Nowadays, there is a vast number of mixtures of Latin American and North American music: "Latin rock," "Latin soul," "rock salsa," in dozens of different combinations. After the mambo, the boogaloo was the second Latin dance to be created in the United States—the latter, however, with English lyrics, not Spanish like the mambo. The boogaloo is a mixture of mambo with rock 'n' roll and, depending on who is playing, with undercurrents of jazz and blues. An especially successful, highly differentiated combination of rhythms from the spheres of rock and Latin music (above all salsa) was created on the West Coast during the early seventies by Carlos Santana, who originally came from Mexico. The rock group Earth, Wind, and Fire is so successful mainly because it includes conga and timbales players, producing a ravishing mixture of soul (or gospel) elements with salsa rhythms. Percussionist Ralph MacDonald (born in Harlem in a family of Trinidad calypso musicians) has become successful with his "Latin fusion," also including aspects of the African tradition.

Three musicians have brought a new quality into Latin music since the early eighties: the New York–based exiled Cuban conguero Daniel Ponce, Puerto Rico's Giovanni Hidalgo, and percussionist, trumpeter, and arranger Jerry Gonzalez. Ponce, a particularly striking and powerful percussionist, is unequalled in the way that he breaks with the self-indulgent and often almost clichéd patterns of the salsa scene. He has played contemporary "Cuban jazz" with altoist Paquito D'Rivera as well as no wave with Bill Laswell and hip-hop with Herbie Hancock, and he was involved in Kip Hanrahan's style-crossing musical encounters.

Hanrahan's projects in the eighties were in fact also a launching pad for many other percussionists including Milton Cardona, Nicky Marrero, Puntilla Orlando Rios, Richie Flores, John Santos, and the most virtuosic and influential of them all, Giovanni Hidalgo from Puerto Rico.

In his work with David Sànchez, Tito Puente, and Eddie Palmieri, Giovanni Hidalgo has masterfully developed Puerto Rican bomba and plena rhythms in a jazz context. More than anyone else, he has founded a new school of conga playing. With his unbelievable technique and extremely fast playing style, he has established an approach to playing Latin music that "seems to come from another planet" (Bobby Sanabrini). Hidalgo plays congas with the complexity and independence of a trap drummer. For example, one of his specialties is to hold a steady beat with the left hand while playing wonderful tablalike figures against it with the right hand. Hidalgo has a wonderfully singing, melodic sound; for all the speed with which he plays, he's always playing songs on the conga. He moves effortlessly between congas and bongos. Poncho Sanchez says, "Sometimes I hear him and I think, damn, I can't even think that fast."

Under Hidalgo's influence, today many congueros tune their congas very high and play very fast. They've transferred rudiments—the fundamental elements of playing drums that all drummers learn, such as rolls and stick patterns—to their percussion instrument. These players continuing Giovanni Hidalgo's lineage include Cuba's Miguel "Anga" Diaz, who has integrated elements of hip-hop into his virtuosic playing, Richie Flores, Luis Conte, Samuel Torres, and Pernell Santurnio, a stylistically very flexible player who emerged from the band of David Sànchez.

Many of these players play rhythms that are so fast and complex that they seem to ignore the basic metrical element of the clave, abstracting and intensifying the beat in a manner similar to what jazz drummers did with the regular jazz beat in the sixties, questioning and expanding it.

Milton Cardona is highly respected not only as a percussionist (he's one of the most successful session conga players in New York), but also as a Yoruba priest of the Santeria religion. During Santeria ceremonies, the *bata* drums are played ritually under the guidance of a great spirit (Aña) that lives in the drum, which has to be consecrated beforehand by introducing a sacred object, symbolizing the Great Spirit, into it. Adherents of the Santeria religion believe that only a drum that is "alive"—that is not played in a mechanical manner—can create and maintain the connection to the Orisha gods.

Jerry Gonzalez already belongs to the second generation of Latino musicians who grew up in New York. The intermingling of "Latin American" and "U.S. American" influences has by now gone so far that neither, as was once the case, dominates at the expense of the other. His Fort Apache Band, which infectiously brings together the great legacy of Afro-Cuban rhythms with the modern jazz tradition's wealth of experience (from Thelonious Monk by way of Bud Powell to Miles Davis), attracted special attention in the eighties.

Bobby Sanabria, an American of Puerto Rican origin, has a similar ability to play jazz and Latin music on the same level. He plays drum set in the swinging tradition of Buddy Rich and Louis Bellson just as convincingly as he plays Afro–Puerto Rican percussion in the clave style. In the nineties, Sanabria led one of the most successful Latin bands in New York.

Other important percussionists on the contemporary scene are the Colombian Samuel Torres (who has worked with Arturo Sandoval and with Chick Corea), the Venezuelan Pibo Marquez, and Roberto Rodriguez, a Cuban who grew up in New York.

Before his breakthrough success with Carlos Santana, Pibo Marquez traveled in Puerto Rico, Ecuador, Colombia, Peru, and Suriname, and incorporated the rhythms of these countries into his conga playing.

Rodriguez has gone the furthest in integrating the experiments of the New York downtown avant-garde into an Afro-Cuban rhythmic context.

Many of the "Nuyoricans," as the descendants of Puerto Rican immigrants living in New York are sometimes called, play with a particular urban energy, forceful and risk-taking. But most of the other young players from Cuba, Puerto Rico, and Venezuela, hugely influenced by contemporary jazz and rock and by the globalized stylistic mixing of world music, also play with an intensity that sets them apart from the "milder" playing of the old school.

On the one hand, this has greatly increased the soloistic and interactive potential of contemporary Latin percussion. On the other hand, however, this gain in soloistic possibilities also creates a problem of musical space. Cuban alto saxophonist Paquito D'Rivera puts it like this: "There's a tendency in Cuban music for the percussion to overpower."

Poncho Sanchez is a conguero who, with a friendly, good-natured style, defies the "technical overkill" of the younger generation. Sanchez came out of the band of Cal Tjader, and has carried on the quiet, melodic style of Mongo Santamaria, combining Afro-Cuban elements with contemporary mainstream jazz. Sanchez is not only an outstanding conga player, but has also been a successful bandleader for more than two decades. His mainstream-conscious Latin playing proves that vital Latin music is possible on the American West Coast as well, outside the salsa center of New York.

Ray Armando, born in Brooklyn, is another master of measured Latin fire. He has worked with Stan Getz and with Gato Barbieri, and in his own group has created an attractive combination of neobop and Afro–Puerto Rican beats.

A specialist in Caribbean rhythms—especially those from Martinique, his father's birthplace—is French-born Mino Cinelu. He has played in Miles Davis's bands and Weather Report. Apart from excelling on the entire arsenal of percussion, he is also a master of impelling, delicate triangle figurations.

Poncho Sanchez has linked Afro-Cuban elements with the contemporary mainstream in some endearing recordings, demonstrating that vital Latin colors are also possible on the American West Coast—far away from the salsa center of New York.

Latin rhythms are almost ubiquitous on the jazz and rock scenes, certainly also because, as we have shown, rock and fusion rhythms are basically latent Latin rhythms. John Storm Roberts (to whose book *The Latin Tinge* we are indebted in this context) quotes salsa bandleader Ray Barretto: "The whole basis of American rhythm . . . changed from the old dotted-note jazz shuffle rhythm to a straightahead straight-eighth approach, which is Latin." Or, to put it more precisely, it is ambivalent, referring to rhythms from North America as much as to those from Latin America.

"Salsa" has become a sort of catch phrase that should be used with caution. No longer does it refer only to Cuban rhythms, but also to the bomba from Puerto Rico, the meringue from Santo Domingo (which was particularly popular on the eighties New York Latin scene), the Songo from the Caribbean, and to other dances and rhythms from the Caribbean and Mexican sphere. In a 1977 *Down Beat* interview, Mongo Santamaria pointed out that some of these rhythms still are "*nañigo*," that is, "coming from secret religious cults."

Let's move on to Brazil. Guitarist Charlie Byrd, who went there in 1961, instigated the interest of jazz musicians in Brazilian music. In 1962, he recorded the album *Jazz Samba* with Stan Getz, including the famous song "Desafinado" written by João Gilberto and Antonio Carlos Jobim. The Grammy Award for this tune was given not to Charlie Byrd but to Stan Getz, because Byrd's guitar solo was cut from the version shortened for single release! As a result, Charlie Byrd's decisive contribution was neglected, and from that point on Getz stood at the center of the bossa nova wave. The Brazilian musicians defined the bossa as "samba plus cool jazz." A first hint of the potential of the combination of Brazilian music with jazz improvisation was given on the West Coast as early as 1953 by the album *Brazilliance*, recorded by a quartet featuring Brazilian-born guitarist Laurindo Almeida and alto saxophonist and flutist Bud Shank (the two are still collaborating in this field).

But the percussive side of Brazilian music was realized on the American scene only beginning in 1967, when Brazilian percussion player Airto Moreira and his wife, singer Flora Purim, moved to New York. Airto was a member of Miles Davis's pathbreaking jazz-rock collective, and played on two tunes on Miles Davis's 1971 album *Live Evil*, causing the in-group of jazz musicians to become aware of Brazilian rhythms. Many leading jazz groups since the seventies have used Brazilian percussionists, among them Chick Corea, McCoy Tyner, Dizzy Gillespie, Weather Report, Pat Metheny, Armando Marçal, and others. The percussionists in these groups were (and still are) Airto, Dom Um Romao, Paulhino da Costa, Guilherme Franco, and one of the most sensitive and flexible players, Naná Vasconcelos. Mainly because of his fusion recordings and the albums he made with Flora Purim, Airto became the real initiator of the percussion wave that hit the scene at the beginning of the seventies. Nana is a real master of the berimbau, an instrument that looks like a bow and arrow and is traditionally used to accompany *capoeira*, an acrobatic combination of dance and martial art originally used for self-defense by Afro-Brazilian slaves. The berimbau has a single metal string that is stretched over a staff and is struck with a wooden rod. The pitch is controlled using a stone to shorten the string, and a gourd pressed against the player's body acts as a resonator and modulator. On this simple instrument, which is commonly played in Bahia, the "New

Orleans of Brazilian music," Nana has discovered a fascinating wealth of expressive possibilities. On one of his records, he makes "body music," employing no instruments but using his entire body as a percussion instrument, producing the most diverse sounds with his hands, fingers, and feet on his chest, stomach, and trunk, as well as on his arms, legs, and shoulders. Like Don Cherry, with whom he played in the band Codona, Naná Vasconcelos is a musician of magical simplicity, touching warmth, and a deliberately "naïve" humanity.

Another interesting percussion instrument from Brazilian music is the *cuica*, an open drum with a pipe inside that is rubbed, mostly with a moist cloth, producing a strange "giggling" sound. More than any other country in Latin America, Brazil has an immense wealth of these different instruments, and a vast number of them—typical of Brazilian music—directly connect the rhythmic and the melodic elements.

The Brazilian rhythms are softer, more supple, more elastic, and less aggressive than the Cuban ones. That's why the Brazilian percussion players have been able to create a perfect integration of jazz and Latin rhythms, so perfect that often the constituent elements—jazz here, Brazilian there—can no longer be singled out. There are also stronger ties between the basic rhythm of Brazilian music, the samba, and that of North American jazz than between jazz and Cuban rhythms. The fascination of combinations of jazz with Cuban music lies in the tension between the two, which creates power, aggressiveness, explosiveness. Combinations of jazz and Brazilian music fascinate through their softness and suppleness and an almost unnoticeable blend of their rhythms, which creates elegance and charm.

Guilherme Franco has demonstrated that in especially masterly fashion. In the seventies as a member of the Coltrane-inspired McCoy Tyner group (and later with Keith Jarrett), he established an enormously flexible unity between jazz and Brazilian rhythms.

In the multistylistic jazz of the nineties, Brazilian percussionists such as *pandeiro* player Marcos Suzano, Caito Marcondes, and above all New York's Cyro Baptista have made inspiring contributions. Suzano revolutionized *pandeiro* playing by expanding the classic approach, coming from samba, with the inclusion of styles from the Afro-Brazilian Candomble religion and a large number of alternative techniques. Caito Marcondes studied classical piano and percussion and has composed music for ballet and theater. His ability to think beyond rhythm, and to use his arsenal of percussion like an orchestra, led Airto Moreira to call him the "Villa-Lobos of percussion."

But the most colorful and virtuosic Brazilian percussionist in contemporary music is Cyro Baptista. He has one foot in the rich musical tradition of his native country and the other in the experimental environment of the New York downtown scene. The role that Airto played in the jazz of the seventies was filled by Baptista in the nineties, as the most in-demand Brazilian percussionist in the American jazz scene. He has worked with Arto Lindsay and John Zorn, but also with Herbie Hancock and Wynton Marsalis.

Beyond the many Brazilian percussion instruments, Baptista has also mastered many other percussion instruments. Thus, in addition to *surdos*, *repeniques*, and *caixas*, he plays countless other instruments from Southeast Asia and Africa. His urge to find new sounds is limitless. "Always I have inside me this volcano. . . . My mission as a musician is to do something completely unexpected," he says. As a result, Baptista has invented many percussion instruments himself. One looks like a for-est of plastic tubes chopped up by a fan. Another is his "Cyrimba," a vibraphone-like structure whose tubes are made of cut-up siphons, and that he plays virtuosically using flip-flops. "I go out and try to be myself," says Baptista, "go back to my basics, and then from there, if someone wants to go a little bananas, then I go out there with them. The percus-sion universe is just so vast!"

In the course of the growing new awareness of their African roots, many American jazz musicians have adopted African percussion instruments, rhythms, techniques, and musicians. The forerunner of this development was Art Blakey, who on his record *Orgy in Rhythm* was already form-ing entire drum orchestras as early as the fifties. Wayne Shorter once said: "Dizzy Gillespie's thing was Afro-Cuban. Then Art Blakey took off the Cuban and said 'Afro' and the whole jazz world understood." A Blakey record released in 1962 is entitled *The African Beat*; on it Blakey plays with, among others, the following musicians, most playing African instruments: Solomon Ilori (African talking drum), Chief Bey (conga, telegraph drum, double gong), Montego Joe (*bambara* drum, double gong, corboro drum, log drum), Garvin Masseaux (chekere, African maracas, conga), James Folami (conga), and Robert Crowder (*bata* drum, conga). Later, Max Roach and others formed similar per-cussion groups.

The first African percussionist to gain recognition in the jazz world, as early as in the beginning of the sixties, was Nigerian Babatunde Olatunji (d. 2003), who also worked with John Coltrane. For his recording dates, he employed musicians like Clark Terry, Yusef Lateef, and George Duvivier. For years, his composition entitled "Uhuru"—the Swahili word for "freedom"—with lyrics by the Nigerian poet Adebayo Faleti, was the "in song" of the New York musicians and music fans, intellectuals, and African American politicians, even in United Nations circles.

At the end of the seventies, Mor Thiam came to the United States from Senegal, where, playing with Freddie Hubbard and Don Pullen and teaching at several universities, he did a great deal to create awareness of and respect for the djembe in North America.

Since the seventies, percussionists like Kahil El'Zabar and Don Moye (from the AACM circle), Mokhtar Samba (with the Orchestre National du Jazz), Kimati Dinizulu (with Danilo Perez), and Mtume (made known by Miles Davis), as well as the aforementioned Ralph McDonald, have referred directly to African rhythms. El'Zabar plays the mbira, the old African "thumb piano," which, in a slightly different version, is also called kalimba and, in other parts of Africa, nsimbi or zanza. With his Ethnic Heritage Ensemble, he has created an impressive synthesis of African music and the sounds of the AACM.

At the beginning of the twenty-first century, the South African percussion group Amampondo presented a successful mixture of Coltrane's modal jazz and Zulu rhythms, in exciting dialogues with the English tenor saxophonist Alan Skidmore. Doudou N'Diaye Rose composed the national anthem of Senegal and, as a virtuoso of the sabar (an instrument played with a stick), is one of the most famous percussionists in Africa. In collaboration with David Murray and Jean-Paul Bourelly, he created a powerful symbiosis of contemporary jazz and age-old Senegalese drumming.

Two highly respected Haitian drummers are Ti-Roro (who died in 1980 and was connected with Haitian voodoo cults) and his somewhat younger colleague, Ti-Marcel. Ti-Roro once said that a person cannot understand Haitian (and that means African) drumming without realizing that drums and drummer are "two different beings." The "loa"— the sacred spirits—do not speak to the drummer, but to the drums. A drum must be "baptized," and for the ceremony it is dressed like a baby. The drums are fed and put to bed at night. They have their own will, which can be quite contrary to that of the drummer—to such an extent that they refuse to "talk" to their player on certain days or under certain circumstances. Ti-Roro: "If you don't consider your drums as 'beings,' you can play technical tricks on them at best, but not meaningful music."

The most satisfying integration of Indian rhythms with jazz was achieved by Indian tabla player Zakir Hussain. The son and student of famous tabla drummer Alla Rahka, Hussain grew up with jazz from the beginning: "I heard Charlie Parker when I was twelve. My father made records with Buddy Rich and Elvin Jones, and he also worked with Yusef Lateef. Thus Indian music and jazz came together for me by themselves." Hussain, who is also a great interpreter of North Indian classical music, made groundbreaking jazz recordings with John Handy and Ali Akbar Khan as well as in John McLaughlin's groups Shakti and Remember Shakti. Hussain lives in San Francisco and has greatly expanded the melodic possibilities of the tabla. No other musician has so virtuosically combined the complex rhythms of classical Indian music with the sounds of rock and jazz, techno, and hip-hop. In a way, he integrated Indian tabla rhythms and sounds as perfectly into jazz as did Cyro Baptista (and others) in terms of Brazilian rhythms.

Among the other Indian percussionists who have worked with jazz musicians are Trilok Gurtu, Badal Roy, V. Selvaganesh (with John McLaughlin and others), Ramesh Shotam (with Rabih Abou-Khalil), and T. A. S. Mani. The latter two musicians play the mridanga, a transverse drum with two heads. Mani is director of the Karnataka College of Percussion, which introduced the great tradition of southern Carnatic Indian music into encounters with saxophonist Charlie Mariano. Badal Roy, in his work with Miles Davis, made a decisive contribution to the incorporation of Indian rhythms into jazz-rock. His tabla playing on Miles's album *On the Corner* (1973) helped Miles create trancelike rhythmic effects that anticipated the later loop-based aesthetic of the DJ and remix scene.

American-born Collin Walcott (who died in a car crash in 1984) is, after Don Cherry, the most outstanding pioneer of world jazz. He achieved celebrity in his performances with Oregon and the Codona Trio (with Cherry and Naná Vasconcelos). As an American musician, he is up to now the only non-Indian player of the tabla (and also sitar) to have gained an international reputation as a stylist. Walcott studied the tabla with Alla Rahka and the sitar with Ravi Shankar. His particular achievement consists in having opened up classical Indian tabla playing to other Asian and also African, Brazilian, and Oriental rhythms and drum techniques. Walcott's exceptional musicality is characterized by the fact that with this (as he put it) "nonidiomatic" way of playing, he was able to assimilate and transmit more of the spirit and greatness of non-Western cultures than other musicians no matter how refined their imitations.

Walcott's successor in Oregon in 1986 was Trilok Gurtu from Bombay, not only an excellent tabla player but also a very good jazz drummer, a combination that would have been unthinkable a few years previously. Of all contemporary tabla players, Trilok Gurtu has the deepest understanding of the jazz conception, and has fused Indian rhythms and Western approaches to playing to a greater extent than anyone else. As a drummer, Gurtu plays a set of his own invention that does not include a bass drum, and is played while kneeling. On this instrument, he has developed a linear style that differs in an original manner from the polyphonic sound of conventional jazz drummers. Gurtu has also made recordings with Don Cherry and Charlie Mariano. He has an unusual talent for sharp contrasts and shadings of dynamics.

In South Korea, the percussion group Samul Nori, founded by drummer Kim Duk Soo, has performed in exciting collaborations with jazz musicians including Wolfgang Puschnig, Ronald Shannon Jackson, and Yosuke Yamashita. In the music of Samul Nori, the archaic and the modern coexist alongside one another. On the one hand, the four master percussionists of this group consider themselves to be guardians of traditional Korean music, while on the other hand they also regard themselves as students of the percussion techniques of other musical cultures. The spectrum of the group's music is correspondingly broad, reaching from the rhythms and dances of Korean peasant folklore to contemporary improvisation, from shamanistic rituals to storms of urban percussion.

This "in-between-ness," this improvisation "between" cultures, is characteristic of many percussionists in the age of migration. When Talvin Singh, an Englishman of Indian descent living in London, traveled to India in the early nineties in order to study classical tabla playing there, he had a surprising experience. "I realized that my Indian teacher would never respect me as an Indian musician. He always saw the Englishman in me. On the other hand, in London I was always taken for an Indian." In his improvisations, Singh transcends such one-dimensional perceptions. Singh, who often electrically amplifies his tabla, is the key figure of a group of English musicians of Asian origin who, based in the East Village, have created a strong, self-aware music. In this "Asian Underground" movement, Singh has discovered particularly radical tabla sounds, mixing Indian rhythms with electrobeats and elements from hip-hop and drum 'n' bass.

In view of the cosmopolitan, world music spirit of today's jazz, it goes without saying that percussion techniques from other musical realms and cultures have also been incorporated into jazz. American Andy Narell and Othello Molineaux brought steel drums from Trinidad into the jazz context. Andy Narell is an unusually flexible improviser, who plays outstanding solos of great melodic richness on his chromatic steel drum. Another pioneer of steel drums in jazz is Trinidad's Othello Molineaux. In 1976 he recorded for the first time on an album of electric bassist Jaco Pastorius. Jaco was so enamored of Molineaux's sound that he hired him many times after that for recordings and made the sound of the steel drum one of the signatures of his band concept. Molineaux adapted John Coltrane's musical ideas to the steel drum. His style is also related to the two other modern steel drum players active in jazz in the eighties and nineties: Frances Haynes (with drummer Beaver Harris) and Junior Gill (with Billy Cobham).

Okay Temiz, born near Istanbul, is a European pioneer of world jazz who has carried the rhythms of his native Turkey into jazz with his group Oriental Wind. Temiz has done more than anyone else to expand the Eastern percussion arsenal with South American colors, using timbales, congas, and above all the instrument that he has most thoroughly mastered: the berimbau, which he plays with electric amplification. In the nineties, his band Magnetic Dances celebrated the music of Turkey's Sinti and Roma peoples. Karl Berger is of the opinion that "Turkish music is world music par excellence, because in it Asian, European, and African sources come together."

Swedish-born Bengt Berger studied *balaphon* techniques in Africa and together with his Bitter Funeral Beer Band made impressive recordings combining jazz with ritual burial music from Ghana. And with Mahama Konaté from Burkina Faso and Aly Keita from Mali, there are at least two African masters of *balaphon* playing who are also active in today's jazz, Konaté with trumpeter Jon Hassell and Keita with Hans Lüdemann. Glen Velez, who first worked with Steve Reich and Paul Winter, is a phenomenon. Just a few years ago it seemed impossible that a percussionist should devote himself exclusively to something so specialized as the tambourine (also known as the frame drum), and yet Velez generates such a wealth of rhythms and sounds from the frame drums he has collected from many cultures (the bodhran from Ireland, the Brazilian *pandeiro*, the Afghan doira, the Arab duff, the North African bendir, and the kanjira from southern India) that he fills entire solo albums with them. Jamey Haddad: "Nobody has the sound and articulation and execution that this guy has."

Other important frame drum players include Italy's Carlo Rizzo, Lebanon's Nabil Khaiat (with Rabih Abou-Khalil), the American Hamid Drake (in a post–AACM free-jazz context), and Brazil's Marcos Susano, also mentioned above.

Rizzo is a wizard of jazz tambourine. He learned to play the instrument from a Sicilian shepherd. Since then, in improvisations with Michael Riessler and Renaud Garcia-Fons he has taken the instrument to the limits of its possibilities. He has invented his own instrument, which he calls a "polytonal tambourine," with snares like a snare drum, a stopping device for the jingles, and a cleverly designed muting system that gives the tambourine expanded melodic and sonic possibilities.

His fame as an interpreter of Persian classical music has not dissuaded Djamchid Chemirani, an Iranian living in France, from emancipating the Persian hand drum called the zarb from its role as an accompanist, making it a fully capable solo instrument, for example in his work with Albert Mangelsdorff and Reto Weber. His son, Keyvan Chemirani, has made especially colorful use of the zarb in contemporary French jazz.

The impact and the "totality" of percussive rhythms from many countries of the earth becomes clear when you realize that Weather Report, the most successful fusion group until its dissolution in 1985, employed one or more percussionists in addition to the drummer during most of that decade, as Joe Zawinul also later did with his band Syndicate. The first percussion player in the group was also the first with Miles Davis and Chick Corea: Airto. After him come Dom Um Romao, Alejandro Acuna, Manolo Badrena, Alyrio Lima, Muruga (not only on Latin American but also on Moroccan and Israeli drums), Jose Rossi from Argentina, Burhan Öçal (from Turkey), and Arto Tuncboyacian (an Armenian born in Turkey)—musicians, in other words, who belong to or have mastered the most diverse musical cultures.

Arto Tuncboyacian grew up near Istanbul. In the early eighties, he emigrated to the United States, where he played with Marc Johnson and with Oregon. He then returned to Eriwan in the early 2000s, where he founded the Armenian Navy Band. Asked why he gave the group this name, since Armenia does not have a coastline, he replied: "We can sail the ship even without water. All we need is love, respect, and truth." Arto Tuncboyacian enriches world jazz with Anatolian and Armenian traditions, but also with a global playing style that he has developed himself. He coaxes brilliant percussive colors even out of simple objects such as a kitchen pot or a bottle. On his congas, which he has combined to form a kind of drum set, he plays incredibly soft, rapid slaps, combining great virtuosity with humility. He describes his jazz as his own brand of "avant-garde folk."

Another characteristic of this totality of percussive rhythms is that a new type of percussionist has evolved. He or she is no longer indebted to one of the different musical cultures, but rather feeds on many of them. Musicians like Mino Cinelu, Kenneth Nash, Sue Evans, Armen Halburian, Ayibe Dieng, French-Algerian musician Karim Ziad, Geoffrey Haynes, Steve Kroon, Vietnam's Le Quan Ninh (a master of free percussion), J. A. Deane, Arto Tuncboyacian, Denmark's Marilyn Mazur, Argentina's Marcio Doctor, France's François Verly, England's Paul Clarvis, Norway's Helge Norbakken, Hungary's Kornel Horvath, Italy's Paolo Vinaccia (an expert in the use of electronic percussion), and Germany's Christoph Haberer and Andreas Weiser belong in this category.

By far the most important of these is Mino Cinelu, the most in-demand percussionist of the contemporary New York jazz scene. He combines a sense of elegance and sensibility, rare among percussionists, with great rhythmic drive. Cinelu worked with Gil Evans and Miles Davis. He has roots in Caribbean music (he is from Martinique), which may also be the source of his musical lightness, but at the same time he plays with a strong sense of flow, a forward-storming expressive force, almost as if he were trying to translate John Coltrane's "sheets of sound" playing into the world of percussion. Cinelu combines all this with a sense of spareness and drama reminiscent of Miles Davis. His inventiveness in the combination of unusual percussion colors has been constant—besides the conga, he plays a steel construction welded together from pieces of scrap, and many other percussion instruments.

Denmark's Marilyn Mazur, who was also a member of Miles Davis's band in the mideighties, plays "poetic percussion." She's an expert in "sound painting," a master of the coloring of rhythms. François Verly has worked with Nguyên Lê and Anouar Brahem, playing with the curiosity of a rhythmic alchemist inspired by many different influences—Indian, Balinese, Arabic, and African—in such a way that it's hard to say what predominates in his music, the hybrid character or the story of universal feelings.

A modern percussionist typically uses an arsenal comprising dozens of different instruments. Each of these instruments has its own tradition and requires its own approach to playing it. Today, it is no longer unusual for percussionists to be familiar with Cuban, Brazilian, Indian, Tibetan, Turkish, and Moroccan instruments, so that in order to play these instruments well, or at least professionally, they have to have a certain degree of knowledge about how they were originally played in the cultures from which they come. This is a sign of how universal jazz has become today.

The level of complexity that the mixing of percussion styles has achieved today is illustrated by Jamey Haddad. An American of Lebanese origin, he has studied South Indian Carnatic percussion, and also plays African, Brazilian, and Middle Eastern instruments. Haddad was a member of the group Oregon, and helped to develop the "Hadgini drum"—a double-bulbed instrument made of ceramic, with an electric pickup, on which various international styles can be played.

Like Haddad, many of the drummers named above represent a kind of pan-global percussion. They have all profited from a circumstance that distinguishes their instrument from others—namely, in the case of percussion instruments the mixing of styles is not felt to be as unnatural as is sometimes the case with other instruments. An approach that might be perceived in the realm of melody and harmony as a "crossover" attempt, or as an incoherent patchwork, often seems natural and unified in the sphere of percussion. From the point of view of percussion, even large cultural differences seem to be easier to bridge.

Because of this, jazz percussionists, including almost all the ones named above, have taken a leading role in overcoming cultural and stylistic barriers in the dialogue with other musicians. Percussionists have often functioned as catalysts in the dialogue between the world's cultures.

It would be a misunderstanding to consider all that has been discussed in this chapter a radically new development. It is new in a gradual sense at best. The tendency for the jazz musician to include and incorporate anything he or she is confronted with has been immanent from the beginning of jazz. Many of the things discovered by jazz in the past few years and decades simply were not known by the early jazz musicians—for example, Indian music. But Latin American music was known from the start. The main reason why New Orleans was the most important city in the development of jazz was because it is not only the southernmost city in the North American cultural sphere but also the northernmost city of the Latin American—Latin and Creole—cultural sphere. Both converged there almost as intensely as in Miami or New York's Barrio today. The "Latin tinge" Jelly Roll Morton spoke of in respect to his "New Orleans Blues" was from the start more than just a tinge. It was an integral part of jazz, because the black rhythms of both North and South America were based on African rhythms—mainly from the same African cultures and, above all, from the Yorubas. It is important in this context that African rhythms and instruments were less tainted, kept purer and more alive, in the Latin sphere (above all, in Cuba, Haiti, and Brazil) than in North America, where they underwent stronger changes and mutations, mainly because the white masters suppressed the black heritage of their slaves. At the risk of oversimplification, it can be said that Latin music is "Africanized European dances and melodies," whereas North American music can be considered "Europeanized African rhythms."

It's no accident that a striking number of Latin musicians, not only Danilo Perez and Jerry Gonzalez, but also Ray Barretto and David Sànchez, have recorded compositions by Thelonious Monk—the musician who was the first to "Africanize" the jazz piano. Monk's angular rhythms fit particularly well with the percussive sounds of Latin music. Jerry Gonzalez says, "Monk's music has a rhythmic logic that fits clave perfectly. Whether he was conscious of it or not, most of his music is in clave. The place where Monk lived, there was a heavy Puerto Rican community."

John Storm Roberts has shown that "the Latin ingredients in early New Orleans jazz are more important than has been realized." He writes that Papa Laine, leader of the first known white jazz band, had a trumpeter at the turn of the century named "Chink" Martin, whose parents were Spanish and Mexican. In interviews, Martin said that Royal Street between Dumaine and Esplanade (a central point in New Orleans's old French Quarter) had been inhabited mainly by Spanish and Mexican people. Jelly Roll Morton never saw a duality of only black and white elements, but from the beginning a trinity: "We had Spanish, we had colored, we had white. . . ."

"Spanish" in old New Orleans is what we would call "Latin" today. Jelly Roll Morton went so far as to claim that the "Spanish tinge" was the essential ingredient that differentiated jazz from ragtime. New Orleans author Al Rose believes that ragtime came into being when black bands tried to play Mexican music. And the old journal, *New Orleans*, surmised that the word *jazz* was a bastardization of the Mexican expression *"Musica de jarabe."* We don't have to take all these speculations at face value, but they point to the significance of Latin elements in old New Orleans—a significance neglected by most jazz historians to date.

The Latin elements are not only significant to the music of old New Orleans but also to the New Orleans of today. New Orleans rock, by people like Fats Domino, Professor Longhair, Allen Toussaint, Dr. John, the Neville Brothers, and others is (as we pointed out in the piano section) different from Northern rock music because it is Latinized and Creolized: a "combination of offbeat Spanish beats and Calypso downbeats," as Professor Longhair put it. This, then, is a constant element in the musical tradition of the city. It points not only toward Mexico and Cuba but directly toward the Spanish history of New Orleans—all part of the same cultural sphere, encompassing Cuba and Mexico as well as the entire Creole realm right down to Trinidad and French Guiana.

It has also become clear that in this field (as in all the others) jazz developed according to the law under which it came into being. Everything was *in nuce*—was already potentially present—in the early forms of jazz.

The Violin

What had happened to the flute during the fifties has come true for the violin since the end of the sixties: all of a sudden, it was at the center of attention—there was talk of a "violin wave." This seems particularly paradoxical in view of the inferior role the violin had previously played in the history of jazz. Though the violin is by no means new to jazz—it is as old as the cornets of New Orleans—its softness of sound long kept it from playing an equal role in the swinging consortium of trombones, trumpets, and saxophones.

Early New Orleans and ragtime bands frequently included a violinist, but only because it was a nineteenth-century custom to have a violin in that sort of a band. The violinist in the old New Orleans orchestras was the counterpart of the "stand-up fiddler" of Viennese *kaffeehaus* music. As late as the fifties, this *kaffeehaus* tradition still cast its shadow over the jazz violinists. As soon as they were no longer "modern," they wound up where their instruments (as far as jazz was concerned) came from: in commercial music.

The first important violinist in jazz was Joe Venuti. Venuti came from the Chicago circle of jazz musicians, and became known both for his duos with guitarist Eddie Lang and for his caustic humor. Rediscovered in the decade preceding his death in 1978, the "old man" generated an amazing vitality, outplaying many of the younger violinists—a phenomenon breaking through all generational boundaries, comparable to Earl Hines among the pianists. One of his specialties was a kind of bow technique that would have filled "venerable" conservatory teachers with horror. He often removed the pin from the frog of the bow, wrapping the bow hair around all four strings of his violin, and holding the stick under the body of the instrument, thereby producing unusual four-note chords that would not otherwise be playable. In the twenty-first century, Andy Stein has continued this tradition in a mischievous, highly swinging way.

Eddie South (1904–62), an African American violinist who was born one year after Venuti, in Louisiana, and was classically trained, never achieved Venuti's fame. South had a warm, lyrical sound and developed a passionate way of playing that seamlessly combined elements of Gypsy music with Swing and Latin rhythms. South, who had ties to the European scene as early as the twenties, spent time in Paris during the thirties and played there with Django Reinhardt and Europe's most important jazz violinist, Stephane Grappelli. An amazing recording made by these three is the "Interprétation swing et improvisation swing sur le premier mouvement du concerto en ré mineur pour deux violons par Jean Sebastian Bach." Here, South and Grappelli play the main segment of the first movement of the Bach D-minor concerto for two violins, with Reinhardt taking the orchestra part on guitar. This recording is one of the earliest, and perhaps the most moving, testimonies to the admiration so many jazz musicians have for Bach's work. During World War II, the German occupation authorities in Paris melted down all available copies of this record as a particularly monstrous example of "degenerate art" (*Entartete Kunst*). Fortunately, a number of copies in private hands survived, and the recording was later reissued.

Stephane Grappelli (who died in 1997) is the "grand seigneur" of the jazz violin, with a very French sort of amiability and charm. His charming swing and strong driving quality, combining wit and elegance, made him the ultimate jazz violinist. From 1934 on, Grappelli was, with Django Reinhardt, a key member of the famous Quintet du Hot Club de France, the first important combo in European jazz. In this band, Grappelli played driving riffs with a lot of blue notes, as well as timeless solos. During the German occupation, he lived in England. During the late forties and after, he played with many well-known European and American musicians in Paris. Then he faded from the scene for a while; but when the "violin wave" started in the late sixties, he made a true comeback. Among his most beautiful recordings are those the then (in 1978) seventy-year-old Grand Old Man made with musicians half his age—for example, with Larry Coryell, Philip Catherine, and Gary Burton. Grappelli was a master of melodic flashes of inspiration, improvising from a lyrical flow of ideas that gave the jazz violin a new lightness. One of his trademarks was the integration of surprising harmonics into "normally" bowed lines—shimmering tones that expand his solos, like a fine confection added to an artfully baked cake.

In the meantime, in the United States—beginning with his 1936 record of "I'se a Muggin'"—Stuff Smith had become the great jazz violinist. Smith favored a raw, bluesy attack, using short, abrupt figures that stand in striking contrast to the long, flowing lines of Grappelli. Stuff was one of the hardest-swinging violinists in jazz. He used a heavy vibrato and many strong scoops and falls (sliding into and off of notes), in the manner of a horn player or a singer. To get these effects, and to get more control and attack in the sound, he mainly used the end of the bow. He said a jazz violinist had to use the bow "like a horn player uses his breath."

Smith was the first to use electronic amplification on the violin, and had a sovereign disregard for the rules of the conservatory. A well-bred concert violinist might cringe at Stuff's violent violin treatment, but he achieved more jazzlike, hornlike effects than any other player prior to the "violin wave" of the seventies. Smith, who died in Munich in 1967, was a humorist of the caliber of Fats Waller. During the second half of the thirties, he led a sextet on Fifty-Second Street in New York with trumpeter Jonah Jones that combined jazz and humor in a wonderful way. In the fifties, Norman Granz teamed Smith's violin with the trumpet of Dizzy Gillespie.

For years Ray Nance was a trumpeter in Duke Ellington's orchestra and also played occasional violin solos. But on violin he played mostly moody, sentimental melodies, while his trumpet solos belong with the great examples of the genre in jazz. On the other hand, it is an illustration of the growing importance of the jazz violin that the instrument became increasingly essential to Nance in the years before his death in 1976. He played it with a warm, "romantic" sound, but concisely, without a virtuosic approach. In smaller groups, he played happy, swinging violin solos that showed his roots in terms of style and phrasing to be where he originated as a trumpeter as well: in Louis Armstrong. Claude Williams (who also played guitar for Count Basie) emerged from Andy Kirk's Clouds of Joy. He played with a rhythmic mobility that uses the entire range of the violin. Williams, who died in 2004, brought the charm and humorous lightness of Swing violinists into the nineties, in recordings with Jay McShann and in his own name.

Denmark's Svend Asmussen, who plays both the violin and the viola, is a powerfully swinging player influenced by Stuff Smith and by Joe Venuti. In European jazz, he was such a sought-after improviser that Benny Goodman unsuccessfully tried to convince him to move to America. The record *Violin Summit*, which Asmussen recorded in 1966 with Stuff Smith, Stephane Grappelli, and Jean-Luc Ponty, is one of the outstanding recorded documents of violin jazz: four completely different styles that contrast and fuse with one another in an exciting manner.

Interestingly enough, it was a European who initiated the great success of the violin in the new jazz: Jean-Luc Ponty, born in 1942, the son of a violin professor, really and definitely electrified the violin. His position is thus the same as Charlie Christian's among guitarists, Jimmy Smith's among organists, or Jaco Pastorius's among bassists.

Ponty, who studied classical violin (he was a first-prize winner at the Conservatoire Nationale Supérieur de Paris), began with true, bop-inspired jazz recordings, made for the label Philips under his own name, featuring exciting, angular lines full of rhythmic complexity and wide double-stops (often in intervals of octaves and tenths). He moved to the United States in 1973, where he played first with Frank Zappa, then in John McLaughlin's second Mahavishnu Orchestra. In the late seventies, Ponty developed the impulses he had received there into his own kind of fusion music—"Lighter, warmer, more romantic and more accessible"

(Tim Schneckloth) than McLaughlin's—which made him successful with a wide audience extending beyond the actual realm of fusion, as did his recordings of African-tinged world jazz beginning in the early nineties. But he also developed a tendency, as *Down Beat* put it, to become "quite predictable" and "corral both his playing and arrangements into the most narrow of bags." Ponty uses a vast number of accessories to produce the electronic sounds on his violin and his music has become a case of constant brinkmanship between extramusical effects and high musical quality.

As the musician who actually initiated the contemporary interest in the violin—with his jazz recordings around the turn of the sixties—Ponty was indirectly responsible for the comeback of the music of veteran masters Venuti and Grappelli.

Around the same time as Ponty, Don "Sugar Cane" Harris became known, only to disappear from the scene again, regrettably, after a couple of years. As Ponty stems from the classical violin tradition, Harris comes from the blues. For years he toured the United States with Johnny Otis's Blues Show, where he acquired his funky blues style.

But the list of extraordinary modern violinists only begins with Ponty and Harris. Immediately after, and in part also parallel to them, come Mike White, Jerry Goodman, Poles Zbigniew Seifert, Michal Urbaniak, and Krzesimir Debski, as well as, later, the Americans John Blake, Darol Anger, Marc O'Connor, and Tracy Silverman, French-born Didier Lockwood and Pierre Blanchard, Indians L. Shankar and L. Subramaniam, and, in the realm of free jazz, Leroy Jenkins, Ramsey Ameen, Billy Bang, Charles Burnham, Ali Akbar, Terry Jenoure, Mark Feldman, and Phil Wachsman from England.

White made Coltrane-inspired recordings with Pharoah Sanders. Goodman is an especially eclectic player, uniting jazz-rock, country, and hillbilly music, the Nashville sound, Mingus, gypsy, and classical music. Urbaniak plays a very personal kind of fusion music often revealing traces of the folk music of his native Poland. Since the mideighties he has also played MIDI violins triggering synthesizers. Darol Anger and Marc O'Connor have uncovered, far from all academic traditions, the "white" folk roots (hillbilly, blue grass, Nashville sound) of their instrument, the former in recordings with Alex DeGrassi and William Ackerman, the latter with mandolin player David Grisman and the jazz-rock group Dregs.

Tracy Silverman, who came out of the Turtle Island String Quartet, is a poet of electric violin playing, full of subtle nuances. But even when he plays his six-stringed violin without amplification, he uses his advanced bowing technique to produce such unusual sounds that the instrument sometimes sounds like an Indian *bansuri* flute or a hybrid electronic instrument.

Of particular significance is Zbigniew Seifert, whom critic Patrick Hinely compared directly to John Coltrane: "What links Seifert and

Coltrane, besides total dedication to their instruments, is a quality one might call 'controlled drift' or 'responsible freedom.' In both men's music, there is no way you can tell what is going to happen next, but you can trust them to take it all the way to the edge." And from Seifert himself: "What I play on the violin, I imagine being produced by the saxophone. I admire Coltrane and try to play as he would if his instrument were the violin. That's probably the reason that I avoid playing my instrument in the usual way, with all the well-known effects." And McCoy Tyner said at the 1976 Berlin Jazz Days, "I've never heard a violinist like him before!" Seifert spices his far-ranging improvisations with an aggressive sound and a rare harmonic depth, but also with a spirituality that has increased in his late work. He is among the outstanding Polish jazz musicians who have made their country one of the most interesting jazz nations in the world. His music lives in the tension between his classical roots and his love for Coltrane. There is, in other words, a Zbigniew of chamber music and one who is "Trane-like." Seifert made recordings with Eddie Gomez, Jack DeJohnette, John Scofield, Joachim Kühn, Cecil McBee, Billy Hart, Charlie Mariano, and others. Toward the end of 1978, only a few weeks before his tragic death early in 1979, the members of the group Oregon, who had just become acquainted with his style, invited him to the studio. The resulting record, *Violin*, was dedicated to his memory.

The jazz world had just lost Zbigniew Seifert when another European jazz violinist arrived on the scene and was immediately hailed as "the new Zbiggy": Didier Lockwood, who comes from France, the classical land of great jazz violinists. The first of these was Michel Warlop, as early as the late twenties. When Django Reinhardt and Stephane Grappelli made their first big-band jazz recordings in the early thirties, it was with an orchestra led by Warlop. When Warlop concluded in 1937 that Grappelli was a greater violinist than himself, he gave him one of his violins as a present. By doing so, he initiated a tradition. And since then the most promising French jazz violinist has been presented with the Warlop violin. Grappelli passed it on to Ponty. In early 1979 Ponty and Grappelli decided that Didier Lockwood had become worthy of possessing Warlop's instrument. It was handed on to Lockwood at a Paris concert.

Said Lockwood, "No other violinist has moved and influenced me more than Zbigniew Seifert." In Lockwood's music, too, the Coltrane tradition remains alive, but he is more interested in fusion music than Seifert was. He possesses an elegance and charm matched by only a very few musicians on today's fusion scene. His electric violin playing demonstrates a sharp sense of musical drama and humor, and it is a mark of his great sensitivity that at the beginning of the new century he increasingly found his way back to playing with an acoustic violin sound, at first in encounters with Indian musicians, and later also in his incorporation of African, Brazilian, and Irish influences, or in collaboration with symphony orchestras and the lyric soprano Caroline Casadesus. In 2005 he premiered his opera *Libertad* in Montpellier. Krzesimir Debski, Pierre Blanchard, and Dominique Pifarély impressively extend Seifert's legacy—Debski in his group String Connection, Blanchard in recordings with Martial Solal and Lee Konitz, and Pifarély in his playing with Mike Westbrook and Louis Sclavis.

It is remarkable that Coltrane has had such a strong influence on violinists. However, his legacy led to quite different results with players like Ponty, Mike White, Seifert, and Lockwood. It resulted in yet another style in Philadelphia-born John Blake, who was first presented by McCoy Tyner as a member of his group and has played with Grover Washington. Blake is an improviser with the burning power of the saxophonists who could be heard in Tyner's groups during the seventies; he has a noticeable interest in black soul and funk music. Blake specializes in long, angular lines with vocal colorings and scooped pitches, combining clean articulation with tasteful vibrato.

It is fitting that with the opening up of jazz toward Indian music, two significant Indian violinists have become successful on the jazz and fusion scene: L. Shankar and L. Subramaniam, the former known through his work in John McLaughlin's Shakti, the latter through recordings with Larry Coryell, Herbie Hancock, Maynard Ferguson, John Handy, and Ali Akbar Khan. Shankar plays a two-necked violin with ten strings. Subramaniam has carried on inspiring dialogues with musicians from other cultures—African, South American, Asian. Both Shankar and Subramaniam hail from the same families of southern Indian musicians; that means they belong to the Carnatic musical culture of India (the other being the Hindustani, in the northern part of the country). Subramaniam currently possesses the title "Violin Chakravarti" ("Emperor of the Violinists"), a title given to only one violinist in each generation. Both Shankar and Subramaniam have brought Indian violin techniques to contemporary jazz with great musicality and feeling.

Coming from a different direction, Hungary's Zoltán Lantos invents strong melodic jazz lines that reflect both Western and Indian influences. In his world jazz, European and Eastern stylistic models enter into a hypnotic connection with each other. Lantos studied at the Béla Bartók Conservatory and at the Franz Liszt Academy in Budapest. Supported by a grant, he traveled to India, where he studied classical North Indian violin playing in Delhi for nine years. In addition to conventional violin, he plays an instrument built especially for him: an Indian violin with five strings and sixteen sympathetic strings (resonating strings that are not played directly).

Other important violinists of world jazz include Hungary's Ferenc Kovacs, Lebanon's Claude Chaloub, America's Anand Bennett, and Turkey's Nedim Nalbantoglu.

Anand Bennett is a very rhythmic player with a highly developed harmonic sense. He has integrated elements of Balkan folk music into the fusion band Son of Slavster (led by Miroslav Tadic), treating Eastern melodies and rhythms with unique violinistic effects.

Nedim Nalbantoglu, a Turk living in Paris, has played with the Orchestre National du Jazz. He enriches the language of contemporary jazz violin by charging it with the power and expressive richness of Eastern music. In his virtuosic solos, he draws on the inexhaustible reservoir of Turkish music and Balkan music: from the Gypsy music of the Sinti and Roma, as well as the expressive forms of Ottoman music, the sounds of the *gazinos* (Istanbul's music cafés), and traditional *taqsim* improvisations.

On to free playing: Michael Samson, a Dutchman, played in saxophonist Albert Ayler's group in 1966, in which he not only supplied a folk-music element, but also used double- and triple-stops, arpeggios, harmonics, and pizzicati to create forceful, racing textures that were a radical departure from the conventions of the jazz violin tradition. However, Samson's playing also represents an impressive failure to counterbalance Ayler's massive saxophone assaults with something of equal weight on the violin. His example shows that jazz violinists can never make a complete break with the classical European roots of their instrument. Even when they play the wildest free jazz, their lines always have a trace of a "classical" accent. Leroy Jenkins (d. 2007) was the true innovator of "creative music" on the violin above all because he translated this recognition into freely improvised music in the most logical and virtuosic manner. Even in aggressive free-jazz contexts, his playing is tonally oriented and full of melodies that follow their own inner logic. Jenkins came from Chicago's AACM, and the awareness of structure and use of space in his playing made important contributions to the aesthetic of that musicians' collective.

Especially in the seventies, Jenkins also used the violin as percussion instrument or noise producer, without scrupling about the traditional rules of violin and harmony. Ramsey Ameen became known in the late seventies through his work with Cecil Taylor, and Billy Bang and Charles Burnham through the String Trio of New York. Akbar Ali played with Ronald Shannon Jackson. Terry Jenoure became known for her sensitive playing in clarinetist John Carter's group, and later she phrased free funk with Leroy Jenkins. Mark Feldman is able to play with equal ease the frenetic music of John Zorn and Tim Berne and the stately jazz-influenced classical music of Anthony Davis. He has made thrilling recordings with the Arcado String Trio. But it is Billy Bang who, after Leroy Jenkins, offers one of the most original violin voices in the new jazz. He plays his instrument with an unusually virtuosic bow technique and that raw "percussive" attack more concerned with naturalness and blues quality than with so-called classical norms. In 1986 Bang was one of the founding members of the String Trio of New York, and his energetic, rhythmic playing, originally inspired by Stuff Smith, and incisive intonation contributed a great deal to the revitalization of the violin in the post–free-jazz context.

Following the achievements of Leroy Jenkins and Billy Bang, many violinists in post–free jazz in the nineties expanded the possibilities of their instrument with unusual textures. The most interesting of these players include Mat Maneri, violist Jeff Gauthier, American Jason Kao Hwang, and Germany's Deutsche Harald Kimmig (who worked with Cecil Taylor).

Mat Maneri is a master of violin styles ranging from straight-ahead jazz to the microtonal music pioneered by his father, Joe Maneri. He is an expert in the modification of the sound of the violin using a wide variety of mutes. In his own trio, he favors an acidic approach that avoids the excitedness of the first free-jazz generation, preferring instead sublime, dark textures and a high degree of concentration.

Jason Kao Hwang, who became known through his work with Henry Threadgill and Anthony Braxton, plays unusually melodically, with a preference for pauses and atmospheric colors. He is an expert in the careful examination of textures.

Other violinists inspired by free jazz who have found personal ways of expanding the limits of jazz violin playing in the direction of new music include the Czech Iva Bittova, Portugal's Carlos Zingaro, Australia's Jon Rose, who lives in Berlin, Dutch violist Maurice Horsthuis, and the Japanese violinist Mari Kimura, living in New York. Kimura has achieved particularly exciting results in the field of MIDI and computer violin playing, presented for example in free improvisations with Jim O'Rourke and Robert Dick. She has developed a new bowing technique that she calls "subharmonics"—a way of playing that she uses to play as much as an octave lower than the lowest note on her violin (the open G-string) without having to retune the instrument.

The extent to which rhythmic and tonal self-assurance has increased among jazz violinists can also be indirectly seen in the fact that a "wave" of jazz playing and improvising string quartets has broken onto the jazz scene, in an astonishing parallel development to the rise of "pure" saxophone quartets. Stylistic openness and an imagination that defies categorizations were shared in the eighties and nineties by such groups as the Kronos Quartet, the Black Swan Quartet, the Turtle Island String Quartet, the Soldier String Quartet, and the Modern String Quartet (with German-born Jörg Widmoser). The Kronos Quartet, founded in 1977 (originally with David Harrington and John Sherba, violins; Hank Dutt, viola; and Joan Jeanrenaud, cello), is particularly impressive. For over two decades it has been one of the most highly esteemed groups in modern concert music, and Terry Riley and Phillip Glass are among the many composers who have written for it. The Kronos Quartet may not improvise, but it has so "disrupted" the "comfortable" image of the string quartet (with the sounds of Jimi Hendrix's "Purple Haze," James Brown's "Sex Machine," and pieces by Ornette Coleman, Bill Evans, and Thelonious Monk) and so advanced a new sensibility that jazz musicians have frequently worked with them: Steve Lacy, Max Roach, John Zorn, Anthony Braxton, Cecil Taylor, and others.

The Turtle Island String Quartet, founded in 1986 (originally with David Balakrishna and Evan Pierce, violins; Danny Seidenberg, viola; and Mark Summer, cello) is particularly eclectic, integrating elements from rock, bluegrass, and world music into its jazz. At the same time, it was the first string quartet to achieve real success in the use of the strings in the manner of a rhythm section. Inspired by the wave of jazz string quartets, there quickly developed a large number of string trios playing a kind of chamber jazz. The most important of these include the Trio Arcado (Mark Feldman, violin; Hank Roberts, cello; and Mark Dresser, bass), the Kent Carter String Trio (Carlos Zingaro, violin; François Dréno, viola; and Kent Carter, bass), the Masada String Trio (Mark Feldman, violin; Erik Friedlander, cello; and Greg Cohen, bass), and the Amsterdam String Trio (Maurice Horsthuis, viola; Ernst Reijseger, cello; and Ernst Glerum, bass).

The String Trio of New York, founded by John Lindberg in 1986, was particularly impressive in its development. It was not only a vehicle for advanced string sounds, but also became a springboard for the most important American jazz violinists of the contemporary scene: Billy Bang, Charles Burnham, Regina Carter, and others.

But jazz violin playing experienced its greatest boost as a result of the explosion of the stylistic diversity in the jazz of the nineties. The inclusion of more and more musical genres made it possible for jazz violinists to radically expand the expressive spectrum of their instrument, including the incorporation of approaches to the violin that lie outside of jazz, such as folk fiddling, classical Indian and Arabic violin techniques, or techniques from new music.

Regina Carter, originally from Detroit, developed into the most diverse violinist of the scene in the nineties. She has great facility with the entire legacy of improvised music, from Swing to contemporary straightahead jazz, from Afro-Cuban Latin sounds to free music. Regina Carter, a cousin of saxophonist James Carter, combines the influences of Jean-Luc Ponty and John Blake. She has a great feeling for subtlety and nuance and an affection for Afro-Caribbean grooves. Her soulful ballad playing is reminiscent of the great tenor saxophonists of jazz, Ben Webster and Paul Gonsalves, but also of great jazz singers such as Sarah Vaughan and Betty Carter. On faster pieces she has a fiery rhythmic drive. Regina Carter gives the jazz violin a strong rhythmic foundation; she sees the violin as an extension of the rhythm section. "When I solo, I love to bow rhythms that work against what the drummer and bassist are playing."

In 2001 the Italian city of Genoa invited her to play on a famous Guarneri violin that had been a favorite of Paganini, and that was known as *il cannone* (the cannon) because of its powerful, dark sound. The invitation was an honor that had previously been extended only to classical musicians, and Regina Carter was the first African American to be invited to play the instrument. "People often wonder why there are so many different things going on on my records. It's because I come from Detroit. In Detroit I used to listen to Motown, soul, hard bop, classical music; there was a Greek community, an Arab community, and an Afro-Cuban community."

Other notable multistylists of contemporary jazz violin playing include the Americans Eyvind Kang, Christan Howes, Carla Kihlstedt, and Rob Thomas (with the Jazz Passengers), Israel's Miri Ben-Ari, Japan's Naoko Terai, England's Christian Garrick, France's Dominique Pifarély, Austria's Tscho Theissing (with the band Pago Libre), and Germany's Gregor Huebner.

In Asia, Naoko Terai (who has played with Kenny Barron and with Mal Waldron) is considered Japan's leading jazz violinist. Her vital jazz strikes a powerful balance between standards and fusion. Miri Ben-Ari, who lives in New York, became known through her work with Wynton Marsalis. She has developed an original urban hip-hop approach to the violin.

Christian Howes, who became known playing with D. D. Jackson, is a player comfortable in many different styles (folk, blues, contemporary), whose aggressive lines on the electric violin come perhaps the closest to Jimi Hendrix's sound among violinists.

Garrick, the most visible jazz violinist in England, has mastered Grappelli's Hot Club style and modern approaches in equal measure. Carla Kihlstedt, who lives in San Francisco, is a magician of finely chiseled lines and of quiet, brittle harmonics. In the Tin Hat Trio she uses elements from folk, new music, tango, and free music to create subtly nuanced dynamic shadings, simultaneously grounded in a solid rhythmic foundation.

The most important and exciting violinist of the New York downtown scene is Mark Feldman, a violinist "who is impressive not only for his beautiful tone and his sheer virtuosity, but also for his love of sudden inspiration, genre-changing, and enthusiastic impromptus" (Thomas Steinfeld). Mark began as a session musician in Nashville's country and western bands. In the early nineties, he found his way into the circle of musicians around John Zorn, associated with the New York venue the Knitting Factory.

Feldman is one of those jazz violinists who does not play "against" the classical heritage of his instrument. He doesn't try to "saxophonize" the instrument, as so many violinists try (and generally fail) to do. As part of this approach, Feldman plays the violin completely acoustically, without any electric amplification.

He's a master of genre pivots and of dynamic contrasts, the expressive exploration of musical extremes. On the one hand, like no other contemporary jazz violinist he cultivates the "schmaltzy" side of the instrument. On the other hand, he creates harsh, caustic lines. His sound is instantly recognizable, whether he plays aggressive chords, shimmering, ingratiatingly sweet runs of harmonics, or racing pizzicato lines. Feldman was the most impressive soloist in the Arcado String Trio and in the Masada String Trio—two string trios whose original chamber music was groundbreaking, the former in the field between jazz and new music, and the latter in the field of John Zorn's "radical Jewish music."

Another player close to the downtown scene is Jenny Scheinman (who has worked with Bill Frisell and with Myra Melford). She has a particularly warm, soft sound, and plays with great calm and transparency. She has mastered a range of styles from the gypsy swing of the Hot Club of France to free music, bridging the experimental world of the Rova Saxophone Quartet (with whom she worked) and Stephane Grappelli. The most impressive quality of Scheinman's recordings is that despite their vehement eclecticism, they create the impression of *a single piece*. Scheinman incorporates Indian, Middle Eastern, European, and Brazilian elements, mixing them with American influences. She avoids empty virtuosity, and her solos do not parody the styles to which they refer. Instead, she plays with great understatement, depth, and soulful clarity.

France's Dominique Pifarély is a musician who has exploited the classical European heritage of the instrument for jazz purposes in a particularly productive manner. He became known through his playing with the Vienna Art Orchestra. He combines lucid force with a warm, soft sonic aura. In 1986, together with clarinetist Louis Sclavis, he founded the Acoustic Quartet (also including guitarist Marc Ducret and bassist Bruno Chevillion). One of their CDs is called *Warm Canto*—"warm song"—and in fact this is a good description of Pifarély's inventive, virtuosic violin lines.

Germany's Gregor Huebner, from the Melos Quartet, has also succeeded in making a sensitive combination of classical music and jazz, for example in the band of pianist Richie Beirach, playing jazz treatments of the music of Béla Bartók.

No other instrument in jazz has as many European players as the violin. Among the violinists mentioned in this section, there are nineteen Europeans (plus thirty-one Americans, two Indians, two Japanese musicians, and three from the Levant region of Asia). In addition, the American players Eddie South, Stuff Smith, and Alan Silva all lived in Europe for extended periods; and "Sugar Cane" Harris, L. Subramaniam, and Billy Bang made some of their most important recordings in Europe. The irony is the fact that the very first of the well-known jazz violinists, Joe Venuti, was European by birth. Venuti used to claim that he had been born of Italian parents on the Atlantic Ocean, en route to America. But when Joe was in his seventies, he admitted that he was born in northern Italy, near Lago di Como, where Venutis still live to this day.

Miscellaneous Instruments

For fifty years, until about 1950, only a relatively small "family" of instruments was employed in jazz. They were basically the same instruments that had been used in early New Orleans jazz: two instruments from the brass group (trumpet and trombone), saxophone and clarinet from the reed group, and, of course, the rhythm-section instruments—drums, bass, guitar, and piano.

Nevertheless, there have been shifts in emphasis within jazz instrumentation—to such a degree that the entire history of jazz can be viewed in terms of shifting emphases placed on particular instruments. In this scheme, the piano would stand at the beginning; it ruled the ragtime period. Then the trumpet blew its way to the forefront: first in New Orleans, where the "Kings of Jazz" always were trumpeters (or cornetists), then in the great Chicago period, when trumpeters like King Oliver, Louis Armstrong, and Bix Beiderbecke came to the fore. The Swing era was the time of the clarinet. And with the appearance of Lester Young and Charlie Parker, the saxophone became the main instrument—initially tenor, then for a while alto, and after that tenor again. In the early seventies, finally, electronics became the determining sound factor—first in the shape of the electric guitar but soon to such a degree that the electronic sound has frequently become more important than the original sound of the instruments electronically amplified or manipulated. Only in jazz since the eighties has it been impossible, because of the multitude of values, to find a single instrument dominating the scene.

There have been three major changes in jazz instrumentation: first, through the Lester Young–initiated switch of jazz consciousness from sonority to phrasing; then, as we indicated, through electronics; and, finally, through the opening of jazz to the world's musical cultures.

After Lester Young had cleared the path for the recognition that the jazz essence was no longer tied, for better or worse, to sonority, jazz could be played on practically any instrument offering possibilities for sufficiently flexible, clear jazz phrasing. Thus, instruments were "discovered" for jazz that previously had hardly ever (or never) been in jazz use. The flute, the French horn, and the violin are examples of this phenomenon. Saxophonist Rufus Harley from Philadelphia has shown that you can convincingly improvise jazz on the Scottish bagpipes. Trombonist Steve Turre blows absolutely modern and captivating jazz solos on conch-shells.

And with Christian Marclay the record player becomes a jazz instrument. The wildness of his scratching (moving records rhythmically forward and backward while the needle is in the groove) and the rough and humorous subversions of his sound collages sound like a punky counterpart to the music of John Zorn.

While some of these instruments could be summarily discussed under the heading "Miscellaneous Instruments" in prior editions of this book, they have since become so important that they require sections of their own.

Another motive behind this ongoing process of discovering new instruments for jazz is the musicians' interest in sound. In the chapter "The Elements of Jazz," it was shown that sound is an indispensable jazz element, and in the course of jazz history, the interest in sound has grown continuously. There are musicians and groups today for whom involvement in and joy of sound seem to have become of paramount importance.

Discovering new sounds has been a crucial motivating factor for jazz musicians. In the late sixties it seemed as if electronics were especially suited to take over this function. But then it became clear that precisely the "oversupply" of sound possibilities in electronics (we discussed this in the section on organ and keyboards) caused problems regarding individuality and personal style. As we have seen, the chief aim of the interest in sound is to arrive at a *personal* expression. That is why, paradoxically, the sound consciousness associated with electronics led to a revival of acoustic jazz from the late seventies on.

But let us return to the topic of "miscellaneous instruments." Many of them are used as secondary instruments, and we have mentioned them where a certain musician's primary instrument was discussed: the cello in connection with bassist Oscar Pettiford; the bass clarinet introduced by Eric Dolphy in the clarinet section; oboe and bassoon in connection with Yusef Lateef in the tenor and flute sections. There we also discussed Roland Kirk, who in addition to all his other instruments played two archaic saxophones, used mainly in turn-of-the-century Spanish military bands: the stritch and the manzello.

How the limits of jazz instrumentation have expanded becomes clear when one hears the harp improvisations of Alice Coltrane. In the fifties, Corky Hale from the West Coast and Dorothy Ashby from New York had already attempted to play in a jazz vein on this instrument. (A curiosity: the first traceable jazz harp was played by Caspar Reardon in 1934, on Jack Teagarden's recording of "Junk Man" [with Benny Goodman], and after that by Adele Girard in Joe Marsala's "Jazz Me Blues" [with Eddie Condon and Joe Bushkin!].) But only the modality of the new jazz seems to have cleared the way for this difficult instrument, which has to be constantly retuned. Alice Coltrane was the first to develop a jazz-harp sound into something more than just a curiosity.

A step beyond Alice Coltrane was taken by Zeena Parkins, who became known in the NYC downtown circle around John Zorn, Elliot Sharp, and Wayne Horvitz. Parkins plays splintered clusters of punk-inspired restlessness, so radically electronically alienating the sound of her harp that she literally "picks to pieces" the romantic aura that is associated with this instrument more than any other musician.

Accordion

For a long time the accordion played no part in jazz, even when as early as 1930 Charles Melrose played an accordion solo with the Cellar Boys: "Wailing Blues" with Bud Freeman and Frank Teschemacher. But all the accordionists who followed him—Buster Moten (in the Bennie Moten Orchestra), Joe Mooney (who headed a swing quartet in the second half of the forties), Mat Mathews, and Art van Damme—could only partially diminish the instrument's rigidity and its innate imprecision of phrasing (which is similarly problematic on the pipe organ since both are reed instruments). Astor Piazzolla made remarkable duo recordings with baritone saxophonist Gerry Mulligan, intertwining the tango and jazz. France's Michel Portal (on bandoneon) and Bernard Lubat, as well as Germany's Rüdiger Carl, have introduced the accordion to European avant-garde jazz.

But only in the eighties did the accordion become an absolutely valid jazz instrument. Three musicians brought that about: Argentinian-born Dino Saluzzi (on the bandoneon), New Yorker Guy Klucevsek (on an arsenal of the most diverse types of accordion), and France's Richard Galliano. Saluzzi emancipates the tango from its schematic aspects by enriching the essence of this music—its rebellious melancholy—with the openness and vitality of the whole of Argentinian folklore: with Indian melodies and European waltzes, with the candomblé rhythms of the en-slaved Africans transported to South America, with the milongas of rural gaucho folklore, and also with the romantic and impressionistic music of the nineteenth century. Through such bandoneon players as Saluzzi, Juan José Mosalini, and Luis DiMatteo—tango musicians who, together with and following from Piazzolla, expand the range of world music—Argentina has now found its way onto the music scene (as Brazil did long before).

Guy Klucevsek, who made a name for himself playing with John Zorn, produces the most uncharacteristic of sounds on the accordion. He is a master of really fast tonal breaks and unaccustomed changes of register, conjuring up intense, strange sounds on his instrument, which sometimes take on a fairy-tale-like and folkloristic character—sounds that you might expect from keyboards but scarcely from an accordion. Klucevsek's solos are a tour de force through a wide range of musical styles and genres—polkas, Mahler, Dvorak, spirituals, tango, South

African freedom songs, zydeco, samba, free jazz, noise music—often folding them together in a humorous manner. In 1996 he founded The Accordion Tribe, a band made up of five accordionists.

But it took a musician of the stature of Richard Galliano to win the jazz accordion the recognition it deserves among a wider audience. Galliano, a Frenchman from Cannes, has made the accordion an integral part of jazz contexts by achieving the final breakthrough to a truly flowing, triplet-based jazz phrasing, influenced by Bill Evans, Herbie Hancock, Chick Corea, and Miles Davis. Galliano began as an accompanist to singers such as Yves Montand. His roots are in the joyous melancholy of French bistro waltzes, "musette" music. In his "New Musette," he has brought a particularly wide variety of other styles and musical cultures to his accordion jazz, including the *tango nuevo* of Astor Piazzola (a mentor to Galliano), Brazilian-Latin music, jazz-rock and gypsy music, Maurice Ravel and Bill Evans, Gabriel Fauré and Charlie Parker.

Galliano refers to himself as a "*melomane*" who gives himself over completely to emotion in his music, and in fact his solos are bursting with melodic inventiveness and polychromatic orchestral colors that even his (sometimes somewhat narcissistic) tendency toward virtuosity cannot obscure. "You can play anything on the accordion," he says. "I'm constantly discovering things on the accordion that a few years earlier I'd never have believed are possible to play."

French musicians such as Richard Galliano and Jean-Louis Matinier have made the accordion into a fully valid jazz instrument. Nonetheless, the difference between these two musicians could hardly be greater. Galliano plays an accordion with keys, while Matinier plays one with buttons. And while Galliano is continuing the musette tradition, bringing new influences to it, Matinier represents a radical break with this tradition. He's an adventurous improviser with an open mind, a master of bucolic, frugal "imaginary folklore," combining dynamism and lightness in a particularly flowing style. Matinier's lines walk a tightrope between jazz, folk, and new music, spiritedly crossing the boundaries between folk music traditions, swinging grooves, and experimental improvisation. With bassist Renaud Garcia-Fons, he formed one of the most imaginative duos in European jazz of the nineties. Garcia-Fons says: "For us, the duo is a symphonic orchestra, with thousands of instruments hidden in the heart of the bow and the bellows."

It is striking that it has been in particular the accordionists of the "imaginary folklore" movement who, in the eighties and nineties, liberated their instrument and made it an equal partner in jazz. But this is hardly surprising, given the richness of folk music traditions connected with the accordion. The most important of these players, besides Galliano and Matinier, include the Italians Luciano Biondini and Gianni Coscia, Norway's Stian Carstensen, and the Armenian David Yengibarjan (who has lived in Hungary since 1995). Stian Carstensen, who also plays banjo, bagpipes, and kaval, has created an exciting contemporary mixture of jazz and Balkan music in the Norwegian-Bulgarian band Farmer's Market. Gianni Coscia became known in the nineties for his richly melodic duos on Mediterranean themes with clarinetist Gianluigi Trovesi.

Finland's Kimmo Pohjonen, born in 1964, began playing accordion at the age of eight. He has studied classical music at the Helsinki Conservatory, African music in Tanzania, and tango in Buenos Aires. After being voted Finland's "folk musician of the year" three years running (1996–98), he evolved into an internationally recognized jazz accordionist—one of the most imaginative. Pohjonen plays the (unjustly ridiculed) accordion with a wild, dervishlike energy, compressing gruff, racing passages into dense emotional statements. His dialogues with sampler players such as DJ Samuli Kosminen radicalize the accordion's sound, taking it somewhere between trance, ambient, and heavy metal, ranging from bombastic storms of sound to organlike textures.

Besides Guy Klucevsek, Ted Reichman and Rob Burger (though he lives in San Francisco) have contributed accordion sounds to the New York downtown jazz scene. Burger has a particularly flowing approach to time, and his lyricism and control of the most subtle nuances of tone and touch are remarkable. John Zorn says, "He can do it all—musette, tango, jazz, cajun, blues—but as with all masters he does it in his own unique way, with his own unique sound."

Tuba

Two instruments have come full circle: harmonica and tuba. In old New Orleans, the tuba, as mentioned, was a kind of forerunner of the string bass. Today, musicians like Howard Johnson, Don Butterfield, Bob Stewart, Joe Daley, Earl McIntyre, and in Europe Michel Godard, Larry Fishkind, and Pinguin Moschner are playing tuba solos of almost trumpetlike agility. Dave Bargeron played energetic jazz-rock tuba solos in the band Blood, Sweat & Tears. Blues singer Taj Mahal used an entire tuba section as accompaniment on one of his records.

Howard Johnson, who also plays pennywhistle and baritone saxophone, is the true father figure of the emancipated modern tuba. As early as 1968, he formed the tuba ensemble Substructure, which later evolved into the six-member tuba band Gravity. Johnson, who is, as he says, "100 percent self-taught," played in the bands of Charles Mingus, Dizzy Gillespie, and Gil Evans. He plays tuba solos with a pointedly modern jazz feeling, combining stupendous agility with great authority and fullness of tone. His solos easily encompass a range of four octaves, and when he ascends into the high register of the tuba, it sounds warm and beautiful, almost like a French horn. Johnson says, "The only reason the tuba has a bad reputation is that it is played badly."

Howard Johnson is the "John Coltrane of tuba playing." In early jazz, the tuba was used exclusively as a harmonic and rhythmic point of reference for the bass voice. After Johnson, more and more contemporary tubaists have made the instrument into a melodic equal partner: Jon Sass, Tom Malone, Joe Daley, and Marcus Rojas (who has lent particular weight to the groups of Henry Threadgill), Belgium's Michel Massot, Norway's Line Horntveth, England's Oren Marshall (who also manipulates the instrument's sound electronically), and Germany's Bettina Wauschke.

The American Jon Sass, who has lived in Vienna since the late eighties, has attracted attention for his artful, fundamental brass playing in the Vienna Art Orchestra. He's a master both of funk grooves and classical technique, combining urban rhythms with a fat bass sound. "The sound of the tuba reminds me of the human voice," he says—and he often sings into the horn while playing, down into the low register. The result: even when using overdubbing to accompany himself on recordings, Sass "humanizes" the brass bass.

Independently of Johnson, Bob Stewart, who became known through his work with Carla Bley, found his way to a fascinating jazz tuba style. He has by far the most powerful tuba sound on the contemporary scene, full of spontaneity and emotion, blues feeling, and multistylistic flexibility. His sound, while warm, has nothing soft about it, but rather implores and invokes. Stewart makes the tuba into a many-faceted melodic instrument, blowing bass lines that, in their extraordinary melodic and rhythmic complexity, are truly hip. He's the main reason that jazz tuba players today play figures and ostinatos that truly belong to the tuba, no longer imitating the lines of upright bass players, as tuba players did in earlier jazz styles.

France's Michel Godard can often be heard in "imaginary folklore" contexts. But beyond this, he is Europe's most flexible and individual jazz tuba player. One of his most beautiful recordings was made in Castel del Monte, a medieval castle built by Friedrich II, king of Sicily. In this recording, Godard plays fantastic jazz permutations of the sounds of early music, imaginary allusions to the music of the Renaissance and to Gregorian chants, using the warm, mysterious sound of the serpent—a literally serpentine wind instrument, made of wood, from the sixteenth century, which Godard also plays.

Godard sees the tuba as a "bass bee" (the title of one of his pieces)—capable of flying, buzzing, and humming, but also of suddenly stinging. Godard has also played in the leading new music group Ensemble InterContemporain, under the leadership of Pierre Boulez. For more than ten years, he has been a permanent member of the band of *oud* player Rabih Abou-Khalil. Although the tuba has associations of a kind of sturdy, gruff formality, Godard favors a melodic, poetic approach to the instrument, playing it with a full, round, singing tone similar to the voice.

His lines are strikingly flexible and agile. He says he's learned his most important lessons from Tibetan *dhung* players (the *dhung* is a giant copper trumpet): "If you want to play really low, you have to think high."

Since one tends to forget the man who initiated this whole development, it should be pointed out that as early as the fifties, in Los Angeles, bassist Red Callender, Charles Mingus's teacher, incorporated the tuba into the then-dominant West Coast sounds. Later came Ray Draper, the first to really play bebop solos on the tuba. In the second half of the fifties, he played striking tuba solos in the hard-bop bands of Max Roach, Donald Byrd, and John Coltrane, making him a modernist among the early tuba pioneers.

Harmonica

The harmonica is the "harp" of the folk-blues singer. The two Sonny Boy Williamsons, as well as Sonny Terry, Junior Wells, Shakey Jake, Little Walter, Big Walter Horton, James Cotton, Carey Bell, Whispering Smith, and many others have played marvelously expressive "talking" harmonica solos—usually in the blues groups that existed (and continue to exist) in the South or on Chicago's South Side. Nevertheless, this instrument was always afflicted with the stigma of a certain folklorelike primitiveness. Belgian Toots Thielemans liberated the harmonica from this affliction. He plays it with a mobility and wealth of ideas reminiscent of the great saxophonists of the cool-jazz era, such as Lee Konitz or Stan Getz. His playing has the immediacy of a born musician. "He is very much a feeling musician," says Kenny Werner. He's most at home in the "little space between a smile and a tear," as he once said. Thielemans's inimitable bop-inspired mainstream style was a point of reference for musicians including Bill Evans and—repeatedly—Jaco Pastorius. "It's like painting with pastels. It's not red, it's not black. It's the colors in between."

Since the emergence of electronic amplification, the harmonica has been given equal rights in the family of instruments. It has also made inroads in contemporary blues-rock music, where it is played by white musicians like Paul Butterfield or John Mayall in the style of the great black blues "harp" men. Magic Dick has contributed exciting harmonica solos in a pure rock context. Stevie Wonder has combined Thielemans's refinement with the "harp" sound of the old blues. Mauricio Einhorn has incorporated the Thielemans sound into his native Brazilian music, adding the specific Brazilian rhythm feeling. Germany's Hendrik Meurkens has impressively developed Einhorn's Brazilian style in swinging recordings with guitarist Charlie Byrd.

Toots Thielemans is the doyen of jazz harmonica. For decades, he monolithically dominated the jazz scene on that instrument, to such an extent that it was hard to conceive of an approach to the instrument that went beyond his accomplishments. However, in the nineties, four players emerged who proved that it is after all possible to move "beyond Toots": Howard Levy, Olivier Ker Ourio, Matthias Broede, and Grégoire Maret.

Howard Levy, an American, has adapted John Coltrane's approach (especially the midperiod Coltrane of "Giant Steps") to the jazz harmonica in a particularly thoroughgoing fashion. He plays the instrument with a passion and intensity reminiscent of Coltrane, with similarly long, spacious lines.

Olivier Ker Ourio, a native of the island of Reunion in the Indian Ocean, now living in France, is a self-taught harmonica player. His playing brings his two worlds together—French and Creole culture—in a unique way. He has taken jazz harmonica down unconventional paths by combining Breton folk music with Creole rhythms.

Matthias Broede, a German living in Cologne, is an expert in the combination of jazz and Balkan grooves. He considers himself influenced less by harmonica players than by trumpeters and soprano saxophonists, and above all by pianists.

But it is Switzerland's Grégoire Maret who has the broadest stylistic spectrum among contemporary harmonica virtuosos. He plays exciting lines that seem to grow naturally from all kinds of different stylistic contexts, such as the tension-filled dialogues of the fusion band Dapp Theory, with keyboardist Andy Milne, or navigating the rhythmic labyrinths of Steve Colemans's M-Base music. In 2004 Maret became a permanent member of the Pat Metheny Group, contributing decisively to the band's sparkling sound.

Pathbreaking harmonica players like Maret and Howard Levy have proven that their instrument will continue to have a secure place as jazz moves forward.

French Horn, Oboe, English Horn, Bassoon, Shells

Next are such instruments as French horn, oboe, English horn, and bassoon. Their "fathers" (in terms of jazz) were, as early as the fifties, Julius Watkins and Yusef Lateef. Watkins played the French horn on recordings with important musicians like Kenny Clarke, Oscar Pettiford, and Quincy Jones, reaching a remarkable jazzlike intensity difficult to find on this difficult instrument. His range effortlessly extended an octave beyond the "normal" range of classical players. Watkins was the first to play bebop on the French horn, with a wonderful feeling for the blues. He has a white "counterpart" in John Graas, who transposed the purity of his classical training to cool, swinging West Coast jazz recordings made in the fifties.

Yusef Lateef—who is as outstanding on tenor sax, flute, oboe, and bassoon as he is on diverse exotic instruments such as the argol (an Egyptian kind of oboe)—was the precursor, even before Coltrane, of the opening up of jazz to world music. In the fifties, tenorist Bob Cooper played oboe and English horn on West Coast jazz recordings, including some with Max Roach on drums. Perhaps the most interesting bassoon solos in the free jazz of the sixties and seventies came from Karen Borca.

The bassoon is not loud, which makes it difficult to combine it with other jazz instruments. For this reason, most jazz bassoonists use an electric pickup that makes the sound more penetrating. Another problem in playing jazz on the bassoon is that on the instrument it is not possible to play slurs and scoops, or sliding tones, in the way that this is done on the saxophone. As a result, in fast passages the bassoon can sound somewhat stiff and formal. One musician who has overcome these handicaps is Michael Rabinowitz, who has become known through his playing with Wynton Marsalis and the Mingus Big Band. He plays exuberantly swinging lines in the spirit of John Coltrane and Charlie Parker, full of authority and rhythmic force. Rabinowitz often enjoys playing the game of "stealing" passages from classical music and integrating them into his exciting jazz solos. The bassoon is an instrument that, like the baritone saxophone, can descend into the bass register. At the same time, it has melodic possibilities similar to those of the oboe or the English horn. In a post–free-jazz context, David Novak has applied the wide tonal range of the bassoon to unusual textures, in his work with Anthony Braxton, among others. However, the first musician to play bassoon in jazz was tenor saxophonist Illinois Jacquet, who got surprisingly swinging sounds out of the instrument in 1963, in a track entitled "Bassoon Blues."

Paul McCandless has come to the fore in the group Oregon on oboe and English horn; he is a musician with roots in the romantic tradition of these instruments. Belgium's Emmanuelle Sommer has brought a jazz sensibility to the always somewhat aristocratic, reserved tone of the oboe, in her work with Dave Douglas.

Returning to the French horn: Julius Watkins is the "Charlie Parker of the French horn." His lyrical phrasing and a wealth of ideas going beyond the horn's normal range have influenced all contemporary players of the instrument: Vincent Chancey, Sharon Freeman, and John Clark (all of whom have played with Carla Bley), Peter Gordon (formerly with Jaco Pastorius), and Martin Mayes. *The* French horn voice in contemporary jazz is, however, Tom Varner. On an instrument where intonation is so difficult, he phrases impetuous but outstandingly relaxed free-bop lines whereby free is represented by lack of prescribed chord changes and bop by a regular swinging beat. Varner's virtuosic playing has been influenced above all by saxophonists, primarily Lee Konitz, John Coltrane, and Sonny Rollins.

One reason why the French horn is so infrequently used in jazz is that it has an extremely soft tone quality. A French horn player who has deliberately cultivated this aspect of the instrument, incorporating it into

European jazz, instead of breaking with it, is Russia's Arkady Shilkloper, from the Moscow Art Trio. Shilkloper is a spirited melodist whose intoxicatingly fluid lines often have a folkloristic tinge. Django Bates has achieved a level of agility on the tenor horn—an instrument very rarely seen in jazz—that is almost equal to that of the trumpet. Swiss trumpeter Hans Kennel plays modern jazz solos on the alpenhorn. In the nineties, with his alphorn quartet Mytha, he created a gentle version of "imaginary folklore" that combined contemporary jazz with Alpine culture, the *Kuhreihe* music of the Swiss mountain herders.

Inspired by Rahsaan Roland Kirk, trombonist Steve Turre took up playing conch shells. He sometimes plays two shells at once, producing gorgeous solos with a full sound. In the midnineties, he founded the band Sanctified Shells, a "choir" of shells in which six musicians play on twenty-five different shells of various sizes and provenance, from the Caribbean, Hawaii, Mexico, Polynesia, India, Africa, and Brazil. What led the world's leading jazz trombonist to put down the trombone and pick up such an odd second instrument? "Because the shell is the origin of all brass instruments," says Turre. "Producing notes by blowing air through tensed lips into a hollow space—it all started in prehistoric times, when someone blew into a shell for the first time."

Mandolin, Banjo, Cello, Daxophone

Let's move on to some miscellaneous (Western) string instruments. The mandolin is so engulfed by the serenade sound of Italian mandolin groups that it might seem paradoxical that it has made its way into jazz. But it has happened—characteristically at first by way of musicians close to country and western and bluegrass music (who, at the same time, are real "Swingers"): Tiny Moore and Jethro Burns. The latter made his first mandolin recordings as early as the forties, with Bob Wills's Texas Playboys. In a modern context, guitarist John Abercrombie (especially convincing in his quartet recordings with McCoy Tyner) and above all David Grisman have employed the mandolin. Grisman, who celebrated successes at the start of the eighties with what he calls his "dawg music," creates string sounds that seem like a contemporary counterpart of Django Reinhardt's Quintet du Hot Club de France.

Béla Fleck, who has been successful in crossover and fusion, has brought the banjo into contemporary jazz. In New Orleans jazz, the banjo was a very common accompanying instrument, providing a harmonic foundation and rhythmic drive in the rhythm section. When the Swing era arrived, the "plinking" sound of the banjo fell out of favor, and in modern jazz it was avoided, as a relic of the "old days." The problem with the banjo is that its notes die away very quickly. Béla Fleck plays the banjo "guitaristically"—with bravura lines full of melodic eloquence. It's no accident that he names jazz guitarist Pat Martino as his main inspiration, because, like Fleck, Martino created an entire style based on short-sounding notes.

The "fathers" of cello playing in jazz have already been mentioned in the section about the bass. The most important of them is Oscar Pettiford, who adapted the bebop vocabulary to the cello in an exciting manner. His 1953 recording "My Little Cello," with Julius Watkins and Charles Mingus, marked the beginning of the cellist as jazz leader and composer. Pettiford tuned his cello in fourths, like a bass, rather than the usual fifths. The first jazz cellists—Pettiford, Harry Babasin, Charles Mingus— were originally bass players, and because the bass was generally played pizzicato (i.e., plucked) in modern jazz, these musicians played the cello in the same way. In 1949 Fred Katz was the first, in the Chico Hamilton Quartet, to improvise modern arco (bowed) jazz lines on the cello. With his swinging approach, coming from the classical heritage of the instrument, he was a kind of white counterpart to Oscar Pettiford.

But it was up to Abdul Wadud (who has recorded with quite a few AACM musicians), David Darling, and Hank Roberts to realize the full potential of this instrument in the new jazz—Darling with romanticizing and aestheticizing sounds and a lot of overdubbing, Wadud with convincing jazz feeling and an astonishing talent for improvisation (and yet complete awareness of the classical and romantic cello tradition). In the Julius Hemphill Ensemble, Wadud succeeded in making the cello an integral part of a jazz group. He was the best improvising cellist in the sixties and seventies. Indiana-born Roberts "vocalizes" the cello most intensively, not only figuratively with an absolutely hymnlike sound but also in actual fact. He often complements his cello line with the elegant force of his singing voice, which, like his cello playing, is electronically transformed in a multitude of ways (with a harmonizer, digital delay, headphone microphone, etc.). Another outstanding cellist in the mainstream of contemporary jazz is Jean-Charles Capon from France. Free jazz on the cello is played by Irene Aebi (especially in Steve Lacy's group), Diedre Murray (in the Henry Threadgill Sextet), David Eyges, and Tristan Honsinger. The latter's radically uncompromising playing brings to mind Derek Bailey's guitar style. Tom Cora has represented the cello in the context of "nonidiomatic music" with bizarre distancing of folklore melodies.

The cello is "the human soul transformed into wood," according to Erwin Koch. More and more jazz cellists no longer see the sonic characteristics of their instrument as a limitation, but rather as an opportunity to explore fresh, original sounds. Since the nineties, such players have included, in the post–avant garde, Peggy Lee, Fred Lonberg-Holm, Thomas Ulrich, and Rufus Cappadocia. But musicians like America's Erik Friedlander, Brazil's Jacques Morelenbaum, Germany's Henning Sieverts, and Italy's Paolo Damiani have shown that the cello, although largely ignored by the jazz mainstream, can make significant contributions to the continued development of multi-stylistic jazz. These players understand themselves not as cellists who improvise, but as improvisers who play the cello.

Erik Friedlander is one of the leading string players in the New York downtown scene. Thomas Seinfeld writes, "With Friedlander, you can race through genres like through a ghost train, and in the next moment he gives himself completely to that elegant melancholy that makes the cello the most romantic of all the instruments." Friedlander has played with John Zorn and with the Masada String Trio, as well as with Dave Douglas. With his masterful arco improvisations, he is something like a postmodern Fred Katz, searching for new sound possibilities by consciously adopting the chamber-music aura of the cello and then taking a deliberate step beyond it. "The cello is the perfect musical voice," he says. "You can hear in it the entire range of the human voice, male and female—all inflections, emotions, and different timbres."

For jazz cellists, it is both a problem and a golden opportunity that the instrument has never been dominated by a single great figure. The cello doesn't have its own John Coltrane or Sonny Rollins, musicians who invented styles and inspired schools of followers. But this circumstance gives jazz cellists the freedom to follow their own path in improvised music—in fact, it means that they have to do so. European cellists have particularly distinguished themselves in this respect, above all two musicians who were in great demand in European jazz in the nineties: France's Vincent Courtois and Holland's Ernst Reijseger. In his work with Michael Riessler, Michel Godard, and Rabih Abou-Khalil, Courtois has developed unusual sounds and textures. In his challenging improvisations, he has created new sound possibilities on the instrument, between ethnic music, experimental jazz, and popular music. In Courtois's hands, the cello need not always sound pleasant. Sometimes it sounds rude and insolent; in his playing the cello not only sings but also screams, chirps, murmurs, growls, caresses, buzzes, or tickles.

French cellist Vincent Segal says, "In the world of jazz strings, especially in the European scene, a consciousness of high culture often predominates, in which there's a fear of taking risks." Segal is also seeking to reinvent his instrument. He loves African music, so much that he has played electric bass with Congolese rumba singer Papa Wemba. In his own projects, and in the duo Bumcello with Iranian-French percussionist Cyril Atef, he takes the cello's grooving qualities in new directions, often with the aid of electronics.

With players like Vincent Courtois, Jean-Charles Capon, and Vincent Segal, France has what is perhaps the strongest cello scene in Europe. However, the most important European jazz cellist, Ernst Reijseger, comes from the Netherlands. No other musician has taken the emancipation of the jazz cello beyond stylistic boundaries as far as he has. Reijseger has expanded the spectrum of expression of the cello with unexpected musical turns and a completely unconventional approach to playing the instrument. For more than twenty years, he has been one of the leading figures of the Dutch avant-garde, with the Amsterdam String Trio and the Clusone Trio. He is a nimble, versatile player with remarkable mobility and rhythmic control, able to play several roles in a single group. When he plays solo, it seems as if anything is possible. Sometimes he puts the venerable instrument over his knee like a guitar. He drums on its precious wood as if it were a djembe or a conga. He attacks its strings with a plastic hotel key ring. And if he runs out of fingers to use on the fingerboard, he uses his chin. In Reijseger's playing there is a wonderful balance between precision and imagination, and his solos always have something of the mischievous prankster about them. He says, "For me the cello is the prosthesis that I live with." Han Bennink once called him a "drummer who plays the cello."

France's Pierre Charial has played barrel organ in jazz projects with Michael Riessler and Martial Solal. His barrel organ, equipped with an electric blower, is capable of continuous sound. The barrel organ, a precursor of the player piano, is one of the first mechanically operated musical instruments; its note sequences have to be carefully punched out in cardboard sheets. Charial "orchestrates" note sequences that are too complex to be played by a human musician, overcoming the robotlike character of the instrument as no one else has done.

Guitarist/composer/instrument builder Hans Reichel plays imaginative solos on the "daxophone," an instrument he designed and built himself. In theory, the daxophone is a simple instrument. It is made up of wooden bars clamped into a frame and played with a bow. The player varies the pitch by pressing a piece of wood or metal against the vibrating bar. The resulting sound is reminiscent of a saxophone, but goes well beyond that association. Using overdubbing recording techniques, Reichel has created opulent daxophone "orchestras." On the recording *Yuxo*, for example, on which almost all the sounds are made by the daxophone, he combines an exotic sound full of mysterious beauty with a dash of humor. The wooden bars Reichel uses are mostly unique, and his intimate relationship to them is like that of blues master B. B. King to his guitar, "Lucille." For example, Reichel calls one of his pieces of wood his "million-dollar bass voice." That one is made of green rosewood from India, with a couple of wormholes. "I've tried more than once to make a replica of that piece," he says, "but the result was not satisfactory. It must have something to do with the spirit of the worms."

Non-Western Instruments

The horizon of instruments was extended even further by the non-Western instruments that found their way into jazz in the course of its opening up to the other great musical cultures of the world. Don Cherry, for example, used instruments from Lapland, Africa, Tibet, India, China, and elsewhere. Han Bennink occasionally uses the dhung, a giant Tibetan Alpine horn. Collin Walcott, Bill Plummer, and others have played the Indian sitar for jazz records. Saxophonist Charlie Mariano studied the *nagaswaram*, an oboelike instrument from southern India, for years, first in the city of Kuala Lumpur, then in a small Indian village. He has created a unique union of Karnatic (south Indian) spirituality and the Coltrane tradition.

One of the most interesting among these musicians is Stephan Micus, a meditative "world musician" in the full sense of the term. Micus commands a zither from Bavaria, bamboo flutes from Japan, a *rabab* from Afghanistan and instruments from Bali, India, and Tibet—plus a Scottish bagpipe and steel drums from Trinidad. For years, he traveled in Asia, studying these instruments. He plays them with a profound internationalization of their tradition and spirituality, uniting their sounds in a musical river that makes the stream of inner consciousness audible. The inner space of sounds in search of which so many musicians dared to venture into electronics: Micus not only imagines it, he realizes it—not with electronics, but on instruments thousands of years old.

Because in the "age of migration" since the eighties jazz has become increasingly international, more and more players are appearing on the jazz scene who come from Asia, Africa, the Middle East, and Latin America and who are masters of the instruments of their cultures. These instruments, such as oud, koto, *komungo*, *erhu*, *pipa*, kora, and many others, no longer merely add "exotic" colors to jazz improvisation; now they expand the scope of improvised music by adding fundamental new sonic and playing possibilities.

The Oud

The first of these instruments was the Arab lute called the oud (Arabic for "wood"). Until the seventies, the oud was almost unknown in jazz, but its use is now common in contemporary jazz ensembles. The man responsible for this development is the Lebanese musician Rabih Abou-Khalil, who lives in Munich. He plays the oud with tremendous facility and an élan that transcends boundaries.

Khalil, one of the most successful musicians in world jazz, is a cultural nomad. He has developed a personal language on the oud in which various traditions are expressed in contemporary ways.

Khalil was born and raised in Lebanon and has a close connection to the Middle Eastern musical tradition, which he has wholly assimilated and integrated into contemporary jazz. His music features long, melismatic lines and fast, complicated rhythms, combining to form musical calligraphy of an ornamental beauty.

At the beginning of the eighties, Khalil was almost the only musician playing the oud in jazz. But he was not the first to do so. That distinction is held by Ahmed Abdul-Malik, who played bass with Thelonious Monk. In 1959 Malik, a New York native of Sudanese descent, made the record *East Meets West* with Lee Morgan and Johnny Griffin. On this record he examined his Arab roots, and played the first (somewhat groping) oud jazz solos.

In contemporary jazz, Tunisia's Anouar Brahem is an oud player of great poetry and gentleness. Whereas Rabih Abou-Khalil plays with exuberant virtuosity, Brahem, who had a wonderful trio with Dave Holland and John Surman, favors a simpler approach. He could be regarded as a "Miles Davis of the oud"—a wizard of the expressive omission of everything inessential, a master of spareness and the artful pause. Brahem's playing is characterized by passionate attention to the smallest details and a luxurious enjoyment of the richness of sound. In his solos, the way in which each sound comes into vibrant being and dies away is as important, or even more important, than the choice of notes.

In comparison with this refinement, critics have called the oud playing of Dhafer Youssef (a Tunisian living in Vienna) "awkward" and "coarse." But Youssef's exciting solos and moving Sufi singing place the jazz oud in a space between the mystical and the modern, between East and West. His music is deeply rooted in the Sufi tradition of Islamic mysticism. At the same time, in his collaborations with musicians such as Nguyên Lê and Eivind Aarset he has successfully brought the oud into the realm of digital, electronic sound. Youssef emphatically rejects the "world music" label and has no interest in anything that smacks of "exoticism." "For me, all musicians have the same culture," he says.

Unlike the guitar, the oud has no frets, so that it is difficult to play it in tune. Nonetheless, the instrument has become so popular in jazz that Americans and Europeans are also taking it up. Roman Bunka, former guitarist of the group Embryo, is one of the very few European musicians to have achieved a sensitive mastery of the Arabic art of musical ornamentation. France's Thierry Robert plays the oud in the Breton-flavored folk jazz of the group led by Erik Marchard. Armenia's Ara Dunkjian plays electric oud to great effect, and also uses a MIDI-enabled oud to control a synthesizer. And Tunisia's Smadj (aka Jean-Pierre Smadja) and Algeria's Mehdi Haddab, in their project DuOud, have introduced the oud to the digital universe of drum 'n' bass and electronic breakbeats.

Asian Stringed Instruments

Asian instruments were also used more frequently in jazz in the eighties and nineties. In the tension between age-old tradition and sonic innovation, more and more Asian musicians are pointing the way to new possibilities to contemporary jazz. They bring not only new ideas but also instruments that, despite their ancient traditions, they approach in a personal, unconventional manner. Examples include koto players Miya

Masaoka and Tadao Sawai, *pipa* virtuoso Min Xiao-Fen, Jiebing Chen on the *erhu* (with Max Roach and the Bejing Trio), Xu Feng Xia on the *ghuzeng*, and Korea's Jin Hi Kim on the *komungo*.

Notably, these instruments are used to particularly striking effect in contexts inspired by free jazz. This is due not least to the fact that avant-garde jazz provides an environment in which the sound of these instruments can be investigated and developed in accordance with their own inherent sonic possibilities. Accordingly, these players use not only traditional approaches, but also a range of new ways of playing: experimental bowing techniques, preparing the instrument (in the manner of prepared piano), unorthodox tunings, playing behind the bridge, and so on.

It is certainly no accident that many of the players of non-Western instruments who have made a name for themselves in post–free jazz come from Asia. In Asian musical cultures, there is a strong interest in the "interior life of the sound," just as there is in free improvisation. Conversely, free jazz's emphasis on texture has enabled Asian players to examine and reinvent their instruments in ways that go beyond the traditional approaches to playing them.

The first musician to apply free improvisation to Asian stringed instruments, in the eighties, was Jin Hi Kim, a Korean musician living in New York. She played the *komungo* (a Korean curved zither with six thick silk strings) in downtown avant-garde settings, including work with Elliot Sharp, Malcolm Goldstein, and Henry Kaiser. The strings of the *komungo* are played using a small bamboo plectrum, moving the hand back and forth. Kim uses the overtone-rich, vocal sound of the *komungo* to create improvisations that use highly variable microtonal shadings.

This Asian art of refined differentiation of a vibrating tone through subsequent manipulation, such as artful vibrato and ornamentation, has also been applied to contemporary jazz by Xu Feng Xia, who plays the *ghuzeng*, a twenty-one–stringed curved zither made of sycamore wood whose history reaches back to Chinese dynasties from 700 BCE. She plays slide effects and shimmering overtones so sensitively that the effect is sometimes created of an imaginary version of Delta blues.

Miya Masaoka, a Japanese player of the koto (another twenty-one–stringed curved zither), has made recordings of the music of Thelonious Monk (with Andrew Cyrille and Reggie Workman), finding the tension of stillness in Monk's innovative compositions in a particularly meditative way. The Japanese call this approach to improvising *onkyo* (echo). Masaoka says: "The thing about free improvisation that I find attractive is that you can explore the sound of your instrument on its own terms. I think of the koto very much as a body—a body lying down. It really has its own life and a soul, which is represented by a piece of wood inside it."

Tadao Sawai, a Japanese musician who died in 1997, also explored new territory on the koto. In free duos with bassist Peter Kowald, he extended traditional koto playing to include textural elements such as fluttering sounds, tremolos of harmonics, and a range of plucking techniques of his own devising.

Min Xiao-Fen, a Chinese *pipa* player living in the United States, came to jazz via her collaborations with John Zorn. She made wonderful duo recordings with guitarist Derek Bailey, challenging the master of "nonidiomatic music" to find new conceptions and sounds.

Kora

Improvisers playing non-Western instruments have one distinct advantage over players of more traditional jazz instruments: they don't feel the weight of having to absorb an existing repertoire of established standards for their instrument; they are freer to set these standards for themselves. Xu Feng Xia says, "For me, what is most exciting about playing the *ghuzeng* is reinventing my instrument in free improvisations."

The same is true for the West African musicians who have introduced the kora (a twenty-one–stringed harp) to jazz. The first such player was Guinea's Foday Musa Suso. In 1984, on the Herbie Hancock record *Sound System*, he played the kora in a funk and jazz-rock context.

Tata Dindin has played jazz on the kora in duos with pianist Hans Lüdemann. And Tunde Jegede has done the same with England's Orphy Robinson. Mamadou Diabaté, who lives in New York, played well-known hard-bop compositions by Miles Davis in the nineties, at a festival dedicated to the trumpeter. Bassist Ben Allison has presented Diabaté's kora in his New York Jazz Collective.

Traditionally, the kora is tuned heptatonically (i.e., according to a seven-note scale). In principle, it is not possible to play chromatically between these notes, as in Western music. Confronted with this situation, Senegalese kora player Soriba Kouyaté took measures that would make conservative ethnomusicologists' hair stand on end: he tuned the kora according to a Western scale, somewhat like a guitar, and installed an extra bridge on the instrument, making it fully capable of chromatic playing in the Western sense. This opened up new possibilities for the instrument, which Kouyaté exploits in his jazz-rock–influenced world jazz.

The degree to which the kora has captured the imagination of jazz musicians is well illustrated by the case of free-jazz trombonist Roswell Rudd. "I had a dream," says Rudd, a pioneer of both free jazz and world jazz. "I dreamed of playing with the Charlie Parker of the kora, Toumani Diabaté from Mali." In 2000 the dream came true. The two musicians gave a concert in Bamako, and made the recording *Malicool*. Toumani had previously collaborated with blues singer Taj Mahal. But the seamless compatibility with which his virtuosic kora playing combines with Rudd's earthy trombone shows how far this West African harp has come in jazz.

Mixing Board

In conclusion we must mention two stylists who don't play any instrument in the traditional sense of the word: Kip Hanrahan and Hal Willner. The "instrument" they do play is the recording studio. One could call them—to adapt a term from the visual arts—"conceptualists." That is precisely what they are—shapers of concepts and creators of contexts for ideas, who are much more comprehensively and profoundly creative than is demanded by the role of the usual record producer. Both are masters in bringing about encounters where stylistic divisions are spectacularly surmounted. In his record projects Willner even succeeded in uniting musicians from such "hostile" camps as jazz, pop, chansons, rock, and European concert music. This produced two of the eighties' most original and trailblazing monuments. *That's The Way I Feel Now*, recorded in 1984, is devoted to Thelonious Monk, the incomparable pianist and composer, with fascinating Monk interpretations by such diverse players as John Zorn, Donald Fagen, Arto Lindsay, Joe Jackson, Randy Weston, Bobby McFerrin, Carla Bley, Johnny Griffin. The other album is devoted to Kurt Weill: *Lost in the Stars*, recorded a year later, with unusual interpretations by Lou Reed, Phil Woods, the Armadillo String Quartet, Carla Bley, Tom Waits, Charlie Haden, Sting, Dagmar Krause, and so forth. Willner's recordings have their finger precisely on the pulse of the eclecticism of the eighties and nineties; they are manifestos in opposition to any and all musical ghettoization. Their common thread is that they extend their subject matter, lifting it to another level and opening up new worlds.

Kip Hanrahan, an expert in musical confrontations, even goes a step further in his projects. Here the most divergent of musical worlds collide even more directly and immediately. High friction is generated when the cream of the New York Latin scene encounters avant-garde musicians, rock singers, contemporary jazz makers, Caribbean guitarists, soul musicians, etc. Hanrahan said:

> It's not always putting things together. Sometimes it is putting things apart. I mean, if you have musicians who always play the same things together, you would have to build an obstacle, so that they would have to dismantle their normal way of communicating and build another thing. Sometimes I try very hard to set up a way in which there are tensions between the bands, so that the tensions themselves become the music.

Critics have accused Hanrahan of "charlatanism" and "musical despotism." But, paradoxically, Hanrahan's projects, aiming at contrast and surprising oppositions—his "aesthetic of confrontation"—led to some of the most homogeneous and successful results in eighties and nineties jazz. Particularly successful is his double album *Desire Develops an Edge* (Hanrahan: "The clearest articulation of myself"), which is to multistylistic jazz what Carla Bley's *Escalator over the Hill* was for the jazz of the seventies. Kip Hanrahan tears down barriers between musical ghettos, bringing together what is apparently incompatible. Here that is successful to the utmost degree because Hanrahan doesn't attempt to bring diverging musical styles closer but looks for what they have in common, within their differences.

The Vocalists of Jazz

The Male Singers

Before jazz, there were blues and shouts, work songs and spirituals—the whole treasury of vocal folk music sung by both black and white in the South. There was what Marshall Stearns has called "archaic jazz." From this music jazz developed. In other words, jazz developed from vocal sources. Much about the sounds peculiar to jazz can be explained by the fact that horn blowers imitate the sounds of the human voice on their instruments. This becomes obvious in the growling sounds of trumpets and trombones in the orchestra of Duke Ellington, for example, or in Eric Dolphy's bass clarinet.

On the other hand, jazz today is so exclusively an instrumental music that its standards and criteria derive from the realm of the instrumental, even the standards of jazz singing. The jazz vocalist handles his voice "like an instrument"—like a trumpet or trombone or, today especially, a saxophone. Thus the criteria important to European vocal music, such as purity or range of voice, are inapplicable to jazz. Some of the most important jazz singers have voices that—according to "classical" criteria—are almost ugly. Many have a vocal range so limited that it would hardly encompass a Schubert song.

The dilemma of jazz singing can be expressed as a paradox: all jazz derives from vocal music, but all jazz singing is derived from instrumental music. Significantly, some of the best jazz singers (at least among the males) are also players—above all, Louis Armstrong.

In the literature of jazz, critics of the most diverse persuasions mean to be laudatory when they say of an instrumentalist—such as alto saxo-

549

phonist Johnny Hodges—that his sound "resembles that of the human voice." On the other hand, nothing more flattering can be said of a singer than that he or she knows how to "treat the voice as an instrument."

Only one domain is beyond this dilemma of jazz singing: the blues. But precisely this makes the vicious circle clear. For decades, almost all jazz singers who found favor with the general public were outside the stream of real blues, whereas the first-rate singers of authentic blues and gospel—at least until the big success of blues in rock music from the sixties on—were hardly known. This breakthrough began as early as the late fifties with Ray Charles, a real soul and blues singer in the tradition of folk blues and gospel, who was accepted by the whole world of modern jazz. It has been rightly said that no one did more to assure the return of the blues to the common consciousness of America than Ray Charles in the fifties. But Charles was only the final link (at that time) in an unending chain of soul and blues singers whose earliest representatives disappear somewhere in the darkness of the South of the past century. And simultaneously, he was the first link in the still growing chain of black singers who sing authentic blues and yet have great success even with white audiences.

The first well-known representatives of this blues folklore are probably Blind Lemon Jefferson, a blind street musician from Texas, and Huddie Leadbetter (called Leadbelly), who served time in Angola State Penitentiary in Louisiana, first for murder and a few years later for manslaughter. From them, the line runs via Robert Johnson, who came from Mississippi and was poisoned in Texas, to Big Bill Broonzy and Son House and the many blues singers who made Chicago the blues capital of the United States (though all are natives of the South): Muddy Waters, Little Brother Montgomery, Sunnyland Slim, Sonny Boy Williamson, Little Walter, Memphis Slim, Howlin' Wolf, and many others. John Lee Hooker, who lived in Detroit (and who passed away in 2001), also belongs here, with his dark, hoarse vocal style. Almost all the blues singers are also excellent guitarists. And when they play piano, they accompany themselves with exciting boogie-woogie bass lines. (Other important folk-blues singers are mentioned in the blues section.)

In an unending stream, over the decades, more and more new blues singers became known. There are two main streams in this great blues migration and two main states: Mississippi and Texas. Mississippi-born blues people generally migrate to Chicago; those from Texas go to California. The two streams differ musically, too. The Mississippi stream is rougher, "dirtier"; the Texas stream softer, more flexible and supple. It was the Texas stream that merged with the Midwestern big bands during the Swing era, leading to Swing blues and jazz blues. But here, too, there are, of course, all imaginable kinds of crossings and mixtures.

The blues was as alive in the eighties and nineties as it was during the twenties and thirties. Since the sixties, a new generation of blues singers has appeared, filled with the consciousness of race and social protest that can be found in many contemporary jazz musicians as well. Members of this modern blues generation include singer-harmonica player Junior Wells, singer-guitarists Buddy Guy, Albert King, Albert Collins, Otis Rush, and Luther Allison, as well as Taj Mahal, Robert Cray, and Keb Mo, who have found success with contemporary rock audiences. They no longer hope—as did Trixie Smith and many other twenties blues vocalists, filled with the despair and irony that coexist in the blues—that someday "the sun will shine in their back door." (The irony is in the avoidance of the front door!) Rather, filled with sense of self, they demand—like singer-pianist Otis Spann in 1967—"I Want a Brand-New House."

When Joachim Berendt visited Angola State Penitentiary in the summer of 1960, he heard several young blues singers every bit as good as the well-known Chicago names—among them Robert Pete Williams, who was later released and made a name for himself in blues circles prior to his death in 1980. The day before his visit, there had been a thunderstorm. One of the prisoners told Berendt he had nearly been struck by lightning. He was still under the spell of the fear that had possessed him. Berendt suggested that he might someday write a blues about his experience—and right away, he strummed a few chords on his guitar and improvised his "Lightning Blues." The surprise was the lyrics, which reflected his experience in intensely realistic expression. These blues lyrics are the real "jazz and poetry." Here the difference between "jazz" and "poetry" is one of terminology, not substance.

One of the most successful singer-guitarists of authentic big-city blues for more than forty-five years now is Mississippi-born B. B. King, a cousin of Bukka White, one of the great old folk-blues men. In the 1966 edition of Leonard Feather's *Encyclopedia of Jazz*, it is stated that King "would like to see Negroes become unashamed of blues, their music." Indeed, King himself has been an essential factor in the fulfillment of this wish, though (especially in the middle class) there still are many African Americans who look down on blues as rustic, primitive, and archaic, and want to dissociate themselves from it. The black American will have found the road to full awareness of his own identity—and thus to true equality—only when he takes as much pride in the blues as a German does in Beethoven or an Italian in Verdi.

From the start, the borderline between folk blues as a realm distinct from jazz and the domain of jazz itself has been fluid. A number of singers who are authentic blues singers have been counted as belonging to the jazz world at least as much as to the world of blues. The first of these, and founder of this vocal Swing tradition, was Jimmy Rushing, who died in 1972. Rushing, from Oklahoma (a state that always was within the sphere of Texas blues influence) became *the* blues singer par excellence of Swing style. He was the first not to sing "on the beat," as the folk-blues people did, but in front of or behind the beat, to "sing around" the rhythmic centers and counter them with his own accents, thus creating greater tension. During the thirties and forties, Rushing was Count Basie's singer, and his singing was the exact vocal expression of Basie's instrumental theme of those years: "Swingin' the Blues." Other singers of this brand were Jimmy Witherspoon, active in California, and Big Miller from Kansas City. In the Basie band of the fifties, Joe Williams took the place of Rushing. He was a fine musician, who on the one hand endowed his ballads with a blueslike intensity and on the other sang the blues with the sophistication of a modern jazzman. With his unique phrasing, deep and dark, flexible and charged with the blues, he carried Basie's message into the new mainstream jazz of the eighties. He died in 1999.

Big Joe Turner (1911–85) from Kansas City was the blues shouter of boogie-woogie. In the thirties he worked with the great boogie pianists; a generation later, he had a second round of success—as did many other bluesmen—with the emergence of rock 'n' roll, creating one of its biggest early hits, "Shake, Rattle, and Roll."

One, or even two, steps further was Leon Thomas, combining the blues tradition with the music of the post-Coltrane era in free, cascading falsetto improvisations and yodeled passages, for which he also found inspiration in ethnic music, such as the songs of Central African pygmies. At the end of the sixties, Thomas showed the acute political awareness of the African American civil rights movement in a particularly exemplary manner in his jazz singing. Today such lyrics are unremarkable, but at the time Thomas, who died in 1999, was one of the first to broach such topical subject matter: "How much does it cost to fly a man up to the moon? I think of the hungry children that I see every afternoon."

The line that leads from Blind Lemon Jefferson through the South Side of Chicago to the classic modern blues of Otis Rush and B. B. King is the backbone of all jazz singing. This line could be designated the "blues line" of jazz singing to differentiate it from the "song line." But it is important to see the continuous, intensive interrelationship between these two. This is illustrated by the first and most significant singer of the "song line," Louis Armstrong. Armstrong's music remains related to the blues even when it is not blues—and in the orthodox sense of the word, it rarely is. Armstrong's singing has come to exemplify the basic conception involved not just in jazz but in the whole of pop, rock, and soul music: emotion and personal expression taking precedence over any kind of traditional standards.

Some decades ago, on the occasion of an Armstrong visit, the *London Times* noted, "Of course, this voice is ugly when measured against what Europe calls beautiful singing. But the expression which Armstrong puts into his voice, all the soul, heart, and depth which swing along in every sound, make it more beautiful than most of the technically perfect and pure, but cold and soulless singing in the white world of today."

Trombonist Jack Teagarden sang some of the most humorous and spirited vocal duets in jazz with Armstrong. Teagarden was a master of "sophisticated" blues singing as early as the thirties, long before the ironic sophistication of the blues became "modern" in the late fifties. Later, in a more modern field, one finds in Woody Herman a similar sophistication, tasteful and musicianly, but not as expressive as Teagarden or the great African American vocalists.

Most male singers who have maintained a position in the realm of jazz per se have been instrumentalists. The others who began somewhere within jazz or close to it have gone over to commercial music: Frank Sinatra, Bing Crosby, Frankie Laine, Perry Como, Matt Dennis, and the musically outstanding Mel Tormé. Wavering between jazz and commercial music, Tormé tries to combine both; he belongs among the best and most swinging interpreters of the songs by America's great popular composers.

The question whether Frank Sinatra ought to be considered a jazz singer has been discussed to death by critics. The answer to the question is not really to be found in the fact that in the fifties he was voted the top jazz singer in almost all jazz polls. Rather, the decisive factor is the unique rhythmic quality of his singing. His voice has a seamless, carefully articulated, meaningful substance—and it has an irresistible swing feeling close to that of the Count Basie band, in that it emphasizes the feeling of uniform quarter notes.

In the forties and fifties, commercial singers often used vibrato. Sinatra, on the other hand, developed a sublime legato technique in which he used vibrato only sparingly, and only at the tail end of a note. In this way, he was the antithesis of the "crooners" (though, paradoxically, the designation was later applied to him)—the schmaltzy singers who never tired of using constant vibrato.

Everything Sinatra sang was rooted in a jazz foundation—especially his ballad singing. Even in slow songs, he had a great sense of pulse, earning him the admiration of many jazz musicians, such as Miles Davis and John Scofield. Frank Sinatra was an interactive singer who never sang a song the same way twice. Tenor saxophonist Joe Lovano says, "When Sinatra sang with different bands and singers, his feelings took on the form of the musicians around him."

Appropriately, Nat "King" Cole was a first-rate jazz vocalist as long as he was mainly a pianist. Later, as he became a successful singer in the commercial field, his piano playing and his jazz interest were pushed further and further back. Nevertheless, his jazz roots and a certain jazz *espressivo* remained noticeable in his singing up to his death in 1965. In Cole's singing, rhythm and emotion are in fact one and the same thing. The smoothness of his voice and the swinging brilliance of his lines have influenced generations of singers, Ray Charles to Stevie Wonder to Peter Cincotti. And he influenced instrumentalists as well: Miles Davis wrote in his autobiography that he learned about phrasing from listening to singers like Cole and Sinatra. This is one reason why American commercial music is the world's best: so many of the popular stars have a jazz background and "paid dues" in jazz before attaining commercial success. (Outside the vocal realm, Glenn Miller, Harry James, and Tommy and Jimmy Dorsey are examples of this.)

The jazz instrumentalist, as we said, is especially qualified also to be a good jazz singer. Examples of this can be cited not only from the times of Hot Lips Page and Jack Teagarden, but also in modern jazz: drummer Grady Tate, trombonist Richard Boone, tenor saxophonist George Adams, guitarists George Benson and John Pizzarelli, and trumpeters Chet Baker and Clark Terry are notable singers in their stylistic area—Terry with lots of joy and humor (in his famous "mumbling" style), Boone with a combination of traditional blues and contemporary satire, Baker with an almost "feminine" kind of fragility and a moving understatedness, Benson (he, too!) with a lot of the King Cole tradition of smoothness, Adams with the masculine attack and the fevered falsetto eruptions known from his tenor playing.

In the forties Billy Eckstine was to male singers what Sarah Vaughan was to the females. Eckstine had the greatest vocal gift since Louis Armstrong and Jimmy Rushing. He belonged to the bop circle around Gillespie and Parker and was so full of enthusiasm for their music that he took up an instrument—the valve trombone. "Jelly, Jelly" was the big (and still popular) hit by "Mr. B.," relating bebop to the blues tradition.

With Billy Eckstine we have reached bop, and we should mention Babs Gonzales, whose fun-filled group Three Bips and a Bop was successful in the late forties and who later—as the writer of "Oop-Bop-A-Da," for instance—was one of bebop's entertaining voices; Earl Coleman, whose sonorous baritone was once accompanied by Charlie Parker; and Kenneth "Pancho" Hagood and Joe Carroll, who both worked with Dizzy Gillespie. Carroll reminded people of Dizzy in mobility of voice and sense of humor. Of course, one must not forget Dizzy Gillespie himself when speaking of bop vocalists. Dizzy's high-pitched, slightly Oriental-sounding voice corresponds as closely to Dizzy the trumpeter as Satchmo's voice corresponded to *his* trumpet. Jackie Paris carried the bop vocal conception into cool jazz. Oscar Brown Jr., who worked on Max Roach's *Freedom Now Suite*, was a singer, nightclub artist, and lyricist of great charisma. In 1998, at the age of 72, Brown, who had always thought of himself as part of the black movement with his socially critical lyrics, enjoyed a comeback. Johnny Hartman is a "musicians' singer," whose supple, flowing phrasing (as in his ballad recordings with John Coltrane) has been much admired by connoisseurs. Bill Henderson and (the early) Mark Murphy sing with a healthy, Basie-inspired mainstream conception; the latter has put a whole era of jazz into song with ravishing sophistication. Mose Allison transforms, in a totally personal style, black and white blues and folk songs into his own compositions with a modern soul character. In fact, when soul singing became an "in thing" in the sixties and seventies, some white singers who didn't know the African American tradition at all referred to white Mose Allison—who, to be sure, comes from an overwhelmingly black town in Mississippi and has absorbed black folk music since childhood. Ben Sidran carries the characteristic Allison style into the realms of jazz-rock and fusion.

No doubt the yield of great male jazz singers—aside from the blues singers and Louis Armstrong—is not impressive. This fits our conception of the jazz vocal dilemma. Jazz singing, beyond blues, is the more effective the closer it approximates instrumental use of the voice. The female voice has the greater potential in this respect. It certainly is characteristic that quite a few male singers have had voices that seemed deformed by nature or at least sounded unusual—beginning with Louis Armstrong. Often deformation increases expression.

This aspect is also clear in the style of Jimmy Scott, a vocalist who got his start in 1948 with the Lionel Hampton band, fell into obscurity in the seventies, and then achieved cult status in the nineties, when he was in his seventies. His trademark is an unusually high, fragile sound that by standards of Western singing may seem somewhat flabby and "weepy." But Scott uses these qualities to achieve effects that a "non-deformed" voice would not be able to achieve. Singer Patricia Barber says, "It's like instrumentalists who have too much technique. Listening to them can be less interesting than listening to someone who has limited technique." With his open-hearted, "feminine" singing style, Jimmy Scott combines a feeling of longing and tragedy with a grandiose sense of time.

Also from the realm of bebop stems a development that led to a highly successful vocal group, the Lambert-Hendricks-Ross Ensemble. Eddie Jefferson is the father of "vocalese": he was the first, as early as at the start of the forties, to use the technique of reproducing famous instrumental solos while also providing them with lyrics of his own invention, or "vocalising" them. King Pleasure has often mistakenly been credited with originating this style, because he was the first to present it on record, in 1952. It was not until later that it became known that Pleasure owed his hit "Moody's Mood for Love" to Jefferson, from whom he borrowed this solo, itself taken from a saxophone solo by James Moody.

Eddie Jefferson and King Pleasure were followed by British-born Annie Ross (whose song "Twisted," based on a tenor improvisation by Wardell Gray, was a hit in 1952). Jon Hendricks carried vocalese singing to its peak. He was the actual "poet of the jazz solo," a "James Joyce of Jive," as *Time* magazine called him. Dave Lambert (who died in 1966) had arranged and recorded a group vocal in 1945 with Gene Krupa's big band, "What's This?" which was the first recorded bebop vocal. So in a sense, Dave Lambert, Jon Hendricks, and Annie Ross belonged together musically even prior to forming Lambert, Hendricks, and Ross in 1958. The trio began with vocalizations of Count Basie records and went on from there to develop an entertaining, spirited vocal ensemble style that has remained unique, vocalizing the entire spectrum of modern jazz. When these three sang solos by Charlie Parker, Lester Young, Sonny Rollins, Miles Davis, Oscar Pettiford, John Coltrane, and others to Jon Hendricks's lyrics, one had the feeling that this was what all those great musicians had wanted to say. When Annie Ross returned to England in 1962, Ceylon-born Yolande Bavan took her place until the trio finally broke up in 1964. Hendricks, however, and Eddie Jefferson (who died in 1979) carried on this style—Hendricks also in a musical based on the much-lauded "Evolution of the Blues" he had created for the Monterey Jazz Festival, Jefferson in an inspired collaboration with the alto player Richie Cole.

The extended harmonies of Lambert, Hendricks, and Ross are also a point of reference for the male vocal group who, in the nineties, took a cappella jazz singing to a new level: the six-member vocal collective Take 6, whose de facto leader is Mark Kibble. In the late eighties, when Take 6 appeared on the jazz scene, a cappella groups were not particularly popular—kitschy imitators of Singers Unlimited had given the format a bad reputation. But Take 6, in dynamic songs bridging jazz, gospel, pop, and soul, transformed their voices into instruments, creating the illusion of entire bands complete with vocally produced "bass," "drums," "keyboards," etc., exploiting the capabilities of the human voice to create explosive improvisations that go far beyond what listeners normally expect to hear from vocalists.

Mark Murphy is a "musician's singer" who has modernized swinging mainstream singing like no one else. He is a charismatic, uncompromising improviser, unafraid to take risks. Murphy's chromatic, harmonically ambitious style is based on an unerring sense of rhythm and a stunning ballad style. "They'll ask where they'll get the proper scat syllables from, and I say you'll get them from the drums."

Throughout his career, which has extended over more than forty years, Mark Murphy has remained a "hipster's hipster." After Jon Hendricks, Murphy is the musician who has done the most to keep the flame of bebop alive in male jazz singing—from 1956, when he made his first recording for Decca, through the forty albums that he has recorded under his own name (for the label Muse, among others), to his collaborations with acid-jazz and house musicians such as 4 Hero and U.F.O. His authoritative baritone, with razor-sharp timing and an enormous range, has encompassed everything from blues to samba, tributes to Nat

King Cole, and the beatnik poetry of Jack Kerouac. Liza Minnelli says, "There's a party goin' on in Mark's head, and I want to go to it."

But the "song line," as we called it, of male jazz singing also continues to develop. It has been carried into our times by singers like Bob Dorough, Joe Lee Wilson, Gil Scott-Heron, Lou Rawls, Tony Middleton, and Tom Waits. Dorough sings songs by the great composers of American popular music with the special intensity of contemporary jazz. Wilson is the male singer of the New York avant-garde; he worked with Archie Shepp and Rashied Ali, among others. Scott-Heron is a poet of the ghetto with an acute political and social consciousness. With his hoarse voice, seemingly "eaten up by rust," Tom Waits establishes impressive musical memorials to the outlaws and down-and-outs for whom the American dream has become a nightmare.

We have mentioned the strong influence of Brazilian music on modern jazz, so we ought to name some of the singers from that country: first the two great "father figures" of modern Brazilian music, Antonio Carlos Jobim and the incomparably relaxed João Gilberto; later, among the younger vocalists, Edu Lôbo, Gilberto Gil, Caetano Veloso, Vinicius Cantuaria, and above all Milton Nascimento. They all possess that melodic enchantment and poetry that makes Brazilian music so unmistakable, the younger ones also with a more contemporary manner and socially critical approach. Nascimento's instrumental falsetto singing—floating way up in the heights, "angelically" dreamy and at the same time unusually expressive—attracted astonishingly many followers in jazz, influencing Pedro Aznar, David Blamires, Mark Ledford, and the Cameroonian electric bassist Richard Bona (all four of these in the Pat Metheny Band), Delmar Brown (in the Gil Evans Orchestra), and guitarist Michael "Gregory" Jackson.

Al Jarreau became the most successful and most frequently named singer of the seventies. He says that he took his cues from Billie Holiday and Nat King Cole and especially from the Lambert-Hendricks-Ross trio. That connection is even visible: when Al sings his saxophonelike phrases, he moves his fingers and his hands as if he were playing some imaginary instrument—just the way Jon Hendricks used to do years ago. Jarreau's throat produces an entire orchestra of sounds: drums and saxophones, trumpets and flutes, congas and basses—all from the mouth of one man, from the lowest bass to the highest falsetto, as if he had a dozen or more different male and female voices at his disposal. Later Jarreau went the way of so many male jazz vocalists, but his inimitable jazz feeling remains apparent even in his commercial successes as a pop and soul singer.

Anyone who thought that Jarreau's vocal skills could scarcely be exceeded discovered otherwise at the start of the eighties with the appearance of Bobby McFerrin. McFerrin disposes over an arsenal of vocal possibilities that no other male singer can match. Bobby was the son of an opera singer, began as a pianist, and was influenced by Jon Hendricks, Ornette Coleman, Herbie Hancock, and above all Keith Jarrett. He's capable of effortlessly sustaining unaccompanied solo concerts for hours. But his inventive wit is best revealed in dialogue with other musicians, such as pianist Chick Corea. He exploits his entire vocal range with devastating agility, using his hands to drum the beat on his chest and changing vocal registers so quickly as to create an impression of polyphony. You think that everything is sounding out at the same time: deep bass lines, highest falsetto parts, accompanying voices, the rhythmic sizzling of hi-hat patterns, guitar riffs, and "blown" sounds—all enriched with a panorama of sounds for which you would have to invent a new vocabulary to capture their novelty and unfamiliarity. With Bobby McFerrin the entire body becomes an orchestra. "Other people have to project their sensations and feelings through an instrument," said McFerrin, "but a singer only has to open his mouth." McFerrin achieves this striking multitude of possibilities by singing not just during exhalations (as normal vocalists do) but also when he is breathing in, thereby surmounting the handicap of disruptive pauses for taking breath, a technique that he is the first jazz singer to employ consistently.

Strict jazz fans took amiss McFerrin's hit "Don't Worry, Be Happy," but for the singer, that was the greatest success in his career. For weeks he dominated the international hit parades exclusively through the power of his voice alone. He sang all the parts by way of playback in a realm where synthesizers, computers, and other electronic equipment usually set the style. McFerrin's comment: "I'm my own Walkman."

Strikingly associated with the development of modern male jazz singing was the initially increasing use of the voice as an instrument. The importance of the lyric, of the sung text, clearly receded into the background. Bebop vocalists still aligned their singing with the horns, mainly saxophones and trumpets, which they not infrequently imitated. With Jarreau and McFerrin, however, the "entire" palette of orchestral instruments opened up for the voice: bass, flute, percussion, guitar, saxophone, drums, etc. On the other hand, the vocalese songs of Eddie Jefferson and Jon Hendricks—as sung "copies" of famous jazz solos—may be instrumental in character but they are still very closely linked with texts. For Al Jarreau and Bobby McFerrin, the instrumental aspect predominates to such an extent (except in their pop vocals) that the sung text is of little significance.

At the beginning of the nineties, the pendulum swung in the opposite direction. Suddenly, the possibilities of the voice as an instrument seemed to have been taken as far as they could go, and singers came back to the song line. This was connected with the fact that many older jazz singers, who had toiled in relative obscurity during the seventies, suddenly enjoyed comebacks. These included not only mature masters such as Freddy Cole, Oscar Brown Jr., and Jimmy Scott, but also Andy Bey. Next to Louis Armstrong and Mark Murphy, Bey is one of the four or five singers who can be said to have set the standard for male jazz singing. His soft singing creates an almost mystical, atmospheric effect. "As soon as he opens his mouth, you're transported to another place," says Jamie Cullum.

Even at its most full-throated, Andy Bey's singing radiates a stately mildness. One of his specialties is what he calls his "quiet style," in which he uses his baritone voice to create a tender softness, full of longing. He achieves this through the use of soft, dark, palatal sounds. Astonishingly, his sound seems to gain in power when he uses this technique, whereas many other jazz singers sound thinner and more hemmed-in when they sing softly. Bey says, "Singing in the soft palate is about singing *on your breath*."

Every singer approaches the lyrics of a song differently; this is one of the things that defines his style. The song singers of the eighties and nineties were distinguished by an extraordinary stylistic breadth. "Nu crooners" such as Harry Connick Jr. (entertaining, with a boyish wit), his protégé Peter Cincotte (elegant and personable), and England's Jamie Cullum (cheerful and intelligent) carry on the smooth, smart jazz singing tradition of Nat King Cole and Frank Sinatra while integrating influences from soul, pop, hip-hop, and dance music. Cullum is a particularly nimble musician, who gives jazz standards pop appeal. Cullum says, "Today you can't be a purist any longer. If you are one, it might be that you have certain deficits, that you just haven't been confronted with enough different things."

Turning to singing in free music: English-born Phil Minton (also a wonderful conventional singer) has opened up male jazz singing to the possibilities of noise: squeaking, screeching, groaning, moaning, raving as if he were driving all these "deformed" sounds to the limits of "white noise," but nevertheless organizing and refining them with such musicality and outstanding technical ability that he became the singer most in demand in European free improvisation. Minton could make art out of singing the phone book. Beginning with Minton, a lineage of singers utilize what could be called extended or extreme vocal techniques—radical vocal effects extending up to noise textures and "nonvocal" mouth sounds. One such sound poet is the Dutchman Jaap Blonk, who has used these bizarre textures in improvisation with percussionist Paul Lytton. France's Mederic Collignon is another vocalist whose original, unorthodox vocal sounds—uninhibited sounds made with the lips, tongue, and cheeks—have earned him a place as a mainstay of the French jazz scene in bands led by Louis Sclavis and Andy Emler. Collignan is a master of rapid changes of tempo and register, focusing his virtuosic range of squawks and squeaks, growls and grumbles, rustles and roars to great musical effect.

Two other singers who, like Minton and Collignon, stand beyond the song line, forming a "noise line," are guitarist Arto Lindsay and drummer David Moss—Lindsay with the protest-charged, eruptive rage of punk (softened by his Brazilian-tinged poetry), and Moss with the childlike curiosity of the playful inventor of sounds. Beginning in the eighties, Moss, an American, began to make the intensity and physical presence of his voice the main focus of his music, with eccentric, wild singing, full of postmodern use of pieces that veer between blues and atonality, and lines that sparkle with erratic, surprising ideas.

In world jazz, singers such as Russia's Sergey Starostin, India's Amit Chatterjee, the Basque Beñat Achiary, Italy's Gavino Murcia, and Germany's Simon Jakob Drees have combined contemporary jazz singing with the roots of various folk music traditions.

Gavino Murcia specializes in a particularly rough, guttural, earthy variant of scat singing, inspired by Sardinian folk music; he has made virtuosic use of this technique in the Rabih Abou-Khalil Ensemble. Sergey Starostin has incorporated elements of Russian folklore into the contemporary jazz of the Moscow Art Trio. Amit Chatterjee and Simon Jakob Drees have created a truly global music by using Asian overtone singing in contemporary jazz—Chatterlee with unusual power in Joe Zawinul's Syndicate, and Drees in the band Ahava Raba, inspired by East Asian and Balkan music. Benat Achiary has adapted the Basque vocal tradition to free improvisation.

We have said a great deal about the tradition of black music in this book. Among the instrumentalists, the avant-garde musicians—like those from the AACM circle—have often been the ones who have maintained this tradition. The situation is quite different with the vocalists. Especially among the female singers, avant-garde musicians have had almost nothing to do with the tradition. Here, the black tradition is largely cultivated in a field outside of jazz—the area of pop music. This was already under way with the successful soul singers of the sixties (unthinkable without Ray Charles): Otis Redding leading by way of James Brown (whose cry, "Say it loud, I'm Black and I'm Proud!" did more for the new self-confidence of the black masses than all the words of people like Eldridge Cleaver, Rap Brown, or Stokely Carmichael) and Marvin Gaye ("Save the World—Save the Babies—Save the Children!") to Stevie Wonder and Prince.

What these vocalists sing is, very much in the sense intended by Charles Mingus and Roland Kirk, "black music"—in fact, in particular with Stevie Wonder, "black classical music." Wonder has been compared as a composer with Duke Ellington. His albums, some of them consisting of several records—*Songs in the Key of Life*, *Hotter Than July*, and *Journey through the Secret Life of Plants*—are suitelike compositions conceived as large works with an inner coherence; they summarize and recapitulate the heritage of black music in a way similar to Ellington. Wonder is a musician of fascinating universality and flexibility. He is a composer and arranger as well as a singer, plays almost every imaginable instrument on his records, and commands all the modern studio techniques: overdubbing, all kinds of synthesizers and sound manipulators, etc., as if the studio with all its electronic gadgetry were an additional instrument on which to play music (which, in fact, it is).

It was not until the eighties and nineties that male jazz singers began to discover their own tradition, in a manner strikingly parallel to the "young lions" movement among instrumentalists. At that time, with the reexamination of the timeless standards of the Great American Songbook, there was finally a renaissance of male singers. Young stylists such as Kevin Mahogany, Allan Harris, Miles Griffith, Steve Tyrell, and England's Ian Shaw began to find an enthusiastic audience for swinging mainstream singing, where Jon Hendricks and Mark Murphy had long seemed to be two lone prophets in the wilderness.

Kevin Mahogany is from Kansas City. He was originally a mediocre saxophonist who imagined fantastic solos that he wasn't able to play. He eventually decided to cut out the middleman, as it were, and became a jazz singer. His baritone effortlessly embraces the entire tradition of classic modern jazz singing. Mahogany continues the tradition of romantic African American singers of the forties and fifties, a lineage that began with Herb Jefferies and Billy Eckstine and continued through Al Hibbler and Johnny Hartman. Mahogany's strongest suit is his versatility. He can sing blues like Joe Williams, ballads like Johnny Hartman, can unleash scat solos like Jon Hendricks, and masterfully handles the standards of the Great American Songbook—all with his own sound, "warm and rich as Devon cream" (Jon Hendricks), soulful and beautiful.

Allan Harris is keeping the legacy of Johnny Hartman alive. Miles Griffith sang the part of "Jesse" in Wynton Marsalis's Pulitzer Prize–winning oratorio *Blood on the Fields*. Ian Shaw is a singer who is carrying on the tradition of Mel Tormé in a contemporary context, simultaneously honoring and deconstructing jazz standards.

Germany's Philip Weiss was a pianist before he became a jazz singer; perhaps this explains the unusual sophistication and refinement of his melodic lines. He is also a masterful interpreter of ballads (which cannot be said of all contemporary male jazz singers), finding wonderfully warm, subtle voicings in his work with the trio of pianist Steve Kuhn.

Even an older singer like Giacomo Gates can be situated in the lineage of interesting new mainstream singers, with a particular preference for the bop vocals of Jon Hendricks and the lines of tenor saxophonists. Gates says, "Some of my favorite singers are Dexter Gordon, Ben Webster, and Lester Young. They were singing through the horn. If that isn't singing, I don't know what is!"

Multistylistic contemporary jazz singing has been particularly fruitful in Europe. Here, Belgium's David Linx, England's Cleveland Watkiss, Hungary's Gabor Winand, and Germany's Michael Schiefel and Theo Bleckmann (living in New York since 1989) have found creative freedom in spontaneous treatment of a wide variety of materials. David Linx has made moving recordings with African American poet and novelist James Baldwin. Their collaborative CD *A Lover's Question* (with Steve Coleman) is a sparkling encounter, rich in ideas, between black poetry and contemporary jazz singing, in which music and lyrics swing together on a high level.

Cleveland Watkiss, who emerged from the Jazz Warriors, represents the expressive richness of Afro-British music that jazz musicians grow up with in London. His voice covers an extraordinarily broad stylistic spectrum, from classic mainstream singing to reggae and rock to electronica, dance, and drum 'n' bass, where he works with Project 23.

Michael Schiefel is one of the few German jazz musicians who has a truly original style. He is an enormously gifted solo performer who, in his unaccompanied appearances, extends and denatures his voice with electronics. In group contexts, he creatively undermines the machismo still prevalent in the jazz world with his "gay" singing (as evidenced on his CD *Gay*).

Theo Bleckmann has made a name for himself as an outstanding singer of the New York downtown scene, above all in duos with drummer John Hollenbeck and trumpeter Dave Douglas.

Good voices can't be tamed. In mainstream male jazz singing, Mark Murphy has made great strides in the direction of more freedom. This is probably why so many contemporary jazz singers take his work as a point of reference, much as many female jazz singers relate to Betty Carter. Two of the most exciting of these male singers are Chicago's Kurt Elling and New York's Curtis Stigers, both of whom are highly eclectic. Stigers, who came up through the band of pianist Gene Harris, masterfully transforms pop, folk, and country songs into new jazz standards, leaping modernistically from one stylistic world to the next in the blink of an eye.

Kurt Elling says that he feels particularly influenced by musicians "who exist in the right moment of freedom"—players like Tony Williams, Wayne Shorter, and Keith Jarrett. Elling's wealth of ideas and forward-thinking musicality have made him one of the most original vocalists in contemporary jazz. "He's the sum of all parts that have come before him, and has actually transcended the masters," says Jamie Cullum. Elling has a rich, full voice that extends from the tenor range all the way down to the low baritone, even deeper than Murphy. He has developed an innovative way of breaking up his phrases. He combines the soft sound of the crooner with a willingness to take musical risks, from free scat singing to the fusion of bebop vocalese with the beat poetry of Allen Ginsberg. In this way, Kurt Elling represents a swinging approach to jazz singing in which anything is possible stylistically. Elling says, "I like what trumpeter Cootie Williams said once: 'The material is immaterial.'"

The Female Singers

The history of female blues singing starts later than male blues singing. No female singers from "archaic" times are known to us. Folk-blues singers like Blind Lemon Jefferson, Leadbelly, or Robert Johnson did not have female counterparts. The simple, rural world of folk blues was dominated by man; woman was an object. This changed as soon as the blues moved into the big cities of the North. At that time—in the early twenties—the great era of classic blues, whose "mother" was Ma Rainey and whose "empress" was Bessie Smith, began. In the section on Bessie, we discussed the classic blues period in detail. Singers like Bertha "Chippie" Hill, Victoria Spivey, Sippie Wallace, and Alberta Hunter carried on the message of classical blues, while Big Mama Thornton incorporated it into rhythm 'n' blues. But it is important to note that in the late twenties the musical climate was already changing, shifting the accent away from the blues and toward the song.

The first female singers important in this field (who are worth listening to even today) are Ethel Waters, Ivie Anderson, and Mildred Bailey. Ethel Waters was the first to demonstrate, as early as the twenties, the many possibilities for jazz singing in good commercial tunes. Ivie Anderson became Duke Ellington's vocalist in 1932 and remained for almost twelve years; Duke called her the best singer he ever had. Mildred Bailey, of part-Indian origin, was a successful singer of the Swing era with great sensitivity and mastery of phrasing. She was married to Red Norvo, and with him, Teddy Wilson, and Mary Lou Williams, she made her finest recordings. Her "Rockin' Chair" became a hit of considerable proportions; it was a blues, but an "alienated," ironic blues.

The songs of the female singers in this "song line" were—and are— the ballads and pop tunes of "commercial music," the melodies of the great American popular composers—Cole Porter, Jerome Kern, Irving Berlin, George Gershwin—sometimes even tunes from the "hit parade," all sung with the inflection and phrasing typical of jazz.

In this area, improvisation has retreated to a final, irreducible position. The songs must remain recognizable, and of course the singers are dependent upon the lyrics. But in a very special sense there can be improvisation here, too. It lies in the art of paraphrasing, juxtaposing, transposing—in the alteration of harmonies, and in a certain way of phrasing. There is a whole arsenal of possibilities for enunciating, emphasizing, and modulating words differently—"shaping" them, as it is called—of which Billie Holiday, the most important figure in this area, had supreme command. Billie was the embodiment of a truth first expressed by Fats Waller (and after him by so many others): in jazz it does not matter so much what you do, but *how* you do it. To pick one example among many: in 1935 Billie Holiday recorded (with Teddy Wilson) a banal little song, "What a Little Moonlight Can Do," and what resulted was a completely valid work of art.

Billie Holiday sang blues only incidentally. But through her phrasing and conception, much that she sang seemed to become blues. She made more than one thousand records—among them about seventy with Teddy Wilson. She made her most beautiful recordings in the thirties with Wilson and Lester Young. In the intertwining of the lines sung by Holiday and the lines played by Young, the question of which is lead and which is accompaniment, which line is vocal and which instrumental, becomes secondary.

Billie Holiday is the great songstress of understatement. Her voice has none of the volume and majesty of Bessie Smith. It is a small, supple, sensitive voice; yet Holiday sang a song that, more than anything sung by Bessie Smith or the other female blues singers, became a musical protest against racial discrimination. This song was "Strange Fruit" (1939). The "strange fruit" hanging from the tree was the body of a lynched Negro. Holiday sang this song as if she were stating a fact: that's the way it is. Any blues by Bessie Smith, even a simple, everyday love song, was sung with more emphasis and pathos than this, the most emphatic and most impassioned musical testimony against racism until Abbey Lincoln's interpretation of Max Roach's *Freedom Now Suite* of 1960.

Billie Holiday's range was limited—not much more than two octaves. But she had great control of timbre and tonal color. She was able to create significant changes in mood and meaning through the smallest gradations of musical nuance. Of all the women singers in jazz, she had the greatest ability to turn a song lyric on its head, ironizing and contesting its surface meaning. She took liberties, singing slow songs fast and transforming up-tempo numbers into ballads. She sang happy songs with a soft bitterness that negated the sugary sweetness of Tin Pan Alley. Billie didn't sing or interpret songs so much as she *created* them. She sang songs not only as if she had written them herself, but as if she had just written them that morning.

Charm and urbane elegance, suppleness and sophistication are the chief elements in the understatement of Billie Holiday. These elements can be found everywhere—for example, in "Mandy Is Two" (1942), a song about little Mandy, who is only two years old but already a big girl. And this is expressed so straightforwardly and warmly! How simple and unpretentious it is! Nothing rings false, as is the rule with commercial ditties attempting childlike naïveté. It is almost inconceivable that something seemingly destined by every known law to become kitsch could be transformed into art.

Billie's singing had the elasticity of Lester Young's tenor playing, and she had this elasticity prior to her first encounter with Lester. Billie was the first artist in all of jazz—not just the first woman or the first jazz singer—in whose music the influence of the saxophone as the style and sound-setting instrument became clear. And this took place, only seemingly in paradoxical fashion, before the beginning of the saxophone era, which actually only began with the success of Lester Young in the early forties. The "cool" tenor saxophone sound is apparent already in Billie Holiday's first recording—"Your Mother's Son-in-Law," made in 1933 with Benny Goodman. It can be said that because of Billie Holiday, modern jazz had its beginning in the realm of singing earlier than in the field of any instrument.

It had its beginning with Holiday also because she was the first to realize—certainly subconsciously—that not only was her voice the instrument but also the microphone. Holiday was the first vocalist to understand that a singer using a microphone has to sing in a totally different way from one not using a mike. She humanized her voice by "microphonizing" it, thus making subtleties significant that had been unknown in all singing up to that point—in fact, that had been unnecessary, because they could not have been made audible.

When Billie opened her mouth to sing, the truth emerged. Her voice expressed the damage and vulnerability of her soul with an almost masochistic honesty, from desire and lust, to joy and optimism, to doubt, sadness, and pain. Her mouth was like an open wound; she wore her heart on her tongue. And when she sang about loneliness, she drew the listener irresistibly into *her* loneliness.

Billie Holiday didn't just sing sad or happy songs. That's what women singers in popular music normally do: sing sad and happy songs. In Billie Holiday's singing, on the other hand, contradictory emotions and feelings exist simultaneously, blending with each other while contradicting each other. Or, as rock singer Bryan Ferry remarked, "Her style sings of hope . . . her message is despair."

The life story of Billie Holiday has been told often and even more often has been effectively falsified: from servant girl in Baltimore through rape and prostitution to successful song star, and through narcotics all the way downhill again. In 1938 she worked with Artie Shaw's band, a white group. For months she had to use service entrances, while her white colleagues went in through the front. She had to stay in dingy hotels and sometimes couldn't even share meals with her associates. And she had to suffer all this not only as a black but also as the sole woman in the band. Billie felt she had to go through all this to set an example. If it could work for *one* black artist, others could make it, too. She took it . . . until she collapsed.

Before that, she had appeared with another great band, that of Count Basie, and had suffered the reverse kind of humiliation, possibly even more stinging than what she had to endure in Shaw's band: though Billie was as much an African American as any of Basie's musicians, her skin color might have seemed too light to some customers, and it was unthinkable at that time to present a white female singer with a black band. At a theater appearance in Detroit, Billie had to put on dark makeup.

In the last years of her life—she died at the age of forty-four in 1959—Billie Holiday's voice was often a mere shadow of her great days. She sang without the suppleness and glow of the earlier recordings; her voice sounded worn, rough, and old. Still, even then her singing had magnetic powers. It is extraordinary to discover just how much a great artist has left when voice and technique and flexibility have failed and nothing remains except the spiritual power of creativity and expression. To hear this on recordings made by Billie Holiday in the fifties is an almost eerie experience: a vocalist devoid of all the material and technical attributes of her profession who still remains a great artist.

Rock singer Marianne Faithful said, "Every time I sing, I pray to Billie Holiday to help me: the singers's saint." Holiday stands at the center of great jazz singing. After her comes a host of female singers whose common denominator was, and still is, their application of Billie's accomplishments to the particular stylistic field to which they belong.

Ella Fitzgerald also stemmed from the Swing era. But Fitzgerald, born in 1917 and thus only three years younger than Billie Holiday, was not only a great Swing vocalist but also one of the great voices in all of classic modern jazz. No other singer—and hardly any other jazz musician—commanded a wider range of music. In the thirties, her big hit "A-Tisket, A-Tasket," done with the Chick Webb band, was a naively playful song dressed up in the Swing sounds of the day. In the forties, her scat vocals (discussed later) on such themes as "How High the Moon" or "Lady Be Good" led to the core of bop. In the fifties, Ella developed a mature ballad conception. Her interpretations of the "songbooks" of the great American songwriters—Gershwin, Kern, Porter, Berlin, Arlen—are among the great, lasting documents of American music. Much of the reverence that listeners today have for the classic American popular songs has its origin in the way Ella Fitzgerald sang them. From the sixties to the eighties she retained supreme mastery of all the different styles through which she lived and sang.

Until her death in 1996, Ella still had, with her pure, beautiful tone, something of the simplicity and lightheartedness of the fifteen-year-old girl who was discovered in January 1934 in an amateur contest at Harlem's Apollo Theatre—as were so many other great jazz talents (for example, her greatest competitor, Sarah Vaughan). The "prize" Ella won back then was a "short" engagement with Chick Webb's band, but the engagement did not end even with Webb's death five years later. In 1939 Ella took over nominal leadership of the Webb band for a while.

June Christy was *the* voice of Stan Kenton's band, and the warm, human climate of her singing won her many friends time and again, even when one could not go along with her all the way as far as intonation was concerned. June Christy replaced Anita O'Day with Kenton in 1947. O'Day (who died in 2006) is still considered to be the "greatest white female jazz vocalist in classic modern jazz," with a musical assurance of virtuoso caliber and great improvisational capacity. Her riff-based, cool singing style had great forward momentum and a strong personality. O'Day: "If you want to sing jazz, it has to have a heart—and the tempo *is* the heart."

Even more important female vocalists came from the circle surrounding Charlie Parker and Dizzy Gillespie: Sarah Vaughan, Carmen McRae, and somewhat later, because she initially was with Lionel Hampton's band, Betty Carter. Like so many jazz singers, Sarah Vaughan (1924–90) received her first impulses in a gospel church. She said, "You have to have a little soul in your singing, the kind of soul that's in the spiritual. . . . It's a part of my life." In 1943 she became the singer of Earl Hines's band; in 1944 of Billie Eckstine's. Both bands were "talent cradles" for the important bebop musicians of those years, and Sarah knew immediately: "I thought Bird and Diz were the end. I still do. I think their playing influenced my singing."

Sarah Vaughan was the first real jazz singer with a vocal range equal to that of an opera singer. In fact, "Sassy" (her nickname) had a vocal flexibility and richness of modulation in comparison with which many a coloratura soprano might seem somewhat bland. She invented blazing lines that covered her entire vocal range in two beats. She tailored her vibrato to the needs of the moment every time she used it, like a new sculpture. Her rich, dark contralto brought a new sound into jazz singing. Her ability to change this sound in the most diverse manner and to literally charge it with emotional content surpassed anything done by any other female jazz singer.

Sarah Vaughan's voice has a richness of colors that borders on the extravagant. In her many-faceted music, she had the luxury of ignoring stylistic boundaries, whether she was singing gospel, pop, or jazz. She was devoted to the song and to the story. With her voice, "she could go wherever she happened to think about," says Karrin Allyson.

Vaughan's stature is so towering that other singers of her generation remained in her shadow. This is particularly regrettable with Carmen McRae (who was once married to Kenny Clarke, the creator of bebop drum style). She is also one of the great individualists of classic modern jazz singing. Especially impressive is the way McRae (who died in 1994) sounds so robust and resolute. She was a master of swing who knew how to give even cheerful songs a dark, sarcastic tinge. Her improvisations are statements, definitive and powerful. "Sing the song—just make the statement and leave it alone," was her advice to younger jazz singers, who, with all their quasi-instrumental vocal virtuosity, sometimes seemed to forget what the lyrics were actually about. Nat Hentoff once compared McRae with a "sternly exotic figurehead over the cutwater of a New England whaling ship," referring both to her personality *and* to the powerful individualism of her singing.

McRae's junior by eight years, Betty Carter was recognized only relatively late by the jazz world as belonging among the great bop singers. Only in the course of the seventies did she become an embodiment of bebop singing—in fact, of jazz vocalizing in general. Betty Carter upholds the standards, the great songs of American popular music, by fragmenting and adapting them in the most subtle and original fashion. She said: "If you want to interpret a standard that's already been played many times, don't do it the way everyone else did. Change it. Sing it your way." For this reason, she gives standards introductions and extensions that completely transform the song. Even though you're never in doubt about what song this is, you nevertheless think she's inventing, here and now, a completely new piece. Her interpretations are peppered with atmospheric transformations and unexpected changes of mood, with explosive fluctuations of rhythm and sudden variations of tempo. Yet they are all presented with the sovereign assurance of a musician who has carried forward and further developed the best of classical jazz singing, creating an absolutely individual language of her own. Her own groups, which she led from the eighties until her death in 1998, were an inexhaustible breeding ground for young talents of the new mainstream jazz. Important players such as pianists John Hicks and Benny Green, or drummers Clarence Penn, Kenny Washington, and Gregory Hutchinson, came from her bands.

Jazz singers such as Betty Carter, Ella Fitzgerald, and Carmen McRae have an immediate intensity that is reflected and radiated by their rhythm sections. It's important to realize that this rhythmic energy largely comes from the singing, because these singers phrase in a way that makes the entire band swing. Ronald Shannon Jackson, formerly one of Betty Carter's drummers, says:

> The role of the drum in Betty Carter's group was not just a time-keeping device. It was to accent what she was singing. She scatted and phrased the words of the songs with such finesse and style, with such rhythmic pull, that it was like the drum and her voice were one thing. . . . We were still calling her Betty Bebop at that time, because she could sing the same rudiments with her voice that you could play on the drums.

Other female singers of this generation are Chris Connor, Jackie Cain, Dakota Staton, Ernestine Anderson, Abbey Lincoln, Helen Merrill,

Carol Sloane, Nina Simone, Shirley Horn, Nancy Wilson, and Sheila Jordan. Ernestine Anderson's comment, "If I had my way, I'd sing true like Ella and breathe like Sarah Vaughan," is in many ways the musical creed of most of them: they want to sound like Ella Fitzgerald in terms of expression and like Sarah in terms of phrasing, though some of them also want it the other way around, combining Ella's phrasing with Sarah's expression.

Jackie Cain first became known in Charlie Ventura's band. With her husband, pianist-arranger Roy Kral, she forms perhaps the most perfect vocal duo in jazz history—spirited, pleasant, humorous. Helen Merrill is a much underrated singer. She has often been accompanied by John Lewis, the former leader of the Modern Jazz Quartet, and indeed has some of his sensitivity and sophistication. Nina Simone's was an especially passionate voice in the struggle for black dignity and identity, a struggle she supported as a woman, singer, pianist—as an entire human being. She once referred to the blues as "racial memory," and this memory is the source for her songs, however entertaining they may sound. Abbey Lincoln has also addressed the social problems facing African Americans, especially in songs by Max Roach, her former husband, whose *Freedom Now Suite* she sang with poignant and moving emotion. She transformed the cry of Billie Holiday into a modern jazz idiom in the most individual way, and contributed many original songs, with interesting melodies, to the repertoire of jazz. "I think young singers today should . . . not sing these old standards, which are great . . . but they have been done and done and done." Her seriousness about this is attested by the fact that long after she attained fame, she began taking composition lessons in order to write her own songs. Continuing into the twenty-first century, she has demonstrated great feeling for the combination of outstanding musicians and unusual instrumentations.

Shirley Horn (d. 2005), with her dreamlike ballad singing, was a master of spareness and economy, making her in this regard a kind of Miles Davis of jazz singers. Mark Murphy says: "I tell my students to listen to her and Miles for their use of *space*."

Sheila Jordan is of special significance. She has "emancipated" song singing, thus paving the way for all the female vocalists in free jazz whom we will discuss later. Sheila became known through her work with George Russell—above all, in the grandiose, satirical "You Are My Sunshine," a spoof full of sharp, cynical criticism of American society.

Once more, we have to backtrack: In his uncompromising endeavors to use the human voice as instrumentally as possible, Duke Ellington first employed Adelaide Hall, then Kay Davis, the former in the twenties, the latter in the forties. Kay Davis's voice was used as a kind of coloratura above the orchestra, often scored in parallels with clarinet, creating a fascinating meshing of sounds. Later, this combination of a jazz voice with the sound of an ensemble or full band was used by others, but few remember that this, too, began with Duke.

One result of the instrumental conception of jazz singing is the development of scat vocals: stringing together "nonsense" syllables with complete absence of lyrics. Louis Armstrong "invented" scat singing way back in the twenties; the story goes that he hit upon it when he forgot the lyrics while recording the song "Heebie Jeebies" in 1926. Anita O'Day, June Christy, Sarah Vaughan, Carmen McRae, Dakota Staton, Jackie Cain, Annie Ross, Betty Roché, Betty Carter, Dianne Reeves, Maria João, and others have created excellent scat vocals; but the mistress of this domain, often also referred to as "bebop vocal," still is Ella Fitzgerald.

It is important to see that scatting—wordless singing of "arbitrarily" combined syllables—has nothing to do with "nonsense vocalizing." The scat vocals of well-known jazz singers cannot simply be interchanged with each other. Not every syllable is suitable for every musical situation. As one critic put it, "Scat singers select their favorite syllables as a countess might select pearls at the jeweler's."

Some syllables are used by singers to imitate particular qualities of various instruments, while other syllables embody the individual sound that the singer develops as a trademark. Thus, each of the great scat vocalists has developed a personal way of handling syllables, as Carmen Mundy explains:

> Certain scat singers use the syllable *dwee* a lot. Ella doesn't really use a lot of *dwee*. She uses a little more *bee-bop-bop-bah-ooo-bee-doo-bee*. She uses more of the *bee* and *dee* sounds. But then I came to listen to Betty Carter, and she would use more of the *louie-ooie-la-la-la*, like it was more of a tongue thing with her. Sarah Vaughan would be *shoo-bee-oo-bee shoo-doo-shoo-bee-ooo-bee*. She had more of this *shoo-eee-bee-deee* sound. . . . One time Betty Carter told me, "What you have to do is find your own syllables."

Scat singing moves beyond the song line and the words of the lyrics. It tries to rattle the bars of the cage of semantic meaning, to escape the limits of verbal logic, rationality, and everyday meaning. The syllables dance their own dance, independent of the gravity of the words. The components of words are no longer saddled with the task of carrying the meaning of the text; now they behave like free subjects, concerned only with themselves and with the sheer, pure joy of sound.

Both vocalizing and scat singing necessarily led to today's "free" singing (to be discussed later).To be sure, there is also a "blues line" among the female vocalists, which refers back to the blues singers mentioned at the beginning of this section. The last of the great classic blues singers, Alberta Hunter, made some wonderfully expressive recordings in 1980—at age eighty-five!—which is even more astounding when you realize that it was Alberta who wrote "Down Hearted Blues," Bessie Smith's first hit, in 1923! In the twenties, she sang with Louis Armstrong, Sidney Bechet, and Fletcher Henderson. She died in 1984.

Among the female singers, too, the blues proves to be the constant element of African American music, always changing but always the blues, whose message is passed on from one generation to the next. Among those who have specialized in the blues are Helen Humes (with Count Basie in the late thirties; she, too, unusually expressive until her death in 1981), Dinah Washington (who died in 1963), Betty Carter (who began with the blues as Dinah Washington's successor in Lionel Hampton's band), Ruth Brown, LaVern Baker, Etta Jones (combining Sarah Vaughan's vibrato with Billie Holiday's diction and phrasing), Koko Taylor, Shemekia Copeland, and many others. Dinah Washington was called the "Queen of the Blues." She, too, had her start in gospel music, and these gospel roots remained audible in many of her blues recordings. Her voice, always somewhat bright and cutting, mixed blues expressiveness with a jazz sensibility, making unique use of a very fast vibrato. Everything Dinah Washington sang had soul. Her sardonic humor, sometimes even cynicism, gave her performances an additional dimension.

Janis Joplin carried the art of classical blues into rock. Almost nothing she sang can be thought of without Bessie Smith; yet Janis's singing always sounded harder, cruder, louder, more obtrusive. She was driven by a fierce will to live and love, up to her untimely death in 1970, which prompted the media to all sorts of wild speculations. Joplin's singing made particularly clear how many white performers—often even those who appear "authentic" in their relationship to black music—have vulgarized and coarsened the message of their African American models.

In the course of the sixties, the heritage of the black spiritual and gospel tradition entered even more strongly into the mainstream of female singing. The white world had become conscious of this heritage through the recordings of Mahalia Jackson, who died in 1972, but Jackson was only one of the many wonderful singers of African American religious music. Others are Dorothy Love Coates, Marion Williams, the late Clara Ward, Bessie Griffin, and Queen Esther Marrow (see the section on spirituals).

When the gospel tradition finally made its way into popular music, soul music came into being. Its representatives are singers like Tina Turner, Diana Ross, Chaka Kahn, and, above all, Aretha Franklin. Aretha is the daughter of Rev. C. L. Franklin, the preacher of New Bethel Baptist Church in Detroit. From childhood on, she heard the rousing gospel songs in her father's church. When she was able to carry a tune, she joined the church choir; and at twelve or thirteen, she became a soloist. As her first important influence she named Mahalia Jackson; later, she pointed in particular to the significance of jazz musicians in her musical development: Oscar Peterson, Erroll Garner, and Art Tatum. Aretha herself is also a good, soul-inspired pianist.

Franklins's hit records are among the best that seventies and eighties pop music has to offer, but one of her recordings is of exceptional interest from a jazz point of view: *Amazing Grace*, recorded in 1972 at the New Temple Missionary Baptist Church in Los Angeles, in front of and with the congregation. It is nothing less than a swinging, ecstatic gospel service. This was not only a homecoming to the musical and spiritual world from which she originates—that alone would have meant much—but a conscious, jubilant rediscovery of her own roots. She repeated that affirmation with the 1987 double album *One Lord, One Faith, One Baptism*, another gospel service recorded in the New Bethel Baptist Church, Detroit.

Rachelle Ferrell sometimes seems to actually be somewhat handicapped by her amazing vocal abilities. In her singing, constantly moving between soul, funk, and jazz, she demonstrates so much technique that she sometimes seems unsure what to do with it all. Nonetheless, her interpretations of standards are breathtaking.

Lizz Wright, from Atlanta, also has strong roots in gospel singing. She has a wonderful natural vibrato, and even when she sings pure contemporary jazz songs her voice has a "thick," powerful quality that stems from the music of the black churches. Patti Cathcart, the vocal half of the duo Tuck & Patti for more than twenty years, combines the spiritual and gospel tradition of Mahalia Jackson with the resolute style of Carmen McRae in her warm, open-hearted singing.

It is only a short step from the female vocalists just mentioned to those in fusion and on the borderline between jazz and fusion. There are so many singers of the most diverse directions in this field that they can be named here only summarily: Phoebe Snow, Ricky Lee Jones, Bonnie Herman (the rich, "sensual" voice of the vocal group Singers Unlimited), Marlena Shaw, Ann Burton, Jean Carn, Patti Austin, Lorraine Feather, Gayle Moran (known through her recordings with Chick Corea), Janis Siegel (from the Manhattan Transfer vocal ensemble; her beautiful, clear voice and sweetness of sound evince a certain affinity for Broadway and cabaret singing), and Meshell Ndegeocello, also known as a soulful, funky electric bassist.

Betty Carter pointed out in the seventies that it had become almost impossible to be a female jazz singer: "I guess I'm the last of the Mohicans. It's understandable: jazz singing is not profitable. Young singers tend toward commercial singing—and let's face it, it's one way or the other: if what you're singing becomes commercial, it's no longer jazz." Many of the singers we just named have discovered this—often quite painfully. One example is Dee Dee Bridgewater. She became known with the Thad Jones–Mel Lewis big band in the early seventies and made some breathtaking records, some of them along avant-garde lines, such as a duet with bass player Reginald Workman. By the end of the seventies, she was working in jazz contexts only infrequently. For economic reasons, Bridgewater turned more to musicals and to soul music; finally, frustrated with working conditions in America, she moved to France in 1983, where her jazz career found new life.

No jazz singer today swings as powerfully as Dee Dee Bridgewater. She has continued the great legacy of Ella Fitzgerald's scat singing in contemporary straight-ahead jazz more convincingly than any other singer, not as an obligatory exercise, but rather as an expression of a vital, abundantly rich musical imagination. Her long improvisations are radical reinventions of the material, in which she makes a fresh re-examination of every song by bringing out its inner emotional content. She says, "Most young singers today have to learn how to tell a story."

Bridgewater's performances are characterized by risk-taking, theatrical flair and high energy. Of all contemporary jazz singers, she has the greatest stage presence, and she is unequaled among contemporary jazz singers in her ability to interact with an audience.

Among folk singers, too, there are some of interest to the jazz scene. Just as the African American singers refer back to the gospel, soul, and blues tradition, so the folk singers have their roots in white Anglo-American music. The two representatives of this direction of most interest from a jazz viewpoint are Judy Collins and the highly influential singer-songwriter Joni Mitchell. Collins did a superb job of incorporating the wistful songs, cries, and signals of whales into her song "Farewell to Tarwathie." Mitchell's album *Mingus*, released in 1979, is the most beautiful, moving memorial to this great jazz musician to date. Critics have called Mitchell's singing much too ethereal and fragile to have anything to do with Mingus's music, yet this very fact makes it clear how far Mingus's message carries. Mitchell has always been fond of employing jazz musicians on her studio dates, among them bassist Jaco Pastorius and saxophonist Wayne Shorter. Her strong, poetic singing and unconventional guitar harmonies go well beyond the conventional chord structures of pop music. She sings with great authenticity; the words come from within her as she gives herself over completely to a lyric. Just how much Mitchell is associated with jazz is illustrated by her statement that the most important record in her musical development was the Count Basie album by Lambert, Hendricks, and Ross.

Annette Peacock's crystal-clear, lyrical voice gives her a rare capacity to penetrate into the music, sounding its depth and subtlety. For eight years, she was married to pianist Paul Bley, for whom she wrote compositions, creating a world of space and breadth that enabled Bley to become, at that time, the most romantic poet of the piano. Later, in England, Peacock moved into an involvement with rock music, but kept a profound jazz sensibility in her fragile, vulnerable singing. "The most important events in a person's life are framed by silence," she has said.

In the context of American performance art, Laurie Anderson achieved cult status in the eighties and nineties. She sings her "magical" songs, harmonically simple and full of mystery, in a wonderful, "speech-like" voice. She specializes in bending pitches subtly upward. Robin Holcomb, married to keyboardist Wayne Horvitz and formerly active in the avant-garde circle around the New York Composers Orchestra, has also created, in the singer-songwriter genre, a floating, delicate atmosphere in which melodiousness coexists peacefully alongside breaks with tradition.

In the nineties, Madeleine Peyroux found success by combining Billie Holiday's approach with roots in folk, blues, and rock. Holly Cole and Norah Jones (further discussed below) also belong in this area of music influenced by folk and pop styles.

What the tradition of Anglo-American folk music is to singers like Collins and Mitchell, the samba tradition (which, in turn, is rooted in African music) is to the Brazilian singers. Flora Purim became the most famous in the northern hemisphere because she moved to the United States in 1968. But back home in Brazil there are even more-impressive voices who did not become known in the States or in Europe until later: Elis Regina and Maria Bethânia—the former having Ella Fitzgerald's flexibility, the latter Billie Holiday's emotional energy.

Astrud Gilberto, with her otherworldly charm and melancholy fragility, became the personification of bossa nova singing. She originally came along as an interpreter when tenor saxophonist Stan Getz met with Brazilian musicians Antonio Carlos Jobim and João Gilberto in New York in 1963. Jobim had brought eight songs with him on that trip. One of these, "Garota de Ipanema," had been partially translated into English with an eye to the international market, but the unfamiliar language proved too much for João to handle comfortably. As this became apparent in the studio, the musicians finally turned to Gilberto's wife, Astrud. In this way, she found herself in front of a microphone for the first time in her life. Today, her version of Jobim's "Girl from Ipanema" is the second-most-played pop song in history, after the Beatles' "Yesterday."

Purim and her husband, percussionist Airto Moreira, were at the center of a "Brazilian movement" on the American scene of the seventies. Flora was first introduced by Stan Getz and Gil Evans, then by Chick Corea (in his first Return to Forever group of the early seventies). One of her most beautiful recordings is *Open Your Eyes, You Can Fly* (1976), the entire record being a triumphant song of liberty. One senses that the song mirrors personal experience. Flora had just been released from jail, where she had been incarcerated for a drug charge that was never proven.

Tania Maria sings Latin-colored scat vocals with a supple feel for Brazilian rhythms, all in unison with her piano playing. Marlui Miranda has brought the music of Brazil's aboriginal inhabitants, the Indians of the Amazon, into the contemporary jazz of the band Pau Brasil. Luciana Souza, who comes from São Paulo and now lives in New York, is a Brazilian singer who is a master of the standard song repertoire. She uses her stunning timbre to examine the moods and feelings of jazz songs, deliberately simplifying their melodies in order to come closer to the meaning of the lyrics, instead of ornamenting them. Souza also frequently combines jazz and poetry on her recordings, including interpretations of poems by South American authors such as Chile's Pablo Neruda.

Flora Purim sometimes sang in free-jazz contexts early in her career, and thus leads us to the group of female vocalists who sing free jazz and post–free jazz. The first to do so, as early as the sixties, were American Jeanne Lee and Norwegian Karin Krog. Then came the British singers Norma Winstone, Julie Tippetts, and Maggie Nicols; Polish Urszula Dudziak; American Jay Clayton; Holland's Greetje Bijma; Russian-born Valentina Ponomareva and Sainkho Namchylak; Uschi Brüning from the former East Germany; Greek-American Diamanda Galas; and Americans Lauren Newton and Shelley Hirsch. These singers have extended the "voice as an instrument" into realms that would have seemed inaccessible only a few years earlier. Singing to them is not only vocalizing songs, but everything else: screaming, laughing, and crying; the moaning of sexual experience and childlike babbling. The entire body, from the abdomen to the sinuses and the skull, becomes an instrument, a vibrating source of sounds, a "body of sound." The entire range of human—and specifically female—sounds is employed; nothing human or organic seems to be alien to it. These singers are unrestrained in the way they scream, moan, and belt out whatever fits the particular song, the mood, or the atmosphere; and yet this lack of restraint is only an apparent one, because all these sounds have to be formed, mastered, and musically integrated in order to become meaningful.

"The voice as an instrument"—this expression can be used sensibly only in relative terms. What seemed a ne plus ultra of instrumental vocalizing in the twenties with Adelaide Hall in Duke Ellington's band was surpassed by Ella Fitzgerald in the forties, by Indian singer Yma Sumac in the fifties, by Jeanne Lee and Karin Krog in the sixties, by Urszula Dudziak in the seventies, by Lauren Newton and Diamanda Galas in the eighties, and by Sainkho Namchylak in the nineties. In their time, each of these voices was hailed as the unbeatable final stage of the development—and that's the way it will continue to be.

Jeanne Lee (who died in 2000) has become known primarily through the artful musical textures she wove in the group of her husband, multi-instrumentalist Gunter Hampel. Lee was a master of the spatialization of sound. She seemed to dance with the words—her voice had an honest, direct sound that changed unspectacularly and movingly between song and speech. Her singing flows from a musical as much as from a literary feeling. Jeanne has vocalized modern poetry. There is no other singer with her acute and detailed sense for words, listening and following the sound of each word, each single syllable.

Karin Krog made one of her most beautiful albums in a duo with tenorist Archie Shepp. As paradoxical as it may sound, the young woman from cool Scandinavia and Shepp with his highly developed consciousness of black music play together in perfect empathy. For the sake of a few tunes, band leader Don Ellis had Karin Krog flown in from Oslo to Hollywood. Said Ellis, "There is no singer in the States who could have done what she does." With her lucid, cool voice and spacious approach to improvising, she became an expert in the chamber-music-like duo format, which she has pursued particularly sensitively since 1978 in dialogues with saxophonist and bass clarinetist John Surman.

Norma Winstone combines the experiences of free jazz with classical European song forms, above all the ballad. She has done so particularly impressively in the group Azimuth, with pianist John Taylor (Winstone's husband) and trumpeter Kenny Wheeler.

Julie Tippetts's career went against the current. She didn't move from jazz to pop music, but from pop to free jazz. In the second half of the sixties, singing as Julie Driscoll, in recordings with organist Brian Auger—including her hit "This Wheel's on Fire"—she was one of the most frequently heard and most sensitive and musically flexible of female rock singers. In the eighties, it often seemed as if she (now under the name Julie Tippetts) was hiding from her old identity in a music of a most demanding and complex kind of abstractness.

Maggie Nicols, who became known for her work with pianist Irène Schweizer, specializes in deliberately hyped-up, agitated vocal acrobatics, driven with enormous inspiration right up to the very top of her alto voice. Polish-born Urszula Dudziak electronicizes and "percussionizes" her voice. She channels it through a number of different synthesizers and uses a custom-built electronic percussion instrument. An American critic wrote, "Imagine that the 'Girl from Ipanema' comes from Warsaw instead of Rio and is now living in New York—then you'll have an idea of how she sounds."

Jay Clayton's singing is clearly influenced by techniques of vocal alteration found in advanced concert music, accompanied, however, by an inimitable jazz feeling. Her rich, dark sound communicates a deep sense of song and of life. Together with Jeanne Lee, Lauren Newton, Urszula Dudziak, and Bobby McFerrin, she formed (at the start of the eighties during the New Jazz Meeting Baden-Baden) Vocal Summit, at that time perhaps the most original and "complete" vocal ensemble on the contemporary scene. Uschi Brüning has recorded witty and exciting duos with saxophonist Ernst Ludwig Petrowsky. Coming from a Betty Carter influence, Gabriele Hasler has gradually developed her versatile voice into a unique, sound-oriented, universal instrument. She has developed her own language of sound painting, adapted to her singing, which she calls Esperango, and also uses difficult texts of Gertrude Stein and Oskar Pastior. Her chamber-musical duos with saxophonist Roger Hanschel (since 1984) show a fascinatingly unorthodox attitude toward jazz singing, as in her avant-garde transformations of songs by Renaissance composer John Dowland. In recent years she has begun to work more frequently in her solo performances with electronic loops and soundscapes, which she uses to create space for new vocal freedoms, approaching the realm of contemporary composed music.

Valentina Ponomareva, from the former Soviet Union, vocalizes with an unusual feel for the impact of sounds—veiled, mysterious, magical. Greetje Bijma from Holland has a vivacious talent for improvisation. In Noodband's free funk she produced ravishingly strident sounds full of sensitivity. Lauren Newton from Oregon, who made a name for herself with the Vienna Art Orchestra, commands what is perhaps the largest range of styles among all these singers. She has studied baroque music as well as modern concert music—Schoenberg and Ligeti, for instance—and she includes all these experiences in an immensely light and witty kind of improvisation that sparkles with fresh ideas. Said Lauren, "I can dare to do things in jazz that you just wouldn't think of doing in modern concert music. Jazz gives you more freedom, but jazz is also more demanding."

On the New York downtown music scene, Shelley Hirsch has made particularly impressive use of the extended techniques of free singing, with head-over-heels, revved-up improvisations full of irony and refined changes of register. She says, "I don't think the voice has any limits." Diamanda Galas (from San Diego) starts where other singers usually leave off. Immediately, without requiring any time to arrive, she reaches a level of almost insane, shocklike intensity, assaulting her listeners' ears with her screams and vocalized eruptions. She is like a raving bacchante from Greek mythology transposed into modern times (and indeed she does have a Greek family background!). And if one Diamanda isn't enough for you, she's singing to multiple tapings and samplings of her own voice, creating a persona as "a goddess of revenge, Cassandra, and a Fury rolled into one" (Harry Lachner).

Sainkho Namchylak travels between East and West. Born in a small gold-mining town in the former Soviet republic of Tuva (an eastern region of Siberia, close to the Mongolian border), she has explored the combination of East Asian overtone and throat singing (which enables sound possibilities of two to four notes at once), as well as many other world folk music techniques, with the extended vocal techniques of free singing. She uses sounds ranging from piercing high tones to guttural low sounds, creating a unique vocal universe. For all the striking innovations in her vocal experiments, Sainkho has maintained close contact to the roots of Tuvan culture. In Tuvan throat singing, there are two main traditional elements: on the one hand, the "light everyday singing," in which songs are sung to the beauty of nature, and whose work songs are intended to create a close connection to farm animals such as yaks, donkeys, and sheep. On the other hand, there are the "spirit songs," which are directed to the spirits of the ancestors and the spirits in nature. These are shamanistic songs that are repeated freely, in the manner of mantras. There are also ritual "lama songs," sung to the Buddha and his bodhisattvas. Today, Sainkho lives in Vienna, and has become one of the most sought-after voices in European free improvised music, having worked with musicians such as Evan Parker and Peter Kowald.

Thirty years ago, jazz singing (as strictly defined) was said to be dying. It really was difficult during the seventies to find a young woman singer who simply sang swinging jazz music, in the vein of Mark Murphy or Bob Dorough among the male vocalists. At the start of the eighties, however, female vocalists experienced an astonishing renaissance as part of jazz classicism (not unlike the situation when some critics rushed to write off big bands only to be surprised by a wave of new, vital groups).

What is special about this comeback for mainstream singing is the versatility of these women vocalists (sometimes concealing a degree of stylistic uncertainty). The important singers—all individually following Betty Carter and developing the mainstream, often in conjunction with other styles inclusive of fusion and contemporary jazz—were, beginning in the eighties, Cassandra Wilson, Dianne Reeves, Diane Schuur, Carmen Lundy, Michele Hendricks, Portugal's Maria João, Italian-born Tiziana Ghiglioni, and Gabriele Hasler from Germany.

Diane Schuur made some compelling recordings in 1987, mainly blues, with the Count Basie Orchestra headed by Frank Foster, uniting the robustness of Dinah Washington with Ella Fitzgerald's agility and childlike playfulness.

Cassandra Wilson's contralto possesses something of the smokiness and robustness of women singers in her home state of Mississippi, and she also commands the most imposing range of style: from M-Base free funk with Steve Coleman (with whom she worked in the late eighties) by way of neoclassicism with New Air (successor to the celebrated trio Air) to standards à la Betty Carter.

Cassandra Wilson has the most mature, darkest, and most sensitive voice in contemporary jazz. With her preference for moderate tempos, she is a great storyteller focused on the lyrics, a true communicator. She sings with great emotion and is not primarily concerned with showing off her technical ability. In fact, when hearing Wilson one often has the feeling that, as Jane Monheit puts it, "The point is not to be a singer; the point is to be a strong, powerful, expressive musician."

One of the most surprising things about Wilson is the quality with which she managed to make it to the top of the charts. In 1993, her album *Blue Light 'Til Dawn* was a sensational success. Her jazz is a stirring celebration of the sounds of atmospheres of the Mississippi Delta and the Caribbean, of archaic blues and Louisiana folk music. With her seemingly unlimited choice of repertoire, including songs by Jobim and Van Morrison, Son House, Robert Johnson, Joni Mitchell, and Bob Dylan—all transformed into the typically bittersweet Wilson mood—she has set new standards for freedom in female jazz singing. "I always say, I don't decide on the songs, they decide on me."

The dreamy, emotional mood of Cassandra Wilson's CD *New Moon Daughter* inspired Norah Jones to create her bluesy pop-folk-jazz. Until then, the big record labels had always assumed that young people wanted to hear heavy, loud, even violent music. And then came a singer-songwriter from Texas who proved the opposite. With her intimate singing and her natural phrasing, she won an audience of millions, and her CD *Come Away with Me*, released in 2003 on Blue Note, won a total of eight Grammys. Critics have constantly raised doubts about Norah Jones's status as a jazz singer. But even as scrupulous a jazz vocalist as Patricia Barber has recognized that "you can't argue with the style of a singer who sells millions of records."

Before this, at the end of the nineties, a trend had already begun whose beginning was marked by the popular success of Diana Krall, and that grew into a vogue for women jazz singers of a size that no one foresaw. The "song jazz" revival brought with it an astonishing rediscovery of the love of standards and the classical song structures of jazz. The interpretation of the melodies from the Great American Songbook became fashionable again, giving female jazz singers an enormous career boost.

As was just mentioned, Canadian singer Diana Krall stood at the beginning of this trend. She cleared a path for countless singers after her by breathing new life into old jazz standards, with a slightly understated phrasing full of surprises. Krall succeeded in reinterpreting the tradition of American jazz standards with a deep understanding of the texts and an irresistible articulation. Her style represents a very attractive, unaffected type of singing. Krall has a phenomenal feeling for using her voice to explore the depths of the emotional presence in a song's lyrics. She makes room for all the facets of human feelings and passions, with fragility, a slight coarseness, seductiveness, and little vocal growls, all filtered through her typical coolness. Later, she wrote fragile-sounding original pop songs, and interpreted songs by her husband Elvis Costello.

Diana Krall is perhaps just as significant as a pianist as she is as a vocalist. She expands and comments on her singing with a piano style that sparkles with improvisational wit and spontaneous lightness. "I owe all that to Jimmy Rowles," she says. From Rowles, Ella Fitzgerald's long-time accompanist, Krall learned that good piano accompaniment is more than just providing harmonic information. The piano helps the singing "catch fire"—and at its best it does this by itself becoming a kind of singer.

Diana Krall's sales figures and concert audiences prove that at the beginning of the twenty-first century there is still a large audience for straight-ahead jazz singing. To critics who accused her of riding a wave of nostalgia with her interpretations of classic American songs, she responded: "The stories of love and romance, loss and loneliness don't change. Those song lyrics stand for a whole range of feelings and relationships that never really change."

Immediately following Diana Krall came Jane Monheit, who became popular through a mixture of standards and youthful sex appeal. Her strengths lie in slow tempos and ballads, which she gives both an erotic charge and a pure, swinging sweetness of sound. But in her singing, one also constantly hears the fact that she came to jazz from a background in Broadway singing—there's something refined and calculated in her passionate, warm sound, in the perfect quickness with which she can move from intimacy to the dramatic chest register. On the other hand, she feels no compulsion to ornament every song with vocal gymnastics, and she allows herself to be influenced by other genres in her approach to singing standards. "Standards are true American treasures," she says. "All these composers—George Gershwin, Jerome Kern, Irving Berlin, Richard Rodgers—have had a permanent influence on popular music; they changed everything. I'll never get tired of this music. It will always have an audience because of its content and its quality."

With the success of Diana Krall, Jane Monheit, and Norah Jones, female jazz singing became by far the most commercially successful branch of contemporary jazz. Record companies and agents immediately jumped on this trend, introducing great numbers of new "talents" whose singing ability often amounted to nothing more than a kind of dreaminess suitable for use in TV commercials. And much of the boom in female jazz singing showed signs of a kind of "girl craziness" in which youth and beauty were more important than singing. "As a jazz singer, the pressure is enormous for *what* you're supposed to sing, *how* you're supposed to sing, and *when* you're supposed to sing it," says Patti Cathcart.

Diana Krall and Jane Monheit made space in jazz singing for intimate, introspective, quiet music. Their tasteful singing satisfies a desire for quieter sounds and melodic reticence. But singers such as Ella Fitzgerald, Sarah Vaughan, and Betty Carter set standards against which younger vocalists have to measure themselves when it comes to improvisational ability and range of expression. A shocking number of today's young singers (though not Krall and Monheit) fall far short of these standards, proving capable only of repeating a few familiar vocal effects. Critic Nat Hentoff says, "To merit being called a jazz singer, you have to have something to say." Nate Chinen remarks, "It's no secret that nostalgia sells. Maturity isn't about having a good wardrobe—it comes from experience."

Beyond the negative effects of the vogue for female vocalists, there were musicians who succeeded in transforming the Great American Songbook into contemporary jazz singing in a personal manner. There are so many of them that we can only name the most important here. These include Melissa Walker (who expands and updates jazz classics in a particularly imaginative way), Jeri Southern, Lynne Arriale, Aina Kemanis, Jeri Brown (strongly influenced by Sarah Vaughan), Laurie Wheeler, Dena DeRose, Jodi Stevens (characterized by a relaxed nonchalance), Carla Cook, Jenny Evans, the German-Nigerian singer Lyamiko, and Germany's Ulita Knaus and Lisa Bassenge. All of these singers have brought a fresh perspective to the traditional song format. The great public success that some of these musicians have enjoyed is due above all to the accessible and intelligent way in which they have created modern-day reinterpretations of the standards of classic modern jazz.

This is also true of Renee Olstead, who was at first marketed as "the girl wonder from Texas" after making her debut on the jazz scene in 2004 at the age of fourteen. Since then, her sophisticated arrangements and outstanding technique have thrilled audiences internationally. She has a pronounced consciousness of tradition, combining the thorough refinement of Dinah Washington with the earthy blues feeling of Etta James.

Measured against the publicity that younger singers have received, in many cases their older colleagues have a harder time of it. Jazz singers such as Carmen Lundy, Susannah McCorkle, Meredith D'Ambrosio, Thierney Sutton, Connie Crothers, and Patricia Barber have radiated a maturity and mastery that eludes many of the "jazz stars" promoted by the record companies. Sheila Jordan explains the difference: "What makes for greatness is something in that player that communicates that thing in the moment. You just hear it and you can't deny it. It's not about having a big voice and kinds of chops. There's another kind of chops: a vulnerability that sits beside the skill and experience."

Thierney Sutton's ultra-cool style comes from Chris Connor and June Christy. The crystal-clear flow of her lines has great rhythmic freedom. In contrast, Susannah McCorkle (d. 2001) sang with a strong consciousness of tradition. She was drawn to the songs of the twenties, thirties, and forties, combining Billie Holiday with blues, bossa, and Broadway songs. Meredith D'Ambrosio has a supple phrasing that comes close to the articulation of trumpeter Chet Baker, almost "like a flugelhorn," as Dee Dee Bridgewater has said. In her grooving songs, she tells her own stories.

Patricia Barber, from Chicago, has particular character. She interprets standards and originals with an intellectual seriousness seldom found in jazz singing. Her father was a saxophonist who worked with the Glenn Miller band. When Barber accompanies herself on the piano, she maintains a wonderful balance between a singer-songwriter approach and classic jazz singing in her (mostly slow) songs. Her compositions target the neuroses of the affluent societies of the contemporary Western world with sarcasm and biting irony. She says, "I don't have to look for irony—it follows me everywhere I go."

But the most individual and virtuosic of these singers is undoubtedly Dianne Reeves, the "Sarah Vaughan of the twenty-first century," as she has been called. There is something uplifting and overpowering in her singing. Critics have ranked her alongside the great singers of jazz such as Ella Fitzgerald and Betty Carter, due to her joyful, melodious voice, her great feeling for dynamics, and her impeccable timing. In the process, Reeves has become a personification of modernity, deconstructing standards only to immediately reconstruct them in the same musical process.

Dianne Reeves has a rare awareness of the power of the words in her songs. Her sparkling voice, a rich contralto with a range of more than five octaves, and her developed harmonic sense allow her to explore melodies in long improvisational flights of ideas, from passionate fortes to passages of great delicacy—not as a display of technique, but in pursuit of genuine feelings.

Dianne Reeves is the great eclecticist of contemporary jazz singing. Despite some stylistically questionable decisions, for example in fusion contexts, her singing remains extremely open to influences from other stylistic areas, particularly African and Brazilian music. At the same time, she always sings from a deep knowledge of straight-ahead approaches to jazz.

Women singers in jazz fundamentally tend toward one of two poles. On the one hand, there are the storytellers, whose primary interest is in the lyrics. These singers are mainly concerned with the musical communication of the emotion contained in the text. On the other hand, there are the scat singers, who use their voice in a predominantly instrumental manner—that is, they are interested above all in the improvisational possibilities of the vocal instrument.

This tension between emotion and chops, between the interpretation of lyrics on the one hand and the instrumental use of the voice on the other hand, seems no longer to exist for contemporary singers such as Dianne Reeves, Carmen Lundy, René Marie, Ann Dyer, Jeri Brown, and Karrin Allyson. These musicians have succeeded in mastering both stylistic registers with equal brilliance.

For example, Karrin Allyson, from the Midwest, is a hip improviser who is simultaneously also able to internalize a song and sing its story. Her repertoire ranges from John Coltrane ballads to Kansas City blues shouting.

Many contemporary jazz singers sing without using vibrato, or use it only sparingly. But Carmen Lundy, who lives in Los Angeles, revels in her "championship tone," animated by the individuality with which she applies a wide variety of vibratos to her "romantic" singing of standards. Ann Dyer, from San Francisco, is not afraid to take stylistic risks. A former dancer, in her intense yet relaxed singing she seeks dark, dramatic ideas, such as recasting classic Beatles songs in new, strange stylistic contexts, as on her CD *Revolver: A New Spin*. René Marie sings triumphant, fiery statements of women's emancipation. She constructs lines with great assuredness, and her eclectic singing is largely vibratoless.

The revival of standard singing has brought with it new reflection on the classic modern song format. As an alternative to this line, marked strongly by the American popular song, there is also a song branch innovated by European women jazz singers. Although much of the improvisation of these European singers remains related to American singing of standards, the musical solutions found by the Europeans are also distinguished by breaks with, and sometimes critical questioning of, this tradition. Important European women jazz singers who have found creative new solutions here include, most significantly, Portugal's Maria João; followed by Christine Tobin (an Irishwoman living in London); Swiss singers Erika Stucky and Susanne Abbuehl; Italy's Maria Pia De Vito, Tiziana Ghiliogne, and Francesca Simone; Greece's Savina Yannatou; and Germany's Celine Rudolph and Sonja Kandels.

For more than two decades, Maria João has been one of the most original and independent European jazz singers. Born in Lisbon, she got her start singing in Dixieland bands and in traditional big bands, before finding her way to modern jazz via fado, the "blues of Portugal." In her music, she shows a rare sensitivity to all the sounds that surround her. She has developed scat singing perhaps more virtuosically than anyone else in European jazz, mixing jazz with influences from rock, folk, Portuguese, Brazilian, and African music (her mother is from Mozambique) with a childlike lightness and playfulness, and seemingly "with an entire orchestra somewhere in her larynx, vocal cords, and mouth," as Bert Noglik put it. Her spirited duo performances with Japanese pianist Aki Takase were highlights of jazz festivals in the eighties and nineties. Later, she also performed duo concerts with keyboardist Joe Zawinul. "For me, singing is something like dancing—not in the conventional sense, but rather dancing with the songs, with the words, with the breath, with the other musicians, with the music."

Christine Tobin, born in Ireland, sings without pretension and without flourishes, "like a voice from heaven, like an angel" (John Taylor). She writes many of her intelligent, melancholy songs herself. Originally a folk singer, in 1984 in London she made contact with musicians including Django Bates, Billy Jenkins, and Ian Bellamy, and developed into a contemporary jazz singer of unusual stylistic flexibility.

Switzerland's Erika Stucky also operates beyond the routine singing of standards. In her performances, her stage presence is a unique combination of Alpine maid and jazz sophisticate. She explores new sound possibilities by celebrating a multicolored stylistic mixture of songs from the seventies and eighties, combining Jimi Hendrix, poetry, and video art. Her songs span a bewildering, thrilling arc between homey Alpine folklore and urban nightmares. Kitsch and the rupture with tradition are side by side in her music, an oblique, beautiful, fresh, pointed American-Swiss stylistic schizophrenia full of parody and reverence. This unique character may be explained to some extent by Stucky's biography: her family had to move from San Francisco to a strongly traditional Catholic village in Oberwallis, Switzerland.

A surprising number of successful European female jazz singers come from Scandinavia. Building on the success of Karin Krog, in the nineties and afterward hosts of Nordic singers appeared on the European jazz scene; here as well, we can mention only the most important of them. These include Norway's Rebekka Bakken, Sidsel Endresen, and Silje Neergard; Sweden's Silvia Tolstoy and Rigmor Gustafsson; Denmark's Susi Hyldgaard and Caecilia Norby; and, creating a kind of world jazz by combining the traditional songs (joiks) of the nomads of Lapland with jazz, Finland's Mari Boine.

In 2002 Silje Neergard made the top of the charts in her native Norway. "She creates interfaces where others glue things together," wrote Germany's *Süddeutsche Zeitung*. Silje combines intensity with clarity in her personal approach to jazz standards. She says, "These songs are timeless."

Rebekka Bakken, in her glamorous singing, cultivates a unique ability to slip into the different roles demanded by her songs. She says, "As soon as there's a text, the text is what it's all about. We're just the delivery personnel." Bakken combines the unusual with the simple in a subtle way, for example in her wonderful duo recordings with guitarist Wolfgang Muthspiel. The surefootedness of her intonation has been praised by critics as "supernatural."

Sweden's Rigmor Gustafsson, who studied with Sheila Jordan in New York, sings standards and soul-jazz lines with a clear, present sound, full of sparkling perfection. She often sounds as if she's modeling her phrasing after the lines of guitarists, and in fact the guitar was previously her main instrument. Also from Sweden is Viktoria Tolstoy, a great-niece of Russian novelist Leo Tolstoy. She has interpreted the very melodic music of pianist Esbjörn Svensson. Her CD *White Russian* was the first album by a Scandinavian artist to appear on the renowned label Blue Note. Her tendency toward a Scandinavian dreaminess is also audible in her pop-jazz recordings, which have found a large audience. "People need beautiful songs in order to survive in a world that has become hard."

"Unfortunately, in today's vocal scene there are a lot of stylistic clichés that are limiting," says Norway's Sidsel Endresen, who has made moving duo recordings with keyboardist Bugge Wesseltoft and with trumpeter Nils Petter Molvaer. Her melancholy singing, often subtly manipulated electronically, opens up wonderfully spacious sound worlds. She is one of those musicians who can create something magical from three or four notes. In the search for new ways to use the voice as an instrument, ethnic influences have been a great source of inspiration for her. She cultivates a simple, lean approach to singing, full of minor chords, reducing sounds and melodies with contemplative calmness instead of inflating them. Endresen is also inspired by the American singer-songwriter tradition and by soul and rhythm 'n' blues, but also is attracted to folk elements, paying great attention to detail without worrying too much about complexity. She seeks to discover what one can create from just a few possibilities, and acknowledges that she learned this approach from Billie Holiday and Chet Baker.

Susanne Abbuehl is also a singer who gets to the bottom of the notes. A native of Switzerland living mostly in the Netherlands, she studied classical North Indian singing in Amsterdam, and later studied in Bombay under Prabha Atre, one of the master women singers of India. In North Indian music, each note has great significance. The language of tonal gestures in that music is very rich and highly differentiated—there are specific ways of attacking, sustaining, and releasing tones. Abbuehl has brought this attentiveness to the individual note to contemporary European jazz singing, cultivating a hypnotic, soft, open sound with great sensitivity.

Huong Thanh, a Vietnamese singer living in Paris, has translated the multicultural experience of Paris's Barbes neighborhood (where she lives) into jazz singing in exemplary fashion in her work with guitarist Nguyên Lê and with Algeria's Karim Ziad, mixing her Vietnamese musical heritage with influences from Algeria, Africa, the Caribbean, and European jazz.

Today, the landscape of women singers in jazz has become overwhelmingly large. The contemporary scene includes so many creative singers that even experts have a hard time keeping track of all of them. This is a striking contrast with the seventies, when Betty Carter had to speak of herself as "the last of the Mohicans." By now her message is being passed on by so large (and ever increasing) a "tribe" of female vocalists that no one would think of asking whether jazz singing had died out.

The Big Bands of Jazz

It is difficult to determine where big bands begin. What a moment ago was New Orleans music in the next moment has become big-band jazz, and we stand at the doorstep of the Swing era. In "The Chant" by Jelly Roll Morton's Red Hot Peppers (recorded in 1926), there are traces of big-band sounds, though the idiom is purest New Orleans jazz. And when King Oliver yielded his band to Luis Russell in 1929, the orchestra, though it had scarcely changed, turned from a New Orleans group into a Swing band. How fluid these transitions were can be clearly seen in the case of Fletcher Henderson. The real big-band history of jazz begins with him. From the early twenties through 1938, he led large orchestras and exerted an influence comparable only to Duke Ellington. (We are omitting Ellington from this section because his music and his spirit run through nearly all stages of big-band jazz; an entire section about Duke may be found in the first part of the book.)

At the outset, Fletcher Henderson played a kind of music that differed little from the New Orleans music of the time. Between 1925 and 1928, he fittingly made records under the name of the Dixie Stompers. Slowly and almost imperceptibly, sections were formed, joining related instruments in groupings. From that point on, the sections were to be the characteristic of the classical jazz big bands. Among the first "sections" were the clarinet trios. They can be found in Henderson and in Jelly Roll Morton as well, and, of course, in Duke Ellington. The development from the nine or ten men Henderson had at the start—a lineup that today would not be considered a big band, but then was the ultimate in "bigness"—to the typical ensemble work of the compact trumpet, trombone, and saxophone sections of the height of his career, is smooth and barely perceptible.

Fletcher Henderson and the Beginning

Fletcher Henderson had a real instinct for trends. He was not a man like Ellington, who spearheaded evolution. He followed, but not without giving format and content to what the trend happened to be. It is fitting that he did not retain his musicians for long periods of time, as Ellington did, but changed personnel frequently.

Henderson, who died in 1952, was a great arranger; there are experts who rate him as the most important arranger of traditional jazz, next to Duke Ellington. At any rate, he and Duke were the first who knew how to write for big bands with a sure feeling for jazz improvisation.

The versatility of the Henderson band was great.

Henderson always had an amazing knack for using the right soloists. Musicians who played in his band have been mentioned in almost every section on instruments in this book. Among the most important are alto saxophonists Don Redman and Benny Carter; tenorists Coleman Hawkins, Ben Webster, and Chu Berry; clarinetist Buster Bailey; trumpeters Tommy Ladnier (the one with the blues sound), Rex Stewart, Red Allen, Roy Eldridge, and Joe Smith; trombonists Jimmy Harrison, Charlie Green, Benny Morton, and Dickie Wells; drummers Kaiser Marshall and Sid Catlett; and Fletcher's brother Horace Henderson, who played piano (as did Fletcher) and often lent his name to the band. Many of these musicians later became band leaders, most prominently Redman and Carter.

Don Redman is one of the names that might well be offered in answer to the oft-asked question about the most underrated musician in jazz history. "I changed my way of arranging after hearing Armstrong," he said. From 1928 on he made recordings with McKinney's Cotton Pickers; from 1931 to 1940 (and intermittently after that until his death in 1964) he led his own band. Many of the musicians who played with Henderson were also with Redman's bands. Redman refined the music of Henderson. But then, this is a common denominator for the whole evolution of orchestral jazz: a steady, uninterrupted refinement of the "classical" ideas of Fletcher Henderson.

In 1931, Redman put together the first big-band lineup in a modern sense. It consisted of three trumpets, three trombones, a four-piece saxophone section and a rhythm section of piano, guitar, bass, and drums. The four saxophones soon grew to five, for the first time in Benny Carter's band in 1933. This constitutes the standard big-band instrumentation—with the qualification that the brass section, occasionally in the late thirties and generally from the forties on, might consist of four or even five trumpets and four trombones. That would add up to a total of seventeen or eighteen musicians, and it is characteristic of the nature of jazz that such an instrumentation is conceived of as a "big" band. From the stand-point of European music, this is still a chamber ensemble. "Big" would mean the hundred-man apparatus of the symphony orchestra. Thus the reproach of overdone trappings certainly does not fit jazz. The impressive multiplication of the same voices, employed in the great symphonic forms—a multiplication often purely for the sake of volume—is contrary to the nature of jazz. Jazz tends toward linear instrumentation of each voice: each instrument has a distinctive, perceivable musical sound; it is used as a "personality."

Benny Carter briefly led McKinney's Cotton Pickers (the manager was named McKinney) after Redman had left. Carter became the prototype of the band leader as he would appear with increasing frequency from then on: leaders who were first and foremost arrangers and who led bands primarily because they wanted to hear their ideas translated into the kind of sounds they had in mind. Carter's career as a band leader, accordingly, was unhappy and full of interruptions, and yet he became the true specialist of the saxophone section and a master of melodic delineation. No one knows how to make a saxophone section "sing" like Carter, like a multivoiced "saxophone-organ." The saxophone sounds discovered by Carter in 1933—on such recordings as "Symphony in Riffs" or "Lonesome Nights"—signified an entirely new tone color, which was to gain ever-increasing importance in jazz. It is in no small measure due to the wealth of possibilities discovered by Carter in the five-piece saxophone section that some modern band leaders have made do with a trombone or a trumpet less rather than without one of their saxophonists.

The Goodman Era

From Fletcher Henderson came the most successful big-band leader of the thirties—Benny Goodman, the King of Swing. Then came all the Henderson- and Goodman-influenced big white orchestras of those years, such as the bands of Tommy and Jimmy Dorsey, and the Artie Shaw band mentioned later. They combined the Henderson influence with that of white bands of the twenties more or less close to the Chicago style: Ben Pollack, the Wolverines, Jean Goldkette.

The Goodman band played a polished Henderson music, cleansed of "impurities" of intonation and precision. It became the symbol of the Swing era. The crest of the B. G. wave (which began in California in 1935 when Goodman and his musicians had almost given up hope of ever breaking through) was the famous 1938 Carnegie Hall concert—the decisive entrance of jazz into the hallowed halls of "serious" music. This success in New York's sanctum of culture gave Goodman a foundation for the recognition of jazz as an art form. Goodman (and John Hammond) had hired members of the Duke Ellington and Count Basie bands for this concert. They performed alongside the well-known soloists of the big Goodman band: trumpeters Harry James and Ziggy Elman, drummer Gene Krupa, pianist Jess Stacy; and the soloists of Goodman's small groups: pianist Teddy Wilson and vibraphonist Lionel Hampton. In point of fact Goodman, Artie Shaw, and Charlie Barnet were the first who, in the era of racial segregation, dared to feature black musicians in white bands, if at first only in the "diplomatic" form of added solo attractions, so that racists would not have to face the fact that white and black musicians were sitting side by side in the same band.

In its early years, Fletcher Henderson was the most important arranger for the Benny Goodman orchestra, and the band actually retained its Henderson stamp, no matter how many other arrangers Goodman employed. Only Eddie Sauter gave the Goodman band of the early forties a "new sound"—in such pieces as "Superman," with Cootie Williams as trumpet soloist, "Clarinet à la King," a showcase for Benny's clarinet, and "Moonlight on the Ganges." Sauter no longer used the sections in contrasting opposition throughout, as had Henderson, but sometimes merged them and sometimes created new "sections" by combining instruments from different sections only to dissolve them again—all according to the flow of the music. Here Sauter began what he would carry to greater perfection, in collaboration with arranger Bill Finegan, in the Sauter-Finegan Band of the fifties. In this band, much of the artistry of concert music—not least the frequent use of percussion instruments beyond the jazz beat—was combined with a thoroughly Americanized, jazz-minded sense of humor. (It should be understood, however, that this process of "dissolving" sections was just beginning with Eddie Sauter. It was to be continued, in a much more radical way, by orchestra leaders like Gil Evans and Sun Ra.)

Clarinetist Artie Shaw, after a not very successful 1936 attempt to use a string quartet within a big band, played the most refined and subtle big-band jazz of the late thirties and forties—with the exception of Duke Ellington, of course. Shaw liked a certain impressionistic sensitivity and yet, often enough, retained the powerhouse vigor of the big Swing bands. Again and again, he used African American musicians in his band: Billie Holiday and trumpeters Hot Lips Page and Roy Eldridge. The indignities these musicians had to suffer during the successful tours of the Shaw band have been touched on before, when speaking of Billie Holiday.

Three white Swing bands are outside the Henderson-Goodman circle in certain respects: the Casa Loma Band and the orchestras of Bob Crosby and Charlie Barnet. The Casa Loma Band, run as a collective but marketed under Glen Gray's name, was a hit with the college crowd before Benny Goodman. In the stiffness of its arrangements and its mechanical ensemble playing, it was a forerunner of the Stan Kenton band of the late forties—the band for which Pete Rugolo was the arranger and that was connected with the "progressive jazz" slogan. Gene Gifford was the "Rugolo" of the Casa Loma Band. He wrote pieces that then seemed as imposing and compact as did the Kenton "Artistry" recordings fifteen years later: "White Jazz," "Black Jazz," "Casa Loma Stomp."

Bob Crosby played Dixieland-influenced Swing, pointing back to the Ben Pollack band (which he took over in 1935) and the New Orleans Rhythm Kings, and pointing ahead to the modern brand of commercialized Dixieland music. He had an ideal Dixieland rhythm section consisting of Nappy Lamare (guitar), Bob Haggart (bass), and Ray Bauduc (drums). Since the late sixties, the World's Greatest Jazz Band has been bringing the old Bob Crosby tradition back to life.

Charlie Barnet founded his first big band in 1932 and led bands almost continuously until the sixties—bands that were all shaped by Barnet's strong feeling for the music of Duke Ellington. Perhaps it is fair to say that Barnet's relationship to Ellington corresponds to that of Goodman to Henderson. "Cherokee," recorded in 1939, was the theme song of the Barnet band, also used as a theme by dozens of radio programs the world over. Later, the musicians of modern jazz transformed it into one of the anthems of bop, invariably played at a fast tempo.

The Black Kings of Swing

Fletcher Henderson not only influenced most of the successful white bands of the thirties but himself led the first successful Harlem band. This concept, the "Harlem" band, became a stamp of quality for jazz bands, just as the word "New Orleans" is a stamp of quality for traditional jazz. Even Benny Goodman had the desire to play for the expert and excited—and exciting—audiences of Harlem, which had made the Savoy Ballroom into a famous center for music and dance in the Swing era. In 1937 Goodman played a musical battle with the then most popular band in Harlem, that of Chick Webb—and lost! Four thousand people jammed the Savoy Ballroom, and five thousand more stood outside on Lenox Avenue to witness this friendly battle.

From Henderson the Harlem line leads straight through Cab Calloway, Chick Webb, and Jimmie Lunceford to Count Basie and the various Lionel Hampton bands; and beyond these to the bebop big bands of Harlem in the forties and finally to the jump bands of the fifties à la Buddy Johnson; or to the back-up band for Ray Charles's appearances.

Cab Calloway, the comedian of scat singing, took over a band in 1929 that had come to New York from the Midwest: the Missourians. From then on through the late forties, he led consistently good bands of which the later ones are important primarily for the musicians who played in them: Ben Webster, Chu Berry, Jonah Jones, Dizzy Gillespie, Hilton Jefferson, Milt Hinton, Cozy Cole.

Tiny, hunchbacked Chick Webb presided over Harlem's Savoy Ballroom. Duke Ellington said, "Webb was always battle-mad, and those guys used to take on every band that came up to play there. And most times they did the cutting, regardless of the fact that half the time the other bands were twice the size. But the unforgettable and lovable Chick ate up any kind of fight, and everybody in the band played like mad at all times." Gene Krupa, who was "drummed out" by Webb while with Benny Goodman, said, "I was never cut by a better man." And pianist-arranger Mary Lou Williams remembered:

> One night, scuffling around Harlem, I fell in the Savoy. After dancing a couple of rounds, I heard a voice that sent chills up my spine. . . I almost ran to the stand to find out who belonged to the voice, and saw a pleasant-looking, brown-skinned girl standing modestly and singing the greatest. I was told her name was Ella Fitzgerald and that Chick Webb had unearthed her from one of the Appollo's amateur hours.

Of at least equal importance was Jimmie Lunceford, orchestra leader par excellence. Through him "precision" started to gain ever-increasing significance in the playing of large jazz bands. From the late twenties until his death in 1947, he led a band whose style was mainly developed by arranger Sy Oliver, who also played trumpet in the band. This style is marked by a two-beat "disguised" behind the 4/4 swing meter, and by the effective unison work of the saxophone section, with its tendencies toward glissandos. Both the Lunceford rhythm and the Lunceford sax sound were widely copied by commercial dance bands in the fifties, most of all by Billy May. The Lunceford beat was so potent in its effect that the general designation of Swing did not seem to suffice. The Lunceford beat became "bounce." Lunceford's music bounced from beat to beat in a way that emphasized the moment of "lassitude," as Erroll Garner did, for example, in his piano playing. Oliver's section writing was the first really new treatment of the sax section since the work of Redman and Carter. From this developed the first typical orchestra sound—aside from Ellington's growl sounds and the clarinet trios of Fletcher Henderson's and Ellington's bands. Such sounds and tricks of instrumentation, which stuck to a band like a trademark and made it identifiable after just a few bars, now became increasingly popular.

With Count Basie, the stream of Kansas City bands merges with that of the successful Harlem bands. To Kansas City belong the Bennie Moten band (which Basie himself took over in 1935); the bands of Jay McShann and Harlan Leonard, in both of which Charlie Parker played; and, prior to these, primarily Andy Kirk and His Twelve Clouds of Joy. All were blues- and boogie-oriented, with a well-developed riff technique, using short, reiterated blues phrases as themes or to heighten tension, or employing such riff phrases as contrasting elements. Andy Kirk's pianist and arranger was Mary Lou Williams, and it was mainly due to her influence that the Kirk band developed beyond the simple blues-riff formula of the other Kansas City bands.

At first (and in some of his recordings until his death in 1984), Basie retained the Kansas City blues-riff formula, but he made much more than a formula of it. In it, he found the substance that gives his music (which in the course of the years has absorbed many of the elements brought forth by the evolution of big-band jazz) its power. Basie led big bands from 1935, with but a few short interruptions. In the Basie bands of the thirties and forties, the emphasis was on a string of brilliant soloists: Lester Young and Herschel Evans (tenors); Harry Edison and Buck Clayton (trumpets); Benny Morton, Dickie Wells, and Vic Dickenson (trombones); and the previously mentioned "All American Rhythm Section." In the modern Basie bands, the emphasis is on an effortless, resilient kind of precision, but of a sort that develops in the most natural way from swing. Basie's band swung with a vigor, lightness, and collective presence that led critic Whitney Balliett to remark that Basie "put the beat on wheels." No other band before or since has achieved that flowing feeling. As precise as it was, the timing of the Basie band was not metronomic: its vitality came from the brilliant perfection with which it encompassed the human tendency to fluctuate between relaxation and restlessness. It has been said that Basie is "orchestrated swing." The Basie band of the fifties also had good soloists: trumpeters Joe Newman and Thad Jones; saxophonists Frank Foster, Frank Wess, and Eddie "Lockjaw" Davis; trombonists Henry Coker, Bennie Powell, and Quentin Jackson; and, last but not least, Basie himself, whose spare piano swings a band as no other pianist can.

In the seventies Basie presented recordings with arrangements by Bill Holman and Sam Nestico. Basie's indestructible "Swing machine" consisted of trumpeters Sonny Cohn, Frank Szabo, and Bobby Mitchell; trombonists Al Grey, Curtis Fuller, and Bill Hughes; saxophonists Eric Dixon, Bobby Plater, and the late Jimmy Forrest and Charlie Fowlkes. Freddie Green was still lending the band his unmistakable guitar sounds, and with Butch Miles, Basie had again found an outstanding Swing drummer.

Above all, Count made a number of excellent combo recordings: jam sessions with Eddie "Lockjaw" Davis, Joe Pass, Clark Terry, and Benny Carter; quartet efforts with Zoot Sims; a date with blues singer Joe Turner; and, especially remarkable, a trio album featuring Basie the pianist.

Count Basie achieved what only Duke Ellington has otherwise managed. He became an institution. This institution hasn't been forgotten since the Count's death, thanks in particular to three musicians from the Basie orchestra who have brought it forward into our own times: first, in 1985 and 1986, Thad Jones; then, when Jones became too ill to carry on directing the orchestra (he died soon afterward), Frank Foster; finally, in the nineties trombonist Grover Mitchell took over this job. All these musicians perpetuated the Basie tradition with that relaxation that is today still this orchestra's trademark, making sensuously accessible what the Count signifies for jazz: a symbol of swing pure and simple.

Woody Herman and Stan Kenton

Elements of the Swing era have remained more important for the styles of modern big bands than for the improvisations of individual soloists. In 1936 Woody Herman became front man for a collective of musicians from the disbanded Isham Jones orchestra. Swing à la Benny Goodman was the last word then. Nevertheless, Herman did not play conventional Swing but blues. He called his band The Band That Plays the Blues. "The Woodchopper's Ball" was their most successful record. When the war broke out, the band that played the blues began to dissolve, but soon thereafter the brilliant line of Herman Herds began. The First Herd was perhaps the most vital white jazz band ever. "Caldonia" was its biggest hit. When Igor Stravinsky heard this piece on the radio in 1945, he asked Herman if he could write a composition for his band. Thus the "Ebony Concerto" came into being: a piece in three movements in which Stravinsky, in his own way, combines his classicist ideas with the language of jazz.

Bassist Chubby Jackson was the backbone of the First Herd. The drummers were first Dave Tough, then Don Lamond. Flip Phillips was on tenor; Bill Harris established himself with one stroke as a significant new trombone voice with his solo on "Bijou"; John La Porta played alto; Billy Bauer, guitar; Red Norvo, vibraphone; and Pete Candoli and Shorty Rogers were among the trumpets—in short, a star lineup which no other jazz band of the time could match.

Indicative of the spirit of this band is Chubby Jackson's recollection that the musicians frequently would congratulate each other on their solos after a night's work.

In 1947 came the Second Herd. It grew into the Four Brothers Band, mentioned in our sections on the tenor sax and saxophone ensembles. This, too, was a bebop band—with Shorty Rogers and Ernie Royal (trumpets); Earl Swope (trombone); Lou Levy (piano); Terry Gibbs (vibraphone); the previously mentioned tenor men, and singer Mary Ann McCall. "Early Autumn," written by Ralph Burns, was the big hit of the Four Brothers sound. George Wallington's "Lemon Drop" was characteristic of the Second Herd bop music.

In the fifties came the Third and Fourth Herman Herds and so on; the transitions are blurred. Herman himself once said, "My three Herds? I feel as if there'd been eighty." Ralph Burns wrote a "book" (i.e., library of arrangements) for the Third Herd in which the Four Brothers sound became the trademark of the band. (This had not been the case in the actual Four Brothers band, where the typical Brothers section of three tenors and one baritone was used alongside the traditional five-voiced sax section with the alto as lead.)

In spite of all the talk about the end of the big bands, Woody Herman's music swung so successfully through the sixties, seventies, and eighties that even his closest followers have stopped counting Herds. Herman adapted the more musical rock themes to his big-band conception—pieces like the Doors' "Light My Fire" or Chick Corea's Latin hit "La Fiesta." And he discovered a fascinating new arranger: New Zealand–born Alan Broadbent, a musician who studied at the Berklee School in Boston and with Lennie Tristano and who proved that new, exciting sounds can still be generated from the tried and true big-band instrumentation. In 1986 Herman undertook a "50th Anniversary Tour" (thereby outstripping even Count Basie as big-band leader). He also managed to keep his band together after discovering that its manager had embezzled money, leaving debts of millions of dollars. Woody Herman died in poverty in 1987.

Stan Kenton, who died in 1979, has also led various bands of differing styles, and so more space must be devoted to him than to any single band. Perhaps the most typical Kenton piece is "Concerto to End All Concertos"—typical in title as well. It opens with poorly copied Rachmaninoff-like bass figures by pianist Kenton. The whole late-romantic musical climate lurks behind these figures, along with the notion that sheer size and volume equal expressive power—this seemed to be the peculiar Kentonian world of ideas. From this climate sprang Kenton's first well-known piece, "Artistry in Rhythm," in 1942. It was followed in subsequent years by a series of other "Artistries": in Percussion, in Tango, in Harlem Swing, in Bass, in Boogie. Arranger Pete Rugolo is often linked with this effect-laden and elaborate style, but Kenton himself clearly had already established the "Artistry" style when Rugolo, then still in the army, first offered him an arrangement in 1944. Rugolo, who studied with Darius Milhaud, the important modern French classical composer, is primarily responsible for the second phase of Kenton's music, progressive jazz in the narrower sense, even more powerful and elaborate, laden with massive chords and multilayered clusters of sound. During the late forties—the main period of Rugolo's influence—Kenton was enormously successful. His soloists led in the jazz polls: drummer Shelly Manne; bassist Eddie Safranski; tenorman Vido Musso; trombonist Kai Winding; and most of all, singer June Christy. Hers was the most engaging voice in the band.

In 1952–53 came the most significant Kenton band from a jazz standpoint. Kenton seemed to have forgotten some of his past and decided to make swinging music, perhaps not directly influenced by Count Basie, but nevertheless extremely well suited to a time in which the Basie spirit had come to life to a degree that hardly anyone in jazz could escape it. Kenton had many gifted soloists in this band, and the emphasis was on swinging solo work as never before in Kenton's career. Zoot Sims and Richie Kamuca played tenors; Lee Konitz was on alto; Conte Candoli on trumpet; Frank Rosolino on trombone. Gerry Mulligan wrote such arrangements as "Swinghouse" and "Young Blood," and Bill Holman, obviously inspired by Mulligan, furnished artfully simple examples of sections employed in contrapuntal ensemble play. Bill Russo maintained the Kenton tradition of a highly demanding music based on complex section interplay.

In the following years Kenton involved himself more and more deeply in work at American colleges and universities. He established "Kenton Clinics," in which he and his musicians acquainted thousands of young students with the fundamentals of classic modern jazz, particularly of big-band music. In the process, Kenton did not shrink from personal sacrifices, often furnishing arrangements and musicians free of charge or below usual rates. "Stan is the driving force in jazz education in America," said Dr. Herb Patnoe of De Anza College in California.

Toward the end of the sixties and in the early seventies, Kenton experienced a comeback hardly anyone had expected. He surrounded himself with young, contemporary musicians (including drummer Peter Erskine), with whom he played more direct, simple, and straightforward music than in his "Progressive" and "Artistry" periods, if still with the Kentonian power and his own incomparable pathos. He recorded some of his best later work at concerts held at universities, such as Redlands and Brigham Young.

In the meantime, Kenton had severed relations with Capitol Records, the label with which he had been affiliated since the start of his career, and began to market his records by mail on his own "Creative World of Stan Kenton" label. This prompted an entire wave of independent record companies run by musicians.

Bebop Big Bands

In the meantime, bebop had arrived, and there were various attempts at big-band bebop. The first signs could be discovered in the Earl Hines big band of the forties. The great pianist, identified with the trumpet style of piano in Louis Armstrong's second Hot Five, led big bands almost uninterruptedly from 1928 to 1948—along lines in which Harlem Jump and bop could merge smoothly. Billy Eckstine, a Hines alumnus, made the first deliberate attempt to play big-band bop when he formed a band in 1944. He and Sarah Vaughan were the vocalists (see the chapter on singers). Dizzy Gillespie, Fats Navarro, and Miles Davis successively played in the band—the three most important modern trumpet voices; Art Blakey was on drums; and the saxophones at various times included Charlie Parker, Gene Ammons, Dexter Gordon, and Leo Parker.

In 1947 the orchestra had to disband, but by then Dizzy Gillespie, who for a time had been musical director of the Eckstine band, had brought about the final transformation of bop into big-band jazz. Gillespie, Tadd Dameron, John Lewis, and Gil Fuller furnished the arrangements. Lewis was at the piano, Kenny Clarke on drums, Milt Jackson on vibraphone, Al McKibbon (later Percy Heath) on bass, James Moody and Cecil Payne among the saxes; and Chano Pozo added the incredibly exciting Cuban rhythms so characteristic of this band—rhythms that remind one of the Machito band, which must be cited among the important big bands of the time. It was the witches' cauldron in which the mixture of Cuban rhythms and jazz phrases was most thoroughly brewed. Its musical director was Mario Bauzá, also known as a trumpeter (working with Chick Webb and others), who engaged a number of arrangers for the great jazz orchestras (out of the Cab Calloway and Chick Webb bands) to work for the Machito band. Bauzá thus became the real originator of salsa big bands. Though he was not well-known at the time, behind the scenes he was a mastermind of Afro-Cuban jazz, greatly respected by musicians. It was Bauzá who introduced Dizzy Gillespie to Chano Pozo, and who pioneered a new art of arranging that brought Latin music into its modern, jazz-conscious form. Shortly before his death in 1993, Bauzá released three albums with his Afro-Cuban Jazz Orchestra, again demonstrating the power of this institution of Latin jazz, and featuring charts by, among others, Chico O'Farrill, the Cuban arranger who was also responsible for many of the works of Stan Kenton's "Latin-American" period. Gillespie was in the process of forming his big band when President Truman warned the Japanese in the summer of 1945 that they must surrender or experience "ultimate destruction." When the first atomic bomb was dropped, the Gillespie band was just about ready to play. This fact takes on almost ghostly symbolism when listening to a piece like "Things to Come." This is the Gil Fuller "Apocalypse in Jazz" mentioned in our Parker-Gillespie montage, with its jabbing, hectic, decaying phrases.

It is illuminating that the accents of "Things to Come" were not taken up again until twenty years later, in the big-band attempts of free jazz.

A string of bands worth mentioning existed in the realm between Kenton and Herman. Les Brown provided dance music, but it was so sophisticated and musical that jazz fans, especially jazz musicians, often responded to it. Claude Thornhill played his calm, atmospheric piano solos amid a big-band sound that inspired the conception of the Miles Davis Nonet in the late forties.

Boyd Raeburn led a band in the midforties that in many respects paralleled Kenton's. "Boyd Meets Stravinsky" was a representative title. Soloists such as pianist Dodo Marmaroso, bassist Oscar Pettiford, and drummer Shelly Manne (on one occasion even Dizzy Gillespie) brought much jazz feeling to the complex arrangements by, among others, George Handy and Johnny Richards. The latter wrote the arrangements for Dizzy Gillespie's 1950 recordings with strings—the most jazz-oriented string arrangements created up to that time—and in the midfifties he put together a band that attempted to extend the ideas of progressive jazz. The Richards band featured huge, piled-up blocks of sound and focused on irregular meters.

Basie as Basis

In the midfifties, the conviction that the contradiction between swing and elaborate production effects cannot be bridged beyond a certain point seemed to gain ground everywhere. This conviction is quite in line with what we have called "Basie classicism." Big bands of this persuasion make music beyond experimentation. Maynard Ferguson, who emerged in 1950–53 from the Kenton band, organized his "Dream Band" in the midfifties for an engagement at Birdland in New York. It really was a dream band. Every musician in it was a famous exponent of his instrument, and all these musicians had the same musical ideal: to play swinging, blues-based jazz, vital and musically interesting in equal measure. Jimmy Giuffre, Johnny Mandel, Bill Holman, Ernie Wilkins, Manny Albam, Marty Paich, and others furnished the arrangements. Eventually, Ferguson decided to form a permanent band instead of a studio orchestra whose members were unable or unwilling to leave New York. He found a bunch of excellent young musicians who made a brand of big-band jazz as fiery and wild as Woody Herman's First Herd, yet more clearly rooted in the language of modern Basie-Young classicism. "Fugue," written by trombonist-arranger Slide Hampton for Ferguson, is perhaps the most swinging fugue yet to have emerged from jazz.

Ferguson lived in Great Britain during the sixties (where he also led a successful band), but in the seventies he had a commercial comeback in America. Ferguson said, "I'm not interested in nostalgia. You have to move along with the times. . . . You just have to take and use the current rhythms. In the so-called golden era of the big bands, the great bandleaders of the day all played the better tunes of the day—so why not now?" And so Ferguson played contemporary pop tunes in jazz-rock arrangements filled with effects that hardly elicited applause from the jazz crowd, but reached a large young audience. In the midnineties, Ferguson returned to a compact, robust, hard-swinging orchestra sound in the various editions of his Big Bop Nouveau band.

But back to the fifties, when Basie's influence was stronger than Ellington's. Shorty Rogers made a kind of Basie jazz with a West Coast conception, full of original, spirited inventiveness. Arranger Quincy Jones, bassist Oscar Pettiford, trombonist Urbie Green, Boston trumpeter Herb Pomeroy, and others made big-band recordings in which the Basie influence is strongly apparent.

Quincy Jones called his first orchestral album—with such marvelous soloists as Art Farmer (muted trumpet), Lucky Thompson and Zoot Sims (tenors), Phil Woods (alto), Herbie Mann and Jerome Richardson (flutes), Jimmy Cleveland (trombone), Milt Jackson (vibraphone), Hank Jones and Billy Taylor (pianos), and Charles Mingus and Paul Chambers (bass)—*This Is How I Feel About Jazz*. He wrote in the liner notes that the music reflected his feelings about "the less cerebral and more vital or basic elements contained in jazz."

Jones always had a great liking for Europe. In 1959 he brought to the Old World the first modern American big band to be permanently based in Europe. The band was to supply the music for the show *Free and Easy*, but the show folded. With great difficulty, Quincy managed to keep the band together for a time with work in Paris, Sweden, Belgium, and Germany. Among the members were Phil Woods, Sahib Shihab, Budd Johnson, and Jerome Richardson in the sax section; Quentin Jackson, Melba Liston, Jimmy Cleveland, and Sweden's Ake Persson in the trombone section. The music was moving and healthy, simple and honest; in many ways the most enjoyable big-band jazz of the turn of the fifties next to Ellington and Basie. To be sure, Quincy offered nothing very new. But he perfected the old, and made it shine as hardly anyone managed to do. Too bad that Jones, after his band returned from Europe and continued to work for several months in the United States, gave up fighting for its survival in the face of the lack of commercial possibilities.

Meanwhile, Jones has become one of Hollywood's most successful producers of pop music (Michael Jackson, Brothers Johnston) and film and television composers. One can feel the jazz tradition in everything he writes and produces, and occasionally a big-band or fusion record by Quincy is released, joining commercialism and jazz quality with a cleverness and "hipness" totally Quincy's own.

Of similar interest in this context are the big-band recordings of Gerry Mulligan—almost like a "sophistication" of Basie, but with much additional contrapuntal work. Around the same time, Bill Holman was the first to attempt something on the order of a big-band realization of hard bop, with intense and concentrated arrangements of such bop themes as Sonny Rollins's "Airegin." His trademark lines, running through all the sections of the band, set the standard for writing for mainstream big bands. Holman is one of the most original and adventurous big-band composers and arrangers. Since founding his own big band, the Bill Holman Orchestra, in 1975, in countless arrangements he has made a distinctive contribution to a development that characterizes contemporary mainstream big bands—a movement away from the five-voiced arrangements of the dance bands and from the conventional big-band format, toward more modern, freer forms of expression. This trend toward more orchestral colors is demonstrated particularly impressively on the CD *Brilliant Corners—The Music of Thelonious Monk*, on the strength of which Holman was voted "Best Arranger" in *Down Beat* magazine's 1998 Critics' Poll. On that recording, Holman creates an exciting bridge between Monk's brilliant compositions and the musical language of Bartók and Stravinsky.

Today, the leader and organizer of a big band is also his own main arranger and composer. This is a sign of the changes that have taken place in the jazz landscape. Bill Holman: "Bands in the States aren't buying arrangements any more. . . . If you want to learn, there aren't many bands to write for. You just about have to go out and get a group."

On the West Coast, since the sixties Gerald Wilson has come to the fore with a big band that found great admiration among musicians. Wilson, who had written arrangements for Lunceford, Basie, Gillespie, and other important orchestras, also did not want to "prove anything new," but rather summed up with power and brilliance the "mainstream" of the development of orchestral jazz up to that time, relating it to the tradition of Fletcher Henderson and Don Redman in a contemporary way.

Gil Evans and George Russell

The one man whose big-band jazz really seemed new in this period was Gil Evans. Gil, who emerged from the Claude Thornhill band, wrote for the Miles Davis Nonet. He once again teamed up with Davis in 1957 to produce those warmly glowing, impressionist orchestral sounds discussed in the Miles Davis section. Davis gave Evans a reason to emerge from his quasi-mystical withdrawnness, and gave Evans's textures an exceptional solo voice. In turn, Gil Evans's arrangements helped Davis to move away from the short bebop trumpet solos he had played with Charlie Parker, toward elaborate melodic lines constructed in long arcs. The Dark Prince and the introverted white man: together they formed one of the iconic partnerships in jazz. Their collaboration was total. As soloist, Davis didn't just empathize with Evans's scores; he helped to shape their form and mood. Conversely, as an arranger Evans went beyond an understanding of the soloist to an intuitive knowledge of how to create contexts that expanded on Davis's stylistic characteristics.

The Evans band became the big-band realization of Miles Davis's trumpet sound. Occasionally—regrettably much too seldom—Evans also created similar sounds for other soloists, among them trumpeter Johnny Coles and guitarist Kenny Burrell.

Later, Evans—a gray-haired veteran by the early seventies—opened himself to free music and even to the compositions of rock guitarist Jimi Hendrix. But Gil, who broke up the classic big-band sections in a very sound-conscious way, was not a "diligent" arranger as, say, Quincy Jones is. He let his music ripen within himself and seldom wrote anything finished and final. Even during recording sessions, he often whittled away at changes and reconstructed entire compositions and arrangements. In many cases, his music was born while it was being played—almost in the sense of the early Ellington.

Gil's arrangements are unequaled in their sonic refinement and atmosphere. He considered Lester Young, Louis Armstrong, and Jimi Hendrix to be "sound innovators," because no one before or after them sounded the way they did. In the field of big-band orchestration, Evans himself was such a sound innovator. He thought of himself primarily not as a songwriter but as an arranger and a discoverer of new orchestral colors. Evans was the first arranger to exploit the possibilities of the recording studio as an instrument in its own right. The many-faceted originality of the instrumental combinations that he discovered came to full fruition in his recordings. The atmospheric enchantment of his sonic inventions and the instrumental combinations that he discovered, in their countless mixtures of sound, were something new not only in jazz but in orchestral music overall. One of the reasons for this is that Evans was able to use the studio to bring certain instrumental combinations into balance with one another in a way that would be very difficult to achieve purely acoustically.

No other composer and arranger in jazz, not even Duke Ellington, did as much to transcend the traditional divisions of the instrumental sections of the big band as Gil Evans did. He loved to create unconventional groupings of unusual instruments, including the use of extreme registers. The bright, shimmering colors of the piccolo and the harp mesmerized him just as much as did the extreme depths of the bass trombone, tuba, bass clarinet, and bassoon. And Evans often inverted the instruments' traditional roles, making traditionally low instruments play in the high register and higher instruments in the low register.

His arrangements go beyond the conventional understanding of that concept. They are recompositions of the material that stand on their own. Nonetheless, for the famous arrangements that he wrote for Miles Davis's albums, Gil Evans received from Columbia only a lump-sum fee—for example, a one-time payment of $2,400 for *Sketches of Spain*, a figure that is a bad joke in view of the fact that the recording has sold millions of copies and still earns large sums in royalties. "Economically I've been living a loser's life," said Gil Evans. "I've been an arranger, and you can't get any royalties from arranging."

That is why there are, regrettably, far too few records by this incomparable musician who, until his death in 1988, was closely linked with Miles Davis. In the eighties Evans, the great laissez-faire arranger, collected together a big band (the Monday Night Orchestra) with the best jazz musicians at New York's Sweet Basil club every Monday night, offering them every possible freedom to improvise. The musical outcome—freer and "more open" than anything the then over seventy-year-old Gil Evans had ever achieved during his rich career—is among the best orchestral music ever produced in the realm of jazz-rock. Slide Hampton: "Gil used as few notes in the chord as possible, which makes a lot of sense. He might use only three notes in a chord, where others would use five. . . . You might have all these dissonant intervals that set up a different harmonic system. . . . I used to ask Miles questions about Gil, and Miles would say Gil was off somewhere for the last week trying to work out two bars of music."

The other great loner among arrangers is George Russell, already mentioned several times. In 1947 the Dizzy Gillespie Big Band premiered its arrangement of "Cubana-Be, Cubana-Bop," a work co-composed by Dizzy Gillespie and Chano Pozo, for which George Russell "custom-tailored" such exciting modern sounds that the piece became a milestone of big-band Cuban jazz. Russell also emerged from the jazz revolution of the forties. During the fifties he created his "Lydian Chromatic Concept of Tonal Organization," the first work deriving a theory of jazz harmony from the immanent laws of jazz, not from the laws of European music. Russell's concept of improvisation, "Lydian" in terms of medieval church scales yet chromatic in the modern sense, was the great pathbreaker for Miles Davis's and John Coltrane's "modality." Russell's 1968 composition *Electric Sonata for Souls Loved by Nature* is one of the early innovative works of electronic jazz—an orchestral suite in which Russell combined prepared tape music and free improvisation (by Manfred Schoof and Jan Garbarek) with fully composed ensemble sounds. Russell came to Europe for the first Berlin Jazz Days in 1964 and subsequently lived in Scandinavia, mainly in Stockholm. It would be difficult to overestimate his influence on the development of modern European jazz, especially in Scandinavia. George Russell's Lydian Chromatic Concept of Tonal Organization was one of the major influences that spurred musicians like Jan Garbarek, Terje Rypdal, and Palle Mikkelborg to find their own forms of expression.

Although George Russell is indisputably one of the innovators of the orchestral jazz avant-garde, he has stubbornly refused to take the final step into a complete departure from any reference to tonality. He says, "The sound system of the blues cannot be atonally resolved, because the implication of tonality is an indispensable part of the blues." In the eighties and nineties, he began to integrate African drum languages and rock influences into his still-uncompromising, ambitious jazz arrangements for his Living Time Orchestra.

With European as well as American musicians, he has created numerous works that are as individual, as different from the mainstream of what most jazz arrangers write, as the works of Gil Evans.

Free Big Bands

Meanwhile, free jazz had entered the scene, and the question was, What does the new free jazz sound like when played by big bands?

The musician who stood out most clearly in the transition from tonal to free tonal orchestral jazz was bassist Charles Mingus with his big-band concerts. These infrequent concerts occasionally bordered on chaos in terms of organization and yet produced results—above all, exciting collective improvisations—that moved the jazz world for years to follow.

Mingus built freedom into his writing. He was able to move from gospel to blues to free jazz within a single piece, and to do so with great humor or with great solemnity. He is the definitive multistylist of the jazz orchestra. Probably for this reason, in the nineties Mingus had—after Duke Ellington—the strongest influence on jazz composition for groups from quintets all the way up to big bands. The way in which he combines disparate elements of the big-band tradition in order to create his own orchestral language—from the basics à la Fletcher Henderson to Duke Ellington's mastery of tone color up to the "crazy forms" of the Sun Ra Arkestra (discussed below)—has a brilliant logic. Something about his process of writing transcends stylistic differences. Mingus is a master of dividing the orchestra into smaller formations, using it as an open space for new groupings.

The most highly praised big band of Mingus's career was probably the band with which he recorded his 1971 album *Let My Children Hear Music*. Mingus commented:

> Jazz is black classical music. . . . Let my children hear music, for God's sake—we've heard enough noise. . . . Now I, myself, came to enjoy the players who didn't only just swing, who invented new rhythmic patterns, along with new melodic concepts. And those people are Art Tatum, Bud Powell, Max Roach, Sonny Rollins, Lester Young, Dizzy Gillespie, and Charlie Parker, who is the greatest genius of all to me because he changed the whole era around. But there is no need to compare composers. If you like Beethoven, Bach, or Brahms, that's okay. They were all pencil composers. I always wanted to be a spontaneous composer.

In 1965 composer (and pianist) Carla Bley and trumpeter-composer Mike Mantler presented their Jazz Composers Workshop first in New York and then at the 1965 Newport Festival.

From this, the Jazz Composers Orchestra evolved, with soloists such as Don Cherry, Roswell Rudd, Cecil Taylor, Pharoah Sanders, Larry Coryell, Charlie Haden, Gato Barbieri—in general, the cream of the New York avant-garde—under Mike Mantler's direction. If one realizes how difficult it is to find an audience for such avant-garde productions in the United States—definitely much more difficult than in Europe—he or she can speak of Mantler's personal contribution with only the greatest respect. In the composition "Communications," he developed a remarkable ability to incorporate independent free-jazz voices such as those of Taylor, Cherry, and Rudd without obscuring their personalities.

The Jazz Composers Orchestra was also involved in the large-scale work *Escalator Over the Hill*, by Carla Bley and Paul Haines, which was mentioned in the section on pianists. In the meantime Carla Bley had become increasingly prominent with medium-sized groups of her own, in increasingly tonal settings. Her compositions and orchestrations are imaginative collages of swinging jazz elements and national anthems (ridiculed, of course!), of world music and children's songs and massive clusters—all this permeated with sensitive, often socially critical humor (as in a piece she wrote in 1980, after Ronald Reagan had been elected to the U.S. presidency).

During the eighties Carla Bley made many recordings with smaller ensembles, usually sensitized fusion music but not compositionally ambitious like her work in the seventies. Her sensitive and delicate duos with bassist Steve Swallow are particularly remarkable. Unforgettable are the arrangements she created, mainly outside her own band, during this period: for Charlie Haden's Liberation Music Orchestra; for Hal Willner; for Nino Rota's "8½," where she "celebrates" (with much melancholy) and simultaneously sardonically parodies Italian fairground, march, and circus music; and for Thelonious Monk's "Misterioso," where tenorist Johnny Griffin's lines fall like a "bebop light" in the gloom of strange, punky, weird sounds. In the nineties Bley returned more frequently to working with larger ensembles. The musicians and interpretations of her orchestras vary greatly, but the compositions always retain their force, a brilliance and luminosity that come from the particular unconventionality that distinguishes Bley's world of sound.

The other, perhaps even more important name in free big-band jazz is Sun Ra (who died in 1993). As early as the midfifties, Sun Ra, who had learned his trade thoroughly as relief pianist with the Fletcher Henderson band of the late forties, had formed a big band in Chicago, incorporating percussive and other sounds totally new for the time—sounds that their composer and creator perceived as "cosmic sounds," as "music of the outer galaxies" and of the "heliocentric worlds." On one of his album covers, Sun Ra had himself depicted with Pythagoras, Tycho Brahe, and Galileo.

Sun Ra's music is more than just avant-garde, free big-band jazz. It certainly is that, but behind it stands the whole black tradition: Count Basie's swing riffs and Duke Ellington's saxophone sounds; Fletcher Henderson's voicings; old blues and black songs; African highlife dances and Egyptian marches; black percussion music from South, Central, and North America and from Africa; Negro show and voodoo ritual; trance and black liturgy—celebrated by a band leader who strikes one as an African medicine-man skyrocketed into the space age.

Sun Ra's music is even freer from the sections common to conventional big bands than that of Gil Evans or the Jazz Composers Orchestra. The instruments play together in ever-changing combinations. Especially notable are the saxophone players of the Sun Ra Cosmic Arkestra, among them John Gilmore, Marshall Allen, Pat Patrick, and Danny Davis. Their saxophone and woodwind sounds are as new and revolutionary as Benny Carter's saxophone sections were in the early thirties. The Arkestra includes, among other rarely used instruments, original constructions by band members, such as the "Sun Horn," as well as oboe, bassoon, bass clarinet, English horn, violin, viola, cello, and a group of dancers, occasionally even a fire-eater.

Sun Ra's compositions have titles like "Next Stop Mars," "Outer Spaceways Incorporated," "Saturn," "It's After the End of the World," "Out in Space," etc. Many uninitiated listeners have smirked at such titles and at the show Sun Ra puts on as naïve. They joke about the dancers and acrobats Sun Ra had jumping all over the stage or about a film he showed with his music: Sun Ra as a Christ figure, a dozen times in twenty minutes. They mock the glittering "Saturn gowns," "galaxy caps," and "cosmic rosaries" that the Sun Ra musicians and dancers wear. Occasionally, the culmination of a Sun Ra show involved a telescope that the master set up next to his organ, and through which he searched for his "home planet Saturn" during special "cosmic climaxes."

But naïveté does not exist where black art is concerned. It did not exist when the chorus girls of the Cotton Club in Harlem during the twenties took on the hullaballoo of white Broadway musicals, accompanied by Duke Ellington's jungle sounds; it does not exist when the preacher of a black Revivalist church expresses his hope that his parishioners may "go to Heaven tonight! right now! by subway"; it did not exist when Louis Armstrong sang "I Hope Gabriel Likes My Music." It existed only in the heads of white critics; and while they diagnose him as a naïf or even a charlatan, they say nothing about Sun Ra's music—and definitely nothing about the man Sun Ra—but a lot about themselves. Sun Ra's music, to LeRoi Jones, is the most precise expression of ancient black existence today. And Sun Ra himself said, "I paint pictures of infinity with my music, and that's why a lot of people can't understand it." He often told the musicians of his Arkestra, "I don't want you to play what you know, I want you to play what you don't know. What you don't know is much greater than what you think you know."

Unlike the United States, Europe offers a mass of free big-band jazz—by Alexander von Schlippenbach, for instance. His "Globe Unity" evolved from the 1965 New Jazz Meeting Baden-Baden and was only given a chance for a short life span back then. Yet up to the present day it has continued sporadically to play its arrangements, which often satirize the jazz tradition while at the same time paying tribute to it, and its wild, liberatory collective improvisations. Schlippenbach's Berlin Contemporary Jazz Orchestra, founded in 1988, is more interested in composition-based and formally structured possibilities. As composers (alongside himself) for this big ensemble, the pianist won over Carla Bley, Misha Mengelberg, Willem Breuker, Kenny Wheeler, and others.

The gap between free jazz and modern concert music is bridged by the London Jazz Composers Orchestra of bassist Barry Guy, who structures his music almost in the sense of classical compositions. As composer and orchestra leader, Barry Guy has succeeded in creating room for the indeterminate with the highest degree of precision. Many of his works for the London Jazz Composers' Orchestra are scored graphically—that is, in the manner of drawings rather than conventional musical notation. "The way the pen moves over the paper, creating spaces, contains a certain energy that can't be captured in words." In this way, he moves in several steps from the image to the sound. The London Jazz Composers' Orchestra is distinguished by the coexistence of composition and soloists, a certain dramatic element, and the unfolding and investigation of sounds.

John Coltrane's pathbreaking *Ascension* and the preceding double-quartet record *Free Jazz* by Ornette Coleman (both cited in the section on Coleman and Coltrane) have been key experiences for many free big bands. Here the form was created: exciting, heated collective improvisations, from which emerges a solo that in turn intensifies to the point that the next collective improvisation (which, again, will "give birth" to a new solo) comes into existence. This form has been further developed by others—differentiated, sublimated, and structured—with especially personal results, indicating future directions by musicians like Anthony Braxton (with his Creative Music Orchestra), Karl Berger (with his Woodstock Workshop Orchestra), Leo Smith, and Roscoe Mitchell; and in Europe by Willem Breuker, Misha Mengelberg, Mike Westbrook, Keith Tippett, Tony Oxley, and Ulrich Gumpert.

Anthony Braxton's Creative Music Orchestra links particularly far-reaching abstractions and distancings with allusions to bebop and march music. From Karl Berger comes some of the most interesting and integrated big-band realizations of world music. Leo Smith has opened up orchestral "free" jazz, sensitizing it to "space," pauses, and stillness. Willem Breuker is *the* master of parody. Following Kurt Weill and Hanns Eisler, he distances the popular music of the nineteenth and early twentieth centuries—marches, opera and operetta, polkas, waltzes, tangos—filling it with farcical burlesque humor, often accompanied by his Kolektief's turbulent music theater. Misha Mengelberg's Instant Composers Pool Tentet presented this principle of parodistic exaggeration in a "more relaxed," compositionally less determined (less "drilled") context. His droll, idiosyncratic compositions have become the trademark of the ICP Orchestra. The Instant Composers Pool (ICP), founded in 1967, has been an important showcase of the Dutch avant-garde improvising scene, with musicians including Han Bennink, Tobias Delius, Tristan Honsinger, and Michael Moore, yet it has always also had organic connections to the tradition of American free jazz. Keith Tippett is a specialist in massive, magical agglomerations of sound in which spirituality, and occasionally also African melodies and rhythms, play a central part. At the start of the seventies his fifty-one-player Centipede Orchestra achieved some powerful, innovative combinations of jazz, rock, and modern concert music.

Mike Westbrook, on the other hand, is a master of large-scale orchestral refurbishings of European tradition, from Rossini by way of Stravinsky to Brecht/Weill. He also makes considerable use of theater and literary texts (William Blake, Goethe, Wilhelm Busch, etc.). Westbrook has particularly convincingly transferred Ellington's compositional principle of long, expansive suites to the European scene. People have justly talked of his composing as "Europeanized Duke." Pianist Ulrich Gumpert (from the former East Germany) and his Workshop Band make especially impressive use of elements of European popular music (marches, waltzes, and polkas) but also of swing and bebop rhythms, diversely disrupting and satirizing them through "free" music. At the end of the eighties, percussionist Tony Oxley founded his Celebration Orchestra, for which he often writes graphic scores, and which is one of the original large ensembles of free-improvised music.

In the nineties a striking number of the orchestras based in free playing combined the tradition of the free big bands with contemporary multistylistic approaches. These included, in the United States, the Aardvark Orchestra, Ken Vandermark's Territory Band, Butch Morris's various "conduction" orchestras, the Satoko Fuji Big Band, and the Asian-American Orchestra of San Francisco percussionist Anthony Brown; in Europe, Italy's Instabile Orchestra, the group La Marmite Infernale, and various other orchestras from Lyon's musicians' initiative A.R.F.I.; and, in Japan, the Shibusa Shirazu Orchestra.

The Aardvark Jazz Orchestra (led by American trumpeter Mark Harvey) has brought the "crazy" stylistic attacks of postmodern jazz into free improvised music in intelligent encounters with, among others, Jaki Byard, Sheila Jordan, and Jimmy Giuffre. The Italian Instabile Orchestra is "the most democratic orchestra in the world" (according to one of its leaders, Pino Minafra), largely because in this band the leaders change faster than the Italian government of the seventies and eighties—namely, every couple of minutes. This big band is not just a collection of Italy's jazz elite, but is also a place where exponents of different regions and generations can meet, including pianist Giorgio Gaslini, clarinetist Gianluigi Trovesi, trumpeter Pino Minafra, and drummer Tiziano Tononi.

The Italian Instabile Orchestra operates without the discipline of the Globe Unity Orchestra and without the serious air of sonic research of the London Jazz Composers' Orchestra, but in its turbulent, humorous, sometimes completely chaotic stylistic mixtures it presents a fantastic panorama of contemporary Mediterranean jazz. The group offers a kind of fresco of styles: combining the European and the American, concert music and folklore, postbop and melodic melodrama, Kurt Weill and outbreaks of dissonance, strictly notated suites and joyous arrangements of folk music. The result is music in which lasting stylistic stability is always avoided, and yet since its founding in 1990 the Italian Instabile Orchestra has remained the most stable fixture of Italian big-band jazz.

Butch Morris, who first made a name for himself as cornetist, composer, and conductor on many albums by David Murray, has devoted the last twenty years to developing his concept of "conduction," an approach in which he completely redefines the roles of the composer, the conductor, the arranger, and the improvising musician. Instructions and attacks are given solely by the conductor (i.e., Butch Morris), who shapes a piece of music from the reactions of the improvising musicians in real time. The effect is that of a real-time variant of digital deconstruction and reconstruction. Guillermo E. Brown: "I saw this Butch Morris—conducted improvisation . . . I thought, that's it! He's sampling the orchestra." However, Morris's conductions, which he has presented all over the world with improvisers from many different cultures, also come at a price: the concept of free improvisation as "multiminded composition," as Evan Parker has called it, is given up in favor of the assumption of a kind of Western formal concept.

The high-energy performances of the Shibusa Shirazu Orchestra, led by Japanese electric bassist Daisuke Fuwa, are a high point of Japanese underground jazz. This band is known for its power improvisations, in which thirty or more musicians blur the lines between jazz, "happenings," and multimedia events. *Butoh* dancing meets pop, magicians encounter free funk, lounge melodies coexist with traditional Japanese *enka* music. This is a shrill collision between trash and high art, between Eastern tradition and everyday culture, filtered through wild, ecstatic collective improvisations.

All of the big bands of free jazz, led by such different personalities as Misha Mengelberg, Alexander von Schlippenbach, Anthony Braxton, Barry Guy, or Ken Vandermark, have created from the spirit of free improvisation compositions in which the tension between the individual and the collective is creatively exploited, just as it was in the great arrangements of tonal jazz. Here lines of connection are also created to the great figures of the European compositional tradition, to composers such as Xenakis, Schoenberg, Ligeti, and Penderecki, and techniques are incorporated that come from new music, such as graphic notation, aleatoric elements, and stochastic procedures, allowing room for chance within the framework of the composition.

Nonetheless, it is not really possible to maintain, as some neotraditionalist musicians have done, that free jazz is a kind of "European classical music." Jazz composition, including free-jazz composition, requires an approach that is fundamentally different from the classical Western tradition of writing for instrumentalists. The art of composing for improvisers does not consist in guessing what they will play, nor does it consist in concentrating entirely on their respective specialties. Rather, the principle is to write music that inspires the improvisers to do something that they would not have thought of themselves. For this reason, the practice of jazz composition also demands the "humility of the non-knower," as John Corbett has written. "It means that you have to believe in something unknown, in something that is as fragile as improvisation." All jazz composers, including free-jazz composers, adhere more or less to a maxim ultimately traceable to Duke Ellington: "discover the identity of a band in the voices of its members, and then bundle these to create something new."

Chicago saxophonist and composer Ken Vandermark: "My approach to composition is to take certain things that I like and to see if I can apply them to a group context in order to get people to improvise in a way that they would never improvise otherwise." In his Territory Band—a trans-Atlantic ensemble of American and European musicians—he builds on the contrasts between the soloists, drawing together improvisational strategies from disparate sources to form a unity—European extended techniques, open improvisation, classic jazz, and other styles and idioms. "There isn't nearly enough composition in the music coming out of free jazz. I think that free improvisation is going to change through composition. I believe that composition is the thing that's going to take improvisation to a new place."

Rock Big Bands

There were three main currents in the big-band jazz of the early seventies:

1. Continued development of free big-band jazz

2. Continued development of conventional big bands, utilizing contemporary themes and tendencies

3. So-called rock big bands

And of course there were widely varying combinations of the three.

Let us first discuss rock big bands, ensembles like Blood, Sweat & Tears, Chicago, Dreams, or The Flock. The word *big* should actually have been put in quotation marks because we are here dealing mostly with groups of seven to eleven members—in other words, relatively small according to the conventions of big-band jazz. Still, it became customary to call them "big bands," because with the help of electronics, they show tendencies to play in "sections." Keep in mind, too, that the big jazz band, in its early stages, also consisted of no more than eight to eleven musicians. Quite possibly, an evolution could have come full circle here. At least theoretically, there was a possibility for a while that the rock big band was standing at the beginning of a development similar to that of the jazz big band from the twenties on, but the reality was a different matter.

Rock big bands frequently strike the listener as being strangely stiff and inflexible, reminiscent in many respects of Stan Kenton during the forties. Since so many young big-band rock musicians have emerged from the university and college bands shaped by Kenton and his clinics, one might perhaps find a connection here.

The musical results often are in grotesque contrast to the effort involved. Unlike most other forms of rock, its big bands have failed to utilize and update tradition, particularly the jazz tradition. On the whole, their horn parts are hardly more than orchestrated guitar riffs. The use of horns is often so primitive that the impression is that beginners who do not have the slightest idea of the mysteries of orchestral arrangement, neither in jazz nor concert music, are at work here.

Until the second half of the seventies, only Frank Zappa had found in rock music—in real rock, that is—musical avenues that reached the level and complexity of big-band jazz. Significantly, Zappa did not start with jazz or blues or rock, as did all the others. In interviews he has repeatedly said he was prompted to become a musician by the works of Edgar Varese, the great modern composer who as early as the twenties treated and solved many problems relevant to modern classical music in the fifties and sixties: problems of noise integration, electronics, percussion, collage techniques, musical density, etc. In the early fifties, Zappa, then unknown and unnoticed, attended the *Kurse für Zeitgenössische Musik* (Courses in Contemporary Music) in Darmstadt, Germany, where many of the composers who so radically changed the contemporary avant-garde music scene at that time lectured or studied: Boulez, Stockhausen, Nono, Zimmermann, Ligeti, Henze, Kagel, Berio, etc. That is the world that shaped Zappa—and that he continued to long for, though one was not supposed to notice. Thus his eccentricity, his bizarre humor, his pose were at once ironic and sincere. In his day and age, didn't he seem like a Don Quixote struggling against windmills? And didn't he love to appear this way?

At the end of his career, the circle was completed: shortly before his death in 1993, he gave concerts with the Ensemble Moderne and with the Kronos Quartet—two of the leading ensembles in composed new music.

Zappa's music has a turbulence that attacks all preconceived notions, and these attacks are directed just as much against mediocre rock musicians as they are against the clichés of jazz. Zappa was an arranger who did not make distinctions in his mind between Charles Ives, the Orioles, Arnold Schoenberg, and Lightnin' Hopkins. His long, technically accomplished guitar solos were the crowning touch on a music for which the adjective "Zappaesque" had to be invented. Superficially chaotic, in fact Zappa's bands and music were precisely choreographed, using intricate rhythms and complicated changes of meter to demand the utmost from his musicians, while simultaneously giving them a great deal of space for improvisation.

Many critics feel that with the album *The Grand Wazoo*, released in 1972, Zappa's music reached its culmination. The production is said to show influences by—we will simply list the names—Miles Davis, John McLaughlin, Manitas de Plata, Gil Evans, Kodaly, Prokofiev, Stravinsky, Kurt Weill, etc. Critic Harvey Siders calls one of the pieces from *The Grand Wazoo* one of the "most successful weddings of jazz and rock in the book."

Big Bands Forever: The Seventies

Anyone who realizes how few convincing rock big-band records have ever appeared, and on the other hand takes into account the excellent productions featuring the conventional big-band setup released in growing numbers from the early seventies on, certainly cannot speak of the "end of big bands." Many outstanding leaders and arrangers have proven that the big band still has noteworthy possibilities. Among these musicians were, in the seventies, Don Ellis, Buddy Rich, Louie Bellson, Thad Jones–Mel Lewis, Oliver Nelson, Doc Severinsen, Toshiko Akiyoshi–Lew Tabackin, and, in Europe, Kenny Clarke–Francy Boland and Chris McGregor and his Brotherhood of Breath. In addition, there is a whole line of arrangers and band leaders who have been active for decades and have kept their music alive as times changed—among them Woody Herman, Count Basie, Maynard Ferguson, and so on.

The scope of big-band music became so broad because on the one hand new possibilities were continually being discovered, while on the other nearly all the possibilities that had been discovered in forty years of big-band history up to that time remained alive.

Don Ellis (who died in 1978) came out of the George Russell sextet of the early sixties and later studied Indian music with Hari Har Rao. He was especially interested in using new meters and rhythmic sequences. Other musicians, to be sure, had employed asymmetrical meters in jazz before Ellis—Thelonious Monk and Max Roach, then Dave Brubeck and Sonny Rollins, and as early as in the thirties, Fats Waller and Benny Carter. But nobody went as far as Ellis, who said:

> I reasoned that since it was possible to play in a meter such as a 9, divided 2-2-2-3, it would then be possible to play in meters of even longer length, and this led to the development of such meters as 3-3-2-2-2-1-2-2-2 (19). To arrive at this particular division of 19, I tried many different patterns, but this was the one that swung the most. The longest meter I have attempted to date is a piece in 85.

Some of Ellis's meters look like mathematical equations—for instance, the blues in 11 that Ellis played as three times $3\,^{2}/_{3}/4$ with natural, swinging ease. Ellis once said, ironically, that if his orchestra had to play a traditional 4/4 beat, one had best explain it to the band as "5/4 minus 1," otherwise it would be no fun.

Buddy Rich (d. 1987), on the other hand, did not experiment at all. His big band "celebrated" his spectacular drum artistry effectively. An evening with the Rich Big Band was show business in the conventional sense, but in its utmost perfection. The band's repertoire included evergreens, classic jazz themes, originals, and good contemporary tunes.

Another famous drummer who made big-band recordings in the seventies and eighties is Louis Bellson. He does not appear so much as the star in the center, but takes on a functional role on drums in order to present musicianly, convincing arrangements (frequently his own) that combine the great big-band tradition with, sometimes, the seventies' rock atmosphere.

Many of these bands—those of Rich, Bellson, and Maynard Ferguson, for example—recruited and still recruit their musicians among the graduates of jazz courses at American colleges and universities. In a sense, it can be said that with the fine training of these young musicians, the bands tend to reach an even higher professional level than most of their forerunners. There is nothing in terms of technique they cannot handle. They are unbeatable readers and can play higher and faster than ever. But strangely enough, what often is lacking is the magic goal of the jazz musician: individuality. A basic problem of music education is revealed here: individuality cannot be taught. It has to grow organically, like a plant. In our modern world of media, with radio and television programs and video clips all sounding alike, the plant called "individuality" has a hard time thriving. The American educational system, a model for the world, and its jazz educators should address themselves more strongly to this problem.

But we have to backtrack once more by a couple of years—to Europe. Here, the Clarke-Boland Big Band proved how alive the big-band tradition can be even when no concessions are made to the *Zeitgeist*. In the sixties, under the co-leadership of drum patriarch Kenny Clarke and Belgian arranger Francy Boland, some of the best-known American expatriates—among them trumpeters Benny Bailey, Art Farmer, and Idrees Sulieman and saxophonists Herb Geller and Sahib Shihab—united with European musicians of the caliber of Swedish trombonist Ake Persson, German trumpeter Manfred Schoof, and British sax men Ronnie Scott and Tony Coe. The band's second drummer was a British musician similar to the famous Clarke not only in playing, but also in name: Kenny Clare. He impressively supplemented Clarke's musicianship and stylistic feeling with his professional dependability, occasionally also disguising a lack of stamina in Clarke, the grand old master.

For years, pianist Francy Boland's arrangements were considered the "most traditional contemporary big-band arrangements" on the jazz scene, carrying on the tradition of classic modern jazz. Especially characteristic of this are the albums *Sax No End* (with tenorists Johnny Griffin and Eddie "Lockjaw" Davis) and *Faces* (with musical portrait sketches of the band members). It is too bad that just when the orchestra was becoming successful with a larger audience in the early seventies, it disbanded.

About that time, Peter Herbolzheimer (d. 2002) formed his Rhythm Combination & Brass. All through the seventies and eighties, and into the nineties, this was Europe's most professional big band—certainly making many concessions to fads of the day, but again and again showing a high degree of musicianship and a swinging power generated by some of the best musicians in Europe and a few American guests. Herbolzheimer's arrangements are characterized by a seamless connection of the swinging jazz tradition with Latin American rhythms and elements of jazz-rock.

In 1972 Swiss pianist George Gruntz founded his Concert Jazz Band, originally simply called The Band. This group is an all-star orchestra that is oriented primarily not toward American sound ideals, but rather toward contemporary European classical principles of composition. As arranger, Gruntz has a gift for new sound combinations and for transcending existing contexts, for example in collaboration with the Basel Pipers or with Scottish Highland bagpipers, in his projects with composer Rolf Liebermann, or in projects such as *Jazz Goes Baroque* and *Percussion Profiles*. Gruntz's Concert Jazz Band is a cheerful musical collective that puts the emphasis on "serious fun," emphasizing individual expression over conformity and rigid sectional discipline. The band has continued to develop this idea of an "orchestra of soloists" up to the present day. The history of the band, which has issued more than thirteen recordings and has had more than 150 members, with featured soloists including Joe Henderson, Lew Soloff, Ray Anderson, Tom Harrell, and Steve Turre, reads like a Who's Who of contemporary jazz.

The musically most convincing of all more recent big bands was, for most of the seventies, the Thad Jones–Mel Lewis Orchestra. For many years, it played New York's Village Vanguard every Monday night. Without making compromises with the rock spirit of the times, the two co-leaders, trumpeter, composer, and arranger Thad Jones and drummer Mel Lewis, managed to appeal to a large audience and to create an orchestral jazz that, as swinging as it was in the traditional sense, was full of sounds and ideas never heard before. Jazz from all periods—including the jazz of the sixties and the music of John Coltrane and the post-Coltrane era—merged in the compositions and arrangements, furnished mainly by Thad Jones and played by an elite troupe of New York's finest musicians. Thad Jones's compositions and arrangements are full of wonders, scintillating with ideas and surprises, full of contrasts and unexpected changes of course, opening up new harmonic, melodic, rhythmic, and also technical worlds without losing sight of the big-band mainstream.

Regrettably Jones and Lewis separated in 1979. For seven years Jones headed the Danish Radio Big Band in Copenhagen, one of the most swinging in Europe. Then in 1985, a year after the Count's death, Jones took charge of the Basie Orchestra. A year later, he was also dead. Mainstream jazz thus lost one of its most important composers and arrangers.

It was Mel Lewis who most vitally carried on the tradition of the New York band, with its compact, dense sound, through the eighties until his death in 1990, adding new arrangers such as Bob Brookmeyer and Bob Mintzer. Thad Jones's unmistakable "composer's touch" is still to be felt: not only in his well-known, artfully woven, swinging pieces, presented time and again, but also in everything the band otherwise played. Lewis used riffs and long solos to give his big band the flexible spirit of a small group. Today, the Thad Jones–Mel Lewis tradition, with its powerful sound and difficult charts, is continued by the Vanguard Jazz Orchestra, in swinging arrangements contributed by "composer-in-residence" Jim McNeely.

Meanwhile, however, another orchestra had made its breakthrough, the Toshiko Akiyoshi–Lew Tabackin Big Band in Los Angeles. Most of the critics voted it the number one big band from 1978 to the first half of the eighties. The orchestra gets its stamp from the compositions and arrangements of Japanese-born pianist Toshiko Akiyoshi. She writes long pieces, seventeen to twenty minutes, that are not suites in the conventional sense but rather continuous orchestral stories. This idea of "programmatic music" she first developed in 1974 in the work *Tales of a Courtesan*, and she has continued to build on the concept in her compositions since then. "Long pieces are very unusual in jazz. Traditionally, jazz is connected with the song form, so the pieces tend to be short. Even Duke Ellington's suites are rare in comparison to the number of songs that he wrote," says Toshiko. "When I look back and analyze what I've done, I find that in many cases I seem to have had a tendency to write in what you might call layers of sound. In other words, I will have one thing, then I will hear another that goes along with it. It's just like a photograph with a double exposure, you know?" Characteristic of Akiyoshi arrangements are the wealth and refinement of harmonic color. Particularly original is a five-part flute section that Toshiko formed with members of her orchestra, with her husband Lew Tabackin taking the lead voice. She has also been successful in widening the scope of the sax section by adding different kinds of flutes and clarinets in new and original combinations. In some of her pieces, she has drawn on Japanese tradition, including *gagaku*, the ancient court music of the Japanese emperors.

Back to the Basics and Postmodernism: The Eighties

The stream of the great big-band tradition continues to flow. Many orchestras all over the world are a part of it. Some of the more important ones in the eighties were Jaki Byard's Apollo Stompers, Ed Shaughnessy's Energy Force, Nat Pierce and Frank Capp's Juggernaut, Rob McConnell's Boss Brass, Charli Persip's Superband, the Bob Mintzer Big Band, the Illinois Jacquet Orchestra, and the American Jazz Orchestra (headed by pianist John Lewis).

All in all, clearly a comeback of tradition can be found on the big-band scene since the early eighties. It is no longer free-jazz orchestras or rock big bands, but the conventional big-band instrumentation (four trumpets, four trombones, a five-piece saxophone section, with minor deviations, alterations, and additions) that has returned to the focal point of big-band attention—forty years after the first talk of the "death" of the big bands.

And finally, there are also big bands that put rock elements to creative use, without the stiffness and lack of inspiration we talked about earlier.

The most important of such ensembles was the Gil Evans Monday Night Orchestra (see the section on Evans); but Bob Moses, the Bob Mintzer Big Band, the Jaco Pastorius Big Band, Edward Wilkerson's Shadow Vignettes, and in Europe the United Jazz & Rock Ensemble, England's Loose Tubes, and Young Power from Poland have also vitalized and expanded jazz-rock with the palette of contemporary jazz feeling. Drummer and composer Bob Moses, who played with Gary Burton and Pat Metheny, creates out of an unusually picturesque tonal imagination. He writes less in "movements" than in "textures"—gentle, pastel-colored, shimmering layers of sound in which there lives the magic of African and Indian music, permeated by the motoric élan of jazz-rock (mainly Miles) and modern jazz (Gil Evans, Monk, but also much Ellington). The titles of pieces on his much-praised albums *When Elephants Dream of Music* (1982) and *Visit with the Great Spirit* (1983) already reflect something of his music's exceptionally visual impact: "Black Orchid," "Lava Flow," "Machupicchu," and "Visit with the Great Spirit."

For a long time, the virtuosic abilities of electric bassist Jaco Pastorius overshadowed his talents as composer and arranger. This was unjust, because the jazz orchestra that he led toward the end of his career created a brilliant stylistic panorama between mainstream jazz and jazz-rock. Like Quincy Jones, Jaco had good arrangers working for him as ghostwriters. But the harmonic ideas of Jaco's big-band compositions are complex and highly developed. They show that Jaco the big-band leader was a logical continuation of Jaco the soloist and electric bassist, because his musical thinking and playing was always primarily orchestral.

Tenor saxophonist Bob Mintzer was the first big-band composer to do something really individual in the fusion area, influenced both by jazz-rock and by the new mainstream jazz. He succeeded in bringing the solid, compact qualities of the swinging big-band into a jazz-rock aesthetic. Mintzer began writing for Buddy Rich, and contributed important arrangements for Louis Bellson and Jaco Pastorius. He founded his own orchestra at the beginning of the eighties, calling on New York musicians who were tired of the studio business. With soloists including trumpeter Randy Brecker, pianist Don Grolnick, and bassist Lincoln Goines, the Bob Mintzer Big Band was an oasis of creativity in the desert of the New York commercial studios.

In the eighties England's Mike Gibbs was in such demand as composer and arranger that he traveled regularly between the United States, where he wrote arrangements for Pat Metheny and John McLaughlin, and London, where he realized his own orchestral projects. His compositions combine influences from Gil Evans and Olivier Messiaen with powerful rock rhythms and asymmetrical lines. With his broad writing, reveling in luxuriant sound colors, Mike Gibbs has cultivated a sound that has influenced many other European jazz orchestras. This open, quasi-symphonic sound is strikingly different from the sound of most American big bands, which tend more toward the taut, exciting Thad Jones–Mel Lewis sound.

From its establishment in 1975 until its disbanding in 2003, with such musicians as Barbara Thompson, Charlie Mariano, Albert Mangelsdorff, Eberhard Weber, and Jon Hiseman, the United Jazz & Rock Ensemble (initiated by pianist Wolfgang Dauner) was the most popular and successful big European orchestra. The reason is that the Ensemble endowed orchestral jazz-rock with something only seldom to be found in that sphere: warmth and communicativeness, and *melos* without affected pathos. The band drew its vitality from the great individuality of its individual members. Over the course of its twenty-seven years of existence, throughout which it kept almost the same personnel, the United Jazz & Rock Ensemble remained a workshop band, without the mechanical precision of other big bands or the polish of a band of outstanding readers, but making up for this with the unusually democratic character of its communicative structures.

Stylistically a step further, marking the transition to postmodern jazz, was Loose Tubes—the twenty-one–member British group around keyboarder Django Bates. This band whirls with turbulent wit through a colorful "chaos" of styles, interweaving South African music, Weather Report, bebop, Arab music, country and western, and free jazz, expressing sheer joy in life.

Bates's adventurous love of musical risk-taking has made him one of the great arrangers of contemporary European jazz. In the eighties, he was a member of Bill Bruford's Earthworks. In 1991, he founded the nineteen-member orchestra Delightful Precipice. There's method in his fresh, well-thought-out "madness." His daring stylistic patchworks combine Bach, soul, African township music, jazz-rock, and free elements to form a music full of absurd humor and emotional presence. "There's not enough laughter in music," he says.

Just as, in the eighties, Loose Tubes became the germ of the contemporary white British jazz scene, producing players such as Steve Arguelles, Ian Ballamy, and Django Bates, the big band Jazz Warriors, founded by Courtney Pine and Gary Crosby, developed into a springboard for the elite players in Afro-British jazz. With soloists like Steve Williamson, Cleveland Watkiss, and Julian Joseph, the Jazz Warriors created a strong, groove-oriented orchestral language from which an original Afro-British black music emerged, moving between reggae and soul, American and European big-band tradition.

Young Power, the eighteen-piece orchestra headed by Polish flutist Krzysztof Popek, has transposed Ornette Coleman's "harmolodic" concept of free funk into especially powerful and expressive multistyle realizations.

But even beyond the integration of rock elements, there are a multitude of results outside the conventional big-band lineup. The significance of David Murray's big ensembles for contemporary jazz has already been covered in the section devoted to the saxophonist. But even more important in that context was probably the work of pianist, composer, and AACM initiator Muhal Richard Abrams. He has most consistently drawn on the entire palette of "classical" big-band sounds for free jazz: following the roots of African American music from Duke Ellington by way of Benny Carter, Don Redman, and Fletcher Henderson, and then further through archaic jazz back to Africa—all of which is to be felt in his abstractly shimmering compositions, nevertheless saturated with enormous feeling for the blues. Astonishingly, Abrams's orchestrations, based on compositional structures and traditional big-band know-how, produce a more modern and vital impact than many a "free" orchestra still radically assailing all the musical norms. Anthony Braxton: "In Muhal's music I hear voices about the future—from the ancients."

Two other unusual orchestras came from Europe in the eighties: the Vienna Art Orchestra, established in the Austrian capital by Swiss composer Mathias Rüegg in 1977, and Pierre Dørge's New Jungle Orchestra. With neo-Dadaist wit, unpredictable perverseness, and a portion of "Viennese mockery," the Vienna Art Orchestra reflects European and American traditions as being of equal stature: Mozart and Mingus, Satie and Ellington, Stravinsky and Basie, with multitudinous references to Alpine folklore (predominantly the *Ländler*). As one critic wrote, "Very few European big bands have combined the American jazz tradition with the achievements of European modernity in such a refined, lighthearted manner." Masterly, too, is the high degree of amalgamation of composition and improvisation, which often results in the ensemble's long suites. The Vienna Art Orchestra has become the leading European big band in postmodern jazz, acclaimed on numerous tours not least because of its "unity," which is not just musical but also human. This success has been achieved together with such soloists as alto saxophonist Wolfgang Puschnig, flugelhorn player Herbert Joos, clarinetist Klaus Dickbauer, and trombonist Christian Muthspiel. Another trademark of the Vienna Art Orchestra is the organic integration of vocal and noise acrobatics into the big-band context, brilliantly realized by American Lauren Newton and France's Anne Lauvergnac, who sing even more freely in this orchestra than in their own groups. As a composer Rüegg is pointing European big-band jazz in new directions, finding unorthodox effects through freakish experimentation and the integration of unusual sound groupings, using alphorns, marimbas, Tibetan horns, melodicas, piccolo, and synthesizer. He has gone furthest, beyond all superficial parody, in developing the art of quotation, and yet he is completely himself in every note he writes. His "wit" and wealth of ideas seem inexhaustible.

Equally far removed from the usual big-band sound is Danish guitarist Pierre Dørge's New Jungle Orchestra, whose "open" way of playing and whose hybrids of jazz and world music became the most visible orchestral exponent of European world jazz—an ebullient, vital celebration of African, Asian, and Latin American music, filtered through the European jazz experience. From 1993 to 1996, the New Jungle Orchestra held the title of State Ensemble of Denmark. Dørge began to study the great musical cultures of the world in the midseventies, after John Tchicai made him aware of the fact that many of the things that Dørge, a free-jazz adherent at that time, took to be a product of experimental Western music had in fact already long been practiced in African, Latin American, and Asian music. In Gambia, Dørge studied the *balaphon* and kora music of the griots. For close to thirty years, the vital, joyful world jazz of the New Jungle Orchestra has been one of the mainstays of the contemporary Danish jazz scene. Most of the arrangements are by Dørge, but saxophonist John Tchicai also writes for the orchestra with such soloists as Harry Beckett, Johnny Dyani (d. 1986), and percussionist Marilyn Mazur.

Of importance too is Irakere, headed by pianist-composer Chucho Valdes. The group became known in 1979 through CBS Records' *Havana Jam* in Cuba, and since then it has attracted worldwide attention. Irakere creates a unique synthesis of jazz, rock, *son*, and the *bata* rhythms of the Afro-Cuban Santeria religion. In the view of Latin American critics, the foundation of the group in 1973 coincided with the beginning of contemporary jazz in Cuba. Chucho Valdés's "Missa Negra" is a ritual of black music that refers at the same time back to Africa and ahead to a new type of Latinized big-band sound. With its virtuosic Afro-Caribbean orchestral jazz, Irakere was the model for countless other Cuban large groups, including the band Cubanismo, led by trumpeter Jesús Alemañy. Up to the present day, the big band has continued to forge many generations of excellent Cuban musicians. The list of players who came through Irakere reads like a Who's Who of the Cuban jazz elite: alto saxophonist Paquito D'Rivera, trumpeter Arturo Sandoval, flutist Orlando "Maraca" Valle, drummer Ignacio Berroa, percussionist Miguel "Anga" Diaz.

Repertory Orchestras, Europe, and the Diversity of Styles: The Nineties

The rediscovery of the jazz tradition has led, in the big-band context as elsewhere, to a renewed appreciation of classical elements and the value of the great repertoire of jazz standards. For this reason, it is not surprising that in the nineties a large number of big bands came into existence, continuing the great heritage of the jazz orchestras in a neotraditional manner.

A striking trend in the nineties was the development of "repertory orchestras," that is, big bands playing updated versions and orchestral arrangements of jazz classics. *The* model for such bands, preserving the heritage of jazz in a consciously conservative manner, is the Lincoln Center Jazz Orchestra, whose artistic director is Wynton Marsalis. Although Wynton himself vehemently rejects the label "repertory orchestra," the LCJO sometimes radiates the aura of a Swing-era (or neo-Swing) big band that has rigidified into a kind of monument. Nonetheless, the band is full of exciting, virtuosic soloists, and in countless concerts has assumed the role of defending big-band excellence in straight-ahead jazz. The results are something of a mixed bag. On the one hand, the LCJO succeeds in uniting the Duke Ellington sound with up-to-date soloing in a contemporary manner, in arrangements by Wynton Marsalis, Wycliffe Gordon, and Andy Farber. On the other hand, they rarely succeed in stimulating anything more in the listener than a longing to hear the originals. In 1998 the LCJO spent seven months on the road, performing concerts in seventy-five countries on five continents.

Inspired by the success of the Lincoln Center Jazz Orchestra, in the nineties a wave of repertory orchestras emerged with the aim of celebrating and continuing the classical heritage of the big bands in a contemporary manner. Despite the technical brilliance of these orchestras, many critics remarked that it is not enough to internalize the sounds of Ellington and Basie without creating something new. "If you really want to play Duke Ellington," says Uri Caine, "you also have to hear how relaxed and open Duke Ellington was. Then you can't sound like a high school big band playing Duke Ellington charts. Which just makes Duke Ellington all the more mysterious. He always found a way to make the old sound new again."

Bands including the John Fedchock Big Band, the Clayton-Hamilton Jazz Orchestra with bassist John Clayton and drummer Jeff Hamilton, the American Jazz Orchestra, the Vanguard Jazz Orchestra (successor to the Thad Jones–Mel Lewis band), the Bill Kirchner Nonet, the Robert Farnon Band, the Carnegie Hall Jazz Band led by trumpeter Jon Faddis, the Gary Wofsey Orchestra, and Mike Holober and the Gotham Jazz Orchestra have all proved that it's possible to create exciting sounds in the area of the new, swinging mainstream big-band jazz.

The John Fedchock Big Band is a sixteen-piece ensemble that maintains a balance between standards and original compositions, and whose tight voicings and lightly swinging lines move between the mainstream and more modern forms of acoustic straight-ahead playing. Mike Holober, in his Gotham Jazz Orchestra, creates unconventional, beautiful colors.

Tenor saxophonist Joe Lovano says, "Big bands demand and promote a group consciousness like no other ensemble in jazz." In fact, a jazz orchestra draws its life from the strength of character and discipline of its members. Nowhere else are the standards of instrumental technique that have developed over the decades put so realistically to the competitive test as in the precision playing of a big band. Probably for this reason, the resurgence of jazz pedagogy has gone hand in hand with a new interest in the jazz orchestra.

Here it is appropriate to recognize that there is a big-band scene that is "underground" in both senses of that word: all the big bands at America's high schools, colleges, and universities. There are hundreds of big bands of all imaginable (and certainly also some unimaginable) shadings. These orchestras form the vital "underground," the basis, for tomorrow's professional big bands. Some of them are good enough to bear comparison with some of the best-known big bands of today.

The problem, however, with many university big bands is a certain lack of musical vision. Jim McNeely says:

> University bands are a reflection of the person at the top, and there are only a few directors like those at Miami, North Texas, and the New England Conservatory with both the vision and the funds to commission creative music. . . . You could say that university bands are comparable to the European scene in terms of numbers, but they are not comparable in terms of budgets or consistent quality.

In the nineties, for reasons of economics, professional big bands became comparatively scarce on the American scene. In contrast, the big-band scene in Europe is more vital, diverse, and stable, thanks above all to state support and the network of radio big bands. Today, it's considered a matter of course for all the great American arrangers and jazz composers—Bill Holman, Bob Brookmeyer, Vince Mendoza, Maria Schneider—to come to Europe three or four times a year to work with radio big bands and other jazz orchestras, such as the Metropole Orchestra in Holland, the Danish Radio Jazz Orchestra in Copenhagen, the UMO Big Band in Finland, the WDR Big Band in Cologne, and the NDR Big Band in Hamburg.

The radio big bands and the state-supported jazz orchestras form the backbone of the European orchestral jazz scene. In Hamburg, for example, the NDR Big Band, under the direction of Dieter Glawischnig and in collaboration with composers such as Colin Towns and lyricist Ernst Jandl, has developed a remarkable stylistic openness. Also remarkable is the power with which the NDR Big Band has built a homogenous orchestral sound from great individual voices of German jazz like Christof Lauer, Claus Stötter, and Reiner Winterschladen.

In pursuing its mission of performing previously little-known material, the WDR Big Band Cologne has developed an individual identity.

It has become a specialist in world premieres and first performances, in projects with Vince Mendoza, Maria Schneider, Clare Fischer, and Lalo Schifren, and in performances at all the major international jazz festivals.

The Finnish UMO Big Band, founded in 1975, has achieved a similarly significant extension and refinement of the big-band vocabulary. Their repertoire comprises more than a thousand compositions, and the band has worked with artists as diverse as Natalie Cole, Muhal Richard Abrams, Billy Eckstine, and Anthony Braxton. Dizzy Gillespie enthused, "One of the best big bands I ever played with."

But for more than forty years, the outstanding European radio jazz orchestra has been the Danish Radio Jazz Orchestra. Founded in 1964, this band has profited like no other European big band from collaboration with an illustrious series of prominent guest arrangers, including Frank Foster, Oliver Nelson, George Russell, Michael Gibbs, and Mike Westbrook. Its international reputation is built largely on an impressively continuous lineage of important artistic directors, including Palle Mikkelborg, Thad Jones, Bob Brookmeyer, and Jim McNeely, who took over as director in 1998.

The extent to which the emphasis in the area of mainstream big bands has moved from America to Europe is seen also in the fact that one of the greatest American jazz arrangers, valve trombonist Bob Brookmeyer, leads his own large ensemble, the New Art Orchestra, in Europe. This big band was founded in 1994 on the occasion of a composition workshop at the Schleswig-Holstein Music Festival. The New Art Orchestra is made up of young Dutch, American, and German musicians—eighteen players realizing Brookmeyer's music in marvelous fashion. Since the seventies Brookmeyer has developed into one of the most important arrangers in the new mainstream jazz, in his arrangements for the Thad Jones–Mel Lewis Orchestra, for Gerry Mulligan's Concert Jazz Band, and for his own band. In the eighties his music also reflected influences from modern European concert music. Brookmeyer specializes in arrangements featuring detailed treatment of motifs and absorbing streams of thought, while still providing inspiration for the soloists. With humorous understatement, Brookmeyer remarks: "I'm lazy. I like to write out slash marks and whole-note melodies for cats to play."

But Brookmeyer is also a sharp observer of the European big-band scene, who points out a shortcoming of many European (and American) big bands: "The tendency, especially with European bands, is to get carried away and just write, write, write, instead of allowing things to open up."

One of Brookmeyer's students is Maria Schneider, who is perhaps the most original composer and orchestra leader in contemporary jazz since Carla Bley. Her pieces have the narrative flow of a novel that takes the listener to new places, using a kind of orchestral storytelling to draw the listener in and transport him or her through a wide variety of moods, colors, and feelings. In the last years of Gil Evans's life, Maria Schneider was his assistant, and she learned a great deal from him about refined coloration, shimmering voices, and a taste for woodwinds and muted brass. Schneider thus represents a continuation of the Gil Evans / George Russell lineage. Her orchestra, which performed every Monday in New York's Club Visiones in the early nineties, provides highly coloristic realizations of the music. Schneider has an excellent ear for timbre, and is especially attentive to individual lines.

Maria Schneider's compositions are not structured around a verse/chorus form, but rather develop in long arcs in which sound mixtures are investigated and delicate, intoxicating original sounds are developed. Her "landscapes of sound" make skillful use of colors and textures. This is an orchestral Impressionism, in which shimmering colors and dramatic crescendos are used to create structures that ebb and flow dynamically. "I think of my pieces as little personalities. They're like my kids. After I finish a piece, it takes a while for me to forget the struggle of composing it. Then, all of a sudden, it becomes something separate from me, and the band takes control of it, and shapes and develops it, and it has its own life."

Other important big bands of contemporary jazz in America in the nineties included the Dave Holland Big Band, Peter Apfelbaum's Hieroglyphic Ensemble, the Either/Orchestra (which produced John Medeski and Matt Wilson), Orange Then Blue, the McCoy Tyner Big Band, the Mingus Big Band, the Jason Lindner Ensemble, and the orchestra of Guillermo Klein, an Argentinian living in New York.

The Hieroglyphic Ensemble, based in San Francisco and led by tenor saxophonist Peter Apfelbaum, creates an exciting world jazz in a big-band format, using hypnotic riffs that move between Afrobeat, reggae, and west African drum languages. "Peter Apfelbaum composes exactly the way I would if I was writing for big bands," said trumpeter Don Cherry.

"A big band is at its best when it sounds like a small group," Herb Pomeroy once said. The McCoy Tyner Big Band, in existence since 1980, plays with great power and emotion and with a strong Ellington influence. It has the loose feeling of a small group, reflecting the personality of its pianist and leader, McCoy Tyner, in its shout choruses, riffs, and briefly sketched ensemble passages.

Guillermo Klein's big-band music combines influences from Steve Reich and Johann Sebastian Bach with the rich heritage of Argentinian folklore, from tangos and milongas to the rhythms and melodies of the gauchos. Klein uses the art of baroque counterpoint, fugati, and canons, together with the superposed patterns of African music and minimalist music to transpose his Argentinian roots into contemporary jazz. Klein's trademark is the layering of contrapuntal ideas, such as riffs. He has his musicians play two- or three-part rhythmic/melodic cells in any tempo they wish, resulting in exciting rhythmic layerings and superpositions, reminiscent of a very contemporary version of the Don Ellis band of the seventies.

The Mingus Big Band, with its raw, rough, powerful interpretations of the music of Charles Mingus, has been thrilling audiences since the nineties. This jazz orchestra, assembled by Mingus's widow Sue Evans, is not purveying the kind of musical necrophilia often observed in orchestras formally led by dead jazz greats. Instead, the Mingus Big Band is a collective bursting with vitality and the joy of playing, whose harmonically challenging, dissonant music makes an essential contribution to keeping Mingus's legacy fresh and continually relevant. In the ecstatic playing of this big band, which has included Randy Brecker, Frank Lacy, Craig Handy, and Chris Potter, there reigns a spirit of creative competition among New York's top soloists. Chris Potter says, "It's not like all the solos are specified. Everyone in the band wants to be soloing and everyone can, but it takes a certain amount of confidence to stand up and be heard."

The band led by bassist Dave Holland (whose contribution to the expansion of the form and content of the jazz idiom has already been addressed in the chapter on the bass) is also dedicated to a progressive treatment of the big-band tradition.

In the triangle between fusion, mainstream jazz, and Western concert music, arranger Vince Mendoza has brought unusual stylistic multiplicity to the traditional jazz orchestra, incorporating minimalist and twelve-tone elements as well as synthesizers and sequencers. Mendoza has strong roots both in jazz and in classical music, and his inspirations range from Johannes Brahms to Joe Zawinul. Mendoza completed a course of study in classical guitar, but then changed to trumpet and studied composition at Ohio State University. In 1983 he moved to Los Angeles, where he began to study computer music (still a novelty at that time) and the use of sequencers. His greatest strength lies in an extreme richness of sonic modulation, which he has demonstrated in arrangements for Joni Mitchell, Peter Erskine, and the WDR Big Band (in the project *Jazzpaña*, *Spanish Night*, a combination of the voicings and dance forms of flamenco with big-band jazz). Mendoza's arrangements are a delicate dance between improvised and composed music. The subtle colors of his ideas are exceptional. No composer and arranger in the nineties managed to show up on so many albums by other jazz musicians as Vince Mendoza. The musicians who have profited from his love of dark, deeply shadowed colors and surprising turns include Michael Brecker, Gary Burton, John Abercrombie, John Scofield, and Charlie Haden. "When you think of a composer, you normally envision someone sitting in an armchair with a lamp on the desk and a pipe in his mouth. But I would rather have an awareness of the musicians. The people I most enjoy working with are the ones who see me as a player. I want to do something that inspires people to improvise."

Bob Belden is another arranger who left his mark on the American big-band landscape of the nineties. Belden began as a tenor saxophonist in the big band of Woody Herman, and in the nineties became an in-demand arranger, record producer, and reissue editor (e.g., of Miles Davis Blue Note recordings) on the New York scene. As a composer, Bob Belden has opened up the classic big-band format to the diversity of multistylistic jazz like no one else. He seems to have absorbed every note ever played by the big bands of Maynard Ferguson, Stan Kenton, Bill Holman, and Don Ellis. His big-band interpretations of popular music by Sting and Prince do not reduce the sonic world of the big band, but rather expand it to include new sound possibilities. He also created lush dream worlds in his jazz treatment of the Puccini opera *Turandot* (whose publication was prevented in the United States by the Puccini estate, but which appeared in Japan and which Belden promoted internationally).

Belden combines a precise knowledge of form and harmony with an adventurous "let's see what happens" attitude. This "perfect balance between the academic and the intuitive sides" (Bob Blumenthal) has made him one of the most sought-after arrangers in contemporary jazz. At the end of the nineties, he became less and less interested in the big-band format. With his colleague of many years, trumpeter Tim Hagans, he created a project in which he combined jazz sounds with the breakbeats of house and drum 'n' bass music. "I define jazz as a pure feeling. It's one of the few forms of music that lets you listen deeply into your heart—for no other reason than to say what you have to say."

As one critic remarked, "Anyone who leads a big band today has to be crazy. Keeping a large ensemble afloat financially is a Herculean task." Nonetheless, in the nineties there were hundreds of such "crazy" people. Despite all the pessimism, the big bands, the "dinosaurs of jazz," enjoyed an unexpected renaissance. In the area of contemporary jazz, particularly original contributions came from Europe. Important European large ensembles that found creative solutions include the Andy Emler MegaOctet and the Orchestre National de Jazz in France, the Colin Towns Mask Orchestra and the Matthew Herbert Big Band in England, the Budapest Jazz Orchestra (under the direction of Kornél Fekete-Kovács) in Hungary, the Geir Lysne Listening Ensemble and Jaga Jazzist from Norway, the Norbotten Big Band in Sweden, the Concert Jazz Band Vienna (led by American arranger Ed Partyka) in Austria, and the Klaus König Orchestra in Germany.

Pianist Andy Emler, who came from the band of Michel Portal, is the father of postmodern French big-band jazz. His arrangements, slipping sideways through styles and genres, inspire unconventional improvisations. In 1992 his MegaOctet was awarded the Django d'Or Prize as the best French jazz band. Under normal circumstances, it would be difficult to call this eight-piece ensemble a big band, but the stylistic turbulence that Emler provokes in his MegaOctet has an orchestral weight, and has made multistylistic improvisation respectable in orchestral French jazz. Emler completed a course of study in classical composition at the Paris Conservatory, and was awarded a prize in counterpoint. He's a fanciful, daring composer who brings together things in his mini-big band, bursting with jubilant energy, that one would never believe would fit together: Bartók and hard bop, Indian ragas and Basque folk music, the Beatles and Stravinsky, Ars Nova and funk, African music and free jazz. Despite all its stylistic diversity, in Emler's music two poles of reference are striking: first, the sarcastic rhythmic sawtooth structures of Frank Zappa (Emler is a huge Zappa fan), and, second, a tendency toward the playing with language and the sonic jokes of neo-Dadaism (with singers such as Beñat Achiary and Mederic Collignon).

The Orchestre National de Jazz, founded in 1986 by the French Ministry of Culture, has as one of its founding principles the rule that its leadership is rotating. Its sounds and arrangements are accordingly varied, written at first by François Jeanneau, later by André Herve, Denis Baudault, and Claude Barthelemy. Despite, or perhaps because of, these changes in color, the Orchestre National de Jazz has become a font of creativity for the modern young French jazz scene, producing such soloists as Nguyên Lê, Stephane Bellmondo, Julien Loureau, and Nedim Nalbantoglu.

England's Colin Towns specializes in sharp dissonances, abrupt brass, and sumptuous melodies. He was in demand as a film composer, for example for the movie *Full Circle*, starring Mia Farrow, before starting his own Colin Towns Mask Orchestra. Towns is the "Stan Kenton of postmodernity"—his lush arrangements make liberal use of theatrical gestures and dramatic crescendos. His music, a mixture of beauty and darkness, shows him to be an expert in the use of cutting brass and bittersweet saxophones. "Music should not radiate comfort—it has to have energy. I want to drive things to the extreme and carry the audience along. I don't write film music for my jazz orchestra, but I think cinematically and I hear visually."

The Matthew Herbert Big Band, in England, and Norway's Jaga Jazzist have made convincing, attractive music in the area between digital electronics and big-band jazz. Herbert has done this by elevating elements of house music to the artistic level of big-band jazz, while Jaga Jazzist has integrated elements of techno and drum 'n' bass into the big-band sound. The Norbotten Big Band, from Sweden, under the direction of American trumpeter Tim Hagans, has achieved a balance between the jazz orchestra and digital breakbeats.

Norwegian saxophonist Geir Lysne, in his Listening Ensemble, has also convincingly expanded the traditional big-band sound with electronics. His suite *Aurora Borealis*, an homage to the Northern Lights, depicts the splendor of this natural phenomenon in daring arrangements. Lysne has brought the "Nordic sound," previously associated with small groups, to an orchestral context, using a very broad, "spacious" sonic language that calls on motifs from folk music as well as loops from techno and drum 'n' bass, intricate meters, and modal passages.

"The composer is an architect," says Klaus König, who has run his own orchestra since 1989, and who is one of the most imaginative jazz composers in Europe. His arrangements are extravagant layerings of fundamentally contradictory elements, full of stylistic comments on contemporary modernity, rock, and strict abstraction. In 1991 he released *At the End of the Universe* (an homage to author Douglas Adams and his *Hitchhiker's Guide to the Galaxy*), an amusing, subtle play on musical set pieces and elements from science fiction. In 1993 he released *The Song of Songs*, with Jay Clayton, Phil Minton, and the Montreal Jubilation Gospel Choir—a "jazz oratorio" for which König took the libretto from the Biblical *Song of Solomon*, brilliantly putting it in a setting with banal and surrealistic elements. "Sometimes I'm interested in taking clichés and turning them into something else," he says. As a composer, König creates unity in multiplicity. His works bring order to a deliberately chaotic musical universe, with humor and a richness of ideas. Elements from punk, blues, funk, twelve-tone music, gospel, folk, and free jazz are combined with clever lunacy to form multiple, interwoven references, finally creating a kind of postmodern burlesque.

Critic Nat Hentoff: "In all of jazz, there's probably no more uplifting sound than that of a big band in full cry—it can't be compared to any other sound." Trumpeter Wynton Marsalis says, "The orchestra is our most sophisticated instrument in jazz. It has a great tradition, and you won't find a richer sound." As precarious as the economic situation may be for many jazz orchestras, the contemporary big-band landscape has undimmed vitality. If you know this scene, with its volcanic vitality, you have to laugh when someone asks if big bands are dead.

The Small Bands of Jazz

Jazz is initially a music of small ensembles. Jazz was a combo music long before the word *combo* existed. This word came into being when it became necessary to distinguish between big bands and small groups. Before that, any jazz band was automatically a combo. If one did not know from hindsight what would evolve from the bands of Fletcher Henderson and Duke Ellington in the twenties, these ensembles, too, could be regarded as "combos."

Since jazz from the start has been an art of small ensembles, a history of small groups must be written differently from a history of big bands. Since practically every jazz man has played in small ensembles, such a history would turn into an endless listing of names. The required selective principle rests in the fact that a small band should be more than merely a group of musicians who have come together to play. By way of the Modern Jazz Quartet and John Lewis, "integration" has become a key term in jazz criticism. Here indeed is the key to our history of the small band in jazz. Integration means that everything belongs to a whole, that all elements are subordinate to one main idea.

In this sense, Dave Brubeck made a relevant statement about the situation: "The important thing about jazz right now is that it's keeping alive the feeling of the group getting together. Jazz, to make it, has got to be a group feeling." This describes what we have referred to as the sociological situation of jazz—as at the beginning of the section dealing with Swing style and in that about the arrangement. Jazz is at once music of the individual and music of the collective. No other art has attained both in such extreme measure. In such simultaneity the sociologist may find philosophical, political, and historical aspects. With jazz, this simultaneity of the individual and the collective, of—if you will—freedom and necessity, has acquired musical aspects for the first time. Rarely can jazz be seen so clearly as a legitimate artistic expression of our time as in this point. And since this is so, the small-band history of jazz is almost something like a concentration of jazz history per se.

In the selective sense in which we wish to present this history, Jelly Roll Morton's Red Hot Peppers (1926–30) and Louis Armstrong's second Hot Five with Earl Hines (1928) are the first significant small jazz bands. Morton was the first to map out pieces from beginning to end and give them the stamp of a formative personality. Armstrong's Hot Five recordings achieved integration through the telepathic rapport between Louis and his musicians, above all pianist Earl Hines.

Orrin Keepnews writes in the liner notes to a Morton album:

> This is complex, intricate music. The musicians reputedly did not play from written scores but each number was preceded by perhaps a half-hour of studying the tunes, deciding on the placements of solos, memorizing the basic arrangements. It is the definitive answer to anyone who would claim that jazz is deficient in counterpoint or in depth of musical structure. It is a remarkable combination of improvisation and arrangement. . . . These are all talented musicians, but nevertheless, the voice that is heard here, the single, unified sound, is Morton's. This is the mark of his greatness.

Phil Schaap has called the recordings of Louis Armstrong's Hot Five (1925–28) and Hot Seven (1927) the "Rosetta Stone of jazz itself." From them, it is possible to decipher the archetypal essence of jazz. These bands not only made swing the indispensible lifeblood of improvised music, they also established *togetherness* as the standard of improvising. They put central emphasis both on the free voice of the soloist and on the productive relationship of tension between the individual and the group.

In the Armstrong Hot Five with Hines (they consisted of six and sometimes even seven musicians) and in the Morton Red Hot Peppers we see for the first time a coming together of elements that previously had only existed separately: the collective improvisation of the old New Orleans bands in which soloistic achievement, and the individuality of the improviser in general, had barely begun to develop; this soloistic achievement itself; and, lastly, the conscious or intuitive creation of form through an outstanding personality.

The Small Swing Bands

The thirties brought a permanent expansion of soloistic abilities. In 1935 Benny Goodman formed his Benny Goodman Trio (with Teddy Wilson and Gene Krupa). It became the germ cell and model not only for all the other Goodman small bands—the quartet with Lionel Hampton and eventually the sextets with Charlie Christian and Cootie Williams—but also for all the small bands that developed as "bands within bands" in all the important large orchestras. Thus, Artie Shaw formed his Gramercy Five with himself on clarinet and first Billy Butterfield and then Roy Eldridge on trumpet. Tommy Dorsey, Bob Crosby, and Jimmy Dorsey formed Dixieland bands within their big bands. Chu Berry recruited his Stompy Stevedores primarily from the ranks of Cab Calloway's band, of which he was a member. Count Basie's band had its Kansas City Six and Seven and Woody Herman his Woodchoppers.

The most important of these "bands within the bands" originated in the Duke Ellington orchestra. Trumpeters Cootie Williams and Rex Stewart, clarinetist Barney Bigard, and altoist Johnny Hodges all made recordings in which the atmosphere of Ellington's music was, amazingly, projected into ever-changing small instrumental combinations. The "Ellington spirit" served as the integrating factor. It was so strong that even some records made by Lionel Hampton with musicians drawn mainly from this band acquired a noticeable Ellington aura.

The opposite of the integration that permeates the recordings made by the Ellington musicians can be found in the recording groups put together by Teddy Wilson from 1935 on. In a sense, these groups should not be mentioned here, in view of our selective principles. Here solo follows solo, but precisely on this account it is amazing how often the musical climate creates its own unity—especially when Billie Holiday and Lester Young are among the participants. In a song like "Easy Living" (1937) there is certainly nothing "integrated," and yet, from first note to last, we are in the unifying climate created by the tune, the lyrics, and the way in which Billie Holiday sings and the musicians, obviously, feel with her.

It is remarkable how the turning point in jazz evolution, which came toward the end of the thirties and beginning of the forties, not only involved the harmonic, melodic, and rhythmic innovations of the bop musicians but also initiated new concepts of integration. In 1938 bassist John Kirby formed an ensemble that in every respect made Swing music in the best sense of the term, yet it was a small band in a sense that did not become the rule until the fifties. Its precise ensemble playing, melodic finesse, and chamber-musical brilliance anticipated many developments that did not become widespread in jazz until twenty years later. With Kirby—and with the Nat King Cole Trio as well—begins the real "integration" line of small-band history that leads through the Art Tatum Trio and the Red Norvo Trio to the characteristic small bands of the fifties and sixties: the Gerry Mulligan Quartet, the Modern Jazz Quartet, the Jimmy Giuffre Trio, the Max Roach–Clifford Brown Quintet, the Miles Davis Quintet, the Horace Silver Quintet, Art Blakey's Jazz Messengers, the various Charles Mingus groups, and the Ornette Coleman groups.

Kirby's "Biggest Little Band in the Land" created airy, complementary frameworks of sound within which trumpeter Charlie Shavers, clarinetist Buster Baily, altoist Russell Procope, and pianist Billy Kyle improvised pretty and pleasing solos. The band had a clearly identifiable sound. It was the first ensemble to find success as a completely integrated small band in the sense that the Gerry Mulligan Quartet or the Modern Jazz Quartet achieved fifteen years later.

Many of these successful later bands sprang up on the West Coast, and perhaps it is fitting that the band that, alongside Kirby, initiated this whole development also started there: the Nat King Cole Trio. It is the first modern piano trio: not merely a pianist accompanied by a rhythm section, but three instruments constituting a single entity. The Nat King Cole Trio was formed in 1940, with Oscar Moore on guitar and Wesley Prince on bass. Later, Cole had guitarist Irving Ashby and bassist Johnny Miller. But in the course of the forties, the success of Cole the singer gradually began to overshadow the pianist, until Nat gave up his trio and became a singer of popular songs.

In Europe, the Quintette du Hot Club de France (1936–37), with its string-centric music—guitar and violin plus bass and two rhythm guitars—became the model for an original conception of integrated, swinging band music. Guitarist Django Reinhardt and violinist Stephane Grappelli were the leading soloists of the ensemble. The quintet almost broke up due to fights about the name and leadership of the group. But as soon as these two musicians played together, they were inseparable. Each awakened certain qualities that were dormant in the other: Django inspired Grappelli to impetuous risk-taking, harmonic modernity, and anarchic imagination; Grappelli brought out qualities of elegance, cultivation, and a sense for rational details in Django's playing. Together in the Quintette du Hot Club de France they created the first masterpieces of European jazz. And their example makes it clear that the cohesive integration of a jazz group arises from a constant give-and-take—through permanent musical communication.

Bop and Cool

In the meantime, bop had arrived. The Charlie Parker Quintet, with Miles Davis on trumpet, set the standard for both the music itself and for the format of the bands who played this music. For the first time it was again as it had been in the old Dixieland jazz: music and structure belonged together. Then it had been the free counterpoint of trumpet, trombone, and clarinet over a two-beat rhythm; now it was trumpet and saxophone in unison over the new legato rhythm. This unity of music and structure remained obligatory for the bands of hard bop: Art Blakey's Jazz Messengers, the Horace Silver Quintet, the Clifford Brown–Max Roach Quintet, and, above all, from the midfifties to the end of the sixties, the

Miles Davis Quintet; and then again (that's how durable this structure has proven) in seventies and eighties neobop and classicism, in groups like Dexter Gordon's, Woody Shaw's, Wynton Marsalis's, and, in the nineties, the bands of Roy Hargrove, Joshua Redman, and many others.

It is only natural that in the course of this long time span many musicians have tried to widen and vary song and group structures, while at the same time preserving their basic format. In the midfifties, pianist Horace Silver was especially successful in this respect through the individualistic construction of his themes. Thus, he might use two twelve-bar blues phrases, follow them up with an eight-bar bridge taken from song form, and then repeat the blues phrase, thus combining blues and song form; or he might combine a fifteen-bar main theme with a sixteen-bar interlude— "even though it's not even, it sounds even," as Horace has said—and so on in many similarly conceived compositions. If today's music, even in the more demanding forms of rock, has often become free of the schematic nature of the conventional thirty-two-bar song form, this is due in no small measure to Silver, who was the first to pave the way for this development. To be sure, there were unique forms deviating from conventions even in the early days of jazz—as in Jelly Roll Morton's music or in William Christopher Handy's (e.g., "St. Louis Blues")—but awareness of this had meanwhile been buried. Horace Silver unearthed it.

A number of years before the first Silver success in this field, around the turn of the forties, Lennie Tristano had already refined and abstracted the Parker format. He also had two horns, but they were both saxophones—Lee Konitz (alto) and Warne Marsh (tenor)—and to this he added a third hornlike line through Billy Bauer's guitar. In the Lennie Tristano Sextet could be found a very mobile linearity, moving over highly differentiated harmonies. After bop had broadened the harmonic material, Lennie Tristano "widened" the line—in the conscious conviction that jazz musicians had been concerned enough with harmonic problems for years and that the time had come to strengthen this awareness of line and melody. There were recordings such as "Wow," with a vigor that only hard bop would return to the general jazz consciousness in the late fifties; but above all there was a thoughtful, inspiring coolness with something of the atmosphere of the medieval cloisters in which scholastic debates were held at dusk.

Even before Tristano, bop musicians had attempted to broaden the structure of the Parker Quintet, in terms of sound. Primarily, Tadd Dameron, James Moody, and Charlie Ventura were involved in this effort—Dameron in his recordings for Blue Note, James Moody with his significant and much-too-neglected recording of "Cu-Ba" (also on Blue Note); and, most successfully, Charlie Ventura with his Bop for the People band, in which vocalist Jackie Cain and pianist Roy Krai (later to become her husband) sang humorous, spirited vocal duets. All this culminated in the Miles Davis Nonet. In it, sound became definitively established as a structuring element. (In the Davis section, the ensemble is discussed in detail.)

What followed consists of manifold combinations and developments of these three elements: the harmonic, connected with the name of Charlie Parker; the element of sound, for which Miles Davis's Nonet created an ideal; and the element of integration, for which the John Kirby Band and the Nat King Cole Trio had already broken ground.

On the West Coast, for example, Shorty Rogers with his Giants and Gerry Mulligan with his Tentette made recordings that further perfected the sound of the Davis Nonet, though sterilizing it a bit in the process. Later, Rogers reduced the Giants to the size of a quintet and created polished West Coast music within the Parker format, as did drummer Shelly Manne. He was one of the few West Coast musicians flexible enough to keep his own musical concept alive by continually reorienting himself in the changing musical stream until his death in 1984.

On the East Coast, J. J. Johnson and Kai Winding found an impressive solution. They joined their two trombones in a quintet; thus on the one hand they preserved the two-horn format of bop and on the other discovered a structuring sound in the subtleties of differentiated trombone tones. This structure was so intriguingly simple that it was frequently copied. Winding himself did it—after the original band disbanded—by combining four trombones instead of two. Al Cohn and Zoot Sims followed suit, combining two tenors—and on occasion, two clarinets—instead of trombones. Phil Woods and Gene Quill did something similar when they teamed up on alto saxophones. Tenormen Eddie "Lockjaw" Davis and Johnny Griffin projected the idea into the world of hard bop around the turn of the fifties. In the early seventies, drummer Elvin Jones transplanted this concept of the "duplicated instrument" into the post-Coltrane era, using two tenor players. In Jack DeJohnette's Special Edition, this principle of "horn doubling" became particularly vital in eighties jazz. And in the nineties, drummer Paul Motian used two guitar voices, with contrasting styles, in his Electric Bebop Band.

First High Points of Integration

As early as the late forties, vibraphonist Red Norvo formed a trio with guitarist Tal Farlow and bassist Charlie Mingus that basically established the concept of "chamber jazz." In light, relaxed, transparent interplay, the lines of vibraphone, guitar, and bass flowed into, opposite, and around each other. If Norvo, as a representative of the older jazz generation, didn't play quite as "modern" as Farlow and Mingus, the twofold stylistic plateau thus created lent an added charm. The linear function Norvo had assigned to the bass of Mingus (later Red Mitchell) was adopted in Gerry Mulligan's successful quartet from 1953 on. Gerry did away with the piano, let the changes be indicated by a single bass line that took on additional contrapuntal significance, and set the lines of his baritone sax and Chet Baker's trumpet above that. After Chet Baker (who became famous almost overnight through his playing in this quartet) had made himself independent, valve trombonist Bob Brookmeyer or trumpeters Jon Eardley and Art Farmer took his place. In a manner that has been described as "busy," Mulligan played contrapuntal countermelodies or riffs on his baritone behind the improvisations of the second horn in his quartet. So it became apparent that even the riff—one of the most rudimentary of jazz elements—could be used structurally in terms of modern band integration. Of course, after some time it became obvious that the more one became used to the surprising sound of this quartet, the more clearly the formulalike nature of its music was revealed. So Gerry Mulligan, who was not only a great musician but also a farsighted man, enlarged his quartet to a sextet. And it is this lineup to which he returned again and again.

The most often cited of all these bands was pianist John Lewis's Modern Jazz Quartet, with Milt Jackson, vibraphone; Percy Heath, bass; and first Kenny Clarke, then Connie Kay, drums. Founded in 1951, disbanded in 1974, reestablished in 1981, and continuing until the early nineties, it was by far the longest-lived band in jazz history. Lewis, one of the melodically most gifted of all jazz composers, found much stimulation in the contrapuntal art of Johann Sebastian Bach. At the beginning, he often took over classical forms almost literally—above all in "Vendome," a precise and knowledgeable version of a baroque invention, with the one difference that in the place of the "episodes" in the form of the invention are put improvisations by the members of the Modern Jazz Quartet. Later, Lewis discovered contrapuntal possibilities more germane to jazz than to old music. As he said:

> In the little piece entitled "Versailles," which also used a "classical" form—the fugue—as a model, I don't feel that this has anything to do with the model, the best-known examples of which are Bach's. We have started to work on some new concepts of playing which give freer rein to the creativity of the improviser and yet produce an even stronger form.

In those terms, Lewis also worked on an incorporation of the percussion part into the linear and contrapuntal play of his quartet. His percussionist, Connie Kay, was equipped with a whole arsenal of auxiliary rhythm instruments: finger cymbals, triangles, small Chinese drum, etc. And if drum instrumentation in general has become increasingly enlarged since the sixties, Connie Kay was among those who gave this direction its first impetus.

Characteristic of Lewis's jazz-minded relationship to baroque music are these thoughts, expressed by him in connection with his suite

"Fontessa": "'Fontessa' is a little suite inspired by the Renaissance Commedia dell'Arte. I had particularly in mind their plays, which consisted of a very sketchy plot and in which the details—the lines, etc.— were improvised."

The MJQ—as Lewis's band is abbreviated—had gone through a clearly perceivable development. During the sixties, the Bach elements became rare, but this was compensated for by a much more swinging jazz intensity. Lewis's "Django," for example, became less and less melancholy in the successive recordings available, and more and more swinging and intense.

The MJQ had great influence. Even in the hard-bop bands with their Parker quintet structure, one suddenly could detect echoes of John Lewis's will to form. And even Oscar Peterson, whose trio at first was a kind of modernized Nat King Cole or Art Tatum trio, paid respect to John Lewis's integration principle.

A similarly long development was undergone by the Dave Brubeck Quartet, formed in 1951, after Brubeck had first gained experience with a highly interesting octet (1946) and a trio (1949). Brubeck has probably had more hits than any other jazz musician of his generation, yet—and certainly because of this—he has been harshly criticized; but Brubeck has charisma, which has carried him from one success to another (see the piano section).

Brubeck's most important partner was Paul Desmond, a "poet of the alto saxophone," whose crystal-clear improvisations have been valued much more highly by critics than Brubeck's piano playing. When Desmond withdrew in the late sixties, Gerry Mulligan stepped into his place. Mulligan had always been an immensely swing-oriented, "busy" improviser, and through his participation the until-then somewhat pastoral, cool Brubeck Quartet definitely became a more intense, "hotter" group.

From Hard Bop to Free

We have already mentioned hard-bop bands in connection with the Charlie Parker Quintet. It is apparent that an evolution toward greater integration took place here as well. Even the most vital hard-bop group, the Jazz Messengers—thrust forward by Art Blakey's wild percussion work—tends to have at least one (sometimes even two) musical "integrator" in the sense of the function of John Lewis within the MJQ, if in hard-bop terms. Horace Silver, then Benny Golson, Bobby Timmons, Wayne Shorter, Cedar Walton, Bobby Watson, Wynton Marsalis, Christian McBride, etc., had this function of musical director with Blakey, whose groups were of central significance right into the eighties. (More about contemporary bop and neoclassicism later in this section.)

Marvelous integration is also a characteristic of the various groups Max Roach led after his work with Clifford Brown and Sonny Rollins in the midfifties—ensembles partially with full, rich three-part horn sounds, without piano; later with pianist Ron Mathews and trumpeter Freddie Hubbard; frequently also with Roach's then wife, Abbey Lincoln. Max's main work, the *Freedom Now Suite*, is exemplary not only for content but also in structure, as a large-form composition for small ensemble.

The more harmonically free a jazz improvisation is, the more it requires interaction among the musicians. No band exemplified this more than the second Miles Davis Quintet (1964–68)—with Wayne Shorter (saxophone), Herbie Hancock (piano), Ron Carter (bass), and Tony Williams (drums). This band combined a maximum of integration with a maximum of individual expressivity. The quintet made exemplarily clear that jazz involves a musical dialogue: an ongoing exchange of ideas both serving the whole and making individual demands. On the one hand, the group still improvised with "time" (i.e., over a regular beat, which was, however, interpreted very freely), but on the other, without a rigid principle of "changes" (prescribed harmonic successions) that had exclusively determined jazz improvisation until the end of the fifties. It's fascinating when listening to the quintet's records to follow how this principle of "time but no changes" almost inevitably led to an ever-greater degree of interaction and integration between the musicians, culminating in a "togetherness" only comparable with Louis Armstrong's Hot Five, the Charlie Parker Quintet, the John Coltrane Quartet, and the Ornette Coleman Quartet. The second Miles Davis Quintet represented an increasing abstraction away from hard bop, without losing sight of the core of that music: a flexible, blues-inflected way of swinging.

From the point of view of our band-selection principle, it is important also to see that the concept of "modality," introduced by Miles and John Coltrane, creates a high degree of connection, and thus integration. The integration factor here is the "scale"—no longer many, continuously varying chord changes, but only a single chord (or very few chords).

John Coltrane transplanted this principle into "freer" jazz, in a sense shown in the section about him (and elsewhere throughout the book). When drummer Art Taylor was asked how he and other musicians reacted to Coltrane's constant musical growth when they made recordings with him, he said: "It was no problem, because all of us were growing right beside him. We were all involved in innovation." One of the most beautiful recordings of the "classic" Coltrane Quartet—with McCoy Tyner on piano, Jimmy Garrison on bass, and Elvin Jones on drums—is the famous *A Love Supreme*, which combines spiritual fervor with formal completeness in a way not heretofore achieved in jazz. This group, with its high standards of improvisation and interplay, with the lasting value of its themes (composed mostly by its leader) and its "togetherness," has remained a model for many jazz groups ever since. McCoy Tyner: "That group was like four pistons in an engine."

Among the groups that paved the way for the new jazz, three are important: the Jimmy Giuffre Trios of the fifties, and the groups of Charles Mingus and George Russell. In the early fifties, Jimmy Giuffre recorded his "Tangents in Jazz," in which the drummer, as percussionist, is drawn into the melodic and structural development of the music to such an extent that a continuous beat is largely dispensed with. In the trio organized by Giuffre in 1954 there was no drummer at all, and one may surmise that this outcome was near at hand: once the drums are used more or less as melody instrument, there surely must be other instruments capable of serving this purpose better. In this trio, Giuffre used guitarist Jim Hall and bassist Ralph Pena. Giuffre went one step further when he joined with pianist Paul Bley and bassist Steve Swallow in a trio that created an exhilarating web of lines that elaborated on both chamber music and folk music. Giuffre: "It has been said that when jazz gets soft it loses its gusto and funkiness. It is my feeling that soft jazz can retain the basic flavor and intensity that it had at a louder volume, and at the same time perhaps reveal some new dimensions of feeling that loudness obscures."

Even more important for further developments were the various groups led by George Russell from the second half of the fifties on—above all, his sextets with musicians like trombonist Dave Baker, multi-instrumentalist Eric Dolphy, and trumpeter Don Ellis. In the freely swinging modality of Russell's music a hymnic tone is achieved—a tone that reached a larger audience only years later through John Coltrane's *A Love Supreme*—but also shows an aspect of abstraction that often seems like a premonition of Anthony Braxton's work.

The most important pathbreaker for free jazz, however, was Charles Mingus. As we discussed earlier, his music returned the feeling of collective improvisation to jazz. To be sure, there has always been collective improvising in jazz, but ever since jazz had given up the three-part New Orleans counterpoint, the emphasis had shifted to solo improvisation, the work of single players accompanied by a rhythm section. Through Mingus, improvising became collective again to an extent unknown since the days of New Orleans jazz, which was not only indicative of a process in music but also in society. It is no accident that the revolutionary Mingus recordings we are referring to were made around the turn of the fifties (i.e., immediately preceding the new awakening of social and political awareness in the sixties). Again and again, jazz has anticipated and heralded such social developments. "Polyphonic music says: we," is what Theodor Adorno, the philosopher, once wrote. In those terms, New Orleans and Dixieland jazz on the one hand, and Charles Mingus and the free, collective jazz of the sixties and seventies on the other, all say "we."

The music of the great individuals—of, for instance, Charlie Parker, Lee Konitz, and, earlier, Coleman Hawkins and Lester Young—says "I."

Among Charles Mingus's most important recordings are "Better Git Hit in Your Soul," "Goodbye Pork Pie Hat," "Open Letter to Duke," "What Love" (with Eric Dolphy), "Ysabel's Table Dance" (with Clarence Shaw, trumpet), and "Solo Dancer" (with Charlie Mariano). Drummer Dannie Richmond played a crucial part in the success of almost all of Mingus's productions. With the assurance of a sleepwalker he kept up with his leader's many tempo changes (still rather new and unusual in jazz at the time), and thus held the music together.

Ornette and After

Aside from Lennie Tristano's "Intuition" and "Digression" (which, in 1949, were lone precursors of much later developments), the Ornette Coleman Quartet of 1959–60 was the first group to play "free" yet from the start meet the integration criteria of this section. Appearing at a New York club, the Five Spot, Coleman and his trumpeter Don Cherry enraptured audiences night after night for months. The many musicians always present in the audience were fascinated by the precision with which Ornette and Don entered in unison after their long, free solo excursions, though it wasn't recognizable to the majority of even the specialists why they came in at this particular spot and not somewhere else. One of the musician-listeners said then, "You can't hear it, but there is no doubt: Ornette and his men know what they're doing. In a couple of years, everybody else will know it, too" (which, of course, has become true). Bassist Charlie Haden had an especially integrating effect in this group, with his totally free bass lines that dispensed with predetermined chord sequences, yet created tonal connection and structure. The integrating factor within the Coleman quartet was communication pure and simple. The dialogic character of the Coleman quartet was so pronounced above all because of the constant give-and-take in the band. As one saxophonist summed up the spirit of the Ornette Coleman ensembles, "Ninety percent of the music that we play consists in listening to each other. If you can't lay back and listen to what's going on, you're in trouble in this group." The success of this integrated unity depends on a selflessness that is rare even in jazz.

A few years later, Ornette did away with the second horn, forming a trio. It may certainly be surmised that he himself took on the roles of trumpeter and violinist—however much he was criticized in them—in addition to his alto work because he needed further sound colorations but nevertheless wanted to mold the music of his group as directly and immediately as possible. Only toward the end of the sixties did Coleman succeed in finding another congenial horn partner in tenor saxophonist Dewey Redman.

From Coleman and Coltrane spring all the free-jazz groups that emphasize the collective experience of their music to an extent heretofore unknown. Dismayed by the isolation of the individual in modern society, these musicians feel that their improvisations unite them to a degree "as otherwise, among humans, only love can do" (Don Cherry). Cherry's piece "Complete Communion," realized in 1965, first in Paris and then in New York, indicates this concept of "total communication" even in its title.

Other groups that compensated for the isolation of the individual expressing himself without restraint (which is where a music that knows no harmonic or formal ordering factor may easily lead), with much stronger and more intensely personal collective relationships, were the Archie Shepp Quintet with trombonist Roswell Rudd; the New York Art Quartet with altoist John Tchicai (and also with Rudd); the Albert Ayler Quintet; and in Europe the Brotzmann/van Hove/Bennink Trio (with tenorist Peter Brotzmann, pianist Fred van Hove, and drummer Han Bennink); the group AMM with guitarist Keith Rowe; drummer John Stevens's Spontaneous Music Ensemble; the trio of Alexander von Schlippenbach, Evan Parker, and Paul Lovens; and the Manfred Schoof Quintet.

In England at that time an approach to improvising arose that critic John Corbett has called "insect music"—playing with rapidly changing textures, sounds, and pitches, as originally explored in groups of Evan Parker, Derek Bailey, and the Spontaneous Music Ensemble. This music was highly influential for the second and third generations of free-jazz musicians in America and Europe.

Roughly speaking, we can recognize two procedures that have been used to create integration in European free-improvised music, using two terms to designate them that were coined by English theorist Nick Couldry. On the one hand, there is the "group voice" approach, heard for example in the Spontaneous Music Ensemble. This refers to the idea of collective improvising with the goal of achieving a tight, dense meshing of lines and textures. The short, reduced figures played by the individual musicians are given meaning by their place in the ensemble of voices. In contrast to this, there is the approach of "parallel voices" improvisation—a procedure exemplified by the long-standing trio of Evan Parker, Barry Guy, and Paul Lytton. In this approach, textures and virtuosic lines unfold in parallel, so that the listener may decide to follow these textures and lines individually.

The band AMM, featuring guitarist Keith Rowe, displays infinite patience in the exploration and investigation of individual sonic events. This quasi-microscopic examination of the smallest details of the sound is what gives this music its life and meaning.

The trio of Alexander von Schlippenbach, Evan Parker, and Paul Lovens, a lineup that has worked together since 1972 and is thus probably the longest-lived working band in European free jazz, also eschews an emphasis on foreground soloing and surface dramatics. The dense, concentrated improvisations of this trio demonstrate that long-term co-operation is possible in free jazz through an ongoing process of melding, distillation, and refinement, achieving a constant transmutation of the materials.

The Seventies

Between the early seventies and the early eighties, the band situation was similar to that of the big bands. There were four streams and various cross-connections between them:

1. The bands playing along the lines of contemporary mainstream jazz, among which the hard-bop and neobop groups occupied a special place, of growing significance around the turn of the seventies

2. The groups playing free music around Chicago's AACM

3. The jazz-rock and fusion groups, whose development was initiated by Miles Davis's *Bitches Brew*

4. Chamber-music-like groups, who further refined the tradition of the Red Norvo Trio or the Jimmy Giuffre Trio. The prototype of these was Oregon with Ralph Towner (guitar and piano), Paul McCandless (oboe and English horn), Glen Moore (bass), and Collin Walcott (sitar, tabla, percussion). In a sense, Oregon constituted *the* culmination of integrated, chamber-music-like jazz playing in all of jazz history so far. Similar coherence was achieved by pianist Keith Jarrett's two quartets: both the American group (with Dewey Redman, saxophone; Charlie Haden, bass; and Paul Motian, drums) and the "European" (with saxophonist Jan Garbarek, bassist Palle Danielsson, and drummer Jon Christensen). The American ensemble was more powerful and hard-driven but also closer to the ideas of world music, whereas the phrasing of Jarrett's "European" quartet was more elegiac, impressionistic, and balladlike.

Neobop

Among the groups of the mainstream of the seventies, there are, on the one hand, those whose "first editions" were formed twenty-five years ago (and thus have been mentioned already) and on the other, newly formed ensembles. Of course, the groups whose leaders had formed ensembles in the fifties integrated the subsequent musical experiences as much as those groups that were first formed in the seventies. For this reason, we list both kinds of groups together: Art Blakey's Jazz Messengers, the Dizzy Gillespie Quintet, the Max Roach Quartet, the Cannonball Adderley Quintet, McCoy Tyner's group, the Phil Woods Quartet, and Herbie Hancock's VSOP. Most of these were groups with ever-changing lineups. McCoy Tyner was a central figure among them, as a source of strength and inspiration for the entire scene.

In all these groups, the bop character was alive, but this character gained a new significance after the turn of the seventies that not even farsighted observers had expected. It initially appeared as if bebop were slowly fading away, but suddenly the exact opposite seemed to be occurring: bop was coming back with full force. Neobop of the seventies (of which we have repeatedly spoken) produced a host of new groups. Towering above them all were the bands of the great veteran tenorist Dexter Gordon, the initiator of this whole movement. Also of great importance was the quintet formed by trumpeter Woody Shaw (d. 1989), which made a decisive contribution toward reconciling bebop and modal playing (the latter still viewed at that time as tending toward free performance). Shaw so successfully introduced modality (improvisation over scales) into the language of bebop that a style that was by then over thirty years old suddenly sounded refreshingly different, contemporary and topical.

AACM

As early as 1961 pianist Muhal Richard Abrams founded the Experimental Band in Chicago, a free-jazz orchestra that gave rise (formally in 1965) to the AACM, the Association for the Advancement of Creative Musicians—a grouping of musicians that has had much significance, not only musically, but also in terms of consciousness in the self-identification process of black musicians. Roscoe Mitchell: "We were musicians who wanted to have better control over our destiny. That's what the AACM is about." The AACM first met with real success in Europe, aside from the much too limited local resonance it found in Chicago. In the late sixties, in a deliberate reaction against the lack of interest in free music on the part of the American public (and against its political and social implications!), some of the most important AACM musicians moved to Paris—among them saxophonists Joseph Jarman and Roscoe Mitchell, trumpeter Lester Bowie, bassist Malachi Favors, and multi-instrumentalist Anthony Braxton. From there, the Art Ensemble of Chicago quickly became known all over Europe. Since Jarman, Mitchell, Bowie, and Favors did not have a regular drummer (Phillip Wilson, Don Moye, and Steve McCall worked only briefly with the group), they soon began to play percussion themselves: Bowie on the bass drum and Mitchell, Jarman, and Favors on the entire range of various percussion instruments that, around that time, became customary in the new jazz. In this way, the percussion parts—played alternately by musicians whose main instruments were trumpet, saxophone, and bass—were integrated completely in the melodic activity. This was also a crucial contribution of the Art Ensemble of Chicago. Don Moye has been the band's drummer since 1969. The increased level of percussive intensity is also indicated by the fact that the other AEC musicians continue to play percussion parts alongside their usual instruments. The Art Ensemble of Chicago is characterized by an exciting mixture of energy, humor, multi-instrumentalism, silence, sonic research, and extended collective improvisation. Years before the arrival of postmodern jazz, the Art Ensemble combined elements of free playing with allusions to reggae, bebop, soul, South African songs, minimalism, New Orleans jazz, *musique concrète*, voodoo, and theatrical performances. In this way, the band created long, durable, pause-filled arcs of "Great Black Music," in which the structure of the music was formed by the communication of the musicians.

After Lester Bowie's death in 1999, the Art Ensemble of Chicago continued at first as a trio of Roscoe Mitchell, Malachi Favors, and Don Moye, but without the self-conscious, often-ironic, and sometimes sarcastic characteristics of the earlier version of the group.

As far as we know, there has never been a jazz band that had so many different instrumental colors at its disposal as the Art Ensemble. On their European tours, the four musicians carried whole busloads of instruments. Particularly versatile are Mitchell (who plays alto, soprano, tenor, and bass saxophone; clarinet, flute, piccolo, sirens, whistles, bells, steel drum, congas, gongs, cymbals, etc., etc.) and Jarman (whose instruments include sopranino, alto, soprano, and tenor sax; alto clarinet; oboe; flute; piano; harpsichord; guitar; marimba; accordion; vibraphone; and several dozen percussion instruments). With this instrumentation, the AACM players made numerous records in France, Germany, and Great Britain, including the first big-band realization of AACM music, at the 1969 New Jazz Meeting Baden-Baden.

The majority of the American jazz audience became aware of the significance of the AACM almost ten years later. It was a slow process, beginning with Anthony Braxton's success and resulting in many AACM musicians being rated in top positions of the 1979 *Down Beat* critics' poll.

In the meantime, another group rooted in the AACM had been formed: Air (Henry Threadgill on saxes and flutes; Fred Hopkins, bass; Steve McCall, drums, who was succeeded in 1982 by Pheeroan AkLaff). This trio, established in 1971, was at that time one of the few avant-garde bands where oneness wasn't just proclaimed, but all the instrumental parts really did flow together in complete equality. *Air Lore*, the 1979 album with ragtime compositions by Scott Joplin and New Orleans pieces by Jelly Roll Morton, was the most courageous and undisguised declaration of a seventies avant-garde group's indebtedness to the great legacy of jazz.

Of course, there has also been band music on a high level by other AACM musicians (and also by members of a similar grouping founded in St. Louis, BAG [Black Artists' Group], as well as by musicians close to these two groupings). These include players like saxophonist Oliver Lake; trumpeter Leo Smith; Muhal Richard Abrams, the great innovative spirit of the AACM; and the best-known AACM musician, Anthony Braxton. Braxton came to the fore particularly with his quartets, which included trombonist George Lewis, later his colleague Ray Anderson, and in the eighties pianist Marilyn Crispell, in a gradual process of abstracting music to the limit.

The attitude of most of these musicians toward tradition is illuminated by a motto formulated by the players of the Chicago Art Ensemble: "Ancient to the future." This not only means (in the Western rationalistic sense) "pointing toward the future from the ancient past," but it also refers (in the sense of ancient concepts of African mythology) to a "suspension of time." Said Abrams, "My thoughts . . . are my . . . future . . . now and forever . . . symbolizing . . . the past . . . present . . . and future . . . in the eternal now." This is an African thought. Or Asian. Definitely not Western.

It fits in with the initially mentioned process of sensitization that Muhal Richard Abrams influenced the musicians of the AACM not just in terms of music. Trombonist George Lewis said that he was even prompted to his extramusical studies—mainly German philosophy— by Muhal. And Joseph Jarman stated that before meeting Abrams he had been "like all the rest of the 'hip' ghetto niggers" on the streets of Chicago's South Side. Quite possibly, his future would have been bleak, as it is for so many young people trapped in the ghettos. But then he met Muhal, and his life acquired a sense of direction. It seems that Abrams, who remained more or less in the background for years, was much more interested in furthering the careers of other AACM musicians than his own. Only since the second half of the seventies—in fact, after his appearance at the 1978 Montreux Festival—has he found the recognition as a pianist and composer that other, much younger AACM players had gained earlier.

Jazz-Rock and Fusion

The integration of jazz and rock—long awaited, often prematurely announced during the sixties, and accomplished by Miles Davis's *Bitches Brew*—shaped the style of the best-known (and best-selling) jazz groups of the seventies. The groups that broke ground for this development in the United States and in Britain have already been discussed in the section on the seventies. The outstanding jazz-rock and fusion groups of the decade were Weather Report; Larry Coryell's Eleventh House; John McLaughlin's Mahavishnu Orchestra; Lifetime, led by drummer Tony

Williams; Chick Corea's Return to Forever; Herbie Hancock's Sextet of the first half of the seventies; the Pat Metheny Quartet in the second half; trumpeter Ian Carr's Nucleus and saxophonist Barbara Thompson's Paraphernalia in Britain; the Association P.C. of drummer Pierre Courbois and keyboard player Jasper van't Hof's Pork Pie in Germany and the Netherlands; Magma in France; and, finally, the groups of guitarist Volker Kriegel.

In the early seventies it was mostly former Miles Davis players who carried forward the development beyond *Bitches Brew*. They include soprano and tenor saxist Wayne Shorter; keyboard players Joe Zawinul, Chick Corea, and Herbie Hancock; drummer Tony Williams; guitarist John McLaughlin, etc.

Some of the first steps in this direction—surprising in light of how little was to follow from this great musician as composer and arranger—were taken by Wayne Shorter with his two albums *Super Nova* and *Odyssey of Iska*. Shorter is the only hornman (on tenor and soprano) on both records; with him are guitarists, bassists, a vibraphonist, percussionists. The *Odyssey of Iska* is the mythical journey of a black explorer—a Nigerian Ulysses—who becomes a symbol of the human soul. Shorter said about the album, "Perhaps you can relate the enclosed [music] to the journey of your own soul."

Odyssey of Iska is an impressive "tone poem" in jazz, calling to mind the Herbie Hancock tone poems mentioned in the piano section. And, indeed, since Hancock's *Maiden Voyage*, there has been an increasing tendency toward compositions in larger forms, complete within themselves, whether suites or tone poems. This is reflected, for instance, by Zappa's *Grand Wazoo* (mentioned in the big-band section) or by *Zawinul*, released around the same time as Shorter's two records: "Impressions of Joe Zawinul's days as a shepherd boy in Austria. . . . A tone poem reminiscent of his grandfather's funeral on a cold winter day in an Austrian mountain village. . . . Zawinul's first impressions of New York when he arrived here as a boy on a ship from France."

Great things were expected when Joe Zawinul and Wayne Shorter founded the group Weather Report in 1970. At first, Miroslav Vitous played bass and Alphonse Mouzon drums, but elemental Mouzon and intellectual Vitous did not fit together. During most of the seventies, the rhythm players of the group kept changing, until a consolidation was reached toward the end of the decade when bassist Jaco Pastorius became the most important member of the group next to Zawinul, while Shorter no longer seemed to function as coleader. Shorter's friends have often regretted that he was featured so rarely on the various Weather Report albums in solos commensurate with his significance as an outstanding saxophonist.

No doubt, after Miles's *Bitches Brew* and along with John McLaughlin's Mahavishnu Orchestra, Weather Report was the most important and the most influential group in fusion. But time and again "WR" polarized the scene, until its dissolution in 1985. After publishing a devastating review of its album *Mr. Gone* in 1979, *Down Beat* was inundated for months with letters from fans and adversaries of the group. The review of *Mr. Gone* said, in part:

> Weather Report has done to jazz in the seventies what Paul Whiteman did to it in the twenties. Like Whiteman, Weather Report has over-orchestrated its sound. Where Whiteman's band made hot jazz saccharine, Weather Report has made experimentation sound processed. . . . By not taking chances they have nothing to lose, but conversely they have nothing to gain.

Zawinul, on the other hand, emphasized that his Weather Report music is embedded in the tradition of jazz, above all, in bebop. His most famous composition is "Birdland," named after the legendary jazz club on Broadway, which in turn was named for Charlie Parker. Around the turn of the fifties, Zawinul was in Birdland almost daily. Twenty years later, in 1980, he said, "The old Birdland was the most important place in my life." In fact, the bop element, albeit veiled and transposed into electronic music, is to be felt during all the stages of Weather Report's development.

No other band succeeded in such a flexible, original way in combining electronic sounds with the acoustic sounds of conventional instruments, layering them and anchoring them in grooves, as did Weather Report. After the album *Black Market* (1976), the incorporation of world music elements into Weather Report's mixture of complex rhythms, catchy melodies, and polished sounds became increasingly important. The extent to which Weather Report had become a mainstay of the scene is also seen in the fact that they were the main influence on one of the most successful jazz-rock formations of the eighties and nineties, namely the Yellowjackets (with Jimmy Haslip, electric bass; Russell Ferrante, keyboards; Bob Mintzer, saxophone; and Will Kennedy, drums). They expanded the Weather Report legacy with refined textures and grooves full of delicate metrical irregularity.

Herbie Hancock (see also the piano and keyboards sections) had left Miles Davis before *Bitches Brew*. In 1972 his sextet created the record *Crossings*, with its rich electronic instrumentation (electric piano, melotron, Moog synthesizer), into which three horns are interwoven: Benny Maupin (soprano saxophone, alto flute, bass clarinet, piccolo), Eddie Henderson (trumpet), and Julian Priester (trombone). With his electronics and the three horns, Hancock achieved sounds reminiscent of Gil Evans's rich orchestral palette. "Quasar," the title of one of his pieces, is representative of the music: mystical, primordial, cosmic explosions, in which time seems to be standing still. The strong rhythmic interlocking of drum patterns made the innovative sounds of the Herbie Hancock Sextet a high point of integrative funk.

Drummer Tony Williams had also left Miles Davis in 1969 to devote himself more intensely to the integration of jazz and rock than seemed possible to him with Miles at the time. The different ensembles he formed under the heading of Lifetime were advanced jazz-oriented rock groups, whose integration problems Williams failed to solve—less for musical than for psychological reasons. Only one Lifetime could satisfy the strict principle of integration applied in this section: the first Lifetime with guitarist John McLaughlin (who here assembled the experience he needed for his Mahavishnu Orchestra) and organist Larry Young (aka Khalid Yasin). This produced cooking, wildly surrealistic improvisations, opening up to jazz-rock a sense of freedom and an avant-garde consciousness that was only to return in eighties free funk.

Later versions of Lifetime—and Weather Report and the Mahavishnu Orchestra, too—illuminate particularly well the complexity of the musical and human (and technical!) mechanisms of such groups. It is truly a stroke of luck when such organisms produce great music: a string quartet has it much easier.

The process of attrition to which jazz-rock and fusion groups are subject can also be seen in Chick Corea's music. In the opinion of most critics, of the various groups he has led—at first under the name Return to Forever—the first, of 1972 (with singer Flora Purim, percussionist Airto Moreira, saxophonist and flutist Joe Farrell, and bassist Stanley Clarke), was by far the best. It was one of the happiest, lightest products of seventies jazz. Here the integration of jazz and rock also included Latin and quasi-Baroque elements, in a playful, magical way. But his later groups have also retained the communicative aspect so characteristic of Corea's music.

Possibly the most dense, artistically most satisfying fusion music so far has come from guitarist John McLaughlin, with his Mahavishnu Orchestra—here, too, with the first (1971–72) of the Mahavishnu groups (with Jan Hammer, keyboards; Billy Cobham, drums; Jerry Goodman, violin; and Rick Laird, bass). Nowhere else has it been demonstrated so convincingly, what astounding, liberating, delightful, and spiritual effects fusion music can create.

The tunes by the first Mahavishnu Orchestra had titles like "The Dance of Maya," "A Lotus on Irish Streams," "Sapphire Bullets of Pure Love," "Meeting of the Spirits," "Awakening," "Sanctuary," and "Vital Transformation," characterizing the meditative spirit at the core of those pieces. To the strength of this meditative spirit belonged (which only seems to be a paradox) the high volume at which this music was played; it brought forth a kind of stillness precisely by virtue of being so overpowering. The Mahavishnu music created a "cathedral of sounds" that admitted nothing but these sounds.

One negative result of the density of this music was that within a short time, the musicians had worn each other out in personal and musical tensions and conflicts, causing the group to break apart. With his later Mahavishnu groups, McLaughlin never again reached the level of this first orchestra. From 1976 on, he began to appear with the outstanding Shakti group (see the section on world jazz in this chapter).

There was something frightening about the process of wear and tear involved in jazz-rock and fusion. Never before in the history of jazz had anything similar occurred. Basically only a single new group of artistic stature developed during the second half of the seventies: the Pat Metheny Band with keyboardist Lyle Mays. With its elegant, harmonically sophisticated fusion and its warm, sensuous, lush electronic timbres, it reached a public of millions. The Pat Metheny Band commands an almost "symphonic" feel for a great range of dynamic shadings. No other jazz-rock group constructs such rounded, expansive, and far-reaching arches of tension. On the other hand, Metheny's music has been charged with a leaning toward kitsch and pathos, overprettification and excessive polish. Nevertheless, the legacy of jazz tradition—alongside much Brazilian music and a touch of country and western—also remain apparent in everything the Metheny Band plays. Other groups (such as Spyro Gyra) brought fusion so close to commercialized funk and muzak that it was often difficult to tell the difference. They were concerned with creating products for the market to such an extent that they themselves became throw-away products.

The Eighties

The eighties brought such a high degree of stylistic overlapping and amalgamation that only very broad and oversimplified generalizations can be made about five strands of development that shaped the small-band scene. They were accompanied by a multitude of superimpositions and interlinkings.

1. *New straight-ahead jazz:* groups refining, through a broad range of styles, the development that started in the seventies with neobop. These groups had strong neoclassicist leanings, emphasizing the legacy of bop-inspired playing from a conservative, contemporary perspective.

2. Bands reflecting and updating elements of traditional jazz in the light of "freer" ways of playing. These groups emphasized the fact that the jazz tradition arose as a continuum of innovation.

3. *Free-funk bands:* expanding funk and jazz-rock by adding aspects of avant-garde styles.

4. *World jazz:* bands amalgamating elements from the world's great musical cultures with contemporary jazz via dialogues.

5. *Nonidiomatic and postmodern bands, or No Wave:* the "style" here consisted in an absence of any one style. These bands were structuring, differentiating, and extending avant-garde jazz by combining it with punk, heavy metal, ethnic music, minimal music, and many other stylistic elements.

New Straight-Ahead Jazz

Neoclassicist groups didn't simply copy bebop, as some people claimed. For a start, they seemed more integrated than the typical forties bebop band. The reason was to be found in the rhythm section's new way of playing, particularly the drummer's: more aggressive, wilder, harsher, and—of particular relevance with regard to our criterion of integration—more interactive and communicative. In that context, neoclassicist jazz groups didn't reflect a single style. They worked on the entire jazz tradition viewed in the light of bebop and post-bebop approaches.

Art Blakey and his diverse Jazz Messengers acted as the backbone of new mainstream jazz. Although never essentially changing his hard-bop concept throughout the seventies and eighties, Blakey gave young musicians so much freedom that his Jazz Messengers became a real springboard for the groups that refined and extended bop-oriented playing multistylistically: the Wynton Marsalis Band, the Branford Marsalis Quartet, the Terence Blanchard–Donald Harrison Quintet, the Mulgrew Miller Band, the Wallace Roney Group, and even in some respects the eighties' Tony Williams Quintet playing "swinging" pure jazz (where many young ex-Messengers musicians gained additional experience). Strikingly, all these groups put the emphasis—as a deliberate countermovement to the hypertrophied results of jazz-rock and fusion—on the concept of musical integration. The "key" to such playing is what is viewed as a "classical" law governing jazz: a band can only sound good when every individual musician phrases "as if he were playing through all of the band's instruments" (Stanley Crouch).

The two most successful bands in that respect were the Wynton Marsalis Group and the Terence Blanchard–Donald Harrison Quintet. Wynton Marsalis is one of the few trumpeters who can produce coherence and rich communication within a group merely through the lines he plays. But members of his group—including pianist Marcus Roberts, bassist Bob Hurst, and drummer Jeff "Tain" Watts—also made their contribution to a togetherness that has stimulated numerous other neoclassicist groups (see also the section on Wynton Marsalis and David Murray).

Like the early Marsalis groups, the Terence Blanchard–Donald Harrison Quintet refined and differentiated in its own particular way the "message" transmitted by the celebrated second Miles Davis Quintet. It played "controlled freedom" on a bop foundation but, unlike the Miles group, added a powerful shot of New Orleans tradition whose African, Spanish, and French *tinge* very much came to life.

In general it's striking how many neoclassicist musicians came from New Orleans. Never since the twenties—since Louis Armstrong, Jelly Roll Morton, and Sidney Bechet—had musicians from the Crescent City exerted such lasting influence on the current jazz scene as during the eighties and nineties. For the second time in the history of jazz New Orleans was a source of renewed energy: with such musicians as trumpeters Wynton Marsalis, Terence Blanchard, and Marlon Jordan; saxophonists Branford Marsalis, Donald Harrison, and Tony Dagradi; flutist Kent Jordan; bassist Reginald Veal; drummer Herlin Riley; and the players in the Dirty Dozen Brass Band. The latter perform in the archaic tradition of the New Orleans marching bands, with Mardi Gras exuberance and joie de vivre. But the Dirty Dozen Brass Band does something that was previously strictly taboo among such groups in the Crescent City. It plays funk, bebop, jump, and soul arrangements—all with contemporary drive at unusually fast speeds for brass bands. That had never happened before: after the funeral dirge and burial of a corpse, a brass band returned to the city to the bebop sounds of Charlie Parker's "Bongo Beep." "Right from the start the other brass bands told us that wouldn't work," said trumpeter Gregory Davis. "When we were in a street parade and the people in front played marches, we struck up with Thelonious Monk's 'Blue Monk' or with pieces by Charlie Parker, Miles Davis, or Duke. . . . They came to us afterward and said, 'Man, you shouldn't play such stuff in parades.'"

In the meantime dozens of New Orleans brass bands started to play like that: the Rebirth Brass Band, the Pair-A-Dice Brass Band, the All Stars Brass Band, etc.—all part of an astonishing revitalization of the venerable tradition of New Orleans brass bands in a dialogue with modern jazz. That too is the achievement of the Dirty Dozen Brass Band.

Viewed overall, it is questionable whether eighties/nineties classicism would ever have exerted such influence on playing styles and the jazz scene if crucial impulses hadn't come from Crescent City musicians. Jazz had certainly come full circle. New Orleans was back.

The Avant-Garde Discovers the Tradition

By the start of the eighties the AACM groups (and the closely connected Black Artists Group) had structured and formally organized free jazz to such an extent that the label "avant-garde," as used with such emphasis in the sixties, became invalid. Traditional forms of playing, often concealed or merely ironically referred to in free jazz, then became simply essential. The freedom that had once been gained wasn't, however, renounced but rather differentiated, refined, and enriched.

Among the important groups that updated the great legacy of jazz tradition, making it contemporary by way of "free" styles, are the World Saxophone Quartet, the David Murray Octet (see the section on David Murray), the Arthur Blythe Quartet, Lester Bowie's Brass Fantasy, the

George Adams–Don Pullen Quartet, the Tim Berne–Herb Robertson Quintet, and the Chico Freeman Group.

Perhaps the most unified neoclassicist band is the World Saxophone Quartet (see also the section on saxophone ensembles). What welds the quartet so closely together are two integrating factors that generate mounting intensity within the band's vital jump style. The WSQ gains its unusual degree of unity from constant interaction between, on the one hand, the fundamental freedom underlying its collective improvisation and, on the other, the unifying principle provided by riffs (the unceasingly repeated figures, derived from swing and rhythm and blues bands, which both support a soloist and provoke his efforts).

The World Saxophone Quartet's influence is also demonstrated by the fact that the group did more than inspire an entire wave of saxophone ensembles. If since the eighties there have been hundreds of bands where musicians playing the same instruments came together to form "pure" groups (string ensembles, brass bands, etc.), and if more and more groups play without a rhythm section so that the instrumentalists themselves become responsible for beat and meter, then it was the World Saxophone Quartet that made such developments possible.

The Henry Threadgill Sextet (in fact a septet) grappled with the New Orleans tradition particularly intensively, reflecting and transforming the music of the start of the century—dirges, marches, and archaic blues, full of dark, sarcastic, and both joyous and morbid sounds. Henry Threadgill achieved unity within his group (with trombonist Craig Harris, cellist Diedre Murray, and drummer Pheeroan AkLaff) through his compositions rather than his interventions as soloist. He ingeniously embedded his musicians' improvisations in the notated parts simultaneously performed by other players so that the compositional elements seemed to be natural continuations of the solos.

A similarly high degree of interaction was also achieved by Henry Threadgill's band Very Very Circus, a septet featuring two electric guitars and two tubas. This ensemble achieved such orchestral effects that Threadgill was asked whether their recordings made use of overdubs—which they did not.

"A golden constant" within this trend—and yet much of what the band plays points the way ahead—came from Jack DeJohnette's Special Edition. He calls his music "multidirectional," stylistically open to all sides, with probably the most imposing range on the scene at that time: contemporary jazz, bebop, modalism, impressionism, jazz-rock, free jazz, funk, reggae, etc. Something of Jack DeJohnette's integrative power, not just as a drummer but also as band leader and composer, is revealed by the fact that many famous jazz musicians have sometimes played more economical and focused solos in Special Edition than in their own groups: Arthur Blythe, David Murray, Chico Freeman, Greg Osby, Gary Thomas, and others.

World Jazz

World jazz, initiated in the sixties by John Coltrane and then taken up by many groups in the seventies, experienced its first real high points of integration around 1980. Catalyst in chief was trumpeter Don Cherry with his various bands. His poetry and magic accompanied many of the groups playing world jazz, and inspired even more (basically all of them): above all, Codona (with tabla and sitar virtuoso Collin Walcott and Brazilian percussionist Naná Vasconcelos), Old and New Dreams (with tenorist and musette player Dewey Redman and drummer Ed Blackwell), and Nu with altoist Carlos Ward. Of importance in Europe were the groups around Charlie Mariano, the grand old master of saxophone playing, American drummer Mark Nauseef's band, Bengt Berger's Bitter Funeral Beer Band in Sweden, and the group around Lebanese-born Rabih Abou-Khalil, who plays the oud, the Arab lute.

The first successful implementations of world jazz took place in the seventies, particularly impressively in Shakti, established by John McLaughlin in 1976 as an astonishing change of direction after the electronic high-energy phase of the Mahavishnu Orchestra. The four musicians in Shakti—John McLaughlin (guitar) and three Indians, including violinist L. Shankar and tabla virtuoso Zakir Hussain—played gentle acoustic music. This was an encounter between jazz and both Indian music (from the south as well as the north) and Indian spirituality and religiosity, at a level of perfection even surpassing another important musical constellation: the earlier cooperation between Ali Akbar Khan, the Indian sarod player, and altoist John Handy, celebrated for his playing in Charles Mingus's groups.

Shakti was criticized for an "abrupt break" with John McLaughlin's Mahavishnu music, but the guitarist's dedication to Indian music and spirituality was already apparent during the Mahavishnu period. Above all, Shakti's music was similarly rich and as interwoven as the Mahavishnu performances. According to John McLaughlin, "India is part of my home on this planet. . . . India is a part of me, not only physically but also psychologically." That also becomes clear from the names of the two bands. Mahavishnu means "divine compassion, power, and justice" and Shakti "female creative intelligence, love, and beauty."

Just as the Charlie Parker Quintet with Dizzy Gillespie brought together the prototypes of bebop, so too did the Codona Trio ideally unite the progenitors of contemporary world jazz: both Don Cherry (on trumpet, numerous flutes, and the African doussn' gouni long-necked lute) and American sitar and tabla virtuoso Collin Walcott as well as Brazilian percussionist Naná Vasconcelos. Walcott once said, "I first studied African music, and then Indian. Before that, I did American Swing. Moving between them I only had to take a very short step." That's just how Codona sounded. Three musicians here built bridges between musical cultures and continents—between Brazilian, African, Arabian, Tibetan, and Indian music—with such poetry and playfulness that the listener heard what they have in common, not the differences between them.

Established in 1970 by four former members of the Paul Winter Consort, Oregon with its sensitive, introspective, acoustic playing marks the high point to date in chamber-music-like integration in jazz. The four musicians played over eighty different instruments: Ralph Towner (guitar, trumpet, piano, French horn, etc.), Collin Walcott (tabla, sitar, percussion, etc.), Paul McCandless (oboe, English horn, soprano sax, bass clarinet, etc.), and Glen Moore (bass, violin, flutes, etc.). Hence the wealth of melodies and tonal color with which this band plays world jazz par excellence, combining ethnic music from all over the globe with romantic, impressionistic, and contemporary concert music as well as free jazz and folklore.

After Walcott's death in 1984, Oregon never recovered the unity and magic the quartet had achieved with the sitar and tabla virtuoso, but even today the group's great chamber-music-like sensitivity still captivates. Its music has become more exciting with Trilok Gurtu from India, and the use of electronic instruments (various synthesizers and drum machines) has opened up additional dimensions of tonal coloring.

Strikingly, the first integrative high points in world music came at the start of the eighties with groups like Shakti, Oregon, Codona, and Old and New Dreams. Since then, jazz groups have so much accepted world music that they no longer deliberately seek to amalgamate elements from different musical cultures but instead allow world-musical influences to enter their multistylistic jazz as one element among many others. "World music" has become an established force in the pop business, but wherever ethnic music flows into rock or pop, that derives—whether consciously or not—from the pioneering work and the advances achieved by such jazzmen as John Coltrane, Don Cherry, and Collin Walcott.

Free Funk

When jazz-rock's problems with integration became ever more obvious during the midseventies, little hope seemed left for this style. All that suddenly changed in 1977 with the appearance of Ornette Coleman's *Dancing in Your Head*: a cooking, bubbling brew of rock rhythms, free jazz, and North African music, the first satisfactorily unified realization of free funk. But only at the start of the eighties was Ornette's "message" understood, taken up, and refined by other jazz groups.

All free-funk ensembles are thus directly or indirectly linked with the music of Ornette Coleman's groups. In that respect, the part played by Ornette in free funk is indeed very reminiscent of Miles Davis's influence on seventies jazz-rock. Directly from Coleman's "harmolodic" Prime Time Band came Shannon Jackson's Decoding Society, the James

"Blood" Ulmer Group, and the Jamaaladeen Tacuma Band. But other musicians who haven't played with the altoist are also linked more or less directly with Coleman's music: the Steve Coleman Band, Ray Anderson's Slickaphonics, Defunkt (around trombonist Joseph Bowie), the Greg Osby Group, and the Gary Thomas Band.

Critics have reproached Coleman for turning away from free jazz, but his "harmolodic" music has only changed since the sixties to the extent that the Prime Time Band now implements this concept in a contemporary framework of rock-oriented and electronic music. They are the same great collective improvisations of a "harmolodic" nature. All the musical developments involve elaboration and modulation of a *single* melody—but without being bound in terms of key, functional harmony, or meter, or even by any reference to the unifying tonal system provided by Western tempered tuning. The "cement" that holds the band together is communication by way of the initial melody. All the players' actions are based on that, even in their wildest "free" moments.

Whereas Ornette Coleman's Prime Time Band has achieved free funk's most melodically integrated performances, Ronald Shannon Jackson's Decoding Society stands for the most rhythmically impulsive solutions. In the first half of the eighties (but later seldom) Shannon Jackson and his group succeeded in creating integrated band jazz of stormy intensity by "melodifying" the polyrhythmic patterns of his powerful drumming and transferring them to the ensemble playing. James "Blood" Ulmer's groups have transposed the language of the blues and its archaic precursors into particularly robust free funk, giving vent to raw expression and unrestrained vitality. Free-funk groups have made jazz-rock more communicative and interactive by linking it with elements from free jazz. The outcome is that such ensembles are often more integrated and "together" than the usual fusion bands. On the other hand, it became ever more apparent during the second half of the eighties that the rock beat can only be "emancipated" to a limited extent. Otherwise this music loses precisely what characterizes it: its "groove," its physical directness.

Since 1990: Stylistic Diversity and the Art of Interaction

In the jazz of the nineties, no single general stylistic dictum dominated band concepts, no hierarchical arrangement of scenes. Instead, an extreme diversity of styles and playing approaches existed alongside one another. The nineties brought another explosion of stylistic diversity to jazz, and a combination of so many different ways of playing and sets of values that it became difficult to maintain an overview of them all. What was considered up-to-date in jazz expanded more and more, or, as historian Ulrich Gumbrecht put it, the present became wider and wider. The era of avant-garde movements, with their radical breaks and clearly defined upheavals, was over. Instead, plurality came to dominate the scene.

Of course, stylistic layers and groupings were also to be found in nineties jazz. But they were marked by such a clear tendency toward combination and overlapping of different styles that bands cannot be assigned to rigidly separated groupings without some degree of violence. Thus, in considering the nineties, the procedure of assigning bands to individual stylistic groups has to be abandoned.

The "collapse of clear genre orderings" (George Lewis) led to a freedom of stylistic options that is unparalleled in the century-long history of jazz bands. The degree of mastery with which musicians learned to handle this diversity and to bring it into integrated group contexts is fascinating. Nowhere was this tendency toward stylistic diversity so colorful and emphatic as in the bands of New York's downtown scene. The downtown bands were united by only one common characteristic: the refusal of any musical categorization. Most of these bands achieved integration by assimilating and combining a wide variety of different influences, going far beyond conventional groupings of styles, genres, and idioms, in such a convincing manner that they succeeded in finding a personal sound.

Inevitably, this resulted in extremely different small-band concepts and playing methods. These range from provocative cut-up techniques, realized virtuosically in the ensembles of John Zorn or Uri Caine, to stylistic layering techniques, mastered and cultivated in groups led by Wayne Horvitz or Ben Allison.

The challenge of multistylistic playing is to look for compatibilities, affinities, and common elements in divergent ways of playing, and to find in them a basis for a dialogue in which these elements can then be combined in order to give life to the music. The various ensembles of alto saxophonist and composer John Zorn were groundbreaking in working with this polyphony of textures and idioms. Zorn has been the single most important catalyst and integrating figure of the New York downtown scene. But only two of his bands have succeeded in satisfying the strict definition formulated above of successful integration: Naked City and the quartet Masada (now in existence for more than fifteen years).

In the early nineties, Naked City became the synonym and the symbol of multistylistic improvising. The highly compressed miniatures of this quintet (with guitarist Bill Frisell, keyboardist Wayne Horvitz, bassist Fred Frith, drummer Joey Baron, and vocalist Yamatsuka Eye) were "an acoustic trip around the world in thirty seconds" (Thomas Miessgang). The music of this group was like an entire city crammed into two- or three-minute outbursts, a frenzy of styles and idioms that changed from one to the next so quickly that Simon Hopkins remarked: "Anyone who doesn't enjoy these pieces is just thinking about it too much."

Masada, on the other hand, cultivates an approach to improvising that emphasizes organic development, inventing and drawing out continuous narrative lines with remarkable logic and consistency. This quartet (with trumpeter Dave Douglas, bassist Greg Cohen, and percussionist Joey Baron) is the most successful, intensive working band of the Radical Jewish Culture movement. In this group, Zorn combines the Ornette Coleman approach with elements from klezmer, Balkan music, soul, and free music.

Other important ensembles of the New York downtown scene include Tim Berne's Bloodcount (with Chris Speed and Jim Black), the band Sex Mob (led by trumpeter Steven Bernstein), Dave Douglas's Tiny Bell Trio, the Jazz Passengers, Ben Allison's Medicine Wheel, and the Balkan jazz group Pachora.

This decidedly polystylistic scene stands in only apparent contradiction to another historical development that was important for the evolution of bands in the nineties: the passionate rediscovery of the jazz tradition. Under the de facto leadership of trumpeter Wynton Marsalis and the "young lions" who emulated him, this movement introduced a more conservative valuation of the heritage of jazz, emphasizing classic straight-ahead jazz elements such as blues, standards, song form, and triplet-based swing.

The neoclassicist bands led or inspired by Wynton Marsalis took advantage of the fact that the concept of modernity, held up as a standard by the jazz avant-garde for twenty or thirty years, was understood too narrowly. "For me, Dizzy Gillespie was the most modern player, period," says saxophonist Joe Lovano, a veteran of this scene. "He made so many young trumpeters sound old. Modern doesn't mean young. Modern means having a concept and developing a way of playing that is free. Free, because you have a deep conception of melody, harmony, and rhythm that enables you to be creative. No limits! Jazz is about expression and imagination."

Powerful musical group identities do not develop in a vacuum—they come from the fact that improvising musicians react to and build on the knowledge of earlier players. The stimulus provided by the study of the jazz tradition lies in the integrative force of comparison. An understanding of the tradition gives the musician a better ability to take risks. The past is reevaluated, but this reevaluation does not stand on its own; it has to be placed into a conscious relationship to the standards and values of fundamental ways of playing jazz. Anyone who seeks a serious engagement with the legacy of jazz is deliberately putting himself or herself to the test. "You can't mess with tradition," says Jacky Terrasson.

Despite the clichés and imitations that the "young lions" groups often produced, an astonishing number of bands succeeded in achieving integration in neo–hard bop and new mainstream approaches—often going back beyond bop, to approaches from the Swing era and from New Orleans jazz, and sometimes from other idioms such as Latin, soul, and rock music. The most important of these bands were Wynton Marsalis's septet (decidedly conservative in its approach), the (much freer) Branford Marsalis Trio (with Jeff "Tain" Watts), the Roy Hargrove Quintet, and the Joshua Redman Quartet (with Brian Blade on drums).

"You should never get on the bandstand with someone you're not willing to get into a foxhole with," says Wynton Marsalis. "The whole band must swing. You can't have weak links in your thing." Although the music of the Wynton Marsalis Septet was highly tailored to its leader's virtuosic trumpet playing, and emphasized the discipline with which its members interpreted Wynton's compositions, this band played with an exciting unity. This unity consisted less in the soloistic abilities of its individual members (including trombonist Wycliffe Gordon, tenor saxophonist Victor Goines, and drummer Herlin Riley) than in a particularly well-developed interaction and the dynamic way in which the individuals subordinated themselves to the overall aim—the exciting updating of older ways of playing jazz.

It would be hard to overstate the ferocity of the so-called New York jazz wars that took place in the nineties between neoconservative jazz musicians and post–avant-gardists coming from free jazz. But in these battles, and in the raw ideological clash of styles and positions, it was often overlooked that the two sides were in some respects not so far from each other.

"Traditional" jazz musicians and ambitious, "forward-thinking" musicians sometimes have more in common than they realize. Both situate themselves relative to the heritage of jazz in a reflective, contemporary manner. Both bring new appreciation of the jazz tradition. But they do so from different perspectives. Whereas the "traditional" players put more emphasis on the conservation of elements of the history of jazz, the "more modern" players emphasize the possibilities for innovation of the same jazz tradition. Both seek, in dialogue with older ways of playing, a new stylistic mixture.

Neither of these approaches is inherently superior to the other. As one critic wrote, "Someone who, in the manner of Zorn, assembles ready-made pieces from the secondhand shop of postmodernity is not, a priori, making better or more contemporary music than someone who, like Branford Marsalis, is creatively confronting the personal styles of his precursors. *What* is played is not as important as *how*."

Innovation in jazz is not measured primarily by an inventory of the materials used, but rather by the possibilities for finding new ways of expressing individuality in an improvised group music. The great bands of neo–hard bop, such as the Joshua Redman Quartet or the Roy Hargrove Quintet, have exploited these possibilities. Pianist Brad Mehldau says, "If we're interested in innovation, we should look at the possibilities for more subtlety." The jazz of the nineties showed that new developments in jazz were not a matter of big, abstract stylistic questions, but rather of differentiated individual ways of playing.

This is also clear in another genre of band in which the rediscovery of the jazz tradition in the nineties spurred a remarkable upswing: the piano trio. Thirty years earlier, Bill Evans provided the model with his trio. By redefining the division of labor between the piano, bass, and drums, he introduced something to the piano trio that became the standard for successful musicmaking in this context: the freshness of dialogue between equals.

A leading band in this area was the trio of Keith Jarrett (piano), Gary Peacock (bass), and Jack DeJohnette (drums), founded in the early eighties, with its interpretation of standards, followed in the early twenty-first century by increasingly freer improvisations. It's true that over the decades some aspects of this trio's improvisations have become routine, but the way in which these three musicians are able to "read" each others' playing results in a level of musical understanding that goes beyond what can be transcribed. The trio simply "speaks." It plays nothing insignificant.

A similar musical density was achieved by The Bad Plus (Ethan Iverson, piano; Reid Anderson, bass; and Dave King, drums) in their jazz "deconstructions" of pop and rock tunes; by the Brad Mehldau Trio (with Larry Grenadier and Jorge Rossy), with its open, polyphonic improvisation and the patient manner in which it lets things develop; the Jacky Terrasson Trio, with virtuosic grooves and a revitalization of traditional jazz elements; the Bill Charlap Trio, creating the effect of an updated Oscar Peterson Trio; Jason Moran's Bandwagon, moving stylistically between Björk, Brahms, and Jaki Byard; and, in Europe, the trio E.S.T. (Esbjörn Svensson, piano; Dan Berglund, bass; and Magnus Öström, drums), the Chano Dominguez Trio, and the Jean-Michel Pilc Trio.

Brad Mehldau says:

What makes jazz so special for me is that it has an essentially social character. Whatever it is that I admire about Miles Davis or John Coltrane is not primarily Miles as soloist, or Coltrane as soloist, but the bands that they had. When I think of them, I think of the whole band, and the way that they relate to each other as a group. That's the spirit of jazz music. That's how it came into being—as collective improvisation.

All the great European small bands of the nineties—the Sclavis/Texier/Romano Trio, the Clusone Trio (with Michael Moore, Ernst Reijseger, and Han Bennink), the Nils Wogram Quartet, Lucas Niggli's Zoom, the Gianluigi Trovesi Octet, the Moscow Art Trio, Renaud Garcia Fons's Oriental Bass, the Nguyên Lê Group, and the Kühn/Humair/Jenny-Clark Trio—gained their power from the fact that they made a group music that reflected, in each case, their own cultural and regional roots. Louis Sclavis: "The band builds the house, we erect it together. The music is

like a house or a castle, or sometimes just a tent, it depends. We all live together in the building that we build ourselves."
Jean-Michel Pilc:

> When I play, I'm part of a larger whole that includes me and my musicians. This larger whole has its own life. It's not "I" that plays with [bassist] François Moutin and [drummer] Ari Hoenig. The three of us are embedded in a musical ceremony that develops. It's like making love, it's a fusing. You don't think about yourself, you become part of something bigger. That's the key when we play together. I wouldn't even say that "we" play together. The "we" itself plays, as a unit. When we make music together, each of us doesn't hear "himself" and "the others." We hear the whole. Sometimes we don't even know any more what instrument we are playing. Then, for me, it feels as if I'm playing everything. Then I'm away from the piano, somewhere else. We're transported, we're outside ourselves.

Interaction in a jazz band does not mean communication at any price. It serves a clearly defined purpose. The central element in a functioning jazz band is cooperation and mutual help. It's a group approach, in which each member of the ensemble has made an individual decision to help the others sound good. Or, as Miles Davis put it: "A good band demands sacrifice and compromise from each of its members—without that, nothing happens."

The Dave Holland Quintet (with Chris Potter, saxophone; Robin Eubanks, trombone; Steve Nelson, vibraphone; and Billy Kilson, drums) has achieved its extraordinary integration and intensity through an extremely unfettered, progressive group handling of predetermined forms—a "freedom within the structural combination" (Steve Coleman).

One thing that was rare in the jazz of the nineties was fixed ensembles. "There are a large number of good individual instrumentalists, who often have technical reserves of ability that goes beyond that of the jazz greats of the past. But there are only a few dozen interesting ensembles that have a common history and development as a working group," says Greg Osby. "Individual and technical development have accelerated, but as far as group logic and knowledge go, and how musicians interact in the context of a performance, we're decades behind."

In the forties and fifties, jazz clubs offered possibilities for bands to play in one venue for weeks, sometimes even months, at a time. This promoted the growth of fixed ensembles. Today, as a rule bands play one-nighters in clubs or single festival performances, a circumstance that makes it more difficult to build working bands. Drummer Jack DeJohnette laments the decline of the jam session, in which new ideas could be tried out spontaneously and without the pressure of judgment: "It's a shame that jamming no longer exists, because that's where the basic work was done." Drummer Dave King says, "I think it's so important for jazz to get back to those working ensembles. So often I'll hear a record and you'll have all these great players, and they just sound like islands stuck together."

Nonetheless, in the jazz of the nineties and beyond, many bands achieved integration, in the sense defined above, on the highest level: the Joe Lovano Quartet, the John Scofield Group, the Bill Frisell Band, Paul Motian's Electric Bebop Band, Charlie Haden's Quartet West (with saxophonist Ernie Watts), the Wayne Shorter Quartet (with Danilo Perez, piano; John Patitucci, bass; and Brian Blade, drums), the James Carter Quartet, and the Charlie Hunter Trio.

"Trying to make potential chaos coherent, moment to moment. That's a jazz band. Continuous musical adjustment to solve problems that never existed"—this is Wynton Marsalis's description of the state of an improvising group. In jazz, teams work particularly well when older, experienced players play together with young, new players. Jazz needs more working bands, not more jazz schools. Trumpeter Michael Weiss says, "I think the continuum of apprentices playing with the masters and gaining recognition and exposure by touring regularly with working bands and the great players and eventually becoming a leader off of that exposure is the proper channel for development."

Pianist Paul Bley:

> In a small jazz group, everyone is responsible for the playing of each individual musician. If you sound good, but someone else doesn't, that's your fault. Here's an interpersonal example: if you're eating at a table, and there's a woman who's shy and doesn't want to speak, while everyone else there isn't shy—if that were a musical situation, then all the people who are talking a lot would have to be quiet at some point, until the silence became so unbearable to the shy woman that she began to speak. And if she were to withdraw again, then the others would have to again lay out, in order to ensure that she had the chance to play an equal role in the conversation. Because equality is the ideal.

This egalitarian principle can be achieved only through permanent interaction between the members of a band. Some rock-oriented ways of playing have the drawback that the rhythmic structure limits interaction and makes it more difficult. All the more astonishing, then, that so many bands in the areas of crossover between drum 'n' bass, hip-hop, digital electronics, and acoustic jazz approaches have achieved musical unity. These include: in the United States, the trio Medeski, Martin & Wood, Steve Coleman's Five Elements, and Dave Binney's Lost Tribe; in Europe: Erik Truffaz's Electric Ladyland, the Nils-Petter Molvaer Group, and Bugge Wesseltoft's New Conception of Jazz.

Medeski, Martin & Wood, with their slow, deliberate development of electronic grooves, have achieved a remarkable unity. Exciting also is the openness with which the group bonds free elements with dub, drum 'n' bass, and retro grooves from soul, funk, and rock.

Steve Coleman has achieved a particularly successful integration of rock-oriented playing, contemporary jazz forms, and world-music influences in his group Five Elements. The logical consistency with which Coleman's Five Elements has brought the sounds of "street music" into metrically intricate M-Base music is remarkable. The fact that Coleman, as well as M-Base groups led by Gary Thomas and Greg Osby, has made such a convincing success of this is due not only to the musical solutions with which funk, rap, and jazz have been seamlessly fused with one another, but also to the social and political implications of their group concepts. Hip-hop, funk, rap, and jazz have a deep message in common. For marginalized, oppressed people all over the world, black music is not only a balm for the heart and soul, but is also the embodiment of freedom and the triumph of hope.

"Jazz is harmony through conflict—like a good discussion," says Wynton Marsalis. Interaction is indispensable for a jazz group. Every musical action that a musician makes at any time in a piece makes a decisive contribution to the music. This is what makes a band swing and gives the music its groove. Ideally, the interaction within a group brings it about that the work of a jazz musician is at its most individual when it sounds the most collective. Stanley Crouch remarks: "A jazz band means that we hear collective art in which there is never anything like a 'solo' unless one is playing alone. Otherwise it is always a group effort in which each member of the ensemble has chosen to help everyone else sound good. Help is the essential aspect of the art." Without trusting each other, without mutual support, bands cannot improvise. All of the great ensembles of jazz, from the very beginning, are distinguished by this mutual reliance among the members. This provides the basis that lets the individual musicians experiment. "The trust has to be there," says Brad Mehldau. "Without trust, it doesn't happen." Bob Belden explains: "The band doesn't have an ego. It has a sound."

Toward a Definition of Jazz

Jazz is a form of art music that originated in the United States through the confrontation of African Americans with European music. The instrumentation, melody, and harmony of jazz are in the main derived from Western musical tradition. Rhythm, phrasing, and production of sound, and the elements of blues harmony are derived from African music and from the musical conception of African Americans. Jazz differs from European music in three basic elements, which all serve to increase intensity:

1. A special relationship to time, defined as "swing"

2. A spontaneity and vitality of musical production in which improvisation plays a role

3. A sonority and manner of phrasing that mirror the individuality of the performing jazz musician

These three basic characteristics, whose essentials have been—and will continue to be—passed on orally from one generation to the next, create a novel climate of tension. In this climate, the emphasis is no longer on great arcs of tension, as in European music, but on a wealth of tension-creating elements, which continuously rise and fall.

A history of jazz could certainly be written from the point of view of the three jazz characteristics—swing, improvisation, and sound/phrasing—and their relation to each other. All these characteristics are important, to be sure, but their relationships change, and these changing relationships are a part of jazz evolution.

That jazz sound and jazz phrasing stand in dialectic opposition has been pointed out already. In old New Orleans jazz, phrasing still largely corresponded to European folk and circus music. On the other hand, typical jazz sonority was particularly highly developed here. Later, this kind of sonority came to be regarded as exaggerated. No major musician in any phase of jazz has had a purely European sonority; nevertheless, jazz sonority and the sonorities of European music occasionally have come very close. By way of compensation, jazz phrasing has become increasingly important. Thus, modern jazz, since cool jazz, is as far removed from European music in terms of phrasing as old jazz was in terms of sonority.

In their extremes, jazz phrasing and jazz sonority seem mutually exclusive. Where jazz sonority is at its strongest—for example, in the "jungle" solos of Tricky Sam Nanton, Bubber Miley, and Cootie Williams with Duke Ellington's band, or in the free-jazz solos of Albert Ayler—jazz phrasing stops. The "jungle" sound or the high-energy playing dictates the phrasing, and this sound exists for its own sake, beyond jazz's flexible, triplet-based phrasing. On the other hand, where jazz phrasing appears at its most highly cultivated stage—as in the tenor improvisations of Stan Getz, the flute solos of Hubert Laws, or the alto lines of the Lee Konitz of the fifties—jazz sonority seems largely suspended. The musical proceedings are so unilaterally dictated by the phrasing that it does not appear possible to produce sounds that have an expressive meaning outside the flow of the phrase.

A similar, if not quite so precise, relationship exists between swing and improvisation. Both are factors of spontaneity. Thus it may come about that when spontaneity is expressed in the extreme through the medium of swing, improvisation will recede. Even when a record by Count Basie's band does not contain a single improvised solo, no one questions its jazz character. But if improvisation is given too free a rein, swing recedes, as in many unaccompanied solos or in some free-jazz recordings. This suppression of swing by freedom is already illustrated by the very first totally "free" record in jazz history—Lennie Tristano's "Intuition."

Thus the relationships among the elements of jazz change constantly. In the thirties, when sonority in terms of New Orleans jazz had already receded and fluent phrasing in terms of modern jazz had not as yet been fully developed, swing celebrated such unquestioned victories that swing (the element) and Swing (the style) were not even differentiated in terminology. There have always been forms of jazz that seek to project the jazz essence into a single element of jazz. The ragtime pianists had swing, but hardly any improvisation and no sonority. The early New Orleans bands did have jazz sonority, but they had more march rhythm than swing and a form of collective improvisation that sooner or later led to ever-repeated head arrangements. In the realm of Swing style there is a kind of big-band music in which improvisation, sonority, and sometimes even soloistic phrasing largely take a backseat—and yet it swings marvelously. During the fifties Jimmy Giuffre often projected the whole jazz essence into a single Lester Young–inspired phrase. On the other hand—as is made clear by just these "exceptional examples"—at the real peaks of jazz, all three jazz elements are present simultaneously, if in varying relationship to one another: from Louis Armstrong through Coleman Hawkins and Lester Young to Charlie Parker, Miles Davis, and John Coltrane, up to David Murray and Wynton Marsalis.

It is important to note, too, that swing, improvisation, and sonority (or phrasing) are elements of intensity. As much as they may differ from each other, just so much do they concur in creating intensity.

Swing creates intensity through friction and superimposition of the levels of time.

Improvisation creates intensity through the fact that the road from musician to sound is shorter and more direct than in any other type of musical production.

In sonority and phrasing, intensity is produced by the immediacy and directness with which a particular human personality is projected into sound. Intensity results from the degree to which an improvising jazz musician succeeds in developing a "signature sound." This intensification through the personalization of sound is what Don Cherry had in mind when he said, "It's not the notes that swing, it's the sound."

The sound is essential. It is the carrier of an urgent message. As one jazz musician said, "No sound, no message." And Peter Niklas Wilson rightly observed: "The vibrato of a Sidney Bechet, the breathy, richly modulated tone of a Ben Webster, a dry piano attack by Thelonious Monk, Jimi Hendrix's howling feedback: each of these says as much as the theme of a Beethoven symphony."

It may thus be assumed that the main task and real meaning of the basic jazz elements rest in the creation of structured intensity. This understanding is also contained in free jazz with its ecstatic heat, as idiosyncratic as the interpretation of the three basic elements in this music may often appear. Even when, as in much of Europe's free-improvised music, free jazz comes close to classical "new music," it has a vital intensity and energy that is not present in the same way in European composed music.

In all these differentiations the question of quality—stature—is decisive. One might almost be tempted to adopt it as a fourth "element of jazz" within our definition. If, for example, Dave Brubeck or Stan Kenton or Keith Jarrett or Derek Bailey or Weather Report has found a place in jazz—a place that was perhaps disputed at some points of their development but nevertheless basically is accepted—this is due to the quality and stature of their music, which are indisputable, even though much might be said against these musicians in terms of jazz essentials. Moreover, this point similarly applies to the European, or to any other, musical culture.

Even if it were possible to give a precise definition of what "classical" music is, a music that contained all the elements of this definition and yet lacked the stature—the quality—of the great classical works would still not be "classical."

It is important in this context to discuss some thoughts that were developed by the American writer and scholar Robert M. Pirsig. Pirsig (in his book *Zen and the Art of Motorcycle Maintenance*) has shown that definitions are "square," because quality is defined "entirely outside the analytic process." Thus the aspect of quality, necessarily, is excluded from any attempt at definition. Pirsig: "When you subtract quality you get squareness."

This explains why we are left strangely dissatisfied with any attempt at definition. Jazz scholars may develop ever more extensive and refined definitions, but the real point eludes them; indeed, it *must* necessarily elude them, for reasons that Pirsig has shown (more extensively than can be summarized here). What remains excluded from the range of the definition musicians know better than all scholars. We have quoted Fats Waller before: "It's not *what* you play, but *how* you play it."

This state of affairs explains why thousands of cocktail, pop, and rock groups all over the world play a kind of music that might fulfill all—or almost all—requirements of all definitions to date, and that yet cannot be called jazz. In countless "commercial" groups, there *also* is improvisation, sometimes even jazz phrasing and jazz sounds; they often even swing, and yet their music is not jazz. On the other hand, as we have shown, with genuine jazz musicians the presence of only *one* element of "jazzness" is often sufficient to insure the jazz character of their music.

It is necessary to understand this: jazz has to do with quality. Quality is felt rather than rationally comprehended. This has been realized subconsciously by musicians for as long as jazz has existed. Louis Armstrong: "If you have to ask what jazz is, you'll never know." For the musicians, music has to be first and foremost "good" to be perceived as jazz. All other criteria play a secondary role, however important they may be.

There is another fact that must be considered in this context. The constant use of the elements, styles, musicianship, techniques, and ideas of jazz in commercial music forces the jazz musician unceasingly to create something new. In this sense, André Hodeir remarked that today's innovation is tomorrow's cliché.

The flair for the cliché, however, is not only connected with the abuses of jazz in commercial music; it lies in the nature of jazz itself. Almost every blues strophe has been turned into a cliché. All the famous blues lines exist as ever-recurring "entities": "I've been drinkin' muddy water, sleepin' in a hollow log . . . ," "My baby treats me like a low-down dog . . . ," "Broke and hungry, ragged and dirty too . . . ," "'cause the world is all wrong . . . ," "But the meanest blues I ever had . . . ," "I'm just as lonely, lonely as a man can be . . . ," "Can't eat, can't sleep . . . ,"

"I wanna hold you, baby, hold you in my arms again . . . ," "I'm gonna buy myself a shotgun . . . ," "Take me back, baby . . . ," "I love you, baby, but you sure don't treat me right . . . ," and so forth. The great blues singers used them as they pleased, taking a line from here and another from there, adapting them to each other, and often not even that.

What holds true for the lyrics also applies to the music. When Jimmy Smith, Horace Silver, or Wynton Marsalis records a blues, both the arrangement and the improvised solos are saturated with structural elements from half a century of blues and jazz history. Everything played by exponents of neobop is saturated with elements from Charlie Parker records that, though not in themselves clichés, certainly lend themselves to cliché making. Or, to reach back into jazz tradition: in every third or fourth blues by Bessie Smith one hears phrases, or even entire lines, that might just as easily have been heard in other contexts from other blues singers. Every boogie consists of nothing but a constantly changing montage of "entities" made up of ostinatos and largely standardized melodic phrases. Almost every improvised break on old records by the Hot Five or Hot Seven, by Johnny Dodds or King Oliver, by Jimmie Noone or Kid Ory, is mutually interchangeable. So are the breaks that set off the four-bar blues phrases from each other—whether they are played by singers accompanying themselves on the guitar or by the most famous of jazz musicians. There are half a hundred, perhaps not even that many, "model breaks" from which all others are derived.

The further one goes back, the more apparent this model character becomes. What Marshall Stearns, Alan Lomax, and Alfons M. Dauer discovered of African elements in jazz consists almost without exception of such connective models and "entities"; they were not only taken over from African music as "entities" but often had this character within African music itself. Their model nature is so compact that they have survived through centuries almost without changing. Consider the tango: the rhythm was brought by the slaves from Africa, and today it exists in African folklore as much as in the great Argentinian tango tradition, in temperamental folk dances, lasciviously slow dance and bar music, in boogie-woogie basses, and in hundreds of intermittent stages. Everywhere there is the identical ostinato figure—the model with its tendency toward the cliché.

All jazz consists of such "models." They are fragments—such as the downward-descending lines of old blues or modern funk—that have something of the aura of the words with which fairy tales begin: "Once upon a time . . ." This, too, is a model element. And as it is in the fairy tales, where elements-turned-symbols become content, so it is in jazz: the evil witch casts a spell on the noble prince, and the hard-hearted king turns soft when he catches sight of the lovely shepherdess, and at last prince and shepherdess find each other and the shepherdess turns out to be a bewitched princess. Witch and prince, magic and hard-heartedness, king and shepherdess . . . all of these are elements of motives that can be joined together in inexhaustible combinations. It is thanks to postmodern jazz that the model character of such elements has been clearly revealed.

No matter how "modern" and "new" a way of playing is felt to be, it always has—unavoidably—connections to earlier periods of jazz, through such models and elements. Duke Ellington: "The other night I heard a cat on the radio talking about 'modern' jazz and playing a record to illustrate his point, but it had devices I heard cats using in the 1920s. These large words like *modern* don't mean anything. Everybody who's had anything to say in this music—all the way back—has been an individualist."

Innovation in jazz is a relative concept. The "new" consists less in something coming to light that was previously hidden than in a reconsideration by musicians of something they already knew. The decisive factor for the greatness of a jazz musician is not primarily the musical material, but rather the personal way it is made to sound.

While Western concert music in the process of its ever-increasing tendency toward abstraction has lost almost all the old models and entities; while there is hardly a structural and formal element that has not been questioned—theme and variation, the sonata form, the triad—while we now long for the attainment of new and connective models and elements in concert music, and can only attain them by taking up once again the old models and elements that in the meantime have become questionable; and while in doing this we are historicizing—meanwhile, all these things are present in jazz in the most natural, self-evident, and living way.

Model, element, entity, cliché, may coincide—literally and note for note. But as model, as element, and as entity they have meaning; as cliché they are meaningless. But *since* they can coincide there is a constant tendency toward the cliché inherent in the models, elements, and entities. To a great extent, it is on the basis of this tendency that jazz constantly renews itself. The most fascinating thing about jazz is its aliveness. Jazz runs counter to all academicism—that very academicism that has made great European music the exclusive concern of the well-bred bourgeoisie, and also the academicism that has become part of the business of jazz education.

The aliveness of jazz is such that standards are constantly overthrown—even where the old models and entities remain relevant. This complicates the position of jazz criticism. It has been reproached for being without standards.

In reality, it is remarkable that jazz criticism has so many standards. Often the evolution of jazz proceeds so rapidly that the kind of standards arrived at in European music, frequently formed one or two generations after the particular music has been alive, are meaningless. Jazz standards without flexibility tend to acquire violent and intolerant aspects.

We insist: the point is not to define standards and to test an art form against them; the point is to have the art and constantly reorient the standards in its image. Since this is inconvenient, one attempts to avoid it—within and outside of jazz. But it is above all jazz, as a music of revolt against all that is too convenient, which can demand of its listeners that they revise standards valid years ago and be prepared to discover new norms.

The aesthetic of otherness, the consciousness of freedom, also belong to jazz. Keith Jarrett says: "If you manage to liberate yourself through expression in music, that's necessarily jazz. Even the greatest players can consider themselves lucky if they experience that freedom for a few minutes. Jazz is the only music in the Western world in which the greatest risk-taking brings the greatest results."

Nearly one hundred years after it began, jazz is still what it was then: a music of protest; that, too, contributes to its aliveness. It cries out against social and racial and spiritual discrimination, against the clichés of picayune bourgeois morality, against the functional organization of modern mass society, against the depersonalization inherent in this society, and against that categorization of standards that leads to the automatic passing of judgments wherever these standards are not met.

Many American musicians, particularly African American ones, understand protest as a matter of race. No doubt it is that. But their music would not have been understood all over the world, and it would not have received almost immediate acceptance by musicians of all cultures, colors, and political systems, if the racial aspect were the crucial factor. Here as elsewhere the racial element of jazz has long transcended itself and become universal. It has become part of the worldwide protest against a domination-oriented society that is perceived as a threat by millions of cultured people in all fields around the world in every country and social system—in short, by those who are shaping the judgment to be passed on our epoch by future generations: a threat not only to themselves and their creative productivity but to essential human dignity and worth.

Discography

Instrument Abbreviations

acc	accordion	keyb	misc. keyboard instruments
as	alto saxophone	ld	bandleader
b	bass	org	organ
bcl	bass clarinet	p	piano
bs	baritone saxophone	perc	percussion
cl	clarinet	sax	misc. saxophone
co	cornet	ss	soprano saxophone
dm	drums	synth	synthesizer
elec	sampler, electronics	tb	trombone
fl	flute	tp	trumpet
flh	flugelhorn	ts	tenor saxophone
frh	french horn	tt	turntables
g	guitar	vib	vibraphone
harm	harmonica	viol	violin
harp	harp	voc	vocal

Eivind Aarset (g, elec)
Electronique Noir 1998; Jazzland

Susanne Abbuehl (voc)
April 2001; ECM

Ahmed Abdul-Malik (b, oud)
Jazz Sounds of Africa (with Andrew Cyrille, Tommy Turrentine, et al.) 1961/1962;
Original Jazz Classics

John Abercrombie (g, mandolin)
Gateway (with Jack DeJohnette, Dave Holland) 1986; ECM
Open Land (with Kenny Wheeler, Joe Lovano, Mark Feldman, Dan Wall, Adam
Nussbaum) 1998; ECM
SEE ALSO Marc Copland, Gil Evans, Charles Lloyd, Enrico Rava, Collin Walcott,
Kenny Wheeler

Rabih Abou-Khalil (oud)
The Cactus of Knowledge (with Tom Varner, Dave Bargeron, Michel Godard,
Gabriele Mirabassi, Ellery Eskelin, et al.) 2001; Enja
Blue Camel (with Charlie Mariano, Kenny Wheeler, Steve Swallow, Milton Cardona,
Nabil Khaiat, Ramesh Shotham) 1992; Enja
SEE ALSO Luciano Biondini, Vincent Courtois, Michel Godard, Gabriele Mirabassi,
Glen Moore

Muhal Richard Abrams (p, ld)
Think All, Focus One (with David Gilmore, Eddie Allen, Brad Jones, Reggie
Nicholson, et al.) 1994; Black Saint
SEE ALSO Leroy Jenkins

Benat Achiary (voc)
The Seven Circles—Dedicated to Peter Kowald 2004; FMP

George Adams (ts, fl, voc)
More Sightings 2005; Enja
SEE ALSO Charles Mingus, Don Pullen

Pepper Adams (bs)
10 to 4 at the 5-Spot (with Donald Byrd, Bobby Timmons, Doug Watkins, Elvin
Jones) 1958; Original Jazz Classics
SEE ALSO Gene Ammons, Chet Baker, Donald Byrd, Charles Mingus

Cannonball Adderley (as)
Somethin' Else (with Miles Davis, Hank Jones, Sam Jones, Art Blakey) 1958; Blue
Note
Mercy, Mercy, Mercy (with Nat Adderley, Joe Zawinul, Viktor Gaskin, Roy
McCurdy) 1966; Capitol
SEE ALSO Miles Davis, Horace Silver

Nat Adderley (tp, co)
Work Song (with Wes Montgomery, Sam Jones, Percy Heath, et al.) 1960; Original
Jazz Classics
SEE ALSO Cannonball Adderley

Air (band)
Air Lore (with Fred Hopkins, Steve McCall, and Henry Threadgill) 1979;
    Bluebird/RCA

Noël Akchoté (g)
Sonny II 2004; Winter & Winter

Toshiko Akiyoshi (p, ld)
Toshiko Akiyoshi Jazz Orchestra Wishing Peace (with Brian Lynch, Lew Tabackin,
    et al.) 1986; Ascent

Pheeroan AkLaff (dm)
SEE ALSO Craig Harris, Julius Hemphill, Oliver Lake

Howard Alden (g)
SEE John Lewis

Ralph Alessi (tp)
Circa (with Michael Cain, Peter Epstein) 1996; ECM
SEE ALSO Fred Hersch

Monty Alexander (p)
Three Originals: Love and Sunshine / Estade / Cobilimbo 1974–77; MPS

Don Alias (dm, perc)
SEE Kenny Kirkland, Jaco Pastorius

Geri Allen (p, keyb)
In the Year of the Dragon (with Charlie Haden, Paul Motian) 1989; JMT
SEE ALSO Oliver Lake, Wallace Roney

Ben Allison (b)
Riding the Nuclear Tiger (with Michael Blake, Ted Nash, Jeff Ballard, et al.) 2000;
    Palmetto
SEE ALSO Michael Blake

Mose Allison (p, voc)
The Mose Chronicles—Live in London, Vol. 1 & 2 2000; Blue Note
SEE ALSO Al Cohn

Laurindo Almeida (g)
Stan Getz: Stan Getz Group Feat. Laurindo Almeida 1963; Verve
SEE ALSO Stan Kenton

Mikhail Alperin (p)
At Home 2001; ECM
SEE ALSO Moscow Art Trio

Franco Ambrosetti (tp)
European Legacy 2003; Enja

Scott Amendola (dm)
Cry (with Jenny Scheinman, Nels Cline, et al.) 2003; Cryptogramophone

AMM (band)
It Had Been an Ordinary Enough Day in Pueblo, Colorado (with Eddie Prevost)
    1979; Japo

Albert Ammons (p)
V.A.: From Spirituals to Swing (3 CD) 1938/1939; Vanguard
SEE ALSO Pete Johnson

Gene Ammons (ts)
Blue Gene (with Pepper Adams, Mal Waldron, Ray Barretto, et al.) 1958; Original
    Jazz Classics

Amsterdam String Trio (band)
Winter Theme (with Ernst Reijseger, Maurice Horsthuis, Ernst Glerum) 2000;
    Winter & Winter

Arild Andersen (b)
Electra 2005; ECM
SEE ALSO Jan Garbarek, Albert Mangelsdorff, Roswell Rudd, Markus Stockhausen

Fred Anderson (ts)
DKV Trio (with Hamid Drake, Ken Vandermark, Kent Kessler) 1996; Okka Disk

Ray Anderson (tb)
Where Home Is (with Lew Soloff, Bobby Previte) 1998; Enja
SEE ALSO Karl Berger, Barbara Dennerlein, Bobby Previte, Hank Roberts, Erika
    Stucky, Bennie Wallace

Arcado String Trio (band)
Arcado String Trio (with Mark Feldman, Hank Roberts, Mark Dresser) 1989; JMT
    Edition / Winter & Winter

Louis Armstrong (co, tp, voc)
The Complete Hot Five and Hot Seven Recordings (4 CD) 1925–29; Columbia
Carnegie Hall Concert 1947; Ambassador
Louis Armstrong Plays W. C. Handy (with Trummy Young, Barney Bigard, Philly
    Kyle, Arvell Shaw, et al.) 1954–56; Columbia
Ella and Louis (with Ella Fitzgerald, Oscar Peterson, Herb Ellis, Ray Brown, Buddy
    Rich) 1957; Verve
Complete Sessions (with Duke Ellington, Barney Bigard) 1960; Roulette
SEE ALSO King Oliver, Kid Ory, Bessie Smith

Art Ensemble of Chicago (band)
Les Stances a Sophie (with Lester Bowie, Don Moye, Malachi Favors, Fontella Bass,
    Roscoe Mitchell, Joseph Jarman) 1970; Universal Sound
Urban Bushmen (2 CD) 1980; ECM

Gilad Atzmon (ts, cl)
Musik—Re-Arranging the 20th Century 2004; Enja

Albert Ayler (ts)
Live in Greenwich Village—The Complete Impulse Recordings 1966; Impulse
Holy Ghost—Rare & Unissued Recordings 1962–1970 (9 CD), Revenant

The Bad Plus (band)
These Are the Vistas (with Ethan Iverson, Reid Anderson, Dave King) 2002; Columbia

Benny Bailey (tp)
Big Brass (with Julius Watkins, Phil Woods, Les Spann, Tommy Flanagan, et al.)
    1960; Candid

Derek Bailey (g)
Pieces for Guitar 1966–67; Tzadik
Outcome (with Steve Lacy) 1983; Ictus
SEE ALSO Peter Kowald, Manfred Schoof, Spontaneous Music Ensemble

Chet Baker (tp, voc)
Chet (with Herbie Mann, Pepper Adams, Bill Evans, Kenny Burrell, Paul Chambers,
    Connie Kay, Phillie Joe Jones) 1959; Original Jazz Classics
The Last Concert Vol. I & II (with NDR Big Band & Radio Orchester Hannover)
    1988; Enja
SEE ALSO Philip Catherine, NDR Big Band

Jon Balke (p)
Jon Balke & Magnetic North Orchestra: Diverted Travels 2004; ECM

Billy Bang (viol)
A Tribute to Stuff Smith 1993; Soulnote

Cyro Baptista (perc)
Beat the Donkey 2002; Tzadik
SEE ALSO Cassandra Wilson, John Zorn

Denys Baptiste (ts)
Let Freedom Ring 2005; Dune Records
SEE ALSO Jazz Jamaica All Stars

Patricia Barber (voc)
Modern Cool 1998; Blue Note

Gato Barbieri (ts)
El Pampero (with Lonnie Liston Smith, Naná Vasconcelos, et al.) 1971; RCA
SEE ALSO Carla Bley, Don Cherry, Charlie Haden

Joey Baron (dm)
We'll Soon Find Out (with Arthur Blythe, Bill Frisell, Ron Carter) 1999;
     Intuition
SEE ALSO Uri Caine, Anthony Coleman, Bill Frisell, Naked City, Michel Portal,
     Bobby Previte, Herb Robertson, John Taylor, Toots Thielemans, John Zorn

Ray Barretto (perc)
La Cuna (with Tito Puente, Joe Farrell, et al.) 1979; Sony
SEE ALSO Gene Ammons, Kenny Burrell, Lou Donaldson

Kenny Barron (p, keyb)
Canta Brazil 2002; Emarcy
SEE ALSO J. J. Johnson, Abbey Lincoln

Gary Bartz (ss, as, ts)
Libra / Another Earth (with Jimmy Owens, Richard Davis, Billy Higgins, Pharoah
     Sanders, et al.) 1967–68; Milestone
SEE ALSO McCoy Tyner

Count Basie (p, org, ld)
The Complete American Decca Recordings (with Lester Young, Hershel Evans,
     Jimmy Rushing, Buck Clayton, Harry Edison, et al.) (3 CD) 1937–39;
     MCA/GRP
April in Paris 1955–56; Verve
Atomic Swing (with Eddie Jones, Freddie Green, et al.) 1957–62; Blue Note
SEE ALSO Benny Goodman, Billie Holiday

Bass Desires (band)
SEE Marc Johnson

Django Bates (keyb, frh, ld)
Winter Truce (And Homes Blaze) 1995; JMT / Winter & Winter

Conrad Bauer (tb)
Hummelsummen 2002; Intakt

Sidney Bechet (cl, ss)
The Complete RCA Victor Sessions (with Tommy Ladnier and the New Orleans
     Feetwarmers, et al.) (3 CD) 1932–43; RCA
The Fabulous Sidney Bechet 1951–53; Blue Note
SEE ALSO King Oliver

Bix Beiderbecke (co)
Singin' the Blues Vol. 1 (with Frankie Trumbauer, Eddie Lang, Jimmy Dorsey, Bill
     Rank, Don Murray, et al.) 1927; Columbia

Richie Beirach (p)
Round About Bartók (with Gregor Huebner) 1999; ACT

Louie Bellson (dm, ld)
Louie Bellson Big Band: Inferno! 1969–70; Concord Jazz
SEE ALSO Art Tatum, Sarah Vaughan

Han Bennink (dm)
SEE ALSO Peter Brötzmann, Clusone 3, Globe Unity Orchestra, ICP Orchestra, Misha
    Mengelberg

George Benson (g, voc)
Anthology (2 CD) 1964–98; Warner

Karl Berger (vib, p, ld)
Conversations (with Carlos Ward, Dave Holland, James "Blood" Ulmer, Mark
    Feldman, Ray Anderson, Ingrid Sertso) 1994; In+Out Records

Tim Berne (as)
Big Satan: I Think They Liked It Honey (with Marc Ducret, Tom Rainey) 1997;
    Winter & Winter
SEE ALSO Julius Hemphill, Hank Roberts, Herb Robertson

Steven Bernstein (tp, slide-tp)
Diaspora Soul 1999; Tzadik
SEE ALSO Michael Blake; Lounge Lizards; Medeski, Martin & Wood; Sex Mob

Andy Bey (voc, p)
American Song 2004; Minor Music

Barney Bigard (cl)
Barney Bigard & Art Hodes: Bucket's Got a Hole in It 1968; Delmark
SEE ALSO Louis Armstrong, Duke Ellington

David Binney (as)
Balance 2002; ACT
SEE ALSO Uri Caine, Joel Harrison

Luciano Biondini (acc)
Luciano Biondini & Javier Girotto: Terra Madre 2005; Enja
SEE ALSO Gabriele Mirabassi

Jim Black (dm)
Habyor (with Skuli Sverisson, Chris Speed) 2004; Winter & Winter
SEE ALSO Ellery Eskelin, Pachora, Tiny Bell Trio

Ed Blackwell (dm)
What It Is? (with Graham Haynes, Carlos Ward, Mark Helias) 1992; Enja
SEE ALSO Don Cherry, Ornette Coleman, Dewey Redman, Bob Stewart

Brian Blade (dm)
Perceptual 1999; Blue Note
SEE ALSO Chris Potter, Joshua Redman, Wayne Shorter, Mark Turner

Michael Blake (ts, ss)
Drift (with Steven Bernstein, Tony Scherr, Ben Allison, Matt Wilson, et al.) 1999;
    Intuition
SEE ALSO Ben Allison, Lounge Lizards

Ran Blake (p)
Ran Blake & Jeanne Lee: The Newest Sound Around 1961; RCA

Art Blakey (dm)
Moanin' (with Benny Golson, Lee Morgan, Bobby Timmons, et al.) 1958; Blue Note
Indestructible (with Lee Morgan, Cedar Walton, Wayne Shorter, et al.) 1964; Blue
    Note
Keystone 3 (live) (with Wynton Marsalis, Branford Marsalis, Bill Pierce, et al.) 1982;
    Concord
SEE ALSO Cannonball Adderley, Hank Mobley, Herbie Nichols

Terence Blanchard (tp)
Flow 2005; Blue Note
SEE ALSO McCoy Tyner

Carla Bley (p, org, ld)
Escalator over the Hill (with Gato Barbieri, Don Cherry, Paul Motian, John
    McLaughlin, et al.) (2 CD) 1968–71; ECM
Social Studies (with Carlos Ward, Gary Valente, Steve Swallow, et al.) 1980; ECM
Looking for America (with Lew Soloff, Gary Valente, Wolfgang Puschnig, Andy
    Sheppard, Steve Swallow, et al.) 2002; ECM
SEE ALSO Charlie Haden, Jazz Composers' Orchestra, Glen Moore, Hal Willner

Paul Bley (p, keyb)
Open, to Love 1972; ECM
SEE ALSO Jimmy Giuffre

Jane Ira Bloom (ss)
As One (with Fred Hersch) 1985; JMT / Winter & Winter

Hamiet Bluiett (bs, bcl)
The Calling (with D. D. Jackson, Kahil El'Zabar) 2001; Justin Time
SEE ALSO Lester Bowie, David Murray, World Saxophone Quartet

Arthur Blythe (as)
Nightsong (with Bob Stewart, Gust Tsilis, Chico Freeman, Arto Tuncboyaciyan, et
    al.) 1997; Clarity
SEE ALSO Joey Baron, Jack DeJohnette, Eric Dolphy, McCoy Tyner

Francy Boland (p, ld)
All Smiles (with Clarke-Boland Big Band) 1968; MPS
SEE ALSO Kenny Clarke

Stefano Bollani (p)
Smat Smat 2003; Label Bleu
SEE ALSO Enrico Rava

Richard Bona (b)
Munia—The Tale 2002; Universal
SEE ALSO Mino Cinelu, Mike Stern

Lester Bowie (tp)
The Great Pretender (with Hamiet Bluiett et al.) 1981; ECM
I Only Have Eyes for You (with Craig Harris, Steve Turre, Bob Stewart, et al.) 1985; ECM
SEE ALSO Art Ensemble of Chicago, Hamiet Bluiett

JoAnne Brackeen (p)
Turnaround (with Donald Harrison, Cecil McBee, Marvin "Smitty" Smith) 1992; Evidence

Anouar Brahem (oud)
Thimar (with Dave Holland, John Surman) 1988; ECM

Anthony Braxton (sax, cl, bcl, contrabass clarinet)
For Alto (solo) 1968; Delmark
Dortmund (Quartet) 1976 (with George Lewis, Dave Holland, Barry Altschul) 1976; Hat Hut Records
Charlie Parker Project (with Ari Brown, Joe Fonda, Misha Mengelberg, Paul Smoker, et al.) 1993; Hat
SEE ALSO Chick Corea, Circle, Gunter Hampel, Max Roach

Michael Brecker (ts)
Tales from the Hudson (with Stanley Turrentine, Dan Grolnick, Pat Metheny, et al.) 1996; Impulse
Nearness of You—The Ballad Book (with Herbie Hancock, Pat Metheny, Charlie Haden, Jack DeJohnette) 2001; Verve
SEE ALSO Randy Brecker, Marc Copland, John McLaughlin, Pat Metheny, Caecilie Norby, Jaco Pastorius, Dave Sanborn, Horace Silver, Kenny Wheeler

Randy Brecker (tp)
34th N Lex (with Michael Brecker, David Sanborn, Fred Wesley, et al.) 2004; ESC
SEE ALSO Paul Chambers, Larry Coryell, Jazz Composers' Orchestra, Herbie Mann, Caecilie Norby, Jaco Pastorius

Willem Breuker (sax, bcl, ld)
Hunger! (with Willem Breuker Kollektief) 1999; BVHaast
SEE ALSO Peter Brötzmann

Dee Dee Bridgewater (voc)
J'ai Deux Amours 2005; Emarcy

Till Brönner (tp)
That Summer 2004; Universal

Bob Brookmeyer (tb, ld)
Back Again 1978; Universal
Get Well Soon (with New Art Orchestra) 2004; Challenge
SEE ALSO Al Cohn, Stan Getz, Gerry Mulligan

Big Bill Broonzy (voc, g)
Treat Me Right 1951–52; Rykodisc

Peter Brötzmann (sax, cl)
Machine Gun (with Han Bennink, Willem Breuker, Evan Parker, et al.) 1968; FMP
Little Birds Have Fast Hearts No. 1 (with William Parker, Hamid Drake, Toshinori
    Kondo) 1997; FMP
SEE ALSO Globe Unity Orchestra, Manfred Schoof

Clifford Brown (tp)
The Clifford Brown Sextet in Paris (with Gigi Gryce, Jimmy Gourley, Pierre
    Michelot, et al.) 1953; Prestige
The Complete Clifford Brown on Emarcy (10 CD) 1954–56; Emarcy
SEE ALSO Max Roach, Sonny Rollins

Ray Brown (b)
Best of the Concord Years 1974–92; Concord
Super Bass (with Christian McBride, John Clayton) 1997; Telarc
SEE ALSO Louis Armstrong, Herb Ellis, Lionel Hampton, Coleman Hawkins, Milt
    Jackson, J. J. Johnson, Barney Kessel, Phineas Newborn, Oscar Peterson, Bud
    Powell, Sarah Vaughan, Ben Webster, Lester Young

Dave Brubeck (p)
Time Out (with Paul Desmond, Joe Morello, Eugene Wright) 1962; CBS
London Flat, London Sharp (with Bobby Militello, Michael Moore, Randy Jones,
    et al.) 2005; Telarc

Bill Bruford (dm)
Random Act of Happiness (with Earthworks) 2004; Voiceprint

Rainer Brüninghaus (keyb)
Continuum (with Markus Stockhausen and Fredy Studer) 1983; ECM

Jane Bunnett (ss, fl)
Red Dragonfly (with Larry Cramer, David Virelles, et al.) 2005; Blue Note

Kenny Burrell (g)
Midnight Blue (with Stanley Turrentine, Ray Barretto, et al.) 1963; Blue Note
SEE ALSO Chet Baker, Red Garland, Jay Hoggard, Jimmy Smith

Gary Burton (vib)
Throb (with Keith Jarrett) 1969–70; Rhino
Native Sense—The New Duets (with Chick Corea) 2003; Concord
SEE ALSO Larry Coryell, Stephane Grappelli, NDR Big Band, Steve Swallow,
    Eberhard Weber

Jaki Byard (p)
Blues for Smoke (solo) 1960; Candid
The Jaki Byard Experience (with Roland Kirk, Richard Davis, Alan Dawson) 1968;
    Prestige
SEE ALSO Stephane Grappelli, NDR Big Band, Steve Swallow, Eberhard Weber

Charlie Byrd (g)
Brazilian Byrd 1964; Columbia

Donald Byrd (tp)
Donald Byrd at the Halfnote Cafe (with Pepper Adams, Duke Pearson, Laymon
    Jackson, Lex Humphries) 1960; Blue Note
SEE ALSO Pepper Adams, Gigi Gryce, Jackie McLean, Sonny Rollins

Don Byron (cl)
Bug Music (with Steve Wilson, Craig Harris, Uri Caine, et al.) 1997; Nonesuch
Ivey Divey (with Jason Moran, Jack DeJohnette, et al.) 2005; Blue Note
SEE ALSO Bill Frisell, Craig Harris

Uri Caine (p)
Primal Light / Urlicht (with Joey Baron, Dave Binney, Dave Douglas, Mark
    Feldman, et al.) 1997; Winter & Winter
Live at the Village Vanguard (with Drew Gress, Ben Perowsky) 2004; Winter &
    Winter
SEE ALSO Don Byron, Dave Douglas

Candido (perc)
Candido 1956; Impulse

Harry Carney (bs, bcl)
SEE Duke Ellington, Benny Goodman

Terri Lyne Carrington (dm)
Jazz Is a Spirit (with Herbie Hancock, Gary Thomas, Kevin Eubanks, Bob Hurst,
    Wallace Roney, et al.) 2001; ACT
SEE ALSO Robin Eubanks, Caecilie Norby, Danilo Perez, Gary Thomas

Benny Carter (as, ts, tp, cl, ld)
Further Definitions (with Coleman Hawkins, Jo Jones, Phil Woods, Jimmy Garrison,
    Charles Rouse, et al.) 1961; GRP
Jazz Giant (with Ben Webster, Barney Kessel, Shelly Manne, et al.) 1957;
    Contemporary
SEE ALSO Coleman Hawkins, Charlie Parker, Art Tatum

Betty Carter (voc)
The Audience With (2 CD) 1979; Verve
I'm Yours, You're Mine 1996; Verve

James Carter (bs, ts, ss)
In Carterian Fashion (with Craig Taborn, Tani Tabbal, et al.) 1998; Atlantic

Live at Baker's Keyboard Lounge (with Ralphe Armstrong, Leonard King, et al.)
2001; Warner
SEE ALSO Regina Carter, Decoding Society, Julius Hemphill, Steve Turre

Regina Carter (viol)
Motor City Moments (with James Carter, Lewis Nash, Russell Malone, et al.) 2000;
Verve

Ron Carter (b)
Telephone (with Jim Hall) 1984; Concord
Mr. Bow-Tie (with Gonzalo Rubalcaba, Edwin Russell, Javon Jackson, Joe
Henderson, Steve Kroon) 1995; Blue Note
SEE ALSO Joey Baron, Miles Davis, Gil Evans, Dexter Gordon, Herbie Hancock,
Barry Harris, Donald Harrison, Bobby Hutcherson, Jazz Composers' Orchestra,
Frank Morgan, Sam Rivers, Horace Silver

Philip Catherine (g)
Summer Night (with Philippe Aerts, Joost van Schalk, Bert Joris) 2002; Dreyfus
SEE ALSO Charles Mingus

Dennis Chambers (dm)
Outbreak (with John Scofield, Michael and Randy Brecker, Jim Beard, Gary Willis)
2002; ESC

Paul Chambers (b)
Outbreak (with John Scofield, Michael and Randy Brecker, Jim Beard, Gary Willis)
2002; ESC
SEE ALSO John Coltrane, Miles Davis, Red Garland, Milt Jackson, Hank Mobley,
Oliver Nelson, Art Pepper, Bud Powell, Sonny Rollins

Pierre Charial (barrel organ)
SEE ALSO Michael Riessler

Ray Charles (voc, p, org)
What'd I Say 1952–58; Atlantic

Vladimir Chekasin (sax)
SEE *Ganelin Trio*

Don Cherry (tp, fl, perc)
The Avant-Garde (with John Coltrane) 1961; Atlantic
Complete Communion (with Gato Barbieri, Henry Grimes, Ed Blackwell) 1965;
Blue Note
El Corazón (with Ed Blackwell) 1982; ECM
SEE ALSO Carla Bley, Codona, Ornette Coleman, Heiner Goebbels, Jazz Composers'
Orchestra, Dewey Redman, Archie Shepp

Jon Christensen (dm)
SEE Jan Garbarek, Keith Jarrett, Dino Saluzzi, Tomasz Stanko, Bobo Stenson, Ralph
Towner

Charlie Christian (g)
The Genius of the Electric Guitar (4 CD) 1939/40; Columbia
SEE ALSO LesterYoung

Mino Cinelu (perc)
Cinelu (with Richard Bona et al.) 2000; Blue Thumb

Circle (band)
SEE Chick Corea

Kenny Clarke (dm, ld)
Clarke-Boland Big Band (RTE) 1969; RTE
SEE ALSO Modern Jazz Quartet

Stanley Clarke (b)
Journey to Love (with Chick Corea, Lenny White, John McLaughlin, et al.) 1975;
    Epic
SEE ALSO Chick Corea, Airto Moreira, Flora Purim

Buck Clayton (tp)
Copenhagen Concert (with Emmett Berry, Earle Warren, Buddy Tate, et al.) 1959;
    Steeple Chase
SEE ALSO Count Basie, Lester Young

Jay Clayton (voc)
Soundsongs (with Jerry Granelli) 1985; JMT / Winter & Winter

Clusone 3 (band)
Love Henry (Michael Moore, Ernst Reijseger, Han Bennink) 1996; Gramavision

Billy Cobham (dm)
Spectrum (with Jan Hammer, Tommy Bolin, Lee Sklar, et al.) 1973; Atlantic
SEE ALSO Donald Harrison, Mahavishnu Orchestra, John McLaughlin

Codona (band)
Codona, Vol. 1 (Don Cherry, Collin Walcott, Naná Vasconcelos) 1978; ECM

Al Cohn (ts)
Al Cohn Quartet (with Bob Brookmeyer, Mose Allison, Teddy Kotick, Nick
    Stabulas) 1956; Coral
Standards of Excellence (with Herb Ellis, Monty Budwig, Jimmie Smith) 1983;
    Concord
SEE ALSO Stan Getz

Holly Cole (voc)
Shade (with David Piltch, Aaron Davis) 2003; Tradition & Moderne

Nat King Cole (p, voc)
Live at Circle Room (with Nat King Cole Trio) 1946; Capitol
SEE ALSO Lester Young

Anthony Coleman (p, keyb)
Sephardic Tinge (with Joey Baron, Greg Cohen) 1995; Tzadik
SEE ALSO John Zorn

Ornette Coleman (as)
The Shape of Jazz to Come (with Billy Higgins, Don Cherry, Charlie Haden) 1959;
    Atlantic
Free Jazz (with Ed Blackwell, Don Cherry, Eric Dolphy, Charlie Haden, Billy
    Higgins, Freddie Hubhard, Scott LaFaro) 1960; Atlantic
Dancing in Your Head (with Charlie Ellerbee, Bern Nix, Jamaaladeen Tacuma,
    Ronald Shannon Jackson) 1975; Caravan Dream Productions
Tone Dialing (with Denardo Coleman, Badal Roy, Dave Bryant, et al.) 1995;
    Harmolodic/Universal
SEE ALSO Pat Metheny

Steve Coleman (as)
The Tao of Mad Phat: Fringe Zones (with Gene Lake, Ziggy Modeliste, George
    Porter, David Gilmore, Andy Milne, Josh Roseman, Roy Hargrove) 1993;
    Novus/RCA
On the Rising of 64 Paths (with Sean Rickman, Andy Milne, Anthony Tidd, Malik
    Mezzadri, et al.) 2003; Label Bleu
SEE ALSO Robin Eubanks

Buddy Collette (fl, cl, ts)
Man of Many Parts (with Gerald Wilson, Barney Kessel, Gerald Wiggins) 1956;
    Original Jazz Classics

Scott Colley (b)
Trouble in Paradise 2001; Palmetto
SEE ALSO Jim Hall, Andrew Hill, Rick Margitza, Chris Potter

Alice Coltrane (harp)
Journey in Satchidananda (with Pharoah Sanders, Charlie Haden, Cecil McBee,
    Rashied Ali, et al.) 1970; Impulse

John Coltrane (ts, ss)
Blue Train (with Lee Morgan, Curtis Fuller, Philly Joe Jones, et al.) 1957; Blue Note
Giant Steps (with Paul Chambers, Tommy Flanagan, Art Taylor, et al.) 1959;
    Atlantic
A Love Supreme (with Jimmy Garrison, Elvin Jones, McCoy Tyner) 1964; Impulse
Ascension (with Jimmy Garrison, Freddie Hubbard, Elvin Jones, Pharoah Sanders,
    Archie Shepp, et al.) 1965; Impulse
SEE ALSO Don Cherry, Miles Davis, Duke Ellington, Milt Jackson

Ravi Coltrane (ts)
In Flux (with Luis Perdomo, Drew Gress, E. J. Strickland) 2004; Savoy Jazz

Marc Copland (p)
Marc Copland And . . . (with John Abercrombie, Michael Brecker) 2002; HATology

Chick Corea (p, synth)
Circle-Paris Concert (with Barry Altschul, Anthony Braxton, Dave Holland) (2 CD)
    1971; ECM
Return to Forever (with Stanley Clarke, Joe Farrell, Airto Moreira, Flora Purim)
    1972; ECM
Inside Out (with John Patitucci, Dave Weckl, Eric Marienthal, Frank Gambale) ca.
    1990; GRP
SEE ALSO Gary Burton, Stanley Clarke, Miles Davis, Joe Farrell, Eddie Gomez, Herbie
    Hancock, Airto Moreira, John Patitucci, Wayne Shorter, Miroslav Vitous

Larry Coryell (g)
Introducing the 11th House (with Randy Brecker, Mike Mandel, Alphonse Mouzon)
    1972; Vanguard
SEE ALSO Charles Mingus, Bob Moses

Eddie Costa (p, vib)
Eddie Costa Quintet (with Art Farmer, Phil Woods) 1957; Mode
SEE ALSO Tal Farlow

Vincent Courtois (cello)
The Fitting Room (with Marc Ducret, Dominique Pifarély) 2000; Enja
SEE ALSO Louis Sclavis

Sylvie Courvoisier (p)
SEE Mark Feldman

Marilyn Crispell (p)
Nothing Ever Was, Anyway: The Music of Annette Peacock (with Paul Motian,
    Gary Peacock) 2004; ECM

Bob Crosby (ld)
Palesteena (with Yank Lawson, Billy Butterfield, Warren Smith, Eddie Miller, et al.)
    1937–42; Naxos

Gary Crosby (b, ld)
Migrations (with Nu Troop) 1997; Dune
See also Jazz Jamaica Allstars

Jamie Cullum (voc, p)
Twentysomething 2004; Verve

Andrew Cyrille (dm)
C/D/E (with Mark Dresser, Marty Ehrlich) 2001; Jazz Magnet
SEE ALSO Ahmed Abdul-Malik, Charlie Haden, Jazz Composers' Orchestra, Peter Kowald

Tadd Dameron (p, ld)
The Magic Touch of Tadd Dameron (with Bill Evans, Johnny Griffin, Charlie Shavers,
    Clark Terry, Julius Watkins, Philly Joe Jones, et al.) 1962; Original Jazz Classics
SEE ALSO Fats Navarro, Lennie Tristano

Eddie Daniels (ts, cl)
Breakthrough 1986; GRP

Olu Dara (co, g, voc)
In the World: From Natchez to New York 1998; Atlantic
SEE ALSO Cassandra Wilson

David Darling (cello)
Cycles (with Collin Walcott, Steve Kuhn, Jan Garbarek, Oscar Castro-Neves, Arild
    Andersen) 1981; ECM

Matt Darriau (cl)
Gambit (with Brad Shepik, Rufus Cappadocia, Seido Salifoski, Theodosii Spassov)
    2005; Enja

Carlo Actis Dato (as, ts, bs, cl)
Garibaldi 2003; Leo Records
SEE ALSO Italian Instabile Orchestra

Wolfgang Dauner (p, synth)
Solo Piano 1989; Mood
SEE ALSO Hans Koller, United Jazz Rock Ensemble

Anthony Davis (p)
Hemispheres (with Leo Smith, George Lewis) 1983; Gramavision
SEE ALSO George Lewis, David Murray

Eddie "Lockjaw" Davis (ts)
The Eddie "Lockjaw" Davis Cookbook Vol. 1–3 (with Shirley Scott, Jerome
    Richardson, George Duvivier, et al.) 1958; Prestige
SEE ALSO Johnny Griffin, J. J. Johnson, Jo Jones

Miles Davis (tp)
Birth of the Cool (with Kai Winding, Gerry Mulligan, Lee Konitz, Max Roach,
    et al.) 1949–50; Blue Note
Kind of Blue (with Bill Evans, John Coltrane, Cannonball Adderley, Paul Chambers,
    Jimmy Cobb) 1959; Columbia
Sketches of Spain (with Gil Evans and His Orchestra) 1959–60; Columbia
Miles Smiles (with Wayne Shorter, Herbie Hancock, Ron Carter, Tony Williams)
    1966; Columbia
Bitches Brew (with Joe Zawinul, Wayne Shorter, Airto Moreira, John McLaughlin,
    Chick Corea, Jack DeJohnette, Dave Holland, et al.) (2 CD) 1969–70; Columbia
Amandla (with Marcus Miller, Kenny Garrett, Omar Hakim, et al.) 1989; Warner
SEE ALSO Cannonball Adderley, Coleman Hawkins, Lee Konitz, Charlie Parker

Richard Davis (b)
Live at Sweet Basil (with Cecil Bridgewater, Ricky Ford, et al.) 1991; Evidence
SEE ALSO Gary Bartz, Jaki Byard, Eric Dolphy, Booker Ervin, Andrew Hill, Archie
    Shepp, Lucky Thompson

Wild Bill Davison (co)
Wild Bill in Denmark, Vol. 2 (with Papa Bue's Viking Jazz Band) 1974–75; Storyville

Decoding Society (band)
Live in Warsaw (with Ronald Shannon Jackson, James Carter, Jef Lee Johnson, Ngolle Pokossi) 1994; Knitting Factory
SEE ALSO Ronald Shannon Jackson

Joey DeFrancesco (org)
Incredible! (with Jimmy Smith, Paul Bollenbeck, Byron Landham) 2000; Concord
SEE ALSO Miles Davis, Didier Lockwood, Pat Martino, John McLaughlin, Jimmy Smith

Buddy DeFranco (cl)
Cooking the Blues 1955; Verve
SEE ALSO Lionel Hampton

Jack DeJohnette (dm)
Special Edition (with Arthur Blythe, David Murray, Peter Warren) 1979; ECM
SEE ALSO John Abercrombie, Michael Brecker, Don Byron, Miles Davis, Keith Jarrett, Charles Lloyd, Lyle Mays, Pat Metheny, Sonny Rollins, Gonzalo Rubalcaba, Wayne Shorter, Collin Walcott, Bennie Wallace, Ernie Watts, Kenny Wheeler, Joe Zawinul

Christopher Dell (vib)
D.R.A. Real (with Christian Ramond, Felix Astor) 2004; Edition Niehler Werft
SEE ALSO Theo Jörgensmann, Klaus König

Barbara Dennerlein (org)
Straight Ahead (with Ray Anderson, Mitch Watkins, Ronnie Burrage) 1988; Enja

Paul Desmond (as)
Easy Living (with Jim Hall et al.) 1963–65; Bluebird
SEE ALSO Dave Brubeck

Roberto Di Gioia (p, keyb)
Marsmobil: Strange World (with Till Brönner, Klaus Doldinger, Nils Landgren, Frank Möbus, et al.) 2003; ACT
SEE ALSO Johannes Enders

Al DiMeola (g)
Elegant Gypsy (with Jan Hammer, Barry Miles, Anthony Jackson, Lenny White, Steve Gadd, Mingo Lewis) 1976; Columbia
Flesh on Flesh (with Gumbi Ortiz, Mario Parmisano, Gonzalo Rubalcaba, Anthony Jackson, et al.) 2002; Telarc
SEE ALSO John McLaughlin

Dirty Dozen Brass Band (band)
Funeral for a Friend 2004; Ropeadope

Bill Dixon (tp, flh)
Berlin Abbozzi (with Matthias Bauer, Klaus Koch, Tony Oxley) 2000; FMP

DJ Logic (elec, tt)
The Anomaly (with John Medeski et al.) 2002; Ropeadope
SEE ALSO Wayne Horvitz

DJ Spooky (Paul D. Miller) (elec, tt)
Drums of Death 2005; Thirsty Ear

Johnny Dodds (cl)
Paramount Recordings, Vol. 2 1926–29; Black Swan
SEE ALSO King Oliver

Eric Dolphy (as, fl, bcl)
Outward Bound (with Freddie Hubbard, Jaki Byard, Roy Haynes, et al.) 1960;
     Original Jazz Classics
At the Five Spot Vols. 1 and 2 (with Booker Little, Mal Waldron, Richard Davis, Ed
     Blackwell) 1961; Prestige
Out to Lunch (with Richard Davis, Freddie Hubbard, Bobby Hutcherson, Tony
     Williams) 1964; Blue Note
SEE ALSO Andrew Hill, Booker Little, Oliver Nelson, George Russell, Ornette
     Coleman

Chano Dominguez (p)
Hecho a Mano 2002; Sunnyside

Lou Donaldson (as)
Blues Walk (with Ray Barretto) 1958; Blue Note

Kenny Dorham (tp)
Una Mas (with Joe Henderson, Herbie Hancock, Butch Warren, Tony Williams)
     1963; Blue Note
SEE ALSO Joe Henderson, Andrew Hill, J. J. Johnson, Abbey Lincoln

Bob Dorough (voc)
Who's on First (live) (with Dave Frishberg) 1999; Blue Note

Jimmy Dorsey (as, cl)
SEE ALSO Bix Beiderbecke, Red Norvo

Tommy Dorsey (tb, ld)
Yes, Indeed! (with Buddy Rich, Ziggy Elman, Johnny Mince, et al.) 1939–45;
     Bluebird/RCA

Dave Douglas (tp)
Charms of the Night Sky (with Guy Klucevsek, Mark Feldman, Greg Cohen) 1998;
     Winter & Winter

Strange Liberation (with Bill Frisell, Chris Potter, Uri Caine, James Genus, Clarence
     Penn) 2003; Bluebird
SEE ALSO Misha Mengelberg, Tiny Bell Trio, John Zorn

Mark Dresser (b)
Aquifer (with Matthias Ziegler, Denman Maroney) 2002; Cryptogramophone
SEE ALSO Arcado String Trio, Andrew Cyrille

Paquito D'Rivera (as, cl)
Portraits of Cuba 1996; Chesky
The Clarinetist, Vol. 1 2000; Peregrina
SEE ALSO Omar Sosa

Marc Ducret (g)
Qui Parle? (with Bruno Chevillon, Éric Échampard, Dominique Pifarély, et al.)
     2003; Sketch
SEE ALSO Daniel Humair, Christof Lauer, Tim Berne, Vincent Courtois

Lajos Dudas (cl)
Talk of the Town 2002; Doublemoon

George Duke (keyb)
Cool (with Flora Purim, Philip Bailey, et al.) 2000; Warner

Billy Eckstine (ld, voc)
Billy's Best! 1958; Mercury

Harry "Sweets" Edison (tp)
Edison, Davis & Boone with Leonardo Pedersen's Jazzkapel 1977; Storyville
SEE ALSO Count Basie, Jo Jones, Anita O'Day, Buddy Rich, Art Tatum

Teddy Edwards (ts)
Midnight Creeper (with Virgil Jones, Buster Williams, et al.) 1997; High Note
SEE ALSO Milt Jackson

Marty Ehrlich (ss, as, cl, bcl, fl)
Line on Love (with Craig Taborn, Michael Formanek, Billy Drummond) 2003;
     Palmetto
SEE ALSO Andrew Cyrille, Julius Hemphill, Andrew Hill, Bobby Previte

Roy Eldridge (tp)
Montreux 1977 (live) (with Oscar Peterson, Niels-Henning Ørsted Pedersen, Bobby
     Durham) 1977; Original Jazz Classics
SEE ALSO Jo Jones, Teddy Wilson, Lester Young

Kurt Elling (voc)
Man in the Air (with Stefon Harris, Laurence Hobgood, et al.) 2003; Blue Note
SEE ALSO Bob Mintzer

Duke Ellington (p, ld)

Early Ellington (with Barney Bigard, Harry Carney, Johnny Hodges, Bubber Miley, Joe Norton, et al.) (3 CD) 1926-31; MCA/GRP

The Blanton/Webster Years (with Barney Bigard, Jimmy Blanton, Lawrence Brown, Rex Stewart, Billy Strayhorn, Ben Webster, et al.) (3 CD) 1940–42; RCA Bluebird

Ellington at Newport (with Paul Gonsalves, Harry Carney, Jimmy Grissomu, et al.) 1956; Columbia

Duke Ellington & John Coltrane (with Jimmy Garrison, Elvin Jones, Aaron Bell, Sam Woodyard) 1962; Impulse

The Intimate Ellington (with Cat Anderson, Lawrence Brown, Johnny Hodges, Harry Carney, Paul Gonsalves, John Lamb, Rufus "Speedy" Jones) 1969–71; Original Jazz Classics

70th Birthday Concert (with Cootie Williams, Johnny Hodges, Wild Bill Davis, Cat Anderson, et al.) 1969; Blue Note

SEE ALSO Louis Armstrong, Ella Fitzgerald

Herb Ellis (g)

Nothing But the Blues (with Roy Eldrigde, Stan Getz, Ray Brown, Stan Levey) 1957; Verve

SEE ALSO Louis Armstrong, Al Cohn, Coleman Hawkins, Oscar Peterson

James Emery (g)

Luminous Cycles 2001; Between the Lines

SEE ALSO String Trio of New York

Johannes Enders (ts)

Home Ground (with Roberto Di Gioia, Thomas Stabenow, Guido May) 1999; Enja

Enders Room: Human Radio (with Rebekka Bakken, Roberto Di Gioia, Joo Kraus, et al.) 2004; Enja

Sidsel Endresen (voc)

Undertow (with Bugge Wesseltoft, Nils Petter Molvaer, Audun Kleive, et al.) 2000; Jazzland

SEE ALSO Trygve Seim

Peter Erskine (dm)

Juni (with Palle Danielsson, John Taylor) 1997; ECM

SEE ALSO Jan Garbarek, Marc Johnson, Stanley Jordan, Jaco Pastorius

Booker Ervin (ts)

The Blues Book (with Carmell Jones, Gildo Mahones, Richard Davis, Alan Dawson) 1964; Original Jazz Classics

SEE ALSO Charles Mingus

Ellery Eskelin (ts)

Ten (with Andrea Parkin, Jim Black, Marc Ribot, et al.) 2004; hatOLOGY

SEE ALSO Rabih Abou-Khalil, Daniel Humair

Kevin Eubanks (g)
Turning Point (with Dave Holland, Marvin "Smitty" Smith) 1991; Blue Note
SEE ALSO Terri Lyne Carrington, Oliver Lake

Robin Eubanks (tb)
Different Perspectives (with Steve Coleman, Slide Hampton, Terri Lyne Carrington,
    Jeff "Tain" Watts, David Gilmore, et al.) 1988; JMT / Winter & Winter
SEE ALSO Dave Holland, Hank Roberts, Marvin "Smitty" Smith

Bill Evans (p, keyb)
Sunday at the Village Vanguard (with Scott LaFaro, Paul Motian) 1961; Riverside /
    Original Jazz Classics
Intuition (with Eddie Gomez) 1974; Fantasy / Original Jazz Classics
SEE ALSO Chet Baker, Tadd Dameron, Miles Davis, Marian McPartland, Oliver
    Nelson, Tony Scott

Bill Evans (ts, ss)
Big Fun (with Vinnie Colaiuta, Ricky Peterson, Hiram Bullock, et al.) 2002; ESC

Gil Evans (p, ld)
Gil Evans & Ten (with Jimmy Cleveland, Steve Lacy, Lee Konitz, et al.) 1957;
    Prestige / Original Jazz Classics
Out of the Cool (with Ron Carter, Elvin Jones, Jimmy Knepper, et al.) 1960;
    Impulse
Gil Evans Orchestra Plays the Music of Jimi Hendrix (with Howard Johnson, David
    Sanborn, Marvin "Hannibal" Peterson, John Abercrombie, et al.) 1974–75;
    Bluebird/RCA
SEE ALSO Miles Davis

Tal Farlow (g)
The Swinging Guitar of Tal Farlow (with Eddie Costa, Vinnie Burke) 1956; Verve
SEE ALSO Red Norvo

Art Farmer (tp, flh)
Meet the Jazztet (with Curtis Fuller, Benny Golson, McCoy Tyner, et al.) 1960; MCA
Blame It on My Youth (with James Williams, Rufus Reid, Victor Lewis) 1988;
    Contemporary
SEE ALSO Eddie Costa, Horace Silver

Joe Farrell (fl, ts)
Outback (with Elvin Jones, Chick Corea, Airto Moreira) 1971; CTI
SEE ALSO Ray Barretto, Elvin Jones

Pierre Favre (dm)
Singing Drums (with Paul Motian, Fredy Studer, Naná Vasconcelos) 1984; ECM
Ulrichsberg (with Irène Schweizer)
SEE Albert Mangelsdorff

Mark Feldman (viol)
Music for Piano and Violin (with Sylvie Courvoisier) 1999; Avant
SEE ALSO John Abercrombie, Arcado String Trio, Karl Berger, Uri Caine, Dave
    Douglas, Masada String Trio, Josh Roseman

Maynard Ferguson (tp, tb, ld)
One More Trip to Birdland (with Tom Garling, Matt Wallace, et al.) 1996; Concord
SEE ALSO Stan Kenton

Glenn Ferris (tb)
Chrominance (with Jeff Boudreaux et al.) 2001; Enja
SEE ALSO Henri Texier

Clare Fischer (p, org)
Just Me 1995; Concord

Ella Fitzgerald (voc)
Sings the Rodgers and Hart Song Book (2 CD) 1956; Verve
Sings the Duke Ellington Song Book (3 CD) (with Duke Ellington and His
    Orchestra) 1957; Verve
Mack the Knife—Ella in Berlin (with Jim Hall et al.) 1960; Verve
Newport Jazz Festival: Live at Carnegie Hall 1973; Columbia
SEE ALSO Louis Armstrong, Chick Webb

David Fiuczynski (g)
Amandala (with Daniel Sadownick, Gene Lake, Fima Ephron) 2001; FuzeLicious

Five Elements (band)
SEE ALSO Steve Coleman

Tommy Flanagan (p)
Jazz Poet (with George Mraz, Kenny Washington) 1989; Timeless
SEE ALSO Benny Bailey, John Coltrane, Curtis Fuller, Jo Jones, Wes Montgomery, Joe
    Newman, Sonny Rollins

Ricky Ford (ts)
Hot Brass (with Lew Soloff, Claudio Roditi, Steve Turre, Christian McBride, Carl
    Allen, Danilo Perez) 1991; Candid
SEE ALSO Charles Mingus

Al Foster (dm)
SEE ALSO Tony Lakatos, Carmen McRae, Frank Morgan, McCoy Tyner

Aretha Franklin (voc)
Lady Soul 1968; Atlantic/Rhino

Chico Freeman (ts)
Peaceful Heart, Gentle Spirit (with James Newton, Kenny Kirkland, et al.) 1980;
    Contemporary
SEE ALSO Arthur Blythe, Kip Hanrahan, Wynton Marsalis, Cecil McBee

Paolo Fresu (tp, flh)
Metamorfosi (with Nguyên Lê, Furio Di Castri, Roberto Gatto, Antonello Salis)
    1998; BMG
SEE ALSO Ngûyen Lê, Enrico Rava, Jens Thomas

Erik Friedlander (voc)
Quake (with Stomu Takeishi, Satoshi Takeishi, et al.) 2002; Cryptogramophone
SEE ALSO Julius Hemphill, Masada String Trio, Ned Rothenberg

David Friedman (vib)
Birds of a Feather 2000; Traumton

David Friesen (b)
Three to Get Ready (with Clark Terry, Bud Shank) 1994; ITM

Bill Frisell (g)
Have a Little Faith (with Don Byron, Guy Klucevsek, Kermit Driscoll, Joey Baron)
    1992; Nonesuch
The Intercontinentals (with Jenny Scheinman, Greg Leisz, Vinicius Cantuaria, et al.)
    2003; Nonesuch
SEE ALSO Joey Baron, Dave Douglas, Wayne Horvitz, Marc Johnson, Paul Motian,
    Naked City, Bobby Previte, Hank Roberts, John Zorn

Fred Frith (g)
Traffic Continues (with Ensemble Modern, Ikue Mori, Zeena Parkins) 2000; Winter
    & Winter
SEE ALSO Heiner Goebbels, Henry Kaiser, Peter Kowald, Naked City, Aki Takase

Curtis Fuller (tb)
Blues-ette, Pt. 2 (with Benny Golson, Tommy Flanagan, Ray Drummond, Al
    Harewood) 1993; Savoy
SEE ALSO John Coltrane, Art Farmer

Diamanda Galás (voc)
La Serpenta Canta 2002; Mute
SEE ALSO Peter Kowald

Frank Gambale (g)
SEE ALSO Chick Corea

Ganelin Trio (band)
Con Affetto (with Vyacheslav Ganelin, Vladimir Tarasow, Vladimir Chekasin) 1983;
    Golden Years of New Jazz / Leo Records

Jan Garbarek (ts, ss)
Afric Pepperbird (with Jon Christensen, Terje Rypdal, Arild Andersen) 1970; ECM
Star (with Miroslav Vitous, Peter Erskine) 1990; ECM
In Praise of Dreams (with Manu Katché, Kim Kashkashian) 2004; ECM
SEE ALSO David Darling, Keith Jarrett, Ralph Towner, Miroslav Vitous, Eberhard
    Weber, Kenny Wheeler

Renaud Garcia-Fons (b)
Oriental Bass 1997; Enja
SEE ALSO Michel Godard, Jean-Louis Matinier

Red Garland (p)
Red Garland Revisited! (with Paul Chambers, Art Taylor, Kenny Burrell) 1959;
    Prestige / Original Jazz Classics

Erroll Garner (p)
Concert by the Sea (with Eddie Calhoun, Denzil Best) 1955; Columbia
SEE ALSO Charlie Parker

Kenny Garrett (as)
Standard of Language (with Chris Dave, Charnett Moffett, Vernell Brown) 2003; Warner
SEE ALSO Miles Davis, Freddie Hubbard, Mike Stern

Jimmy Garrison (b)
SEE Benny Carter, John Coltrane, Duke Ellington, Elvin Jones

Stan Getz (ts)
The Brothers (with Zoot Sims, Al Cohn, Brew Moore, Allen Eager) 1949–52;
    Original Jazz Classics
Stan Getz at the Shrine (with Bob Brookmeyer, John Williams, Bill Anthony, Art
    Mardigan) 1954; Norgran
Getz/Gilberto (with Astrud Gilberto, João Gilberto, Antonio Carlos Jobim, et al.)
    1963; Verve
SEE ALSO Laurindo Almeida, Herb Ellis, Al Haig, Lionel Hampton

Dizzy Gillespie (tp, voc, ld)
The Complete RCA Victor Recordings: 1937–1949 (2 CD) (with Teddy Hill and
    His Orchestra, Lionel Hampton, Don Byas, Milt Jackson, Ray Brown, James
    Moody, Cecil Payne, Chano Pozo, Yusef Lateef, Miles Davis, Fats Navarro,
    Kai Winding, J. J. Johnson, Charlie Parker, Lennie Tristano, Billy Bauer, Shelly
    Manne, et al.); RCA Victor
School Days (with Joe Carroll, Milt Jackson, Wynton Kelly, Percy Heath, et al.)
    1951; Savoy
At Newport (with Al Grey, Billy Mitchell, Mary Lou Williams) 1957; Verve
Max & Dizzy, Paris 1989 (with Max Roach) 1989; A&M
SEE ALSO Charlie Parker

Jimmy Giuffre (cl, ts)
1961 (with Paul Bley, Steve Swallow) 1961; ECM
SEE ALSO Shelly Manne

Globe Unity Orchestra (big band)
Globe Unity 67 & 70 (with Alexander von Schlippenbach, Peter Brötzmann, Han
    Bennink, Fred van Hove, et al.) 1967–70; Atavistic
Globe Unity Orchestra 2002 (live) (with Alexander von Schlippenbach, Peter
    Brötzmann, Manfred Schoof, Evan Parker, Paul Rutherford, et al.) 2002; Intakt

Michel Godard (tuba, serpent)
Castel Del Monte (with Gianluigi Trovesi, Pino Minafra, Jean-Louis Matinier, Renaud Garcia-Fons, et al.) 2002; Enja
See also Rabih Abou-Khalil, Luciano Biondini, Vincent Courtois, Christof Lauer, Gabriele Mirabassi

Heiner Goebbels (keyb)
Der Mann im Fahrstuhl (with Don Cherry, Fred Frith, George Lewis, Arto Lindsay, et al.) 1988; ECM

Larry Goldings (org, p)
Sweet Science (with Peter Bernstein, Bill Stewart) 2002; Palmetto
See also Javon Jackson

Jean Goldkette (ld)
Jean Goldkette Bands 1924–1929; Timeless

Eddie Gomez (b)
Next Future (with Chick Corea, Rick Margitza, Lenny White, Jeremy Steig, et al.) 1992; Stretch
See also Bill Evans, Jazz Composers' Orchestra, Bennie Wallace

Paul Gonsalves (ts)
Paul Gonsalves Meets Earl Hines (with Earl Hines, Al Hall, Jo Jones) 1972; Black Lion
See also Duke Ellington, Johnny Hodges

Jerry Gonzalez (perc, tp)
Rumba Para Monk (with Carter Jefferson, Larry Willis, et al.) 1988; Sunnyside
See also Giovanni Hidalgo

Benny Goodman (cl, ld)
The Complete RCA Victor Small Group Recordings (with Lionel Hampton, Teddy Wilson, Gene Krupa, Dave Tough) (3 CD) 1935–39; RCA Victor
Carnegie Hall Concert (with Count Basie, Harry Carney, Buck Clayton, Bobby Hackett, Lionel Hampton, Johnny Hodges, Harry James, Cootie Williams, Teddy Wilson, Lester Young, et al.) (2 CD) 1938; CBS
See also Billie Holiday, Red Norvo, Bessie Smith

Dexter Gordon (ts)
Go! (with Sonny Clark, Billy Higgins, Butch Warren) 1962; Blue Note
The Other Side of Round Midnight (with Ron Carter, Herbie Hancock, Palle Mikkelborg, et al.) 1985; Blue Note

Stephane Grappelli (viol)
Limehouse Blues (with Barney Kessel, Nini Rosso, Michel Gaudry, Jean-Louis Viale) 1969; Black Lion
Paris Encounter (with Gary Burton) 1976; Atlantic
See also Django Reinhardt

Frank Gratkowski (as)
Facio (with Wolter Wierbos, Dieter Manderscheid, Gerry Hemingway) 2004; Leo
SEE ALSO Gerry Hemingway

Benny Green (p)
Bluebird (with Russell Malone) 2004; Telarc
SEE ALSO J. J. Johnson

Grant Green (g)
Matador (with McCoy Tyner, Bob Cranshaw, Elvin Jones) 1964; Blue Note

Johnny Griffin (ts)
Tough Tenors Back Again! (with Eddie "Lockjaw" Davis, Kenny Washington, et al.)
    1984; Storyville
SEE ALSO Tadd Dameron, Niels-Henning Ørsted Pedersen

Gigi Gryce (as)
Gigi Gryce and the Jazz Lab Quintet (with Donald Byrd, Art Taylor, et al.) 1957;
    Riverside / Original Jazz Classics
SEE ALSO Clifford Brown

Trilok Gurtu (perc, dr)
Broken Rhythms 2004; Exil
SEE ALSO John McLaughlin

Mats Gustafsson (bs)
Windows: The Music of Steve Lacy 1999; Blue Chopsticks
SEE ALSO Barry Guy

Barry Guy (b, ld)
Inscape . . . Tableaux (with Mats Gustafsson, Evan Parker, Marilyn Crispell, Herb
    Robertson, et al.) 2000; Intakt
SEE ALSO London Jazz Composers' Orchestra, Evan Parker

Bobby Hackett (tp)
Hello Louis (with Steve Lacy et al.) 1964; Epic
SEE ALSO Benny Goodman

Charlie Haden (b)
Liberation Music Orchestra (with Carla Bley, Sam Brown, Gato Barbieri, Andrew
    Cyrille, et al.) 1969; Impulse
Quartet West (with Ernie Watts, Alan Broadbent, Billy Higgins) 1986; Polygram
Land of the Sun (with Gonzalo Rubalcaba) 2003; Verve
SEE ALSO Geri Allen, Michael Brecker, Ornette Coleman, Alice Coltrane, Jim Hall,
    Keith Jarrett, Jazz Composers' Orchestra, Pat Metheny, Paul Motian, Dewey
    Redman, Gonzalo Rubalcaba

Al Haig (p)
Trio and Sextet (with Stan Getz, Wardell Gray, et al.) 1954; Original Jazz Classics

Edmond Hall (cl)
Profoundly Blue (with Billie Holiday, Lionel Hampton, Coleman Hawkins, et al.) MCA
SEE ALSO Art Tatum

Jim Hall (g)
Jim Hall & Basses (with Dave Holland, Charlie Haden, Scott Colley, George Mraz, Christian McBride) 2001; Telarc
SEE ALSO Ron Carter, Paul Desmond, Ella Fitzgerald, Quincy Jones, Lee Konitz, Michel Petrucciani, Sonny Stitt

Scott Hamilton (ts)
Red Door: Remember Zoot Sims (with Bucky Pizzarelli) 1995; Concord

Gunter Hampel (vib, fl, cl, bcl, p)
The 8th of July 1969 (with Jeanne Lee, Anthony Braxton, et al.) 1969; Birth
Legendary (with Alexander von Schlippenbach, Manfred Schoof, Pierre Courbois, et al.) 1998; Birth

Lionel Hampton (vib, p, dm, ld)
Air Mail Special (with Oscar Peterson, Ray Brown, Buddy Rich, Buddy DeFranco) 1953; Clef
Hamp and Getz (with Stan Getz, Lou Levy, Leroy Vinnegar, Shelly Manne) 1955; Verve
As Time Goes By (with Svend Asmussen, Niels-Henning Ørsted Pedersen, Ed Thigpen) 1978; Sonet
SEE ALSO Benny Goodman, Edmond Hall, Jimmy Scott

Slide Hampton (tb)
Roots (with Clifford Jordan, Cedar Walton, Billy Higgins) 1985; Criss Cross
SEE ALSO Philly Joe Jones

Herbie Hancock (p, synth)
Maiden Voyage (with Ron Carter, George Coleman, Freddie Hubbard, Tony Williams) 1965; Blue Note
Thrust (with Benny Maupin, Bill Summers, et al.) 1974; Columbia
Gershwin's World (with Chick Corea, Joni Mitchell, Stevie Wonder, et al.) 1998; Verve
SEE ALSO Michael Brecker, Terri Lyne Carrington, Miles Davis, Kenny Dorham, Dexter Gordon, Grachan Moncur III, Airto Moreira, Jaco Pastorius, Sam Rivers, Steve Turre

Kip Hanrahan (ld, producer)
Desire Develops an Edge (with Jack Bruce, Chico Freeman, Arto Lindsay, Steve Swallow, et al.) 1982; American Clavé

Roy Hargrove (tp, flh)
Approaching Standards (with Ron Blake, Marc Cary, Rodney Whitaker, Gregory Hutchinson) 1994; Verve
SEE ALSO Steve Coleman

Tom Harrell (tp)
Live at the Village Vanguard (with Jimmy Greene, Quincy Davis, et al.) 2001;
    Bluebird
SEE ALSO Mark Murphy

Barry Harris (p)
Magnificient (with Ron Carter, Leroy Williams) 1969; Prestige / Original Jazz
    Classics
SEE ALSO Thad Jones, Lee Morgan

Bill Harris (tb)
Bill Harris and Friends (with Ben Webster, Jimmy Rowles, Red Mitchell, et al.)
    1957; Original Jazz Classics

Craig Harris (tb)
Shelter (with Pheeroan AkLaff, Don Byron, Anthony Cox, et al.) 1986; JMT /
    Winter & Winter
SEE ALSO Lester Bowie, Don Byron

Eddie Harris (sax)
Eddie Who 1986; Timeless
SEE ALSO Les McCann

Stefon Harris (vib)
Evolution (with Marc Cary, Casey Benjamin, Daryl Hall, et al.) 2003; Blue Note
SEE ALSO Kurt Elling

Donald Harrison (as)
Heroes (with Billy Cobham, Ron Carter, et al.) 2002; Nagel-Heyer
SEE ALSO JoAnne Brackeen, Rodney Jones

Joel Harrison (g)
So Long 2nd Street (with Dave Binney et al.) 2002–04; ACT

Antonio Hart (as)
All We Need (with Jimmy Heath, Lonnie Plaxico, Billy Kilson, Nasheet Waits, et al.)
    2003; Downtown
SEE ALSO Dave Holland

Gabriele Hasler (voc)
Flow 2004; Foolish Music

Jon Hassell (tp)
Fourth World, Vol. 1: Possible Musics (with Brian Eno) 1980; EG

Coleman Hawkins (ts)
Body & Soul (with Benny Carter, J. C. Higginbotham, Hank Jones, Fats Navarro,
    Max Roach, Charlie Shavers, et al.) 1939–56; RCA Bluebird

Hollywood Stampede (with Howard McGhee, Vic Dickenson, Miles Davis, et al.)
1944; Capitol
Coleman Hawkins Encounters Ben Webster (with Ray Brown, Herb Ellis, Oscar
Peterson, Ben Webster, et al.) 1957; Verve
SEE ALSO Benny Carter, Edmond Hall, Max Roach, Bessie Smith

Roy Haynes (dm)
Fountain of Youth (with Marcus Strickland, John Sullivan, et al.) 2002; Dreyfus
SEE ALSO Bud Powell, Sonny Rollins, McCoy Tyner

Percy Heath (b)
SEE ALSO Milt Jackson, Modern Jazz Quartet, Sonny Rollins, Sarah Vaughan

Thomas Heberer (tp)
What a Wonderful World (with Dieter Manderscheid) 2001; Jazz Haus Musik
SEE ALSO ICP Orchestra

Gerry Hemingway (dm)
Double Blues Crossing (with Frank Gratkowski, Wolter Wierbos, Kermit Driscoll,
et al.) 2005; Between the Lines
SEE ALSO Frank Gratkowski

Julius Hemphill (as, ss)
Fat Man and the Hard Blues (with Marty Ehrlich, James Carter, et al.) 1991; Black
Saint
One Atmosphere (with Erik Friedlander, Marty Ehrlich, Tim Berne, Pheeroan
AkLaff, et al.) 2003; Tzadik
SEE ALSO World Saxophone Quartet

Fletcher Henderson (p, ld)
1926–1927: Classics (several titles available, various years)

Joe Henderson (ts)
Page One (with Kenny Dorham, McCoy Tyner, Butch Warren, Pete La Roca) 1963;
Blue Note
Lush Life: The Music of Billy Strayhorn (with Wynton Marsalis, Christian McBride,
et al.) 1991; Verve
SEE ALSO Kenny Dorham, Andrew Hill, Lee Konitz, Lee Morgan, Flora Purim,
Horace Silver

Jimi Hendrix (g)
Are You Experienced? 1967; Universal

Matthew Herbert (ld)
Goodbye Swingtime 2003; Accidental

Peter Herbolzheimer (tb, ld)
Masterpieces 1972–77; MPS

Woody Herman (d, as, ss, voc, ld)
Thundering Herds 1945–1947 (with Flip Phillips, Bill Harris, et al.) Columbia
The Raven Speaks (with Harold Danko, Gregory Herbert, et al.) 1972; Fantasy

Fred Hersch (p)
Trio + 2 (with Nasheet Waits, Drew Gress, Ralph Alessi, Tony Malaby) 2003;
    Palmetto
SEE ALSO Jane Ira Bloom, Toots Thielemans

Giovanni Hidalgo (perc)
Time Shifter (with Jerry Gonzalez et al.) 1995; Sony

Billy Higgins (dm)
Billy Higgins Quintet (with Harold Land, Cedar Walton, et al.) 1997; Evidence
SEE ALSO Gary Bartz, Ornette Coleman, Dexter Gordon, Charlie Haden, Slide
    Hampton, Milt Jackson, Charles Lloyd, Lee Morgan, Art Pepper, Joshua
    Redman, Cedar Walton

Andrew Hill (p)
Point of Departure (with Eric Dolphy, Joe Henderson, Richard Davis, Tony
    Williams, Kenny Dorham) 1964; Blue Note
Dusk (with Greg Tardy, Marty Ehrlich, Scott Colley, Billy Drummond) 2000;
    Palmetto

Earl Hines (p, ld)
Blues in Thirds 1965; Black Lion
SEE ALSO Paul Gonsalves

Milt Hinton (b)
SEE Joe Venuti

Johnny Hodges (as, ss)
Everybody Knows (with Cat Anderson, Ray Nance, Harold Ashby, Paul Gonsalves,
    Lawrence Brown) 1965; GRP/Impulse
SEE ALSO Duke Ellington, Benny Goodman, Charlie Parker, Teddy Wilson

Jay Hoggard (vib)
The Fountain (with Kenny Burrell, James Weidman) 1991; Muse

Billie Holiday (voc)
Lady Day—The Complete Billie Holiday on Columbia 1933–1944 (10 CD) (with
    Benny Goodman & His Orchestra, Teddy Wilson & His Orchestra, Count
    Basie & His Orchestra, et al.) Columbia
All or Nothing at All 1955; Verve
Lady in Satin 1958; Columbia
SEE ALSO Edmond Hall, Teddy Wilson

Dave Holland (b, vc)
Not for Nothin' (with Robin Eubanks, Chris Potter, Steve Nelson, Billy Kilson)
2000; ECM
Overtime (with Robin Eubanks, Duane Eubanks, Chris Potter, Antonio Hart, Steve
Nelson, Josh Roseman, Billy Kilson, Taylor Haskins, Gary Smulyan, Jonathan
Arons, Alex Spiagin) 2002; Sunnyside
SEE ALSO John Abercrombie, Karl Berger, Anouar Brahem, Anthony Braxton, Chick
Corea, Miles Davis, Kevin Eubanks, Jim Hall, Jeanne Lee, Chris Potter, Collin
Walcott, Kenny Wheeler

Richard "Groove" Holmes (org)
Groove (with Les McCann, Ben Webster, et al.) 1961; Pacific

John Lee Hooker (g)
This Is Hip 1980; Charly
The Healer 2000; EMI

Paul Horn (fl)
Inside the Taj Mahal 1968; Rykodisc

Shirley Horn (voc)
You're My Thrill (with Wynton Marsalis, Russell Malone, et al.) 2000; Verve

Wayne Horvitz (keyb)
Film Music 1998–2001 (with Bill Frisell, DJ Logic, Julian Priester, et al.) Tzadik
SEE ALSO Naked City, Bobby Previte

Freddie Hubbard (tp)
Open Sesame (with Sam Jones, McCoy Tyner, et al.) 1960; Blue Note
Freddie Hubbard / Woody Shaw Sextet—Double Take (with Carl Allen, Cecil
McBhee, Kenny Garrett, Mulgrew Miller) 1985; Blue Note
SEE ALSO Eric Dolphy, Herbie Hancock, Bobby Hutcherson, Quincy Jones, Oliver
Nelson, Sam Rivers, McCoy Tyner

Daniel Humair (dm)
Liberté Surveillé (with Marc Ducret, Bruno Chevillon, Ellery Eskelin) (2 CD) 2001; Sketch
SEE ALSO Phil Woods

Alberta Hunter (voc)
Songs We Taught Your Mother 1961; Original Blues Classics

Charlie Hunter (g)
Friends Seen and Unseen (with Derrek Phillips, John Ellis) 2004; Ropeadope

Zakir Hussain (perc)
SEE ALSO John McLaughlin, Shakti, L. Shankar

Bobby Hutcherson (vib)
Components (with Joe Chambers, Herbie Hancock, Freddie Hubbard, James
    Spaulding, Ron Carter) 1965; Blue Note
SEE ALSO Eric Dolphy, Jackie McLean, McCoy Tyner

Abdullah Ibrahim (Dollar Brand) (p)
African Magic 2002; Enja

ICP Orchestra (band)
Jubilee Varia (with Misha Mengelberg, Michael Moore, Han Bennink, Thomas
    Heberer, Ernst Reijseger, Tristan Honsinger, et al.) 1997; hatOLOGY

Irakere (big band)
Misa Negra (with Chucho Valdés, Carlos Morales, et al.) 1986; Rounder
SEE ALSO Chucho Valdés

Italian Instabile Orchestra (band)
Litania Sibilante (with Gianluigi Trovesi, Pino Minafra, Carlo Actis Dato, et al.)
    2002; Enja

Itchy Fingers (band)
Live (Mike Mower, John Graham, Nigel Hitchcock, Howard Turner) 1982;
    Enja

Javon Jackson (ts)
Pleasant Valley (with Dave Stryker, Larry Goldings, Billy Drummond) 1999; Blue
    Note
SEE ALSO Ron Carter

Mahalia Jackson (voc)
Live at Newport 1958; Columbia

Milt Jackson (vib)
Bags and Trane (with John Coltrane, Hank Jones, Connie Kay, Paul Chambers)
    1959; Atlantic
Milt Jackson at the Kosei Nenkin (with Ray Brown, Teddy Edwards, Billy Higgins,
    Cedar Walton) 1976; Pablo
SEE ALSO Dizzy Gillespie, Quincy Jones, Modern Jazz Quartet, Oscar Peterson

Ronald Shannon Jackson (dm)
Barbeque Dog (with Vernon Reid et al.) 1983; Antilles
SEE ALSO Decoding Society

Illinois Jacquet (ts, bassoon)
The Blues: That's Me! (with Wynton Kelly, Tiny Grimes, Buster Williams, Oliver
    Jackson) 1969; Original Jazz Classics

Jaga Jazzist (band)
What We Must 2005; Ninja Tune

Ahmad Jamal (p)
Ahmad Jamal at the Pershing: But Not for Me 1958; Chess
In Search of Momentum (with Idris Muhammad, James Cammack) 2002; Dreyfus

Al Jarreau (voc)
Tenderness (with Joe Sample, Steve Gadd, Eric Gale, Marcus Miller) 1993; Warner

Keith Jarrett (p)
Death and the Flower (with Dewey Redman, Charlie Haden, Paul Motian,
    Guillerme Franco) 1975; Impulse
The Köln Concert (solo) 1975; ECM
Nude Ants (with Jan Garbarek, Palle Danielsson, Jon Christensen) 1979; ECM
At the Blue Note—The Complete Recordings (with Gary Peacock, Jack DeJohnette)
    (6 CD) 1994; ECM
SEE ALSO Gary Burton, Charles Lloyd, Bob Moses

Jazz Composers' Orchestra (band)
Communications (with Michael Mantler, Cecil Taylor, Don Cherry, Roswell Rudd,
    Carla Bley, Randy Brecker, Howard Johnson, Andrew Cyrille, Ron Carter, Steve
    Lacy, Lew Tabackin, Steve Swallow, Charlie Haden, Reggie Workman, Eddie
    Gomez, et al.) 1968; ECM

Jazz Jamaica All Stars (band)
Massive (with Gary Crosby, Denys Baptiste, Andy Sheppard, Guy Barker, Annie
    Whitehead, et al.) 2001; Dune Records

Jazz Passengers (band)
Live in Spain (with Debbie Harry, Roy Nathanson, Rob Thomas, et al.) 1997; 32
    Jazz

Leroy Jenkins (viol)
Lifelong Ambitions (with Muhal Richard Abrams) 1977; Black Saint

Maria João (voc)
Fábula (with Ralph Towner, Manu Katché, Dino Saluzzi, et al.) 1996; Verve
SEE ALSO Aki Takase

Howard Johnson (tuba, bs, fl)
Gravity! (with Dave Bargeron, Marcus Rojas, et al.) 1995; Verve
SEE ALSO Gil Evans, Jazz Composers' Orchestra, NDR Big Band

James P. Johnson (p)
Piano Solos 1942–1945, Smithsonian

J. J. Johnson (tb)
Early Bones (with Kai Winding, Benny Green, Sonny Rollins, Kenny Dorham, Gerry
    Mulligan, Eddie "Lockjaw" Davis, et al.) 1949–54; Prestige
Things Are Getting Better All the Time (with Kenny Barron, Ray Brown, Mickey
    Roker) 1983; Original Jazz Classics

Marc Johnson (b)
Bass Desires (with Bill Frisell, John Scofield, Peter Erskine) 1985; ECM
SEE ALSO John Lewis, Lyle Mays, John Scofield, John Taylor, Toots Thielemans

Pete Johnson (p)
Atomic Boogie: The National Recordings 1945–1947 (with Big Joe Turner) Savoy
    Jazz

Robert Johnson (voc, g)
The Complete Recordings 1936–37; Columbia

Elvin Jones (dm)
Puttin' It Together (with Jimmy Garrison, Joe Farrell) 1968; Blue Note
It Don't Mean a Thing (with Nicholas Payton, Sonny Fortune, Delfeayo Marsalis,
    Cecil McBee, Kevin Mahogany, Willie Pickens) 1993; Enja
SEE ALSO John Coltrane, Duke Ellington, Gil Evans, Joe Farrell, Grant Green, Albert
    Mangelsdorff, David Murray, Sonny Sharrock,

Hank Jones (p)
Groovin' High (with Thad Jones, Sam Jones, Mickey Roker, Charlie Rouse) 1978;
    Muse
Sarala (with Cheikh Tidiane-Seck & The Mandinkas) 1995; Verve
SEE ALSO Cannonball Adderley, Coleman Hawkins, Milt Jackson, Joe Lovano,
    Warne Marsh, Lucky Thompson

Jo Jones (dm)
The Main Man (with Harry "Sweets" Edison, Roy Eldridge, Eddie "Lockjaw"
    Davis, Tommy Flanagan, et al.) 1976; Original Jazz Classics
SEE ALSO John Coltrane, Duke Ellington, Gil Evans, Joe Farrell, Jimmy Garrison,
    Grant Green, Albert Mangelsdorff, David Murray, Sonny Sharrock

Norah Jones (voc)
Come Away with Me 2002; Blue Note

Philly Joe Jones (dm)
Drum Songs (with Blue Mitchell, Cedar Walton, Slide Hampton, et al.) 1978;
    Galaxy
SEE ALSO John Coltrane, Tadd Dameron, Abbey Lincoln, Art Pepper

Quincy Jones (ld)
Smackwater Jack (with Freddie Hubbard, Milt Jackson, Toots Thielemans, Jim Hall,
    et al.) 1971; A&M

Rodney Jones (g)
The Undiscovered Few (with Donald Harrison, Greg Osby, Mulgrew Miller, Lonnie
    Plaxico, Eric Harland, et al.) 1999; Blue Note

Sam Jones (b, cello)
SEE ALSO Cannonball Adderley, Nat Adderley, Freddie Hubbard, Hank Jones, Abbey
    Lincoln, Oscar Peterson, Bobby Timmons, Cedar Walton

Thad Jones (tp, flh, ld)
The Magnificent Thad Jones (with Billy Mitchell, Barry Harris, Percy Heath, Max
    Roach) 1956; Blue Note
SEE ALSO Hank Jones, Sarah Vaughan

Herbert Joos (tp, flh)
Aspects (with Wolfgang Puschnig, Klaus Dickbauer, et al.) 2000; Pao
SEE ALSO Bernd Konrad, Vienna Art Orchestra

Sheila Jordan (voc)
Portrait of Sheila (with Steve Swallow, Denzil Best, et al.) 1962; Blue Note
SEE ALSO Roswell Rudd

Stanley Jordan (g)
Magic Touch (with Omar Hakim, Peter Erskine, et al.) 1984; Blue Note

Theo Jörgensmann (cl)
Snijbloemen (with Christopher Dell, Christian Ramond, Klaus Kugel) 1999;
    hatOLOGY

Henry Kaiser (g)
Who Needs Enemies (with Fred Frith) 1981; Metalanguage

Wynton Kelly (p)
Smokin' at the Half Note (with Wes Montgomery et al.) 1965; Verve
SEE ALSO Dizzy Gillespie, Illinois Jacquet, Hank Mobley

Stan Kenton (p, ld)
New Concepts of Artistry in Rhythm (with Maynard Ferguson, Gerry Mulligan, Bill
    Russo, Lee Konitz, et al.) 1952; Capitol
Retrospective (with Lee Konitz, Laurindo Almeida, Pete Rugolo, Shelly Manne,
    Maynard Ferguson, et al.) (4 CD) 1943–68; Capitol

Barney Kessel (g)
The Poll Winners (with Shelly Manne, Ray Brown) 1957; Original Jazz Classics
SEE ALSO Benny Carter, Buddy Collette, Stephane Grappelli, Anita O'Day, Oscar
    Peterson, Art Tatum, Lester Young

David Kikoski (p)
Details (with Larry Grenadier, Bill Stewart) 2004; Criss Cross

B. B. King (g, voc)
Live in Cook County Jail 1971; MCA

Rahsaan Roland Kirk (sax, fl)
The Inflated Tear (with Ron Burton, Steve Novosel, Jimmy Hopps) 1967; Atlantic
SEE ALSO Jaki Byard, Charles Mingus

Kenny Kirkland (p, keyb)
Kenny Kirkland (with Branford Marsalis, Don Alias, et al.) 1991; GRP

Ryan Kisor (tp)
Awakening (with Sam Yahel, Peter Bernstein, et al.) 2002; Criss Cross

Guy Klucevsek (acc)
Tales from the Cryptic (with Phillip Johnston) 2000; Winter & Winter
SEE ALSO Dave Douglas, Bill Frisell, Bobby Previte

Koch-Schütz-Studer (band)
Life Tied (with Hans Koch, Martin Schütz, Fredy Studer) 2004; Intakt

Hans Koller (ts, ld)
Kunstkopfindianer (with Wolfgang Dauner, Zbigniew Seifert, et al.) 1974; MPS
SEE ALSO Oscar Pettiford

Kölner Saxophon Mafia (band)
Spaceplayer (with Wollie Kaiser, Joachim Ulrich, Roger Hanschel, Steffen Schorn)
    2004; Jazz Haus Musik

Klaus König (tb, ld)
Songs and Solos (with Roger Hanschel, Claudio Puntin, Reiner Winterschladen,
    Christopher Dell, et al.) 2002; Enja

Lee Konitz (as)
Ess-thetic (with Miles Davis, Sal Mosca, Billy Bauer) 1951–53; Prestige
The Lee Konitz Duets (with Marshall Brown, Joe Henderson, Jim Hall, et al.) 1967;
    Original Jazz Classics
SEE ALSO Miles Davis, Gil Evans, Stan Kenton, Lennie Tristano

Bernd Konrad (ss, ts, bs, bcl)
Phonolith (with Didier Lockwood, Kenny Wheeler, Herbert Joos, et al.) 1980/1994;
    hatOLOGY

Peter Kowald (b, tuba)
Duos 2—Europa America Japan (with Derek Bailey, Fred Frith, Michihiro Sato,
    Andrew Cyrille, Diamanda Galás, et al.) 1986–90; FMP

David Krakauer (cl)
The Twelve Tribes 2002; Label Bleu

Diana Krall (voc, p)
Live in Paris (with Anthony Wilson, John Clayton, Jeff Hamilton, et al.) 2002;
    Verve

Volker Kriegel (g)
SEE ALSO United Jazz + Rock Ensemble

Karin Krog (voc)
Where You At (with Steve Kuhn, David Finck, Billy Drummond) 2002; Enja

Kronos Quartet (band)
Caravan 2000; Nonesuch
SEE ALSO John Zorn

Gene Krupa (dm)
The Drum Battle (with Buddy Rich) 1952; Verve
SEE ALSO Benny Goodman, Red Norvo

Joachim Kühn (p)
Famous Melodies 1993; Label Bleu

Steve Kuhn (p)
Promises Kept (w/Strings) 2004; ECM
SEE ALSO David Darling, Karin Krog

Frank Lacy (tb)
Tonal Weights and Blue Fire 1990; Tutu Records

Steve Lacy (ss)
Hooky 1976; Emanem
Steve Lacy / Roswell Rudd Quartet: Monk's Dream (with Irène Aebi, Jean-Jacques
    Avenel, John Betsch) 1998; Verve
SEE ALSO Derek Bailey, Gil Evans, Bobby Hackett, Jazz Composers' Orchestra,
    Misha Mengelberg, Mal Waldron

Tony Lakatos (ts)
Recycling (with Al Foster) 2000; Jazzline

Oliver Lake (as, ss, fl)
Expandable Language (with Kevin Eubanks, Geri Allen, Fred Hopkins, Pheeroan
    AkLaff) 1984; Black Saint
SEE ALSO World Saxophone Quartet

Nils Landgren (tb, voc)
Paint It Blue 1997; ACT
SEE ALSO Roberto Di Gioia

Bill Laswell (b)
Invisible Design 1999; Tzadik

Yusef Lateef (ts, fl, oboe, frh, bassoon)
Eastern Sounds (with Connie Kay, Ernie Farrow, et al.) 1961; Original Jazz Classics
SEE ALSO Dizzy Gillespie

Christof Lauer (ts)
Fragile Network (with Marc Ducret, Michel Godard, Anthony Cox, Gene Jackson)
    1999; ACT
SEE ALSO United Jazz + Rock Ensemble, NDR Big Band, Colin Towns

Nguyên Lê (g)
Tales from Vietnam (with Paolo Fresu, Steve Argüelles, Joel Allouche, et al.) 1996; ACT
SEE ALSO Paolo Fresu

Leadbelly (g, voc)
Take This Hammer (The Secret Story of Rock & Roll) 1940; Bluebird/RCA

Joelle Léandre (b)
Joelle Léandre Project (with Marilyn Crispell, Paul Lovens, et al.) 1999; Leo Records

Jeanne Lee (voc)
Natural Affinities (with Dave Holland, Leo Smith, Mark Whitecage) 1992; Sunnyside
SEE ALSO Ran Blake, Gunter Hampel

George Lewis (tb)
Homage to Charles Parker (with Anthony Davis et al.) 1979; Black Saint
SEE ALSO Anthony Braxton

John Lewis (p)
Evolution II (with Howard Alden, George Mraz, Marc Johnson, Lewis Nash, et al.)
    2000; Atlantic
SEE ALSO Anthony Davis, Heiner Goebbels, Misha Mengelberg, Modern Jazz
    Quartet, David Murray

Mel Lewis (dm, ld)
Naturally (with Jim McNeely, Dick Latts, John Marshall, et al.) 1979; Telarc
SEE ALSO Thad Jones / Mel Lewis Orchestra, Warne Marsh

Dave Liebman (ts, ss)
Colors 2003; hatOLOGY
SEE ALSO John McLaughlin, Niels-Henning Ørsted Pedersen

Abbey Lincoln (voc)
Abbey Is Blue (with Max Roach, Kenny Dorham, Sam Jones, Philly Joe Jones, et al.)
    1959; Original Jazz Classics
It's Me (with Kenny Barron, Cedar Walton, et al.) 2003; Verve

John Lindberg (b)
Winter Birds 2005; Between the Lines
SEE ALSO String Trio of New York

Arto Lindsay (g, voc)
Salt 2004; Righteous Babe
SEE ALSO Heiner Goebbels, Kip Hanrahan

Booker Little (tp)
Out Front (with Eric Dolphy, Max Roach) 1961; Candid
SEE ALSO Eric Dolphy, Max Roach

Charles Lloyd (ts)
Dream Weaver (with Keith Jarrett, Jack DeJohnette, Cecil McBee) 1966; Atlantic
The Water Is Wide (with Billy Higgins, John Abercrombie, Brad Mehldau, Larry
    Grenadier) 1999; ECM

Didier Lockwood (viol)
Storyboard (with Joey DeFrancesco, James Genus, Steve Wilson, et al.) 1996;
    Dreyfus
SEE ALSO Bernd Konrad

Frank London (tp)
Brotherhood of Brass 2001; Piranha

London Jazz Composers' Orchestra (big band)
Double Trouble (with Barre Phillips, Paul Rutherford, Trevor Watts, Evan Parker,
    et al.) 1989; Intakt

Lounge Lizards (band)
Live in Berlin Vol. 1 & 2 (with John Lurie, Michael Blake, Steven Bernstein, Jane
    Scarpantoni, et al.) 1991; Intuition

Joe Lovano (ts)
Joyous Encounter (with Hank Jones, George Mraz, Paul Motian) 2004; Blue Note
SEE ALSO John Abercrombie, Paul Motian, John Scofield, Tommy Smith

Jimmie Lunceford (as, ld)
Stomp It Off 1934–35; GRP

Geir Lysne (ts, ld)
Korall (with the Listenig Ensemble) 2003; ACT

Machito (perc, ld)
Latin Soul Plus Jazz 1957; Charly
SEE ALSO Charlie Parker

Magic Malik (Malik Mezzadri) (fl)
13 XP Song S Book (2 CD) 2005; Label Bleu

Rudi Mahall (bcl)
SEE ALSO Der Rote Bereich, Aki Takase

Mahavishnu Orchestra (band)
The Inner Mounting Flame (with John McLaughlin, Jerry Goodman, Jan Hammer,
    Rick Laird, Billy Cobham) 1971; Columbia

Kevin Mahogany (voc)
Pride & Joy (with James Weidman, Jon Faddis, Dave Stryker) 2001; Telarc
SEE ALSO Elvin Jones

Mike Mainieri (vib)
SEE ALSO Steps Ahead

Joe Maneri (ss)
Angles of Repose (with Barre Phillips, Mat Maneri) 2004; ECM

Mat Maneri (viol)
Sustain (with William Parker, Joe McPhee, Craig Taborn, et al.) 2002; Thirsty Ear
SEE ALSO Joe Maneri, Matthew Shipp, Craig Taborn

Albert Mangelsdorff (tb)
Tension! (with Ralf Hübner, Günther Kronberg, Günter Lenz, Heinz Sauer) 1963;
    L+R Records
Albert Mangelsdorff and His Friends 1967–69; MPS
Three Originals (with Palle Danielsson, Elvin Jones, Jaco Pastorius, Ronald Shannon
    Jackson, et al.) (2 CD) 1975–80; MPS
Triplicity (with Arild Andersen, Pierre Favre) 1979; Skip
Live at Montreux Jazz Festival (with Reto Weber's Percussion Orchestra) 2004;
    Doublemoon
SEE ALSO NDR Big Band, United Jazz + Rock Ensemble

Herbie Mann (fl, ts)
America / Brasil (with Randy Brecker, Claudio Roditi, Romero Lubambo, Jim Pugh)
    1995; Lightyear
SEE ALSO Chet Baker

Shelly Manne (dm)
The West Coast Sound, Vol. 1 (with Art Pepper, Jimmy Giuffre, Shorty Rogers,
    et al.) 1955; Original Jazz Classics
SEE ALSO Benny Carter, Lionel Hampton, Stan Kenton, Barney Kessel, Howard
    McGhee

Rick Margitza (ts)
Heart of Hearts (with Joey Calderazzo, Scott Colley, et al.) 1999; Palmetto
SEE ALSO Eddie Gomez, Maria Schneider

Charlie Mariano (as, ss, fl, nagaswaram)
Boston All Stars 1951–53; Original Jazz Classics
Bangalore (with Karnataka College of Percussion et al.) 2000; Intuition
SEE ALSO Rabih Abou-Khalil, Charles Mingus, United Jazz + Rock Ensemble,
    Edward Vesala

Branford Marsalis (ts, ss)
Eternal (with Joey Calderazzo, Jeff "Tain" Watts, et al.) 2003; Rounder
SEE ALSO Art Blakey, Kenny Kirkland

Wynton Marsalis (tp, ld)
Marsalis Standard Time Vol. 1 (with Bob Hurst, Marcus Roberts, Jeff "Tain" Watts)
    1987; Columbia

The Majesty of the Blues (with Wes Anderson, Herlin Riley, et al.) 1988;
    Columbia
Citi Movement (2 CD) (with Wycliffe Gordon, Eric Reed, Herlin Riley, et al.) 1992;
    Columbia
Wynton Marsalis Septet—Live at the Village Vanguard (8 CD) 1990–94;
    Columbia
SEE ALSO Art Blakey, Joe Henderson, Shirley Horn

Warne Marsh (ts)
Star Highs (with Hank Jones, George Mraz, Mel Lewis) 1982; Criss Cross
SEE ALSO Art Pepper, Lennie Tristano

Pat Martino (g)
Live At Yoshi's (with Joey DeFrancesco, Billy Hart) 2000; Blue Note

Masada String Trio (band)
50th Birthday Celebration, Vol. 1 (with Mark Feldman, Erik Friedlander, Greg
    Cohen) 2004; Tzadik

Jean-Louis Matinier (acc)
Confluences (with Renaud Garcia-Fons et al.) 2003; Enja
SEE ALSO Michel Godard, Michael Riessler, Louis Sclavis

Lyle Mays (keyb, p)
Fictionary (with Marc Johnson, Jack DeJohnette) 1992; Geffen
SEE ALSO Pat Metheny

Cecil McBee (b)
Compassion (with Chico Freeman, Joe Gardner, Dennis Moorman, Don Moye, Steve
    McCall) 1983; Enja
SEE ALSO JoAnn Brackeen, Alice Coltrane, Elvin Jones, Charles Lloyd, Grachan
    Moncur III

Christian McBride (b)
A Family Affair (with Tim Warfield, Gregory Hutchinson, et al.) 1998; Warner
SEE ALSO Ray Brown, Ricky Ford, Jim Hall, Joe Henderson, Joshua Redman,
    McCoy Tyner

Les McCann (p)
Swiss Movement (with Eddie Harris) 1969; Atlantic
SEE ALSO Richard "Groove" Holmes

Bobby McFerrin (voc)
Circlesongs 1997; Columbia

Howard McGhee (tp)
Maggie's Back in Town (with Phineas Newborn, Leroy Vinnegar, Shelly Manne)
    1961; Original Jazz Classics
SEE ALSO Coleman Hawkins, Charlie Parker

Chris McGregor (p, ld)
Bremen to Bridgewater (with Brotherhood of Breath) 1971–75; Cuneiform

John McLaughlin (g)
My Goal's Beyond (with Dave Liebman, Billy Cobham, Jerry Goodman, Airto
    Moreira) 1970; Rykodisc
Friday Night in San Francisco (with Al DiMeola, Paco de Lucia) 1980; Philips
The Promise (with Jeff Beck, Dennis Chambers, Joey DeFrancesco, Michael Brecker,
    Paco De Lucia, Al DiMeola, Zakir Hussain, Trilok Gurtu) 1995; Verve
Thieves and Poets (Deutsche Kammerphilharmonie, cond. Renato Rivolta; Aighetta
    Quartet) 2002; Verve
SEE ALSO Carla Bley, Stanley Clarke, Miles Davis, Mahavishnu Orchestra, Shakti,
    Wayne Shorter, Miroslav Vitous, Tony Williams

Jackie McLean (as)
4, 5 and 6 (with Donald Byrd, Hank Mobley, Mal Waldron, et al.) 1956; Original
    Jazz Classics
One Step Beyond (with Bobby Hutcherson, Tony Williams, et al.) 1963; Blue Note
SEE ALSO Charles Mingus

Marian McPartland (p)
Piano Jazz: McPartland/Evans (with Bill Evans) 1978; Jazz Alliance

Carmen McRae (voc)
Carmen Sings Monk (with Clifford Jordan, Eric Gunnison, George Mraz, Al Foster)
    1988; Novus

Medeski, Martin & Wood (band)
End of the World Party (Just in Case) (with John Medeski, Billy Martin, Chris
    Wood, Marc Ribot, Steven Bernstein, et al.) 2004; Blue Note

Brad Mehldau (p)
The Art of the Trio, Vol. 3: Songs (with Jorge Rossy, Larry Grenadier) 1998; Warner
Live in Tokyo (solo) 2004; Nonesuch
SEE ALSO Charles Lloyd, Joshua Redman, Mark Turner

Misha Mengelberg (p, ld)
Change of Season: The Music of Herbie Nichols (with Steve Lacy, George Lewis,
    Harjen Gorter, Han Bennink) 1984; Soul Note
Four in One (with Han Bennink, Dave Douglas, Brad Jones) 2000; Songlines
SEE ALSO Anthony Braxton, ICP Orchestra

Helen Merrill (voc)
Jelena Ana Milcactic a.k.a. Helen Merrill 1999; Gitanes

Pat Metheny (g)
Bright Size Life (with Bob Moses, Jaco Pastorius) 1975; ECM
Song X (with Denardo Coleman, Ornette Coleman, Jack DeJohnette, Charlie
    Haden) 1985; Geffen Records
We Live Here (with Lyle Mays, Steve Rodby, Paul Wertico) 1994; Geffen
Trio (with Larry Grenadier, Bill Stewart) 1999; Warner
SEE ALSO Michael Brecker, Joshua Redman, Gary Thomas, Eberhard Weber

Palle Mikkelborg (tp)
The Voice of Silence (with the Danish Radio Jazz Orchestra) 2002; Stunt
SEE ALSO Dexter Gordon, Terje Rypdal

Bubber Miley (co, tp)
SEE ALSO Duke Ellington

Marcus Miller (b)
The Ozell Tapes: The Official Bootleg 2003; Telarc
SEE ALSO Miles Davis

Mulgrew Miller (p)
Live At Yoshi's Vol. 1 & 2 (with Derrick Hodge, Karriem Riggins) 2003; Max
    Jazz
SEE ALSO Freddie Hubbard, Rodney Jones, Frank Morgan, Diane Reeves, Woody
    Shaw, Lew Soloff, Eric Watson, Tony Williams

Charles Mingus (b, vc, ld)
Passions of a Man (with George Adams, Pepper Adams, Philip Catherine, Larry
    Coryell, Booker Ervin, Ricky Ford, John Handy, Rahsaan Roland Kirk, Jimmy
    Knepper, Jackie McLean, Don Pullen, Dannie Richmond, Mal Waldron, et al.)
    1956–77; Atlantic
Mingus Ah Um (with John Handy, Jimmy Knepper, Dannie Richmond, et al.) 1959;
    CBS
The Black Saint and the Sinner Lady (with Jaki Byard, Charlie Mariano, Dannie
    Richmond, et al.) 1963; Impulse
The Great Concert Paris 1964 (2 CD) 1964; Emarcy
SEE ALSO Charlie Parker

Phil Minton (voc)
Drainage (with Roger Turner) 1998–2003; Emanem

Bob Mintzer (bcl, ts, ld)
Bob Mintzer Big Band Live at MCG (with Kurt Elling, Rufus Reid, et al.) 2002,
    Telarc
SEE ALSO Jaco Pastorius

Gabriele Mirabassi (cl)
Latakia Blend (with Luciano Biondini, Michel Godard) 2001; Enja
SEE ALSO Rabih Abou-Khalil

Hank Mobley (ts)
Soul Station (with Art Blakey, Paul Chambers, Wynton Kelly) 1960; Blue Note
SEE ALSO Jackie McLean, Max Roach, Horace Silver

Modern Jazz Quartet (band)
Modern Jazz Quartet (with Kenny Clarke, Percy Heath, Milt Jackson, Connie Kay,
    John Lewis) 1951–52; Original Jazz Classics
Lonely Woman (with John Lewis, Percy Heath, Milt Jackson, Connie Kay) 1962;
    Atlantic
For Ellington (with John Lewis, Percy Heath, Milt Jackson, Connie Kay) 1988; East
    West

Nils Petter Molvaer (tp, elec)
Khmer 1998; ECM
SEE ALSO Sidsel Endresen

Grachan Moncur III (tb)
Some Other Stuff (with Herbie Hancock, Wayne Shorter, Cecil McBee, Tony
    Williams) 1964; Blue Note

Jane Monheit (voc)
Taking a Chance on Love 2004; Sony

Thelonious Monk (p)
Brilliant Corners (with Sonny Rollins, Oscar Pettiford, Ernie Henry, Max Roach)
    1956; Original Jazz Classics
Monk's Dream (with Charlie Rouse, John Ore, Frankie Dunlop) 1962; Columbia
SEE ALSO Charlie Parker

Wes Montgomery (g)
The Incredible Jazz Guitar of Wes Montgomery (with Tommy Flanagan, Percy
    Heath, Albert Heath) 1960; Original Jazz Classics
SEE ALSO Nat Adderley, Wynton Kelly

Tete Montoliu (p)
The Music I Like to Play, Vol. 1 1986; Soul Note

James Moody (as, ts, fl)
Don't Look Away Now 1969; Original Jazz Classics

Glen Moore (b)
Nude Bass Ascending (with Rabih Abou-Khalil, Carla Bley, Steve Swallow, Arto
    Tuncboyaciyan) 1999; Intuition
SEE Oregon

Michael Moore (b)
SEE ALSO Dave Brubeck

Michael Moore (as, cl)
SEE Clusone 3, ICP Orchestra

Jason Moran (p, keyb)
The Bandwagon (with Tarus Mateen, Nasheet Waits) 2003; Blue Note
SEE ALSO Don Byron, Greg Osby

Airto Moreira (perc)
Killer Bees (with Chick Corea, Herbie Hancock, Mark Egan, Stanley Clarke) 1989;
    B&W
SEE ALSO Chick Corea, Miles Davis, Joe Farrell, Flora Purim, Wayne Shorter

Frank Morgan (as)
Yardbird Suite (with Mulgrew Miller, Ron Carter, Al Foster) 1988; Contemporary

Lee Morgan (tp)
The Sidewinder (with Bob Cranshaw, Barry Harris, Joe Henderson, Billy Higgins)
    1963; Blue Note
SEE ALSO Art Blakey, John Coltrane

Ikue Mori (elec)
Labyrinth 2000; Tzadik

Butch Morris (co, ld)
Butch Morris Conducts Berlin Skyskraper (2 CD) 1995; FMP

Jelly Roll Morton (p)
The Complete Victor Recordings (5 CD) 1926–39; RCA/Bluebird

Moscow Art Trio (band)
Once Upon a Time (with Misha Alperin, Arkady Shilkloper, Sergey Starostin, Eli
    Kristin Hovdsveen Hagen) 2000; Jaro

Bob Moses (dm, ld)
Love Animal (with Larry Coryell, Steve Swallow, Keith Jarrett) 1967–68; Amulet
Time Stood Still (with Miles Evans, Brian Carrot, Bill Martin, et al.) 1993;
    Gramavision
SEE ALSO Pat Metheny

David Moss (dm, voc)
My Favorite Things 1990; Intakt

Bennie Moten (ld)
Classics 1929–1930; Classics

Paul Motian (dm)
On Broadway, Vol. 1 (with Bill Frisell, Joe Lovano, Charlie Haden) 1988; JMT /
    Winter & Winter
I Have the Room Above Her (with Bill Frisell, Joe Lovano) 2004; ECM
SEE ALSO Geri Allen, Carla Bley, Marily Crispell, Bill Evans, Keith Jarrett, Joe
    Lovano, Tony Scott

George Mraz (b)
SEE ALSO Tommy Flanagan, Jim Hall, John Lewis, Joe Lovano, Warne Marsh,
    Carmen McRae, Lew Soloff

Gerry Mulligan (bs)
Pleyel Concert Vol. 1 & 2 (with Bob Brookmeyer, Red Mitchell, Frank Isola) 1954;
    BMG/Vogue
Gerry Mulligan Meets Ben Webster 1959; Verve
SEE ALSO Miles Davis, J. J. Johnson, Stan Kenton

Mark Murphy (voc)
The Latin Porter (with Tom Harrell, Peter Schimke, Daniel Ganzales) 2000;
    Go Jazz

David Murray (ts, bcl, ld)
Ming (with Anthony Davis, George Lewis, Henry Threadgill, et al.) 1980; Black Saint
Special Quartet (with McCoy Tyner, Fred Hopkins, Elvin Jones) 1990; Columbia
Now Is Another Time (with Hugh Ragin, Hamiet Bluiett, et al.) 2002; Justin Time
SEE ALSO Jack DeJohnette, World Saxophone Quartet

Amina Claudine Myers (org, p)
Women in (E)motion (with Reggie Nicholson, Jerome Harris) 1988; Tradition &
    Moderne

Simon Nabatov (p)
The Move (with Nils Wogram) 2005; Between the Lines
SEE ALSO Perry Robinson, Nils Wogram

Naked City (band)
Naked City (with John Zorn, Bill Frisell, Wayne Horvitz, Fred Frith, Joey Baron,
    Yamatsuka Eye) 1989; Nonesuch

Ray Nance (tp, viol)
SEE Johnny Hodges

Fats Navarro (tp)
Fats Navarro with Tadd Dameron (with Kai Winding, Allan Eager, et al.) 1948;
    Milestone
SEE ALSO Bud Powell, Coleman Hawkins

NDR Big Band (big band)
Bravissimo (with Chet Baker, Gary Burton, Johnny Griffin, Howard Johnson, Albert
    Mangelsdorff, et al.) 1980–95; ACT
SEE ALSO Colin Towns

Oliver Nelson (as, ts)
The Blues and the Abstract Truth (with Eric Dolphy, Freddie Hubbard, George
    Barrow, Bill Evans, Paul Chambers) 1961; Impulse

Phineas Newborn (p)
Look Out: Phineas Is Back (with Ray Brown, Jimmy Smith) 1976; Original Jazz
    Classics
SEE ALSO Howard McGhee

New Conception of Jazz (band)
Live (with Bugge Wesseltoft, Audun Kleive, John Scofield, et al.) 2002; Jazzland

Joe Newman (tp)
Good 'N' Groovy (with Frank Foster, Tommy Flanagan, Eddie Jones, Bill English)
    1961; Original Jazz Classics

New Orleans Rhythm Kings (band)
1922–1923; Original Jazz Classics

Herbie Nichols (p)
Complete Blue Note Recordings (with Art Blakey, Max Roach, Al McKibbon, et al.)
(3 CD) 1955–56; Blue Note

Lucas Niggli (dm)
Zoom—Rough Ride (with Nils Wogram, Philipp Schaufelberger) 2003; Intakt

Jimmie Noone (cl)
Apex Blues 1928–30; Decca/GRP

Caecilie Norby (voc)
My Corner of the Sky (with David Kikoski, Joey Calderazzo, Terri Lyne Carrington,
Randy Brecker, Michael Brecker) 1997; Blue Note

Red Norvo (vib)
Dance of the Octopus (with Benny Goodman, Jimmy Dorsey, Artie Shaw, Charlie
Barnet, Chu Berry, Teddy Wilson, Gene Krupa, et al.) 1933–36; HEP
The Red Norvo Trios (with Jimmy Raney, Tal Farlow, Red Mitchell) 1953–55;
Prestige

Anita O'Day (voc)
Pick Yourself Up (with Buddy Bregman Orchestra, Harry Edison, Barney Kessel, et
al.) 1956; Verve

Old & New Dreams (band)
SEE ALSO Dewey Redman

King Oliver (co, tp)
King Oliver—Louis Armstrong (with Louis Armstrong, Sidney Bechet, Johnny
Dodds, Jelly Roll Morton, et al.) 1923–24; Milestone

Oregon (band)
Music of Another Present Era (with Collin Walcott, Ralph Towner, Paul
McCandless, Glen Moore) 1972; Vanguard
Northwest Passage (with Ralph Towner, Paul McCandless, Glen Moore, Arto
Tuncboyaciyan, Mark Walker) 1996; Intuition

Original Dixieland Jazz Band (band)
75th Anniversary 1917–21; Bluebird/RCA

Niels-Henning Ørsted Pedersen (b)
Dancing on the Tables (with John Scofield, Billy Hart, Dave Liebman) 1979;
Steeplechase
Those Who Were (with Ulf Wakenius, Johnny Griffin, et al.) 1996, Verve
SEE ALSO Roy Eldridge, Lionel Hampton, Oscar Peterson, Aki Takase, Ben
Webster

Kid Ory (tb)
Kid Ory's Creole Jazz Band 1944–45; Good Time Jazz

Greg Osby (as, ss)
Banned in New York (with Rodney Green, Jason Moran, Atsushi Osada) 1998; Blue
    Note
SEE ALSO Rodney Jones

Pachora (band)
Astereotypical (with Jim Black, Chris Speed, Brad Shepik, Skuli Sverisson) 2003;
    Winter & Winter

Pago Libre (band)
Cinemagique (with Arkady Shilkloper, John Wolf Brennan, Tscho Theissing, Daniele
    Patumi) 1999–2000; TCB

Charlie Parker (as)
The Complete Savoy Studio Sessions (with Miles Davis, Dizzy Gillespie, John Lewis,
    Bud Powell, Max Roach, et al.) (5 CD) 1944–48; Savoy
Bird: Complete Charlie Parker on Verve (with Machito's Cuban Orchestra, JATP,
    Miles Davis, Charles Mingus, Thelonious Monk, Dizzy Gillespie, Johnny
    Hodges, Benny Carter, et al.) (10 CD) 1946–54; Verve
The Legendary Dial Masters, Vols. 1 & 2 (with Earl Coleman, Errol Garner,
    Howard McGhee, Wardell Gray, et al.) 1946–47; Jazz Classics
The Greatest Jazz Concert Ever (with Dizzy Gillespie, Bud Powell, Charles Mingus,
    Max Roach) 1953; Prestige

Evan Parker (ss, ts)
Monoceros 1978; Incus
Toward the Margins (with Walter Prati, Marco Vecchi, Paul Lytton, Philipp
    Wachsmann, Barry Guy) 1996; ECM
SEE ALSO Peter Brötzmann, Barry Guy, London Jazz Composers' Orchestra, Manfred
    Schoof, Spontaneous Music Ensemble, Alexander von Schlippenbach

Joe Pass (g)
Virtuoso No. 2 1976; Pablo
SEE ALSO Oscar Peterson, Zoot Sims, Sarah Vaughan

Jaco Pastorius (b)
Jaco Pastorius (with Don Alias, Herbie Hancock, Hubert Laws, Lenny White, et al.)
    1976; Epic
Birthday Concert (with Peter Erskine, Don Alias, Michael Brecker, Randy Brecker,
    Bob Mintzer, et al.) 1981; Warner
Invitation (with Toots Thielemans, Othello Molineaux, Peter Erskine, et al.) 1981;
    Warner
SEE ALSO Albert Mangelsdorff, Pat Metheny, Weather Report

John Patitucci (b)
Heart of the Bass (with Chick Corea, Alex Acuna, et al.) 1991; Stretch
SEE ALSO Wayne Shorter, Tommy Smith

Nicholas Payton (tp)
Sonic Trance (with Tim Warfield, Kevin Hays, Adonis Rose, et al.) 2003; Warner
SEE ALSO Elvin Jones

Gary Peacock (b)
Oracle (with Ralph Towner) 1993; ECM
SEE ALSO Marilyn Crispell, Keith Jarrett

Art Pepper (as)
The Way It Was (with Paul Chambers, Philly Joe Jones, Warne Marsh, et al.)
    1956–60; Contemporary
Straight Life (with Tommy Flanagan, Billy Higgins, et al.) 1979; Galaxy
SEE ALSO Shelly Manne, Buddy Rich

Danilo Perez (p)
Panamonk (with Terri Lyne Carrington, Avishai Cohen, et al.) 1996; Impulse
SEE ALSO Ricky Ford, Wayne Shorter

Oscar Peterson (p)
Compact Jazz: Oscar Peterson Plays Jazz Standards (with Ray Brown, Herb Ellis, Ed
    Thigpen) 1953–62; Verve
The History of an Artist (with Ray Brown, Herb Ellis, Louis Hayes, Sam Jones,
    Barney Kessel, et al.) 1972–74; Pablo
If You Could See Me Now (with Joe Pass, Niels-Henning Ørsted Pedersen, et al.)
    1983; Pablo
Live at the Blue Note (with Milt Jackson, Ray Brown) 1998; Telarc
SEE ALSO Roy Eldridge, Lionel Hampton, Coleman Hawkins, Zoot Sims, Sarah
    Vaughan, Ben Webster, Lester Young

Michel Petrucciani (p)
Power of Three (with Jim Hall, Wayne Shorter) 1986; Blue Note
Solo Live 1999; Dreyfus

Oscar Pettiford (b, vc)
Vienna Blues: The Complete Sessions (with Hans Koller, Attila Zoller, Jimmy Pratt)
    1959; Black Lion
SEE ALSO Thelonious Monk, Sonny Rollins

Dominique Pifarély (viol)
Poros (with Francois Couturier) 1997; ECM
SEE ALSO Marc Ducret, Louis Sclavis

Jean-Michel Pilc (p)
Cardinal Points (with Sam Newsome, James Genus, Ari Hoenig, et al.) 2002;
    Dreyfus

Courtney Pine (ts, ld)
Devotion (with Cameron Pierre, Robert Fordjour, Peter Martin, et al.) 2003;
    Creative People

Jean-Luc Ponty (viol)
The Very Best of Jean-Luc Ponty (with Allan Holdsworth, Daryl Stuermer, Steve
    Smith, Paulinho Da Costa, et al.) 1975–85; Rhino
Jean-Luc Ponty in Concert (with William Lecomte, Guy Nsangué Akwa, et al.)
    2004; J. L. P. Productions

Michel Portal (sax, bcl, bandoneon)
Dejarme Solo! 1979; Dreyfus
Dockings (with Joey Baron, Steve Swallow, Markus Stockhausen, Bruno Chevillon, Bojan Zulfikarpasic) 1998; Label Bleu

Chris Potter (ts, ss)
Gratitude (with Kevin Hays, Scott Colley, Brian Blade) 2000; Verve
SEE ALSO Dave Douglas, Dave Holland, Josh Roseman, Jochen Rückert

Bud Powell (p)
The Genius of Bud Powell (with Ray Brown, Max Roach, Buddy Rich, Curly Russell) 1949–51; Verve
The Amazing Bud Powell Vol. 2 (with Roy Haynes, Art Taylor, et al.) 1949–51; Blue Note
The Scene Changes (with Paul Chambers, Art Taylor) 1958; Blue Note
SEE ALSO Charlie Parker, Oscar Pettiford

Bobby Previte (dm)
Claude's Late Morning (with Ray Anderson, Joey Baron, Bill Frisell, Wayne Horvitz, Guy Klucevsek, et al.) 1988; Gramavision
Counterclockwise (with Marty Ehrlich, Curtis Fowlkes, Wayne Horvitz, Steve Swallow) 2003; Palmetto
SEE ALSO Ray Anderson, Wayne Horvitz, John Zorn

Don Pullen (p, org)
Random Thoughts (with Lewis Nash, James Genus) 1990; Blue Note
SEE ALSO Charles Mingus

Claudio Puntin (cl, bcl)
Mondo Live (with Marcio Doctor, Gerdur Gudmundsdottir, Wang Yong) 1999–2000; JazzHausMusik
SEE ALSO Klaus König

John Purcell (ss, ts, bcl, oboe)
Third Kind of Blue 1986; Minor Music
SEE ALSO World Saxophone Quartet

Flora Purim (voc)
Butterfly Dreams (with Stanley Clarke, Joe Henderson, George Duke, Airto Moreira) 1973; Original Jazz Classics
Perpetual Emotion (with Airto Moreira, Gary Meek, Oscar Castro Neves, et al.) 2001; Narada
SEE ALSO Chick Corea, George Duke, Airto Moreira

Wolfgang Puschnig (as)
Then Comes the White Tiger (with Samul Nori, Jamaaladeen Tacuma, Linda Sharrock, et al.) 1994; ECM
Roots & Fruits (with Amstettener Musikanten, Linda Sharrock, Samul Nori, Andy Scherer, Bumi Fian, Jamaaladeen Tacuma, et al.) 1997; Amadeo
SEE ALSO Carla Bley, Herbert Joos, Saxofour, Vienna Art Orchestra

Quintet du Hot Club de France (band)
SEE Django Reinhardt

Sun Ra (p, key, ld)
Greatest Hits: Easy Listening for Intergalactic Travel (with Hobart Dotson, John Gilmore, Marshall Allen, et al.) 1956–73; Evidence
Lanquidity 1978; Evidence
Mayan Temples (with John Gilmore, Michael Ray, Ahmed Abdullah, Marshall Allen) 1990; Black Saint

Ma Rainey (voc)
Ma Rainey 1928; Riverside

Enrico Rava (tp)
The Pilgrim and the Stars (with John Abercrombie, Palle Danielsson, Jon Christensen) 1975; ECM
Montreal Diary / A: Plays Miles Davis (with Paolo Fresu, Roberto Gatto, Stefano Bollani, et al.) 2004; Label Bleu

Dewey Redman (ts, musette)
Old and New Dreams (with Don Cherry, Charlie Haden, Ed Blackwell) 1979; ECM
In London (with Rita Marcotulli, Cameron Brown, Matt Wilson) 1996, Palmetto
SEE ALSO Keith Jarrett, Steve Turre

Joshua Redman (ts)
Wish (with Pat Metheny, Charlie Haden, Billy Higgins) 1993; Warner
Moodswing (with Brad Mehldau, Christian McBride, Brian Blade) 1994; Warner

Diane Reeves (voc)
I Remember (with Mulgrew Miller, Charnett Moffett, Billy Kilson, Marvin "Smitty" Smith, et al.) 1990–92; Blue Note

Hans Reichel (g, daxophone)
Yuxo: A New Daxophone Opera 2002; a/l/l

Ernst Reijseger (voc)
Colla Parte 1997; Winter & Winter
SEE ALSO Amsterdam String Trio, Clusone 3, ICP Orchestra

Django Reinhardt (g)
Django Reinhardt & Stephane Grappelli: The Quintet of the Hot Club of France (with Stephane Grappelli et al.) 1936–37; Pearl Flapper
Pêche à la Mouche (with Quintet of the Hot Club of France et al.) 1947–53; Verve

Marc Ribot (g)
Marc Ribot y los Cubanos Postizos (with E. J. Rodriguez et al.) 1998; Atlantic
Saints 2001; Atlantic
SEE ALSO Ellery Eskelin; Medeski, Martin & Wood; John Zorn

Buddy Rich (dm, ld)
This One's for Basie (With Harry "Sweets" Edison, Frank Rosolino, Jimmy Rowles, et al.) 1956; Verve
Mercy, Mercy (with Don Menza, Art Pepper, Phil Wilson, et al.) 1968; World Pacific
SEE ALSO Tommy Dorsey, Lionel Hampton, Gene Krupa, Bud Powell, Art Tatum

Michael Riessler (ss, as, cl, bcl)
Orange (with Elise Caron, Pierre Charial, Jean-Louis Matinier) 2000; ACT

Sam Rivers (ts, ss, fl)
Contours (with Freddie Hubbard, Herbie Hancock, Ron Carter, Joe Chambers) 1965; Blue Note
Tangens (with Alexander von Schlippenbach) 1998; FMP

Max Roach (dm)
Standard Time (with Clifford Brown, Kenny Dorharn, Hank Mobley, Sonny Rollins, et al.) 1954–59; Emarcy
We Insist: Freedom Now Suite (with Coleman Hawkins, Abbey Lincoln, Booker Little, et al.) 1960; Candid
The Max Roach Trio, Feat. the Legendary Hasaan (with Hasaan Ibn Ali, Art Davis) 1964; Atlantic
One in Two, Two in One (with Anthony Braxton) 1979; HatHUT
SEE ALSO Miles Davis, Dizzy Gillespie, Coleman Hawkins, Thad Jones, Abbey Lincoln, Booker Little, Thelonious Monk, Herbie Nichols, Charlie Parker, Bud Powell, Sonny Rollins

Hank Roberts (voc)
Black Pastels (with Ray Anderson, Robin Eubanks, Tim Berne, Bill Frisell, Joey Baron, et al.) 1987; JMT / Winter & Winter
SEE ALSO Arcado String Trio

Herb Robertson (tp)
X-cerpts: Live at Willisau (with Joey Baron, Tim Berne, et al.) 1987; JMT / Winter & Winter

Perry Robinson (cl)
Call to the Stars (with Simon Nabatov, Ed Schuller, Ernst Bier) 1990; WestWind

Sonny Rollins (ts)
Saxophone Colossus (with Clifford Brown, Kenny Dorharn, Tommy Flanagan, Max Roach, et al.) 1957; Original Jazz Classics
Freedom Suite (with Paul Chambers, Roy Haynes, Percy Heath, Oscar Pettiford, Max Roach, et al.) 1957–58; Original Jazz Cassics
Don't Stop the Carnival (with Donald Byrd, Tony Williams, et al.) 1978; Milestone
Sonny Rollins Plus Three (with Tommy Flanagan, Stephen Scott, Bob Cranshaw, Al Foster, Jack DeJohnette) 1996; Milestone
SEE ALSO J. J. Johnson, Thelonious Monk, Max Roach

Wallace Roney (tp)
No Room for Argument (with Lenny White, Geri Allen, Adam Holzman) 2000;
  Concord
SEE ALSO Terri Lyne Carrington, Marvin "Smitty" Smith, Tony Williams

Josh Roseman (tb)
Treats for the Nightwalker (with Peter Apfelbaum, Ben Monder, Billy Kilson, Chris
  Potter, Mark Feldman, et al.) 2002; Enja
SEE ALSO Steve Coleman, Dave Holland

Florian Ross (p)
Home and Some Other Place (with Claus Stötter, Matthias Erlewein, Dietmar Fuhr,
  Stephane Huchard) 2005; Intuition

Der Rote Bereich (band)
Live in Montreux (with Frank Möbus, Rudi Mahall, John Schröder) 2004; ACT

Ned Rothenberg (ss, ts)
Ghost Stories (With Min Xiao-Fen, Erik Friedlander, Satoshi Takeishi, et al.) 2000;
  Tzadik

Rova Saxophone Quartet (band)
The Works, Vol. 3 1997; Black Saint

Keith Rowe (g)
SEE AMM

Gonzalo Rubalcaba (p, keyb)
The Blessing (with Charlie Haden, Jack DeJohnette) 1991; Blue Note
Supernova Blue Note, 2001
SEE ALSO Charlie Haden

Jochen Rückert (dm)
Introduction (with Chris Potter, Ben Monder, et al.) 1997; Jazzline
SEE ALSO Nils Wogram

Roswell Rudd (tb)
Flexible Flyer (with Hod O'Brien, Arild Andersen, Barry Altschul, Sheila Jordan)
  1974; Black Lion
Malicool (with Toumani Diabaté et al.) 2003; Sunnyside
SEE ALSO Jazz Composers' Orchestra, Steve Lacy, Misha Mengelberg, Sex Mob

Mathias Rüegg (ld)
SEE Vienna Art Orchestra

Jimmy Rushing (voc)
SEE Count Basie

George Russell (p, ld)
Ezz-thetics (with Don Ellis, Dave Baker, Eric Dolphy, Steve Swallow, Joe Hunt)
    1961; Original Jazz Classics

Terje Rypdal (g)
Odyssey 1975; ECM
Lux Aeterna (with Palle Mikkelborg, Bergen Chamber Ensemble) 2000; ECM
SEE ALSO Jan Garbarek, Tomasz Stanko, Markus Stockhausen

Dino Saluzzi (bandoneon)
Senderos (with Jon Christensen) 2002; ECM
SEE ALSO Maria João

David Sanborn (as)
Straight to the Heart (with Michael Brecker, Marcus Miller, et al.) 1984; Warner
SEE ALSO Randy Brecker, Gil Evans, Jimmy Scott

David Sànchez (ts)
Melaza (with Miguel Zenón, Antonio Sánchez, William Cepeda, et al.) 2000; Columbia
SEE ALSO Steve Turre

Pharoah Sanders (ts, ss)
Karma (with Leon Thomas, Billy Hart, Lonnie Liston Smith, Reggie Workman,
    et al.) 1969; Impulse
Welcome to Love (with William Henderson, Stafford James, Eccleston W.
    Wainwright) 1990; Timeless
SEE ALSO Gary Bartz, Alice Coltrane, John Coltrane, Steve Turre

Heinz Sauer (ts)
Melancholia (with Michael Wollny) 2005; ACT
SEE ALSO Albert Mangelsdorff

Saxofour (band)
Saxofour: Streunende Hörner (with Wolfgang Puschnig, Klaus Dickbauer, Florian
    Bramböck, Christian Maurer) 1998; PAO

Jenny Scheinman (viol)
The Rabbi's Lover 2002; Tzadik
SEE ALSO Scott Amendola, Bill Frisell

Maria Schneider (ld)
Evanescence (with Rick Margitza, Rich Perry, Tim Hagans, Tim Ries, Kenny Werner,
    et al.) 1994; Enja

Daniel Schnyder (sax, ld)
Tarantula (with Hubert Laws, Thomas Chapin, Michael Formanek, John Clark,
    et al.) 1998; Enja

Manfred Schoof (tp)
European Echoes (with Derek Bailey, Evan Parker, Peter Brötzmann, Fred van Hove,
    Alexander von Schlippenbach) 1969; Atavistic
SEE ALSO Globe Unity Orchestra, Gunter Hampel

Irène Schweizer (p)
Irène Schweizer & Günter Sommer 1987; Intakt
Where's Africa (with Omri Ziegele) 2005; Intakt

Louis Sclavis (cl, bcl, ss)
Trio de Clarinettes (with Armand Angster, Jacques Di Donato) 1990; Intakt
Dans la Nuit (with Vincent Courtois, Dominique Pifarély, Jean-Louis Matinier,
    Francois Merville) 2002; ECM

John Scofield (g)
Shinola (with Steve Swallow, Adam Nussbaum) 1981; Enja
Meant to Be (with Joe Lovano, Marc Johnson, Bill Stewart) 1990; Blue Note
Überjam (with Avi Bortnick et al.) 2002; Verve
SEE ALSO Paul Chambers, Marc Johnson, Pat Metheny, New Conception of Jazz,
    Niels-Henning Ørsted Pedersen, Tommy Smith, Jeremy Steig, Steve Swallow,
    Bennie Wallace

Jimmy Scott (voc)
Someone to Watch over Me (with Lionel Hampton, David Sanborn, Jools Holland,
    et al.) 1950–98; Warner

Tony Scott (cl)
A Day in New York (with Bill Evans, Paul Motian, et al.) 1959; Fresh Sound
Music for Zen Meditation (with Hozan Yamamoto, Shiniche Yuize) 1964; Verve

Trygve Seim (ss, ts, ld)
Different Rivers (with Arve Henriksen, Stian Carstensen, Sidsel Endresen, Nils
    Jansen, et al.) 1999; ECM

Sex Mob (band)
Dime Grind Palace (with Steven Bernstein, Briggan Krauss, Tony Scherr, Roswell
    Rudd) 2003; Ropeadope

Shakti (band)
Shakti (with John McLaughlin, Zakir Hussain, L. Shankar, et al.) 1974; Columbia
Saturday Night in Bombay: Remember Shakti (with John McLaughlin, Zakir
    Hussain, U. Shrinivas, V. Selvaganesh, et al.) 2001; Verve

Bud Shank (as, fl)
At Jazz Alley 1986; Contemporary
SEE ALSO David Friesen

L. Shankar (viol)
Eternal Light (with Zakir Hussain, T. H. Vinayakram) 2000; Moment
SEE ALSO Shakti

Elliott Sharp (g)
Figure Ground 1997; Tzadik

Sonny Sharrock (g)
Black Woman (with Linda Sharrock, Milford Graves, Teddy Daniel) 1969; Vortex
Ask the Ages (with Pharoah Sanders, Elvin Jones, Charnett Moffett) 1991; Axiom

Artie Shaw (cl, ld)
Begin the Beguine: Classic Jazz (with Buddy Rich, Billie Holiday, Ray Conniff)
  1938–41; RCA, Bluebird
The Complete Gramercy Five Sessions (with Johnny Guarneri, Billy Butterfield,
  Barney Kessel, Roy Eldridge) 1940–45; Bluebird

Woody Shaw (tp)
Song of Songs (with George Cabies, Bennie Maupin, et al.) 1972; Original Jazz Classics
Time Is Right—Woody Shaw Quintet Live in Europe (with Stafford James, Mulgrew
  Miller, Tony Reedus, Steve Turre) 1983; Red Records
SEE ALSO Freddie Hubbard, Joe Zawinul

George Shearing (p)
Live at the Cafe Carlyle 1984; Concord

Brad Shepik (g)
SEE Matt Darriau, Pachora, Tiny Bell Trio

Archie Shepp (ts, ss)
Archie Shepp & the New York Contemporary Five (with Don Cherry, John Tchicai,
  et al.) 1963; Storyville
Trouble in Mind (with Horace Parlan) 1980; SteepleChase
St. Louis Blues (with Richard Davis, Sunny Murray) 1998; PAO
SEE ALSO John Coltrane, Cecil Taylor

Arkady Shilkloper (frh, alphorn)
Presente Para Moscow (with Alegre Correa, Dhafer Youssef, et al.) 2003; Jaro
SEE ALSO Moscow Art Trio, Pago Libre

Matthew Shipp (p)
Gravitational Systems (with Mat Maneri) 1998; hatOLOGY
Equilibrium (with William Parker, Gerald Cleaver, Khan Jamal, FLAM) 2002;
  Thirsty Ear
SEE ALSO Mat Maneri

Wayne Shorter (ts, ss)
Super Nova (with Chick Corea, Jack DeJohnette, John McLaughlin, Airto Moreira,
  Miroslav Vitous, et al.) 1969; Blue Note
Atlantis 1985; CBS
Beyond the Sound Barrier (with Danilo Perez, John Patitucci, Brian Blade) 2005;
  Verve
SEE ALSO Art Blakey, Miles Davis, Grachan Moncur III, Michel Petrucciani, Weather
  Report, Joe Zawinul

Horace Silver (p)
The Stylings of Silver (with Art Farmer, Hank Mobley, et al.) 1957; Blue Note
Song for My Father (with Joe Henderson, Carmell Jones, Gene Taylor, et al.) 1964;
  Blue Note
The Hardbop Grandpop (with Claudio Roditi, Michael Brecker, Steve Turre, Ron
  Carter, Ronnie Cuber, Lewis Nash) 1996; GRP

Zoot Sims (ts, ss, cl)
Zoot Sims and the Gershwin Brothers (with Joe Pass, Oscar Peterson, et al.) 1975;
 Pablo
SEE ALSO Stan Getz, Joe Venuti

Bessie Smith (voc)
The Essential Bessie Smith (with Louis Armstrong, Coleman Hawkins, Benny
 Goodman, et al.) 1923–33; Columbia

Jimmy Smith (org)
Back at the Chicken Shack (with Kenny Burrell et al.) 1960; Blue Note
Root Down 1972; Verve
Legacy (with Joey DeFrancesco) 2004; Concord
SEE ALSO Joey DeFrancesco, Phineas Newborn

Marvin "Smitty" Smith (dm)
The Road Less Traveled (with Wallace Roney, Robin Eubanks, Ralph Moore, Steve
 Coleman, James Williams) 1989; Concord
SEE ALSO JoAnne Brackeen, Kevin Eubanks

Tommy Smith (ts)
Evolution (with Joe Lovano, John Scofield, John Taylor, John Patitucci, Bill Stewart)
 2003; ESC

Wadada Leo Smith (tp)
Red Sulphur Sky 2001; Tzadik

Martial Solal (p)
Martial Solal Trio at Newport 1963; RCA
Plays Ellington (with Sylvain Beuf, Francois Merville, Denis Leloup, et al.) 1997;
 Dreyfus

Lew Soloff (tp)
With a Song in My Heart (with Mulgrew Miller, George Mraz, Victor Lewis, et al.)
 1998; Milestone
SEE ALSO Ray Anderson, Carla Bley, Ricky Ford

Günter "Baby" Sommer (dm)
Sächsische Schatulle—Hörmusik II 1988; Intact
SEE ALSO Irène Schweizer

Omar Sosa (p)
Mulatos (with Paquito D'Rivera, Dhafer Youssef, Philippe Foch, et al.) 2004; Otá

Special Edition (band)
SEE Jack DeJohnette

Spontaneous Music Ensemble (band)
Quintessence 2 (with John Stevens, Trevor Watts, Evan Parker, Derek Bailey, Kent
 Carter, et al.) 1973–74; Emanem

Tomasz Stanko (tp)
Litania: The Music of Krysztof Komeda (with Bernt Rosengren, Bobo Stenson, Palle
   Danielsson, Jon Christensen, Terje Rypdal) 1997; ECM

Jeremy Steig (fl)
Firefly (with Dave Matthews, Eric Gale, Hiram Bullock, John Scofield, Steve Gadd,
   et al.) 1973; CTI
SEE ALSO Eddie Gomez

Norbert Stein (ts)
Pata Maroc (with Michael Heupel, Klaus Mages, Michael Rüsenberg, et al.)
   1998–99; Pata Music

Bobo Stenson (p)
Serenity (with Anders Jormin, Jon Christensen) 2000; Enja
SEE ALSO Tomasz Stanko

Steps Ahead (band)
Vibe 1994; NYC

Mike Stern (g)
These Times (with Richard Bona, Vinnie Colaiuta, Kenny Garrett, Jim Beard, et al.)
   2003; ESC

John Stevens (dm)
SEE Spontaneous Music Ensemble

Bob Stewart (tuba)
Goin' Home (with James Zoller, Steve Turre, Jerome Harris, Ed Blackwell, et al.)
   1988; JMT / Winter & Winter
SEE ALSO Arthur Blythe, Lester Bowie

Sonny Stitt (as, ts)
Stitt Plays Bird (with Jim Hall, John Lewis, et al.) 1963; Atlantic

Markus Stockhausen (tp, flh)
Karta (with Arild Andersen, Patrice Heral, Terje Rypdal) 1999; Enja
SEE ALSO Rainer Brüninghaus, Michel Portal, Gianluigi Trovesi

String Trio of New York (band)
Gut Reaction (with Rob Thomas, James Emery, John Lindberg) 2003; Omnitone

Erika Stucky (voc)
Bubbles + Bones (with Ray Anderson, Art Baron, et al.) 2001; Traumton

John Surman (bs, ss, bcl, synth)
Upon Reflection 1979; ECM
Coruscating (with Chris Laurence et al.) 1999; ECM
SEE ALSO Anouar Brahem

Esbjörn Svensson (p)
Strange Place for Snow (with Dan Berglund, Magnus Öström) 2001; ACT
SEE ALSO Viktoria Tolstoy

Steve Swallow (b)
Swallow (with Gary Burton, John Scofield) 1991; ECM
L'Histoire du Clochard: The Bum's Tale (with Ohad Talmor, Russ Johnson, Greg
    Tardy, et al.) 2002; Palmetto
SEE ALSO Rabih Abou-Khalil, Carla Bley, Jimmy Giuffre, Kip Hanrahan, Jazz
    Composers' Orchestra, Sheila Jordan, Glen Moore, Bob Moses, Michel Portal,
    Bobby Previte, George Russell, John Scofield

Lew Tabackin (ts, fl)
SEE Toshiko Akiyoshi

Craig Taborn (p, org)
Junk Magic (Aaron Stewart, David King, Mat Maneri) 2004; Thirsty Ear
SEE ALSO James Carter, Marty Ehrlich, Mat Maneri

Jamaaladeen Tacuma (b)
Jukebox (with Byard Lancaster, Dennis Alston, et al.) 1987; Gramavision
SEE ALSO Ornette Coleman, Wolfgang Puschnig

Aki Takase (p)
Alice (with Maria João, Niels-Henning Ørsted Pedersen) 1990; Enja
St. Louis Blues (with Fred Frith, Rudi Mahall, Paul Lovens, Nils Wogram) 2001;
    Enja

Take 6 (band, voc)
Take 6 1988; Warner

Vladimir Tarasov (dm)
SEE Ganelin Trio

Art Tatum (p)
Pure Genius (with Tiny Grimes, Edmond Hall, Slam Stewart, et al.) 1937–44; Affinity
The Art Tatum Solo Masterpieces (7 CD) 1953–54; Pablo
The Art Tatum Group Masterpieces (6 CD) (with Louie Bellson, Benny Carter,
    Buddy DeFranco, Harry Edison, Roy Eldrige, Lionel Hampton, Jo Jones,
    Barney Kessel, Buddy Rich, Ben Webster, et al.) 1954–56; Pablo

Cecil Taylor (p)
The World of Cecil Taylor (with Archie Shepp et al.) 1960; Candid
Unit Structures (with Eddie Gale, Jimmy Lyons, Henry Grimes, Alan Silva, et al.)
    1966; Blue Note
One Too Many Salty Swift and Not Goodbye (2 CD) (with Ronald Shannon
    Jackson, Jimmy Lyons, et al.) 1978; HatArt
The Willisau Concert 2000; Intakt
SEE ALSO Jazz Composers' Orchestra

John Taylor (p, org)
Rosslyn (with Marc Johnson, Joey Baron) 2002; ECM
SEE ALSO Peter Erskine, Tommy Smith

Jack Teagarden (tb, voc)
The Indispensable 1928–1957 (with Roger Wolf Kahn's Orchestra, Eddie Condon's
    Hot Shots, Ben Pollack, Paul Whiteman's Orchestra, et al.); RCA

Clark Terry (tp, co, flh, voc)
Clark Terry–Red Mitchell 1986; Enja
SEE ALSO Tadd Dameron, David Friesen

Henri Texier (b)
Mosaïc Man (with Glenn Ferris, Bojan Zulfikarpasic, Sebastien Texier, Tony
    Rabeson) 1998; Label Bleu
SEE ALSO Phil Woods

Toots Thielemans (harm, g)
Only Trust Your Heart (with Joey Baron, Fred Hersch, Marc Johnson, Harvie
    Swartz) 1988; Concord
SEE ALSO Quincy Jones

Gary Thomas (ts, fl)
Till We Have Faces (with Pat Metheny, Tim Murphy, Anthony Cox, Terri Lyne
    Carrington, et al.) 1992; JMT / Winter & Winter
SEE ALSO Terri Lyne Carrington

Jens Thomas (p)
Plays Ennio Morricone (with Paolo Fresu, Antonello Salis) 2000; Act

Lucky Thompson (ts, ss)
Lucky Strikes (with Richard Davis, Hank Jones, Connie Kay) 1964; Original Jazz
    Classics

Henry Threadgill (as, fl, bs)
Rag, Bush and All (with Ted Daniels, Bill Lowe, Reggie Nicholson, et al.) 1988;
    Novus/RCA
Up Popped the Two Lips (with Liberty Ellman, Dafnis Prieto, et al.) 2001; PI
SEE ALSO Air, David Murray

Steve Tibbetts (g)
A Man About a Horse (with Marc Anderson, Jim Anton, et al.) 2002; ECM

Bobby Timmons (p)
This Here Is Bobby Timmons (with Sam Jones, Jimmy Cobb) 1960; Original Jazz
    Classics
SEE ALSO Pepper Adams, Art Blakey

Tiny Bell Trio (band)
Constellations (with Dave Douglas, Jim Black, Brad Shepik) 1995; HatHUT

Viktoria Tolstoy (voc)
Shining on You (with Esbjörn Svensson et al.) 2003; ACT

Ralph Towner (g)
Solstice (with Jan Garbarek, Jon Christensen, Eberhard Weber) 1974; ECM
Anthem 2000; ECM
SEE ALSO Maria João, Oregon, Gary Peacock, Weather Report, Eberhard Weber

Colin Towns (p, ld)
The Theatre of Kurt Weill (with NDR Big Band) 2000; ACT

Lennie Tristano (p)
Lennie Tristano / Tadd Dameron (with Billy Bauer, Lee Konitz, Warne Marsh, et al.)
     1949; Affinity
Requiem (with Lee Konitz et al.) 1955–61; Atlantic

Gianluigi Trovesi (ss, as, cl, bcl)
In Cerca di Cibo (with Gianni Coscia) 1999; ECM
Dedalo (with Markus Stockhausen, Tom Rainey, WDR Big Band) 2001; Enja
SEE ALSO Michel Godard

Erik Truffaz (tp)
Walk of the Giant Turtle (with Marc Erbetta, Marcello Giuliani, Patrick Muller)
     2003; Blue Note

Arto Tuncboyacian (perc, dr)
SEE Arthur Blythe, Glen Moore, Oregon

Mark Turner (ts)
In This World (with Brad Mehldau, Larry Grenadier, Brian Blade, et al.) 1996; Warner

Steve Turre (tb, shells)
Rhythm Within (with Herbie Hancock, Pharoah Sanders, et al.) 1995; Verve
TNT (Trombone-N-Tenor) (with James Carter, Dewey Redman, David Sànchez)
     2000; Telarc
SEE ALSO Lester Bowie, Ricky Ford, Woody Shaw, Horace Silver, Bob Stewart

McCoy Tyner (p, ld)
Reaching Fourth (with Henry Grimes, Roy Haynes) 1962; Impulse
Song of the New World 1973; Milestone
Four Times Four (with Arthur Blythe, Al Foster, Freddie Hubbard, Bobby
     Hutcherson, Cecil McBee) 1980; Milestone
Illuminations (with Terence Blanchard, Gary Bartz, Christian McBride, Lewis Nash)
     2003; Telarc
SEE ALSO John Coltrane, Art Farmer, Grant Green, Joe Henderson, Freddie
     Hubbard, David Murray

James "Blood" Ulmer (g)
Forbidden Blues (with Amin Ali, Calvin Weston, et al.) 1996; DIW
SEE ALSO Karl Berger

Underkarl (band)
Second Brain (with Sebastian Gramss, Nils Wogram, et al.) 2003; Enja

United Jazz + Rock Ensemble (big band)
Plays Albert Mangelsdorff (with Albert Mangelsdorff, Wolfgang Dauner, Christof
    Lauer, Charlie Mariano, Volker Kriegel, Barbara Thompson, Eberhard Weber,
    Kenny Wheeler, et al.) 1998; Mood

Chucho Valdés (p, keyb)
Solo—Live in New York 2001; Blue Note
SEE ALSO Irakere

Ken Vandermark (ts, as, ld)
Design in Time (with Tim Mulvenna, Robert Barry) 1999; Delmark
SEE ALSO Fred Anderson

Jasper van't Hof (keyb)
At the Concertgebouw—Solo 1993; Challenge

Tom Varner (frh)
Second Communion (with Tony Malaby, Pete McCann, Cameron Brown, Matt
    Wilson) 2000; Omnitone
SEE ALSO Rabih Abou-Khalil

Naná Vasconcelos (perc)
SEE Gato Barbieri, Codona, Pierre Favre

Sarah Vaughan (voc)
Sarah Vaughan Live! (with Roy Haynes, Thad Jones, Frank Wess, Buster Williams,
    et al.) 1957–63; Mercury
How Long Has This Been Going On (with Louis Bellson, Ray Brown, Joe Pass,
    Oscar Peterson) 1978; Pablo

Glen Velez (perc)
Rhythmcolor Exotica (with Art Baron et al.) 1996; Ellipsis Arts

Joe Venuti (viol)
Stringing the Blues (with Eddie Lang et al.) 1926–31; Naxos
Joe Venuti & Zoot Sims (with John Bunch, Milt Hinton, et al.) 1975;
    Chiaroscuro

Edward Vesala (dm, ld)
Nan Madol (with Charlie Mariano, Juhani Aaltonen, et al.) 1974; ECM

Vienna Art Orchestra (big band)
Tango from Obango (with Mathias Rüegg, Wolfgang Puschnig, Wolfgang
    Reisinger, Herbert Joos, Lauren Newton, Werner Pirchner, et al.) 1980;
    Extraplatte
Art & Fun (with Mathias Rüegg, Anna Lauvergnac, Bumi Fian, Klaus Dickbauer,
    Harry Sokal, Martin Koller, et al.) (2 CD) 2002; Emarcy

Miroslav Vitous (b)
Universal Syncopations (with John McLaughlin, Jan Garbarek, Chick Corea, Jack DeJohnette) 2003; ECM
SEE ALSO Jan Garbarek, Wayne Shorter, Weather Report, Joe Zawinul

Alexander von Schlippenbach (p, ld)
Complete Combustion (with Paul Lovens, Evan Parker) 1998; FMP
SEE ALSO Globe Unity Orchestra, Gunter Hampel, Sam Rivers, Manfred Schoof

Cuong Vu (tp)
Come Play with Me 2001; Knitting Factory Works
SEE ALSO Nils Wogram

Collin Walcott (perc, sitar)
Cloud Dance (with John Abercrombie, Jack DeJohnette, Dave Holland) 1975; ECM
SEE ALSO Codona, David Darling, Oregon

Mal Waldron (p)
Mal / 4 Trio (with Addison Farmer, Kenny Davis) 1958; Original Jazz Classics
Live at the Dreher, Paris (with Steve Lacy) 1981; HatHUT
One More Time (with Jean-Jacques Avenel, Steve Lacy) 2002; Sketch
SEE ALSO Gene Ammons, Eric Dolphy, Jackie McLean, Charles Mingus

Bennie Wallace (ts)
Twilight Time (with Ray Anderson, Jack DeJohnette, Eddie Gomez, John Scofield, et al.) 1985; Blue Note

Fats Waller (p, org)
1939 Transcriptions, Vol. 2 (with John Hamilton, Gene Sedric, et al.) Naxos
The Centennial Collection (with Alberta Hunter et al.) 1927–43; RCA

Cedar Walton (p)
Eastern Rebellion (with George Coleman, Sam Jones, Billy Higgins) 1975; Timeless
SEE ALSO Art Blakey, Slide Hampton, Billy Higgins, Milt Jackson, Philly Joe Jones, Abbey Lincoln

Dinah Washington (voc)
What a Difference a Day Makes! 1959; Mercury
The Definitive Dinah Washington (with Hal Mooney's Orchestra, Terry Gibbs, Brook Benton, et al.) 1943–62; Universal

Muddy Waters (g, voc)
His Best 1947–55; Chess

Julius Watkins (frh)
SEE Benny Bailey, Tadd Dameron

Bobby Watson (as)
Horizon Reassembled (with Edward Simon, Essiet Essiet, Victor Lewis, Terell Stafford) 2004; Palmetto

Eric Watson (p)
Reaching Up (with Mulgrew Miller, Charles Fambrough, Jack DeJohnette) 1993;
    JVC

WDR Big Band (big band)
SEE Gianluigi Trovesi

Weather Report (band)
I Sing the Body Electric (with Miroslav Vitous, Wayne Shorter, Joe Zawinul, Ralph
    Towner, et al.) 1972; Columbia
Heavy Weather (with Jaco Pastorius, Wayne Shorter, Joe Zawinul, et al.) 1977; CBS

Chick Webb (dm, ld)
The Quintessence / New York (with Ella Fitzgerald et al.) 1929–39; Fremeaux &
    Associes

Eberhard Weber (b)
Selected Recordings (with Gary Burton, Pat Metheny, Ralph Towner, Jan Garbarek,
    et al.) 1974–2000; ECM (:rarum XVIII)
SEE ALSO Ralph Towner, United Jazz + Rock Ensemble

Ben Webster (ts)
Ben Webster with the Oscar Peterson Trio (with Ray Brown, Ed Thigpen) 1959;
    Verve
Stormy Weather (with Niels-Henning Ørsted Pedersen et al.) 1965; Black Lion
SEE ALSO Benny Carter, Duke Ellington, Bill Harris, Coleman Hawkins, Richard
    "Groove" Holmes, Gerry Mulligan, Art Tatum, Teddy Wilson

Dave Weckl (dm)
SEE Chick Corea

Bugge Wesseltoft (p, keyb)
SEE ALSO New Conception of Jazz (band)

Kenny Wheeler (tp, flh)
Deer Wan (with Jan Garbarek, John Abercrombie, et al.) 1978; ECM
Double, Double You (with Michael Brecker, Jack DeJohnette, Dave Holland, John
    Taylor) 1983; ECM
SEE ALSO John Abercrombie, Rabih Abou-Khalil, Bernd Konrad, United Jazz + Rock
    Ensemble

Cootie Williams (tp)
SEE ALSO Duke Ellington, Benny Goodman

Mary Lou Williams (p)
Solo Recital, Montreux 1978; Pablo
SEE ALSO Dizzy Gillespie

Tony Williams (dm)
Emergency! (with John McLaughlin, Larry Young) 1969; Polydor

Civilization (with Mulgrew Miller, Charnett Moffett, Billy Pierce, Wallace Roney)
  1986; Blue Note
SEE ALSO Miles Davis, Kenny Dorham, Herbie Hancock, Jackie McLean, Sonny Rollins

Hal Willner (producer)
Lost in the Stars—The Music of Kurt Weill (with Carla Bley, Lou Reed, Sting, Tom
  Waits, Phil Woods, John Zorn, et al.) 1985; A&M

Cassandra Wilson (voc)
Blue Light 'Til Dawn (with Brandon Ross, Lonnie Plaxico, Olu Dara, Cyro Baptista,
  Lance Carter, Kenneth Davis, et al.) 1993; Blue Note

Matt Wilson (dm)
Smile (with Joel Frahm, Andrew D'Angelo, Yosuke Inoue) 1999; Palmetto
SEE ALSO Michael Blake, Dewey Redman

Teddy Wilson (p)
Too Hot for Words (with Roy Eldridge, Johnny Hodges, Billie Holiday, Ben Webster,
  et al.) 1935; Hep
The Impeccable Mr. Wilson (with Jo Jones, Al Lucas) 1957; Verve
SEE ALSO Benny Goodman, Billie Holiday, Red Norvo, Lester Young

Kai Winding (tb)
Cleveland June 1957 (with Wayne Andre, Carl Fontana, et al.) 1957; Storyville
SEE ALSO Miles Davis, J. J. Johnson, Fats Navarro

Reiner Winterschladen (tp)
Nighthawks: Metrobar (with Dal Martino) 2001; Intuition
SEE ALSO Klaus König, NDR Big Band

Nils Wogram (tb)
Odd and Awkward (with Cuong Vu, Hayden Chisholm, Jochen Rückert, Steffen
  Schorn, Simon Nabatov, Chris Speed, Henning Sieverts) 2002; Enja
SEE ALSO Simon Nabatov, Lucas Niggli, Aki Takase, Undercarl

Phil Woods (as)
At the Montreux Jazz Festival (with George Gruntz, Henri Texier, Daniel Humair)
  1969; Verve
Ornithology: Phil Salutes Bird (with Franco D'Andrea et al.) 1994; Philology
SEE ALSO Benny Bailey, Benny Carter, Eddie Costa, Hal Willner

World Saxophone Quartet (band)
Live in Zürich (with Julius Hemphill, Oliver Lake, Hamiet Bluiett, David Murray)
  1981; Black Saint
Requiem for Julius (with Oliver Lake, Hamiet Bluiett, David Murray, John Purcell)
  2000; Justin Time

Lester Young (ts, cl)
The Kansas City Sessions (with Buck Clayton, Eddie Durham, Charlie Christian,
  Freddie Green, Walter Page, Jo Jones) 1938–44; GRP

The Complete Aladdin Sessions (2 CD) (with Nat "King" Cole, Red Callendar, et al.) 1942–48; Blue Note
The Complete Savoy Recordings 1944; Savoy Jazz
Lester Young with the Oscar Peterson Trio (with Barney Kessel, Ray Brown) 1952; Verve
The Jazz Giants '56 (with Roy Eldridge, Vic Dickenson, Teddy Wilson, Freddie Green, Gene Ramey, Jo Jones) 1956; Verve
SEE ALSO Count Basie, Benny Goodman

Joe Zawinul (keyb)
Zawinul (with Wayne Shorter, Miroslav Vitous, Woody Shaw, Jack DeJohnette) 1970; Atlantic
World Tour (with Manolo Badrena, Victor Bailey, Paco Sery, et al.) 1997; Zebra
SEE ALSO Cannonball Adderley, Miles Davis, Weather Report

John Zorn (as, mouthpieces, ld)
Spillane (with Kronos Quartet, Ronald Shannon Jackson, Bill Frisell, Bobby Previte, et al.) 1986–87; Nonesuch
Film Works Vol. 8 (with Masada String Trio, Marc Ribot, Anthony Coleman, Cyro Baptista, Kenny Wollesen) 1997; Tzadik
Masada: Live in Sevilla 2000 (with Dave Douglas, Greg Cohen, Joey Baron) 2000; Tzadik
SEE ALSO Naked City, Hal Willner

Bojan Zulfikarpasic (p)
Koreni (with Julien Lourau, Kudsi Erguner, Tony Rabeson, Karim Ziad) 1998; Label Bleu
SEE ALSO Michel Portal, Henri Texier

Index

AACM, 32–33, 46, 62, 145, 259, 276, 279, 300, 306, 309, 329–30, 354, 381, 394, 485, 498, 512

Aaltonen, Juani, 331

Åarset, Eivind, 414, 430, 544

Abdul-Malik, Ahmed, 460, 544

Abercrombie, John, 40, 431, 437, 439, 493, 539, 623

Åberg, Lennart, 331

Abou-Khalil, Rabih, 51, 291, 357, 513, 515, 535, 541, 543–44, 560, 650

Abrams, Muhal Richard, 32, 46, 57, 98, 205, 288, 368, 380–81, 384, 459, 617, 621, 640, 642

Achiary, Beñat, 560, 625

acid jazz, 69–70, 189, 432, 526, 556

Ackerman, William, 432, 522

Adams, George, 328–29, 354, 381, 554, 649

Adams, Pepper, 220, 286, 340–42

Adderley, Cannonball, 119, 127, 165, 305, 312, 335, 373, 505, 640

Adderley, Nat, 245, 252

Afro-Cuban Rhumba All-Stars, 297

Ahmad Jamal Trio, 392

Air, 46, 307, 343, 458, 486, 578, 641

Akchoté, Noel, 433–34

Akiyoshi, Toshiko, 98, 297, 314, 356, 372, 611, 614

Alden, Howard, 334, 436–37

Ali, Rashied, 49, 70, 140, 148, 237, 478, 481, 557

Alias, Don, 505

All Stars Brass Band, 648

Allen, Geri, 380, 382, 384, 406

Allen, Henry "Red," 249, 588

Allison, Ben, 348, 459, 546, 653–54

Allison, Mose, 372–73, 555

Allyson, Karrin, 567, 582

Almeida, Laurindo, 418, 509

Altena, Maarten, 456–57

Altschul, Barry, 33, 306, 481, 485–86

Amampondo, 331, 512

AMM, 28–29, 434, 638

Andersen, Arild, 453, 456–57

Anderson, Cat, 250

Anderson, Ivie, 563

Anderson, Laurie, 574

Anderson, Ray, 50, 271, 277–78, 459, 613, 642, 652

Anderson, Wes, 313

Anger, Darol, 522

Apfelbaum, Peter, 338, 622

Arcado String Trio, 459, 525, 527, 529

Argüelles, Steve, 498–99, 616

Armando, Ray, 508

Armstrong, Louis, 6, 11, 12–13, 15–16, 22, 41, 77, 78–86, 88, 90, 103, 110, 114, 120, 124, 126, 130, 134, 156, 165, 168, 174, 194, 196, 199, 202–3, 205, 234, 236, 246–47, 249–51, 255–56, 262, 268–69, 271, 280–81, 295–96, 302, 335, 358, 366, 369, 416, 442, 468, 470–71, 521, 530, 549, 552–55, 559, 570–71, 588, 596, 600, 605, 628, 635, 648, 663–64

Art Ensemble of Chicago, 145, 294, 306, 457, 485, 640–42

Asmussen, Svend, 521

atonality, 21–22, 223, 226, 560

Atzmon, Gilad, 338
Auld, Georgie, 315, 317
Avenel, Jean-Jacques, 454
Avital, Omer, 461
Ayler, Albert, 20, 22, 25, 28,
    47, 49, 59, 81, 109, 148,
    167, 170–71, 203, 227,
    327–29, 333, 337, 450,
    480, 489, 525, 638, 662

Baars, Ab, 65, 291, 293
Bach, Johann Sebastian, 20, 30,
    104, 120, 154, 165–66,
    169, 196–97, 230, 233,
    240–41, 333, 351, 373,
    378, 381, 387–88, 396–
    97, 400, 409, 419, 459,
    472, 520, 603, 616, 622,
    633–34
Bad Plus, The, 392, 460, 656
Bailey, Benny, 612
Bailey, Buster, 588
Bailey, Derek, 413, 431, 433–
    34, 540, 546, 638, 663
Bailey, Mildred, 563
Bailey, Victor, 463–64
Baker, Chet, 248, 251, 281,
    341, 554, 581, 585, 633
Baker, Ginger, 35, 155, 483–84
Bakken, Rebekka, 584
Baldwin, James, 24, 562
Balkan music, 62, 64–67, 191,
    241, 265, 292, 352, 357,
    363, 396–97, 439–40,
    495, 525, 534, 537, 560,
    654
Ballou, Dave, 260
Bang, Billy, 40, 522, 525–27,
    530
Baptista, Cyro, 61, 510–11,
    513
Baptiste, Denys, 65, 336–37
Barber, Patricia, 555, 579,
    581–82
Bargeron, Dave, 273, 534
Barker, Danny, 165, 221
Barker, Guy, 257
Barnet, Charlie, 113, 295,
    590–91
Baron, Art, 277
Baron, Joey, 61–62, 185, 190,
    493–95, 499, 653–54
Barrett, Dan, 277
Barretto, Ray, 504–5, 508, 518

Barron, Kenny, 318, 356, 390,
    409, 528
Barthelmes, Johannes, 331
Basie, Count, 4, 13, 17–20, 91,
    102, 104–6, 112, 152,
    171, 196, 203, 238, 244,
    249, 252, 268, 271, 284,
    315–16, 318–21, 340–41,
    348, 350, 367, 382,
    398, 416–17, 420, 443,
    470–71, 477, 501, 521,
    552–54, 556, 566, 571,
    573, 578, 589, 591–93,
    595, 598–600, 604, 611,
    613, 617, 619, 629, 662
Bates, Django, 405, 539, 584,
    616
Bauer, Conrad, 274–75
Bauer, Johannnes, 274
Baum, Jamie, 355
Bauzá, Mario, 261, 502–3, 597
Beard, Jim, 406–7
Beatles, 35, 83, 181, 214, 325,
    333, 574, 583, 625
bebop, 2, 14–17, 18, 21, 28,
    30, 33, 39, 43–48, 55–58,
    68, 77, 102–3, 108–9,
    114–17, 120–21, 127–28,
    147, 149, 153, 164, 170–
    71, 173–74, 179–80, 188,
    208, 221–25, 234–37,
    255, 259, 262, 269–72,
    275, 283, 289, 291, 296,
    303, 310, 312–13, 316,
    319, 323, 332, 334–35,
    340–41, 346, 348, 351,
    358–59, 366, 371, 385,
    388, 394, 400, 403, 420,
    422, 428, 430–32, 436,
    444, 460, 466, 472–73,
    478, 483, 496, 500, 505,
    536–37, 540, 554–56,
    558, 563, 567–68, 570,
    591, 594, 600, 604, 606–
    7, 616, 640–41, 647–50
Bechet, Sidney, 295–96, 298–302,
    325, 442, 571, 648, 663
Beiderbecke, Bix, 12, 23, 77,
    89–94, 199, 203, 221,
    247–48, 251–52, 271,
    281, 303, 470, 530
Beirach, Richie, 386, 529
Belden, Bob, 67–69, 264, 624,
    659

Bellson, Louie, 101, 470, 477,
    507, 611–12, 615
Bennett, Anand, 524–25
Bennink, Han, 29, 383, 414,
    487–88, 492, 499, 501,
    542–43, 606, 638, 656
Benson, George, 278, 422–24,
    437, 554
Berg, Alban, 22, 33, 301
Berg, Bob, 331, 333, 335
Berg, Henning, 272
Berger, Bengt, 51, 515, 650
Berger, Karl, 40, 42, 52, 138,
    361, 381, 514, 606
Bergin, Fred, 93
Bergman, Borah, 380
Berigan, Bunny, 13, 247
Berlin, Jeff, 463–64
Berne, Tim, 70, 260, 306–9,
    436, 495, 525, 649, 654
Bernstein, Peter, 402, 437
Bernstein, Steven, 174, 265–66,
    654
Berroa, Ignacio, 500, 618
Berry, Chu, 13–14, 88, 199,
    315, 588, 591, 629
Berry, Chuck, 213–14
Best, Denzil, 477
Bey, Andy, 559
Bickert, Ed, 427–28
Bigard, Barney, 8, 79, 281,
    291, 629
Bill Evans Trio, 376, 387, 392,
    448, 450–51, 656
Binney, David, 309–10, 658
Bishop, Jeb, 276
Black Artist Group, 46, 300,
    306, 343, 642, 648
black diaspora, 72, 176, 217,
    309, 362
Black, Jim, 495, 654
Blackman, Cindy, 495, 497–98
Blackwell, Ed, 142, 145, 479–
    80, 491, 493, 496, 650
Blade, Brian, 493–94, 655, 658
Blake, Eubie, 5
Blake, John, 524, 527
Blake, Michael, 300, 338
Blake, Ran, 28, 348, 380
Blake, Seamus, 334, 336–37
Blakey, Art, 19, 24, 48, 67,
    126, 168–69, 237, 253,
    255, 257, 264, 279, 298,
    311, 322–23, 337, 373,

389–90, 392, 456, 460, 473–75, 477–78, 494, 496, 499, 501, 503–4, 511, 522, 596, 629, 630, 634, 640, 647
Blanchard, Terence, 48, 178, 255–57, 311, 474, 647–48
Blanton, Jimmy, 15, 98–99, 442, 444–47, 467, 483
Bley, Carla, 25, 28, 98, 205, 277, 313, 331, 380, 401, 408, 448, 462–63, 535, 538, 547–48, 603–5, 621
Bley, Paul, 28, 37, 259, 377, 380, 384, 404, 410, 573, 636, 658
Blonk, Jaap, 559
Blood, Sweat & Tears, 35, 157, 273, 534, 609
Bloom, Jane Ira, 299–300
Bloomfield, Mike, 216, 425
blue notes, 11, 62, 81, 147, 208–9, 221, 224, 226, 294, 321, 520
Bluiett, Hamiet, 288, 339, 343–46, 349
Blythe, Arthur, 33, 46, 119, 310–11, 347, 648–49
Bobo, Willie, 504–5
Boland, Francy, 611–12
Bolden, Buddy, 79, 246, 467
Bollani, Stefano, 387–88
Boltro, Flavio, 257
Bona, Richard, 464–65, 557
Bonano, Sharkey, 247
Bond, Graham, 35, 154–55
Borca, Karen, 538
bossa nova, 261, 299, 320–21, 419, 509, 574
Bostic, Earl, 137, 303
Bourelly, Jean-Paul, 435, 512
Bowie, Joseph, 50, 273, 652
Bowie, Lester, 46, 56, 59, 256, 258–60, 278, 337, 485, 640–41, 648
Brackeen, JoAnne, 389, 474
Braden, Don, 336
Braff, Ruby, 249, 436
Brahem, Anouar, 516, 544
Brand, Dollar. See Ibrahim, Abdullah
Brandlmayer, Martin, 65
Braud, Wellman, 98, 443

Braxton, Anthony, 16, 40, 119, 145, 206, 276–77, 288–89, 294, 300, 306–7, 330, 346–47, 381, 459, 473, 486, 526–27, 538, 606, 608, 617, 621, 636, 640–42
Brecker, Michael, 264, 278, 285, 315, 331–34, 339, 402, 431, 437, 494, 623
Brecker, Randy, 35, 254, 263–64, 278, 285, 355, 437, 615, 623
Breuker, Willem, 29, 286, 329, 487, 605–6
Bridgewater, Dee Dee, 572–73, 581
Brignola, Nick, 342
Broadbent, Alan, 373, 595
Brody, Paul, 63, 265
Broede, Matthias, 537
Brönner, Till, 257–58, 264
Bronson, Art, 106
Brooklyn All Stars, 219
Brookmeyer, Bob, 19, 271–72, 320, 428, 614, 620–21, 633
Broonzy, Big Bill, 19, 271–72, 320, 428, 614, 620–21, 633
Brötzmann, Peter, 28–29, 59, 181, 329–30, 343, 486–87, 638
Brown, Clifford, 19, 48, 168, 251–53, 256–58, 261, 325, 472, 629–30, 635
Brown, Garnett, 270, 273
Brown, Guillermo E., 486, 500, 608
Brown, James, 124, 127, 220, 272, 310, 490, 497, 527, 560
Brown, Lawrence, 268
Brown, Les, 255, 597
Brown, Marion, 142, 306
Brown, Ray, 372, 400, 411, 419, 437, 444–46, 451, 456, 458, 467, 491
Brown, Tom, 10
Brubeck, Dave, 66, 206, 215, 289, 304, 341, 377–78, 474, 483, 611, 627, 634, 663
Bruce, Jack, 35, 130, 463, 484

Bruford, Bill, 483, 498, 616
Brüninghaus, Rainer, 406–7, 575–77
Bryant, Ray, 372–73
Buckner, Milt, 377, 399–400
Buckner, Teddy, 247
Bullock, Hiram, 430
Bunnett, Jane, 297, 354
Burkhardt, Ingolf, 261
Burns, Ralph, 98, 205, 594
Burrell, Kenny, 422, 425, 440, 600
Burton, Abraham, 312
Burton, Gary, 35, 40, 333, 358–62, 428, 460, 491, 520, 615, 623
Butcher, John, 301
Butler, Henry, 389
Byard, Jaki, 59, 126, 306, 377, 607, 614, 656
Byas, Don, 49, 114, 315–18, 325, 329–30, 337, 469
Byrd, Donald, 19, 252, 536
Byron, Don, 56, 61, 290–91, 343, 495

Caceres, Ernie, 340
Cain, Jackie, 568–90, 630
Caine, Uri, 61k, 101, 397, 619, 653
Calhoun, Will, 484
call and response, 13, 174, 232, 379
Callender, Red, 442, 536
Calloway, Cab, 112–13, 221, 470, 503, 591, 597, 629
Camilo, Michel, 394–95
Campbell, Roy, 260
Cantuária, Vinicius, 419, 557
Cardew, Cornelius, 27
Cardona, Milt, 506–7
Carisi, Johnny, 121
Carl, Rüdiger, 532
Carlos, Walter, 37, 409–10
Carmichael, Hoagy, 92
Carney, Harry, 94, 96–97, 285, 339–40, 343–44
Carr, Ian, 122, 263, 643
Carrington, Terri Lyne, 484, 497–98
Carrott, Bryan, 361–62
Carstensen, Stian, 533
Carter, Benny, 13, 113, 271, 302–4, 306, 344, 471,

588–89, 592–93, 604, 611, 617

Carter, Betty, 392, 423, 497, 527, 562, 567–68, 570–72, 576, 578, 580, 582, 585

Carter, James, 297, 337, 338, 344–45, 400, 527, 658

Carter, John, 166, 283, 289–90, 525

Carter, Regina, 527–28

Carter, Ron, 123, 126, 168, 242, 386, 444, 449–50, 635

Carver, Wayman, 350

Casa Loma Band, 590–91

Cathcart, Patti, 572, 580

Catlett, Sid, 13, 79, 470, 477–78, 480–81, 487, 493, 588

Celestin, Papa, 246

Cepeda, William, 278

Chadbourne, Eugene, 433–34

Chakasin, Vladimir, 301, 330

Chaloff, Serge, 319, 340–43

Chambers, Dennis, 484

Chambers, Paul, 122–23, 446–47, 451, 455, 598

Charial, Pierre, 542

Charlap, Bill, 391–92, 656

Charles, Ray, 20, 37, 213, 220, 399, 550, 554, 560, 591

Chatterjee, Amit, 560

Cheatham, Doc, 116, 256

Chemirani, Djamchid, 515

Chemirani, Keyvan, 515

Cherry, Don, 24–25, 41, 51, 72, 138, 142, 152, 168, 258, 260, 328–29, 333, 338, 356, 415, 433, 448, 480, 510, 513, 542, 603, 622, 637–38, 650–51, 663

Chestnut, Cyrus, 57, 391–92

Chicago style, 2, 10, 12–13, 77, 82, 90–92, 103–4, 108, 234, 247–48, 267, 281–82, 293, 303, 317, 358, 364, 417, 469, 589

Christensen, Jon, 242, 388, 452, 490, 492, 498, 639

Christian, Charlie, 15, 36, 113, 224, 231–32, 282, 371, 400, 416–17, 420–24,

431, 443–44, 471, 473, 521, 629

Christlieb, Pete, 322, 339

Christmann, Günter, 274, 488

Christy, June, 567, 570, 581, 595

Cinelu, Mino, 508, 516

Clapton, Eric, 40, 130, 155, 214, 216, 427

Clark, Sonny, 188

Clarke, Kenny, 15, 108, 113, 121, 231, 350, 471, 473, 475–78, 537, 567, 596, 611–12, 633

Clarke, Stanley, 451, 462, 467, 645

Clay, James, 316

Clayton, Buck, 33, 249, 593

Clayton, Jay, 575–76, 626

Cleveland, Jimmy, 271, 598–99

Cobb, Arnett, 315–16, 337

Cobham, Billy, 38, 159, 236–37, 332, 431, 437, 478, 482, 493, 501, 514, 645

Codona, 51, 510, 513, 650–51

Coe, Tony, 288–89, 612

Cohen, Greg, 190, 459, 527, 654

Cohn, Al, 19, 196, 319–21, 593, 632

Cole, Cozy, 13, 470–71, 477, 481, 493, 591

Cole, Holly, 574

Cole, Nat King, 369, 553–54, 557, 559, 629–30, 632, 634

Cole, Ritchie, 119, 305, 556

Coleman, Anthony, 62, 189, 407

Coleman, Ornette, 22–25, 28, 41, 47, 49–50, 51, 64, 77, 119, 136–53, 163, 165–67, 169, 180, 183, 187, 190, 225, 258, 276, 285, 290, 305–7, 311, 314, 315, 326, 328, 330, 335, 360, 374, 380, 412, 431, 434, 448, 466, 479, 489, 527, 558, 606, 617, 629, 635, 637–38, 651–52, 654

Coleman, Steve, 50, 59, 71–72, 119, 279, 309–10, 357, 382, 408, 490, 494, 537, 562, 578, 652, 657–59

Coles, Johnny, 251, 600

Colina, Javier, 453

Collette, Buddy, 19, 284, 319, 321, 350

Colley, Scott, 460

Collignon, Médéric, 559–60, 625

Collins, Albert, 181, 425, 551

Collins, Cal, 33, 436

Collins, Nicolas, 276

Colosseum, 35

Coltrane, Alice, 140, 148–49, 531–32

Coltrane, John, 19, 23–25, 27–28, 33, 42, 48–49, 52, 59, 77, 109, 123, 125, 127, 136–53, 162, 165–66, 168, 170, 176, 179, 199, 203, 205, 219, 225, 228, 239, 242, 252, 254–55, 262, 265–66, 270, 277–78, 288, 292, 295–99, 301, 304, 310–12, 314, 321, 323, 326–27, 339, 349, 360, 374, 381, 387–90, 393, 401, 403, 415, 427–28, 436, 447–48, 452, 466, 474–76, 478, 482, 505, 510–12, 514, 516, 522–24, 527–28, 535–38, 541, 543, 552, 554, 556, 582, 602, 606, 613, 632, 635–36, 638, 650–51, 656, 663

Condon, Eddie, 90, 283, 417, 531

Cooder, Ry, 432

cool jazz, 2, 17–20, 24, 28, 33, 77, 102, 108, 121, 127, 132, 215, 221–23, 234–35, 248, 252, 268, 284, 289, 296, 305, 319, 321–22, 340, 343, 373, 422, 472, 474, 504, 509, 536, 554, 662

Cooper, Bob, 319, 350, 538

Corea, Chick, 37, 39-40, 127, 135, 153, 156, 199, 205, 272, 306, 318, 377, 382, 386-7, 391-2, 396k, 405, 451, 464, 474, 482–83, 507, 509, 515, 533, 558, 572, 574, 595, 643, 645

Coryell, Larry, 35, 40, 158, 418, 422, 428–29, 482, 520, 524, 603, 642
Coscia, Gianni, 533–34
Cosey, Pete, 428
Courbois, Pierre, 236, 482–83, 643
Courtois, Vincent, 444, 541
Courvoisier, Sylvie, 383
Cox, Anthony, 458–59
Cox, Ida, 88
Crane, Thomas, 494
Cranshaw, Bob, 456
Cray, Robert, 425, 551
Crayton, Pee Wee, 137
Cream, 35, 463, 483
Creative Music Studio, 42, 52, 138, 361, 381
Crispell, Marilyn, 380–81, 642
Criss, Sonny, 304
Crosby, Bob, 590–91, 629
Crosby, Gary, 461, 616
Crouch, Stanley, 56, 84, 145, 163, 172, 177, 448, 468, 647, 659
Cullum, Jamie, 559, 562
Cyrille, Andrew, 481, 501, 545

Dalto, Jorge, 389
Daly, Claire, 344–45
Dameron, Tadd, 17, 322, 596, 631
Damiani, Paolo, 453, 540
Daniels, Eddie, 289
Danielsson, Lars, 453
Danielsson, Palle, 242, 449, 452–53, 639
Danish Radio Jazz Orchestra (aka Danish Radio Big Band), 613, 620–21
Dara, Olu, 46, 172, 260
Darling, David, 540
Darriau, Matt, 191, 292
Dauer, Alfons M., 210, 297, 665
Dauner, Wolfgang, 386, 404, 406, 410, 616
Davern, Kenny, 282, 295, 301
Davis, Anthony, 44, 59, 172, 380–81, 525
Davis, Art, 140, 142
Davis, Eddie "Lockjaw," 315, 329, 337, 593, 612, 632
Davis, Kay, 97, 569

Davis, Miles, 7, 17–19, 25, 35–37, 39, 48, 50, 67, 70, 77, 92, 100–101, 104, 115–16, 120–36, 137–39, 152–54, 163, 168–70, 173, 192, 194, 199–200, 203, 205, 225, 227–28, 236–37, 242, 248–49, 251–52, 255–56, 258, 261–65, 270, 277, 286, 298–99, 305, 311, 313, 319, 322, 324–25, 327, 333, 335, 340, 373, 376, 378, 385–86, 403, 405, 415, 426, 428, 430–32, 447, 449, 458, 463–65, 472, 474, 478–79, 483, 491, 505, 507–9, 512–13, 515–16, 533, 544, 546, 553–54, 556, 569, 596–97, 600–602, 611, 624, 629, 630–32, 635, 639, 642–45, 647–48, 651, 656, 656–57, 663
Davis, Richard, 449
Davis, Steve, 140, 271–72, 278, 363, 474
Davis, Wild Bill, 37, 303, 399–400
Davison, Wild Bill, 245
de Souza, Raul, 272
Decoding Society, 50–51, 361, 466, 489, 651–52
DeFrancesco, Joey, 401–4
DeFranco, Buddy, 283–84, 289, 340
Defunkt, 50, 273, 465, 652
DeGruy, Philip, 429–30
Deitch, Adam, 484–85
DeJohnette, Jack, 124, 134, 152, 156, 167, 237, 288, 301, 310, 431, 437, 456, 460, 478, 484, 492–94, 499–501, 523, 632, 649, 656–57
Delbecq, Benoit, 383
DeLisle Nelson, Louis, 8
DeLisle Nelson, Papa, 8
Delius, Tobias, 65, 90, 330, 606
Dell, Christopher, 242, 363
Dennerlein, Barbara, 401–2
Desmond, Paul, 304, 307, 341, 378, 427, 634

di Battista, Stefano, 119, 300, 312
Di Meola, Al, 427–28
Diabaté, Toumani, 440, 546
Dick, Robert, 355, 526
Dickbauer, Klaus, 291, 293, 348, 617
Dickenson, Vic, 107, 268–69, 271, 593
Dickerson, Walt, 359–61
Diddley, Bo, 241
Dieuf Dieul, 176
Dindin, Tata, 397, 546
Dirty Dozen Brass Band, 648
Dixieland, 2, 9–10, 16, 91, 110, 202, 221, 234–35, 237, 245, 247, 249, 271, 273, 280, 283, 293, 296, 317, 340, 469–70, 501, 583, 591, 629–30, 636
Dixon, Bill, 258–59
DJ Logic, 411
DJ Olive, 411–12
DJ Soul Slinger, 411
DJ Spooky, 411–13
Dodds, Baby, 79, 234, 468, 470, 487, 496, 501
Dodds, Johnny, 11, 79, 280, 302, 468, 665
Dolphy, Eric, 8, 48, 64, 125–26, 140, 142, 167, 239, 253–54, 285–86, 288, 305–7, 352, 354, 374, 429, 446, 448, 531, 549, 636–37
Dominguez, Chano, 396, 656
Domino, Fats, 213–14, 260, 364–65, 518
Doran, Christy, 430
Dorge, Pierre, 617–18
Dorham, Kenny, 188, 229, 251, 258
Dörner, Axel, 259
Dorsey, Jimmy, 90, 113, 255, 281–82, 554, 589, 629
Dorsey, Thomas A., 221
Dorsey, Tommy, 90, 118, 267, 271–72, 351, 470, 477, 501, 629
double coding, 43
Douglas, Dave, 57, 61, 66, 71, 98, 158, 190–91, 265–66, 355, 414, 440, 495, 497, 538, 541, 562, 654

downtown scene, 60–63, 66,
    184, 265–66, 337–38,
    397, 403, 406–7, 419,
    435, 440–41, 459, 466,
    494–95, 510, 528–29,
    541, 562, 653–54
Drake, Hamid, 31, 57, 485–86,
    515
Draper, Ray, 536
Drees, Simon Jakob, 560
Dréno, François, 527
Dresch, Mihaly, 338
Dresser, Mark, 355, 458–59,
    527
D'Rivera, Paquito, 119, 288,
    297, 310, 362, 419, 506,
    508, 618
Drummond, Anne, 356
drums 'n' bass, 60, 68–69,
    257–58, 264–65, 276,
    328, 357, 393, 406–7,
    413–14, 426, 432–33,
    485–86, 498, 514, 544,
    562, 624–26, 658–59
Ducret, Marc, 309, 435–36,
    529
Dudek, Gerd, 331
Dudziak, Urszula, 575–76
Dulfer, Candy, 310
Dunkjian, Ara, 544
Dupree, Cornell, 417
Durham, Eddie, 420
Duval, Dominic, 458
Duvivier, George, 446, 448,
    511
Dylan, Bob, 214, 425, 579

Earland, Charles, 399–400
East Coast jazz, 18
Eckstine, Billy, 113–15, 318,
    323, 554, 561, 567, 596,
    621
Edison, Harry, 33, 249, 340,
    593
Ehrlich, Marty, 288, 354
Eldridge, Roy, 13, 15, 107,
    110, 112, 194–95, 236,
    249–51, 269, 283, 560,
    588, 590, 629
Ellerbee, Charles, 150, 435
Elling, Kurt, 562–63
Ellington, Duke, 14, 46–47,
    77–79, 94–101, 113,
    118, 126, 130, 141, 164,

170–72, 174–75, 179–80,
    184, 196, 202, 205, 248,
    250, 268, 281–82, 285,
    290, 295, 302–3, 308,
    313, 316–17, 325, 327,
    339–40, 344, 346, 348,
    354, 365, 369, 375, 379,
    382, 385, 391, 395, 418,
    443–44, 447, 469, 477,
    504, 521, 549, 560–61,
    563, 569, 575, 587–93,
    598–601, 603–5, 607,
    609, 614–15, 617, 619,
    622, 627, 629, 662, 666
Ellington, Mercer, 101, 344
Ellis, Don, 25, 66, 258, 576,
    611, 623–24, 638
El'Zabar, Kahil, 512
Emler, Andy, 559, 624–25
Enders, Johannes, 332
Endresen, Sidsel, 584–85
Eno, Briank, 129, 261, 406
Erguner, Kudsi, 72, 356
Erskine, Peter, 242, 285, 334,
    437, 482–83, 493, 596,
    623
Ertegun, Nesuhi, 206
Ervin, Booker, 220, 323–24
Eskelin, Ellery, 331, 338, 363
Eubanks, Robin, 277, 279,
    474, 657
Evans, Bill (pianist), 123, 127,
    156, 360, 373, 375–77,
    386–88, 391–93, 395–96,
    407, 409, 448, 450–51,
    464, 492, 527, 533, 536,
    656
Evans, Bill (saxophonist), 299,
    331
Evans, Gil, 25, 98, 120–22,
    124, 127–28, 130, 133,
    135, 154, 156, 254–55,
    297, 329, 422, 426, 430,
    465, 516, 534, 557, 574,
    590, 600–602, 604, 611,
    615–16, 622, 644
Evans, Herschel, 315–16, 593
Evans, Orrin, 391
Evans, Sue, 516, 623
Eye, Yamatsuka, 187, 653

Faddis, Jon, 250, 254–55, 619
Fahey, John, 432
Fahn, Mike, 272

Fania All Stars, 504
Farlow, Tal, 154, 420–22, 426,
    632
Farmer, Art, 19, 246, 251–52,
    257, 494, 598, 612, 633
Farroukh, Toufic, 338
Fauré, Gabriel, 533
Favors, Malachi, 456–57,
    640–41
Favre, Pierre, 487, 499, 501
Feather, Leonard, 99, 109,
    114, 117–18, 126, 195,
    206, 283–84, 289, 297,
    551, 572
Fedchock, John, 272, 619
Feidman, Giora, 292
Feldman, Mark, 61, 522, 525,
    527–29
Fennesz, Christian, 65, 412–13
Fenton, Nick, 113
Ferguson, Maynard, 250, 272,
    524, 598, 611–12, 624
Ferrell, Rachelle, 572
Ferris, Glenn, 272
field hollers, 22, 212, 327
Finegan, Bill, 590
Fischer, Clare, 373, 376, 398,
    401, 621
Fitzgerald, Ella, 374, 378, 436,
    566, 568–70, 573–75,
    578–80, 582, 592
Fiuczynski, Dave, 428–29
Five Elements, 50, 71, 309,
    490, 658–59
Flanagan, Tommy, 372–73,
    437, 460
flatted fifth, 14–15, 97, 147,
    208–9, 222, 224, 229
Fleck, Béla, 466, 539–40
Flory, Chris, 436
Fontana, Carl, 271
Ford, Ricky, 335
Foster, Al, 133, 135, 482–83,
    490–91
Foster, Frank, 315, 318, 578,
    593, 621
Foster, Pops, 442–43
four-beat jazz, 12, 34
Four Brothers sound, 102, 284,
    319–21, 346, 594
Fowlkes, Curtis, 277, 593
Franco, Guilherme, 509–10
Franklin, Aretha, 220–21, 571
free electronics, 70

free funk, 45, 49–51, 54, 132,
150–52, 273, 361, 427,
434–35, 438, 466, 489–
90, 525, 577–78, 608,
617, 645–46, 651–52
free jazz, 2–3, 16, 20–34, 38,
40–41, 44–51, 53–56,
59, 62–63, 70, 108–9,
123, 125, 127, 141–42,
144, 147, 149–51, 162,
166–67, 169–73, 180,
185, 187, 195–96, 198,
203–4, 206, 221, 225–28,
230–31, 233, 235, 237,
242–44, 245, 249, 258–
59, 261–62, 266, 273–74,
276, 283–85, 287–90,
294, 296–97, 299–301,
305–6, 308, 317, 322,
327–30, 333, 335, 337,
343, 346–47, 360, 369,
373–75, 379–84, 386,
397–98, 403–4, 411, 422,
426, 431, 433–36, 442,
450, 453, 456–59, 465,
473–74, 480–81, 485–90,
493, 496, 499, 515, 522,
525–26, 533, 538, 540,
545–46, 569, 575–76,
597, 602–3, 605–6, 608–
9, 615–17, 625–26, 636,
638–40, 648–49, 651–52,
655, 662–63
Freeman, Bud, 90–91, 108,
317, 532
Freeman, Chico, 47, 327–28,
649
Fresu, Paolo, 261, 263
Friedlander, Erik, 195, 527,
540–41
Friesen, David, 51, 449, 452,
466
Frisell, Bill, 184, 187, 265,
419–20, 431–32, 437–39,
529, 653, 658
Frith, Fred, 53, 187, 435, 653
Fuchs, Wolfgang, 301
Fuller, Curtis, 270–71, 474,
593
fusion. See jazz rock
Fuwa, Daisuke, 608

Gadd, Steve, 482
Galas, Diamanda, 575, 577

Galliano, Richard, 532–33
Galper, Hal, 304, 389
Ganelin, Vyacheslav, 383, 489
Garbarek, Jan, 59, 64, 66, 194,
242, 265, 301–2, 333,
387, 419, 452–53, 492,
602, 639
Garcia-Fons, Renaud, 64–65,
453–54, 533, 656
Garcia, Phillipe, 484–85
Garland, Red, 123, 139, 372–
73, 474
Garner, Erroll, 115, 196,
377–78, 392, 395, 399,
572, 592
Garrett, Kenny, 310–11
Garrison, Jimmy, 140, 142,
148, 242, 448, 466, 635
Gayle, Charles, 31, 327
Geller, Herb, 304, 612
Gentet, Christian, 454
Getz, Stan, 126, 129, 194, 199,
215, 236, 272, 319–20,
321–22, 341, 389–90,
422, 475, 503, 505,
508–9, 536, 574, 662
Gibbs, Melvin, 466
Gibbs, Mike, 616, 621
Gibbs, Terry, 149, 283, 359,
594
Gifford, Gene, 590
Gil, Gilberto, 557
Gilberto, Astrud, 422, 574
Gilberto, João, 509, 557, 574
Gillespie, Dizzy, 14–17, 19, 30,
48, 65, 77–78, 109–20,
122, 125, 137, 143, 163,
168, 194, 224–25, 231,
236–37, 249–52, 255,
257, 261, 269, 271, 278,
303, 305, 317–18, 322,
340, 358–59, 390, 400,
419, 422, 444–45, 471,
491, 495, 502–5, 509,
511, 521, 534, 554, 567,
591, 596–97, 600, 602–3,
621, 640, 650, 654
Gisbert, Greg, 257
Gismonti, Egberto, 42, 419
Giuffre, Jimmy, 18–19, 98, 195,
205, 225, 239, 271, 281,
283–84, 290, 319, 321,
422, 598, 607, 629, 636,
639, 663

Globe Unity Orchestra, 206,
262, 286, 383, 488, 605,
607
Godard, Jean-Luc, 183, 186
Godard, Michel, 534–35, 541
Goldberg, Ben, 62–63, 292
Goldings, Larry, 402
Goldkette, Jean, 90, 92, 443, 589
Golson, Benny, 312, 315, 317,
634
Gomez, Eddie, 353, 418,
449–50, 523
Gonsalves, Paul, 99, 167, 170,
316, 318, 334, 527
Gonzales, Andy, 461
Gonzalez, Jerry, 506–7, 518
Goodman, Benny, 13, 36, 88,
90–91, 105, 194–95, 215,
270–71, 281–84, 289–90,
318, 358, 369–70, 416,
422, 444, 469, 521, 531,
565, 589–91, 592, 594,
628–29
Goodman, Jerry, 159–60, 522,
645
Gordon, Bob, 341
Gordon, Dexter, 33, 153,
254, 270, 319, 322–23,
334–35, 452, 496, 561,
596, 631, 640
Gordon, Wycliff, 175, 277–78,
619, 655
Gordon, Wycliffe, 175, 277–78,
619, 655
Gorn, Steve, 357
gospel, 20, 40, 87, 162–63,
166, 171–73, 177, 179,
216–21, 260, 297, 329,
373, 391–92, 399–400,
425, 433, 446, 494, 506,
550, 556, 567, 571–73,
603, 626
Graham Bond Organisation,
35, 154
Graham, Larry, 462
Gramss, Sebastian, 454
Granz, Norman, 105, 107, 116,
283, 317, 436, 445, 477,
503, 521
Grappelli, Stéphane, 154,
520–23, 528–29, 630
Gratkowski, Frank, 313–14
Graves, Milford, 237, 259,
481, 486

Gräwe, Georg, 314, 382, 384
Gray, Glen, 590
Gray, Wardell, 318–19, 555
Green, Benny, 57, 391–92, 437, 568
Green, Charlie, 88, 267–69, 588
Green, Freddie, 244, 416–17, 420, 443, 471, 593
Green, Grant, 422, 437, 440
Green, Rodney, 489–90
Green, Urbie, 271, 598
Greene, Jimmy, 300, 336
Greer, Sonny, 96, 469
Gregory, Ed. See Shihab, Sahib
Grenadier, Larry, 394, 460, 656
Gress, Drew, 459
Grey, Al, 271, 593
Griffin, Johnny, 323–24, 544, 547, 604, 612, 632
Grisman, David, 418, 522, 539
Grofé, Ferde, 95
Grolnick, Don, 390, 615
groove, 13, 26, 56, 65, 67, 69–70, 128–29, 132, 176, 232–44, 252, 265, 279, 293, 310, 313, 344, 347, 349, 362, 372, 374, 379, 385, 390, 392–93, 404, 406, 423, 429, 441, 443, 451, 461–62, 464, 483–87, 490–91, 494–96, 498, 527, 531, 533, 535, 537, 617, 644, 652, 656, 659
Gruntz, George, 24–25, 465, 613
Gryce, Gigi, 19, 110, 304
Gullin, Lars, 341
Gumpert, Ulrich, 382, 606–7
Gunn, Russell, 264
Gurtu, Trilok, 357, 513, 651
Gustafsson, Mats, 343
Gustafsson, Rigmor, 584
Guthrie, Woody, 214
Guy, Barry, 206, 456–57, 605–6, 608, 638
Guy, Joe, 113

Hackett, Bobby, 78, 247–48
Haddad, Jamey, 515, 517
Haden, Charlie, 104, 142, 145, 152, 289, 332, 395, 419,

431, 447–49, 459, 547, 603–4, 623, 637, 639, 658
Haffner, Wolfgang, 484–85, 491, 498
Hagans, Tim, 69, 264, 624–25
Haggart, Bob, 443, 591
Haley, Bill, 213–14
Hall, Adelaide, 97, 569, 575
Hall, Edmond, 282–83
Hall, Jim, 377, 422, 427, 431, 439, 460, 636
Hamilton, Chico, 19, 305, 351, 422, 540
Hamilton, Jeff, 419, 490–91, 619
Hamilton, Jimmy, 282–83
Hamilton, Scott, 33, 334, 436
Hammer, Jan, 159–60, 405–6, 437, 482, 645
Hampel, Gunter, 29, 40, 155, 286, 289, 361, 426, 575
Hampton, Lionel, 196, 217, 252, 271, 282–83, 315, 317, 350, 358, 360, 368, 377, 445, 470, 555, 567, 571, 590–91, 629
Hampton, Slide, 59, 270, 272, 278, 474, 598, 601
Hancock, Herbie, 37, 39–40, 123, 126–27, 135, 153, 156, 174, 205, 244, 270, 318, 326, 385–86, 391–92, 395–97, 406, 415, 423, 449, 465, 505–6, 511, 524, 533, 546, 558, 635, 640, 643–45
Handy, John, 310, 512, 524, 650
Handy, William Christopher, 7, 268, 631
Hanrahan, Kip, 463, 506, 547–48
hard bop, 2, 17–20, 23, 28, 33, 43, 48–49, 56, 70, 108, 119, 123, 127, 132, 181, 188, 196, 251–53, 255–59, 261, 264, 266, 270, 279, 288, 294, 304–5, 311–12, 317, 323, 326, 332, 356, 373–75, 390–91, 402–3, 422–23, 429, 447, 456, 472, 474–75, 497, 528, 536, 546, 599,

625, 630–32, 634–37, 639, 647, 654–55
Hardwicke, Otto, 96
Hargrove, Roy, 57, 246, 257, 264, 631, 655
Harland, Eric, 497
Harlem, 12, 14, 112, 217, 219, 282, 303, 474, 502, 505–6, 566, 596, 605
  bands, 95–96, 108, 113, 316
  pianists, 113, 365–67, 370, 372, 591–92
harmolodics, 138, 151–52, 446, 489, 617, 651–52
harmony, 9, 11, 22, 28, 34, 43, 53, 58–59, 63, 92, 95, 98, 120, 138, 140, 151, 169, 172, 197, 221–26, 227, 229, 236, 262, 267, 300, 325, 328, 336, 342, 349, 366, 373–74, 394, 420, 432, 435, 444, 448, 459, 472–73, 506, 517, 525, 602, 624, 652, 654, 659, 661
  modal, 25, 48, 125, 127, 138, 180, 225–26, 254, 262, 265, 279, 290, 296, 311, 324, 331–32, 335, 376, 401, 415, 423, 499, 512, 531, 602, 626, 635–36, 640, 649
Harrell, Tom, 254, 613
Harriott, Joe, 306
Harris, Barry, 113, 372, 374, 391
Harris, Beaver, 49, 481, 514
Harris, Bill, 269, 271, 273, 594
Harris, Craig, 277–78, 649
Harris, Don "Sugar Cane," 522, 529
Harris, Eddie, 325
Harris, Mick, 187
Harris, Stefon, 363
Harrison, Donald, 48, 256, 310–11, 474, 647–48
Harrison, Jimmy, 267–68, 473, 588
Harrison, Joel, 432–33
Hart, Antonio, 119, 312
Hart, Billy, 490–91, 523
Hart, Clyde, 15
Harth, Alfred, 330

Hartman, Johnny, 554, 561
Harvey, Mark, 607
Haskins, Taylor, 265
Hasler, Gabriele, 576, 578
Hasselgard, Stan, 283, 341
Hassell, Jon, 51, 260, 357, 515
Hawkins, Coleman, 13–14, 33, 40, 77, 101–9, 126, 167, 170–72, 194, 197, 199, 205, 207, 228, 236, 295, 315–18, 322, 324, 327, 328, 339, 342, 350, 366, 478, 588, 637, 663
Hayes, Louis, 475
Haynes, Graham, 69, 264
Haynes, Roy, 48, 337, 392, 475–77
Hazeltine, David, 391
head arrangements, 203, 662
Heard, J. C., 477
Heath, Percy, 446, 596, 633
Heberer, Thomas, 261–62
Heckstall-Smith, Dick, 35, 155
Hedges, Michael, 432–33
Hefti, Neal, 196
Helias, Mark, 458–59
Hemingway, Gerry, 314, 485–86
Hemphill, Julius, 33, 300, 306–8, 343, 345–47, 466, 540
Henderson, Eddie, 131, 254, 644
Henderson, Fletcher, 13–14, 79, 82, 88, 97, 102–4, 106, 109, 137, 171, 195, 202–3, 248, 267–68, 443, 471, 473, 571, 587, 588–92, 600, 603–4, 617, 627
Henderson, Joe, 49, 278, 326, 335, 389, 391, 456, 461, 613
Henderson, Michael, 463
Henderson, Wayne, 272
Hendricks, Jon, 555–58, 561, 573
Hendrix, Jimi, 35, 63, 124, 127–28, 166–67, 292, 355, 401–2, 406, 421, 424–28, 430–32, 434–35, 438–39, 476, 527–28, 584, 600, 663
Heral, Patrice, 492, 498–99

Herbert, Matthew, 69, 414, 624–25
Herbolzheimer, Peter, 613
Herman, Bonnie, 572
Herman Herds, 203, 470, 594–95, 598
Herman, Woody, 102, 113, 203, 231, 255, 269, 271, 282, 295, 302, 317–19, 334, 340, 342, 346, 359, 470, 477, 553, 594–98, 611, 624, 629
Hersch, Fred, 376–77, 387, 459, 490
Herwig, Conrad, 278
Hicks, John, 389, 568
Hidalgo, Giovanni, 506–7
Higginbotham, J. C., 268–69
Higgins, Billy, 142, 152, 479–80
Hill, Andrew, 355, 384–85, 498
Hill, Bertha "Chippie," 88, 563
Hill, Teddy, 110–11
Hindemith, Paul, 118, 224
Hines, Earl, 22, 41, 79, 113–14, 318, 369, 473, 519, 567, 596, 628
Hinton, Milt, 77, 112, 443, 591
Hinze, Chris, 352
hip-hop, 1, 56, 60, 67–69, 83, 127, 135, 169, 176, 213, 215, 219, 252, 256–58, 264, 290, 309, 312, 335, 337, 348, 363, 385, 394, 397, 429, 435, 486, 489–90, 498, 506–7, 512, 514, 528, 559, 658–59
Hirsch, Shelley, 575, 577
Hiseman, Jon, 35, 483, 616
Ho, Fred, 74, 343
Hodges, Johnny, 13, 97, 99–100, 113, 137, 295, 302–3, 311, 313–14, 316, 341, 550, 629
Hoggard, Jay, 361
Holcomb, Robin, 574
Holdsworth, Allan, 428–30
Holiday, Billie, 37, 63, 85, 105, 325, 375, 557, 564–66, 569, 571, 574, 581, 585, 590, 629

Holland, Dave, 46, 103, 135, 156, 270, 279, 306, 309, 333, 363, 444, 448, 458, 466, 494, 541, 544, 622–23, 657
Holman, Bill, 593, 595, 598–600, 620, 624
Holtzman, Adam, 405
Hooker, John Lee, 207, 212–13, 425, 440, 550
Hopkins, Fred, 456–58, 641
Hopkins, Lightnin', 212, 610
Hopper, Hugh, 463
Horn, Paul, 42, 304, 350–53, 452
Horn, Shirley, 569
Hornweb Saxophone Quartet, 348
Horton, Ron, 260, 536
Horvitz, Wayne, 53, 185, 187, 403, 406–7, 411, 415, 532, 574, 653
Hot Five, 11, 79–80, 82, 114, 280, 596, 628, 635, 665
hot intonation, 194, 246
Hot Seven, 11, 79–80, 82, 90, 280, 468, 628, 665
Howard, George, 299
Howlin' Wolf, 213, 550
Hubbard, Freddie, 40, 142, 168, 252–54, 256–58, 261, 313, 385, 447, 474, 511, 635
Huebner, Gregor, 528–29
Humair, Daniel, 389, 454, 490–92, 656
Humphrey, Bobbi, 353
Hunter, Alberta, 211, 216, 563, 570
Hunter, Charlie, 428–29, 658
Huong Thanh, 585
Hussain, Zakir, 160, 427, 512, 650
Hutcherson, Bobby, 359–61, 363
Hyman, Dick, 405

Ibarra, Susie, 61, 74, 485–86
Ibrahim, Abdullah, 385
Ilg, Dieter, 449, 451, 453
imaginary folklore, 56, 60, 62, 64–65, 287, 291–92, 338, 436, 452–53, 533, 535, 539

Indian music, 24–26, 45, 51–52, 66, 73, 129, 140, 160–62, 225, 233, 235, 241, 258–59, 296, 298, 302, 304, 310–11, 314, 328, 345, 352, 357, 382, 415, 426–27, 432, 453, 490, 512–17, 522–34, 527, 529, 543, 585, 611, 615, 625, 650–51

Instant Composers Pool, 383, 606

International Association of Jazz, 58

Irakere, 250, 310, 353, 395, 401, 618

Italian Instabile Orchestra, 607

Itchy Fingers, 348

Iverson, Ethan, 392, 656

Iyer, Vijay, 72, 380, 382

Izenzon, David, 143, 259, 448

Izmailov, Enver, 439–40

Jackson, Ali, 495–96

Jackson, Anthony, 430, 464

Jackson, Chubby, 340, 594

Jackson, Gene, 475, 489–90

Jackson, Mahalia, 87, 216, 218, 571–72

Jackson, Michael, 124, 133, 599

Jackson, Michael "Gregory," 433–34, 557

Jackson, Milt, 20, 137, 196, 220, 350, 358–61, 363, 596, 598, 633

Jackson, Ronald Shannon, 50–51, 146, 150, 274, 361, 466, 482, 489, 501, 513, 525, 568, 651–52

Jacky Terrasson Trio, 392–93, 496, 654, 656

Jacquet, Illinois, 274, 315–17, 481, 538, 614

Jaga Jazzist, 65, 69, 414, 485, 624–25

Jamal, Ahmad, 124, 378–79, 392

Jang, Jon, 74

Jarman, Joseph, 294, 297, 300, 306, 640–42

Jarreau, Al, 557–58

Jarrett, Keith, 31–32, 40, 58, 124, 127–28, 133–34,

146, 153, 169, 226, 377, 380, 384, 386–88, 391–92, 396, 450, 452, 474, 492, 510, 558, 562, 639, 656, 663, 667

Jaume, André, 330

Jazz at Lincoln Center (JALC), 56, 177–79

Jazz Composers Orchestra, 289, 603–7

Jazz Messengers, 168, 253, 255, 264, 279, 311, 323, 474, 504, 629, 630, 634, 640, 647

jazz rock, 2, 32, 35–36, 38–40, 45, 48–51, 55–56, 70, 77, 124, 130, 132–34, 160, 180, 234, 236, 254–55, 264, 270, 272–73, 286, 299, 310, 313–14, 323–26, 332–33, 348, 351–53, 360–61, 386, 388, 401, 403, 404, 406, 417, 426–32, 437, 439, 451, 456, 462–63, 466, 479, 482–86, 490, 493, 496, 498, 500, 509, 513, 522, 533–34, 546, 555, 598, 601, 613, 615–16, 639, 642–46, 647, 649, 651–52

Jazz Warriors, 337, 562, 616

Jazzmatazz, 70

Jeanneau, François, 331, 625

Jefferson, "Blind" Lemon, 147, 212, 550, 552, 563

Jefferson, Eddie, 555–56, 558

Jenkins, Leroy, 145, 149, 522, 525–26

Jenny-Clark, Jean-François, 389, 449, 454, 656

Jensen, Christine, 300

Jensen, Ingrid, 257

Jin Hi Kim, 545

João, Maria, 383, 570, 578, 583

Jobim, Antonio Carlos, 299, 509, 557, 574, 579

Johansson, Sven-Åke, 488

Johnson, Alphonso, 463

Johnson, Bill, 79, 441

Johnson, Budd, 295, 318, 599

Johnson, Bunk, 246, 280

Johnson, Dewey, 142

Johnson, Howard, 534–35

Johnson, J. J., 121, 134, 199, 269–73, 277–78, 340, 632

Johnson, James P., 6, 40, 88, 365, 372

Johnson, Lonnie, 212, 416–17, 424

Johnson, Marc, 437, 449, 451, 516

Johnson, Mark, 489

Johnson, Richard Leo, 432

Johnson, Robert, 212, 416, 550, 563, 579

Jones, Darryl, 299, 463, 465

Jones, Elvin, 19, 38, 48, 139–40, 142, 228, 242, 256, 274, 298, 312, 334, 475–78, 489, 491–92, 496, 501, 512, 632, 635

Jones, Hank, 350, 371, 403, 494, 598

Jones, Jo, 15, 105, 112, 233, 237–38, 443, 470–71, 473, 477, 494, 499, 501

Jones, Jonah, 247, 521, 591

Jones, Leroi, 23, 139, 141, 605

Jones, Norah, 60, 574, 579–80

Jones, Philly Joe, 123, 447, 474–75, 496

Jones, Quincy, 19, 124, 135, 297, 305, 452, 491, 537, 598–99, 600, 615

Jones, Ricky Lee, 572

Jones, Thad, 246, 252, 254, 271, 297, 572, 593, 611, 613–14, 616, 619, 621

Joos, Herbert, 261, 617

Joplin, Janis, 35, 89, 571

Joplin, Scott, 4–6, 46, 364–65, 641

Jordan, Duke, 237, 372–73

Jordan, Kent, 356, 648

Jordan, Louis, 303

Jordan, Marlon, 255, 648

Jordan, Sheila, 569, 581, 584, 607

Jordan, Stanley, 428–29, 440

Jörgensmann, Theo, 289–90

Kaiser, Henry, 411, 435, 545

Kamuca, Richie, 319–20, 595

Kandirali, Mustafa, 292

Kansas City jazz, 231, 243

Kao Hwang, Jason, 526
Kassap, Sylvain, 330
Katz, Fred, 540–41
Kaufmann, Achim, 382, 384
Keepnews, Orrin, 5, 117–18,
    628
Kelly, Wynton, 372–73
Kelsey, Bishop, 219
Kennel, Hans, 261, 539
Kent Carter String Trio, 527
Kenton, Stan, 250, 268, 270–
    71, 314, 341, 350, 419,
    482, 502–3, 567, 590–91,
    594–96, 597–98, 609–10,
    624–25, 663
Keppard, Freddie, 8, 246, 442,
    467
Kessel, Barney, 421
Kikoski, David, 391–92
Killian, Al, 250
Kilson, Billy, 475, 493–94, 657
Kim Duk Soo, 513
Kimura, Mari, 526
Kinch, Soweto, 65, 312
King, Albert, 213, 425, 551
King, B. B., 40, 207, 213, 325,
    420, 424–26, 431, 542,
    551–52
King, Martin Luther, Jr., 85
Kirby, John, 442–43, 629–30,
    632
Kirk, Andy, 369, 521, 592
Kirk, Rahsaan Roland, 298,
    323, 325, 337, 344, 350,
    353, 377, 425, 452, 531,
    539, 560
Kirkland, Kenny, 299, 391,
    406
Klein, Guillermo, 73, 622
Kleive, Audun, 498
klezmer jazz, 61–63, 181,
    189–90, 192, 265, 290,
    292, 397, 654
Klucevsek, Guy, 185, 532, 534
Knepper, Jimmy, 220, 270
Koch, Hans, 301, 330
Koenig, Lester, 137, 144
Koller, Hans, 321–22
Kölner Saxophon Mafia, 348
Kondo, Toshinori, 258
König, Klaus, 98, 205, 624, 626
Konitz, Lee, 18, 37, 119, 121,
    126, 227, 273, 304, 307,
    313, 322, 341, 377, 421,

    452, 472, 524, 536, 538,
    595, 631, 637, 662
Korner, Alexis, 154, 215, 368
Kottke, Leo, 432
Kouyaté, Soriba, 546
Kowald, Peter, 456–57, 466,
    545, 578
Koyama, Shota, 489
Krakauer, David, 63, 292
Kral, Roy, 569
Krall, Diana, 60, 437, 491,
    579–80
Kraslow, George, 94
Kriegel, Volker, 430, 643
Krog, Karin, 575–76, 584
Kronos Quartet, 526–27, 610
Krupa, Gene, 13, 90, 282,
    469–70, 495, 556, 590,
    592, 628
Kühn, Joachim, 389, 454, 523,
    656
Kühn, Rolf, 284–85
Kuhn, Steve, 377, 386, 561

La Rocca, Nick, 247
Lacy, Frank, 277, 279, 623
Lacy, Steve, 40, 273, 296–98,
    300, 346, 527, 540
Ladnier, Tommy, 88, 246, 267,
    271, 588
LaFaro, Scott, 376, 446–48,
    450, 462
Laine, "Papa" Jack, 9, 518
Laird, Rick, 159–60, 645
Lake, Gene, 488–90
Lake, Oliver, 33, 300, 306,
    345–46, 348, 354, 642
Lambert, Dave, 555–57, 573
Landgren, Nils, 275
Lang, Eddie, 88, 90, 417, 424,
    473, 519
Lantos, Zoltán, 524
Laswell, Bill, 45, 53, 70, 187,
    328, 385, 463–65, 506
Lateef, Yusef, 24–25, 323–24,
    350, 353, 511–12, 531,
    537
Lauer, Christof, 331, 620
Laws, Hubert, 351, 353, 356,
    662
Laws, Ronnie, 299
Leadbelly, 154, 207, 212, 215,
    416, 550, 563. See also
    Leadbetter, Huddie

Leadbetter, Huddie, 147, 550.
    See also Leadbelly
Léandre, Joelle, 456–57
Lebovich, Avi, 277
Ledru, Jean, 107
Lee, Jeanne, 575–76
Leloup, Denis, 275
Levy, Howard, 372–537, 594
Lewis, George, 40, 72, 75, 172,
    185, 276, 280, 410–11,
    642, 653
Lewis, John, 17, 20, 22, 98,
    121–22, 137, 204–5, 305,
    359, 367, 418, 452, 569,
    596, 614, 627, 633–34
Lewis, Meade Lux, 368
Lewis, Mel, 252, 254, 271,
    334, 341, 470, 477–78,
    572, 611, 613–14, 616,
    619, 621
Lewis, Victor, 337, 495–98
Liebman, David, 148, 298,
    301, 339, 386, 397, 476
Lifetime, 35, 157, 401, 482,
    642, 645
Lincoln, Abbey, 564, 568–69,
    635
Lincoln Center Jazz Orchestra,
    178–80, 344, 396, 619
Lindberg, John, 456, 458–59,
    527
Lindsay, Arto, 53, 185, 413,
    419, 435, 511, 547, 560
Linx, David, 562
Little, Booker, 252–53, 306,
    313
Little Richard, 214, 220
Lloyd, Charles, 35, 148, 326–
    27, 377, 453, 498
Lôbo, Edu, 557
Locke, Joe, 363
Lockwood, Didier, 552–54
London, Frank, 62–63, 265
London Jazz Composers'
    Orchestra, 605–7
Loose Tubes, 337, 615–16
loudness, 37, 41, 61, 107, 151,
    294, 415, 636
Louis Armstrong All Stars, 79,
    82, 85, 269, 281
Louiss, Eddy, 401
Lovano, Joe, 103, 119, 333–34,
    492, 553, 620, 654, 658
Lovens, Paul, 488, 638

Lubambo, Romero, 419
Lubat, Bernard, 532
Lucas, Gary, 440
Lüdemann, Hans, 397, 515, 546
Lunceford, Jimmie, 12, 269, 271, 420, 591–92, 600
Lundy, Carmen, 578, 581–83
Lurie, John, 53
Lussier, René, 435
Lynch, Brian, 261, 504
Lysne, Geir, 624–26
Lytton, Paul, 488, 559, 638

M-Base, 60, 71–72, 279, 300, 309–10, 332, 337, 357, 382, 408, 466, 489–90, 537, 578, 659
Maarten Rehak, Frank
Macero, Teo, 128–29
Machito, 116, 359, 502–3
Machito Band, 116, 503, 597
Magnarelli, Joe, 257
Mahall, Rudi, 286, 383
Mahanthappa, Rudresh, 309–10
Mahavishnu Orchestra, 36, 38–39, 159–61, 406, 426–27, 482, 521, 642–43, 645–46, 650
Mahogany, Kevin, 561
Majumdar, Ronu, 357
Makowicz, Adam, 370, 372
Malach, Bob, 333
Malone, Russell, 422, 437
Malone, Tom, 272, 535
Mandel, Johnny, 19, 598
Maneri, Joe, 301, 526
Maneri, Mat, 526
Mangelsdorff, Albert, 40, 228, 271, 273–75, 304, 331, 451, 485, 515, 616
Mangelsdorff, Emil, 352
Mangione, Chuck, 263
Mani, T. A. S., 52, 513
Mann, Herbie, 24, 350–51, 503, 598
Manne, Shelly, 18–19, 40, 104, 446, 478, 595, 597, 632
Manring, Michael, 464
Mantilla, Ray, 504–5
Mantler, Mike, 258, 603
Marclay, Christian, 53, 185, 531

Marcondes, Caito, 510
Maret, Grégoire, 537
Mariano, Charlie, 51, 119, 298, 310, 314, 463, 513, 523, 543, 616, 637, 650
Marsalis, Branford, 49, 55, 59, 299, 335–36, 455, 474, 647–48, 655
Marsalis, Ellis, 57
Marsalis, Wynton, 32, 43, 48, 55–56, 78, 81, 84, 98, 101, 162–80, 188, 199, 245, 254, 260, 265–66, 278, 289–90, 313, 335–37, 339, 363, 374, 390–91, 396, 451, 456, 494, 496, 511, 528, 538, 561, 619, 626, 631, 634, 647–48, 654–55, 658–59, 663, 665
Marsh, Warne, 18, 322, 336, 421, 631
Martignon, Hector, 394
Martin, Stu, 490–91
Martino, Pat, 423, 437, 539–40
Martland, Steve, 75
Marwedel, Dick, 301
Masada, 63, 185, 189–92, 266, 308, 407, 653
Masada String Trio, 459, 527, 529, 541
Masaoka, Miya, 74, 544–45
Matinier, Jean-Louis, 533
Matta, Nilson, 461
Mayall, John, 215–16, 536
Mayfield, Irvin, 255–56
Mays, Lyle, 406–7, 415, 646
Mazur, Marilyn, 498, 516, 618
Mazurek, Rob, 259
McBride, Christian, 455–56, 474, 634
McCall, Steve, 172, 485–86, 640–41
McCandless, Paul, 538, 639, 651
McCann, Les, 372–73
McFerrin, Bobby, 547, 557–58, 576
McGhee, Howard, 251, 503
McLaughlin, John, 35, 40, 47, 77, 127, 135, 153–62, 401, 403, 408, 420, 426–28, 431, 441, 476,

482, 512–13, 521–22, 524, 611, 616, 642–43, 645–46, 650
McLean, Jackie, 119, 272, 305
McLean, René, 298
McPartland, Jimmy, 89–90, 92, 247, 296
McPartland, Marian, 370
McPhee, Joe, 327–28
McPherson, Charles, 304
McRae, Carmen, 495, 567–68, 570, 572
McShann, Jay, 110–11, 113, 147, 521, 592
Medeski, John, 402, 432, 460, 622, 658–59
Mehldau, Brad, 59, 387, 392–94, 460, 498, 655–56, 659
Mehta, Rajesh, 259
Melford, Myra, 380–81, 529
melody, 5, 8, 46, 92, 98, 105, 112, 120, 122, 129, 133–34, 138–40, 151, 197–98, 221, 226–33, 235–36, 240, 251, 253, 298, 320, 323–24, 340, 387, 403, 420, 423, 427, 430–31, 448, 453, 462, 464, 466, 472–73, 506, 517, 631, 652, 654, 661
Melton, Bob, 81
Memphis Slim, 367, 550
Mendoza, Vince, 205, 620–21, 623
Mengelberg, Misha, 29, 31, 201, 206, 375, 382–83, 605–6, 608
Menza, Don, 319, 321
Metheny, Pat, 146, 152, 199, 407, 420, 422, 430–33, 475, 500, 509, 537, 557, 615–16, 643, 646
Mezzadri, Malik "Magic," 357
Mezzrow, Mezz, 90, 281
Micus, Stephan, 42, 543
Mikkelborg, Palle, 263, 602, 621
Miles Davis Capitol Band, 270
Miles, Ron, 265
Miley, Bubber, 96, 99, 130, 194, 228, 248, 260, 328, 662
Miller, Glenn, 90, 283, 469, 554, 582

Miller, Marcus, 133, 243, 286, 463–65
Miller, Mulgrew, 48, 390–91, 474, 479, 647
Min Xiao-Fen, 545–46
Mingus, Charles, 21, 33, 38, 46, 68, 98, 123, 126, 167, 170–71, 173, 179–80, 196, 205, 220, 225, 251–52, 254, 257, 270, 277, 290, 305, 308, 314, 324–25, 329, 335, 343, 346, 377, 418, 429, 444–46, 450, 452, 458, 461, 475, 522, 534, 536, 538, 540, 560, 573, 598, 602–3, 617, 622–23, 629, 632, 636–37, 650
Minton, Phil, 559–60, 626
Minton's Playhouse, 14–15, 113–14, 128, 371, 416, 420, 471
Mintzer, Bob, 288, 333, 614–15, 644
Mirabassi, Gabriele, 291–92
Mitchell, Joni, 333, 573–74, 579, 623
Mitchell, Nicole, 354–55
Mitchell, Red, 244, 289, 446, 632
Mitchell, Roscoe, 294, 297, 300, 306, 606, 640–41
Mitterer, Wolfgang, 411, 413–15
Mobley, Hank, 19, 188, 323–24
modality, 25, 48, 138, 226, 279, 296, 311, 331, 415, 531, 602, 635–36, 640
Modern Jazz Quartet, 20–21, 137, 204, 359, 367, 418, 446, 475, 499, 569, 627, 629–30, 633
Moffett, Charles, 451, 480–81
Moffett, Charnett, 48, 451, 479
Mole, Miff, 267
Molineaux, Othello, 514
Molvær, Nils Petter, 65, 69, 264–65, 414, 485, 585, 658
Monheit, Jane, 578, 580
Monk, Thelonious, 15, 48, 113–14, 124–25, 137,

139, 165, 168, 179, 183, 205, 224, 231, 259, 273, 296–97, 322–24, 335, 362, 374–75, 380, 382–83, 385, 390–91, 395–96, 423, 447, 460–61, 471, 496, 507, 518, 527, 544–45, 547, 599, 604, 611, 615, 648, 663
Montgomery, Wes, 422–26, 428, 431, 436–37, 462
Montrose, Jack, 201, 204, 319, 341
Moody, James, 229, 318–20, 322, 350–51, 555, 596, 631
Moore, Brew, 320, 322, 503
Moore, Glen, 449, 452, 639, 651
Moore, Michael, 289, 313, 606, 656
Moore, Oscar, 421, 630
Moran, Gayle, 572
Moran, Jason, 59, 392, 394, 466, 490, 656
Moran, Matt, 362
Moreira, Airto, 501, 509–10, 515, 574, 645
Morello, Joe, 474, 483
Morgan, Frank, 313
Morgan, Lee, 19, 252–53, 261, 474, 544
Mori, Ikue, 61, 185, 412–13
Moriyama, Takeo, 489
Morris, Butch, 172, 206, 245, 258, 607–8
Morris, Wilbur, 172
Morrison, James, 250
Morrison, Jim, 35
Morton, Benny, 268–69, 588, 593
Morton, Jelly Roll, 6, 8, 11, 14, 19, 46, 79, 90, 111, 165, 171, 202, 205, 262, 268, 281, 285, 364–65, 416, 470, 517–18, 587, 628, 631, 641, 648
Moses, Bob, 354, 490–91, 615
Moss, David, 43–44, 53–54, 490, 560
Mossman, Michael Philip, 261
Most, Sam, 350–51, 353
Moten, Bennie, 13, 532, 592

Motian, Paul, 334, 376, 432, 490, 492, 632, 639, 658
Moutin, François, 454, 657
Mouzon, Alphonse, 38, 274, 482, 493, 643
Moye, Don, 485, 512, 640–41
Mozdzer, Leszek, 387
Mrubata, McCoy, 338
Muhammad, Idris, 490–91, 496
Mulligan, Gerry, 19, 98, 121–22, 143, 196, 206, 251, 340–41, 343–44, 464, 532, 595, 599, 621, 629–30, 632–34
multiphonics, 162, 259, 274–75, 330, 355
Murcia, Gavino, 560
Murphy, Mark, 554, 556, 559, 561–62, 569, 578
Murray, Diedre, 540, 649
Murray, Albert, 56, 164, 177–78
Murray, David, 43, 46, 57, 77, 98, 162–79, 193, 217, 239, 255, 260, 278, 283, 285, 288, 323, 327–28, 336, 345, 494, 512, 608, 617, 647–49, 663
Murray, Sunny, 23, 29, 38, 237, 289, 478, 480–81, 501

Nabatov, Simon, 459
Naked City, 185–87, 189, 403, 435, 538, 653
Nalbantoglu, Nedimm, 524–25, 625
Namchylak, Sainkho, 575, 577
Namyslowski, Zbigniew, 313
Nance, Ray, 174, 248, 521
Nanton, Joe "Tricky Sam," 59, 96, 99, 268, 278, 328, 662
Napoleon, Phil, 247, 267
Narell, Andy, 514
Nascimento, Milton, 557
Nat King Cole Trio, 629–30, 632, 634
Nathanson, Roy, 338
Naughton, Bobby, 361
Navarro, Fats, 17, 48, 251–52, 322, 596
N'Diaye Rose, Doudou, 176, 435, 512

NDR Big Band, 620
Neergard, Silje, 584
Nelson, Oliver, 98, 205–6, 253, 297, 304, 405, 611, 621
Nelson, Steve, 361, 363, 657
neobop, 45–48, 54, 152, 252–56, 278, 305, 332, 334–35, 339, 342, 373, 389, 391, 427, 431, 436, 438, 472, 493–94, 496–97, 508, 631, 639–40, 646, 665
New Art Saxophone Quartet, 348
New Jungle Orchestra, 617–18
New Orleans, 4, 5, 6–9, 10–12, 13–16, 22–23, 30, 43–44, 46–47, 51, 54, 56, 66, 72, 77–82, 86, 90–92, 100, 102–3, 106, 110, 145, 148, 164–66, 169–72, 174, 176, 179, 196, 198, 202, 211, 218, 221–23, 234, 237, 245–47, 255–56, 260, 264, 266–68, 279–81, 285, 288, 293–96, 308, 311, 327, 346–47, 356, 363–65, 395, 416, 441–43, 462, 468, 470, 473–74, 480, 483, 487, 491, 496, 501, 517–19, 530, 534, 539, 587, 591, 628, 636, 641, 647–49, 654, 662
New Orleans Rhythm Kings, 9–10, 202, 280–81, 293, 469, 591
New Orleans Wanderers, 11
New York downtown scene. See downtown scene
Newman, David "Fathead," 58, 316
Newman, Joe, 19, 78, 593
Newton, James, 46–47, 354, 382, 459
Newton, Lauren, 575–77, 617
Nguyên Lê, 72, 74, 439, 516, 544, 585, 625, 656
Nicholas, Albert, 8, 280–81
Nichols, Herbie, 375, 383
Nichols, Red, 247, 267
Nicols, Maggie, 575–76
Niewood, Gerry, 353
Niggli, Lucas, 498–99, 656

No Jazz, 69, 152
no wave, 45, 53–54, 330, 413, 427, 435–36, 465, 490, 506, 647. See also noise music
Nock, Mike, 35
noise music, 45, 53–54, 60, 132, 276, 308, 412, 419, 438, 490, 533. See also no wave
Noodband, 50, 577
Noone, Jimmie, 280, 302, 665
Norvo, Red, 358, 445, 563, 594, 629, 632, 639
nu jazz, 69–70
Nureyev, Rudolf, 105
Nuss, Ludwig, 272

Öçal, Burhan, 515
O'Connor, Marc, 522
O'Day, Anita, 567, 570
O'Farrill, Chico, 116, 597
off-beat, 239
Olatunji, Babatunde, 511
Oliver, King, 11, 79, 82, 103, 110, 146, 171, 174, 194, 199, 202–3, 206, 246, 248–49, 271, 281, 416, 442, 468, 530, 587, 665
Oliver, Sy, 592
Olstead, Renee, 581
Orchestre National de Jazz, 624–25
Oregon, 42, 51, 438, 452, 513, 516–17, 523, 538, 639, 651
Original Creole Jazz Band, 441
Original Dixieland Jazz Band, 9, 91, 247, 469, 501
O'Rourke, Jim, 61, 433–34, 526
Ørsted Pedersen, Niels-Henning, 449, 452, 455
Ory, Kid, 8, 78–79, 194, 267, 442, 445, 473, 665
Osborne, Mike, 306, 346
Osby, Greg, 50, 119, 299–300, 309–10, 363, 394, 490, 646, 652, 657, 659
Ostertag, Bob, 411–12
Öström, Magnus, 498, 656
Ourio, Oliver Ker, 537
Owens, Jimmy, 78, 246, 254

Oxley, Tony, 27, 29, 156, 488, 499, 606–7

Pacheco, Johnny, 504–5
Page, Hot Lips247, 554, 590
Page, Walter, 443, 471
Palmieri, Eddie, 261, 278, 504–6
Papasov, Ivo, 292
Parker, Charlie, 15–17, 48, 64, 67, 77, 81, 91, 108, 109–20, 121–22, 124, 126–27, 130, 135–37, 143, 147, 149, 168, 173, 199, 203, 205, 221, 224, 228–29, 236, 255, 270, 277, 283, 288–89, 292, 303–5, 309, 312–14, 319–22, 325, 335, 340–41, 371, 373, 380, 402, 420, 446, 460, 462–63, 467, 471–72, 475–76, 502–3, 512, 530, 533, 538, 546, 554, 556–57, 592, 596–97, 600, 603, 630–32, 634–35, 637, 644, 648, 650, 663, 665
Parker, Evan, 29, 31, 59, 70, 203, 274, 297, 300–301, 327–28, 330, 346, 412, 414, 488, 578, 608, 638
Parker, Leo, 340, 344, 495, 596
Parker, Leon, 495–97
Parker, Maceo, 272, 310–11, 402
Parker, William, 70, 456–58
Parkins, Zeena, 53, 532
Pascoal, Hermeto, 127, 353–54
Pass, Joe, 436–37, 593
Pastorius, Jaco, 242, 462–67, 483, 514, 521, 536, 538, 573, 615, 643
Pat Metheny Group, 537
Patitucci, John, 450–51, 462, 464, 658
Paul, Les, 421–22
Payton, Nicholas, 57, 255–57
Peacock, Annette, 573
Peacock, Gary, 124, 449–50, 656
Pege, Aladár, 449, 452
Pelt, Jeremy, 250, 257

Penn, Clarence, 474, 497, 568
Peplowski, Ken, 288–89
Pepper, Art, 304, 312
Pepper, Jim, 326–27
Perez, Danilo, 394–95, 512, 518, 658
Perkins, Bill, 319–20
Perowsky, Ben, 495
Peterson, Hannibal Marvin, 254–55
Peterson, Oscar, 21, 40, 283, 371–72, 392, 421–22, 436, 445, 452, 572, 634, 656
Peterson, Ralph, 48, 290, 361
Peterson, Ralph, Jr., 493–94, 498
Petrella, Gianluca, 275
Petrowsky, Ernst-Ludwig, 306, 576
Petrucciani, Michel, 304, 326, 376–77, 387
Pettiford, Oscar, 98, 104, 444–47, 450, 462, 478, 531, 537, 540, 556, 597–98
Peyroux, Madeleine, 574
Phillips, Barre, 449–50, 457
Phillips, Flip, 107, 315, 317–18, 594
phrasing, 9, 39, 81–82, 151, 174, 193–95, 198, 226–28, 235, 239, 242, 249–52, 260, 264, 272, 279, 281, 288, 291, 301, 306–7, 311–13, 318, 321, 334, 337, 347–50, 358–59, 361, 364, 383, 391, 409, 423, 430, 435, 441, 456, 462, 464, 466, 472, 521, 530, 532–33, 538, 552, 554, 563–64, 569, 571, 579, 581, 584, 639, 661–64
Piazzolla, Astor, 532
Pickett, Wilson, 220
Picou, Alphonse, 8, 199, 279–80
Pieranunzi, Enrico, 376–77
Pieronczyk, Adam, 331
Pifarély, Dominique, 524, 528–29
Pilc, Jean-Michel, 392–93, 656–57
Pilz, Michel, 286

Pine, Courtney, 65, 332, 336–37, 616
Pizzarelli, Bucky, 436
Pizzarelli, John, 436, 554
Plaxico, Lonnie, 443, 451, 455–56, 465
Pohjonen, Kimmo, 534
Ponce, Daniel, 506
Ponty, Jean-Luc, 24–25, 159–60, 521–24, 527
Portal, Michel, 286, 532, 624
Position Alpha, 348
Potter, Chris, 301, 333–34, 446, 623, 657
Powell, Baden, 419
Powell, Bud, 17, 48, 322, 325, 334, 365, 369, 371–74, 377, 380, 382, 384, 390, 394, 396, 452, 504, 507, 603
power trio, 392–93
Pozo, Chano, 116, 237, 359, 501–3, 505, 597, 602
Prado, Perez, 503
Presencer, Gerard, 257
Presley, Elvis, 213–14
Previte, Bobby, 184, 189, 493, 495, 498
Priester, Julian, 270, 644
Prieto, Dafnis, 489–90
Prime Time, 49–51, 150–52, 466, 651–52
Printup, Marcus, 250, 257
Puente, Tito, 353, 503, 506
Pukwana, Dudu, 306
Pullen, Don, 354, 380–81, 384, 403, 511, 649
Puntin, Claudio, 291–92
Purcell, John, 288, 301, 306, 328, 347
Purim, Flora, 509, 574–75, 645
Purviance, Douglas, 273
Puschnig, Wolfgang, 313, 348, 513, 617
Pyysalo, Severi, 362

Quinichette, Paul, 107, 322
Quintette du Hot Club de France, 630

Ra, Sun, 258, 278, 342, 380, 404, 410, 415, 440, 457, 590, 603–5

Rabinowitz, Michael, 538
Radovan, Christian, 275
Raeburn, Boyd, 293, 318, 597
ragtime, 2, 4–6, 10, 12, 19, 23, 40, 46, 49, 81, 92, 99, 154, 221–22, 234, 238, 246, 363–65, 367, 381, 391, 394, 518–19, 530, 641, 662
Rainey, "Ma," 88, 563
Rainey, Tom, 495
Randolph, Robert, 425
Raney, Jimmy, 305, 320, 421–22, 427
Rappolo, Leon, 10, 203
Rava, Enrico, 261–62, 388
Ravel, Maurice, 89–90, 93, 377, 533
Red Garland Trio, 139
Red Hot Peppers, 11, 79, 90, 285, 587, 628
Redding, Otis, 213, 220, 560
Redman, Dewey, 33, 145, 166, 274, 327–28, 335, 431, 480, 637, 650, 689
Redman, Don, 295, 303, 588–89, 592, 600, 617
Redman, Joshua, 57, 334–36, 437, 493, 631, 655
Reed, Eric, 175, 391–92
Reed, Lou, 151, 192, 547
Reedus, Tony, 495–97
Reeves, Dianne, 419, 570, 578, 582
register, 86, 98, 108, 163, 246, 249–50, 254, 266, 280–81, 284, 289–90, 299–300, 307, 310, 320, 327–29, 332, 342–43, 353, 355, 361, 375, 394, 399, 448, 450, 452, 454, 463–64, 469, 532, 534–35, 538, 558–59, 577, 580, 582, 601
Rehak, Frank, 271
Reich, Steve, 37, 120, 412, 415, 463, 515, 622
Reichel, Hans, 433–34, 542
Reid, Rufus, 449, 460
Reid, Vernon, 57, 431, 435
Reijseger, Ernst, 527, 541–42, 656
Reinhardt, Django, 28, 65, 103–4, 154, 283, 341,

417–19, 426, 520, 523,
539, 630
Return to Forever, 39, 386,
451, 483, 574, 643, 645
Ribot, Marc, 61, 185, 440–41
Rich, Buddy, 320–21, 470,
477–78, 507, 512, 611–
12, 615
Richardson, Jerome, 295, 350,
598–99
Richmond, Dannie, 475, 637
Rickman, Sean, 489–90
Riessler, Michael, 291, 301,
515, 541–42
riffs, 13, 50, 110, 131, 174,
205, 229, 231–32, 243,
249, 303, 310, 346, 349,
358, 374, 399, 463, 466,
520, 558, 567, 592–93,
604, 610, 614, 622, 633,
649
Riley, Herlin, 175, 495–96,
648, 655
Riley, Terry, 260, 410, 415–16,
527
Rizzo, Carlo, 515
Roach, Max, 16, 19, 48, 68,
121, 137, 229, 237, 253,
270, 330, 347, 350, 385,
471–75, 477, 487, 491,
494, 496–97, 501, 504,
511, 527, 536, 538, 545,
554, 564, 569, 603, 611,
629–30, 635, 640
Robert, Thierry, 544
Robert, Yves, 275
Roberts, Hank, 444, 527, 540
Roberts, John Storm, 508, 518
Roberts, Marcus, 170, 175,
391, 647
Robertson, Herb, 260, 649
Robinson, Janice, 271–72
Robinson, Orphy, 361–62, 546
Robinson, Perry, 34, 285, 289
Robinson, Scott, 294, 342
Roditi, Claudio, 261, 461
Rodney, Red, 255, 333
Rodriguez, Arsenio, 441, 505
Rodriguez, Roberto, 61, 261,
507–8
Rogers, Adam, 437
Rogers, Barry, 278
Rogers, Shorty, 18–19, 200,
594, 598, 632

Rolling Stones, 35, 154, 215–25,
368
Rollins, Sonny, 19, 49, 67, 74,
107–8, 166–67, 205,
228–29, 312, 317–19,
321–23, 325–26, 328–29,
332, 335–37, 339, 344,
379, 421, 452, 456, 494,
538, 541, 556, 599, 603,
611, 635
Romano, Aldo, 65, 288,
452, 482–83, 492, 498,
656
Roney, Wallace, 119, 474, 479,
497, 647, 2547
Roseman, Josh, 277, 279
Rosengren, Bernt, 331
Rosenwinkel, Kurt, 432, 492
Rosewoman, Michele, 382
Rosnes, Renee, 392
Rosolino, Frank, 271, 278,
595
Ross, Annie, 555–56, 570
Ross, Brandon, 440
Rossy, Jorge, 394, 498, 656
Rothenberg, Ned, 301, 328,
355
Rouse, Charlie, 323–24
Rova Saxophone Quartet, 297,
346–47, 529
Rowe, Keith, 433–34, 638
Roy, Badal, 513
Rubalcaba, Gonzalo, 394–95,
405, 500
Rudd, Roswell, 41, 52, 259,
273, 275, 277, 279, 289,
296, 546, 603, 638
Rüegg, Mathias, 98, 617
Rugolo, Pete, 590, 595
Ruiz, Hilton, 389
Rumsey, Howard, 137
Rush, Otis, 207, 213, 424–25,
551–52
Rushing, Jimmy, 551–52, 554
Russell, George, 21, 98, 103,
126, 138, 225, 258, 569,
600–602, 611, 621–22,
636
Russell, Luis, 110, 249, 281,
587
Russell, Pee Wee, 90, 93, 281
Russo, Bill, 98, 101, 137, 205,
268, 596
Rutherford, Paul, 273

Rypdal, Terje, 40, 430, 498,
602

Saft, Jamie, 61, 407
Sakata, Akira, 306
salsa, 43, 261, 278, 353,
504–9, 597
Saluzzi, Dino, 532
Samson, Michel, 525
Samuels, Clarence, 147
Samuels, David, 360
Sanabria, Bobby, 73, 507
Sanborn, David, 244, 310, 313,
430, 504
Sanchez, Antonio, 500
Sánchez, David, 73–74, 314,
338–39, 506–7, 518
Sanchez, Poncho, 505, 507–8
Sanders, Pharoah, 22, 109,
142–43, 148–49, 297,
327–28, 331, 433, 486,
522, 603
Sandoval, Arturo, 250, 261,
507, 618
Santamaria, Mongo, 504–5,
508–9
Santana, Carlos, 128, 427, 476,
506–7
Sass, Jon, 535
Satoh, Masahiko, 40
Sauer, Heinz, 331
Sauter, Eddie, 590
Savage, John, 355
Sawai, Tadao, 545
Saxofour, 348
Scheinman, Jenny, 529
Schiefel, Michael, 562
Schlippenbach, Alexander
von, 25, 40, 206, 259,
380, 382–83, 488, 605,
608, 638
Schneider, Maria, 98, 205, 257,
297, 620–22
Schnyder, Daniel, 330
Schoenberg, Arnold, 86, 89,
98, 118, 384, 438, 577,
608, 610
Schoof, Manfred, 29, 31, 261–
62, 602, 612, 638
Schorn, Steffen, 293, 344–45,
349
Schuller, George, 331, 485–86
Schuller, Gunther, 22, 124, 137,
331, 378–79

Schulte, Frank, 411–12
Schweizer, Irène, 383, 576
Sclavis, Louis, 43, 64–65, 275, 286–88, 291–92, 302, 396, 452, 492, 524, 529, 559, 657
Scofield, John, 39, 133–35, 326, 430–32, 436, 438, 484–85, 499, 523, 553, 623, 658
Scott, Jimmy, 555, 559
Scott, Tom, 299, 331, 353
Scott, Tony, 42, 114, 204, 283–85
Seck, Cheick Tidiane, 403
Segal, Vincent, 541
Seifert, Zbigniew, 40, 195, 522–24
Shakti, 160–61, 426–27, 512, 524, 646, 650–51
Shank, Bud, 304, 350, 353, 419, 509
Shankar, L., 160, 522, 524, 650
Shankar, Ravi, 140, 142, 155, 160, 304, 513
Sharp, Elliott, 53, 191, 435, 532, 545
Sharpe, Avery, 449, 452
Sharrock, Sonny, 433
Shavers, Charlie, 199, 250, 630
Shaw, Artie, 215, 282, 477, 565–66, 589–90, 629
Shaw, Charles Bobo, 49
Shaw, Ian, 561
Shaw, Woody, 252–54, 257, 277, 474, 496, 631, 640
Shea, David, 412
Shearing, George, 377, 477, 504
Shepik, Brad, 66, 439–40
Shepp, Archie, 16, 22, 40, 109, 141–42, 146–47, 167, 274, 297, 327, 330–31, 333, 337–38, 360, 473, 557, 576, 638
Sheppard, Andy, 300, 331
Shibusa Shirazu Orchestra, 607–8
Shihab, Sahib, 24–25, 341, 350, 353, 599, 612
Shilkloper, Arkady, 539
Shipp, Matthew, 31, 70, 380, 382, 412

Shorter, Wayne, 40, 48, 123, 126–27, 135, 153, 156–57, 159, 205, 278–79, 296, 298–301, 310, 313, 323–24, 331–32, 335, 337, 339, 386, 391, 395, 432, 451, 463, 474, 493, 511, 562, 573, 634–35, 643, 658
Shterev, Simeon, 352
Sickler, Don, 257
Siddik, Rasul, 260
Silver, Horace, 19–20, 122, 205, 220, 254, 261, 264, 266, 317–18, 326, 372, 374, 629–31, 634, 665
Silverman, Tracy, 522
Simeon, Omer, 202, 281, 285
Simone, Nina, 569
Sims, Zoot, 284, 298, 319–21, 503, 593, 595, 598, 632
Sinatra, Frank, 78, 214, 249, 325, 553–54, 559
Singh, Talvin, 514
Singleton, Zutty, 468
Sipiagin, Alex, 250, 257
Skidmore, Alan, 331, 346, 512
Slawe, Jan, 239
Smith, Bessie, 11, 77, 86–89, 106, 207, 216, 221, 255, 267, 365, 563–64, 571, 665
Smith, Clara, 88
Smith, Jimmy, 37, 399–402, 405, 422, 429, 521, 665
Smith, Johnny, 421
Smith, Leo, 40, 145, 258–59, 606, 642
Smith, Mamie, 103, 109
Smith, Marvin "Smitty," 48, 494
Smith, Stuff, 520–21, 526, 529
Smith, Trixie, 551
Smith, Willie "The Lion," 6, 14, 365
Snow, Phoebe, 572
Socarras, Alberto, 349
Soft Machine, 35, 401, 415, 428, 463, 483
Solal, Martial, 40, 370–72, 524, 542
Soloff, Lew, 254, 613
Sommer, Emmanuelle, 538
Sommer, Günter "Baby," 398, 488

Sonneck, Ronny, 191
SOS, 131, 346
soul, 2, 20, 40, 49, 55–57, 68–72, 92, 149, 171, 173, 174–76, 213, 216, 219–20, 244, 253, 257, 258, 266, 270, 272, 279, 305–6, 310, 312–13, 317, 324–25, 327, 336–38, 348, 359, 362, 368, 373–74, 385, 399–401, 404, 417, 425, 431, 440, 442, 454, 456, 463, 473, 489, 495, 498, 506, 524, 527–29, 540, 547, 550, 552–53, 555–57, 559–61, 567, 571–73, 572–73, 584–85, 616–17, 641, 648, 654, 659
South, Eddie, 519–20, 529
Souza, Luciana, 575
Spanier, Muggsy, 90, 245, 247
Spann, Otis, 367, 551
Spassov, Theodosii, 64, 357
Spaulding, James, 304, 347, 350
Special Edition, 492, 632, 649
Speed, Chris, 291–92, 338, 654
spirituals, 216-21, 1, 7, 40, 71, 87, 94, 177, 179, 223, 232, 387, 398, 416, 481, 489, 532, 549, 567, 571–72, 635, 645
Sri Chinmoy, 158–60
Stafford, Terrell, 257
Stalling, Carl W., 181, 183
standards, 9, 56, 59–60, 162, 168–69, 173–76, 194, 197, 199, 229, 248, 250, 272, 304, 313, 317, 325, 336, 387, 390, 393, 396, 430, 441, 450, 484, 528, 552, 559, 561–62, 568–69, 572, 578–84, 619–20, 654, 656, 666–67
Stanko, Tomasz, 261–62, 275
Starostin, Sergey, 560
Stefanoski, Vlatko, 67
Steig, Jeremy, 35, 353
Stein, Norbert, 338
Stenson, Bobo, 326, 386–87
Stern, Mike, 133, 430
Stevens, John, 300, 487–88, 492, 638

Steward, Herbie, 319
Stewart, Bill, 402, 493, 501
Stewart, Bob, 278, 313,
    534–35
Stewart, Rex, 13, 84, 92, 174,
    245, 248, 260, 296, 588,
    629
Stewart, Sid, 92
Stewart, Slam, 443
Stief, Bo, 463–64
Stigers, Curtis, 562
Stitt, Sonny, 37, 57–58, 119,
    135, 172, 303, 318–20,
    322
Stivín, Jirí, 352
Stockhausen, Karlheinz, 24, 33,
    185, 263, 287, 610
Stockhausen, Markus, 261,
    263, 499
Stone, Sly, 124, 127, 456
Stötter, Claus, 246, 261, 620
Strayhorn, Billy, 94, 99–100
Strickland, Marcus, 58,
    336–37
stride piano, 366–67, 370, 374,
    377, 391
String Trio of New York, 459,
    525–27
Strozier, Frank, 304
Stucky, Erika, 583–84
Studer, Fredy, 482–83
Subramaniam, L., 522, 524,
    529
Sullivan, Ira, 252, 255
Sullivan, Jim, 155
Sullivan, Joe, 90
Sulsbrük, Birger, 505
Sumac, Yma, 575
Sun Ra Cosmic Arkestra, 604
Surman, John, 40, 156, 286,
    297, 301–2, 342–43, 346,
    406–7, 544, 576
Suzano, Marcos, 510
Svensson, Esbjörn, 275, 387,
    393, 498, 584, 656
Swallow, Steve, 331, 436, 449–
    50, 462, 604, 636
Swing (era), 1–2, 12–13, 14–
    15, 23, 28, 32–33, 39, 43,
    47, 77, 82, 91, 103, 106,
    112–13, 171, 195, 215,
    221–22, 233–35, 246,
    249–50, 255, 266, 268–
    70, 279, 281–83, 301–2,

310, 334, 340, 343–44,
    348–50, 358, 367,
    369–70, 391, 402, 420,
    436–37, 442–43, 469–71,
    491, 521, 527, 530, 539,
    550–51, 563, 566, 587,
    589–95, 619, 628–30,
    650, 654, 662–63
swing (style), 12–13, 81–82,
    180, 195–96, 233–35,
    237–41, 289, 307, 311,
    340, 342, 346–47, 366,
    374, 378, 389, 428, 433,
    446–47
Szukalski, Tomasz, 331

Tabackin, Lew, 322, 339, 356,
    611, 614
Tacuma, Jamaaladeen, 50, 150,
    313, 466, 652
Takase, Aki, 286, 382–83, 583
Take 6, 556
Tarasov, Vladimir, 488–89
Tardy, Greg, 293, 336
Tate, Buddy, 49, 315–16, 335
Tate, Grady, 477
Tate, Greg, 67, 167
Tatum, Art, 40, 168, 316, 364,
    366, 370–72, 377–78,
    392, 395–96, 572, 603,
    629, 634
Taylor, Art, 122, 312, 475, 635
Taylor, Billy, 206–7, 344, 371,
    598
Taylor, Cecil, 16, 28, 40, 81,
    100, 126, 157, 166, 225,
    296, 327, 330, 363, 369,
    375, 379–84, 388, 457–
    58, 473, 481–82, 486,
    488–89, 525–27, 603
Taylor, John, 386, 401, 406,
    576, 583
Tchamitchian, Claude, 454
Teagarden, Jack, 79, 88, 90,
    267–69, 469, 531,
    553–54
Temiz, Okay, 51, 514
Temperley, Joe, 344
Terai, Naoko, 528
Terrasson, Jacky, 392–93, 496,
    654, 656
Terry, Clark, 126, 165, 245–46,
    248, 256, 258, 511, 554,
    593

Terry, Sonny, 212, 536
Teschemacher, Frank, 90–91,
    281, 532
Texier, Henri, 65, 288, 396,
    449, 452, 454, 492,
    656
Thelin, Eje, 273–74
Thiam, Mor, 511
Thielemans, Toots, 536
Thigpen, Ed, 52, 372
Thomas, Gary, 56, 68, 331–32,
    354, 649, 652, 659
Thomas, Jens, 331, 384
Thomas, Leon, 219, 552
Thompson, Barbara, 299, 353,
    616, 643
Thompson, Lucky, 294, 315,
    598
Thornhill, Claude, 120–22,
    340, 597, 600
Threadgill, Henry, 46, 98, 172,
    205, 227, 260, 306–8,
    343, 354, 440, 458, 526,
    535, 540, 641, 649
Ti-Roro, 512
Tibbetts, Steve, 432
Timmons, Bobby, 372–73, 634
Tippett, Keith, 382–83, 606
Tippetts, Julie, 575–76
Tizol, Juan, 97, 268
Tjader, Cal, 359, 504–5, 508
Tobin, Christine, 583
Togashi, Masahiko, 357, 489
Tolstoy, Viktoria, 584
Torn, David, 429–30
Torres, Nestor, 353
Torres, Samuel, 507
Tough, Dave, 15, 90, 231, 469–
    70, 477–78, 501, 594
Toure, Ali Farka, 440
Towner, Ralph, 40, 42, 437–38,
    639, 652
Towns, Colin, 620, 624–25
Tristano, Lennie, 18–19, 21,
    66, 126, 225, 227,
    304–5, 317, 322, 372–73,
    384, 389, 421–22, 427,
    595, 631, 639, 662
Tronzo, David, 440–41
Trovesi, Gianluigi, 64, 205,
    286–87, 291–92, 302,
    534, 607, 656
Truffaz, Erik, 69, 264–65, 485,
    658

Trumbauer, Frankie, 90–93, 108, 303
Tuncboyacian, Arto, 64, 515–16
Turner, Big Joe, 326, 368, 370, 552, 593
Turner, Mark, 334, 336
Turre, Steve, 254, 270, 277–78, 530, 539, 613
Turrentine, Stanley, 323–24
Turtle Island String Quartet, 522, 526–27
29th Street Saxophone Quartet, 347–48
two-beat jazz, 82
Tyner, McCoy, 40–41, 140, 142, 153, 166, 279, 388–89, 391, 452, 478, 482, 504, 509–10, 523–24, 539, 622, 635–36, 640

U.F.O., 70, 556
Ullmann, Gebhard, 286, 330–31, 348
Ulmer, James "Blood," 50–51, 138, 167, 434–35, 440, 489, 652
Umezu, Kazutoki, 50
UMO Big Band, 620–21
United Jazz and Rock Ensemble, 483, 615–16
United Nations Orchestra, 119, 278, 511
Urbaniak, Michal, 522
Urcola, Diego, 73, 261

Vaché, Warren, 33, 250, 436
Valdés, Carlos "Patato," 503
Valdés, Chucho, 394–95, 618
Valente, Gary, 277–79
Valentin, Dave, 353, 356
Valle, Orlando "Maraca," 353, 356, 618
Van Kemenade, Paul, 313
Vandermark, Ken, 31, 330, 343, 607–9
van't Hof, Jasper, 386, 643
Vapirov, Anatoly, 300, 330, 357
Varner, Tom, 538
Vasconcelos, Naná, 51, 509–10, 513, 650
Vaughan, Sarah, 159, 221, 362, 527, 554, 566–67, 569–71, 580–82, 596
Vega, Ray, 261, 318

Velez, Glen, 357, 515
Veloso, Caetano, 557
Ventura, Charlie, 315, 317–18, 569, 631
Venuti, Joe, 90, 519, 521–22, 530
Verly, François, 516
Very Very Circus, 308, 649
Vidal, Carlos, 502–3
Vienna Art Orchestra, 275, 313, 529, 535, 577, 617
Vinnegar, Leroy, 446
Vitous, Miroslav, 159, 449, 452, 643
Vloeimans, Eric, 261–62
V.S.O.P., 40, 385
Vysniauskas, Petras, 301

Wadud, Abdul, 444, 540
Waits, Nasheet, 394, 490–91
Waits, Tom, 547–57
Walcott, Collin, 42–43, 52, 72, 513–43, 639, 650–51
Walden, Myron, 312
Waldron, Mal, 375, 528
Walker, T-Bone, 207, 213, 217, 424
Wallace, Bennie, 328–29
Waller, Fats, 13, 40, 205, 228, 265–67, 325, 372, 378, 397–98, 521, 564, 611, 664
Walrath, Jack, 254
Wamble, Doug, 432–33
Ware, Bill, 362
Ware, David S., 31, 327, 382, 486
Ware, Wilbur, 446–47
Warlop, Michel, 523
Washington, Dinah, 221, 318, 571, 578, 581
Washington, Grover, 299, 524
Washington, Kenny, 58, 392, 475, 477, 495, 497, 568
Washingtonians, The, 96
Waters, Ethel, 563
Waters, Muddy, 154, 213–14, 216, 424–25, 550
Watkins, Julius, 537–38, 540
Watkiss, Cleveland, 562, 616
Watrous, Bill, 271, 276
Watson, Bobby, 48, 148, 299, 310–11, 332, 348, 474, 634, 658

Watts, Ernie, 148, 299, 310–11, 332, 658
Watts, Jeff "Tain," 48, 170, 237, 335, 495–96, 501, 647, 655
Watts, Trevor, 306, 346
WDR Big Band, 271, 451, 620, 623
Weather Report, 36, 38–39, 159, 242, 299, 324, 332, 405, 452, 462–65, 482, 486, 508–9, 515, 616, 642–45, 663
Webb, Chick, 350, 470, 478, 503, 566–67, 591–92, 597
Weber, Eberhard, 438, 463, 616
Webster, Ben, 167, 170, 172, 199, 315–17, 324, 327–30, 340, 344, 452, 527, 561, 588, 591, 663
Weiss, David, 257
Weiss, Michael, 658
Weiss, Philip, 561
Wells, Dickie, 111, 268, 588, 593
Wells, Junior, 536, 551
Wesley, Fred, 272
Wess, Frank, 315, 350, 593
Wesseltoft, Bugge, 65, 69, 414–15, 485, 585, 658
West Coast jazz, 18, 304, 321, 341, 373, 446, 478, 537–38
Westbrook, Mike, 524, 606–7, 621
Weston, Calvin, 150, 489
Weston, Randy, 24, 314, 375, 547
Wettling, George, 90, 469
Wheeler, Kenny, 205, 246, 261–62, 414, 576, 605
Whetsol, Arthur, 96
White, Bukka, 212, 551
White, Lenny, 482–83
White, Mike, 522, 524
Whitehead, Annie, 275
Whiteman, Paul, 89–90, 92–95, 443, 644
Whitfield, Mark, 437
Wickman, Putte, 288–89
Wierbos, Wolter, 65, 275
Wilber, Bob, 282, 295, 301

Wilkins, Ernie, 19, 598
Wilkins, Jack, 427–28
Williams, Big Joe, 212, 214
Williams, Clarence, 88, 202, 281, 349
Williams, Claude, 521
Williams, Cootie, 97, 100, 130, 174, 247–48, 260, 563, 590, 629, 662
Williams, James, 390
Williams, Joe, 552, 561
Williams, Martin, 86, 137, 166, 170, 236
Williams, Mary Lou, 231, 369, 563, 592
Williams, Robert Pete, 551
Williams, Tony, 35, 38, 40, 48, 68, 123, 126, 139, 156–58, 228, 237, 242, 257, 386, 390, 401, 425, 449, 476, 478–79, 482, 492–94, 496–97, 501, 562, 635, 643, 645, 647
Williamson, Claude, 372–73
Williamson, Sonny Boy, 536, 550
Willner, Hal, 547, 604
Wilson, Cassandra, 71, 440, 578–79
Wilson, Gerald, 600
Wilson, Joe Lee, 557
Wilson, Matt, 304, 493–94, 498, 622
Wilson, Peter Niklas, 27, 29, 62, 125, 151, 327, 411, 488, 663
Wilson, Phillip, 485, 640
Wilson, Steve, 301, 312
Wilson, Teddy, 13, 91, 107, 146, 282, 369–70, 563–64, 590, 628–29
Winchester, Lem, 359–62
Winding, Kai, 121, 270, 273, 340, 595, 632
Windmill Saxophone Quartet, 348

Winstone, Norma, 575–76
Winterschladen, Reiner, 261, 263, 620
Wogram, Nils, 275, 278, 656
Wollesen, Kenny, 486, 495
Wonder, Stevie, 266, 310, 333, 423, 536, 554, 560
Wood, Chris, 460
Woods, Phil, 119, 254, 305, 311–12, 547, 598–99, 632, 640
Wooten, Victor, 466
Workman, Reginald, 140, 444, 447, 545, 573
world jazz, 45, 51–54, 56, 60, 64, 66, 74, 153, 177, 258, 260, 278, 292, 313–14, 338, 356, 394, 396, 403, 405, 427, 437, 439, 460, 473, 500, 513–14, 516, 522, 524, 543, 546, 560, 584, 618, 622, 646, 650–51
world music, 21, 23, 25–26, 34, 41–42, 44, 51–53, 57, 72, 122, 129, 132, 176, 191, 260, 263, 276, 292, 309, 314, 331, 352–53, 361, 381, 419, 441, 452, 457, 483, 499–500, 508, 514, 527, 532, 538, 544, 604, 606, 618, 639, 644, 651, 659
World Saxophone Quartet, 47, 167, 172, 301, 306, 308, 311, 343, 345–47, 648–49
Wright, Lizz, 572
Wyatt, Robert, 483

Xenakis, Iannis, 457, 608
Xu Feng Xia, 545–46

Yamamoto, Hozan, 356
Yamashita, Yosuke, 382–83, 513
Yellowjackets, 463, 484, 644

Yoshihide, Otomo, 411–12
Young, Larry, 127, 156–58, 401–2, 429, 482, 645
Young, Lester, 4, 15, 17–19, 74, 77, 101–9, 110, 124, 137, 146, 152, 167, 171–72, 194, 199, 205–6, 228, 236, 271, 281–82, 284, 303, 315, 317–22, 325, 333–34, 344, 350, 420, 427, 530, 556, 561, 564–65, 593, 600, 603, 629, 637, 663
young lions, 55–57, 60, 62, 152, 164, 169, 178, 256, 305, 312, 336, 338–39, 390, 436–37, 445, 456, 497, 561, 654
Young, Snooky, 250
Young, Trummy, 268–69, 271
Your Neighborhood Saxophone Quartet, 348
Youssef, Dhafer, 73, 357, 499, 544

Zadeh, Aziza Mustafa, 396
Zadlo, Leszek, 331
Zappa, Frank, 384, 427, 434, 521, 610, 625, 643
Zawinul, Joe, 39, 127, 135, 153, 156–57, 159, 318, 404–7, 415, 438, 463, 465, 500, 515, 560, 583, 623, 643–44
Zenón, Miguel, 73, 314
Ziegler, Matthias, 355
Ziporyn, Evan, 292
Zoller, Attila, 40, 427
Zorn, John, 31, 43, 53–54, 60–63, 78, 180–93, 206, 266, 307–8, 355, 397, 403, 407, 435, 438, 441, 459, 495, 511, 525, 527–29, 531–32, 534, 541, 546–47, 653–55
Zulfikarpasic, Bojan, 66, 396–97